the best brands in one harbour
Dometic GROUP
From air conditioning and refrigeration to galley equipment and sanitation, Dometic products ensure that all the best brands are in one harbour

Make a winning decision
Your choice of marine electronics is one of the most important decisions you will have to make as a boat owner, next to choosing the boat itself of course.
When you buy Raymarine equipment, you are buying into world-class performance, top-notch integration, and the latest proven design technologies. Years of research and development, and customer feedback have resulted in the 'simple-on-the-outside, sophisticated-on-the-inside' design philosophy that is behind all our intuitive easy-to-use equipment.
Worldwide support and warranty
That's why Raymarine has a worldwide network of product-trained distributors and service dealers and offers a comprehensive warranty to handle the unexpected… wherever you decide to go.
Raymarine
Raymarine
Raymarine
Raymarine
For product information, visit your local stockist or go to www.raymarine.co.uk
Lifestyle photo: Joe McCarthy
Raymarine®
…world leaders in marine electronics.

REEDS WESTERN ALMANAC 2010

ADLARD COLES NAUTICAL

EDITORS Andy Du Port and Rob Buttress

Free updates are available at www.reedsalmanac.co.uk

Published by Adlard Coles Nautical 2009

IMPORTANT SAFETY NOTE AND LEGAL DISCLAIMER

This Almanac is intended as an aid to navigation only and to assist with basic planning for your passage. The information, charts, maps and diagrams in this Almanac should not be relied on for navigational purposes and should always be used in conjunction with current official hydrographic data. Whilst every care has been taken in its compilation, this Almanac may contain inaccuracies and is no substitute for the relevant official hydrographic charts and data, which should always be consulted in advance of, and whilst, navigating in the relevant area. Before setting out you should also check local conditions with the harbourmaster or other appropriate office responsible for your intended area of navigation.

Before using any waypoint or coordinate listed in this Almanac it must first be plotted on an appropriate official hydrographic chart to check its usefulness, accuracy and appropriateness for the prevailing weather and tidal conditions.

To the extent that the editors or publishers become aware that corrections are required, these will be published on the website www.reedsalmanac.co.uk. Readers should therefore regularly check the website for any such corrections. Data in this Almanac is corrected up to Weekly Edition 26/2009 of Admiralty Notices to Mariners.

The publishers, editors and their agents accept no responsibility for any errors or omissions, or for any accident, loss or damage (including without limitation any indirect, consequential, special or exemplary damages) arising from the use or misuse of, or reliance upon, the information contained in this Almanac.

The decision to use and rely on any of the data in this Almanac is entirely at the discretion of, and is the sole responsibility of, the Skipper or other individual in control of the vessel in connection with which it is being used or relied upon.

Adlard Coles Nautical
36 Soho Square
London, W1D 3QY
Tel: +44 (0)207 758 0200
Fax: +44 (0)207 758 0222/0333
Email: info@reedsalmanac.co.uk
www.reedsalmanac.co.uk

Almanac manager
Chris Stevens

Cartography
Chris Stevens, Garold West

Cover photograph
Dun Laoghaire
www.dlmarina.com

ISBN 978 1 4081 1367 7 – Reeds Western Almanac 2010

A CIP catalogue record for this book is available from the British Library.

Printed in the UK.

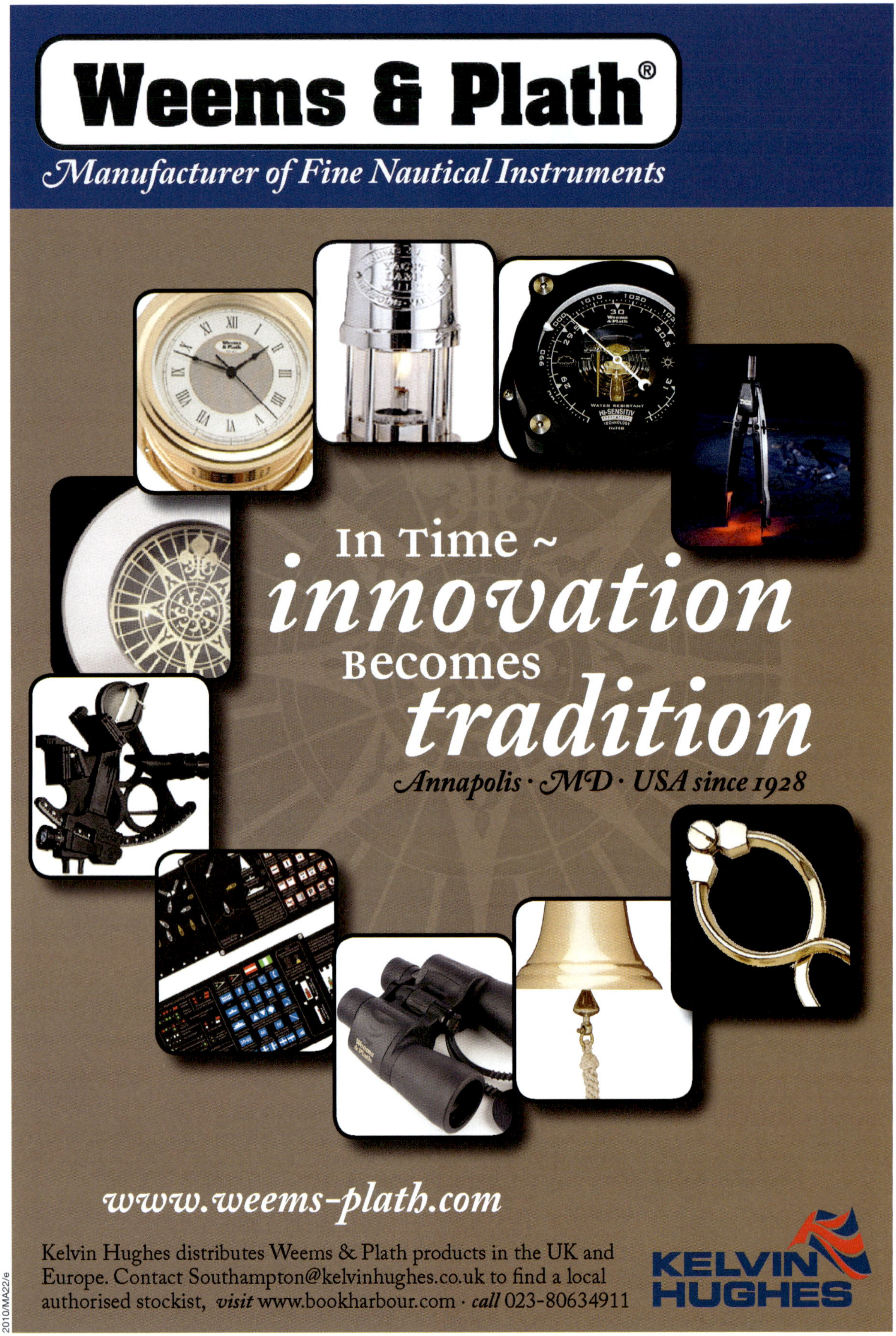

Weems & Plath®
Manufacturer of Fine Nautical Instruments
In Time ~
innovation
Becomes
tradition
Annapolis · MD · USA since 1928
www.weems-plath.com
Kelvin Hughes distributes Weems & Plath products in the UK and Europe. Contact Southampton@kelvinhughes.co.uk to find a local authorised stockist, visit www.bookharbour.com · call 023-80634911
KELVIN HUGHES

2010/MA22/e

Reference Contents

Navigational Contents

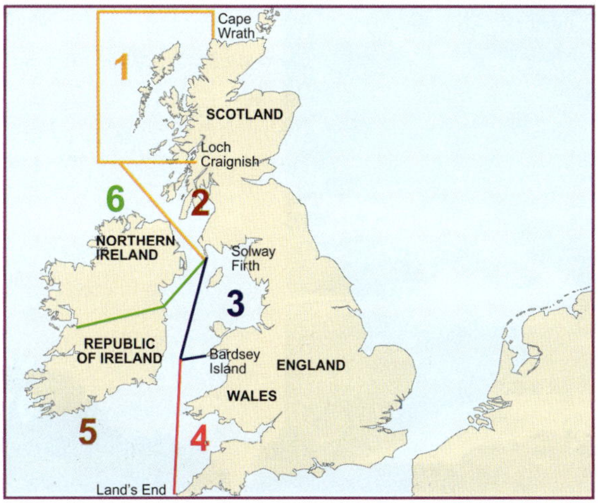

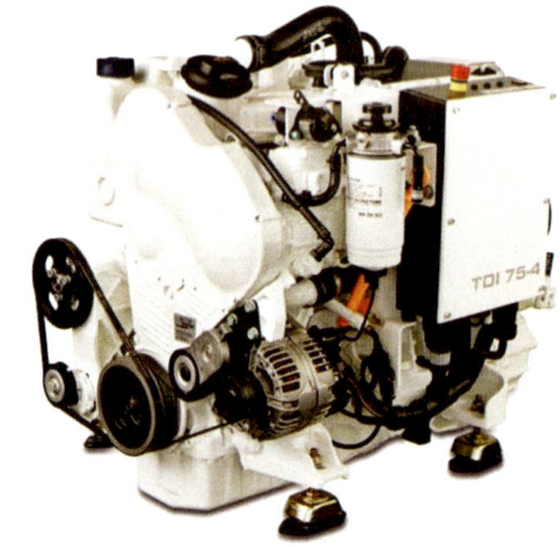

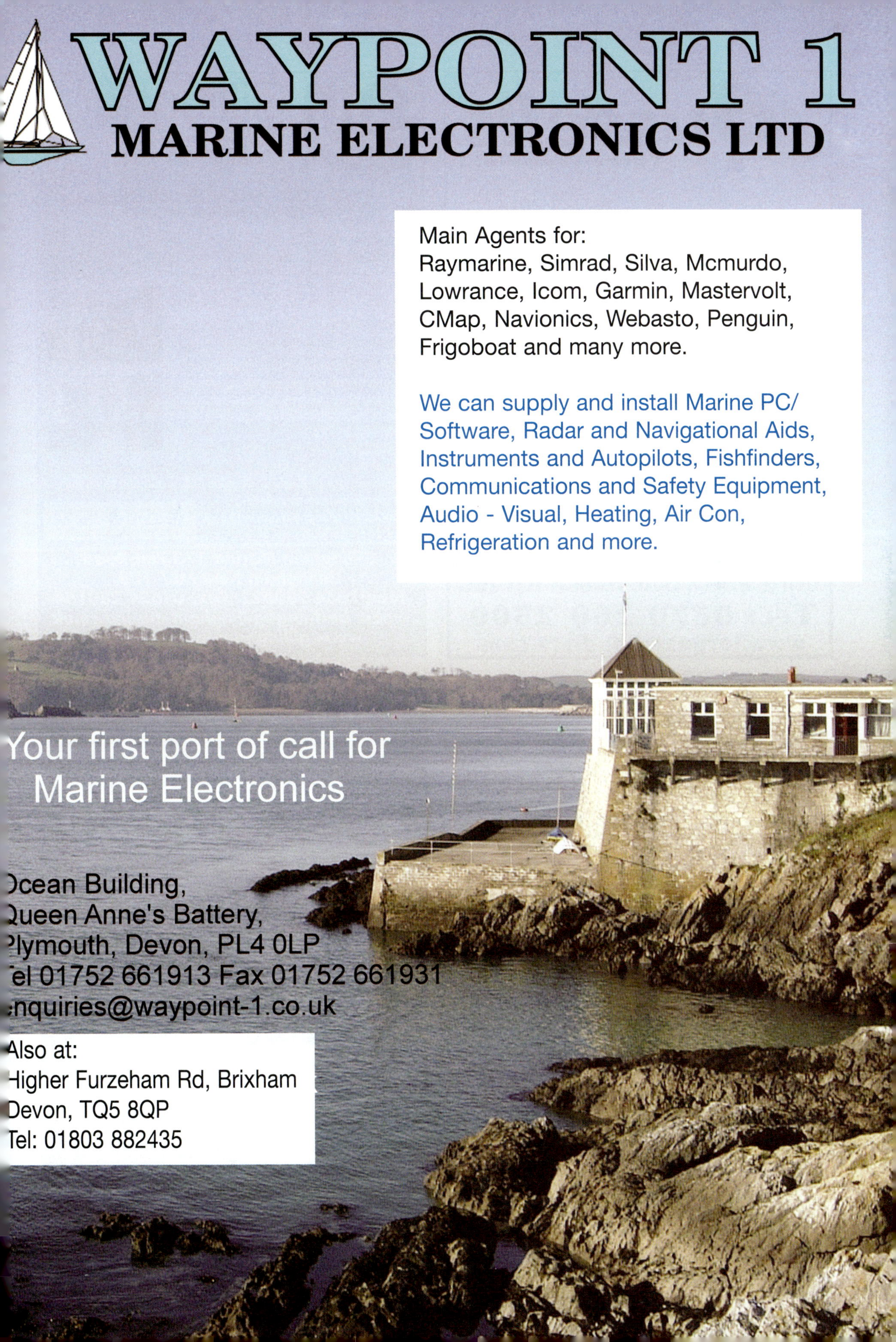
WAYPOINT 1
MARINE ELECTRONICS LTD
Main Agents for:
Raymarine, Simrad, Silva, Mcmurdo, Lowrance, Icom, Garmin, Mastervolt, CMap, Navionics, Webasto, Penguin, Frigoboat and many more.
We can supply and install Marine PC/ Software, Radar and Navigational Aids, Instruments and Autopilots, Fishfinders, Communications and Safety Equipment, Audio - Visual, Heating, Air Con, Refrigeration and more.
Your first port of call for Marine Electronics
cean Building,
ueen Anne's Battery,
lymouth, Devon, PL4 0LP
el 01752 661913 Fax 01752 661931
nquiries@waypoint-1.co.uk
Also at:
igher Furzeham Rd, Brixham
Devon, TQ5 8QP
Tel: 01803 882435

CELERITAS

A. JEDYNAK ELECTRICS
(Marine Electronics)
Andrew Jedynak
Island Street, Salcombe, S. Devon TQ8 8DP
Tel: 01548 843321 • Mobile: 0777 5626134
2010/MA51/e

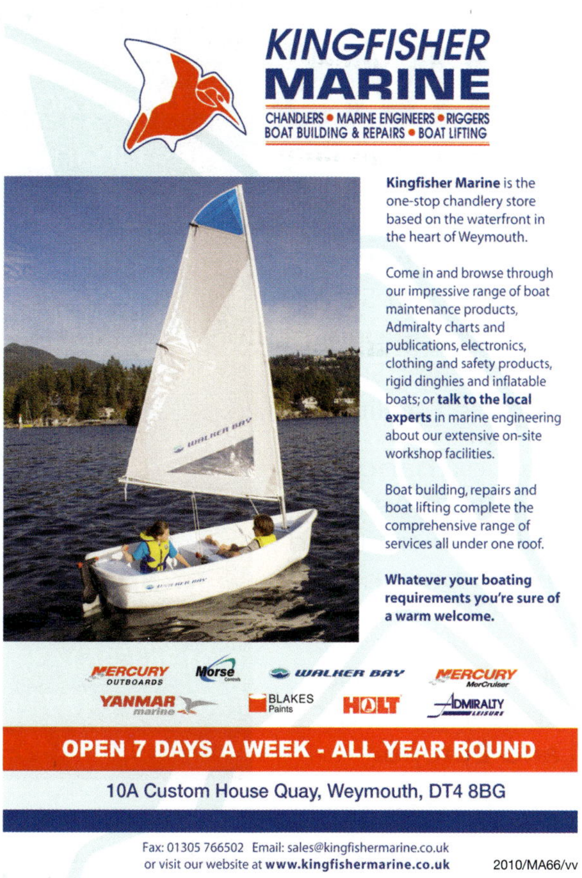
KINGFISHER MARINE
CHANDLERS • MARINE ENGINEERS • RIGGERS
BOAT BUILDING & REPAIRS • BOAT LIFTING
Kingfisher Marine is the one-stop chandlery store based on the waterfront in the heart of Weymouth.
Come in and browse through our impressive range of boat maintenance products, Admiralty charts and publications, electronics, clothing and safety products, rigid dinghies and inflatable boats; or talk to the local experts in marine engineering about our extensive on-site workshop facilities.
Boat building, repairs and boat lifting complete the comprehensive range of services all under one roof.
Whatever your boating requirements you're sure of a warm welcome.
MERCURY OUTBOARDS
Morse
WALKER BAY
MERCURY MerCruiser
YANMAR marine
BLAKES Paints
HOLT
ADMIRALTY LEISURE
OPEN 7 DAYS A WEEK - ALL YEAR ROUND
10A Custom House Quay, Weymouth, DT4 8BG
Fax: 01305 766502 Email: sales@kingfishermarine.co.uk
or visit our website at www.kingfishermarine.co.uk
2010/MA66/vv

PREMIER CLASS
INVESTING IN YOUR FUTURE BOATING
PREMIER
MARINAS
First Class marina facilities with great customer service in fantastic locations.
Helping you to get the most out of your boating.
www.premiermarinas.com
CHICHESTER MARINA
8 fantastic Marinas along the South Coast:
Brighton Marina
Chichester Marina
Falmouth Marina
Gosport Marina
Port Solent Marina
Sovereign Harbour, Eastbourne
Southsea Marina
Swanwick Marina
Marinas | Boat Yards | Yacht Sales & Brokerage | Insurance
2010/MA52/e

Peterhead
PORT AUTHORITY

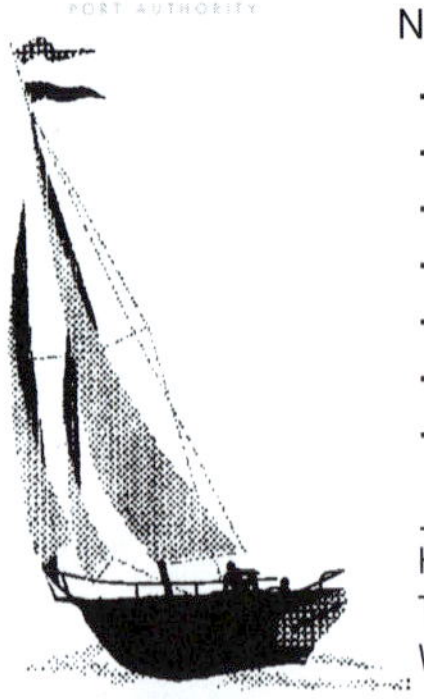

SET SAIL FOR
PETERHEAD BAY MARINA
North East Scotland's Finest Marina

- Fully serviced pontoons
- Shower and toilet facilities
- Access at all states of the tide
- Visiting yachtsmen welcome
- Secure on shore storage
- Comprehensive local services
- Annual berths from £444

(for a 6 metre vessel)

Harbour Office, West Pier, Peterhead, AB42 1DW.
Tel: 01779 483600. Fax: 01779 475715
Web: www.peterheadport.co.uk

2010/MA99/v

HOLMAN RIGGING
Professional rigging services

- Visual rig checks
- Electronic non-destructive rig checks
- Roller reefing
- In-mast reefing
- In-boom reefing
- Single line reefing
- Masts
- Life lines
- Guard wires

Contact Chris Holman
Chichester Marina
Chichester, West Sussex PO20 7EJ
Email: enquiries@holmanrigging.co.uk
Web: www.holmanrigging.co.uk
Tel/Fax: (01243) 514000

Agents for Hyde Sails and all major mast and reefing suppliers.

2010/MA98/d

Howth Marina

The marina is owned and managed by Howth Yacht Club. It is a perfect stopping off point being situated just north of Dublin Bay, mid way through the Irish Sea; it is 30 minutes from Dublin city centre and from Dublin International Airport, both accessible by public transport.

The marina is extremely safe in all weather conditions and there is access at all stages of the tide. Facilities include water and electricity to all berths, diesel pump, 24 hour reception and security, a drying out pad and 15 ton crane. Overnight rates are exceptionally good value. The full facilities of Howth Yacht Club are available to the crews of visiting boats including changing rooms, showers, laundry, bar and catering.

2010/MA19/e

FOX'S
SINCE 1927
MARINE SERVICE CENTRE

- Heated Workshops
- Osmosis Treatment
- Masts & Rigging
- Stainless Steel
- Fabrication
- Insurance Repairs
- Yacht Spray Centre
- Electronics
- Sales & Service
- Engineering
- Boat Hoist to 70 tons
- Large Chandlery

Fox's Marina Ipswich Ltd
Ipswich Suffolk IP2 8SA
T: +44 (0) 1473 689111
F: +44 (0) 1473 601737
E: foxs@foxsmarina.com
www.foxsmarina.com

2010/MA9/e

HMS
Hutchins
Marine Sales Ltd

Independent specialist in Sealine
30 Years Experience
Full Dealer Sales & Service Facilities

Part exchange available on selected craft and boats bought for cash

A friendly service covering the UK and Europe.

Quality Used & Brokerage sales Finance
Insurance
Transportation
Training
Electronics
Fitting
Repairs
Canopies
and more....

T: 01344 861432
F: 01344 647924
M: 07766 051455

sales@hutchins-marine.co.uk
www.hutchins-marine.co.uk

Sealand Boat Deliveries Ltd
Nationwide and worldwide yacht transport 36 years.
Storage, salvage. lifting
24/7 ops room **01254 705225** fax 776582
ros@poptel.org
www.btx.co.uk

2010/MA66/s

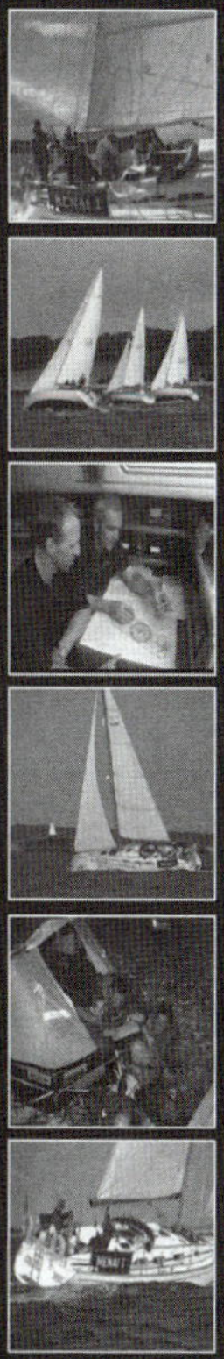

Sailing HOLIDAYS IN IRELAND
CALL US NOW FOR 2010
KILRUSH MARINA & BOATYARD +353-65-9052072
BANGOR MARINA 028 9145 3297
FENIT HARBOUR MARINA +353-66-7136231
CARLINGFORD MARINA +353-4293-73073
DINGLE MARINA +353-66-9151629
MALAHIDE MARI +353-1-8454129
LAWRENCE COVE MARINA +353-27-75044
DUBLIN CITY MOOR +353-1-818 330
SALVE MARINE +353-21-831145
DUN LAOGHAIRE MAR +353-1-2020040
CASTLEPARK MARINA +353-21-4774959
WATERFORD CITY MARINA +353-51-309900
KILMORE QUAY MARINA +353-53-29955
LARNE
DONEGAL
BELFAST
SLIGO
GALWAY
R. Shannon
DUBLIN
Lough Derg
LIMERICK
ROSSLARE
KILLARNEY
CORK
Sail in Ireland and enjoy the experience of a lifetime
Further information: Sailing Holidays in Ireland, Trident Hotel, Kinsale, Co. Cork, Ireland. Tel +353-21-477 2927.
www.sailingireland.com www.irelandwatersports.net Email:sailirl@indigo

Reference data

Reference data

0.1 THE ALMANAC

• Acknowledgements

The Editors thank the many official bodies and individuals for information and advice given in the compilation of this Almanac. These include: UKHO, Trinity House, HM Nautical Almanac Office, SHOM, HMSO, HM Revenue & Customs, Meteorological Office, BBC, IBA, MCA, RNLI, ABP, countless Harbourmasters and our many individual Harbour Agents.

• Permissions

Chartlets, tidal stream diagrams and curves are reproduced from Admiralty charts and publications (ALL, ASD, ATT and ALRS) by permission of the UKHO (Licence No GB DQ – 001 – Adlard Coles) and the Controller of HMSO.

UK and foreign tidal predictions are supplied by and with the permission of UKHO.

Extracts from the *International Code of Signals 1969* and *Meteorological Office Weather Services for Shipping* are published by permission of the Controller of HMSO.

Ephemerides are derived from HM Nautical Almanac by permission of HM Nautical Almanac Office and the Council for the Central Laboratory of the Research Councils.

• Disclaimer

No National HO has verified the information in this product and none accepts liability for the accuracy of reproduction or any modifications made thereafter. No National HO warrants that this product satisfies national or international regulations regarding the use of the appropriate products for navigation.

Chartlets in this Almanac are not intended for navigational use, only for reference. Always consult fully updated navigational charts for the latest information.

• Improvements

This edition contains many hundreds of corrections. Tide Tables for 2 new Standard Ports (Tarbert Island and River Foyle) have been included, and many of the harbour chartlets have been revised and brought up to date.

Readers' suggestions for improving the content or layout are always most welcome, especially those based on experience and practical use at sea. Not every suggestion can be implemented, but all are carefully considered.

Please send your comments, by email if possible, to: updates@reedsalmanac.co.uk. Otherwise a note to Adlard Coles Nautical (see page v) will be forwarded to the relevant Editor.

• Notifying errors

Although the Almanac has been very carefully compiled from countless sources, a few errors may still occur. Please let us know if you spot any.

• Harbour Agents

Our harbour agents provide invaluable local information which may not appear in official sources. Vacancies are advertised on our website www.reedsalmanac.co.uk. If you would like to earn a free copy of Reeds Nautical Almanac every year, please apply to Adlard Coles Nautical (page v) with a brief summary of your nautical qualifications.

• Sources of corrections

This Almanac is corrected to Weekly edition No. 26/2009 of Admiralty Notices to Mariners.

Corrections to Admiralty charts and publications can be downloaded from the UKHO website or obtained from Admiralty Chart Agents (ACA) and certain Port Authorities.

• Updates

Free monthly updates, from January to June, can be downloaded at www.reedsalmanac.co.uk/updates. Please register online if you would like to receive an email reminder when the updates are available for download.

0.2 ABBREVIATIONS AND SYMBOLS

The following more common abbreviations and symbols feature in Reeds Almanacs. Other Admiralty chart symbols are on the flap of the inside back cover. Chart 5011 (a booklet) is the complete reference for Symbols and Abbreviations on charts.

@	Internet café/access
AB	Alongside berth
ABP	Associated British Ports
AC,	Shore power (electrical)
AC, ACA	Admiralty Chart, AC Agent
ACN	Adlard Coles Nautical (Publisher)
Aff Mar	Affaires Maritimes
AIS	Automatic Identification System
aka	Also known as
ALL	Admiralty List of Lights
ALRS	Admiralty List of Radio Signals
Al	Alternating light
AM	Amplitude Modulation
ANWB	Association of road & waterway users (Dutch)
Appr	Approach(es)
ASD	Admiralty Sailing Directions (Pilot)
ATM	Automatic telling machine, cashpoint
ATT	Admiralty Tide Tables
ATT	Atterisage (landfall/SWM) buoy
Auto	Météo Répondeur Automatique
B.	Bay, Black
Bar,	Licensed bar, Public house, Inn
BH	Boat Hoist (+ tons)
Bkwtr	Breakwater
BMF	British Marine Federation
BMS	Bulletin Météorologique Spécial
Bn, bcn(s)	Beacon, beacon(s)
BSH	German Hydrographic Office/chart(s)
BST	British Summer Time (= DST)
Bu	Blue
BWB	British Waterways Board
By(s)	Buoy, buoys
BY,	Boatyard
C.	Cape, Cabo, Cap
C	Crane (+ tons)
©	National Coastwatch Institution station
ca	Cable (approx 185m)
Cas	Castle
CD	Chart datum (vertical)
CEVNI	Code Européen de Voies de la Navigation Intérieure (inland waterways signs etc)
cf	Compare, cross-refer to
CG	Coastguard
CH,	Chandlery
chan	Channel (navigational)
Ch	Channel (VHF)
Ch,	Church
Chy	Chimney
COG	Course Over the Ground

Col	Column, pillar, obelisk
CPA	Closest Point of Approach
CROSS	Centre Régional Opérationnel de Surveillance et Sauvetage (= MRCC)
CRS	Coast Radio Station
D	Diesel (supply by hose)
Dec	Declination (of the Sun)
dest	Destroyed
DG	De-gaussing (range)
DGPS	Differential GPS
Dia	Diaphone (fog signal)
discont	Discontinued
Dn(s)	Dolphin(s)
DR	Dead Reckoning
DSC	Digital Selective Calling
DST	Daylight Saving Time
DW	Deep Water (route)
DYC	Dutch Yacht Chart(s)
DZ	Danger Zone (buoy)
E	East
ECM	East cardinal mark (buoy/beacon)
ED	Existence doubtful, European Datum
EEA	European Economic Area
El	Electrical repairs
Ⓔ	Electronic repairs
Elev	Elevation
Ent	Entrance, entry, enter
EP, △	Estimated position
ETA	Estimated Time of Arrival
ETD	Estimated Time of Departure
F	Fixed light
f	Fine (eg sand)
F&A	Fore and aft (berth/mooring)
Fcst	Forecast
FFL	Fixed and Flashing light
Fl	Flashing light
FM	Frequency Modulation
Foc	Free of charge
Fog Det lt	Fog Detector light
Freq, Fx	Frequency
FS	Flagstaff, Flagpole
ft	Foot, feet
Ft	Fort
FV	Fishing vessel
FW,	Fresh water supply
G	Gravel, Green
Gas	Calor Gas
Gaz	Camping Gaz
GC	Great Circle
GDOP	Geometrical Dilution of Precision (GPS)
GHA	Greenwich Hour Angle
GLA	General Lighthouse Authority
GMDSS	Global Maritime Distress & Safety System
grt	Gross Registered Tonnage
Gy	Grey
H, h, Hrs	Hour(s)
H–, H+	Minutes before/after the whole hour
H24	Continuous
HAT	Highest Astronomical Tide
HF	High Frequency
HFP	High Focal Plane (buoy)
HIE	Highlands & Islands Enterprise
HJ	Day service only, sunrise to sunset
HM	Harbour Master
HMRC	HM Revenue & Customs
HMSO	Her Majesty's Stationery Office
HN	Night service only, sunset to sunrise
HO	Office hours, Hydrographic Office
(hor)	Horizontally disposed (lights)
hPa	Hectopascal (= 1millibar)
HT	High Tension (overhead electricity line)
HW	High Water
HX	No fixed hours
IALA	International Association of Lighthouse Authorities
iaw	In accordance with
ICAO	International Civil Aviation Organisation
IDM	Isolated Danger Mark (buoy/beacon)
IHO	International Hydrographic Organisation
IMO	International Maritime Organisation
INMARSAT	International Maritime Satellite Organisation
intens	Intensified (light sector)
IPTS	International Port Traffic Signals
IQ	Interrupted quick flashing light
IRPCS	International Regulations for the Prevention of Collisions at Sea
Is, I	Island, Islet
ISAF	International Sailing Federation
Iso	Isophase light
ITU	International Telecommunications Union
ITZ	Inshore Traffic Zone (TSS)
IUQ	Interrupted ultra quick flashing light
IVQ	Interrupted very quick flashing light
kn	knot(s)
Kos	Kosangas
kW	Kilowatts
L	Lake, Loch, Lough, Landing place
Lat	Latitude
LAT	Lowest Astronomical Tide
Lanby,	Large automatic navigational buoy
LB,	Lifeboat, inshore lifeboat
Ldg	Leading (light)
LF	Low frequency
L Fl	Long flash
LH	Left hand
L/L	Latitude/Longitude
LNG	Liquefied Natural Gas
LNTM	Local Notice To Mariners
LOA	Length overall
Long	Longitude
LPG	Liquefied Petroleum Gas
LT	Local time
Lt(s), ☆ ☆	Light(s)
	Light float, minor
Lt V,	Light vessel; Lt float, major; Lanby
M	Moorings, nautical (sea) mile(s), Mud
m	Metre(s)
Mag	Magnetic, magnitude (of Star)
mb	Millibar (= 1 hectopascal, hPa)
MCA	Maritime and Coastguard Agency
ME	Marine engineering repairs
Météo	Météorologie (weather)
MHWN	Mean High Water Neaps
MHWS	Mean High Water Springs
MHz	Megahertz
ML	Mean Level (tidal)

MLWN	Mean Low Water Neaps
MLWS	Mean Low Water Springs
MMSI	Maritime Mobile Service Identity
Mo	Morse
Mon	Monument, Monday
MRCC	Maritime Rescue Co-ordination Centre
MSI	Maritime Safety Information
N	North
Navi	Navicarte (French charts)
NB	Nota Bene, Notice Board
NCI, ©	National Coastwatch Institution
NCM	North Cardinal Mark (buoy/beacon)
NGS	Naval Gunfire Support (buoy)
NM	Notice(s) to Mariners
nps	Neap tides
NP	Naval Publication (plus number)
NT	National Trust (land/property)
Obscd	Obscured
Obstn	Obstruction
Oc	Occulting light
ODAS	Ocean Data Acquisition System (buoy)
Or	Orange
OT	Other times
OWF	Offshore wind farm
P	Petrol (supply by hose), Pebbles
(P)	Preliminary (NM)
PA	Position approximate
Pax	Passenger(s)
PC	Portuguese chart
PD	Position doubtful
PHM	Port-hand Mark (buoy/beacon)
PLA	Port of London Authority
PO, ✉	Post Office
prom	Prominent
PSSA	Particularly Sensitive Sea Area
Pt(e), Pta	Point(e), Punta
	Pump-out facility
Q	Quick flashing light
QHM	Queen's Harbour Master
R	Red, Restaurant ✕, River, Rock
Racon	Radar transponder beacon
Ramark	Radar beacon
RCD	Recreational Craft Directive
RG	Emergency RDF station
RH	Right hand
Rk, Rky	Rock, Rocky
RMG	Reeds Marina Guide
RNLI	Royal National Lifeboat Institution
ROI	Republic of Ireland
R/T	Radiotelephony
Ru	Ruins
RYA	Royal Yachting Association
S	South, Sand
S, St, Ste	Saint(s)
SAMU	Service d'Aide Médicale Urgente (ambulance)
SAR	Search and Rescue
SC	Sailing Club, Spanish chart
SCM	South Cardinal Mark (buoy/beacon)

SD	Sailing Directions, Semi-diameter (of sun)
SD	Sounding of doubtful depth
sf	Stiff
Sh	Shells, Shoal
SHM	Simplified Harmonic Method (tides),
SHM	Starboard-hand Mark (buoy/beacon)
SHOM	French Hydrographic Office/Chart
Si	Silt
SIGNI	Signalisation de la Navigation Intérieure
SM	Sailmaker
	Shipwright (esp wooden hulls)
SMS	Short Message Service (mobile texting)
SNSM	Société Nationale de Sauvetage en Mer
so	Soft (eg mud)
SOG	Speed over the Ground
SOLAS	Safety of Life at Sea (IMO Convention)
sp	Spring tides
SPM	Special Mark (buoy/beacon)
SR	Sunrise
SRR	Search and Rescue Region
SS	Sunset, Signal Station
SSB	Single Sideband (Radio)
Stbd	Starboard
subm	Submerged
SWM	Safe Water Mark (buoy/beacon)
(T), (Temp)	Temporary
tbc	To be confirmed
tbn	To be notified
TD	Temporarily discontinued (fog signal)
TE	Temporarily extinguished (light)
tfn	Till further notice
Tr, twr	Tower
T/R	Traffic Report (tells the CG your route etc)
TSS	Traffic Separation Scheme
≠	In transit with, ie ldg marks/lts
u/mkd	Unmarked (feature/hazard)
UQ	Ultra Quick flashing light
UT	Universal Time (= approx GMT)
Var	Variation (magnetic)
Vel	Velocity
(vert)	Vertically disposed (lights)
Vi	Violet
VLCC	Very large crude carrier (Oil tanker)
VNF	Voie Navigable de France (canals)
VQ	Very Quick flashing light
VTS	Vessel Traffic Service
W	West, White
WCM	West Cardinal Mark (buoy/beacon)
	Wind turbine
wef	With effect from
WGS	World Geodetic System (GPS datum)
WIP	Work in progress
Wk	Wreck
WPT, ⊕	Waypoint
Wx	Weather
WZ	Code for UK coastal navigation warning
Y	Yellow, Amber, Orange
YC	Yacht Club

0.3 PASSAGE PLANNING FORM

DATE .... FROM ....ETD .... VIA .... TO .... ETA ....

TIMES OF SUNRISE .... SUNSET .... MOON RISE .... MOONSET .... WATCH SYSTEM ☐

CHARTS ☐ DOCUMENTS ☐ CUSTOMS ☐ PAY DUES ☐ CG (T/R) ☐ FUEL ☐ WATER ☐ FOOD ☐

WEATHER FORECAST ....

DEPARTURE PORT VHF .... HM ☎ ....

BRIDGE TIMES ....

LOCK/GATE TIMES...

BAR CROSSING TIMES ....

DEPARTURE WINDOW ....

DEPARTURE PROCEDURE ....

....

....

VTS DETAILS ....

....

....

STANDARD PORT, TIDES (SP/NP, HW/LW TIMES & HEIGHTS)

....

....

....

DEPARTURE PORT TIDES (HW/LW TIMES & HEIGHTS)...........

....

....

....

TIDAL STREAMS ON DEPARTURE ....

....

....

EN ROUTE

TIDAL STREAM ANALYSIS ....

....

....

....

....

TIDAL GATES (TIMES) ....

....

TIDE RACES ....

....

TRAFFIC SEPARATION SCHEMES..

....

PROHIBITED AREAS/DANGERS ....

PRINCIPAL LIGHTS/MARKS ....

....

....

LEG DETAILS

FROM	TO	WPT	TRK°M	DIST	TIME	REMARKS

DESTINATION PORT VHF .... HM ☎ ....

ARRIVAL PROCEDURE ....

....

BAR CROSSING TIMES ....

LOCK/GATE/SILL TIMES ....

BRIDGE TIMES ....

ACCESS WINDOW ....

ALTERNATE PORT VHF .... HM ☎ ....

ARRIVAL PROCEDURE ....

....

BAR CROSSING TIMES ....

LOCK/GATE/SILL TIMES ....

BRIDGE TIMES ....

ACCESS WINDOW ....

0.4 PASSAGE PLANNING

Before you start to navigate you need to plan: where you are going, how to get there and what factors may influence the plan. To most people this is commonsense; it is also the law. Guidance is given to small craft skippers in the MCA's *Pleasure Craft Information Pack* at www.mcga.gov.uk/c4mca/mcga-safety_information.htm.

SOLAS V Regulation 34 requires that all passages outside sheltered waters should be pre-planned. At the least, the following should be considered:

- **Limitations of the vessel.** Seaworthiness; suitably equipped and provisioned (food, water, fuel).
- **Limitations of the crew.** Experience, ability and stamina.
- **Navigational dangers**. Awareness and avoidance; use of up-to-date charts and publications.
- **Tides.** Times and heights; best use of tidal streams.
- **Weather.** Suitability for passage; forecast updates.
- **Contingency plan.** Deteriorating weather; gear failure; accident or injury.
- **GPS.** Equipment failure; ability to navigate 'manually'.
- **Information ashore.** Shore contact; CG66 - Voluntary Identification Scheme.

Although the passage plan need not be recorded on paper, in the event of legal action a written plan is clear proof that planning has been done. It can also be referred to during the passage. A suggested passage planning form is on the previous page. When completed this would constitute a reasonable passage plan. The blank form may be photocopied and modified to suit individual needs.

Before completing the form:

- Decide the aim; it is not always obvious.
- Gather the facts; time consuming but essential.
- Assess all available information.
- Formulate the plan; think of all contingencies.

0.5 HORIZONTAL DATUMS

GPS uses the World Geodetic System 84 datum (WGS84). With the exception of much of the coast of Ireland and the west coast of Scotland, Admiralty charts of UK waters have now been converted to WGS84. All harbour chartlets in this Almanac are referenced to WGS84.

GPS fixes can be plotted directly onto charts which are referenced to WGS84 but not onto charts which are still referenced to another datum. Before plotting WGS84 coordinates read from the GPS receiver, they must be converted to the datum of the chart in use. The datum used is always printed on the chart, normally under 'SATELLITE-DERIVED POSITIONS' which gives the Lat/Long corrections (which can amount to several hundred metres) to be applied.

Most receivers contain many datums. The navigator has two options:

- Set the receiver to WGS84. Before plotting positions, manually apply the corrections given on the chart. This option is advised by UKHO.
- Set the receiver to the datum of the chart in use. The datum corrections will automatically be applied by the receiver's software. This method is convenient but not the most accurate due to the random nature of the differences and software limitations.

0.6 COMMUNICATIONS

Radio Telephony (R/T)

VHF gives a range about 30-40M depending on the aerial heights of both the shore station and the yacht.

Give your position in Lat/Long or as the yacht's bearing and distance **from** a charted object, eg 'My position 225° Start Point 4M' means you are 4M SW of the Start Point. Use the 360° True bearing notation and the 24 hour clock (0000 to 2359), specifying UT, LT, etc.

VHF sets may be Simplex, ie transmit and receive on the same frequency, so that only one person can talk at a time; Semi-Duplex, ie transmit and receive on different frequencies; or Duplex, ie simultaneous semi-duplex, so that conversation is normal.

Marine VHF frequencies are in the band 156·00 –174·00 MHz. Frequencies are known by their international channel number (Ch), as shown below.

Channels are grouped according to three main purposes, but some can be used for more than one purpose.

- ***Public correspondence:*** (via Coast Radio Stations). Ch 26, 27, 25, 24, 23, 28, 04, 01, 03, 02, 07, 05, 84, 87, 86, 83, 85, 88, 61, 64, 65, 62, 66, 63, 60, 82, 78, 81. All channels can be used for duplex.

- ***Inter-ship:*** Ch **06**, **08**, 10, 13, 09, **72**, 73, 69, **77**, 15, 17. These are all simplex channels. It is as well to remember the **recommended** channels so that, if called on Ch 16, you can nominate an inter-ship working channel without delay.

- ***Port Operations:***
Simplex: Ch 12, 14, 11, 13, 09, 68, 71, 74, 69, 73, 17, 15.
Duplex: Ch 20, 22, 18, 19, 21, 05, 07, 02, 03, 01, 04, 78, 82, 79, 81, 80, 60, 63, 66, 62, 65, 64, 61, 84.

The following channels have one specific purpose:

Ch 0 (156·00 MHz): SAR ops, not available to yachts.

Ch 10 (156·50 MHz), **23** (161·750 MHz), **84** (161·825 MHz) and **86** (161·925 MHz): MSI broadcasts. The optimum channel number is stated on Ch 16 in the announcement prior to the broadcast itself.

Ch 13 (156·650 MHz): Inter-ship communications relating to safety of navigation; a possible channel for calling a merchant ship if no contact on Ch 16.

Ch 16 (156·80 MHz): Distress, Safety and calling. Ch 16, in parallel with DSC Ch 70, will be monitored by ships, CG rescue centres (and, in some areas, any remaining Coast radio stations) for Distress and Safety until further notice.

Yachts should monitor Ch 16. After an initial call, stations concerned **must** switch to a working channel, except for Distress and Safety matters.

Ch 67 (156·375 MHz): Small craft safety channel used by all UK CG centres, accessed via Ch 16.

Ch 70 (156·525 MHz): Digital Selective Calling for Distress and Safety purposes under GMDSS.

Ch 80 (157·025 MHz): Primary working channel between yachts and UK marinas.

Ch M (157·85 MHz): Secondary working channel, formerly known as Ch 37, but no longer.

Ch M2 (161·425 MHz): for race control, with Ch M as standby. YCs may apply to use Ch M2.

0.7 DISTRESS CALLS

Distress signal - MAYDAY

Distress only applies to a situation where a vessel or person is in ***grave and imminent danger and requires immediate assistance***. A MAYDAY call should usually be sent on VHF Ch 16 or MF 2182 kHz, but any frequency may be used if help would thus be obtained more quickly.

Distress, Urgency and Safety messages from vessels at sea are free of charge. A Distress call has priority over all other transmissions. If heard, cease all transmissions that may interfere with the Distress call or messages, and listen on the frequency concerned.

Brief your crew so they are all able to send a Distress message. The MAYDAY message format (below) should be displayed near the radio. Before making the call:

- Switch on radio (check main battery switch is ON)
- Select HIGH power (25 watts)
- Select VHF Ch 16 (or 2182 kHz for MF)
- Press and hold down the transmit button, and say slowly and distinctly:

- **MAYDAY MAYDAY MAYDAY**
- **THIS IS** ....
  (name of boat, spoken three times)
- **MAYDAY** ....
  (name of boat spoken once)
- **MY POSITION IS** ....
  (latitude and longitude, true bearing and distance *from* a known point, or general location)
- **Nature of distress** ....
  (sinking, on fire etc)
- **Help required** ....
  (immediate assistance)
- **Number of persons on board** ....
- **Any other important, helpful information** ....
  (you are taking to the liferaft; distress rockets are being fired etc)
- **OVER**

On completion of the Distress message, release the transmit button and listen. The boat's position is of vital importance and should be repeated if time allows.

Vessels with GMDSS equipment should make a MAYDAY call on Ch 16 *after* sending a DSC Distress alert on VHF Ch 70 or MF 2187·5 kHz.

0.7.1 MAYDAY acknowledgement

In coastal waters an immediate acknowledgement should be expected, as follows:

MAYDAY ....
(name of station sending the Distress message, spoken three times)

THIS IS ....
(name of station acknowledging, spoken three times)

RECEIVED MAYDAY

If an acknowledgement is not received, check the set and repeat the Distress call.

If you hear a Distress message, write down the details and, if you can help, acknowledge accordingly - but only after giving an opportunity for the nearest Coastguard station or some larger vessel to do so.

0.7.2 MAYDAY relay

If you hear a Distress message from a vessel, and it is not acknowledged, you should pass on the message as follows:

MAYDAY RELAY ....
(spoken three times)

THIS IS ....
(name of vessel re-transmitting the Distress message, spoken three times), followed by the intercepted message.

0.7.3 Control of MAYDAY traffic

A MAYDAY call imposes general radio silence until the vessel concerned or some other authority (eg the nearest Coastguard) cancels the Distress. If necessary the station controlling Distress traffic may impose radio silence as follows:

SEELONCE MAYDAY, followed by its name or other identification, on the Distress frequency.

If some other station nearby believes it necessary to do likewise, it may transmit:

SEELONCE DISTRESS, followed by its name or other identification.

0.7.4 Relaxing radio silence

When complete radio silence is no longer necessary, the controlling station may relax radio silence as follows, indicating that restricted working may be resumed:

MAYDAY

ALL STATIONS, ALL STATIONS, ALL STATIONS

THIS IS ....
(name or callsign)

The time ....

The name of the vessel in distress ....

PRUDONCE

Normal working on the Distress frequency may then be resumed, having listened carefully before transmitting. Subsequent calls from the casualty should be prefixed by the Urgency signal (0.8).

If Distress working continues on other frequencies these will be identified. For example, PRUDONCE on 2182 kHz, but SEELONCE on VHF Ch 16.

0.7.5 Cancelling radio silence

When the problem is resolved, the Distress call must be cancelled by the co-ordinating station using the prowords SEELONCE FEENEE as follows:

MAYDAY

ALL STATIONS, ALL STATIONS, ALL STATIONS

THIS IS ....
(name or callsign)

The time ....

The name of the vessel in distress ....

SEELONCE FEENEE

0.8 URGENCY AND SAFETY CALLS

Urgency signal - PAN PAN

The radio Urgency prefix, consisting of the words PAN PAN spoken three times, indicates that a vessel, or station, has ***a very urgent message concerning the safety of a ship or person***. It may be used when urgent medical advice is needed.

This is an example of an Urgency call:

PAN PAN, PAN PAN, PAN PAN

ALL STATIONS, ALL STATIONS, ALL STATIONS

THIS IS YACHT SEABIRD, SEABIRD, SEABIRD

Two nine zero degrees Needles lighthouse two miles

Dismasted and propeller fouled

Drifting east north east towards Shingles Bank

Require urgent tow

OVER

PAN PAN messages take priority over all traffic except Distress, and are sent on Ch 16 or 2182 kHz. They should be cancelled when the urgency is over.

If the message is long (eg a medical call) or communications traffic is heavy, it may be passed on a working frequency after an initial call on Ch 16 or 2182 kHz. At the end of the initial call you should indicate that you are switching to a working frequency.

If you hear an Urgency call react in the same way as for a Distress call.

0.8.1 Safety signal - SÉCURITÉ

The word SÉCURITÉ (pronounced SAY-CURE-E-TAY) spoken three times, indicates that the station is about to transmit an important navigational or meteorological warning. Such messages usually originate from a CG Centre or a Coast Radio Station, and are transmitted on a working channel after an announcement on the distress/calling channel (Ch 16 or 2182 kHz).

Safety messages are usually addressed to 'All stations', and are often transmitted at the end of the first available silence period. An example of a Sécurité message is:

SÉCURITÉ, SÉCURITÉ, SÉCURITÉ ....

THIS IS ....
(CG Centre or Coast Radio Station callsign, spoken three times)

ALL STATIONS ....
(spoken three times) followed by instructions to change channel, then the message.

0.9 GMDSS

The Global Maritime Distress and Safety System (GMDSS) is a sophisticated, but complex, semi-automatic, third-generation communications system. Although not compulsory for yachts, its potential for saving life, particularly when far offshore and out of VHF range, is so great that every yachtsman should consider it. Equipment costs continue to fall. Training courses, leading to the award of the Short Range Certificate (SRC) of Competence, are widely available.

0.9.1 Purpose

GMDSS enables a coordinated SAR operation to be mounted rapidly and reliably anywhere at sea. To this end, terrestrial and satellite communications and navigation equipment is used to alert SAR authorities ashore and ships in the vicinity to a Distress incident or Urgency situation. GMDSS also promulgates MSI (Maritime Safety Information).

0.9.2 Sea areas

For the purposes of GMDSS, the world's sea areas are divided into 4 categories (A1-4), defined mainly by the range of radio communications. These are:

A1 An area within R/T coverage of at least one VHF Coastguard or Coast radio station in which continuous VHF alerting is available via DSC. Range: 20–50M from the CG/CRS.

A2 An area, excluding sea area A1, within R/T coverage of at least one MF CG/CRS in which continuous DSC alerting is available. Range: approx 50–250M from the CG/CRS.

A3 An area between 70°N and 70°S, excluding sea areas A1 and A2, within coverage of HF or an Inmarsat satellite in which continuous alerting is available.

A4 An area outside sea areas A1, A2 and A3, ie the polar regions, within coverage of HF.

In each category certain types of radio equipment must be carried. In A1 areas VHF DSC; A2 areas MF or HF DSC; A3 areas SatCom; A4 MF/HF.

0.9.3 Digital Selective Calling

DSC is a vital component of GMDSS. It is so called because information is sent by a burst of digital code; selective because it can be addressed to a specific DSC-equipped vessel or to a selected group of vessels.

In GMDSS every vessel and shore station has a 9-digit number, or MMSI (Maritime Mobile Service Identity), which is in effect an automatic, electronic callsign.

DSC is used to transmit Distress alerts from ships, and to receive Distress acknowledgements from ships or shore stations. DSC is also used to send Urgency and Safety alerts; to relay Distress alerts; and for routine calling and answering. A thorough working knowledge is needed. A typical VHF/DSC Distress alert might be sent as follows:

- Briefly press the (red, guarded) Distress button. The set automatically switches to Ch 70 (DSC Distress channel). Press again for 5 seconds to transmit a basic Distress alert with position and time. The radio then reverts to Ch l6.
- If time permits, select the nature of the distress from the menu, eg Collision, then press the Distress button for 5 seconds to send a full Distress alert.

A CG/CRS should automatically send an acknowledgement on Ch 70 before replying on Ch 16. Ships in range should reply directly on Ch 16. When a DSC Distress acknowledgement has been received, or after about 15 seconds, the vessel in distress should transmit a MAYDAY message by voice on Ch 16, including its MMSI.

Fig 0(4) Distress and life saving signals

(1) Signals to be used by Ships, Aircraft or Persons in Distress

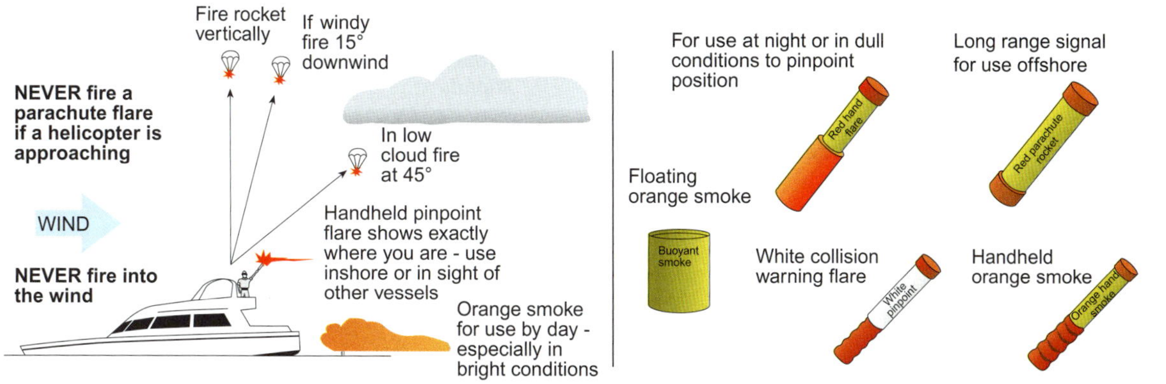

(2) Replies from life-saving stations etc. to distress signals made by ships or persons

Orange smoke signal

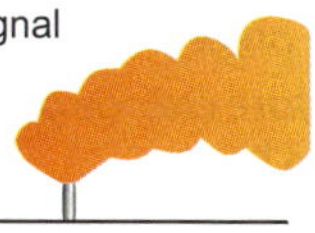

White star rocket - three single signals fired at intervals of about one minute

Meaning
'You are seen - assistance will be given as soon as possible'

(3) Surface to Air Signals

Message	International Code of Signals			ICAO Visual Signals
'I require assistance'	'V'		(• • • —)	V
'I require medical assistance'	'W'		(• — —)	X
'No' or 'negative'	'N'		(— •)	N
'Yes' or 'affirmative'	'C'		(— • — •)	Y
'Proceed in this direction'				↑

(4) Air to Surface replies

'Message understood'

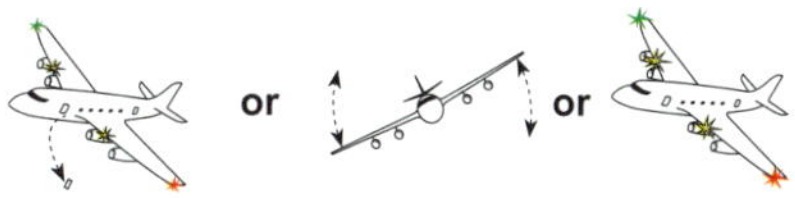

Drop a message **or** Rocking wings **or** Flash landing or navigation lights twice **or 'T'** (—) **or 'R'** (• — •) Morse code signal by light

'Message not understood - repeat'

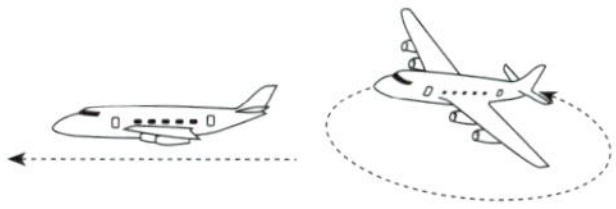

Straight and level flight — Circling — **or 'RPT'** (• — — • • — — — • — —) Morse code signal by light

(5) Air to Surface Direction Signals

Sequence of 3 manœuvres meaning proceed in this direction

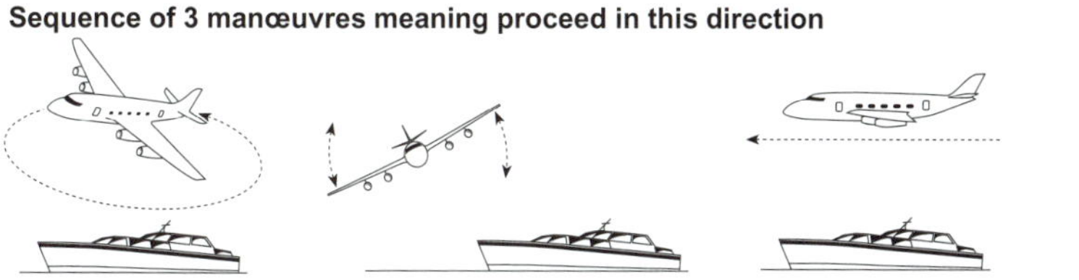

(1) Circle Vessel at least once

(2) Cross low ahead of vessel, rocking wings

(3) Overfly vessel and head in required direction

Your assistance is no longer required

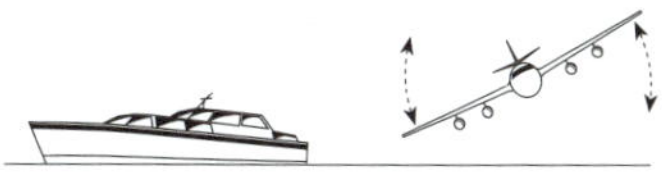

Cross low astern of vessel rocking wings

Note: as an alternative to rocking wings, the aircraft engine pitch or volume may be varied

(6) Surface to Air replies

'Message understood - I will comply'

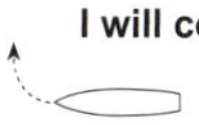

Change course or direction

or

'T' (—) Morse Code signal by light

or

Code and answering pennant 'Close up'

'I am unable to comply'

'N' (— •) Morse Code signal by light

or

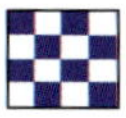

International flag 'N'

0.10 WEATHER BROADCASTS IN THE UK

BBC Radio 4 Shipping forecast

BBC Radio 4 broadcasts shipping forecasts at:

0048 LT[1]	LW, MW, FM
0520 LT[1]	LW, MW, FM
1201 LT	LW only
1754 LT	LW, FM (Sat/Sun)

[1] Includes weather reports from coastal stations

Frequencies

LW		198 kHz
MW	**London and N Ireland:**	720 kHz
	Redruth:	756 kHz
	Plymouth & Enniskillen:	774 kHz
	Carlisle:	1485 kHz
FM	**England:**	92·4–94·6 MHz
	Scotland:	91·3–96·1 MHz 103·5–104·9 MHz
	Wales:	92·8–96·1 MHz & 103·5–104·9 MHz
	N Ireland	93·2–96·0 MHz 103·5–104·6 MHz

Contents of the Shipping forecast

The forecast contains:

A summary of gale warnings in force at time of issue; a general synopsis of weather systems and their expected development over the next 24 hours; and a forecast of wind direction/force, weather and visibility in each sea area for the next 24 hours.

Gale warnings are also broadcast at the earliest juncture in Radio 4 programmes after receipt, as well as after the next news bulletin. Sea area Trafalgar is only included in the 0048 forecast.

Strong Wind Warnings are issued by the Met Office whenever winds of Force 6 or more are expected over coastal waters up to 5M offshore.

Shipping forecasts cover large sea areas, and rarely include the detailed variations that may occur near land. The Inshore waters forecast (see 0.10.1) can be more helpful to mariners on coastal passages.

Weather reports from coastal stations follow the 0048 and 0520 forecasts. They include wind direction and force, present weather, visibility, and sea-level pressure and tendency, if available. The stations are shown below in 0.10.1 and in Fig 0(2).

0.10.1 BBC Radio 4 Inshore waters forecast

A forecast for inshore waters (up to 12M offshore) around the UK and N Ireland, valid until 1800, is broadcast after the 0048 and 0520 coastal station reports.

It includes a general synopsis, forecasts of wind direction and force, visibility and weather for stretches of inshore waters, extending from Land's End to Cape Wrath. Areas are defined by well-known places such as St David's Hd, Great Ormes Hd, Mull of Galloway and Ardnamurchan Pt.

Reports of actual weather at the stations below are only broadcast after the 0048 inshore waters forecast: *Scilly**, Milford Haven, Aberporth, Valley, Liverpool (Crosby), *Ronaldsway*, Larne, Machrihanish*, Greenock and *Stornoway*. These stations are shown in Fig 0(2). Asterisk* denotes an automatic station. Stations in italics also feature in the 0048 and 0520 shipping forecasts.

0.10.2 Terms used in weather bulletins

Speed of movement of pressure systems	
Slowly	< 15 knots
Steadily	15–25 knots
Rather quickly	25–35 knots
Rapidly	35–45 knots
Very rapidly	> 45 knots
Visibility	
Good	> 5 miles
Moderate	2–5 miles
Poor	1000 metres–2 miles
Fog	Less than 1000 metres
Timing of gale warnings	
Imminent:	Within 6 hrs from time of issue
Soon:	6–12 hrs from time of issue
Later:	>12 hrs from time of issue

Barometric pressure changes (tendency)

Rising or falling slowly: Pressure change of 0·1 to 1·5 hPa/mb in the preceding 3 hours.

Rising or falling: Pressure change of 1·6 to 3·5 hPa/mb in the preceding 3 hours.

Rising or falling quickly: Pressure change of 3·6 to 6 hPa/mb in the preceding 3 hours.

Rising or falling very rapidly: Pressure change of more than 6 hPa/mb in the preceding 3 hours.

Now rising (or falling): Pressure has been falling (rising) or steady in the preceding 3 hours, but at the observation time was definitely rising (falling).

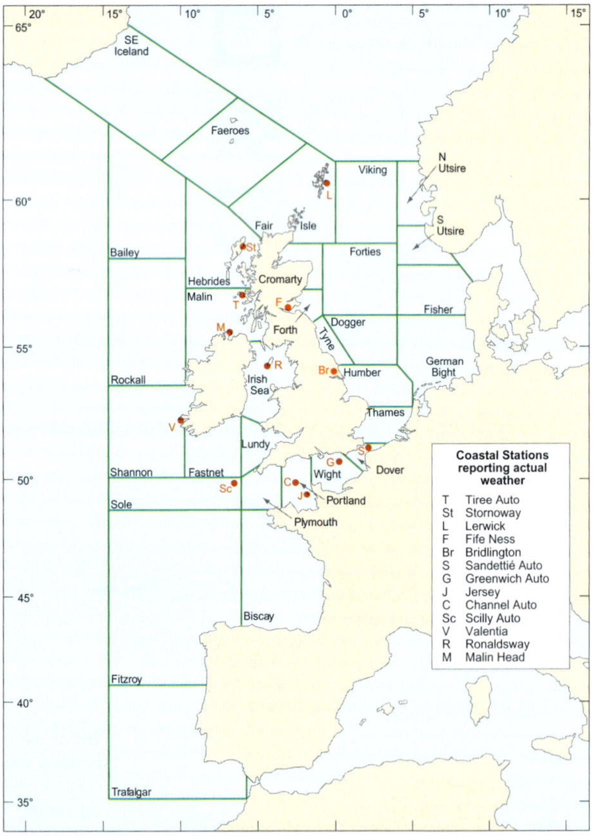

Fig 0(2) UK – Forecast areas

0.11 NAVTEX

Navtex is the prime method of disseminating MSI, with coverage to 270 miles around the UK. A dedicated receiver is used. Radio telephony complements the service with HM Coastguard providing VHF and MF coverage to 30M and 150M respectively. The user selects which stations and message types are recorded for automatic display or printing.

518 kHz and 490 kHz are used. On 518 kHz, messages are in English (occasionally in the national language as well), with excellent coverage of Europe. Interference between stations is minimised by time sharing and by limiting transmission power; see Fig 6(4). Navtex information applies only to the geographic area for which each station is responsible.

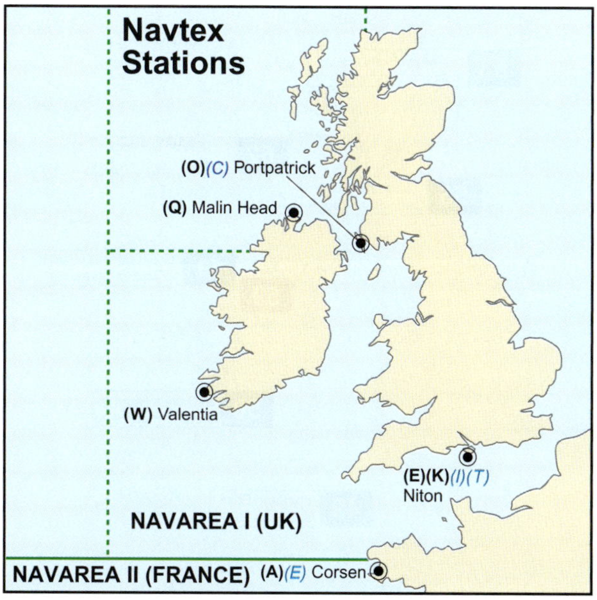

Fig 0(3) Navtex stations/areas – UK & Ireland

490 kHz (for clarity shown in red throughout this chapter) is used abroad for transmissions in the national language. In the UK it is used for inshore waters forecasts in English. 490 kHz and 518 kHz stations have different identification letters.

0.11.1 Message numbering

Each message is prefixed by a group of 4 characters:

The 1st is the ident letter of the station (eg **E** for Niton).

The 2nd is the message category, see 0.11.2.

The 3rd and 4th are message serial numbers, from 01 to 99 then re-starting at 01. Serial number 00 is an urgent message which is always printed.

Messages which are corrupt or have already been printed are rejected. Weather messages, and certain other message types, are dated and timed. All Navtex messages end with NNNN.

0.11.2 Message categories

A*	Navigational warnings
B*	Meteorological warnings
C	Ice reports
D*	SAR info and Piracy attack warnings
E	Weather forecasts
F	Pilot service
G	AIS
H	LORAN
I	Spare
J	SATNAV
K	Other electronic Navaids
L	Navwarnings additional to **A**
M-U	Spare
V-Y	Special services – as allocated
Z	No messages on hand

* These categories cannot be rejected by the receiver.

0.11.3 UK 518 kHz stations

Weather message times (UT) are in bold. Extended outlook times (2-3 days beyond the shipping forecast period) are in italics.

O –	**Portpatrick** Lundy clockwise to SE Iceland.	*0220*	**0620**	1020	1420	**1820**	2220
E –	**Niton** Thames clockwise to Fastnet, excluding Trafalgar.	*0040*	0440	**0840**	1240	1640	**2040**

0.11.4 UK 490 kHz stations

These provide forecasts for UK inshore waters (to 12M offshore), a national 3 day outlook for inshore waters and, at times in bold, reports of actual weather at the places listed below. To receive these reports select message category 'V' (0.11.2) on your Navtex receiver. Times (UT) of transmissions are listed in chronological order.

Actual Met data includes: Sea level pressure (mb), wind direction and speed (kn), weather, visibility (M), air and sea temperatures (°C), dewpoint temperature (°C) and mean wave height (m).

C –	**Portpatrick** Land's End to Shetland	**0020**	**0420**	0820	**1220**	**1620**	2020

North Rona, Stornoway, South Uist, Lusa (Skye bridge), Tiree, Macrihanish, Belfast, Malin Head, Belmullet, St Bees Head, Ronaldsway, Crosby (Liverpool), Valley, Aberporth, Roches Point, Valentia, St Mawgan.

0.11.5 Navtex coverage in Ireland and Brittany

Times of weather messages are shown in **bold**. Gale warnings are usually transmitted 4 hourly.

METAREA I (Co-ordinator – UK)		**Transmission times (UT)**					
Q –	**Malin Head,** Ireland	0240	**0640**	**1040**	1440	**1840**	**2240**
W –	**Valentia,** Ireland	0340	**0740**	**1140**	1540	**1940**	**2340**
METAREA II (Co-ordinator – France)							
A –	**Corsen,** France	**0000**	0400	0800	**1200**	1600	2000

0.12 WEATHER BY TELEPHONE

MARINECALL offer 3 types of recorded weather bulletins. Call from any landline or mobile network within the UK (inc Channel Islands). In case of difficulty contact Customer Services on 0871 200 3985.

0.12.1 Actual weather

Current weather, updated hourly, gives hourly summaries for next 6 hours at over 160 locations around the UK. Dial **09068 969** + the required area number, in green on Fig 0(4).

0.12.2 5-day forecasts for Inshore waters

For any of 15 UK inshore areas, call **09068 9696 + the Area number** shown in green on Fig 0(4). For an inshore waters forecast covering the whole UK for 3 to 5 days ahead, dial **09068 9696** 40.

Forecasts cover the waters out to 12M offshore for up to 5 days and include: General situation, strong wind or gale warnings in force, wind, weather, visibility, sea state, max air temp and mean sea temp.

The initial 2-day forecast is followed by a forecast for days 3 and 4 and outlook for day 5. Forecasts are updated at 0700 daily. The Channel Islands area (656) is additionally updated at 1300.

The local inshore forecast for Shetland is only available from Shetland CG on ☎ 01595 692976.

09068 calls cost 60p/min from a landline. Calls from mobiles may be subject to network charges.

Discounts are available via Marinecall Club, ie., 10 forecasts £20; 20 for £40; 30 for £55; and 40 for £70. Pay in advance and dial a Marinecall freefone number using a unique PIN.

0.12.3 Offshore planning forecasts

For 2- to 5-day planning forecasts for offshore areas, updated by 0700 daily, call **09068 9696** + the number for the offshore area, shown in red on Fig 0(4), ie:

57	English Channel	61	NW Scotland
59	Irish Sea	62	Northern North Sea
60	Biscay		

These forecasts contain elements similar to those in 0.12.2.

0.12.4 Contacting Marinecall

For further information contact: Marinecall Customer Services, iTouch (UK) Ltd, Avalon House, 57-63 Scrutton Street, London EC2A 4PF. ☎ 0871 200 3985; 📠 0870 600 4229. www.marinecall.co.uk marinecall@itouch.co.uk

0.13 WEATHER BY FAX

Fax forecasts contain the same data as those listed under 0.12, but are updated thrice daily. The Advance forecast (📠 09065 @ £1.50/min) contains slightly more detail than the Standard forecast (📠 09060 @ £1/min). The Fax numbers in Fig 0(9) are for the Advance service.

To obtain a forecast dial 📠 09065 22 23 plus the 2 digit area number in Fig 0(4), either green for inshore waters or red for offshore. After dialling press the Start or Receive button to start the transmission; be prepared for a slight delay as the data is downloaded to your fax machine.

0.13.1 Marinecall FaxDirect

Discounts to regular users of the Advance services include, for example over 3 months: 1 fax per week costs £38.76 inc VAT; 3 faxes per week £102.23; and 7 faxes per week £211.50. Monthly and annual subscriptions are available.

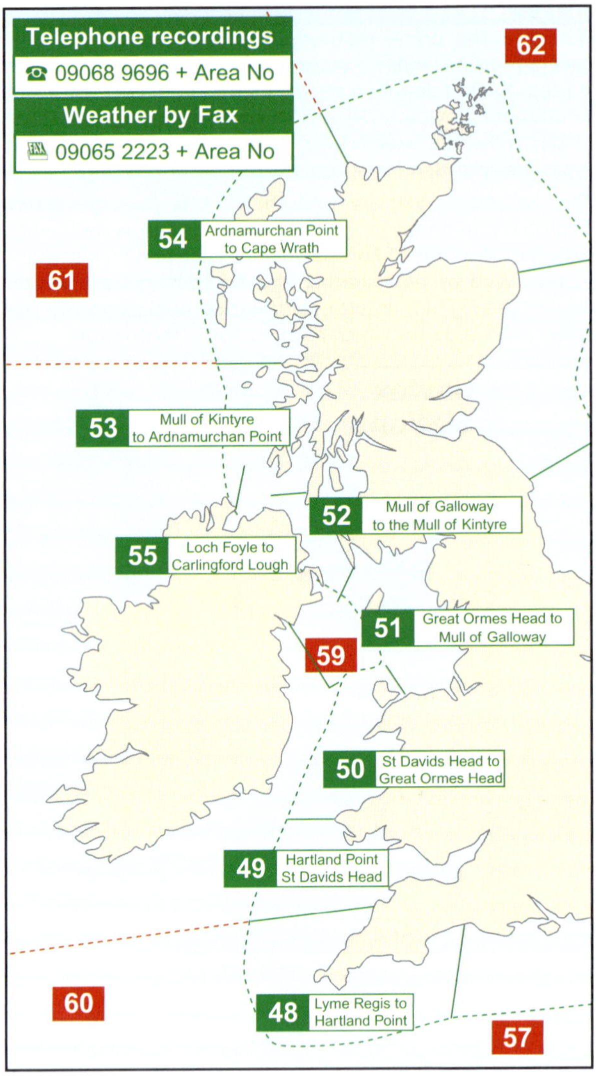

Fig 0(4) Inshore/Offshore forecast areas by Telephone and Fax

EUROPEAN WEATHER BY TELEPHONE & FAX

0.13.2 4-digit codes

Over 200 such codes give quicker, cheaper access to a required area or port by reducing the preamble. They apply to Tel and Fax messages for UK and Europe. Dial ☎ 09068 96 96 or 📠 09065 22 23, and the 2 digit area code, ie the offshore areas 57-62 shown in red in Fig. 0(4). Add the 4-digit code, eg 6360 for Oban, as soon as the call connects or you are prompted to do so. A full listing of 4-digit codes is in the Marinecall Handbook or visit www.marinecall.co.uk.

For European coastal locations dial ☎ 09068 96 96 or 📠 09065 22 23, and the 2 digit area code; add the 4-digit code as stated above. For example for Dublin 59 2928.

Other 2-digit Area codes include:

Northern Ireland Area code 59, + 4 digits, ie: Lough Foyle 6560; Portrush 6562; Ballycastle 6563; Larne 6564; Bangor 6565; Portavogie 6566; Strangford Lough 6567.

Republic of ireland Area code 59: Carlingford Lough 2924; Dublin 2928; Wicklow Head 2925; Mine Head 2926; Baltimore 2927, Malin Head 6561. W coast locations are not covered.

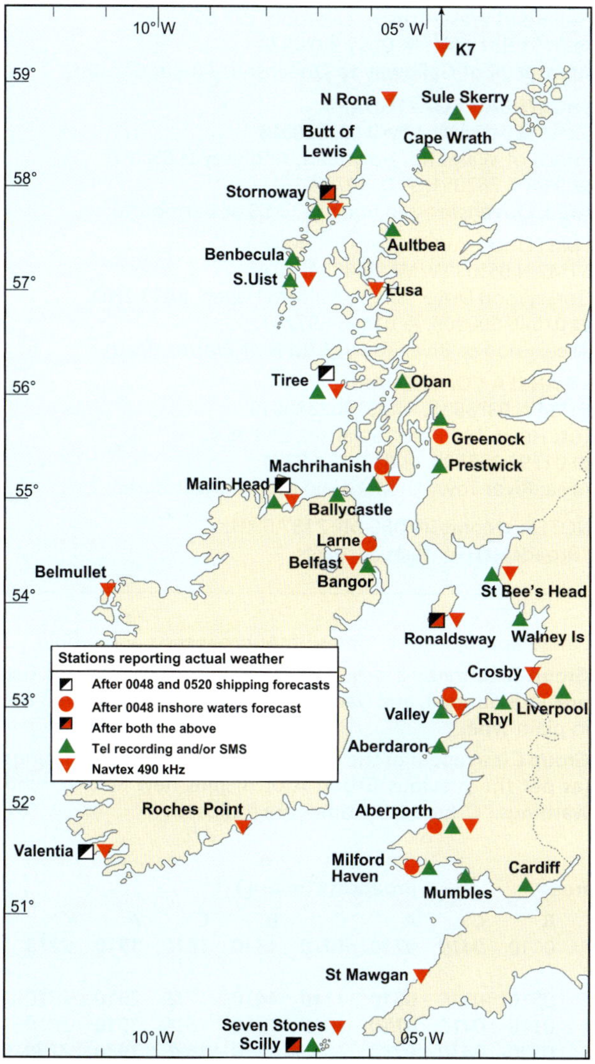

Fig 0(5) Stations reporting actual weather via BBC Radio 4, SMS or telephone recordings

0.14 WEATHER BY MOBILE PHONE

Mobile phones that have Internet access can receive the BBC Shipping Forecast as long as they have signal coverage. Texting the word WEATHER to 81010 results in a link to a BBC shipping forecast mobile site.

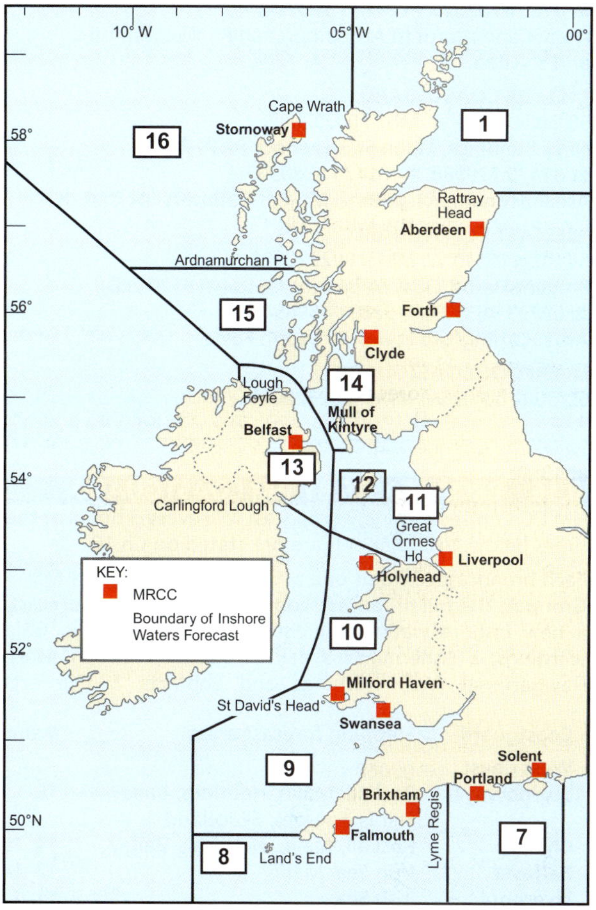

Fig 0(6) Boundaries of the areas used by the CG for forecasts covering inshore waters

0.15 HM COASTGUARD - CONTACT DETAILS OF CG CENTRES

†*STORNOWAY COASTGUARD
58°12'N 06°22'W. MMSI 002320024
Battery Point, Stornoway, Isle of Lewis H51 2RT.
☎ 01851 702013. 📠 01851 706796.
Area: Cape Wrath to Ardnamurchan Pt, Western Isles and St Kilda.

†*CLYDE COASTGUARD
55°58'N 04°48'W. MMSI 002320022
Navy Buildings, Eldon St, Greenock PA16 7QY.
☎ 01475 729988. 📠 01475 888095.
Area: Ardnamurchan Pt to Mull of Galloway inc islands.

***BELFAST COASTGUARD**
54°40'N 05°40'W. MMSI 002320021
Bregenz House, Quay St, Bangor, Co Down BT20 5ED.
☎ 02891 463933. 📠 02891 469854.
Area: Carlingford Lough to Lough Foyle.

LIVERPOOL COASTGUARD
53°30'N 03°03'W. MMSI 002320019
Hall Road West, Crosby, Liverpool L23 8SY.
☎ 0151 9313341. 📠 0151 9320978
Area: Mull of Galloway to Queensferry (near Chester).

†HOLYHEAD COASTGUARD
53°19'N 04°38'W. MMSI 002320018
Prince of Wales Rd, Holyhead, Anglesey LL65 1ET.
☎ 01407 762051. 📠 01407 761613
Area: Queensferry to Friog (1·6M S of Barmouth).

†MILFORD HAVEN COASTGUARD
51°42'N 05°03'W. MMSI 002320017
Gorsewood Drive, Hakin, Milford Haven, SA73 2HD.
☎ 01646 690909. 📠 01646 697287.
Area: Friog to River Towy (11M N of Worms Head).

SWANSEA COASTGUARD
51°34'N 03°58'W. MMSI 002320016
Tutt Head, Mumbles, Swansea SA3 4EX.
☎ 01792 366534. 📠 01792 368371.
Area: River Towy to Marsland Mouth (near Bude).

NOTES: †Monitors DSC MF 2187.5 kHz.
*Broadcasts Gunfacts/Subfacts.

0.16 BROADCASTS BY HM COASTGUARD

HM CG Centres routinely broadcast MSI every 3 hours at the times below. VHF channels are pre-stated on Ch 16.

Each broadcast contains one of 3 different Groups of MSI:
Group A, the full broadcast, contains the Shipping forecast, a new Inshore waters forecast and 24 hrs outlook, Gale warnings, a Fisherman's 3 day forecast* (1 Oct-31 Mar), Navigational (WZ) warnings and Subfacts & Gunfacts where appropriate ‡. Times of '**A**' broadcasts are in bold.

Group B contains a new Inshore waters forecast, plus the previous outlook, and Gale warnings. '**B**' broadcast times are in plain type.

Group C is a repeat of the Inshore forecast and Gale warnings (as per the previous Group A or B) plus new Strong wind warnings. '**C**' broadcast times are italicised.

Coastguard	Shipping forecast areas	Inshore areas	Broadcast times LT							
West Coast			B	*C*	**A**	*C*	B	*C*	**A**	*C*
Stornoway‡*	Rockall, Malin, Hebrides, Bailey, Fair Is, Faeroes, SE Iceland	16	0110	*0410*	**0710**	*1010*	1310	*1610*	**1910**	*2210*
Clyde‡	Rockall, Malin, Hebrides, Bailey	14, 15	0210	*0510*	**0810**	*1110*	1410	*1710*	**2010**	*2310*
Belfast‡	Irish Sea, Malin	12–14	0110	*0410*	**0710**	*1010*	1310	*1610*	**1910**	*2210*
Liverpool	Irish Sea	11, 12	0130	*0430*	**0730**	*1030*	1330	*1630*	**1930**	*2230*
Holyhead	Irish Sea	10, 11	0150	*0450*	**0750**	*1050*	1350	*1650*	**1950**	*2250*
Milford Haven	Lundy, Fastnet, Irish Sea	9, 10	0150	*0450*	**0750**	*1050*	1350	*1650*	**1950**	*2250*
Swansea	Lundy, Fastnet, Irish Sea	9, 10	0150	*0450*	**0750**	*1050*	1350	*1650*	**1950**	*2250*

TABLE 0(1) Remote Coastguard transmitters and their VHF working channels

Stornoway CG		
Butt of Lewis	*1743kHz*, 86	58°28'N 06°14'W
Portnaguran (Stornoway)	84	58°15'N 06°10'W
Forsnaval (W Lewis)	23	58°13'N 07°00'W
Melvaig (Loch Ewe)	23	57°51'N 05°47'W
Rodel (S Harris)	86	57°45'N 06°57'W
Clettreval (N Uist)	84	57°37'N 07°27'W
Skriag (Portree, Skye)	84	57°23'N 06°14'W
Drumfearn (SE Skye)	86	57°12'N 05°48'W
Barra	10	57°01'N 07°30'W
Arisaig (S of Mallaig)	23	56°55'N 05°50'W
Clyde CG		
Glengorm (N Mull)	23	56°38'N 06°08'W
Tiree	*1883kHz*, 86	56°30'N 06°59'W
Torosay (E Mull)	10	56°27'N 05°44'W
Clyde CG (Greenock)	84	55°58'N 04°48'W
South Knapdale (Loch Fyne)	23	55°55'N 05°28'W
Kilchiaran (W Islay)	84	55°46'N 06°27'W
Lawhill (Ardrossan)	86	55°42'N 04°50'W
Rhu Staffnish (Kintyre)	10	55°22'N 05°32'W
Belfast CG		
Navar (Lower Lough Erne)	86	54°28'N 07°54'W
Limvady (Lough Foyle)	84	55°06'N 06°53'W
West Torr (Fair Head)	86	55°12'N 06°06'W
Black Mountain (Belfast)	23	54°35'N 06°01'W
Orlock Point (Bangor)	84	54°40'N 05°35'W
Slievemartin (Rostrevor)	86	54°06'N 06°10'W
Liverpool CG		
Caldbeck (Carlisle)	23	54°46'N 03°05'W
Snaefell (Isle of Man)	86	54°16'N 04°28'W
Langthwaite (Lancaster)	84	54°02'N 02°46'W
Moel-y-Parc (N Wales)	23	53°13'N 03°18'W
Holyhead CG		
Great Ormes Head	86	53°20'N 03°51'W
South Stack (Holyhead)	23	53°19'N 04°41'W

Remote Coastguard transmitters and their VHF working channels contd

Milford Haven CG		
Blaenplwyf (Aberystwyth)	84	52°22'N 04°06'W
Dinas Hd (Fishguard)	86	52°00'N 04°54'W
St Ann's Head	84	51°41'N 05°11'W
Monkstone (Tenby)	84	51°42'N 04°41'W

Swansea CG		
Mumbles	86	51°34'N 03°59'W
St Hilary (Barry)	23	51°27'N 03°25'W
Severn Bridges	86	51°37'N 02°39'W
Combe Martin	23	51°10'N 04°03'W
Hartland Point	86	51°01'N 04°31'W

0.17 REPUBLIC OF IRELAND

Met Éireann (the Irish Met Office) is at Glasnevin Hill, Dublin 9, Ireland. ☎ 1 806 4250, 📠 1 806 4250, www.met.ie. General forecasting division (H24, charges may apply) ☎ 1 806 4255, 📠 1 806 4275.

0.17.1 Irish Coast Radio Stations

CRS and their VHF channels are listed below (anti-clockwise from Malin Head) and shown on Fig 0(7). Weather bulletins for 30M offshore and the Irish Sea are broadcast on VHF at 0103, 0403, 0703, 1003, 1303, 1603, 1903 and 2203UT after an announcement on Ch 16. Broadcasts are made 1 hour earlier when DST is in force. Bulletins include gale warnings, synopsis and a 24-hour forecast.

MALIN HEAD	23	**Bantry**	23
Glen Head	24	**Mizen Head**	04
Donegal Bay	02	**Cork**	26
Belmullet	83	**Mine Head**	83
Clifden	26	**Rosslare**	23
Galway	04	**Wicklow Head**	02
Shannon	28	**DUBLIN**	83
VALENTIA	24	**Carlingford**	04

Gale warnings are broadcast on these VHF channels on receipt and at 0033, 0633, 1233 and 1833 UT, after an announcement on Ch 16.

MF Valentia Radio broadcasts forecasts for sea areas Shannon and Fastnet on 1752 kHz at 0833 & 2033 UT, and on request.

Gale warnings are broadcast on 1752 kHz on receipt and at 0303, 0903, 1503 and 2103 (UT) after an announcement on 2182 kHz.

Malin Head does not broadcast weather information on 1677 kHz. At Dublin there is no MF transmitter.

0.17.2 Weather by telephone

The latest sea area forecasts and gale warnings are available H24 from Weatherdial as recorded messages. Dial ☎ 1550 123 plus the following suffixes:

850 Munster; 851 Leinster; 852 Connaught; 853 Ulster; 854 Dublin (plus winds in Dublin Bay and HW times); 855 Coastal waters and Irish Sea.

0.17.3 Weather by fax

Similar information, plus isobaric, swell and wave charts and any Small craft warnings (>F6 up to 10M offshore; Apr–Sep inc) is available H24 by Weatherdial Fax.

Dial 📠 1570 131 838 (from within ROI only). From the menu below select the required 4-digit product code (see code 0400 for full listing):

- 0015: Latest analysis chart
- 0016: Forecast valid for next 24 hrs
- 0017: Forecast valid for next 36 hrs
- 0018: Forecast valid for next 48 hrs
- 0021: Forecasts for coastal waters and Irish Sea
- 0031, 0032, 0033, 0034: Forecast (days 1–4) for sea and swell wave heights and periods
- 5-day forecasts (plain language, farming/national) 0001: Munster. 0002: Leinster. 0003: Connaught. 0004: Ulster. 0005: Dublin.

Sea Planners provide graphic forecasts for up to 5 days (updated at 0430 daily) of expected winds and waves at the following seven offshore positions:

0041: 53°N 05° 30'W.	0045: 54°N 11°W.
0042: 51°N 06°W.	0046: 55°N 10°W.
0043: 51°N 10°30'W.	0047: 56°N 08°W.
0044: 53°N 11°W.	

0.17.4 Radio Telefís Éireann (RTE) Radio 1

RTE Radio 1 broadcasts weather bulletins daily at 0602, 1255, 1657 & 2355LT (1hr earlier when DST is in force) on 567kHz (Tullamore), 729kHz (Cork) and FM (88·2–95·2MHz).

Bulletins contain a situation, forecast and coastal reports for Irish Sea and coastal waters. The forecast includes: wind, weather, vis, swell (if higher than 4m) and a 24 hrs outlook.

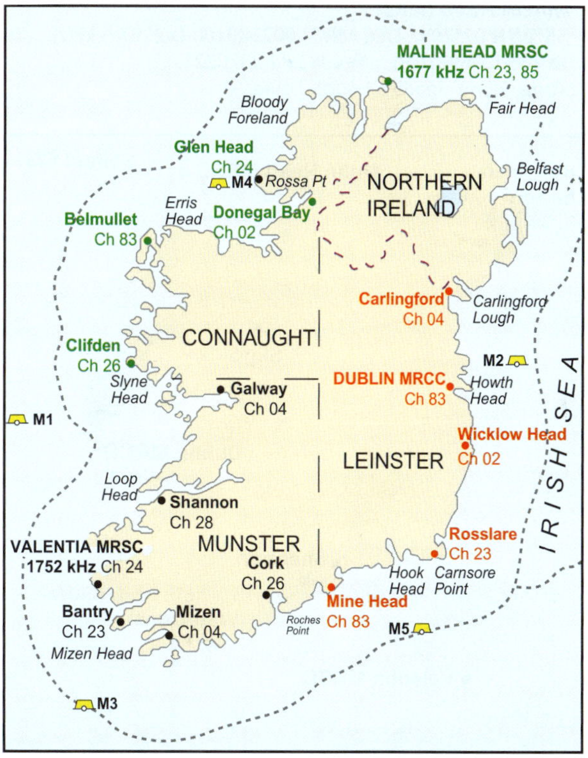

Fig 0(7) shows CRS, Met buoys M1–M5, PROVINCES and headlands named in forecasts

Gale warnings are included in hourly news bulletins on FM & MF.

Coastal reports include wind, weather, visibility, pressure, with pressure change over the last 3 hrs described as:

Steady	=	0–0·4 hPa change
Rising/falling slowly	=	0·5–1·9
Rising/falling	=	2·0–3·4
Rising/falling rapidly	=	3·5–5·9
Rising/falling very rapidly	=	> 6·0

0.18 REPUBLIC OF IRELAND (COASTGUARD)

The Irish CG co-ordinates SAR operations around the coast of Eire via Dublin MRCC, Malin Head and Valentia MRSCs and remote sites. It may liaise with the UK and France during any rescue operation within 100M of the Irish coast. It is part of the Dept of Marine, Leeson Lane, Dublin 2. ☎ (01) 6620922; 📠 (01) 6620795. The Irish EPIRB Registry is at the same address; ☎ (01) 6199280; 📠 (01) 6621571.

The MRCC/MRSCs are co-located with the Coast radio stations of the same name and manned by the same staff. All stations keep watch H24 on VHF Ch 16 and DSC Ch 70. If ashore dial 999 or 112 in an emergency and ask for Marine Rescue.

Details of the MRCC/MRSCs are as follows:

DUBLIN (MRCC)
53°20'N 06°15W. DSC MMSI 002500300 (+2187·5 kHz).
☎ +353 1 662 0922/3; 📠 +353 1 662 0795.
Area: Carlingford Lough to Youghal.

VALENTIA (MRSC)
51°56'N 10°21'W.DSC MMSI 002500200 (+2187·5 kHz).
☎ +353 669 476 109; 📠 +353 669 476 289.
Area: Youghal to Slyne Head.

MALIN HEAD (MRSC)
55°22'N 07°20W. DSC MMSI 002500100 (+2187·5 kHz).
☎ +353 74 9370103; 📠 +353 74 9370221.
Area: Slyne Head to Lough Foyle.

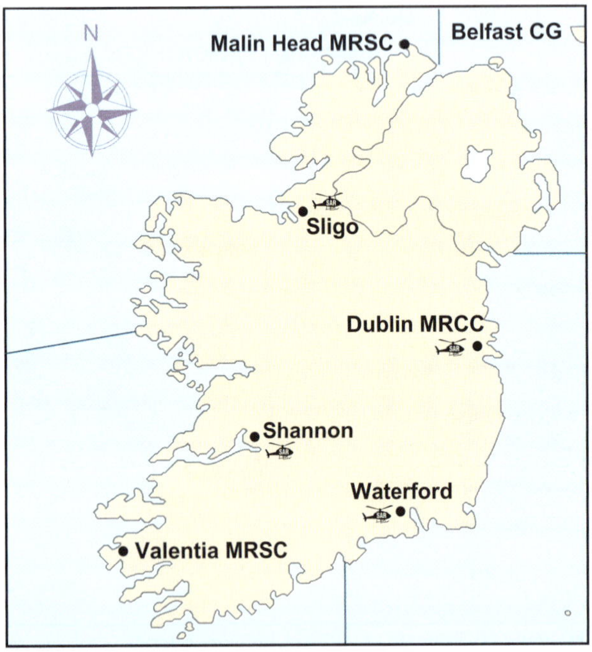

Fig 0(8) Irish CG centres and boundaries

0.18.1 SAR resources

The Irish coastguard provides some 50 units around the coast and is on call H24. The RNLI maintains four stations around the coast and operates 42 lifeboats. Additionally, six community-run inshore rescue boats are available.

Sikorsky S-61 helicopters, based at Dublin, Waterford, Shannon and Sligo, can respond within 15 to 45 minutes and operate to a radius of 200M. They are equipped with infrared search equipment and can uplift 30 survivors.

Military and civilian aircraft and vessels, together with the Garda and lighthouse service, can also be called upon.

Some stations provide specialist cliff climbing services. They are manned by volunteers, who are trained in first aid and equipped with inflatables, breeches buoys, cliff ladders etc. Their ☎ numbers (the Leader's residence) are given, where appropriate, under each port.

0.19 AUTOMATIC IDENTIFICATION SYSTEM (AIS)

Automatic Identification System (AIS) was originated to monitor SOLAS traffic in key areas (in the Minches, for example, to safeguard the marine environment), and in choke points (for example, the Dover Strait). It is also widely used to assist in collision avoidance by automatically and continuously identifying, tracking and displaying other vessels' movements.

Each ship's course and speed vector is shown by a tadpole-like symbol on an AIS screen or overlaid on radar, chart plotter or PC. This data may also appear in a text box as heading, COG & SOG, range, CPA (in some sets); Lat/Long, ship's name (derived from its MMSI), and her status - under power or sail, anchored, constrained by draught, restricted in her ability to manoeuvre, not under command, fishing etc. Range scales are usually 1, 2, 4, 8, 16 and 32M.

AIS must be fitted in passenger ships and all commercial vessels >300 GRT.

AIS is not mandatory for leisure craft, but it is worth considering. Accurate and continuous display of a target's COG and SOG removes any doubts when these parameters are derived solely from basic radar information. Receive-only equipment (basically a VHF dual frequency transceiver, aerial, GPS input and a mini-computer) is available for small craft. Note: AIS is not a radar despite what some advertisements may imply!

Caveats: Some ships do not switch on their AIS; some only display 3 lines of text, not a plot; in busy areas only the strongest signals may be shown; AIS may distract a bridge watchkeeper from his radar watch (yachts may therefore not be detected); unlike eyes and radar, AIS does not yet feature in IRPCS; GPS/electronic failures invalidate AIS.

Reference data

0.20 CALCULATING CLEARANCES BELOW OVERHEAD OBJECTS

A diagram often helps when calculating vertical clearance below bridges, power cables etc. Fig 0(9) shows the relationship to CD. The height of such objects as shown on the chart is usually measured above HAT, so the actual clearance will almost always be more. The height of HAT above CD is given at the foot of each page of the tide tables. Most Admiralty charts now show clearances above HAT, but check the **Heights** block below the chart title.

To calculate clearances, insert the dimensions into the following formula, carefully observing the conventions for brackets:

Masthead clearance = (Height of object above HAT + height of HAT above CD) minus (height of tide at the time + height of the masthead above waterline)

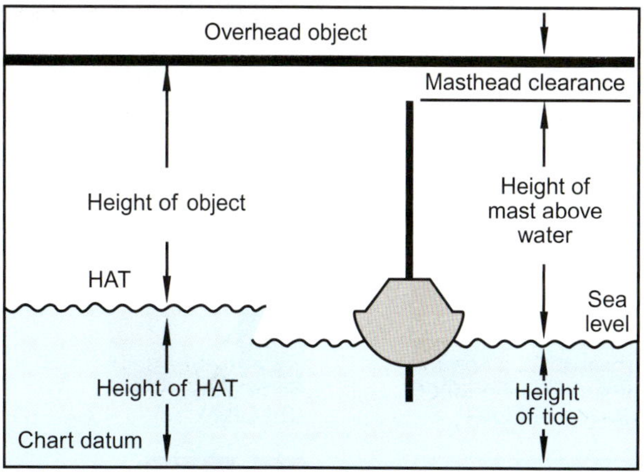

Fig 0(9) Calculating masthead clearance

0.21 IALA BUOYAGE

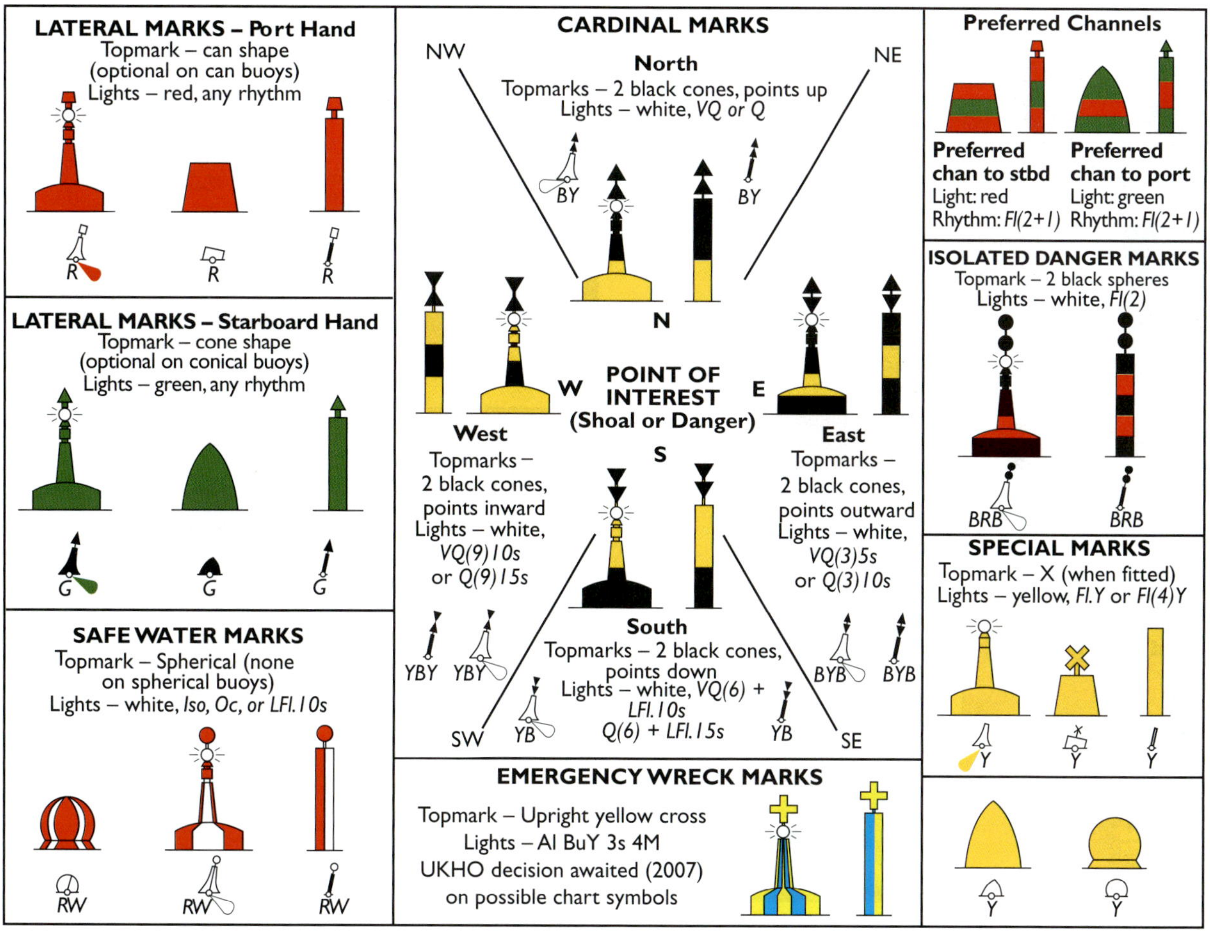

0.22 FLAGS AND ENSIGNS

UK WHITE ENSIGN

UK BLUE ENSIGN

UK RED ENSIGN

AUSTRALIA

BASQUE FLAG

BELGIUM

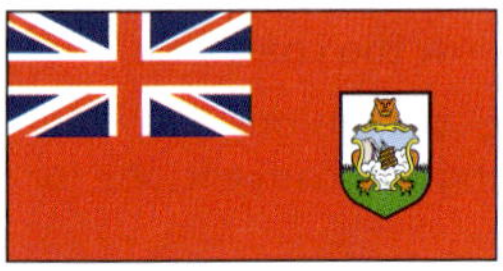
BERMUDA

CANADA

CYPRUS

DENMARK

EU

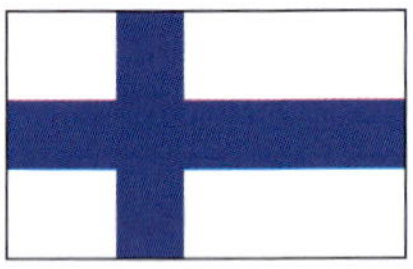
FINLAND

FRANCE

GERMANY

GREECE

GUERNSEY

IRELAND

ISRAEL

ITALY

LIBERIA

MALTA

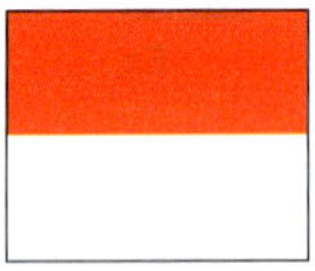
MONACO

MOROCCO

NETHERLANDS

NEW ZEALAND

NORWAY

PANAMA

POLAND

PORTUGAL

SOUTH AFRICA

SPAIN

SWEDEN

SWITZERLAND

TUNISIA

TURKEY

USA

0.23 LIGHTS AND SHAPES

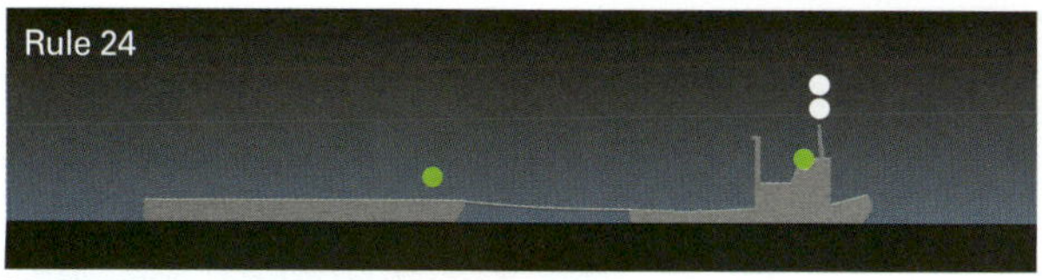

Vessels being towed and towing

Vessel towed shows sidelights (forward) and sternlight

Tug shows two masthead lights, sidelights, sternlight, yellow towing light

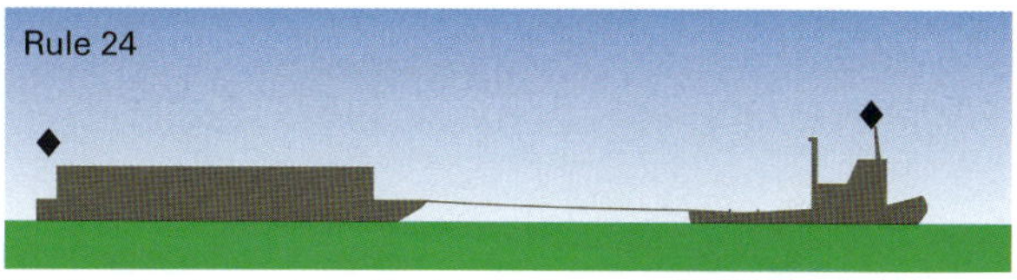

Towing by day — Length of tow more than 200m

Towing vessel and tow display diamond shapes. By night, the towing vessel shows three masthead lights instead of two as for shorter tows

---

Motor sailing

Cone point down, forward. At night the lights of a power-driven vessel underway

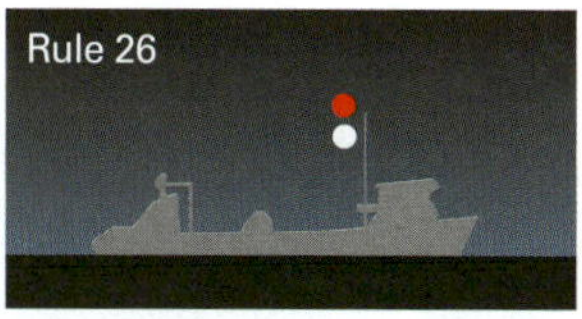

Vessel fishing

All-round red light over all-round white, plus sidelights and sternlight when making way

Fishing/Trawling

A shape consisting of two cones point to point in a vertical line one above the other

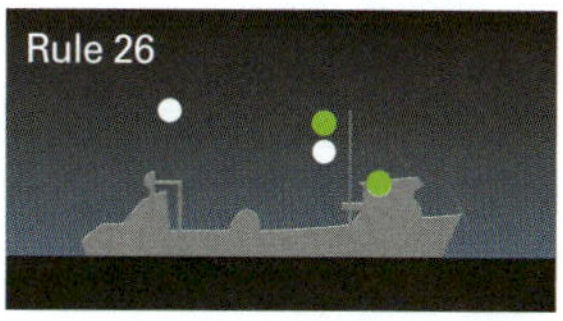

Vessel trawling

All-round green light over all-round white, plus sidelights and sternlight when making way

---

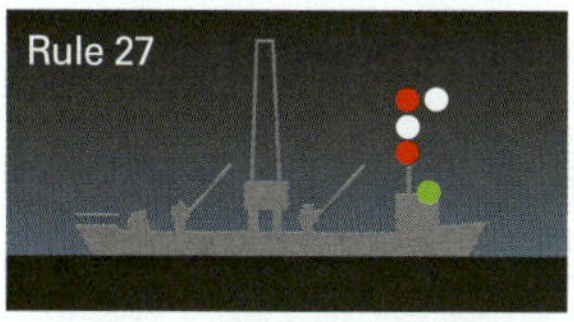

Vessel restricted in her ability to manoeuvre

All-round red, white, red lights vertically, plus normal steaming lights when making way

Three shapes in a vertical line: ball, diamond, ball

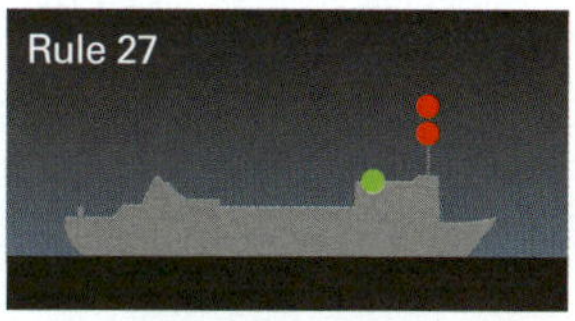

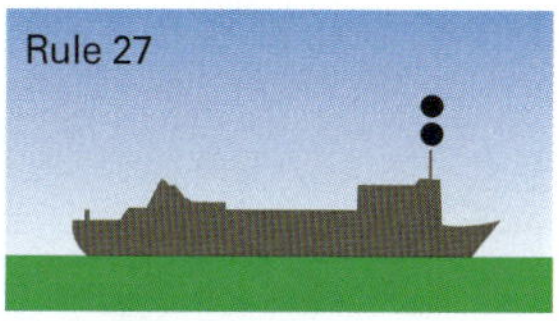

Not under command

Two all-round red lights, plus sidelights and sternlight when making way

Two balls vertically

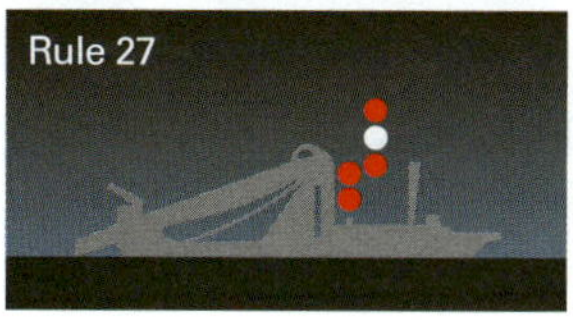

Dredger

All round red, white, red lights vertically, plus two all-round red lights (or two balls) on foul side, and two all-round green (or two diamonds) on clear side

Divers down

Letter 'A' International Code

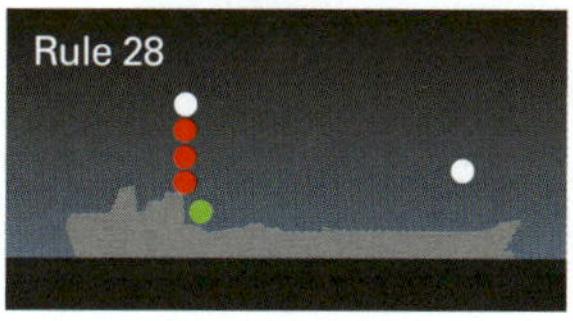

Constrained by draught

Three all-round red lights in a vertical line, plus normal steaming lights. By day — a cylinder

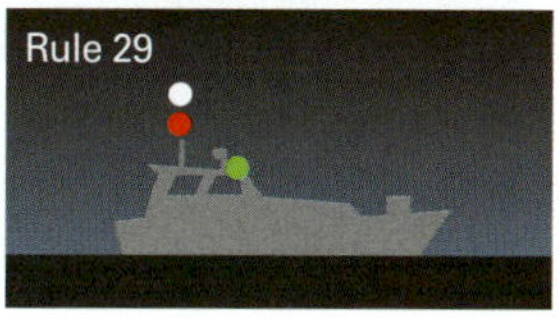

Pilot boat

All-round white light over all-round red, plus sidelights and sternlight when underway, or anchor light

---

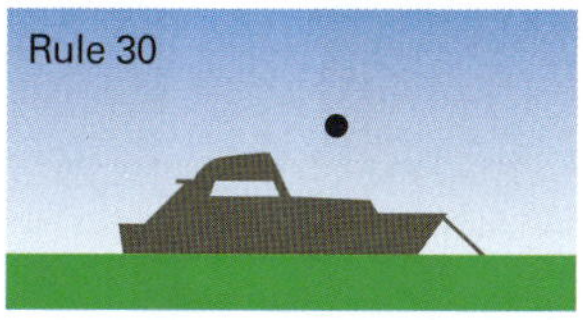

Vessel at anchor

All-round white light; if over 50m, a second light aft and lower

Ball forward

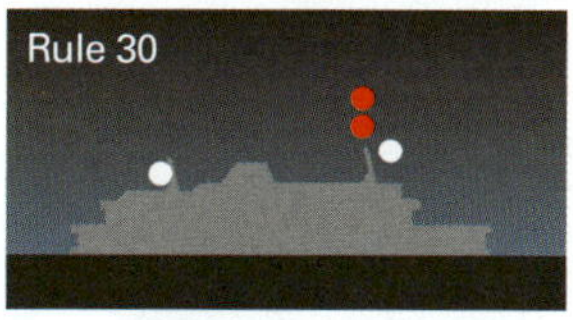

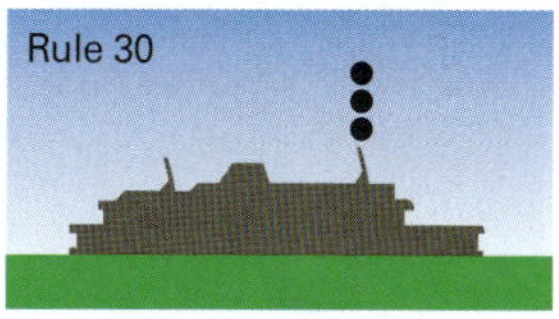

Vessel aground

Anchor light(s), plus two all-round red lights in a vertical line

Three balls in a vertical line

0.24 NAVIGATION LIGHTS

LIGHTS FOR TYPICAL YACHT WITH 3 OPTIONAL VARIANTS

C: If < 12m LOA: Masthead and sternlights may be combined into one all-round light.

Stern light

Two side lights

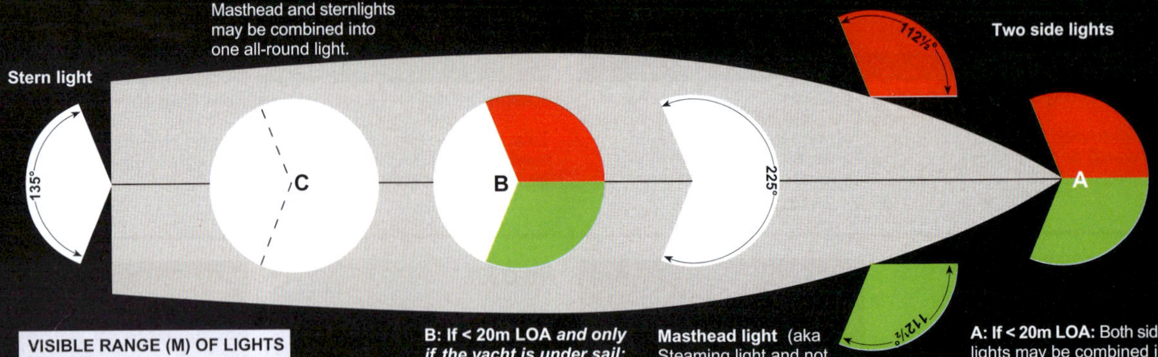

VISIBLE RANGE (M) OF LIGHTS (Rule 22)			
Light/LOA	**<12m**	**<50m**	**>50m**
All-round	2	2	3
Masthead	2	3*, 5	6
Side	**1**	**2**	**3**
Stern	2	2	3
		*<20m	

B: If < 20m LOA *and only if the yacht is under sail:* The side and sternlights may be combined in a single tricolour light atop the mast

Masthead light (aka Steaming light and not usually placed at the masthead) *Shown by vessels under power only*

A: If < 20m LOA: Both side lights may be combined in one centreline R/G light

PLAN VIEWS OF LIGHTS FOR SAILING VESSELS UNDERWAY AND UNDER SAIL ONLY

Note: If motor-sailing, the lights appropriate for a power-driven vessel must be shown, as below

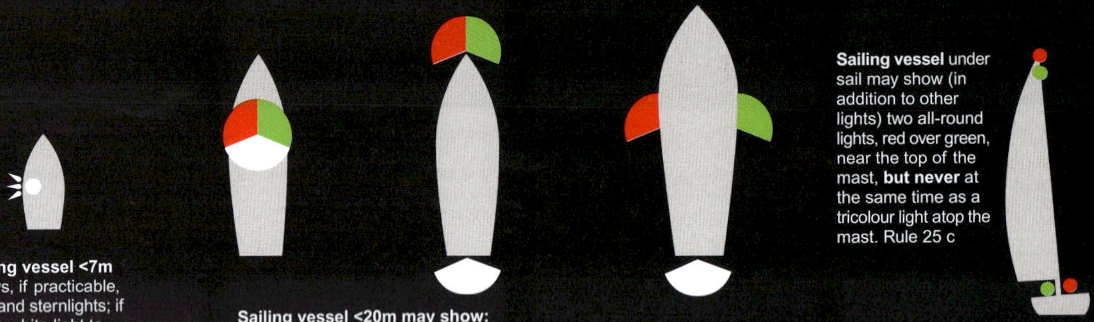

Sailing vessel <7m shows, if practicable, side and sternlights; if not, a white light to prevent collision. Rule 25 d i

Sailing vessel <20m may show:

Either tricolour light atop the mast. Rule 25 b

Or combined centreline side lights plus stern light. Rule 25 a

Sailing vessel >20m Separate sidelights and sternlight. Rule 25 a

Sailing vessel under sail may show (in addition to other lights) two all-round lights, red over green, near the top of the mast, **but never** at the same time as a tricolour light atop the mast. Rule 25 c

PLAN VIEWS OF LIGHTS FOR POWER-DRIVEN VESSELS UNDERWAY AND SAILING CRAFT UNDER POWER

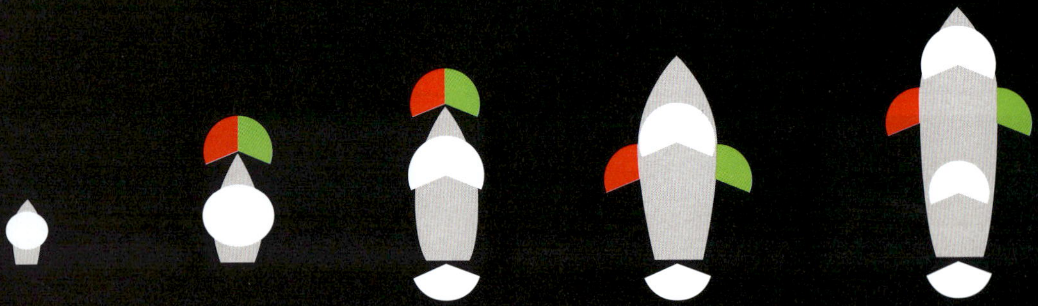

<7m and <7 knots (all-round light and, if practicable, side lights). Rule 23 d ii

<12m (combined masthead & sternlight). Rule 23 d i

<20m (sidelights combined in one centreline light). Rule 21 b

>20m showing masthead, stern and separate sidelights. Rule 21 a, b, c

>50m with two masthead lights, the aft one higher. Rule 23 a i & ii

Times are in UT - add 1 hour in non-shaded areas to convert to BST

0.25 SUNRISE/SET TIMES 2010

The table shows times of Sunrise (SR) and Sunset (SS) for every 4th day as the times of Sunrise and Sunset never change by more than 8 minutes (and often by only 1–3 minutes) between the given dates.

The table is based on Longitude 0°, so longitude corrections are required, ie add 4 minutes of time for every degree West of Greenwich; subtract if East.

LATITUDE 56°N

	JANUARY Rise	JANUARY Set	FEBRUARY Rise	FEBRUARY Set	MARCH Rise	MARCH Set	APRIL Rise	APRIL Set	MAY Rise	MAY Set	JUNE Rise	JUNE Set
1	08 31	15 36	07 55	16 33	06 52	17 34	05 31	18 38	04 17	19 39	03 22	20 34
4	08 30	15 40	07 49	16 39	06 44	17 40	05 23	18 44	04 10	19 45	03 19	20 38
7	08 29	15 44	07 43	16 46	06 37	17 47	05 15	18 50	04 03	19 51	03 17	20 42
10	08 26	15 49	07 37	16 53	06 29	17 53	05 08	18 56	03 57	19 57	03 15	20 44
13	08 24	15 54	07 30	16 59	06 21	17 59	05 00	19 02	03 51	20 03	03 14	20 47
16	08 20	16 00	07 23	17 06	06 13	18 05	04 52	19 09	03 46	20 08	03 13	20 49
19	08 16	16 06	07 16	17 12	06 05	18 11	04 45	19 15	03 40	20 14	03 13	20 50
22	08 12	16 12	07 09	17 19	05 57	18 18	04 38	19 21	03 36	20 19	03 13	20 51
25	08 07	16 18	07 02	17 25	05 50	18 24	04 30	19 27	03 31	20 24	03 14	20 51
28	08 02	16 24	06 54	17 32	05 42	18 30	04 23	19 33	03 27	20 29	03 16	20 50
31	07 57	16 31			05 34	18 36			03 23	20 33		

	JULY Rise	JULY Set	AUGUST Rise	AUGUST Set	SEPTEMBER Rise	SEPTEMBER Set	OCTOBER Rise	OCTOBER Set	NOVEMBER Rise	NOVEMBER Set	DECEMBER Rise	DECEMBER Set
1	03 18	20 49	04 04	20 08	05 04	18 55	06 03	17 36	07 07	16 20	08 07	15 31
4	03 21	20 47	04 09	20 02	05 10	18 47	06 09	17 28	07 13	16 13	08 11	15 29
7	03 24	20 45	04 15	19 55	05 16	18 39	06 15	17 20	07 19	16 07	08 16	15 27
10	03 28	20 42	04 21	19 49	05 21	18 31	06 21	17 12	07 26	16 01	08 20	15 26
13	03 32	20 39	04 27	19 42	05 27	18 23	06 27	17 05	07 32	15 56	08 23	15 25
16	03 36	20 35	04 33	19 35	05 33	18 15	06 33	16 57	07 38	15 51	08 26	15 25
19	03 41	20 31	04 38	19 28	05 39	18 07	06 39	16 50	07 44	15 46	08 28	15 26
22	03 46	20 26	04 44	19 20	05 45	18 00	06 45	16 43	07 50	15 41	08 30	15 27
25	03 51	20 21	04 50	19 13	05 51	17 52	06 52	16 36	07 56	15 37	08 31	15 29
28	03 56	20 16	04 56	19 05	05 57	17 44	06 58	16 29	08 01	15 34	08 32	15 31
31	04 02	20 10	05 02	18 57			07 04	16 22			08 31	15 35

0.26 MOONRISE/SET TIMES 2010

The table gives the times of Moonrise (MR) and Moonset (MS) for every 4th day; interpolation is necessary for other days. The aim is simply to indicate whether the night in question will be brightly moonlit, partially moonlit or pitch black – depending, of course, on cloud cover. The table is based on Longitude 0°. To correct for longitude, add 4 minutes of time for every degree West; subtract if East. ** Indicates that the phenomenon does not occur.

LATITUDE 56°N

	JANUARY Rise	JANUARY Set	FEBRUARY Rise	FEBRUARY Set	MARCH Rise	MARCH Set	APRIL Rise	APRIL Set	MAY Rise	MAY Set	JUNE Rise	JUNE Set
1	16 39	09 07	20 27	08 20	19 22	06 37	22 51	05 41	23 53	05 20	23 42	07 36
4	21 27	10 02	** **	08 56	23 56	07 18	01 15	07 30	01 02	08 39	00 05	11 18
7	00 24	10 35	03 37	10 06	02 31	08 46	03 01	10 56	01 48	12 22	00 35	15 00
10	04 34	11 31	06 09	12 53	04 37	11 55	03 42	14 38	02 17	16 04	01 25	19 02
13	07 34	13 53	07 05	16 37	05 24	15 38	04 10	18 23	03 00	20 05	03 52	21 57
16	08 44	17 34	07 33	20 18	05 52	19 21	04 57	22 24	04 59	23 22	08 19	23 03
19	09 14	21 16	08 04	** **	06 29	23 18	07 07	00 39	09 05	00 23	12 47	23 41
22	09 42	** **	09 20	02 50	08 08	01 47	11 18	02 18	13 32	01 08	17 05	00 12
25	10 43	03 51	12 56	05 27	12 03	03 54	15 49	03 01	17 56	01 48	20 25	01 54
28	13 57	06 59	17 47	06 25	16 45	04 43	20 20	03 43	21 42	03 12	21 48	05 18
31	18 53	08 07			21 23	05 22			23 25	06 20		

	JULY Rise	JULY Set	AUGUST Rise	AUGUST Set	SEPTEMBER Rise	SEPTEMBER Set	OCTOBER Rise	OCTOBER Set	NOVEMBER Rise	NOVEMBER Set	DECEMBER Rise	DECEMBER Set
1	22 23	09 02	21 14	11 40	21 04	14 25	22 18	14 47	00 25	14 11	02 34	13 00
4	22 53	12 41	22 24	15 31	** **	16 49	01 16	15 52	04 56	14 55	06 57	14 12
7	23 52	16 36	00 18	18 21	03 49	17 48	05 56	16 35	09 23	16 19	09 59	17 04
10	01 29	19 51	04 51	19 29	08 34	18 31	10 32	17 46	12 03	19 26	11 08	20 53
13	05 52	21 09	09 35	20 10	12 59	19 50	13 35	20 32	13 03	23 11	11 43	** **
16	10 30	21 49	14 00	21 13	15 38	22 44	14 44	** **	13 36	01 35	12 20	02 55
19	14 53	22 41	17 04	23 43	16 38	01 12	15 19	02 38	14 16	05 15	13 40	06 41
22	18 22	** **	18 17	02 08	17 11	04 50	15 54	06 17	15 48	08 59	16 58	09 20
25	19 54	03 04	18 52	05 49	17 47	08 30	17 07	10 03	19 18	11 20	21 25	10 26
28	20 32	06 48	19 23	09 27	19 05	12 14	20 06	12 46	23 39	12 18	00 20	11 08
31	21 02	10 25	20 25	13 14			** **	13 56			04 40	12 12

0.27 INTERNATIONAL CODE OF SIGNALS

Code flags, phonetic alphabet, Morse code, single-letter signals. IALA buoyage system 'A'. International Port Traffic Signals.

A – Alpha
I have a diver down; keep well clear at slow speed
• ▬

***B – Bravo**
I am taking in, or discharging, or carrying dangerous goods
▬ • • •

***C – Charlie**
Yes
▬ • ▬ •

***D – Delta**
Keep clear of me; I am manoeuvring with difficulty
▬ • •

***E – Echo**
I am altering course to starboard
•

F – Foxtrot
I am disabled; communicate with me
• • ▬ •

***G – Golf**
I require a pilot. When made by fishing vessels 'I am hauling in nets'
▬ ▬ •

***H – Hotel**
I have a pilot on board
• • • •

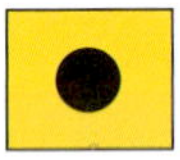
***I – India**
I am altering my course to port
• •

J – Juliett
I am on fire and have dangerous cargo aboard; keep well clear of me
• ▬ ▬ ▬

K – Kilo
I wish to communicate with you
▬ • ▬

L – Lima
You should stop your vessel instantly
• ▬ • •

***M – Mike**
My vessel is stopped and making no way through the water
▬ ▬

N – November
No
▬ •

O – Oscar
Man overboard
▬ ▬ ▬

P – Papa
Vessel about to put to sea. By fishing vessels 'My nets are caught fast'
• ▬ ▬ •

Q – Quebec
My vessel is 'healthy' and I request free pratique
▬ ▬ • ▬

R – Romeo
• ▬ •

***S – Sierra**
My engines are going astern
• • •

***T – Tango**
Keep clear of me; I am engaged in pair trawling
▬

U – Uniform
You are running into danger
• • ▬

V – Victor
I require assistance
• • • ▬

W – Whiskey
I require medical assistance
• ▬ ▬

X – X-ray
Stop carrying out your intentions and watch for my signals
▬ • • ▬

Y – Yankee
I am dragging my anchor
▬ • ▬ ▬

***Z – Zulu**
I require a tug. By fishing vessels 'I am shooting nets'
▬ ▬ • •

1 Wun
• ▬ ▬ ▬ ▬

2 Too
• • ▬ ▬ ▬

3 Tree
• • • ▬ ▬

4 Fow-er
• • • • ▬

5 Fife
• • • • •

6 Six
▬ • • • •

7 Sev-en
▬ ▬ • • •

8 Ait
▬ ▬ ▬ • •

9 Nin-er
▬ ▬ ▬ ▬ •

0 Zero
▬ ▬ ▬ ▬ ▬

Code and answering pennant

First Substitute

Second Substitute

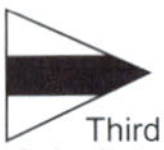
Third Substitute

INTERNATIONAL PORT TRAFFIC SIGNALS

No	Lights		Main message
1		Flashing	Serious emergency – all vessels to stop or divert according to instructions
2		Fixed or Slow Occulting	Vessels shall not proceed (*Note:* Some ports may use an exemption signal, as in 2a below)
3			Vessels may proceed. One-way traffic
4			Vessels may proceed. Two-way traffic
5			A vessel may proceed only when she has received specific orders to do so. (*Note:* Some ports may use an exemption signal, as in 5a below)
			Exemption signals and messages
2a		Fixed or Slow Occulting	Vessels shall not proceed, except that vessels which navigate outside the main channel need not comply with the main message
5a			A vessel may proceed when she has received specific orders to do so, except that vessels which navigate outside the main channel need not comply with the main message
			Auxiliary signals and messages
White and/or yellow lights, displayed with the main lights			Local meanings, as promulgated in local port orders

0.28 AREA INFORMATION

The 6 geographic Areas are arranged as follows:

A map of the area showing the positions of harbours, principal lights, emergency RDF stations, CG Centres with their boundaries, magnetic variation and a distance table.

Tidal stream chartlets showing hourly rates and set.

Lights, buoys and waypoints listing characteristics of selected lights, their daytime appearance, fog signals, Racons and position. Arcs of visibility and alignment of leading lights are true bearings as seen from seaward. Lights are white unless otherwise stated. Any colours are shown between the bearings of the relevant arcs.

Passage information is threaded between the harbours in each Area and briefly describes the coast, offlying dangers, tidal gates, tide races, selected anchorages, recommended routes and any local weather patterns.

Special notes giving data specific to that country or Area.

0.29 HARBOUR INFORMATION

Below the **harbour name**, the County or Unitary Council (or foreign equivalent) is given, followed by the lat/long of the harbour entrance for use as the final waypoint.

The **harbour ratings**, which are inevitably subjective, grade a port for ease of access, facilities and attractiveness as a place to visit, based on the following criteria:

Ease of access:

❁❁❁ *Can be entered in gales from most directions and at all states of tide, by day or night.*

❁❁ *Accessible in strong winds from most directions; possible tidal or pilotage constraints.*

❁ *Only accessible in calm, settled conditions by day with little or no swell; possible bar and difficult pilotage.*

Facilities available:

👍👍👍 *Good facilities for vessel and crew.*

👍👍 *Most domestic needs catered for, but limited boatyard facilities.*

👍 *Possibly some domestic facilities, but little else.*

Attractiveness:

✿✿✿ *An attractive place; well worth visiting.*

✿✿ *Average for this part of the coast.*

✿ *Holds no particular attraction.*

Chart numbers show Admiralty (AC), Imray and Stanford (Stan) charts, all smallest scale first, and Admiralty Leisure Folios (56XX). Some ACs are available as Leisure Editions (prefix: SC), printed on wet strength paper and with additional useful information on the back of each chart.

Tide tables and tidal curves are given for Standard Ports and the differences for Secondary Ports.

Harbour chartlets are based on AC or relevant foreign charts.

> They are not intended to be used for navigation, although great care has been taken to ensure that they accurately portray the harbour. The publisher and editors disclaim any responsibility for resultant accidents or damage if they are so used. The largest scale official chart, properly corrected, should always be used.

Drying areas and the 5m depth contour are coloured as follows: Dries   <5m   >5m

Due to their scale, chartlets do not always cover the whole area referred to in the text nor do they show every depth, mark, feature or the approach waypoint (⊕).

Shelter assesses how protected a harbour is from wind, sea, surge and swell. It warns of access difficulties and advises on safe berths and anchorages.

Navigation gives the lat/long of an approach waypoint with its bearing and distance to the harbour entrance or next significant feature; some waypoints may be off the harbour chartlet. Approach channels, buoyage, speed limits and hazards are also described.

Access times, if quoted, are based on a nominal 1·5m draft, plus a safety margin, for an average tide. Any significant swell may affect these times. Lock and bridge opening times are in local time.

Wrecks around the UK which are of archaeological or historic interest are protected by law. Sites are listed under the nearest harbour or in Passage Information. Unauthorised interference, including anchoring and diving on such sites, may lead to a substantial fine.

Lights and Marks describe, in more detail than is shown on the chartlets, any unusual characteristics of marks, their appearance by day and features not listed elsewhere.

IPTS (International Port Traffic Signals) are shown at 0.27.

R/T lists VHF channels related to the port, marina or VTS. Callsigns, if not obvious, are in *italics*.

Telephone gives any area code in brackets (which is not repeated for individual telephone numbers unless different or additional codes apply). International calls from/to the UK are described in Special Notes, as are national numbers for marine emergencies abroad including Ambulance, Fire, Police. In the EU 112 is the main emergency number; in the UK it is 999.

Facilities describe man-made features: pontoons, ♁s, quays, pile moorings, etc at harbours, YCs and marinas (see also the free **Reeds Marina Guide**), followed by commercial services. Most YCs welcome bona fide crews who belong to a recognised club and arrive by sea. Town facilities are listed, with rail, ferry and air links.

The overnight cost of a visitor's alongside berth (AB), *at the previous year's rates*, is the average charge per metre LOA (unless otherwise stated) during high season, usually June to Sept. It includes harbour dues, if applicable, and VAT. The cost of pile moorings, ♁s or ⚓s, where these are the norm, may also be given. Shore electricity is usually free abroad, but extra in the UK.

The number of Ⓥ berths is a marina's estimate of how many visitors may be accommodated at any one time. It is always advisable to call the marina beforehand.

Slipways. Access and launch/recovery fees per day, eg Slip HW±2 (£6.00), are given where possible for craft <6.5m LOA.

0.30 FACILITIES FOR DISABLED PEOPLE

RYA Sailability operates under the RYA's auspices to open up sailing and its related benefits to disabled sailors. Facilities include car parking, wheelchair ramps to buildings and pontoons and purpose-built toilets and showers. Facilities for those with sight or hearing disabilities are becoming more widely available. Standard symbols (♿ ◉ ⓓ ⓓ) are used.

0.31 ENVIRONMENTAL GUIDANCE

- Comply with regulations for navigation and conduct within Marine Nature Reserves, Particularly Sensitive Sea Areas (PSSA) and National Water Parks.
- In principle never ditch rubbish at sea, keep it on board and dispose of it in harbour refuse bins.
- Readily degradable foodstuffs may be ditched at sea when >3M offshore (>12M in the English Channel).
- Foodstuffs and other materials which are not readily degradable should never be ditched at sea.
- Sewage. If you do not have a holding tank, only use the onboard heads when well offshore. A holding tank should be fitted as soon as possible as many countries require them. Pump-out facilities (⚓) are shown in the text. Do not pump out holding tanks until more than 3M offshore.
- Do not discharge foul water into a marina, anchorage or moorings area and minimise on washing-up water.
- Deposit used engine oil and oily waste ashore at a recognised facility. Do not allow an automatic bilge pump to discharge oily bilge water overboard.
- Dispose of toxic waste, (eg some antifoulings, cleaning chemicals, old batteries) at an approved disposal facility.
- Row ashore whenever possible – to minimise noise, wash and disturbance. Land at recognised places.
- Respect wild birds, plants, fish and marine animals. Avoid protected nesting sites and breeding colonies.
- Do not anchor or dry out on vulnerable seabed species, eg soft corals, eel grass.

0.32 DISTANCES (M) ACROSS THE IRISH SEA

Approximate distances in nautical miles are by the most direct route, avoiding dangers and allowing for TSS.

Ireland / Scotland England Wales	Port Ellen (Islay)	Campbeltown	Troon	Portpatrick	Mull of Galloway	Kirkcudbright	Maryport	Fleetwood	Pt of Ayre (IOM)	Port St Mary (IOM)	Liverpool	Holyhead	Pwllheli	Fishguard	Milford Haven	Swansea	Avonmouth	Ilfracombe	Padstow	Longships
Tory Island	75	107	132	119	134	170	185	215	156	171	238	207	260	279	307	360	406	355	372	399
Malin Head	45	76	101	88	103	139	154	184	125	140	207	176	229	248	276	329	375	324	341	368
Lough Foyle	38	61	86	73	88	124	139	169	110	125	192	161	214	233	261	314	360	309	326	353
Portrush	31	50	76	64	80	116	131	161	102	117	184	153	206	225	253	306	352	301	318	345
Carnlough	42	35	57	32	45	81	96	126	67	78	149	115	168	187	215	268	314	363	280	307
Larne	51	39	58	24	37	72	88	118	58	70	141	106	159	178	206	259	305	254	271	298
Carrickfergus	64	48	65	26	34	69	85	115	55	66	138	101	154	173	201	254	300	249	266	293
Bangor	63	48	64	22	30	65	81	111	51	62	134	97	150	169	197	250	296	245	262	289
Strangford L.	89	72	84	36	30	63	76	97	41	37	107	69	121	141	167	219	265	214	231	258
Carlingford L.	117	100	112	64	60	90	103	112	70	51	118	67	111	124	149	202	248	197	214	241
Dun Laoghaire	153	136	148	100	93	119	126	120	93	69	119	56	82	94	109	162	208	157	174	201
Wicklow	170	153	165	117	108	133	140	127	108	83	123	56	67	71	90	143	189	138	155	182
Arklow	182	165	177	129	120	144	149	133	117	93	131	64	71	65	79	132	179	128	144	167
Rosslare	215	202	208	161	154	179	180	164	152	125	156	90	83	55	58	109	157	110	119	137
Tuskar Rock	216	203	209	162	155	179	182	165	152	126	152	91	82	48	51	105	150	103	112	130
Dunmore East	250	237	243	196	189	213	216	199	186	160	189	127	116	79	76	130	177	124	127	136
Youghal	281	268	274	227	220	244	247	230	217	191	220	158	147	110	103	156	200	148	139	138
Crosshaven	300	287	293	246	239	263	266	249	236	210	239	177	166	131	118	170	216	163	151	144
Baltimore	346	333	339	292	285	309	312	295	282	256	285	223	212	172	160	209	254	198	178	161
Fastnet Rock	354	341	347	300	293	317	320	303	290	264	293	231	220	181	169	216	260	207	185	170

West Scotland

Cape Wrath to Solway Firth

AREA 1 – NORTH WEST SCOTLAND

AREA 2 – SOUTH WEST SCOTLAND

1.	Mull of Kintyre	232	203	189	175	159	133	143	121	105	120	89	87	98	72	78	62	57	54	51	**1**
2.	Crinan	187	157	158	129	112	95	95	74	63	97	42	30	54	25	45	14	9	6	**2**	
3.	Loch Craignish	188	158	159	131	118	95	96	76	64	98	44	31	55	26	46	17	14	**3**		
4.	Craobh Haven	184	155	155	117	114	93	92	70	60	93	40	27	50	21	43	5	**4**			
5.	Loch Melfort	184	154	155	117	114	92	93	69	61	92	40	27	45	18	45	**5**				
6.	Loch Lathaich	160	130	124	98	91	62	67	49	35	56	31	53	77	48	**6**					
7.	Oban	169	138	139	111	100	76	77	56	44	77	24	13	29	**7**						
8.	Fort William	198	161	162	134	121	99	98	75	63	96	43	34	**8**							
9.	Loch Aline	157	127	128	100	87	65	66	45	33	66	13	**9**								
10.	Tobermory	144	114	115	87	74	52	53	32	20	53	**10**									
11.	Castlebay (Barra)	133	105	92	69	97	43	76	59	46	**11**										
12.	Eigg	123	98	97	75	54	34	35	14	**12**											
13.	Mallaig	112	82	83	84	42	33	21	**13**												
14.	Kyle of Lochalsh	91	63	62	63	21	53	**14**													
15.	Loch Harport	110	82	65	45	66	**15**														
16.	Portree	83	57	53	42	**16**															
17.	East Loch Tarbert	75	56	33	**17**																
18.	Stornoway	53	45	**18**																	
19.	Ullapool	54	**19**																		
20.	*Cape Wrath*	**20**																			

DISTANCE TABLE

Approximate distances in nautical miles are by the most direct route, keeping East of Skye and Mull where appropriate, and avoiding dangers. Places in *italics* are in adjoining areas.

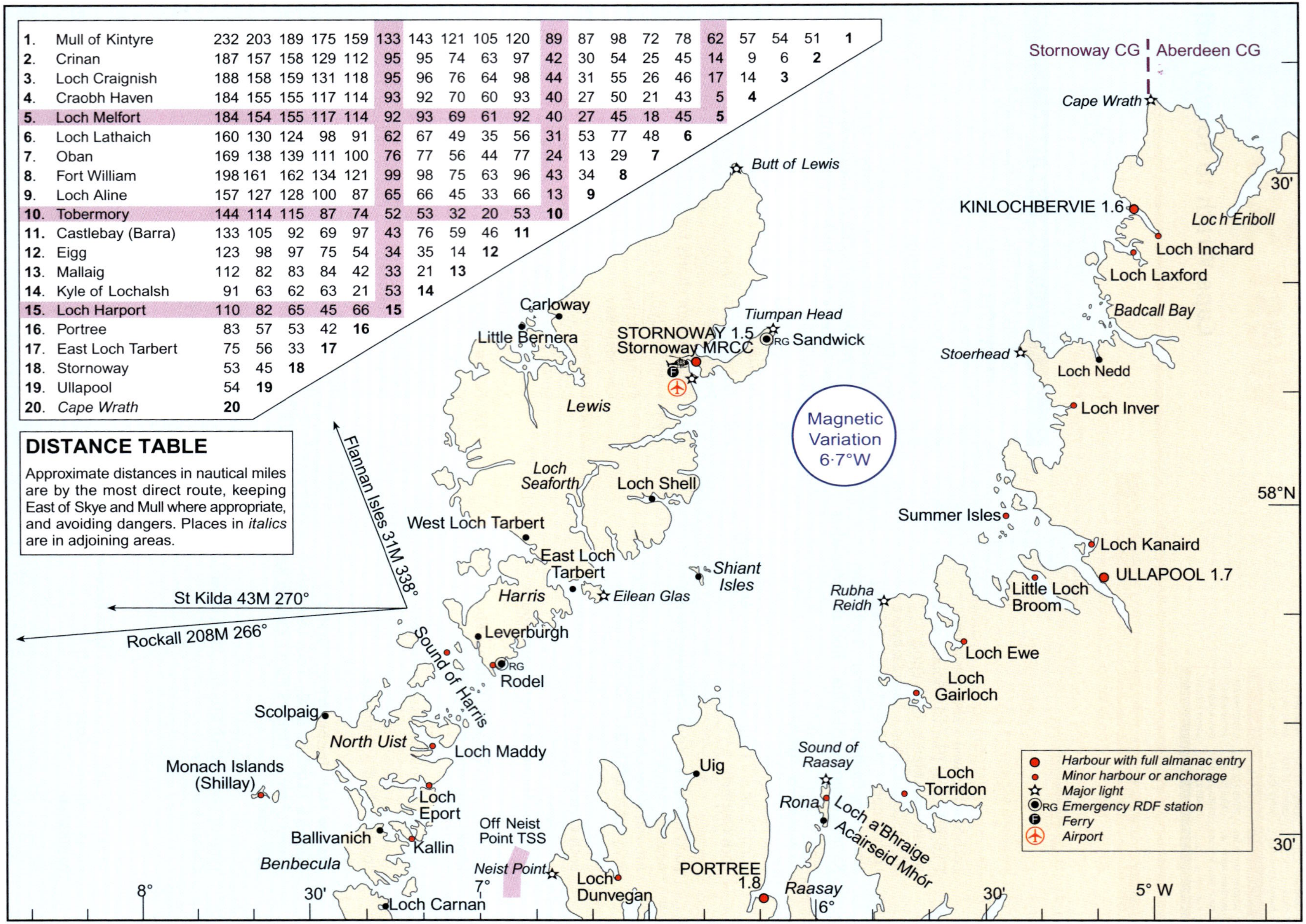

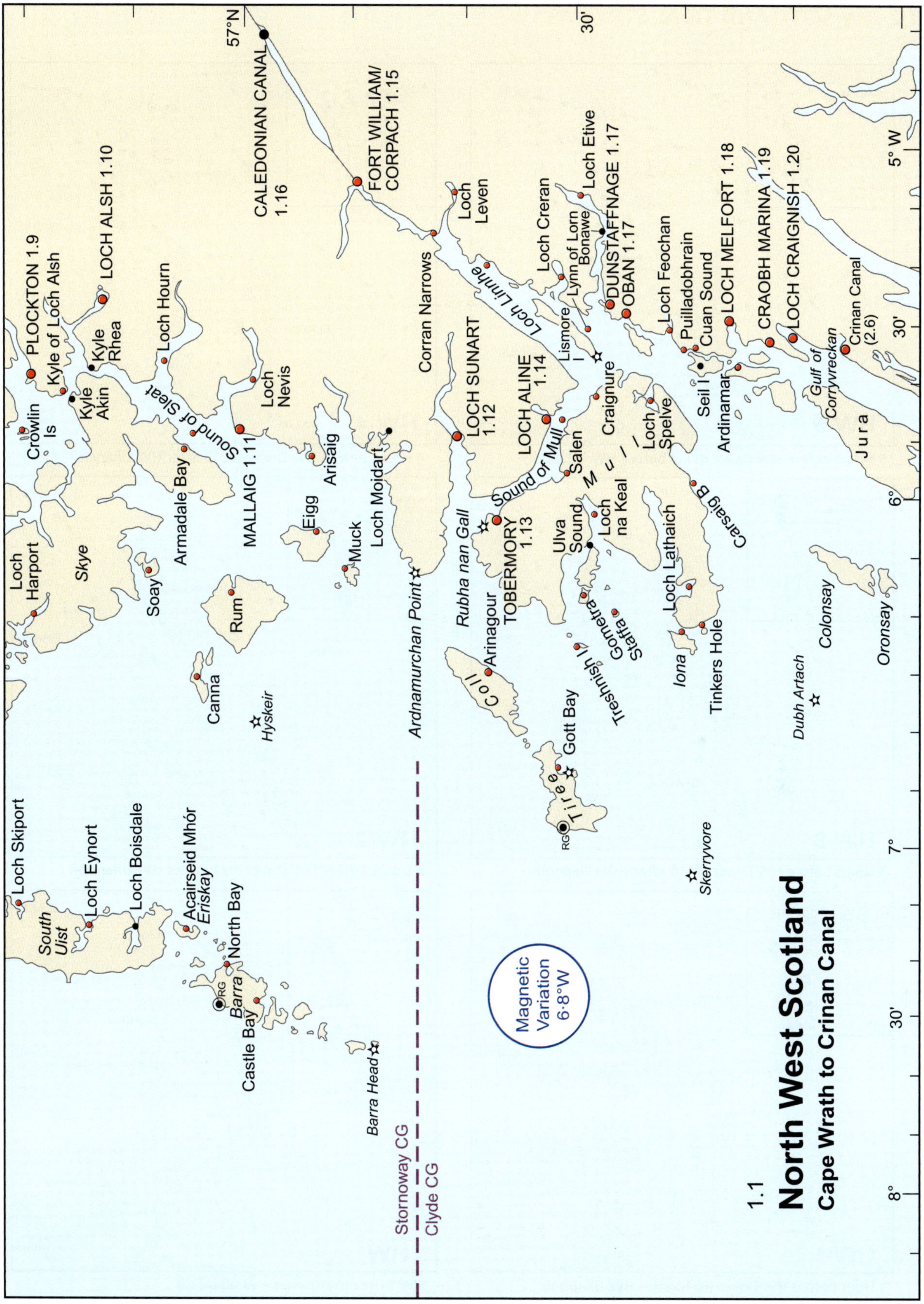

1.1

North West Scotland

Cape Wrath to Crinan Canal

1.2 NW SCOTLAND TIDAL STREAMS

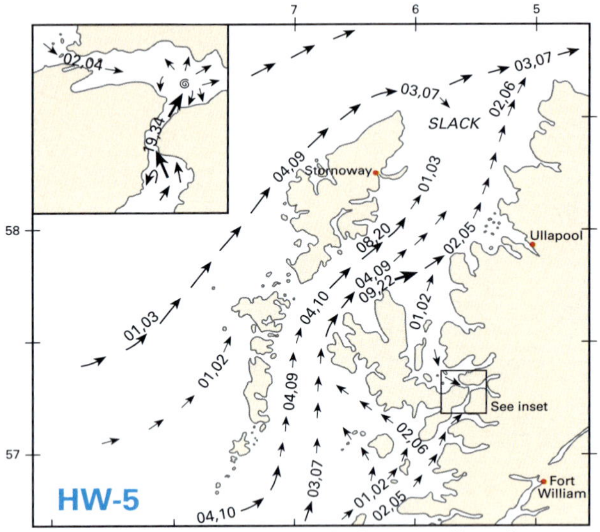

5 Hours before HW Dover (0050 before HW Ullapool)

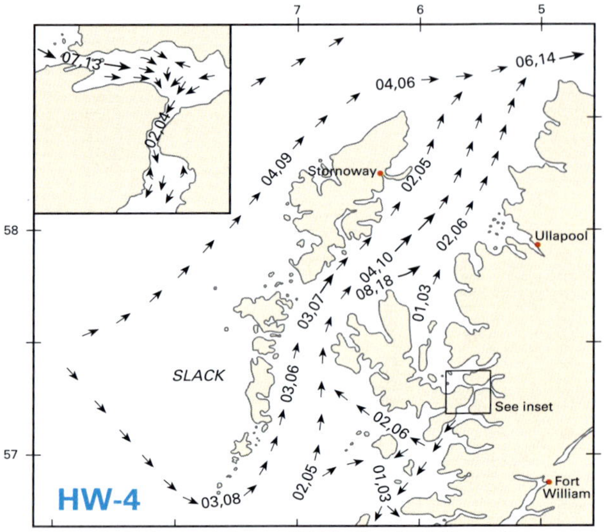

4 Hours before HW Dover (0010 after HW Ullapool)

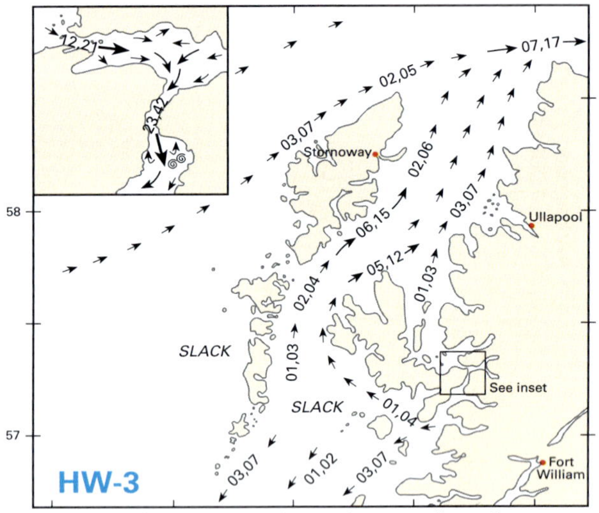

3 Hours before HW Dover (0110 after HW Ullapool)

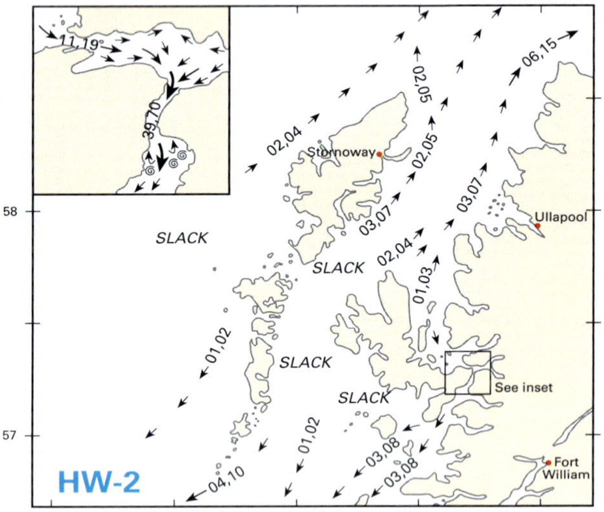

2 Hours before HW Dover (0210 after HW Ullapool)

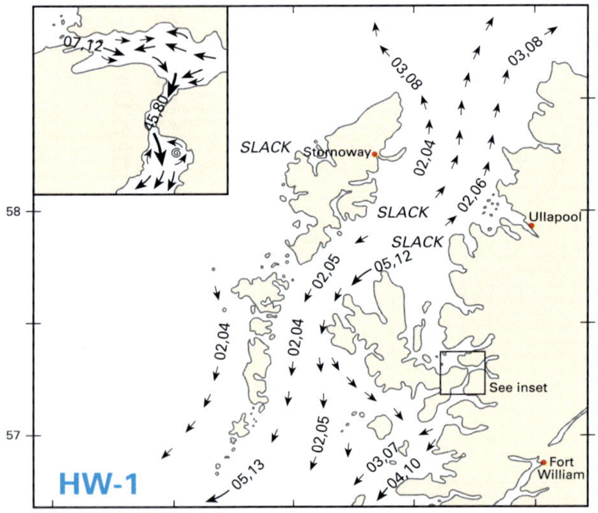

1 Hour before HW Dover (0310 after HW Ullapool)

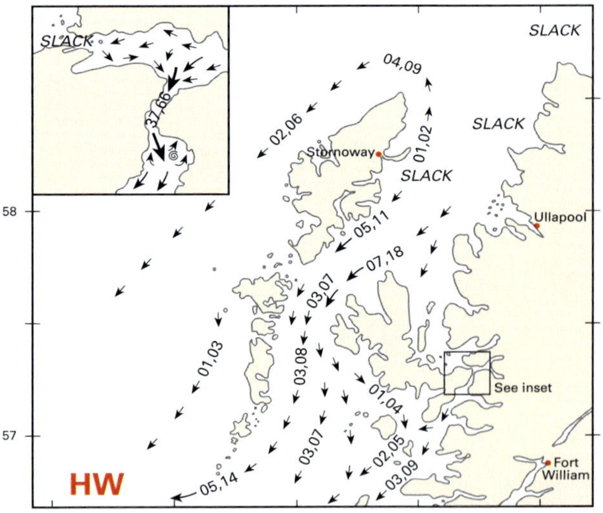

HW Dover (0410 after HW Ullapool)

Southward 2.2 Mull of Kintyre 2.9

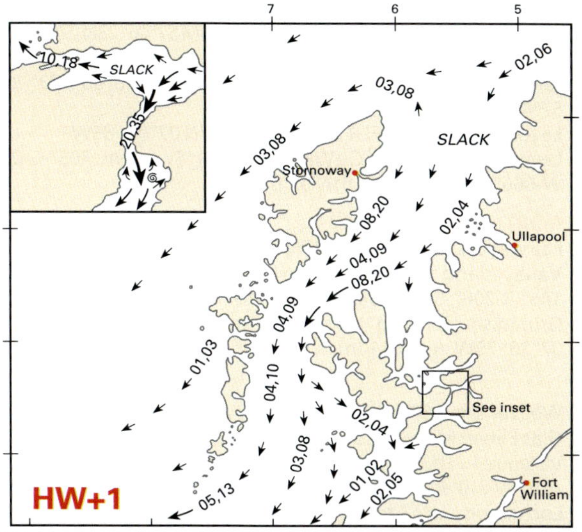

1 Hour after HW Dover (0510 after HW Ullapool)

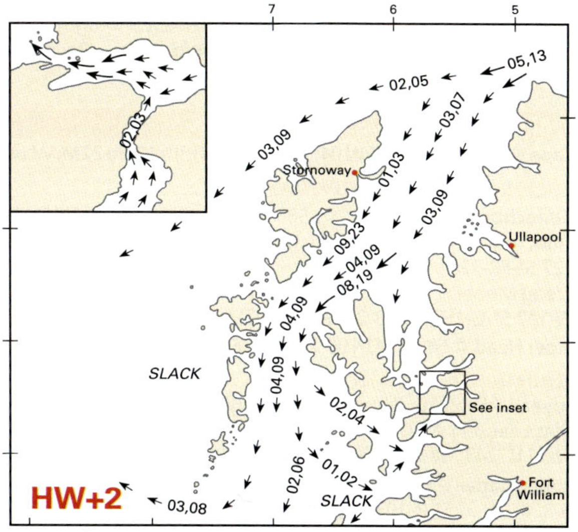

2 Hours after HW Dover (0615 before HW Ullapool)

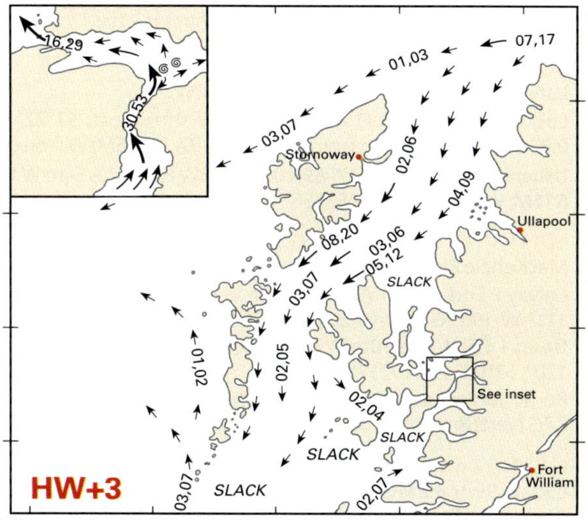

3 Hours after HW Dover (0515 before HW Ullapool)

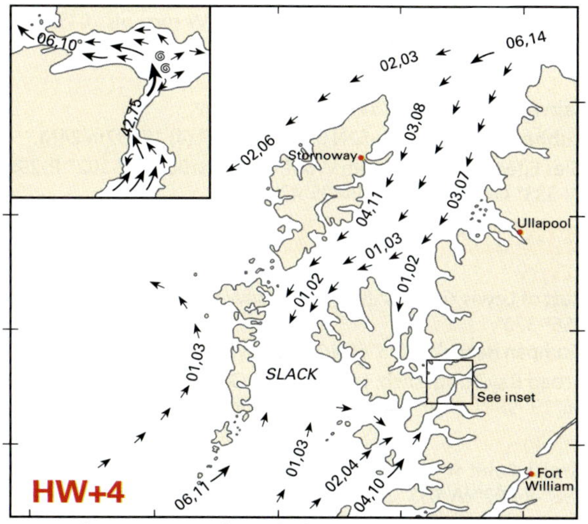

4 Hours after HW Dover (0415 before HW Ullapool)

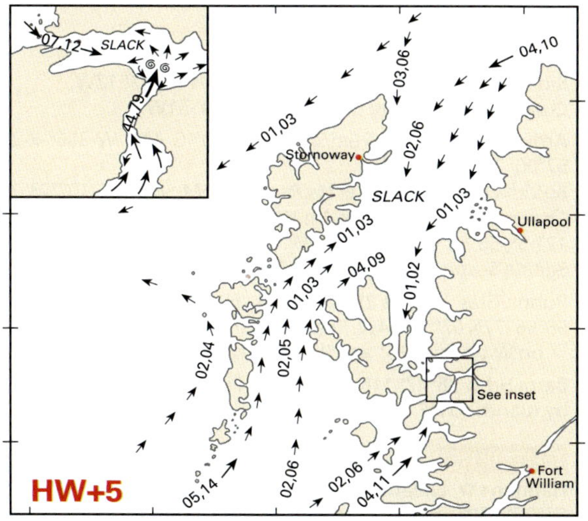

5 Hours after HW Dover (0315 before HW Ullapool)

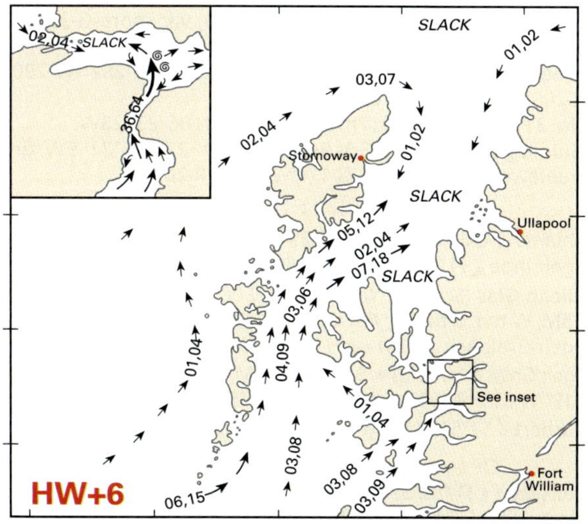

6 Hours after HW Dover (0215 before HW Ullapool)

1.3 LIGHTS, BUOYS AND WAYPOINTS

Bold print = light with a nominal range of 15M or more. CAPITALS = place or feature. *CAPITAL ITALICS* = light-vessel, light float or Lanby. *Italics* = Fog signal. ***Bold italics*** = Racon. See 0.2 for Abbreviations.

CAPE WRATH TO LOCH TORRIDON

Cape Wrath ☆ 58°37'·54N 04°59'·99W Fl (4) 30s 122m **22M**; W twr.

LOCH INCHARD and LOCH LAXFORD

Kinlochbervie Dir lt 327° ☆. 58°27'·49N 05°03'·08W WRG 15m **16M**; vis: 326°-FG-326·5°-Al GW-326·75°-FW-327·25°-Al RW-327·5°-FR-328°.

Creag Mhòr Dir lt 147°; Iso WRG 2s 16m 4M; vis: 136·5°-R -146·5°-W-147·5°-G-157·5°; 58°26'·99N 05°02'·45W.

Stoer Head ☆ 58°14'·43N 05°24'·07W Fl 15s 59m **24M**; W twr.

LOCH INVER, SUMMER ISLES and ULLAPOOL

Soyea I Fl (2) 10s 34m 6M; 58°08'·56N 05°19'·67W.

Glas Leac Fl WRG 3s 7m 5M; vis: 071°- W-078°-R-090°-G-103°-W-111°, 243°-W-247°-G-071°; 58°08'·68N 05°16'·36W.

Rubha Cadail Fl WRG 6s 11m W9M, R6M, G6M; W twr; vis: 311°-G-320°-W-325°-R-103°-W-111°-G-118°-W-127°-R-157°-W-199°; 57°55'·51N 05°13'·40W.

Ullapool Pt Iso R 4s 8m 6M; W twr; vis: 258°-108°; 57°53'·59N 05°09'·93W.

Cailleach Head Fl (2) 12s 60m 9M; W twr; vis: 015°-236°; 57°55'·81N 05°24'·23W.

LOCH EWE and LOCH GAIRLOCH

Fairway L Fl 10s; 57°51'·98N 05°40'·09W.

Rubha Reidh ☆ 57°51'·52N 05°48'·72W Fl (4) 15s 37m **24M**.

Glas Eilean Fl WRG 6s 9m W6M, R4M; vis: 080°-W-102°-R-296°-W-333°-G-080°; 57°42'·79N 05°42'·42W.

OUTER HEBRIDES – EAST SIDE

LEWIS

Butt of Lewis ☆ 58°30'·89N 06°15'·84W Fl 5s 52m **25M**; R twr; vis: 056°-320°.

Tiumpan Head ☆ 58°15'·66N 06°08'·29W Fl (2) 15s 55m **25M**; W twr.

Broad Bay Tong Anch. Ldg Lts 320°, Oc R 8s 8m 4M; 58°14'·48N 06°19'·98W. Rear, 70m from front, Oc R 8s 9m 4M.

STORNOWAY

Arnish Point ☆ Fl WR 10s 17m W9M, R7M; W ○ twr; vis: 088°-W-198°-R-302°-W-013°; 58°11'·50N 06°22'·16W.

Sandwick Bay, NW side Oc WRG 6s 10m 9M; vis: 334°-G-341°-W-347°-R-354°; 58°12'·20N 06°22'·11W.

No. 1 Pier SW corner Q WRG 5m 11M; vis: shore-G-335°-W-352°-R-shore; 58°12'·36N 06°23'·43W.

Creed Estuary Iso WRG 10s 24m 5M; vis: 277°-G-282°-W-290°-R-295°; 58°12'·03N 06°23'·47W.

No. 3 Pier Q (2) G 10s 7m 2M 58°12'·31N 06°23'·28W.

Glumaig Hbr Iso WRG 3s 8m 3M; 58°11'·27N 06°22'·9W; grey framework twr; vis: 150°-G-174°-W-180°-R-205°.

LOCH ERISORT, LOCH SHELL and EAST LOCH TARBERT

Shiants QG; 57°54'·57N 06°25'·70W.

Sgeir Inoe Fl G 6s; ***Racon (M) 5M***; 57°50'·93N 06°33'·93W.

Eilean Glas (Scalpay) ☆ 57°51'·41N 06°38'·55W Fl (3) 20s 43m **23M**; W twr, R bands; ***Racon (T) 16-18M***.

Sgeir Graidach Q (6) + L Fl 15s; 57°50'·36N 06°41'·37W.

Sgeir Ghlas Iso WRG 4s 9m W9M, R6M, G6M; W ○ twr; vis: 282°-G-319°-W-329°-R-153°-W-164°-G-171°; 57°52'·36N 06°45'·24W.

Tarbert 57°53'·82N 06°47'·93W Oc WRG 6s 10m 5M

SOUND OF HARRIS, LEVERBURGH and BERNERAY

Fairway L Fl 10s; 57°40'·35N 07°02'·15W.

No.1 QG; 57°41'·20N 07°02'·67W.

No. 3 Fl G 5s; 57°41'·86N 07°03'·44W.

No. 4 Fl R 5s; 57°41'·76N 07°03'·63W.

Suilven Fl (3)R 10s; 57°41'·68N 07°04'·36W.

Cabbage Fl (2) R 6s; ***Racon (T) 5M (3cm)***; 57°42'·13N 07°03'·96W.

Leverburgh Ldg Lts 014·7°. Front, Q 10m 4M 57°46'·23N 07°02'·04W. Rear, Oc 3s 12m 4M.

Jane's Tower Q (2) G 5s 6m 4M; vis: obscured 273°-318°; 57°45'·76N 07°02'·12W.

Leverburgh Reef Fl R 2s 4m 57°45'·97N 07°01'·86W.

Leverburgh Pier Hd Oc WRG 8s 5m 2M; Gy col; vis: 305°-G-059°-W-066°-R-125°; 57°46'·01N 07°01'·62W.

NORTH UIST

Fairway L Fl 10s; 57°40'·23N 07°01'·39W.

Vallay Island Fl WRG 3s 4m 8M; vis: 206°-W-085°-G-140°-W-145°-R-206°; 57°39'·69N 07°26'·42W.

Griminish Hbr Ldg Lts 183°. Front, QG 6m 4M; 57°39'·38N 07°26'·75W. Rear, 110m from front, QG 7m 4M.

LOCH MADDY and GRIMSAY

Weaver's Pt 57°36'·49N 07°06'·00W Fl 3s 24m 7M; W hut.

Glas Eilean Mòr 57°35'·95N 07°06'·70W Fl (2) G 4s 8m 5M.

Vallaquie I Fl (3) WRG 8s 11m W7M, R5M, G5M; W pillar; vis: shore-G-205°-W-210°-R-240°-G-254°-W-257°-R-shore; 57°35'·50N 07°09'·40W.

Lochmaddy Ldg Lts 298°. Front, Ro-Ro Pier 2 FG (vert) 8m 4M. Rear, 110m from front, Oc G 8s 10m 4M; vis: 284°-304°; 57°35'·76N 07°09'·36W.

Grimsay No. 1 Fl (2) R 8s; 57°28'·26N 07°11'·82W.

SOUTH UIST and LOCH CARNAN

Landfall L Fl 10s; 57°22'·27N 07°11'·52W.

Ldg Lts 222°. Front Fl R 2s 7m 5M; W ◊ on post; 57°22'·00N 07°16'·34W. Rear, 58m from front, Iso R 10s 11m 5M; W ◊ on post.

Ushenish ☆ (S Uist) 57°17'·89N 07°11'·58W Fl WR 20s 54m **W19M, R15M**; W twr; vis: 193°-W-356°-R-018°.

LOCH BOISDALE

MacKenzie Rk Fl (3) R 15s 3m 4M; 57°08'·24N 07°13'·71W.

Calvay E End Fl (2) WRG 10s 16m W7M, R4M, G4M; W twr; vis: 111°-W-190°-G-202°-W-286°-R-111°; 57°08'·53N 07°15'·38W.

Gasay I Fl WR 5s 10m W7M, R4M; W twr; vis: 120°-W-284°-R-120°; 57°08'·93N 07°17'·39W.

Ro-Ro Jetty Head Iso RG 4s 8m 2M; vis: shore-G-283°-R-shore; 2 FG (vert) 8m 3M on dn; 57°09'·12N 07°18'·22W.

LUDAIG and ERISKAY

Ludaig Bwtr 2 FR (vert) 6m 3M; 57°06'·17N 07°19'·49W.

Acairseid Mhor Ldg Lts 285°. Front, Oc R 6s 9m 4M; 57°03'·89N 07°17'·25W. Rear, 24m from front, Oc R 6s 10m 4M.

BARRA, CASTLEBAY and VATERSAY SOUND

Drover Rocks Q (6) + L Fl 15s; 57°04'·08N 07°23'·54W.

Binch Rock Q (6) + L Fl 15s; 57°01'·60N 07°17'·12W.

Curachan Q (3) 10s; 56°58'·56N 07°20'·51W.

Ardveenish Oc WRG 6m 9/6M; vis: 300°-G-304°-W-306°-R-310°; 57°00'·21N 07°24'·43W.

Bo Vich Chuan Q (6) + L Fl 15s; ***Racon (M) 5M***; 56°56'·15N 07°23'·31W.

Channel Rk Fl WR 6s 4m W6M, R4M; vis: 121·5°-W-277°-R-121·5°; 56°56'·24N 07°28'·94W.

Sgeir a Scape Fl (2) G 8s; 56°56'·25N 07°27'·21W.

Rubha Glas. Ldg Lts 295°. Front FBu 9m 6M; Or △ on W twr; 56°56'·77N 07°30'·64W. Rear, 457m from front, FBu 15m 6M; Or ▽ on W twr; vis: 15° and 8° respectively either side of ldg line.

Barra Hd ☆ 56°47'·11N 07°39'·26W Fl 15s 208m **18M**; W twr; obsc by islands to NE.

OUTER HEBRIDES – WEST SIDE

Flannan I ☆, Eilean Mór Fl (2) 30s 101m **20M**; W twr; 58°17'·32N 07°35'·23W, obsc in places by Is to W of Eilean Mór.

Rockall Fl 15s 19m 8M (unreliable); 57°35'·76N 13°41'·27W.

WGS84 DATUM

Plot waypoints on chart before use

Gasker Lt ☆ Fl (3) 10s 38m 10M; 57°59′·05N 07°17′·20W.
Whale Rock ⫝ Q (3) 10s 5m 5M; ***Racon (T)***; 57°54′·40N 07°59·91W.
Haskeir I ☆ 57°41′·98N 07°41·36W Fl 20s 44m **23M**; W twr; ***Racon (M) 17–15M.***
Monach Isles ☆ Fl (2) 15s 47m **18M**; R brick twr; 57°31′·55N 07°41′·68W.

EAST LOCH ROAG

Aird Laimishader Carloway ☆ Fl 6s 63m 8M; W hut; obsc on some brgs; 58°17′·06N 06°49′·50W.
Ardvanich Pt ☆ Fl G 3s 4m 2M; 58°13′·48N 06°47′·68W.
Tidal Rk ☆ Fl R 3s 2m 2M (synch with Ardvanich Pt above); 58°13′·45N 06°47′·57W.
Grèinam ☆ Fl WR 6s 8m W8M, R7M; W Bn; vis: R143°-169°, W169°-143°; 58°13′·30N 06°46′·16W.

NORTH UIST and SOUTH UIST

Vallay I ☆ Fl WRG 3s 8M; vis: 206°-W-085°-G-140°-W-145°-R-206°; 57°39′·70N 07°26′·34W.
Falconet twr ☆ FR 25m 8M (3M by day); shown 1hr before firing, changes to Iso R 2s 15 min before firing until completion; 57°22′·04N 07°23′·58W.

ST KILDA

Ldg Lts 270°. Front, Oc 5s 26m 3M; 57°48′·32N 08°34′·31W. Rear, 100m from front, Oc 5s 38m 3M; synch.

LOCH TORRIDON TO MALLAIG

LITTLE MINCH and W SKYE

Eugenie Rock t Q 6 + LF 15s; 57°46′·47N 06°27′·28W.
Eilean Trodday ☆ Fl (2) WRG 10s 52m W12M, R9M, G9M; W Bn; vis: W062°-R088°-130°-W-322°-G-062°; 57°43′·64N 06°17′·89W.
Uig, Edward Pier Hd ☆ 57°35′·09N 06°22′·29W Iso WRG 4s 9m W7M, R4M, G4M; vis: 180-W-006°-G-050°-W-073°-R-180°.
Waternish Pt ☆ Fl 20s 21m 8M; W twr; 57°36′·48N 06°37′·99W.
Loch Dunvegan, Uiginish Pt ☆ Fl WRG 3s 16m W7M,R5M,G5M; W metal-framed Twr; vis: 041°-G-132°-W-145°-R-148°-W-253°-R-263°-W-273°-G-306°, obsc by Fiadhairt Pt when brg > 148°; 57°26′·84N 06°36′·53W.
Neist Point ☆ 57°25′·41N 06°47′·30W Fl 5s 43m **16M**; W twr.
Loch Harport, Ardtreck Pt ☆ 57°20′·38N 06°25′·80W Fl 6s 18m 9M; small W twr.

RONA, LOCH A'BHRAIGE and INNER SOUND

Na Gamhnachain ⫝ Q; 57°35′·89N 05°57′·71W.
Rona NE Point ☆ 57°34′·68N 05°57′·56W Fl 12s 69m **19M**; W twr; vis: 050°-358°.
Loch A'Bhraige, Sgeir Shuas ☆ Fl R 2s 6m 3M; vis: 070°-199°; 57°35′·02N 05°58′·61W.
Ldg Lts 136·5°. Front, ⫝ Q WRG 3m W4M, R3M; vis: 135°-W- 138°-R-318°-G-135°; 57°34′·41N 05°58′·09W. Rear, ⫝ Iso 6s 28m 5M.
Ru Na Lachan ☆ Oc WR 8s 21m 10M; twr; vis: 337°-W-022°- R-117°-W-162°; 57°29′·02N 05°52′·15W.

SOUND OF RAASAY, PORTREE and CROWLIN ISLANDS

Sgeir Mhór ▲ Fl G 5s; 57°24′·57N 06°10′·53W.
Eilean Beag ☆ Fl 6s 32m 6M; W Bn; 57°21′·21N 05°51′·42W.

RAASAY and LOCH SLIGACHAN

Suisnish ☆ 2 FG (vert) 8m 2M; 57°19′·87N 06°03′·91W.
Eyre Point ☆ Fl WR 3s 6m W9M, R6M; W twr; vis: 215°-W-266°-R-288°-W-063°; 57°20′·01N 06°01′·29W.

KYLEAKIN and KYLE OF LOCH ALSH

Carragh Rk ▲ Fl (2) G 12s; ***Racon (T) 5M***; 57°17′·18N 05°45′·36W.
Bow Rk ◼ Fl (2) R 12s; 57°16′·71N 05°45′·85W.
Fork Rks ▲ Fl G 6s; 57°16′·85N 05°44′·93W.
Black Eye Rk ◼ Fl R 6s; 57°16′·72N 05°45′·31W.
Eileanan Dubha East ☆ Fl (2) 10s 9m 8M; vis: obscured 104°-146°; 57°16′·56N 05°42′·32W.
8 Metre Rock ☆ Fl G 6s 5m 4M; 57°16′·60N 05°42′·69W.
String Rock ◼ Fl R 6s; 57°16′·50N 05°42′·89W.

Sgeir-na-Caillich ☆ Fl (2) R 6s 3m 4M; 57°15′·59N 05°38′·90W.

SOUND OF SLEAT

Kyle Rhea ☆ Fl WRG 3s 7m W8M, R5M, G5M; W Bn; vis: shore-R-219°-W-228°-G-338°-W-346°-R-shore; 57°14′·22N 05°39′·93W.
Sandaig I, NW point ☆ Fl 6s 13m 8M; W twr; 57°10′·05N 05°42′·29W.
Ornsay, SE end ☆ 57°08′·59N 05°46′·88W Oc 8s 18m **15M**; W twr; vis: 157°-030°.
Pt. of Sleat ☆ Fl 3s 20m9M; W twr; 57°01′·08N06°01′·08W.

MALLAIG and LOCH NEVIS ENTRANCE

Sgeir Dhearg ▲ QG; 57°00′·74N 05°49′·50W.
Northern Pier E end ☆ Iso WRG 4s 6m W9M, R6M, G6M; Gy twr; vis: 181°-G-185°-W-197°-R-201°. Fl G 3s 14m 6M; same structure; 57°00′·47N 05°49′·50W.
Sgeir Dhearg ☆ 57°00′·63N 05°49′·61W Fl (2) WG 8s 6m 5M; Gy Bn; vis: 190°-G-055°-W-190°.

SMALL ISLES AND WEST OF MULL

CANNA and RUM

Canna, E end Sanday Is ☆ Fl 10s 32m 9M; W twr; vis: 152°-061°; 57°02′·82N 06°28′·02W.
Loch Scresort ⫝ Q; 57°00′·79N 06°14′·61W.

HYSKEIR, EIGG, MUCK and ARISAIG

Humla ▲ Fl G 6s 3m 4M 57°00′·46N 06°37′·39W.
Hyskeir ☆ 56°58′·14N 06°40′·87W Fl (3) 30s 41m **24M**; W twr. ***Racon (T) 14-17M***.
SE point Eigg (Eilean Chathastail) ☆ Fl 6s 24m 8M; W twr; vis: 181°-shore; 56°52′·25N 06°07′·28W.
Eigg, Sgeir nam Bagh (Ferry Terminal) ☆ Dir 245°; Fl WRG 3s 9m W14, R11, G11; H24; steel pole; vis: 242·5°-G-244°-W-246°-R-247·5°. 2FR(vert) on same structure; 56°52′·80N 06°07′·60W.
Isle of Muck (Port Mor) ☆ Dir Fl WRG 3s 7m W14, R11, G11, by day W1, R1, G1; steel twr; vis: 319·5°-G-321°-W-323°-R-324·5°; 56°49′·96N 06°13′·64W.
Bogha Ruadh ☆ Fl G 5s 4m 3M; 56°49′·56N 06°13′·05W.
Bo Faskadale ▲ Fl (3) G 18s; 56°48′·18N 06°06′·37W.
Ardnamurchan ☆ 56°43′·63N 06°13′·58W Fl (2) 20s 55m **24M**; Gy twr; vis: 002°-217°.
Cairns of Coll, Suil Ghorm ☆ Fl 12s 23m 10M; W twr; 56°42′·26N 06°26′·75W.

TIREE, COLL and ARINAGOUR

Loch Eatharna, Bogha Mór ▲ Fl G 6s; 56°36′·65N 06°30′·90W.
Roan Bogha ⫝ Q (6) + L Fl 15s 3m 5M; 56°32′·23N 06°40′·18W.
Placaid Bogha ▲ Fl G 4s; 56°33′·22N 06°44′·06W.
Scarinish ☆, S side of ent 56°30′·01N 06°48′·27W Fl 3s 11m **16M**; W□twr; vis: 210°-030°.
Cairn na Burgh More (Treshnish Is), Fl (3) 15s 36m 8M; solar panels on framework tr; 56°31′·05N 06°22′·95W.
Gott Bay Ldg Lts 286·5°. Front FR 8m; 56°30′·61N 06°47′·82W. Rear 30m from front FR 11m.
Cairn na Burgh More (Treshnish Is), Fl (3) 15s 36m 8M; solar panels on framework tr; 56°31′·05N 06°22′·95W.
Skerryvore ☆ Fl 10s 46m **23M**; Gy twr; ***Racon (M) 18M***. 56°19′·36N 07°06′·88W

LOCH NA LÀTHAICH (LOCH LATHAICH)

Eileanan na Liathanaich, SE end ☆ Fl WR 6s 12m W8M, R6M; vis: R088°- W108°-088°; 56°20′·56N 06°16′·38W.
Loch Eatharna, Pier Head ☆ Dir Oc WRG 7s 6m 2M; vis: 316°-G-322°-W-328°-R-334°; 56°36′·86N 06°31′·29W.
Dubh Artach ☆ 56°07′·94N 06°38′·08W Fl (2) 30s 44m **20M**; Gy twr, R band.

SOUND OF MULL

LOCH SUNART, TOBERMORY and LOCH ALINE

Ardmore Pt ☆ Fl (2) 10s 18m 13M; 56°39′·37N 06°07′·70W.
New Rks ▲ Fl G 6s 56°39′·05N 06°03′·30W.

WGS84 DATUM

Plot waypoints on chart before use

Rubha nan Gall ☆ 56°38'·33N 06°04'·00W Fl 3s 17m **15M**; W twr.
Eileanan Glasa (Dearg Sgeir) 56°32'·25N 05°54'·80W Fl 6s 7m 8M; W ○ twr.
Fiunary Spit 56°32'·66N 05°53'·17W Fl G 6s.
Lochaline Ldg Lts 356°. Front, F 2m; 56°32'·39N 05°46'·49W. Rear, 88m from front, F 4m; both H24.

Ardtornish Pt Fl (2) WRG 10s 8m W8M, R6M, G6M; W twr; vis: G shore- 302°-W-308°-R-342°-W-057°-R-095°-W-108°-G-shore; 56°31'·10N 05°45'·23W.

Craignure Ldg Lts 240·9°. Front, FR 10m; 56°28'·26N 05°42'·28W. Rear, 150m from front, FR 12m; vis: 225·8°-255·8°.

MULL TO CALEDONIAN CANAL AND OBAN

Lismore ☆, SW end 56°27'·34N 05°36'·45W Fl 10s 31m **17M**; W twr; vis: 237°-208°.

Lady's Rk Fl 6s 12m 5M; 56°26'·92N 05°37'·05W.
Duart Pt Fl (3) WR 18s 14m W5M, R3M; vis: 162°-W-261°-R-275°-W-353°-R-shore; 56°26'·84N 05°38'·77W.

LOCH LINNHE

Corran Shoal QR 56°43'·69N 05°14'·39W.
Ent W side, Corran Pt Iso WRG 4s 12m W10M, R7M, G7M; W twr; vis: shore-R-195°-W-215°-G-020-W-030°-R-shore;56°43'·25N 05°14'·54W.
Corran Narrows NE Fl 5s 4m 4M; W twr; vis: S shore-214°; 56°43'·62N 05°13'·90W.
Clovullin Spit Fl (2) R 15s; 56°42'·29N 05°15'·56W.
Cuil-cheanna Spit Fl G 6s; 56°41'·17N 05°15'·72W.

FORT WILLIAM and CALEDONIAN CANAL

Corpach, Caledonian Canal Lock ent Iso WRG 4s 6m 5M; W twr; vis: G287°- W310°- R335°-030°; 56°50'·52N 05°07'·44W.

LYNN OF LORN

Sgeir Bhuidhe Appin Fl (2) WR 7s 8m W9M R6M; W Bn; vis: W013·5°- R184°-220°; 56°33'·63N 05°24'·65W.
Appin Point Fl G 6s; 56°32'·69N 05°25'·97W.
Dearg Sgeir, off Aird's Point Fl WRG 2s 2m W3M, R1M, G1M; vis: 196°-R-246°-W-258°-G-041°-W-058°-R-093°-W-139°; 56°32'·20N 05°25'·22W.
Rubha nam Faoileann (Eriska) QG 2m 2M; G col; vis 128°-329°; 56°32'·20N 05°24'·11W.

DUNSTAFFNAGE BAY/OBAN

N spit of Kerrera Fl R 3s 9m 5M; W col, R bands; 56°25'·49N 05°29'·56W.
Dunollie Fl (2) WRG 6s 6m W8M, R6M, G6M; vis: 351°-G- 020°-W-047°-R-120°-W-138°-G-143°; 56°25'·37N 05°29'·05W.
Corran Ledge VQ (9) 10s; 56°25'·19N 05°29'·11W.

OBAN TO LOCH CRAIGNISH

Kerrera Sound, Dubha Sgeirean Fl (2) 12s 7m 5M; W ○ twr; 56°22'·81N 05°32'·27W.
Bogha Nuadh Q (6) + LFl 15s; 56°21'·69N 05°37'·88W.
Bono Rock Q (9) 15s; 56°16'·21N 05°41'·22W.
Fladda Fl (2) WRG 9s 13m W11M, R9M, G9M; W twr; vis: 169°-R-186°-W-337°-G-344°-W-356°-R-026°; 56°14'·89N 05°40'·83W.
Dubh Sgeir (Luing) Fl WRG 6s 9m W6M, R4M. G4M; W twr; vis: W000°- R010°- W025°- G199°-000°; ***Racon (M) 5M***; 56°14'·76N 05°40'·20W.
The Garvellachs, Eileach an Naoimh, SW end Fl 6s 21m 9M; W Bn; vis: 240°-215°; 56°13'·04N 05°49'·06W.

LOCH MELFORT and CRAOBH HAVEN

Melfort Pier Dir FR 6m 3M; (Apr -Nov); 56°16'·14N 05°30'·19W.
56°12'·88N 05°33'·59W.
Craobh Marina Bkwtr Hd Iso WRG 5s 10m, W5M, R3M, G3M; vis:114°-G-162°-W-183°-R-200°; 56°12'·78N 05°33'·52W.

1.4 PASSAGE INFORMATION

It is essential to carry large scale charts and current Pilot Books: Admiralty *W Coast of Scotland Pilot*; Clyde Cruising Club's *Sailing Directions, Pt 2 Kintyre to Ardnamurchan* and *Pt 3 Ardnamurchan to Cape Wrath*; and the *Yachtsman's Pilot to W Coast of Scotland; Vol 2 Crinan to Canna, Vol 3 The Western Isles, Vol 4 Skye & NW Scotland* (Lawrence/Imray).

Scotland's west coast provides splendid, if boisterous, sailing and matchless scenery. In summer the long daylight hours and warmth of the Gulf Stream compensate for the lower air temperatures and higher wind speeds experienced when depressions run typically north of Scotland. Inshore winds are often unpredictable, due to geographical effects of lochs, mountains and islands offshore; calms and squalls can alternate rapidly.

Good anchors, especially on kelp/weed, are essential. 🅥s are listed but it should not be assumed that these will always be available. Particularly in N of area, facilities are very dispersed. A *'Rover Ticket'* from Highland Council allows berthing for 15 days; the scheme includes: Kinlochbervie, Lochinver, Gairloch, Kyle of Lochalsh, Kyleakin, Portree and Uig. VHF communications with shore stations may be limited by high ground. Beware ever more fish farms in many inlets. Local magnetic anomalies occur in Kilbrannan Sound, Passage of Tiree, Sound of Mull, Canna, and East Loch Roag. Submarines exercise throughout these waters.

More Passage Information is threaded between the harbours in this Area.

OUTER HEBRIDES

(AC 1785, 1794, 1795) The E sides of these Is have many good, sheltered anchs, but W coasts give little shelter. The CCC's *Outer Hebrides SDs* or *The Western Isles* (Imray) are advised.

▶ *The Minches and Sea of the Hebrides can be very rough, particularly in the Little Minch between Skye and Harris, and around Shiant Is where tide runs locally 4kn at sp, and heavy overfalls can occur. The NE going stream on both shores begins at HW Ullapool -0340 (HW Dover +0430), with the strongest flow from mid channel to the Skye coast. There is a W going counter tide E of Vaternish Pt.*

The SW going stream on both shores begins at HW Ullapool +0240 (HW Dover –0130), with the strongest flow from mid channel to the Skye coast, sp rates 2·5kn. The E going stream in Sound of Scalpay runs at up to 2k.The E going flood and W going ebb in Sound of Scalpay run at up to 2k.◀

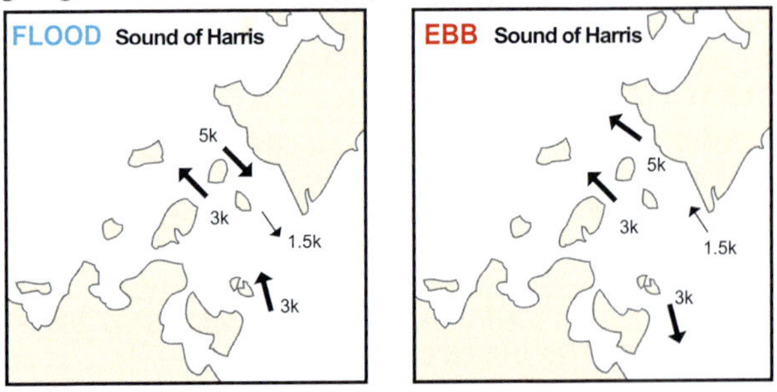

▶ ***Sound of Harris.*** *The behaviour of tidal streams is complicated and varies from day to night, springs to neaps, and winter to summer. In the NE part of the Sound, at springs, the stream sets SE from Ullapool +0535 to –0035. At neaps, in the summer, the stream sets SE during the day and NW during the night. To the SW of the Sound, the NW stream starts at Ullapool –0545; the SE stream starts at Ullapool +0025. The approximate maximum rates are as shown. For more detailed information refer to the Admiralty West Coast of Scotland Pilot.*◀

From N to S, the better harbours in Outer Hebrides include:

Lewis. Stornoway; Loch Grimshader (beware Sgeir a'Chaolais, dries in entrance); Loch Erisort; Loch Odhairn; Loch Shell. Proceeding S from here, or to E Loch Tarbert beware Sgeir Inoe (dries 2·3m) 3M ESE of Eilean Glas lt ho at SE end of Scalpay.

Harris. E Loch Tarbert; Loch Scadaby; Loch Stockinish; Loch Finsby; W Loch Tarbert; Loch Rodel (ⓥ). A well marked ferry chan connects Leverburgh (South Harris) to Berneray.

N Uist. Loch Maddy (ⓥ); Loch Eport, Kallin Hbr (ⓥ).

S Uist. Loch Carnan (ⓥ); Loch Skiport; Loch Eynort; Loch Boisdale (ⓥ).

Barra. Castlebay (ⓥ), and Berneray, on N side, E of Shelter Rk.

Activity at the Hebrides Range, S. Uist ☎ (01870) 604441, is broadcast daily at 0950LT and Mon-Fri 1100-1700LT on VHF Ch **12** (Ch 73 in emergency) and on MF 2660 kHz.

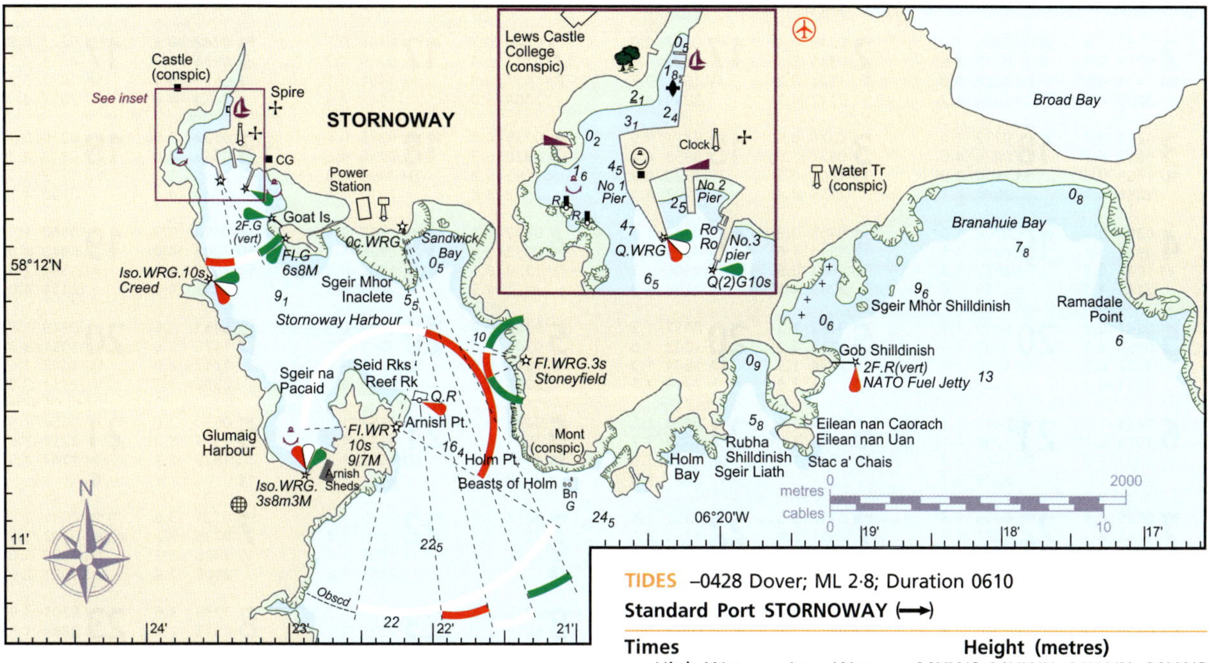

1.5 STORNOWAY

Lewis (Western Isles) **58°11'·58N 06°21'·82W** ❁❁❁✋✋✿✿

CHARTS AC 1785, 1794, 2529; Imray C67.

SHELTER Good. A small marina, max LOA 12m, at the N end of the Inner Hbr, beyond the LB berth, has depths 1·4–3·3m. Or AB for larger boats on adjacent Cromwell St Quay, close S; or lie alongside FVs in the inner hbr. Visitors should report to HM. Ferries use W side No 3 pier, and commercial vessels on Nos 1 and 2 Piers. S'ly swells can make anchoring uncomfortable.

⚓s as on chartlet at: Poll nam Portan on the W side of inner chan, opposite No 1 Pier; Glumaig Hbr is best ⚓, and in bay NW of Goat Island (Eilean na Gobhail).

NAVIGATION WPT 58°09'·98N 06°20'·87W, 343°/2·3M to Oc WRG lt. Reef Rk, N of Arnish Pt on W side of ent, is marked by PHM buoy, QR. At the E side of ent an unlit G bn marks the Beasts of Holm, a rky patch off Holm Pt, on which is a conspic memorial. A local magnetic anomaly exists over a small area in mid-hbr, 1·75ca N of Seid Rks PHM bn.

LIGHTS AND MARKS Arnish sheds are conspic 3ca SW of Arnish Pt lt, W sector 302°-013° covers ent. Then in turn follow W sectors of: Sandwick Bay lt (close E of water tr, 3 power stn chys; all conspic), then Creed Estuary, Iso WRG 10s, across the harbour, and finally No 1 Pier, Q WRG.

R/T VHF Ch 12 16 (H24).

TELEPHONE (Code 01851) HM 702688; MRCC 702013; ⊖ 703626; Marinecall 09068 969654; Police 702222; Dr 703145.

FACILITIES **Marina** 27 berths, inc 8 ⓥ, £9.40 via HM Ch 12; FW. **Nos 1 & 2 Piers** FW, C (10 ton), CH, AB, Slip, P. **No3 Pier** AB(E side), FW, C (Mobile10+ ton), D(road tanker) **Services:** ACA, ME, El, ⚒. **Town** P (cans), D, El, 🛒, ⊡, R, Bar, Gas, ✉, Ⓑ, ⇌ (Ferry to Ullapool, bus to Garve), ✈.

TIDES –0428 Dover; ML 2·8; Duration 0610

Standard Port STORNOWAY (⟶)

Times				Height (metres)			
High Water		Low Water		MHWS	MHWN	MLWN	MLWS
0100	0700	0300	0900	4·8	3·7	2·0	0·7
1300	1900	1500	2100				
East side of Outer Hebrides, N to S							
Differences LOCH SHELL (Harris)							
–0013	0000	0000	–0017	0·0	–0·1	–0·1	0·0
EAST LOCH TARBERT (Harris)							
–0025	–0010	–0010	–0020	+0·2	0·0	+0·1	+0·1
LOCH MADDY (N Uist)							
–0044	–0014	–0016	–0030	0·0	–0·1	–0·1	0·0
LOCH CARNAN (S Uist)							
–0050	–0010	–0020	–0040	–0·3	–0·5	–0·1	–0·1
LOCH SKIPORT (S Uist)							
–0100	–0025	–0024	–0024	–0·2	–0·4	–0·3	–0·2
LOCH BOISDALE (S Uist)							
–0055	–0030	–0020	–0040	–0·7	–0·7	–0·3	–0·2
BARRA (North Bay)							
–0103	–0031	–0034	–0048	–0·6	–0·5	–0·2	–0·1
CASTLE BAY (Barra)							
–0115	–0040	–0045	–0100	–0·5	–0·6	–0·3	–0·1
BARRA HEAD (Berneray)							
–0115	–0040	–0045	–0055	–0·8	–0·7	–0·2	+0·1
West side of Outer Hebrides, N to S							
CARLOWAY (W Lewis)							
–0040	+0020	–0035	–0015	–0·6	–0·5	–0·4	–0·1
LITTLE BERNERA (W Lewis)							
–0021	–0011	–0017	–0027	–0·5	–0·6	–0·4	–0·2
WEST LOCH TARBERT (W Harris)							
–0015	–0015	–0046	–0046	–1·1	–0·9	–0·5	0·0
SCOLPAIG (W North Uist)							
–0033	–0033	–0040	–0040	–1·0	–0·9	–0·5	0·0
SHILLAY (Monach Islands)							
–0103	–0043	–0047	–0107	–0·6	–0·7	–0·7	–0·3
BALIVANICH (W Benbecula)							
–0103	–0017	–0031	–0045	–0·7	–0·6	–0·5	–0·2

TIME ZONE (UT)
For Summer Time add ONE hour in **non-shaded areas**

STORNOWAY LAT 58°12′N LONG 6°23′W

TIMES AND HEIGHTS OF HIGH AND LOW WATERS

Dates in red are SPRINGS
Dates in blue are NEAPS

YEAR 2010

JANUARY

Date	Day	Time	m	Date	Day	Time	m
1	F	0050 0652 1327 1923	0.9 5.0 0.7 4.8	16	SA	0132 0724 1358 1945	1.0 4.6 1.0 4.2
2	SA	0135 0737 1414 2009	0.8 5.1 0.5 4.8	17	SU	0205 0755 1429 2014	1.0 4.6 0.9 4.2
3	SU	0219 0822 1459 2054	0.7 5.2 0.4 4.7	18	M	0237 0826 1500 2044	1.0 4.6 0.9 4.1
4	M	0303 0908 1545 2141	0.8 5.1 0.5 4.5	19	TU	0308 0857 1532 2115	1.0 4.5 1.0 4.0
5	TU	0347 0957 1632 2233	0.9 4.9 0.7 4.3	20	W	0340 0930 1606 2148	1.2 4.3 1.1 3.9
6	W	0433 1053 1721 2333	1.2 4.6 1.0 4.0	21	TH	0415 1006 1643 2228	1.4 4.1 1.3 3.7
7	TH ◑	0525 1158 1816	1.5 4.3 1.3	22	F	0453 1051 1725 2321	1.6 3.9 1.5 3.6
8	F	0042 0624 1311 1918	3.8 1.7 4.0 1.6	23	SA ◐	0539 1150 1814	1.8 3.8 1.7
9	SA	0156 0738 1428 2033	3.7 1.9 3.8 1.8	24	SU	0032 0635 1301 1914	3.5 2.0 3.7 1.8
10	SU	0308 0906 1541 2150	3.7 2.0 3.7 1.8	25	M	0148 0750 1418 2029	3.5 2.0 3.7 1.9
11	M	0410 1024 1643 2250	3.8 1.8 3.8 1.7	26	TU	0303 0920 1536 2150	3.7 1.9 3.8 1.7
12	TU	0500 1123 1731 2338	4.0 1.6 3.8 1.5	27	W	0411 1038 1644 2258	4.0 1.6 4.0 1.5
13	W	0541 1209 1811	4.2 1.4 3.9	28	TH	0508 1138 1739 2352	4.3 1.2 4.3 1.2
14	TH	0019 0618 1250 1844	1.3 4.4 1.2 4.0	29	F	0557 1230 1827	4.7 0.8 4.6
15	F ●	0057 0652 1325 1916	1.2 4.5 1.1 4.1	30	SA ○	0039 0641 1316 1910	0.8 5.0 0.4 4.8
				31	SU	0124 0723 1400 1951	0.6 5.3 0.2 4.9

FEBRUARY

Date	Day	Time	m	Date	Day	Time	m
1	M	0205 0804 1441 2031	0.4 5.4 0.1 4.9	16	TU	0214 0757 1432 2012	0.7 4.7 0.7 4.3
2	TU	0246 0845 1522 2112	0.4 5.3 0.2 4.7	17	W	0242 0825 1501 2039	0.8 4.6 0.7 4.2
3	W	0326 0927 1604 2155	0.6 5.0 0.5 4.4	18	TH	0311 0853 1532 2107	0.9 4.4 0.9 4.1
4	TH	0408 1014 1647 2245	0.9 4.6 0.9 4.1	19	F	0343 0924 1606 2138	1.1 4.2 1.1 3.9
5	F ◑	0453 1113 1734 2352	1.2 4.2 1.3 3.8	20	SA	0417 1002 1644 2219	1.3 4.0 1.3 3.7
6	SA	0544 1234 1830	1.6 3.8 1.7	21	SU	0458 1059 1729 2327	1.6 3.7 1.6 3.5
7	SU	0117 0651 1404 1947	3.5 2.0 3.5 2.0	22	M ◐	0551 1227 1828	1.8 3.6 1.8
8	M	0239 0837 1526 2127	3.5 2.1 3.5 2.1	23	TU	0109 0710 1400 1953	3.5 2.0 3.5 2.0
9	TU	0350 1019 1635 2237	3.6 2.0 3.5 1.9	24	W	0239 0905 1526 2134	3.6 1.9 3.7 1.8
10	W	0445 1118 1724 2325	3.9 1.7 3.7 1.6	25	TH	0355 1029 1634 2245	3.9 1.5 4.0 1.5
11	TH	0527 1200 1759	4.1 1.4 3.8	26	F	0454 1126 1726 2338	4.3 1.0 4.4 1.1
12	F	0005 0602 1235 1828	1.4 4.3 1.2 4.0	27	SA	0542 1214 1810	4.8 0.6 4.7
13	SA	0041 0634 1307 1856	1.1 4.5 1.0 4.1	28	SU ○	0023 0624 1258 1850	0.7 5.1 0.2 4.9
14	SU ●	0114 0703 1336 1921	0.9 4.6 0.8 4.3				
15	M	0145 0731 1404 1946	0.8 4.7 0.7 4.3				

MARCH

Date	Day	Time	m	Date	Day	Time	m
1	M	0106 0704 1338 1928	0.4 5.3 0.0 5.0	16	TU	0118 0703 1333 1918	0.8 4.7 0.7 4.5
2	TU	0146 0742 1417 2005	0.3 5.4 0.0 5.0	17	W	0146 0729 1401 1943	0.7 4.7 0.6 4.5
3	W	0225 0820 1455 2042	0.3 5.3 0.2 4.8	18	TH	0215 0756 1430 2010	0.7 4.6 0.6 4.4
4	TH	0303 0859 1534 2121	0.5 5.0 0.5 4.5	19	F	0245 0826 1502 2038	0.8 4.5 0.8 4.3
5	F	0343 0941 1614 2205	0.8 4.5 0.9 4.2	20	SA	0317 0859 1535 2110	0.9 4.3 1.0 4.1
6	SA	0425 1033 1657 2305	1.2 4.1 1.4 3.8	21	SU	0352 0941 1613 2152	1.2 4.0 1.3 3.9
7	SU ◑	0513 1200 1747	1.6 3.6 1.9	22	M	0435 1044 1658 2303	1.4 3.7 1.6 3.6
8	M	0038 0614 1340 1902	3.6 2.0 3.4 2.2	23	TU ◐	0531 1220 1759	1.7 3.5 1.9
9	TU	0206 0808 1506 2056	3.5 2.2 3.3 2.3	24	W	0052 0701 1353 1934	3.6 1.9 3.5 2.0
10	W	0320 1002 1618 2213	3.6 2.0 3.4 2.0	25	TH	0222 0855 1515 2118	3.7 1.7 3.7 1.9
11	TH	0419 1058 1705 2302	3.8 1.7 3.6 1.7	26	F	0337 1012 1618 2226	4.0 1.3 4.0 1.5
12	F	0503 1136 1737 2341	4.0 1.5 3.8 1.4	27	SA	0435 1106 1707 2317	4.4 0.9 4.4 1.1
13	SA	0538 1209 1805	4.2 1.2 4.0	28	SU	0522 1152 1749	4.8 0.5 4.7
14	SU	0016 0609 1239 1830	1.2 4.4 1.0 4.2	29	M	0002 0603 1234 1827	0.8 5.0 0.3 4.9
15	M ●	0049 0637 1307 1854	0.9 4.6 0.8 4.4	30	TU ○	0044 0642 1314 1904	0.5 5.2 0.2 5.0
				31	W	0124 0719 1351 1940	0.4 5.2 0.2 5.0

APRIL

Date	Day	Time	m	Date	Day	Time	m
1	TH	0203 0757 1429 2016	0.4 5.0 0.4 4.8	16	F	0150 0735 1403 1948	0.8 4.6 0.7 4.6
2	F	0242 0836 1506 2054	0.6 4.7 0.7 4.6	17	SA	0223 0809 1437 2021	0.8 4.5 0.8 4.5
3	SA	0322 0918 1545 2138	0.9 4.4 1.1 4.3	18	SU	0259 0849 1513 2100	0.9 4.3 1.0 4.3
4	SU	0404 1008 1626 2233	1.3 4.0 1.6 4.0	19	M	0340 0940 1554 2151	1.1 4.0 1.3 4.0
5	M	0451 1126 1713 2356	1.6 3.6 2.0 3.7	20	TU	0429 1051 1642 2311	1.3 3.8 1.6 3.8
6	TU ◑	0550 1304 1820	2.0 3.3 2.3	21	W ◐	0534 1217 1747	1.5 3.6 1.9
7	W	0121 0725 1428 2008	3.6 2.2 3.3 2.4	22	TH	0041 0703 1339 1921	3.8 1.6 3.6 2.0
8	TH	0236 0913 1541 2132	3.6 2.1 3.4 2.2	23	F	0201 0833 1453 2051	3.9 1.5 3.8 1.8
9	F	0338 1015 1631 2225	3.8 1.8 3.6 1.9	24	SA	0311 0945 1555 2157	4.1 1.2 4.0 1.5
10	SA	0427 1057 1706 2307	4.0 1.6 3.8 1.6	25	SU	0410 1039 1644 2250	4.4 0.9 4.3 1.2
11	SU	0505 1132 1734 2344	4.2 1.3 4.0 1.4	26	M	0459 1126 1726 2337	4.6 0.7 4.5 1.0
12	M	0538 1203 1800	4.3 1.1 4.3	27	TU	0542 1208 1805	4.8 0.6 4.7
13	TU	0017 0606 1232 1824	1.1 4.5 0.9 4.4	28	W ○	0021 0621 1249 1841	0.8 4.9 0.5 4.8
14	W ●	0048 0634 1301 1850	1.0 4.6 0.8 4.6	29	TH	0103 0700 1328 1918	0.7 4.8 0.6 4.8
15	TH	0118 0703 1331 1918	0.8 4.6 0.7 4.6	30	F	0144 0739 1406 1956	0.7 4.7 0.7 4.7

Chart Datum: 2·71 metres below Ordnance Datum (Newlyn). HAT is 5·5 metres above Chart Datum; see 0.20

TIME ZONE (UT)
For Summer Time add ONE hour in **non-shaded areas**

STORNOWAY

LAT 58°12′N LONG 6°23′W

TIMES AND HEIGHTS OF HIGH AND LOW WATERS

Dates in red are SPRINGS
Dates in blue are NEAPS

YEAR 2010

MAY

Date	Day	Time	m	Time	m	Time	m	Time	m	Moon
1	SA	0225	0.8	0820	4.5	1443	1.0	2035	4.6	
2	SU	0306	1.0	0903	4.2	1522	1.3	2119	4.4	
3	M	0349	1.3	0952	3.9	1602	1.6	2211	4.1	
4	TU	0435	1.6	1053	3.6	1648	1.9	2315	3.9	
5	W	0528	1.8	1209	3.4	1745	2.1			
6	TH	0025	3.8	0635	2.0	1329	3.3	1904	2.3	◑
7	F	0137	3.7	0758	2.0	1444	3.4	2031	2.2	
8	SA	0242	3.7	0912	1.9	1543	3.5	2135	2.1	
9	SU	0338	3.9	1004	1.7	1625	3.8	2223	1.8	
10	M	0422	4.0	1045	1.5	1657	4.0	2304	1.6	
11	TU	0500	4.2	1121	1.3	1725	4.2	2340	1.4	
12	W	0534	4.3	1155	1.1	1754	4.4			
13	TH	0016	1.2	0607	4.4	1230	1.0	1825	4.5	
14	F	0052	1.0	0643	4.5	1306	0.9	1858	4.6	●
15	SA	0130	0.9	0721	4.5	1342	0.8	1935	4.6	
16	SU	0210	0.8	0803	4.5	1421	0.9	2015	4.6	
17	M	0253	0.9	0850	4.3	1501	1.0	2100	4.5	
18	TU	0339	1.0	0945	4.1	1545	1.2	2157	4.3	
19	W	0433	1.1	1049	3.9	1636	1.5	2306	4.1	
20	TH	0536	1.3	1200	3.8	1740	1.7			◐
21	F	0021	4.0	0646	1.3	1312	3.7	1857	1.8	
22	SA	0133	4.0	0759	1.3	1422	3.8	2015	1.7	
23	SU	0241	4.1	0909	1.2	1526	3.9	2124	1.6	
24	M	0343	4.2	1009	1.1	1619	4.1	2223	1.4	
25	TU	0437	4.3	1100	1.0	1704	4.3	2315	1.2	
26	W	0524	4.4	1146	0.9	1745	4.5			
27	TH	0003	1.1	0607	4.4	1229	0.9	1824	4.6	○
28	F	0049	1.0	0648	4.4	1310	0.9	1902	4.6	
29	SA	0133	1.0	0729	4.3	1349	1.0	1941	4.6	
30	SU	0214	1.0	0809	4.2	1427	1.1	2021	4.6	
31	M	0255	1.1	0850	4.1	1505	1.3	2102	4.4	

JUNE

Date	Day	Time	m	Time	m	Time	m	Time	m	Moon
1	TU	0335	1.2	0933	3.9	1544	1.4	2146	4.3	
2	W	0417	1.4	1019	3.7	1625	1.7	2236	4.1	
3	TH	0501	1.6	1111	3.5	1712	1.9	2330	3.9	
4	F	0549	1.7	1211	3.4	1807	2.1			◑
5	SA	0028	3.8	0643	1.8	1319	3.4	1910	2.2	
6	SU	0129	3.7	0743	1.9	1429	3.5	2020	2.1	
7	M	0230	3.7	0847	1.8	1526	3.6	2123	2.0	
8	TU	0326	3.8	0945	1.7	1610	3.8	2216	1.8	
9	W	0416	3.9	1035	1.5	1648	4.0	2302	1.6	
10	TH	0502	4.1	1120	1.3	1726	4.3	2347	1.4	
11	F	0546	4.3	1203	1.2	1804	4.5			
12	SA	0032	1.1	0630	4.4	1246	1.0	1844	4.6	●
13	SU	0118	0.9	0714	4.5	1329	0.9	1925	4.8	
14	M	0203	0.7	0800	4.5	1411	0.8	2009	4.8	
15	TU	0249	0.6	0847	4.5	1454	0.9	2056	4.7	
16	W	0336	0.7	0937	4.3	1539	1.0	2147	4.6	
17	TH	0426	0.7	1032	4.1	1627	1.2	2246	4.4	
18	F	0519	0.9	1132	3.9	1722	1.4	2352	4.2	
19	SA	0618	1.1	1238	3.8	1825	1.6			◐
20	SU	0101	4.1	0721	1.3	1347	3.7	1936	1.7	
21	M	0212	4.0	0829	1.4	1455	3.8	2052	1.7	
22	TU	0320	3.9	0939	1.4	1556	3.9	2203	1.6	
23	W	0421	4.0	1039	1.3	1648	4.1	2303	1.5	
24	TH	0514	4.0	1131	1.3	1732	4.2	2356	1.3	
25	F	0601	4.0	1216	1.2	1813	4.4			
26	SA	0043	1.2	0642	4.1	1258	1.1	1850	4.5	○
27	SU	0125	1.0	0720	4.1	1336	1.1	1927	4.6	
28	M	0204	1.0	0756	4.1	1413	1.0	2003	4.6	
29	TU	0240	1.0	0831	4.1	1448	1.1	2039	4.5	
30	W	0315	1.0	0906	4.0	1523	1.2	2116	4.4	

JULY

Date	Day	Time	m	Time	m	Time	m	Time	m	Moon
1	TH	0350	1.1	0943	3.9	1559	1.4	2156	4.2	
2	F	0427	1.3	1023	3.7	1637	1.6	2240	4.0	
3	SA	0507	1.4	1111	3.6	1720	1.8	2330	3.8	
4	SU	0551	1.6	1205	3.5	1809	2.0			◑
5	M	0026	3.7	0640	1.7	1306	3.5	1906	2.1	
6	TU	0126	3.6	0737	1.8	1411	3.5	2013	2.1	
7	W	0230	3.7	0842	1.8	1515	3.7	2126	2.0	
8	TH	0336	3.8	0951	1.7	1612	3.9	2231	1.7	
9	F	0437	3.9	1052	1.5	1702	4.2	2328	1.4	
10	SA	0531	4.2	1144	1.3	1748	4.5			
11	SU	0019	1.1	0619	4.4	1233	1.0	1831	4.7	●
12	M	0107	0.8	0705	4.6	1317	0.8	1914	5.0	
13	TU	0153	0.5	0749	4.7	1400	0.7	1957	5.1	
14	W	0237	0.3	0833	4.7	1442	0.6	2040	5.1	
15	TH	0321	0.3	0917	4.6	1525	0.7	2127	4.9	
16	F	0405	0.4	1005	4.4	1609	0.9	2218	4.7	
17	SA	0452	0.7	1059	4.1	1657	1.2	2319	4.3	
18	SU	0543	1.0	1203	3.9	1751	1.5			◐
19	M	0031	4.0	0641	1.4	1315	3.7	1858	1.7	
20	TU	0149	3.8	0751	1.6	1429	3.7	2025	1.9	
21	W	0307	3.7	0914	1.7	1539	3.8	2155	1.8	
22	TH	0416	3.7	1027	1.7	1637	3.9	2302	1.6	
23	F	0512	3.8	1121	1.5	1722	4.1	2353	1.4	
24	SA	0556	3.9	1205	1.3	1801	4.3			
25	SU	0035	1.2	0632	4.0	1245	1.2	1836	4.5	
26	M	0113	1.0	0705	4.1	1321	1.0	1909	4.6	○
27	TU	0146	0.9	0735	4.1	1355	0.9	1941	4.6	
28	W	0218	0.8	0805	4.2	1427	0.9	2011	4.6	
29	TH	0248	0.8	0834	4.1	1458	1.0	2042	4.5	
30	F	0318	0.9	0905	4.0	1528	1.2	2114	4.3	
31	SA	0350	1.0	0938	3.9	1601	1.4	2150	4.1	

AUGUST

Date	Day	Time	m	Time	m	Time	m	Time	m	Moon
1	SU	0426	1.2	1016	3.8	1637	1.6	2231	3.9	
2	M	0505	1.4	1104	3.6	1720	1.8	2328	3.7	
3	TU	0550	1.7	1207	3.5	1812	2.0			◑
4	W	0037	3.6	0644	1.8	1319	3.5	1919	2.1	
5	TH	0153	3.6	0753	1.9	1434	3.6	2049	2.0	
6	F	0312	3.7	0918	1.9	1545	3.8	2213	1.8	
7	SA	0422	3.9	1033	1.7	1643	4.2	2314	1.4	
8	SU	0518	4.2	1129	1.3	1732	4.6			
9	M	0005	0.9	0605	4.5	1217	1.0	1816	4.9	
10	TU	0051	0.6	0649	4.8	1301	0.7	1858	5.2	●
11	W	0135	0.2	0730	4.9	1343	0.5	1938	5.4	
12	TH	0216	0.1	0810	5.0	1423	0.4	2019	5.3	
13	F	0257	0.1	0851	4.8	1504	0.5	2101	5.1	
14	SA	0338	0.3	0935	4.6	1545	0.8	2148	4.8	
15	SU	0421	0.7	1025	4.3	1630	1.1	2246	4.3	
16	M	0508	1.2	1129	4.0	1720	1.5			◐
17	TU	0007	3.9	0602	1.6	1248	3.7	1825	1.9	
18	W	0135	3.7	0715	1.9	1408	3.7	2009	2.1	
19	TH	0258	3.6	0856	2.1	1523	3.7	2156	2.0	
20	F	0413	3.6	1015	1.9	1623	3.9	2259	1.7	
21	SA	0508	3.7	1107	1.7	1709	4.1	2342	1.4	
22	SU	0546	3.9	1148	1.5	1745	4.4			
23	M	0018	1.2	0615	4.0	1226	1.2	1816	4.5	
24	TU	0051	1.0	0643	4.2	1259	1.0	1846	4.7	○
25	W	0120	0.9	0709	4.3	1331	0.9	1914	4.7	
26	TH	0148	0.8	0735	4.4	1400	0.9	1941	4.7	
27	F	0215	0.8	0801	4.4	1428	0.9	2008	4.6	
28	SA	0243	0.8	0828	4.3	1457	1.0	2037	4.4	
29	SU	0314	1.0	0856	4.2	1528	1.2	2106	4.2	
30	M	0348	1.2	0927	4.0	1601	1.5	2141	4.0	
31	TU	0424	1.4	1006	3.8	1640	1.7	2234	3.8	

Chart Datum: 2·71 metres below Ordnance Datum (Newlyn). HAT is 5·5 metres above Chart Datum; see 0.20

TIME ZONE (UT)
For Summer Time add ONE hour in **non-shaded areas**

STORNOWAY LAT 58°12′N LONG 6°23′W

TIMES AND HEIGHTS OF HIGH AND LOW WATERS

Dates in red are SPRINGS
Dates in blue are NEAPS

YEAR **2010**

SEPTEMBER

Date	Day	Time	m	Time	m	Time	m	Time	m
1	W	0507	1.7	1113	3.6	1730	2.0	◑	
2	TH	0006	3.6	0602	1.9	1246	3.6	1843	2.1
3	F	0136	3.5	0718	2.1	1409	3.7	2031	2.1
4	SA	0259	3.7	0858	2.0	1525	3.9	2200	1.7
5	SU	0408	4.0	1016	1.7	1625	4.3	2258	1.3
6	M	0501	4.3	1110	1.4	1715	4.7	2346	0.8
7	TU	0546	4.7	1157	1.0	1758	5.1		
8	W	0029	0.4	0627	5.0	1240	0.7	● 1838	5.4
9	TH	0111	0.2	0707	5.1	1321	0.5	1917	5.5
10	F	0151	0.1	0745	5.2	1401	0.4	1956	5.4
11	SA	0230	0.2	0824	5.0	1441	0.6	2037	5.2
12	SU	0310	0.5	0906	4.8	1522	0.8	2121	4.8
13	M	0351	0.9	0954	4.4	1605	1.2	2218	4.3
14	TU	0435	1.4	1058	4.1	1655	1.7	2346	3.9
15	W	0527	1.9	1221	3.9	1759	2.1	◐	
16	TH	0117	3.6	0640	2.2	1341	3.8	1951	2.2
17	F	0241	3.5	0831	2.3	1456	3.8	2143	2.1
18	SA	0359	3.6	0952	2.1	1558	4.0	2239	1.8
19	SU	0450	3.8	1042	1.9	1644	4.2	2317	1.6
20	M	0523	3.9	1122	1.6	1720	4.4	2350	1.3
21	TU	0551	4.1	1158	1.4	1752	4.6		
22	W	0020	1.1	0616	4.3	1232	1.2	1820	4.7
23	TH	0048	1.0	0641	4.5	1303	1.0	○ 1846	4.8
24	F	0115	0.9	0704	4.6	1331	0.9	1912	4.8
25	SA	0142	0.8	0729	4.6	1400	1.0	1939	4.7
26	SU	0211	0.9	0756	4.5	1429	1.1	2008	4.6
27	M	0242	1.0	0824	4.4	1500	1.2	2039	4.3
28	TU	0316	1.2	0855	4.2	1535	1.4	2117	4.1
29	W	0352	1.4	0935	4.0	1615	1.7	2217	3.8
30	TH	0436	1.7	1046	3.8	1708	1.9	2356	3.6

OCTOBER

Date	Day	Time	m	Time	m	Time	m	Time	m
1	F	0533	2.0	1226	3.7	1830	2.1	◑	
2	SA	0125	3.6	0657	2.2	1349	3.8	2018	2.0
3	SU	0243	3.8	0839	2.1	1503	4.1	2140	1.6
4	M	0348	4.1	0953	1.8	1603	4.5	2235	1.2
5	TU	0440	4.5	1046	1.4	1653	4.8	2322	0.8
6	W	0524	4.8	1133	1.1	1736	5.2		
7	TH	0004	0.5	0604	5.0	1217	0.8	● 1816	5.4
8	F	0045	0.4	0642	5.2	1259	0.6	1856	5.4
9	SA	0125	0.4	0721	5.2	1340	0.6	1935	5.3
10	SU	0204	0.5	0800	5.1	1421	0.8	2016	5.0
11	M	0244	0.8	0841	4.9	1502	1.0	2102	4.6
12	TU	0324	1.2	0929	4.6	1546	1.4	2158	4.2
13	W	0407	1.6	1030	4.3	1636	1.7	2319	3.8
14	TH	0457	2.0	1148	4.0	1738	2.1	◐	
15	F	0045	3.6	0604	2.4	1303	3.9	1910	2.3
16	SA	0205	3.5	0745	2.5	1413	3.9	2053	2.2
17	SU	0320	3.6	0910	2.3	1517	4.0	2156	2.0
18	M	0414	3.8	1005	2.1	1608	4.2	2238	1.8
19	TU	0450	4.0	1049	1.8	1648	4.3	2313	1.5
20	W	0520	4.2	1126	1.6	1722	4.5	2344	1.3
21	TH	0547	4.4	1200	1.4	1752	4.6		
22	F	0013	1.2	0611	4.5	1233	1.2	1819	4.7
23	SA	0042	1.0	0636	4.7	1303	1.1	○ 1847	4.7
24	SU	0112	1.0	0704	4.7	1334	1.1	1918	4.7
25	M	0144	1.0	0733	4.7	1407	1.1	1951	4.6
26	TU	0217	1.0	0805	4.6	1442	1.2	2028	4.4
27	W	0253	1.2	0842	4.4	1521	1.4	2115	4.2
28	TH	0332	1.5	0929	4.2	1606	1.5	2220	3.9
29	F	0417	1.7	1042	4.0	1705	1.7	2346	3.8
30	SA	0517	2.0	1208	3.9	1825	1.8	◑	
31	SU	0105	3.8	0640	2.1	1325	4.0	1952	1.8

NOVEMBER

Date	Day	Time	m	Time	m	Time	m	Time	m
1	M	0218	3.9	0809	2.0	1435	4.2	2108	1.5
2	TU	0321	4.1	0922	1.8	1537	4.5	2206	1.2
3	W	0414	4.4	1019	1.5	1629	4.7	2255	1.0
4	TH	0500	4.7	1108	1.2	1715	4.9	2339	0.8
5	F	0542	4.9	1154	1.0	1758	5.0		
6	SA	0021	0.7	0621	5.0	1239	0.9	● 1839	5.1
7	SU	0103	0.7	0700	5.1	1323	0.9	1920	4.9
8	M	0143	0.9	0741	5.0	1406	1.0	2003	4.7
9	TU	0223	1.1	0823	4.9	1449	1.1	2048	4.5
10	W	0303	1.3	0909	4.7	1533	1.4	2139	4.2
11	TH	0346	1.6	1001	4.4	1620	1.6	2240	3.9
12	F	0432	2.0	1103	4.2	1713	1.9	2352	3.7
13	SA	0528	2.2	1209	4.1	1817	2.1	◐	
14	SU	0107	3.6	0642	2.4	1316	4.0	1934	2.2
15	M	0220	3.6	0806	2.4	1422	3.9	2050	2.1
16	TU	0323	3.7	0915	2.2	1520	4.0	2146	1.9
17	W	0410	3.9	1007	2.0	1608	4.1	2229	1.8
18	TH	0446	4.1	1050	1.8	1648	4.3	2305	1.6
19	F	0516	4.3	1128	1.6	1722	4.4	2339	1.4
20	SA	0544	4.5	1203	1.4	1756	4.5		
21	SU	0012	1.2	0613	4.6	1239	1.3	○ 1829	4.6
22	M	0048	1.1	0644	4.7	1316	1.1	1905	4.6
23	TU	0124	1.0	0719	4.7	1354	1.1	1944	4.6
24	W	0201	1.1	0756	4.7	1434	1.1	2027	4.5
25	TH	0240	1.2	0838	4.6	1517	1.1	2115	4.3
26	F	0321	1.3	0928	4.5	1605	1.2	2214	4.1
27	SA	0408	1.5	1030	4.3	1701	1.4	2323	3.9
28	SU	0505	1.7	1141	4.2	1806	1.5	◑	
29	M	0034	3.9	0614	1.9	1253	4.2	1916	1.5
30	TU	0143	3.9	0731	1.9	1402	4.2	2028	1.5

DECEMBER

Date	Day	Time	m	Time	m	Time	m	Time	m
1	W	0249	4.0	0845	1.8	1508	4.3	2133	1.3
2	TH	0348	4.2	0951	1.6	1607	4.4	2229	1.2
3	F	0438	4.4	1048	1.4	1659	4.5	2319	1.1
4	SA	0524	4.6	1140	1.2	1746	4.6		
5	SU	0004	1.0	0606	4.8	1229	1.1	● 1829	4.6
6	M	0047	1.0	0647	4.9	1314	1.0	1912	4.6
7	TU	0129	1.0	0727	4.9	1357	1.0	1953	4.5
8	W	0209	1.1	0807	4.8	1439	1.1	2034	4.3
9	TH	0248	1.2	0848	4.7	1519	1.2	2115	4.2
10	F	0327	1.4	0931	4.6	1600	1.4	2158	4.0
11	SA	0408	1.6	1017	4.4	1642	1.6	2247	3.8
12	SU	0453	1.9	1109	4.2	1728	1.8	2346	3.6
13	M	0544	2.1	1206	4.0	1820	1.9	◐	
14	TU	0055	3.5	0645	2.2	1308	3.8	1919	2.0
15	W	0211	3.6	0756	2.3	1412	3.8	2026	2.0
16	TH	0316	3.7	0908	2.2	1515	3.8	2130	1.9
17	F	0404	3.9	1006	2.0	1608	3.9	2222	1.8
18	SA	0443	4.1	1054	1.8	1654	4.1	2307	1.6
19	SU	0518	4.3	1138	1.6	1736	4.2	2349	1.4
20	M	0554	4.5	1221	1.3	1817	4.4		
21	TU	0030	1.2	0631	4.7	1303	1.1	○ 1858	4.5
22	W	0110	1.0	0709	4.8	1345	0.9	1939	4.6
23	TH	0151	0.9	0749	4.9	1428	0.8	2021	4.6
24	F	0231	0.9	0831	4.9	1511	0.7	2105	4.5
25	SA	0313	1.0	0916	4.8	1556	0.8	2154	4.3
26	SU	0357	1.1	1007	4.6	1645	0.9	2250	4.1
27	M	0447	1.3	1108	4.4	1738	1.1	2354	3.9
28	TU	0543	1.5	1216	4.2	1838	1.3	◑	
29	W	0104	3.8	0650	1.7	1329	4.1	1945	1.5
30	TH	0216	3.8	0807	1.8	1442	4.0	2100	1.5
31	F	0324	3.9	0928	1.7	1551	4.0	2209	1.5

Chart Datum: 2·71 metres below Ordnance Datum (Newlyn). HAT is 5·5 metres above Chart Datum; see 0.20

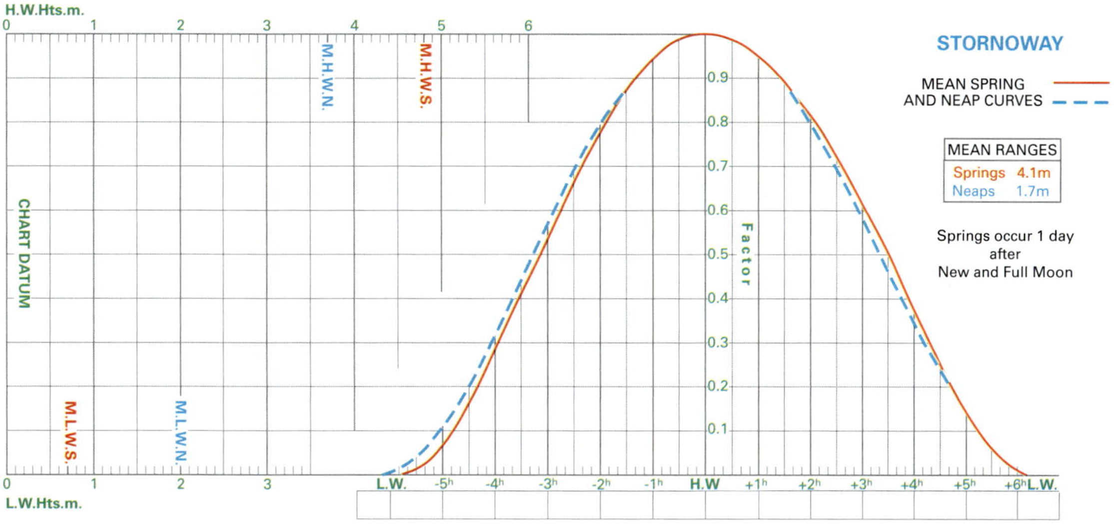

HARBOURS AND ANCHORAGES ON THE EAST SIDE OF THE OUTER HEBRIDES, from N to S:

Visitor moorings mentioned in this section are inspected annually, have pick up buoys, can take yachts <15tons, and there is no charge <7days. Refer to www.w-isles.gov.uk/harbour master.

LOCH SHELL, Lewis, **57°59′·98N 06°25′·07W**. AC 1794. HW –0437 on Dover; ML 2·7m. See 1.5. Pass S of Eilean Iuvard; beware rks to W of Is. ⚓ in Tob Eishken, 2½M up loch on N shore (beware rk awash on E side of ent), or at head of loch (exposed to E winds; dries some distance). **Facilities:** ✉/Stores at Lemreway.

SHIANT ISLANDS, Lewis, **57°53′·68N 06°21′·37W**. AC 1794, 1795. Tides as Loch Shell 1.5. Beware strong tidal streams and overfalls in Sound of Shiant. Strictly a fair weather ⚓ ; in W winds ⚓ E of Mol Mor, isthmus between Garbh Eileen (159m) and Eileen an Tighe. In E winds ⚓ W of Mol Mor. No lights or facilities.

EAST LOCH TARBERT, Harris, **57°49′·98N 06°41′·07W**. AC 2905. HW –0446 on Dover; ML 3·0m; Duration 0605. See 1.5. Appr via Sound of Scalpay; beware Elliot Rk (2m) 2½ca SSW of Rubha Crago. A bridge (20m clearance) at 57°52′·80N 06°41′·73W joins Scalpay to Harris. Bridge lts: Centre Oc 6s; N side Iso G 4s 35m; S side Iso R 4s 35m. Eilean Glas lt ho at E end of Scalpay, Fl (3) 20s 43m 23M; W tr, R bands. In Sound of Scalpay, stream sets W from HW +3, and E from HW –3. ⚓ off Tarbert WSW of steamer pier in about 2·5m. ☎ (01589) 502444. Facilities: Bar, D, Dr, FW, P, ✉, R, 🛒, ferry to Uig. Alternatively Scalpay N Hbr gives good shelter. Beware rk 5ca off Aird an Aiseig, E side of ent. SHM buoy marks wk off Coddem; 5ca E of the buoy is a rk, depth 1·1m. Ldg Lt Oc WRG 6s 10m 5M. Both piers have 2FG (vert) lts; ⚓ 7ca N, in about 3m. **Facilities:** FW at pier, ✉, 🛒, Ferry to Harris.

SOUND OF HARRIS, 57°43′N 06°58′W. Passages through this difficult Sound are detailed in the *W Coast of Scotland Pilot*. The Stanton and Outer Stromay Chans off the Harris shore are the most feasible for yachts. AC 2802 shows the ferry routes from Leverburgh to Berneray.

LOCH RODEL, Harris. AC 2802. 3 Ⓜs at **57°44′·2N 06°57′·4W** in Poll an Tigh-mhàil; enter from SW past jetties. No lts.

LOCH MADDY, North Uist, **57°35′·98N 07°06′·07W**. AC 2825. HW –0500 on Dover. See 1.5. With strong wind against tide there can be bad seas off ent. Appr clear, but from S beware submerged rk ½ca N of Leacnam Madadh. Lts: Weaver's Pt Fl 3s 21m 7M; Glas Eilean Mor Fl (2) G 4s 8m 5M; Rubna Nam Pleac Fl R 4s 7m 5M. Inside loch: Ruigh Liath QG 6m 5M; Vallaquie Is Dir Fl (3) WRG 8s. Ferry pier ldg lts 298°: front 2FG(vert) 4M; rear Oc G 8s 10m 4M, vis 284°-304°. 2 Ⓜs Bagh Aird nam Madadh; 2 Ⓜs W of and 4 Ⓜs SW of ferry pier ☎ (01870) 602425; 2 Ⓜs E of Oronsay. ⚓s: clear S of ferry pier; NE of Vallaquie Is; Charles Hbr; Oronsay (⚓ not advised due to moorings), tidal berth on private pier; Sponish Hbr; Loch Portain. VHF Ch 12 16. Port Manager ☎ (01876) 5003337 (day), 5003226 (night). **Facilities:** Lochmaddy, Shop, Ⓑ, Gas, ✉, P, D, FW; Loch Portain ✉, Shop.

LOCH EPORT, North Uist, **57°33′·45N 07°08′·12W**. AC 2825, but not the head of loch. Tides, approx as L Maddy; 3kn sp stream. On the S side of ent are rks, some drying. The ent proper is clean but very narrow (about 100m) for 5ca, then widens. Follow the charted clearing line 082°. Best ⚓s are: Bàgh a' Bhiorain (S of chan; line up cairn and Bu boulder on 129°); and Acairseid Lee (N bank) E or W of Deer Is. 🛒, R, Bar, ✉ at Clachan, hd of loch.

KALLIN, Grimsay. **57°28′·9N 07°12′·2W**. AC 2904. 1 Ⓜ in NE of hbr. 3 chan lt buoys and 2 FR (vert) on hbr bkwtr. ☎ (01870) 602425.

LOCH CARNAN, South Uist, **57°22′·03N 07°16′·39W**. AC 2825. Tides, see 1.5. SWM buoy, L Fl 10s, at 57°22′·30N 07°11′·57W is almost 2M E of app chan proper, marked by Nos 1 and 2 buoys, Fl G 2·5s and Fl R 2s, at 57°22′·45N 07°14′·90W. Round No 3 PHM buoy, Fl R 5s, between Gasay and Taigh Iamain, then pick up ldg lts 222° to Sandwick Quay; front Fl R 2s, rear Iso R 10s, both 5M, W ◇s on posts. Power stn and 2 chys are conspic close to SE of quay. ☎ (01870) 602425 for permission to berth on the quay (MoD property). There is ⚓ or 2 Ⓜs about 2ca WNW of the quay in deep water. ☎ (01870) 610238. The passage S of Gasay is unmarked and needs careful pilotage. FW, D available.

LOCH SKIPPORT, South Uist, **57°19′·98N 07°13′·67W**. AC 2904, 2825. HW –0602 on Dover; see 1.5. Easy ent 3M NNE of Hecla (604m). No lights, but 2¼M SSE is Usinish lt ho Fl WR 20s 54m 19/15M. ⚓s at: Wizard Pool in 7m; beware Float Rk, dries 2·3m; on N side of Caolas Mor in 7m; Bagh Charmaig in 5m. Linne Arm has narrow ent, many fish farms and poor holding. No facilities.

LOCH EYNORT, South Uist, **57°13′·13N 07°16′·87W**. AC 2825. Tides: interpolate between Lochs Skipport and Boisdale, see 1.5. ⚓s in the outer loch at Cearcdal Bay and on the N side just before the narrows are exposed to the E. The passage to Upper L Eynort is very narrow and streams reach 5-7kn; best not attempted unless local fishermen offer guidance. Good ⚓ inside at Bàgh Lathach.

Continued overleaf

LOCH BOISDALE, South Uist, **57°08′·78N 07°16′·07W**. AC 2770. HW –0455 on Dover; ML 2·4m; Duration 0600. See 1.5. Good shelter except in SE gales when swell runs right up the 2M loch. From N, appr between Rubha na Cruibe and Calvay Is; ldg line 245°: Hollisgeir (0·3m) on with pier (ru). From S beware Clan Ewan Rk, dries 1·2m, and McKenzie Rk (2·4m), marked by PHM lt buoy Fl (3) R 15s. Chan to Boisdale Hbr lies N of Gasay Is; beware rks off E end. ⚓ off pier in approx 4m, or SW of Gasay Is in approx 9m. 4 Øs NE of pier ☎ (01870) 602425. There are fish cages W of Rubha Bhuailt. Lts: E end of Calvay Is Fl (2) WRG 10s 16m 7/4M. Gasay Is Fl WR 5s 10m 7/4M. N side of loch, opp Gasay Is, Fl G 6s. Ro-Ro terminal Iso RG 4s 8m 2M; and close SE, Fl (2) R 5s. See 1.3. ☎ (0187) 700288. **Facilities:** Bar, FW (on pier), P, ✉, R, Ferry to mainland.

ACAIRSEID MHÓR, Eriskay, ⊕ **57°03′·78N 07°16′·35W**. AC 2770. Tides approx as for North Bay (Barra), see 1.5. Ben Scrien (183m) is conspic, pointed peak N of hbr. Ldg lts 285°, both Oc R 6s 9/10m 4M, W △ ▽ on orange posts, lead for 0·5M from the above lat/long between two drying rks into the outer loch. A SHM buoy, Fl G 6s, marks a rk drying 3m. Possible AB on pontoon; 2 Øs (perhaps submerged at HW) are at 57°03′·95N 07°17′·40W on S side of inner loch, opp pier, 2 FG (vert). ☎ (01870) 602425. 🛒, R, Bar, ✉ at Haun, 1·5M at N end of island.

NORTH BAY, Barra, **57°00′·11N 07°24′·67W**. AC 2770. Tides see 1.5. Well marked approach to inlet sheltered from S and W winds. WPT 56°58′·68N 07°20′·31W is about 200m NE of Curachan ECM buoy, Q (3) 10s, and in the white sector (304°-306°) of Ardveenish dir ☆ 305°, Oc WRG 3s, 2·5M to the WNW. ⚓ 1ca WNW of Black Island or in N part of Bay Hirivagh where there are Øs; or tempy AB on the quay in 4·5m. FW, Bar, 🛒, bus to Castlebay.

CASTLEBAY, Barra, **56°56′·78N 07°29′·67W**. AC 2769. HW –0525 on Dover; ML 2·3m; Duration 0600. See 1.5. Very good shelter & holding. Best ⚓ in approx 8m NW of Kiessimul Castle (on an island); NE of castle are rks. About 20 Øs lie to W of the pier; they may be encroaching on the recommended anchorage NW of Kiessimul Castle. ☎ (01870) 602425. Or ⚓ in Vatersay Bay in approx 9m. W end of Vatersay Sound is closed by a causeway. Beware rks NNW of Sgeir Dubh a conspic W/G tr, Q(3)G 6s 6m 5M, which leads 283° in transit with Sgeir Liath bn. Chan Rk, 2ca to the S, is marked by Fl WR 6s 4m 6/4M. Close-in ldg lts 295°, both FBu 6M on W framework trs: front 9m Or △ on Rubha Glas; rear, 457m from front, 15m Or ▽, vis: 15° and 8° respectively either side of ldg line. ☎ (01871) 810306. **Facilities:** Bar, D, FW, P, ✉, R, 🛒, Ferry to mainland.

ISLANDS WEST OF THE OUTER HEBRIDES (N to S)

TIDES

Standard Port STORNOWAY (⟵)

Times				Height (metres)			
High Water		Low Water		MHWS	MHWN	MLWN	MLWS
0100	0700	0300	0900	4·8	3·7	2·0	0·7
1300	1900	1500	2100				
Differences FLANNAN ISLES							
–0026	–0016	–0016	–0026	–0·9	–0·7	–0·6	–0·2
VILLAGE BAY (St Kilda)							
–0040	–0040	–0045	–0045	–1·4	–1·2	–0·8	–0·3
ROCKALL							
–0055	–0055	–0105	–0105	–1·8	–1·5	–0·9	–0·2

FLANNAN ISLES, Western Isles, centred on **58°17′·28N 07°35′·27W** (Eilean Mór). AC 2524, 2721. Tides, as above. Uninhabited group of several rky islets, 18M WNW of Gallan Head (Lewis). The main islet is Eilean Mór where landing can be made on SW side in suitable conditions. Lt ho, Fl (2) 30s 101m 20M, is a 23m high W tr on NE tip of Eilean Mór; the lt is obscured by islets to the W which are up to 57m high. No recommended ⚓s and the few charted depths are by lead-line surveys.

ST KILDA, Western Isles, **57°48′·28N 08°33′·07W**. AC 2721, 2524. Tides at Village Bay, Hirta: HW –0510 on Dover; ML 1·9m; Duration 0615; see above. A group of four isles and three stacks, the main island is Hirta from which the Army withdrew in April 1998 after 30 years. The facility is now manned by a civilian company, Qinetiq ☎ (01870) 604443, based at South Uist. Hirta is owned by National Trust for Scotland and leased to Scottish National Heritage who employ a Seasonal Warden, ☎ 01870 604628. ⚓ in Village Bay, SE-facing, in approx 5m about 1·5ca off the pier. Ldg lts 270°, both Oc 5s 26/38m 3M. If wind is between NE and SSW big swells enter the bay; good holding, but untenable if winds strong. Levenish Is (55m) is 1·5M E of Hirta with offlying rks. Call *Kilda Radio* VHF Ch 16 **12** 73 (HJ) for permission to land; ☎ (01870) 604406 (HO), 604612 (OT). Alternative ⚓ at Glen Bay on N side is only safe in S & E winds. Facilities: FW from wells near landings.

ROCKALL, 57°35′·7N 13°41′·2W. AC 1128, 2524. Tides, as above. A 19m high granite rock, 200M W of N Uist. Best access by helicopter. Lt, Fl 15s 13M, is often extinguished for long periods due to weather damage. Helen's Reef, 1·4m, on which the sea breaks is 2M ENE.

MONACH ISLANDS (Heisker Is), centred on **57°31′·28N 07°38′·07W**. AC 2721, 2722. Tides, see 1.5 Shillay. The group lies 5M SW of N Uist and 8M WNW of Benbecula. The 5 main islands (W-E) are Shillay, Ceann Iar, Shivinish, Ceann Ear and Stockay; all uninhabited. Many rky offliers from NW through N to SE of the group. On Shillay there is a conspic red brick lt ho, Fl (2) 15s. ⚓s at: E of lt ho; Croic Hbr, bay N of Shivinish; and S Hbr on W side of Shivinish.

CAPE WRATH TO ULLAPOOL

(AC 1785, 1794) C Wrath (lt, fog sig) is a steep headland (110m). ▶ *To N of it the E-going stream begins at HW Ullapool – 0350, and W-going at HW Ullapool + 0235, sp rates 3kn. Eddies close inshore cause almost continuous W-going stream E of Cape, and N-going stream SW of it. Where they meet is turbulence, with dangerous seas in bad weather.* ◀ Duslic Rk, 7ca NE of lt ho, dries 3·4m. 6M SW of C Wrath, islet of Am Balg (45m)is foul for 2ca around.

There are anchorages in Loch Inchard (AC 2503), the best shelter being in Kinlochbervie on N shore; also good anchs among Is along S shore of Loch Laxford, entered between Ardmore Pt and Rubha Ruadh. Handa Is to WSW is a bird sanctuary. Handa Sound is navigable with care, but beware Bogha Morair in mid-chan and associated overfalls. ▶ *Tide turns 2hrs earlier in the Sound than offshore. Strong winds against tide raise a bad sea off Pt of Stoer.* ◀ The best shelter is 8M S at Loch Inver (AC 2504), with good anch off hotel near head of loch. Anchorages to the N of Loch Inver may be found at Kylesku, Culkein Drumbeg, Drumbeg, Loch Nedd and Loch Roe. To the S lies Enard Bay.

1.6 KINLOCHBERVIE

Highland **58°27′·26N 05°02′·78W** ❂❂❂✿✿✿

CHARTS AC 1954, 1785, 2503; Imray C67.

TIDES –0400 Dover; ML 2·7; Duration 0610

Standard Port ULLAPOOL (⟶)

Times				Height (metres)			
High Water		Low Water		MHWS	MHWN	MLWN	MLWS
0000	0600	0300	0900	5·2	3·9	2·1	0·7
1200	1800	1500	2100				
Differences LOCH BERVIE							
+0020	+0010	+0010	+0020	–0·4	–0·3	–0·2	0·1
LOCH LAXFORD							
+0015	+0015	+0005	+0005	–0·3	–0·4	–0·2	0·0
BADCALL BAY							
+0005	+0005	+0005	+0005	–0·7	–0·5	–0·5	+0·2
LOCH NEDD							
0000	0000	0000	0000	–0·3	–0·2	–0·2	0·0
LOCH INVER							
–0005	–0005	–0005	–0005	–0·2	0·0	0·0	+0·1

SHELTER Very good in Kinlochbervie Hbr off the N shore of Loch Inchard. A useful passage port, only 14.5 track miles S of Cape Wrath. It is an active FV port, but yachts AB on pontoon (contact HM for details); NE side is shoal/foul. If full, ⚓ at Loch Clash, open to W; landing jetty in 2·7m. Other ⚓s at: Camus Blair on S shore, 5ca SW of hbr ent, and up the loch at L Sheigra, Achriesgill Bay and 5ca short of the head of the loch.

NAVIGATION WPT 58°27′·34N 05°05′·08W (at mouth of Loch Inchard), 100°/1·3M to hbr ent. The sides of the loch are clean, but keep to N side of Loch Inchard to clear Bodha Ceann na Saile NCM and rk (3m depth) almost in mid-chan.

LIGHTS AND MARKS From offshore in good vis Ceann Garbh, a conspic mountain 900m (6M inland), leads 110° toward ent of Loch Inchard. Rubha na Leacaig, Fl (2) 10s 30m 8M, marks N side of loch ent. Dir ☆ WRG (H24) 15m 16M, Y framework tr (floodlit) leads 327° into hbr; see 1.3 for vis sectors. The 25m wide ent chan (and hbr) is dredged 4m and marked by 2 PHM poles, Fl R 4s and QR, and by a SHM pole, Fl G 4s. On S shore of loch Creag Mhòr, Dir Oc lt WRG 2.8s 16m 9M, is aligned 147°/327° with hbr ent chan; see 1.3.

R/T VHF Ch **14** 16 HX. Ch 06 is used by FVs in the Minches.

TELEPHONE (Code 01971) HM ☎ 521235, mob 07901 514350; MRCC (01851) 702013; ⊖ (0141) 887 9369 (H24); Marinecall 09068 969654; Police 521222; Dr 502002.

FACILITIES AB (pontoon) £1.50<10m for 48hrs, FW, D at FV quay, P (cans), Gas, CH, ME, ✉, Bar, 🛒, R, Showers (Mission & Hbr Office), ♿. In summer, bus to Inverness.

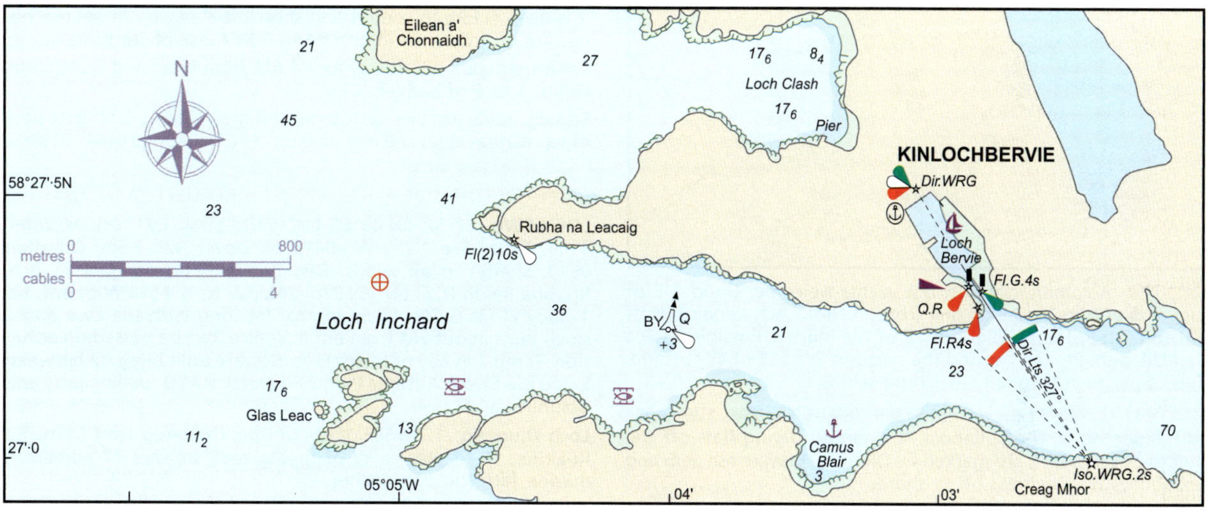

⚓ & HBR BETWEEN KINLOCHBERVIE AND ULLAPOOL

LOCH LAXFORD Highland, **58°24′·78N 05°07′·18W**. AC 2503. HW –0410 on Dover. ML 2·7m. See 1.6. Ent between Rubha Ruadh and Ardmore Pt, 1M ENE, clearly identified by 3 isolated mountains (N-S) Ceann Garbh, Ben Arkle and Ben Stack. The many ⚓s in the loch include: Loch a'Chadh-fi, on N/NE sides of islet (John Ridgeway's Adventure School on Pt on W side of narrows has moorings); Bagh nah-Airde Beag, next bay to E, (beware rk 5ca off SE shore which covers at MHWS); Weaver's Bay on SW shore, 3M from ent (beware drying rk off NW Pt of ent); Bagh na Fionndalach Mor on SW shore (4-6m); Fanagmore Bay on SW shore (beware head of bay foul with old moorings). Beware many fish farming cages. Facilities: none, nearest stores at Scourie (5M).

LOCH INVER Highland, **58°08′·98N 05°15′·08W**. AC 2504. HW –0433 on Dover; ML 3·0m. See 1.6. Good shelter in all weathers at head of loch in busy fishing hbr on S side. Appr N or S of Soyea Is, Fl (2) 10s 34m 6M; beware rock drying 1·7m about 50m off Kirkaig Point (S side of ent). Glas Leac, a small islet 7ca WSW of hbr, may be passed on either side. Its ☆, Fl WRG 3s, has 3 WRG sectors (see 1.3) covering the chans N and S of Soyea Is and into the hbr. The church, hotel (S side) and white ho (N side) are all conspic. A 22-berth marina is between the breakwater (QG) and the first FV pier. Or, in W'ly gales, ⚓ in the lee of bkwtr in about 8m; or where HM directs. Other ⚓s on S shore of Loch Inver. VHF Ch 12 16. HM ☎ (01571) 844247; mob 07958 734610. Health Centre 01571 844452. **Facilities:** FW, P, D, ⊡, showers (Leisure Centre), CH, 🛒, ✉, Gas.

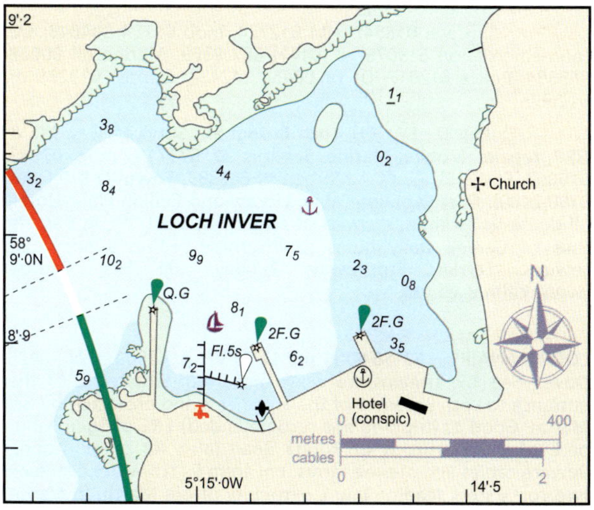

1.7 ULLAPOOL

Highland **57°53′·70N 05°09′·38W** ✿✿✿⚓⚓✿✿

CHARTS AC 1794, 2500, 2501, 2509; Imray C67.

TIDES –0415 Dover; ML 3·0; Duration 0610

Standard Port ULLAPOOL (⟶)

Times				**Height (metres)**			
High Water		Low Water		MHWS	MHWN	MLWN	MLWS
0000	0600	0300	0900	5·2	3·9	2·1	0·7
1200	1800	1500	2100				
Differences SUMMER ISLES (Tanera Mor)							
–0005	–0005	–0010	–0010	–0·1	+0·1	0·0	+0·1
LOCH EWE (Mellon Charles, 57°51′N 05°38′W)							
–0005	–0010	–0005	–0005	–0·5	–0·5	–0·5	0·5
LOCH GAIRLOCH							
–0020	–0020	–0010	–0010	0·0	+0·1	–0·3	–0·1

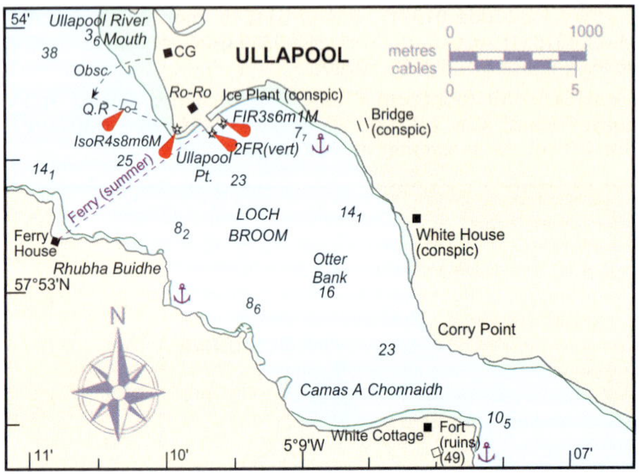

SHELTER A commercial port but yachts welcome. Good ⚓ E of pier, 8 ⓥ or possible AB on pier (consult HM). Loch Kanaird (N of ent to Loch Broom) has good ⚓ E of Isle Martin. Possible ⚓s 6ca S of Ullapool Pt, and beyond the narrows 3ca ESE of W cottage. The upper loch is squally in strong winds.

NAVIGATION WPT L Broom ent 57°55′·78N 05°15′·08W, 129°/3.5M to Ullapool Pt lt. N of Ullapool Pt extensive drying flats off the mouth of Ullapool R are marked by QR buoy. Beware fish pens and unlit buoys SE of narrows off W shore.

LIGHTS AND MARKS Rhubha Cadail, N of L. Broom ent, Fl WRG 6s 11m 9/6M. Cailleach Hd, W of ent, Fl (2) 12s 60m 9M. Ullapool Pt Iso R 4s 8m 6M; grey mast, vis 258°-108°.

R/T *Ullapool Harbour* Ch 14 16 (H24).

TELEPHONE (Code 01854) HM 612724, mob 07734 004843; CG (non-emergency) 613076; ⊖ (0141) 887 9369; Marinecall 09068 969654; Police 612017; Dr Dr 08454 242424; Dentist 613289 or 612660.

FACILITIES **Pier** D, FW, CH; **Loch Broom SC Services:** Gas, ME & GRP repairs Mobile Marine Services ☎ 633719, mob 07866 516067, El, Ⓔ, El, Ⓔ, ⚒ A.Morgan ☎ 666383; **Town** D & P (cans 0700-2100), @ at Captains Cabin, Library and Ceilidh Place Hotel, all domestic facilities, showers at swimming pool, 🛒, R, Bar, ⇌ (bus to Garve). Daily buses to Inverness (✈)(no Sunday bus services. **Ferries:** Stornoway; 2-3/day; 2¾ Hrs; Calmac (www.calmac.co.uk).

ADJACENT ANCHORAGES

LOCH KANAIRD, 57°56′60′N 05°12′20′W. AC 2500. HW –0425 Dover; See 1.7; streams are weak and irreg. Situated E of the entrance to Loch Broom, S of the Summer Is and protected by Isle Martin. Good ⚓s (tripping line recommended) ENE of Sgeir Mhor or E of Isle Martin, N of Rubha Beag (also AB on pontoon). Beware cables and marine farms. Ent from S (1ca wide) between two rocky spits, leading line E extremity of Isle Martin in transit with dark streak on cliff behind brg 000°. Ent from N, deep and clear of dangers. Facilities: Ardmair Boat Centre ☎ P.Fraser (01854) 612054, M, FW, showers, some repairs. Isle Martin, Landing permitted (voluntary donation to Trust, ☎ (01854) 612531).

SUMMER ISLES, 58°01′N 05°25′W. AC 2509, 2501. HW –0425 Dover; See 1.7; streams are weak and irregular. In the N apps to Loch Broom some 30 islands and rks, the main ones being Eilean Mullagrach, Isle Ristol, Glas-leac Mor, Tanera Beg, Eilean a' Char, Eilean Fada Mor. Beware rocks at S end of Horse Sound. ⚓s:

Isle Ristol, ⚓ to S of drying causeway and clear of moorings; beware landings frequented by local FVs. Close to slip is lt Fl G 3s. Facilities: 🛒 (at Polbain 2M).

Tanera Beg, ⚓ in the chan to the E inside Eilean Fada Mor.

Tanera Mor, on E side, ⚓ in bay to N off pier or in W corner off stone jetty ; beware many moorings and fish pens. Also poss ⚓ close NW of Is and close E of Eilean na Saille, but N of drying rock. Facilities: ☎ (01854) 622272 B Wilder for M, showers, FW, Tea Room.

Badentarbat Bay, Temp'y ⚓ NW part of bay ESE of pier which is busy with marina farm activity. Beware N part of bay is shoal. Suitable for Achiltibuie or Polbain on mainland. Facilities: 🛒, R, Gas, FW, D (emerg) ☎ (01854) 622261.

LITTLE LOCH BROOM, 57°54′·98N 05°24′·68W. AC 2500. HW –0415 Dover as per Ullapool, see 1.7; streams are weak (approx 1kn). Between Loch Broom and Gruinard Bay, entered S of Cailleach Hd it is deep (115m in centre) and shoreline steep to. In approaches beware of Ardross Rk (depth 0.6m) 0.38M ENE of Stattic Pt.

Camusnagaul, on S side of loch 1.6M from head and Dundonnel Hotel, ⚓ to E of hamlet.

Scoraig, inside narrows on N shore in N'ly conditions, ⚓ off jetty clear of submarine cables and marine farm. ⚒ C.Dawson ☎ 01845 613380.

⚓s BETWEEN LITTLE LOCH BROOM AND LOCH GAIRLOCH

LOCH EWE, 57°52′·0N 05°40′·0W (SWM buoy, L Fl 10s). AC 2509, 3146. Tides: See 1.7; HW –0415 on Dover; ML 2·6m; Duration 0610. Shelter in all winds. Easy ent with no dangers in loch. Rhubha Reidh lt, Fl (4) 15s 37m 24M, W tr, is 4·5M W of ent. No 1 buoy Fl (3) G 10s. Loch approx 7M long with Isle Ewe and 2 small islets about 2M from ent in centre; can be passed on either side. Temp ⚓ in bay of Isle of Ewe. Beware unlit buoy A2 between E side Isle Ewe & Aultbea Pier, 2 FG (vert). NATO fuelling jetty and dolphins, all Fl G 4s.

Loch Thurnaig, 1.7M SSE of Isle of Ewe, sheltered ⚓ off Ob na Bà Rùaidhe, SE of pier to W of drying reef. Beware of numerous marine farms in approaches.

Aultbea: ⚓ off Aultbea Hotel on E shore or in NW'lies close of pier. N part of bay is shoal. Facilities: Dr, P, ✉, R, 🛒, Bar.

Poolewe Bay ⚓ in SW part of bay in 3·5m, at head of loch: Boor Rks(3m) with drying rocks extending 1ca NW lie off W shore about 9ca NW of Poolewe. Facilities: FW, D, L on pier, P (at garage), ✉, R, Bar, 🛒, Gas.

Inverewe Gdns on NE side of bay, ⚓ to SW of Jetty at Port na Cloiche Gile.

LOCH GAIRLOCH, 57°43′N 05°45′W. AC 228, 2528. HW –0440 on Dover. See 1.7. A wide loch facing W. Ent clear of dangers but Submarine Exercise Area (see 1.21) to S of Longa Is. Quite heavy seas enter in bad weather. Lts: Glas Eilean Fl WRG 6s 9m 6/4M, Gairloch Pier Hd, QR 9m. HM ☎ (01445) 712140.

Badachro, good shelter SW of Eilean Horrisdale on SW side of loch but busy with FVs and local craft. Also ⚓'ge to NNW of Sgeir Dhubh Bheag SSE of Eilean Horrisdale, passage to S of this island is possible with caution. R, Bar, (Bad Inn HM ☎ (01445) 741255 for M availability.

Loch Shieldaig, at SE end of the loch with many moorings for local craft, if congested ⚓ to SSW of Eilean an t-Sabhail. Beware marine farms.

Flowerdale Bay, ⚓ in approx 6m near Gairloch pier or berth on pontoons (2m depth N side, 3m S side) at pier. HM ☎ (01445) 712140. VHF Ch 16 (occas). Gairloch Pier: AB fees charged. P (cans), D, FW, SC, Hotel, Bar, Showers, Gas, 🛒, CH, ✉.

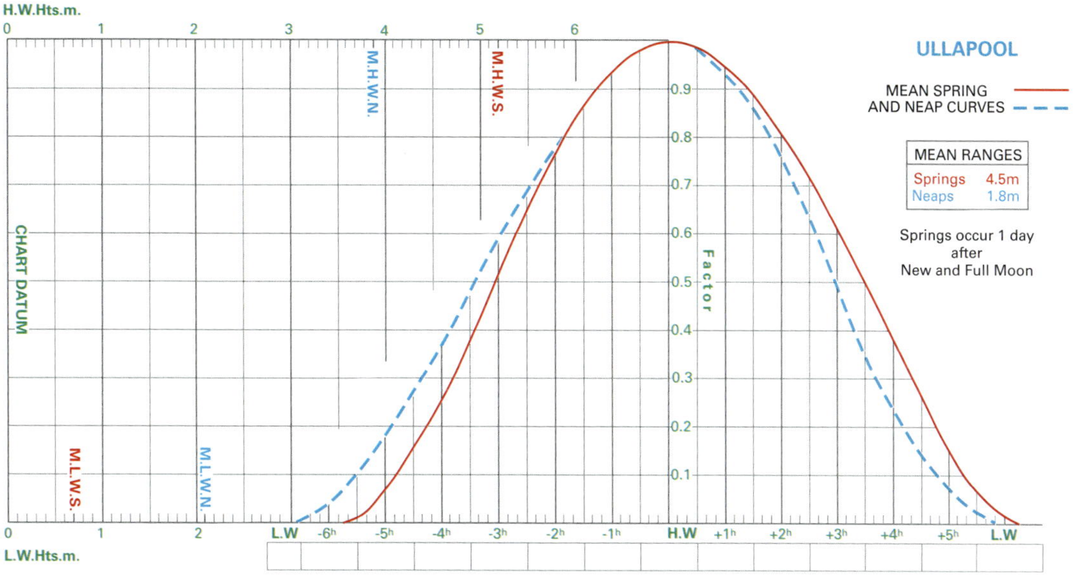

1.8 PORTREE

Skye (Highland) **57°24'·73N 06°11'·07W**

CHARTS AC 2209, 2534; Imray C66.

TIDES –0445 Dover; ML no data; Duration 0610

Standard Port ULLAPOOL (⟶)

Times				Height (metres)			
High Water		Low Water		MHWS	MHWN	MLWN	MLWS
0000	0600	0300	0900	5·2	3·9	2·1	0·7
1200	1800	1500	2100				
Differences PORTREE (Skye)							
–0025	–0025	–0025	–0025	+0·1	–0·2	–0·2	0·0
SHIELDAIG (Loch Torridon)							
–0020	–0020	–0015	–0015	+0·4	+0·3	+0·1	0·0
LOCH A'BHRAIGE (Rona)							
–0020	0000	–0010	0000	–0·1	–0·1	–0·1	–0·2
PLOCKTON							
+0005	–0025	–0005	–0010	+0·5	+0·5	+0·5	+0·2
LOCH SNIZORT (Uig Bay, Skye)							
–0045	–0020	–0005	–0025	+0·1	–0·4	–0·2	0·0
LOCH DUNVEGAN (Skye)							
–0105	–0030	–0020	–0040	0·0	–0·1	0·0	0·0
LOCH HARPORT (Skye)							
–0115	–0035	–0020	–0100	–0·1	–0·1	0·0	+0·1
SOAY (Camus nan Gall)							
–0055	–0025	–0025	–0045	–0·4	–0·2	No data	
KYLE OF LOCHALSH							
–0040	–0020	–0005	–0025	+0·1	0·0	0·0	–0·1
DORNIE BRIDGE (Loch Alsh)							
–0040	–0010	–0005	–0020	+0·1	–0·1	0·0	0·0
GLENELG BAY (Kyle Rhea)							
–0105	–0035	–0035	–0055	–0·4	–0·4	–0·9	–0·1
LOCH HOURN							
–0125	–0050	–0040	–0110	–0·2	–0·1	–0·1	+0·1

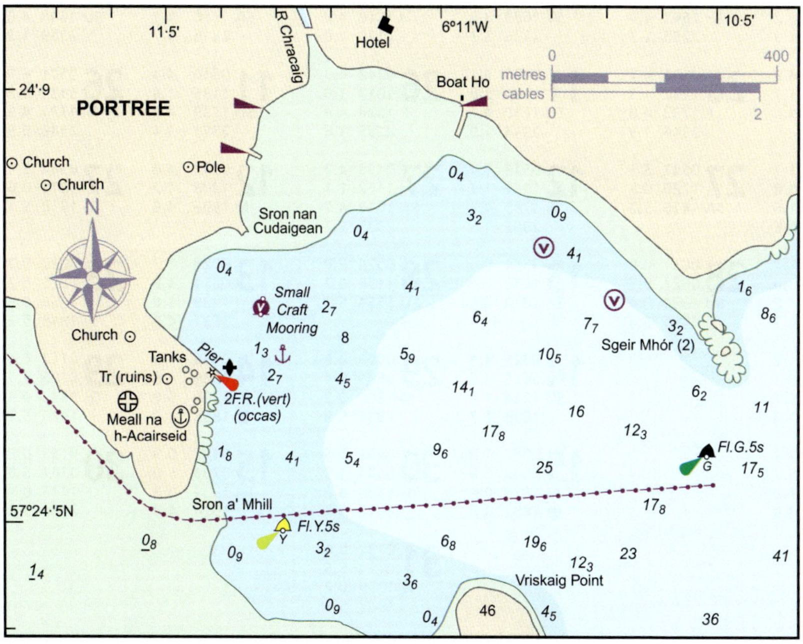

SHELTER Secure in all but strong S to SW'lies, when Camas Bàn is more sheltered. In the NW of the bay there are 8 🅥s for <15 tons. Short stay pontoon on pier.

NAVIGATION WPT 57°24'·58N 06°10'·07W, 275°/0·72M to pier. From the S, avoid rks off An Tom Pt (1·5M to E, off chartlet).

LIGHTS AND MARKS Only lts are a SHM buoy Fl G 5s marking Sgeir Mhór, 2 FR (vert) 6m 4M (occas) on the pier and a SPM buoy Fl Y 5s.

R/T VHF Ch 16 12 (occas).

TELEPHONE (Code 01478) HM ☎ 612926; Moorings 612341; MRCC (01851) 702013; ⊜ (0141) 887 9369; Marinecall 09068 969654; Police 612888; Dr 612013; Ⓗ 612704.

FACILITIES **Pier** AB £14, D (cans), L, FW. **Town** P, 🛒, Gas, Gaz, 🏧, R, Bar, ✉, Ⓑ, bus to Kyle of Lochalsh, ≷.

TIME ZONE (UT)
For Summer Time add ONE hour in **non-shaded areas**

ULLAPOOL LAT 57°54′N LONG 5°10′W

TIMES AND HEIGHTS OF HIGH AND LOW WATERS

Dates in red are SPRINGS
Dates in blue are NEAPS

YEAR **2010**

JANUARY

Date	Day	Time	m	Time	m	Time	m	Time	m	Moon
1	F	0058	1.1	0657	5.4	1332	0.9	1929	5.3	
2	SA	0144	0.9	0741	5.6	1418	0.7	2015	5.3	
3	SU	0229	0.9	0826	5.6	1505	0.6	2103	5.3	
4	M	0314	0.9	0913	5.5	1551	0.7	2152	5.1	
5	TU	0359	1.1	1003	5.3	1639	0.9	2244	4.8	
6	W	0446	1.3	1058	5.0	1728	1.2	2342	4.5	
7	TH	0538	1.6	1201	4.7	1822	1.6			◑
8	F	0047	4.3	0636	2.0	1314	4.4	1925	1.9	
9	SA	0201	4.2	0748	2.2	1435	4.2	2041	2.1	
10	SU	0317	4.2	0913	2.3	1553	4.2	2159	2.1	
11	M	0421	4.3	1032	2.1	1655	4.3	2301	2.0	
12	TU	0512	4.5	1131	1.9	1743	4.4	2350	1.8	
13	W	0554	4.7	1217	1.7	1823	4.6			
14	TH	0031	1.6	0629	4.9	1257	1.5	1856	4.7	
15	F	0108	1.5	0702	5.0	1332	1.4	1927	4.8	●
16	SA	0142	1.4	0732	5.1	1405	1.2	1955	4.8	
17	SU	0214	1.3	0801	5.1	1436	1.2	2023	4.8	
18	M	0245	1.3	0830	5.1	1507	1.2	2051	4.7	
19	TU	0316	1.4	0901	5.0	1538	1.3	2121	4.6	
20	W	0347	1.5	0933	4.9	1610	1.4	2154	4.5	
21	TH	0420	1.7	1010	4.7	1645	1.6	2232	4.3	
22	F	0457	1.9	1052	4.5	1724	1.8	2320	4.1	
23	SA	0541	2.1	1147	4.3	1812	2.0			◐
24	SU	0028	4.0	0639	2.3	1304	4.1	1914	2.2	
25	M	0156	4.0	0801	2.4	1428	4.1	2038	2.2	
26	TU	0316	4.1	0934	2.3	1547	4.2	2203	2.1	
27	W	0423	4.4	1048	1.9	1653	4.5	2308	1.7	
28	TH	0517	4.7	1145	1.5	1746	4.8			
29	F	0000	1.4	0603	5.1	1235	1.0	1832	5.2	
30	SA	0048	1.0	0645	5.5	1321	0.6	1916	5.4	○
31	SU	0132	0.7	0727	5.7	1405	0.3	1958	5.5	

FEBRUARY

Date	Day	Time	m	Time	m	Time	m	Time	m	Moon
1	M	0214	0.6	0809	5.8	1448	0.3	2040	5.4	
2	TU	0256	0.6	0851	5.7	1530	0.4	2123	5.2	
3	W	0338	0.7	0935	5.4	1611	0.7	2208	4.9	
4	TH	0420	1.0	1023	5.0	1654	1.1	2258	4.6	
5	F	0505	1.4	1120	4.6	1740	1.6			◑
6	SA	0001	4.3	0556	1.9	1235	4.2	1835	2.0	
7	SU	0119	4.0	0703	2.3	1407	3.9	1955	2.4	
8	M	0246	4.0	0844	2.4	1538	3.9	2137	2.4	
9	TU	0402	4.1	1023	2.3	1645	4.0	2249	2.2	
10	W	0457	4.3	1123	2.0	1733	4.2	2337	1.9	
11	TH	0538	4.6	1205	1.7	1809	4.4			
12	F	0016	1.7	0612	4.8	1241	1.5	1839	4.6	
13	SA	0051	1.4	0642	5.0	1313	1.2	1906	4.7	
14	SU	0123	1.2	0710	5.1	1343	1.1	1931	4.8	●
15	M	0153	1.1	0737	5.2	1412	1.0	1955	4.9	
16	TU	0221	1.1	0804	5.2	1440	0.9	2021	4.9	
17	W	0250	1.1	0832	5.1	1508	1.0	2048	4.8	
18	TH	0319	1.2	0902	5.0	1538	1.1	2118	4.7	
19	F	0350	1.3	0936	4.8	1610	1.3	2152	4.5	
20	SA	0424	1.6	1015	4.6	1646	1.5	2233	4.3	
21	SU	0505	1.8	1106	4.3	1729	1.8	2332	4.1	
22	M	0558	2.1	1225	4.0	1828	2.1			◐
23	TU	0110	3.9	0720	2.3	1406	3.9	2001	2.3	
24	W	0248	4.0	0914	2.2	1533	4.1	2147	2.1	
25	TH	0405	4.3	1036	1.8	1642	4.4	2255	1.7	
26	F	0501	4.7	1132	1.3	1733	4.8	2346	1.3	
27	SA	0547	5.1	1220	0.8	1816	5.2			
28	SU	0031	0.8	0627	5.5	1304	0.4	1856	5.4	○

MARCH

Date	Day	Time	m	Time	m	Time	m	Time	m	Moon
1	M	0114	0.5	0707	5.7	1345	0.1	1934	5.5	
2	TU	0154	0.4	0746	5.8	1424	0.1	2013	5.5	
3	W	0234	0.4	0826	5.6	1503	0.3	2052	5.3	
4	TH	0314	0.5	0908	5.3	1542	0.6	2133	5.0	
5	F	0354	0.9	0952	4.9	1621	1.1	2218	4.6	
6	SA	0436	1.3	1045	4.4	1703	1.6	2315	4.2	
7	SU	0524	1.8	1201	4.0	1753	2.1			◑
8	M	0036	3.9	0626	2.2	1338	3.7	1908	2.4	
9	TU	0209	3.8	0811	2.4	1514	3.7	2108	2.5	
10	W	0331	3.9	1003	2.3	1623	3.8	2226	2.3	
11	TH	0430	4.1	1100	2.0	1710	4.1	2314	1.9	
12	F	0512	4.4	1139	1.7	1745	4.3	2352	1.6	
13	SA	0546	4.6	1213	1.4	1813	4.5			
14	SU	0025	1.4	0615	4.8	1244	1.1	1838	4.7	
15	M	0057	1.2	0642	5.0	1313	0.9	1902	4.8	●
16	TU	0126	1.0	0709	5.1	1341	0.8	1926	4.9	
17	W	0154	0.9	0736	5.1	1409	0.8	1951	4.9	
18	TH	0223	0.9	0804	5.1	1438	0.8	2018	4.9	
19	F	0253	1.0	0836	5.0	1508	0.9	2049	4.8	
20	SA	0325	1.1	0911	4.8	1541	1.1	2124	4.6	
21	SU	0401	1.4	0954	4.5	1618	1.4	2207	4.3	
22	M	0443	1.6	1052	4.2	1703	1.8	2309	4.1	
23	TU	0539	1.9	1220	3.9	1804	2.1			◐
24	W	0051	3.9	0707	2.1	1355	3.9	1944	2.3	
25	TH	0226	4.0	0900	2.0	1518	4.0	2129	2.0	
26	F	0342	4.3	1017	1.6	1624	4.4	2235	1.6	
27	SA	0439	4.7	1112	1.1	1713	4.7	2325	1.2	
28	SU	0524	5.0	1158	0.7	1754	5.1			
29	M	0009	0.8	0605	5.4	1240	0.3	1832	5.3	
30	TU	0052	0.5	0644	5.5	1320	0.2	1910	5.4	○
31	W	0132	0.4	0724	5.5	1359	0.2	1947	5.4	

APRIL

Date	Day	Time	m	Time	m	Time	m	Time	m	Moon
1	TH	0212	0.4	0804	5.4	1436	0.4	2025	5.2	
2	F	0251	0.6	0845	5.0	1514	0.8	2104	4.9	
3	SA	0331	0.9	0930	4.6	1552	1.2	2148	4.6	
4	SU	0413	1.3	1022	4.2	1633	1.6	2240	4.2	
5	M	0500	1.7	1134	3.8	1721	2.0	2354	4.0	
6	TU	0558	2.1	1300	3.6	1828	2.4			◑
7	W	0119	3.8	0726	2.3	1429	3.6	2016	2.5	
8	TH	0242	3.8	0911	2.2	1543	3.7	2143	2.3	
9	F	0346	4.0	1016	2.0	1633	3.9	2236	2.0	
10	SA	0433	4.2	1059	1.7	1710	4.1	2316	1.7	
11	SU	0510	4.4	1135	1.4	1739	4.4	2351	1.4	
12	M	0542	4.6	1208	1.2	1806	4.6			
13	TU	0024	1.2	0611	4.8	1239	1.0	1831	4.8	
14	W	0056	1.0	0639	4.9	1309	0.8	1856	4.9	●
15	TH	0127	0.9	0709	5.0	1339	0.8	1924	4.9	
16	F	0158	0.9	0741	5.0	1411	0.8	1955	4.9	
17	SA	0231	0.9	0818	4.8	1444	0.9	2029	4.8	
18	SU	0307	1.0	0900	4.7	1520	1.1	2110	4.6	
19	M	0348	1.2	0951	4.4	1602	1.4	2201	4.4	
20	TU	0436	1.5	1059	4.1	1651	1.7	2311	4.2	
21	W	0538	1.7	1221	4.0	1758	2.0			◐
22	TH	0040	4.0	0704	1.8	1341	4.0	1930	2.1	
23	F	0202	4.1	0836	1.7	1455	4.1	2100	1.9	
24	SA	0314	4.3	0948	1.4	1558	4.3	2206	1.6	
25	SU	0412	4.6	1044	1.0	1648	4.6	2259	1.2	
26	M	0501	4.9	1131	0.8	1731	4.9	2346	0.9	
27	TU	0544	5.1	1215	0.6	1810	5.1			
28	W	0029	0.7	0625	5.2	1256	0.5	1848	5.2	○
29	TH	0112	0.6	0706	5.1	1335	0.6	1926	5.2	
30	F	0153	0.6	0747	5.0	1413	0.7	2004	5.0	

Chart Datum: 2·75 metres below Ordnance Datum (Newlyn). HAT is 5·9 metres above Chart Datum; see 0.20

TIME ZONE (UT)
For Summer Time add ONE hour in **non-shaded areas**

ULLAPOOL LAT 57°54′N LONG 5°10′W

TIMES AND HEIGHTS OF HIGH AND LOW WATERS

Dates in red are SPRINGS
Dates in blue are NEAPS

YEAR **2010**

MAY

Date	Time	m	Date	Time	m
1 SA	0233	0.8	16 SU	0217	0.9
	0830	4.7		0810	4.8
	1451	1.0		1428	0.9
	2044	4.8		2021	4.9
2 SU	0314	1.0	17 M	0259	0.9
	0915	4.4		0859	4.7
	1530	1.3		1510	1.1
	2126	4.6		2108	4.8
3 M	0356	1.3	18 TU	0345	1.0
	1006	4.1		0956	4.5
	1611	1.6		1556	1.3
	2215	4.3		2203	4.6
4 TU	0441	1.6	19 W	0437	1.2
	1104	3.9		1100	4.3
	1657	1.9		1649	1.5
	2314	4.1		2310	4.4
5 W	0533	1.8	20 TH ◐	0538	1.4
	1211	3.7		1208	4.2
	1753	2.2		1752	1.7
6 TH ◑	0024	3.9	21 F	0023	4.3
	0638	2.0		0649	1.5
	1324	3.6		1317	4.1
	1911	2.3		1907	1.8
7 F	0137	3.8	22 SA	0135	4.3
	0757	2.1		0803	1.5
	1438	3.6		1425	4.1
	2036	2.3		2024	1.8
8 SA	0244	3.9	23 SU	0243	4.3
	0909	2.0		0912	1.4
	1538	3.8		1529	4.3
	2142	2.1		2132	1.6
9 SU	0340	4.0	24 M	0346	4.5
	1005	1.8		1013	1.2
	1623	4.0		1623	4.5
	2231	1.9		2232	1.4
10 M	0425	4.2	25 TU	0441	4.6
	1048	1.5		1106	1.1
	1659	4.2		1710	4.7
	2312	1.6		2325	1.2
11 TU	0503	4.4	26 W	0530	4.7
	1126	1.3		1153	1.0
	1730	4.4		1753	4.9
	2349	1.4			
12 W	0538	4.6	27 TH ○	0012	1.0
	1202	1.1		0614	4.8
	1800	4.6		1237	0.9
				1832	5.0
13 TH	0025	1.2	28 F	0058	0.9
	0612	4.7		0657	4.8
	1237	1.0		1318	1.0
	1830	4.8		1911	5.0
14 F ●	0101	1.0	29 SA	0140	0.9
	0648	4.8		0739	4.7
	1313	0.9		1357	1.0
	1903	4.9		1950	4.9
15 SA	0138	0.9	30 SU	0221	1.0
	0727	4.8		0820	4.5
	1350	0.9		1435	1.2
	1940	4.9		2028	4.8
			31 M	0300	1.1
				0901	4.4
				1513	1.3
				2107	4.7

JUNE

Date	Time	m	Date	Time	m
1 TU	0340	1.2	16 W	0341	0.7
	0943	4.2		0947	4.7
	1552	1.5		1550	1.1
	2149	4.5		2156	4.9
2 W	0421	1.4	17 TH	0431	0.9
	1027	4.0		1043	4.6
	1633	1.7		1640	1.2
	2235	4.3		2253	4.7
3 TH	0504	1.6	18 F	0524	1.0
	1118	3.9		1143	4.4
	1719	1.9		1735	1.5
	2328	4.1		2357	4.6
4 F ◑	0553	1.8	19 SA ◐	0622	1.2
	1216	3.7		1246	4.2
	1813	2.1		1837	1.6
5 SA	0030	4.0	20 SU	0105	4.4
	0648	1.9		0725	1.4
	1321	3.7		1353	4.2
	1918	2.2		1946	1.8
6 SU	0136	3.9	21 M	0215	4.3
	0751	1.9		0835	1.6
	1426	3.7		1500	4.2
	2030	2.2		2059	1.8
7 M	0238	3.9	22 TU	0326	4.3
	0856	1.9		0944	1.6
	1524	3.9		1603	4.3
	2134	2.1		2210	1.7
8 TU	0334	4.0	23 W	0430	4.3
	0953	1.8		1045	1.5
	1613	4.1		1656	4.5
	2227	1.9		2311	1.5
9 W	0423	4.2	24 TH	0525	4.4
	1043	1.6		1138	1.4
	1654	4.3		1742	4.7
	2314	1.6			
10 TH	0508	4.4	25 F	0004	1.4
	1128	1.4		0611	4.5
	1732	4.5		1225	1.3
	2358	1.4		1823	4.8
11 F	0551	4.6	26 SA ○	0050	1.2
	1211	1.2		0653	4.5
	1810	4.8		1306	1.2
				1901	4.9
12 SA ●	0041	1.1	27 SU	0131	1.1
	0634	4.7		0731	4.6
	1253	1.0		1344	1.2
	1849	4.9		1937	4.9
13 SU	0124	0.9	28 M	0210	1.1
	0719	4.8		0806	4.5
	1336	0.9		1421	1.2
	1931	5.0		2011	4.9
14 M	0208	0.8	29 TU	0246	1.1
	0806	4.9		0840	4.5
	1419	0.9		1456	1.3
	2015	5.1		2045	4.8
15 TU	0254	0.7	30 W	0321	1.1
	0855	4.8		0913	4.4
	1504	0.9		1531	1.4
	2103	5.0		2119	4.7

JULY

Date	Time	m	Date	Time	m
1 TH	0356	1.2	16 F	0413	0.6
	0948	4.3		1016	4.8
	1606	1.5		1622	1.0
	2156	4.5		2227	5.0
2 F	0432	1.4	17 SA	0459	0.8
	1026	4.1		1110	4.6
	1644	1.7		1710	1.2
	2238	4.3		2327	4.7
3 SA	0510	1.5	18 SU ◐	0550	1.2
	1111	4.0		1212	4.3
	1725	1.9		1805	1.6
	2327	4.2			
4 SU ◑	0553	1.7	19 M	0036	4.4
	1207	3.9		0647	1.6
	1814	2.1		1322	4.1
				1910	1.9
5 M	0028	4.0	20 TU	0153	4.1
	0642	1.9		0757	1.9
	1315	3.8		1436	4.1
	1915	2.2		2031	2.0
6 TU	0136	3.9	21 W	0316	4.0
	0744	2.0		0920	2.0
	1423	3.8		1548	4.2
	2029	2.2		2159	2.0
7 W	0244	3.9	22 TH	0428	4.1
	0855	2.0		1033	1.9
	1527	4.0		1647	4.4
	2143	2.1		2307	1.8
8 TH	0348	4.0	23 F	0523	4.2
	1003	1.9		1129	1.7
	1623	4.2		1733	4.6
	2245	1.8		2359	1.5
9 F	0446	4.2	24 SA	0607	4.4
	1101	1.6		1214	1.5
	1711	4.5		1812	4.7
	2338	1.5			
10 SA	0537	4.5	25 SU	0041	1.3
	1152	1.4		0642	4.5
	1755	4.8		1254	1.4
				1846	4.9
11 SU ●	0026	1.1	26 M ○	0119	1.2
	0623	4.8		0714	4.6
	1239	1.1		1329	1.2
	1837	5.0		1918	5.0
12 M	0113	0.8	27 TU	0153	1.0
	0709	5.0		0743	4.7
	1324	0.9		1403	1.2
	1920	5.3		1948	5.0
13 TU	0158	0.5	28 W	0224	1.0
	0754	5.1		0811	4.7
	1408	0.7		1434	1.1
	2003	5.4		2017	5.0
14 W	0243	0.4	29 TH	0255	1.0
	0839	5.1		0839	4.6
	1452	0.7		1505	1.2
	2048	5.4		2047	4.9
15 TH	0328	0.4	30 F	0325	1.0
	0926	5.0		0908	4.5
	1536	0.8		1536	1.3
	2136	5.2		2119	4.7
			31 SA	0357	1.2
				0940	4.4
				1608	1.5
				2154	4.6

AUGUST

Date	Time	m	Date	Time	m
1 SU	0430	1.4	16 M ◐	0516	1.3
	1016	4.2		1136	4.4
	1644	1.7		1734	1.6
	2235	4.3			
2 M	0506	1.6	17 TU	0010	4.2
	1101	4.1		0609	1.8
	1725	1.9		1252	4.1
	2327	4.1		1838	2.0
3 TU ◑	0549	1.8	18 W	0139	3.9
	1203	3.9		0722	2.2
	1817	2.2		1415	4.0
				2010	2.2
4 W	0040	3.9	19 TH	0309	3.9
	0645	2.1		0902	2.3
	1329	3.8		1533	4.1
	1931	2.3		2155	2.1
5 TH	0205	3.9	20 F	0422	4.0
	0803	2.2		1023	2.1
	1449	3.9		1633	4.3
	2107	2.2		2301	1.9
6 F	0323	4.0	21 SA	0514	4.2
	0933	2.1		1116	1.9
	1558	4.1		1718	4.5
	2225	1.9		2346	1.6
7 SA	0430	4.2	22 SU	0552	4.4
	1043	1.8		1158	1.6
	1654	4.5		1754	4.7
	2323	1.5			
8 SU	0524	4.5	23 M	0023	1.4
	1137	1.4		0623	4.5
	1740	4.9		1234	1.4
				1825	4.9
9 M	0012	1.0	24 TU ○	0057	1.2
	0609	4.9		0650	4.7
	1225	1.1		1307	1.2
	1821	5.2		1853	5.0
10 TU ●	0058	0.6	25 W	0127	1.0
	0652	5.2		0716	4.8
	1309	0.7		1338	1.1
	1902	5.5		1921	5.1
11 W	0141	0.3	26 TH	0156	0.9
	0733	5.4		0740	4.8
	1351	0.5		1407	1.1
	1943	5.7		1948	5.1
12 TH	0223	0.1	27 F	0225	0.9
	0815	5.4		0806	4.8
	1433	0.4		1436	1.1
	2025	5.7		2016	5.0
13 F	0305	0.2	28 SA	0253	1.0
	0857	5.3		0832	4.8
	1515	0.5		1505	1.2
	2109	5.4		2045	4.9
14 SA	0347	0.4	29 SU	0322	1.1
	0943	5.0		0901	4.6
	1558	0.8		1536	1.3
	2158	5.1		2118	4.7
15 SU	0430	0.8	30 M	0353	1.3
	1034	4.7		0934	4.5
	1643	1.2		1609	1.6
	2255	4.7		2156	4.5
			31 TU	0428	1.5
				1014	4.3
				1648	1.8
				2246	4.2

Chart Datum: 2·75 metres below Ordnance Datum (Newlyn). HAT is 5·9 metres above Chart Datum; see 0.20

TIME ZONE (UT)
For Summer Time add ONE hour in **non-shaded areas**

ULLAPOOL LAT 57°54′N LONG 5°10′W

TIMES AND HEIGHTS OF HIGH AND LOW WATERS

Dates in red are SPRINGS
Dates in blue are NEAPS

YEAR **2010**

SEPTEMBER

Date	Day	Time	m	Time	m	Time	m	Time	m	Moon
1	W	0509	1.8	1109	4.0	1738	2.1			◑
2	TH	0003	3.9	0602	2.1	1245	3.9	1853	2.3	
3	F	0142	3.8	0725	2.3	1421	3.9	2043	2.3	
4	SA	0307	4.0	0913	2.2	1537	4.2	2208	1.9	
5	SU	0415	4.3	1027	1.8	1634	4.6	2305	1.4	
6	M	0507	4.7	1119	1.4	1720	5.0	2353	0.9	
7	TU	0550	5.0	1205	1.0	1801	5.4			
8	W	0036	0.5	0630	5.4	1248	0.6	1840	5.7	●
9	TH	0118	0.2	0709	5.5	1329	0.4	1920	5.8	
10	F	0159	0.1	0748	5.5	1410	0.4	2001	5.7	
11	SA	0239	0.2	0828	5.4	1451	0.5	2043	5.4	
12	SU	0319	0.5	0911	5.1	1533	0.8	2130	5.0	
13	M	0400	1.0	0958	4.8	1617	1.2	2227	4.5	
14	TU	0444	1.5	1059	4.4	1707	1.7	2348	4.1	
15	W	0535	2.0	1221	4.1	1811	2.1			◐
16	TH	0121	3.8	0648	2.4	1349	4.0	1949	2.3	
17	F	0252	3.8	0838	2.5	1509	4.1	2138	2.2	
18	SA	0403	3.9	1002	2.3	1609	4.2	2239	2.0	
19	SU	0452	4.1	1052	2.0	1653	4.5	2320	1.7	
20	M	0528	4.4	1132	1.7	1728	4.7	2355	1.4	
21	TU	0556	4.6	1207	1.5	1758	4.9			
22	W	0026	1.2	0622	4.7	1239	1.3	1825	5.0	
23	TH	0056	1.0	0646	4.9	1310	1.1	1852	5.1	○
24	F	0125	0.9	0710	5.0	1339	1.1	1919	5.1	
25	SA	0153	0.9	0735	5.0	1408	1.1	1947	5.1	
26	SU	0221	1.0	0801	4.9	1437	1.1	2017	5.0	
27	M	0251	1.1	0830	4.8	1509	1.3	2052	4.8	
28	TU	0323	1.3	0904	4.7	1544	1.5	2132	4.5	
29	W	0358	1.5	0945	4.4	1625	1.8	2227	4.2	
30	TH	0441	1.8	1043	4.2	1717	2.0	2352	4.0	

OCTOBER

Date	Day	Time	m	Time	m	Time	m	Time	m	Moon
1	F	0537	2.2	1220	4.0	1836	2.2			◑
2	SA	0127	3.9	0704	2.4	1356	4.1	2024	2.1	
3	SU	0247	4.1	0852	2.2	1511	4.3	2145	1.8	
4	M	0353	4.4	1003	1.8	1609	4.7	2242	1.3	
5	TU	0445	4.8	1055	1.4	1656	5.1	2329	0.9	
6	W	0528	5.1	1141	1.0	1738	5.4			
7	TH	0012	0.5	0606	5.4	1225	0.7	1818	5.7	●
8	F	0054	0.3	0645	5.6	1307	0.5	1858	5.7	
9	SA	0134	0.3	0723	5.6	1348	0.5	1940	5.6	
10	SU	0214	0.5	0803	5.4	1430	0.6	2023	5.3	
11	M	0253	0.8	0844	5.2	1512	0.9	2110	4.9	
12	TU	0334	1.2	0930	4.8	1557	1.3	2207	4.4	
13	W	0417	1.6	1026	4.5	1646	1.7	2322	4.1	
14	TH	0507	2.1	1142	4.2	1747	2.1			◐
15	F	0047	3.8	0614	2.4	1307	4.0	1911	2.3	
16	SA	0214	3.8	0751	2.5	1426	4.0	2048	2.3	
17	SU	0326	3.9	0919	2.4	1530	4.2	2156	2.1	
18	M	0417	4.1	1015	2.1	1617	4.4	2241	1.8	
19	TU	0455	4.3	1058	1.9	1655	4.6	2318	1.6	
20	W	0525	4.5	1134	1.6	1727	4.8	2351	1.4	
21	TH	0552	4.7	1208	1.4	1757	4.9			
22	F	0022	1.2	0617	4.9	1240	1.3	1825	5.0	
23	SA	0053	1.1	0642	5.0	1311	1.2	1854	5.1	○
24	SU	0123	1.0	0709	5.1	1342	1.1	1925	5.1	
25	M	0153	1.1	0738	5.1	1415	1.2	1959	5.0	
26	TU	0226	1.1	0810	5.0	1450	1.3	2038	4.8	
27	W	0301	1.3	0848	4.8	1528	1.5	2125	4.6	
28	TH	0340	1.5	0934	4.6	1613	1.7	2226	4.3	
29	F	0426	1.8	1036	4.4	1710	1.9	2345	4.1	
30	SA	0525	2.1	1202	4.2	1826	2.0			◑
31	SU	0106	4.1	0647	2.3	1327	4.3	1956	1.9	

NOVEMBER

Date	Day	Time	m	Time	m	Time	m	Time	m	Moon
1	M	0220	4.2	0819	2.2	1439	4.4	2112	1.7	
2	TU	0325	4.5	0931	1.9	1540	4.7	2212	1.3	
3	W	0419	4.8	1028	1.5	1632	5.0	2302	1.0	
4	TH	0505	5.1	1117	1.2	1718	5.3	2348	0.8	
5	F	0546	5.3	1203	0.9	1801	5.4			
6	SA	0031	0.7	0625	5.4	1248	0.8	1843	5.4	●
7	SU	0113	0.7	0705	5.5	1331	0.8	1927	5.3	
8	M	0153	0.8	0745	5.4	1414	0.9	2011	5.1	
9	TU	0233	1.1	0826	5.2	1457	1.1	2057	4.8	
10	W	0314	1.4	0910	4.9	1541	1.4	2148	4.5	
11	TH	0356	1.7	0959	4.7	1627	1.7	2246	4.2	
12	F	0443	2.0	1057	4.4	1719	2.0	2352	3.9	
13	SA	0538	2.3	1206	4.2	1821	2.2			◐
14	SU	0106	3.8	0648	2.5	1320	4.1	1935	2.3	
15	M	0222	3.8	0810	2.5	1430	4.1	2048	2.2	
16	TU	0325	4.0	0921	2.4	1528	4.2	2148	2.0	
17	W	0412	4.2	1014	2.1	1614	4.4	2234	1.8	
18	TH	0449	4.4	1057	1.9	1653	4.6	2313	1.6	
19	F	0521	4.6	1135	1.7	1728	4.7	2348	1.5	
20	SA	0551	4.8	1211	1.5	1802	4.9			
21	SU	0023	1.3	0620	5.0	1247	1.4	1835	5.0	○
22	M	0058	1.2	0650	5.1	1323	1.2	1911	5.0	
23	TU	0133	1.2	0724	5.1	1400	1.2	1951	5.0	
24	W	0210	1.2	0801	5.1	1439	1.2	2034	4.9	
25	TH	0249	1.3	0843	5.0	1522	1.3	2124	4.8	
26	F	0331	1.4	0931	4.9	1610	1.4	2221	4.6	
27	SA	0419	1.7	1029	4.7	1704	1.6	2326	4.4	
28	SU	0515	1.9	1138	4.6	1808	1.7			◑
29	M	0036	4.3	0623	2.0	1253	4.5	1920	1.8	
30	TU	0146	4.3	0739	2.1	1405	4.5	2033	1.7	

DECEMBER

Date	Day	Time	m	Time	m	Time	m	Time	m	Moon
1	W	0253	4.4	0854	2.0	1512	4.6	2139	1.6	
2	TH	0354	4.6	0959	1.8	1612	4.8	2237	1.4	
3	F	0446	4.9	1057	1.5	1706	4.9	2328	1.2	
4	SA	0532	5.1	1148	1.3	1754	5.1			
5	SU	0015	1.1	0614	5.2	1237	1.1	1838	5.1	●
6	M	0058	1.1	0654	5.3	1321	1.1	1921	5.1	
7	TU	0140	1.1	0734	5.3	1404	1.1	2003	5.0	
8	W	0219	1.2	0813	5.2	1445	1.2	2043	4.8	
9	TH	0258	1.4	0852	5.1	1525	1.3	2124	4.6	
10	F	0337	1.6	0932	4.9	1606	1.5	2205	4.4	
11	SA	0418	1.8	1014	4.6	1648	1.7	2251	4.2	
12	SU	0501	2.0	1103	4.4	1733	1.9	2346	4.0	
13	M	0550	2.3	1204	4.2	1825	2.1			◐
14	TU	0054	3.9	0650	2.4	1313	4.1	1926	2.2	
15	W	0207	3.9	0803	2.5	1421	4.1	2035	2.2	
16	TH	0314	4.0	0916	2.4	1523	4.2	2139	2.1	
17	F	0407	4.2	1015	2.2	1616	4.3	2232	2.0	
18	SA	0450	4.4	1104	2.0	1702	4.5	2317	1.8	
19	SU	0527	4.7	1147	1.7	1743	4.7	2359	1.5	
20	M	0602	4.9	1228	1.5	1823	4.9			
21	TU	0039	1.4	0637	5.1	1309	1.3	1902	5.0	○
22	W	0119	1.2	0714	5.2	1350	1.1	1944	5.1	
23	TH	0159	1.1	0754	5.3	1432	1.0	2027	5.1	
24	F	0240	1.1	0836	5.3	1515	0.9	2114	5.0	
25	SA	0323	1.1	0922	5.3	1601	1.0	2203	4.9	
26	SU	0409	1.3	1012	5.1	1649	1.2	2259	4.7	
27	M	0458	1.5	1110	4.9	1742	1.4			
28	TU	0001	4.5	0554	1.8	1218	4.7	1842	1.6	◑
29	W	0109	4.4	0659	2.0	1331	4.5	1951	1.8	
30	TH	0221	4.3	0816	2.1	1448	4.4	2107	1.9	
31	F	0332	4.4	0935	2.0	1602	4.5	2218	1.8	

Chart Datum: 2·75 metres below Ordnance Datum (Newlyn). HAT is 5·9 metres above Chart Datum; see 0.20

ULLAPOOL TO LOCH TORRIDON

(AC 1794, 2210) The Summer Isles (AC 2501), 12M NW of the major fishing port of Ullapool, offer some sheltered anchorages and tight approaches. The best include the bay on E side of Tanera Mor; off NE of Tanera Beg (W of Eilean Fada Mor); and in Caolas Eilean Ristol, between the island and mainland.

Loch Ewe (AC 3146) provides good shelter and easy access. Best anchorages are in Poolewe Bay (beware Boor Rks off W shore) and in SW corner of Loch Thuirnaig (entering, keep close to S shore to avoid rocks extending from N side). Off Rubha Reidh (lt) seas can be dangerous.

▶ *The NE-going stream begins at HW Ullapool –0335; the SW-going at HW Ullapool +0305. Sp rates 3kn, but slacker to SW of point.* ◀

Longa Is lies N of ent to Loch Gairloch (AC 2528). The channel N of it is navigable but narrow at E end. Outer loch is free of dangers, but exposed to swell. Best anchorage is on S side of loch in Caolas Bad a' Chrotha, W of Eilean Horrisdale.

Entering L Torridon (AC 2210) from S or W beware Murchadh Breac (dries 1·5m) 3ca NNW of Rubha na Fearna. Best anchorages are SW of Eilean Mor (to W of Ardheslaig); in Loch a 'Chracaich, 7ca further SE; E of Shieldaig Is; and near head of Upper L Torridon. ▶ *Streams are weak except where they run 2-3kn in narrows between L Shieldaig and Upper L Torridon.* ◀

SKYE TO ARDNAMURCHAN

(AC 1795, 2210, 2209, 2208, 2207) Skye and the islands around it provide many good and attractive anchorages, of which the most secure are: Acairseid Mhor on the W side of Rona; Portree (1.8); Isleornsay; Portnalong, near the entrance to Loch Harport, and Carbost at the head; Loch Dunvegan; and Uig Bay in Loch Snizort. 🅥s at Stein (Loch Dunvegan), Portree, Acairseid Mhor (Rona), Churchton Bay (Raasay) and Armadale Bay (S tip).

▶ *Tides are strong off Rubha Hunish at N end of Skye, and heavy overfalls occur with tide against fresh or strong winds.* ◀ Anchorage behind Fladday Is near the N end of Raasay can be squally and uncomfortable; and Loch Scavaig (S. Skye, beneath the Cuillins) more so, though the latter is so spectacular as to warrant a visit in fair weather. Soay Is has a small, safe harbour on its N side, but the bar at entrance almost dries at LW springs.

Between N Skye and the mainland there is the choice of Sound of Raasay or Inner Sound. **The direction of buoyage in both Sounds is Northward.** In the former, coming S from Portree, beware Sgeir Chnapach (3m) and Ebbing Rk (dries 2·9m), both NNW of Oskaig Pt. Beware McMillan's Rk (0·4m depth) in mid-channel, marked by SHM lt buoy. ▶ *At the Narrows (chart 2534) the SE-going stream begins at HW Ullapool –0605, and the NW-going at HW Ullapool +0040; sp rate 1·4kn in mid-chan, but more near shoals each side.* ◀

The channel between Scalpay and Skye narrows to 2.5ca with drying reefs each side and least depth 0·1m. ▶ *Here the E-going stream begins at HW Ullapool +0550, and W-going at HW Ullapool –0010, sp rate 1kn.* ◀

Inner Sound, which is a Submarine exercise area, is wider and easier than Sound of Raasay; the two are connected by Caol Rona and Caol Mor, respectively N and S of Raasay. Dangers extend about 1M N of Rona, and Cow Is lies off the mainland 8M to S; otherwise approach from N is clear to Crowlin Is, which should be passed to W. There is a good anch between Eilean Mor and Eilean Meadhonach.

A torpedo range in the Inner Sound does not normally restrict passage, but vessels may be requested to keep to the E side of the Sound if the range is active. Range activity is broadcast at 0800 and 1800LT first on VHF Ch 16 and then on Ch 8, and is indicated by Red Flags flown at the range building at Applecross, by all range vessels and at the naval pier at Kyle of Lochalsh, ☎ (01599) 534262.

Approaching Kyle Akin (AC 2540) from W, beware dangerous rks to N, off Bleat Is (at S side of entrance to Loch Carron); on S side of chan, Bogha Beag (dries 1·2m) and Black Eye Rk (depth 3·2m), respectively 6ca and 4ca W of bridge. Pass at least 100m N or S of Eileanan Dubha in Kyle Akin. On S side of chan String Rk (dries) is marked by PHM lt buoy.

Kyle Rhea connects Loch Alsh with NE end of Sound of Sleat. ▶ *The tidal streams are very strong: N-going stream begins HW Ullapool + 0600, sp rate 6-7kn; S-going stream begins at HW Ullapool, sp rate 8kn. N-going stream in Kyle Rhea begins HW Dover +0140 (HW Ullapool +0555) and runs for 6 hours. The E-going stream in Kyle Akin begins (Sp) HW Dover +0350 (HW Ullapool –0415). (Nps) HW Dover –0415 (HW Ullapool).*

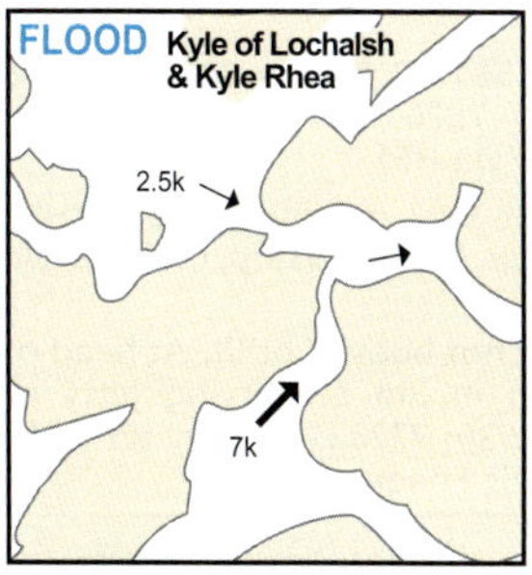

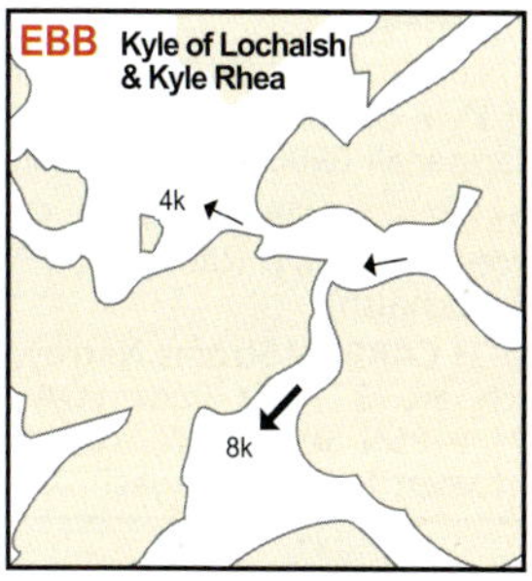

S-going stream in Kyle Rhea begins HW Dover –0415 (HW Ullapool) and runs for 6 hours. The W-going stream in Kyle Akin begins (Sp) HW Dover –0015 (HW Ullapool +0400). (Nps) HW Dover +0140 (HW Ullapool +0555). Eddies form both sides of the Kyle and there are dangerous overfalls off S end in fresh S'ly winds on S-going stream. ◀ Temp anch in Sandaig Bay, 3M to SW.

The Sound of Sleat widens to 4M off Point of Sleat and is exposed to SW winds unless Eigg and Muck give a lee. Mallaig is a busy fishing and ferry hbr, convenient for supplies. Further S the lochs require intricate pilotage. 6M NE of Ardnamurchan Pt (lt, fog sig) are Bo Faskadale rks, drying 0·5m and marked by SHM lt buoy, and Elizabeth Rock with depth of 0·7m. ▶ *Ardnamurchan Pt is an exposed headland onto which the ebb sets. With onshore winds, very heavy seas extend 2M offshore and it should be given a wide berth. Here the N-going stream begins at HW Oban –0525, and the S-going at HW Oban + 0100, sp rates 1·5kn.* ◀

THE SMALL ISLES

(AC 2207, 2208) These consist of Canna, Rum, Eigg and Muck. The hbrs at Eigg (SE end), Rhum (Loch Scresort) and Canna (between Canna and Sanday) are all exposed to E'lies; Canna has best shelter and is useful for the Outer Hebrides. Dangers extend SSW from Canna: at 1M Jemina Rk (depth 1·5m) and Belle Rk (depth 3·6m); at 2M Humla Rk (5m high), marked by buoy and with offlying shoals close W of it; at 5M Hyskeir (lt, fog sig), the largest of a group of small islands; and at 7M Mill Rks (with depths of 1·8m). ▶ *The tide runs hard here, and in bad weather the sea breaks heavily up to 15M SW of Canna. Between Skerryvore and Neist Pt the stream runs generally N and S, starting N-going at HW Ullapool + 0550, and S-going at HW Ullapool –0010. It rarely exceeds 1kn, except near Skerryvore, around headlands of The Small Isles, and over rks and shoals.* ◀

1M off the N side of Muck are Godag Rks, some above water but with submerged dangers extending 2ca further N. Most other dangers around the Small Isles are closer inshore, but there are banks on which the sea breaks heavily in bad weather. A local magnetic anomaly exists about 2M E of Muck.

1.9 PLOCKTON

Highland **57°20′·52N 05°38′·47W**

CHARTS AC 2209, 2528; Imray C66.

TIDES –0435 Dover; ML 3·5m; Duration 0600; See 1.8

SHELTER Good, exposed only to N/NE'lies. 9 Y Ⓥs or ⚓ in centre of bay in approx 3·5m. Inner part of bay shoals and dries to the SW.

NAVIGATION WPT 57°21′·16N 05°39′·44W; thence towards Bogha Dubh Sgeir PHM bn, between Cat Is disused Lt ho and Sgeir Golach PHM Bcn and High Stone (1m) to the N. Hawk (0.1m) will be cleared when Duncraig Castle bears 158°. Alter S to the ⚓. Beware Plockton Rks (3·1m) on E side of bay.

LIGHTS AND MARKS See 1.3 and chartlet. Old lt ho (13m) on Cat Is is conspic, as is Duncraig Castle. Plockton Rks marked by lit PHM Bcn.

R/T None.

TELEPHONE HM (01599) 534589, 📠 534167, Mobile 07802 367253 (at Kyle of Lochalsh); MRCC (01851) 702013; ⊜ (0141) 887 9369; Marinecall 09068 969654; Police/Dr via HM.

FACILITIES **Village** FW, M £5, L at 50m dinghy pontoon (H24 except MLWS), D (cans), CH, 🛒, R, Bar, ✉, ⇌, airstrip, (bus to Kyle of Lochalsh).

LOCH CARRON Strome Narrows are not buoyed or lit. At head of loch are 3 Y Ⓥs (max LOA 14m) in 3m off drying jetty at 57°23′·95N 05°29′·0W; call ☎ 01520 722321. Appr on 328° between Sgeir Chreagach and Sgeir Fhada.

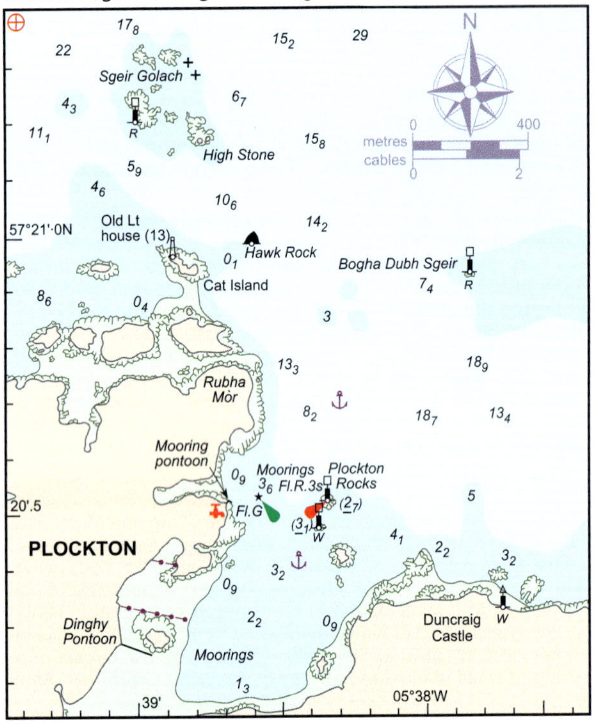

ANCHORAGES AROUND OR NEAR SKYE

LOCH TORRIDON Highland, **57°36′N 05°49′W**. AC 2210. Tides, see 1.8. Three large lochs: ent to outer loch (Torridon) is 3M wide, with isolated Sgeir na Trian (2m) almost in mid-chan; ⚓s on SW side behind Eilean Mór and in L Beag. L Sheildaig is middle loch with good ⚓ and 2 Ⓥs (up to 10 tons) between the Is and village. 1M to the N, a 2ca wide chan leads into Upper L Torridon; many fish cages and prone to squalls. Few facilities, except Shieldaig: FW, 🛒, R, Bar, ✉, Garage.

LOCH A'BHRAIGE Rona (Highland), **57°34′·6N 05°57′·9W**. AC 2479, 2534. HW –0438 on Dover; ML 2·8m; Duration 0605. See 1.8. A good ⚓ in NW of the island, safe except in NNW winds. Beware rks on NE side up to 1ca off shore. Hbr in NE corner of loch head. Ldg lts 137°, see 1.3. Facilities: jetty, FW and a helipad, all owned by MOD (DRA). Before ent, call *Rona* Range Control VHF Ch 13.

Acarseid Mhór is ⚓ on W of Rona. One Ⓥ £12, ☎ 07831 293963. App S of Eilean Garbh marked by W arrow. SD sketch of rks at ent is necessary. FW (cans), showers. At **Churchton Bay**, SW tip of Raasay, there are 4 HIE Ⓥs; ☎ (01478) 612341; Slip, showers, R, ◙.

LOCH DUNVEGAN 4 Ⓥs off Stein, **57°30′·9N 06°34′·5W**. 3 Ⓥs off Dunvegan, 57°26′·3N 06°35′·2W. Fuel, FW, R. ☎ (01478) 612341.

LOCH HARPORT Skye (Highland), **57°20′·6N 06°25′·8W**. AC 1795. HW –0447 (sp), –0527 (np) on Dover. See 1.8. On E side of Loch Bracadale, entered between Oronsay Is and Ardtreck Pt (W lt ho, Fl 6s 18m 9M). SW end of Oronsay has conspic rk pillar, called The Castle; keep ¼M off-shore here and off E coast of Oronsay which is joined to Ullinish Pt by drying reef. ⚓ Oronsay Is, N side of drying reef (4m), or on E side, but beware rk (dries) 0·5ca off N shore of Oronsay. Fiskavaig Bay 1M S of Ardtreck (7m); Loch Beag on N side of loch, exposed to W winds; Port na Long E of Ardtreck, sheltered except from E winds (beware fish farm); 1 Ⓥ off the distillery and 2 Ⓥ off *The Old Inn* at Carbost on SW shore. Facilities: (Carbost) 🛒, Bar, R, P (garage), ✉, FW. (Port na Long) Bar, FW, 🛒.

SOAY HARBOUR Skye (Highland), **57°09′·5N 06°13′·4W**. AC 2208. Tides see 1.8. Narrow inlet on NW side of Soay; enter from Soay Sound above half flood to clear bar, dries 0·6m. Appr on 135° from 5ca out to avoid reefs close each side of ent. Cross bar slightly E of mid-chan, altering 20° stbd for best water; ent is 15m wide between boulder spits marked by W poles with Or tops. ⚓ in 3m mid-pool or shoal draft boats can enter inner pool. Good shelter and holding. Camas nan Gall (poor holding); no other facilities.

ARMADALE BAY Skye (Highland), 4M NW of Mallaig. AC 2208. 6 Ⓥs £12 at **57°04′·0N 05°53′·6W**, ☎ (01471) 844216. Bay is sheltered from SE to N winds but subject to swell in winds from N to SE. From S, beware the Eilean Maol & Sgorach rocks. Ferry pier, Oc R 6s 6m 6M, with conspic W shed. Facilities, Skye Yachts ☎ 01471 844216, M (£12), FW at pontoon or by hose to charter M's, D, 🛒 (not Sat pm or Sun), showers, Gas, free pontoon for tenders, ferry to Mallaig for ⇌. Ardvasar ¾ mile: Slip HW±3 at BY (launching/parking £5), P (cans) (not Sun), showers, WC; Gaz at ¼ mile; R, Bar.

CROWLIN ISLANDS Highland, **57°21′·1N 05°50′·6W**. AC 2209, 2498. HW –0435 on Dover, –0020 on Ullapool; HW +0·3m on Ullapool. See 1.7. ⚓ between Eilean Meadhonach and Eilean Mor, appr from N, keep E of Eilean Beg. Excellent shelter except in strong N winds. There is an inner ⚓ with 3½m but ent chan dries. Eilean Beg lt ho Fl 6s 32m 6M, W tr. No facilities.

ANCHORAGES IN THE SOUND OF SLEAT (see also 1.8)

SOUND OF SLEAT There are ⚓s at: **Glenelg Bay (57°12′·57N 05°37′·95W)** SW of pier out of the tide, but only moderate holding. Usual facilities in village. At **Sandaig Bay** (57°10′·0N 05°41′·4W), exposed to SW. Sandaig Is are to NW of the bay; beware rks off Sgeir nan Eun. Eilean Mór has lt Fl 6s. At **Isleornsay Hbr** (57°09′N 05°48′W) 2ca N of pier, 2FR (vert) and floodlit. Give drying N end of Ornsay Is a wide berth. Lts: SE tip of Ornsay, Oc 8s 18m 15M, W tr; N end, Fl R 6s 8m 4M. Facilities: FW, ✉, Hotels. 5 Ⓥs at Duisdale (NW corner).

LOCH HOURN Highland, **57°08′N 05°42′W**. AC 2208, 2541. Tides see 1.8. Ent is S of Sandaig Is and opposite Isle Ornsay, Skye. Loch extends 11M inland via 4 narrows to Loch Beag; it is scenically magnificent, but violent squalls occur in strong winds. Sgeir Ulibhe, drying 2·1m, bn, lies almost in mid-ent; best to pass S of it to clear Clansman Rk, 2·1m, to the N. ⚓s on N shore at Eilean Ràrsaidh and Camas Bàn, within first 4M. For pilotage further E, consult SDs. Facilities at Arnisdale (Camas Bàn): FW, 🛒, R, Bar, ✉. Doune Marine (01687 462667) FW, D.

LOCH NEVIS Highland, **57°02′·2N 05°43′·3W**. AC 2208, 2541. HW –0515 on Dover. See 1.8. Beware rks Bogha cas Sruth (dries 1·8m), Bogha Don and Sgeirean Glasa both marked by bns. ⚓ NE of Eilean na Glaschoille, good except in S winds; or 9 Or Ⓥs off Inverie, £5 (free if dining), 10m max LOA. Call *Old Forge* VHF Ch 16, 12; FW, Bar, R, showers, ◙. In strong winds expect violent unpredictable squalls. Enter the inner loch with caution, and ⚓ N or SE of Eilean Maol.

ANCHORAGES IN THE SMALL ISLES

CANNA The Small Isles, **57°03′·3N 06°29′·4W**. AC 1796, 2208. HW –0457 (Sp), –0550 (Np) on Dover; HW –0035 and –0·4m on Ullapool; Duration 0605. Good shelter, except in strong E'lies, in hbr between Canna and Sanday Is but holding is poor due to kelp. Appr along Sanday shore, keeping N of Sgeir a' Phuirt, dries

4·6m. Ldg marks as in SDs. ⚓ in 3–4m W of Canna pier, off which beware drying rky patch. ⚓ Lt is advised due to FVs. Conspic W lt bn, Fl 10s 32m 9M, vis 152°-061°, at E end of Sanday Is. Magnetic anomaly off NE Canna. Facilities: FW, shower at farm, R(☎01687 462937) with limited 🛒, ✉, Note: NT manage island.

RUM The Small Isles, **57°00′·1N 06°15′·7W**. AC 2207, 2208. HW –0500 on Dover; –0035 and –0·3m on Ullapool; ML 2·4m; Duration 0600. SNH owns Is. The mountains (809m) are unmistakable. Landing is only allowed at L Scresort on E side; no dogs beyond village limit. Beware drying rks 1ca off N point of ent and almost 3ca off S point. The head of the loch dries 2ca out; ⚓ off slip on S side or further in, to NE of jetty. Hbr is open to E winds/swell. Facilities: ✉, FW, 🛒 (limited), R, Bar, ferry to Mallaig.

EIGG HARBOUR The Small Isles, **56°52′·6N 06°07′·6W**. AC 2207. HW –0523 on Dover. See 1.11. Entering from N or E use Sgeir nam Bagh (Ferry Terminal) Dir lt 245° Fl WRG 3s, leads between Garbh Sgeir Bn Fl (2) G 10s & Flod Sgeir Bn Fl R 5s. An Sgùrr is a conspic 391m high peak/ridge brg 281°/1·3M from Sgeir nam Bagh. Most of hbr dries, but good ⚓ 1ca NE of Galmisdale Pt pier, except in NE winds when yachts should go through the narrows and ⚓ in South Bay in 6–8m; tide runs hard in the narrows. Also ⚓ in 2·5m at Poll nam Partan, about 2ca N of Flod Sgeir. SE point of Eilean Chathastail Fl 6s 24m 8M, vis 181°-shore, W tr. VHF Ch 08 *Eigg Hbr*. HM ☎ via (01687) 482428. FW, repairs. **Pierhead** Showers, ✉, R, 🛒, Gas. **Cleadale village** (2M to N) Bar.

MUCK The Small Isles, **56°49′·8N 06°13′·3W**. AC 2207. Tides approx as Eigg, 1.11. Port Mór at SE end is the main hbr, with a deep pool inside offlying rks, but open to S'lies. Approach: Dir lt Fl WRG 3s 7m vis 1M by day leads between Dubh Sgeir (Fl(2) R 10s) and Bogha Ruadh (Fl G 5s) rks; see 1.3. ⚓ towards the NW side of inlet; NE side has drying rks. To N of Is, Bagh a' Ghallanaich is ⚓ protected from S. Few facilities.

1.10 LOCH ALSH

Highland **57°16′·68N 05°42′·87W**

CHARTS AC 2540; Imray C66.

TIDES –0450 Dover; ML 3·0m; Duration 0555; See 1.8

SHELTER **Kyle of Lochalsh:** AB on Railway Pier, with FVs, or on 40m L-shaped pontoon (seasonal), close W of Railway Pier; or ⚓ off the hotel there in 11m. **Kyle Akin:** 3 free Ⓥs are subject to tidal stream. Lit pontoon on NW side of hbr, shoal on N side.

⚓s, safe depending on winds, are (clockwise from Kyle): Avernish B, (2ca N of Racoon Rk) in 3m clear of power cables, open to SW; NW of Eilean Donnan Cas (conspic); in Ratagan B at head of L Duich in 7m; in Totaig B facing Loch Long ent in 3·5m; on S shore in Ardintoul B in 5·5m; at head of Loch na Béiste in 7m close inshore and W of fish cages.

NAVIGATION WPT (from Inner Sound) 57°16′·98N 05°45′·77W, 123°/0·75M to bridge. Chan to bridge is marked by 2 PHM and 2 SHM lt buoys. Bridge to Skye, 29m clearance, is lit Oc 6s in centre of main span, Iso R 4s on S pier and Iso G4s on N pier. The secondary NE span is lit, but has only 3.7m clearance.

LIGHTS AND MARKS See chartlet. Direction of buoyage is N in Kyle Rhea, thence E up Loch Alsh; but W through Kyle Akin and the bridge, ie SHMs are on N side of chan.

R/T VHF Ch 11 16.

TELEPHONE (Code 01599) HM 534589, Mobile 07802 367253; MRCC (01851) 702013; ⊖ (0141) 887 9369; Marinecall 09068 969654; Police, Dr, Ⓗ: via HM. Skye br ☎ 534844.

FACILITIES **Kyle of Lochalsh**: AB pontoon, £14 (second day free), FW, D (Fish pier via HM), P (cans), ME, Ⓔ, CH, ✉, Ⓑ, R, Bar, 🛒, Gas, ⇌ (useful railhead), Bus to Glasgow & Inverness; buses every ½hr to/from Kyleakin. **Kyleakin:** ☎ 534167 or VHF Ch 11, 120m AB (£14/craft) depth varies from 3m to drying, M, FW, 🛒, R, Bar.

1.11 MALLAIG

Highland **57°00′·47N 05°49′·47W**

CHARTS AC 2208, 2541; Imray C65, C66.

TIDES –0515 Dover; ML 2·9; Duration 0605

Standard Port OBAN (⟶)

Times				Height (metres)			
High Water		Low Water		MHWS	MHWN	MLWN	MLWS
0000	0600	0100	0700	4·0	2·9	1·8	0·7
1200	1800	1300	1900				
Differences MALLAIG							
+0017	+0017	+0017	+0017	+1·0	+0·7	+0·3	+0·1
INVERIE BAY (Loch Nevis)							
+0030	+0020	+0035	+0020	+1·0	+0·9	+0·2	0·0
BAY OF LAIG (Eigg)							
+0015	+0030	+0040	+0005	+0·7	+0·6	–0·2	–0·2
LOCH MOIDART							
+0015	+0015	+0040	+0020	+0·8	+0·6	–0·2	–0·2
LOCH EATHARNA (Coll)							
+0025	+0010	+0015	+0025	+0·4	+0·3	No data	
GOTT BAY (Tiree)							
0000	+0010	+0005	+0010	0·0	+0·1	0·0	0·0

SHELTER Good in SW'lies but open to N. Access H24. ⚓ in SE part of hbr or find a berth on Fish Pier. No Ⓥs. Hbr is often full of FVs; also Skye ferry.

Continued overleaf

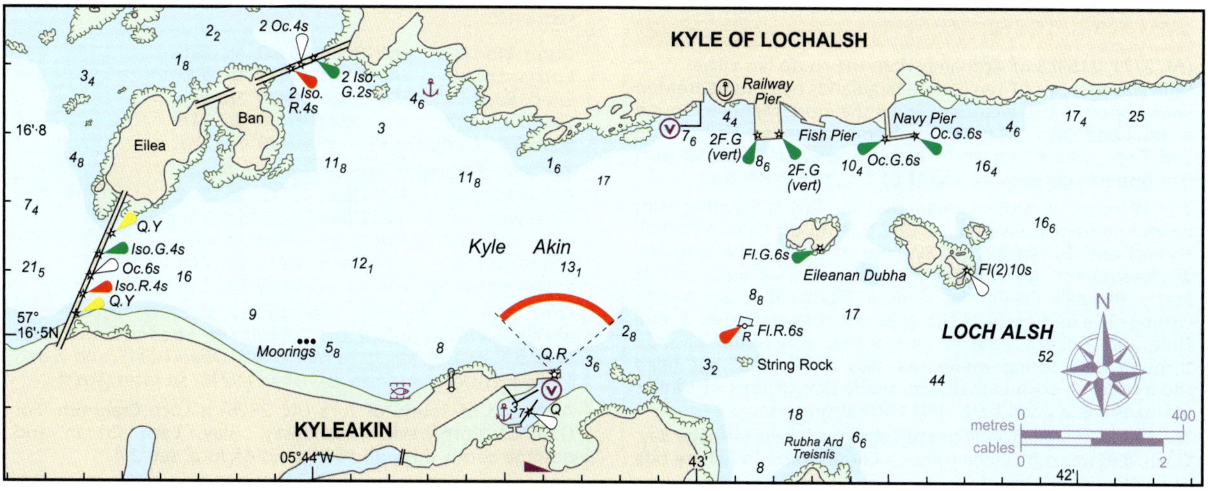

MALLAIG *continued*

NAVIGATION WPT 57°00′·75N 05°49′·40W, 191°/0·3m to Steamer Pier lt, passing E of Sgeir Dhearg lt bn. The former W chan is now permanently closed to navigation.

LIGHTS AND MARKS As chartlet & 1.3. Town lts may obscure Sgeir Dhearg lt. Outer Hbr Pier Hds floodlit. IPTS (3 FR vert at pier hd) when ferries manoeuvring, no other traffic allowed except by HM's permission.

R/T Call: *Mallaig Hbr Radio* VHF Ch 09 16 (HO).

TELEPHONE (Code 01687) HM 462154, outside office hrs 462411; MRCC (01851) 702013; ⊖ (0141) 887 9369; Marinecall 09068 969654; Police 462177.

FACILITIES **Hbr** AB £6 whenever alongside for FW/fuel/stores (⚓ is free), M, P (cans), D, FW, ME, El, ⚒, C (mobile 10 ton), CH, Ⓔ, ACA, Slip; a busy FV hbr, yacht berths may be provided at a later date near root of the Fish Pier. **Town** Dr 462202. 🛒, R, Gas, Gaz, Bar, ✉, Ⓑ, ⇌.

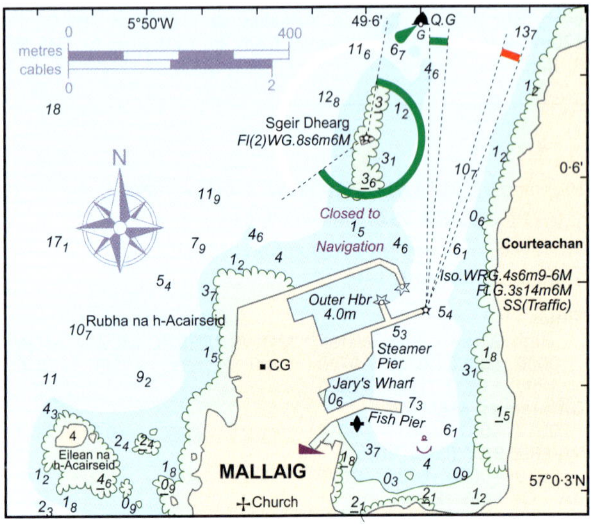

ADJACENT ANCHORAGE

ARISAIG, (Loch nan Ceall), Highland, **56°53′·64N 05°55′·77W** (ent). AC 2207. HW –0515 on Dover; +0030 and +0·9m on Oban. S side of ent is identifiable by W mark on Rubh' Arisaig. SDs essential. S Chan is winding, but marked by 8 perches; each must be identified. Appr HW±4 to avoid strongest streams LW±1½. Caution: many unmarked rks; no lts. Sheltered ⚓ at head of loch, clear of moorings. Call **Arisaig Marine** ☎ (01687) 450224, VHF Ch 16, M; few Øs, C (10 ton), CH, D & FW at ferry pier (HW), P (cans), El, ME, ⚒, Slip. **Village** FW at hotel, Bar, ✉, R, Gas, 🛒, ⇌.

ARDNAMURCHAN TO CRINAN

(AC 2171, 2169) S of Ardnamurchan the route lies either W of Mull via Passage of Tiree (where headlands need to be treated with respect in bad weather); or via the more sheltered Sound of Mull and Firth of Lorne. The former permits a visit to Coll and Tiree, where best anchs are at Arinagour (Øs) and Gott Bay respectively. Beware Cairns of Coll, off the N tip.

The W coast of Mull is rewarding in settled weather, but careful pilotage is needed. Beware tide rip off Caliach Pt (NW corner) and Torran Rks off SW end of Mull (large scale AC 2617 required). Apart from the attractions of Iona and of Staffa (Fingal's Cave), the remote Treshnish Is are worth visiting. The best anchs in this area are at Ulva, Gometra, Bull Hole and Tinker's Hole in Iona Sound. The usual passage through Iona Sound avoids overfalls W of Iona, but heed shoal patches. Loch Lathaich on the N side of Ross of Mull is 5M to the E; a good base with anch at Bunessan.

The Sound of Mull gives access to Tobermory, Dunstaffnage Bay, Oban, and up Loch Linnhe through Corran Narrows (where tide runs strongly) to Fort William and to Corpach for the Caledonian Canal. Apart from these places, there are dozens of lovely anchs in the sheltered lochs inside Mull, as for example in Loch Sunart with Øs at Kilchoan.

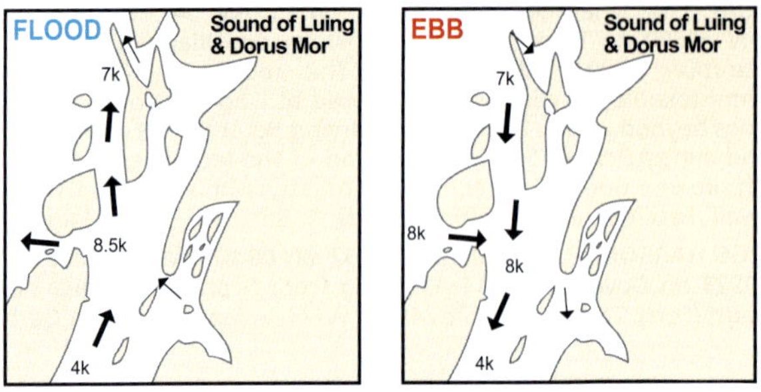

▶ *Firth of Lorne: the N-going stream begins at HW Oban +0430 (HW Dover –0100). The W-going stream in the Sound of Mull begins at HW Oban –0550 (HW Dover +0105). The ingoing tides at Lochs Feochan, Etive and Creran begin at HW Oban –0350, +0430 and +0600.*

The S-going stream in the Firth of Lorne begins at HW Oban –0155 (HW Dover +0500). The E-going stream in the Sound of Mull begins at HW Oban –0025 (HW Dover +0555).◀

On the mainland shore Puilladobhrain is a sheltered anch. Cuan Sound is a useful short cut to Loch Melfort, and Craobh Marina. Good shelter, draft permitting, in Ardinamar B, SW of Torsa.

Sound of Luing (AC 2326) between Fladda (lt), Lunga and Scarba on the W side, and Luing and Dubh Sgeir (lt) on the E side, is the normal chan to or from Sound of Jura, despite dangers at the N end and strong tidal streams. ▶ *The N- and W-going flood begins at HW Oban +0430; the S- and E-going ebb at HW Oban –0155. Sp rates are 2·5kn at S end of Sound, increasing to 6kn or more in Islands off N entrance, where there are eddies, races and overfalls.* ◀

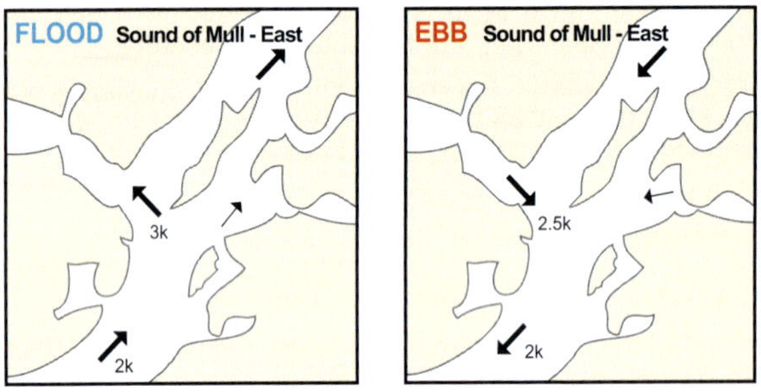

▶ *The N- or W-going stream begins in the following sequence:*

Dorus Mor:	*HW Oban +0330. Sp: 8kn.*
Corryvreckan:	*HW Oban +0410. Sp: 8.5kn.*
Cuan Sound:	*HW Oban +0420. Sp: 6kn.*
Sound of Jura:	*HW Oban +0400. Sp: 4kn.*
Sound of Luing:	*HW Oban +0430. Sp: 7kn.*

The S- or E-going stream begins as follows:

Dorus Mor:	*HW Oban –0215. Sp: 8kn.*
Corryvreckan:	*HW Oban –0210. Sp: 8.5kn.*
Cuan Sound:	*HW Oban –0200. Sp: 6kn.*
Sound of Jura:	*HW Oban –0205. Sp: 4kn.*
Sound of Luing:	*HW Oban –0155. Sp: 7kn.*

From the N, beware very strong streams, eddies and whirlpools in Dorus Mór, off Craignish Pt. Streams begin to set W and N away from Dorus Mór at HW Oban +0345, and E and S towards Dorus Mór at HW Oban –0215, sp rates 7kn.◀

At N end of Sound of Jura (AC 2326) is Loch Craignish. For Gulf of Corryvreckan, Colonsay, Islay, Loch Crinan and passage south through the Sound of Jura, see 2.4.

1.12 LOCH SUNART

Highland **56°39'·49N 06°00'·07W**

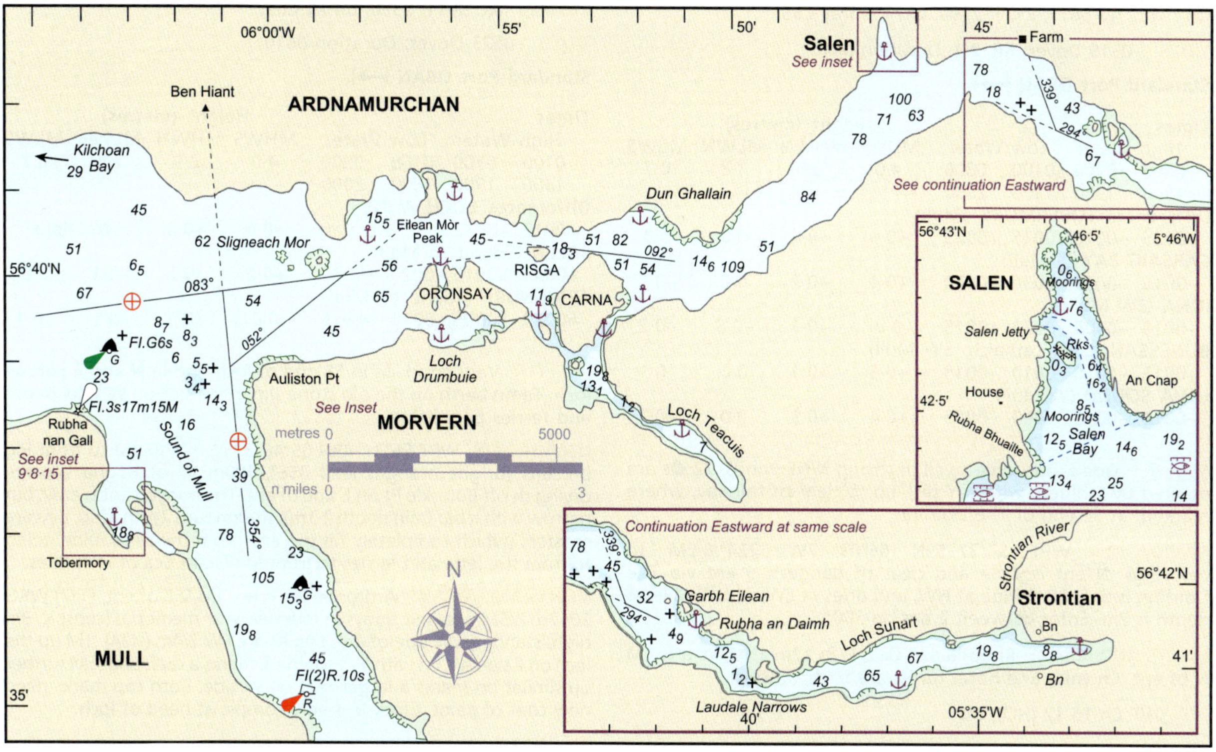

CHARTS AC 5611, 2171, 2392, 2394; Imray C65.

TIDES Salen –0500 Dover; ML 2·0

Standard Port OBAN (⟶)

Times				Height (metres)			
High Water		Low Water		MHWS	MHWN	MLWN	MLWS
0100	0700	0100	0800	4·0	2·9	1·8	0·7
1300	1900	1300	2000				
Differences SALEN (Loch Sunart)							
–0015	+0015	+0010	+0005	+0·6	+0·5	–0·1	–0·1

SHELTER 8 ✪s at Kilchoan Bay (56°41'·5N 06°07'·3W); ☎ (01972) 510209. ⚓s in Loch Drumbuie (S of Oronsay) sheltered in all winds; in Sailean Mór (N of Oronsay) convenient and easy ent; between Oronsay and Carna; in Loch Teacuis (very tricky ent); E of Carna; Salen Bay, with ✪s and jetty, open only to SSE (see facilities); Garbh Eilean (NW of Rubha an Daimh), and E of sand spit by Strontian R.

NAVIGATION **West WPT**, 56°39'·69N 06°03'·07W, 083°/3·7M to Creag nan Sgarbh (NW tip of Orinsay). **South WPT**, 56°38'·00N 06°00'·65W, 1M S of Auliston Pt; there are extensive rky reefs, The Stirks W of this pt. AC 2394 and detailed directions are needed to navigate the 17M long loch, particularly in its upper reaches. Beware Ross Rk, S of Risga; Broad Rk, E of Risga; Dun Ghallain Rk; shoals extending 3ca NNW from Eilean mo Shlinneag off S shore; drying rock 1ca W of Garbh Eilean and strong streams at sp in Laudale Narrows. Fish farms on both sides of the loch.

LIGHTS AND MARKS Unlit. Transits as on the chart: from W WPT, Risga on with N tip of Oronsay at 083°; N pt of Carna on with top of Risga 092°. From S WPT, Ben Hiant bearing 354°, thence Eilean Mor Peak at 052°. Further up the loch, 339° and 294°, as on chartlet, are useful. Many other transits are shown on AC 2394.

R/T None, except under Salen Bay opposite.

TELEPHONE (Code 01967) MRCC (01475) 729014; ⊖ (0141) 887 9369; Marinecall 09068 969653; Dr 431231.

FACILITIES **Salen Bay** jetty (56°42'·39N 05°46'·17W). ☎ 01967 431333. VHF Ch 16 (occas). Access HW±2 to jetty, keeping on E side of ent to avoid a drying reef on W side; two R ✪s (15 ton) £10 (other moorings are private); ⚓ buoy advised as bottom is generally foul. L (£2 unless on ✪), FW, D by hose, ⚡, Slip, SM, ME, El, CH, Gas, Gaz, Diver, ☐, 🛒, R, Bar. **Acharacle** (2½M), P, 🛒, ✉, Ⓑ (Tues/Wed, mobile), ⇌ (bus to Loch Ailort/Fort William), ✈ (Oban). **Strontian** FW, P, 🛒, hotel, ✉, Gas, Gaz, Bar. Bus to Fort William.

ANCHORAGES IN COLL AND TIREE (Argyll and Bute)

ARINAGOUR, Loch Eatharna, Coll, **56°37'·0N 06°31'·2W**. AC 5611, 2171, 2474. HW –0530 on Dover; ML 1·4m; Duration 0600; see 1.11. Good shelter except with SE swell or strong winds from ENE to SSW. Enter at SHM buoy, Fl G 6s, marking Bogha Mòr. Thence NW to Arinagour ferry pier, 2 FR(vert) 10m and Dir Oc WRG 7s. Beware McQuarrie's Rk (dries 2·9m) 1ca E of pier hd and unmarked drying rks further N on E side of fairway. Ch and hotel are conspic ahead. Continue N towards old stone pier; ⚓ S of it or pick up a buoy. Six ✪s on W side of hbr, between the two piers. Also ⚓ E of Eilean Eatharna. Piermaster ☎ (01879) 230347; VHF Ch 31. **Facilities**: HIE Trading Post ☎ 230349, M, D, FW, Gas, 🛒, CH, R. **Village** ☐, FW, P, ✉, Ferry to Oban (⇌).

GOTT BAY, Tiree, **56°30'·74N 06°48'·07W**. AC 5611, 2474. Tides as 1.11; HW –0540 on Dover. HM ☎ (01879) 230337, VHF Ch 31. Adequate shelter in calm weather, but exposed in winds ENE to S. (in which case use Wilson hbr in Balephetrish Bay IM W, Ldg lts F.G/Oc.G). The bay, at NE end of island, can be identified by conspic latticed tr at Scarinish about 8ca SW of ent, with lt Fl 3s 11m 16M close by (obscd over hbr). Appr on NW track, keeping to SW side of bay which is obstructed on NE side by Soa Is and drying rks. The ferry pier at S side of ent has FR ldg lts 286½°. ⚓ 1ca NW of pier head in 3m on sand; L at pier. Facilities: P & D (cans), Gas, 🛒, R, Bar, ✉ at Scarinish (½M), Ferry to Oban (⇌).

1.13 TOBERMORY

Mull (Argyll and Bute) **56°37'·19N 06°03'·87W** ❁❁❁◊◊✿✿✿

CHARTS AC 5611, 2171, 2390, 2474; Imray C65.

TIDES –0519 Dover; ML 2·4; Duration 0610

Standard Port OBAN (⟶)

Times				Height (metres)			
High Water		Low Water		MHWS	MHWN	MLWN	MLWS
0100	0700	0100	0800	4·0	2·9	1·8	0·7
1300	1900	1300	2000				
Differences TOBERMORY (Mull)							
+0025	+0010	+0015	+0025	+0·4	+0·4	0·0	0·0
CARSAIG BAY (S Mull)							
–0015	–0005	–0030	+0020	+0·1	+0·2	0·0	–0·1
IONA (SW Mull)							
–0010	–0005	–0020	+0015	0·0	+0·1	–0·3	–0·2
BUNESSAN (Loch Lathaich, SW Mull)							
–0015	–0015	–0010	–0015	+0·3	+0·1	0·0	–0·1
ULVA SOUND (W Mull)							
–0010	–0015	0000	–0005	+0·4	+0·3	0·0	–0·1

SHELTER Good, but some swell in strong N/NE winds. 22 Ⓥs are marked by a blue ⌂ with a Y pick-up. ⚓ clear of fairway, where marked; at SE end of The Doirlinn.

NAVIGATION WPT 56°37´·59N 06°03´·17W, 224°/0·5M to moorings. N ent is wide and clear of dangers. S ent via The Doirlinn is only 80m wide at HW, and dries at LW; at HW±2 least depth is 2m. Enter between 2 bns on 300°.

LIGHTS AND MARKS Rhubha nan Gall, Fl 3s 17m 15M, W tr is 1M N of ent. Ch spire and hotel turret are both conspic.

R/T VHF Ch 16 12 (HO), M.

TELEPHONE (Code 01688) Piermaster 302017; MRCC (01475) 729014; Local CG 302200; Marinecall 09068 969653; Police 302016; Dr 302013.

FACILITIES **Cal-Mac Pier**, only short stay AB for P, D; landing stage FW £2; **Western Isles YC** ☎ 302371; **Services:** Ⓥ £9 <8m £12 >8m or, 10 nights/£70-£90, ME, CH, ACA, Gaz, Gas, Divers. **Town** FW, P, Dr, 🛒, R, Bar, ✉, Ⓑ, ⇌ (ferry to Oban), ✈ (grass strip; helipad on golf course).

SOUND OF MULL (Mull, **56°31'·44N 05°56'·82W**). Beware drying rocks 6ca E of the bay; ent on SE side. **Salen Jetty,** Ⓥs £10. Landing from yacht at ⚓ £1 per person/H24. FW , D. **Village,** 🛒, ME, Ⓔ, CH, R, Dr, ✉. Land at jetty in SW corner.

CRAIGNURE, (Mull, **56°28'·37N 05°42'·25W**) ldg lts 241°, both FR 10/12m. Facilities: 🛒, Bar, ✉, Gas, Ferry to Oban. Tides, see 1.14.

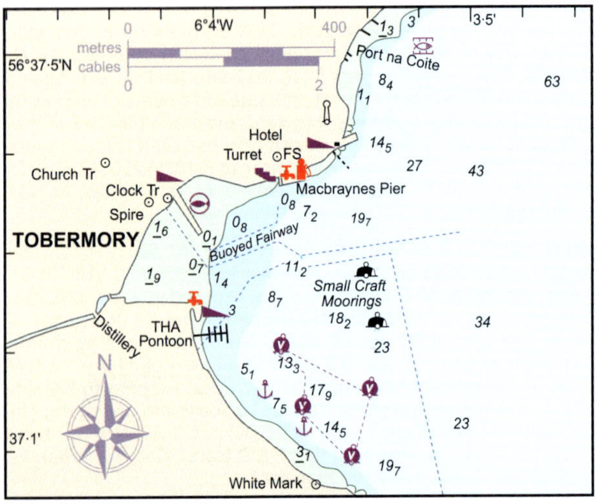

1.14 LOCH ALINE

Highland **56°32'·09N 05°46'·47W** ❁❁❁◊✿✿✿

CHARTS AC 5611, 2390; Imray C65.

TIDES –0523 Dover; Duration 0610

Standard Port OBAN (⟶)

Times				Height (metres)			
High Water		Low Water		MHWS	MHWN	MLWN	MLWS
0100	0700	0100	0800	4·0	2·9	1·8	0·7
1300	1900	1300	2000				
Differences LOCH ALINE							
+0012	+0012	No data		+0·5	+0·3	No data	
SALEN (Sound of Mull)							
+0045	+0015	+0020	+0030	+0·2	+0·2	–0·1	0·0
CRAIGNURE (Sound of Mull)							
+0030	+0005	+0010	+0015	0·0	+0·1	–0·1	–0·1

SHELTER Very good. ⚓s in SE end of loch and in N and E part of loch. Temp berth on the old stone slip in the ent on W side, depth and ferries permitting.

NAVIGATION WPT 56°31´·49N 05°46´·37W, 176°/0·9M to front ldg bn. Bns (bright orange) lead 356°, 100m W of Bogha Lurcain, drying rk off Bolorkle Pt on E side of ent. The buoyed ent is easy, but narrow with a bar (min depth 2·1m); stream runs 2½kn at sp. Beware coasters (which completely fill the ent) from the sand mine going to/from the jetty and ferries to/from Mull. Last 5ca of loch dries.

LIGHTS AND MARKS Ardtornish Pt lt ho, 1M SSE of ent, Fl (2) WRG 10s 7m 8/5M. Lts and buoys as chartlet. War memorial (conspic, 9m high) stands on W side of ent. Ldg lts are FW 2/4m (H24). 1M up the loch on E side a Y bn with Y ● topmark marks a reef, and ½M further up similar bn marks a larger reef on W side. Both top marks need new coat of paint. Clock tr is very conspic at head of loch.

R/T None.

TELEPHONE (Code 01967) MRCC (01475) 729014; ⊖ (0141) 887 9369; Marinecall 09068 969653; Ⓗ (01631) 563727; Dr 421252.

FACILITIES **Village** FW at pier, P & D, Gas, 🛒, R, Bar, P, ✉, (Ⓑ, ⇌, ✈ at Oban), Ferry to Fishnish Bay (Mull).

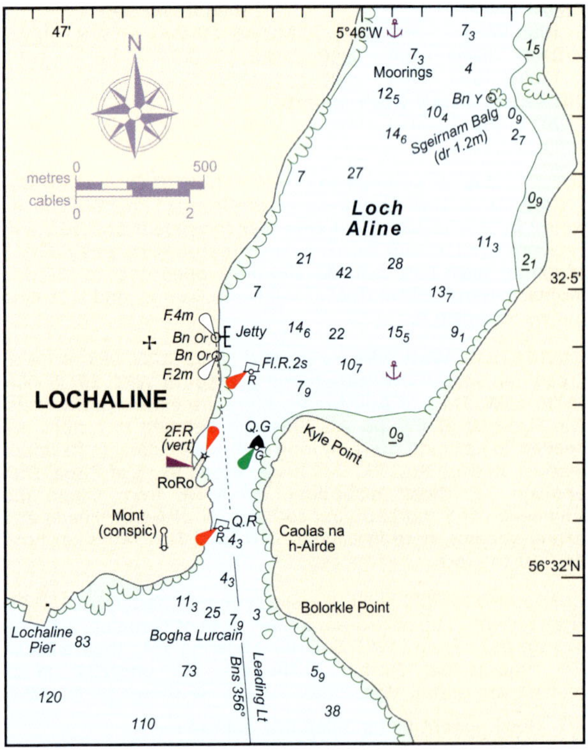

ANCHORAGES on WEST and SOUTH COASTS OF MULL (Anti-clockwise from the north. SDs essential) (See AC *5611*)

TRESHNISH ISLES 56°29'N 06°31'W. AC 2652. The main Is (N to S) are: Cairn na Burgh, Fladda, Lunga, Bac Mòr and Bac Beag. Tides run hard and isles are exposed to swell, but merit a visit in calm weather. Appr with caution on ldg lines as in CCC SDs; temp ⚓ off Lunga's N tip in 4m.

STAFFA 56°25'·96N 06°20'·34W. AC 2652. Spectacular isle with Fingal's Cave, but same caveats as above. Very temp ⚓ off SE tip where there is landing; beware unmarked rks.

GOMETRA 56°28'·85N 06°23'W. AC 2652. Tides as 1.13. The narrow inlet between Gometra and Ulva Is offers sheltered ⚓, except in S'lies. Appr on 020° between Staffa and Little Colonsay, or N of the former. Beware rks drying 3·2m, to stbd and 5ca S of ent. Inside, E side is cleaner.

LOCH NA KEAL 56°26'N 06°18'W (ent). AC 2652. Tides in 1.13. Appr S of Geasgill Is and N of drying rks off **Inch Kenneth**; E of this Is and in **Sound of Ulva** are sheltered ⚓s, except in S'lies. Beware MacQuarrie's Rk, dries 0·8m.

LOCH LATHAICH Mull, **56°19'·29N 06°15'·47W**. AC 2617. HW –0545 on Dover; ML 2·4. See 1.13. Excellent shelter with easy access; good base for cruising W Mull. Eilean na Liathanaich (a group of islets) lie off the ent, marked by a W bn at the E end, Fl WR 6s 12m 8/6M, R088°-108°, W108°-088°. Keep to W side of loch and ⚓ off Bendoran BY in SW, or SE of Eilean Ban off the pier in approx 5m. **Facilities**: (Bunessan) Shop, ✉, Bar, R, FW.

SOUND OF IONA 56°19'·45N 06°23'·12W. AC 2617. Tides see 1.13. From N, enter in mid-chan; from S keep clear of Torran Rks. Cathedral brg 012° closes the Iona shore past 2 SHM buoys and SCM buoy. Beware a bank 0·1m in mid-sound, between cathedral and Fionnphort; also tel cables and ferries. ⚓ S of ferry close in to Iona, or in Bull Hole. Consult SDs. Crowded in season; limited facilities.

TINKER'S HOLE Ross of Mull, **56°17'·49N 06°23'·07W**. AC 2617. Beware Torran Rks, reefs extending 5M S and SW of Erraid. Usual app from S, avoiding Rankin's Rks, drying 0·8m, and rk, dries 2·3m, between Eilean nam Muc and Erraid. Popular ⚓ in mid-pool between Eilean Dubh and Erraid.

CARSAIG BAY Ross of Mull, **56°19'·19N 05°59'·07W**. Tides see 1.13. AC 2386. Temp, fair weather ⚓s to N of Gamhnach Mhòr, reef 2m high, or close into NW corner of bay. Landing at stone quay on NE side. No facilities.

LOCH SPELVE Mull, **56°23'N 05°41'W**. AC 2387. Tides as Oban. Landlocked water, prone to squalls off surrounding hills. Ent narrows to ½ca due to shoal S side and drying rk N side, 56°23'·24N 05°41'·95W, ☆ FlG 5s 3m 2M, G pole. CCC SDs give local ldg lines. ⚓s in SW and NW arms, clear of fish farms. Pier at Croggan; no facilities.

ANCHORAGES ALONG LOCH LINNHE
(AC 5611, 2378, 2379, 2380)

LYNN OF LORN 56°33'N 05°25'·2W. At NE end are ⚓s off **Port Appin**, clear of ferry and cables (beware Appin Rks); and in **Airds Bay**, open to SW. At NW tip of Lismore, **Port Ramsey** offers good ⚓s between the 3 main islets. **Linnhe Marina** ☎ 01631 730401 offers pontoon and mooring berths.

LOCH CRERAN 56°32'·14N 05°25'·22W. Tides 1.15. Ent at Airds Pt, Dir lt 050°, Fl WRG 2s, W vis 041-058°. Chan turns 90° stbd with streams of 4kn. Sgeir Callich, rky ridge extends NE to SHM By, Fl G 3s; ⚓ W of it. Ⓥs (max LOA 7m) off Barcaldine; also 3 Ⓥs max LOA 9m off Creagan Inn, ☎ (01631) 573250. Bridge has 12m clearance. Beware of extensive marine farms in loch.

LOCH LEVEN 56°42'N 05°12'W. (See inset 1.15.) Tides 1.15. Fair weather ⚓s in Ballachulish Bay, at Kentallen B (deep), Onich and off St Brides on N shore. App bridge (17m clnce) on 114°; 4ca ENE of br are moorings and ⚓ at Poll an Dùnan, entered W of perch. Facilities at Ballachulish: Hotels, 🛒, R, ✉, Ⓑ. Loch is navigable 7M to Kinlochleven.

CORRAN NARROWS 56°43'·27N 05°14'·34W. AC 2372. Sp rate 6kn. Well buoyed; Corran Pt lt ho, Iso WRG 4s, and lt bn 5ca NE. ⚓ 5ca NW of Pt, off Camas Aiseig pier/slip.

1.15 FORT WILLIAM/CORPACH

Highland 56°48'·99N 05°07'·07W (off Fort William)

CHARTS AC 5611, 2372, 2380; Imray C65, C23.

TIDES –0535 Dover; ML 2·3; Duration 0610

Standard Port OBAN (⟶)

Times				**Height (metres)**			
High Water		Low Water		MHWS	MHWN	MLWN	MLWS
0100	0700	0100	0800	4·0	2·9	1·8	0·7
1300	1900	1300	2000				
Differences CORPACH							
0000	+0020	+0040	0000	0·0	0·0	–0·2	–0·2
LOCH EIL (Head)							
+0025	+0045	+0105	+0025		No data		No data
CORRAN NARROWS							
+0007	+0007	+0004	+0004	+0·4	+0·4	–0·1	0·0
LOCH LEVEN (Head)							
+0045	+0045	+0045	+0045		No data		No data
LOCH LINNHE (Port Appin)							
–0005	–0005	–0030	0000	+0·2	+0·2	+0·1	+0·1
LOCH CRERAN (Barcaldine Pier)							
+0010	+0020	+0040	+0015	+0·1	+0·1	0·0	+0·1
LOCH CRERAN (Head)							
+0015	+0025	+0120	+0020	–0·3	–0·3	–0·4	–0·3

SHELTER Exposed to winds SW thro' N to NE. ⚓s off Fort William pier; in Camus na Gall; SSW of Eilean A Bhealaidh; and off Corpach Basin, where there is also a waiting pontoon; or inside the canal where it is more sheltered. The sea lock is normally available HW±4 during canal hrs. For Caledonian Canal see 1.16.

NAVIGATION Corpach WPT 56°50'·29N 05°07'·07W, 315°/0·32M to lock ent.

Beware McLean Rk, dries 0·3m, buoyed, 8ca N of Fort William. Lochy Flats dry 3ca off the E bank. In Annat Narrows at ent to Loch Eil streams reach 5kn.

LIGHTS AND MARKS Iso WRG 4s lt is at N jetty of sea-lock ent, W310°-335°. A long pier/viaduct off Ft William is unlit.

R/T Call: *Corpach Lock* VHF Ch **74** 16 (during canal hours).

TELEPHONE (Code 01397) HM 772249; MRCC (01475) 729014; ⊖ 702948; Marinecall 09068 969653; Police 702361; Dr 703136.

FACILITIES **Fort William: Pier** ☎ 703881, AB; **Services:** Slip, L, CH, ACA. **Town:** P, ME, El, ⚒, YC, 🛒, R, Bar, Ⓗ, ✉, Ⓑ, ⇌. **Corpach: Corpach Basin** ☎ 772249, AB, L, FW, D; **Lochaber YC** ☎ 703576, M, FW, L, Slip; **Services:** ME, El, ⚒, D (cans), M, CH, Slip, Divers. **Village:** P, 🛒, R, Bar, ✉, Ⓑ, ⇌.

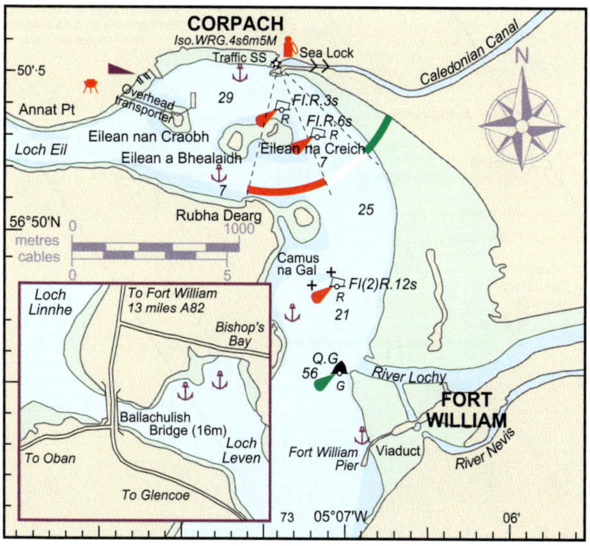

1.16 CALEDONIAN CANAL

Highland

CHARTS AC 1791; Imray C23; *BWB Skippers Guide*

TIDES Tidal differences: Corpach –0455 on Dover; See 1.15. Clachnaharry: +0116 on Dover.

SHELTER Corpach is at the SW ent of the Caledonian Canal, see 1.15; the sea locks at both ends do not open LW±2 at springs. For best shelter transit the sea lock and lie above the double lock. Numerous pontoons along the canal; cost is included in the canal dues.

NAVIGATION The 60M canal consists of 38M through 3 lochs, (Lochs Lochy, Oich and Ness), connected by 22M of canal.

Loch Oich is part of a hydro-electric scheme which may vary the water level. The passage normally takes two full days, possibly longer in the summer; absolute minimum is 14 hrs. Speed limit is 5kn in the canal sections. There are 10 swing bridges; road traffic has priority at peak hrs. Do not pass bridges without the keeper's instructions.

LOCKS There are 29 locks: 14 between Loch Linnhe (Corpach), via Lochs Lochy and Oich up to the summit (106ft above sea level); and 15 locks from the summit down via Loch Ness to Inverness.

2005 information

Hours: Winter Mon-Fri 0900-1600
Spring Mon-Sun 0830-1730
Summer Mon-Sun 0800-1730
Autumn Mon-Sun 0830-1730

Dues payable at Corpach: transit/lock fee Outward £16 per metre for 8 day passage or less; Return £12 per metre. £20 per metre is charged for a 2 week sojourn. For regulations and useful booklet *BWS Skipper's Guide* apply: Canal Manager, Canal Office, Seaport Marina, Muirtown Wharf, Inverness IV3 5LE, ☎ (01463) 233140, or download from: www.waterscape.com

LIGHTS AND MARKS See 1.15 for ent lts. Channel is marked by posts, cairns and unlit buoys, PHM on the NW side of the chan and SHM on the SE side.

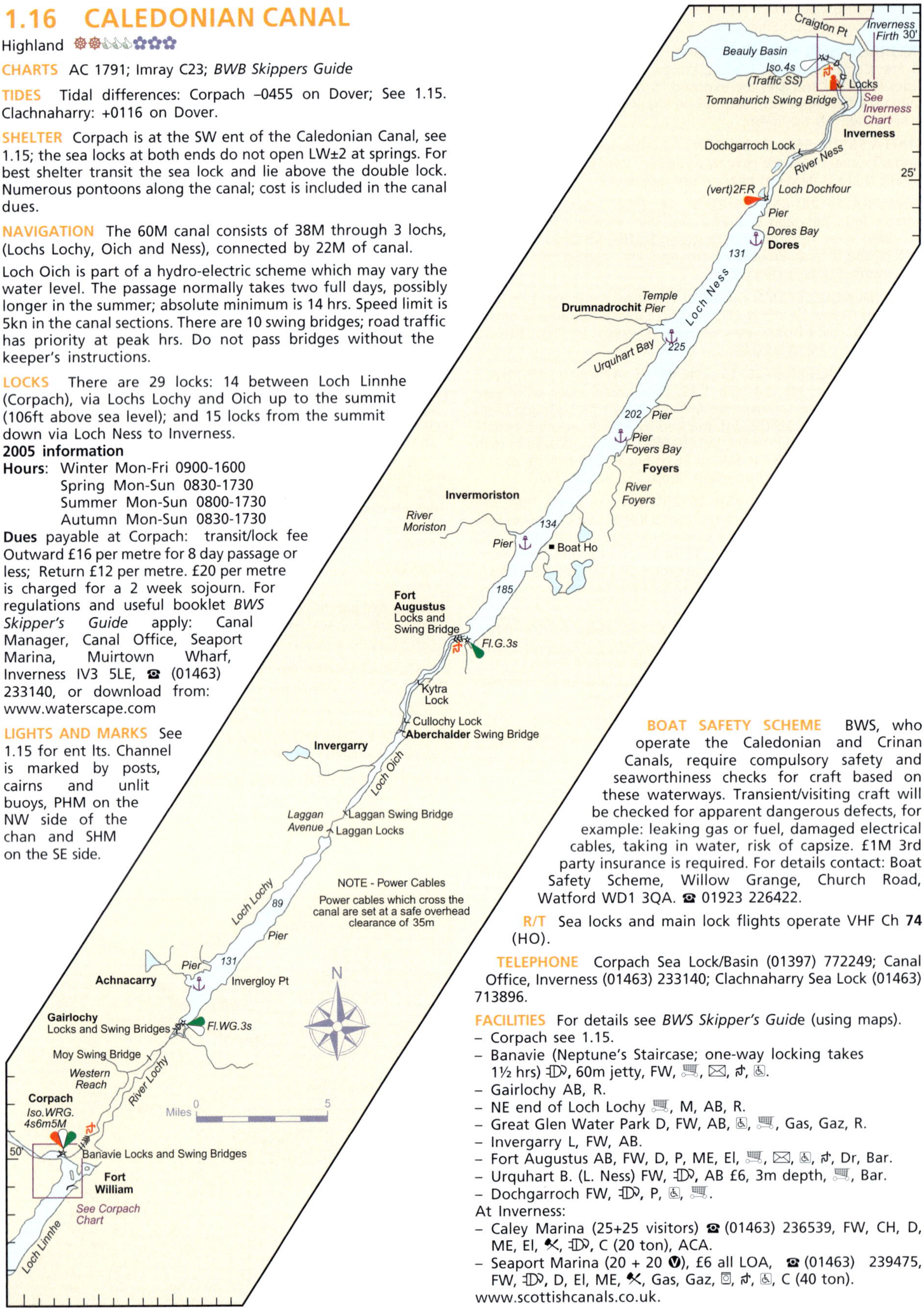

BOAT SAFETY SCHEME BWS, who operate the Caledonian and Crinan Canals, require compulsory safety and seaworthiness checks for craft based on these waterways. Transient/visiting craft will be checked for apparent dangerous defects, for example: leaking gas or fuel, damaged electrical cables, taking in water, risk of capsize. £1M 3rd party insurance is required. For details contact: Boat Safety Scheme, Willow Grange, Church Road, Watford WD1 3QA. ☎ 01923 226422.

R/T Sea locks and main lock flights operate VHF Ch **74** (HO).

TELEPHONE Corpach Sea Lock/Basin (01397) 772249; Canal Office, Inverness (01463) 233140; Clachnaharry Sea Lock (01463) 713896.

FACILITIES For details see *BWS Skipper's Guide* (using maps).

- Corpach see 1.15.
- Banavie (Neptune's Staircase; one-way locking takes 1½ hrs), 60m jetty, FW.
- Gairlochy AB, R.
- NE end of Loch Lochy, M, AB, R.
- Great Glen Water Park D, FW, AB, Gas, Gaz, R.
- Invergarry L, FW, AB.
- Fort Augustus AB, FW, D, P, ME, El, Dr, Bar.
- Urquhart B. (L. Ness) FW, AB £6, 3m depth, Bar.
- Dochgarroch FW, P.

At Inverness:

- Caley Marina (25+25 visitors) ☎ (01463) 236539, FW, CH, D, ME, El, C (20 ton), ACA.
- Seaport Marina (20 + 20 Ⓥ), £6 all LOA, ☎ (01463) 239475, FW, D, El, ME, Gas, Gaz, C (40 ton).

www.scottishcanals.co.uk.

TIME ZONE (UT)
For Summer Time add ONE hour in **non-shaded areas**

OBAN LAT 56°25'N LONG 5°29'W

TIMES AND HEIGHTS OF HIGH AND LOW WATERS

Dates in red are SPRINGS
Dates in blue are NEAPS

YEAR **2010**

JANUARY

Day	Time	m	Day	Time	m
1 F	0543 1216 1814	4.0 0.9 4.0	16 SA	0023 0621 1249 1833	1.1 4.0 1.3 3.8
2 SA	0019 0627 1304 1856	0.6 4.2 0.8 4.0	17 SU	0058 0655 1322 1905	1.1 4.0 1.3 3.8
3 SU	0105 0710 1350 1937	0.5 4.2 0.8 3.9	18 M	0131 0728 1354 1935	1.1 4.0 1.3 3.8
4 M	0152 0754 1437 2020	0.5 4.1 0.9 3.7	19 TU	0201 0759 1425 2002	1.2 3.9 1.4 3.7
5 TU	0239 0839 1524 2105	0.6 3.9 1.0 3.5	20 W	0227 0828 1452 2029	1.3 3.8 1.5 3.6
6 W	0328 0925 1613 2153	0.7 3.7 1.3 3.3	21 TH	0252 0858 1521 2100	1.4 3.6 1.6 3.4
7 TH	0419 1016 1708 ◑ 2250	1.0 3.4 1.5 3.1	22 F	0321 0931 1559 2137	1.6 3.5 1.7 3.3
8 F	0515 1118 1810	1.3 3.2 1.7	23 SA	0401 1014 1652 ◐ 2223	1.7 3.3 1.9 3.1
9 SA	0010 0618 1251 1922	3.0 1.5 3.0 1.8	24 SU	0458 1114 1803 2328	1.9 3.1 1.9 3.0
10 SU	0139 0731 1431 2043	3.0 1.7 3.0 1.8	25 M	0621 1310 1920	1.9 3.0 1.9
11 M	0251 0853 1553 2146	3.1 1.7 3.1 1.7	26 TU	0122 0753 1503 2033	3.0 1.9 3.2 1.7
12 TU	0346 1004 1627 2233	3.3 1.6 3.2 1.5	27 W	0309 0925 1602 2137	3.2 1.6 3.4 1.3
13 W	0429 1056 1656 2312	3.5 1.5 3.4 1.4	28 TH	0408 1034 1648 2233	3.5 1.3 3.7 1.0
14 TH	0507 1137 1727 2348	3.7 1.4 3.6 1.2	29 F	0455 1126 1729 2322	3.9 0.9 3.9 0.6
15 F	0545 1214 1800 ●	3.9 1.3 3.7	30 SA	0538 1211 1807 ○	4.1 0.7 4.0
			31 SU	0008 0619 1255 1844	0.4 4.3 0.5 4.1

FEBRUARY

Day	Time	m	Day	Time	m
1 M	0053 0659 1336 1922	0.2 4.3 0.5 4.0	16 TU	0108 0705 1327 1910	0.9 4.0 1.0 3.9
2 TU	0137 0738 1416 1959	0.2 4.2 0.6 3.9	17 W	0133 0732 1353 1934	1.0 3.9 1.1 3.8
3 W	0220 0817 1456 2037	0.3 4.0 0.8 3.7	18 TH	0154 0757 1414 1958	1.1 3.8 1.2 3.7
4 TH	0304 0855 1538 2116	0.6 3.7 1.1 3.5	19 F	0215 0823 1440 2027	1.2 3.7 1.3 3.6
5 F	0350 0935 1624 ◑ 2200	0.9 3.4 1.4 3.2	20 SA	0244 0854 1516 2102	1.3 3.5 1.5 3.4
6 SA	0439 1021 1718 2259	1.2 3.1 1.7 3.0	21 SU	0322 0933 1606 2145	1.5 3.3 1.7 3.2
7 SU	0537 1129 1826	1.6 2.8 1.9	22 M	0416 1030 1718 ◐ 2247	1.7 3.0 1.8 3.0
8 M	0049 0650 1514 2002	2.8 1.8 2.7 1.9	23 TU	0553 1230 1848	1.9 2.8 1.8
9 TU	0231 0841 1623 2132	2.9 1.9 2.9 1.8	24 W	0056 0746 1459 2010	2.9 1.8 3.0 1.6
10 W	0341 1006 1653 2223	3.1 1.7 3.1 1.5	25 TH	0303 0926 1555 2122	3.2 1.5 3.3 1.3
11 TH	0419 1052 1654 2302	3.3 1.5 3.3 1.3	26 F	0359 1027 1639 2219	3.5 1.1 3.6 0.9
12 F	0454 1128 1716 2336	3.6 1.4 3.5 1.1	27 SA	0443 1114 1716 2308	3.9 0.8 3.8 0.5
13 SA	0529 1159 1745	3.8 1.2 3.7	28 SU	0523 1156 1751 ○ 2353	4.2 0.5 4.0 0.2
14 SU	0008 0603 1229 ● 1816	1.0 4.0 1.1 3.8			
15 M	0039 0635 1258 1845	0.9 4.0 1.0 3.9			

MARCH

Day	Time	m	Day	Time	m
1 M	0602 1235 1825	4.3 0.4 4.1	16 TU	0010 0608 1227 1816	0.8 4.0 0.9 3.8
2 TU	0036 0639 1313 1859	0.1 4.3 0.4 4.1	17 W	0038 0637 1255 1840	0.8 4.0 0.8 3.8
3 W	0118 0715 1350 1934	0.1 4.2 0.5 4.0	18 TH	0102 0703 1320 1904	0.8 3.9 0.9 3.8
4 TH	0159 0750 1427 2009	0.3 4.0 0.7 3.8	19 F	0125 0728 1344 1931	0.9 3.8 1.0 3.7
5 F	0240 0824 1505 2044	0.5 3.7 1.0 3.5	20 SA	0150 0756 1414 2002	1.0 3.6 1.1 3.6
6 SA	0323 0859 1548 2123	0.9 3.3 1.3 3.3	21 SU	0222 0830 1453 2039	1.2 3.4 1.3 3.4
7 SU	0409 0937 1640 ◑ 2212	1.3 3.0 1.6 3.0	22 M	0304 0912 1543 2126	1.4 3.2 1.5 3.2
8 M	0506 1028 1746 2355	1.7 2.7 1.8 2.8	23 TU	0405 1014 1656 ◐ 2235	1.6 2.9 1.6 3.0
9 TU	0619 1455 1917	1.9 2.5 1.9	24 W	0555 1239 1826	1.8 2.7 1.6
10 W	0210 0834 1603 2106	2.8 1.9 2.7 1.7	25 TH	0051 0746 1439 1949	2.9 1.7 2.9 1.5
11 TH	0322 0952 1627 2159	3.0 1.7 2.9 1.5	26 F	0242 0912 1534 2101	3.2 1.4 3.2 1.1
12 F	0358 1031 1628 2238	3.3 1.5 3.2 1.3	27 SA	0337 1008 1617 2158	3.6 1.0 3.5 0.8
13 SA	0431 1103 1650 2312	3.5 1.3 3.4 1.1	28 SU	0421 1052 1654 2247	3.9 0.7 3.8 0.5
14 SU	0504 1131 1719 2342	3.7 1.1 3.6 0.9	29 M	0501 1132 1727 2333	4.1 0.5 3.9 0.2
15 M	0537 1159 1749 ●	3.9 0.9 3.8	30 TU	0539 1210 1801 ○	4.2 0.4 4.1
			31 W	0015 0614 1247 1835	0.2 4.2 0.4 4.1

APRIL

Day	Time	m	Day	Time	m
1 TH	0057 0650 1323 1909	0.2 4.1 0.5 4.0	16 F	0033 0636 1251 1839	0.8 3.9 0.8 3.8
2 F	0138 0724 1359 1944	0.4 3.9 0.7 3.8	17 SA	0104 0706 1323 1911	0.9 3.7 0.8 3.7
3 SA	0218 0757 1438 2019	0.7 3.6 1.0 3.6	18 SU	0138 0740 1359 1948	1.0 3.6 0.9 3.6
4 SU	0259 0831 1520 2059	1.1 3.3 1.3 3.3	19 M	0218 0821 1443 2031	1.1 3.4 1.1 3.5
5 M	0346 0908 1611 2147	1.4 2.9 1.5 3.1	20 TU	0310 0911 1537 2125	1.3 3.1 1.3 3.3
6 TU	0441 0957 1713 ◑ 2305	1.7 2.7 1.8 2.8	21 W	0423 1019 1646 ◐ 2239	1.5 2.9 1.4 3.1
7 W	0551 1324 1830	1.9 2.5 1.8	22 TH	0556 1225 1805	1.6 2.8 1.4
8 TH	0130 0741 1453 2013	2.8 1.9 2.6 1.8	23 F	0031 0729 1407 1923	3.1 1.5 2.9 1.3
9 F	0241 0910 1525 2119	3.0 1.8 2.8 1.6	24 SA	0209 0845 1504 2033	3.3 1.3 3.2 1.1
10 SA	0323 0952 1547 2201	3.2 1.5 3.1 1.3	25 SU	0308 0940 1549 2132	3.5 1.0 3.4 0.8
11 SU	0358 1024 1615 2236	3.4 1.3 3.3 1.2	26 M	0354 1025 1627 2224	3.7 0.8 3.6 0.6
12 M	0432 1053 1646 2306	3.6 1.1 3.5 1.0	27 TU	0436 1106 1701 2310	3.9 0.7 3.8 0.5
13 TU	0505 1122 1716 2335	3.8 0.9 3.7 0.9	28 W	0514 1144 1737 ○ 2355	4.0 0.6 3.9 0.5
14 W	0538 1151 1745 ●	3.9 0.8 3.8	29 TH	0551 1221 1812	4.0 0.6 4.0
15 TH	0004 0608 1221 1811	0.8 3.9 0.8 3.8	30 F	0037 0627 1258 1848	0.5 3.9 0.7 3.9

Chart Datum: 2·10 metres below Ordnance Datum (Newlyn). HAT is 4·5 metres above Chart Datum; see 0.20

TIME ZONE (UT)
For Summer Time add ONE hour in **non-shaded areas**

OBAN LAT 56°25′N LONG 5°29′W

TIMES AND HEIGHTS OF HIGH AND LOW WATERS

Dates in red are SPRINGS
Dates in blue are NEAPS

YEAR 2010

MAY

Date	Day	Time	m	Time	m	Time	m	Time	m	Moon
1	SA	0119	0.7	0702	3.7	1336	0.9	1925	3.8	
2	SU	0159	1.0	0737	3.5	1415	1.1	2002	3.6	
3	M	0241	1.2	0813	3.2	1458	1.3	2043	3.4	
4	TU	0326	1.5	0853	3.0	1545	1.5	2130	3.2	
5	W	0418	1.7	0941	2.8	1639	1.7	2230	3.0	
6	TH	0519	1.9	1053	2.6	1741	1.8	2359	2.9	◑
7	F	0633	1.9	1313	2.6	1852	1.8			
8	SA	0138	3.0	0751	1.8	1417	2.8	2006	1.7	
9	SU	0234	3.1	0849	1.6	1457	3.0	2103	1.6	
10	M	0316	3.3	0931	1.4	1533	3.2	2145	1.4	
11	TU	0354	3.5	1007	1.2	1608	3.4	2221	1.2	
12	W	0432	3.6	1041	1.1	1642	3.5	2257	1.1	
13	TH	0508	3.7	1116	0.9	1715	3.7	2333	1.0	
14	F	0543	3.8	1151	0.8	1748	3.7			●
15	SA	0012	0.9	0617	3.8	1228	0.7	1823	3.8	
16	SU	0053	0.9	0654	3.7	1308	0.7	1901	3.8	
17	M	0137	0.9	0734	3.6	1351	0.8	1944	3.7	
18	TU	0226	1.0	0820	3.4	1439	0.9	2032	3.6	
19	W	0321	1.2	0913	3.2	1532	1.0	2128	3.4	
20	TH	0426	1.3	1016	3.0	1633	1.1	2234	3.3	◐
21	F	0540	1.4	1144	2.9	1740	1.2	2358	3.2	
22	SA	0658	1.4	1321	2.9	1852	1.2			
23	SU	0128	3.2	0810	1.3	1427	3.1	2001	1.1	
24	M	0235	3.4	0909	1.2	1518	3.3	2104	1.0	
25	TU	0329	3.5	0958	1.1	1601	3.5	2200	0.9	
26	W	0414	3.6	1041	1.0	1639	3.7	2251	0.9	
27	TH	0456	3.7	1121	0.9	1717	3.8	2337	0.9	○
28	F	0534	3.7	1200	0.9	1756	3.9			
29	SA	0021	0.9	0611	3.6	1239	0.9	1833	3.9	
30	SU	0103	1.0	0648	3.6	1318	1.0	1911	3.8	
31	M	0144	1.2	0724	3.5	1357	1.1	1949	3.7	

JUNE

Date	Day	Time	m	Time	m	Time	m	Time	m	Moon
1	TU	0225	1.3	0801	3.3	1437	1.2	2029	3.6	
2	W	0307	1.5	0840	3.2	1519	1.4	2111	3.4	
3	TH	0351	1.6	0922	3.0	1603	1.6	2157	3.2	
4	F	0441	1.8	1010	2.9	1651	1.7	2251	3.1	◑
5	SA	0536	1.8	1109	2.8	1744	1.8	2358	3.0	
6	SU	0635	1.8	1229	2.8	1840	1.8			
7	M	0116	3.1	0735	1.8	1347	2.9	1940	1.8	
8	TU	0223	3.2	0830	1.6	1443	3.0	2039	1.6	
9	W	0316	3.3	0919	1.4	1530	3.2	2134	1.5	
10	TH	0403	3.5	1004	1.2	1613	3.4	2225	1.3	
11	F	0446	3.6	1046	1.0	1655	3.6	2313	1.1	
12	SA	0528	3.7	1129	0.8	1735	3.7			●
13	SU	0000	0.9	0608	3.7	1212	0.7	1816	3.8	
14	M	0048	0.8	0649	3.7	1256	0.6	1858	3.9	
15	TU	0135	0.8	0731	3.6	1342	0.6	1943	3.9	
16	W	0225	0.8	0816	3.5	1430	0.6	2029	3.8	
17	TH	0316	0.9	0905	3.3	1520	0.7	2120	3.6	
18	F	0412	1.1	0959	3.2	1614	0.9	2215	3.4	
19	SA	0512	1.3	1104	3.0	1713	1.1	2321	3.3	◐
20	SU	0619	1.4	1226	3.0	1818	1.2			
21	M	0043	3.1	0729	1.4	1345	3.0	1926	1.3	
22	TU	0204	3.1	0838	1.4	1449	3.1	2036	1.3	
23	W	0311	3.2	0936	1.4	1542	3.3	2142	1.3	
24	TH	0405	3.3	1025	1.3	1626	3.5	2238	1.2	
25	F	0449	3.4	1108	1.2	1706	3.7	2327	1.2	
26	SA	0528	3.5	1147	1.1	1745	3.8			○
27	SU	0010	1.2	0604	3.5	1226	1.0	1822	3.9	
28	M	0051	1.2	0639	3.6	1304	1.0	1859	3.9	
29	TU	0130	1.2	0713	3.6	1340	1.1	1935	3.8	
30	W	0207	1.3	0747	3.5	1416	1.1	2011	3.7	

JULY

Date	Day	Time	m	Time	m	Time	m	Time	m	Moon
1	TH	0243	1.4	0821	3.4	1451	1.3	2046	3.6	
2	F	0320	1.5	0854	3.3	1525	1.4	2122	3.5	
3	SA	0359	1.6	0929	3.2	1601	1.6	2201	3.3	
4	SU	0442	1.7	1009	3.1	1643	1.7	2246	3.2	◑
5	M	0534	1.8	1059	2.9	1736	1.8	2346	3.1	
6	TU	0633	1.8	1207	2.9	1839	1.9			
7	W	0120	3.0	0736	1.7	1348	2.9	1949	1.8	
8	TH	0245	3.1	0838	1.6	1503	3.1	2101	1.6	
9	F	0346	3.3	0935	1.3	1558	3.3	2209	1.4	
10	SA	0436	3.5	1026	1.1	1645	3.6	2306	1.1	
11	SU	0521	3.7	1114	0.8	1729	3.8	2356	0.9	●
12	M	0603	3.8	1159	0.5	1812	4.0			
13	TU	0043	0.7	0642	3.8	1245	0.4	1853	4.1	
14	W	0129	0.6	0722	3.8	1330	0.3	1935	4.1	
15	TH	0213	0.6	0803	3.7	1416	0.3	2017	4.0	
16	F	0259	0.7	0845	3.6	1502	0.5	2101	3.8	
17	SA	0346	0.9	0931	3.4	1552	0.7	2148	3.5	
18	SU	0438	1.2	1025	3.1	1645	1.0	2242	3.2	◐
19	M	0536	1.4	1135	3.0	1745	1.3	2356	3.0	
20	TU	0645	1.6	1307	2.9	1854	1.5			
21	W	0141	2.9	0807	1.6	1430	3.0	2013	1.6	
22	TH	0327	2.9	0923	1.6	1536	3.2	2136	1.6	
23	F	0431	3.1	1017	1.4	1620	3.4	2237	1.5	
24	SA	0456	3.2	1100	1.2	1657	3.6	2322	1.3	
25	SU	0523	3.4	1138	1.1	1734	3.8			
26	M	0000	1.2	0553	3.5	1214	1.0	1808	3.9	○
27	TU	0036	1.1	0625	3.7	1248	0.9	1843	4.0	
28	W	0109	1.1	0656	3.7	1320	0.9	1915	4.0	
29	TH	0142	1.1	0726	3.7	1351	1.0	1947	3.9	
30	F	0214	1.2	0754	3.6	1419	1.2	2016	3.8	
31	SA	0244	1.3	0821	3.5	1445	1.3	2045	3.6	

AUGUST

Date	Day	Time	m	Time	m	Time	m	Time	m	Moon
1	SU	0314	1.5	0850	3.4	1512	1.5	2115	3.5	
2	M	0347	1.6	0924	3.2	1547	1.7	2152	3.3	
3	TU	0435	1.7	1007	3.1	1636	1.8	2242	3.1	◑
4	W	0541	1.8	1105	2.9	1752	1.9			
5	TH	0009	2.9	0656	1.8	1256	2.9	1921	1.9	
6	F	0236	3.0	0810	1.7	1454	3.1	2053	1.7	
7	SA	0342	3.2	0916	1.4	1552	3.4	2208	1.4	
8	SU	0430	3.5	1012	1.0	1638	3.7	2302	1.0	
9	M	0512	3.7	1101	0.7	1719	4.0	2348	0.7	
10	TU	0550	3.9	1146	0.4	1800	4.2			●
11	W	0030	0.5	0626	4.0	1230	0.2	1838	4.3	
12	TH	0112	0.4	0703	4.0	1314	0.1	1917	4.3	
13	F	0153	0.5	0740	3.9	1357	0.2	1956	4.1	
14	SA	0234	0.6	0819	3.7	1441	0.4	2034	3.8	
15	SU	0316	0.9	0900	3.5	1528	0.7	2115	3.5	
16	M	0403	1.2	0946	3.2	1618	1.1	2200	3.1	◐
17	TU	0458	1.5	1048	3.0	1716	1.4	2304	2.8	
18	W	0606	1.7	1237	2.8	1826	1.7			
19	TH	0142	2.7	0738	1.8	1424	2.9	2003	1.8	
20	F	0400	2.8	0909	1.6	1540	3.1	2142	1.7	
21	SA	0442	3.0	1004	1.4	1612	3.3	2232	1.5	
22	SU	0450	3.2	1045	1.2	1641	3.6	2309	1.4	
23	M	0503	3.4	1121	1.0	1713	3.8	2341	1.2	
24	TU	0531	3.6	1154	0.9	1747	4.0			○
25	W	0011	1.1	0601	3.8	1225	0.8	1818	4.0	
26	TH	0042	1.0	0630	3.8	1255	0.9	1849	4.1	
27	F	0112	1.0	0657	3.9	1322	1.0	1918	4.0	
28	SA	0141	1.1	0722	3.8	1346	1.1	1944	3.9	
29	SU	0207	1.2	0747	3.7	1407	1.3	2009	3.7	
30	M	0231	1.3	0814	3.5	1432	1.4	2037	3.5	
31	TU	0303	1.5	0847	3.4	1506	1.6	2112	3.3	

Chart Datum: 2·10 metres below Ordnance Datum (Newlyn). HAT is 4·5 metres above Chart Datum; see 0.20

TIME ZONE (UT)
For Summer Time add ONE hour in **non-shaded areas**

OBAN LAT 56°25′N LONG 5°29′W

TIMES AND HEIGHTS OF HIGH AND LOW WATERS

Dates in red are SPRINGS
Dates in blue are NEAPS

YEAR **2010**

SEPTEMBER

Day	Time	m	Day	Time	m
1 W	0348 0929 1554 ◑ 2200	1.7 3.2 1.8 3.0	16 TH	0531 1210 1803	1.7 2.9 1.9
2 TH	0457 1027 1724 2331	1.8 3.0 2.0 2.8	17 F	0208 0702 1410 2000	2.6 1.8 3.0 2.0
3 F	0625 1235 1915	1.8 2.9 2.0	18 SA	0340 0842 1517 2129	2.8 1.7 3.1 1.8
4 SA	0233 0747 1447 2055	2.9 1.7 3.2 1.7	19 SU	0415 0938 1547 2210	3.0 1.5 3.4 1.6
5 SU	0331 0858 1539 2200	3.2 1.3 3.5 1.3	20 M	0416 1019 1615 2242	3.2 1.3 3.6 1.4
6 M	0416 0955 1621 2247	3.5 1.0 3.9 0.9	21 TU	0433 1055 1646 2311	3.4 1.1 3.8 1.2
7 TU	0454 1044 1700 2329	3.8 0.6 4.1 0.6	22 W	0501 1127 1718 2339	3.6 1.0 4.0 1.0
8 W ●	0529 1128 1739	4.0 0.3 4.3	23 TH ○	0532 1156 1750	3.8 0.9 4.1
9 TH	0009 0603 1212 1816	0.4 4.1 0.1 4.4	24 F	0009 0600 1224 1820	0.9 3.9 0.9 4.1
10 F	0048 0638 1254 1852	0.4 4.1 0.1 4.3	25 SA	0039 0626 1251 1847	0.9 3.9 1.0 4.0
11 SA	0126 0714 1336 1929	0.4 4.0 0.2 4.1	26 SU	0107 0651 1315 1913	1.0 3.9 1.1 3.9
12 SU	0205 0751 1419 2005	0.6 3.9 0.5 3.8	27 M	0133 0717 1338 1940	1.1 3.8 1.3 3.7
13 M	0246 0829 1504 2042	0.9 3.6 0.9 3.5	28 TU	0201 0747 1406 2010	1.2 3.7 1.4 3.5
14 TU	0331 0912 1553 2122	1.2 3.3 1.3 3.1	29 W	0236 0822 1444 2048	1.4 3.5 1.6 3.3
15 W	0424 1009 1651 ◐ 2215	1.5 3.1 1.6 2.7	30 TH	0322 0906 1540 2141	1.6 3.3 1.8 3.0

OCTOBER

Day	Time	m	Day	Time	m
1 F	0430 1011 1723 ◑ 2323	1.7 3.1 2.0 2.8	16 SA	0100 0615 1330 1917	2.6 1.9 3.0 2.0
2 SA	0557 1224 1913	1.8 3.0 1.9	17 SU	0237 0753 1432 2047	2.7 1.8 3.2 1.9
3 SU	0212 0720 1423 2040	2.9 1.6 3.3 1.6	18 M	0313 0859 1511 2131	2.9 1.6 3.4 1.7
4 M	0308 0833 1515 2138	3.2 1.3 3.6 1.3	19 TU	0332 0945 1543 2204	3.2 1.4 3.6 1.5
5 TU	0353 0931 1557 2223	3.5 1.0 3.9 0.9	20 W	0358 1022 1614 2234	3.4 1.3 3.8 1.3
6 W	0430 1021 1636 2304	3.8 0.6 4.2 0.7	21 TH	0428 1054 1647 2304	3.6 1.2 3.9 1.1
7 TH	0503 1107 1713 ● 2343	4.0 0.4 4.3 0.5	22 F	0500 1123 1720 2334	3.8 1.1 4.0 1.0
8 F	0537 1151 1751	4.1 0.3 4.4	23 SA ○	0530 1152 1751	3.9 1.1 4.0
9 SA	0021 0612 1234 1827	0.5 4.2 0.3 4.3	24 SU	0006 0557 1222 1820	1.0 3.9 1.1 4.0
10 SU	0059 0649 1316 1902	0.6 4.1 0.5 4.1	25 M	0037 0625 1252 1849	1.0 3.9 1.2 3.9
11 M	0138 0726 1359 1938	0.7 4.0 0.8 3.8	26 TU	0108 0656 1322 1921	1.0 3.8 1.3 3.7
12 TU	0219 0805 1443 2014	1.0 3.7 1.1 3.4	27 W	0142 0730 1358 1957	1.1 3.7 1.4 3.5
13 W	0303 0848 1531 2053	1.2 3.5 1.5 3.1	28 TH	0222 0810 1444 2042	1.3 3.6 1.6 3.3
14 TH	0355 0941 1628 ◐ 2142	1.5 3.2 1.8 2.8	29 F	0311 0900 1548 2140	1.4 3.4 1.8 3.1
15 F	0457 1112 1737	1.7 3.0 2.0	30 SA	0413 1007 1719 ◑ 2308	1.6 3.3 1.9 2.9
			31 SU	0530 1148 1851	1.6 3.2 1.8

NOVEMBER

Day	Time	m	Day	Time	m
1 M	0134 0648 1344 2010	3.0 1.5 3.4 1.6	16 TU	0200 0753 1426 2030	2.9 1.8 3.3 1.9
2 TU	0237 0801 1443 2108	3.2 1.3 3.6 1.3	17 W	0242 0855 1505 2115	3.1 1.7 3.5 1.7
3 W	0324 0903 1530 2156	3.5 1.1 3.9 1.1	18 TH	0318 0940 1541 2152	3.3 1.6 3.6 1.5
4 TH	0403 0957 1611 2238	3.7 0.8 4.1 0.9	19 F	0354 1016 1617 2227	3.5 1.5 3.8 1.3
5 F	0438 1045 1650 2318	3.9 0.7 4.2 0.8	20 SA	0429 1050 1653 2302	3.6 1.4 3.9 1.2
6 SA	0514 1131 1728 ● 2357	4.1 0.6 4.2 0.7	21 SU	0503 1124 1729 ○ 2337	3.8 1.3 3.9 1.0
7 SU	0552 1215 1806	4.2 0.7 4.1	22 M	0536 1200 1802	3.9 1.2 3.9
8 M	0036 0629 1259 1842	0.8 4.1 0.8 3.9	23 TU	0012 0609 1238 1836	1.0 3.9 1.2 3.9
9 TU	0116 0708 1342 1919	0.9 4.0 1.0 3.7	24 W	0050 0644 1317 1912	1.0 3.9 1.2 3.8
10 W	0157 0748 1426 1956	1.1 3.9 1.3 3.5	25 TH	0130 0723 1401 1953	1.0 3.9 1.3 3.6
11 TH	0241 0830 1512 2035	1.3 3.7 1.6 3.2	26 F	0213 0807 1450 2039	1.1 3.8 1.4 3.4
12 F	0328 0918 1603 2121	1.5 3.4 1.8 3.0	27 SA	0302 0857 1548 2133	1.2 3.6 1.6 3.2
13 SA	0422 1018 1702 ◐ 2222	1.7 3.2 2.0 2.8	28 SU	0357 0957 1657 ◑ 2240	1.3 3.5 1.7 3.1
14 SU	0523 1153 1812	1.8 3.1 2.1	29 M	0502 1111 1813	1.4 3.4 1.7
15 M	0030 0634 1335 1928	2.8 1.9 3.2 2.0	30 TU	0015 0612 1248 1928	3.0 1.4 3.4 1.6

DECEMBER

Day	Time	m	Day	Time	m
1 W	0151 0724 1407 2034	3.1 1.4 3.5 1.5	16 TH	0118 0726 1416 2012	3.0 2.0 3.3 1.9
2 TH	0251 0833 1505 2128	3.3 1.3 3.6 1.3	17 F	0228 0832 1509 2105	3.1 1.9 3.4 1.7
3 F	0338 0934 1553 2215	3.6 1.1 3.8 1.2	18 SA	0319 0932 1554 2151	3.3 1.7 3.6 1.5
4 SA	0419 1028 1635 2258	3.8 1.0 3.9 1.1	19 SU	0404 1021 1635 2233	3.5 1.6 3.7 1.3
5 SU	0459 1117 1715 ● 2339	3.9 1.0 3.9 1.0	20 M	0444 1105 1715 2314	3.7 1.4 3.8 1.1
6 M	0538 1203 1753	4.1 1.0 3.9	21 TU	0523 1148 1753 ○ 2354	3.8 1.2 3.9 0.9
7 TU	0020 0617 1247 1830	1.0 4.1 1.1 3.8	22 W	0602 1230 1830	3.9 1.1 3.9
8 W	0100 0656 1329 1906	1.0 4.1 1.2 3.7	23 TH	0035 0639 1313 1906	0.8 4.0 1.0 3.9
9 TH	0140 0735 1410 1943	1.1 4.0 1.4 3.6	24 F	0118 0719 1357 1945	0.7 4.0 1.0 3.8
10 F	0221 0814 1451 2020	1.2 3.8 1.6 3.5	25 SA	0202 0801 1443 2028	0.7 4.0 1.1 3.6
11 SA	0302 0855 1534 2058	1.4 3.7 1.7 3.3	26 SU	0249 0847 1532 2115	0.8 3.8 1.2 3.4
12 SU	0346 0939 1620 2141	1.6 3.5 1.9 3.1	27 M	0339 0937 1627 2208	0.9 3.7 1.4 3.3
13 M	0433 1030 1712 ◐ 2233	1.7 3.3 2.0 3.0	28 TU	0435 1035 1729 ◑ 2315	1.1 3.5 1.6 3.1
14 TU	0524 1136 1811 2344	1.9 3.2 2.0 3.0	29 W	0538 1151 1840	1.3 3.3 1.7
15 W	0622 1303 1912	2.0 3.2 2.0	30 TH	0047 0649 1329 1954	3.1 1.4 3.2 1.7
			31 F	0215 0803 1449 2103	3.2 1.5 3.3 1.6

Chart Datum: 2·10 metres below Ordnance Datum (Newlyn). HAT is 4·5 metres above Chart Datum; see 0.20

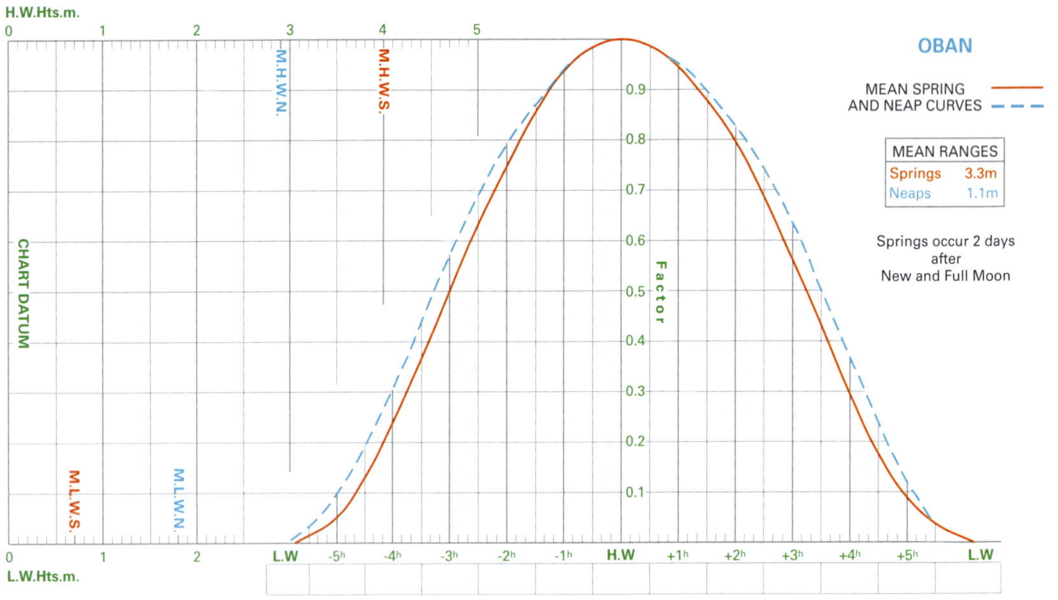

1.17 DUNSTAFFNAGE/OBAN

DUNSTAFFNAGE BAY, Argyll and Bute, **56°27′·04N 05°25′·97W**.

CHARTS AC 2171, 2387, 2388, 1790, 5611; Imray C65.

TIDES –0530 Dover; ML 2·4; Duration 0610

Standard Port OBAN (⟵)

Times				Height (metres)			
High Water		Low Water		MHWS	MHWN	MLWN	MLWS
0100	0700	0100	0800	4·0	2·9	1·8	0·7
1300	1900	1300	2000				
Differences DUNSTAFFNAGE BAY							
+0005	0000	0000	+0005	+0·1	+0·1	+0·1	+0·1
CONNEL							
+0020	+0005	+0010	+0015	–0·3	–0·2	–0·1	+0·1
BONAWE							
+0150	+0205	+0240	+0210	–2·0	–1·7	–1·3	–0·5

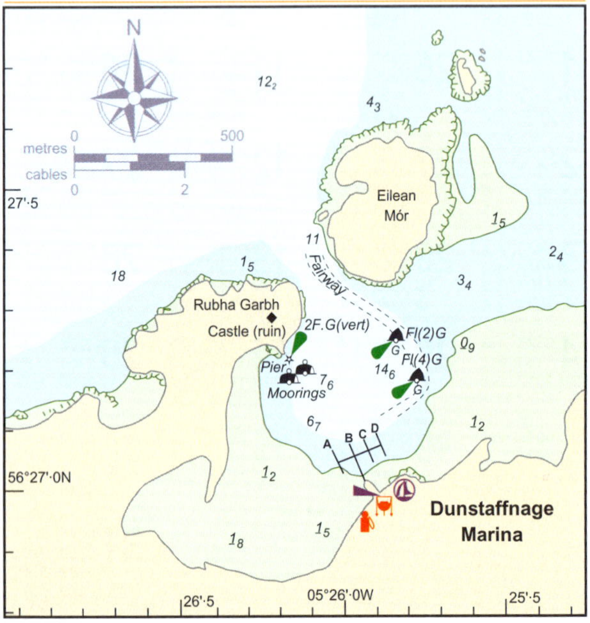

SHELTER Good at marina in SE side of bay, little room to ⚓, within the bay the tidal stream is rotary but sets mainly E through the marina.

NAVIGATION Entered between Rubha Garbh and Eilean Mór. No navigational hazards, spd limit 4kn in bay/⚓. Do not approach marina through moorings, use buoyed fairway. W and SW sides of bay dry.

LIGHTS AND MARKS See 1.3 and chartlet.

R/T Call *Dunstaffnage Marina* VHF Ch M.

TELEPHONE Marinecall 09068 969653; ⊜ 08457231110; MRCC (01475) 729988; Police 510500; Dr 563175.

FACILITIES **Dunstaffnage Marina,** (Code 01631) 566555, 150 inc 10Ⓥ AB £2.00, Wi-fi, D (0830-2000 summer), Gas, Slip (launching H24 except LWS ±2hrs, £9.00 each way) BH (18 ton), CH, C (masting), ME, BY, ⊡, SM, R, Bar; Facilities: P (cans, ¾M), 🛒 (½M), Bus, ⇄ Oban (2M), Glasgow (✈) 2-3hrs and Connel (airstrip).

OBAN, Argyll and Bute **56°24′·99N 05°29′·07W**

CHARTS and TIDES As Dunstaffnage

SHELTER Good shelter in bay except in strong SW/NW winds, but Oban Marina in Ardantrive Bay (Kerrera) is well sheltered from all directions. The only ⚓s convenient for town are in deep water off the Esplanade and NW of Sailing Club, beware of moorings. Alternatively ⚓ at N end of Kerrera to S of Rubh'a Chruidh Is or Horseshoe Bay and Little Horseshoe Bay, Kerrera Sound.

NAVIGATION **WPT (N)** 56°25′·85N 05°30′·0W, 132°/0·7M to Dunollie lt; **WPT (S)** 56°22′N 05°33′W, 035°/1M to 1·5ca E of Sgeirean Dubha, thence through Kerrera Sound to Oban Bay. Ferry Rks (56°24′·0N) can be passed on either side. Note the direction of the buoyage is **NE**, thus pass to the E'ward of PHM unlit buoy or to W'ward of the SHM QG buoy. The N'ly SHM buoy must be passed to the W'ward. In Oban Bay beware Sgeir Rathaid, buoyed, in middle of the bay; also ferries running to/from Railway Pier.

LIGHTS AND MARKS See 1.3 and Oban chartlet.

R/T Call: *North Pier* Ch 12 16 (0900-1700). For Railway Pier, call *CalMac* Ch 06 12 16. **Oban Marina**, call *Oban Yachts* Ch 80.

☎ (Code 01631) Pier 562892; Marinecall 09068 969653; ⊜ 08457231110; MRCC (01475) 729988; Police 510500; Dr 563175.

FACILITIES **Oban Marina** (Ardantrive Bay) www.obanmarina.com ☎ 01631 565333; 94 AB £2.00; 33 Ⓥs £15/day. D (0800-1800), Gas/Gaz, ⊡, Bar, R, Wi-fi, (limited), BH (50T), SM, Ⓔ, El. Free water taxi (2 hourly, 0800-1800) to/from Oban.

ARDANTRIVE BAY, KERRERA Argyll and Bute **56°25'·15N 05°29'·80W** ✿✿✿◊◊✿✿✿ AC 1790. HW -0530 on Dover. **Oban Yachts Marina,** www.obanyachts.com, VHF Ch80/16, ☎ 565333. 56 AB (pontoons,inc 30Ⓥ) £2.20, 30⚲s £1.95; D, FW, Gas, ⛽, ⊡, Showers, WC, ME, BY, ⚒, C (masting), CH, Slip, BH (16 ton), marina water taxi 0800-2200 in season, (call *Oban Yachts* Ch 80 for timetable); 10min crossing to Oban. For Town facilities see previous page.

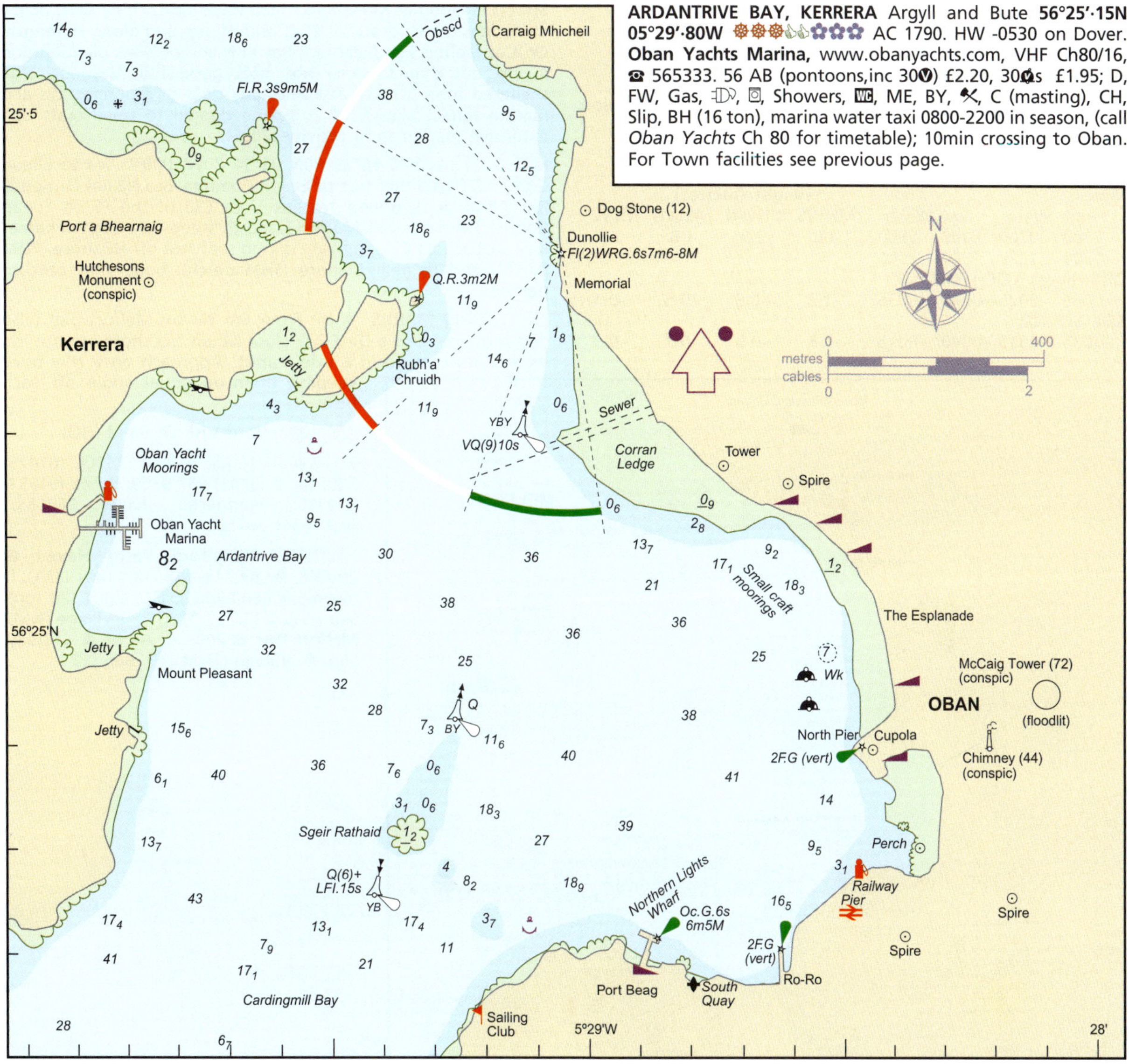

N Pier 562892, L, FW, C (15 ton mobile) via Piermaster; **Rly Pier,** L, Slip, D (H24, ☎ 562849), FW, CH; **Services:** Slip, ACA, Gas, ME, El, divers. **Town** P (cans, ½M), all facilities, Ⓗ, ⇌, Glasgow (✈) 2-3hrs & Connel (airstrip) 3M, Ferry to Inner & Outer Hebrides.

ANCHORAGES ON MAINLAND SHORE OF FIRTH OF LORN

LOCH FEOCHAN, Argyll and Bute, **56°21'.39N 05°29'·77W.** AC 5611, 2387. HW = HW Oban; flood runs 4 hrs, ebb for 8 hrs. Caution: strong streams off Ardentallan Pt. Good shelter, 5M S of Oban and 1·5M SE of Kerrera. Best appr at local slack LW = LW Oban +0200. Narrow buoyed channel, ⚓ off pier, or moor off **Ardoran Marine** ☎ (01631) 566123, 📠 566611; 4 ⚲s £10 <11m, D, FW, ME, CH, Slip, Showers.

PUILLADOBHRAIN, Argyll and Bute, **56°19'·47N 05°35'·22W.** AC 5611, 2386/2387. Tides as Oban. Popular ⚓ on the SE shore of the Firth of Lorne, approx 7M S of Oban, sheltered by the islets to the W of it. At N end of Ardencaple Bay identify Eilean Dùin (18m) and steer SE keeping 1½ca off to clear a rk awash at its NE tip. Continue for 4ca between Eilean nam Beathach, with Orange drum on N tip, and Dun Horses rks drying 2·7m. Two W cairns on E side of Eilean nam Freumha lead approx 215° into the inner ⚓ in about 4m. Landing at head of inlet. Nearest facilities: Bar, ☎, at Clachan Br (½M); ☎, ✉ at Clachan Seil.

CUAN SOUND, Argyll and Bute, **56°15'·84N 05°37'·47W.** AC 2386, 2326. Tides see 1.18 SEIL SOUND. Streams reach 6kn at sp; N-going makes at HW Oban +0420, S-going at HW Oban –2. The Sound is a useful doglegged short cut from Firth of Lorne to Lochs Melfort and Shuna, but needs care due to rks and tides. There are ⚓s at either end to await the tide. At the 90° dogleg, pass close N of Cleit Rk onto which the tide sets; it is marked by a Y △ perch. The chan is only ¾ca wide here due to rks off Seil. Overhead cables (35m) cross from Seil to Luing. There are ⚓s out of the tide to the S of Cleit Rk. No lts/facilities. See CCC SDs.

ARDINAMAR, Luing/Torsa, **56°14'·92N 05°37'·04W.** AC 2326. HW –0555 on Dover; ML 1·7m; see 1.18 SEIL SOUND. A small cove and popular ⚓ between Luing and Torsa, close W of ent to L. Melfort. Appr on brg 290°. Narrow, shallow (about 1m CD) ent has drying rks either side, those to N marked by 2 SHM perches. Keep about 15m S of perches to ⚓ in 2m in centre of cove; S part dries. Few facilities: 🛒, ✉, ☎, at Cullipool 1·5M WNW. Gas at Cuan Sound ferry 2M NNW.

1.18 LOCH MELFORT

Argyll and Bute **56°14'·59N 05°34'·07W** ❀❀❀◊◊◊✿✿✿

CHARTS AC 5611, 2169, 2326; Imray C65.

TIDES Loch Shuna –0615 Dover; ML Loch Melfort 1·7; Duration Seil Sound 0615

Standard Port OBAN (⟵)

Times				Height (metres)			
High Water		Low Water		MHWS	MHWN	MLWN	MLWS
0100	0700	0100	0800	4·0	2·9	1·8	0·7
1300	1900	1300	2000				
Differences LOCH MELFORT							
–0055	–0025	–0040	–0035	–1·2	–0·8	–0·5	–0·1
SEIL SOUND							
–0035	–0015	–0040	–0015	–1·3	–0·9	–0·7	–0·3

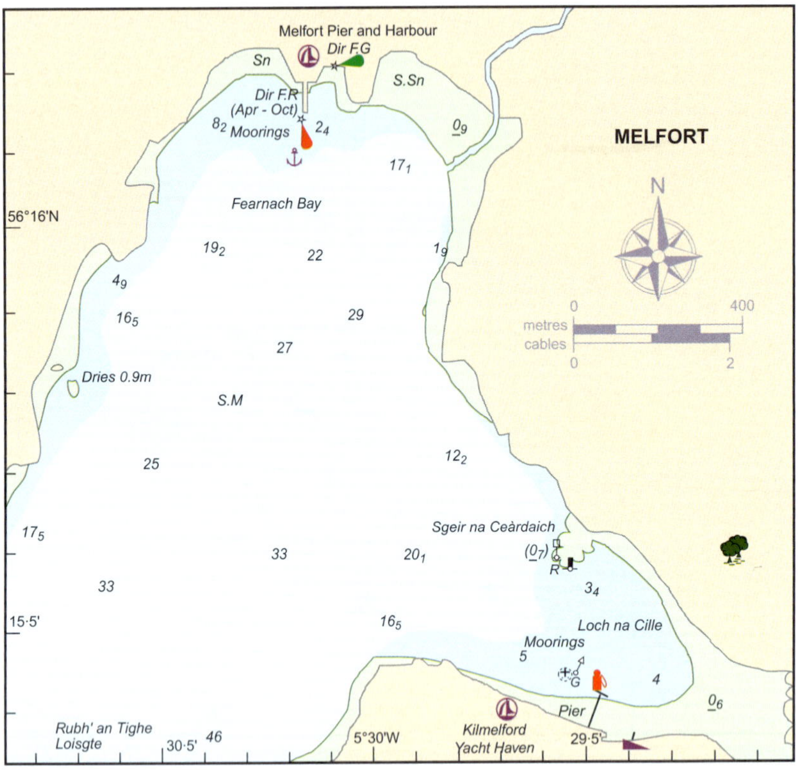

SHELTER Good at Kilmelford Yacht Haven in Loch na Cille; access at all tides for 3m draft, W lts at end of pier and along its length. Or lt at Melfort Pier (Fearnach Bay at N end of loch): pier/pontoon in 2m, but chan to inner hbr dries; good ⚓ in N winds. ⚓'ge sheltered from S to W at Kames Bay clear of moorings, rks and marine farms. ⚓'ge N of Arduaine denied to small craft due extensive marine farm activity (2005).

NAVIGATION WPT 56°13'·90N 05°34'·80W, 000°/3·5ca to Eilean Gamhna. Pass either side of Eilean Gamhna. 8ca NE lies Campbell Rk (1·8m). A rk drying 1m lies 1½ca ESE of the FS on Eilean Coltair. The S side of L Melfort is mostly steep-to, except in Kames Bay. At Loch na Cille, beware drying reef ¾ca off NE shore (PHM perch), and rk near S shore (SHM perch); boats may obscure perches.

LIGHTS AND MARKS A Dir FR ☆ 6m 3M on Melfort pier (also depth gauge) and a Dir FG ☆ close NE on the shore are not ldg lts, nor do they form a safe transit. Approach on a N'ly track keeping them an equal angle off each bow.

R/T Kilmelford VHF Ch **80** M (HO).

TELEPHONE (Code 01852) MRCC (01475) 729014; ⊖ (0141) 887 9369; Police (01631) 510500; Marinecall 09068 969653; Ⓗ (01631) 567500.

FACILITIES **Kilmelford Yacht Haven** ☎ 200248, 🖷 200343, £16/craft (any LOA), D (Mon-Sat 0800-2000), FW, ⊡,BH (20 ton), Slip HW±4, ME, El, ⚒, Gas, ♿ village (¾M); **Melfort Pier** ☎ 200333, AB or ⚓ £12/day, Slip, @. **Village** (1¼M) 🛒, Bar, ✉.

1.19 CRAOBH MARINA (L SHUNA)

Argyll & Bute **56°12′·80N 05°33′·54W** ❁❁❁◊◊◊✿✿✿

CHARTS AC 5611, 2169, 2326; Imray C65.

TIDES HW Loch Shuna –0100 Oban; –0615 Dover; Seil Sound Duration 0615, ML 1·4. For tidal figures see 1.18.

SHELTER Very good. Craobh (pronounced Croove) Marina (access H24) on SE shore of Loch Shuna is enclosed by N and S causeways between islets. The ent is between 2 bkwtrs on the N side. In the marina, a shoal area S of the E bkwtr is marked by 9 PHM and 2 SHM buoys. A Y perch in W corner of hbr marks a spit; elsewhere ample depth. There are ⚓s in Asknish Bay 1M to the N, and in the bays E of Eilean Arsa and at Bàgh an Tigh-Stòir, S of Craobh.

NAVIGATION WPT 56°13′·01N 05°33′·57W, 173°/2ca to ent. Tidal streams in Loch Shuna are weak. Beware fish farm 2ca N of Shuna, lobster pots in appr's and unmarked rks (dr 1·5m) 4ca NNE of ent. An unlit SHM buoy marks a rk (1m) 150m NNW of the W bkwtr. 1M N of marina, Eich Donna, an unmarked reef (dr 1·5m), lies between Eilean Creagach and Arduaine Pt.

LIGHTS AND MARKS The W sector, 162°-183°, of Dir Lt, Iso WRG 5s 10m 5/3M, on E bkwtr hd leads 172° between the close-in rks above. Multi coloured marina buildings are conspic.

R/T VHF Ch M, 80 (summer 0830-2000; winter 0830-1800).

TELEPHONE (Code 01852) HM 500222; MRCC (01475) 729014; ⊖ (0141) 887 9369; Marinecall 09068 969653; Police (01546) 602222; 🏥 (01546) 602323.

FACILITIES **Craobh Marina** (200+50 Ⓥ) ☎ 500222; £2.00, D, SM, BY, CH, Slip (launch/recovery £3.70/m), BH (15 ton), C (12 ton), Gas, Gaz, ME, El, ⚒, R, SC, Ⓔ, ⊡, Divers. **Village** 🛒, Bar, Ⓑ (Fri), ✉ (Kilmelford), ⇄ (Oban by bus), ✈ (Glasgow).

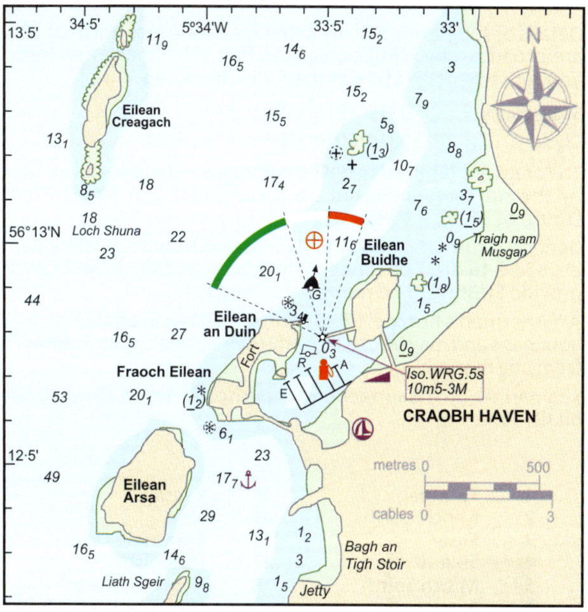

1.20 LOCH CRAIGNISH

Argyll and Bute **56°07′·99N 05°35′·07W** (Ardfern) ❁❁❁◊◊◊✿✿✿

CHARTS AC 5611, 2169, 2326; Imray C65, C63.

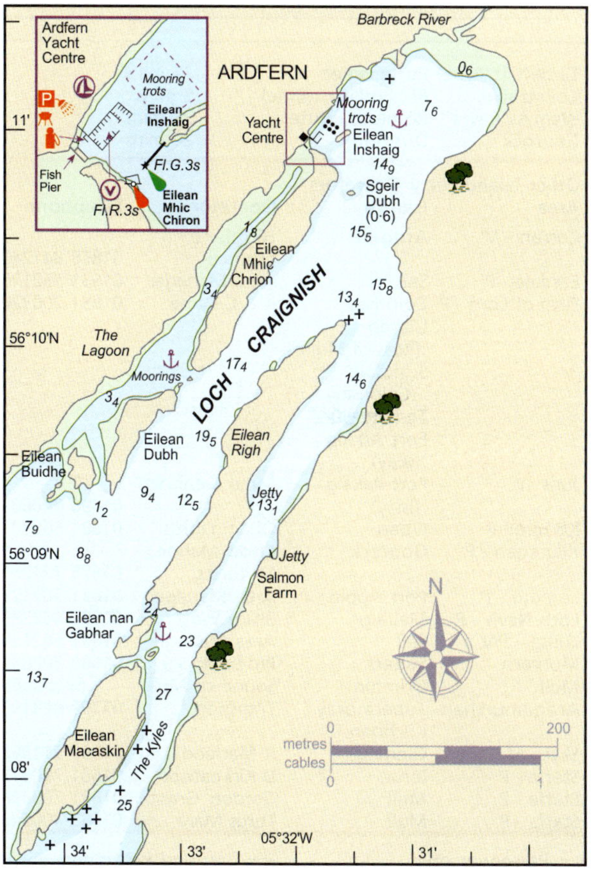

TIDES +0600 Dover; ML (Loch Beag)1·2; Duration (Seil Sound) 0615

Standard Port OBAN (⟵)

Times				Height (metres)			
High Water		Low Water		MHWS	MHWN	MLWN	MLWS
0100	0700	0100	0800	4·0	2·9	1·8	0·7
1300	1900	1300	2000				
Differences LOCH BEAG (Sound of Jura)							
–0110	–0045	–0035	–0045	–1·6	–1·2	–0·8	–0·4

NOTE: HW Ardfern is approx HW Oban –0045; times/heights much affected by local winds and barometric pressure

SHELTER Good at Ardfern, 56°11′·0N 05°31′·8W, access H24; ⚓s at:

- Eilean nan Gabhar; appr from E chan and ⚓ E of island.
- Eilean Righ; midway up the E side of the island.
- Eilean Dubh in the 'lagoon' between the Is and mainland.
- Beware squalls in E'lies, especially on E side of loch.

NAVIGATION **See 1.4.** WPT 56°07′·59N 05°35′·37W (off chartlet) between Dorus Mór and Liath-sgier Mhòr.

Beware: strong tidal streams (up to 8kn) in Dorus Mór see 1.4; a reef extending 1ca SSW of the SE chain of islands; rk 1½ca SSW of Eilean Dubh; fish cages especially on E side of loch; a drying rock at N end of Ardfern ⚓ with a rock awash ¼ca E of it. (These 2 rks are ½ca S of the more S'ly of little islets close to mainland.) The main fairway is free from hazards, except for Sgeir Dhubh, an unmarked rk 3½ca SSE of Ardfern, with a reef extending about ½ca all round. Ardfern is 1ca W of Eilean Inshaig.

LIGHTS AND MARKS Ent to Ardfern Yacht Centre marked by PHM buoy, Fl R 3s, and end of floating breakwater, Fl G 3s, which extends 90m SW from Eilean Inshaig.

R/T Ardfern Yacht Centre VHF Ch 80 M (office hrs).

TELEPHONE (Code 01852) HM (Yacht Centre) 500247, www.ardfernyacht.co.uk, MRCC (01475) 729014; Marinecall 09068 969653; ⊖ (0141) 887 9369; Dr (01546) 602921; 🏥 (01546) 602449.

FACILITIES **Ardfern Yacht Centre** (87+20 AB; 80+12 Ⓥ) AB £1.95, M £1.30, Wi-fi, D (HO), BH (20 ton), Slip (HW±3, £1.50/m inc parking), ME, El, ⚒, SM, ACA, C (12 ton), CH, ♿, Gas, Gaz. **Village** R, 🛒, Ⓑ (Fri), ✉, ⇄ (Oban), Bar, ✈ (Glasgow).

1.21 SUBMARINE EXERCISE AREAS (SUBFACTS)

Details of submarine activity in the Exercise Areas north of Mull are broadcast by MRCCs on a specified VHF Ch after an initial announcement on Ch 16 at the following times:

Stornoway 0710 1910 UT
Clyde 0810 2010 UT

The areas are referred to by the names given below, rather than by the numbers indicated on the chartlet. For Areas 22–81 (South of Mull), see page 472.

General information on SUBFACTS is also broadcast twice daily at 0620 & 1820 UT on Navtex. Stornoway and Clyde MRCCs will provide SUBFACTS on request; call on Ch 16.

A 'Fisherman's hotline' (☎ (01436) 677201) is available on a 24 hour basis and may be used for any queries relating to SUBFACTS from any mariner.

Submarines on the surface and at periscope depth always listen on Ch 16.

1	Tiumpan	**14**	Raasay
2	Minch North	**15**	Neist
3	Stoer	**16**	Bracadale
4	Shiant	**17**	Ushenish
5	Minch South	**18**	Hebrides North
6	Ewe	**19**	Canna
7	Trodday	**20**	Rhum
8	Rona West	**21**	Sleat
9	Rona North	**22**	Barra
10	Lochmaddy	**23**	Hebrides Central
11	Dunvegan	**24**	Hawes
12	Portree	**25**	Eigg
13	Rona South	**26**	Hebrides South

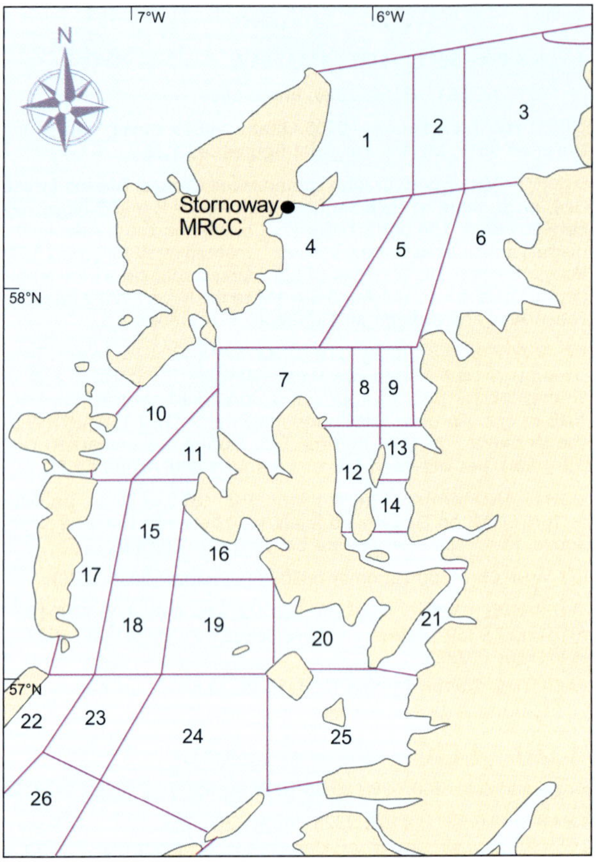

1.22 FERRIES

Many ferries ply between mainland and island harbours. This summary may prove useful when plans or crews change in remote places. It covers Areas 1 and 2. The major operator is Caledonian MacBrayne: Head Office, The Ferry Terminal, Gourock PA19 1QP. For reservations: ☎ 08000 665000; www.calmac.co.uk. Many routes are very short and may not be pre-bookable; seasonal routes are marked *.

From	To	Time	Remarks
Area 8			
Berneray	Leverburgh	1¼	
Ullapool	Stornoway	2¾ hrs	
Uig (Skye)	Tarbert (Harris)	1¾ hrs	Not Sun
Uig	Lochmaddy (N Uist)	1¾ hrs	
Oban	Castlebay/Lochboisdale	5-7 hrs	
Sconser (Skye)	Raasay	15 mins	Not Sun
Mallaig*	Armadale (Skye)	20 mins	
Mallaig	Eigg-Muck-Rum-Canna	Varies	Not Sun
Oban	Coll-Tiree	Varies	Not Thurs
Tobermory	Kilchoan	35 mins	
Fionnphort	Iona	5 mins	
Lochaline	Fishnish (Mull)	15 mins	
Oban	Craignure (Mull)	45 mins	
Oban	Lismore	50 mins	Not Sun
Areas 8/9			
Oban	Colonsay	2¼ hrs	Sun/W/Fri
Area 9			
Kennacraig	Port Askaig/Colonsay	Varies	Wed
Kennacraig	Port Ellen	2h 10m	
Kennacraig	Port Askaig	2 hrs	
Tayinloan	Gigha	20 mins	
Ardrossan	Brodick	55 mins	
Claonaig	Lochranza (Arran)	30 mins	
Largs	Cumbrae Slip	10 mins	
Tarbert (L Fyne)	Portavadie*	25 mins	
Colintraive	Rhubodach (Bute)	5 mins	
Wemyss Bay	Rothesay (Bute)	35 mins	
Gourock	Dunoon	20 mins	

Other Island Ferry Operators

Area	From	Operator	Telephone
Corran - V	Ardgour	Highland Council	01855 841243
Easdale - P	Seil	Area Manager	01631 562125
Firth of Lorn - P	Colonsay	K & C Byrne	01951 200320
	Uisken (Ross of Mull)		
	Scalasaig (Colonsay)		
	Tarbert (Jura)		
	Port Askaig (Islay)		
Jura - V	Port Askaig (Islay)	Serco Denholm	01496 840681
Kerrara - P	Oban	Oban Yachts	01631 565333
Kilgregan - P	Gourock	Clyde Marine Motoring	01475 721281
Lismore - P	Port Appin	Area Manager	01631 562125
Loch Nevis - P	Mallaig	Bruce Watt	01687 462233
Luing - P/V	Seil	Area Manager	01631 562125
Morvern	Sunart	Pre-book via	01688 302851
Mull	Drimnin	Sound of Mull	or mobile
Ardnamurchan	Tobermoray Kilchoan	Transport	07799 608199
Skye - V	Gleneig	R Macleod	01599 511302
Staffa - P	Iona	D Kirkpatrick	01681 700373
Staffa - P	Mull	Gordon Grant	01681 700338
Staffa - P	Mull	Turus Mara	01688 400242

P = Passenger only V = Cars and Passengers

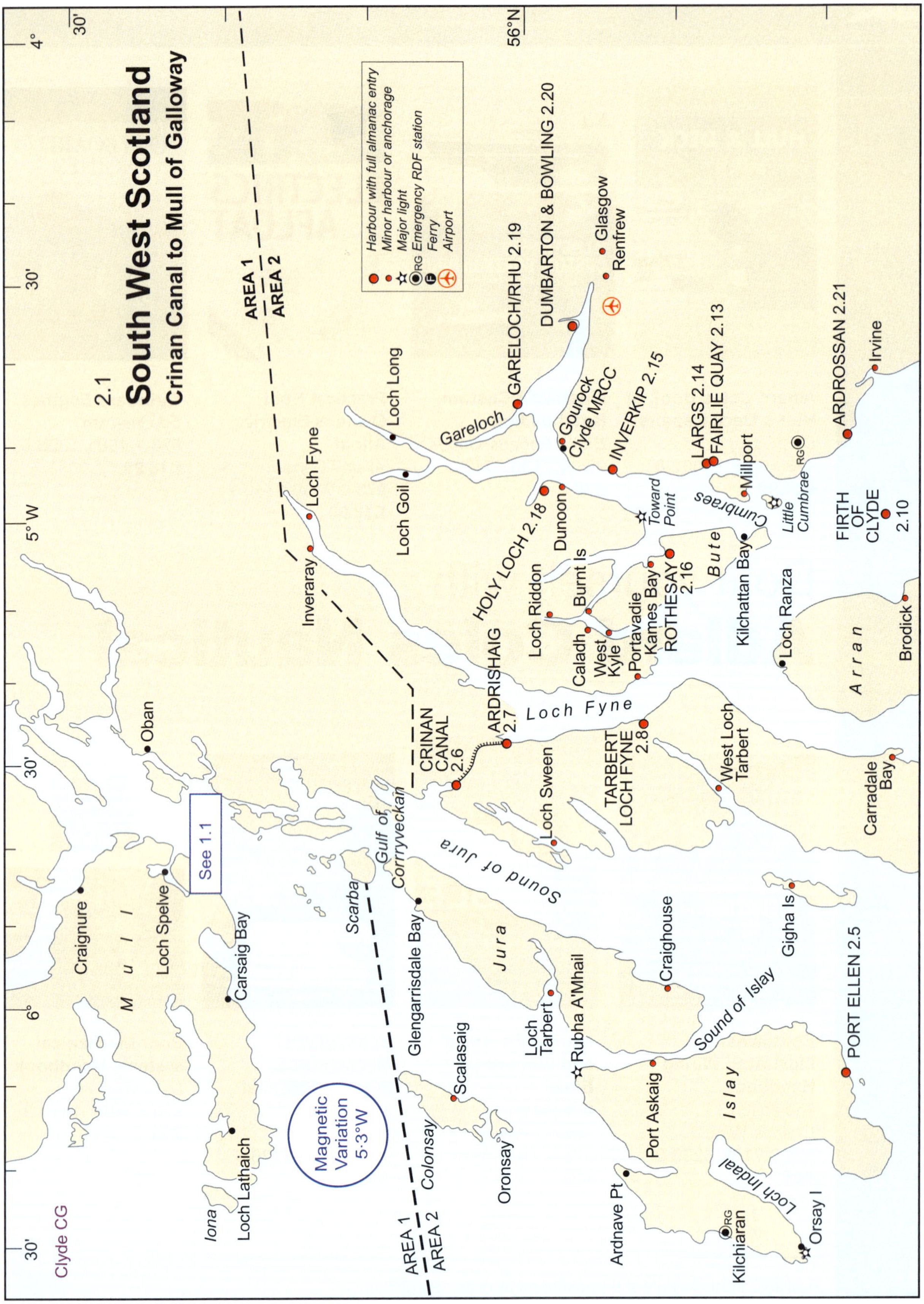
2.1
South West Scotland
Crinan Canal to Mull of Galloway
Harbour with full almanac entry
Minor harbour or anchorage
Major light
RG Emergency RDF station
Ferry
Airport
AREA 1
AREA 2
4°
30'
5° W
6°
56°N
Clyde CG
Magnetic Variation 5·3°W
See 1.1
Oban
Craignure
Mull
Loch Spelve
Carsaig Bay
Loch Lathaich
Iona
Colonsay
Scalasaig
Oronsay
Scarba
Gulf of Corryvreckan
Glengarrisdale Bay
Jura
Sound of Jura
Loch Tarbert
Rubha A'Mhail
Craighouse
Sound of Islay
Islay
Port Askaig
Ardnave Pt
Kilchiaran
Loch Indaal
Orsay I
PORT ELLEN 2.5
Gigha Is
CRINAN CANAL 2.6
ARDRISHAIG 2.7
Loch Sween
Loch Fyne
TARBERT LOCH FYNE 2.8
West Loch Tarbert
Carradale Bay
Arran
Brodick
Loch Ranza
Inveraray
Loch Fyne
Loch Goil
Loch Long
Gareloch
GARELOCH/RHU 2.19
DUMBARTON & BOWLING 2.20
Glasgow
Renfrew
Gourock Clyde MRCC
INVERKIP 2.15
LARGS 2.14
FAIRLIE QUAY 2.13
Millport
Cumbraes
Little Cumbrae
ARDROSSAN 2.21
Irvine
FIRTH OF CLYDE 2.10
HOLY LOCH 2.18
Dunoon
Toward Point
Loch Riddon
Burnt Is
Caladh
West Kyle
Portavadie
Kames Bay
ROTHESAY 2.16
Bute
Kilchattan Bay

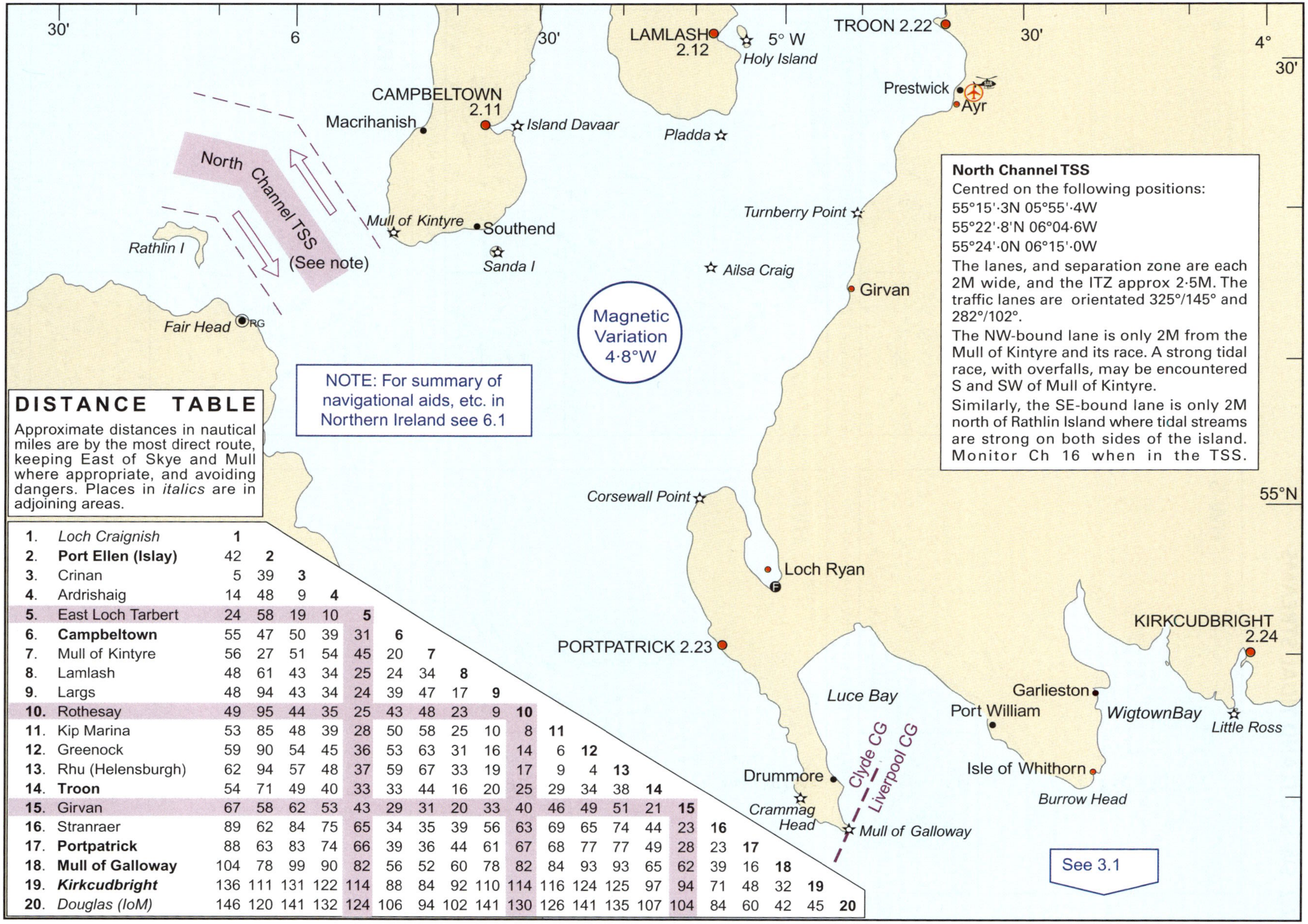

North Channel TSS

Centred on the following positions:
55°15'·3N 05°55'·4W
55°22'·8'N 06°04·6W
55°24'·0N 06°15'·0W

The lanes, and separation zone are each 2M wide, and the ITZ approx 2·5M. The traffic lanes are orientated 325°/145° and 282°/102°.

The NW-bound lane is only 2M from the Mull of Kintyre and its race. A strong tidal race, with overfalls, may be encountered S and SW of Mull of Kintyre.

Similarly, the SE-bound lane is only 2M north of Rathlin Island where tidal streams are strong on both sides of the island. Monitor Ch 16 when in the TSS.

NOTE: For summary of navigational aids, etc. in Northern Ireland see 6.1

DISTANCE TABLE

Approximate distances in nautical miles are by the most direct route, keeping East of Skye and Mull where appropriate, and avoiding dangers. Places in *italics* are in adjoining areas.

1.	*Loch Craignish*	1																			
2.	**Port Ellen (Islay)**	42	2																		
3.	Crinan	5	39	3																	
4.	Ardrishaig	14	48	9	4																
5.	East Loch Tarbert	24	58	19	10	5															
6.	**Campbeltown**	55	47	50	39	31	6														
7.	Mull of Kintyre	56	27	51	54	45	20	7													
8.	Lamlash	48	61	43	34	25	24	34	8												
9.	Largs	48	94	43	34	24	39	47	17	9											
10.	Rothesay	49	95	44	35	25	43	48	23	9	10										
11.	Kip Marina	53	85	48	39	28	50	58	25	10	8	11									
12.	Greenock	59	90	54	45	36	53	63	31	16	14	6	12								
13.	Rhu (Helensburgh)	62	94	57	48	37	59	67	33	19	17	9	4	13							
14.	**Troon**	54	71	49	40	33	33	44	16	20	25	29	34	38	14						
15.	Girvan	67	58	62	53	43	29	31	20	33	40	46	49	51	21	15					
16.	Stranraer	89	62	84	75	65	34	35	39	56	63	69	65	74	44	23	16				
17.	**Portpatrick**	88	63	83	74	66	39	36	44	61	67	68	77	77	49	28	23	17			
18.	**Mull of Galloway**	104	78	99	90	82	56	52	60	78	82	84	93	93	65	62	39	16	18		
19.	***Kirkcudbright***	136	111	131	122	114	88	84	92	110	114	116	124	125	97	94	71	48	32	19	
20.	*Douglas (IoM)*	146	120	141	132	124	106	94	102	141	130	126	141	135	107	104	84	60	42	45	20

2.2 SW SCOTLAND TIDAL STREAMS

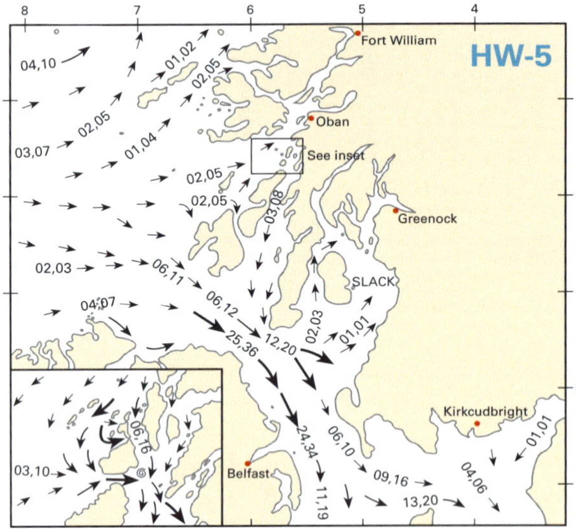

5 Hours before HW Dover (0605 after HW Greenock)

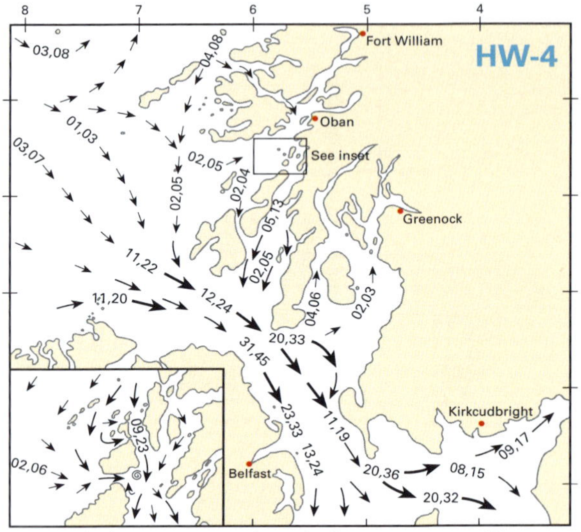

4 Hours before HW Dover (0520 before HW Greenock)

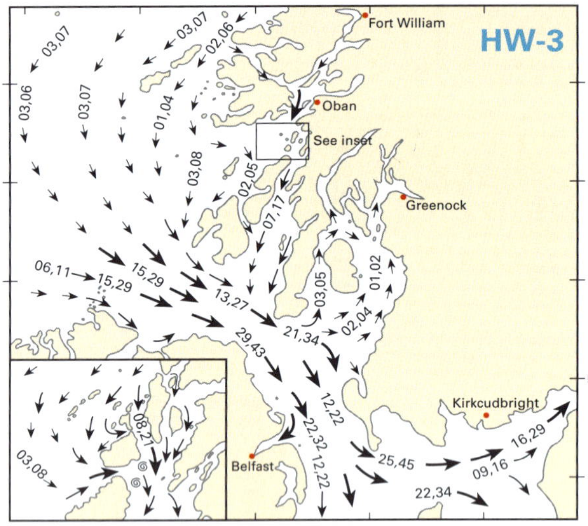

3 Hours before HW Dover (0420 before HW Greenock)

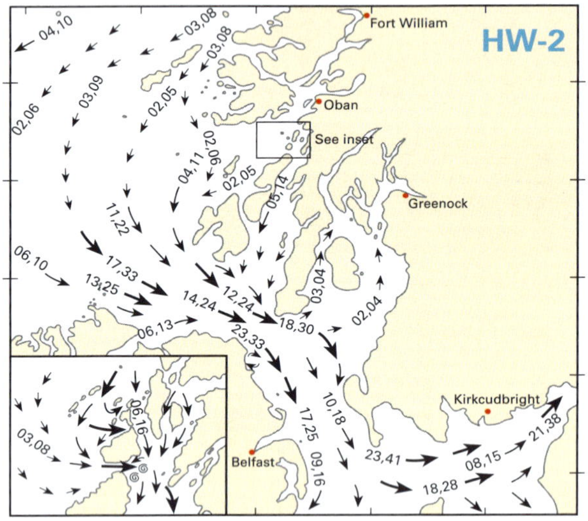

2 Hours before HW Dover (0320 before HW Greenock)

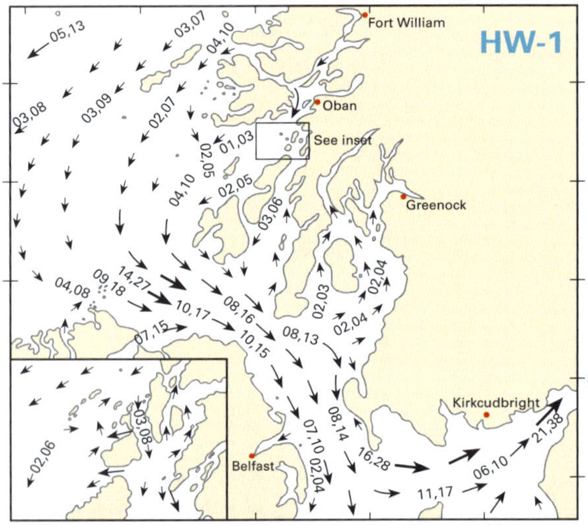

1 Hour before HW Dover (0220 before HW Greenock)

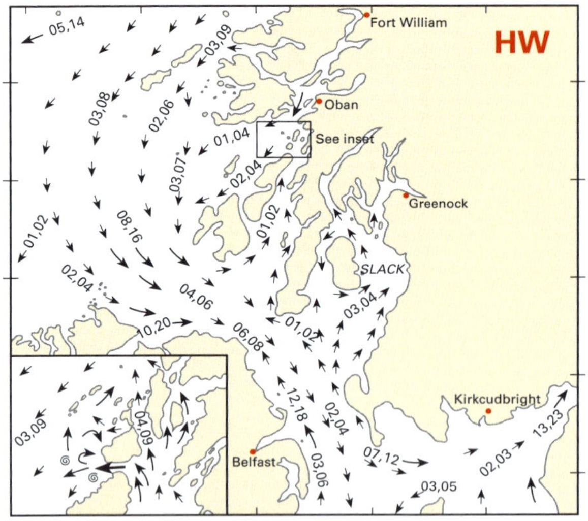

HW Dover (0120 before HW Greenock)

Northward 1.2 Mull of Kintyre 2.9 Irish Sea 3.2, 4.2 Northern Ireland 6.2

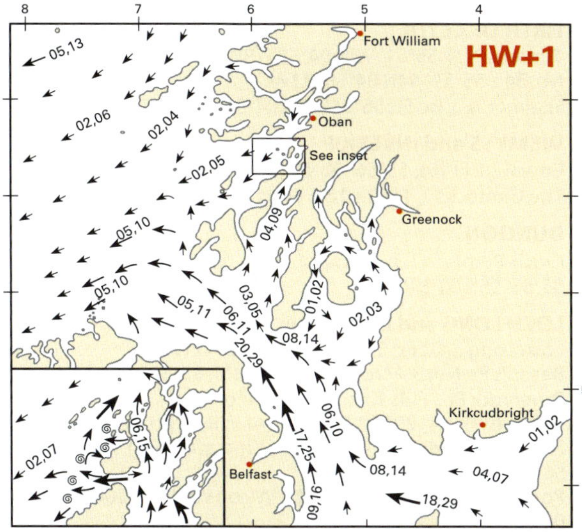

1 Hour after HW Dover (0020 before HW Greenock)

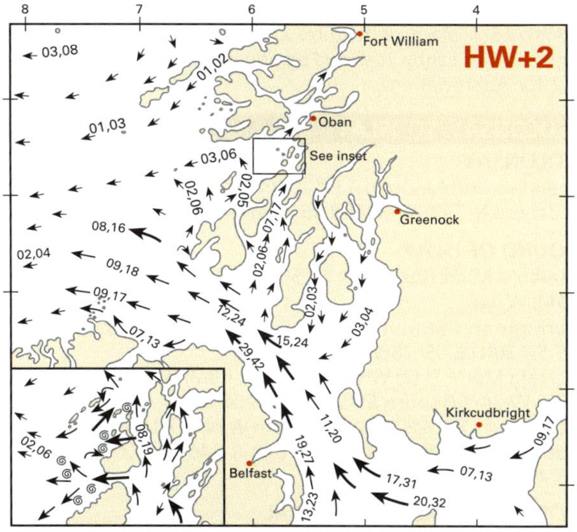

2 Hours after HW Dover (0040 after HW Greenock)

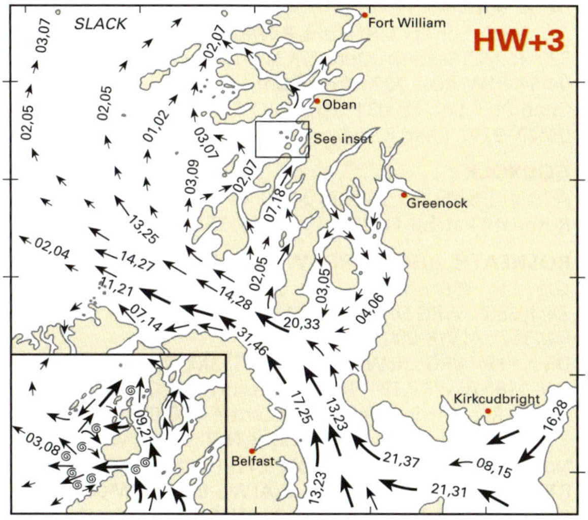

3 Hours after HW Dover (0140 after HW Greenock)

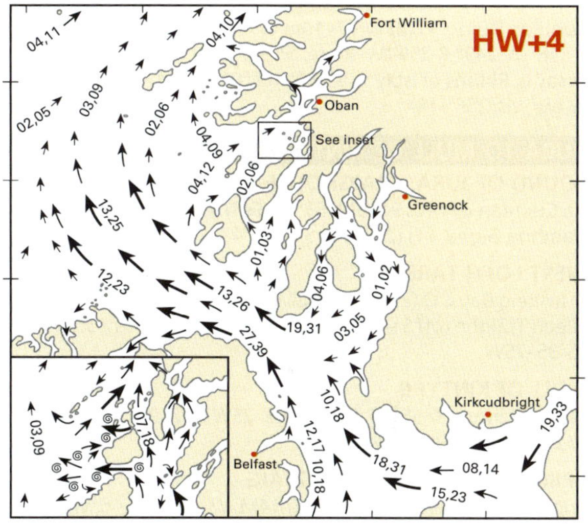

4 Hours after HW Dover (0240 after HW Greenock)

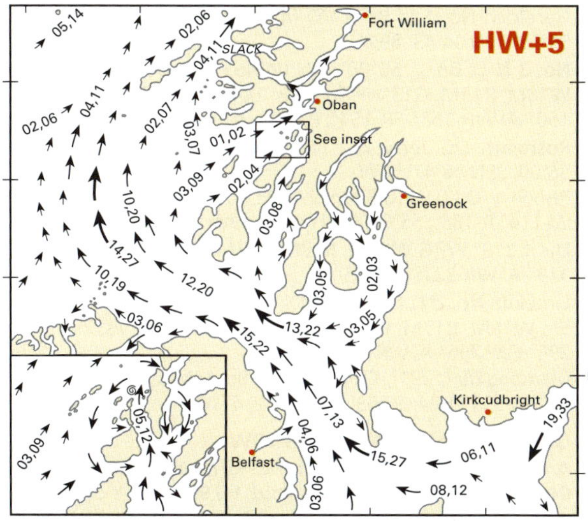

5 Hours after HW Dover (0340 after HW Greenock)

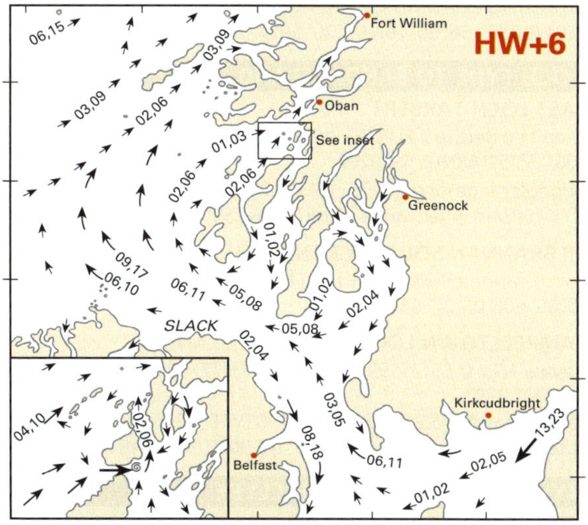

6 Hours after HW Dover (0440 after HW Greenock)

2.3 LIGHTS, BUOYS AND WAYPOINTS

Bold print = light with a nominal range of 15M or more. CAPITALS = place or feature. *CAPITAL ITALICS* = light-vessel, light float or Lanby. *Italics* = Fog signal. ***Bold italics*** = Racon. See 0.2 for Abbreviations.

COLONSAY TO ISLAY

COLONSAY

Scalasaig, Rubha Dubh Fl (2) WR 10s 8m W8M, R6M; W bldg; vis: shore-R- 230°-W-337°-R-354°; 56°04'·01N 06°10'·90W.

SOUND OF ISLAY

Rhubh' a Mháil (Ruvaal) ☆ 55°56'·18N 06°07'·46W Fl (3) 15s 45m **19M**; W twr.

Carragh an t'Struith Fl 3s 8m 9M; W twr; vis: 354°-180°; 55°52'·30N 06°05'·78W.

Carraig Mòr Fl (2) WR 6s 7m W8M, R6M; W twr; vis: shore-R-175°-W-347°-R-shore; 55°50'·42N 06°06'·13W.

McArthur's Hd Fl (2) WR 10s 39m W14M, R11M; W twr; W in Sound of Islay from NE coast,159°-R-244°-W-E coast of Islay; 55°45'·84N 06°02'·90W.

PORT ELLEN and LOCH INDAAL

Carraig Fhada Fl WRG 3s 20m W8M, R6M, G6M; W □ twr; vis: W shore- 248°-G-311°-W-340°-R-shore; 55°37'·22N 06°12'·71W.

Rubh'an Dùin Fl (2) WR 7s 15m W11M, R8M; W twr; vis: shore-R-218°-W-249°-R-350°-W-shore; 55°44'·70N 06°22'·28 W.

Orsay Is, **Rhinns of Islay** ☆ 55°40'·40N 06°30'·84W Fl 5s 46m **24M**; W twr; vis: 256°-184°.

JURA TO MULL OF KINTYRE

SOUND OF JURA, CRAIGHOUSE, L SWEEN and GIGHA

Na Cùiltean Fl 10s 9m 9M; 55°48'·64N 05°54'·90W.
Gamhna Gigha Fl (2) 6s 7m 5M; 55°43'·78N 05°41'·08W.

WEST LOCH TARBERT

Dunskeig Bay Q (2) 10s 11m 8M; 55°45'·22N 05°35'·00W.
Eileen Tráighe (off S side) Fl (2) R 5s 5m 3M; R post; 55°45'·37N 05°35'·75W.

MULL OF KINTYRE

Mull of Kintyre ☆ 55°18'·64N 05°48'·25W Fl (2) 20s 91m **24M**; W twr on W bldg; vis: 347°-178°.

CRINAN CANAL and ARDRISHAIG

Crinan, E of lock ent Fl WG 3s 8m 4M; W twr, R band; vis: shore-W-146°-G-shore; 56°05'·48N 05°33'·37W.

Ardrishaig Bkwtr Hd L Fl WRG 6s 9m 4M; vis: 287°-G-339°-W-350°-R-035°; 56°00'·76N 05°26'·59W.

LOCH FYNE TO SANDA ISLAND

EAST LOCH TARBERT

Eilean na Beithe Fl WRG 3s 7m 5M; vis: G036°- W065°- R078°-106°; 55°52'·68N 05°19'·62W.

Skipness range Iso R 8s 7m 10M; Y ◇ on bldg; vis 292·2°-312·2°. Oc (2) Y 10s **24M** when range in use (occas); 55°46'·72N 05°19'·06W.

KILBRANNAN SOUND, CRANNAICH and CARRADALE BAY

Port Crannaich Bkwtr Hd Fl R 10s 5m 6M; vis: 099°-279°; 55°35'·60N 05°27'·84W.

CAMPBELTOWN LOCH to SANDA ISLAND

Davaar N Pt ☆ 55°25'·69N 05°32'·42W Fl (2) 10s 37m **23M**; W twr; vis: 073°-330°.
Sanda Island ☆ 55°16'·50N 05°35'·01W Fl 10s 50m **15M**; W twr.
Patersons Rock Fl (3) R 18s; 55°16'·90N 05°32'·48W.

KYLES OF BUTE TO RIVER CLYDE

KYLES OF BUTE and CALADH

Ardlamont Point No. 47 W Fl R 4s; 55°49'·59N 05°11'·76.

Ardmaleish Point No. 41 Q (3) 10s; 55°53'·02N 05°04'·70W.
Bogany Point No. 36 Fl R 4s; 55°50'·78N 05°01'·41W.

FIRTH OF CLYDE

Toward Pt ☆ 55°51'·73N 04°58'·79W Fl 10s 21m **22M**; W twr.
No. 34 55°51'·44N 04°59'·11W.
Skelmorlie Iso 5s; 55°51'·65N 04°56'·34W.

WEMYSS and INVERKIP

Cowal L Fl 10s; 55°56'·00N 04°54'·83W.
The Gantocks Fl R 6s 12m 6M; ○ twr; 55°56'·45N 04°55'·08W.

DUNOON

Cloch Point Fl 3s 24m 8M; W ○ twr, B band, W dwellings; 55°56'·55N 04°52'·74W.

LOCH LONG and LOCH GOIL

Loch Long Oc 6s; 55°59'·15N 04°52'·42W.
Baron's Pt No. 3 Oc (2) Y 10s 5m 3M; 55°59'·18N 04°51'·12W.
Ravenrock Pt Fl 4s 12m 10M; W twr on W col. Dir lt 204°, WRG 9m (same twr); vis: 201·5°-F R-203°-Al WR(W phase incr with brg)-203·5°-FW-204·5°-Al WG(G phase incr with brg)-205°-FG-206·5°; 56°02'·14N 04°54'·39W.
Port Dornaige Fl 6s 8m 11M; W col; vis: 026°-206°; 56°03·75N 04°53'·65W.
Rubha Ardnahein Fl R 5s 3m 3M; vis: 132°-312°; 56°06'·15N 04°53'·60W.
The Perch, Ldg Lts 318° Front, F WRG 3m 5M; vis: 311°-G-317°-W-320°-R-322°. Same structure, Fl R 3s 3m 3M; vis: 187°-322°; 56°06'·90N 04°54'·31W. Rear, 700m from front, F 7m 5M; vis: 312°-322·5°.
Cnap Pt Ldg Lts 031°. Front, Q 8m 10M; W col; 56°07'·40N 04°49'·97W. Rear, 87m from front F 13m; R line on W twr.

GOUROCK

Ashton Iso 5s; 55°58'·10N 04°50'·65W.
Rosneath Patch Fl (2) 10s 5m 10M; 55°58'·52N 04°47'·45W.

ROSNEATH, RHU NARROWS and GARELOCH

Ldg Lts 356°. **Front, No. 7N** 56°00'·05N 04°45'·36W Dir lt 356°. WRG 5m **W16M**, R13M, G13M; vis: 353°-Al WG- 355°-FW-357°-Al WR-000°-FR-002°.

Dir lt 115° WRG 5m **W16M**, R13M, G13M; vis: 111°-Al WG-114°-FW- 116°-Al WR-119°-FR-121°. Passing lt Oc G 6s 6m 3M; G △ on G pile . Rear, Ardencaple Castle Centre 56°00'·54N 04°45'·43W 2 FG (vert) 26m 12M; twr on Castle NW corner; vis: 335°-020°.

No. 8N Lt Bn 55°59'·09N 04°44'·21W Dir lt 080° WRG 4m; **W16M**, R13M,G13M;vis: 075°-FG-077·5°-Al WG-079·5°-FW-080·5°-AltWR-082·5°-FR-085°. **Dir lt 138°** WRG 4m **W16M**, R13M, G13M; vis: 132°-FG-134°-Al WG- FW137°-139°-Al WR-142°. Passing lt Fl Y 3s 6m 3M.

Gareloch No. 1 Lt Bn VQ (4) Y 5s 9m; Y 'X' on Y structure; 55°59'·12N 04°43'·89W.

No. 3 N Lt Bn 56°00'·07N 04°46'·72W Dir lt 149° WRG 9m **W16M**, R13M, G13M F & Al; vis: 144°-FG-145°-Al WG-148°-FW-150°-Al WR-153°-FR-154°. Passing lt Oc R 8s 9m 3M.

Rosneath DG Jetty 2 FR (vert) 5M; W col; vis: 150°-330°; 56°00'·39N 04°47'·51W.

Rhu Pt Q (3) WRG 6s 9m W10M, R7M, G7M; vis: 270°-G-000°-W-114°-R-188°; 56°00'·95N 04°47'·19W.

Dir lt 318° WRG **W16M**, R13M,G13M; vis: 315°-Al WG-317°-F-319°-Al WR-321°-FR-325°.

Limekiln No. 2N Lt Bn 56°00'·67N 04°47'·64W Dir lt 295° WRG 5m **W16M**, R13M, G13M F & Al; R □ on R Bn; vis: 291°-Al WG-294°-FW- 296°-Al WR-299°-FR-301°.

Mambeg Dir lt 331°, Q (4) WRG 8s 10m 14M; vis: 328·5°-G-330°-W-332°-R-333°; H24; 56°03'·74N 04°50'·47W.

GREENOCK and PORT GLASGOW

Anchorage Lts in line 196°. Front, FG 7m 12M; Y col; 55°57'·62N 04°46'·58W. Rear, 32m from front, FG 9m 12M. Y col.

Lts in line 194·5°. Front, FG 18m; 55°57'·45N 04°45'·91W. Rear, 360m from front, FG 33m.

Steamboat Quay, W end FG 12m 12M; B&W chequered col; vis 210°-290°; 55°56'·25N 04°41'·44W. From here to Glasgow Lts on S bank are Fl G and Lts on N bank are Fl R.

CLYDE TO MULL OF GALLOWAY

LARGS and FAIRLIE

Approach L Fl 10s; 55°46'·40N 04°51'·85W.
Fairlie Patch Fl G 1·5s; 55°45'·38N 04°52'·34W.

MILLPORT and GREAT CUMBRAE

Ldg Lts 333°. Pier Head front, 55°45'·04N 04°55'·85W FR 7m 5M. Rear, 137m from front, FR 9m 5M.
Mountstuart L Fl 10s; 55°48'·00N 04°57'·57W.
Runnaneun Pt (Rubha'n Eun) Fl R 6s 8m 12M; W twr; 55°43'·79N 05°00'·23W.
Little Cumbrae Is, Cumbrae Elbow Fl 6s 28m 14M; W twr; vis: 334°-193°; 55°43'·22N 04°58'·06W.

ARDROSSAN

Approach Dir lt 055°, WRG 15m W14M, R11M, G11M; vis: 050°-F G-051·2°-Alt WG(W phase inc with Brg)- 053·8°-FW-056·2°-Alt WR(R phase inc with brg)-058·8°-FR-060°; 55°38'·66N 04°49'·22W. Same structure FR 13m 6M; vis: 325°-145°.
Lt ho Pier Hd Iso WG 4s 11m 9M; W twr; vis: 035°-W-317°-G-035°; 55°38'·47N 04°49'·57W.

IRVINE

Ldg Lts 051°. Front, FG 10m 5M; 55°36'·40N 04°41'·57W. Rear, 101m from front, FR 15m 5M; G masts, both vis: 019°-120°.

TROON

Troon Approach Fl R 2s 4m 3M; 55°33'·06N 04°41'·35W.
W Pier Hd Fl (2) WG 5s 11m 9M; W twr; vis: 036°-G-090°-W-036°; 55°33'·07N 04°41'·02W.
Lady I Fl 2s 19m 11M; W Tr R vert stripes; ***Racon (T) 13-11M***; 55°31'·63N 04°44'·05W.

ARRAN, RANZA, LAMLASH and BRODICK

Pillar Rk Pt ☆ (Holy Island), 55°31'·04N 05°03'·67W Fl (2) 20s 38m **25M**; W □ twr.
Holy I SW end Fl G 3s 14m 10M; W twr; vis: 282°-147°; 55°30'·73N 05°04'·21W.
Pladda ☆ 55°25'·50N 05°07'·12W Fl (3) 30s 40m **17M**; W twr.

AYR and AILSA CRAIG

S Pier Hd Q 7m 7M; R twr; vis: 012°-161°. Also FG 5m 5M; vis: 012°-082°; 55°28'·17N 04°38'·74W.
Ldg Lts 098°. Front, FR 10m 5M; Tfc sigs; 55°28'·15N 04°38'·38W. Rear, 130m from front Oc R 10s 18m 9M.
Turnberry Point ☆, near castle ruins 55°19'·56N 04°50'·71W Fl 15s 29m **24M**; W twr.
Ailsa Craig ☆ 55°15'·12N 05°06'·52W Fl 4s 18m **17M**; W twr; vis: 145°-028°.

GIRVAN

S Pier Hd 2 FG (vert) 8m 4M; W twr; 55°14'·72N 04°51'·90W.

LOCH RYAN and STRANRAER

Milleur Point Q; 55°01'·28N 05°05'·66W.
Forbes Shoal QR; 54°59'·47N 05°02'·96W.
Loch Ryan W QG;54°59'·23N 05°03'·24W .
Cairn Pt Fl (2) R 10s 14m 12M; W twr; 54°58'·46N 05°01'·85W.
Cairnryan Fl R 5s 5m 5M; 54°57'·77N 05°00'·99W.
Stranraer No.1 Oc G 6s; 54°56'·67N 05°01'·32W.
No. 3 QG; 54°55'·87N 05°01'·60W.
No. 5 Fl G 3s; 54°55'·08N 05°01'·86W.
E Pier Hd 2 FR (vert) 9m; 54°54'·61N 05°01'·60W.
Corsewall Point ☆ 55°00'·41N 05°09'·58W Fl (5) 30s 34m **22M**; W twr; vis: 027°-257°.
Black Head Old Lighthouse (disused); W tower, 22m; 54°51'·70N 05°08'·80W.

PORTPATRICK

Ldg Lts 050·5°. Front, FG (occas); 54°50'·50N 05°07'·02W. Rear, 68m from front, FG 8m (occas).
Crammag Hd ☆ 54°39'·90N 04°57'·92W Fl 10s 35m **18M**; W twr.
Mull of Galloway ☆, SE end 54°38'·08N 04°51'·45W Fl 20s 99m **28M**; W twr; vis: 182°-105°.

MULL OF GALLOWAY and WIGTOWN BAY

Port William Ldg Lts 105°. Front, Pier Hd Fl G 3s 7m 3M; 54°45'·66N 04°35'·28W. Rear, 130m from front, FG 10m 2M.
Whithorn Ldg Lts 335°. Front, Oc R 8s 7m 7M; Or ♦; 54°42'·01N 04°22'·05W. Rear, 35m from front, Oc R 8s 9m 7M; Or ♦, synch.
Little Ross Fl 5s 50m 12M; W twr; obsc in Wigtown B when brg more than 103°; 54°45'·93N 04°05'·10W.

KIRKCUDBRIGHT BAY and KIPPFORD

Little Ross NNE end of Is Fl (2) 5s 21m 5M; Stone bcn; 54°46'·06N 04°05'·02W.
Hestan I, E end Fl (2) 10s 42m 9M; 54°49'·95N 03°48'·53W.

2.4 PASSAGE INFORMATION

Conditions in the SW of Scotland are generally less rugged south of Mull. Some of the remarks at the start of 1.4 are equally applicable to this area. The area is covered by Admiralty Leisure Folios 5610, 5611 and, to the south, 5613. Refer to the Clyde Cruising Club's SDs, Admiralty *West Coast of Scotland Pilot* and to *Yachtsman's Pilot to the W Coast of Scotland, Clyde to Colonsay* (Imray/Lawrence). Submarines exercise throughout these waters; see Subfacts for information on active areas.

More Passage Information is threaded between the harbours of this Area.

Some of the following more common *Gaelic* terms may help with navigation: *Acairseid*: anchorage. *Ailean*: meadow. *Aird, ard*: promontory. *Aisir, aisridh*: passage between rocks. *Beag*: little. *Beinn*: mountain. *Bo, boghar, bodha*: rock. *Cala*: harbour. *Camas*: channel, bay. *Caol*: strait. *Cladach*: shore, beach. *Creag*: cliff. *Cumhamn*: narrows. *Dubh, dhubh*: black. *Dun*: castle. *Eilean, eileanan*: island. *Garbh*: rough. *Geal, gheal*: white. *Glas, ghlas*: grey, green. *Inis*: island. *Kyle*: narrow strait. *Linn, Linne*: pool. *Mor, mhor:* large. *Mull*: promontory. *Rinn, roinn*: point. *Ruadh*: red, brown. *Rubha, rhu*: cape. *Sgeir*: rock. *Sruth*: current. *Strath*: river valley. *Tarbert*: isthmus. *Traigh*: beach. *Uig*: bay.

CORRYVRECKAN TO CRINAN

(AC 2326, 2343) ▶ *Between Scarba and Jura is the Gulf of Corryvreckan (AC 2343) which is best avoided, and should never be attempted by small craft except at slack water and in calm conditions. (In any event the Sound of Luing is always a safer and not much longer alternative.) The Gulf has a least width of 6ca and is free of dangers apart from its very strong tides which, in conjunction with a very uneven bottom, cause extreme turbulence. This is particularly dangerous with strong W winds over a W-going (flood) tide which spews out several miles to seaward of the gulf, with overfalls extending 5M from the W of ent (The Great Race). Keep to the S side of the gulf to avoid the worst turbulence and the whirlpool known as The Hag, caused by depths of only 29m, as opposed to more than 100m in the fairway.*

The W-going stream in the gulf begins at HW Oban + 0410, and the E-going at HW Oban – 0210. Sp rate W-going is 8·5kn, and E-going about 6kn. The range of tide at sp can vary nearly 2m between the E end of the gulf (1·5m) and the W end (3·4m), with HW 30mins earlier at the E end. Slack water occurs at HW Oban +0400 and –0230 and lasts almost 1 hr at nps, but only 15 mins at sps. On the W-going (flood) stream eddies form both sides of the gulf, but the one on the N (Scarba) shore is more important. Where this eddy meets the main stream off Camas nam Bairneach there is violent turbulence, with heavy overfalls extending W at the division of the eddy and the main stream.

◀ There are temp anchs with the wind in the right quarter in Bàgh Gleann a' Mhaoil in the SE corner of Scarba, and in Bàgh Gleann nam Muc at N end of Jura but the latter has rks in approaches E and SW of Eilean Beag.

SE of Corryvreckan is Loch Crinan, which leads to the Crinan Canal. Beware Black Rk, 2m high and 2ca N of the canal sea lock, and dangers extending 100m from the rock.

WEST OF JURA TO ISLAY

(AC 2481, 2168) The W coasts of Colonsay and Oronsay (AC 2169) are fringed with dangers up to 2M offshore. The two islands are separated by a narrow chan which dries and has an overhead cable (10m). There are HIE ♦s at Scalasaig.

The Sound of Islay presents no difficulty; hold to the Islay shore, where all dangers are close in. ▶ *The N-going stream begins at HW Oban +0440, and the S-going at HW Oban –0140. Main flood begins HW Oban +0545. Streams turn approx 1 hr earlier in Gigha Sd and at Kintyre and Jura shores. S going stream for 9hrs close inshore between Gigha and Machrihanish starting HW Oban –0530.*

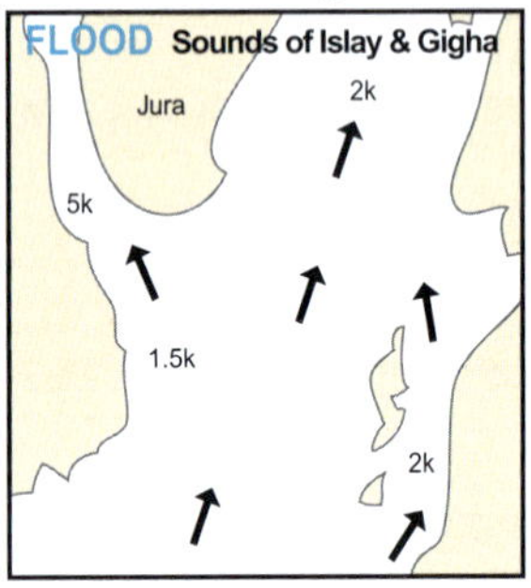

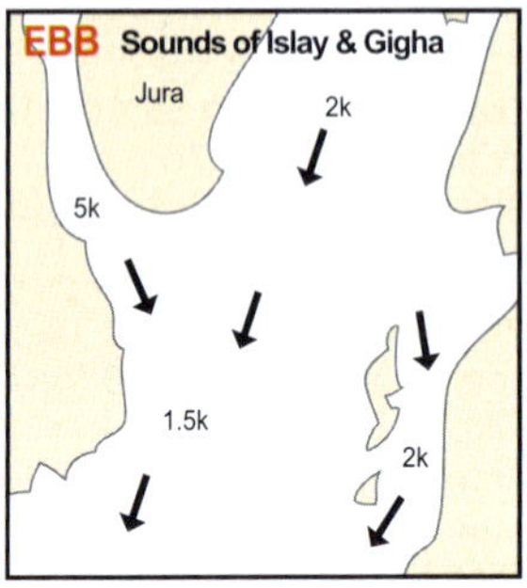

Main ebb begins HW Oban –0015. Streams turn 1 hr earlier in Gigha Sd, Kintyre and Jura shores. Overfalls off McArthur's Hd. The sp rates are 2·5kn at N entrance and 1·5kn at S entrance, ***but reaching 5kn in the narrows off Port Askaig.*** ◀ There are anchs in the Sound, but holding ground is mostly poor. The best places are alongside at Port Askaig, or at anch off the distillery in Bunnahabhain B, 2·5M to N. ▶ *There are overfalls off McArthur's Hd (Islay side of S entrance) during the S-going stream.* ◀

The N coast of Islay and Rhinns of Islay are very exposed. In the N there is anch SE of Nave Island at entrance to Loch Gruinart; beware Balach Rks which dry, just to N. ▶ *To the SW off Orsay (lt), Frenchman's Rks and W Bank there is a race and overfalls which should be cleared by 3M. Here the NW-going stream begins at HW Oban +0530, and the SE-going at HW Oban –0040;* ***sp rates are 6-8kn inshore,*** *but decrease to 3kn 5M offshore.* ◀ Loch Indaal gives some shelter; beware rks extending from Laggan Pt on E side of ent. Off the Mull of Oa there are further overfalls. Port Ellen, the main hbr on Islay, has HIE ♦s; there are some dangers in approach, and it is exposed to S; see AC 2474.

SOUND OF JURA TO GIGHA

(AC 2397, 2396, 2168) From Crinan to Gigha the Sound of Jura is safe if a mid-chan course is held. Ruadh Sgeir (lt) are rocky ledges in mid-fairway, about 3M W of Crinan. Loch Sween (AC 2397) can be approached N or SE of MacCormaig Islands, where there is an attractive anch on NE side of Eilean Mor, but exposed to NE. Coming from N beware Keills Rk and Danna Rk. Sgeirean a Mhain is a rk in fairway 1·5M NE of Castle Sween (conspic on SE shore). Anch at Tayvallich, near head of loch on W side.

W Loch Tarbert (AC 2477) is long and narrow, with good anchs and lts near ent, but unmarked shoals. On entry give a berth of at least 2½ca to Eilean Traighe off N shore, E of Ardpatrick Pt. Dun Skeig, an isolated hill, is conspic on S shore. Good anch near head of loch, 1M by road from E Loch Tarbert, Loch Fyne.

On W side of Sound, near S end of Jura, are The Small Is (AC 2396) across the mouth of Loch na Mile. Beware Goat Rk (dries 0·3m) 1.5ca off s'most Is, Eilean nan Gabhar, behind which is good anch. Also possible to go alongside Craighouse Pier (HIE ♦). Another anch is in Lowlandman's B, about 3M to N, but exposed to S winds; Ninefoot Rks with depth of 2·4m and ECM lt buoy lie off ent. Skervuile (lt) is a reef to the E, in middle of the Sound.

S of W Loch Tarbert, and about 2M off the Kintyre shore, is Gigha Is (AC 2475). Good anchs on E side in Druimyeon B and Ardminish B (HIE ♦s), respectively N and S of Ardminish Pt. Outer and Inner Red Rks (least depth 2m) lie 2M SW of N end of Gigha Is. Dangers extend 1M W off S end of Gigha Is. Gigalum Is and Cara Is are off the S end. Gigha Sound needs very careful pilotage, since there are several dangerous rks, some buoyed/lit, others not. ▶ *The N-going stream begins at HW Oban +0430, and S-going at HW Oban –0155, sp rates 1·3kn.* ◀

HARBOURS AND ANCHORAGES IN COLONSAY, JURA, ISLAY AND THE SOUND OF JURA

SCALASAIG, Colonsay, **56°04'·14N 06°10'·86W**. AC 2169. HW +0542 on Dover; ML 2·2m. See 2.5. Conspic monument ½M SW of hbr. Beware group of rks N of pier hd marked by bn. 2 HIE Ⓥ berths on N side of pier, inner end approx 2·5m. Inner hbr to SW of pier is safe, but dries. Ldg lts 262°, both FR 8/10m on pier. Also ⚓ clear of cable in **Loch Staosnaig**; SW of Rubha Dubh lt, Fl (2) WR 10s 8m 8/6M; shore-R-230°-W-337°-R-354°. Facilities: D, P, 🛒 (all at ✉), FW, Hotel ☎ (01951) 200316, Dr (0951) 200328.

LOCH TARBERT, W Jura, **55°57'·69N 06°00'·06W**. AC 2169, 2481. Tides as Rubha A'Mhàil (N tip of Islay). See 2.5. HW –0540 on Dover; ML 2·1m; Duration 0600. Excellent shelter inside the loch, but subject to squalls in strong winds; ⚓ outside in Glenbatrick Bay in approx 6m in S winds, or at Bagh Gleann Righ Mor in approx 2m in N winds. To enter inner loch via Cumhann Beag, there are four pairs of ldg marks (W stones) at approx 120°, 150°, 077°, and 188°, the latter astern, to be used in sequence; pilot book required. There are no facilities.

PORT ASKAIG, Islay, **55°50'·87N 06°06'·26W**. AC 2168, 2481. HW +0610 on Dover; ML 1·2m. See 2.5. Hbr on W side of Sound of Islay. ⚓ close inshore in 4m or secure to ferry pier. Beware strong tide/eddies. ☆ FR at LB. Facilities: FW (hose on pier), Gas, P, R, Hotel, 🛒, ✉, ferries to Jura and Kintyre. Other ⚓s in the Sound at: Bunnahabhain (2M N); Whitefarland Bay, Jura, opp Caol Ila distillery; NW of Am Fraoch Eilean (S tip of Jura); Aros Bay, N of Ardmore Pt.

CRAIGHOUSE, SE Jura, **55°49'·99N 05°56'·31W**. AC 2168, 2481, 2396. HW +0600 on Dover; ML 0·5m; Duration 0640 np, 0530 sp. See 2.5. Good shelter, but squalls occur in W winds. Enter between lt bn on SW end of Eilean nan Gabhar, Fl 5s 7m 8M vis 225°-010°, and unlit bn close SW. There are 8 HIE ♦s N of pier (☎ (01496) 810332), where yachts may berth alongside; or ⚓ in 5m in poor holding at the N end of Loch na Mile. Facilities: very limited, Bar, FW, ✉, R, 🛒, Gas, P & D (cans). **Lowlandman's Bay** is 1M further N, with ECM buoy, Q (3) 10s, marking Nine Foot Rk (2·4m) off the ent. ⚓ to SW of conspic houses, off stone jetty.

LOCH SWEEN, Argyll and Bute, **55°55'·69N 05°41'·26W**. AC 2397. HW +0550 on Dover; ML 1·5m; Duration = 0610. See 2.6 Carsaig Bay. Off the ent to loch, **Eilean Mòr** (most SW'ly of MacCormaig Isles) has tiny ⚓ on N side in 3m; local transit marks keep clear of two rks, 0·6m and 0·9m. Inside the loch, beware Sgeirean a'Mhain, a rk in mid-chan to S of Taynish Is, 3M from ent. Good shelter in Loch a Bhealaich (⚓ outside **Tayvallich** in approx 7m on boulders) or enter inner hbr to ⚓ W of central reef. There are no lts. Facilities: Gas, Bar, ✉, FW (🚰 by ✉), R, 🛒. Close to NE are ⚓s at **Caol Scotnish** and **Fairy Is**, the former obstructed by rks 3ca from ent.

WEST LOCH TARBERT, Argyll and Bute, (Kintyre), **55°45'N 05°36'W**. AC 2476. Tides as Gigha Sound, 2.5. Good shelter. Ent is S of Eilean Traighe, Fl (2) R 5s, and NW of Dun Skeig, Q (2) 10s, where there is also conspic conical hill (142m). Loch is lit for 5M by 3 bns, QG, QR and QG in sequence, up to Kennacraig ferry pier, 2FG (vert). PHM buoy, QR, is 2½ca NW of pier. Caution: many drying rks and fish farms outside the fairway and near head of loch. ⚓s are NE of Eilean Traighe (beware weed and ferry wash); near Rhu Pt, possible ♦s; NE of Eilean dà Gallagain, and at loch hd by pier (ru). Tarbert (2.8) is 1·5M walk/bus.

GIGHA ISLAND, Argyll and Bute, **55°40′·6N 05°44′·0W**. AC 2168, 2475. HW +0600 on Dover; ML 0·9m; Duration 0530. See 2.5. Main ⚓ is **Ardminish Bay**: 12 HIE Ⓜs in the centre. Reefs extend off both points, the S'ly reef marked by an unlit PHM buoy. Kiln Rk (dries 1·5m) is close NE of the old ferry jetty. **Druimyeon Bay** is more sheltered in E'lies, but care needed entering from S. ⚓s sheltered from winds in Kilnaughton Bay, Port Mór (S-W), Bàgh na Dòirlinne (SE-S), W Tarbert Bay (NE). Caolas Gigalum (⚓ 50m SE of pier) is safe in all but NE-E winds. Beware many rks in Gigha Sound. Lts: Fl (2) 6s, on Gamhna Gigha (off NE tip); WCM buoy Fl (9) 15s marks Gigalum Rks, at S end of Gigha. **Ardminish** ☎ (01583) 505254: FW, Gas, P & D (cans), ▣, ✉, Bar, R, 🛒.

2.5 PORT ELLEN

Islay (Argyll and Bute) **55°37′·29N 06°12′·26W**

CHARTS AC 2168, 2476; Imray C64

TIDES HW +0620 np, +0130 sp on Dover; ML 0·6. Sea level is much affected by the weather, rising by 1m in S/E gales; at nps the tide is sometimes diurnal and range negligible.

Standard Port OBAN (⟵)

Times				Height (metres)			
High Water		Low Water		MHWS	MHWN	MLWN	MLWS
0100	0700	0100	0800	4·0	2·9	1·8	0·7
1300	1900	1300	2000				
Differences PORT ELLEN (S Islay)							
−0530	−0050	−0045	−0530	−3·1	−2·1	−1·3	−0·4
SCALASAIG (E Colonsay)							
−0020	−0005	−0015	+0005	−0·1	−0·2	−0·2	−0·2
GLENGARRISDALE BAY (N Jura)							
−0020	0000	−0010	0000	−0·4	−0·2	0·0	−0·2
CRAIGHOUSE (SE Jura)							
−0230	−0250	−0150	−0230	−3·0	−2·4	−1·3	−0·6
RUBHA A'MHÀIL (N Islay)							
−0020	0000	+0005	−0015	−0·3	−0·1	−0·3	−0·1
ARDNAVE POINT (NW Islay)							
−0035	+0010	0000	−0025	−0·4	−0·2	−0·3	−0·1
ORSAY ISLAND (SW Islay)							
−0110	−0110	−0040	−0040	−1·4	−0·6	−0·5	−0·2
BRUICHLADDICH (Islay, Loch Indaal)							
−0105	−0035	−0110	−0110	−1·8	−1·3	−0·4	+0·1
PORT ASKAIG (Sound of Islay)							
−0110	−0030	−0020	−0020	−1·9	−1·4	−0·8	−0·3
GIGHA SOUND (Sound of Jura)							
−0450	−0210	−0130	−0410	−2·5	−1·6	−1·0	−0·1
MACHRIHANISH							
−0520	−0350	−0340	−0540	Mean range 0·5 metres.			

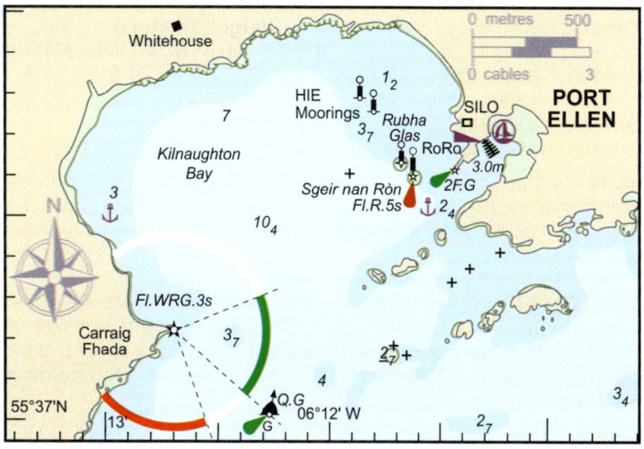

SHELTER Good shelter on pontoons (3m at MLWS), but in S winds swell sets into the bay. 10 HIE Ⓜs to W of Rubha Glas; adjacent rks marked by 3 bcns with reflective topmarks. In W'lies ⚓ in Kilnaughton Bay, N of Carraig Fhada lt ho; or 4M ENE at Loch-an-t-Sàilein.

NAVIGATION WPT 55°36′·69N 06°12′·06W, 326°/0·63M to Carraig Fhada lt ho. Beware Otter Rk 4M SE of hbr, rks on both sides of ent and in NE corner of bay. Keep close to pier.

LIGHTS AND MARKS On W side 10 Radio masts (103m) and Carraig Fhada lt ho (conspic), Fl WRG 3s 20m 8/6M; keep in W sector until past the SHM lt buoy. Sgeir nan Ròn Bn Fl R 5s, Ro-Ro Pier 2 FG (vert) and Marina pontoon Fl G 4s. Limits of dredged area around Ro-Ro Pier and pontoon area marked by buoys.

TELEPHONE Moorings (01496)300301/mob 07732191333; MRCC (01475) 729988.

FACILITIES **Marina** (30 inc Ⓥ – welcome, Ⓜ in bay), ☎ 300301 for fuel and assistance, dredged to 3m, £12<10m, £14 >10m, D, Slip; **Village** Bar, FW, ✉, R, 🛒, Gas.

MULL OF KINTYRE

(AC 2126, 2199, 2798) From Crinan to Mull of Kintyre is about 50M. Passage round the Mull of Kintyre within 2 or 3 miles of the coast requires great care. Races exist S and SW of the Mull, and fresh to strong S winds cause dangerous breaking seas especially during E-going (flood) tidal streams. Best to keep at least 3 miles offshore and S of Sanda Island. ▶ *In Sanda Sound the W-going stream starts HW Dover −0110, and the E-going stream starts HW Dover +0500. Sp rates 5kn. Close W of the Mull the N-going stream starts at HW Dover −0130, and the S-going stream at HW Dover +0430. Sp rates 5kn. Careful timing is needed, especially W-bound.* ◀ The Traffic Separation Scheme in the North Channel, is only 2M W of the Mull and limits sea-room in the ITZ.

Sanda Sound separates Sanda Island and its rocks and islets from Kintyre. On the mainland shore beware Macosh Rks (dry, PHM lt buoy), forming part of Barley Ridges, 2ca offshore; and Arranman's Barrels, drying and submerged, marked by PHM lt buoy. Sanda Is provides useful stopping point while waiting for the tide. Beware Paterson's Rk (9ca E, dries). There is good anchorage on N side in Sanda Roads. Approach with Boat Ho bearing 155°; beware strong TS across entrance, and drying rocks in middle of bay. See Plan on AC 2126.

MULL OF KINTYRE TO UPPER LOCH FYNE

(AC 2126, 2383, 2381, 2382). ▶ *Once E of Mull of Kintyre, tidal conditions and pilotage much improve.* ◀ Campbeltown is entered N of Island Davaar (lt). 1·5M N off lt ho is Otterard Rk (depth 3·8m), with Long Rk (dries 1·1m) 5ca W of it; only Otterard Rock is buoyed. ▶ *E of Island Davaar tide runs 3kn at sp, and there are overfalls.* ◀

Kilbrannan Sound runs 21M from Island Davaar to Skipness Pt, where it joins Inchmarnock Water, Lower Loch Fyne and Bute Sound. ▶ *There are few dangers apart from overfalls on Erins Bank, 10M S of Skipness, on S-going stream.* ◀ Good anch in Carradale Bay, off Torrisdale Castle. ▶ *There are overfalls off Carradale Pt on S-going stream.* ◀

Lower L Fyne (AC 2381) is mainly clear of dangers to East L Tarbert. On E shore beware rks off Ardlamont Pt; 4M to NW is Skate Is which is best passed to W. 3M S of Ardrishaig beware Big Rk (depth 2·1m). Further N, at entrance to Loch Gilp (mostly dries), note shoals (least depth 1·5m) round Gulnare Rk, PHM lt buoy; also Duncuan Is with dangers extending SW to Sgeir Sgalag (depth 0·6m), buoyed.

Where Upper L Fyne turns NE (The Narrows) it is partly obstructed by Otter Spit (dries 0·9m), extending 8ca WNW from E shore and marked by lt bn. The stream runs up to 2kn here. A buoyed/lit rk, depth less than 2m, lies about 7ca SW of Otter Spit bn. In Upper L Fyne (AC 2382) off Minard Pt, the chan between rks and islands in the fairway is buoyed/lit.

2.6 CRINAN CANAL

Argyll and Bute **56°05'·50N 05°33'·38W** Crinan

CHARTS AC 2326, 2320; Imray C65.

TIDES –0608 Dover; ML 2·1; Duration 0605; HW Crinan is at HW Oban –0045

Standard Port OBAN (⟵)

Times				Height (metres)			
High Water		Low Water		MHWS	MHWN	MLWN	MLWS
0100	0700	0100	0800	4·0	2·9	1·8	0·7
1300	1900	1300	2000				
Differences CARSAIG BAY (56°02'N 05°38'W)							
–0105	–0040	–0050	–0050	–2·1	–1·6	–1·0	–0·4

NOTE: In the Sound of Jura, S of Loch Crinan, the rise of tide occurs mainly during the 3½ hrs after LW; the fall during the 3½ hrs after HW. At other times the changes in level are usually small and irregular.

SHELTER Complete shelter in canal basin; yachts are welcome. Good shelter in Crinan Hbr (E of Eilean da Mheinn) but full of moorings. Except in strong W/N winds, ⚓ E of the canal ent, clear of fairway. Gallanach Bay on N side of L Crinan has good holding in about 3m.

NAVIGATION WPT 56°05'·70N 05°33'·64W, 146°/0·27M to Fl WG 3s lt. Beware Black Rock (2m high) in appr NE of ldg line 146° to dir Fl WG 3s lt. Off NW corner of chartlet, no ⚓ in a nearly rectangular shellfish bed, 6ca by 6ca. SPM lt buoys mark each corner: Fl (4) Y 12s at the NE and NW corners, Fl Y 6s at the SW and SE corners; the latter being about 100m NE of Black Rock.

CANAL Canal is 9M long with 15 locks and 7 opening bridges. Least transit time is 5 to 6 hrs, observing 4kn speed limit. Entry at all tides. Max LOA: 26·82m, 6.09m beam, 2·89m draft (add 0.10m to your salt water draft), mast 28.95m. Vessels NW-bound have right of way. **Lock hrs**: The canal operates 7 days a week during the summer but during the winter periods of closure or partial closure can be expected. Contact the Canal Office for current operating schedule. The lock can be turbulent; have ready long warps and plenty of fenders. The canal is normally closed from Christmas to the New Year. Do not pump out bilge water or toilets in the canal. Contact canal staff if reqd.

BOAT SAFETY SCHEME Transit craft liable to safety checks on gas, fuel, electrics; £1M 3rd party insurance required. Resident craft subject to full safety checks. See 1.16.

LIGHTS AND MARKS Crinan Hotel is conspic W bldg. A conspic chy, 3ca SW of hotel, leads 187° into Crinan Hbr. E of sea-lock: Dir Fl WG 3s 8m 4M, vis 114°-W-146°-G-280°. Ent: 2 FG (vert) and 2FR (vert).

R/T VHF Ch **74** 16 only at sea locks.

TELEPHONE (Code 01546) Sea lock 830285; Canal HQ 603210; MRCC (01475) 729988; Marinecall 09068 500463; Police 702201; Dr 462001.

FACILITIES **Canal HQ** ☎ 603210, www.waterscape.com. All fees are under review; contact office for details. M, L, FW, *Skippers Guide* is essential reading; **Sea Basin** AB (overnight rate available). **Services:** BY, D, Slip, ME, El, ⚒, Gas, ACA, C (5 ton), ▣, CH, P (cans), 🛒, R, Bar. Use shore toilets, not yacht heads, whilst in canal. **Village** ✉, Ⓑ (Ardrishaig), ⇌ (Oban), ✈ (Glasgow or Macrihanish). There is a wintering park, plus BY and CH, at Cairnbaan for yachts <10m LOA.

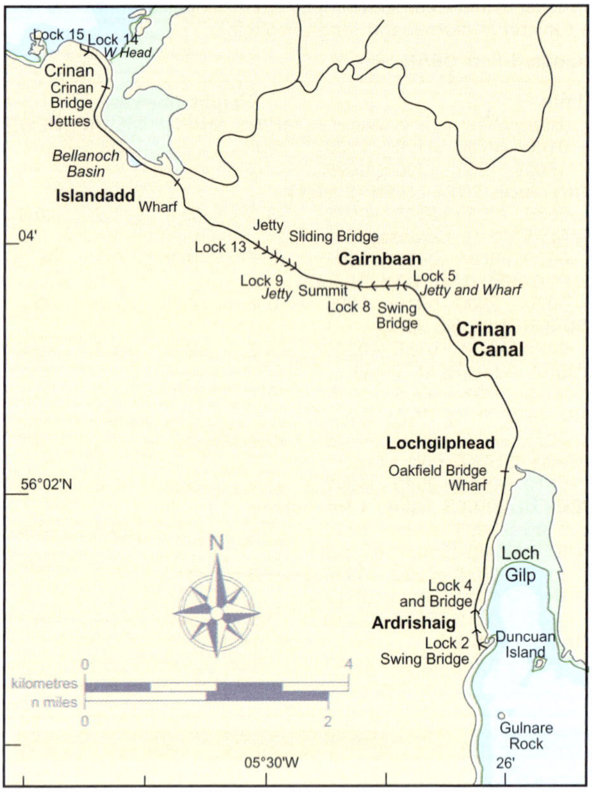

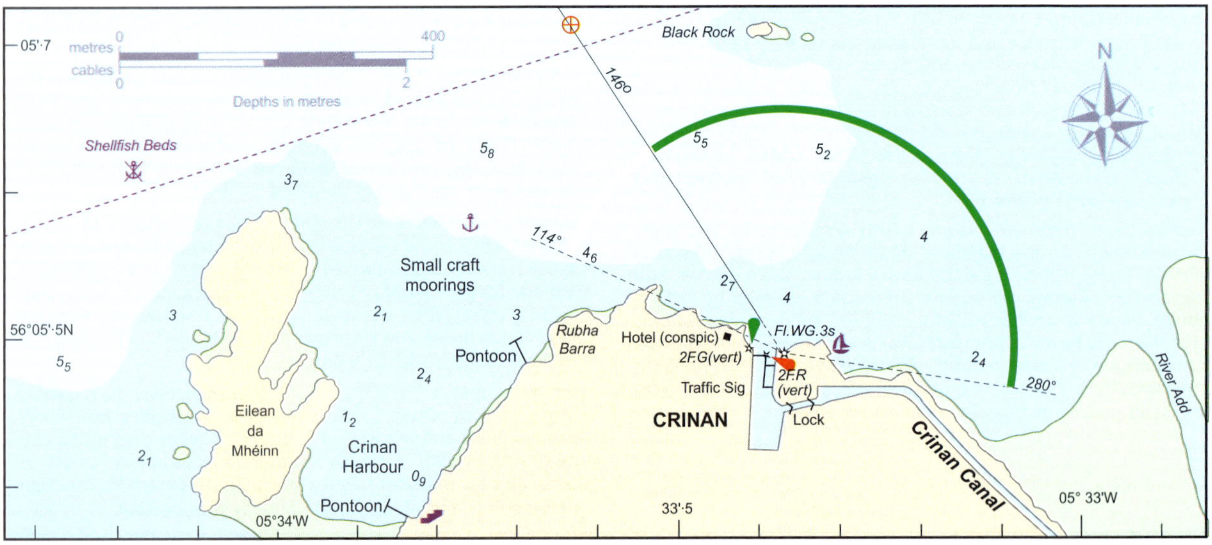

2.7 ARDRISHAIG

Argyll and Bute **56°00′·78N 05°26′·62W** ❁❁⚓⚓✿✿

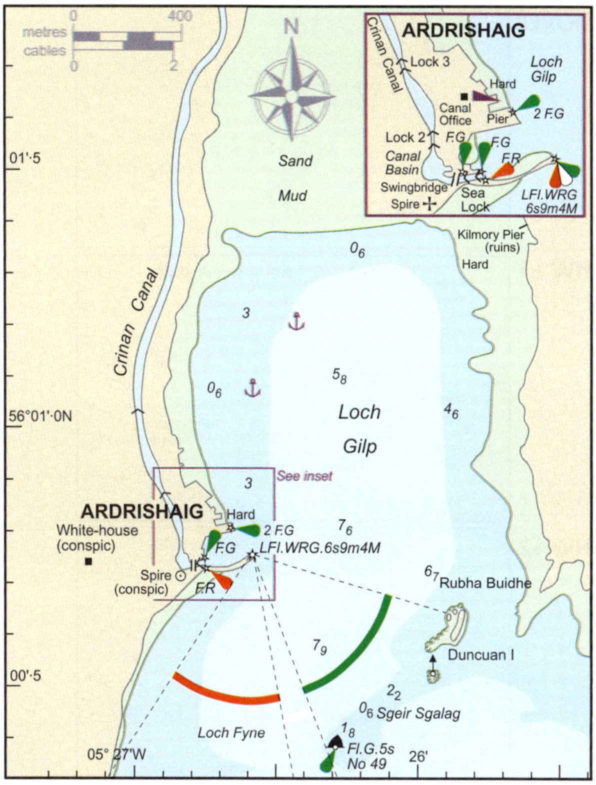

CHARTS AC 5610, 2131, 2381; Imray C63.

TIDES +0120 Dover; ML 1·9; Duration 0640

Standard Port GREENOCK (⟶)

Times				Height (metres)			
High Water		Low Water		MHWS	MHWN	MLWN	MLWS
0000	0600	0000	0600	3·4	2·8	1·0	0·3
1200	1800	1200	1800				
Differences ARDRISHAIG							
+0006	+0006	-0015	+0020	0·0	0·0	+0·1	–0·1
INVERARAY							
+0011	+0011	+0034	+0034	–0·1	+0·1	–0·5	–0·2

SHELTER Hbr is sheltered except from strong E'lies; do not berth on pier or ⚓ due to commercial vessels H24. Sea lock into the Crinan Canal is usually left open, however, a waiting pontoon has been installed outside the lock, with restricted depth, for use in fair weather only. Access at all tides. Complete shelter in the canal basin, or beyond lock No 2; see 2.6. Also ⚓ 2ca N of hbr, off the W shore of L Gilp. Head of Loch dries for nearly 1M.

NAVIGATION WPT No 48 PHM lt buoy, 56°00′·18N 05°26′·31W, 345°/0·6M to bkwtr lt. Dangerous drying rocks to E of appr chan are marked by No 49 Fl.G.5s SHM buoy.

LIGHTS AND MARKS Conspic W Ho on with block of flats leads 315°between Nos 48 and 49 buoys. Bkwtr lt, L Fl WRG 6s, W339°-350°. Pier is floodlit. Other lights as plan.

R/T VHF Ch **74** 16.

TELEPHONE (Code 01546) HM 603210; Sea lock 602458; MRCC (01475) 729988; Marinecall 09068 969652; Police 702201; Dr 462001.

FACILITIES **Pier/Hbr** ☎ 603210, AB (fees under review), Slip, FW; **Sea Lock** ☎ 602458; **Crinan Canal** www.scottishcanals.co.uk/crinan/index.html, AB, M, L, FW, R, Bar; dues, see 2.6. **Services:** BY, ME, El, ⚒, CH, D (cans), Gas. **Village** P & D (cans), 🛒, R, Bar, ✉, Ⓑ, 🚆 (bus to Oban), ✈ (Glasgow or Campbeltown).

2.8 TARBERT, LOCH FYNE

Also known as East Loch Tarbert

Argyll and Bute **55°52′·05N 05°24′·22W** ❁❁❁⚓⚓⚓✿✿

CHARTS AC 5610, 2131, 2381; Imray C63.

TIDES +0120 Dover; ML 1·9; Duration 0640

Standard Port GREENOCK (⟶)

Times				Height (metres)			
High Water		Low Water		MHWS	MHWN	MLWN	MLWS
0000	0600	0000	0600	3·4	2·8	1·0	0·3
1200	1800	1200	1800				
Differences EAST LOCH TARBERT							
–0005	–0005	0000	–0005	+0·2	+0·1	0·0	0·0

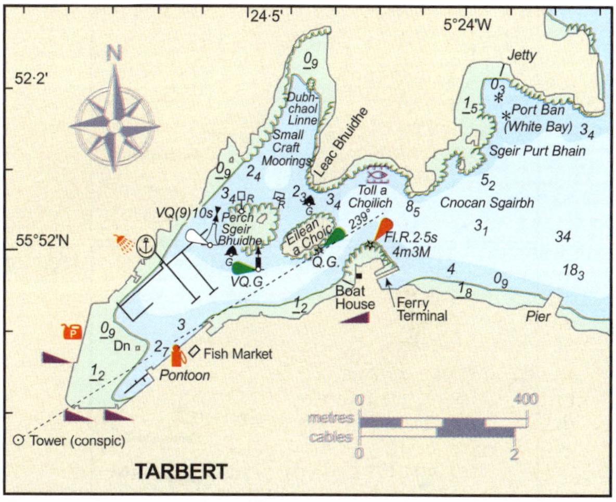

SHELTER Very good in all weathers but gets crowded. Access H24. 120 Ⓥ AB on pontoons; only use Fish Quay if directed by HM. See also Portavadie Marina, below.

NAVIGATION WPT 55°52′·02N 05°23′·03W, 270°/0·7M to Fl R 2·5s lt. Ent is very narrow. Cock Isle divides the ent in half: Main hbr to the S, Buteman's Hole to the N, where ⚓s are fouled by heavy moorings and lost chains. Speed limit 3kn.

LIGHTS AND MARKS Outer ldg lts 252° to S ent: Fl R 2·5s on with Cock Is lt QG. Inner ldg line 239°: same QG, G column, on with conspic ✠ tr. Note: The W sector, 065°-078°, of Eilean na Beithe ☆, Fl WRG 3s 7m 5M (on E shore of Lower Loch Fyne), could be used to position for the initial appr to Tarbert.

R/T Call VHF Ch **14** (0900-1700LT).

TELEPHONE (Code 01880) HM 820344, tarbertharbour@btconnect.com; MRCC (01475) 729988; Marinecall 09068 969652; Police 820200; ⊞ (01546) 602323.

FACILITIES **Yacht Berthing Facility** 99 visitors, AB £2.10, FW, AC; **Fish Quay** D (Mon-Fri 0800-1800), FW; **Tarbert YC** Slip, L; **Services:** SM, 🗐, ACA, ⚒, CH. **Town** P & D (0800-1800 cans), Gas, Gaz, L, 🛒, R, Bar, ✉, Ⓑ, Wi-fi, 🚆 (bus to Glasgow), ✈ (Glasgow/Campbeltown). See also **Portavadie Marina**, below.

PORTAVADIE MARINA (55°52′·23N 05°18′·98W)
3M east of Tarbert; ☎ (01700) 811075, www.portavadiemarina.com, 230 inc Ⓥ, £1.80; D, BH (18 ton), Gas, Gaz, Wi-fi, 🗐. Entrance marked by Fl R 2s and Fl (2) G 8s lights. Local shops at Kames (2.5M).

ANCHORAGES IN LOCH FYNE

• ***Beware discarded wires on seabed throughout the area.***

In Lower L Fyne there is a ⚲ at Kilfinan Bay, ☎ (01700) 821201. In Upper Loch Fyne: 4 ⚲ for patrons of the Oyster Bar at Inverary; ⚓ SSW of pier in 4m or dry out NW of the pier; FW (on pier), ✉, 🛒, R, Bar, Gas, bus to Glasgow. On NW bank at Port Ann, Loch Gair and Minard Bay; and on SE bank at Otter Ferry, Strachur Bay (5 ⚲s off Creggans Inn, ☎ (01369) 860279) and St Catherine's.

2.9 TIDAL STREAMS AROUND THE MULL OF KINTYRE

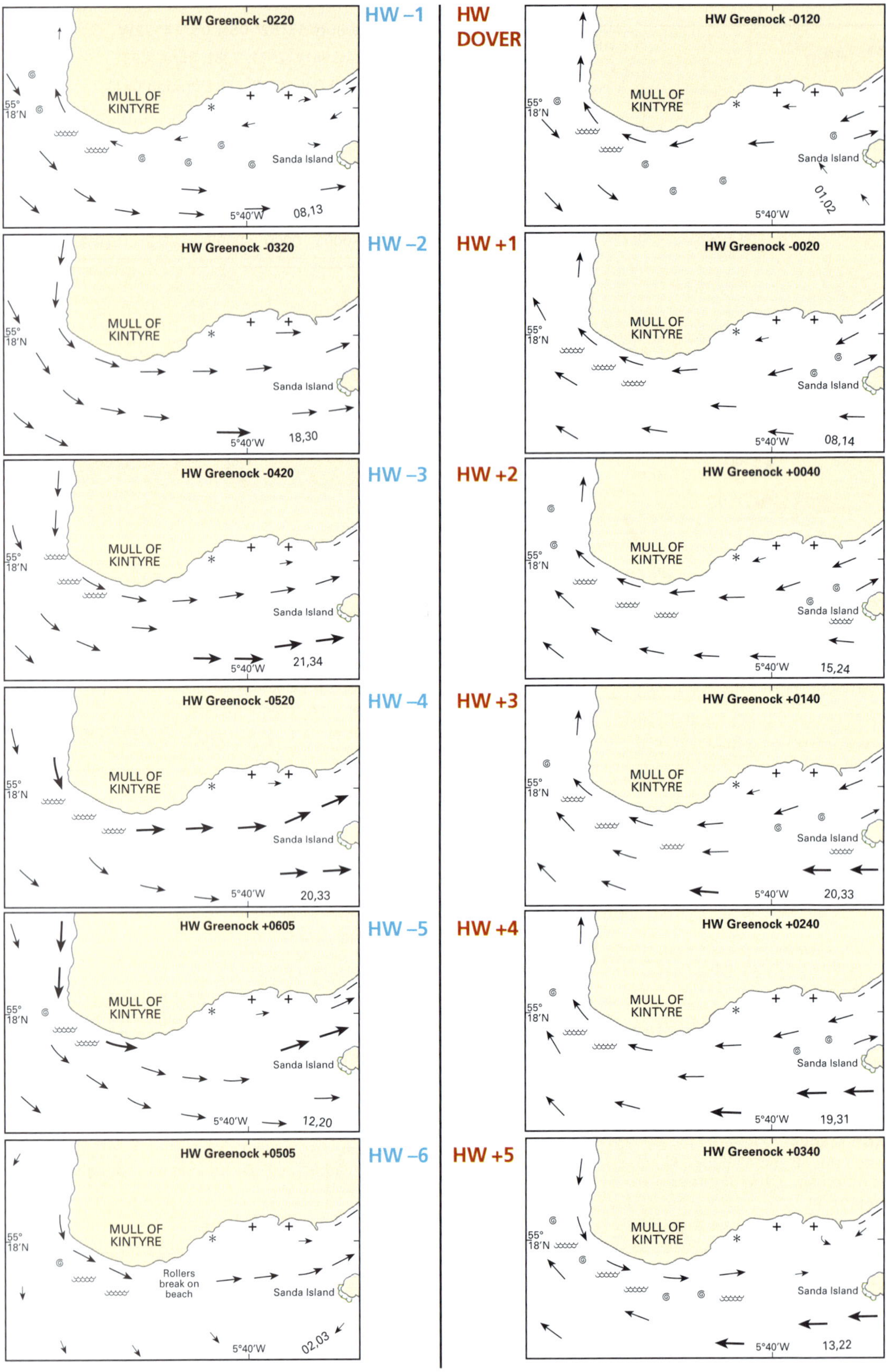

2.10 FIRTH OF CLYDE AREA

2.11 CAMPBELTOWN

Argyll & Bute **55°25'·90N 05°32'·56W** Hbr ent

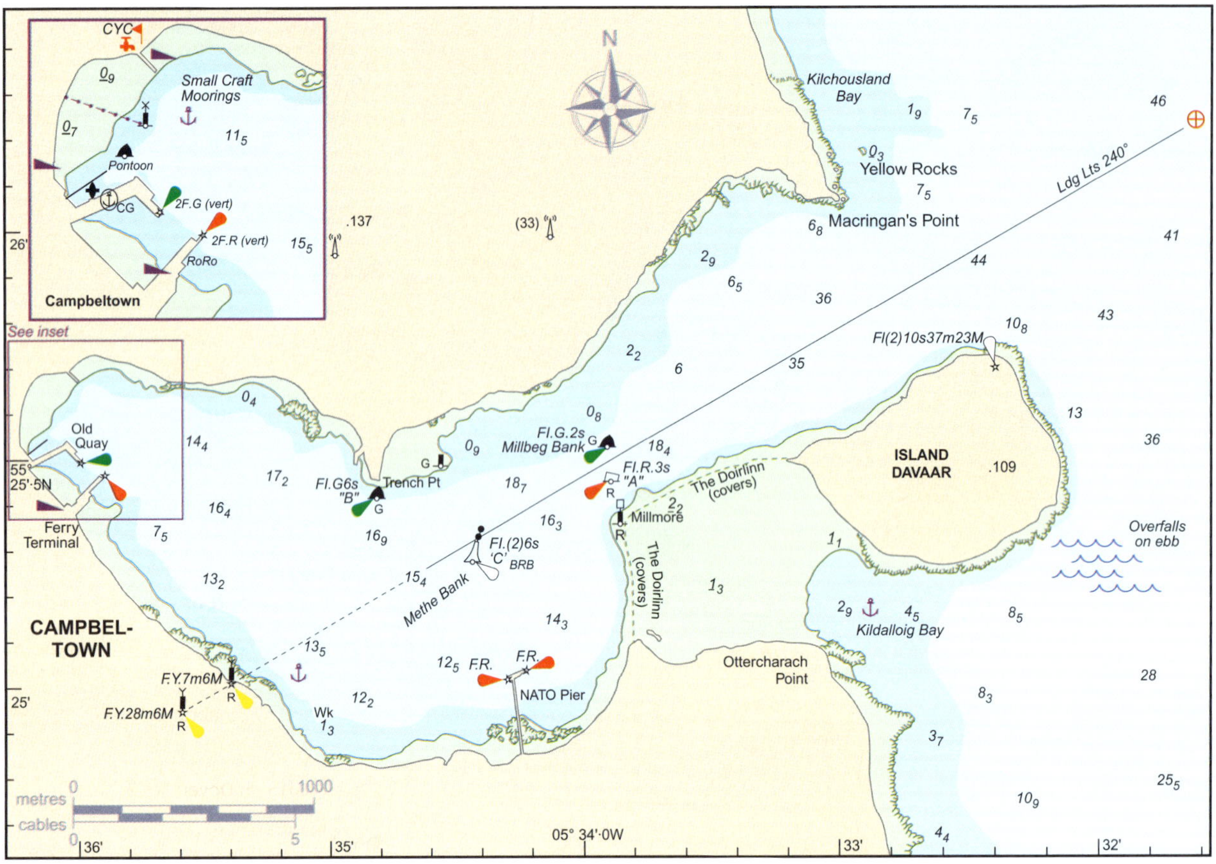

CHARTS AC 5610, 2126, 1864; Imray C63;.

TIDES +0125 Dover; ML 1·8; Duration 0630

Standard Port GREENOCK (⟶)

Times				Height (metres)			
High Water		Low Water		MHWS	MHWN	MLWN	MLWS
0000	0600	0000	0600	3·4	2·8	1·0	0·3
1200	1800	1200	1800				
Differences CAMPBELTOWN							
–0025	–0005	–0015	+0005	–0·5	–0·3	+0·1	+0·2
CARRADALE BAY							
–0015	–0005	–0005	+0005	–0·3	–0·2	+0·1	+0·1
SOUTHEND, (Mull of Kintyre)							
–0030	–0010	+0005	+0035	–1·3	–1·2	–0·5	–0·2

SHELTER Good, but gusts off the hills in strong SW'lies. Yacht pontoon (10+20Ⓥ) dredged 3·0m is close NW of Old Quay and gives excellent sheltered berthing. Yachts >12m LOA should notify ETA to Berthing Master by ☎ (below). Excellent ⚓ close E of front ldg lt (240°); ⚓ near moorings NNE of the hbr is cluttered and exposed to SE winds: use only in settled conditions and do not pick up private mooring buoys. S of Island Davaar there is a temp ⚓ in Kildalloig Bay, but no access to the loch.

NAVIGATION WPT 55°26'·24N 05°31'·61W, 240°/1·4M to first chan buoys. The ent is easily identified by radio masts N and NE of Trench Pt and conspic lt ho on N tip of Island Davaar off which streams are strong (4kn sp). Caution: The Dhorlin, a bank drying 2·5m which covers at HW, is close S of the ldg line.

LIGHTS AND MARKS See 2.4 and chartlet. Otterard Rk (3·8m depth, off chartlet, 1·5M NNE of Island Davaar), is marked by ECM lt buoy.

R/T VHF Ch 12 13 16 (Mon-Fri 0900-1700).

TELEPHONE (Code 01586) HM ☎ 552552; Yacht pontoon Berthing Master ☎ (mobile) 07798 524821; MRCC (01475) 729988; Marinecall 09068 969652; Police 862000; Dr 552105.

FACILITIES **Yacht pontoon** £1.40, FW, ⚡; **Aqualibrium** – dedicated facilities for yacht crews, opposite yacht pontoon: @, showers, toilets, ▣, R. Also swimming pool, gym, sauna, creche and library. **Old Quay** D (and by cans from across road, opposite pontoon), FW, AB, LB; **Ferry Terminal** used by commercial vessels. No berthing alongside without HM's permission. The attached public slipway has a drying out berth (with timber keel blocks and upright leaning posts) for FVs and yachts, FW, ⚡; **Campbeltown SC** Slip (dinghies), Bar, regular racing.

Town ME, ACA, C (10 ton), P & D (cans), El, CH, Ⓔ, Gas, Gaz, 🛒 (2 supermarkets), R, Bar, ✉, Ⓑ, ▣, Ⓗ, ♿ toilet about 100m from yacht pontoon, key at Tourist office or police station (H24). Bus 3/day to Glasgow, ✈ twice daily to Glasgow, ⇄ (nearest is Arrochar, 90 miles N by road). Car hire/taxi.

ADJACENT ANCHORAGE IN KILBRANNAN SOUND

CARRADALE BAY, Argyll and Bute, **55°34'·40N 05°28'·66W.** AC 5610, 2131, HW+0115 on Dover. ML 1·8m. See 2.11. Good ⚓ in 7m off Torrisdale Castle in SW corner of Carradale Bay. In N & E winds ⚓ in NE corner of bay, W of Carradale Pt 3ca E of this Pt, a PHM buoy Fl (2) R 12s marks Cruban Rk. With S & SE winds a swell sets into bay, when good shelter can be found 1M N in **Carradale Harbour** (Port Crannaich); if full of FVs, ⚓ 100m N of Hbr. Bkwtr lt, Fl R 10s 5m 6M. Piermaster ☎ (01583) 431228. Facilities: FW on pier, D (cans), Gas, 🛒, R, Bar, ✉.

2.12 LAMLASH

Isle of Arran, N Ayrshire **55°32'·00N 05°07'·06W**

CHARTS AC 5610, 2131, 2220, 1864; Imray C63.

TIDES +0115 Dover; ML no data; Duration 0635

Standard Port GREENOCK (⟶)

Times				Height (metres)			
High Water		Low Water		MHWS	MHWN	MLWN	MLWS
0000	0600	0000	0600	3·4	2·8	1·0	0·3
1200	1800	1200	1800				
Differences LAMLASH							
–0016	–0036	–0024	–0004	–0·2	–0·2	No data	
BRODICK BAY							
–0013	–0013	–0008	–0008	–0·2	–0·1	0·0	+0·1
LOCH RANZA							
–0015	–0005	–0010	–0005	–0·4	–0·3	–0·1	0·0

SHELTER Very good in all weathers. Lamlash is a natural hbr with sheltered anchorages as follows: off Lamlash except in E'lies – depth may be 20m but shoals rapidly to the W; off Kingscross Point, good except in strong N/NW winds; off the NW of Holy Island in E'lies. Ⓐ off Lamlash Pier. Dry out against pier if in need of repairs. See also Brodick 5M N, and Loch Ranza 14M N (RH col).

NAVIGATION WPT 55°32'·63N 05°03'·06W, 270°/1M to N Chan buoy (Fl R 6s).

Beware: submarines exercise frequently in this area (see 2.15), and also wreck of landing craft (charted) off farmhouse on Holy Is.

LIGHTS AND MARKS See 2.4 and chartlet.

R/T None.

TELEPHONE (Code 01770) MRCC (01475) 729988; Marinecall 09068 969652; Police 302573; Ⓗ 600777.

FACILITIES **Lamlash Old Pier** Slip (£3–£5), L, FW, CH, ⚒; **Arran YC** 25 Ⓐ £10 via: ☎ 01770 600333. **Village** (Lamlash/Brodick); ME, P & D (cans), Bar, R, 🛒, ✉, ⇌ (bus to Brodick, Ferry to Ardrossan), ✈ (Glasgow or Prestwick).

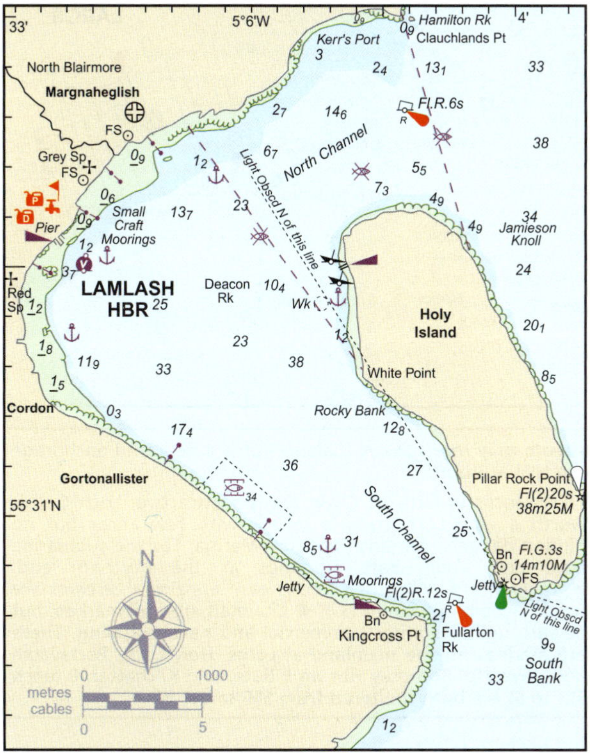

OTHER HARBOURS ON ARRAN (See AC 5610)

BRODICK, Arran, **55°35'·50N 05°08'·66W**. AC 2131, 2220, 1864. HW +0115 on Dover; ML 1·8m; Duration 0635. See 2.12. Shelter is good except in E winds. ⚓ W of ferry pier in 3m; on NW side just below the Castle in 4·5m, or further N off Merkland Pt in 3-4m. Also 5 Ⓐs. There are no navigational dangers but the bay is in a submarine exercise area; see 2.15. Only lts are 2FR (vert) 9/7m 4M on pier hd and Admiralty buoy, Fl Y 2s, 5ca N of pier. Facilities: Ⓑ, Bar, P & D (cans), FW (at pier hd), ME, ✉, R, 🛒. Ferry to Ardrossan.

LOCH RANZA, Arran, **55°42'·60N 05°17'·96W**. AC 2131, 2383, 2221. HW +0120 on Dover; ML 1·7m; Duration 0635. See 2.12. Good shelter, but swell enters loch with N'lies. The 850m mountain 4M to S causes fierce squalls in the loch with S winds. Beware Screda Reef extending SW off Newton Pt. 12 Ⓐs. ⚓ in 5m off castle (conspic); holding is suspect in soft mud. Dinghy landing pontoon at Lochranza. 2F.G lts on RoRo pier at Coillemore. S shore dries. Facilities: Bar, FW at ferry slip, ✉, R, 🛒. Ferry to Claonaig.

HARBOURS AND ANCHORAGES AROUND BUTE (Clockwise from Garroch Head, S tip of Bute) (See AC 5610)

ST NINIAN'S BAY, Bute, **55°48'·15N 05°07'·86W**. AC 2221, 2383. Inchmarnock Is gives some shelter from the W, but Sound is exposed to S'lies. At S end, beware Shearwater Rk, 0·9m, almost in mid-sound. ⚓ in about 7m, 2ca E of St Ninian's Pt; beware drying spit to S of this Pt. Or ⚓ off E side of Inchmarnock, close abeam Midpark Farm.

WEST KYLE, Bute, **55°54'N 05°12'·7W**. AC1906. Tides, see 2.16 (Tighnabruaich). On W bank PHM buoys, each Fl R 4s, mark Ardlamont Pt, Carry Pt and Rubha Ban; N of which are two Fl Y buoys (fish farms). ⚓ close off Kames or Tighnabruaich, where space allows; or in Black Farland Bay (N of Rubha Dubh). Some Ⓐs off Kames and Royal Hotels, maintained by them on a 'use at own risk basis': Kames Hotel ☎ (01700) 811489; Kyles of Bute Hotel 811350; Royal Hotel 811239; and Tighnabruaich Hotel 811615. Facilities: FW, D (cans), BY, 🛒.

CALADH HARBOUR, Argyll and Bute, **55°56'·00N, 05°11'·73W**. AC 1906. HW (Tighnabruaich) +0015 on Dover; ML 2·1m. See 2.16. Perfectly sheltered natural hbr on W side of ent to Loch Riddon. Enter Caladh Hbr to N or S of Eilean Dubh; keep to the middle of the S passage. When using the N ent, keep between R and G bns to clear a drying rk marked by perch. ⚓ in the middle of hbr clear of moorings. No facilities/stores; see West Kyle above.

LOCH RIDDON, Argyll and Bute, **55°57'N 05°11'·6W**. AC 1906. Tides, see 2.16. Water is deep for 1·3M N of Caladh and shore is steep-to; upper 1·5M of loch dries. ⚓ on W side close N of Ormidale pier; on E side at Salthouse; off Eilean Dearg (One Tree Is); and at NW corner of Fearnoch Bay.

BURNT ISLANDS, Bute, **55°55'·76N 05°10'·39W**. AC 1906. Tides, see 2.16. The three islands (Eilean Mor, Fraoich and Buidhe) straddle the East Kyle. There are 2 channels: North, between Buidhe and the other 2 islets, is narrow, short and marked by 2 SHM buoys (the NW'ly one is Fl G 3s), and one PHM buoy, Fl R 2s. South chan lies between Bute and Fraoich/Mor; it is unlit, but marked by one PHM and two SHM buoys. Depths may be less than charted. A SHM buoy, Fl G 3s, is off Rubha a' Bhodaich, 4ca ESE. Direction of buoyage is to SE. Sp streams reach 5kn in N Chan and 3kn in S Chan. ⚓ in Wreck Bay, Balnakailly Bay or in the lee of Buidhe and Mor in W'lies; also W of Colintraive Pt, clear of ferry and cables. There are 6 Ⓐs off the hotel, ☎ (01700) 841207.

KAMES BAY, Bute, **55°51'·7N 05°04'·81W**. AC 1906, 1867. Tides as Rothesay. Deep water bay, but dries 2ca off head of loch and 1ca off NW shore. AB in marina, 55 inc Ⓥ, £1.85/m, on S side of bay at Port Bannatyne. P & D in cans, CH, Gas, BY, BH (25 ton). ⚓ off Port Bannatyne (clear of moorings) W of unmarked ruined jetty. Beware drying rks 1ca off Ardbeg Pt. No lts. Facilities: BY, FW, Gas, 🛒, Bar, ✉.

KILCHATTAN BAY, Bute, **55°45'N 05°01'·1W**. AC 1907. Bay is deep, but dries 3ca off the W shore. Temp ⚓s only in offshore winds: off the village on SW side, or on N side near Kerrytonlia Pt. 4 Ⓐs for hotel guests. Rubh' an Eun Lt, Fl R 6s, is 1·1M to SSE. Facilities: FW, 🛒, ✉, bus Rothesay.

2.13 FAIRLIE QUAY

N Ayrshire **55°46'·07N 04°51'·78W**

CHARTS AC 5610, 2131, 1907, 1867; Imray C63, 2900 Series.

TIDES +0105 Dover; ML 1·9; Duration 0640

Standard Port GREENOCK (⟶)

Times				Height (metres)			
High Water		Low Water		MHWS	MHWN	MLWN	MLWS
0000	0600	0000	0600	3·4	2·8	1·0	0·3
1200	1800	1200	1800				
Differences MILLPORT							
−0005	−0025	−0025	−0005	0·0	−0·1	0·0	0·1

SHELTER Access H24 with at least 2.6m at berths. Poor shelter; pontoon subject to swell in fresh conditions and wash from passing vessels. Craft should not be left unsupervised unless calm settled weather is forecast. Cumbrae Island gives shelter from westerlies; Largs Channel is open to S or N winds.

NAVIGATION WPT 55°46'·08N 04°51'·84W. From S beware Hunterston Sands, Southannan Sands and outfalls from Hunterston Power Stn (conspic).

LIGHTS AND MARKS Lts as on chartlet. Fairlie Quay, 2 FG (vert) N & S ends of Pier.

R/T *Fairlie Quay Marina* Ch **80** M (H24).

TELEPHONE (Code 01475) Fairlie Quay 568267; MRCC 729988; Dr 673380; Ⓗ 733777; Marinecall 09068 969652; Police 674651.

FACILITIES **Fairlie Quay** Some Ⓥ £12/yacht, Fuel H24: D, SM, BY, ME, El, ⚒, BH (80 ton), CH, Gas. **Fairlie YC**; **Town** 🛒, R, Bar, ✉, Ⓑ, ⇌ (Fairlie & Largs; 50 mins to Glasgow), ✈.

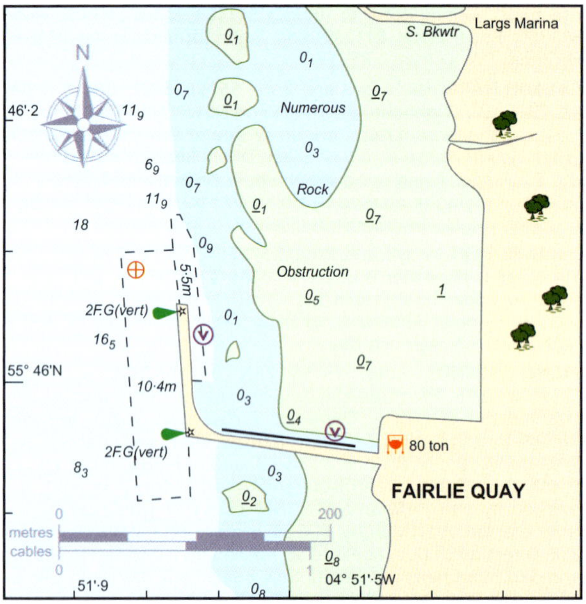

2.14 LARGS

N Ayrshire **55°46'·40N 04°51'·84W**

CHARTS AC 5610, 2131, 1907, 1867; Imray C63, 2900 Series.

TIDES +0105 Dover; ML 1·9; Duration 0640

Standard Port GREENOCK (⟶)

Times				Heights (metres)			
High Water		Low Water		MHWS	MHWN	MLWN	MLWS
0000	0600	0000	0600	3·4	2·8	1·0	0·3
1200	1800	1200	1800				
Differences MILLPORT							
−0005	−0025	−0025	−0005	0·0	−0·1	0·0	+0·1

SHELTER Excellent in Largs Yacht Haven, access all tides (2·5m in ent; 3m deep berths). 7 pontoons; Ⓥ on 'C/D'. Cumbrae Is gives shelter from W'lies; Largs Chan is open to S or N winds.

NAVIGATION WPT 55°46'·40N 04°51'·84W, SWM lt buoy, off ent. From S beware Hunterston Sands, Southannan Sands and outfalls from Hunterston Power Stn (conspic). From the S bkwtr to Fairlie Quay is a restricted, no ⚓ area.

LIGHTS AND MARKS 'Pencil' monument (12m) conspic 4ca N of ent. Lts as on chartlet. Largs Pier, 2 FG (vert) when vessel expected.

R/T *Largs Yacht Haven* Ch **80** M (H24).

TELEPHONE (Code 01475) Largs Yacht Haven 675333, www.yachthavens.com; Largs SC 670000; MRCC 729988; Dr 673380; Ⓗ 733777; Marinecall 09068 969652; Police 674651.

FACILITIES **Largs Yacht Haven** (755, some Ⓥ), £2.58, Wi-fi, Fuel H24: D, P, ♿, SM, BY, C (17 ton), ME, El, ⚒, BH (70 ton), Divers, Ⓔ, CH, 🗑, Ice, Gas, Gaz, Slip (access H24), Bar, R. **Town** 🛒, R, Bar, ✉, Ⓑ, ⇌ (dep Largs every H −10; 50 mins to Glasgow), ✈.

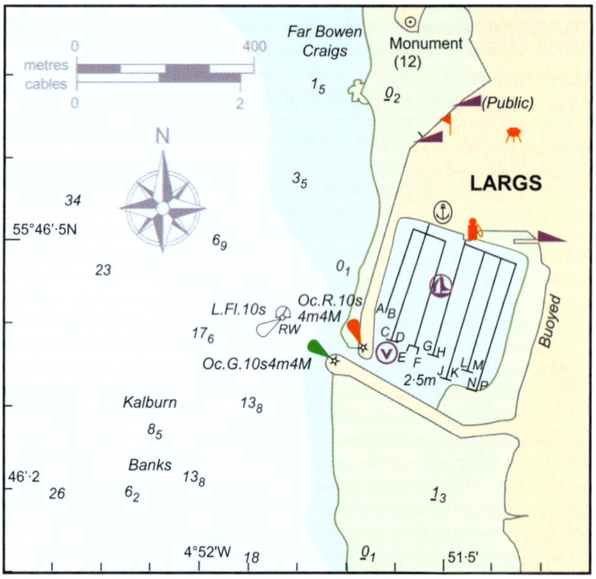

ARRAN, BUTE AND FIRTH OF CLYDE

(AC1906, 1907) Arran's mountains tend to cause squalls or calms, but there are good anchorages at Lamlash, Brodick and Loch Ranza. Sannox Rock (depth 1·5m) is 2½ca off Arran coast 8M N of Lamlash. 1ca off W side of Inchmarnock is Tra na-h-uil, a rock drying 1·5m. In Inchmarnock Sound, Shearwater Rk (depth 0·9m) lies in centre of S entrance.

The Kyles of Bute are attractive channels N of Bute, and straightforward apart from the Burnt Islands where it is best to take the north channel, narrow but well buoyed, passing between Eilean Buidhe and Eilean Fraoich/Eilean Mor. ►*Spring stream may reach 5kn.*◄ Caladh Hbr is a beautiful anchorage 7ca NW of Burnt Is.

The N lochs in Firth of Clyde are less attractive. Loch Goil is worth a visit; Loch Long is squally with few anchs but no hidden dangers; Gareloch has Rhu Marina, Faslane submarine base and small craft moorings at the northern end. ►*Navigation in Firth of Clyde is easy since tidal streams are weak, seldom exceeding 1kn.*◄ Channels are well marked; but beware unlit moorings commercial and naval shipping. There are marinas on the mainland at Largs, Holy Loch, Portavadie and Inverkip. Rothesay Hbr on E Bute, and Kilchattan B (anch 6M to S) are both sheltered from SSE to WNW.

2.15 SUBMARINE EXERCISE AREAS

Submarines on the surface and at periscope depth keep a constant listening watch on Ch 16. Submarines on the surface will comply strictly with IRPCS; submarines at periscope depth will not close to within 1500 yds of a FV without her express agreement. See 3.13.1 for more guidance.

Details of submarine activity in the Exercise Areas between Barra and the Isle of Man are broadcast by MRCCs on a specified VHF Ch after an initial announcement on Ch 16 at the following times:

Stornoway	0710	1910	UT
Clyde	0810	2010	UT
Belfast	0710	1910	UT

The areas are referred to by the names given in the table on the right, rather than by the numbers indicated on the chartlet on Page 490. For Areas 1–26 (North of Mull), see 1.21.

General information on SUBFACTS is also broadcast twice daily at 0620 & 1820 UT on Navtex. Stornoway and Clyde MRCCs will provide SUBFACTS on request; call on Ch 16.

A 'Fisherman's hotline' (☎ (01436) 677201) is available on a 24 hour basis and may be used for any queries relating to SUBFACTS from any mariner.

22	Barra	**52**	Boyle
23	Hebrides Central	**53**	Orsay
24	Hawes	**54**	Islay
25	Eigg	**55**	Otter
26	Hebrides South	**56**	Gigha
27	Ford	**57**	Earadale
28	Tiree	**58**	Lochranza
29	Staffa	**59**	Davaar
30	Mackenzie	**60**	Brodick
31	Mull	**61**	Irvine
32	Linnhe	**62**	Lamlash
33	Jura Sound	**63**	Ayr
34	Fyne	**64**	Skerries
35	Minard	**65**	Rathlin
36	Tarbert	**66**	Kintyre
37	Skipness	**67**	Sanda
38	West Kyle	**68**	Stafnish
39	Striven	**69**	Pladda
40	East Kyle	**70**	Turnberry
41	Goil	**71**	Torr
42	Long	**72**	Mermaid
43	Cove	**73**	Ailsa
44	Gareloch	**74**	Maiden
45	Rosneath	**75**	Corsewall
46	Cumbrae	**76**	Ballantrae
47	Garroch	**77**	Magee
48	Laggan	**78**	Londonderry
49	Blackstone	**79**	Beaufort
50	Place	**80**	Ardglass
51	Colonsay	**81**	Peel

2.16 ROTHESAY

Isle of Bute, Argyll and Bute **55°50´·32N 05°03´·08W**

CHARTS AC 5610, 2131, 1907, 1906, 1867; Imray C63, 2900 Series;.

TIDES +0100 Dover; ML 1·9; Duration 0640

Standard Port GREENOCK (⟶)

Times				Height (metres)			
High Water		Low Water		MHWS	MHWN	MLWN	MLWS
0000	0600	0000	0600	3·4	2·8	1·0	0·3
1200	1800	1200	1800				
Differences ROTHESAY BAY							
−0020	−0015	−0010	−0002	+0·2	+0·2	+0·2	+0·2
RUBHA BHODACH (Burnt Is)							
−0020	−0010	−0007	−0007	−0·2	−0·1	+0·2	+0·2
TIGHNABRUAICH							
+0007	−0010	−0002	−0015	0·0	+0·2	+0·4	+0·5

SHELTER Good in Outer and Inner Harbours, and on pontoons S of West Arm, but beware of very strong easterly flow towards the rocks on the E side of the harbour due to wash during ferry manoeuvres (and whilst berthed). No berthing on north and east faces of Main Pier. 20 🅥, and good ⚓ off Isle of Bute SC, in Rothesay Bay. Exposed to N/NE when Kyles of Bute or Kames Bay offer better shelter.

NAVIGATION WPT 55°51´·00N 05°02´·76W, 194°/0·69M to Outer hbr ent. From E keep 1ca off Bogany Pt PHM buoy, Fl R 4s. Call HM for bridge openings to Inner Harbour.

LIGHTS AND MARKS Lts as chartlet, hard to see against shore lts. Conspicuous church spire leads 190° to outer hbr; at night beware large, unlit Admiralty buoy 'MK' on this bearing 5½ca from harbour. 3½ca N of hbr is Rothesay 'A' mooring buoy, Fl Y 2s.

R/T *Bute Berthing* Ch 16 **M**; *Rothesay Harbour* Ch **16**.

TELEPHONE (Code 01700) HM 503842; Bute Berthing Co 07799

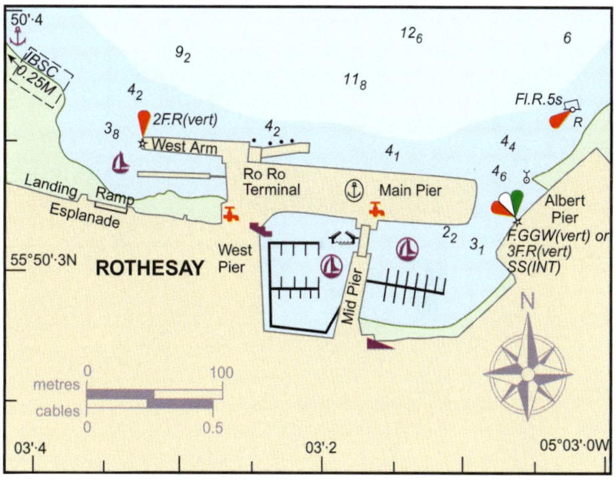

724225; MRCC (01475) 729988; Marinecall 09068 969652; Police 894000; Dr 503985; Ⓗ 503938.

FACILITIES 60 🅥 AB (Bute Berthing Co) £14 for 8m LOA, £19 for 11m LOA, Slip, L, FW, ME, ♿; showers/toilets on Rothesay Pier; D by arrangement week days only (min 200 galls). 🅥s £7/night. **Town** P & D (closes 1800), @ (0900-1700), R, Bar, ✉, Ⓑ, ⇌ (Ferry to Wemyss Bay), ✈ (Glasgow).

GREAT CUMBRAE ISLAND

MILLPORT, Great Cumbrae, N Ayrshire, **55°45´·00N 04°55´·82W**. AC 5610, 1867, 1907. HW +0100 on Dover; ML 1·9m; Duration 0640. See 2.16. Good shelter, except in S'lies. ⚓ in approx 3m S of pier or E of the Eileans. 12 🅥s 1½ca SSE of pier. Ldg marks: pier hd on with ✠ twr 333°; or ldg lts 333°, both FR 7/9m 5M, between the Spoig and the Eileans, QG. Unmarked, drying rk is close E of ldg line. HM ☎ (01475) 530826. **Town** CH, Bar, Gas, D, P, FW, ✉, R, Slip. Possible temporary AB on pontoon belonging to SportScotland off NE of island (approx 55°47´·1N 04°53´·8W) in 3.5m–4.5m; no services.

WGS84 DATUM

SUBMARINE EXERCISE AREA MAP

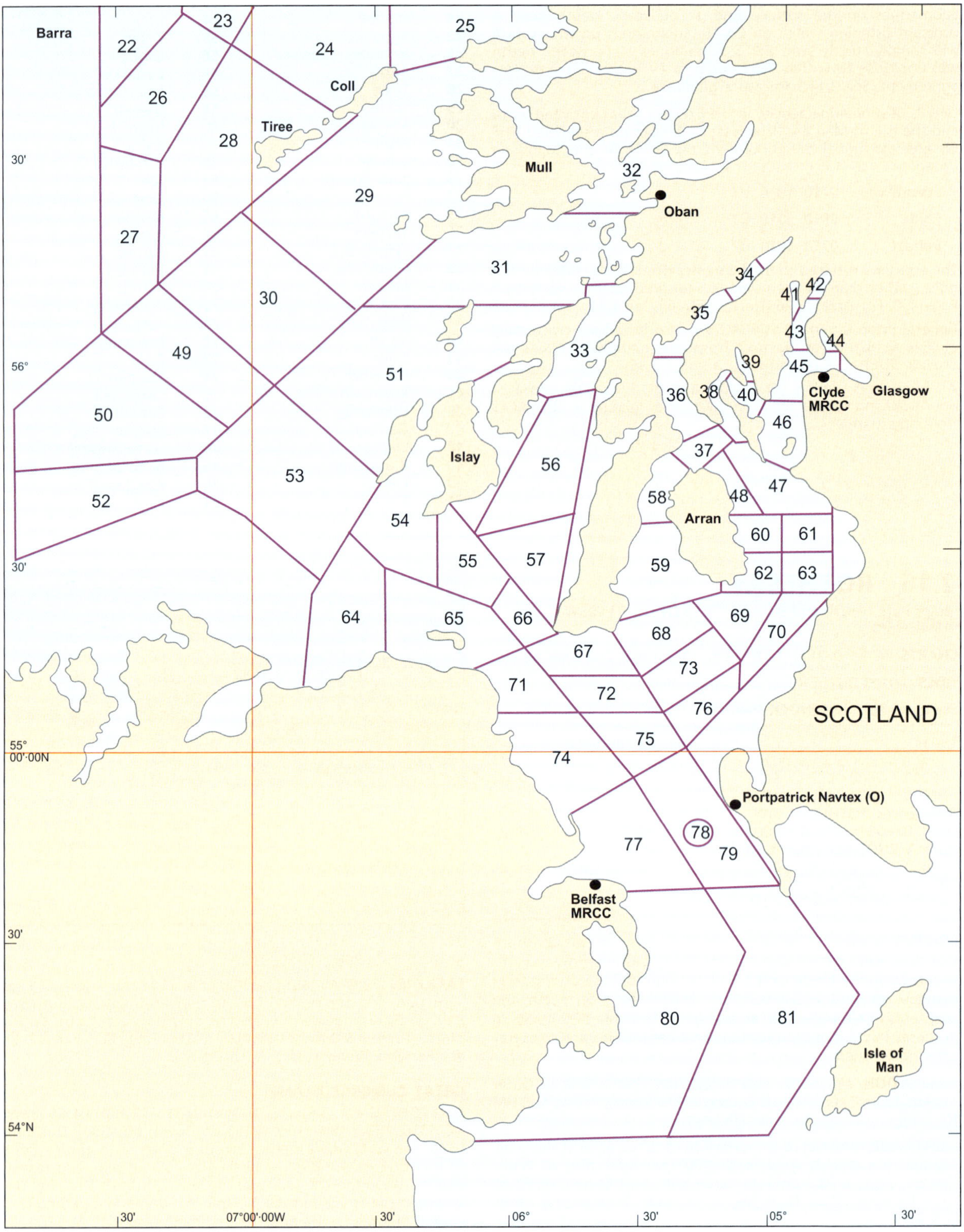

2.17 INVERKIP (KIP MARINA)

Inverclyde **55°54'·50N 04°53'·00W**

CHARTS AC 5610, 2131, 1907; Imray C63, 2900 Series.

TIDES +0110 Dover; ML 1·8; Duration 0640

Standard Port GREENOCK (⟶)

Times				Height (metres)			
High Water		Low Water		MHWS	MHWN	MLWN	MLWS
0000	0600	0000	0600	3·4	2·8	1·0	0·3
1200	1800	1200	1800				
Differences WEMYSS BAY							
–0005	–0005	–0005	–0005	0·0	0·0	+0·1	+0·1

SHELTER Excellent inside marina. Chan and marina are dredged 3·5m; accessible H24. Inverkip Bay is exposed to SW/NW winds.

NAVIGATION WPT 55°54'·49N 04°52'·95W, Kip SHM buoy, Fl G 5s, at ent to buoyed chan; beware shifting bank to the N.

LIGHTS AND MARKS SHM 55°54'·55N 04°54'·47W Fl G 1·06M 093° to entr which is ½M N of conspic chmy (238m). SPM buoy marks sewer outfall off Ardgowan Pt. From Kip SHM buoy, 3 SHM and 3 PHM buoys mark 365m long appr chan.

R/T *Kip Marina* Ch **80** M (H24). *Clydeport Estuary Radio* VHF Ch **12** 16 (H24). Info on weather and traffic available on request.

TELEPHONE (Code 01475) MRCC 729988; Marinecall 09068 969652; Police 521222; Dr 520248; Ⓗ 33777.

FACILITIES **Kip Marina** ☎ 521485, www.scottishmarinas.co.uk; (700 + Ⓥ) £2.15, £12 <5hrs), Wi-fi, D, P (cans), ⚒, C, ME, El, Ⓔ, SM, CH, Diver, BH (50 ton), 🛒, R, Bar, ⊡, Gas, Gaz, YC. **Town** ✉, Ⓑ (Gourock), ⇌, ✈ (Glasgow).

ADJACENT ANCHORAGE

DUNOON, Argyll and Bute, **55°56'·70N 04°55'·20W**. AC 5610, 2131, 1907, 1994. Use Greenock tides. Temp ⚓ in West or East Bays (S and N of Dunoon Pt). The former is open to the S; the latter more shoal. Six HIE Ⓥs (free, but condition uncertain) in each bay; call ☎ (01369) 703785. The Gantocks, drying rks 3ca SE of Dunoon Pt, have W ○ bn tr, Fl R 6s 12m 6M. 2FR (vert) on ferry pier. Facilities: P & D (cans), 🛒, R, Bar, ✉, Gas, ferry to Gourock. 3 Ⓥs off Inellan, 3·7M S of Dunoon, ☎ (01369) 830445.

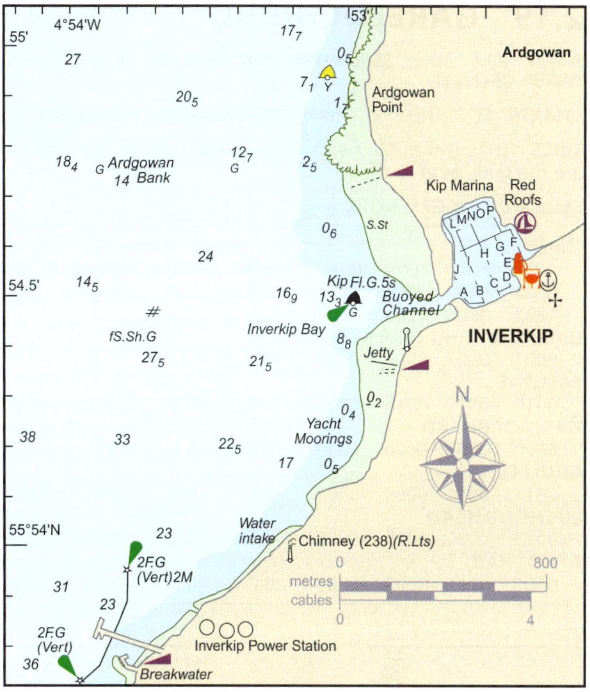

ANCHORAGE IN THE UPPER FIRTH OF CLYDE

GOUROCK, Inverclyde, **55°58'·00N 04°49'·00W**. AC 5610, 2131, 1994, Imray C63, 2900 Series; OS 63. Use Greenock tides. ⚓ in West Bay, beware of moorings. It is exposed in NW/NE'lies. Beware foul ground in Gourock Bay. No navigational dangers, but much shipping and ferries in the Clyde. The S edge of the Firth of Clyde recommended channel lies 2ca N of Kempock Pt. The pier at the S end of Gourock Bay is disused and unsafe. Facilities: Royal Gourock YC ☎ 632983 M, L, FW, ME, Slip, 🛒, R, Bar. Services: SM. Town: P, D (cans), 🛒, R, Bar, ✉, Ⓑ, ⇌, Ferry (to Dunoon) ✈ (Glasgow).

2.18 HOLY LOCH

Argyll **55°59'·03N 04°56'·82W**

CHARTS AC 5610, 2131, 1994; Imray C63, 2900 Series.

TIDES +0122 Dover; ML 2·0; Duration 0640

Standard Port GREENOCK (⟶)

SHELTER Good, but exposed to to E/NE.

NAVIGATION WPT 55°59'·03N 04°55'·75W 270° to marina ent 0.60M. No offshore dangers. Holy Loch is controlled by QHM Clyde but navigation is not restricted; keep well clear of ferries when entering or leaving the loch.

LIGHTS AND MARKS No 30 SCM 55°58'·75N 04°53'·82W off Strone Pt. 2FR at SE end of pier. Marina floodlit.

R/T *Holy Loch Marina* Ch 80 M.

TELEPHONE (Code 01369) MRCC (01475) 729988; Marinecall 09068 969652; Police 702222; Dr 703279; Ⓗ 704341.

FACILITIES **Marina** (270 + Ⓥ in 3m) £2.00, short stay £5. ☎ 701800, www.holylochmarina. co.uk, D, P, C, BH (25 ton), BY, CH, Gas, Wi-fi, ⊡ ✕. Possible AB on breakwater pontoon for larger yachts in depth >5m, but open to the E. **Holy Loch SC** ☎ 702707.

Sandbank (town) PO, 🛒. Ferries from Sandbank to Gourock connecting with trains and coaches to Glasgow Airport.

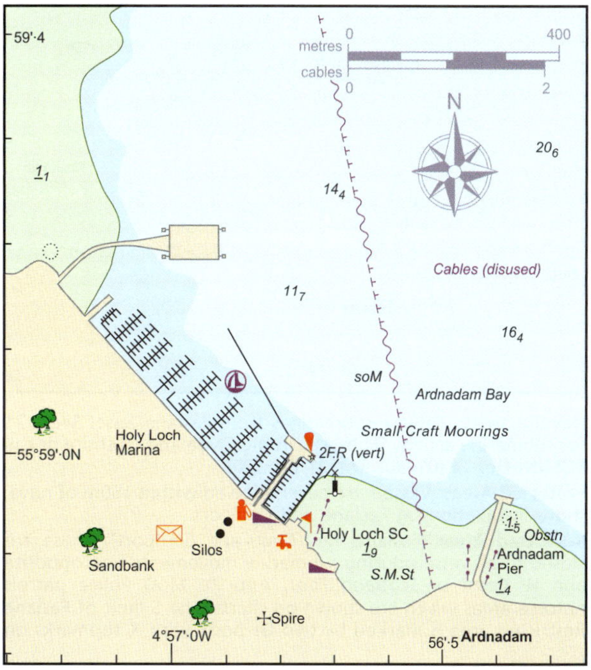

2.19 GARELOCH/RHU

Argyll and Bute **56°00'·70N 04°46'·57W** (Rhu Marina)

CHARTS AC 5610, 2131, 1994, 2000; Imray C63, 2900 Series.

TIDES +0110 Dover; ML 1·9; Duration 0640. Tides at Helensburgh are the same as at Greenock

Standard Port GREENOCK (⟶)

Times				Height (metres)			
High Water		Low Water		MHWS	MHWN	MLWN	MLWS
0000	0600	0000	0600	3·4	2·8	1·0	0·3
1200	1800	1200	1800				
Differences RHU MARINA							
−0007	−0007	−0007	−0007	−0·1	−0·1	−0·1	−0·2
FASLANE							
−0010	−0010	−0010	−0010	0·0	0·0	−0·1	−0·2
GARELOCHHEAD							
0000	0000	0000	0000	0·0	0·0	0·0	−0·1
COULPORT							
−0011	−0011	−0008	−0008	0·0	0·0	0·0	0·0
LOCHGOILHEAD							
+0015	0000	−0005	−0005	−0·2	−0·3	−0·3	−0·3
ARROCHAR							
−0005	−0005	−0005	−0005	0·0	0·0	−0·1	−0·1

BYELAWS Loch Long and Gareloch are Dockyard Ports under the jurisdiction of the Queen's Harbour Master. All submarines and other warships at anchor or underway have an Exclusion Zone around them enforced by MOD Police.

SHELTER Rhu Marina is entered between low, floating wavebreaks on its S and W sides, not easy to find at night; beware cross-tides. On E/SE sides a rock bkwtr 1m above MHWS protects from strong SE'lies. Helensburgh Pier is a temp'y drying berth, rather exposed, used by occas steamers. ⚓ E of marina or in Rosneath Bay. Moorings N of the narrows at Stroul B & Clynder; and at the head of the loch. Clyde Naval Base at Faslane must be avoided by yachts.

NAVIGATION WPT 55°59'·29N 04°45'·26W, 356°/1·3M to bn No 7. Beaches between Cairndhu Pt and Helensburgh Pier are strewn with large boulders above/below MLWS. Gareloch ent is via Rhu Narrows. Beware submerged breakwater between new breakwater and Fl G SHM buoy S of marina entrance. There are large unlit MoD buoys and barges off W shore of Gareloch; for Garelochhead keep to W shore until well clear of Faslane Naval Base.

LIGHTS AND MARKS Ldg/dir lts into Gareloch 356°, 318°, 295°, 329° and 331°. Conspic ✠ tr at Rhu.

R/T VHF Ch 16. Rhu Marina Ch **80** M (H24 in season).

TELEPHONE (Code 01436) Marina 820238; Queen's HM 674321; MRCC (01475) 729014; Marinecall 09068 969652; Police 672141; Ⓗ (01389) 754121; Dr 672277.

FACILITIES **Rhu Marina** (200) ☎ 820238, AB £2.20 (£11 for 5Hrs), @, D, M, BH (35 ton), CH, ME, El, Slip, M, C hire, Gas, Gaz, Wi-fi; **Royal Northern and Clyde YC** ☎ 820322. Possible Øs, L, R, Bar; **Helensburgh SC** ☎ 672778 Slip (dinghies) L, FW; **Town** (1M) all services, ⇌, ✈ (Glasgow). **DRB Marine** (Rosneath) ☎ 831231, no AB but some Øs, BH (40 ton), Slip, Wi-fi (ashore only).

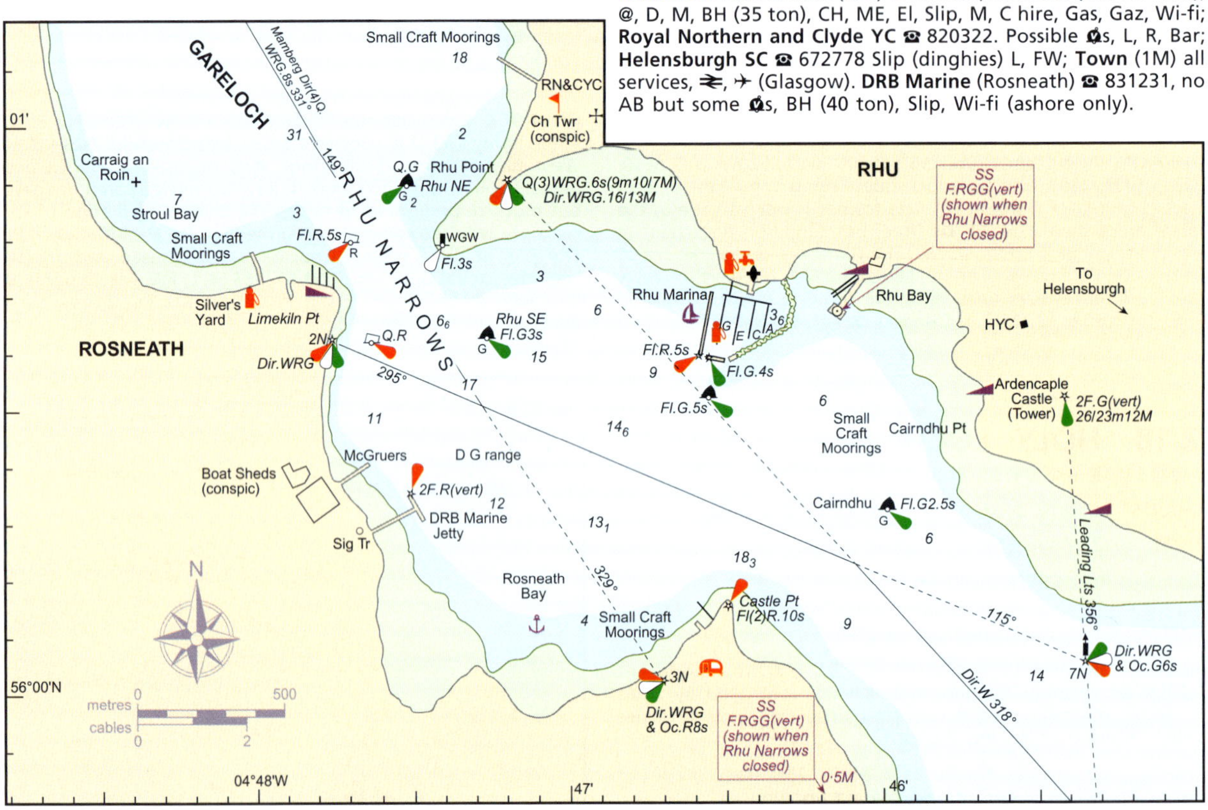

Naval activity: Beware submarines from Faslane Base. See 2.21 for submarine activity (Subfacts) in the Clyde and offshore or call FOSNNI Ops ☎ (01436) 674321 Ext 3206.

Protected Areas: Vessels are never allowed within 150m of naval shore installations at Faslane and Coulport.

Restricted Areas (Faslane, Rhu Chan and Coulport): These are closed to all vessels during submarine movements (see opposite and *W Coast of Scotland Pilot*, App 2). MoD Police patrols enforce areas which are shown on charts. The S limit of Faslane Restricted area is marked by two Or posts with X topmarks on Shandon foreshore. The W limit is marked by Iso WRG 4s, vis W356°-006°, at Gareloch Oil fuel depot N jetty. The following signals are shown when restrictions are in force:

Entrance to Gareloch
Day & Night: ● ● ● (vert), supplemented by R flag with W diagonal bar.

Faslane and Coulport
Day & Night: ● ● ● (vert), supplemented by International Code pendant over pendant Nine.

LOCH LONG/LOCH GOIL, Argyll and Bute, approx 56°00′N 04°52′·5W to 56°12′·00N 04°45′·00W. AC *5610,* 3746. Tides: See 2.19 for differences. ML 1·7m; Duration 0645.

SHELTER Loch Long is about 15M long. Temp ⚓s (south to north)at: Cove, Blairmore (not in S'lies), Ardentinny, Portincaple, Coilessan (about 1M S of Ardgartan Pt), and near head of loch (Arrochar) on either shore. In Loch Goil ⚓ at Swines Hole and off Carrick Castle (S of the pier, in N'lies a swell builds). Avoid ⚓ near Douglas Pier. The head of the loch is crowded with private/dinghy moorings, and is either too steep-to or too shallow to ⚓. The loch is frequently closed to navigation due to the trial range half way down.

LIGHTS Coulport Jetty, 2FG (vert) each end and two Fl G 12s on N jetty; Port Dornaige Fl 6s 8m 11M, vis 026°-206°; Dog Rock (Carraig nan Ron) Fl 2s 11M; Finnart Oil Terminal has FG lts and ldg lts 031° QW/FW on Cnap Pt. Upper Loch Long is unlit. Loch Goil ent is marked by 2 PHM buoys (Fl R 3s and QR), a SHM buoy (QG) and ldg lts 318°: front (The Perch) Dir FWRG and Fl R 3s; rear FW. Rubha Ardnahein Fl R5s.

FACILITIES Loch Long (Cove), Cove SC, FW, Bar; 🛒, FW (pier); (Portincaple) shops, hotel, ✉, FW; (Ardentinny) shop, 🛒, R, hotel, M; (Blairmore) shops, ✉, Slip, FW; (Arrochar) shops, hotel, FW, Gas, ✉. Loch Goil (Carrick Castle) has one blue 🅜 (£10/night, max 15 ton) ✉, WC, shop; (Lochgoilhead) has a store, ✉, FW, Gas.

2.20 DUMBARTON (SANDPOINT) AND BOWLING HARBOUR

Dunbartonshire **55°56′·50N 04°34′·27W** ✿✿✿◊✿

CHARTS AC 5610, 2131, 1994, 2007*:* BW Skipper's Guide for Forth and Clyde Canal, BW Skipper's Brief for Lowland Canals; Imray 63, 2900 Series.

TIDES +0122 Dover; ML 2·0; Duration 0640

Standard Port GREENOCK (⟶)

Times				Height (metres)			
High Water		Low Water		MHWS	MHWN	MLWN	MLWS
0000	0600	0000	0600	3·4	2·8	1·0	0·3
1200	1800	1200	1800				
Differences PORT GLASGOW (55°56′·10N 04°40′·50W)							
+0010	+0005	+0010	+0020	+0·2	+0·1	0·0	0·0
DUMBARTON							
+0015	+0010	+0020	+0040	+0·4	+0·3	+0·1	0·0
BOWLING							
+0020	+0010	+0030	+0055	+0·6	+0·5	+0·3	+0·1
RENFREW							
+0025	+0015	+0035	+0100	+0·9	+0·8	+0·5	+0·2
GLASGOW							
+0025	+0015	+0035	+0105	+1·3	+1·2	+0·6	+0·4

SHELTER Good at Dumbarton (Sandpoint Marina) and Bowling Hbr 3M further east. Hbrs are controlled by Clyde Port Authority.

NAVIGATION WPT 55°57′·61N 04°45′·96W, No 1 SHM buoy, 2ca NNW of Clydeport container terminal (conspic blue cranes). No navigational dangers, but much shipping and ferries in the Clyde. Keep just inboard of chan lateral marks as depths shoal rapidly outboard. For Dumbarton cross the river at 90° abeam No 39 SHM buoy. Depths in R Leven may be less than charted. For Bowling Hbr cross abeam No 45 SHM buoy. Follow ldg marks as charted.

LIGHTS AND MARKS The R Clyde is well buoyed/lit.

R/T Call *Clydeport Estuary Radio* Ch **12** 16 (H24) when abm No 1 buoy E-bound. Weather and traffic info on request. Marina Ch M. Bowling lockkeeper Ch 74, HW±2.

TELEPHONE (Codes: Greenock 01475; Glasgow 0141, followed by 7 digit Tel No). HM 725775; Estuary Control 726221; British Waterways Board 332 6936; MRCC 729988; Police 01389 822000; Dr 634617; Marinecall 09068 969652; Ⓗ 01389 754121.

FACILITIES Sandpoint Marina 55°56′·48N 04°34′·07W. ☎ 01389 762396/731500. Limited visitors berths, £10 per night. VHF Ch M. BH (40 ton), Slip, BY, D (can), CH ☎ 01389 742438. **Town** 🛒, R, Bar, Ⓑ, ✉, ⇌ 30 mins to Glasgow.

Bowling Basin 55°55′·8N 04°29′·0W, W end of Forth & Clyde Canal, ☎ 01389 877969. Lock access HW±2 to Basin and Canal. For lock hrs call VHF Ch 74 asap for latest schedule. *Skipper's Brief* essential obtain from www.scottishcanals.co.uk. **Facilities** AB £30/night, FW, Showers, WC, D by prior notice, C (mast), Wi-fi. **Town** P&D (cans), 🛒, R, Bar, ✉, Ⓑ, ⇌ .

There are no yachting facilities on R Clyde E of Bowling Basin.

GLASGOW 55°55′·94N 04°34′·25W; Clyde Yacht Clubs Association is at 8 St James St, Paisley. ☎ 8878296. Clyde Cruising Club is at Suite 408, Pentagon Centre, 36 Washington Street, Glasgow G3 8AZ, ☎ 221 2774. **Services:** ACA, CH.

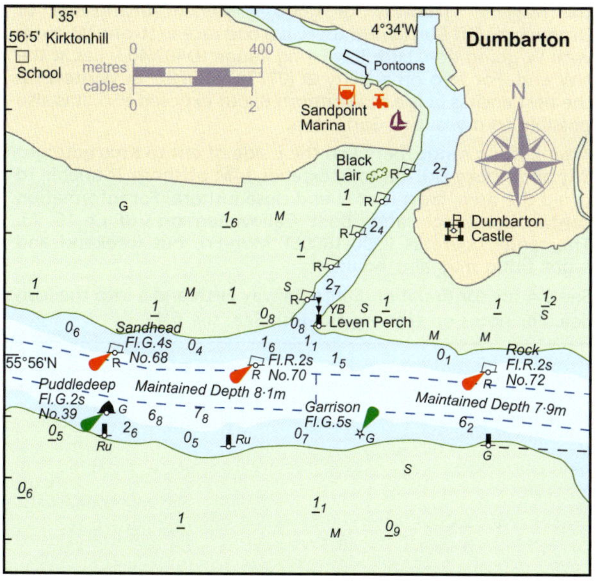

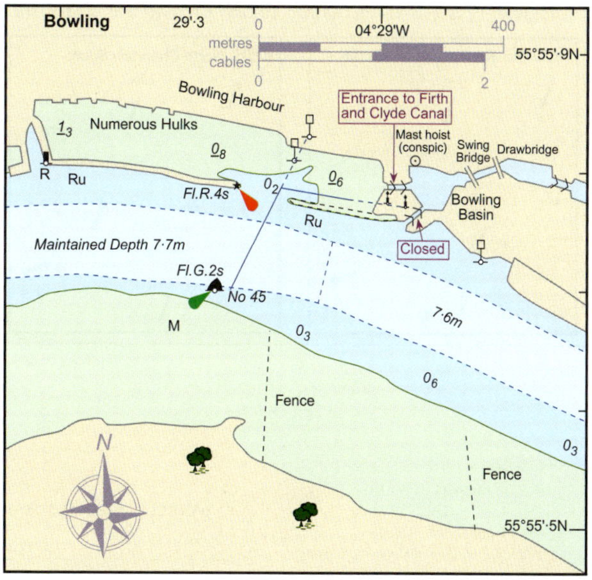

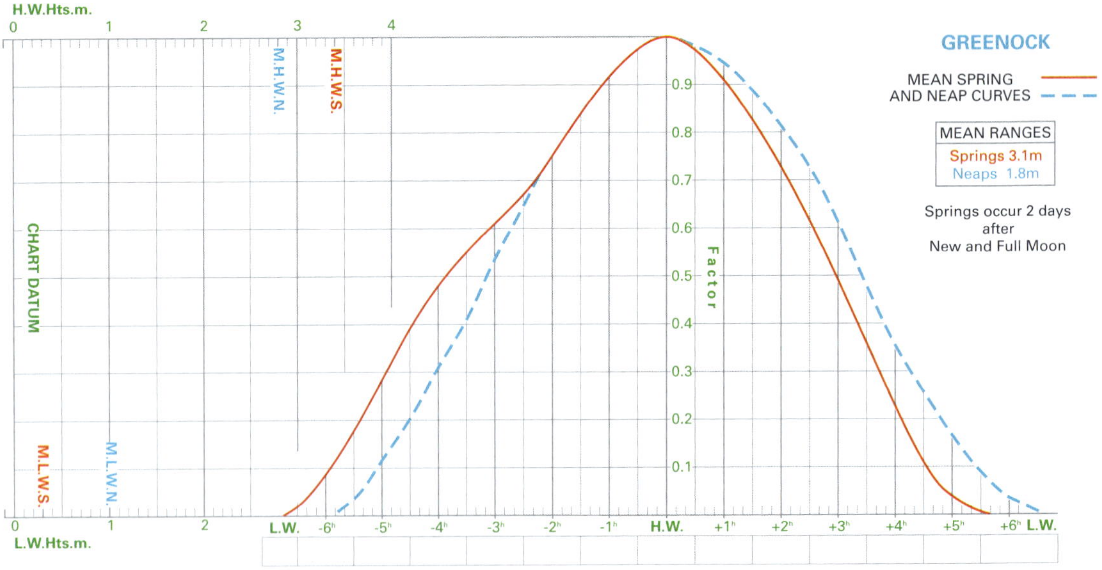

FIRTH OF CLYDE TO MULL OF GALLOWAY

(AC 2131, 2126, 2199, 2198) Further S the coast is less inviting, with mostly commercial hbrs until reaching Ardrossan and Troon, NW of which there are various dangers: beware Troon Rk (depth 5·6m, but sea can break), Lappock Rk (dries 0·6m, marked by bn), and Mill Rk (dries 0·4m, buoyed). Lady Isle (lt, racon), shoal to NE, is 2M WSW of Troon.

▶ *There is a severe race off Bennane Hd (8M SSE of Ailsa Craig, conspic) when tide is running strongly.*◀ Loch Ryan offers little for yachtsmen but there is anch S of Kirkcolm Pt, inside the drying spit which runs in SE direction 1·5M from the point. There is also a useful anch in Lady Bay, sheltered except from NE. Portpatrick is a useful passage hbr, but not in onshore winds.

▶ ***North Channel South*** *(6.4 for N.Chan N): Irish coast – the S-going flood begins HW Belfast –0600 (HW Dover +0610). Counter tide off Donaghadee and Island Magee for last 3 hrs of flood. Scottish coast between Corsewall Pt and Mull of Galloway – HW Greenock +0310 (HW Dover +0430). Sp rate off Corsewall Pt is 2–3kn, increasing* ***to 5kn off and S of Black Hd.***

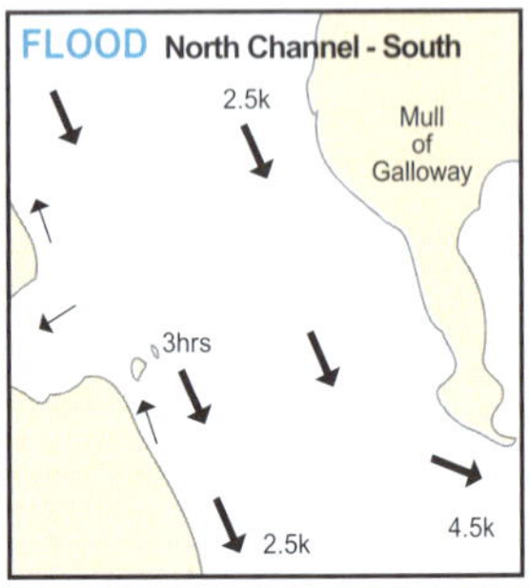

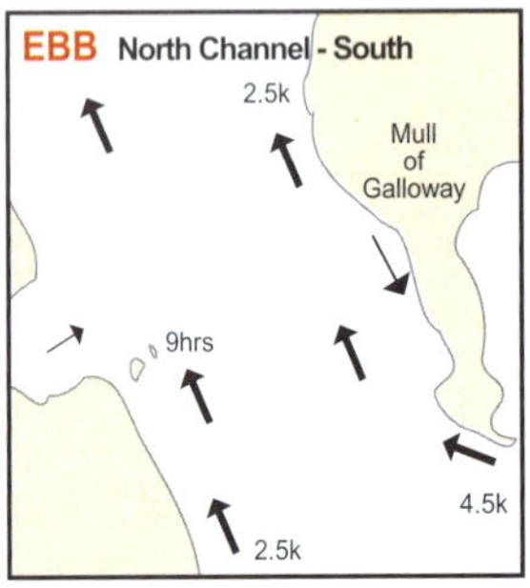

Races occur off Copeland Is. Morroch B, Money Hd Mull of Logan and Mull of Galloway.

Irish coast – N-going ebb begins at HW Belfast (HW Dover –0015). Scottish coast – HW Greenock –0250 (HW Dover –0130). Races off Copeland Is and Mull of Galloway. Flood begins 2 hrs early close inshore N of Mull of Galloway. A race SSE of Crammag Hd is bad if wind against tide. Mull of Galloway (lt) is a high (82m), steep-to headland with ***a dangerous race extending nearly 3M to S.*** *On E-going stream it extends NNE into Luce B; on W-going stream it extends SW and W. Give the race a wide berth, or pass close inshore at slack water nps and calm weather. SW wind >F4 against W-going stream, do not attempt inshore route.*◀

SCOTLAND – SW COAST

The Scares, two groups of rocks, lie at the mouth of Luce Bay which elsewhere is clear more than 3ca offshore; but the whole bay is occupied by a practice bombing range, marked by 12 DZ SPM lt buoys. Good anch at E Tarbert B to await the tide around the Mull of Galloway, or good shelter in drying hbr of Drummore. Off Burrow Hd there is a bad race in strong W winds with W-going tide. Luce Bay Firing Range (D402/403) lies at the NW end. For info on activity ☎ (01776) 888792. In Wigtown B the best anch is in Isle of Whithorn B, but exposed to S. It is also possible to dry out in Garlieston.

A tank firing range, between the E side of ent to Kirkcudbright Bay and Abbey Hd, 4M to E, extends 14M offshore. If unable to avoid the area, cross it at N end close inshore. For information contact the Range safety boat 'Gallovidian' on VHF Ch 16, 73. The range operates 0900-1600LT Mon-Fri, but weekend and night firing may also occur.

See 3.4 for continuation E into Solway Firth and S into the Irish Sea. For notes on crossing the Irish Sea, see 6.4.

TIME ZONE (UT)
For Summer Time add ONE hour in **non-shaded areas**

GREENOCK LAT 55°57′N LONG 4°46′W

TIMES AND HEIGHTS OF HIGH AND LOW WATERS

Dates in red are SPRINGS
Dates in blue are NEAPS

YEAR **2010**

JANUARY

Day	Time	m	Day	Time	m
1 F	0019	3.4	16 SA	0100	3.1
	0539	0.5		0617	0.7
	1225	3.7		1313	3.6
	1800	0.3		1843	0.5
2 SA	0111	3.4	17 SU	0133	3.2
	0627	0.4		0649	0.7
	1311	3.8		1345	3.6
	1848	0.2		1914	0.5
3 SU	0202	3.4	18 M	0206	3.2
	0715	0.4		0719	0.7
	1357	3.9		1416	3.6
	1936	0.1		1946	0.5
4 M	0251	3.4	19 TU	0239	3.2
	0804	0.4		0751	0.7
	1443	3.9		1447	3.6
	2025	0.2		2018	0.5
5 TU	0339	3.4	20 W	0312	3.2
	0853	0.4		0826	0.7
	1528	3.9		1521	3.5
	2116	0.2		2053	0.6
6 W	0425	3.3	21 TH	0346	3.2
	0944	0.5		0904	0.7
	1615	3.8		1556	3.4
	2209	0.4		2133	0.6
7 TH	0512	3.2	22 F	0422	3.2
	1039	0.7		0946	0.8
	1703	3.6		1635	3.3
◑	2307	0.6		2219	0.7
8 F	0601	3.1	23 SA	0500	3.1
	1139	0.8		1033	0.9
	1754	3.4		1718	3.1
			◐	2312	0.8
9 SA	0011	0.7	24 SU	0543	3.0
	0657	3.0		1129	1.1
	1249	0.9		1812	3.0
	1850	3.2			
10 SU	0124	0.9	25 M	0015	1.0
	0808	2.9		0636	2.9
	1403	1.0		1236	1.1
	2009	3.0		1923	2.8
11 M	0232	0.9	26 TU	0128	1.0
	0925	3.0		0754	2.9
	1510	0.9		1355	1.1
	2142	3.0		2055	2.9
12 TU	0331	0.9	27 W	0245	0.9
	1027	3.2		0923	3.0
	1605	0.7		1512	0.9
	2248	3.0		2218	3.0
13 W	0421	0.9	28 TH	0348	0.7
	1117	3.4		1031	3.2
	1652	0.6		1612	0.5
	2339	3.1		2320	3.2
14 TH	0505	0.8	29 F	0440	0.5
	1200	3.5		1125	3.4
	1733	0.5		1702	0.3
15 F	0022	3.1	30 SA	0013	3.3
	0543	0.8		0527	0.3
	1239	3.6		1214	3.6
●	1809	0.5	○	1747	0.1
			31 SU	0104	3.4
				0613	0.2
				1301	3.7
				1832	0.0

FEBRUARY

Day	Time	m	Day	Time	m
1 M	0152	3.4	16 TU	0144	3.2
	0658	0.2		0652	0.6
	1346	3.8		1355	3.5
	1917	-0.1		1916	0.4
2 TU	0237	3.4	17 W	0213	3.2
	0743	0.2		0721	0.5
	1431	3.9		1424	3.5
	2002	0.0		1944	0.4
3 W	0318	3.4	18 TH	0243	3.3
	0829	0.2		0755	0.5
	1513	3.9		1456	3.5
	2048	0.1		2018	0.4
4 TH	0357	3.4	19 F	0313	3.3
	0916	0.3		0832	0.5
	1555	3.8		1530	3.4
	2135	0.3		2057	0.4
5 F	0435	3.3	20 SA	0346	3.3
	1004	0.4		0914	0.5
	1636	3.6		1606	3.3
◑	2225	0.5		2142	0.6
6 SA	0514	3.1	21 SU	0421	3.2
	1059	0.6		1000	0.7
	1719	3.3		1646	3.1
	2324	0.8		2235	0.7
7 SU	0559	3.0	22 M	0501	3.1
	1210	0.8		1056	0.8
	1807	3.0		1736	2.9
			◐	2338	0.9
8 M	0045	1.0	23 TU	0551	2.9
	0656	2.8		1203	1.0
	1337	0.9		1846	2.7
	1906	2.7			
9 TU	0210	1.1	24 W	0054	1.0
	0848	2.8		0701	2.8
	1451	0.9		1327	0.9
	2135	2.6		2037	2.7
10 W	0314	1.1	25 TH	0225	1.0
	1009	3.0		0853	2.9
	1548	0.7		1454	0.7
	2244	2.8		2214	2.9
11 TH	0406	0.9	26 F	0334	0.7
	1101	3.2		1015	3.1
	1634	0.5		1557	0.4
	2330	2.9		2312	3.1
12 F	0449	0.8	27 SA	0426	0.4
	1144	3.4		1110	3.4
	1714	0.4		1646	0.1
13 SA	0009	3.0	28 SU	0001	3.3
	0526	0.7		0511	0.2
	1222	3.5		1159	3.5
	1749	0.3	○	1729	-0.1
14 SU	0043	3.1			
	0558	0.6			
	1256	3.5			
●	1820	0.4			
15 M	0114	3.1			
	0626	0.6			
	1326	3.5			
	1849	0.4			

MARCH

Day	Time	m	Day	Time	m
1 M	0048	3.4	16 TU	0046	3.1
	0554	0.1		0558	0.5
	1245	3.7		1259	3.3
	1811	-0.2		1818	0.3
2 TU	0132	3.4	17 W	0115	3.2
	0637	0.0		0622	0.5
	1330	3.8		1328	3.3
	1853	-0.1		1843	0.3
3 W	0213	3.4	18 TH	0143	3.3
	0720	0.0		0651	0.4
	1413	3.8		1359	3.4
	1935	-0.1		1913	0.3
4 TH	0250	3.4	19 F	0212	3.3
	0802	0.0		0726	0.3
	1453	3.8		1432	3.4
	2018	0.1		1950	0.3
5 F	0325	3.4	20 SA	0243	3.4
	0845	0.1		0805	0.3
	1532	3.6		1508	3.4
	2101	0.3		2032	0.4
6 SA	0359	3.3	21 SU	0316	3.4
	0931	0.3		0849	0.4
	1610	3.4		1545	3.3
	2147	0.6		2119	0.5
7 SU	0436	3.2	22 M	0352	3.3
	1023	0.5		0938	0.5
	1651	3.1		1627	3.1
◑	2240	0.9		2213	0.7
8 M	0518	3.0	23 TU	0432	3.2
	1133	0.8		1036	0.7
	1737	2.8		1718	2.9
	2357	1.2	◐	2318	0.9
9 TU	0610	2.8	24 W	0523	3.0
	1310	0.9		1146	0.8
	1833	2.5		1831	2.7
10 W	0141	1.2	25 TH	0037	1.0
	0741	2.6		0634	2.8
	1424	0.8		1313	0.8
	2120	2.5		2036	2.7
11 TH	0250	1.1	26 F	0206	0.9
	0942	2.8		0830	2.8
	1521	0.6		1436	0.5
	2224	2.7		2201	2.9
12 F	0342	0.9	27 SA	0315	0.7
	1035	3.1		0954	3.1
	1607	0.4		1537	0.2
	2305	2.9		2254	3.1
13 SA	0425	0.7	28 SU	0407	0.4
	1117	3.2		1050	3.3
	1646	0.3		1625	0.0
	2341	3.0		2340	3.3
14 SU	0501	0.6	29 M	0452	0.1
	1154	3.3		1138	3.5
	1720	0.3		1708	-0.1
15 M	0014	3.1	30 TU	0024	3.3
	0532	0.5		0534	0.0
	1228	3.3		1225	3.6
●	1751	0.3	○	1748	-0.1
			31 W	0106	3.4
				0615	-0.1
				1309	3.6
				1828	-0.1

APRIL

Day	Time	m	Day	Time	m
1 TH	0144	3.4	16 F	0112	3.3
	0655	-0.1		0626	0.3
	1351	3.6		1334	3.3
	1909	0.1		1849	0.3
2 F	0219	3.4	17 SA	0144	3.4
	0736	0.0		0704	0.3
	1431	3.6		1411	3.3
	1950	0.2		1930	0.3
3 SA	0253	3.4	18 SU	0218	3.5
	0818	0.1		0746	0.3
	1509	3.4		1451	3.3
	2032	0.4		2016	0.4
4 SU	0328	3.4	19 M	0254	3.5
	0902	0.2		0833	0.3
	1547	3.2		1532	3.2
	2117	0.6		2107	0.5
5 M	0405	3.2	20 TU	0333	3.4
	0953	0.5		0926	0.4
	1628	3.0		1619	3.0
	2207	0.9		2204	0.7
6 TU	0447	3.0	21 W	0416	3.3
	1101	0.7		1027	0.5
	1715	2.7		1715	2.9
◑	2313	1.2	◐	2309	0.8
7 W	0538	2.8	22 TH	0509	3.1
	1232	0.8		1139	0.6
	1812	2.5		1833	2.7
8 TH	0053	1.3	23 F	0023	0.9
	0651	2.6		0625	2.9
	1346	0.7		1258	0.5
	1957	2.4		2020	2.7
9 F	0209	1.2	24 SA	0141	0.8
	0852	2.7		0806	2.9
	1443	0.6		1411	0.4
	2137	2.6		2133	2.9
10 SA	0306	1.0	25 SU	0248	0.6
	0955	2.9		0927	3.1
	1530	0.4		1510	0.2
	2223	2.8		2226	3.1
11 SU	0351	0.8	26 M	0343	0.4
	1039	3.1		1024	3.3
	1610	0.3		1600	0.1
	2301	3.0		2313	3.2
12 M	0428	0.6	27 TU	0431	0.2
	1117	3.2		1114	3.4
	1645	0.3		1644	0.0
	2337	3.1		2356	3.3
13 TU	0459	0.6	28 W	0514	0.1
	1152	3.2		1201	3.5
	1717	0.3		1725	0.1
			○		
14 W	0010	3.1	29 TH	0037	3.4
	0526	0.5		0555	0.0
	1226	3.2		1246	3.5
●	1744	0.3		1805	0.1
15 TH	0042	3.2	30 F	0116	3.4
	0554	0.4		0635	0.0
	1259	3.2		1329	3.4
	1814	0.3		1846	0.3

Chart Datum: 1·62 metres below Ordnance Datum (Newlyn). HAT is 4·0 metres above Chart Datum; see 0.20

TIME ZONE (UT)
For Summer Time add ONE hour in **non-shaded areas**

GREENOCK LAT 55°57′N LONG 4°46′W

TIMES AND HEIGHTS OF HIGH AND LOW WATERS

Dates in red are SPRINGS
Dates in blue are NEAPS

YEAR **2010**

MAY

Date	Time	m	Date	Time	m
1 SA	0152	3.4	16 SU	0121	3.5
	0715	0.1		0649	0.2
	1409	3.3		1355	3.3
	1927	0.4		1917	0.4
2 SU	0227	3.4	17 M	0159	3.6
	0756	0.1		0735	0.2
	1448	3.2		1440	3.2
	2010	0.5		2007	0.4
3 M	0302	3.4	18 TU	0240	3.6
	0840	0.3		0824	0.2
	1527	3.1		1526	3.2
	2054	0.7		2100	0.5
4 TU	0340	3.3	19 W	0322	3.5
	0930	0.4		0919	0.3
	1609	2.9		1617	3.1
	2143	0.9		2156	0.6
5 W	0421	3.1	20 TH	0409	3.4
	1029	0.6		1020	0.3
	1657	2.8		1716	2.9
	2238	1.0		◐ 2257	0.7
6 TH	0510	2.9	21 F	0504	3.2
	1141	0.7		1127	0.4
	1753	2.6		1828	2.9
	◑ 2345	1.2			
7 F	0612	2.8	22 SA	0002	0.7
	1252	0.7		0612	3.1
	1902	2.6		1235	0.4
				1946	2.9
8 SA	0102	1.2	23 SU	0111	0.7
	0733	2.7		0735	3.1
	1353	0.6		1342	0.4
	2019	2.6		2055	2.9
9 SU	0210	1.1	24 M	0217	0.6
	0854	2.8		0854	3.1
	1444	0.5		1442	0.3
	2123	2.8		2153	3.0
10 M	0303	0.9	25 TU	0318	0.5
	0949	2.9		0956	3.2
	1527	0.4		1535	0.3
	2213	2.9		2244	3.2
11 TU	0346	0.8	26 W	0410	0.3
	1033	3.0		1050	3.3
	1606	0.4		1622	0.3
	2255	3.1		2330	3.3
12 W	0422	0.6	27 TH	0456	0.2
	1112	3.1		1139	3.3
	1641	0.3		1706	0.3
	2333	3.2		○	
13 TH	0456	0.5	28 F	0013	3.3
	1150	3.2		0539	0.1
	1714	0.3		1226	3.3
				1748	0.4
14 F	0008	3.3	29 SA	0054	3.4
	0530	0.4		0620	0.1
	1230	3.2		1310	3.2
	● 1750	0.3		1829	0.5
15 SA	0044	3.4	30 SU	0131	3.4
	0607	0.3		0659	0.2
	1312	3.2		1351	3.1
	1831	0.3		1910	0.5
			31 M	0206	3.4
				0739	0.2
				1430	3.1
				1951	0.6

JUNE

Date	Time	m	Date	Time	m
1 TU	0242	3.4	16 W	0229	3.7
	0821	0.3		0815	0.1
	1510	3.0		1523	3.2
	2034	0.7		2048	0.4
2 W	0319	3.4	17 TH	0314	3.6
	0906	0.4		0908	0.1
	1551	2.9		1614	3.1
	2117	0.8		2141	0.4
3 TH	0358	3.2	18 F	0401	3.6
	0955	0.5		1004	0.2
	1636	2.9		1708	3.1
	2204	0.8		2236	0.5
4 F	0441	3.1	19 SA	0453	3.4
	1051	0.6		1104	0.3
	1724	2.8		1804	3.0
	◑ 2254	1.0		◐ 2335	0.6
5 SA	0531	2.9	20 SU	0550	3.3
	1151	0.7		1206	0.4
	1816	2.8		1905	2.9
	2350	1.0			
6 SU	0629	2.8	21 M	0039	0.6
	1251	0.7		0656	3.1
	1913	2.8		1311	0.4
				2011	2.9
7 M	0054	1.1	22 TU	0147	0.7
	0731	2.8		0815	3.0
	1348	0.6		1415	0.5
	2014	2.8		2118	3.0
8 TU	0159	1.0	23 W	0254	0.6
	0843	2.8		0930	3.0
	1439	0.6		1514	0.5
	2115	2.9		2218	3.1
9 W	0257	0.9	24 TH	0353	0.5
	0943	2.9		1032	3.1
	1525	0.5		1606	0.5
	2209	3.0		2310	3.2
10 TH	0346	0.7	25 F	0443	0.4
	1034	3.0		1126	3.1
	1608	0.4		1653	0.5
	2255	3.1		2356	3.3
11 F	0429	0.6	26 SA	0528	0.3
	1121	3.1		1215	3.1
	1649	0.4		1737	0.6
	2338	3.3		○	
12 SA	0511	0.4	27 SU	0038	3.4
	1208	3.2		0609	0.2
	1732	0.4		1259	3.0
	●			1816	0.6
13 SU	0020	3.4	28 M	0116	3.4
	0553	0.3		0647	0.2
	1256	3.2		1338	3.0
	1818	0.3		1854	0.6
14 M	0102	3.5	29 TU	0151	3.5
	0638	0.2		0723	0.3
	1344	3.2		1415	3.0
	1906	0.3		1931	0.6
15 TU	0145	3.6	30 W	0225	3.4
	0725	0.1		0759	0.3
	1433	3.2		1451	3.0
	1956	0.3		2009	0.6

JULY

Date	Time	m	Date	Time	m
1 TH	0259	3.4	16 F	0303	3.8
	0837	0.4		0847	0.0
	1528	3.0		1559	3.2
	2047	0.6		2118	0.2
2 F	0333	3.3	17 SA	0348	3.7
	0918	0.4		0938	0.1
	1607	3.0		1644	3.2
	2127	0.7		2210	0.3
3 SA	0410	3.2	18 SU	0434	3.6
	1002	0.5		1033	0.2
	1647	3.0		1730	3.1
	2210	0.8		◐ 2305	0.5
4 SU	0451	3.1	19 M	0522	3.3
	1051	0.6		1133	0.4
	1730	2.9		1819	3.0
	◑ 2257	0.9			
5 M	0539	2.9	20 TU	0008	0.6
	1146	0.7		0615	3.1
	1816	2.9		1242	0.6
	2352	1.0		1919	2.9
6 TU	0636	2.8	21 W	0121	0.7
	1246	0.7		0724	2.9
	1910	2.8		1354	0.8
				2042	2.8
7 W	0055	1.1	22 TH	0236	0.7
	0743	2.8		0911	2.8
	1348	0.7		1459	0.8
	2014	2.8		2158	3.0
8 TH	0206	1.0	23 F	0340	0.6
	0857	2.8		1027	2.8
	1447	0.7		1555	0.7
	2122	2.9		2256	3.1
9 F	0312	0.8	24 SA	0432	0.4
	1005	2.9		1122	2.9
	1541	0.6		1643	0.7
	2223	3.1		2343	3.3
10 SA	0408	0.6	25 SU	0516	0.3
	1102	3.0		1208	3.0
	1630	0.4		1725	0.6
	2314	3.3			
11 SU	0456	0.3	26 M	0025	3.4
	1154	3.1		0554	0.2
	1717	0.3		1249	3.0
	●			○ 1802	0.6
12 M	0001	3.4	27 TU	0102	3.4
	0540	0.1		0629	0.2
	1246	3.2		1323	3.0
	1803	0.3		1835	0.6
13 TU	0047	3.6	28 W	0135	3.5
	0626	0.0		0702	0.3
	1336	3.2		1354	3.0
	1851	0.2		1907	0.6
14 W	0133	3.7	29 TH	0205	3.5
	0711	-0.1		0733	0.3
	1426	3.2		1425	3.1
	1939	0.2		1938	0.6
15 TH	0218	3.7	30 F	0235	3.4
	0759	-0.1		0804	0.3
	1513	3.2		1458	3.1
	2028	0.2		2013	0.5
			31 SA	0307	3.4
				0838	0.4
				1531	3.1
				2049	0.6

AUGUST

Date	Time	m	Date	Time	m
1 SU	0340	3.3	16 M	0411	3.6
	0915	0.5		0958	0.4
	1606	3.1		1650	3.2
	2129	0.6		◐ 2234	0.5
2 M	0417	3.2	17 TU	0454	3.3
	0957	0.6		1056	0.6
	1644	3.1		1734	3.0
	2214	0.7		2339	0.7
3 TU	0458	3.0	18 W	0541	3.0
	1049	0.7		1213	0.9
	1727	3.0		1828	2.9
	◑ 2306	0.9			
4 W	0549	2.9	19 TH	0101	0.8
	1150	0.8		0639	2.7
	1818	2.9		1338	1.0
				2000	2.8
5 TH	0008	1.0	20 F	0220	0.8
	0657	2.7		0909	2.6
	1301	0.9		1445	1.0
	1923	2.8		2142	2.9
6 F	0124	1.0	21 SA	0323	0.6
	0822	2.7		1024	2.7
	1417	0.8		1541	0.8
	2042	2.9		2239	3.2
7 SA	0245	0.9	22 SU	0414	0.4
	0949	2.8		1112	2.9
	1521	0.7		1627	0.7
	2156	3.1		2325	3.3
8 SU	0350	0.6	23 M	0456	0.3
	1053	3.0		1152	3.0
	1614	0.5		1707	0.6
	2255	3.3			
9 M	0440	0.2	24 TU	0005	3.4
	1145	3.1		0533	0.2
	1701	0.3		1227	3.0
	2345	3.5		○ 1741	0.6
10 TU	0525	0.0	25 W	0041	3.5
	1235	3.2		0605	0.3
	1746	0.2		1257	3.1
	●			1811	0.6
11 W	0032	3.6	26 TH	0112	3.5
	0608	-0.1		0635	0.3
	1323	3.3		1326	3.1
	1831	0.1		1837	0.6
12 TH	0119	3.7	27 F	0140	3.4
	0651	-0.2		0702	0.4
	1409	3.3		1354	3.2
	1917	0.1		1905	0.5
13 F	0204	3.8	28 SA	0209	3.4
	0735	-0.1		0729	0.4
	1452	3.3		1424	3.2
	2003	0.1		1937	0.5
14 SA	0247	3.8	29 SU	0239	3.4
	0821	0.0		0800	0.4
	1532	3.3		1455	3.3
	2050	0.1		2014	0.5
15 SU	0329	3.8	30 M	0313	3.4
	0908	0.1		0836	0.5
	1611	3.3		1529	3.3
	2140	0.3		2054	0.6
			31 TU	0348	3.3
				0919	0.6
				1605	3.3
				2140	0.7

Chart Datum: 1·62 metres below Ordnance Datum (Newlyn). HAT is 4·0 metres above Chart Datum; see 0.20

TIME ZONE (UT)
For Summer Time add ONE hour in **non-shaded areas**

GREENOCK LAT 55°57′N LONG 4°46′W

TIMES AND HEIGHTS OF HIGH AND LOW WATERS

Dates in red are SPRINGS
Dates in blue are NEAPS

YEAR **2010**

SEPTEMBER

Day	Time	m	Day	Time	m
1	0426	3.1	16	0515	2.9
	1010	0.8		1141	1.1
W	1646	3.1	TH	1750	2.9
◑	2232	0.9			
2	0514	2.9	17	0043	0.9
	1111	1.0		0613	2.6
TH	1736	3.0	F	1316	1.2
	2336	1.0		1914	2.8
3	0622	2.7	18	0158	0.9
	1227	1.1		0858	2.5
F	1842	2.9	SA	1423	1.1
				2114	2.9
4	0055	1.0	19	0258	0.7
	0758	2.7		1004	2.7
SA	1354	1.0	SU	1518	1.0
	2009	2.9		2212	3.2
5	0225	0.8	20	0347	0.5
	0943	2.8		1047	2.9
SU	1504	0.8	M	1604	0.8
	2135	3.1		2257	3.4
6	0331	0.5	21	0428	0.3
	1043	3.1		1123	3.1
M	1557	0.5	TU	1642	0.6
	2236	3.4		2336	3.5
7	0421	0.2	22	0505	0.3
	1131	3.2		1154	3.2
TU	1643	0.3	W	1715	0.6
	2327	3.6			
8	0505	0.0	23	0010	3.5
	1216	3.3		0536	0.3
W	1727	0.1	TH	1224	3.2
●			○	1742	0.6
9	0014	3.7	24	0042	3.5
	0546	-0.1		0605	0.4
TH	1301	3.4	F	1253	3.3
	1809	0.1		1807	0.6
10	0101	3.8	25	0111	3.5
	0627	-0.1		0631	0.4
F	1343	3.4	SA	1322	3.3
	1852	0.0		1834	0.6
11	0145	3.8	26	0141	3.5
	0710	-0.1		0658	0.5
SA	1422	3.4	SU	1351	3.4
	1936	0.1		1907	0.5
12	0228	3.8	27	0214	3.5
	0753	0.1		0730	0.5
SU	1500	3.4	M	1423	3.5
	2022	0.2		1945	0.5
13	0308	3.7	28	0249	3.4
	0837	0.3		0809	0.5
M	1536	3.4	TU	1458	3.5
	2109	0.3		2028	0.6
14	0348	3.5	29	0326	3.3
	0924	0.6		0854	0.7
TU	1615	3.3	W	1534	3.4
	2203	0.5		2115	0.7
15	0429	3.2	30	0406	3.2
	1019	0.9		0946	0.9
W	1658	3.1	TH	1615	3.3
◐	2313	0.8		2210	0.8

OCTOBER

Day	Time	m	Day	Time	m
1	0454	3.0	16	0011	0.9
	1048	1.1		0556	2.7
F	1705	3.1	SA	1236	1.4
◑	2316	1.0		1835	2.9
2	0603	2.8	17	0124	0.9
	1206	1.2		0746	2.6
SA	1812	3.0	SU	1348	1.3
				2023	3.0
3	0037	1.0	18	0223	0.8
	0746	2.7		0919	2.8
SU	1333	1.1	M	1445	1.1
	1942	3.0		2132	3.1
4	0203	0.8	19	0312	0.6
	0927	2.9		1005	3.0
M	1443	0.8	TU	1532	0.9
	2111	3.2		2219	3.3
5	0308	0.5	20	0355	0.5
	1023	3.2		1043	3.2
TU	1537	0.6	W	1611	0.8
	2214	3.4		2259	3.4
6	0358	0.2	21	0432	0.4
	1109	3.4		1117	3.3
W	1623	0.3	TH	1644	0.7
	2305	3.6		2335	3.4
7	0442	0.0	22	0505	0.4
	1152	3.5		1150	3.4
TH	1706	0.2	F	1713	0.7
●	2353	3.7			
8	0523	0.0	23	0008	3.5
	1234	3.5		0535	0.5
F	1748	0.1	SA	1221	3.4
			○	1740	0.7
9	0039	3.8	24	0042	3.5
	0604	0.0		0603	0.5
SA	1315	3.5	SU	1252	3.5
	1830	0.1		1810	0.6
10	0124	3.8	25	0116	3.5
	0645	0.1		0633	0.6
SU	1353	3.6	M	1324	3.6
	1912	0.1		1845	0.6
11	0207	3.7	26	0153	3.5
	0728	0.3		0710	0.6
M	1430	3.6	TU	1358	3.7
	1956	0.2		1925	0.6
12	0247	3.6	27	0231	3.5
	0811	0.5		0752	0.7
TU	1507	3.5	W	1435	3.7
	2043	0.4		2010	0.6
13	0327	3.4	28	0312	3.4
	0857	0.8		0840	0.8
W	1546	3.4	TH	1514	3.6
	2136	0.6		2059	0.7
14	0409	3.2	29	0355	3.2
	0949	1.0		0933	0.9
TH	1630	3.2	F	1556	3.5
◐	2245	0.8		2156	0.8
15	0457	2.9	30	0447	3.1
	1059	1.3		1034	1.1
F	1722	3.1	SA	1647	3.4
			◑	2303	0.9
			31	0554	2.9
				1147	1.2
			SU	1753	3.2

NOVEMBER

Day	Time	m	Day	Time	m
1	0019	0.9	16	0136	0.9
	0728	2.9		0759	2.8
M	1305	1.1	TU	1356	1.3
	1915	3.2		2027	3.1
2	0135	0.7	17	0230	0.8
	0856	3.0		0904	3.0
TU	1414	0.9	W	1450	1.2
	2041	3.3		2129	3.2
3	0240	0.5	18	0316	0.7
	0954	3.2		0955	3.2
W	1512	0.7	TH	1534	1.0
	2148	3.5		2216	3.3
4	0333	0.4	19	0356	0.6
	1042	3.4		1038	3.3
TH	1602	0.5	F	1612	0.9
	2242	3.6		2258	3.3
5	0419	0.2	20	0433	0.6
	1127	3.5		1117	3.4
F	1647	0.3	SA	1646	0.8
	2331	3.7		2336	3.4
6	0503	0.2	21	0507	0.6
	1209	3.6		1152	3.5
SA	1730	0.2	SU	1718	0.7
●			○		
7	0019	3.7	22	0015	3.4
	0544	0.3		0540	0.6
SU	1250	3.6	M	1226	3.6
	1812	0.2		1752	0.7
8	0105	3.7	23	0055	3.4
	0626	0.4		0616	0.6
M	1329	3.7	TU	1302	3.7
	1854	0.3		1830	0.6
9	0149	3.6	24	0136	3.4
	0708	0.5		0656	0.6
TU	1407	3.7	W	1340	3.8
	1937	0.3		1912	0.6
10	0230	3.5	25	0218	3.4
	0751	0.7		0741	0.7
W	1445	3.6	TH	1419	3.8
	2023	0.5		1959	0.5
11	0311	3.3	26	0302	3.4
	0836	0.9		0830	0.7
TH	1525	3.5	F	1501	3.8
	2113	0.6		2049	0.6
12	0354	3.2	27	0349	3.3
	0924	1.1		0922	0.8
F	1608	3.4	SA	1546	3.7
	2211	0.8		2145	0.6
13	0441	3.0	28	0441	3.2
	1019	1.2		1019	0.9
SA	1657	3.2	SU	1636	3.6
◐	2321	0.9	◑	2246	0.7
14	0537	2.8	29	0541	3.1
	1128	1.4		1123	1.0
SU	1756	3.1	M	1735	3.4
				2353	0.7
15	0033	0.9	30	0656	3.0
	0644	2.8		1232	1.0
M	1248	1.4	TU	1845	3.4
	1908	3.0			

DECEMBER

Day	Time	m	Day	Time	m
1	0102	0.7	16	0134	1.0
	0815	3.1		0755	3.0
W	1342	1.0	TH	1346	1.3
	2004	3.3		2018	3.0
2	0209	0.6	17	0230	0.9
	0921	3.2		0900	3.0
TH	1447	0.8	F	1448	1.2
	2119	3.4		2125	3.1
3	0308	0.6	18	0320	0.8
	1016	3.3		0957	3.2
F	1543	0.6	SA	1538	1.1
	2220	3.5		2222	3.2
4	0400	0.5	19	0403	0.8
	1104	3.5		1045	3.3
SA	1632	0.5	SU	1620	0.9
	2314	3.5		2310	3.3
5	0447	0.5	20	0443	0.7
	1150	3.6		1126	3.5
SU	1717	0.4	M	1659	0.7
●				2355	3.3
6	0004	3.5	21	0522	0.6
	0530	0.5		1205	3.6
M	1233	3.7	TU	1738	0.6
	1800	0.3	○		
7	0052	3.5	22	0040	3.4
	0613	0.6		0602	0.6
TU	1313	3.7	W	1245	3.7
	1842	0.3		1818	0.5
8	0136	3.4	23	0125	3.4
	0655	0.7		0644	0.6
W	1352	3.7	TH	1325	3.8
	1923	0.4		1902	0.4
9	0217	3.4	24	0210	3.4
	0735	0.8		0730	0.5
TH	1429	3.7	F	1408	3.9
	2005	0.5		1948	0.3
10	0257	3.3	25	0255	3.4
	0817	0.8		0817	0.5
F	1507	3.6	SA	1451	3.9
	2049	0.6		2036	0.3
11	0338	3.2	26	0341	3.3
	0858	0.9		0906	0.6
SA	1547	3.5	SU	1536	3.8
	2136	0.7		2128	0.4
12	0421	3.1	27	0428	3.3
	0943	1.0		0959	0.7
SU	1630	3.4	M	1623	3.7
	2229	0.8		2223	0.5
13	0507	3.0	28	0519	3.2
	1031	1.2		1055	0.8
M	1716	3.3	TU	1714	3.6
◐	2328	0.9	◑	2323	0.6
14	0557	3.0	29	0616	3.1
	1127	1.3		1159	0.9
TU	1809	3.1	W	1812	3.4
15	0031	1.0	30	0029	0.7
	0652	2.9		0725	3.0
W	1235	1.4	TH	1310	0.9
	1909	3.0		1920	3.2
			31	0141	0.8
				0843	3.0
			F	1423	0.9
				2049	3.2

Chart Datum: 1·62 metres below Ordnance Datum (Newlyn). HAT is 4·0 metres above Chart Datum; see 0.20

SW Scotland

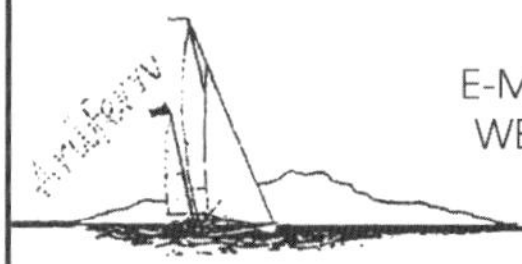

Crinan Boatyard Ltd
Chandlery, Boat repairs, Moorings, Slipway.
YAMAHA VOLVO PENTA
Marine Hardware
Antique books
Charts
Clothing
Footwear
And other things of interest!
Chandlery - 01546 830133
Tel: 01546 830 232
e-mail: info@crinanboatyard.co.uk
Listening on Channels 12 and 16

2.21 ARDROSSAN

N Ayrshire **55°38'·50N 04°49'·61W** ✵✵◊◊◊✿✿

CHARTS AC 5610, 2126, 2221, 2491, 1866; Imray C63.

TIDES +0055 Dover; ML 1·9; Duration 0630

Standard Port GREENOCK (⟵)

Times				Height (metres)			
High Water		Low Water		MHWS	MHWN	MLWN	MLWS
0000	0600	0000	0600	3·4	2·8	1·0	0·3
1200	1800	1200	1800				
Differences ARDROSSAN							
–0020	–0010	–0010	–0010	–0·2	–0·2	+0·1	+0·1
IRVINE							
–0020	–0020	–0030	–0010	–0·3	–0·3	–0·1	0·0

SHELTER Good in marina (formerly Eglinton Dock), access at all tides over sill, 5·2m least depth. A storm gate is fitted; max acceptable beam is 8·6m (28ft). Strong SW/NW winds cause heavy seas in the apprs and the hbr may be closed in SW gales. Ferries berth on both sides of Winton Pier.

NAVIGATION WPT 55°38'·13N 04°50'·55W, 055°/0·65M to hbr ent. From the W/NW keep clear of low-lying Horse Isle (conspic W tower on its S end) ringed by drying ledges. The passage between Horse Isle and the mainland is obstructed by unmarked drying rks and should not be attempted. Be aware of following dangers: From the S/SE, Eagle Rk 3ca S of hbr ent, marked by SHM buoy, Fl G 5s. 3ca SE of Eagle Rk lies unmarked Campbell Rk (0·2m). W Crinan Rk (1·1m) is 300m W of hbr ent, marked by PHM buoy, Fl R 4s.

LIGHTS AND MARKS Dir lt WRG 15m W14M, R/G11M (see 2.3); W sector leads 055° to hbr ent between lt ho and detached bkwtr. Lt ho Iso WG 4s 11m 9M, 317°-G-035°, W elsewhere. On S end of detached bkwtr, Fl R 5s 7m 5M.

Traffic Signals, shown H24 from control twr at ent to marina:

3 F ● lts (vert) = hbr and marina closed; no entry/exit for commercial and pleasure vessels.

3 F ● lts (vert) = marina open, hbr closed; pleasure craft may enter/exit the marina, no commercial movements.

2 F ● lts over 1 F ● = hbr open, marina closed; in severe weather marina storm gate is closed. Commercial vessels may enter/exit hbr, subject to approval by Hbr Control on VHF. Pleasure craft must clear the approach channel, ferry turning area (between the detached bkwtr and Winton Pier) and the outer basin. Yachts may not manoeuvre under sail alone until seaward of the outer breakwater.

R/T *Clyde Marina* VHF Ch **80** M. *Hbr Control* Ch 12 14 16 (H24).

TELEPHONE (Code 01294) Marina 607077, www. clyde marina.com; Ardrossan Hbr 469468; MRCC (01475) 729988; Marinecall 09068 969652; Police 404500; Dr 463011.

FACILITIES **Clyde Marina** (252 inc 50 Ⓥ) £2.35, short stay £10<4hrs, access H24, Marina Office hrs 0900-1800, Wi-fi, D, ME, El, Ⓔ, CH, BH (50 ton), R. **Town** 🛒, R, Bar, ▣, Gas, ✉, Ⓑ, Wi-fi. ⇌, ✈ (Prestwick/Glasgow). Ferry to Brodick (Arran).

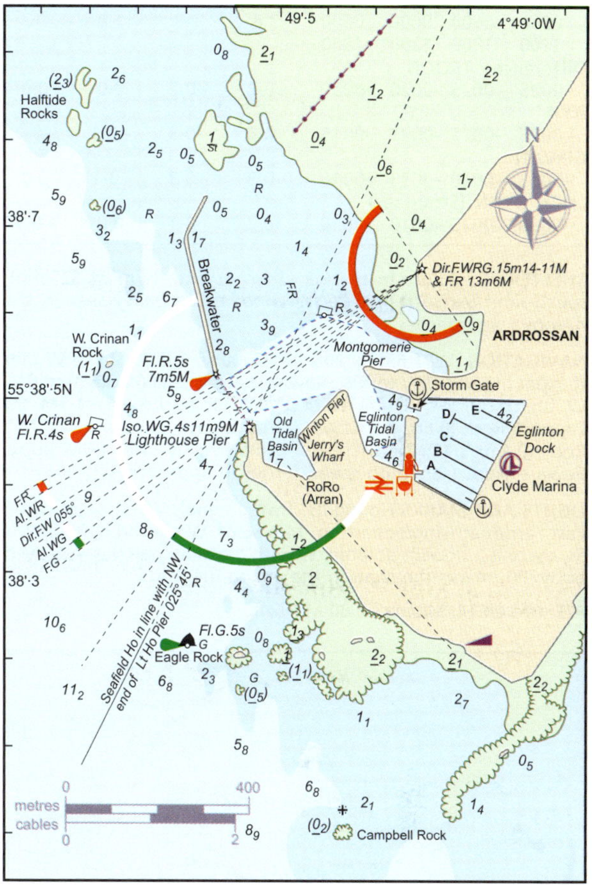

HARBOUR BETWEEN ARDROSSAN AND TROON

IRVINE, N Ayrshire, **55°36'·17N 04°42'·07W**. AC 2126, 2220, 1866. HW +0055 on Dover. Tides: see 2.21.

- Do not attempt ent in heavy onshore weather.
- Good shelter once across the bar (0·5m CD); access approx HW ±3½ for 1·4m draft.

The IB-B SPM buoy, Fl Y 3s, is 1·15M from hbr ent, close NW of ldg line. 5 blocks of flats and chys are conspic ENE of ent. Ldg lts 051°: front, FG 10m 5M; rear, FR 15m 5M. The S ent groyne is lit, Fl G 3s; groynes inside the ent have unlit perches. White Pilot tr with mast is conspic 3ca inside ent. Visitors' pontoons on N side or on S side at visitors' quay (2·2m). ⚓ prohib. VHF Ch 12 (0800-1600 Tues and Thurs; 0800-1300 Wed). HM ☎ (01294) 487286, 📠 487111. Berths available above opening footbridge which opens at 5 mins notice ☎ 08708 403123 or VHF Ch 12 (call *Irvine Bridge*). Facilities: **Quay** AB < 5m £4, >5m <10m £6, >10m <15m £9, FW, Slip, C (3 ton), Showers, SM. **Town** P & D (cans, 1·5km), Gas, 🛒, R, ⇌, ✈ (Prestwick).

2.22 TROON

S Ayrshire **55°33'·10N 04°40'·97W** ❀❀◇◇✿✿

CHARTS AC 5610, 2126, 2220, 1866; Imray C63.

TIDES +0050 Dover; ML 1·9; Duration 0630

Standard Port GREENOCK (⟵)

Times				Height (metres)			
High Water		Low Water		MHWS	MHWN	MLWN	MLWS
0000	0600	0000	0600	3·4	2·8	1·0	0·3
1200	1800	1200	1800				
Differences TROON							
–0025	–0025	–0020	–0020	–0·2	–0·2	0·0	0·0
AYR							
–0025	–0025	–0030	–0015	–0·4	–0·3	+0·1	+0·1
GIRVAN							
–0025	–0040	–0035	–0010	–0·3	–0·3	–0·1	0·0
LOCH RYAN (Stranraer)							
–0030	–0025	–0010	–0010	–0·2	–0·1	0·0	+0·1

SHELTER Complete in marina (2·4m at ent, 1·6m at SE end); speed limit 5kn. *Strong SW/NW winds cause heavy seas in the harbour approaches.*

NAVIGATION WPT 55°33'·20N 04°42'·00W, 103°/0·6M to W pier lt. Appr in sector SW to NW. Beware Lady Isle, Fl (4) 30s 19m 8M, W bn, 2·2M SW; Troon Rock (5·6m, occas breaks) 1·1M W; Lappock Rock (0·6m, bn with G barrel topmark) 1·6M NNW; Mill Rock (0·4m) ½M NNE of hbr ent, marked by unlit PHM buoy. Beware wash from high speed ferries in approaches.

LIGHTS AND MARKS No ldg lts. Traffic signals VQ.Y. occas when Fast Ferries arriving/departing. 14m SE of W pier hd lt, Fl (2) WG 5s, there is a floodlit dolphin, W with dayglow patches. A SHM lt buoy, FG, marks the chan in the ent to marina.

R/T HM Ch 14. Marina Ch **80** M (H24).

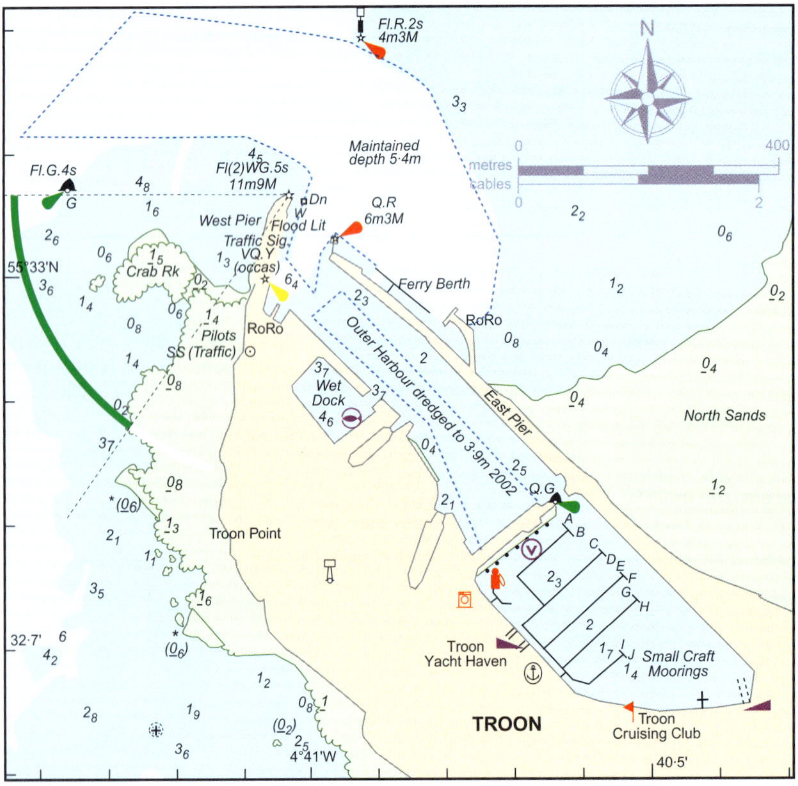

TELEPHONE (Code 01292) HM 281687; Troon CC 311865; Troon YC 316770. MRCC (01475) 729988; Marinecall 09068 969652; Police 313100; Dr 313593; ⊞ 610555 (Ayr).

FACILITIES Troon Yacht Haven (300+50 ⓥ), £2.35, access all tides. ☎ 315553, www.yachthavens.com ⓥ berths on pontoon A, first to stbd. AB for LOA 36m x 3m draft at hammerheads. Wi-fi, D (H24), ME, El, Ⓔ, CH, ⚒, SM (daily pick-up), BH (50 ton), C (20 ton), Slip, 🛒, R ☎ 311523, Bar, ▣, Gas, Gaz. **Town** ✉, Ⓑ, ⇌, ✈ (Prestwick/Glasgow). Fast RoRo ferry to Belfast.

HARBOURS ON THE FIRTH OF CLYDE SOUTH OF TROON

AYR, S Ayrshire, **55°28'·22N 04°38'·78W.** AC 5610, 2126, 2220, 1866. HW +0050 on Dover; ML 1·8m. Duration 0630. See 2.22. After heavy rains large amounts of debris may be washed down the R Ayr. From the W, hbr ent lies between conspic gasholder to the N and townhall spire to the S. Outer St Nicholas SHM buoy, Fl G 2s, warns of shoals and Rk (0·8m) 150m S of ent. Ldg lts 098°: front, by Pilot Stn, FR 10m 5M R tr, also tfc sigs; rear (130m from front), Oc R 10s 18m 9M. N bkwtr hd, QR 9m 5M. S pier hd, Q 7m 7M, vis 012°-161°, and FG 5m 5M, same structure, vis 012°-082°, over St Nicholas Rk. Tfc sigs (near front ldg lt): 2 ● (vert) = hbr closed to incoming traffic. HM ☎ (01292) 281687; VHF Ch 14 16. **Ayr Y & CC** at S dock, limited AB on pontoon on N side of hbr (access key, £10 deposit) from Ship Inn), M. **Services:** ⚒, ME, El, CH. **Town** Ⓑ, Bar, Gas, P & D, FW, ✉, R, ⇌, 🛒.

GIRVAN, S Ayrshire, **55°14'·77N 04°51'·87W.** AC 2199, 1866. HW +0043 on Dover; ML 1·8m; Duration 0630. See 2.22. Good shelter at inner hbr for 16 yachts on 60m pontoon (1·7m) beyond LB. Coasters and FVs berth on adjacent quay. No access LW±2 over bar 1·5m. Beware Girvan Patch, 1·7m, 4ca SW of ent, and Brest Rks, 3·5M N of hbr extending 6ca offshore. Ch spire (conspic) brg 104° leads between N bkwtr, Fl R 4s 5m 2M, and S pier, 2 FG (vert) 8m 4M. Inner N groyne, Iso 4s 3m 4M. Tfc sigs at root of S pier: 2 B discs (hor), at night 2 ● (hor) = hbr shut. VHF Ch 12 16 (HO). HM ☎ (01465) 713648; FW, Slip. **Town** Ⓑ, ✉, 🛒, R, ⇌, P & D (cans).

ANCHORAGES WITHIN LOCH RYAN

(See chartlet on next page)

LOCH RYAN, Dumfries and Galloway, **55°01'N 05°05'W.** AC 2198, 1403. HW (Stranraer) +0055 on Dover; ML 1·6m; Duration 0640. See tides 2.22. See adjacent chartlet. Very good shelter except in strong NW winds. Ent between Milleur Pt and Finnarts Pt. Beware The Beef Barrel rock, 1m high 6ca SSE of Milleur Pt, and The Spit running 1·5M to SE from W shore opposite Cairn Pt lt ho Fl (2) R10s 14m 12M. **Lights:** Cairnryan ferry terminal Fl R 5s 5m 5M; Stranraer, centre pier hd 2FBu (vert), E pier hd 2FR (vert). ⚓s in Lady Bay, 1·3M SSE of Milleur Pt, but exposed to heavy wash from HSS; in The Wig in 3m (avoid weed patches); or off Stranraer 3ca NW of W Pier hd. Larger yachts berth on NE side of E pier, by arrangement with HM, VHF Ch **14** (H24) or ☎ (01776) 702460. There is a small marina ☎ (07734 073421) to the west of West Pier with 8 AB for visitors. Max LOA 27m; craft >23m must book in advance. Facilities (Stranraer): Ⓑ, Bar, D, FW, P, ✉, R, ⇌, 🛒.

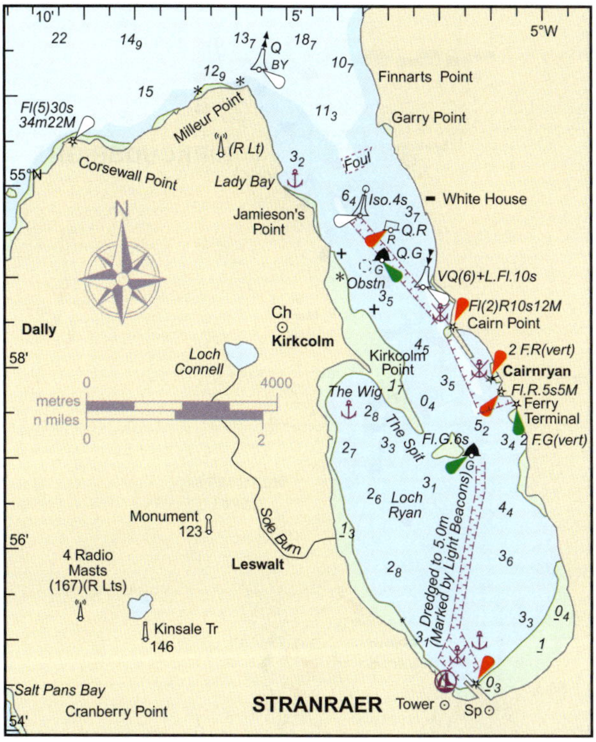

HARBOURS FROM MULL OF GALLOWAY TO WIGTOWN BAY

DRUMMORE, Dumfries and Galloway, **54°41′·57N 04°53′·49W.** AC 2094, 5613. HW +0040m on Dover; ML 3.3m; Duration 0610. Recently acquired from MOD by Drummore Hbr Trust ☎ 01557 330337. Good shelter from all conditions in small drying harbour convenient for awaiting weather/tidal conditions for rounding Mull of Galloway westbound. Temp'y ⚓ 5.5ca NNE of hbr ent in 4m. Access HW ±0245; approach entrance heading 140° from 1ca off. Depth in hbr varies due to silting but suitable for craft of <1.3m draft. Berth on pier (fender board required with fenders). Facilities FW, Slip, P (cans), Gas, 🛒, R, Bar, ✉, ⇄ (bus to Stranraer), ✈ (Carlisle).

ISLE OF WHITHORN, Dumfries and Galloway, **54°41′·91N 04°21′·88W**. AC 1826, 2094, 5613. HW +0035 on Dover; ML 3·7m; Duration 0545. See 2.24. Shelter good but hbr dries, having approx 2·5m at HW±3. On W side of ent beware the Skerries ledge. St Ninian's Tr (Fl WR 3s 20m 6/4M viz: 310°-W-005°-R-040°; W □ tr) is conspic at E side of ent. E pier hd has QG 4m 5M; ldg lts 335°, both Oc R 8s 7/9m 7M, synch, Or masts and ◊. HM ☎ (01988) 500468, www.isleofwhithorn.com; Facilities: AB on quay £4.83/yacht, 2 Slips (launching £1.00), P, D (by arrangement with HM), FW, ME, ⚒, CH, 🛒, Bar, ✉, VHF Ch 08 (occas).

GARLIESTON, Dumfries and Galloway, **54°47′·36N 04°21′·83W**. AC 1826, 2094, 5613. HW +0035 on Dover; ML no data; Duration 0545. See 2.24. Hbr affords complete shelter but dries. Access (2m) HW±3. Pier hd lt 2FR (vert) 5m 3M. Beware rky outcrops in W side of bay marked by a perch. HM ☎ (01988) 600295, Mobile 07734 073422. Facilities: M £3, FW, AC on quay, Slip. **Town:** 🛒, ME, P, D. ⚓s NE or W of Hestan Is to await tide. VHF: Ch M call *Kippford Startline* (YC) HW±2 in season. Ch 16 *Kippford Slipway* (Pilotage). Facilities: **Solway YC** (01556) 600221, www.thesyc.com; AB, ⛽, FW, M; **Services:** AB £6, M, Slip, D (cans), CH, Gaz, BY *Kippford Slipway Ltd*(01556) 620249, ME. **Town** P, SM, 🛒, ✉, Bar, Slip.

2.23 PORTPATRICK

Dumfries and Galloway **54°50′·42N 05°07′·18W** ❁❁❁⚓⚓⚓✿✿

CHARTS AC 2724, 2198; Imray C62.

TIDES +0032 Dover; ML 2·1; Duration 0615

Standard Port LIVERPOOL (⟶)

Times				Heights (metres)			
High Water		Low Water		MHWS	MHWN	MLWN	MLWS
0000	0600	0200	0800	9·3	7·4	2·9	0·9
1200	1800	1400	2000				
Differences PORTPATRICK							
+0018	+0026	0000	−0035	−5·5	−4·4	−2·0	−0·6

SHELTER Good in tiny Inner harbour, but entrance is difficult in strong SW/NW winds.

NAVIGATION WPT 54°50′·00N 05°08′·07W, 055°/0·7M to ent. Ent to outer hbr by short narrow chan with hazards either side, including rky shelf covered at HW. Beware cross tides off ent, up to 3kn springs. Barrel buoy (a mooring buoy) marks end of Half Tide Rk; do not cut inside.

LIGHTS AND MARKS Old Lt Ho (W tower, 22m) on Black Head is 1·6M north of entrance. Ldg lts 050°, FG (H24) 6/8m: Front on sea wall; rear on bldg; 2 vert orange stripes by day. Conspic features include: TV mast 1M NE, almost on ldg line; large hotel on cliffs about 1½ca NNW of hbr ent; Dunskey Castle (ru) 4ca SE of hbr.

R/T None.

TELEPHONE (Code 01776) HM 810355; MRCC (01475) 729988; Marinecall 09068 969652; Police 702112; Ⓗ 702323; RNLI Coxswain (for local advice) 07771 741717.

FACILITIES **Hbr** Slip (small craft), AB £12, M, FW, L. **Village** P (cans), D (bulk tanker), Gas, 🛒, R, Bar, ✉, Ⓑ (Stranraer), ⇄ (bus to Stranraer), ✈ (Prestwick).

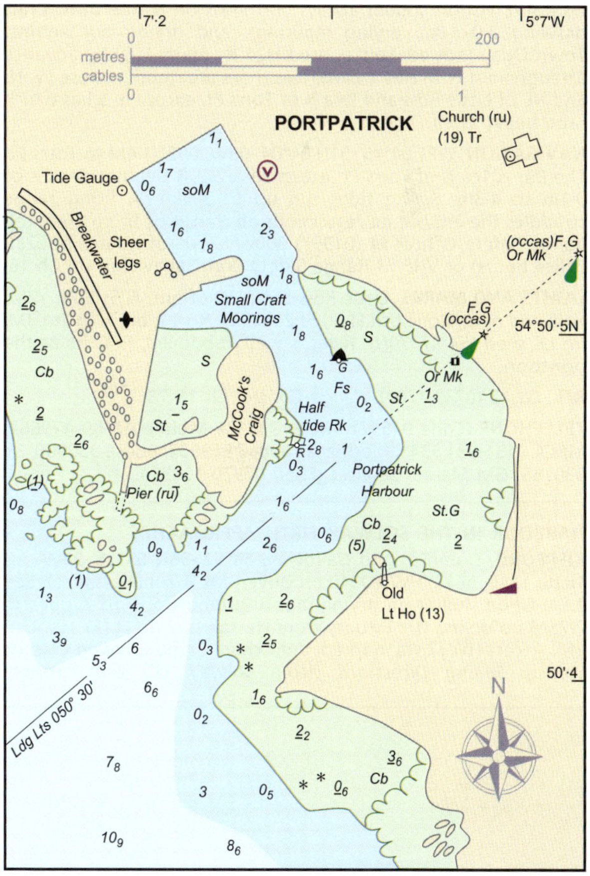

2.24 KIRKCUDBRIGHT

Dumfries and Galloway **54°50'·33N 04°03'·47W** ❁❁❁❁❁❁

CHARTS AC 1826, 2094, 1346, 1344, 5613; Imray C62.

TIDES +0030 Dover; ML 4·1; Duration 0545

Standard Port LIVERPOOL (3.16) (⟶)

Times				Height (metres)			
High Water		Low Water		MHWS	MHWN	MLWN	MLWS
0000	0600	0200	0800	9·3	7·4	2·9	0·9
1200	1800	1400	2000				
Differences KIRKCUDBRIGHT BAY							
+0015	+0015	+0010	0000	−1·8	−1·5	−0·5	−0·1
DRUMMORE							
+0030	+0040	+0015	+0020	−3·4	−2·5	−0·9	−0·3
PORT WILLIAM							
+0030	+0030	+0025	0000	−2·9	−2·2	−0.8	No data
GARLIESTON							
+0025	+0035	+0030	+0005	−2·3	−1·7	−0·5	No data
ISLE OF WHITHORN							
+0020	+0025	+0025	+0005	−2·4	−2·0	−0.8	−0.2
HESTAN ISLET (Kippford)							
+0025	+0025	+0020	+0025	−1·0	−1·1	−0.5	0.0
SOUTHERNESS POINT							
+0030	+0030	+0030	+0010	−0·7	−0·7	No data	
ANNAN WATERFOOT							
+0050	+0105	+0220	+0310	−2·2	−2·6	−2·7	*
TORDUFF POINT							
+0105	+0140	+0520	+0410	−4·1	−4·9	*Not below CD	
REDKIRK							
+0110	+0215	+0715	+0445	−5·5	−6·2	*Not below CD	

NOTES: At Annan Waterfoot, Torduff Pt and Redkirk the LW time differences are for the start of the rise, which at sp is very sudden. *At LW the tide does not usually fall below CD.

SHELTER Very good. Depths at LW: 1·0–2·0m at the floating pontoon, visitors should always berth/raft on N side of it. Craft drawing 2·0–3·0m, drying moorings, and drying out against Town Quay (not advised as used H24 by many FVs) by advance arrangement with HM. Down-river there are good ⚓s close W, N, and NE of Little Ross and ½ca N of Torrs Pt, except in S'lies which raise heavy swell.

NAVIGATION WPT 54°45'·51N 04°04'·08W, 005°/1·4M to Torrs Pt. The Bar is 1ca N of Torrs Pt; access HW±2½. R Dee has depths of 0·1m to 4·3m. Spring tides run up to 3–4kn. A firing range straddles the ent but no restrictions on transit of firing area; call Range Safety Officer ☎ (01557) 500271 (out of hours), 830236 office hours) or VHF 73 Range Safety Craf Gallavidian on Ch 16.

LIGHTS AND MARKS Little Ross Lt ho, W of ent, Fl 5s 50m 12M, NNE end of Is, Stone bcn Fl (2) 5s 21m 5M. No 1 lt bn, Fl 3s 7m 3M, on LB shed (54°47'·70N). River is well lit/buoyed, Fl G lts at the pontoon.

R/T Ch 12 (0730-1700). *Range Control* Ch 16 73.

TELEPHONE (Code 01557) HM ☎ 331135 Mobile 07709 479663; MRCC 0151-931 3341; Marinecall 09068 969652; Police 330600; Dr 330755; GM Marine Services (Fuel) 07970 109814.

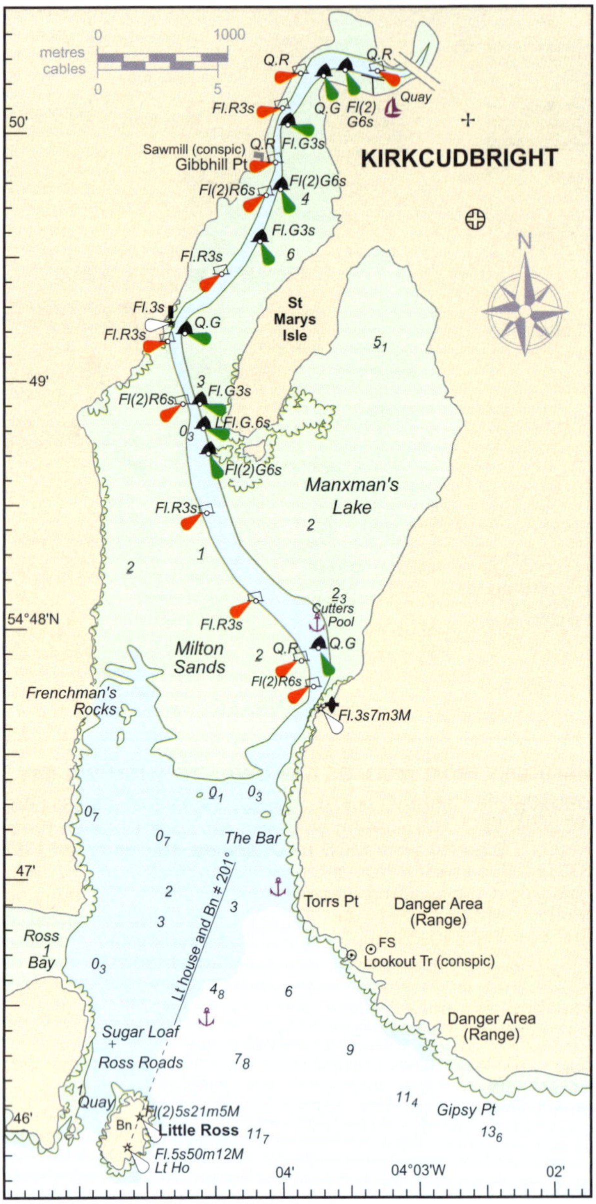

FACILITIES **Pontoon/jetty** £1.40 inc showers & ⊐D, FW; **Town Quay** P (hose), D (stictly by arrangement with HM), FW, El, C (15 ton) CH, ME. **KYC** ☎ 330963; **SC** ☎ 330032, Slip, M, FW; **Town** 🛒, R, Bar, ✉, Ⓑ, ≥ (Dumfries 30M), ✈ (Glasgow 100M).

HARBOUR IN THE SOLWAY FIRTH APPROACHES

KIPPFORD, Dumfries and Galloway, **54°52'·36N 03°48'·93W**. AC 1826, 1346, 5613. HW +0040 on Dover; ML 4·2m (Hestan Is). See 2.24. Good shelter on drying moorings/pontoons off Kippford, 2·75M up drying Urr Estuary from Hestan Is lt ho Fl (2) 10s 42m 9M. Access HW±2 via marked, unlit chan. *Clyde Cruising Club* or *Solway Sailing Directions* (from Solway YC) are strongly advised. Beware Craig Roan on E side of ent. Temp ⚓s NE or W of Hestan Is to await tide. VHF: Ch M call *Kippford Startline* (YC) HW±2 in season. Ch 16 *Kippford Slipway* (Pilotage). Facilities: **Solway YC** (01556) 600221, www.thesyc.com; AB, ⊐D, FW, M; **Services:** AB £6, M, Slip, D (cans), CH, Gaz, BY *Kippford Slipway Ltd* (01556) 620249, ME. **Town** P, SM, 🛒, ✉, Bar, Slip.

Make a winning decision
Your choice of marine electronics is one of the most important decisions you will have to make as a boat owner, next to choosing the boat itself of course.
When you buy Raymarine equipment, you are buying into world-class performance, top-notch integration, and the latest proven design technologies. Years of research and development, and customer feedback have resulted in the 'simple-on-the-outside, sophisticated-on-the-inside' design philosophy that is behind all our intuitive easy-to-use equipment.
Worldwide support and warranty
That's why Raymarine has a worldwide network of product-trained distributors and service dealers and offers a comprehensive warranty to handle the unexpected… wherever you decide to go.
HD DIGITAL
Raymarine
Raymarine
Raymarine
Raymarine
For product information, visit your local stockist or go to www.raymarine.co.uk
Lifestyle photo: Joe McCarthy
Raymarine®
…world leaders in marine electronics.

West England, IoM & Wales

Solway Firth to Land's End

AREA 3 – NW ENGLAND, IOM & N WALES

AREA 4 – S WALES & BRISTOL CHANNEL

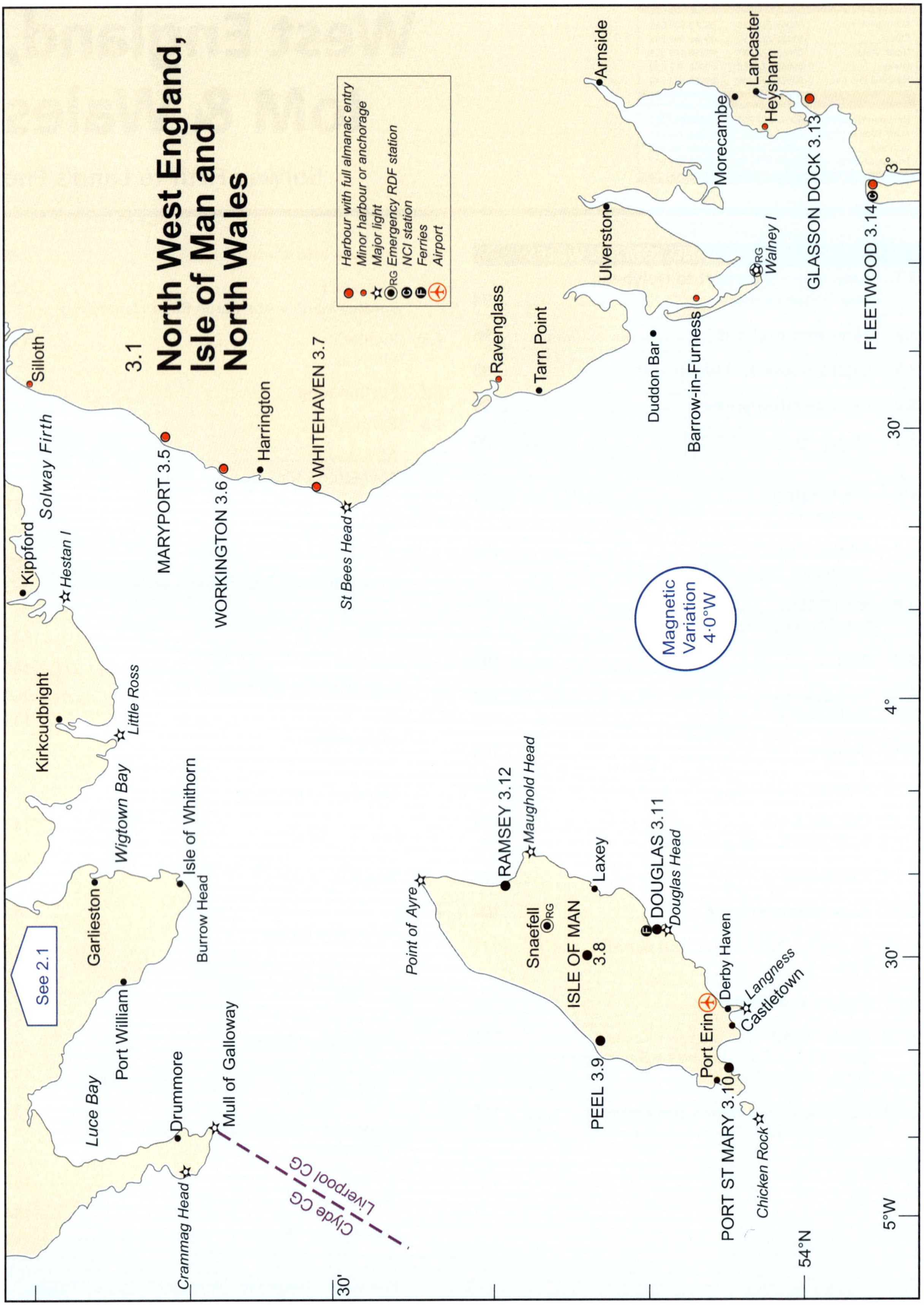
3.1
North West England, Isle of Man and North Wales
Harbour with full almanac entry
Minor harbour or anchorage
Major light
RG Emergency RDF station
NCI station
Ferries
Airport
Silloth
Solway Firth
Kippford
Hestan I
Kirkcudbright
Little Ross
Wigtown Bay
Garlieston
Isle of Whithorn
Burrow Head
Port William
Luce Bay
Drummore
Mull of Galloway
Crammag Head
See 2.1
Clyde CG
Liverpool CG
MARYPORT 3.5
WORKINGTON 3.6
Harrington
WHITEHAVEN 3.7
St Bees Head
Ravenglass
Tarn Point
Duddon Bar
Barrow-in-Furness
Walney I
RG
Ulverston
Arnside
Morecambe
Lancaster
Heysham
GLASSON DOCK 3.13
FLEETWOOD 3.14
Magnetic Variation 4·0°W
Point of Ayre
RAMSEY 3.12
Maughold Head
Snaefell
RG
Laxey
DOUGLAS 3.11
Douglas Head
ISLE OF MAN 3.8
PEEL 3.9
Derby Haven
Langness
Castletown
Port Erin
PORT ST MARY 3.10
Chicken Rock
54°N
30'
5°W
4°
3°

Off Skerries TSS
Centred on:
53°22·8'N 04°52'·0W
53°31'·3N 04°41'·7W
53°32'·1N 04°31'·6W

The separation zone and traffic lanes are 2M wide and orientated 263°-083° and 216°-036°.

The passage outside the Skerries is preferable to the inside passage, except in strong offshore winds. The inside passage should not be used at night. When passing outside the Skerries allow a distance off of at least 1M to avoid the worst of the strong tidal stream.

Monitor Ch 16 when in the TSS.

1. ***Fishguard***	171	158	175	175	169	160	153	140	126	134	144	153	147	136	100	88	78	89	45	**1**
2. Bardsey Island	127	113	129	129	123	114	107	94	80	88	98	107	101	90	53	41	31	43	**2**	
3. **Holyhead**	93	81	94	96	90	69	68	62	46	50	65	79	73	68	36	32	26	**3**		
4. Caernarfon	117	103	104	105	99	82	81	73	68	68	80	76	70	59	22	10	**4**			
5. Beaumaris	109	93	94	95	89	72	71	73	58	58	70	66	60	49	12	**5**				
6. **Conwy**	111	95	95	92	86	58	72	72	57	59	68	62	56	46	**6**					
7. **Liverpool**	118	102	97	89	83	60	80	86	76	70	77	52	46	**7**						
8. **Fleetwood**	95	79	68	59	53	30	58	80	63	57	55	10	**8**							
9. Glasson Dock	101	85	74	66	60	37	64	85	69	63	61	**9**								
10. Ramsey	44	28	34	41	35	34	6	24	27	15	**10**									
11. Douglas	60	42	46	50	44	39	19	30	13	**11**										
12. **Port St Mary**	56	41	61	63	57	50	35	18	**12**											
13. Peel	41	26	46	55	49	52	18	**13**												
14. **Point of Ayre**	38	22	28	37	31	34	**14**													
15. Ravenglass	70	54	40	30	23	**15**														
16. Workington	63	47	25	6	**16**															
17. **Maryport**	65	49	26	**17**																
18. **Kirkcudbright**	48	32	**18**																	
19. ***Mull of Galloway***	16	**19**																		
20. ***Portpatrick***	**20**																			

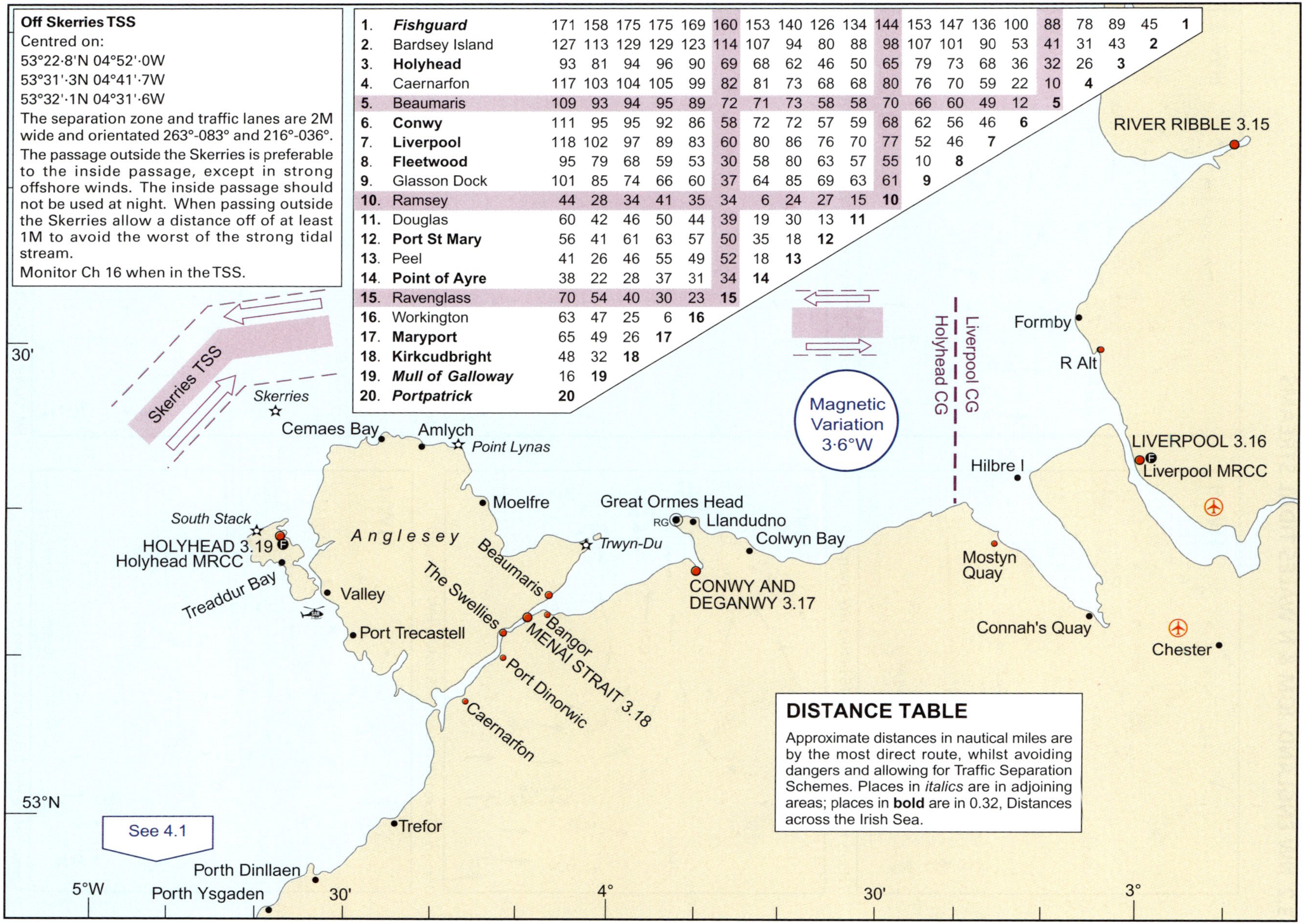

DISTANCE TABLE

Approximate distances in nautical miles are by the most direct route, whilst avoiding dangers and allowing for Traffic Separation Schemes. Places in *italics* are in adjoining areas; places in **bold** are in 0.32, Distances across the Irish Sea.

3.2 NW ENGLAND, IOM & N WALES TIDAL STREAMS

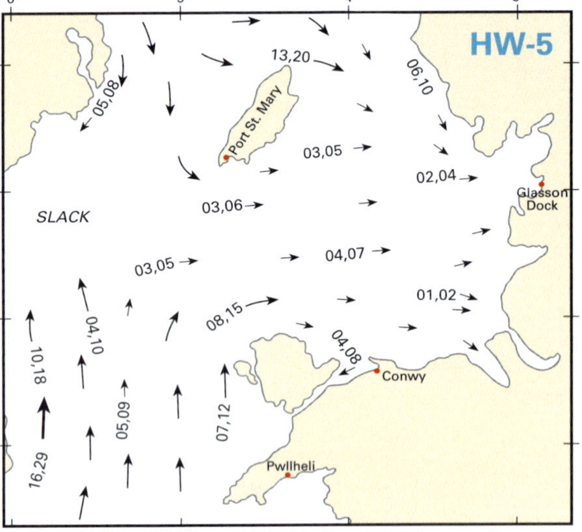

5 Hours before HW Dover (0515 before HW Liverpool)

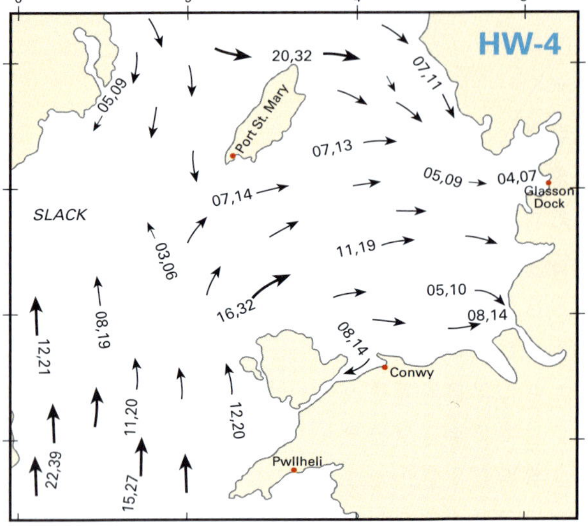

4 Hours before HW Dover (0415 before HW Liverpool)

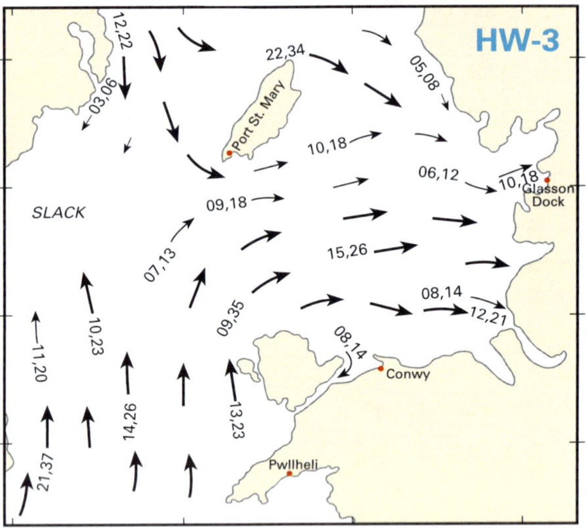

3 Hours before HW Dover (0315 before HW Liverpool)

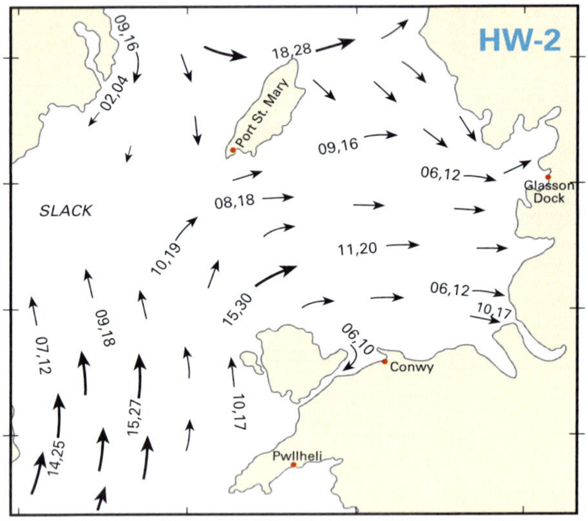

2 Hours before HW Dover (0215 before HW Liverpool)

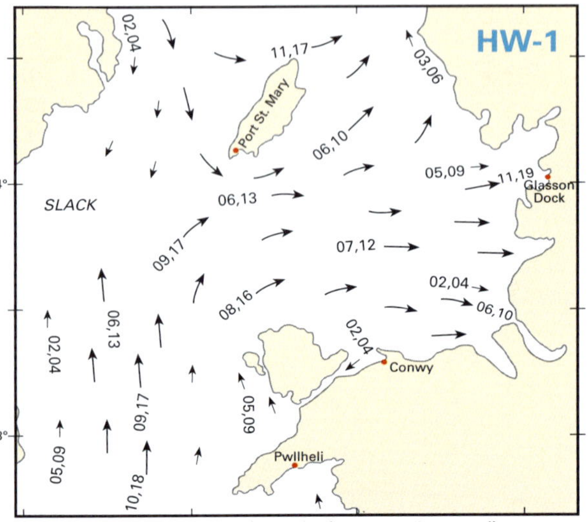

1 Hour before HW Dover (0115 before HW Liverpool)

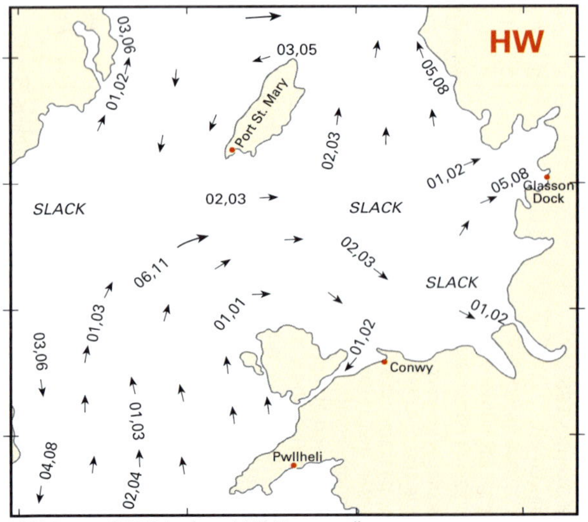

HW Dover (0015 before HW Liverpool)

Northward 2.2 Southward 4.2 North Ireland 6.2 Mull of Kintyre 2.9 South Ireland 5.2

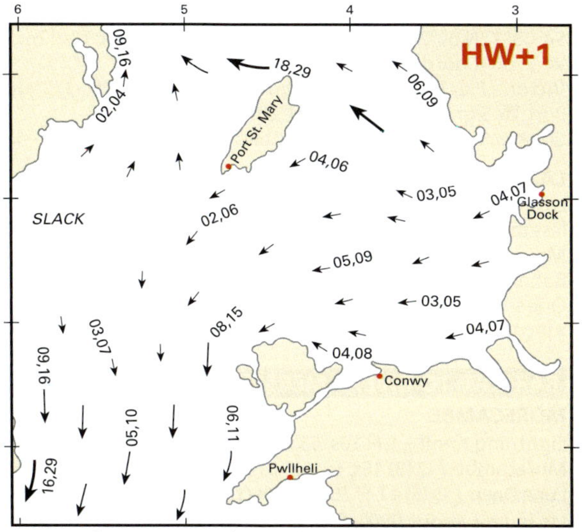

1 Hour after HW Dover (0045 after HW Liverpool)

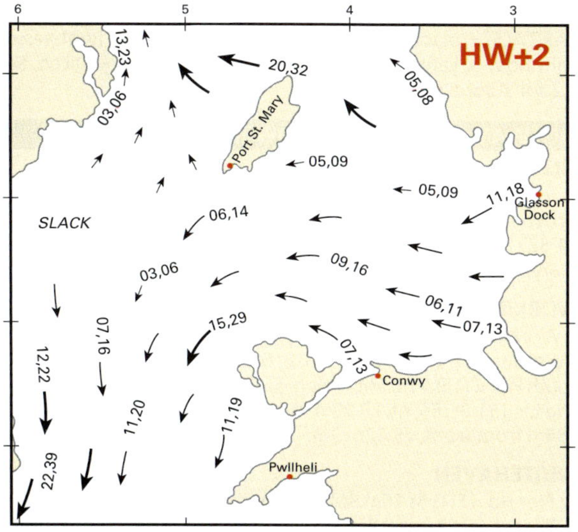

2 Hours after HW Dover (0145 after HW Liverpool)

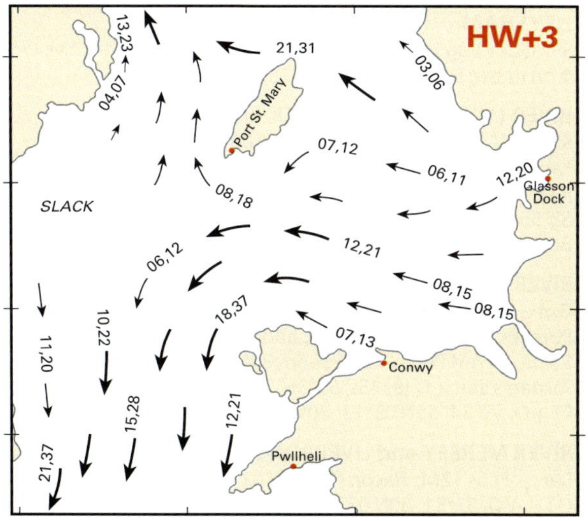

3 Hours after HW Dover (0245 after HW Liverpool)

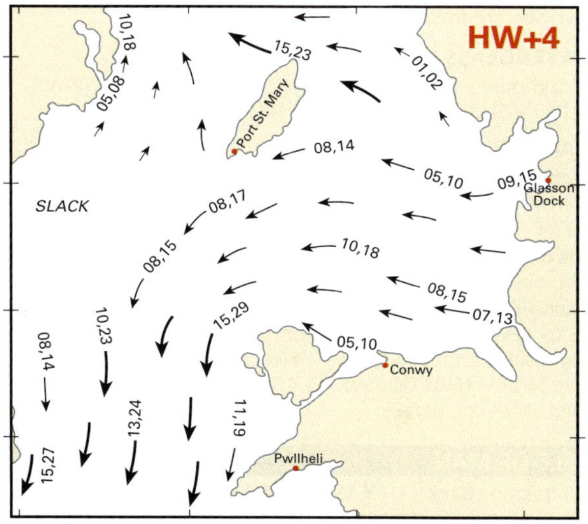

4 Hours after HW Dover (0345 after HW Liverpool)

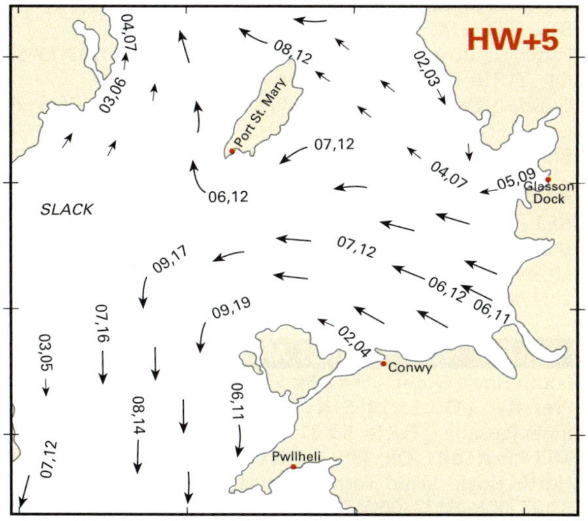

5 Hours after HW Dover (0445 after HW Liverpool)

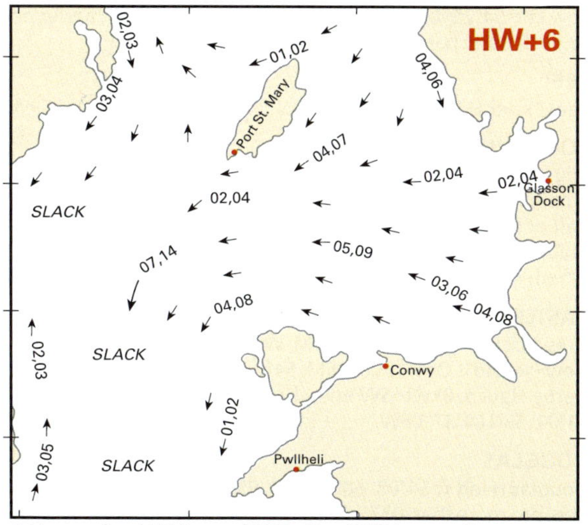

6 Hours after HW Dover (0545 after HW Liverpool)

W England, IoM, Wales

3.3 LIGHTS, BUOYS AND WAYPOINTS

Blue print = light with a nominal range of 15M or more. CAPITALS = place or feature. *CAPITAL ITALICS* = light-vessel, light float or Lanby. *Italics* = Fog signal. ***Bold italics*** = Racon. See 0.2 for Abbreviations.

SOLWAY FIRTH TO BARROW-IN-FURNESS

SILLOTH and MARYPORT

Two Feet Bank Q (9) 15s; 54°42'·90N 03°47'·10W.
Groyne Hd 2 FG (vert) 4m 4M; Fl Bu tfc signals close by; 54°52'·14N 03°23'·93W.
Maryport S Pier Hd .Fl 1·5s 10m 6M;54°43'·07N 03°30'·64W.

WORKINGTON and HARRINGTON

N Workington Q; 54°40'·10N 03°38'·18W.
S Workington VQ (6) + L Fl 10s; 54°37'·01N 03°38'·58W.
South Pier Fl 5s 11m 5M; R bldg; 54°39'·12N 03°34'·67W.
Ldg Lts 131·8°. Front, FR 10m 3M; 54°38'·92N 03°34'·19W. Rear, 134m from front, FR 12m 3M.

WHITEHAVEN

W Pier Hd Fl G 5s 16m 8M; W ○ twr; 54°33'·17N 03°35'·92W.
N Pier Hd 2 FR (vert) 8m 5M; W ○ twr; 54°33'·17N 03°35'·75W.
Saint Bees Hd ☆ 54°30'·81N 03°38'·23W Fl (2) 20s 102m **18M**; W○ twr; obsc shore-340°.

RAVENGLASS

Blockhouse FG; (Eskdale Range); 54°20'·16N 03°25'·34W.
Selker Fl (3) G 10s; *Bell;* 54°16'·14N 03°29'·58W.

BARROW-IN-FURNESS

Lightning Knoll L Fl 10s; 53°59'·83N 03°14'·28W.
Halfway Shoal QR 19m 10s; R&W chequer Bn; ***Racon (B) 10M***; 54°01'·46N 03°11'·88W.
Isle of Walney ☆ 54°02'·92N 03°10'·64W Fl 15s 21m **23M**; stone twr; obsc 122°-127° within 3M of shore.
Walney Chan Ldg Lts 040·7°. No.1 Front , Q 7m 10M; B Pile; 54°03'·19N 03°09'·22W. No. 2 Rear , 0·61M from front, Iso 2s 13m 10M; Pile.
Rampside Sands Ldg Lts 005·1°. No. 3 Front , Q 9m10M; W ○ twr; 54°04'·41N 03°09'·79W. No. 4 Rear , 0·77M from front, Iso 2s 14m 6M; R col, W face.

ISLE OF MAN

Whitestone Bank Q (9) 15s; 54°24'·58N 04°20'·41W.
Point of Ayre ☆ 54°24'·94N 04°22'·13W Fl (4) 20s 32m **19M**; W twr, two R bands, ***Racon (M) 13-15M***.
Low Lt 54°25'·03N 04°21'·86W Fl 3s 10m 8M; R twr, lower part W, on B Base; part obsc 335°-341°.

PEEL

Peel Bkwtr Hd Oc 7s 11m 6M; W twr; 54°13'·67N 04°41'·69W.

PORT ERIN and PORT ST MARY

Ldg Lts 099·1°. Front, 54°05'·23N 04°45'·57W FR 10m 5M; W twr, R band. Rear, 39m from front, FR 19m 5M; W col, R band.
Calf of Man Lighthouse (disused), white 8-sided tower.
Chicken Rk Fl 5s 38m **21M**; twr; 54°02'·27N 04°50'·32W.
Alfred Pier Hd Oc R 10s 8m 6M; W twr, R band; 54°04'·33N 04°43'·82W.

CASTLETOWN and DERBY HAVEN

Dreswick Pt Fl (2) 30s 23m 12M; W twr; 54°03'·29N 04°37'·45W.
New Pier Hd Oc R 15s 8m 5M; 54°04'·33N 04°38'·97W.
Derby Haven, Bkwtr SW end Iso G 2s 5m 5M; W twr, G band; 54°04'·58N 04°37'·06W.

DOUGLAS

Douglas Head ☆ 54°08'·60N 04°27'·95W Fl 10s 32m **24M**; W twr; obsc brg more than 037°. FR Lts on radio masts 1 and 3M West.
No. 1 Q (3) G 5s; 54°09'·04N 04°27'·68W.
Princess Alexandra Pier Hd Fl R 5s 16m 8M; R mast; *Whis (2) 40s;* 54°08'·84N 04°27'·85W.
Ldg Lts 229·3°, Front , Oc 10s 9m 5M; W △ R border on mast; 54°08'·72N 04°28'·25W. Rear , 62m from front, Oc 10s 12m 5M; W ▽ on R border; synch with front.
Victoria Pier Hd Iso G 10s 10m 3M; W col; vis: 225°-327°; Intnl Port Tfc Signals; 54°08'·84N 04°28'·08W.
Conister Rk Refuge twr Q 3M; vis: 234°-312°; 54°09'·03N 04°28'·12W.

LAXEY to RAMSEY

Laxey Pier Hd Oc R 3s 7m 5M; W twr, R band; obsc when brg less than 318°; 54°13'·50N 04°23'·43W.
Maughold Head ☆ 54°17'·72N 04°18'·58W Fl (3) 30s 65m **21M**.
Bahama VQ (6) + L Fl 10s; 54°20'·01N 04°08'·57W.
Queens Pier Dn Fl R 5s; 54°19'·28N 04°21'·95W.
King William Bank Q (3) 10s; 54°26'·01N 04°00'·08W.

BARROW TO RIVERS MERSEY AND DEE

MORECAMBE

Lightning Knoll L Fl 10s; 53°59'·84N 03°14'·28W.
Morecambe Q (9) 15s; 53°52'·01N 03°24'·10W.
Lune Deep Q (6) + L Fl 15s; ***Racon (T);*** 53°56'·07N 03°12·9W.
Lts in line about 090°. Front, FR 10m 2M; G mast; 54°04'·41N 02°52'·63W. Rear, 140m from front, FR 14m 2M; G mast.

HEYSHAM

SW Quay Ldg Lts 102·2°. Front , both F Bu 11/14m 2M; Or & B ♦ on masts; 54°01'·91N 02°55'·22W.

RIVER LUNE, GLASSON DOCK and FLEETWOOD

R Lune Q (9) 15s; 53°58'·63N 03°00'·03W.
Fairway No. 1(Fleetwood) 53°57'·67N 03°02'·03W Q; *Bell*.
Fleetwood Esplanade Ldg Lts 156°. Front, Iso G 2s 14m 9M; 53°55'·71N 03°00'·56W. Rear, 320m from front, Iso G 4s 28m 9M. Both vis on Ldg line only. (H24) (chan liable to change).

RIVER RIBBLE

Gut L Fl 10s; 53°41'·74N 03°08'·98W.
Perches show Fl R on N side, and Fl G on S side of chan.
S side, 14¼M Perch Fl G 5s 6m 3M; 53°42'·75N 03°04'·90W.
Jordan's Spit Q (9) 15s; 53°35'·76N 03°19'·28W.
FT Q; 53°34'·56N 03°13'·20W.

RIVER MERSEY and LIVERPOOL

Bar Fl.5s 12M; ***Racon (T) 10M;*** 53°32'·01N 03°20'·98W.
Q1 VQ; 53°31'·00N 03°16'·72W.
Q2 VQ R; 53°31'·47N 03°14'·95W.
Q3 Fl G 3s; 53°30'·95N 03°15'·10W.
BT Fl (3) G 9s; 53°30'·41N 03°17'·61W.
Formby Iso 4s 11m 6M; R hull, W stripes; 53°31'·13N 03°13'·50W.
C4 Fl R 3s; 53°31'·82N 03°08'·51W.
Crosby Oc 5s 11m 8M; R hull, W stripes; 53°30'·72N 03°06'·29W.
C14 Fl R 3s; R hull; 53°29'·91N 03°05'·34W.
Brazil QG; G hull; 53°26'·84N 03°02'·24W.

RIVER DEE, MOSTYN and CONNAH'S QUAY

HE1 Q (9) 15s; 53°26'·33N 03°18'·08W.
HE2 Q (3) 10s; 53°25'·13N 03°13'·07W.
Mostyn Dir Lt 174°. 53°19'·33N 03°16'·12W Iso WRG 2s 16m 7M vis: 174·8°-G-176·8°-W-177·8°-R-179·8°; H24.

WALES – NORTH COAST AND INNER PASSAGE

South Hoyle Outer Fl R 2·5s; 53°21'·47N 03°24'·70W.
Prestatyn QG; 53°21'·51N 03°28'·51W.
Inner Passage Fl R 5s; 53°21'·91N 03°31'·95W.
Mid Patch Spit QR; 53°22'·25N 03°32'·67W.
North Hoyle Wind Farm (30 turbines, see 3.4) centred on 53°25'·00N 03°27'·00W. NW, NE, SW, SE extremities (F.R Lts) Fl Y 2.5s 5M Horn Mo (U) 30s.

Mast Mo (U) 15s 12m 10M & 2FR (vert); Horn Mo (U) 30s; Mast (80); 53°28'·84N 03°30'·50W.
W Constable Q (9) 15s; ***Racon (M) 10M;*** 53°23'·14N 03°49'·26W.
N Constable VQ; 53°23'·76N 03°41'·42W.

RHYL, LLANDUDNO and CONWY

River Clwyd Outfall 53°19'·59N 03°30'·63W.
Llandudno Pier Hd 2 FG (vert) 8m 4M; 53°19'·90N 03°49'·51W.
Great Ormes Hd Lt Ho, (unlit); 53°20'·56N 03°52'·17W.
Conwy Fairway L Fl 10s; 53°17'·95N 03°55'·58W.
C2 Fl (2) R 10s; 53°17'·64N 03°54'·71W.
Conway R ent S side Fl WR 5s 5m 2M; vis: 076°-W-088°-R- 171°-W-319°-R-076°; 53°18'·07N 03°50'·86W.

ANGLESEY

Point Lynas ☆ 53°24'·98N 04°17'·35W Oc 10s 39m **18M**; W castellated twr; vis: 109°-315°; *Horn 45s;* H24.

AMLWCH to HOLYHEAD BAY

Main Bkwtr Fl G 15s 11m 3M; W mast; vis: 141°-271°; 53°25'·02N 04°19'·91W.
Furlong Fl G 2·5s; 53°25'·41N 04°30'·47W.
Archdeacon Rock Q; 53°26'·71N 04°30'·87W.
Victoria Bank VQ; 53°25'·61N 04°31'·37W.
Coal Rk Q (6) + L Fl 15s; 53°25'·91N 04°32'·79W.
Ethel Rk VQ; 53°26'·64N 04°33'·67W.
The Skerries ☆ 53°25'·27N 04°36'·55W Fl (2) 15s 36m **20M**; W ○ twr, R band; ***Racon (T) 25M***. Iso R 4s 26m 10M; same twr; vis: 233°-253°; *Horn (2) 60s*. H24 in periods of reduced visibility.
Langdon Q (9) 15s; 53°22'·74N 04°38'·74W.
Bolivar FL G 2·5s; 53°21'·51N 04°35'·33W.
Wk Fl (2) R 10s; 53°20'·43N 04°36'·60W.

HOLYHEAD to SOUTH STACK

Bkwtr Head Fl (3) G 10s 21m 14M; W □ twr, B band; Fl Y vis: 174°-226°; *Siren 20s;* 53°19'·31N 04°37'·16W.
Spit Fl G 3s; 53°19'·79N 04°37'·15W.
South Stack ☆ 53°19'·31N 04°41'·98W Fl 10s 60m **24M**; (H24); W ○ twr; obsc to N by N Stack and part obsc in Penrhos bay; *Horn 30s*. Fog Det lt vis: 145°-325°.

MENAI STRAIT TO BARDSEY ISLAND

Ten Feet Bank QR; 53°19'·47N 04°02'·82W.
Dinmor QG; 53°19'·34N 04°03'·32W.
Trwyn-Du Fl 5s 19m 12M; W ○ castellated twr, B bands; vis: 101°-023°; *Bell (1) 30s*, sounded continuously; 53°18'·77N 04°02'·44W. FR on radio mast 2M SW.

APPROACHES to BEAUMARIS and BANGOR

(Direction of buoyage NE to SW)
Perch Rock Fl R 5s; 53°18'·73N 04°02'·09W.

PORT DINORWIC and CAERNARFON

Port Dinorwic Pier Hd 53°11'·18N 04°12'·64W F WR 5m 2M; vis: 225°-R- 357°-W-225°.
(Direction of buoyage SW to NE)
Caernarfon N Pier Hd 2 FG (vert) 5m 2M; 53°08'·72N 04°16'·56W.
Abermenai Point Fl WR 3·5s 6m 3M; W mast; vis: 065°-R-245°-W-065°; 53°07'·62N 04°19'·72W.
C1 Fl G 5s; 53°07'·27N 04°24'·85W.
C2 Fl R 10s; 53°07'·38N 04°24'·87W.
Llanddwyn I Fl WR 2·5s 12m W7M, R4M; W twr; vis: 280°-R-015°-W-120°; 53°08'·05N 04°24'·79W .

PORTH DINLLÄEN

CG Stn FR when firing taking place 10M N; 52°56'·82N 04°33'·89W.
Careg y Chwislen 52°56'·99N 04°33'·51W.
Bardsey I ☆ 52°44'·97N 04°48'·02W Fl (5) 15s 39m **26M**; W □ twr, R bands; obsc by Bardsey Is 198°-250° and in Tremadoc B when brg < 260°; *Horn Mo (N) 45s*; (H24 in poor vis).

3.4 PASSAGE INFORMATION

For detailed directions covering these waters and harbours refer to the Admiralty Pilot *W Coast of England and Wales*; *Lundy and Irish Sea Pilot* (Taylor/Imray). Admiralty Leisure Folio 5609 covers North West Wales from Aberystwyth to Colwyn Bay including Menai Strait; Folio 5613 covers Great Ormes Head to the Mull of Galloway including the Isle of Man.

More Passage Information is threaded between the harbours of this Area.

SOLWAY FIRTH

(AC 1346) Between Abbey Hd and St Bees Hd lies the Solway Firth, most of which is encumbered by shifting sandbanks.The *Solway SDs* are essential. Off the entrances to the Firth, and in the approaches to Workington beware shoals over which strong W winds raise a heavy sea. There are navigable, buoyed chans as far as Annan on the N shore, but buoys are laid primarily for the aid of Pilots. ► *Local knowledge is required, particularly in the upper Firth, where streams run very strongly in the chans when the banks are dry, and less strongly over the banks when covered. In Powfoot chan for example the in-going stream begins at HW Liverpool – 0300, and the outgoing at HW Liverpool + 0100, **sp rates up to 6kn.*** ◄

Between Silloth and Walney Is are Maryport, Workington, Harrington, Whitehaven, and Ravenglass. A windfarm is under construction (2008) approximately 7M WNW of Maryport. South along the Cumbrian coast past St Bees Hd to Walney Is there are no dangers more than 2M offshore, but no shelter except, possibly, in Ramsey bay, IoM.

3.5 MARYPORT

Cumbria **54°43'·03N 03°30'·38W**

CHARTS AC 1826, 1346, 2013, 5613; Imray C62.

TIDES +0038 Dover; ML no data; Duration 0550

Standard Port LIVERPOOL (⟶)

Times				Height (metres)			
High Water		Low Water		MHWS	MHWN	MLWN	MLWS
0000	0600	0200	0800	9·3	7·4	2·9	0·9
1200	1800	1400	2000				
Differences MARYPORT							
+0017	+0032	+0020	+0005	–0·7	–0·8	–0·4	0·0
SILLOTH							
+0030	+0040	+0045	+0055	–0·1	–0·3	–0·6	–0·1

SHELTER Good in marina, access HW ±2½ nps over sill 1·75m; at other times Workington is a refuge. Elizabeth Basin dries 2m, access HW±1½; commercial, not used by yachts.

NAVIGATION WPT 54°43´·09N 03°32´·47W, 090°/1M to S pier. Overfalls at ent with W/SW winds over ebb. At HW–3 1·8m over bar at ent and in river chan; mud banks cover HW –2.

LIGHTS AND MARKS See 3.3 and chartlet. SHM bn Fl G 5s marks outfall 6ca SW of S pier.

R/T Port VHF Ch 12 16. Marina (H24) Ch 12 16.

TELEPHONE (Code 01900) HM 817440; Hbr Authority 604351; CG 812782; MRCC (0151) 931 3341; Marinecall 09068 969651; Police 602422; Dr 815544; Ⓗ 812634.

FACILITIES Maryport Marina (201 inc Ⓥ £14.69/craft inc ⊐D), ☎ 814431, www.maryportmarina.com, BY, BH, El, CH, ⊡, ME, Slip (±3HW), D, P, (fresh fish from Fisherman's Co-op); **Maryport Yachting Ass'n** ☎ 64964. **Town** P, D, ME, 🛒, R, Bar, ✉, Ⓑ, ⇌, ✈ (Newcastle).

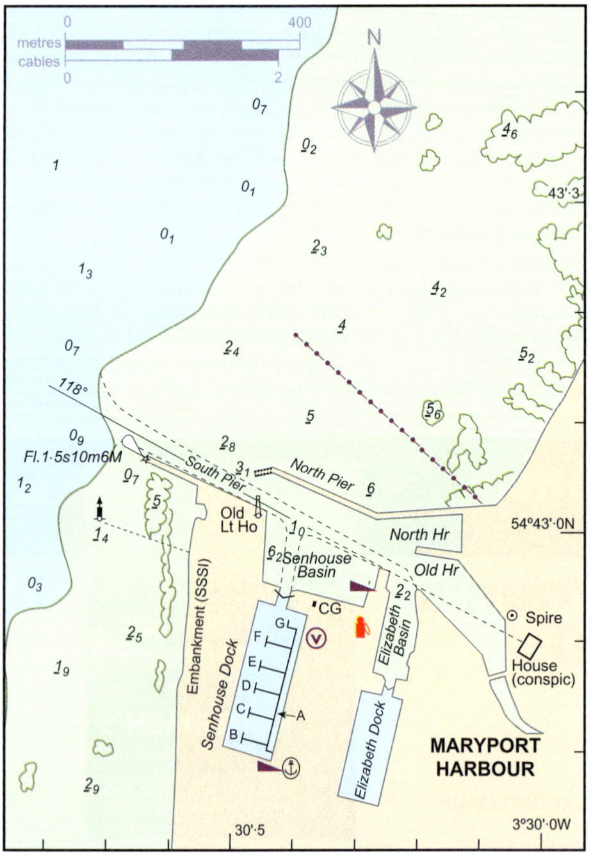

3.6 WORKINGTON

Cumbria 54°39'·03N 03°34'·38W

CHARTS AC 1826, 1346, 2013, 5613; Imray C62.

TIDES +0025 Dover; ML 4·5; Duration 0545

Standard Port LIVERPOOL (⟶)

Times				Height (metres)			
High Water		Low Water		MHWS	MHWN	MLWN	MLWS
0000	0600	0200	0800	9·3	7·4	2·9	0·9
1200	1800	1400	2000				
Differences WORKINGTON							
+0020	+0020	+0020	+0010	–1·2	–1·1	–0·3	0·0

SHELTER Good; ent and chan to Prince of Wales Dock are dredged 1·8m. Berth where you can (free in tidal harbour); no ⚓ in Turning Basin. Lock (HW±1½) into PoW Dock 1·8m (for coasters). Low (1·8m) fixed railway bridge across ent to inner tidal hbr.

NAVIGATION WPT 54°39´·59N 03°35´·38W, 131°/1M to front ldg lt.

- Tide sets strongly across ent. In periods of heavy rain a strong freshet from R Derwent may be encountered in the hbr ent.

LIGHTS AND MARKS Workington Bank, least depth 5·5m, is 2M W of hbr ent; and is marked by NCM and SCM lt buoys (see 3.3). A SHM buoy, Fl G 5s, 1·3M NW of hbr ent is a mark for English Chan. Ldg lts 132°, both FR 10/12m 3M, on W pyramidal trs with R bands. Two sets of F Bu lts in line mark NE and SW edges of chan.

- There are 16 wind-turbines between ¾M and 2M NE of hbr ent.

R/T VHF Ch 14 16 (HW–2½ to HW+2 approx).

TELEPHONE (Code 01900) HM 602301; MRCC (0151) 931 3341; Marinecall 09068 969651; Police 602422; Dr 64866; Ⓗ 602244.

FACILITIES Dock D, FW, ME, El; **Vanguard SC** ☎ 01228 674238, M, FW. **Town** P, 🛒, R, Bar, ✉, Ⓑ, ⇌, ✈ (Carlisle).

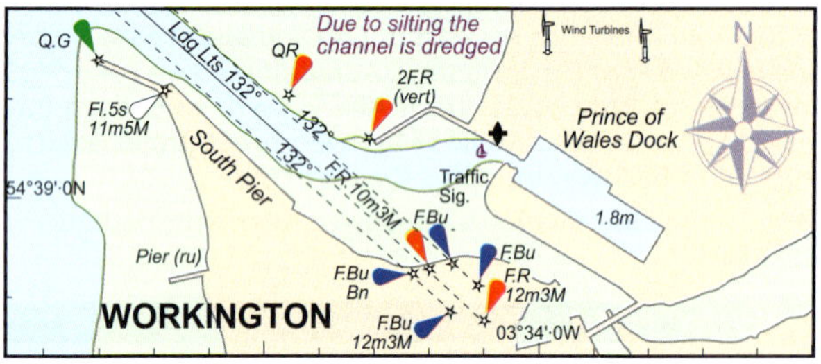

MINOR HARBOUR 10M NNE OF MARYPORT

SILLOTH, Cumbria, **54°52´·16N 03°23´·86W**. AC 1826, 1346, 2013, 5613. HW –0050 on Dover; ML no data; Duration 0520. See 3.5. Appr via English or Middle Chans, approx 8M long, requires local knowledge. Beware constantly shifting chans and banks. Yachts are not encouraged. ⚓ SW of ent in about 4m off Lees Scar, Fl G 10s 11m 2M; exposed to SW winds. Outer hbr dries; lock into New Dock (note sill 1.2 above CD), which is mainly commercial. East Cote Dir lt 052° FG 15m 12M; vis 046°-058°, intens 052°. Ldg lts, both F, 115°. Groyne 2 FG (vert). Tfc sigs on mast at New Dock: must receive permission from Port Authority before proceeding. VHF Ch 16 12 (HW–2½ to HW+1½). HM ☎ (016973) 31358. Facilities: FW, Ⓑ, Bar, ✉, R, 🛒.

MINOR HARBOUR 2M S OF WORKINGTON

HARRINGTON, Cumbria, **54°36´·77N 03°34´·29W**. AC 1826, 1346, 2013, 5613. HW +0025 on Dover; Duration 0540; Use Diff's Workington 3.6. Good shelter in small hbr only used by local FVs and yachts; dries 3ca offshore. Ent difficult in strong W winds. Berth on N wall of inner hbr (free). Call ☎ (01946) 823741 Ext 148 for moorings. Limited facilities. **SC**.

3.7 WHITEHAVEN

Cumbria **54°33´·18N 03°35´·82W** ❀❀❀◊◊✿✿

CHARTS AC 1826, 1346, 2013, 5613; Imray C62.

TIDES +0015 Dover; ML 4·5; Duration 0550

Standard Port LIVERPOOL (⟶)

Times				Height (metres)			
High Water		Low Water		MHWS	MHWN	MLWN	MLWS
0000	0600	0200	0800	9·3	7·4	2·9	0·9
1200	1800	1400	2000				
Differences WHITEHAVEN							
+0005	+0015	+0010	+0005	−1·3	−1·1	−0·5	+0·1
TARN POINT (54°17'N 03°25'W)							
+0005	+0005	+0010	0000	−1·0	−1·0	−0·4	0·0
DUDDON BAR (54°09'N 03°20'W)							
+0003	+0003	+0008	+0002	−0·8	−0·8	−0·3	0·0

SHELTER Very good, entry safe in most weathers. One of the more accessible ports of refuge in NW England, with a new marina in the inner hbr. Appr chan across the outer hbr is dredged to 1·0m above CD giving access approx HW±4. Sea lock (30m x 13.7m), with sill at CD, maintains 7m within inner hbr. Yacht pontoons are in Inner Hbr. Queen's Dock (from which the lock gates have been decommissioned) and N Hbr remain for commercial and FV use.

NAVIGATION WPT 54°33'·34N 03°36'·21W, 133°/4½ca to W pier hd. There are no hazards in the offing. Hold closer to the North Pier, and beware stone bar at end of W Pier.

LIGHTS AND MARKS Several tall chimneys are charted within 1·5M S of hbr. St Bees Head Lt ho is 2·7M SSW of hbr ent. SHM bn, Fl G 2·5s, 4½ca S of W pierhead marks sewer outfall. IPTS sigs 1-3 shown from N side of lock ent to seaward only at present: priority to inward bound vessels.

R/T HM VHF Ch 12 16 (as for access times).

TELEPHONE (Code 01946)HM 692435, 📠 691135; Sealock 694672; MRCC (0151) 931 3341; Police 692616; Marinecall 09068 969651.

FACILITIES **Marina** (200 inc Ⓥ) ☎ 692435, office@whitehaven-harbour.co.uk, <12m £15, <12m £8 on quay wall, contact HM, D, Gas, BY, CH, ME, Ⓔ, El, ⚒, BH, Slip, ▣. **SC**. **Town** Market days Thurs, Sat; P (cans), Bar, Ⓑ, ✉, R, 🛒, ⇌.

MINOR HARBOUR BETWEEN ST BEES HD AND MORECAMBE BAY

RAVENGLASS, Cumbria, **54°20´·00N 03°26´·80W** (drying line). AC 1346, 1826, 5613. HW +0020 on Dover; ML no data; Duration 0545. See 3.7 (Tarn Pt). Large drying hbr, into which R's Mite, Irt and Esk flow; approx 2·5m in ent at HW–2. Sellafield power stn with WCM lt buoy and outfall buoys are 5M NNW. FG ☆ (occas) on blockhouse at S side of ent. *Solway Sailing Directions* with pilotage notes by Ravenglass Boating Ass'n, local knowledge advisable. From N beware Drigg Rk and from S Selker Rks, SHM lt buoy, 5M SSW of ent. Firing range D406 close S at Eskmeals; Mon-Thur 0800-1600LT (1500 Fri). When in use R flags flown, R lts at night; *Eskmeals Gun Range* VHF Ch 16 13, ☎ (01229) 717631 Ext 245/6. **Village**: FW, Slip, Bar, 🛒, ✉.

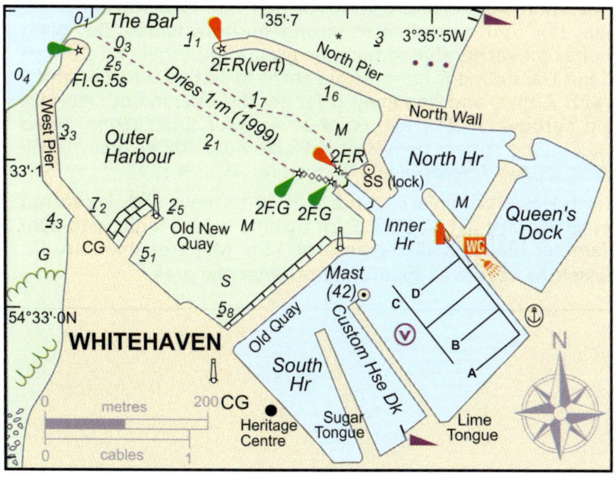

3.8 ISLE OF MAN

Charts AC Irish Sea 1826, 1411; 2094 (small scale); 2696 (ports), 5613 (Folio). Imray, C26, Y70.

The Isle of Man is one of the British Islands, set in the Irish Sea roughly equidistant from England, Scotland, Wales and Ireland but it is not part of the UK. It has a large degree of self-government. Lights are maintained by the Northern Lighthouse Board. Manx harbours are administered by the IOM Government.

Distances See 3.1 for distances between ports in Area 10 and 0.32 for distances across the Irish Sea, North Channel and St George's Channel.

Harbours and anchorages Most of the harbours are on the E and S sides, but a visit to the W coast with its characteristic cliffs is worth while. The four main harbours are described in an anti-clockwise direction from Peel on the W coast to Ramsey in the NE. There are good ⚓s at: Port Erin in the SW, Castletown and Derby Haven in the SE, and Laxey Bay in the E. All IOM harbours charge the same overnight berthing rate, £1.02/m (multi-hulls £1.53/m).

R/T If contact with local Harbour Offices cannot be established on VHF, vessels should call *Douglas Hbr Control* Ch **12** 16 for urgent messages or other info.

Coastguard Call Liverpool MRCC Ch 16 67 86; the Snaefell (IoM) aerial is linked to Liverpool by land line.

Customs The IOM is under the same customs umbrella as the rest of the UK, and there are no formalities on arriving from or returning to the UK.

Weather Forecasts can be obtained direct from the forecaster at Ronaldsway Met Office ☎ 0900 6243 3200, H24. **Douglas Hbr Control** (3.15) can supply visibility and wind info on request.

MINOR HARBOURS IN THE ISLE OF MAN

PORT ERIN, Isle of Man, **54°05´·31N 04°46´·34W**. AC 2094, 2696, 5613. HW –0020 on Dover; ML 2·9m; Duration 0555. See 3.14. From S and W, Milner's Twr on Bradda Hd is conspic. Ldg lts, both FR 10/19m 5M, lead 099° into the bay. Beware the ruined bkwtr (dries 2·9m) extending N from the SW corner, marked by an unlit SHM buoy. A small hbr on the S side dries 0·8m. Raglan Pier (E arm of hbr), Oc G 5s 8m 5M. Two Ⓥs W of Raglan Pier. Good ⚓ in 3-8m N of Raglan Pier, but exposed to W'lies. Call Port St. Mary Harbour (VHF Ch 12) ☎ 833205

CASTLETOWN BAY, Isle of Man, **54°03´·51N 04°38´·57W**. AC 2094, 2696, 5613. HW +0025 on Dover; ML 3·4m; Duration 0555. The bay gives good shelter except in SE to SW winds. From the E, keep inside the race off Dreswick Pt, or give it a wide berth. Beware Lheeah-rio Rks in W of bay, marked by PHM buoy, Fl R 3s, Bell. Hbr dries 3·1m to level sand. Access HW±2½. Berth in outer hbr or go via swing footbridge (manually opened) into inner hbr below fixed bridge. ⚓ between Lheeah-rio Rks and pier in 3m; or NW of Langness Pt. Lts: Langness lt, on Dreswick Pt, Fl (2) 30s 23m 12M. Hbr S (New) Pier, Oc R 15s 8m 5M; Inner S pier (Irish Quay), Oc R 4s 5m 5M, vis 142°-322°. 150m NW is swing bridge marked by 2 FR (hor). N pier, Oc G 4s 3m (W metal post on concrete column). VHF Ch 12 16 (when vessel due). HM ☎ 823549; Dr 823597. Facilities: **Outer hbr** Slip, L, C (mobile), AB; **Irish Quay** AB, C, FW; **Inner hbr** AB, C, FW; **Town** P, D, Gas, ME.

LAXEY, Isle of Man, **54°13´·46N 04°23´·32W**. AC 2094, 5613. HW +0025 on Dover; +0010 and –2·0m on Liverpool; ML 4m; Duration 0550. The bay gives good shelter in SW to N winds. 2 yellow Ⓥs (seasonal) are close E of hbr ent; 2 more are 1M S in Garwick Bay. ⚓ about 2ca S of pier hds or in Garwick Bay. The hbr dries 3·0m to rk and is only suitable for small yachts; access HW±3 for 1·5m draft. Beware rks on N side of the narrow ent. Keep close to pier after entering to avoid training wall on NE side. AB on inside of pier; inner basin is full of local boats. Pier hd lt Oc R 3s 7m 5M, obsc when brg <318°. Bkwtr hd lt Oc G 3s 7m. Harbour Office ☎ 861663. Facilities: FW, R, ✉, Ⓑ, Bar.

ISLE OF MAN

(Charts 2094, 2696, 5613) For general pilotage information, tidal streams and hbr details of IOM, see *IOM Sailing Directions, Tidal Streams and Anchorages*, published by Hunter Publications. For notes on crossing the Irish Sea, see 6.4.

There are four choices when rounding S of IoM:

In bad weather, or at night, keep S of Chicken Rk. In good conditions, pass between Chicken Rk and Calf of Man. With winds of <Force 3 and a reliable engine giving >5kn, and only by day use Calf Sound between Calf of Man and IoM, passing W of Kitterland Is but E of Thousla Rk, which is marked by lt bn and is close to Calf of Man shore. Little Sound, a minor chan, runs E of Kitterland Is.

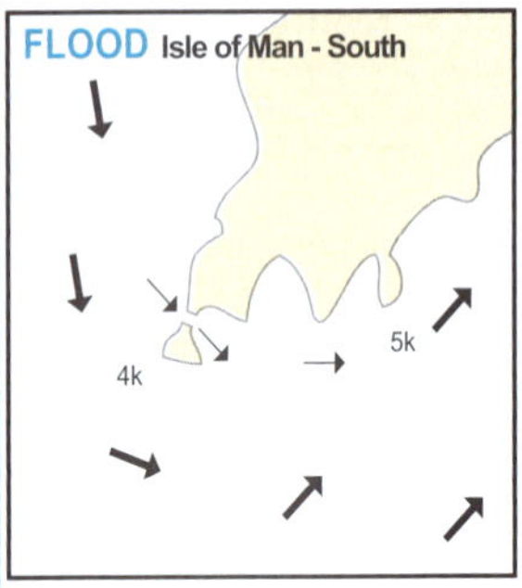

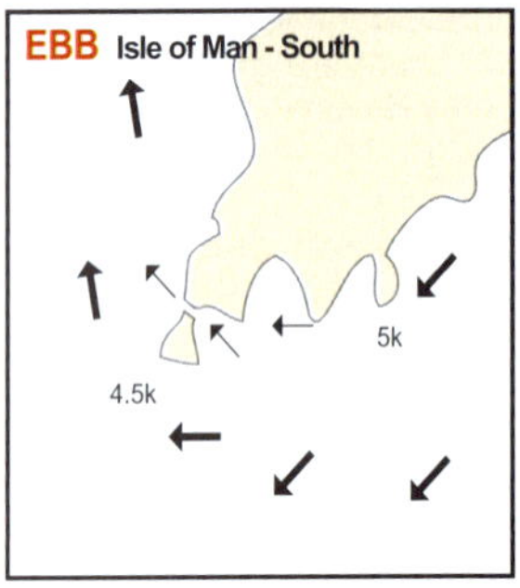

▶ *The stream runs strongly through Calf Sound, starting N-going at HW Liverpool – 0145, and S-going at HW Liverpool + 0345, sp rates 3·5kn. W of Calf of Man the stream runs N and S, but changes direction off Chicken Rk and runs W and E between Calf of Man and Langness Pt 6M to E. Overfalls extend E from Chicken Rk on E-going stream, which begins at HW Liverpool + 0610, and N from the rk on W-going stream, which begins at HW Liverpool.*

Off Langness Pt (lt) the Skerranes (dry) extend 1ca SW, and tidal stream runs strongly, with eddies and a race. E side of Langness peninsula is foul ground, over which a dangerous sea can build in strong winds. Here the NE-going stream begins at HW Liverpool +0545, and the SW-going at HW Liverpool –0415, sp rates 2·25kn. ◀

There is an anchorage in Derby Haven, N of St Michael's Is, but exposed to the E. From here to Douglas and on to Maughold Hd (lt), there are no dangers more than 4ca offshore. ▶ *Near the coast the SW-going stream runs for 9 hours and the NE-going for 3 hours, since an eddy forms during the second half of the main NE-going stream. Off Maughold Hd the NE-going stream begins at HW Liverpool +0500, and the SW-going at HW Liverpool –0415.*◀

SE, E and NW of Pt of Ayre are dangerous banks, on which seas break in bad weather. These are Whitestone Bk (least depth 2·0m), Bahama Bk (1·5m), Ballacash Bk (2·7 m), King William Bks (3·3m), and Strunakill Bk (6·7m).

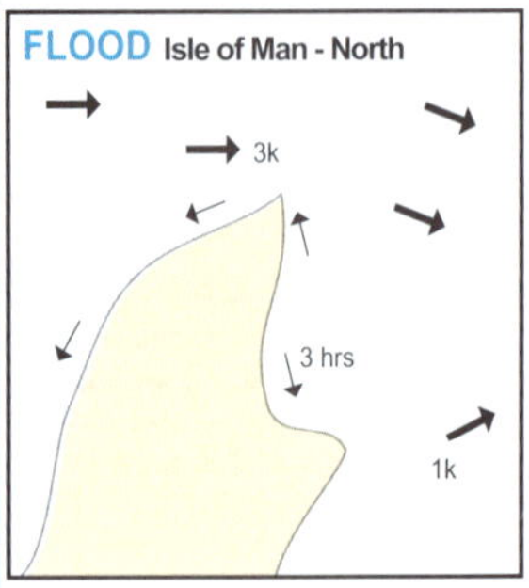

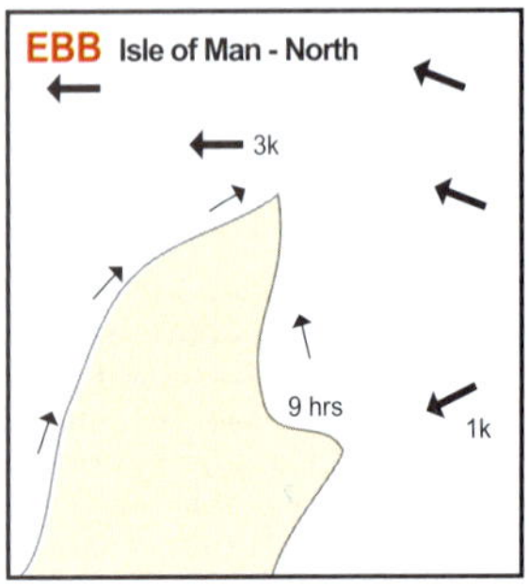

▶ *E-going stream at Point of Ayre begins HW Liverpool –0600 (HW Dover –0545). Counter tide inside banks E of Point. In Ramsey Bay the S-going tide runs for 3 hours from Liverpool +0515 (Dover +0530).*

W-going stream at Point of Ayre begins HW Liverpool (HW Dover +0015). Counter tide inside banks W of Point. In Ramsey Bay the N going tide runs for 9 hours from Liverpool –0345 (Dover –0330).◀

The W coast of IOM has few pilotage hazards. A spit with depth of 1·4m runs 2ca offshore from Rue Pt. Jurby Rk (depth 2·7m) lies 3ca off Jurby Hd. Craig Rk (depth 4 m) and shoals lie 2·5M NNE of Peel.

BARROW TO CONWY

(AC 2010, 1981, 1978, 5613) Ent to Barrow-in-Furness (AC 3164) is about 1M S of Hilpsford Pt at S end of Walney Island where the lt ho is prominent. ▶*The stream sets across the narrow chan, which is well marked but shallow in patches.*◀ W winds cause rough sea in the ent. Moorings and anch off Piel and Roa Islands, but space is limited. ▶ *Stream runs hard on ebb. Coming from the S it is possible with sufficient rise of tide to cross the sands between Fleetwood and Barrow.* ◀

Barrow Wind Farm, consisting of 30 turbines, is marked by FR and Fl Y lights on all structures. The site is centred approx 7·6M SSW of Barrow-in-Furness.

Lune Deep, 2M NW of Rossall Pt, is ent to Morecambe B (chart 2010), and gives access to the ferry/commercial port of Heysham, Glasson Dock, and Fleetwood; it is well buoyed. ▶ *Streams run 3·5kn at sp.*◀ Most of Bay is encumbered with drying sands, intersected by chans which are subject to change. S of Morecambe B, beware shoals and drying outfall (2·0m) extending 3M W of Rossall Pt. Further S, R. Ribble gives access via a long drying chan to the marina at Preston.

Queen's Chan and Crosby Chan (AC 1951 &1978) are entered E of the Bar Lat Buoy SWM. They are well buoyed, dredged and preserved by training banks, and give main access to R Mersey and Liverpool. Keep clear of commercial shipping. From the N the old Formby chan is abandoned, but possible near HW. Towards HW in moderate winds a yacht can cross the training bank (level varies between 2m and 3m above CD) E of Great Burbo Bk, if coming from the W, Rock Chan, which is unmarked and dries in parts, may also be used but beware wrecks.

In good weather at nps, the Dee Estuary (AC 1953, 1978) is accessible for boats able to take the ground. But most of estuary dries and banks extend 6M seaward. Chans shift, and buoys are moved as required. ▶ *Stream runs hard in chans when banks are dry.* ◀ Main ent is Welsh Chan, but if coming from N, Hilbre Swash runs W of Hilbre Is.

Sailing W from the Dee on the ebb, it is feasible to take the Inner Passage (buoyed) S of West Hoyle Spit, which gives some protection from onshore winds at half tide or below. Rhyl is a tidal hbr, not accessible in strong onshore winds, but gives shelter for yachts able to take the ground. Abergele Rd, Colwyn B and Llandudno B are possible anchs in settled weather and S winds. Conwy and Deganwy offer good shelter in both marinas and harbour. ▶ *Between Point of Ayr and Great Ormes Head the E-going stream begins at HW Liverpool +0600, and the W-going at HW Liverpool –0015, sp rates 3kn.* ◀

North Hoyle Wind Farm consists of 30 turbines and is centred on 53°25'·00N 03°27'·00W. Each turbine is 58m high, with 80m diameter blades and clearance of 18m. Many of them are lit. Vessels to keep well clear and not enter the area.

3.9 PEEL

Isle of Man 54°13'·61N 04°41'·68W ❀❀⚓⚓✿✿✿

CHARTS AC 2094, 2696, 5613; Imray C62; Y70.

TIDES +0005 Dover; ML 2·9; Duration 0545

Standard Port LIVERPOOL (⟶)

Times				Height (metres)			
High Water		Low Water		MHWS	MHWN	MLWN	MLWS
0000	0600	0200	0700	9·3	7·4	2·9	0·9
1200	1800	1400	1900				
Differences PEEL							
+0005	+0005	-0015	–0025	–4·1	–3·1	–1·4	–0·5

SHELTER Good, except in strong NW to NE winds when ent should not be attempted. 4 Y Øs (seasonal) off S groyne in about 2m. Fin keelers may be able to berth on N bkwtr in 5m. A new (2009) 120-berth marina is in the Inner Harbour. Approach dries 1·4m; access approx HW±2 when flapgate lowered and through swing bridge. Maintained depth 2·5m.

NAVIGATION WPT 54°13´·97N 04°41´·43W, 200°/0·42M to groyne lt. When close in, beware groyne on S side of hbr ent, submerged at half tide.

LIGHTS AND MARKS Power stn chy (80m, grey with B top) at S end of inner hbr is conspic from W and N; chy brg 203° leads to hbr ent. Groyne lt and Clock Tr (conspic) in transit 200° are almost on same line. Peel Castle and 2 twrs are conspic on St Patrick's Isle to NW of hbr. Ldg lts in transit 207° on Groyne Fl R 5s 4m. Traffic sigs for Inner Hbr.

R/T *Peel Hbr* VHF Ch **12** 16 (HW±2, HO for Swing Bridge – other times call *Douglas Hbr Control* Ch 12 for remote bridge opening).

TELEPHONE (Code 01624) Harbour Office ☎ 842338, Mobile 07624 495036; MRCC 0151-931 3341; Weather 0900 6243 322; Marinecall 09068 969651; Police 697327; Dr 843636.

FACILITIES **Outer Hbr**, AB see 3.8; **Marina** 102 AB inc Ⓥ, £1.53; access via flapgate; M, Slip, FW, D, ME, El, ⚒, C (mobile); **Peel Sailing and Cruising Club** ☎ 842390, Showers (key from Harbour Office), R, ▣, Bar; **Services:** Gas, BY, CH, ACA. **Town** P (cans), 🛒, R, Bar, ✉, Ⓑ, ⇄ (bus to Douglas (and ferry)), ✈ Ronaldsway. Facilities: Bar, D, P, FW, R, Slip, 🛒.

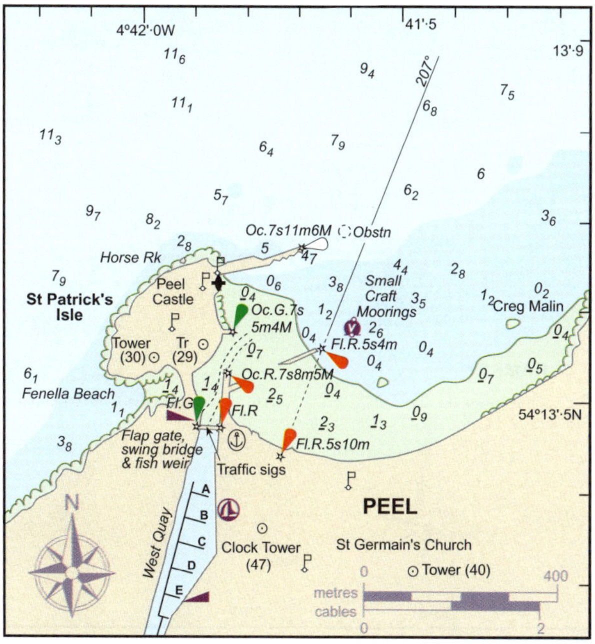

3.10 PORT ST MARY

Isle of Man **54°04'·43N 04°43'·73W** ❀❀⚓⚓✿✿

CHARTS AC 2094, 2696, 5613; Imray C62; Y70.

TIDES +0020 Dover; ML 3·2; Duration 0605

Standard Port LIVERPOOL (⟶)

Times				Height (metres)			
High Water		Low Water		MHWS	MHWN	MLWN	MLWS
0000	0600	0200	0700	9·3	7·4	2·9	0·9
1200	1800	1400	1900				
Differences PORT ST MARY							
+0005	+0015	–0010	–0030	–3·4	–2·6	–1·3	–0·4
CALF SOUND							
+0005	+0005	–0015	–0025	–3·2	–2·6	–0·9	–0·3
PORT ERIN							
–0005	+0015	–0010	–0050	–4·1	–3·2	–1·3	–0·5

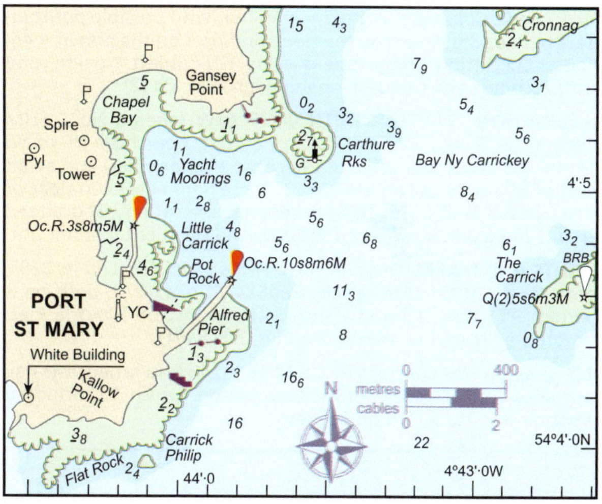

SHELTER Very good except in E or SE winds. ⚓ S of Gansey Pt, but poor holding. 5 yellow Øs (seasonal) between Alfred Pier and Little Carrick.

NAVIGATION WPT 54°04´·21N 04°43´·37W, 295°/0·3M to Alfred Pier lt. Rocky outcrops to SE of pier to 2ca offshore. Beware lobster/crab pots, especially between Calf Island and Langness Pt.

LIGHTS AND MARKS Alfred Pier, Oc R 10s 8m 6M. Inner pier, Oc R 3s 8m 5M; both lts on W trs + R band, in transit 295° lead clear S of The Carrick Rk, in centre of bay, which is marked by IDM bn, Q (2) 5s 6m 3M. A conspic TV mast (133m), 5ca WNW of hbr, in transit with Alfred Pier lt leads 290° towards the hbr and also clears The Carrick rock.

R/T Call *Port St Mary Hbr* VHF Ch 12 16 (when vessel due or through Douglas Hbr Control Ch 12).

TELEPHONE (Code 01624) HM 833205; MRCC 0151 931 3341; Weather 0900 6243 322, Marinecall 09068 969651; Police 697327; Dr 832226.

FACILITIES **Alfred Pier** AB see 3.8, Slip, D, L, FW, C (mobile); **Inner Hbr** dries 2·4m on sand; AB, Slip, D, L, FW; **Isle of Man YC** ☎ 832088, FW, Showers, Bar; **Services:** ME, CH, D, El, SM. **Town** CH, 🛒, R, Bar, ✉, Ⓑ, ⇄ (bus to Douglas, qv for ferries), ✈ Ronaldsway.

MINOR HARBOUR EAST OF CASTLETOWN

DERBY HAVEN, Isle of Man, **54°04´·65N 04°36´·45W**. Tides & charts as above. Rather remote bay exposed only to NE/E winds. ⚓ in centre of bay, NW of St Michael's Island, in 3-5m. A detached bkwtr on NW side of the bay gives shelter to craft able to dry out behind it. Lts: Iso G 2s on S end of bkwtr. Aero FR (occas) at Ronaldsway airport, NW of bay. Facilities: at Castletown (1½M) or Port St Mary.

Isle of Man

3.11 DOUGLAS

Isle of Man **54°08'·87N 04°27'·96W** ❀❀❀◊◊✿✿✿

CHARTS AC 2094, 2696, 5613; Imray C62; Y70.

TIDES +0009 Dover; ML 3·8; Duration 0600

Standard Port LIVERPOOL (⟶)

Times				Height (metres)			
High Water		Low Water		MHWS	MHWN	MLWN	MLWS
0000	0600	0200	0700	9·3	7·4	2·9	0·9
1200	1800	1400	1900				
Differences DOUGLAS							
+0005	+0015	−0015	−0025	−2·4	−2·0	−0·5	−0·1

SHELTER Good except in NE winds. Very heavy seas run in during NE gales. Outer hbr: Victoria and King Edward VIII piers are for commercial vessels/ferries. At inner end of Battery Pier in summer about 18 boats can raft up on pontoon; untenable in NE/E winds. Complete shelter in inner hbr, with possible pontoon berths, flapgate lowers on the flood and rises on the ebb at 4·4m above CD, lifting bridge opens every ½H subject to tide/road traffic conditions (request opening on VHF Ch12).

NAVIGATION WPT 54°09′·01N 04°27′·67W (abeam No 1 SHM buoy, Q (3) G 5s), 229°/0·47M to front ldg lt. Appr from NE of No 1 buoy (to avoid overfalls E of Princess Alexandra Pier) and await port entry sig, or call on VHF Ch 12. There is no bar. Keep clear of large vessels and ferries. Beware concrete step at end of dredged area (◊ mark on King Edward VIII Pier) and cill at ent to inner hbr.

LIGHTS AND MARKS Douglas Head Fl 10s 32m 24M. Ldg lts 229°, both Oc 10s 9/12m 5M, synch; front W △; rear W ▽, both on R border. IPTS Nos 2, 3 and 5 shown from mast on Victoria Pier. Dolphin at N end of Alexandra Pier 2FR (vert).

R/T *Douglas Hbr Control* VHF Ch **12** 16 (H24); also broadcasts nav warnings for IoM ports and coastal waters on Ch 12 including weather and tidal info on request.

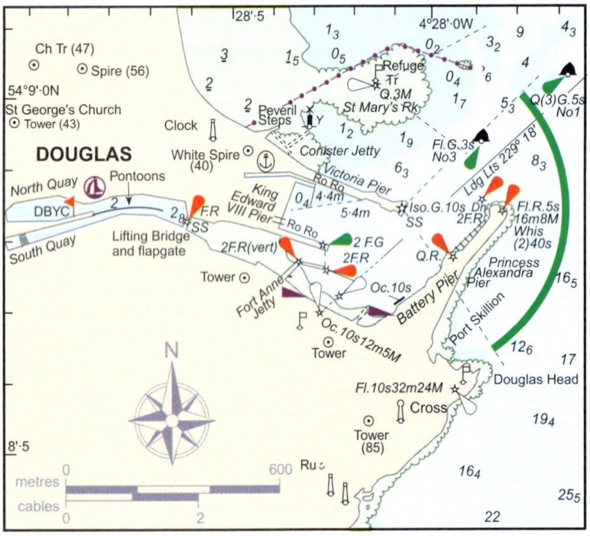

TELEPHONE (Code 01624) Hr Control 686628 (H24); MRCC 0151-931 3341; Weather 0900 6243 322, Marinecall 09068 969651; Police 697327; ⊞ 650000.

FACILITIES **Outer Hbr** AB see 3.8, M, FW at pontoon, D, ME, El, ⚒, C (mobile), Slip; **Inner Hbr (Pontoons and N and S Quays)** (110); Ⓥ according to space (no reservations), M, ⊐D, FW, ME, C, El, ⚒, CH, Slip; **Douglas Bay YC** ☎ 673965, Bar, Slip, L, showers 0930-2300. **Services:** P (cans), D, CH, ACA, El, Divers, Gas, Gaz, Kos. **Town** www.gov.im, 🛒, R, Bar, ✉, Ⓑ, ⊡, ✈ Ronaldsway. **Ferries:** Liverpool; 16/week; 2½ Hrs; IoM Steam Packet (www.steam-packet.com). Heysham; 16/week; 3½ Hrs; Steam Packet. Also to Dublin and Belfast.

3.12 RAMSEY

Isle of Man **54°19'·44N 04°22'·49W** ❀❀◊◊✿✿

CHARTS AC 2094, 2696, 5613; Imray C62; Y70.

TIDES +0020 Dover; ML 4·2; Duration 0545

Standard Port LIVERPOOL (⟶)

Times				Height (metres)			
High Water		Low Water		MHWS	MHWN	MLWN	MLWS
0000	0600	0200	0700	9·3	7·4	2·9	0·9
1200	1800	1400	1900				
Differences RAMSEY							
+0005	+0015	−0005	−0015	−1·9	−1·5	−0·6	0·0

SHELTER Very good except in strong NE winds. Hbr dries 1·8m–6m. Access and ent only permitted HW −2½ to HW +2. Berth on Town quay (S side) or as directed by HM on entry. 4 yellow Ⓥs are close NW of Queen's Pier hd (seasonal). Note: Landing on Queen's Pier is prohibited.

NAVIGATION WPT 54°19′·44N 04°21′·89W, 270°/0·37M to ent. The foreshore dries out 1ca to seaward of the pier hds.

LIGHTS AND MARKS No ldg lts/marks. Relative to hbr ent, Pt of Ayre, Fl (4) 20s 32m 19M, is 5·5M N; Maughold Hd, Fl (3) 30s 65m 21M, is 3M SE; Albert Tr (□ stone tr 14m, on hill 130m) is conspic 7ca S; and Snaefell (617m) bears 220°/5M. Inside the hbr an Iso G 4s, G SHM post, marks the S tip of Mooragh Bank; it is not visible from seaward. 2FR (hor) on each side mark the centre of swing bridge.

R/T *Ramsey Hbr* VHF Ch **12** 16 (0800-1600LT and when a vessel is due); Other times call *Douglas Hbr Control* Ch **12**.

TELEPHONE (Code 01624) Harbour Office 812245, mob 07624 460304; MRCC 0151 931 3341; Weather 0900 6243 322, Marinecall 09068 969651; Police 812234; Dr 813881; ⊞ 811811.

FACILITIES **Outer Hbr: E Quay** ☎ 812245, strictly for commercial vessels (frequent movements H24), no AB for yachts, FW; **Town Quay** (S side) AB see 3.8, ⊐D, FW. **Inner Hbr, W Quay** AB, ⊐D, FW, Slip (Grid); **N Quay** AB, D, FW; **Shipyard Quay** Slip; **Old Hbr** AB, Slip, M; **Manx S&CC:** ☎ 813494 AB; **Services:** P (cans) from garages, D, ME, El, Ⓔ, ⚒, ⓢ. **Town** 🛒, R, Gas, Gaz, Kos, Bar, @ in Library, ⊡, ✉, Ⓑ, ⇌ (bus to Douglas, which see for ferries), ✈ Ronaldsway.

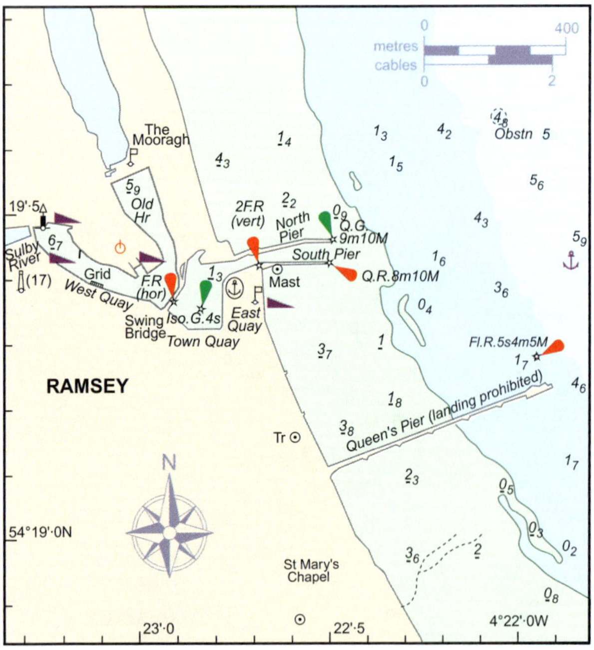

3.13 GLASSON DOCK

Lancashire **53°59'·98N 02°50'·93W** ❁❁◊◊◊✿✿

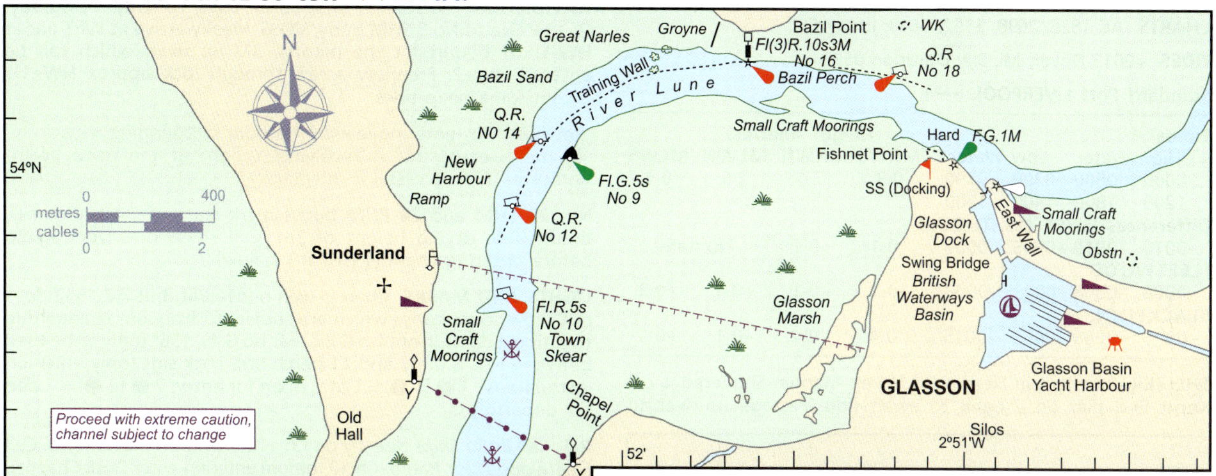

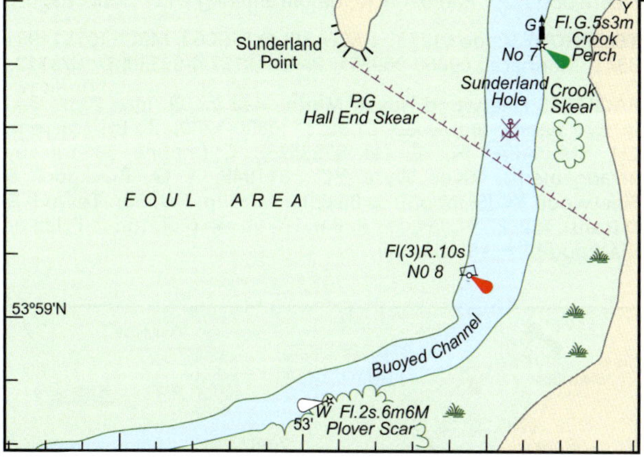

CHARTS AC 1826, 1552, 2010, 5613; Imray C62.

TIDES +0020 Dover; ML No data; Duration 0535

Standard Port LIVERPOOL (⟶)

Times				Height (metres)			
High Water		Low Water		MHWS	MHWN	MLWN	MLWS
0000	0600	0200	0700	9·3	7·4	2·9	0·9
1200	1800	1400	1900				
Differences BARROW-IN-FURNESS (Ramsden Dock)							
+0015	+0015	+0015	+0015	0·0	–0·3	+0·1	+0·2
ULVERSTON							
+0020	+0040	No data		0·0	–0·1	No data	
ARNSIDE							
+0100	+0135	No data		+0·5	+0·2	No data	
MORECAMBE							
+0005	+0010	+0030	+0015	+0·2	0·0	0·0	+0·2
HEYSHAM							
+0005	+0005	+0015	0000	+0·1	0·0	0·0	+0·2
GLASSON DOCK							
+0020	+0030	+0220	+0240	–2·7	–3·0	No data	
LANCASTER							
+0110	+0030	Dries out		–5·0	–4·9	Dries out	

NOTE: At Glasson Dock LW time differences give the end of a LW stand which lasts up to 2 hrs at sp.

SHELTER Very good in marina (lock width 9m); also sheltered ⚓ in R Lune to await sea lock, opens HW–1 to HW (Liverpool) (but daylight hrs only Nov-Mar) into Glasson Dock. Inner lock/swing bridge lead into BWB basin.

NAVIGATION WPT 53°58'·63N 03°00'·03W (R Lune WCM buoy), 4·2M to Plover Scar. Leave WPT at HW–1½ via buoyed/lit chan which is subject to frequent change. For latest info call Port Commission (☎ 01524 751724). ⚓ is prohibited between Sutherland Pt and No 10 PHM lt buoy. Beyond this a training wall, marked by PHM lt buoys/bn, extends to lock ent. R Lune is navigable to Lancaster.

• ***It is dangerous to proceed downriver later than HW +1.***

LIGHTS AND MARKS Plover Scar, Fl 2s, on with Cockersand, FW, leads 084° up to Nos 2/3 buoys; then follow buoyed chan which shifts.

Tfc Sigs at E side of lock from estuary
● = lock manned, but shut
● = lock open, clear to enter

Tfc Sigs inside dock
● = Gate closed or vessel(s) entering dock
● = Gate open. Vessels may leave

R/T VHF Ch 16 69 (HW–1½ to HW Liverpool).

TELEPHONE (Code 01524) HM 751724, 🖷 753601; MRCC 0151 931 3341; Marinecall 09068 969651; Police 63333; Ⓗ 765944.

FACILITIES **Glasson Basin Marina** (240 + 20 Ⓥ) £12.00/craft) ☎ 751491, www.BWML.co.uk. Slip, D (0830-1630), ME, El, Ⓔ, ⚒, BH (35 ton), CH, ♿; **Glasson SC** ☎ 751089 Slip, M, C; **Lune CC** Access HW±2. **Town** P (cans), 🛒, R, Bar, ✉, Ⓑ (Lancaster), ⇌ (bus to Lancaster 4M), ✈ (Blackpool).

ADJACENT HARBOURS IN MORECAMBE BAY

BARROW-IN-FURNESS, Cumbria, **54°05'·64N 03°13'·44W**. AC 1826, 2010, 3164, 5613. HW +0030 on Dover; See 3.13. ML 5·0m; Duration 0530. Good shelter but open to SE winds. Drying moorings off Piel and Roa Islands or ⚓ clear of fairway. Marks/lts: Walney Island Lt ho (conspic stone tr), Fl 15s 21m 23M (obsc 122°-127° within 3M of shore). Directions: From Lightning Knoll SWM lt buoy, ldg lts, front Q 7m 10M; rear (6ca from front), Iso 2s 13m 10M (lattice structures) lead 041°/3·7M past Halfway Shoal bn, QR 16m 10M with RY chequers, Racon, to Bar lt buoy (abeam Walney Island lt ho). Inner Channel ldg lts, front Q 9m 10M, rear Iso 2s 14m 6M, lead 005° past Piel Is with least charted depth 1·7m. Piel Is, conspic ruined castle, slip and moorings on E side. Roa Is, 5ca N, has jetty at S end and moorings on E & W sides. Slip (Roa Is Boat Club ☎ (01229) 825291). Causeway joins to mainland. Commercial docks, 3M NW at Barrow, reached via buoyed/lit Walney Chan, dredged to 2·5m, which must be kept clear. HM (Barrow) ☎ (01229) 822911; VHF *Barrow Port Control* Ch 12 16 (H24). Facilities: Hotel at Rampside, 🛒.

HEYSHAM, Lancashire, **54°02'·01N 02°55'·96W**. AC 1826, 2010, 1552, 5613. HW +0015 on Dover; ML 5·1m; Duration 0545. See 3.13. Good shelter, but yachts not normally accepted without special reason. Beware high speed ferries and oil rig supply ships. Ldg lts 102°, both F Bu 11/14m 2M, Y+B ◊ on masts. S jetty lt 2 FG (vert), Siren 30s. S pier hd ,Oc G 7·5s 9m 6M. N pier hd, 2FR (vert) 11m, obsc from seaward. Ent sigs: R flag or ● = no entry; no sig = no dep; 2 R flags or 2 ● = no ent or dep. VHF Ch 14 74 16 (H24). HM ☎ (01524) 852373. Facilities: Bar, FW, R, 🛒 at Morecambe (2M).

NW England

3.14 FLEETWOOD

Lancashire **53°55'·49N 03°00'·15W** ☸☸☸◊◊◊✿✿

CHARTS AC 1826, 2010, 1552, 5613; Imray C62.

TIDES +0015 Dover; ML 5.2; Duration 0530

Standard Port LIVERPOOL (⟶)

Times				Height (metres)			
High Water		Low Water		MHWS	MHWN	MLWN	MLWS
0000	0600	0200	0700	9·3	7·4	2·9	0·9
1200	1800	1400	1900				
Differences WYRE LIGHTHOUSE							
−0010	−0010	+0005	0000	−0·1	−0·1	No data	
FLEETWOOD							
−0008	−0008	−0003	−0003	−0·1	−0·1	+0·1	+0·3
BLACKPOOL							
−0015	−0005	−0005	−0015	−0·4	−0·4	−0·1	+0·1

SHELTER Excellent in Fleetwood Haven Marina. Sheltered ⚓ off Knott End pier on E bank to await tide. Passage up-river to Skippool (5M) needs local knowledge and shoal draft; access HW±1·5 hrs (if ht of tide is >8·5m).

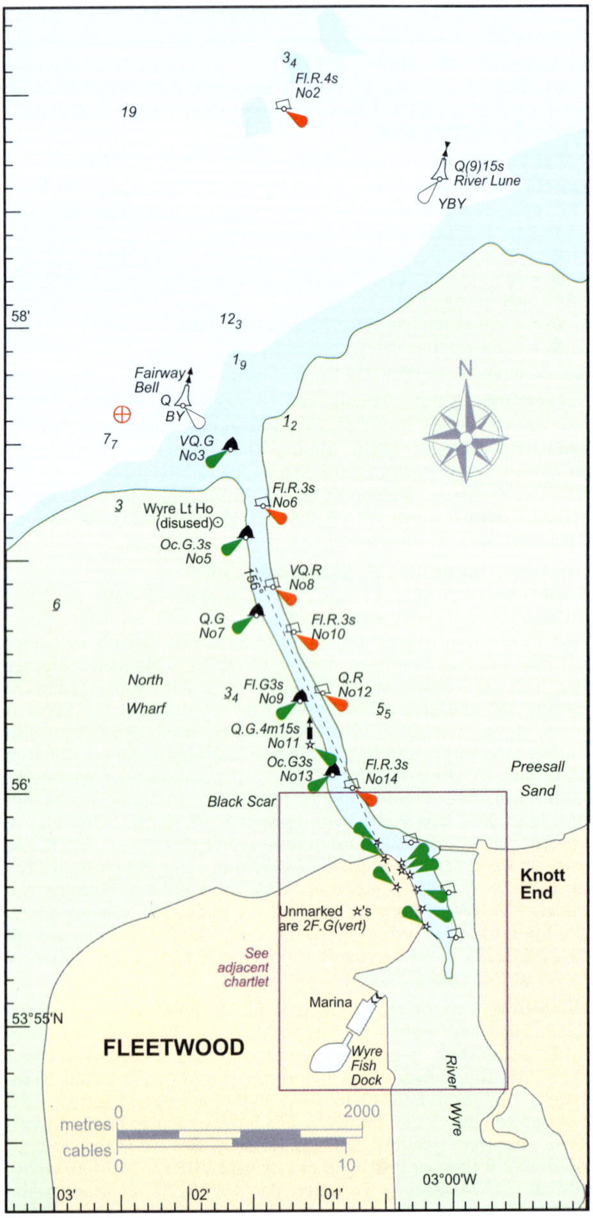

NAVIGATION WPT 53°57´·67N 03°02´·05W, Fairway NCM buoy, Q, 134°/3ca to No 3 SHM buoy, VQ.G. Ideally arrive at WPT about HW-1½ if bound for the marina, 3M up river, which can be entered HW±2. Freeflow access through lock approx HW±1½ except some neap tides.

Beware ships entering/leaving harbour or swinging in vicinity of the river berths. A revolving Y light at the ro-ro berth indicates a large vessel is moving.

Nos 23 SHM and 24 PHM buoys mark start of Dock Channel, dredged to drying height of 3m. Call Fleetwood Dock Radio before entering channel (see R/T below).

LIGHTS AND MARKS Chan is well buoyed/lit, but AC 1552 does not show some buoys which are subject to frequent change due to silting. Ldg lts, front Iso G 2s; rear Iso G 4s, 156° (only to be used between Nos 8 buoy and 11 perch bn). Lock sigs (only enter on instructions): 1 ● (1 ●) = Gates open for entry; 2 ● (2 ●) = open for departures.

R/T Call *RoRo Ships* directly on Ch 11 for info on movements. Call *Fleetwood Dock Radio,* Ch 12, before entering enter Dock Channel.

TELEPHONE (Code 01253) HM (ABP) ☎ 879062; MRCC (0151) 931 3341; Marinecall 09068 969651; Police (01524) 63333; Dr 873312.

FACILITIES Fleetwood Haven Marina 420 inc Ⓥ (max 20m LOA) in two basins, ☎ 879062, £1.96, D (0800-1700), ▣, BH (75 ton), CH, SM, ACA, ⚒, Ⓔ (☎ 8253535), C (mobile 50 ton by arrangement). **River Wyre YC** 811948, 1 Ⓥ. **Blackpool & Fleetwood YC** (Skippool) ☎ 884205, AB, Slip, FW, Bar; **Town** P & D (cans), ME, El, ⚒, CH, ▦, R, Bar, ✉, Ⓑ, ⇌ (Poulton-le-Fylde or Blackpool), ✈ (Blackpool).

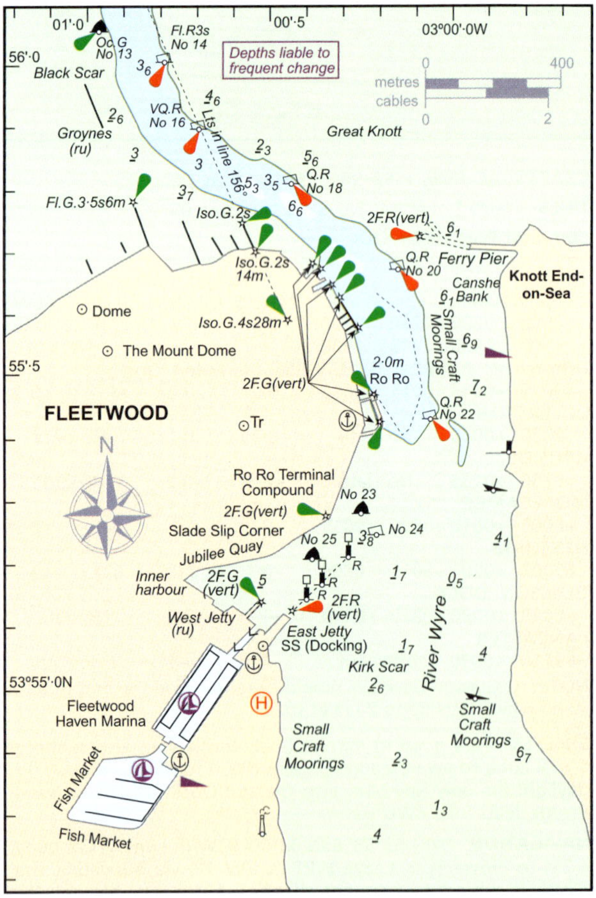

3.15 RIVER RIBBLE/PRESTON

Lancashire **53°43´·51N 03°00´·08W** ❀❀◊◊◊✿✿

CHARTS AC 1826, 1981, 5613; Imray C62.

TIDES +0013 Dover; ML No data; Duration 0520

Standard Port LIVERPOOL (⟶)

Times				Height (metres)			
High Water		Low Water		MHWS	MHWN	MLWN	MLWS
0000	0600	0200	0700	9·3	7·4	2·9	0·9
1200	1800	1400	1900				
Differences PRESTON							
+0010	+0010	+0335	+0310	–4·0	–4·1	–2·8	–0·8
LW time differences give the end of a LW stand lasting 3½ hrs.							
SOUTHPORT							
–0020	–0010	No data		–0·3	–0·3	No data	
FORMBY							
–0015	–0010	–0020	–0020	–0·3	–0·1	0·0	+0·1

SHELTER Good in Preston Marina (5m depth) 15M upriver. Possible drying berths on the N bank at Lytham or Freckleton, or 2M up R Douglas access HW±1.

NAVIGATION WPT **A** 53°41'·75N 03°08'·90W, Gut SWM lt buoy. The chartlet shows only the outer 6M of the estuary. The seaward 2·5M of the Gut chan is silted up. Best water is now via South Gut chan (liable to shift), navigable HW±2.

Leave WPT **A** at HW Liverpool –2. Track 105°/2·9M to WPT **B** 53°40'·96N 03°04'·22W; thence 032°/0·9M to WPT **C** 53°41'·70N 03°03'·43W; thence 026°/1·8M to WPT **D** 53°43'·29N 03°02'·10W.

Enter Gut Chan via the gap, leaving *11½M* perch 100m to port. The river trends 080° between training walls 3m, marked by lit perches. The remaining 15M is straightforward but night appr not advised.

Shortcut if draught < 2m: from WPT **A** track 090°/3·2M to WPT **C**. Then 026°/1·8M to WPT **D** and the transit of the 11½M SCM lt perch with conspic W twr.

LIGHTS AND MARKS 14½M perch is the most seaward chan mark. Up-river of 11½M perch there is a PHM buoy and perch (off chartlet), both Fl R 5s. 4 SHM perches, Fl G 5s, lead to 5M perch, Fl (2) G 10s, marking mouth of unlit R Douglas. 3M and 2M perches are Fl G 5s; 1M perch is Fl G 10s. Warton airfield beacon, Mo (WQ) G 9s occas, is N abeam 6M perch, Fl G 5s.

R/T At Preston, for locks call *Riversway* Ch **16** 14 (HW –1½ to +2); Marina Ch 80 (HO); Douglas BY Ch 16 when vessel due.

TELEPHONE (Code 01772) Preston locks 726871; MRCC (0151) 9313341; Marinecall 09068 969651; Police 203203; Ⓗ 710408.

FACILITIES Waiting berth for 2m draft outside storm gates which are usually open. Tfc lts at lock into marina; see plan below. Lock in HW–1 to +2, 0700-2100 Apr-Sep (Oct-Mar by arrangement with 24Hrs notice). Swing bridge opens in unison with locks.

Preston Marina ☎ 733595, www.prestonmarina. co.uk, £1·60, D, CH, ME, ⚒, Gas, C (25 ton, 45 ton by arrangement), R, 🛒, ACA, ♿.

Douglas BY, ☎ 812462, mob 07740 780899, AB, £0·70, C (20 ton), CH, D, FW, ⚒, Slip, ME.

Freckleton BY ☎ 632439, mob 07957 820881, AB, £5/yacht, slip, FW, CH, ME.

Ribble Cruising Club ☎ (01253) 739983.

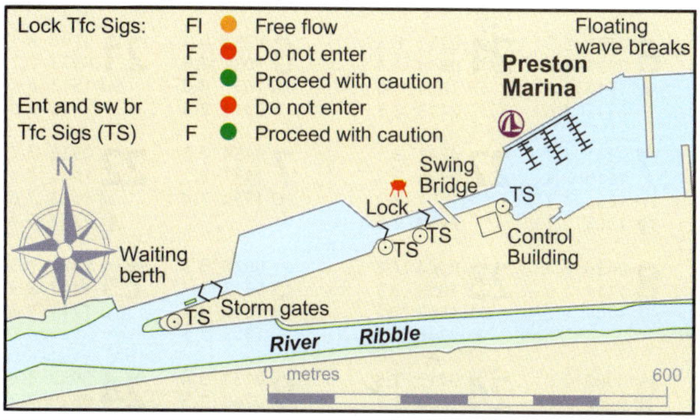

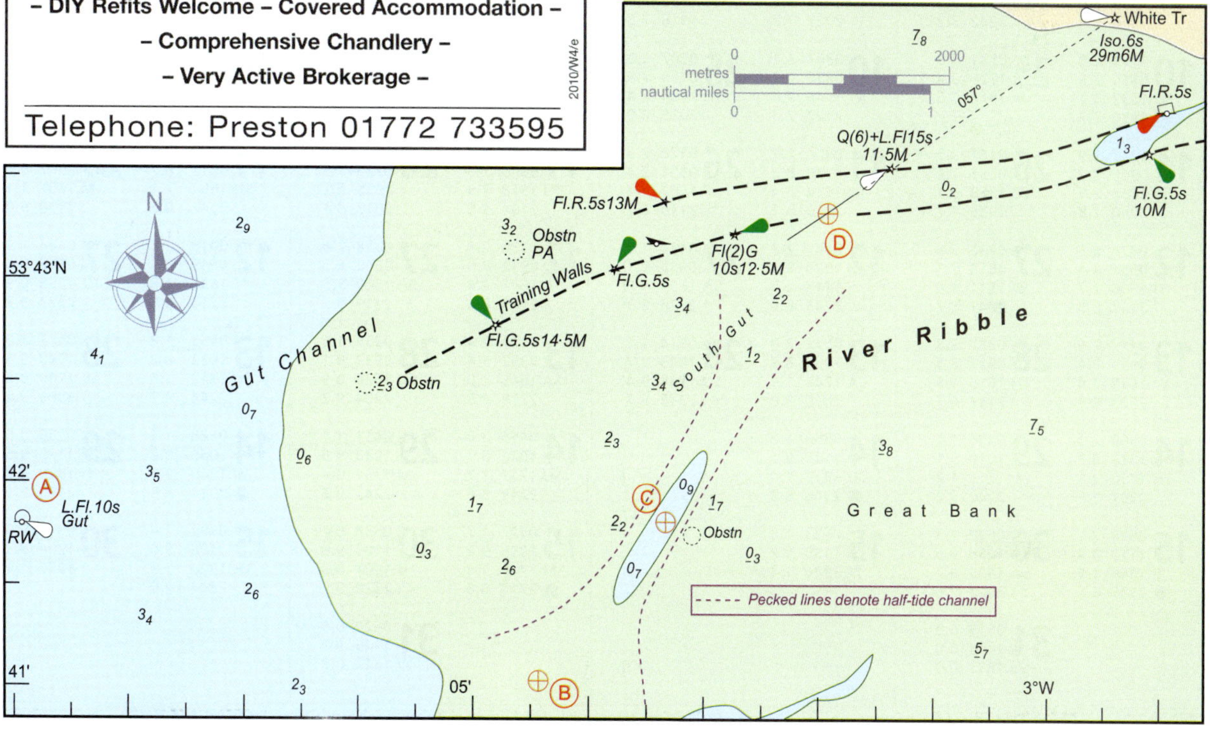

TIME ZONE (UT)
For Summer Time add ONE hour in **non-shaded areas**

LIVERPOOL (GLADSTONE DOCK)

LAT 53°27′N LONG 3°01′W

TIMES AND HEIGHTS OF HIGH AND LOW WATERS

Dates in red are SPRINGS
Dates in blue are NEAPS

YEAR **2010**

JANUARY

Date	Time	m
1 F	0539	1.4
	1110	9.5
	1815	1.1
	2338	9.5
2 SA	0629	1.2
	1158	9.7
	1905	0.8
3 SU	0027	9.6
	0715	1.1
	1246	9.8
	1953	0.7
4 M	0115	9.5
	0801	1.2
	1334	9.8
	2039	0.8
5 TU	0203	9.3
	0846	1.4
	1422	9.5
	2125	1.1
6 W	0251	8.9
	0931	1.8
	1511	9.2
	2212	1.6
7 TH	0341	8.5
	1019	2.2
	1604	8.7
	◑ 2303	2.1
8 F	0436	8.1
	1114	2.6
	1704	8.2
9 SA	0002	2.6
	0540	7.7
	1220	3.0
	1814	7.8
10 SU	0111	2.9
	0654	7.6
	1337	3.1
	1930	7.7
11 M	0221	2.9
	0806	7.7
	1452	2.9
	2040	7.8
12 TU	0324	2.8
	0907	8.1
	1556	2.7
	2137	8.0
13 W	0417	2.5
	0955	8.4
	1648	2.4
	2223	8.3
14 TH	0500	2.3
	1036	8.7
	1730	2.1
	2301	8.5
15 F	0538	2.1
	1112	8.9
	1806	1.9
	● 2335	8.6
16 SA	0610	2.0
	1145	9.0
	1838	1.8
17 SU	0007	8.7
	0641	1.9
	1218	9.1
	1908	1.8
18 M	0038	8.7
	0711	1.9
	1250	9.1
	1937	1.7
19 TU	0108	8.6
	0743	1.9
	1321	8.9
	2008	1.8
20 W	0138	8.5
	0815	2.1
	1352	8.8
	2039	2.0
21 TH	0209	8.3
	0849	2.4
	1424	8.5
	2113	2.3
22 F	0243	8.1
	0926	2.7
	1501	8.2
	2150	2.6
23 SA	0324	7.8
	1008	3.0
	1547	7.9
	◐ 2236	2.9
24 SU	0417	7.5
	1104	3.3
	1650	7.6
	2342	3.2
25 M	0531	7.3
	1226	3.4
	1812	7.5
26 TU	0111	3.2
	0657	7.4
	1358	3.1
	1935	7.7
27 W	0232	2.8
	0814	7.9
	1511	2.6
	2047	8.2
28 TH	0337	2.3
	0917	8.5
	1615	1.9
	2147	8.7
29 F	0436	1.7
	1010	9.1
	1713	1.2
	2240	9.2
30 SA	0529	1.3
	1059	9.6
	1805	0.7
	○ 2328	9.6
31 SU	0618	0.9
	1146	10.0
	1853	0.3

FEBRUARY

Date	Time	m
1 M	0013	9.8
	0703	0.7
	1231	10.1
	1937	0.2
2 TU	0058	9.7
	0746	0.7
	1315	10.1
	2019	0.4
3 W	0140	9.5
	0826	0.9
	1357	9.8
	2059	0.8
4 TH	0222	9.1
	0906	1.3
	1441	9.3
	2139	1.4
5 F	0305	8.6
	0947	1.9
	1527	8.7
	◑ 2221	2.2
6 SA	0353	8.1
	1034	2.6
	1621	8.0
	2313	2.8
7 SU	0454	7.6
	1137	3.1
	1733	7.4
8 M	0026	3.3
	0613	7.2
	1305	3.4
	1903	7.1
9 TU	0153	3.4
	0740	7.3
	1435	3.2
	2027	7.3
10 W	0307	3.1
	0850	7.7
	1545	2.8
	2127	7.7
11 TH	0404	2.7
	0940	8.2
	1636	2.4
	2210	8.1
12 F	0447	2.3
	1020	8.6
	1715	2.0
	2245	8.4
13 SA	0522	2.0
	1054	8.9
	1748	1.8
	2316	8.6
14 SU	0553	1.8
	1125	9.1
	1817	1.6
	● 2346	8.8
15 M	0623	1.6
	1156	9.2
	1846	1.4
16 TU	0014	8.8
	0652	1.5
	1226	9.2
	1914	1.4
17 W	0042	8.8
	0722	1.5
	1255	9.1
	1943	1.5
18 TH	0110	8.7
	0753	1.7
	1323	9.0
	2013	1.7
19 F	0138	8.6
	0824	1.9
	1353	8.7
	2042	2.0
20 SA	0209	8.4
	0856	2.3
	1428	8.5
	2114	2.3
21 SU	0246	8.1
	0933	2.7
	1512	8.1
	2155	2.8
22 M	0336	7.7
	1025	3.1
	1612	7.6
	◐ 2257	3.2
23 TU	0451	7.3
	1147	3.3
	1741	7.3
24 W	0032	3.3
	0629	7.3
	1332	3.1
	1916	7.5
25 TH	0207	3.0
	0755	7.8
	1454	2.4
	2035	8.0
26 F	0320	2.3
	0901	8.4
	1601	1.7
	2136	8.7
27 SA	0421	1.7
	0955	9.1
	1658	0.9
	2226	9.3
28 SU	0514	1.1
	1043	9.7
	1748	0.4
	○ 2310	9.7

MARCH

Date	Time	m
1 M	0601	0.6
	1127	10.0
	1833	0.1
	2353	9.8
2 TU	0644	0.4
	1209	10.2
	1915	0.0
3 W	0033	9.8
	0724	0.4
	1251	10.0
	1953	0.3
4 TH	0113	9.6
	0802	0.7
	1331	9.7
	2029	0.8
5 F	0151	9.2
	0839	1.2
	1411	9.2
	2105	1.5
6 SA	0230	8.7
	0917	1.8
	1453	8.5
	2141	2.3
7 SU	0315	8.1
	1000	2.5
	1544	7.7
	◑ 2226	3.0
8 M	0412	7.5
	1059	3.2
	1654	7.1
	2336	3.6
9 TU	0532	7.1
	1232	3.5
	1831	6.8
10 W	0120	3.7
	0704	7.1
	1409	3.3
	2004	7.0
11 TH	0242	3.4
	0820	7.5
	1518	2.9
	2104	7.5
12 F	0338	2.9
	0912	8.0
	1607	2.4
	2145	8.0
13 SA	0421	2.4
	0952	8.4
	1645	2.0
	2219	8.3
14 SU	0455	2.0
	1026	8.7
	1717	1.7
	2249	8.6
15 M	0527	1.7
	1058	9.0
	1748	1.4
	● 2317	8.8
16 TU	0557	1.5
	1128	9.1
	1817	1.3
	2345	8.9
17 W	0629	1.3
	1157	9.2
	1848	1.2
18 TH	0013	8.9
	0700	1.3
	1227	9.1
	1917	1.3
19 F	0042	8.9
	0731	1.4
	1257	9.0
	1947	1.5
20 SA	0111	8.8
	0803	1.7
	1330	8.8
	2017	1.8
21 SU	0144	8.6
	0836	2.0
	1408	8.5
	2050	2.2
22 M	0224	8.2
	0914	2.4
	1455	8.1
	2133	2.7
23 TU	0317	7.8
	1009	2.8
	1559	7.6
	◐ 2236	3.1
24 W	0436	7.4
	1133	3.1
	1729	7.3
25 TH	0010	3.3
	0612	7.4
	1314	2.8
	1901	7.5
26 F	0145	2.9
	0735	7.9
	1435	2.2
	2018	8.1
27 SA	0258	2.3
	0840	8.5
	1540	1.5
	2116	8.7
28 SU	0359	1.6
	0933	9.1
	1636	0.9
	2204	9.2
29 M	0451	1.1
	1020	9.6
	1724	0.4
	2247	9.6
30 TU	0538	0.7
	1103	9.9
	1807	0.3
	○ 2328	9.7
31 W	0620	0.5
	1145	9.9
	1847	0.3

APRIL

Date	Time	m
1 TH	0007	9.7
	0700	0.5
	1226	9.7
	1924	0.6
2 F	0046	9.5
	0738	0.8
	1306	9.4
	1959	1.1
3 SA	0123	9.2
	0815	1.3
	1345	8.9
	2033	1.8
4 SU	0201	8.7
	0852	1.9
	1426	8.3
	2107	2.5
5 M	0244	8.2
	0932	2.5
	1514	7.6
	2147	3.1
6 TU	0339	7.6
	1026	3.1
	1619	7.0
	◑ 2247	3.6
7 W	0452	7.2
	1150	3.4
	1747	6.7
8 TH	0028	3.8
	0617	7.1
	1323	3.3
	1917	6.9
9 F	0155	3.5
	0732	7.3
	1430	2.9
	2021	7.3
10 SA	0254	3.1
	0828	7.8
	1521	2.5
	2106	7.8
11 SU	0339	2.6
	0912	8.2
	1602	2.1
	2142	8.2
12 M	0418	2.1
	0949	8.5
	1638	1.8
	2214	8.5
13 TU	0453	1.8
	1023	8.8
	1712	1.5
	2244	8.7
14 W	0528	1.5
	1056	9.0
	1746	1.3
	● 2314	8.9
15 TH	0602	1.4
	1128	9.0
	1820	1.3
	2344	9.0
16 F	0637	1.3
	1201	9.1
	1853	1.3
17 SA	0017	9.0
	0712	1.4
	1237	9.0
	1926	1.5
18 SU	0052	8.9
	0747	1.6
	1315	8.8
	2000	1.8
19 M	0131	8.7
	0825	1.9
	1359	8.5
	2038	2.1
20 TU	0217	8.4
	0910	2.2
	1452	8.1
	2126	2.6
21 W	0315	8.0
	1009	2.5
	1559	7.7
	◐ 2230	2.9
22 TH	0432	7.7
	1129	2.6
	1720	7.6
	2354	3.0
23 F	0555	7.8
	1254	2.4
	1842	7.7
24 SA	0118	2.7
	0709	8.1
	1408	2.0
	1952	8.2
25 SU	0229	2.2
	0813	8.6
	1512	1.5
	2050	8.6
26 M	0331	1.7
	0907	9.0
	1607	1.1
	2138	9.0
27 TU	0424	1.3
	0955	9.3
	1656	0.9
	2222	9.3
28 W	0512	1.0
	1040	9.5
	1740	0.8
	○ 2303	9.4
29 TH	0556	0.9
	1123	9.5
	1820	0.9
	2343	9.4
30 F	0637	0.9
	1204	9.3
	1857	1.1

Chart Datum: 4·93 metres below Ordnance Datum (Newlyn). HAT is 10·5 metres above Chart Datum; see 0.20

TIME ZONE (UT)
For Summer Time add ONE hour in **non-shaded areas**

LIVERPOOL (GLADSTONE DOCK)

LAT 53°27'N LONG 3°01'W

TIMES AND HEIGHTS OF HIGH AND LOW WATERS

Dates in red are SPRINGS
Dates in blue are NEAPS

YEAR **2010**

MAY

Date	Day	Time	m	Time	m	Time	m	Time	m
1	SA	0021	9.3	0716	1.2	1245	9.0	1932	1.5
2	SU	0059	9.0	0754	1.5	1324	8.6	2006	2.0
3	M	0138	8.7	0831	2.0	1404	8.1	2040	2.5
4	TU	0220	8.3	0910	2.5	1450	7.7	2117	3.0
5	W	0310	7.8	0956	2.9	1545	7.2	2207	3.4
6	TH	0412	7.4	1058	3.2	1655	6.9	◑ 2319	3.7
7	F	0523	7.3	1215	3.2	1810	6.9		
8	SA	0044	3.6	0632	7.3	1326	3.0	1918	7.2
9	SU	0152	3.3	0732	7.6	1423	2.7	2012	7.5
10	M	0246	2.8	0823	7.9	1511	2.3	2055	7.9
11	TU	0332	2.4	0906	8.2	1555	2.0	2133	8.3
12	W	0415	2.0	0946	8.5	1635	1.7	2208	8.6
13	TH	0457	1.7	1024	8.7	1715	1.5	2243	8.8
14	F	0537	1.5	1101	8.9	1754	1.4	● 2320	9.0
15	SA	0618	1.4	1141	9.0	1832	1.4	2358	9.1
16	SU	0658	1.3	1223	9.0	1911	1.5		
17	M	0040	9.1	0740	1.4	1308	8.9	1951	1.7
18	TU	0126	8.9	0824	1.6	1357	8.7	2034	2.0
19	W	0217	8.7	0914	1.8	1452	8.4	2125	2.3
20	TH	0315	8.4	1012	2.0	1554	8.1	◐ 2226	2.5
21	F	0422	8.2	1119	2.1	1702	7.9	2335	2.6
22	SA	0531	8.2	1228	2.1	1813	8.0		
23	SU	0046	2.5	0639	8.3	1337	1.9	1920	8.1
24	M	0155	2.3	0744	8.5	1440	1.8	2020	8.4
25	TU	0259	2.0	0842	8.7	1537	1.6	2112	8.7
26	W	0357	1.8	0934	8.8	1628	1.5	2159	8.9
27	TH	0449	1.5	1021	8.9	1714	1.4	○ 2242	9.1
28	F	0536	1.4	1106	8.9	1756	1.5	2323	9.1
29	SA	0619	1.4	1148	8.8	1834	1.6		
30	SU	0002	9.1	0659	1.5	1229	8.7	1910	1.8
31	M	0041	8.9	0737	1.7	1307	8.5	1944	2.1

JUNE

Date	Day	Time	m	Time	m	Time	m	Time	m
1	TU	0119	8.7	0813	2.0	1345	8.2	2018	2.4
2	W	0158	8.5	0848	2.2	1425	7.9	2053	2.7
3	TH	0242	8.2	0926	2.5	1510	7.6	2135	3.0
4	F	0331	7.8	1011	2.7	1602	7.3	◑ 2226	3.3
5	SA	0427	7.6	1105	2.9	1702	7.1	2328	3.4
6	SU	0529	7.4	1209	3.0	1806	7.1		
7	M	0038	3.3	0630	7.5	1316	2.9	1907	7.3
8	TU	0146	3.1	0728	7.7	1417	2.7	2002	7.7
9	W	0245	2.7	0821	7.9	1511	2.3	2051	8.0
10	TH	0338	2.3	0910	8.3	1601	2.0	2135	8.4
11	F	0428	2.0	0956	8.6	1647	1.8	2218	8.8
12	SA	0516	1.6	1041	8.8	1732	1.6	● 2301	9.0
13	SU	0603	1.4	1127	9.0	1817	1.4	2346	9.2
14	M	0650	1.2	1213	9.2	1902	1.3		
15	TU	0032	9.3	0737	1.1	1302	9.1	1946	1.4
16	W	0121	9.3	0824	1.1	1352	9.0	2032	1.6
17	TH	0211	9.2	0913	1.2	1443	8.8	2121	1.8
18	F	0304	8.9	1003	1.5	1537	8.5	2212	2.0
19	SA	0401	8.7	1058	1.7	1636	8.2	◐ 2309	2.3
20	SU	0502	8.4	1157	2.0	1740	8.0		
21	M	0013	2.5	0607	8.2	1303	2.2	1847	8.0
22	TU	0123	2.5	0715	8.1	1409	2.2	1952	8.1
23	W	0233	2.4	0821	8.2	1511	2.2	2051	8.3
24	TH	0337	2.2	0919	8.3	1607	2.1	2143	8.5
25	F	0434	2.0	1010	8.4	1655	2.0	2228	8.8
26	SA	0524	1.8	1056	8.6	1738	1.9	○ 2310	8.9
27	SU	0607	1.7	1136	8.6	1817	1.9	2348	9.0
28	M	0646	1.7	1214	8.6	1852	1.9		
29	TU	0024	8.9	0721	1.7	1249	8.5	1925	2.0
30	W	0100	8.9	0753	1.8	1323	8.4	1956	2.1

JULY

Date	Day	Time	m	Time	m	Time	m	Time	m
1	TH	0135	8.7	0824	2.0	1357	8.2	2029	2.3
2	F	0212	8.5	0856	2.1	1434	8.0	2105	2.6
3	SA	0250	8.2	0932	2.4	1513	7.7	2146	2.8
4	SU	0333	7.9	1014	2.6	1559	7.5	◑ 2233	3.1
5	M	0423	7.6	1104	2.9	1655	7.3	2333	3.3
6	TU	0524	7.5	1209	3.0	1802	7.3		
7	W	0047	3.3	0632	7.5	1324	3.0	1911	7.5
8	TH	0202	3.0	0739	7.7	1432	2.7	2014	7.8
9	F	0307	2.6	0841	8.0	1531	2.3	2109	8.3
10	SA	0405	2.1	0936	8.5	1625	1.9	2200	8.8
11	SU	0459	1.6	1027	8.9	1716	1.6	● 2247	9.2
12	M	0552	1.2	1116	9.2	1806	1.3	2334	9.5
13	TU	0642	0.8	1203	9.4	1853	1.1		
14	W	0021	9.7	0729	0.6	1250	9.5	1938	1.0
15	TH	0108	9.8	0814	0.6	1337	9.4	2023	1.1
16	F	0155	9.6	0859	0.8	1423	9.1	2106	1.3
17	SA	0242	9.4	0943	1.1	1511	8.8	2151	1.7
18	SU	0332	8.9	1029	1.7	1603	8.4	◐ 2241	2.2
19	M	0429	8.4	1123	2.2	1703	8.0	2341	2.6
20	TU	0535	8.0	1228	2.6	1814	7.7		
21	W	0055	2.9	0651	7.7	1342	2.8	1929	7.7
22	TH	0216	2.8	0808	7.7	1453	2.7	2037	8.0
23	F	0329	2.6	0912	7.9	1554	2.5	2132	8.3
24	SA	0428	2.3	1004	8.2	1644	2.3	2218	8.6
25	SU	0516	2.0	1046	8.4	1726	2.1	2256	8.9
26	M	0556	1.8	1122	8.6	1802	1.9	○ 2331	9.0
27	TU	0630	1.7	1155	8.7	1833	1.8		
28	W	0004	9.1	0659	1.6	1226	8.7	1903	1.8
29	TH	0037	9.0	0728	1.6	1257	8.6	1933	1.9
30	F	0108	8.9	0756	1.7	1327	8.5	2004	2.0
31	SA	0140	8.8	0826	1.9	1357	8.3	2036	2.2

AUGUST

Date	Day	Time	m	Time	m	Time	m	Time	m
1	SU	0211	8.5	0857	2.1	1430	8.1	2111	2.5
2	M	0246	8.2	0932	2.5	1507	7.8	2151	2.9
3	TU	0328	7.9	1014	2.8	1555	7.5	◑ 2242	3.2
4	W	0425	7.5	1112	3.1	1702	7.3	2355	3.4
5	TH	0542	7.3	1234	3.3	1828	7.3		
6	F	0125	3.2	0706	7.4	1359	3.0	1945	7.7
7	SA	0242	2.7	0820	7.9	1507	2.5	2050	8.3
8	SU	0347	2.1	0922	8.5	1607	2.0	2144	8.9
9	M	0445	1.4	1014	9.0	1701	1.4	2233	9.4
10	TU	0538	0.8	1102	9.5	1752	1.0	● 2318	9.9
11	W	0627	0.4	1147	9.7	1839	0.7		
12	TH	0003	10.1	0712	0.2	1231	9.8	1922	0.6
13	F	0048	10.1	0755	0.3	1314	9.7	2004	0.8
14	SA	0131	9.9	0835	0.6	1357	9.4	2044	1.1
15	SU	0215	9.5	0915	1.2	1441	8.9	2126	1.6
16	M	0302	8.9	0957	1.9	1529	8.4	◐ 2212	2.3
17	TU	0355	8.2	1047	2.6	1627	7.9	2312	2.9
18	W	0504	7.6	1154	3.1	1743	7.5		
19	TH	0034	3.2	0631	7.3	1321	3.3	1908	7.5
20	F	0206	3.1	0759	7.4	1440	3.1	2023	7.8
21	SA	0321	2.7	0905	7.7	1542	2.7	2119	8.2
22	SU	0417	2.3	0952	8.1	1630	2.4	2201	8.6
23	M	0459	2.0	1029	8.4	1708	2.1	2236	8.9
24	TU	0534	1.7	1101	8.7	1740	1.9	○ 2308	9.1
25	W	0604	1.6	1130	8.8	1809	1.7	2339	9.2
26	TH	0632	1.5	1159	8.9	1838	1.6		
27	F	0009	9.2	0659	1.5	1227	8.8	1907	1.7
28	SA	0039	9.1	0727	1.5	1255	8.8	1938	1.8
29	SU	0108	8.9	0756	1.7	1323	8.6	2009	2.0
30	M	0137	8.7	0826	2.0	1353	8.4	2042	2.4
31	TU	0210	8.4	0858	2.4	1428	8.1	2118	2.8

Chart Datum: 4·93 metres below Ordnance Datum (Newlyn). HAT is 10·5 metres above Chart Datum; see 0.20

TIME ZONE (UT)
For Summer Time add ONE hour in **non-shaded areas**

LIVERPOOL (GLADSTONE DOCK) LAT 53°27′N LONG 3°01′W

TIMES AND HEIGHTS OF HIGH AND LOW WATERS

Dates in red are SPRINGS
Dates in blue are NEAPS

YEAR **2010**

SEPTEMBER

Date	Day	Time	m	Time	m	Time	m	Time	m
1	W	0251	8.0	0937	2.8	1514	7.8	◑ 2206	3.1
2	TH	0347	7.6	1032	3.2	1622	7.4	2320	3.4
3	F	0509	7.3	1156	3.4	1757	7.3		
4	SA	0059	3.2	0643	7.4	1332	3.2	1923	7.7
5	SU	0222	2.6	0804	7.9	1446	2.6	2031	8.4
6	M	0329	1.9	0906	8.6	1548	1.9	2125	9.1
7	TU	0427	1.2	0957	9.2	1643	1.3	2213	9.7
8	W	0519	0.6	1042	9.6	1732	0.9	● 2257	10.1
9	TH	0606	0.3	1125	9.9	1818	0.6	2341	10.2
10	F	0649	0.2	1207	9.9	1900	0.6		
11	SA	0023	10.2	0729	0.3	1248	9.8	1941	0.7
12	SU	0106	9.9	0808	0.8	1329	9.4	2020	1.2
13	M	0148	9.4	0846	1.4	1410	9.0	2101	1.8
14	TU	0233	8.7	0925	2.2	1456	8.4	2147	2.4
15	W	0325	8.0	1012	2.9	1554	7.8	◐ 2246	3.1
16	TH	0435	7.3	1119	3.5	1712	7.4		
17	F	0015	3.4	0607	7.0	1256	3.7	1841	7.4
18	SA	0147	3.3	0740	7.2	1418	3.4	1957	7.7
19	SU	0257	2.8	0843	7.6	1518	2.9	2052	8.2
20	M	0348	2.4	0928	8.1	1603	2.5	2133	8.6
21	TU	0428	2.0	1002	8.4	1639	2.2	2208	8.9
22	W	0501	1.8	1033	8.7	1710	1.9	2240	9.1
23	TH	0531	1.6	1101	8.9	1740	1.7	○ 2310	9.2
24	F	0559	1.5	1129	9.0	1810	1.6	2340	9.2
25	SA	0628	1.5	1157	9.0	1842	1.6		
26	SU	0010	9.2	0658	1.5	1225	8.9	1913	1.7
27	M	0040	9.0	0728	1.7	1254	8.8	1946	2.0
28	TU	0111	8.8	0759	2.0	1325	8.6	2019	2.3
29	W	0147	8.5	0832	2.4	1403	8.3	2057	2.7
30	TH	0231	8.1	0913	2.8	1452	7.9	2147	3.0

OCTOBER

Date	Day	Time	m	Time	m	Time	m	Time	m
1	F	0330	7.7	1010	3.2	1603	7.6	◑ 2303	3.2
2	SA	0453	7.4	1133	3.4	1736	7.5		
3	SU	0039	3.1	0625	7.5	1307	3.2	1900	7.9
4	M	0200	2.5	0743	8.1	1422	2.6	2007	8.5
5	TU	0306	1.8	0844	8.7	1524	1.9	2102	9.2
6	W	0403	1.2	0934	9.3	1619	1.4	2150	9.7
7	TH	0454	0.7	1018	9.7	1708	1.0	● 2234	10.0
8	F	0540	0.5	1101	9.9	1754	0.8	2318	10.1
9	SA	0622	0.5	1142	9.9	1837	0.7		
10	SU	0000	10.0	0702	0.7	1222	9.7	1918	0.9
11	M	0043	9.6	0741	1.2	1303	9.4	1959	1.4
12	TU	0125	9.1	0818	1.8	1343	9.0	2040	1.9
13	W	0209	8.5	0856	2.5	1428	8.5	2125	2.6
14	TH	0259	7.9	0940	3.2	1524	7.9	◐ 2222	3.1
15	F	0404	7.3	1042	3.7	1636	7.5	2343	3.4
16	SA	0529	7.0	1214	3.9	1758	7.4		
17	SU	0107	3.4	0656	7.1	1336	3.6	1912	7.6
18	M	0213	3.0	0804	7.5	1436	3.2	2010	8.0
19	TU	0304	2.6	0851	7.9	1522	2.8	2056	8.4
20	W	0345	2.3	0927	8.3	1601	2.4	2133	8.7
21	TH	0421	2.0	0959	8.6	1636	2.1	2208	8.9
22	F	0454	1.8	1029	8.8	1709	1.8	2240	9.1
23	SA	0527	1.6	1059	9.0	1743	1.7	○ 2312	9.1
24	SU	0559	1.6	1129	9.1	1818	1.7	2344	9.1
25	M	0633	1.6	1159	9.1	1853	1.7		
26	TU	0018	9.0	0706	1.8	1233	9.0	1928	1.9
27	W	0055	8.9	0740	2.0	1310	8.8	2006	2.2
28	TH	0136	8.6	0817	2.4	1352	8.5	2049	2.5
29	F	0224	8.3	0901	2.7	1445	8.2	2142	2.7
30	SA	0325	7.9	1000	3.1	1554	7.9	◑ 2255	2.9
31	SU	0441	7.7	1116	3.2	1716	7.9		

NOVEMBER

Date	Day	Time	m	Time	m	Time	m	Time	m
1	M	0017	2.7	0601	7.8	1239	3.0	1832	8.1
2	TU	0132	2.3	0715	8.2	1352	2.6	1939	8.6
3	W	0237	1.8	0817	8.7	1455	2.1	2036	9.1
4	TH	0335	1.4	0909	9.1	1552	1.6	2126	9.4
5	F	0426	1.1	0955	9.4	1643	1.3	2213	9.7
6	SA	0513	1.0	1038	9.6	1731	1.1	● 2258	9.7
7	SU	0557	1.0	1120	9.7	1816	1.1	2342	9.6
8	M	0638	1.2	1201	9.6	1900	1.2		
9	TU	0025	9.3	0717	1.6	1242	9.3	1941	1.6
10	W	0108	8.9	0755	2.1	1323	9.0	2023	2.0
11	TH	0150	8.4	0832	2.6	1406	8.6	2105	2.5
12	F	0236	7.9	0912	3.1	1455	8.2	2153	3.0
13	SA	0330	7.5	1001	3.5	1555	7.8	◐ 2254	3.3
14	SU	0436	7.2	1110	3.8	1703	7.5		
15	M	0005	3.4	0549	7.1	1230	3.8	1812	7.5
16	TU	0112	3.2	0700	7.3	1337	3.5	1915	7.7
17	W	0208	2.9	0758	7.6	1431	3.1	2008	8.0
18	TH	0256	2.6	0843	8.0	1517	2.7	2054	8.3
19	F	0338	2.3	0922	8.3	1559	2.4	2134	8.6
20	SA	0418	2.1	0957	8.7	1639	2.1	2211	8.8
21	SU	0456	1.9	1031	8.9	1719	1.9	○ 2248	9.0
22	M	0534	1.7	1106	9.1	1759	1.7	2325	9.1
23	TU	0612	1.7	1142	9.2	1839	1.7		
24	W	0004	9.1	0650	1.7	1220	9.2	1919	1.7
25	TH	0046	9.0	0729	1.9	1302	9.1	2002	1.8
26	F	0131	8.8	0811	2.1	1348	8.9	2048	2.0
27	SA	0221	8.6	0857	2.4	1441	8.7	2141	2.2
28	SU	0317	8.3	0952	2.6	1542	8.4	◑ 2242	2.4
29	M	0421	8.1	1055	2.8	1650	8.3	2349	2.4
30	TU	0531	8.0	1206	2.8	1800	8.3		

DECEMBER

Date	Day	Time	m	Time	m	Time	m	Time	m
1	W	0058	2.3	0642	8.1	1317	2.7	1908	8.5
2	TH	0206	2.1	0747	8.4	1425	2.4	2010	8.7
3	F	0307	1.9	0844	8.7	1528	2.1	2107	8.9
4	SA	0402	1.7	0935	9.0	1624	1.8	2159	9.1
5	SU	0452	1.6	1022	9.3	1715	1.5	● 2246	9.2
6	M	0537	1.5	1106	9.4	1803	1.4	2331	9.2
7	TU	0620	1.6	1147	9.4	1847	1.5		
8	W	0013	9.0	0659	1.8	1227	9.3	1928	1.7
9	TH	0054	8.8	0736	2.1	1306	9.1	2006	1.9
10	F	0132	8.5	0811	2.4	1345	8.8	2043	2.3
11	SA	0211	8.2	0845	2.7	1426	8.5	2119	2.6
12	SU	0253	7.9	0923	3.1	1513	8.1	2159	2.9
13	M	0341	7.5	1009	3.4	1606	7.8	◐ 2248	3.1
14	TU	0438	7.3	1106	3.6	1706	7.5	2349	3.3
15	W	0543	7.2	1217	3.7	1810	7.5		
16	TH	0058	3.3	0650	7.3	1329	3.5	1913	7.6
17	F	0201	3.0	0751	7.6	1431	3.1	2010	7.8
18	SA	0256	2.7	0842	7.9	1524	2.7	2100	8.2
19	SU	0345	2.4	0927	8.4	1612	2.3	2146	8.5
20	M	0430	2.1	1008	8.7	1659	2.0	2229	8.8
21	TU	0514	1.8	1048	9.0	1745	1.7	○ 2311	9.0
22	W	0557	1.6	1129	9.3	1830	1.4	2353	9.2
23	TH	0640	1.5	1211	9.4	1915	1.3		
24	F	0038	9.3	0723	1.5	1256	9.5	2000	1.3
25	SA	0124	9.2	0806	1.6	1341	9.4	2045	1.4
26	SU	0211	9.0	0851	1.8	1430	9.2	2131	1.6
27	M	0301	8.7	0938	2.1	1521	8.9	2221	1.9
28	TU	0355	8.4	1030	2.4	1619	8.6	◑ 2317	2.2
29	W	0457	8.1	1131	2.6	1725	8.3		
30	TH	0022	2.4	0606	7.9	1242	2.8	1837	8.1
31	F	0134	2.5	0718	8.0	1359	2.7	1950	8.2

Chart Datum: 4·93 metres below Ordnance Datum (Newlyn). HAT is 10·5 metres above Chart Datum; see 0.20

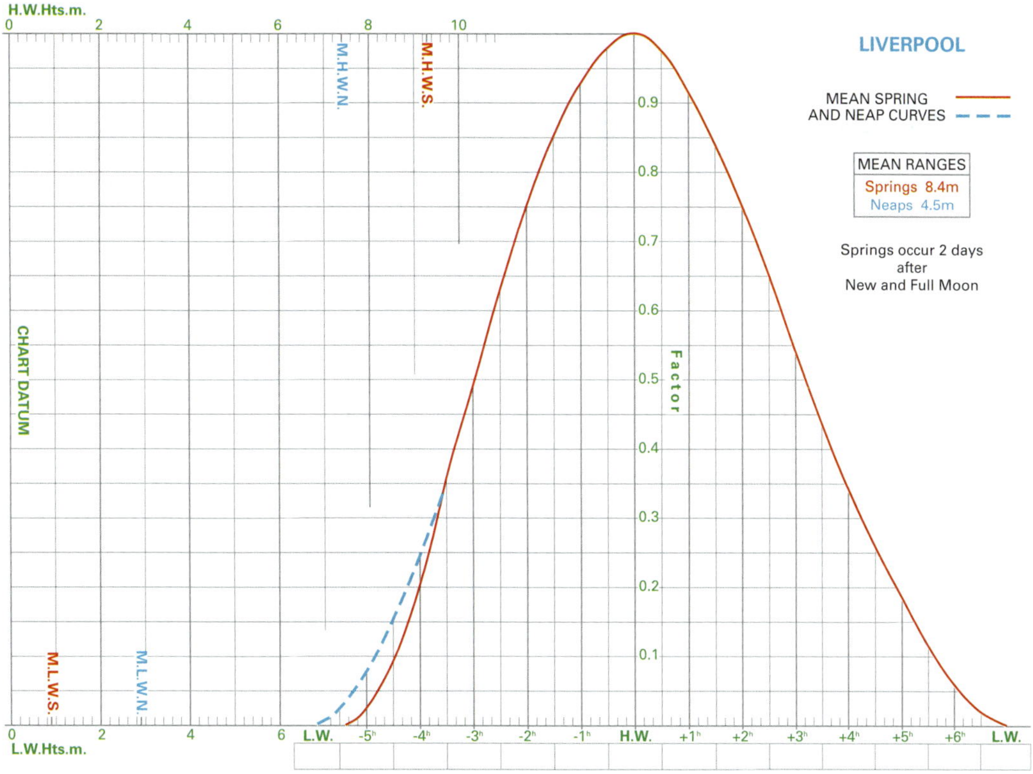

3.16 LIVERPOOL

Merseyside **53°24'·22N 03°00'·28W** (Liver Bldg)

CHARTS AC 1826, 1978, 1951, 3490, 5613; Imray C62.

TIDES +0015 Dover; ML 5·2; Duration 0535

Standard Port LIVERPOOL (GLADSTONE DOCK) (⟵)

Times				Height (metres)			
High Water		Low Water		MHWS	MHWN	MLWN	MLWS
0000	0600	0200	0700	9·3	7·4	2·9	0·9
1200	1800	1400	1900				
Differences EASTHAM (River Mersey)							
+0010	+0010	+0009	+0009	+0·3	+0·1	−0·1	−0·3
HALE HEAD (River Mersey)							
+0030	+0025	No data		−2·4	−2·5	No data	
WIDNES (River Mersey)							
+0040	+0045	+0400	+0345	−4·2	−4·4	−2·5	−0·3
FIDDLER'S FERRY (River Mersey)							
+0100	+0115	+0540	+0450	−5·9	−6·3	−2·4	−0·4
HILBRE ISLAND (River Dee)							
−0015	−0012	−0010	−0015	−0·3	−0·2	+0·2	+0·4
MOSTYN DOCKS (River Dee)							
−0020	−0015	−0020	−0020	−0·8	−0·7	No data	
CONNAH'S QUAY (River Dee)							
0000	+0015	+0355	+0340	−4·6	−4·4	Dries	
CHESTER (River Dee)							
+0105	+0105	+0500	+0500	−5·3	−5·4	Dries	
COLWYN BAY							
−0020	−0020	No data		−1·5	−1·3	No data	
LLANDUDNO							
−0020	−0020	−0035	−0040	−1·7	−1·4	−0·7	−0·3

NOTE: LW time differences at Connah's Quay give the end of a LW stand lasting about 3¾hrs at sp and 5hrs at nps. A bore occurs in the R Dee at Chester.

SHELTER Good at marinas in Brunswick/Coburg docks and in Canning/Albert Docks. Fair weather ⚓ on the SW side of river. In strong NW'lies there is swell on the bar. Wind against tide causes steep, breaking seas in outer reaches of River Mersey. Inside, the buoyed chan is safe; elsewhere local knowledge and great caution needed as the whole area (R Dee, R Mersey to R Alt and N to Morecambe Bay) is littered with sandbanks.

NAVIGATION WPT 53°32´·02N 03°20´·98W, Bar SWM lt buoy, 111°/2·8M to Q1 NCM lt F. From Q1 to marina is 15·5M via Queen's and Crosby Chans. Both chans have training banks which cover and it is unwise to navigate between the floats/buoys and the trng banks. Sp tidal streams exceed 5kn within the river.

Leeds and Liverpool Canal (BWB) gives access to E Coast, ent at Stanley Dock. Max draft 1·0m, air draft 2·2m, beam 4·3m, LOA 18·3m. Liverpool to Goole 161M, 103 locks.

Manchester Ship Canal, ent at Eastham Locks, leads 31M to Salford Quays or R Weaver for boatyards at Northwich. Obtain licence from MSC Co ☎ 0151 327 1461.

R Dee: WPT 53°25´·13N 03°13´·17W, Hilbre Swash HE2 ECM buoy, Q (3) 10s, (chan shifts). From the W use Welsh Chan. The Dee estuary mostly dries.

LIGHTS AND MARKS Bar SWM lt buoy, L Fl 10s Racon. Keep 5ca clear of SPM, 5ca W of Bar lt float. Formby SWM lt F, Iso 4s, is at the ent to Queen's Chan which is marked by PHM lt Flts and SHM buoys, and 3 NCM buoys, numbered Q1-Q12. Crosby Chan is similarly marked, C1-C23. From Crosby SWM lt F, Oc 5s, the track up-river is approx 145°. The Liver Bldg (twin spires) and Port of Liverpool Bldg (dome) are conspic on the E bank opposite Birkenhead Docks.

R/T Monitor *Mersey Radio* VHF Ch **12** 16 (H24). Local nav and gale warnings are broadcast on receipt on Ch 12. Traffic movements, nav warnings and weather reports are broadcast on Ch 09 at HW–3 and –2. Radar Ch 18 covers a radius of 20M and in poor vis can offer continuous fixing. *Liverpool Marina* Ch **M**. Eastham Locks Ch 07 (H24). Manchester Ship Canal Ch 14.

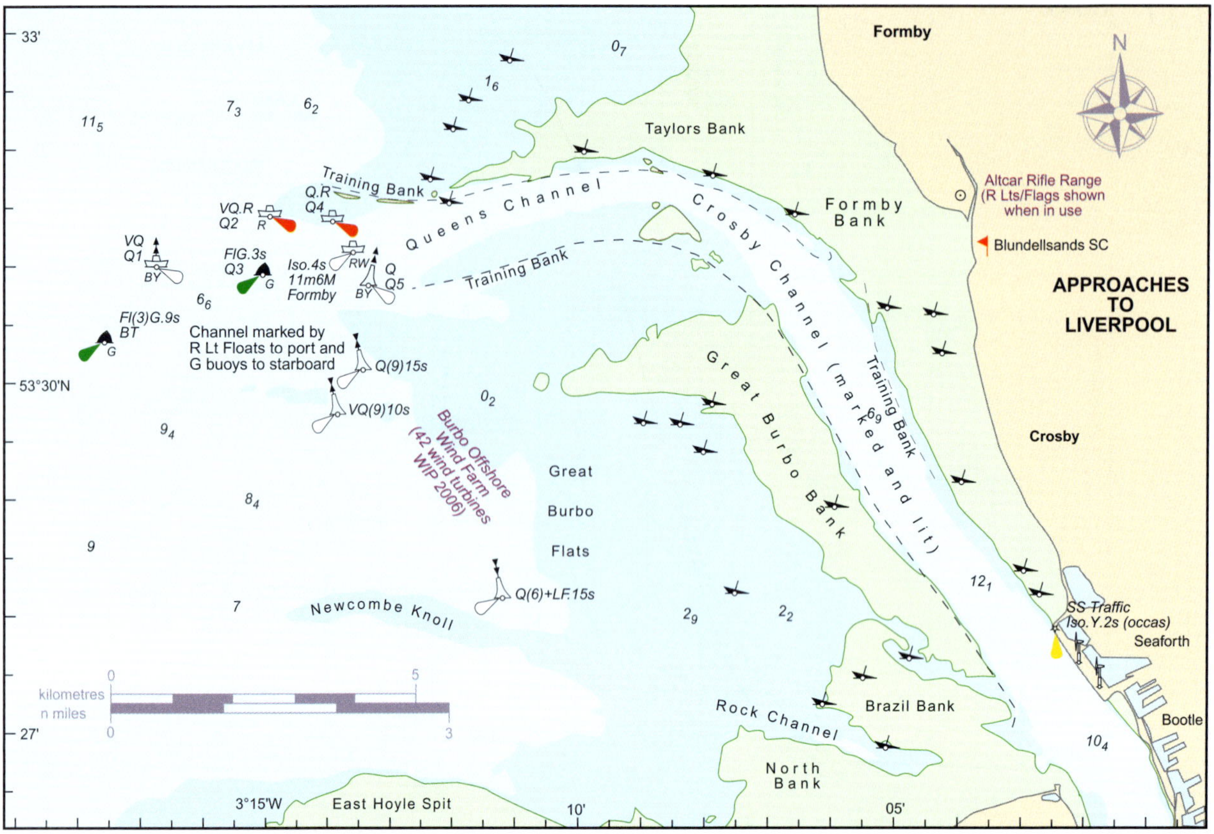

TELEPHONE (Code 0151) Port Ops 949 6134/5; MRCC 931 3341; Marinecall 09068 969651; Police 709 6010; Ⓗ 709 0141.

FACILITIES Liverpool Marina entrance is 1M S of the Liver Bldg, abeam Pluckington Bank WCM buoy. **IPTS** (sigs 2, 3 & 5) from conspic black control bldg at lock ent. Access approx HW ±2¼ sp, ±1½ nps, 0600-2200 Mar-Oct, via Brunswick Dock lock (width 8m), pontoons inside, min depth 3·5m; night locking by arrangement. www.liverpoolmarina.co.uk ☎ 7076777, (0600-2200 Mar–Oct). 350 AB + 50 Ⓥ, £2.42. D, P (½M), BH (60 ton), Slip, CH, SM, ▣, ♿, Bar, R (☎ 7076888).

Albert Dock ☎ 7096558; access HW–2 to HW via Canning Dock, but not on every tide. VHF Ch M when ent manned, AB, FW, AC.

Royal Mersey YC ☎ 6453204, Slip, M, P, D, L, FW, R, Bar.

W Kirby SC ☎ 6255579, AB (at HW), Slip, M (in Dee Est), L, FW, C (30ton), Bar.

Hoylake SC ☎ 6322616, Slip, M, FW, Bar; **Services:** CH, SM, ME, El, ⚒, ACA, Ⓔ.

City all facilities, ⇌, ✈.

ADJACENT ANCHORAGE

RIVER ALT, Merseyside, **53°31´·42N 03°03´·80W**. AC 1978, 1951, 5613. HW –0008 on Dover. Good shelter but only for LOA <8·5m x 1·2m draft on a HW of at least 8m. Mersey E training wall can be crossed HW±2. Ent to chan (shifts frequently) is E of C14 PHM lt float, thence marked by locally-laid Y Fairway buoy and perches on the training wall. Unsafe to ⚓ in R Alt; pick up a free mooring off the SC and contact club. Local knowledge advised. Facilities very limited. **Blundellsands SC** ☎ (0151) 929 2101 (occas), Slip, L (at HW), FW, Bar.

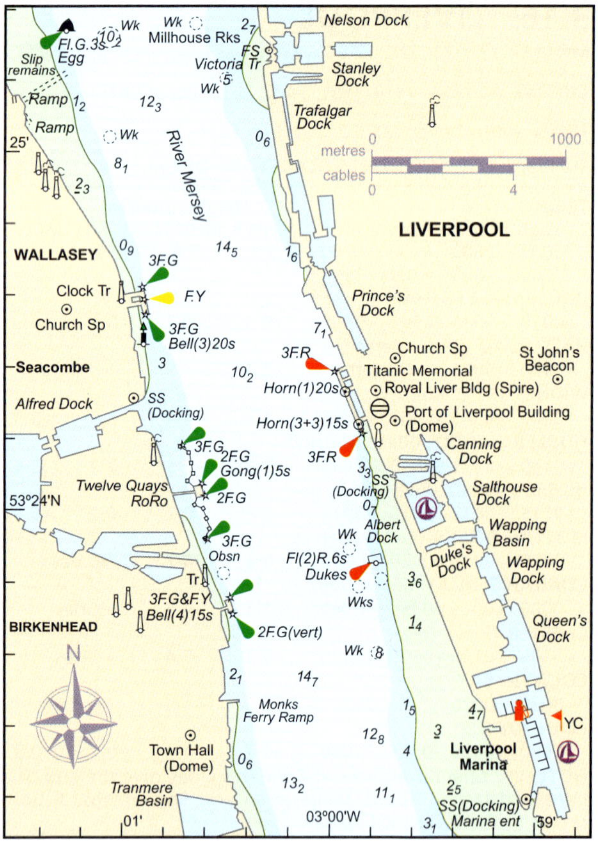

3.17 CONWY AND DEGANWY

Conwy 53°17'·48N 03°50'·23W (marina)
Deganwy 53°17'·41N 03°49'·66W (marina)

CHARTS AC 5609, 1826, 1977, 1978, 1463; Imray C52; Stan 27

TIDES –0015 Dover; ML 4·3; Duration 0545

Standard Port HOLYHEAD (⟶)

Times				Height (metres)			
High Water		Low Water		MHWS	MHWN	MLWN	MLWS
0000	0600	0500	1100	5·6	4·4	2·0	0·7
1200	1800	1700	2300				
Differences CONWY							
+0025	+0035	+0120	+0105	+2·3	+1·8	+0·6	+0·4

NOTE: HW Conwy is approx HW Liverpool –0040 sp and –0020 nps.

SHELTER Good, except in NW gales.

NAVIGATION WPT Fairway buoy, 53°17'·95N 03°55'·58W, 120°/6·5ca to No 2 PHM. Access HW±2; if Conwy Sands (to the N) are covered, there is enough water in chan for a 2m draught boat. A bar, dries 1·0m, forms at The Scabs adjacent to No 6 PHM.

After No C2 PHM buoy the channel up to Deganwy is marked by lt buoys (even Nos = PHM, odd Nos = SHM) in sequence: C1, C4, then paired buoys C3 and C6, C5 and C8, C7 and C10, C9 and C12, C11 and C14. C16 (unlit) at narrows into R Conwy. 10kn speed limit above Perch lt bcn. Sp ebb up to 5kn.

North Deep, a buoyed inshore passage (close SW of Gt Orme's Hd to Deganwy Point), is only advised with local knowledge.

Beware: unlit Beacons Jetty (close N of Conwy marina); unlit moorings off Deganwy; and five unlit pontoons between Bodlondeb Pt and the road/rail bridge.

LIGHTS AND MARKS Penmaenmawr SPM outfall buoy (SW of No 2 buoy) is not a channel mark. The 4 towers of Conwy castle and the 2 adjacent bridge towers are conspic.

R/T HM Ch **14**. Summer 0900-1700LT daily; winter, same times Mon-Fri). Conwy Marina, pre-call Ch 80 (H24) for a berth. Deganwy Quay Ch 80. N Wales CC launch Ch M, water taxi.

TELEPHONE (Code 01492) HM 596253. MRCC (01407) 762051. Marinecall 09068 969650. Police 517171. Dr 592424.

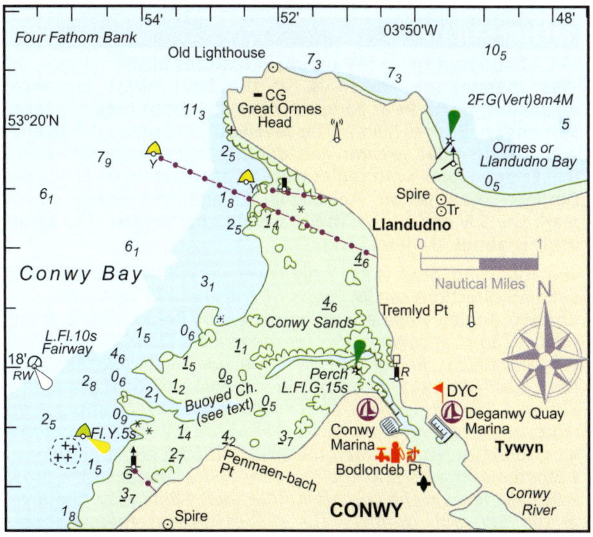

FACILITIES Conwy Marina Access when height of tide above CD exceeds 3·5m, ie approx HW ±3¼. Gate times are on an electronic noticeboard. Waiting pontoon outside. Obey R/G entry lts. ☎ 593000. www.quaymarinas.com, 505 AB inc Ⓥ, £2.25m; < 5hrs, £10. D & P (0700-2200), BH (30 ton), BY, ⚒, ⛭, CH, Gas, SM, Wi-fi, ▣, R, Bar.

Harbour Between Bodlondeb Pt and Conwy bridge contact HM for: Pontoon AB £13; Town Quay AB dries (12·3m max LOA, short stay for loading); and ⚓'s. D (Town Quay/pontoon HW±2, call Ch 14 to confirm), FW, ♿. Slip HW±3 at Beacons Jetty £18/day.

Deganwy Quay Marina Keep close to 3 PHM lt buoys marking the appr channel (see lower chartlet). Min depth in chan is 2·5m when marina gate open. Access when height of tide above CD exceeds 4m, ie approx HW ±3¼. www.deganwyquay.com/marina ☎ 576888. deganwymarina@tiscali.co.uk 200 AB inc Ⓥ, £3.30. ♿, ⚒, ME, El, Ⓔ, Slip, BH (20 ton).

Conwy YC (Deganwy) ☎ 583690, Slip, M, L, FW, R, Bar.

N Wales Cruising Club (in Conwy) ☎ 593481, AB, M, FW, Bar.
Services: ME, Gas, Gaz, ⚒, El, Ⓔ.

Town P & D (cans), 🛒, R, Bar, ✉, Ⓑ, ⇌, ✈ (Liverpool).

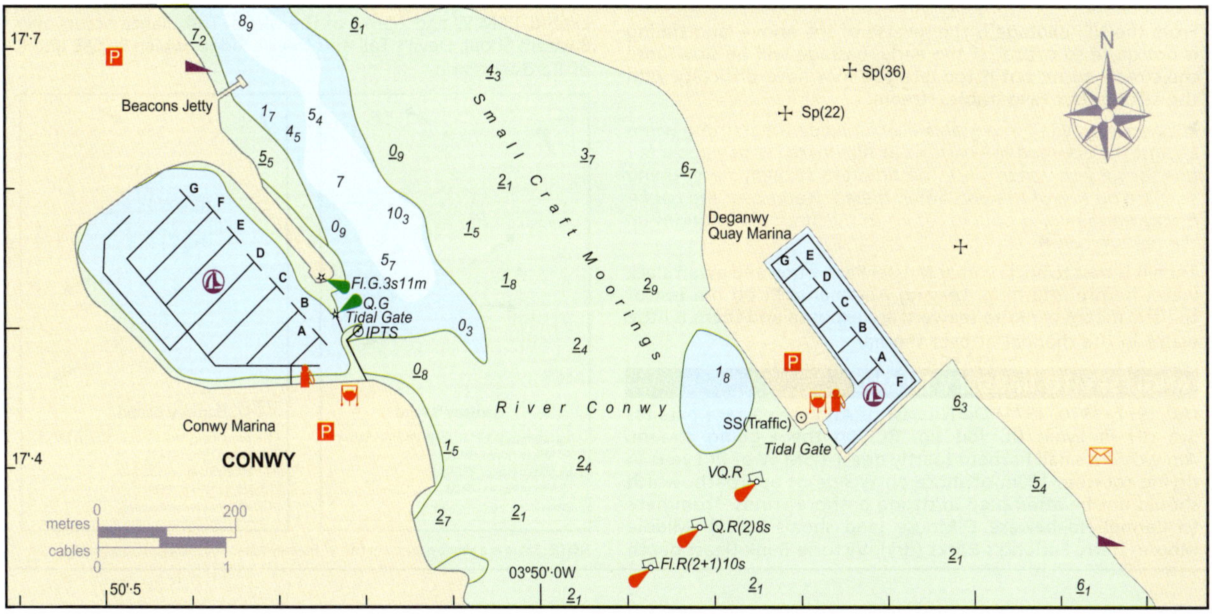

MENAI STRAIT

(AC 1464) From NE to SW the main features of this narrow, 20 mile channel are: Puffin Is, at the North-West Entrance; Beaumaris; Garth Pt at Bangor, where the Strait begins; Menai Suspension Bridge (29m); The Swellies, a narrow 1M stretch with strong tidal streams and dangers mid-stream; Britannia Rail Bridge (26m), with cables close W at elevation of 21m; Port Dinorwic; Caernarfon; Abermenai Pt and Fort Belan, which mark the SW end of the Strait; and Caernarfon Bar. The Strait itself is about 10 miles long.

The following brief notes only cover very basic pilotage. For detailed directions see *W Coasts of England and Wales Pilot*, or *Cruising Anglesey and adjoining waters* by Ralph Morris. ▶ *For tidal streams 'Arrowsmiths' is recommended, from Arrowsmiths, Winterstoke Rd, Bristol, BS3 2NT. The Swellies should be taken near local HW slack, and an understanding of tidal streams is essential. The tide is about 1 hour later, and sp range about 2·7m more, at the NE end of the Strait than at the SW end. Levels differ most at about HW +1, when the level at the NE end is more than 1·8m above the level at the SW end; and at about HW – 0445, when the level at the NE end is more than 1·8m below the level at the SW end. Normally the stream runs as follows (times referred to HW Holyhead). HW –0040 to HW +0420: SW between Garth Pt and Abermenai Pt. HW +0420 to HW +0545: outwards from about The Swellies, ie NE towards Garth Pt and SW towards Abermenai Pt. HW +0545 to HW –0040: NE between Abermenai Pt and Garth Pt. Sp rates are generally about 3kn,* ***but more in narrows, eg 5kn off Abermenai Pt, 6kn between the bridges, and 8kn at The Swellies.*** *The timings and rates of streams may be affected by strong winds in either direction.* ◀ **Note: Direction of buoyage becomes NE off Caernarfon**.

From SW to NE, arrive at the Swellies early (HW Holyhead –0130) to take the last of the E-going tidal stream. Better to arrive too early, and wait, than too late and risk not making it through the narrows before the stream turns to the W. Approach the S arch of Britannia Bridge keeping the white pyramid in line with the centre of the arch. Once through the bridge, head for a point midway between the pyramid and Price's Point. When the pyramid is abeam, look astern and keep the white leading marks (beneath the S arch of the bridge) in line. When Price's Point is abeam, turn to starboard to pass 20-30m S of Swelly Perch rock, then head just S of the Anglesey (ie N) pillar of the Menai Suspension Bridge until clear of the Platters (cottage abeam to starboard). Then head for the centre of the bridge.

From the NE, pilotage is the reverse of the above, and timing is not quite so critical. If too early, passage will be slow until the stream turns; but if too late you may have difficulty with the strong, but favourable, stream.

▶ *Caernarfon Bar is impassable even in moderately strong winds against the ebb, and the narrows at Abermenai Pt demand a fair tide, or slackish water, since the tide runs strongly here. Going seaward on first of the ebb, when there is water over the banks, it may not be practicable to return to the Strait if conditions on the bar are bad.* ◀

Then it is best to anchor near Mussel Bank buoy and await slack water before returning. Leaving Abermenai Pt on the last of the ebb means banks to seaward are exposed and there is little water in the channel or over the bar.

ANGLESEY TO BARDSEY ISLAND

(AC 1977, 1970, 1971) On N coast of Anglesey a race extends 5ca off Pt Lynas (lt, fog sig, RC) on the E-going stream. Amlwch is a small harbour (partly dries) 1·5M W of Pt Lynas. A drying rock lies 100m offshore on W side of approach, which should not be attempted in strong onshore winds. From here to Carmel Hd beware E Mouse (and shoals to SE), Middle Mouse, Harry Furlong's Rocks (dry), Victoria Bank (least depth 1·8m), Coal Rock (awash), and W Mouse (with dangers to W & SW). The outermost of these dangers is 2M offshore. There are overfalls and races at headlands and over the many rocks and shoals along this coast.

The simplest passage, or at night or in bad weather, is to pass 1M off Skerries, in the TSS ITZ. In good conditions by day and at slack water, Carmel Hd can be rounded close inshore; but beware short, steep, breaking seas here in even moderate winds against tide. Holyhead (port of refuge), access H24 in all weathers, within New Harbour; beware fast ferries.

▶ *Between Carmel Hd and The Skerries the NE-going stream begins at HW Holyhead +0550, and the SW-going at HW Holyhead –0010,* ***sp rates 5kn.*** *1M NW of Skerries the stream turns 0130 later, and runs less strongly.* ***Flood tide close to the coast runs at over 5kn springs,*** *and at about 2.5kn 7 miles offshore. The brief period of slack water offshore is HW Dover –0100 (HW L'pool –0115). Slack water lasts longer in Holyhead Bay.*

Ebb tide close to the coast runs at over 5k springs, *and at about 2.5kn 7 miles offshore. Slack water is 5 hours after HW Dover (4¾ hours after HW L'pool). There is no significant counter tide in Holyhead Bay, but the ebb starts first there, giving about 9 hours W-going tide N of the harbour.* ◀

▶ *Races occur off N Stack and (more severe) off S Stack, up to 1·5M offshore on NNE-going stream which begins at HW Holyhead –0605,* ***sp rate 5kn.*** *Races do not extend so far on SSW-going stream which begins at HW Holyhead +0020,* ***sp rate 5kn.*** ◀

The W coast of Anglesey is rugged with rks, some drying, up to 1·5M offshore. There are races off Penrhyn Mawr and Rhoscolyn Hd. Pilot's Cove, E of Llanddwyn Is, is good anch to await the right conditions for Menai Strait.

On the Lleyn Peninsula Porth Dinllaen is good anch, but exposed to N and NE. Braich y Pwll is the steep, rky point at end of Lleyn Peninsula (AC 1971). About 1M N of it and up to 1M offshore lie The Tripods, a bank on which there are o'falls and a bad sea with wind against tide.

▶ *Bardsey Sound, 1·5M wide, can be used by day in moderate winds.* ***Stream reaches 6kn at sp, and passage should be made at slack water,*** *Holyhead –0015 HW or +0035 LW.* ◀

Avoid Carreg Ddu on N side and Maen Bugail Rock (dries 4·1m) on S side of Sound, where there are dangerous races. If passing outside Bardsey Is make a good offing to avoid overfalls which extend 1·5M W and 2·5M S of the island. Turbulence occurs over Bastram Shoal, Devil's Tail and Devil's Ridge, which lie SSE and E of Bardsey Island.

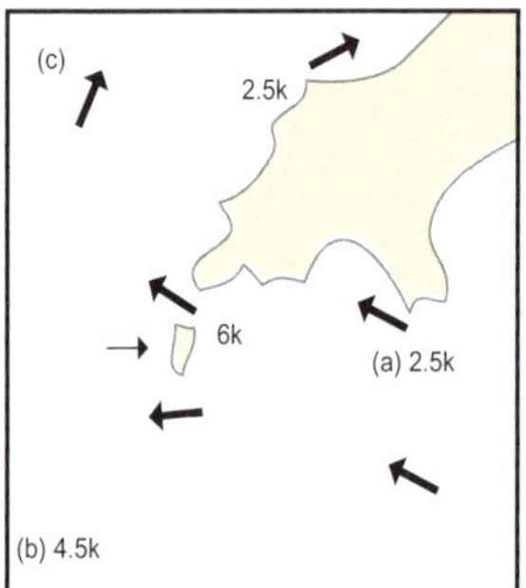

FLOOD Bardsey Sound

The tide turns to the NW or NE (flood) as follows:
(a): Milford Haven +0130;
(b): Milford Haven –0030;
(c): Milford Haven –0100.
These times are approximate.

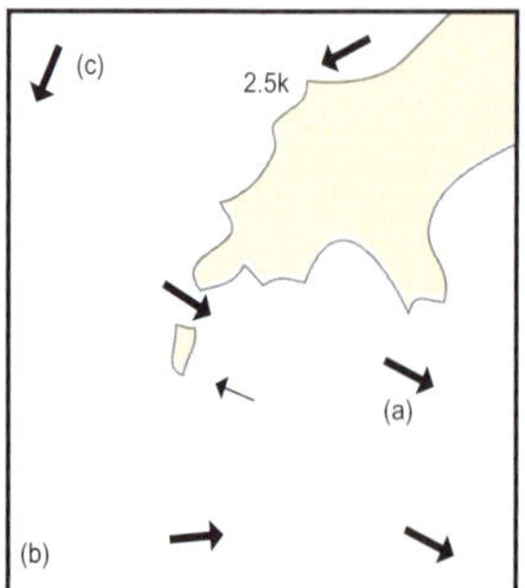

EBB Bardsey Sound

The tide turns to the SW or SE (ebb) as follows:
(a): Milford Haven –0430;
(b): Milford Haven +0530;
(c): Milford Haven +0500.
These times are approximate.

NOTE: There is a strong eddy down tide off Bardsey Island and overfalls throughout the area.

3.18 MENAI STRAIT

Gwynedd/Isle of Anglesey

CHARTS AC 5609, 1464, Imray C52; Stanfords 27. NOTE: The definitive Pilot book is *Cruising Anglesey and adjoining waters* by Ralph Morris.

TIDES Beaumaris –0025 Dover; ML Beaumaris 4·2; Duration 0540

Standard Port HOLYHEAD (⟶)

Times				Height (metres)			
High Water		Low Water		MHWS	MHWN	MLWN	MLWS
0000	0600	0500	1100	5·6	4·4	2·0	0·7
1200	1800	1700	2300				
Differences BEAUMARIS							
+0025	+0010	+0055	+0035	+2·0	+1·6	+0·5	+0·1
MENAI BRIDGE							
+0030	+0010	+0100	+0035	+1·7	+1·4	+0·3	0·0
PORT DINORWIC							
–0015	–0025	+0030	0000	0·0	0·0	0·0	+0·1
CAERNARFON							
–0030	–0030	+0015	–0005	–0·4	–0·4	–0·1	–0·1
FORT BELAN							
–0040	–0015	–0025	–0005	–1·0	–0·9	–0·2	–0·1
LLANDDWYN ISLAND							
–0115	–0055	–0030	–0020	–0·7	–0·5	–0·1	0·0

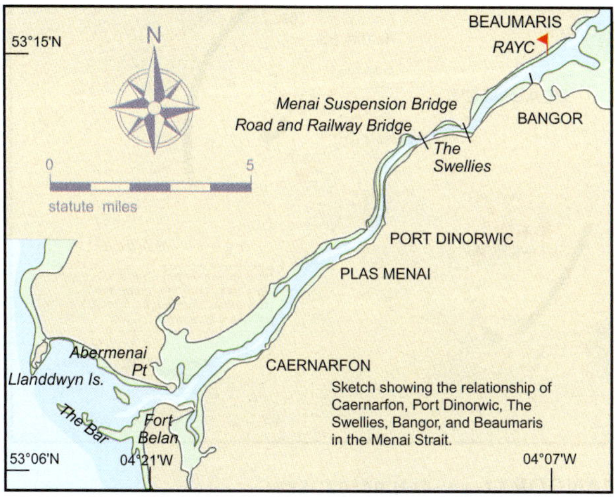

Sketch showing the relationship of Caernarfon, Port Dinorwic, The Swellies, Bangor, and Beaumaris in the Menai Strait.

SOUTH WEST ENTRANCE – CAERNARFON BAR

NAVIGATION WPT 53°06´·70N 04°25´·40W, 6ca WSW of C1 SHM. A dangerous sea can build in even a moderate breeze against tide, especially if a swell is running. Bar Chan should not be used at any time other than HW-3 to HW+3. Caernarfon Bar shifts often and unpredictably.

LIGHTS AND MARKS See 3.3 and chartlet. **Direction of buoyage changes at Caernarfon.**

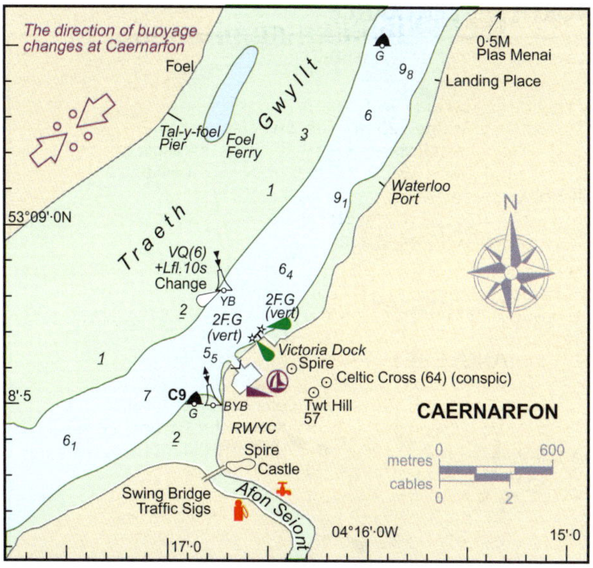

CAERNARFON 53°08'·51N 04°16'·83W

SHELTER Good in Victoria Dock marina, access HW±2 via gates, trfc lts; pontoons at SW end in 2m. Or in river hbr (S of conspic castle), dries to mud/gravel, access HW±3 via swing bridge; for opening sound B (–•••). ⚓ off Foel Ferry, with local knowledge; or temp ⚓ in fair holding off Abermenai Pt, sheltered from W'lies, but strong streams. [mooring] waiting 1½ca SW of C9.

R/T Victoria Dock marina VHF Ch 80. Port Ch 14 16 (HJ).

TELEPHONE (Code 01286) HM 672118, Mobile 07786 730865; Police 673333; [H] 01248 384384; Dr (emergency) 01248 384001.

FACILITIES **Dock** £1·80 **River** £13·50/craft, 0700-2300 (Summer), FW, Slip, C (2 ton), [trolley], ME, El, Ⓔ, [chandlery]; **Caernarfon SC** ☎ (01248) 672861, L, Bar; **Royal Welsh YC** ☎ (01248) 672599, Bar; **Town** P (cans), ✉, Ⓑ.

PORT DINORWIC 53°11'·23N 04°13'·70W

TELEPHONE (Code 01248) Marina 671500; MRCC (01407) 762051; Dr 670423.

FACILITIES **Port Dinorwic Marina** (231 berths in fresh water) [visitors] £21/craft. Call *Dinorwic Marina* VHF Ch **80** M (HO)3 [mooring] 1ca NE of lock. **Tidal basin** dries at sp; lock (width 9·7m) opens HW±2. ☎ 671500, D, P (cans), [pump-out], CH, SM; Pier hd F WR 5m 2M, vis R225°- W357°-225°. **Services:** SM, ME, El, [repairs], Slip, C, CH. Dinas Boatyard ☎ 671642 all BY facilities. **Town** Ⓔ, ✉ (Bangor or Caernarfon), Ⓑ, [rail] (Bangor), ✈ (Liverpool). **Plas Menai** (between Port Dinorwic and Caernarfon), the Sport Council for Wales Sailing and Sports Centre: ☎ 670964. *Menai Base* Ch **80** M; day moorings only; [disabled].

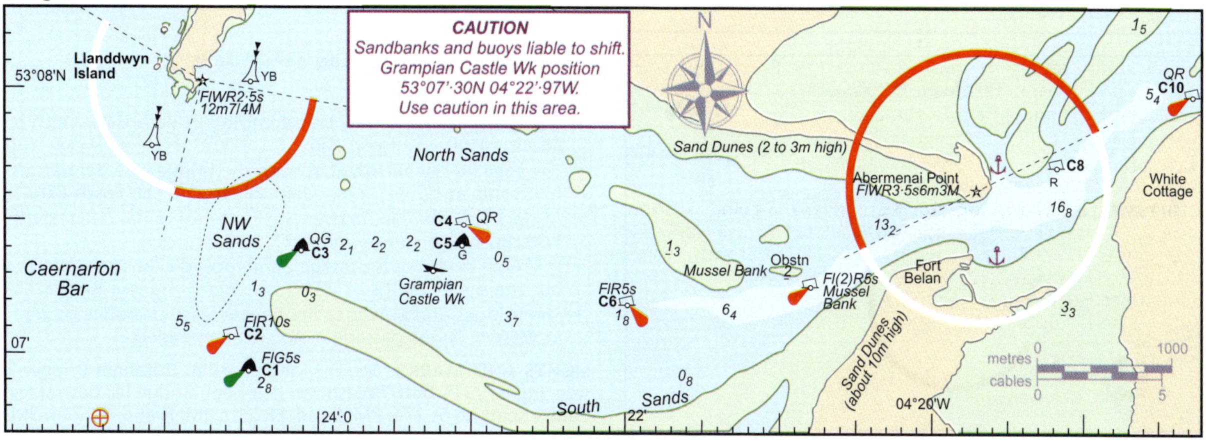

NORTH EAST ENTRANCE

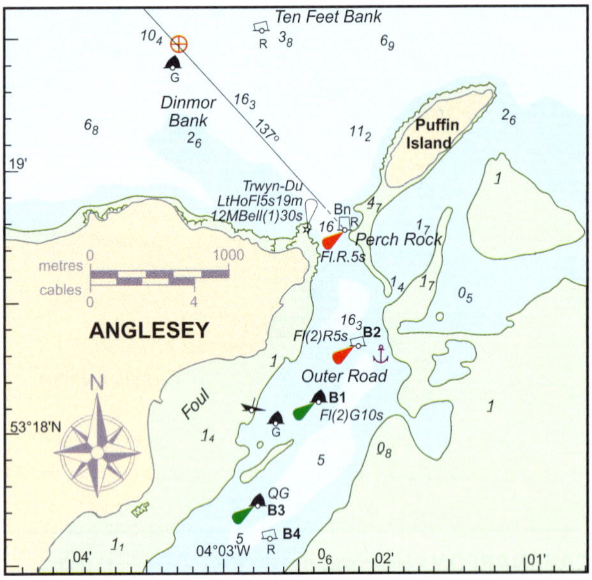

NAVIGATION WPT 53°19´·48N 04°03´·28W, 137°/1M to Perch Rk PHM Bn.

- In N'ly gales seas break on Ten Feet Bank.
- In N Strait keep to buoyed chan, nearer Anglesey.
- Night pilotage not advised due to many unlit buoys/moorings.

LIGHTS AND MARKS See 3.3. and chartlet. At NE end of Strait, Trwyn-Du Lt ho and Conspic tr on Puffin Is. Chan is laterally buoyed, some lit. Beaumaris pier has FWG sectored lt.

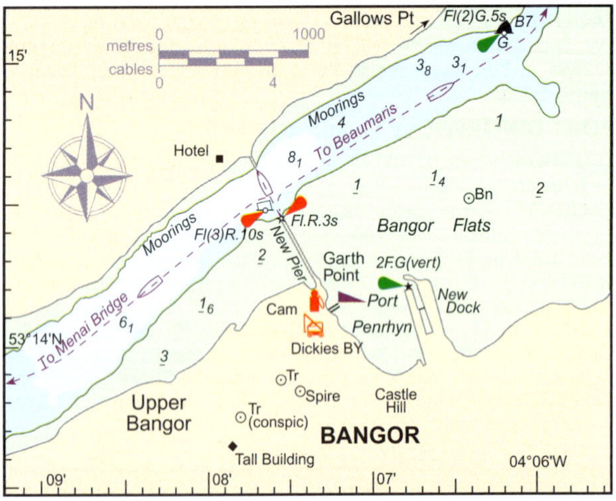

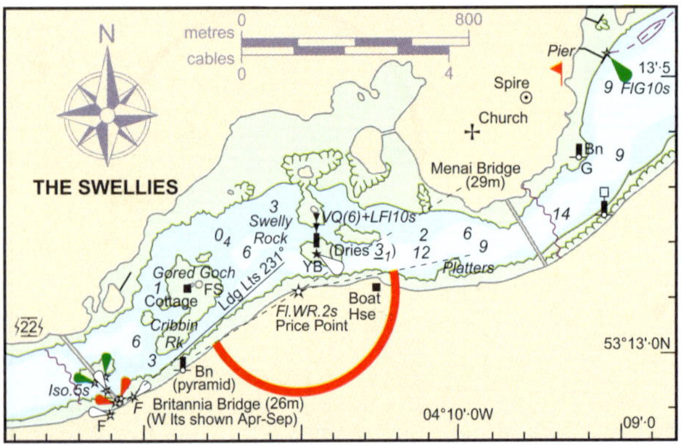

MENAI BRIDGE/BEAUMARIS 53°15'·66N 04°05'·38W

SHELTER Reasonable off Beaumaris except from NE winds. ⚓ S of B10 PHM buoy or call YCs for mooring. At Menai Bridge, call HM VHF Ch 69 16 for mooring or temp'y berth on St George's Pier (S of which a marina is planned).

TELEPHONE (Code 01248) HM Menai 712312, mobile 07990 531595; MRCC (01407) 762051; Marinecall 09068 969650; Police (01286) 673333; Dr (emergency) 01248 384001.

FACILITIES **St George's Pier** (Fl G 10s) L at all tides; **Royal Anglesey YC** ☎ 810295, Slip, M, L, R, Bar, P; **North West Venturers YC** ☎ 810023, M, L, FW, water taxi at w/ends only; **Menai Bridge SC. Services:** Slip, P & D (cans), FW, ME, BH (20 ton), ⚒, C (2 ton), CH, El, Ⓔ, Gas. **Both towns** ✉, Ⓑ, ⇌ (bus to Bangor), ✈ (Liverpool).

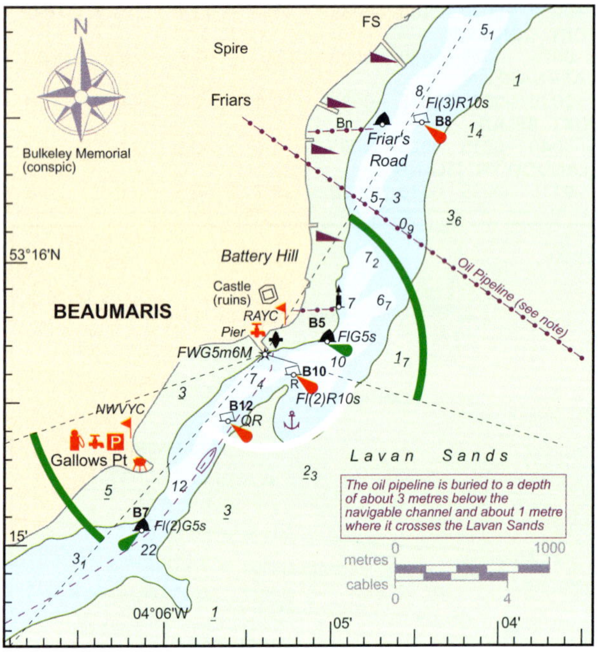

BANGOR 53°14'·46N 04°07'·58W

SHELTER Good, except in E'lies, at Dickies BY or Port Penrhyn dock (both dry; access HW±2).

R/T *Dickies* VHF Ch 09 M 16 (0930-1730), all year.

TELEPHONE (Code 01248) Penrhyn HM 352525; MRCC (01407) 762051; Police (01286) 673333; Dr (emergency) 384001.

FACILITIES **Services:** Slip, D, P (cans), FW, ME, El, ⚒, C, CH, Ⓔ, SM, BH (30 ton), Gas, Gaz, ACA; **Port Penrhyn**, Slip, AB, D. **Town** ✉, Ⓑ, ⇌, ✈ (Chester).

THE SWELLIES 53°13'·14N 04°10'·46W

NAVIGATION

- The passage should only be attempted at slack HW, which is about –0100 HW Holyhead.
- The shallow rky narrows between the bridges are dangerous for yachts at other times, when the stream can reach 8kn.
- At slack HW there is 3m over The Platters and the outcrop off Price Pt, which can be ignored.
- For shoal-draft boats passage is also possible at slack LW nps, but there are depths of 0·5m close E of Britannia Bridge.
- The bridges and power cables have a least clearance of 21m at MHWS. Night passage is not recommended.

LIGHTS AND MARKS See 3.3. and chartlet. Britannia Bridge, E side, ldg lts 231°, both FW (shown Apr-Sep). Bridge lts, both sides: Centre span Iso 5s 27m 3M; S end, FR 21m 3M; N end, FG 21m 3M.

3.19 HOLYHEAD

Isle of Anglesey **53°19'·72N 04°37'·07W**

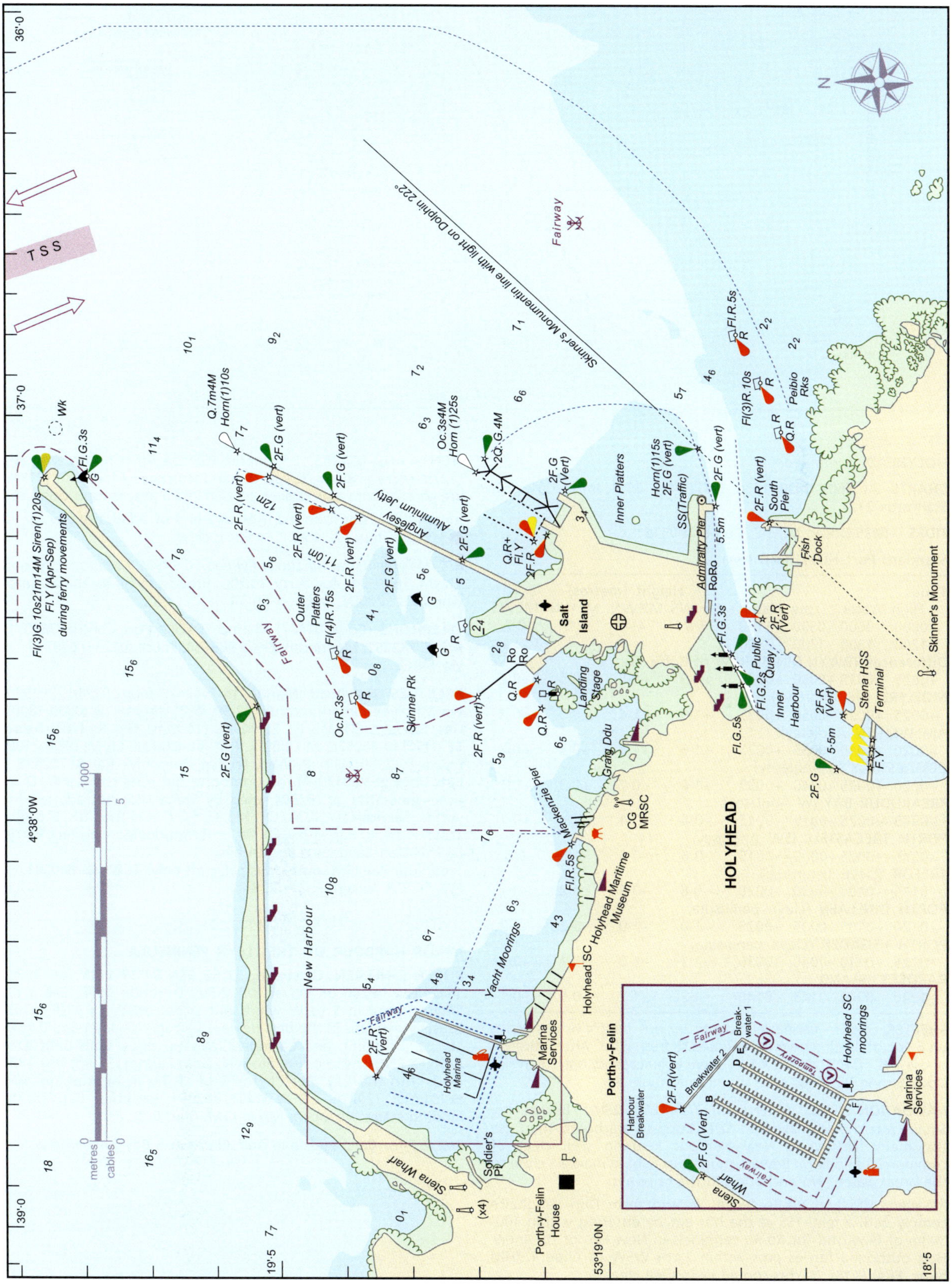

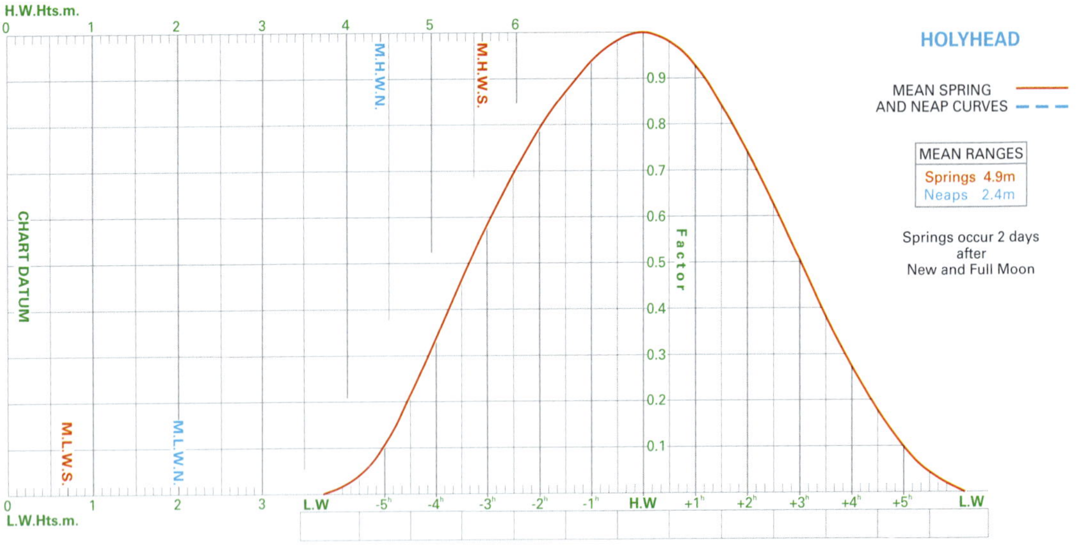

HOLYHEAD *continued*

CHARTS AC 5609, 1826, 1970, 1977, 1413, 2011; Imray C61, C52; Stanfords 27.

TIDES –0035 Dover; ML 3·2; Duration 0615

Standard Port HOLYHEAD (⟶)

Times				Height (metres)			
High Water		Low Water		MHWS	MHWN	MLWN	MLWS
0000	0600	0500	1100	5·6	4·4	2·0	0·7
1200	1800	1700	2300				
Differences TRWYN DINMOR (W of Puffin Is)							
+0025	+0015	+0050	+0035	+1·9	+1·5	+0·5	+0·2
MOELFRE (NE Anglesey)							
+0025	+0020	+0050	+0035	+1·9	+1·4	+0·5	+0·2
AMLWCH (N Anglesey)							
+0020	+0010	+0035	+0025	+1·6	+1·3	+0·5	+0·2
CEMAES BAY (N Anglesey)							
+0020	+0025	+0040	+0035	+1·0	+0·7	+0·3	+0·1
TREARDDUR BAY (W Anglesey)							
–0045	–0025	–0015	–0015	–0·4	–0·4	0·0	+0·1
PORTH TRECASTELL (SW Anglesey)							
–0045	–0025	–0005	–0015	–0·6	–0·6	0·0	0·0
TREFOR (Lleyn peninsula)							
–0115	–0100	–0030	–0020	–0·8	–0·9	–0·2	–0·1
PORTH DINLLAEN (Lleyn peninsula)							
–0120	–0105	–0035	–0025	–1·0	–1·0	–0·2	–0·2
PORTH YSGADEN (Lleyn peninsula)							
–0125	–0110	–0040	–0035	–1·1	–1·0	–0·1	–0·1
BARDSEY ISLAND							
–0220	–0240	–0145	–0140	–1·2	–1·2	–0·5	–0·1

SHELTER Good in marina, least depth 2m, but temp'y visitors berths on E side of floating bwtr are exposed to fresh E'lies. Alternatively ⚓ or use Y ⓥ off HSC; drying AB on bkwtr in emergency only; or in Fish Dock. Strong NE winds raise an uncomfortable sea.

NAVIGATION WPT 53°20´·12N 04°37´·27W, 165°/0·28M to Bkwtr Lt ho. Small craft should leave Spit SHM buoy to starboard then use the main fairway to New Harbour keeping well clear of commercial shipping. Beware numerous fishing markers close to the breakwater. No anchoring in the fairways.

Frequent HSS and Ro-Ro ferries to and from Dun Laoghaire comply with a mini-TSS at the hbr ent by entering within 100-500m of bkwtr hd for Ro-Ro terminals in New Hbr or the Inner Hbr; outbound ferries pass within 2½ca WSW of Clipera PHM buoy, Fl(4) R 15s. Yachts should keep well clear.

LIGHTS AND MARKS Ldg marks 165°: bkwtr lt ho on with chy (127m, grey + B top; R lts); chy and Holyhead Mountain (218m) are conspic from afar. Cranes on aluminium jetty conspic closer to.

Inner hbr tfc sigs from old lt ho at E end of Admiralty pier: ● = Ent is impracticable. ○ = Ent is clear.

R/T *Holyhead Marina* and *Holyhead SC*: Ch **M**. Monitor *Holyhead* Ch 14 16 (H24) for ferry traffic. Broadcast of local nav info/warnings 1200UT daily on Ch 14.

TELEPHONE (Code 01407) Marina 764242; Port Control 763071; MRCC 762051; Marinecall 09068 969650; Police (01286) 673333; Dr via MRCC.

FACILITIES **Holyhead Marina** ☎ 764242, mob 07714 292990, www.holyheadmarina.co.uk, £2.50, ⓥ 21 approx, D (0800-1800), Gas, Gaz, BY, CH, ME, Ⓔ, El, ⚒, BH (14 tons), Slip, R. **Holyhead SC (HSC)** ☎ 762526, M £8.00, L, FW, launch (call Ch M: 0900-2100, Fri/Sat to 2330), Slip, R (Wed, Fri, Sat, Sun only), Bar ☎ 762496. **Fish Dock** ☎ 760139 AB on pontoons, but little room, FW, D by hose. **Inner Hbr** ☎ 762304, used by Stena HSS; not advised for yachts. **Services:** BY, ACA, CH, ME, El, ⚒, C (100 ton), BH, Slip, Ⓔ. **Town** P, 🛒, R, Bar, ⊡, ✉, Ⓑ, ⇌, ✈ (Liverpool/Manchester). Ferry/HSS to Dun Laoghaire and Dublin.
Treaddur Bay (3M south) M (small craft only), L; **BY** ☎ 860501, D, FW, ⚒, CH. **Village** P, 🛒, R, Bar.

MINOR HARBOUR ON THE LLEYN PENINSULA

PORTH DINLLAEN, Gwynedd, **52°56´·68N 04°33´·66W**. AC 1971, 1512. HW –0240 on Dover; ML 2·5m; Duration 0535. See 3.19. Shelter good in S to W winds but strong NNW to NNE winds cause heavy seas in the bay. Beware Carreg-y-Chad (1·8m) 0·75M SW of the point, and Carreg-y-Chwislen (dries, with unlit IDM Bn) 2ca ENE of the point. From N, Garn Fadryn (369m) brg 182° leads into the bay. Best ⚓ 1ca S of LB ho in approx 2m. HM ☎ (01758) 720276; CG ☎ 01407 762051. Facilities: Bar, 🛒 by landing stage. At Morfa Nefyn (1M), Bar, P, R, 🛒.

See 4.5 for Bardsey Island and Aberdaron Bay anchorages.

TIME ZONE (UT)
For Summer Time add ONE hour in **non-shaded areas**

HOLYHEAD

LAT 53°19′N LONG 4°37′W

TIMES AND HEIGHTS OF HIGH AND LOW WATERS

Dates in red are SPRINGS
Dates in blue are NEAPS

YEAR **2010**

JANUARY

Date	Time	m	Date	Time	m
1 F	0405 1021 1637 2250	0.9 5.8 0.7 5.7	16 SA	0448 1057 1712 2320	1.3 5.5 1.1 5.2
2 SA	0452 1107 1725 2338	0.8 6.0 0.5 5.7	17 SU	0519 1129 1743 2351	1.2 5.6 1.1 5.2
3 SU	0538 1154 1813	0.7 6.0 0.4	18 M	0550 1201 1814	1.2 5.5 1.1
4 M	0026 0625 1242 1902	5.7 0.8 6.0 0.5	19 TU	0022 0622 1234 1846	5.1 1.3 5.5 1.2
5 TU	0115 0713 1331 1953	5.5 1.0 5.9 0.7	20 W	0055 0655 1308 1920	5.1 1.4 5.4 1.3
6 W	0205 0803 1423 2046	5.3 1.2 5.6 1.0	21 TH	0129 0730 1344 1956	4.9 1.5 5.2 1.5
7 TH	0259 0859 1519 ◑ 2145	5.0 1.5 5.3 1.4	22 F	0206 0809 1423 2038	4.8 1.7 5.0 1.6
8 F	0400 1002 1624 2251	4.8 1.8 5.0 1.7	23 SA	0249 0857 1511 ◐ 2130	4.6 2.0 4.8 1.9
9 SA	0510 1115 1739	4.6 2.0 4.8	24 SU	0346 0959 1614 2237	4.5 2.1 4.6 2.0
10 SU	0001 0623 1231 1857	1.9 4.6 2.0 4.7	25 M	0504 1119 1738 2357	4.4 2.2 4.5 2.0
11 M	0110 0731 1342 2004	1.9 4.8 1.9 4.8	26 TU	0629 1241 1901	4.5 2.0 4.7
12 TU	0210 0827 1441 2058	1.8 5.0 1.7 4.9	27 W	0111 0739 1350 2008	1.8 4.8 1.6 4.9
13 W	0300 0912 1527 2141	1.7 5.2 1.5 5.0	28 TH	0214 0835 1448 2104	1.5 5.2 1.2 5.3
14 TH	0340 0951 1606 2217	1.5 5.3 1.3 5.1	29 F	0307 0923 1538 2152	1.1 5.5 0.8 5.5
15 F	0416 1025 1640 ● 2250	1.4 5.5 1.2 5.2	30 SA	0354 1008 1625 ○ 2238	0.8 5.9 0.4 5.8
			31 SU	0438 1053 1710 2322	0.6 6.1 0.2 5.8

FEBRUARY

Date	Time	m	Date	Time	m
1 M	0522 1137 1755	0.4 6.2 0.1	16 TU	0525 1136 1746 2354	1.0 5.6 0.9 5.3
2 TU	0006 0605 1222 1839	5.8 0.4 6.2 0.3	17 W	0555 1207 1815	1.0 5.5 1.0
3 W	0050 0649 1307 1924	5.6 0.6 6.0 0.6	18 TH	0024 0626 1239 1845	5.2 1.1 5.4 1.1
4 TH	0135 0735 1354 2012	5.4 0.9 5.6 1.0	19 F	0056 0658 1312 1919	5.1 1.2 5.3 1.2
5 F	0221 0825 1444 ◑ 2104	5.1 1.3 5.2 1.4	20 SA	0130 0735 1349 1958	5.0 1.4 5.1 1.5
6 SA	0314 0923 1544 2207	4.8 1.7 4.8 1.9	21 SU	0209 0820 1434 2047	4.8 1.7 4.8 1.7
7 SU	0421 1037 1704 2324	4.5 2.0 4.4 2.1	22 M	0301 0920 1536 ◐ 2155	4.6 1.9 4.6 2.0
8 M	0545 1205 1840	4.4 2.2 4.3	23 TU	0417 1046 1709 2327	4.4 2.1 4.4 2.1
9 TU	0046 0710 1329 1958	2.2 4.5 2.0 4.5	24 W	0558 1219 1846	4.4 1.9 4.5
10 W	0156 0813 1431 2051	2.0 4.7 1.8 4.7	25 TH	0053 0718 1335 1957	1.9 4.7 1.5 4.9
11 TH	0247 0859 1515 2130	1.8 5.0 1.5 4.9	26 F	0159 0818 1433 2051	1.5 5.1 1.0 5.2
12 F	0326 0935 1550 2202	1.5 5.2 1.3 5.0	27 SA	0252 0906 1522 2137	1.1 5.6 0.6 5.5
13 SA	0359 1007 1620 2230	1.3 5.4 1.1 5.1	28 SU	0337 0950 1606 ○ 2219	0.7 5.9 0.2 5.8
14 SU	0428 1036 1649 ● 2257	1.1 5.5 1.0 5.2			
15 M	0456 1106 1717 2325	1.0 5.6 0.9 5.3			

MARCH

Date	Time	m	Date	Time	m
1 M	0419 1033 1649 2300	0.4 6.1 0.0 5.9	16 TU	0429 1038 1646 2256	0.9 5.5 0.8 5.3
2 TU	0500 1116 1731 2341	0.2 6.2 0.1 5.8	17 W	0458 1108 1715 2325	0.8 5.6 0.8 5.4
3 W	0542 1159 1813	0.3 6.1 0.2	18 TH	0528 1140 1745 2356	0.8 5.5 0.8 5.3
4 TH	0022 0624 1243 1854	5.7 0.4 5.9 0.6	19 F	0600 1212 1816	0.9 5.4 1.0
5 F	0104 0708 1327 1938	5.5 0.8 5.5 1.0	20 SA	0028 0633 1247 1850	5.3 1.1 5.3 1.1
6 SA	0147 0755 1414 2026	5.2 1.2 5.1 1.5	21 SU	0103 0712 1327 1931	5.1 1.3 5.1 1.4
7 SU	0235 0850 1510 ◑ 2124	4.8 1.6 4.6 2.0	22 M	0145 0800 1415 2023	4.9 1.5 4.8 1.7
8 M	0336 1002 1629 2244	4.5 2.0 4.2 2.3	23 TU	0239 0904 1522 ◐ 2134	4.7 1.8 4.5 2.0
9 TU	0500 1135 1816	4.3 2.2 4.1	24 W	0356 1031 1658 2308	4.5 1.9 4.4 2.1
10 W	0015 0636 1303 1938	2.4 4.3 2.1 4.3	25 TH	0535 1202 1833	4.5 1.7 4.5
11 TH	0131 0745 1405 2029	2.2 4.6 1.8 4.5	26 F	0034 0655 1316 1940	1.9 4.8 1.3 4.9
12 F	0222 0832 1448 2106	1.9 4.8 1.5 4.8	27 SA	0139 0755 1412 2031	1.5 5.2 0.9 5.2
13 SA	0301 0908 1522 2136	1.6 5.1 1.2 5.0	28 SU	0230 0844 1500 2115	1.0 5.5 0.5 5.5
14 SU	0332 0939 1551 2203	1.3 5.3 1.0 5.1	29 M	0315 0928 1543 2156	0.7 5.8 0.3 5.7
15 M	0401 1009 1619 ● 2229	1.1 5.4 0.9 5.2	30 TU	0356 1011 1625 ○ 2236	0.4 6.0 0.2 5.8
			31 W	0438 1054 1705 2316	0.3 6.0 0.2 5.8

APRIL

Date	Time	m	Date	Time	m
1 TH	0520 1137 1746 2357	0.3 5.9 0.4 5.7	16 F	0503 1115 1718 2331	0.8 5.5 0.9 5.4
2 F	0602 1220 1827	0.5 5.6 0.8	17 SA	0539 1151 1753	0.9 5.4 1.0
3 SA	0037 0646 1304 1909	5.5 0.8 5.3 1.2	18 SU	0008 0617 1232 1833	5.4 1.0 5.2 1.1
4 SU	0119 0732 1349 1954	5.2 1.2 4.9 1.6	19 M	0048 0702 1317 1918	5.2 1.1 5.0 1.4
5 M	0205 0824 1442 2048	4.9 1.6 4.5 2.0	20 TU	0135 0755 1411 2015	5.0 1.3 4.8 1.7
6 TU	0259 0930 1554 ◑ 2200	4.6 1.9 4.2 2.3	21 W	0233 0901 1521 ◐ 2126	4.8 1.5 4.6 1.9
7 W	0413 1053 1730 2329	4.3 2.1 4.0 2.4	22 TH	0347 1022 1649 2251	4.7 1.6 4.5 1.9
8 TH	0541 1215 1855	4.3 2.0 4.2	23 F	0513 1142 1810	4.7 1.4 4.6
9 F	0045 0656 1320 1950	2.3 4.5 1.8 4.4	24 SA	0008 0627 1250 1914	1.8 4.9 1.2 4.9
10 SA	0142 0749 1407 2029	2.0 4.7 1.6 4.7	25 SU	0112 0728 1346 2006	1.4 5.2 0.9 5.1
11 SU	0223 0830 1443 2101	1.7 4.9 1.3 4.9	26 M	0205 0819 1435 2051	1.1 5.4 0.7 5.4
12 M	0257 0904 1515 2129	1.4 5.1 1.1 5.1	27 TU	0251 0906 1519 2132	0.8 5.6 0.5 5.5
13 TU	0328 0936 1544 2157	1.2 5.3 1.0 5.2	28 W	0335 0950 1601 ○ 2213	0.6 5.7 0.5 5.6
14 W	0358 1007 1614 ● 2226	1.0 5.4 0.9 5.3	29 TH	0418 1034 1643 2254	0.5 5.7 0.6 5.7
15 TH	0430 1040 1645 2258	0.9 5.5 0.8 5.4	30 F	0502 1118 1724 2335	0.6 5.6 0.8 5.6

Chart Datum: 3·05 metres below Ordnance Datum (Newlyn). HAT is 6·3 metres above Chart Datum; see 0.20

TIME ZONE (UT)
For Summer Time add ONE hour in **non-shaded areas**

HOLYHEAD LAT 53°19′N LONG 4°37′W

TIMES AND HEIGHTS OF HIGH AND LOW WATERS

Dates in red are SPRINGS
Dates in blue are NEAPS

YEAR **2010**

MAY

	Time	m		Time	m
1	0545	0.7	16	0525	0.8
	1201	5.4		1138	5.4
SA	1804	1.0	SU	1739	1.0
				2355	5.5
2	0016	5.4	17	0609	0.9
	0628	0.9		1223	5.3
SU	1245	5.1	M	1824	1.1
	1845	1.3			
3	0057	5.2	18	0040	5.4
	0713	1.2		0658	0.9
M	1328	4.8	TU	1314	5.1
	1928	1.6		1913	1.3
4	0140	5.0	19	0131	5.2
	0801	1.5		0754	1.1
TU	1417	4.5	W	1410	4.9
	2017	1.9		2010	1.5
5	0228	4.7	20	0228	5.1
	0856	1.8		0856	1.2
W	1515	4.3	TH	1515	4.7
	2116	2.2	◐	2115	1.7
6	0328	4.5	21	0334	5.0
	1002	1.9		1005	1.3
TH	1629	4.1	F	1628	4.7
◑	2228	2.3		2227	1.7
7	0438	4.4	22	0447	4.9
	1114	2.0		1115	1.3
F	1746	4.2	SA	1740	4.7
	2343	2.3		2338	1.7
8	0550	4.4	23	0557	5.0
	1219	1.9		1220	1.2
SA	1851	4.3	SU	1844	4.8
9	0045	2.1	24	0042	1.5
	0651	4.6		0700	5.1
SU	1312	1.7	M	1319	1.1
	1939	4.5		1939	5.0
10	0134	1.9	25	0140	1.3
	0741	4.8		0756	5.2
M	1355	1.5	TU	1411	1.0
	2017	4.8		2028	5.2
11	0215	1.6	26	0231	1.1
	0823	4.9		0847	5.3
TU	1433	1.3	W	1459	0.9
	2052	5.0		2112	5.3
12	0252	1.4	27	0320	0.9
	0901	5.1		0935	5.4
W	1508	1.1	TH	1543	0.9
	2125	5.1	○	2155	5.5
13	0328	1.1	28	0405	0.9
	0938	5.2		1020	5.3
TH	1543	1.0	F	1625	0.9
	2159	5.3		2237	5.5
14	0405	1.0	29	0449	0.9
	1016	5.3		1104	5.3
F	1619	0.9	SA	1706	1.0
●	2235	5.4		2318	5.5
15	0443	0.9	30	0532	0.9
	1055	5.4		1146	5.1
SA	1658	0.9	SU	1746	1.2
	2313	5.5		2357	5.4
			31	0613	1.0
				1227	5.0
			M	1825	1.3

JUNE

	Time	m		Time	m
1	0036	5.3	16	0032	5.6
	0653	1.2		0652	0.6
TU	1307	4.8	W	1306	5.3
	1904	1.5		1905	1.0
2	0116	5.1	17	0122	5.5
	0735	1.4		0744	0.7
W	1348	4.6	TH	1359	5.1
	1947	1.7		1957	1.2
3	0158	4.9	18	0215	5.4
	0821	1.5		0840	0.9
TH	1434	4.5	F	1455	5.0
	2034	1.9		2054	1.4
4	0245	4.8	19	0313	5.2
	0911	1.7		0940	1.1
F	1528	4.3	SA	1558	4.8
◑	2128	2.1	◐	2157	1.5
5	0340	4.6	20	0417	5.1
	1007	1.8		1044	1.2
SA	1630	4.2	SU	1705	4.7
	2231	2.2		2306	1.6
6	0443	4.5	21	0526	5.0
	1108	1.9		1150	1.4
SU	1736	4.3	M	1812	4.7
	2336	2.2			
7	0547	4.5	22	0014	1.6
	1208	1.8		0636	4.9
M	1837	4.4	TU	1254	1.4
				1915	4.8
8	0036	2.0	23	0120	1.5
	0646	4.6		0741	4.9
TU	1302	1.7	W	1353	1.4
	1928	4.6		2010	5.0
9	0130	1.8	24	0220	1.4
	0740	4.8		0838	5.0
W	1351	1.5	TH	1446	1.3
	2014	4.8		2059	5.1
10	0217	1.6	25	0312	1.2
	0828	4.9		0928	5.0
TH	1435	1.3	F	1532	1.3
	2055	5.0		2143	5.3
11	0302	1.3	26	0359	1.1
	0913	5.1		1012	5.1
F	1517	1.2	SA	1614	1.2
	2135	5.3	○	2224	5.4
12	0345	1.0	27	0440	1.0
	0957	5.3		1053	5.1
SA	1600	1.0	SU	1652	1.2
●	2217	5.4		2302	5.4
13	0429	0.8	28	0518	1.0
	1042	5.4		1130	5.1
SU	1643	0.9	M	1728	1.2
	2300	5.6		2339	5.4
14	0515	0.7	29	0555	1.0
	1128	5.4		1206	5.0
M	1729	0.9	TU	1803	1.2
	2345	5.6			
15	0603	0.6	30	0014	5.4
	1216	5.4		0630	1.1
TU	1816	0.9	W	1241	4.9
				1838	1.3

JULY

	Time	m		Time	m
1	0050	5.3	16	0105	5.8
	0706	1.2		0724	0.5
TH	1316	4.8	F	1337	5.4
	1915	1.5		1935	0.9
2	0127	5.1	17	0154	5.7
	0744	1.3		0814	0.7
F	1354	4.7	SA	1427	5.1
	1955	1.7		2027	1.1
3	0206	5.0	18	0247	5.4
	0824	1.5		0909	1.1
SA	1435	4.6	SU	1523	4.9
	2039	1.9	◐	2126	1.4
4	0250	4.8	19	0347	5.1
	0909	1.7		1011	1.4
SU	1524	4.4	M	1628	4.7
◑	2129	2.0		2235	1.7
5	0342	4.6	20	0458	4.8
	1002	1.8		1121	1.7
M	1624	4.3	TU	1742	4.6
	2230	2.1		2352	1.8
6	0444	4.5	21	0619	4.6
	1104	1.9		1233	1.8
TU	1733	4.4	W	1856	4.7
	2339	2.1			
7	0555	4.5	22	0108	1.8
	1210	1.9		0735	4.6
W	1841	4.5	TH	1341	1.7
				2000	4.8
8	0047	2.0	23	0216	1.6
	0702	4.6		0836	4.7
TH	1313	1.7	F	1438	1.6
	1940	4.7		2051	5.0
9	0148	1.7	24	0308	1.4
	0802	4.8		0924	4.9
F	1409	1.5	SA	1523	1.4
	2031	5.0		2134	5.2
10	0242	1.4	25	0351	1.2
	0855	5.0		1004	5.0
SA	1459	1.3	SU	1601	1.3
	2117	5.3		2211	5.4
11	0330	1.0	26	0427	1.1
	0943	5.3		1038	5.1
SU	1545	1.0	M	1635	1.2
●	2201	5.5	○	2244	5.4
12	0417	0.7	27	0500	1.0
	1029	5.4		1110	5.1
M	1630	0.8	TU	1707	1.1
	2246	5.8		2317	5.5
13	0503	0.4	28	0531	1.0
	1115	5.6		1140	5.1
TU	1715	0.7	W	1738	1.1
	2331	5.9		2349	5.5
14	0549	0.3	29	0602	1.0
	1201	5.6		1210	5.1
W	1801	0.6	TH	1810	1.2
15	0017	5.9	30	0021	5.4
	0636	0.3		0633	1.1
TH	1249	5.5	F	1243	5.0
	1847	0.7		1843	1.3
			31	0055	5.3
				0706	1.2
			SA	1316	4.9
				1917	1.4

AUGUST

	Time	m		Time	m
1	0130	5.1	16	0219	5.4
	0741	1.4		0837	1.2
SU	1352	4.8	M	1449	5.0
	1955	1.7	◐	2057	1.5
2	0207	4.9	17	0318	4.9
	0820	1.6		0937	1.7
M	1432	4.6	TU	1552	4.7
	2040	1.9		2208	1.8
3	0252	4.7	18	0434	4.6
	0907	1.8		1052	2.0
TU	1523	4.5	W	1713	4.5
◑	2137	2.1		2334	2.0
4	0350	4.5	19	0608	4.4
	1009	2.0		1214	2.1
W	1634	4.4	TH	1839	4.6
	2251	2.2			
5	0509	4.4	20	0059	1.9
	1126	2.1		0732	4.5
TH	1759	4.4	F	1329	2.0
				1948	4.8
6	0014	2.1	21	0207	1.7
	0634	4.5		0831	4.7
F	1244	1.9	SA	1425	1.8
	1913	4.7		2038	5.0
7	0126	1.7	22	0256	1.5
	0745	4.7		0913	4.8
SA	1349	1.6	SU	1508	1.5
	2011	5.0		2117	5.2
8	0225	1.3	23	0333	1.3
	0841	5.0		0946	5.0
SU	1442	1.3	M	1542	1.3
	2100	5.4		2150	5.4
9	0315	0.9	24	0405	1.1
	0929	5.3		1016	5.1
M	1529	0.9	TU	1613	1.2
	2144	5.7	○	2220	5.5
10	0400	0.5	25	0434	1.0
	1013	5.6		1043	5.2
TU	1613	0.6	W	1641	1.1
●	2227	6.0		2250	5.5
11	0444	0.2	26	0502	0.9
	1056	5.8		1111	5.2
W	1656	0.4	TH	1710	1.0
	2311	6.1		2320	5.6
12	0528	0.1	27	0530	0.9
	1140	5.8		1139	5.2
TH	1739	0.4	F	1740	1.1
	2356	6.2		2351	5.5
13	0613	0.2	28	0600	1.0
	1224	5.7		1209	5.2
F	1824	0.5	SA	1811	1.2
14	0041	6.0	29	0023	5.4
	0657	0.4		0630	1.1
SA	1309	5.5	SU	1241	5.1
	1910	0.7		1843	1.3
15	0128	5.7	30	0056	5.2
	0745	0.8		0702	1.3
SU	1356	5.2	M	1315	5.0
	1959	1.1		1919	1.5
			31	0132	5.0
				0739	1.5
			TU	1353	4.8
				2002	1.8

Chart Datum: 3·05 metres below Ordnance Datum (Newlyn). HAT is 6·3 metres above Chart Datum; see 0.20

TIME ZONE (UT)
For Summer Time add ONE hour in **non-shaded areas**

HOLYHEAD LAT 53°19′N LONG 4°37′W

TIMES AND HEIGHTS OF HIGH AND LOW WATERS

Dates in red are SPRINGS
Dates in blue are NEAPS

YEAR **2010**

SEPTEMBER

Date	Day	Time	m	Time	m	Time	m	Time	m
1	W	0215	4.8	0825	1.8	1441	4.6	◑ 2059	2.0
2	TH	0313	4.5	0927	2.1	1551	4.4	2218	2.2
3	F	0438	4.4	1053	2.2	1726	4.4	2350	2.1
4	SA	0616	4.5	1221	2.0	1849	4.7		
5	SU	0107	1.7	0729	4.8	1330	1.7	1950	5.1
6	M	0206	1.2	0824	5.1	1423	1.3	2039	5.5
7	TU	0255	0.7	0910	5.5	1509	0.9	2123	5.9
8	W	0339	0.4	0952	5.7	1551	0.5	● 2205	6.1
9	TH	0421	0.1	1033	5.9	1633	0.3	2248	6.3
10	F	0503	0.1	1115	5.9	1716	0.3	2332	6.2
11	SA	0546	0.2	1157	5.8	1759	0.5		
12	SU	0017	6.0	0630	0.5	1241	5.6	1845	0.7
13	M	0104	5.7	0715	1.0	1327	5.3	1934	1.1
14	TU	0154	5.2	0805	1.4	1417	5.0	2032	1.6
15	W	0252	4.8	0905	1.9	1519	4.7	◐ 2144	2.0
16	TH	0412	4.4	1022	2.3	1641	4.5	2313	2.1
17	F	0552	4.3	1149	2.4	1812	4.5		
18	SA	0038	2.0	0715	4.4	1306	2.2	1923	4.7
19	SU	0144	1.8	0810	4.6	1401	1.9	2012	5.0
20	M	0230	1.5	0849	4.9	1442	1.7	2050	5.2
21	TU	0305	1.3	0920	5.0	1515	1.4	2122	5.4
22	W	0335	1.1	0947	5.2	1545	1.2	2152	5.5
23	TH	0403	1.0	1013	5.3	1613	1.1	○ 2221	5.6
24	F	0430	1.0	1040	5.4	1641	1.0	2251	5.6
25	SA	0458	1.0	1109	5.4	1711	1.1	2322	5.5
26	SU	0527	1.0	1139	5.4	1743	1.1	2354	5.4
27	M	0558	1.2	1211	5.3	1817	1.3		
28	TU	0029	5.3	0632	1.3	1246	5.2	1854	1.5
29	W	0107	5.1	0711	1.6	1326	5.0	1939	1.7
30	TH	0153	4.8	0759	1.8	1417	4.8	2039	1.9

OCTOBER

Date	Day	Time	m	Time	m	Time	m	Time	m
1	F	0255	4.6	0904	2.1	1528	4.6	◑ 2200	2.1
2	SA	0423	4.4	1031	2.2	1701	4.6	2330	1.9
3	SU	0558	4.6	1158	2.1	1823	4.9		
4	M	0044	1.5	0708	4.9	1306	1.7	1924	5.2
5	TU	0142	1.1	0802	5.2	1359	1.3	2014	5.6
6	W	0231	0.7	0847	5.6	1445	0.9	2059	5.9
7	TH	0315	0.4	0928	5.8	1528	0.6	● 2142	6.1
8	F	0357	0.3	1009	5.9	1611	0.4	2226	6.2
9	SA	0439	0.3	1051	6.0	1654	0.4	2311	6.1
10	SU	0522	0.5	1133	5.9	1739	0.6	2356	5.9
11	M	0605	0.8	1217	5.7	1825	0.9		
12	TU	0043	5.5	0649	1.2	1302	5.4	1914	1.2
13	W	0133	5.1	0737	1.6	1351	5.1	2010	1.6
14	TH	0229	4.7	0833	2.1	1448	4.8	◐ 2117	2.0
15	F	0342	4.4	0945	2.4	1601	4.6	2238	2.2
16	SA	0513	4.2	1108	2.5	1725	4.6	2357	2.1
17	SU	0636	4.4	1224	2.4	1838	4.7		
18	M	0101	1.9	0732	4.6	1322	2.1	1932	4.9
19	TU	0150	1.7	0813	4.8	1406	1.9	2013	5.1
20	W	0228	1.5	0846	5.0	1442	1.6	2048	5.3
21	TH	0300	1.3	0915	5.2	1513	1.4	2120	5.4
22	F	0329	1.2	0943	5.3	1543	1.2	2151	5.5
23	SA	0358	1.1	1011	5.4	1614	1.1	○ 2223	5.5
24	SU	0428	1.1	1041	5.5	1647	1.1	2257	5.5
25	M	0500	1.1	1114	5.5	1721	1.2	2332	5.5
26	TU	0534	1.2	1149	5.5	1759	1.2		
27	W	0011	5.3	0612	1.3	1228	5.3	1840	1.4
28	TH	0054	5.1	0655	1.6	1312	5.2	1930	1.6
29	F	0145	4.9	0746	1.8	1406	5.0	2031	1.7
30	SA	0248	4.7	0851	2.0	1513	4.9	◑ 2146	1.8
31	SU	0408	4.6	1010	2.1	1635	4.8	2305	1.7

NOVEMBER

Date	Day	Time	m	Time	m	Time	m	Time	m
1	M	0532	4.7	1130	2.0	1752	5.0		
2	TU	0015	1.4	0640	5.0	1237	1.7	1855	5.3
3	W	0114	1.1	0735	5.2	1333	1.4	1948	5.6
4	TH	0205	0.9	0822	5.5	1422	1.1	2037	5.8
5	F	0252	0.7	0906	5.7	1508	0.8	2123	5.9
6	SA	0336	0.6	0948	5.8	1553	0.7	● 2209	6.0
7	SU	0419	0.7	1031	5.9	1638	0.7	2255	5.8
8	M	0502	0.8	1114	5.8	1724	0.8	2341	5.6
9	TU	0545	1.1	1157	5.7	1810	1.0		
10	W	0026	5.4	0628	1.4	1241	5.5	1857	1.3
11	TH	0114	5.0	0713	1.7	1326	5.3	1947	1.6
12	F	0203	4.7	0802	2.0	1416	5.0	2043	1.9
13	SA	0302	4.5	0900	2.3	1514	4.8	◐ 2147	2.1
14	SU	0412	4.3	1009	2.5	1622	4.6	2257	2.1
15	M	0528	4.3	1123	2.5	1732	4.6		
16	TU	0002	2.1	0634	4.5	1227	2.3	1835	4.7
17	W	0057	1.9	0725	4.7	1319	2.1	1926	4.9
18	TH	0142	1.7	0805	4.9	1403	1.9	2010	5.1
19	F	0221	1.6	0840	5.1	1440	1.6	2048	5.2
20	SA	0256	1.4	0913	5.3	1516	1.4	2124	5.4
21	SU	0330	1.3	0945	5.4	1551	1.3	○ 2201	5.4
22	M	0404	1.2	1019	5.5	1628	1.2	2238	5.5
23	TU	0440	1.2	1056	5.6	1707	1.1	2318	5.5
24	W	0519	1.2	1135	5.6	1749	1.1		
25	TH	0000	5.4	0600	1.3	1218	5.6	1834	1.2
26	F	0047	5.3	0646	1.4	1304	5.4	1924	1.3
27	SA	0138	5.1	0737	1.6	1356	5.3	2021	1.4
28	SU	0237	4.9	0837	1.8	1456	5.2	◑ 2125	1.5
29	M	0344	4.8	0944	1.9	1605	5.1	2235	1.5
30	TU	0458	4.8	1056	1.9	1717	5.1	2343	1.4

DECEMBER

Date	Day	Time	m	Time	m	Time	m	Time	m
1	W	0607	4.9	1205	1.8	1825	5.2		
2	TH	0046	1.3	0707	5.1	1307	1.5	1926	5.4
3	F	0142	1.2	0801	5.3	1403	1.3	2021	5.5
4	SA	0234	1.1	0849	5.5	1455	1.1	2111	5.6
5	SU	0321	1.0	0934	5.7	1544	1.0	● 2159	5.6
6	M	0405	1.0	1017	5.8	1630	0.9	2245	5.6
7	TU	0448	1.1	1100	5.8	1714	1.0	2329	5.4
8	W	0529	1.2	1141	5.7	1757	1.1		
9	TH	0011	5.3	0609	1.3	1222	5.6	1838	1.2
10	F	0052	5.1	0649	1.5	1302	5.4	1920	1.4
11	SA	0133	4.9	0731	1.8	1343	5.2	2004	1.6
12	SU	0216	4.7	0816	2.0	1428	5.0	2052	1.8
13	M	0306	4.5	0907	2.2	1519	4.8	◐ 2146	2.0
14	TU	0406	4.4	1007	2.4	1620	4.7	2247	2.1
15	W	0514	4.4	1115	2.4	1726	4.6	2351	2.1
16	TH	0620	4.5	1221	2.3	1831	4.7		
17	F	0049	2.0	0717	4.7	1318	2.1	1929	4.8
18	SA	0140	1.8	0805	4.9	1408	1.9	2018	5.0
19	SU	0225	1.6	0846	5.1	1452	1.6	2102	5.1
20	M	0306	1.4	0924	5.3	1533	1.3	2143	5.3
21	TU	0346	1.2	1003	5.5	1615	1.1	○ 2225	5.4
22	W	0426	1.1	1042	5.7	1656	0.9	2307	5.5
23	TH	0508	1.0	1123	5.8	1740	0.8	2351	5.5
24	F	0551	1.0	1207	5.8	1825	0.8		
25	SA	0036	5.5	0635	1.0	1253	5.8	1912	0.8
26	SU	0125	5.4	0723	1.2	1341	5.6	2003	1.0
27	M	0216	5.2	0815	1.4	1434	5.5	2059	1.2
28	TU	0314	5.0	0914	1.6	1534	5.3	◑ 2202	1.4
29	W	0419	4.8	1021	1.8	1643	5.1	2310	1.5
30	TH	0531	4.8	1135	1.8	1758	5.0		
31	F	0019	1.6	0642	4.9	1247	1.8	1910	5.0

Chart Datum: 3·05 metres below Ordnance Datum (Newlyn). HAT is 6·3 metres above Chart Datum; see 0.20

CELERITAS

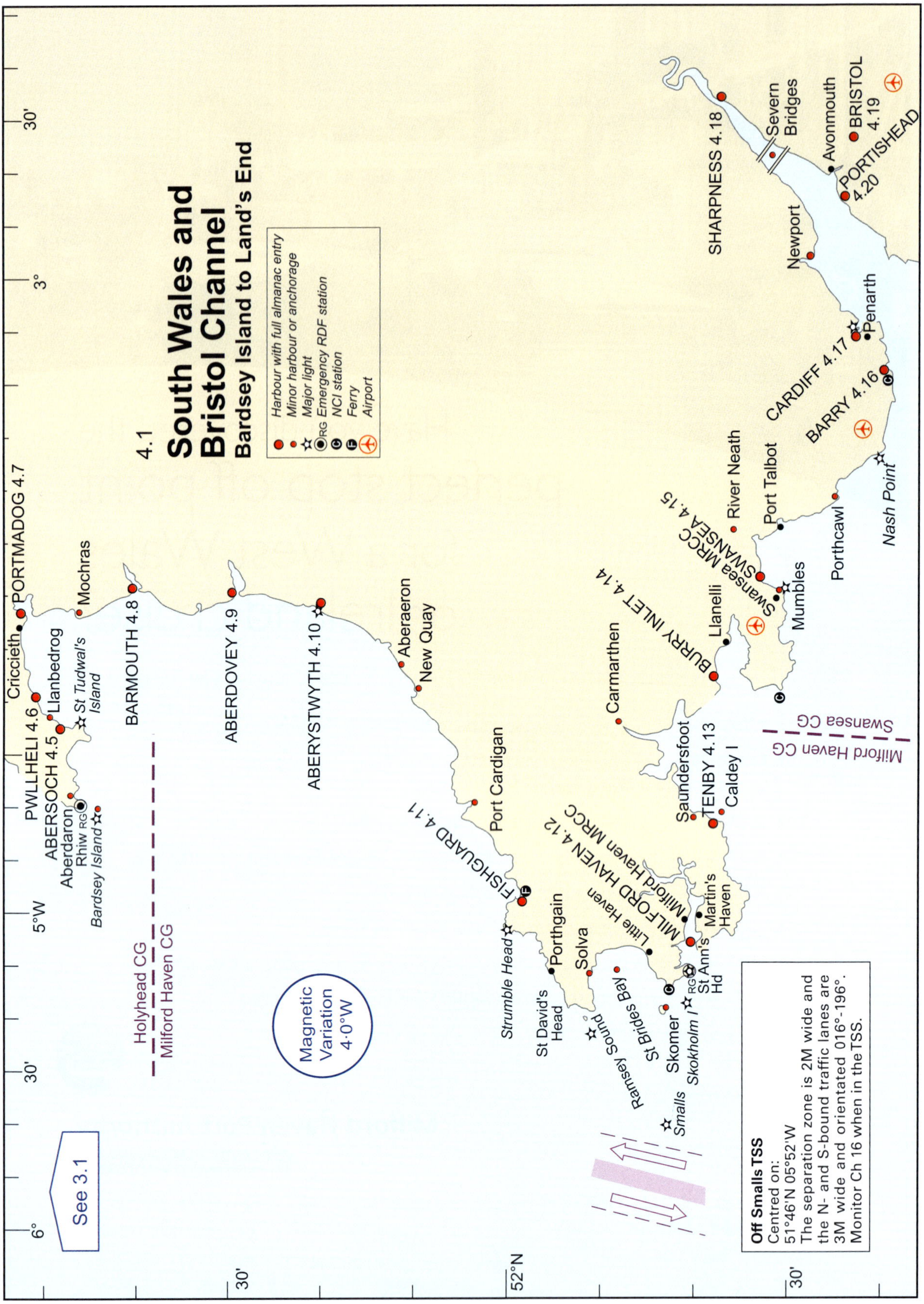
4.1
South Wales and Bristol Channel
Bardsey Island to Land's End
Harbour with full almanac entry
Minor harbour or anchorage
Major light
RG Emergency RDF station
NCI station
Ferry
Airport
PORTMADOG 4.7
Criccieth
PWLLHELI 4.6
Llanbedrog
ABERSOCH 4.5
St Tudwal's Island
Aberdaron
Rhiw RG
Bardsey Island
Mochras
BARMOUTH 4.8
ABERDOVEY 4.9
ABERYSTWYTH 4.10
Aberaeron
New Quay
Port Cardigan
FISHGUARD 4.11
Strumble Head
Porthgain
St David's Head
Solva
Ramsey Sound
St Brides Bay
Skomer
Skokholm I
Smalls
Little Haven
MILFORD HAVEN 4.12
Milford Haven MRCC
St Ann's Hd
RG
Martin's Haven
Saundersfoot
TENBY 4.13
Caldey I
Carmarthen
BURRY INLET 4.14
Llanelli
Swansea MRCC
SWANSEA 4.15
Mumbles
River Neath
Port Talbot
Porthcawl
Nash Point
BARRY 4.16
CARDIFF 4.17
Penarth
Newport
SHARPNESS 4.18
Severn Bridges
Avonmouth
BRISTOL 4.19
PORTISHEAD 4.20
Holyhead CG
Milford Haven CG
Swansea CG
Magnetic Variation 4·0°W
See 3.1
Off Smalls TSS
Centred on:
51°46'N 05°52'W
The separation zone is 2M wide and the N- and S-bound traffic lanes are 3M wide and orientated 016°-196°. Monitor Ch 16 when in the TSS.
30'
3°
5°W
6°
52°N

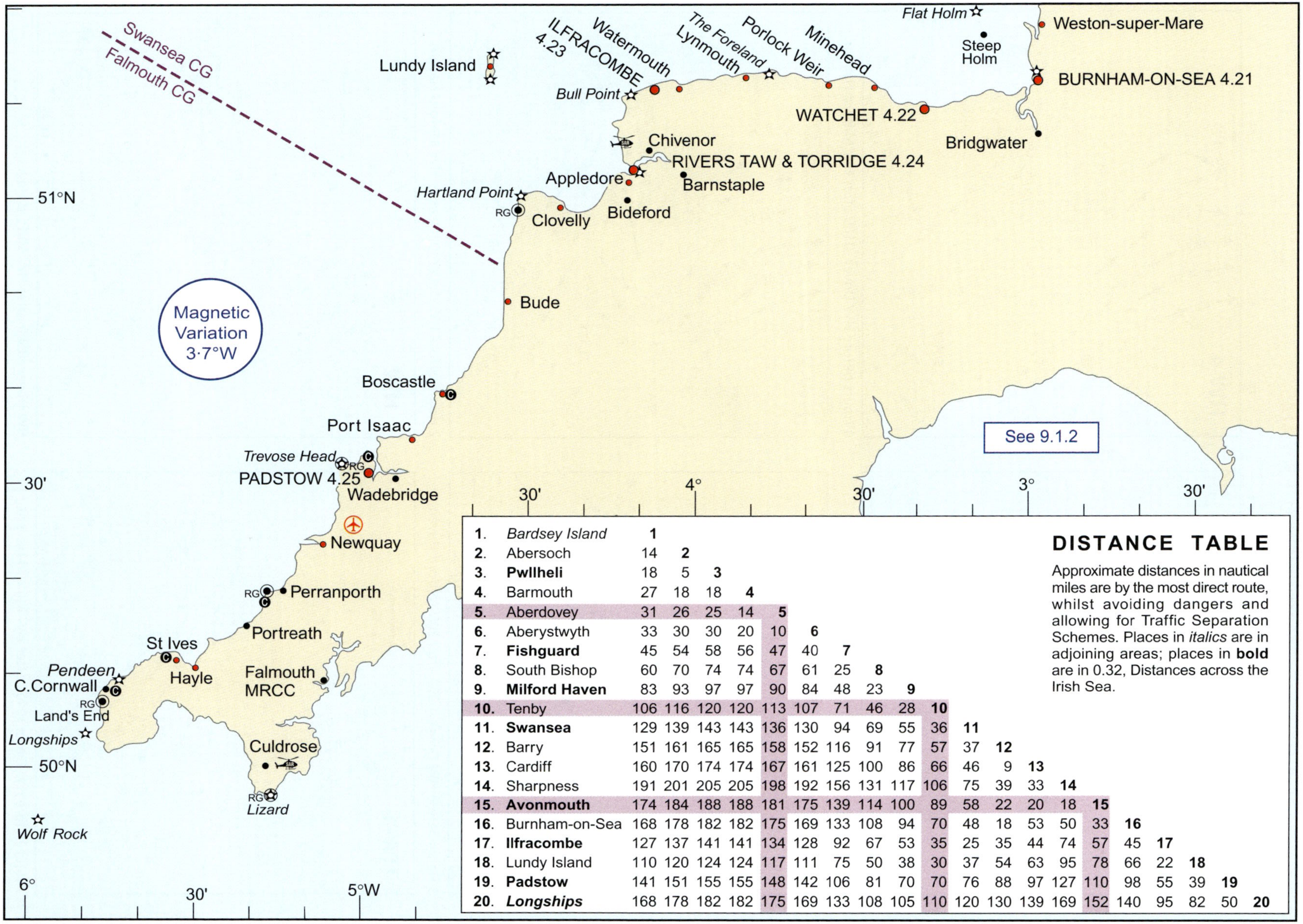

DISTANCE TABLE

Approximate distances in nautical miles are by the most direct route, whilst avoiding dangers and allowing for Traffic Separation Schemes. Places in *italics* are in adjoining areas; places in **bold** are in 0.32, Distances across the Irish Sea.

1. *Bardsey Island*	**1**																			
2. Abersoch	14	**2**																		
3. **Pwllheli**	18	5	**3**																	
4. Barmouth	27	18	18	**4**																
5. Aberdovey	31	26	25	14	**5**															
6. Aberystwyth	33	30	30	20	10	**6**														
7. **Fishguard**	45	54	58	56	47	40	**7**													
8. South Bishop	60	70	74	74	67	61	25	**8**												
9. **Milford Haven**	83	93	97	97	90	84	48	23	**9**											
10. Tenby	106	116	120	120	113	107	71	46	28	**10**										
11. **Swansea**	129	139	143	143	136	130	94	69	55	36	**11**									
12. Barry	151	161	165	165	158	152	116	91	77	57	37	**12**								
13. Cardiff	160	170	174	174	167	161	125	100	86	66	46	9	**13**							
14. Sharpness	191	201	205	205	198	192	156	131	117	106	75	39	33	**14**						
15. **Avonmouth**	174	184	188	188	181	175	139	114	100	89	58	22	20	18	**15**					
16. Burnham-on-Sea	168	178	182	182	175	169	133	108	94	70	48	18	53	50	33	**16**				
17. **Ilfracombe**	127	137	141	141	134	128	92	67	53	35	25	35	44	74	57	45	**17**			
18. Lundy Island	110	120	124	124	117	111	75	50	38	30	37	54	63	95	78	66	22	**18**		
19. **Padstow**	141	151	155	155	148	142	106	81	70	70	76	88	97	127	110	98	55	39	**19**	
20. ***Longships***	168	178	182	182	175	169	133	108	105	110	120	130	139	169	152	140	95	82	50	**20**

4.2 S WALES & BRISTOL CHANNEL TIDAL STREAMS

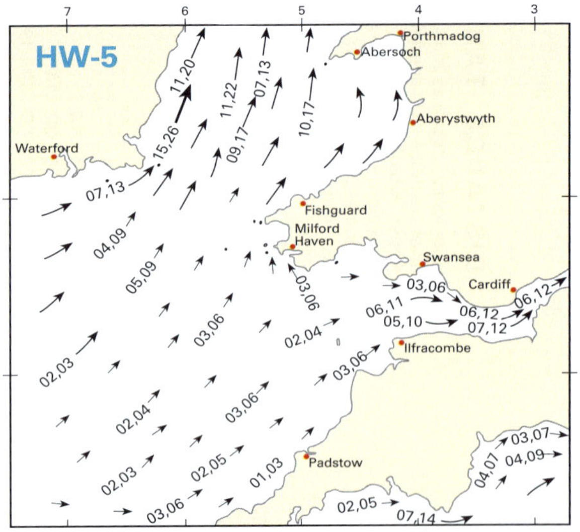

5 Hours before HW Dover (HW Milford Haven)

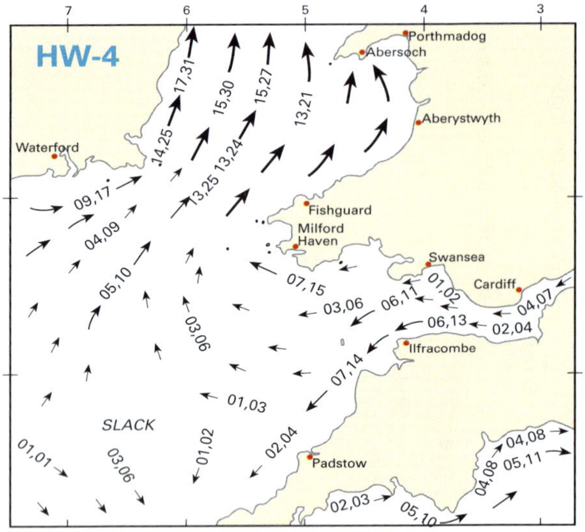

4 Hours before HW Dover (0100 after HW Milford Haven)

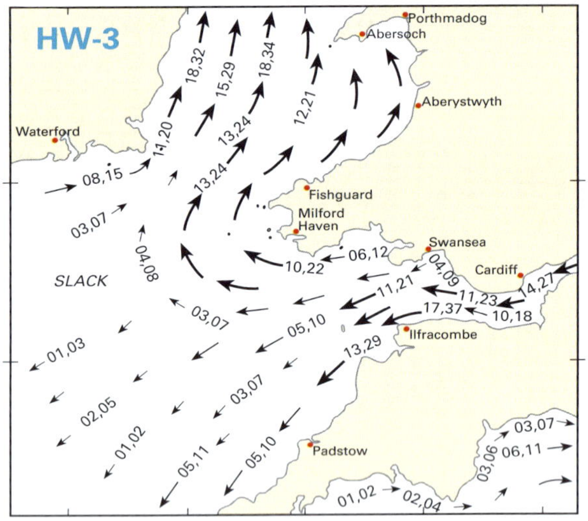

3 Hours before HW Dover (0200 after HW Milford Haven)

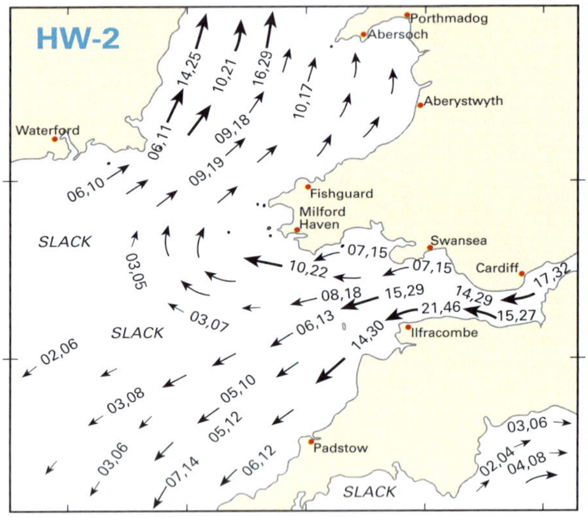

2 Hours before HW Dover (0300 after HW Milford Haven)

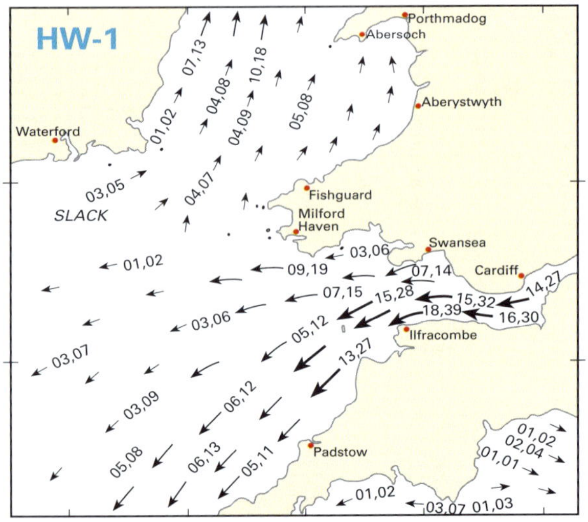

1 Hour before HW Dover (0400 after HW Milford Haven)

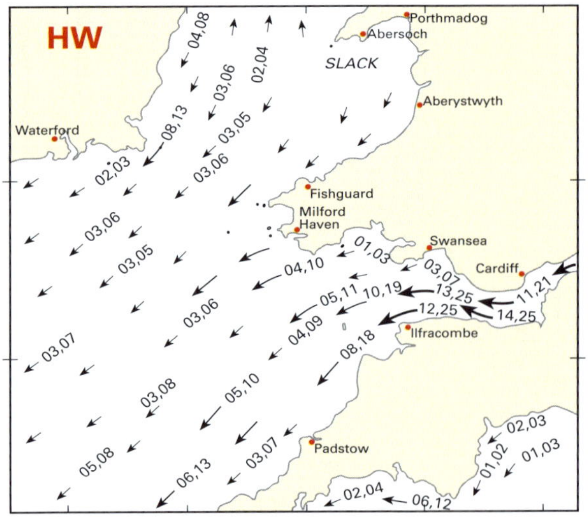

HW Dover (0500 after HW Milford Haven)

Northward 3.2 South Ireland 4.2

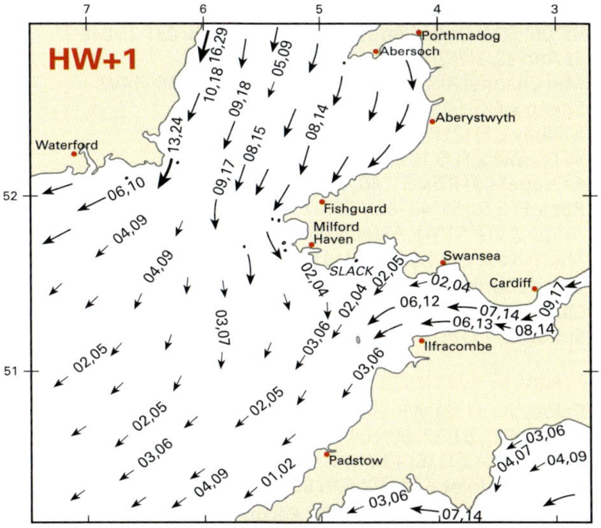

1 Hour after HW Dover (0600 after HW Milford Haven)

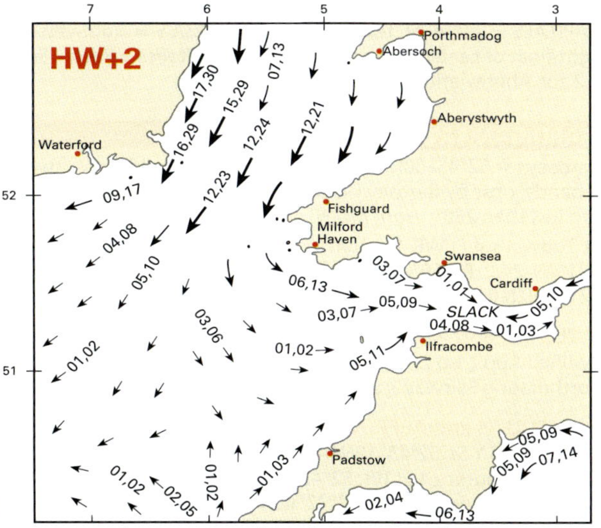

2 Hours after HW Dover (0525 before HW Milford Haven)

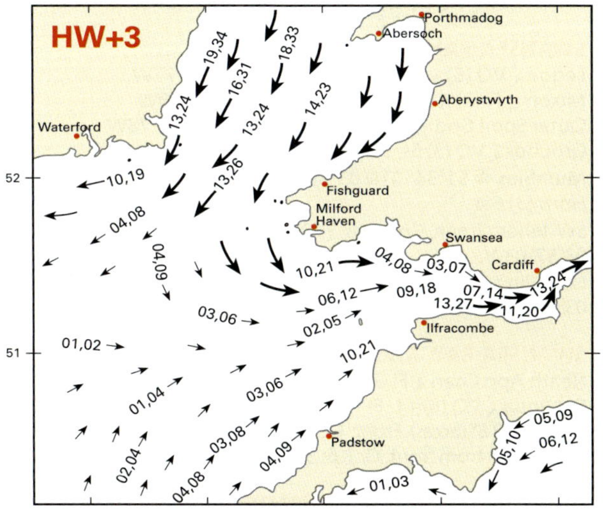

3 Hours after HW Dover (0425 before HW Milford Haven)

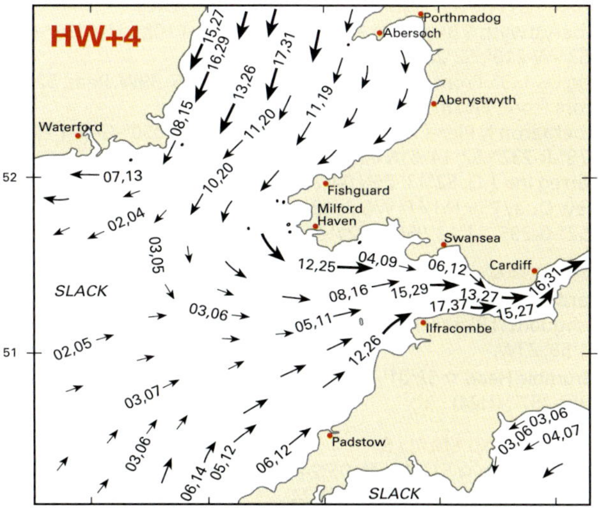

4 Hours after HW Dover (0325 before HW Milford Haven)

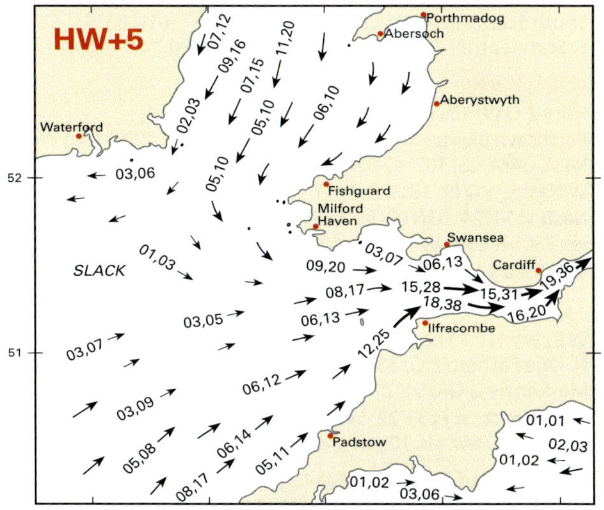

5 Hours after HW Dover (0225 before HW Milford Haven)

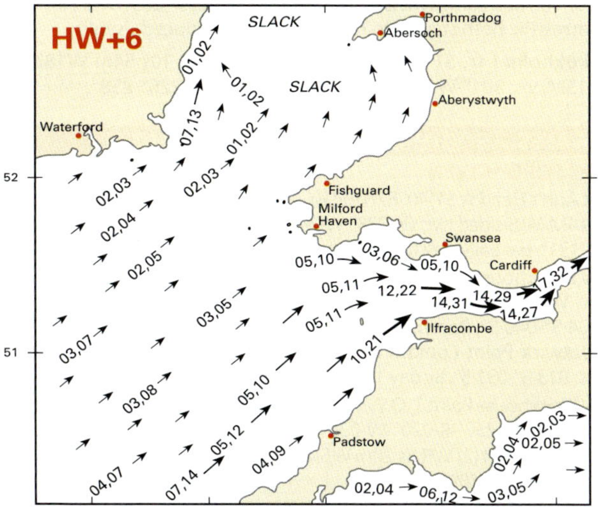

6 Hours after HW Dover (0125 before HW Milford Haven)

S Wales & Bristol Ch

4.3 LIGHTS, BUOYS AND WAYPOINTS

Bold print = light with a nominal range of 15M or more. CAPITALS = place or feature. *CAPITAL ITALICS* = light-vessel, light float or Lanby. *Italics* = Fog signal. ***Bold italics*** = Racon. See 0.2 for Abbreviations.

CARDIGAN BAY (see also 3.3)

Bardsey I ☆ 52°45'·00N 04°47'·98W Fl (5) 15s 39m **26M**; W□ twr, R bands; obsc by Bardsey I 198°-250° and in Tremadoc B when brg less than 260°; *Horn Mo(N) 45s*.

St Tudwal's ☆ Fl WR 15s 46m W14, R10M; vis: 349°-W-169°-R-221°-W-243°-R-259°-W-293°-R-349°; obsc by East I 211°-231°; 52°47'·92N 04°28'·30W.

PWLLHELI and PORTHMADOG

Pwllheli App Iso 2s; 52°53'·02N 04°23'·07W.
Porthmadog Fairway L Fl 10s; 52°52'·97N 04°11'·18W.

BARMOUTH and ABERDOVEY

Diffuser Fl Y 5s; 52°43'·19N 04°05'·38W.
Barmouth Outer L Fl 10s; 52°42'·62N 04°04'·83W.
Aberdovey Outer Iso 4s; 52°32'·00N 04°05'·56W.
Cynfelyn Patches, Patches Q (9) 15s; 52°25'·83N 04°16'·41W.

ABERYSTWYTH, ABERAERON and NEW QUAY

Aberystwyth S Bkwtr Hd ☆ Fl (2) WG 10s 12m 10M; vis: 030°-G-053°-W-210°; 52°24'·40N 04°05'·52W.
Ldg Lts 133°. Front, FR 4m 5M; 52°24'·37N 04°05'·39W. Rear, 52m from front, FR 7m 6M.
Aberaeron N Pier ☆ Fl (4) WRG 15s 10m 6M; vis: 050°-G-104°-W-178°-R-232°; 52°14'·61N 04°15'·87W.
Carreg Ina Q; 52°13'·25N 04°20'·75W.
New Quay Pier Hd ☆ Fl WG 3s 12m W8M, G5M; G △; vis: 135°-W-252°-G-295; 52°12'·95N 04°21'·35W.

CARDIGAN and FISHGUARD

Cardigan Channel Fl (2) 5s; 52°06'·44N 04°41'·43W.
Fishguard N Bkwtr Hd ☆ Fl G 4·5s 18m 13M; *Bell (1) 8s*; 52°00'·76N 04°58'·23W.

Strumble Head ☆ 52°01'·79N 05°04'·43W Fl (4) 15s 45m **26M**; vis: 038°-257°; (H24).

BISHOPS and SMALLS

South Bishop ☆ 51°51'·14N 05°24'·74W Fl 5s 44m **16M**; W ○ twr; *Horn (3) 45s*; ***Racon (O)10M***; (H24).

The Smalls ☆ 51°43'·27N 05°40'·19W Fl (3) 15s 36m **18M**; ***Racon (T)***; *Horn (2) 60s*. Same twr, Iso R 4s 33m 13M; vis: 253°-285° over Hats & Barrels Rk; both Lts shown H24 in periods of reduced visibility.

Skokholm I ☆, 51°41'·64N 05°17'·22W Fl WR 10s 54m **W18M, R15M**; vis: 301°-W-154°-R-301°; partially obsc 226°-258°.

WALES – SOUTH COAST – BRISTOL CHANNEL

MILFORD HAVEN

St Ann's Head ☆ 51°40'·87N 05°10'·42W Fl WR 5s 48m **W18M, R17M**, R14M; W 8-sided twr; vis: 233°-W-247°-R-285°-R(intens)-314°-R-332°-W131°, partially obscured between 124°-129°; *Horn (2) 60s*.

W Blockhouse Point Ldg Lts 022·5°. Front, F 54m 13M; B stripe on W twr; vis: 004·5°-040·5°; intens on lead. By day 10M; vis: 004·5°-040·5°; ***Racon (Q)***; 51°41'·31N 05°09'·56W.
Watwick Point Common Rear ☆, 0·5M from front, F 80m **15M**; vis: 013·5°-031·5°. By day 10M; vis: 013·5°-031·5°; ***Racon (Y)***.

W Blockhouse Point Q WR 21m W9M, R7M; R lantern on W base: vis: 220°-W-250°-R-020°-W-036°-R-049°; 51°41'·31N 05°09'·56W.
Dale Fort ☆ Fl (2) WR 5s 20m W5M, R3M; vis: 222°-R-276°-W-019°; 51°42'·16N 05°09'·01W.
Gt Castle Hd F WRG 27m W5M, R3M, G3M; vis: 243°-R-281°-G-299°-W-029°; also Dir WRG (040°) 038·25°-G-039°-Al WG-039·5°-W-040·5°-AlWR-041°-R-041·75°; 51°42'·67N 05°07'·07W (not used in conjunction with the following front light) also Ldg Lts 039·7°
Front, Oc 4s 27m **15M**; vis: 031·2°-048·2°. **Rear**, 890m from front. 05°06'·60W Oc 8s 53m **15M** (by day 10M) vis: 031·2°-048·2°.
St Ann's Fl R 2·5s; 51°40'·25N 05°10'·51W.
Mid Channel Rks Q (9) 15s; 51°40'·18N 05°10'·14W.
Sheep QG; 51°40'·06N 05°08'·31W.
Millbay Fl (2) R 5s; 51°41'·05N 05°09'·45W.
W Chapel Fl G 10s; 51°40'·98N 05°08'·67W.
E Chapel Fl R 5s; 51°40'·87N 05°08'·15W.
Rat Fl G 5s; 51°40'·80N 05°07'·86W.
Angle VQ; 51°41'·63N 05°08'·27W.
Thorn Rock Q (9) 15s; 51°41'·53N 05°07'·76W.
Turbot Bank VQ (9) 10s; 51°37'·41N 05°10'·08W.
ODAS Fl(5) Y 20s; 51°36'·70N 05°08'·70W
St Gowan Q (6) + L Fl 15s, ***Racon (T) 10M;*** 51°31'·93N 04°59'·77W.

TENBY to SWANSEA BAY

Caldey I ☆ Fl (3) WR 20s 65m W13M, R9M; vis: R173°- W212°-R088°-102°; 51°37'·90N 04°41'·08W.
Woolhouse Q (6) + L Fl 15s; 51°39'·35N 04°39'·69W.
Burry Port Inlet ☆ 51°40'·62N 04°15'·06W Fl 5s 7m **15M**.
W. Helwick (W HWK) (9) 15s; ***Racon (T) 10M***; *Whis;* 51°31'·40N 04°23'·65W Q.
E. Helwick VQ (3) 5s; *Bell;* 51°31'·80N 04°12'·68W.

SWANSEA BAY and SWANSEA

Ledge VQ (6) + L Fl 10s; 51°29'·93N 03°58'·77W.
Mixon Fl (2) R 5s; *Bell;* 51°33'·12N 03°58'·78W.
Outer Spoil Gnd Fl Y 2·5s; 51°32'·11N 03°55'·73W.
Grounds VQ (3) 5s; 51°32'·81N 03°53'·47W.
Mumbles ☆ 51°34'·01N 03°58'·27W Fl (4) 20s 35m **15M**; W twr; *Horn (3) 60s*.
SW Inner Green Grounds Q (6) + L Fl 15s; *Bell;* 51°34'·06N 03°57'·03W.
Lts in line 020°. Jetty Head Front, Oc G 4s 5m 2M; 51°36'·55N 03°55'·52W. Rear, 260m from front, FG 6M.

SWANSEA BAY, RIVER NEATH and PORT TALBOT

Neath App Chan Fl G 5s; 51°35'·71N 03°52'·83W.
Cabenda VQ (6) + L Fl 10s; ***Racon (Q);*** 51°33'·36N 03°52'·23W.
Ldg Lts 059·8° (occas). Front, Oc R 3s 12m 6M; 51°34'·92N 03°48'·10W. Rear, 400m from front, Oc R 6s 32m 6M.

BRISTOL CHANNEL – NORTH SHORE (EASTERN PART)

W Scar Q (9) 15s, *Bell*, ***Racon (T) 10M;*** 51°28'·31N 03°55'·57W.
South Scar (S SCAR) Q (6) + L Fl 15s; 51°27'·61N 03°51'·58W.
E. Scarweather Q (3) 10s; *Bell;* 51°27'·98N 03°46'·76W.

PORTHCAWL

Fairy Q (9) 15s; *Bell;* 51°27'·86N 03°42'·07W.
Porthcawl Bkwtr Hd ☆ 51°28'·39N 03°41'·98W F WRG 10m W6M, R4M, G4M; vis: 302°-G-036°-W-082°-R-122°.
W Nash VQ (9) 10s ; *Bell;* 51°25'·99N 03°45'·95W.
Nash ☆ 51°24'·03N 03°33'·06W Fl (2) WR 15s 56m **W21M, R16M**; vis: 280°-R-290°-W-100°-R-120°-W-128°.
Breaksea L Fl 10s; ***Racon (T) 10M***; 51°19'·88N 03°19'·08W.

BARRY

W Bkwtr Hd ☆ Fl 2·5s 12m 10M; 51°23'·46N 03°15'·52W.
N. One Fathom Q; 51°20'·94N 03°12'·17W.
Mackenzie QR; 51°21'·75N 03°08'·24W.
Flat Holm ☆, SE Pt 51°22'·54N 03°07'·14W Fl (3) WR 10s 50m **W15M**, R12M; W○ twr; vis: 106°-R-140°-W-151°-R-203°-W-106°; (H24).

CARDIFF and PENARTH ROADS

Lavernock Outfall Fl Y 5s; 51°23'·95N 03°09'·50W.
Ranie Fl (2) R 5s; 51°24'·23N 03°09'·39W.

S Cardiff Q (6) + L Fl 15s; *Bell;* 51°24'·18N 03°08'·57W.
Mid Cardiff Fl (3) G 10s; 51°25'·60N 03°08'·09W.
Cardiff Spit QR; 51°24'·57N 03°07'·12W.
N Cardiff QG; 51°26'·52N 03°07'·19W.

PENARTH and CARDIFF

Wrach Chan Dir lt 348·5°. Oc WRG 10s 5m; W3M, R3M, G3M; vis: 344·5°-G-347°-W-350°-R-352°; H24; 51°27'·16N 03°09'·75W.
Outer Wrach Q (9) 15s; 51°26'·20N 03°09'·46W.
Tail Patch QG; 51°23'·53N 03°03'·65W.
Hope Q (3) 10s; 51°24'·84N 03°02'·68W.
NW Elbow VQ (9) 10s; *Bell;* 51°26'·28N 02°59'·93W.
EW Grounds L Fl 10s 7M; *Bell;* ***Racon (T) 7M;*** 51°27'·12N 02°59'·95W.

NEWPORT DEEP, RIVER USK and NEWPORT

Newport Deep Fl (3) G 10s; *Bell;*51°29'·36N 02°59'·12W.
East Usk ☆ 51°32'·40N 02°58'·01W; Fl (2) WRG 10s 11m W11M,R10M, G10M; vis: 284°-W-290° -obscured shore-324°-R- 017°-W-037°-G-115°-W-120°. Also Oc WRG 10s 10m W11M, R9M, G9M; vis: 018°-G-022°-W- 024°-R-028°.
Julians Pill Ldg Lts 062°. Front, FG 5m 4M; 51°33'·30N 02°57'·94W. Rear, 61m from front, FG 8m 4M.

BRISTOL CHANNEL – SOUTH SHORE (EASTERN PART)

BRISTOL DEEP

N Elbow QG; *Bell;* 51°26'·97N 02°58'·65W.
S Mid Grounds VQ (6) + L Fl 10s; 51°27'·62N 02°58'·68W.
E Mid Grounds Fl R 5s; 51°27'·75N 02°54'·98W.
Clevedon VQ; 51°27'·39N 02°54'·93W.
Welsh Hook Q (6) + L Fl 15s; 51°28'·53N 02°51'·86W.
Avon Fl G 2·5s; 51°27'·92N 02°51'·73W.
Black Nore Point ☆ 51°29'·09N 02°48'·05W Fl (2) 10s 11m **17M**; obsc by Sand Pt when brg less than 049°; vis: 044°-243°.
Newcome 51°30'·01N 02°46'·71W Fl (3) R 10s.
Denny Shoal VQ (6) + L Fl 10s; 51°30'·15N 02°45'·45W.
Firefly Fl (2) G 5s; 51°29'·96N 02°45'·35W.
Portishead Point ☆ 51°29'·68N 02°46'·42W Q (3) 10s 9m **16M**; B twr, W base; vis: 060°-262°; *Horn 20s.*

PORTISHEAD

Pier Hd Iso G 2s 5m 3M; 51°29'·69N 02°45'·27W.
Seabank. Lts in line 086·8°. Front, IQ 13m 5M; vis: 070·3°-103·3°; by day 1M vis: 076·8°-096·8°; 51°30'·07N 02°43'·81W. Dir WG 6m 5M; vis: 089·7°-FG-090·6°-AltWG-090·8°-FW-093·6°. Rear, 500m from front, IQ 16m 5M; vis: 070·3°-103·3°; by day 1M, vis: 076·8°-096·8°.
Knuckle Lts in line 099·6°, Oc G 5s 6m 6M; 51°29'·94N 02°43'·67W. Rear, 165m from front, FG 13m 6M; vis: 044°-134°.

AVONMOUTH

Royal Edward Dock N Pier Hd Fl 4s 15m 10M; vis: 060°-228·5°; 51°30'·49N 02°43'·09W.
King Road Ldg Lts 072·4°. N Pier Hd Front, Oc R 5s 5m 9M; W obelisk, R bands; vis: 062°-082°; 51°30'·49N 02°43'·09W. Rear, 546m from front, QR 15m 10M; vis: 066°- 078°.

RIVER AVON, CUMBERLAND BASIN and AVON BRIDGE

S Pier Hd Oc RG 30s 9m 10M and FBu 4m 1M; vis: 294°-R-036°-G-194°; 51°30'·37N 02°43'·10W. *Bell(1) 10s.*
Ldg Lts 127·2°. Front, Iso R 2s 6m 3M, vis: 010°-160°; 51°30'·10N 02°42'·59W. Rear, Iso R 2s10m 3M, vis: 048°-138°.

BRISTOL CHANNEL (SOUTH SHORE)

WESTON-SUPER-MARE

Pier Hd 2 FG (vert) 6m; 51°20'·88N 02°59'·26W.
E Culver Q (3) 10s; 51°18'·00N 03°15'·44W.
W Culver VQ (9) 10s; 51°17'·37N 03°18'·68W.
Gore Iso 5s; *Bell;* 51°13'·94N 03°09'·79W.

BURNHAM-ON-SEA and RIVER PARRETT

Ent Fl 7·5s 7m 12M; vis: 074°-164°; 51°14'·89N 03°00'·36W; Dir lt 076°. F WRG 4m W12M, R10M, G10M; vis: 071°-G- 075°-W-077°-R-081°.
DZ No. 1 Fl Y 2·5s; 51°15'·28N 03°09'·49W.
DZ No. 2 Fl Y 10s; 51°13'·77N 03°17'·19W.
DZ No. 3 Fl Y 5s; 51°15'·52N 03°14'·98W.

WATCHET, MINEHEAD and PORLOCK WEIR

Watchet W Bkwtr Hd Oc G 3s 9m 9M; 51°11'·03N 03°19'·74W.
Watchet E Pier 2 FR (vert) 3M; 51°11'·01N 03°19'·72W.
Minehead Bkwtr Hd Fl (2) G 5s 4M; vis: 127°-262°; 51°12'·81N 03°28'·36W.
Lynmouth Foreland ☆ 51°14'·73N 03°47'·21W Fl (4) 15s 67m **18M**; W ○ twr; vis: 083°-275°; (H24).

LYNMOUTH and WATERMOUTH

River Training Arm 2 FR (vert) 6m 5M; 51°13'·90N 03°49'·83W.
Harbour Arm 2 FG (vert) 6m 5M; 51°13'·92N 03°49'·84W.
Sand Ridge Q G; 51°15'·01N 03°49'·77W.
Copperas Rock Fl G 2·5s; 51°13'·78N 04°00'·60W.
Watermouth Oc WRG 5s 1m 3M; W △; vis: 149·5°-G-151·5°-W-154·5°-R-156·5°; 51°12'·93N 04°04'·60W.

ILFRACOMBE to BAGGY POINT

Ldg Lts 188°. Front, Oc 10s 8m 3M; 51°12'·53N 04°06'·65W. Rear, Oc 10s 6m 3M.
Horseshoe Q; 51°15'·02N 04°12'·96W.
Bull Point ☆ 51°11'·94N 04°12'·09W Fl (3) 10s 54m **20M**; W ○ twr, obscd shore-056°. Same twr; FR 48m 12M; vis: 058°-096°.
Morte Stone Fl G 5s; 51°11'·30N 04°14'·95W.
Baggy Leap Fl G 10s; 51°08'·92N 04°16'·97W.

BIDEFORD, RIVERS TAW and TORRIDGE

Bideford Fairway L Fl 10s; *Bell;* 51°05'·25N 04°16'·25W.
Bideford Bar Q G; 51°04'·89N 04°14'·62W.
Instow ☆ Ldg Lts 118°. **Front,** 51°03'·62N 04°10'·66W Oc 6s 22m **15M;** vis: 103·5°-132°. **Rear,** 427m from front, Oc 10s 38m **15M;** vis: 103°-132·5°; (H24).
Crow Pt Fl WR 2. 5s 8m W6M R5M; vis: 225°-R-232°-W-237°-R-358°-W- 015°-R-045°; 51°03'·96N 04°11'·39W.

LUNDY

Near North Point ☆ 51°12'·10N 04°40'·65W Fl 15s 48m **17M**; vis: 009°-285°.
South East Point ☆ 51°09'·72N 04°39'·37W Fl 5s 53m **15M;** vis: 170°-073°; *Horn 25s.*
Hartland Point ☆ 51°01'·29N 04°31'·59W Fl (6) 15s 37m **25M;** (H24); *Horn 60s.*

NORTH CORNWALL

BUDE, PADSTOW and NEWQUAY

Compass Point twr 50°49'·71N 04°33'·42W.
Stepper Point (Padstow) L Fl 10s 12m 4M; 50°34'·12N 04°56'·72W.
Trevose Head ☆ 50°32'·94N 05°02'·13W Fl 7·5s 62m **21M;** *Horn (2) 30s.*
North Pier Hd (Newquay) 2 FG (vert) 5m 2M; 50°25'·07N 05°05'·19W.

HAYLE and ST IVES

The Stones Q; 50°15'·64N 05°25'·51W.
Godrevy I Fl WR 10s 37m W12M, R9M; vis: 022°-W-101°-R-145°-W-272°; 50°14'·54N 05°24'·04W.
Hayle App QR; 50°12'·26N 05°26'·30W.
Lts in line 180°. Front, F 17m 4M; 50°11'·50N 05°26'·18W. Rear, 110m from front, F 23m 4M.
St Ives App 50°12'·85N 05°28'·42W
Pendeen ☆ 50°09'·90N 05°40'·32W Fl (4) 15s 59m **16M;** vis: 042°-240°; in bay between Gurnard Hd and Pendeen it shows to coast; *Horn 20s.*

4.4 PASSAGE INFORMATION

For directions on this coast refer to the Admiralty *W Coasts of England and Wales Pilot*; *Lundy and Irish Sea Pilot* (Imray/Taylor). The area is well covered by Admiralty Leisure Folios. For additional tidal information east of Ilfracombe/Swansea see *Arrowsmith's Bristol Channel Tide Tables* from J.W. Arrowsmith Ltd ☎ (0117) 9667545.

It is useful to know some Welsh words with navigational significance. *Aber:* estuary. *Afon:* river. *Bach, bychan, fach:* little. *Borth:* cove. *Bryn:* hill. *Careg, craig:* rock. *Coch, goch:* red. *Dinas:* fort. *Ddu:* black. *Fawr, Mawr:* big. *Ffrydiau:* tiderip. *Llwyd:* grey. *Moel:* bare conical hill. *Mor*: sea. *Morfa:* sandy shore. *Mynydd:* mountain. *Penrhyn:* headland. *Porth:* cove. *Ynys, Ynysoedd*: island(s).

There is more Passage Information threaded between the harbours in this Area.

CARDIGAN BAY

(AC 1971, 1972, 1973) Harbours are mostly on a lee shore, and/or have bars which make them dangerous to approach in bad weather. Abersoch and Pwllheli offer best shelter from the prevailing westerlies. There may be overfalls off Trwyn Cilan, SW of St Tudwal's Is (lit). In N part of the bay there are three major dangers to coasting yachts: St Patrick's Causeway (Sarn Badrig) runs 12M SW from Mochras Pt. It is mostly large loose stones, and dries (up to 1·5m) for much of its length. In strong winds the sea breaks heavily at all states of tide. The outer end is marked by a WCM light buoy. At the inner end there is a channel about 5ca offshore, which can be taken with care at half tide.

Sarn-y-Bwch runs 4M WSW from Pen Bwch Pt. It is consists of rocky boulders, drying in places close inshore and with least depth 0·3m over 1M offshore. There is a WCM buoy off the W end. NW of Aberystwyth, Sarn Cynfelyn and Cynfelyn Patches extend 6·5M offshore, with depths of 1·5m in places. A WCM buoy is at the outer end. Almost halfway along the bank is Main Channel, 3ca wide, running roughly N/S but not marked.

Aberporth Range occupies much of Cardigan B. Beware targets and buoys, some unlit. Range activity is broadcast on VHF Ch 16, 0800-1600LT Mon-Fri or ☎ (01239) 813462.

If on passage N/S through St George's Chan (ie not bound for Cardigan B or Milford Haven) the easiest route, and always by night, is W of the Bishops and the Smalls, noting the TSS. If bound to/from Milford Haven or Cardigan Bay, passage inside both the Smalls and Grassholm is possible.

RAMSEY SOUND, THE BISHOPS, THE SMALLS TO MILFORD HAVEN

(AC 1478, 1482) The Bishops and the Clerks are islets and rocks 2·5M W and NW of Ramsey Island, a bird sanctuary SSW of St David's Head. N Bishop is the N'ly of the group, 3ca ENE of which is Bell Rock (depth 1·9m). S Bishop (Lt, fog sig) is 3M to the SSW.

Between South Bishop and Ramsey Island the dangers include Daufraich with offlying dangers to the E and heavy overfalls; Llech Isaf and Llech Uchaf drying rocks are further ENE. Carreg Rhoson and offlying dangers are between Daufraich and N Bishop. The navigable routes between most of these islets and rocks trend NE/SW. Use only by day, in good visibility and with local knowledge. The N/S route close W of Ramsey Island is considered easier than Ramsey Sound.

► *2M W of The Bishops the S-going stream begins at Milford Haven +0400, and the N-going at Milford Haven –0230, sp rates 2kn. Between The Bishops and Ramsey Is the SW-going stream begins at Milford Haven +0330, and the NE-going at Milford Haven –0300,* ***sp rates 5kn.*** *Ramsey Sound should be taken at slack water. The S-going stream begins at Milford Haven +0300, and the N-going at Milford Haven –0330,* ***sp rates 6kn at The Bitches,*** *where the channel is narrowest (2ca), decreasing N and S.* ◄

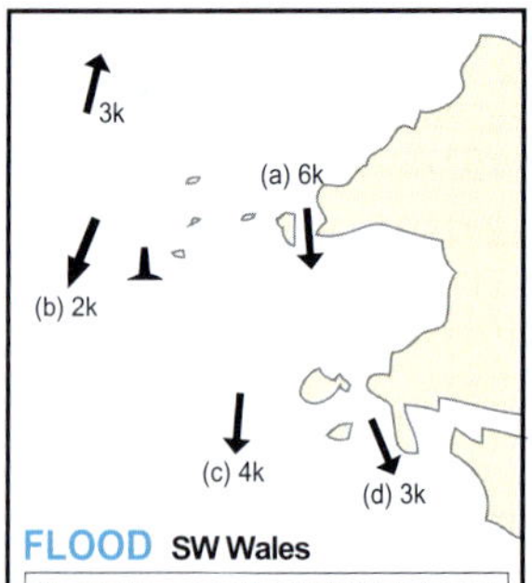

The tide turns to the S or SE (Bristol Channel flood) as follows:
(a): Milford Haven +0330;
(b) & (c): Milford Haven +0400;
(d): Milford Haven +0200.

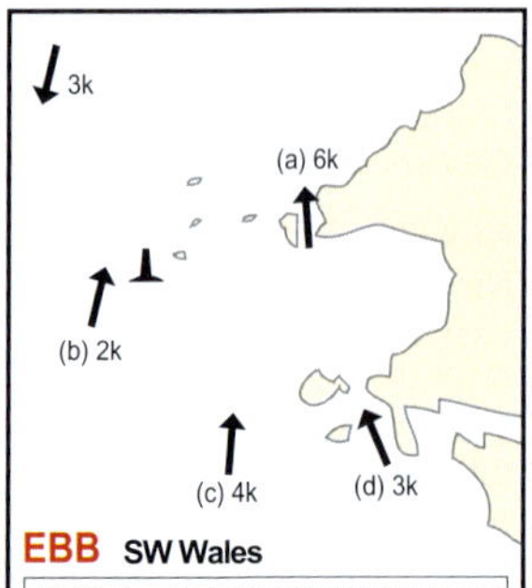

The tide turns to the N or NW (Bristol Channel ebb) as follows:
(a): Milford Haven –0300;
(b) & (c): Milford Haven –0230 ;
(d): Milford Haven –0430.

The Bitches are rocks up to 4m high and extending 2ca from E side of Ramsey Island. Other dangers are: Gwahan and Carreg-gafeiliog, both 3m high at N end of Sound, to W and E; Horse Rock (dries 0·9m) almost in mid-channel about 5ca NNE of The Bitches, with associated overfalls; Shoe Rock (dries 3m) at SE end of channel; and rocks extending 5ca SSE from S end of Ramsey Island.

St Brides Bay provides an anchorage in settled weather/ offshore winds. It is also a regular anchorage for tankers, but is a trap in westerlies. Solva is a little hbr with shelter for boats able to take the ground, or anchor behind Black Rk (dries 3·6m) in the middle of the entrance.

The Smalls Lt, where there is a Historic Wreck (see 0.29) is 13M W of the Welsh mainland (Wooltack Pt). 2M and 4M E of The Smalls are the Hats and Barrels, rocky patches on which the sea breaks.

► *7M E of The Smalls is Grassholm Island with a race either end and strong tidal eddies so that it is advisable to pass about 1M off. The chan between Barrels and Grassholm is 2·5M wide, and here the S-going stream begins at Milford Haven + 0440, and the N-going at Milford Haven – 0135,* ***sp rates 5kn.*** ◄

Five miles of clear water lie between Grassholm and Skomer Is/ Skokholm Is to the E. But Wildgoose Race, which forms W of Skomer and Skokholm is very dangerous, so keep 2M W of these two Islands.

To E of Skomer Island Midland Island, and between here and Wooltack Point is Jack Sound, least width about 1ca. Do not attempt it without AC 1482, detailed pilotage directions, and only at slack water neaps. ► *Correct timing is important. The S-going stream begins at Milford Haven +0200, and the N-going at Milford Haven –0430,* ***sp rates 6-7kn.*** ◄ Rocks which must be identified include, from N to S: On E side of chan off Wooltack Pt, Tusker Rock (2m), steep-to on its W side; and off Anvil Point, The Cable (2·4m), The Anvil and Limpet Rocks (3·7m). On the W side lie the Crabstones (3·7m) and the Blackstones (1·5m).

4.5 ABERSOCH

Gwynedd **52°49'·29N 04°29'·20W**

CHARTS AC 5609, 1410, 1411, 1971, 1512; Imray C61, C52; Stanfords 27.

TIDES –0315 Dover; ML 2·5; Duration 0520; Zone 0 (UT)

Standard Port MILFORD HAVEN (⟶)

Times				Height (metres)			
High Water		Low Water		MHWS	MHWN	MLWN	MLWS
0100	0800	0100	0700	7·0	5·2	2·5	0·7
1300	2000	1300	1900				
Differences ST TUDWAL'S ROADS							
+0155	+0145	+0240	+0310	–2·2	–1·9	–0·7	–0·2
ABERDARON							
+0210	+0200	+0240	+0310	–2·4	–1·9	–0·6	–0·2

SHELTER There are few moorings for visitors. Apply to HM or SC. ⚓ in St Tudwal's Roads clear of moored yachts; sheltered from SSE through S to NE.

NAVIGATION WPT 52°48´·52N 04°26´·13W, 293°/2·4M to YC jetty. There are no navigational dangers, but steer well clear of the drying rks to the E of East Island; Carred y Trai buoy FlR 2·5s is 2ca E of these rks (just off chartlet). St Tudwal's islands themselves are fairly steep-to, except at N ends. St Tudwal's Sound is clear of dangers.

LIGHTS AND MARKS The only lt is on St Tudwal's West Island, Fl WR 15s 46m 14/10M (see chartlet and 4.3).

R/T S Caernarfon YC Ch **80** M.

TELEPHONE (Code 01758) HM 712203; MRCC (01407) 762051; Marinecall 09068 969650; Police (01286) 673333; Dr 612535.

FACILITIES **South Caernarvonshire YC** ☎ 712338, Slip, M, L, FW, R, Bar (May-Sept), D, **Abersoch Power Boat Club** ☎ 812027. **Services** BY, Slip, ME, El, ⚒, ACA, CH, P, C (12 ton), LPG. **Town** CH, 🛒, R, Bar, ✉, Ⓑ, ⇌ (Pwllheli), ✈ (Chester).

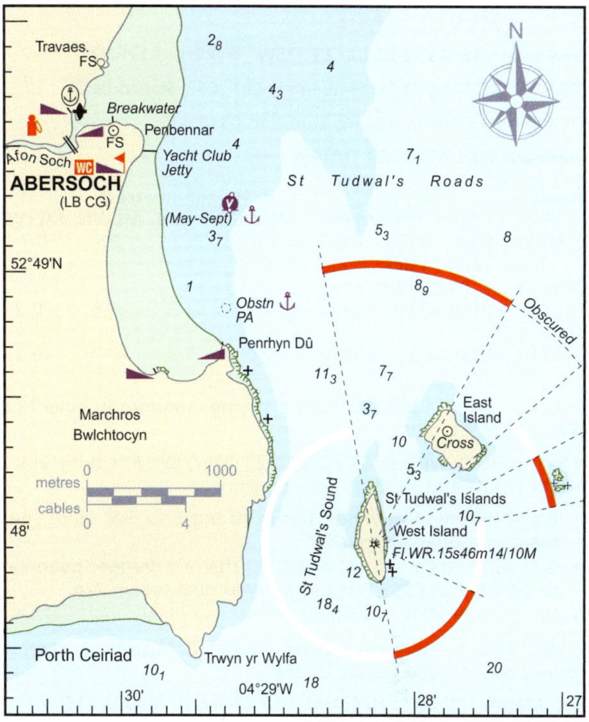

ADJACENT ANCHORAGES

BARDSEY ISLAND – YNYS ENNLI, Gwynedd, **52°45´·00N 04°47´·40W.** AC 5609, 1410, 1411, 1971. HW –0240 on Dover, see 3.19. Lights and Marks see 4.3. ⚓ in settled conditions only, is useful on passage N when awaiting tide through Bardsey Sound, see 3.4. ⚓ to W of Pen Cristin in approach to Henllwyn Cove in 4m. Sheltered in winds from WSW through N to NE but may be subject to swell at times. Possible with caution for smaller craft to anchor in the cove but beware of isolated rocks and shoals. Landing at jetty in rocks at cove marked by small boathouse at top of slip. Island is of historical interest with ruined abbey and religious settlement since 6th century. Now run as managed farm and nature reserve, see 0.31 Environmental Guidance.

ABERDARON BAY, Gwynedd, **52°47´·75N 04°42´·82W.** AC 5609, 1410, 1411, 1971, 5609. HW –0240 on Dover, see 3.19 Bardsey Is. In settled conditions only, is useful on passage N when awaiting tide through Bardsey Sound, see 3.4. In SE appr to bay are 2 islets Ynys Gwylan-fawr and Ynys Gwylan-bâch with a deep water passage between them, also passage between Ynys Gwylan-fawr and Trwyn Gwningaer (shore). ⚓ 4ca SSW of church in 5-10m, limited protection and subject to swell at times but sheltered in winds from W through N to NE. Do not leave craft unattended due to poor holding ground. Dinghy landing with care on shingle beach at Porth Meudwy, W side of bay. **Village** limited facilities: FW, R, Bar, ✉, ⇌ (Pwllheli).

LLANBEDROG, Gwynedd, **52°51´·14N 04°28´·09W.** AC 5609, 1410, 1411, 1971, 1512. HW –0245 on Dover, see 4.5 (St Tudwal's Roads). Good ⚓ N of Trwyn Llanbedrog (steep sided headland 131m) 1.0ca ENE of Bcn PHM in 2-3m. Beach has numerous conspicuous bathing huts. Sheltered in winds from N through W to SW. ⚓ well clear of local craft moorings as they have a long scope. Dinghy landing near boathouse. **Village** limited facilities: P & D (cans ½M), FW , R, Bar, ⇌ (Pwllheli).

4.6 PWLLHELI

Gwynedd **52°53′·23N 04°23′·75W** ❀❀❀⚐⚐⚐✿✿✿

CHARTS AC 1410, 1971, 1512; Imray C61, C52; Stanfords 27

TIDES –0315 Dover; ML 2·6; Duration 0510

Standard Port MILFORD HAVEN (⟶)

Times				Height (metres)			
High Water		Low Water		MHWS	MHWN	MLWN	MLWS
0100	0800	0100	0700	7·0	5·2	2·5	0·7
1300	2000	1300	1900				
Differences PWLLHELI							
+0210	+0150	+0245	+0320	–2·0	–1·8	–0·6	–0·2
CRICCIETH							
+0210	+0155	+0255	+0320	–2·0	–1·8	–0·7	–0·3

SHELTER Good in hbr and marina. Drying moorings in inner hbr (SW and NW bights).

NAVIGATION WPT 52°53'·02N 04°23'·07W, SWM lt buoy 299°/ 0·47M to QG lt at head of Training Arm.

- Ent is safe in most winds, but in strong E to SW winds sea breaks on offshore shoals.
- Ent subject to silting and bar and hbr chan are dredged but only to 0·6m below CD; 3 tide gauges. Max tidal stream 2kn.
- No ⚓ in hbr; 4kn speed limit.

LIGHTS AND MARKS See 4.3 and chartlet. Gimblet Rock (30m) is conspic conical rock 3ca SW of ent.

R/T Marina: Ch **80** M H24. HM: VHF Ch **12** 16 (0900-1715).

TELEPHONE (Code 01758) HM 704081, mob 07879 433145; MRCC (01407) 762051; ⊞ Bangor (A&E) 01248 384384; Marinecall 09068 969650; Police (01286) 673333; Dr 701457.

FACILITIES Marina ☎ 701219, www.hafanpwllheli.co.uk; 400 AB, £2.88, £12.21 <4hrs. Pontoon numbers are 4–12 from S–N. Pile berths on S side of appr chan. Wi-fi, P&D, LPG, BH (40 ton), C, Slip, ⌼, ♿, ⛭; **Boat Club** ☎ 612271, Slip, FW.

Pwllheli SC pwllhelisailingclub@btinternet.com ☎ 614442.

Services: BY, ME, Gas, Gaz, ⚒, CH, ACA, C (14 ton), El, Ⓔ, SM.

Town 🛒, R, Bar, ✉, Ⓑ, ⇌, ✈ (Chester).

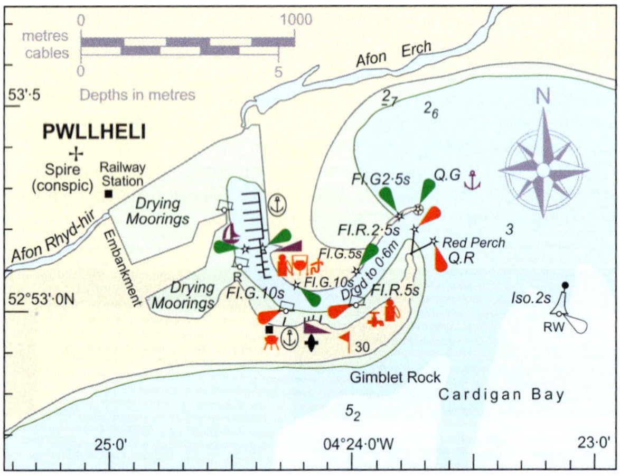

ADJACENT HARBOUR

MOCHRAS, Gwynedd, **52°49′·57N 04°07′·77W**. AC 1971, 1512. HW –0245 on Dover. Small yacht hbr in drying Mochras lagoon on SE side of Shell Is. Bar, about 2ca seaward. Appr advised HW±2. 3 grey posts, R topmarks, mark NE side of chan. Ebb tide runs strongly in the narrow ent between the sea wall and Shell Is (lt Fl WRG 4s, 079°-G-124°-W-134°-R-179°; Mar-Nov); at sp beware severe eddies inside. Inside ent, buoyed chan runs WSW to Shell Island Yacht Hbr ☎ 01341 241453. Facilities: M, FW, Slip, R, Bar, shwrs. Shifting chan, marked by posts and buoys, runs NE to Pensarn, where permanent moorings limit space. Drying AB, ⇌.

4.7 PORTHMADOG

Gwynedd **52°55'·32N 04°07'·77W** ❀⚐⚐⚐✿✿✿

CHARTS AC 1410, 1971, 1512,; Imray C61, C51; Stanfords 27.

TIDES –0247 Dover; ML no data; Duration 0455

Standard Port MILFORD HAVEN (⟶)

Times				Height (metres)			
High Water		Low Water		MHWS	MHWN	MLWN	MLWS
0100	0800	0100	0700	7·0	5·2	2·5	0·7
1300	2000	1300	1900				
Differences PORTHMADOG							
+0235	+0210	No data		–1·9	–1·8	No data	

SHELTER Inner hbr (N of Cei Ballast): Good all year round; visitors' drying AB adjacent Madoc YC or afloat rafted on moored yachts off YC. Outer hbr: Summer only, exposed to S winds. Speed limit 6kn in hbr upstream of No 8 buoy.

NAVIGATION WPT Fairway SWM buoy, 52°52'·97N 04°11'·09W, 041°/1·9M to conspic white Ho at W side of ent.

- Chan shifts and may divide. Bar changes frequently, but is near to No 3 and 4 buoys; dries approx 0·3m.
- In SW'lies, waves are steep-sided and close, especially on the ebb.
- Latest info from HM on request. Advise entering HW±1½.

LIGHTS AND MARKS Fairway buoy RW, L Fl 10s. Chan marker buoys (14) Nos 1–9 lit (May-Oct), have R/G reflective top marks and W reflective numbers. Moel-y-Gest is conspic hill (259m) approx 1M WNW of hbr. Harlech Castle (ru) is about 3M SE of appr chan.

R/T HM Ch 12 16 (HO and when vessel due). Madoc YC Ch M.

TELEPHONE (Code 01766) HM 512927, mobile (07879) 433147; MRCC (01407) 762051; Pilot 530684; Hbr Authority Gwynedd Council (01758) 704066; Marinecall 09068 969650; Police (01286) 673333; Dr 512284.

FACILITIES Hbr (265 berths) ☎ 512927, £7.00 all craft; D, FW, C, Slip access HW±4 (launching £10); **Madoc YC** ☎ 512976, AB, M, FW, Bar; **Porthmadog SC** ☎ 513546, AB, M, FW, Slip; **Services:** CH, ACA, ⚒, D(quay), D & P (cans), C (8 ton), M, BY, El, Pilot. **Town** ✉, Ⓑ, ⇌, ✈ (Chester).

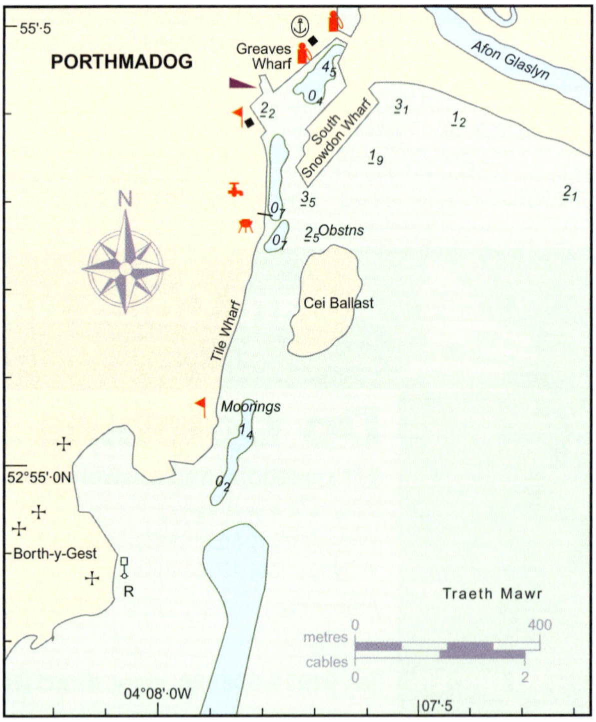

4.8 BARMOUTH

Gwynedd **52°42'·97N 04°03'·07W** ✪✪✥✥✿✿✿

CHARTS AC 5609, 1410, 1971, 1484; Imray C61, C51; Stanfords 27.

TIDES –0305 Dover; ML 2·6; Duration 0515

Standard Port MILFORD HAVEN (⟶)

Times				Height (metres)			
High Water		Low Water		MHWS	MHWN	MLWN	MLWS
0100	0800	0100	0700	7·0	5·2	2·5	0·7
1300	2000	1300	1900				
Differences BARMOUTH							
+0215	+0205	+0310	+0320	–2·0	–1·7	–0·7	0·0

SHELTER Good. Entry HW±2½ safe, but impossible with strong SW'lies. Exposed ⚓ W of Barmouth Outer buoy in 6 to 10m. Serious silting reported. In hbr there are 5 ♁s; secure as directed by HM, because of submarine cables and strong tidal streams. A Ⓥ berth is marked at W end of quay, dries at half-tide. Drying ⚓ inside Penrhyn Pt.

NAVIGATION WPT, Barmouth Outer SWM buoy, 52°42´·72N 04°05´·02W, 082°/0·8M to Y perch lt, QR. Appr from SW between St Patrick's Causeway (Sarn Badrig) and Sarn-y-Bwch. Barmouth can be identified by Cader Idris, a mountain 890m high, 5M ESE. Fegla Fawr, a rounded hill, lies on S side of hbr.

- The Bar, 0·75M W of Penrhyn Pt, with min depth 0·3m is subject to constant change. Chan is marked by buoys (see below) fitted with radar reflectors and reflective tape and moved as required.
- Spring ebb runs 3–5kn.
- The estuary and river (Afon Mawddach) are tidal and can be navigated for about 7M above rly br (clearance approx 5·5m); but chan is not buoyed, and sandbanks move constantly – local knowledge essential.

LIGHTS AND MARKS Outer SWM L Fl 10s; Bar SHM Fl G; No2 PHM Fl R. Inner PHM not lit. Y perch QR 4m 5M on R framework tr, marks S end of stony ledge extending 3ca SW from Ynys y Brawd across N Bank. Ynys y Brawd groyne, SE end, marked by lit bn, Fl R 5s 5M. NW end of rly bridge 2 FR (hor).

R/T Call *Barmouth Hbr* VHF Ch **12** 16 (Apr-Sep 0900-1700 later for HW; Oct-Mar 0900-1600); wind and sea state are available.

TELEPHONE (Code 01341) HM 280671 mob 07795 012747; MRCC (01407) 762051; Marinecall 09068 969650; Police (01286) 673333; Dr 280521. Local information www.barmouthwebcam.co.uk

FACILITIES Quay £9.00/yacht (inc electricity), M (incl 3 drying ♁) contact HM in advance if deep water ♁ required, D, FW, 2 Slips (HW±3, £12/day); Merioneth YC ☎ 280000; Services: CH, ACA. **Town** P, D, 🛒, R, Bar, ✉, @, Ⓑ, ⇌, ✈ (Chester), Ferry to Penrhyn Pt. **Fairbourne** ✉, 🛒, ⇌, Ferry to Barmouth.

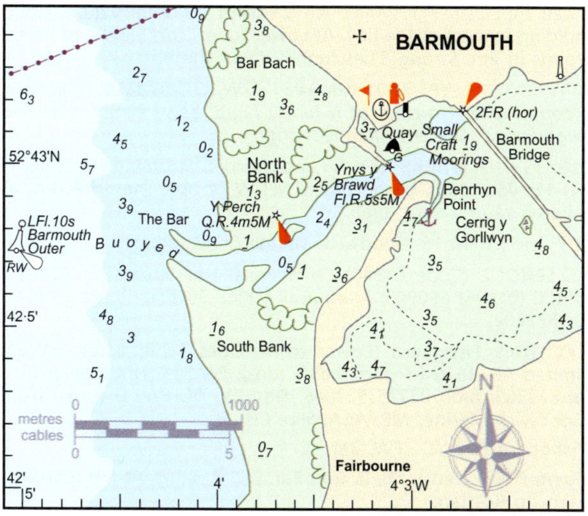

4.9 ABERDOVEY

Gwynedd **52°32'·57N 04°02'·72W** (Jetty) ✪✪✥✥✿✿✿

CHARTS AC 5609, 1410, 1972, 1484; Imray C61, C51; Stanfords 27.

TIDES –0320 Dover; ML 2·6; Duration 0535. For differences see 4.10.

SHELTER Good except in strong W/SW winds. Berth on jetty in 3m; to the E there is heavy silting.

NAVIGATION WPT Aberdovey Outer SWM buoy, 52°32´·00N 04°05´·56W, 093°/0.43M to Bar buoy.

- Bar and channel constantly shift and are hazardous below half-tide; buoys moved accordingly.
- Enter the channel at gateway between Bar SHM and PHM Fl R 5s. Visitors should call HM on VHF before entering.

LIGHTS AND MARKS See 4.3 and chartlet. No daymarks. Lts may be unreliable. Submarine cables (prohib ⚓s) marked by bns with R ◇ topmarks.

R/T Call *Aberdovey Hbr* VHF Ch 12 16.

TELEPHONE (Code 01654) HM 767626, mobile 07879 433148; MRCC (01646) 690909; Marinecall 09068 969650; Police (01286) 673333; Dr 710414; Ⓗ 710411.

FACILITIES **Jetty** AB £7.00 <9m, £10.50 >9m; M, FW; **Wharf** Slip, AB, L, FW, C; **Dovey YC** ☎ 767607, Bar, Slip(launching £4.50 if engine <10hp), L, FW; **Services:** BY, ME, El, ⚒, CH, ACA, Ⓔ. **Town** P & D (cans), ME, El, CH, 🛒, R, Bar, ✉, Ⓑ, ⇌, ✈ (Chester).

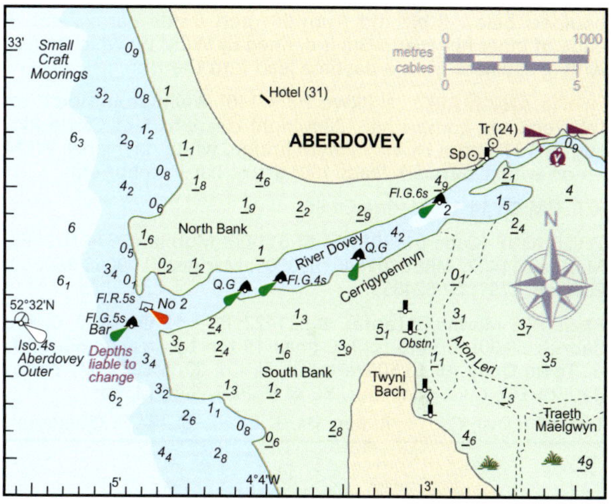

OTHER HARBOURS IN SOUTH PART OF CARDIGAN BAY

ABERAERON, Ceredigion, **52°14´·62N 04°15´·94W**. AC 1410, 1972, 1484. HW –0325 on Dover; +0140 and –1·9m on Milford Haven; ML 2·7m; Duration 0540. A small, popular drying hbr at the mouth of the R Aeron; access HW±1½. Short drying piers extend each side of river ent. In strong NW'lies there is little shelter. AB £8/craft on NW wall, only in calm conditions. Foul ground with depths of 1·5m extend 3ca offshore to SW of Aberaeron. Beware Carreg Gloyn (0·3m) 4ca WSW of hbr, and Sarn Cadwgan (1·8m) shoals 5ca N of the hbr ent. Lts (see 4.3 for sectors): N pier Fl (4) WRG 15s 10m 6M. S pier Fl (3) G 10s 11m 6M. VHF **14** 16. HM ☎ (01545) 571645; FW, D (from fishermen). **YC** ☎ 570077. **Town** P.

NEW QUAY, Ceredigion, **52°12´·92N 04°21´·22W**. AC 1410, 1972, 1484. HW –0335 on Dover; Duration 0540; see 4.10. Good shelter in offshore winds, but untenable in NW'lies. On E side of bay Carreg Ina, rks drying 1·3m, are marked by NCM buoy, Q. Two Y bns mark a sewer outfall running 7ca NNW from Ina Pt. The hbr (dries 1·6m) is protected by a pier with lt, Fl WG 3s 12m 8/5M; 135°-W-252°-G-295°. Groyne extends 80m SSE of pierhd to a SHM bn; close ENE of which is a ECM bn, Q (3) 10s. VHF Ch **14** 16. HM ☎ (01545) 560368. MRCC (01646) 690909; Dr ☎ 560203; YC ☎ 560516. Facilities: FW, D (from fishermen), slip (£6). **Town** P (3M), ✉, R, Bar.

4.10 ABERYSTWYTH

Ceredigion **52°24'·42N 04°05'·47W**

CHARTS AC 5609, 5620, 1410, 1972, 1484; Imray C61, C51; Stanfords 27.

TIDES –0330 Dover; ML 2·7; Duration 0540

Standard Port MILFORD HAVEN (⟶)

Times				Height (metres)			
High Water		Low Water		MHWS	MHWN	MLWN	MLWS
0100	0800	0100	0700	7·0	5·2	2·5	0·7
1300	2000	1300	1900				
Differences ABERDOVEY							
+0215	+0200	+0230	+0305	–2·0	–1·7	–0·5	0·0
ABERYSTWYTH							
+0145	+0130	+0210	+0245	–2·0	–1·7	–0·7	0·0
NEW QUAY							
+0150	+0125	+0155	+0230	–2·1	–1·8	–0·6	–0·1
ABERPORTH							
+0135	+0120	+0150	+0220	–2·1	–1·8	–0·6	–0·1

SHELTER Good, in marina (1·7m) on E side of chan; or dry against Town Quay. Access approx HW±3 (HW±2 for strangers).

NAVIGATION WPT 52°24'·83N 04°06'·22W, 133/0·6M° to ent.

Appr dangerous in strong on-shore winds. The Bar, close off S pier hd, has 0·7m least depth. From N, beware Castle Rks, in R sector of N bkwtr lt; also rks drying 0·5m W of N bkwtr and boulders below S pier hd. Turn 90° port inside narrow ent. E edge of inner hbr chan 0·3m is defined by WCM bn which in line with Y daymark gives a daytime lead into the Hbr.

LIGHTS AND MARKS N Bkwtr Hd ≠ 140° Wellington Mon't (on top Pendinas, conspic hill 120m high) clears to S of Castle Rks. Ldg lts 133°, both FR on Ystwyth Bridge, white daymarks. WCM bn on with Y daymark leads 100° across bar into hbr ent.

R/T HM Ch **14** 16. Marina Ch 80.

TELEPHONE (Code 01970) HM ☎ 611433 Mobile 07974 023965; Marina 611422; MRCC (01646) 690909; Marinecall 09068 969650; Police 612791; Dr 624855.

FACILITIES **Marina (Y Lanfa)**, ☎ 611422. 88 + 15 Ⓥ, £2.60. D, Slip (launch £8.00), BH (10 ton), C (max 15 ton by arrangement), ⛹, ♿. **Town Quay** AB £6.50/craft, FW, El, CH, Ⓔ, ME, ⚒, M, 2 Slips (launch £6), C (25 ton), Gas. **YC** ☎ 612907, Slip, M, Bar.

Town P (cans), CH, 🛒, R, Bar, SM, ♿, 🗑, ✉, Ⓑ, ⇌, ✈ (Swansea).

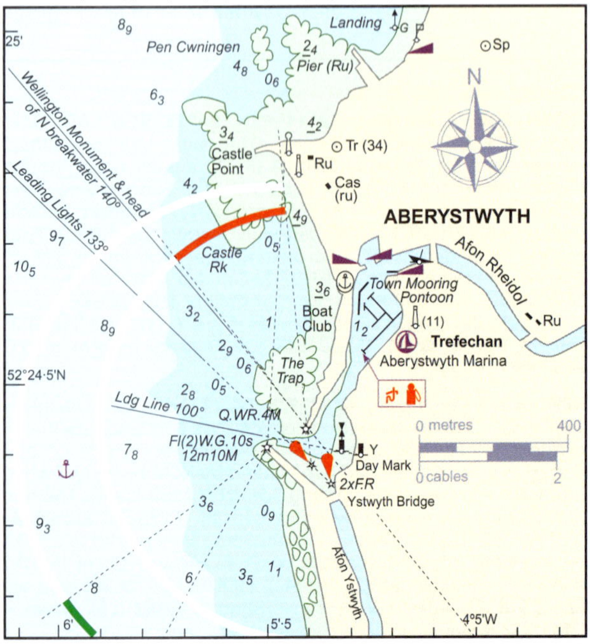

MINOR HARBOUR, 12M NE of Fishguard

PORT CARDIGAN, Ceredigion, **52°07'·02N 04°42'·07W**. AC 1973, 1484. HW –0405 on Dover; ML 2·4m; Duration 0550. Shelter is good, but ent dangerous in strong N/NW winds. Large scale charts are essential; see www.afon-teifi-fairways.com for up to date advice or telephone Mooring Master (see below) before entering. The bar has 0·5m or less. ⚓ near Hotel (conspic) on E side of ent. Chan is usually close to E side; IDM bn, Fl (2) 5s, should be left to stbd when clear of the bar. From Pen-yr-Ergyd to Bryn-Du chan is marked with lit mid channel markers but shifts constantly. St Dogmaels has ⚓ or a Ⓜ via Mooring Master ☎ (01329) 621437 mob 07774 126342. Or ⚓ in pools off Pen-yr-Ergyd. Short stay pontoons in the Teifi; possible Ⓜs off Teifi Boating Club. **Moorings**: administered by Afon Teifi Fairway Committee, Mooring Master ☎ (01239) 613966, mob 07799 284206.
Teifi Boating Club ☎ 613846, FW, Bar; **Services:** ME, ⚒. **Town** Ⓑ, 🛒, CH, P&D (cans), FW, ME, Bar, R.

4.11 FISHGUARD

Pembrokeshire **52°00'·12N 04°58'·40W**
Commercial Hbr ; Lower Hbr

CHARTS AC 5620, 1178, 1410, 1973, 1484; Imray C61, C51, C60; Stanfords 27.

TIDES –0400 Dover; ML 2·6; Duration 0550

Standard Port MILFORD HAVEN (⟶)

Times				Height (metres)			
High Water		Low Water		MHWS	MHWN	MLWN	MLWS
0100	0800	0100	0700	7·0	5·2	2·5	0·7
1300	2000	1300	1900				
Differences FISHGUARD							
+0115	+0100	+0110	+0135	–2·2	–1·8	–0·5	+0·1
PORT CARDIGAN							
+0140	+0120	+0220	+0130	–2·3	–1·8	–0·5	0·0
CARDIGAN (Town)							
+0220	+0150	No data		–2·2	–1·6	No data	
PORTHGAIN							
+0055	+0045	+0045	+0100	–2·5	–1·8	–0·6	0·0
RAMSEY SOUND							
+0030	+0030	+0030	+0030	–1·9	–1·3	–0·3	0·0
SOLVA							
+0015	+0010	+0035	+0015	–1·5	–1·0	–0·2	0·0
LITTLE HAVEN							
+0010	+0010	+0025	+0015	–1·1	–0·8	–0·2	0·0
MARTIN'S HAVEN							
+0010	+0010	+0015	+0015	–0·8	–0·5	+0·1	+0·1
SKOMER IS							
–0005	–0005	+0005	+0005	–0·4	–0·1	0·0	0·0

SHELTER Good, except in strong NW/NE winds. Beware large swell, especially in N winds. No ⚓, except SW of ferry quay. Good holding in most of the bay. At Lower town ⚓ off Saddle or Castle Points in 2m. Strong S'lies funnel down the hbr.

NAVIGATION WPT 52°01'·02N 04°57'·57W, 237°/0·48M to N bkwtr lt. *Keep at least 1ca clear of N bkwtr head; beware of ferries and High-Speed SeaCats manoeuvring.*

LIGHTS AND MARKS See 4.3 and chartlet. Strumble Hd Lt ho, Fl (4) 15s 45m 26M, is approx 4M WNW of hbr. The SHM (bn) at Aber Gwaun is very small.

R/T HM Ch **14** 16. Goodwick Marine Ch M (occas).

TELEPHONE (Code 01348) Commercial Hbr Supervisor 404425; MRCC (01646) 690909; Marinecall 09068 969650; Police 873073; Dr 872802.

FACILITIES **Fishguard** (Lower town) dries 3·2m; access HW±1, limited AB. 15 Ⓜ (drying, max 5 tons), FW. HM (Lower hbr) ☎ 873369; mob 07775 523846. Slip, BY, ⚒, FW, D (cans) from Goodwick Marine, ME, ACA, Slip, CH, El.

Fishguard Bay YC , FW, Bar, ♿.

Town P & D (cans), 🛒, R, Gas, Bar, ✉, 🗑, @, Ⓑ, ⇌, ✈ (Cardiff), Ferry to Rosslare.

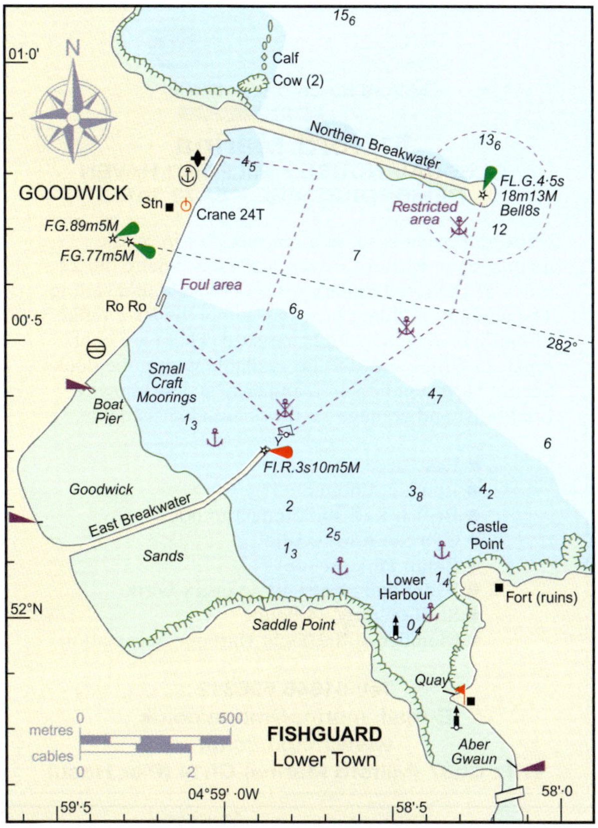

HARBOURS IN ST BRIDES BAY (See AC 5620)

SOLVA, Pembrokeshire, **51°52′02N 05°11′·67W**. AC 1478. HW –0450 on Dover; ML 3·2m; Duration 0555. See 4.11. Good shelter for small boats that can take the ground; access HW±3. Avoid in strong S winds. Black Scar, Green Scar and The Mare are rks 5ca S. Ent via SSE side; best water near Black Rk in centre of ent. Beware stone spit at Trwyn Caws on W just inside ent. There are 9 Or Øs drying on hard sand (£6.00), drying/rafting ABs for <9·5m LOA; or ⚓ behind the rk in approx 3m. Yachts can go up to the quay (£7.50) Facilities: showers, 🛒, Bar, R in village. FW on quay, Slip (launching £5). HM (01437) 721703 mob 07974 020139, VHF Ch 16 8, M, CH. **Solva Boat Owners Assn** ☎ 721489 mob 07974 020139.

ST BRIDES BAY, Pembrokeshire, **51°49′02N 05°10′·07W**. AC 1478. HW (Little Haven) –0450 on Dover; ML 3·2m; Duration 0555. See 4.11. A SPM buoy, Fl (5) Y 20s, is midway between Ramsey and Skomer islands at 51°48′·2N 05°20′·0W. Keep at least 100m offshore 1/9-28/2 to avoid disturbing seals, and ditto nesting sea birds 1/3-31/7. Many good ⚓s, especially between Little Haven and Borough Head in S or E winds or between Solva and Dinas Fawr in N or E winds. In W'lies boats should shelter in Solva, Skomer (below) or Pendinas Bach. Tankers anchor in mouth of B. For apprs from the N or S see 4.4. Facilities: (Little Haven) CH, 🛒, R, Bar, FW (cans).

4.12 MILFORD HAVEN

Pembrokeshire **51°40'·13N 05°08'·16W**

CHARTS AC 5620, 1410, 1178, 1478, 2878, 3273/4/5; Imray C60, C13; Stanfords 27.

TIDES –0500 Dover; ML 3·8; Duration 0605

Standard Port MILFORD HAVEN (⟶)

Times				Height (metres)			
High Water		Low Water		MHWS	MHWN	MLWN	MLWS
0100	0800	0100	0700	7·0	5·2	2·5	0·7
1300	2000	1300	1900				
Differences DALE ROADS							
–0005	–0005	–0008	–0008	0·0	0·0	0·0	–0·1
NEYLAND							
+0002	+0010	0000	0000	0·0	0·0	0·0	0·0
HAVERFORDWEST							
+0010	+0025	Dries out		–4·8	–4·9	Dries out	
LLANGWM (Black Tar)							
+0010	+0020	+0005	0000	+0·1	+0·1	0·0	–0·1

SHELTER Very good in various places round the hbr, especially in Milford Marina and Neyland Yacht Haven. ⚓s in Dale Bay; off Chapel Bay and Angle Pt on S shore; off Scotch Bay, E of Milford marina; and others beyond Pembroke Dock. Free pontoons (May-Oct) include: Dale Bay, Gelliswick Bay; waiting pontoons off Milford Dock and Hobbs Pt (for Pembroke Dock); and drying pontoons at Dale Beach, Hazelbeach, Neyland and Burton; mainly intended for tenders. It is possible to dry out safely at inshore areas of Dale, Sandy Haven and Angle Bay, depending on weather.

NAVIGATION **West Channel** WPT 51°40′·21N 05°10′·28W. **East Channel** WPT 51°40′·12N 05°08′·67W.

- The tide sets strongly across the ent to the Haven particularly at sp. In bad weather avoid passing over Mid Chan Rks and St Ann's Hd shoal, where a confused sea and swell will be found (see AC 3273). Give St Ann's Head a wide berth especially on the ebb, when East Chan by Sheep Island is better.
- Beware large tankers entering/departing the Haven and ferries moving at high speed in the lower Haven. Caution: Only 15m clearance below cables between Thorn Is and Thorn Pt.
- Milford Haven Port Authority has a jetty, Port Control and offices near Hubberston Pt. Their launches have G hulls and W upperworks with 'PILOT' in black letters and fly a Pilot flag while on patrol; Fl Bu lt at night. Their instructions must be obeyed. No vessel may pass within 100m of any terminal or any tanker, whether at ⚓ or under way.

River Cleddau is navigable 6M to Picton Pt, at junction of West and East arms, at all tides for boats of moderate draught. Clearance under Cleddau Bridge above Neyland is 37m; and 25m under power cable 1M upstream. Chan to Haverfordwest has 2m at HW and clearances of only 6m below cables and bridge; only feasible for shoal draft/lifting keel and unmasted craft.

Firing Ranges to the S and SE, see 4.13 and AC 1076.

LIGHTS AND MARKS See 4.3 and chartlets. The ldg lts are specifically for VLCCs entering/leaving hbr and proceeding to/from the oil refineries. The Haven is very well buoyed and lit as far as Cleddau bridge.

Milford Dock ldg lts 348°, both F.Bu, with W ○ daymarks. Dock entry sigs on E side of lock: 2 FG (vert) = gates open, vessels may enter. VHF Ch 18 is normally used for ent/exit by day and night.

R/T Monitor *Milford Haven Port Control* Ch 12 (H24) while underway in the Haven. *Milford Haven Patrol* launches Ch11/12 (H24). To lock in to Milford Dock marina call *Pierhead,* Ch 18, for clearance, then call *Milford Marina,* Ch M, for a berth. Neyland Yacht Haven Ch 80/M.

Broadcasts: Local forecasts on Ch 12 14 at 0300, 0900, 1500 and 2100 (all UT). Nav warnings follow on Ch14. Gale warnings issued on receipt Ch 12 14. Expected shipping movements for next 24 hours on Ch 12, 0800–0830, 2000–2030LT and on request. Tide hts and winds on request. Bcsts on Ch 16 67 at 0335 then every 4 hrs to 2335.

TELEPHONE (Code 01646) Lock 696310; Port Ctrl 696136/7; MRCC 690909; Marinecall 09068 969649; Police (01437) 763355; Ⓗ Haverfordwest (01437) 764545; Dr 690674.

FACILITIES **Marinas/Berthing** (from seaward):

Dale Bay 🛒, FW, R, Slip, Pontoon, YC.

Milford Haven Port Authority jetty ☎ 696133 (occas use by visitors with approval from HM), AB, FW.

Milford Marina (280) ☎ 696312, Pierhead ☎ 696310; £2·05. VHF Ch 14 M. Lock hrs: ent HW–4, exit –3½, free flow HW –2¼ to HW–¼, ent +1½, exit +1¾, ent +2¾, exit +3¼; waiting pontoon or shelter in lock, 3·5m water at MLWS. D (H24), C, BH (16 ton), CH, El, ME, ⚒, Ⓔ, D, Gas, Gaz, 🛒, R, Bar, Ice, ▣, ♿, ✉, Ⓑ,Wi-fi.

Lawrenny Yacht Station (100) ☎ 651212/651065, ⚓ £5, L, FW, BY, CH, D, P, ⚒, C (15 ton), ME, Slip (launching £5.00), ▣, Bar, R, 🛒, ♿, ✉, Gas.

Neyland Yacht Haven (420 inc Ⓥ, £2.06) ☎ 601601, www.yachthavens.com ; Wi-fi, D, CH, Ⓔ, Gas, Gaz, ▣, C (20 ton), SM, SC, ME, El, ⚒, R, 🛒, Wi-fi; Access lower basin H24, upper basin HW±3½ (sill + depth gauges and R/G lit perches); marina and approaches dredged annually Oct/March – proceed with extreme caution.

Services: All marine services available; check with HM, marinas or YC/SC. **Dale Sailing Co** (@ Neyland), BY, CH, ME, ⚒, D, LPG, BH (35T). **East Llannion Marine**: access HW±3, Slip, scrubbing piles, BH (30 ton), fuel. **Rudder's BY**, small but useful, is just upstream of Burton Pt.

Yacht Clubs: Dale YC ☎ 636362; Pembrokeshire YC ☎ 692799; Neyland YC ☎ 600267; Pembroke Haven YC ☎ 684403; Lawrenny YC ☎ 651212.

Towns: Milford Haven, ✉, Ⓑ, ⇌. Pembroke Dock; ✉, Ⓑ, ⇌, Ⓗ. Neyland, ✉, Ⓑ. Haverfordwest, ✉, Ⓗ, Ⓑ, ⇌, ✈ (Swansea or Cardiff). Ferry: Pembroke Dock–Rosslare.

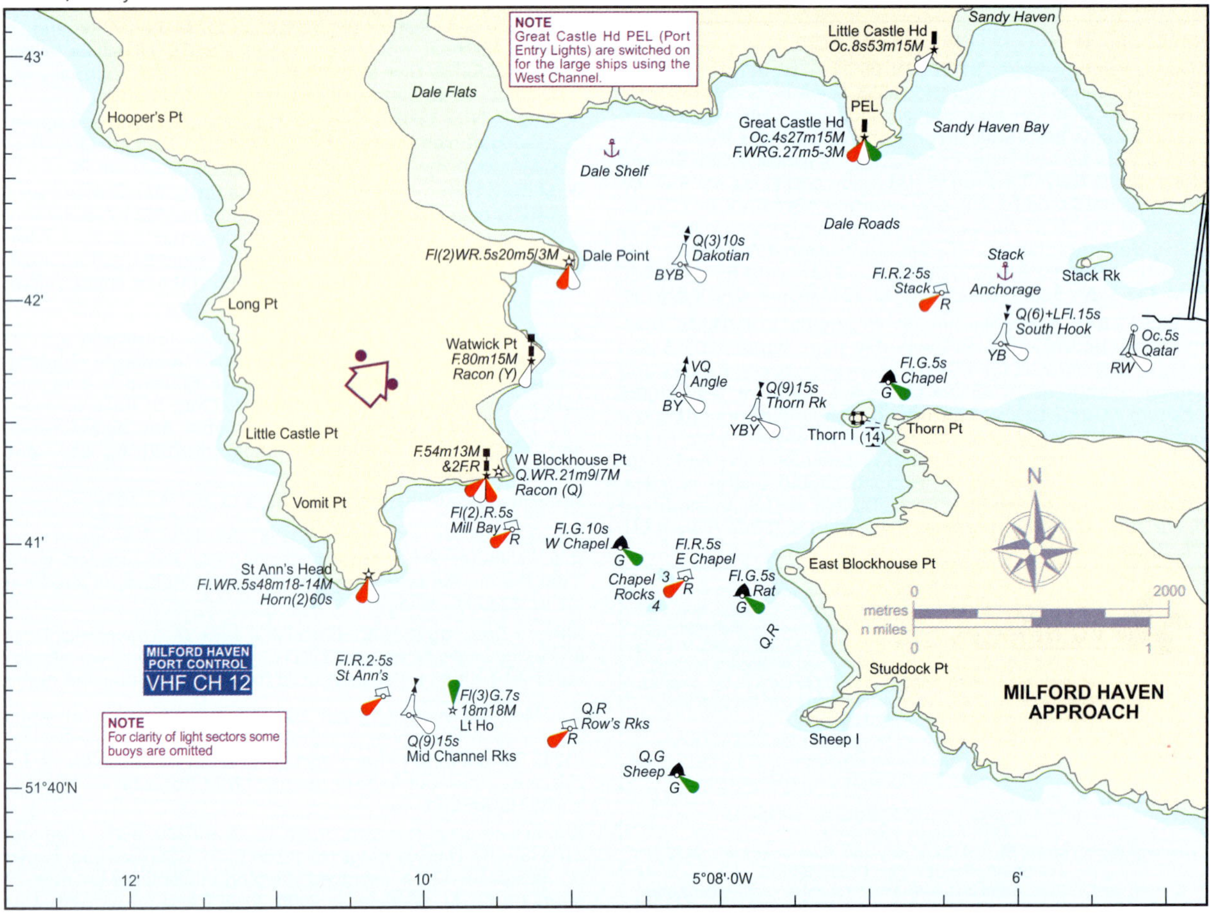

MILFORD HAVEN *continued*

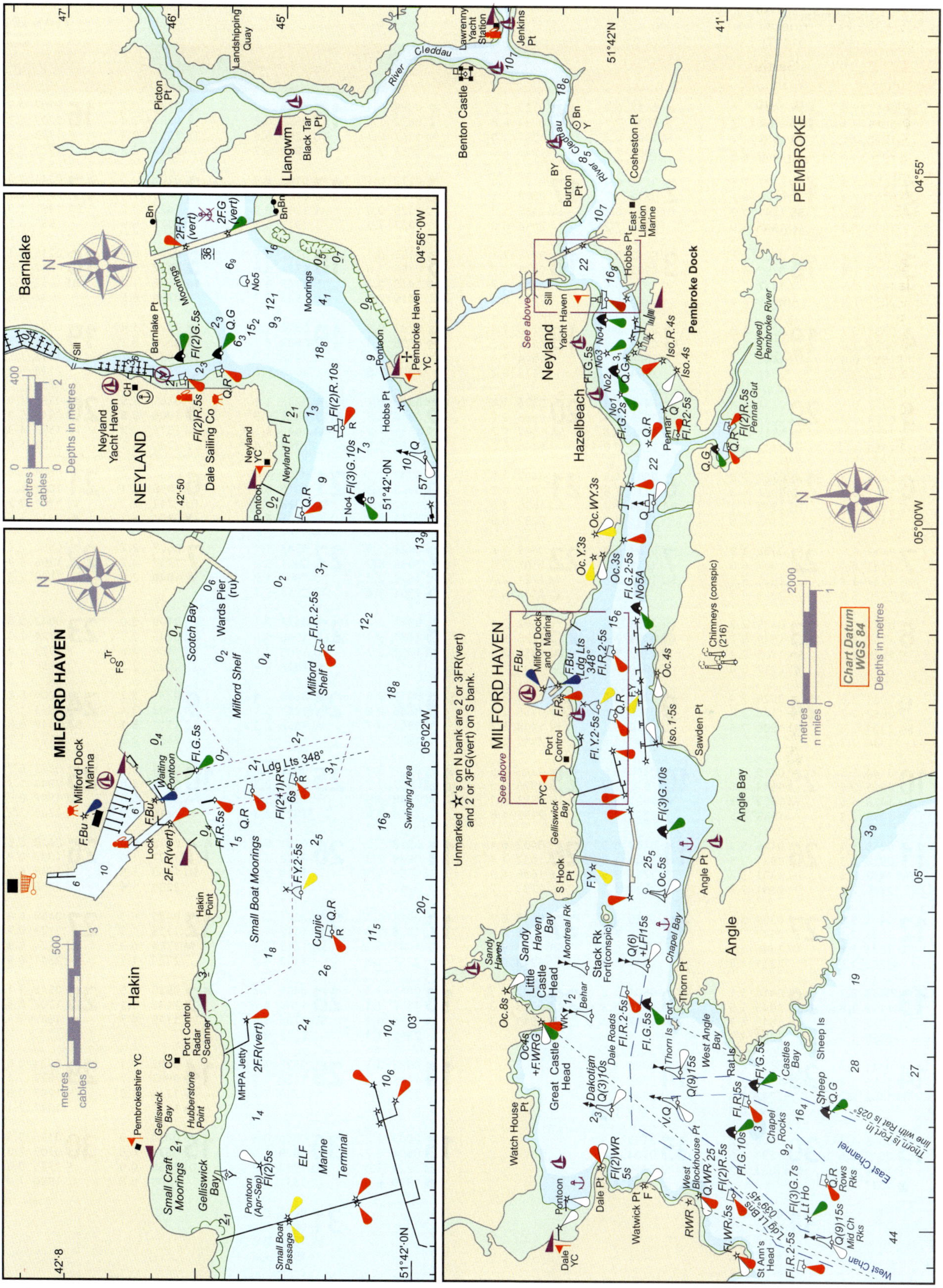

S Wales

TIME ZONE (UT)
For Summer Time add ONE hour in **non-shaded areas**

MILFORD HAVEN   LAT 51°42'N   LONG 5°03'W

TIMES AND HEIGHTS OF HIGH AND LOW WATERS

Dates in red are SPRINGS
Dates in blue are NEAPS

YEAR **2010**

JANUARY

Date	Time	m	Date	Time	m
1 F	0011	1.0	16 SA	0049	1.4
	0614	7.1		0654	6.7
	1240	0.8		1309	1.3
	1842	7.1		1910	6.4
2 SA	0058	0.8	17 SU	0121	1.3
	0702	7.3		0726	6.7
	1328	0.6		1341	1.2
	1930	7.2		1941	6.5
3 SU	0145	0.7	18 M	0151	1.3
	0750	7.4		0757	6.7
	1416	0.5		1412	1.2
	2017	7.1		2011	6.4
4 M	0231	0.7	19 TU	0221	1.3
	0837	7.4		0828	6.6
	1503	0.6		1442	1.3
	2103	7.0		2041	6.3
5 TU	0317	0.9	20 W	0251	1.4
	0924	7.2		0859	6.5
	1549	0.9		1513	1.5
	2150	6.7		2112	6.2
6 W	0403	1.2	21 TH	0322	1.6
	1011	6.8		0931	6.3
	1636	1.3		1546	1.7
	2237	6.3		2145	6.0
7 TH	0452	1.5	22 F	0356	1.9
	1101	6.4		1007	6.0
	1727	1.7		1621	1.9
	◑ 2330	5.9		2223	5.7
8 F	0547	1.9	23 SA	0435	2.2
	1157	6.0		1049	5.7
	1825	2.1		1705	2.2
				◐ 2312	5.4
9 SA	0031	5.6	24 SU	0526	2.4
	0652	2.2		1146	5.5
	1304	5.6		1806	2.5
	1936	2.3			
10 SU	0144	5.5	25 M	0019	5.3
	0811	2.4		0643	2.6
	1418	5.5		1303	5.3
	2053	2.3		1933	2.5
11 M	0258	5.5	26 TU	0146	5.3
	0926	2.3		0821	2.5
	1532	5.6		1431	5.4
	2159	2.2		2101	2.3
12 TU	0405	5.8	27 W	0309	5.6
	1028	2.1		0942	2.1
	1633	5.8		1546	5.8
	2252	1.9		2211	1.8
13 W	0458	6.1	28 TH	0416	6.1
	1117	1.8		1045	1.5
	1722	6.0		1649	6.3
	2335	1.7		2308	1.3
14 TH	0541	6.4	29 F	0513	6.7
	1159	1.6		1140	1.0
	1802	6.2		1742	6.8
				2359	0.8
15 F	0013	1.5	30 SA	0604	7.2
	0619	6.6		1230	0.5
	1236	1.4		1831	7.2
	● 1837	6.4		○	
			31 SU	0047	0.5
				0651	7.5
				1317	0.2
				1916	7.4

FEBRUARY

Date	Time	m	Date	Time	m
1 M	0132	0.3	16 TU	0129	1.0
	0736	7.7		0733	6.8
	1401	0.2		1347	1.0
	2000	7.4		1946	6.6
2 TU	0215	0.3	17 W	0158	1.0
	0819	7.6		0802	6.8
	1443	0.3		1416	1.0
	2042	7.2		2014	6.6
3 W	0257	0.5	18 TH	0226	1.1
	0902	7.4		0831	6.7
	1524	0.6		1445	1.2
	2123	6.9		2042	6.4
4 TH	0337	0.8	19 F	0256	1.3
	0943	7.0		0900	6.5
	1604	1.1		1514	1.4
	2204	6.5		2113	6.2
5 F	0418	1.3	20 SA	0326	1.6
	1026	6.4		0933	6.2
	1645	1.6		1547	1.7
	◑ 2249	6.0		2148	6.0
6 SA	0504	1.9	21 SU	0402	1.9
	1114	5.8		1012	5.9
	1734	2.2		1626	2.0
	2343	5.5		2232	5.6
7 SU	0603	2.4	22 M	0449	2.2
	1215	5.3		1105	5.5
	1843	2.6		1721	2.4
				◐ 2336	5.3
8 M	0058	5.2	23 TU	0602	2.5
	0729	2.7		1225	5.2
	1342	5.0		1853	2.6
	2020	2.7			
9 TU	0231	5.2	24 W	0111	5.2
	0906	2.6		0755	2.5
	1514	5.1		1408	5.2
	2141	2.5		2040	2.4
10 W	0350	5.5	25 TH	0249	5.5
	1015	2.2		0926	2.0
	1621	5.5		1533	5.7
	2238	2.1		2155	1.8
11 TH	0443	5.9	26 F	0402	6.1
	1104	1.9		1032	1.4
	1707	5.9		1636	6.3
	2321	1.7		2253	1.2
12 F	0525	6.3	27 SA	0458	6.7
	1143	1.5		1125	0.8
	1745	6.2		1727	6.9
	2357	1.4		2343	0.7
13 SA	0601	6.5	28 SU	0547	7.3
	1217	1.3		1213	0.3
	1818	6.4		1813	7.3
				○	
14 SU	0030	1.2			
	0633	6.7			
	1249	1.1			
	● 1849	6.5			
15 M	0100	1.1			
	0704	6.8			
	1319	1.0			
	1918	6.6			

MARCH

Date	Time	m	Date	Time	m
1 M	0029	0.3	16 TU	0034	1.0
	0632	7.6		0635	6.8
	1257	0.1		1250	0.9
	1856	7.5		1849	6.7
2 TU	0112	0.1	17 W	0103	0.9
	0715	7.7		0704	6.9
	1339	0.0		1319	0.9
	1937	7.5		1917	6.8
3 W	0153	0.1	18 TH	0132	0.9
	0756	7.6		0734	6.8
	1418	0.2		1349	0.9
	2016	7.3		1946	6.7
4 TH	0232	0.3	19 F	0202	1.0
	0835	7.3		0803	6.7
	1455	0.6		1418	1.0
	2054	7.0		2016	6.6
5 F	0310	0.7	20 SA	0232	1.1
	0914	6.9		0835	6.5
	1531	1.1		1449	1.3
	2132	6.5		2048	6.4
6 SA	0347	1.3	21 SU	0305	1.4
	0953	6.3		0910	6.3
	1607	1.7		1523	1.6
	2213	6.0		2125	6.1
7 SU	0428	1.9	22 M	0343	1.7
	1036	5.7		0951	5.9
	1649	2.2		1604	1.9
	◑ 2301	5.4		2211	5.7
8 M	0521	2.4	23 TU	0433	2.1
	1131	5.1		1048	5.5
	1751	2.7		1703	2.3
				◐ 2318	5.4
9 TU	0013	5.0	24 W	0550	2.4
	0646	2.8		1211	5.1
	1303	4.7		1836	2.5
	1939	2.9			
10 W	0158	5.0	25 TH	0055	5.3
	0837	2.7		0741	2.3
	1448	4.9		1353	5.2
	2114	2.6		2021	2.3
11 TH	0322	5.3	26 F	0231	5.6
	0949	2.3		0908	1.9
	1556	5.3		1515	5.7
	2212	2.2		2135	1.7
12 F	0416	5.7	27 SA	0341	6.2
	1038	1.9		1012	1.3
	1641	5.7		1615	6.3
	2255	1.8		2232	1.2
13 SA	0457	6.1	28 SU	0437	6.8
	1116	1.5		1104	0.7
	1718	6.1		1705	6.8
	2331	1.4		2322	0.7
14 SU	0533	6.5	29 M	0525	7.2
	1149	1.2		1150	0.4
	1750	6.4		1750	7.2
15 M	0003	1.2	30 TU	0006	0.3
	0604	6.7		0609	7.5
	1221	1.0		1233	0.2
	● 1820	6.6		○ 1831	7.4
			31 W	0049	0.2
				0651	7.5
				1313	0.2
				1911	7.4

APRIL

Date	Time	m	Date	Time	m
1 TH	0129	0.2	16 F	0107	0.9
	0731	7.4		0707	6.8
	1351	0.4		1323	0.9
	1949	7.2		1921	6.8
2 F	0207	0.5	17 SA	0141	1.0
	0809	7.1		0741	6.7
	1427	0.8		1357	1.0
	2027	6.9		1955	6.7
3 SA	0244	0.9	18 SU	0216	1.1
	0847	6.6		0817	6.5
	1502	1.2		1432	1.2
	2104	6.5		2032	6.5
4 SU	0321	1.4	19 M	0254	1.3
	0925	6.1		0858	6.3
	1537	1.7		1512	1.5
	2144	6.0		2115	6.2
5 M	0401	1.9	20 TU	0338	1.6
	1006	5.6		0946	5.9
	1616	2.2		1559	1.9
	2230	5.5		2208	5.9
6 TU	0451	2.4	21 W	0435	1.9
	1058	5.1		1047	5.5
	1712	2.7		1701	2.2
	◑ 2334	5.1		◐ 2317	5.6
7 W	0607	2.7	22 TH	0552	2.1
	1217	4.7		1206	5.3
	1846	2.9		1828	2.3
8 TH	0109	5.0	23 F	0042	5.6
	0746	2.7		0724	2.0
	1400	4.8		1333	5.4
	2025	2.7		1956	2.1
9 F	0235	5.2	24 SA	0206	5.8
	0903	2.4		0841	1.7
	1512	5.1		1448	5.8
	2130	2.3		2107	1.7
10 SA	0333	5.6	25 SU	0313	6.2
	0956	2.0		0944	1.3
	1601	5.6		1547	6.3
	2216	1.9		2205	1.2
11 SU	0418	6.0	26 M	0410	6.6
	1037	1.6		1037	0.9
	1640	5.9		1638	6.7
	2254	1.6		2256	0.9
12 M	0455	6.3	27 TU	0459	6.9
	1113	1.3		1123	0.7
	1714	6.3		1724	6.9
	2329	1.3		2341	0.6
13 TU	0530	6.5	28 W	0545	7.1
	1146	1.1		1206	0.6
	1746	6.5		1807	7.1
				○	
14 W	0002	1.1	29 TH	0024	0.6
	0602	6.7		0627	7.1
	1218	1.0		1247	0.6
	● 1817	6.7		1847	7.1
15 TH	0034	1.0	30 F	0106	0.6
	0634	6.8		0707	7.0
	1250	0.9		1325	0.8
	1848	6.8		1926	7.0

Chart Datum: 3·71 metres below Ordnance Datum (Newlyn). HAT is 7·8 metres above Chart Datum; see 0.20

TIME ZONE (UT)
For Summer Time add ONE hour in **non-shaded areas**

MILFORD HAVEN

LAT 51°42′N LONG 5°03′W

TIMES AND HEIGHTS OF HIGH AND LOW WATERS

Dates in red are SPRINGS
Dates in blue are NEAPS

YEAR **2010**

MAY

Date	Time	m	Date	Time	m
1	0145 0747 SA 1402 2004	0.8 6.7 1.0 6.7	16	0125 0726 SU 1342 1943	1.0 6.7 1.0 6.8
2	0223 0825 SU 1438 2043	1.1 6.4 1.4 6.4	17	0207 0809 M 1424 2027	1.0 6.6 1.1 6.7
3	0301 0903 M 1514 2122	1.5 6.0 1.8 6.0	18	0251 0855 TU 1509 2115	1.2 6.4 1.4 6.5
4	0341 0944 TU 1553 2207	1.8 5.6 2.1 5.7	19	0340 0947 W 1559 2210	1.4 6.1 1.6 6.2
5	0427 1031 W 1641 2300	2.2 5.2 2.5 5.4	20	0437 1046 TH 1659 ◐ 2313	1.6 5.8 1.8 6.0
6	0526 1132 TH 1751 ◑	2.5 5.0 2.7	21	0544 1152 F 1811	1.7 5.7 1.9
7	0010 0641 F 1252 1913	5.2 2.5 4.9 2.7	22	0022 0657 SA 1304 1925	5.9 1.8 5.7 1.9
8	0130 0755 SA 1409 2026	5.2 2.4 5.0 2.5	23	0135 0808 SU 1414 2034	6.0 1.7 5.8 1.7
9	0236 0857 SU 1507 2122	5.4 2.2 5.4 2.2	24	0241 0912 M 1515 2136	6.1 1.5 6.1 1.5
10	0327 0947 M 1552 2209	5.7 1.9 5.7 1.8	25	0341 1008 TU 1610 2230	6.3 1.3 6.3 1.3
11	0410 1029 TU 1632 2249	6.0 1.6 6.1 1.6	26	0434 1058 W 1700 2319	6.5 1.2 6.6 1.1
12	0450 1108 W 1709 2328	6.3 1.3 6.4 1.3	27	0523 1143 TH 1746 ○	6.6 1.1 6.7
13	0528 1146 TH 1746	6.5 1.1 6.6	28	0004 0608 F 1225 1828	1.0 6.6 1.1 6.8
14	0006 0606 F 1224 ● 1823	1.1 6.6 1.0 6.8	29	0047 0650 SA 1305 1909	1.0 6.6 1.1 6.7
15	0045 0645 SA 1302 1902	1.0 6.7 1.0 6.8	30	0128 0730 SU 1343 1948	1.1 6.4 1.3 6.6
			31	0206 0808 M 1420 2026	1.3 6.3 1.4 6.4

JUNE

Date	Time	m	Date	Time	m
1	0244 0845 TU 1455 2104	1.5 6.0 1.7 6.2	16	0248 0851 W 1504 2112	0.8 6.7 1.0 6.8
2	0321 0923 W 1531 2143	1.7 5.8 1.9 5.9	17	0337 0940 TH 1553 2202	1.0 6.5 1.2 6.6
3	0401 1003 TH 1612 2227	1.9 5.5 2.1 5.7	18	0428 1032 F 1646 2256	1.2 6.2 1.4 6.4
4	0446 1049 F 1701 ◑ 2317	2.1 5.3 2.4 5.5	19	0524 1128 SA 1744 ◐ 2355	1.4 6.0 1.7 6.1
5	0540 1144 SA 1802	2.3 5.1 2.5	20	0625 1230 SU 1850	1.7 5.8 1.8
6	0016 0643 SU 1249 1911	5.3 2.4 5.1 2.5	21	0100 0731 M 1338 1959	5.9 1.8 5.7 1.9
7	0123 0748 M 1358 2017	5.3 2.3 5.2 2.4	22	0208 0839 TU 1445 2108	5.9 1.8 5.8 1.8
8	0226 0848 TU 1457 2116	5.5 2.1 5.5 2.1	23	0314 0943 W 1547 2210	5.9 1.8 6.0 1.7
9	0322 0942 W 1548 2209	5.7 1.9 5.8 1.8	24	0416 1038 TH 1643 2304	6.0 1.6 6.2 1.5
10	0411 1031 TH 1634 2257	6.0 1.6 6.2 1.5	25	0509 1127 F 1732 2351	6.1 1.5 6.4 1.4
11	0458 1117 F 1719 2343	6.3 1.3 6.5 1.2	26	0556 1210 SA 1816 ○	6.3 1.4 6.5
12	0544 1202 SA 1804 ●	6.5 1.1 6.7	27	0034 0637 SU 1250 1855	1.3 6.3 1.3 6.6
13	0028 0630 SU 1247 1849	1.0 6.7 1.0 6.9	28	0113 0715 M 1327 1932	1.2 6.3 1.3 6.6
14	0114 0716 M 1332 1935	0.9 6.8 0.9 7.0	29	0149 0751 TU 1401 2007	1.3 6.3 1.4 6.5
15	0201 0803 TU 1417 2023	0.8 6.8 0.9 7.0	30	0224 0824 W 1434 2042	1.3 6.2 1.5 6.4

JULY

Date	Time	m	Date	Time	m
1	0257 0858 TH 1506 2116	1.4 6.0 1.6 6.2	16	0322 0923 F 1537 2144	0.6 6.8 0.8 7.0
2	0331 0932 F 1540 2152	1.6 5.9 1.8 6.0	17	0407 1009 SA 1623 2231	0.9 6.5 1.2 6.6
3	0407 1009 SA 1618 2231	1.8 5.7 2.0 5.8	18	0454 1058 SU 1713 ◐ 2323	1.3 6.1 1.6 6.2
4	0447 1050 SU 1702 ◑ 2317	2.0 5.4 2.2 5.5	19	0547 1154 M 1813	1.8 5.8 1.9
5	0536 1141 M 1759	2.2 5.3 2.4	20	0024 0652 TU 1302 1927	5.7 2.1 5.5 2.2
6	0013 0638 TU 1245 1911	5.4 2.4 5.2 2.5	21	0137 0810 W 1419 2049	5.5 2.3 5.5 2.2
7	0122 0750 W 1359 2027	5.3 2.4 5.3 2.4	22	0255 0925 TH 1533 2159	5.4 2.2 5.7 2.0
8	0234 0900 TH 1507 2134	5.4 2.2 5.6 2.1	23	0406 1026 F 1634 2255	5.6 1.9 6.0 1.8
9	0339 1001 F 1607 2233	5.7 1.8 6.0 1.7	24	0501 1115 SA 1722 2341	5.9 1.7 6.3 1.5
10	0436 1056 SA 1700 2326	6.1 1.5 6.4 1.3	25	0545 1157 SU 1803	6.1 1.5 6.5
11	0528 1146 SU 1750 ●	6.5 1.1 6.8	26	0020 0622 M 1234 ○ 1839	1.3 6.3 1.3 6.6
12	0015 0618 M 1234 1838	0.9 6.8 0.8 7.1	27	0055 0657 TU 1308 1912	1.2 6.4 1.2 6.7
13	0104 0705 TU 1321 1925	0.6 7.0 0.6 7.3	28	0128 0729 W 1339 1944	1.1 6.4 1.2 6.7
14	0151 0752 W 1407 2012	0.5 7.1 0.5 7.3	29	0159 0759 TH 1409 2015	1.1 6.4 1.2 6.6
15	0237 0838 TH 1452 2058	0.5 7.0 0.6 7.2	30	0229 0828 F 1438 2045	1.2 6.3 1.3 6.5
			31	0259 0858 SA 1509 2116	1.4 6.2 1.5 6.3

AUGUST

Date	Time	m	Date	Time	m
1	0330 0930 SU 1541 2150	1.6 6.0 1.8 6.0	16	0421 1025 M 1641 ◐ 2250	1.4 6.2 1.6 6.0
2	0404 1005 M 1617 2229	1.8 5.7 2.1 5.7	17	0509 1118 TU 1738 2348	2.0 5.7 2.2 5.5
3	0443 1048 TU 1703 ◑ 2318	2.1 5.5 2.3 5.4	18	0613 1228 W 1859	2.4 5.3 2.5
4	0536 1147 W 1810	2.4 5.2 2.6	19	0109 0746 TH 1358 2036	5.1 2.6 5.2 2.5
5	0028 0655 TH 1309 1945	5.2 2.5 5.2 2.6	20	0243 0913 F 1522 2151	5.1 2.5 5.5 2.2
6	0156 0826 F 1436 2110	5.2 2.4 5.4 2.2	21	0357 1015 SA 1621 2243	5.5 2.1 5.9 1.9
7	0316 0940 SA 1547 2216	5.6 2.0 5.9 1.7	22	0447 1101 SU 1705 2324	5.8 1.7 6.3 1.5
8	0420 1039 SU 1644 2311	6.1 1.5 6.5 1.1	23	0527 1138 M 1743 2359	6.2 1.5 6.5 1.3
9	0514 1130 M 1736	6.6 1.0 7.0	24	0601 1212 TU 1816 ○	6.4 1.3 6.7
10	0001 0603 TU 1219 ● 1823	0.7 7.0 0.6 7.4	25	0031 0632 W 1243 1847	1.1 6.5 1.1 6.8
11	0049 0649 W 1305 1908	0.3 7.3 0.3 7.6	26	0102 0701 TH 1313 1916	1.0 6.6 1.1 6.8
12	0134 0733 TH 1349 1953	0.2 7.4 0.2 7.6	27	0130 0730 F 1341 1945	1.0 6.6 1.1 6.8
13	0217 0816 F 1431 2036	0.2 7.3 0.4 7.5	28	0159 0757 SA 1409 2014	1.1 6.6 1.2 6.6
14	0258 0858 SA 1513 2119	0.5 7.1 0.7 7.1	29	0227 0825 SU 1438 2043	1.2 6.4 1.4 6.4
15	0339 0940 SU 1555 2202	0.9 6.7 1.1 6.6	30	0257 0855 M 1509 2114	1.5 6.2 1.6 6.2
			31	0328 0928 TU 1543 2151	1.7 6.0 2.0 5.8

Chart Datum: 3·71 metres below Ordnance Datum (Newlyn). HAT is 7·8 metres above Chart Datum; see 0.20

TIME ZONE (UT)
For Summer Time add ONE hour in **non-shaded areas**

MILFORD HAVEN LAT 51°42′N LONG 5°03′W

TIMES AND HEIGHTS OF HIGH AND LOW WATERS

Dates in red are SPRINGS
Dates in blue are NEAPS

YEAR **2010**

SEPTEMBER

Day	Time	m	Day	Time	m
1 W ◑	0404 1009 1626 2239	2.1 5.7 2.3 5.5	16 TH	0537 1156 1832	2.7 5.2 2.7
2 TH	0455 1107 1732 2351	2.4 5.3 2.6 5.2	17 F	0041 0719 1334 2017	4.9 2.9 5.1 2.7
3 F	0615 1234 1919	2.7 5.2 2.6	18 SA	0223 0852 1459 2130	5.0 2.6 5.4 2.4
4 SA	0130 0803 1414 2053	5.1 2.5 5.4 2.2	19 SU	0335 0952 1556 2219	5.4 2.2 5.9 1.9
5 SU	0300 0922 1530 2200	5.6 2.0 6.0 1.6	20 M	0422 1036 1638 2257	5.8 1.8 6.3 1.6
6 M	0404 1022 1627 2254	6.2 1.4 6.6 1.0	21 TU	0500 1112 1714 2331	6.2 1.5 6.6 1.3
7 TU	0457 1112 1717 2342	6.7 0.9 7.2 0.5	22 W	0532 1144 1747	6.4 1.3 6.7
8 W ●	0544 1159 1803	7.2 0.5 7.6	23 TH ○	0002 0602 1215 1817	1.1 6.6 1.1 6.8
9 TH	0028 0627 1244 1847	0.2 7.5 0.2 7.8	24 F	0032 0631 1245 1846	1.1 6.7 1.1 6.9
10 F	0111 0710 1326 1929	0.1 7.6 0.2 7.7	25 SA	0101 0659 1313 1915	1.0 6.8 1.1 6.9
11 SA	0152 0751 1407 2011	0.2 7.4 0.3 7.5	26 SU	0130 0728 1343 1945	1.1 6.7 1.2 6.7
12 SU	0232 0831 1448 2052	0.5 7.1 0.7 7.0	27 M	0159 0757 1413 2015	1.2 6.6 1.3 6.6
13 M	0310 0912 1528 2133	1.0 6.7 1.2 6.5	28 TU	0229 0828 1445 2048	1.4 6.4 1.6 6.3
14 TU	0350 0955 1612 2219	1.6 6.2 1.8 5.8	29 W	0302 0903 1521 2127	1.7 6.2 1.9 5.9
15 W ◐	0434 1045 1707 2315	2.2 5.7 2.4 5.3	30 TH	0341 0946 1608 2219	2.1 5.8 2.3 5.5

OCTOBER

Day	Time	m	Day	Time	m
1 F ◑	0435 1047 1718 2335	2.4 5.5 2.6 5.2	16 SA	0003 0634 1252 1932	4.9 2.9 5.2 2.8
2 SA	0557 1216 1904	2.7 5.3 2.5	17 SU	0139 0809 1415 2048	5.0 2.8 5.4 2.5
3 SU	0113 0744 1354 2034	5.2 2.5 5.6 2.1	18 M	0253 0913 1515 2140	5.3 2.4 5.7 2.1
4 M	0240 0901 1508 2139	5.7 2.0 6.1 1.5	19 TU	0344 0959 1601 2221	5.7 2.1 6.1 1.8
5 TU	0343 1000 1605 2232	6.3 1.4 6.7 1.0	20 W	0424 1038 1639 2257	6.1 1.7 6.4 1.5
6 W	0434 1050 1654 2320	6.8 0.9 7.2 0.6	21 TH	0458 1112 1714 2330	6.4 1.5 6.6 1.3
7 TH ●	0520 1137 1740	7.2 0.5 7.5	22 F	0530 1145 1746	6.6 1.3 6.8
8 F	0004 0603 1221 1823	0.4 7.5 0.3 7.7	23 SA ○	0001 0601 1217 1817	1.2 6.7 1.2 6.8
9 SA	0046 0645 1303 1906	0.3 7.5 0.4 7.6	24 SU	0033 0631 1249 1849	1.1 6.8 1.2 6.8
10 SU	0127 0726 1345 1947	0.5 7.4 0.6 7.3	25 M	0104 0703 1321 1922	1.1 6.8 1.2 6.8
11 M	0206 0807 1425 2028	0.8 7.1 0.9 6.8	26 TU	0137 0736 1355 1957	1.2 6.8 1.3 6.6
12 TU	0244 0847 1506 2109	1.3 6.7 1.4 6.3	27 W	0211 0811 1432 2035	1.4 6.6 1.6 6.3
13 W	0323 0930 1549 2153	1.8 6.2 1.9 5.8	28 TH	0249 0851 1514 2119	1.7 6.3 1.8 6.0
14 TH ◐	0406 1019 1642 2247	2.3 5.7 2.4 5.3	29 F	0333 0940 1606 2215	2.0 6.0 2.1 5.7
15 F	0504 1123 1758	2.7 5.3 2.8	30 SA ◑	0430 1043 1715 2328	2.3 5.8 2.3 5.5
			31 SU	0547 1203 1845	2.5 5.6 2.3

NOVEMBER

Day	Time	m	Day	Time	m
1 M	0052 0718 1327 2006	5.5 2.3 5.8 2.0	16 TU	0150 0811 1419 2044	5.1 2.7 5.5 2.4
2 TU	0211 0832 1439 2111	5.8 2.0 6.2 1.6	17 W	0251 0910 1513 2134	5.4 2.4 5.8 2.1
3 W	0314 0933 1538 2206	6.2 1.5 6.7 1.2	18 TH	0339 0957 1558 2217	5.8 2.1 6.1 1.8
4 TH	0408 1026 1630 2256	6.7 1.1 7.0 0.9	19 F	0420 1038 1638 2255	6.1 1.8 6.3 1.6
5 F	0456 1115 1718 2341	7.0 0.8 7.2 0.7	20 SA	0457 1115 1715 2332	6.4 1.6 6.5 1.4
6 SA ●	0541 1200 1803	7.2 0.7 7.3	21 SU ○	0533 1152 1752	6.6 1.4 6.7
7 SU	0024 0624 1244 1846	0.7 7.3 0.7 7.2	22 M	0008 0608 1229 1829	1.3 6.8 1.3 6.8
8 M	0105 0706 1326 1928	0.8 7.2 0.9 7.0	23 TU	0045 0645 1307 1907	1.2 6.9 1.2 6.8
9 TU	0145 0748 1407 2009	1.1 7.0 1.1 6.7	24 W	0123 0723 1346 1948	1.2 6.9 1.2 6.7
10 W	0224 0829 1448 2050	1.4 6.7 1.5 6.3	25 TH	0202 0805 1428 2031	1.3 6.8 1.3 6.5
11 TH	0303 0911 1530 2132	1.8 6.3 1.9 5.8	26 F	0244 0849 1514 2118	1.5 6.6 1.5 6.3
12 F	0344 0956 1617 2219	2.2 5.9 2.3 5.5	27 SA	0331 0940 1605 2212	1.7 6.4 1.7 6.0
13 SA ◐	0432 1048 1714 2317	2.5 5.6 2.6 5.2	28 SU ◑	0425 1037 1706 2314	1.9 6.2 1.9 5.8
14 SU	0537 1154 1826	2.8 5.4 2.7	29 M	0530 1143 1817	2.1 6.0 2.0
15 M	0032 0657 1311 1940	5.0 2.8 5.3 2.6	30 TU	0023 0644 1255 1930	5.7 2.1 6.0 2.0

DECEMBER

Day	Time	m	Day	Time	m
1 W	0136 0758 1405 2039	5.8 2.0 6.1 1.8	16 TH	0140 0801 1412 2035	5.2 2.7 5.4 2.4
2 TH	0243 0905 1510 2140	6.1 1.8 6.3 1.6	17 F	0245 0906 1511 2133	5.4 2.4 5.6 2.2
3 F	0342 1004 1608 2234	6.4 1.5 6.6 1.4	18 SA	0339 1001 1602 2222	5.7 2.1 5.9 1.9
4 SA	0436 1057 1701 2323	6.6 1.3 6.7 1.2	19 SU	0426 1048 1648 2306	6.1 1.8 6.2 1.6
5 SU ●	0525 1145 1749	6.9 1.1 6.8	20 M	0509 1131 1732 2348	6.4 1.5 6.5 1.3
6 M	0008 0611 1231 1834	1.1 7.0 1.0 6.8	21 TU ○	0551 1214 1815	6.7 1.3 6.7
7 TU	0050 0654 1313 1916	1.1 7.0 1.1 6.7	22 W	0030 0633 1257 1857	1.1 6.9 1.1 6.9
8 W	0130 0735 1354 1955	1.2 6.9 1.2 6.6	23 TH	0113 0716 1340 1941	1.0 7.1 0.9 6.9
9 TH	0208 0814 1433 2034	1.4 6.7 1.4 6.3	24 F	0155 0800 1424 2026	1.0 7.1 0.9 6.8
10 F	0245 0852 1510 2111	1.6 6.5 1.7 6.1	25 SA	0239 0845 1509 2112	1.0 7.0 1.0 6.7
11 SA	0321 0931 1549 2150	1.9 6.2 1.9 5.8	26 SU	0324 0932 1555 2159	1.2 6.9 1.2 6.4
12 SU	0359 1012 1630 2233	2.2 5.9 2.2 5.5	27 M	0412 1022 1646 2251	1.4 6.6 1.5 6.2
13 M ◐	0443 1059 1720 2323	2.4 5.7 2.4 5.3	28 TU ◑	0505 1117 1743 2350	1.7 6.3 1.8 5.9
14 TU	0540 1155 1821	2.6 5.4 2.6	29 W	0607 1219 1850	2.0 6.0 2.0
15 W	0026 0649 1302 1929	5.1 2.7 5.3 2.6	30 TH	0057 0720 1331 2004	5.7 2.1 5.9 2.1
			31 F	0211 0837 1444 2117	5.7 2.1 5.9 2.0

Chart Datum: 3·71 metres below Ordnance Datum (Newlyn). HAT is 7·8 metres above Chart Datum; see 0.20

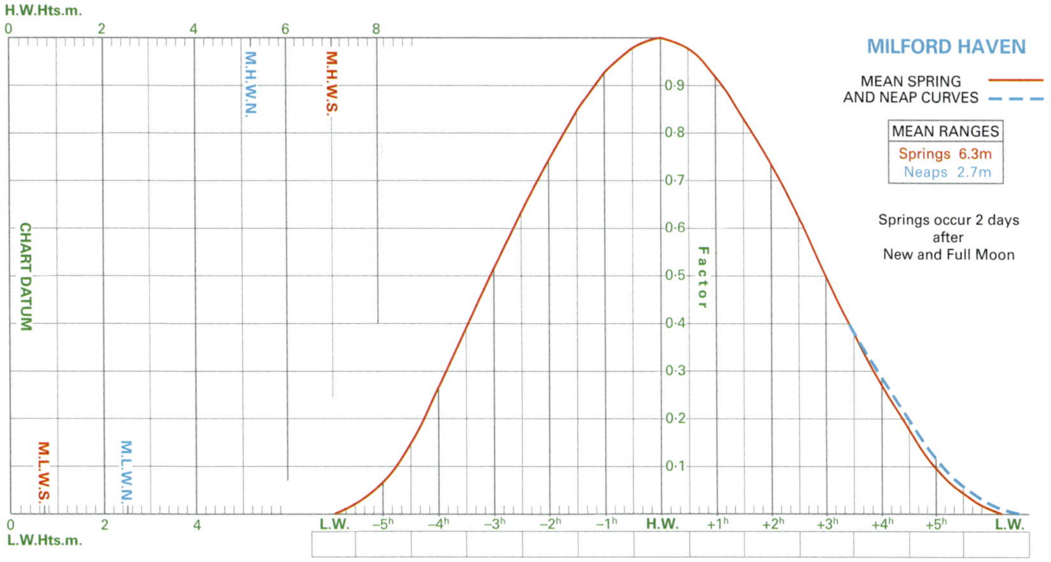

MILFORD HAVEN TO MUMBLES HEAD

(AC 1179, 1076) Milford Haven is a long natural, all-weather harbour with marinas beyond the oil terminals. Beware Turbot Bank (WCM lt buoy) 3M S of the entrance. Crow Rk (dries 5·5m) is 5ca SSE of Linney Hd, and The Toes are dangerous submerged rocks close W and SE of Crow Rock. There is a passage inshore of these dangers. There are overfalls on St Gowan Shoals which extend 4M SW of St Govan's Hd, and the sea breaks on the shallow patches in bad weather. There are firing areas from Linney Hd to Carmarthen Bay.

Caldey Is (lit) lies S of Tenby. Off its NW pt is St Margaret's Is connected by a rocky reef. Caldey Sound, between St Margaret's Is and Giltar Pt (AC 1482), is buoyed, but beware Eel Spit near W end of Caldey Is where there can be a nasty sea with wind against tide, and Woolhouse Rocks (dry 3·6m) 1ca NE of Caldey Is. Saundersfoot harbour (dries) is 2M N of Tenby, with an anchorage well sheltered from N and W but subject to swell. Streams are weak here. Carmarthen Bay has no offshore dangers for yachts, other than the extensive drying sands at head of the bay and on its E side off Burry Inlet.

S of Worms Head, Helwick Sands (buoyed at each end) extend 7M W from Port Eynon Pt; least depth of 1·3m is near their W end. Stream sets NE/SW across the sands. There is a narrow channel inshore, close to Port Eynon Pt.

▶ *Between here and Mumbles Hd the stream runs roughly along coast, sp rates 3kn off headlands, but there are eddies in Port Eynon Bay and Oxwich Bay (both yacht anchorages), and overfalls SSE of Oxwich Pt.* ◀

FIRING RANGES – LINNEY HEAD TO BURRY INLET

For daily info on all range firing times call *Milford Haven CG* Ch 16/67 or ☎ 01646 690909.

Castlemartin Range Danger Area extends 12M WNW from Linney Hd, thence in an anti-clockwise arc to a point 12M S of St Govan's Hd. The exact Danger Area operative on any one day depends on the ranges/ammunition used; it is primarily a tank range. When firing is in progress R flags are flown (Fl R lts at night) along the coast from Freshwater West to Linney Head to St Govan's Head. Yachts are requested to keep clear of ranges when active.

Firing takes place on weekdays 0900–1630, exceptionally to 1700. Night firing takes place on Mon to Thurs, up to 2359, depending on the hours of darkness. In Jan only small arms are usually fired and the danger area is reduced.

Days/times of firing are published locally and can be obtained by VHF from *Castlemartin Range* Ch 16 or ☎ 01646 662367 (H24 answering service); Range safety launches Ch 16 or 12; and Milford Haven CG Ch 16. Also from the Range Office ☎ (01646) 662287 or Warren Tower 01646 662336.

Manorbier Range (further E) covers a sector arc radius 12M centred on Old Castle Head; E/W extent is approximately between St Govan's Hd and Caldey Is (see AC Q6402). It is usually active Mon-Fri 0900-1700LT, occasionally Sat and Sun, and is primarily a surface to air missile range, but active areas depend on the weapons in use on any given day. On firing days warnings are broadcast on Ch 16, 73 at 0830, 1430 and on completion; red flags are flown either side of Old Castle Hd. Yachts on passage should either keep 12M offshore or transit close inshore via Stackpole Hd, Trewent Pt, Priest's Nose and Old Castle Hd. Firing days/times are available from local HMs and YCs. For further info call: *Manorbier Range Control* Ch 16, 73 (also manned by Range safety launches); *Milford Haven CG* Ch 16; or Range Control ☎ (01834) 871282 ext 209, 📠 871283.

Penally Range (further E at Giltar Pt) is for small arms only and seldom interferes with passage through Caldey Sound. Info ☎ (01834) 843522.

Pendine Range (between Tenby and Burry Inlet) is a MOD range for testing explosive devices. It is usually possible to steer the rhumb line course from Tenby to Worms Hd without interference. Info ☎ (01994) 453243. Broadcasts on VHF Ch 16, 73 at 0900 and 1400LT. Range active 0800-1615.

Pembrey Range (approx 5M NW of Burry Inlet) is used for bombing practice by the RAF. Info ☎ (01554) 891224.

4.13 TENBY

Pembrokeshire **51·40'·42N 04°41'·93W**

CHARTS AC 5620, 1179, 1076, 1482; Imray C60; Stanfords 14.

TIDES –0510 Dover; ML 4·5; Duration 0610

Standard Port MILFORD HAVEN (⟵)

Times				Height (metres)			
High Water		Low Water		MHWS	MHWN	MLWN	MLWS
0100	0800	0100	0700	7·0	5·2	2·5	0·7
1300	2000	1300	1900				
Differences TENBY							
–0015	–0010	–0015	–0020	+1·4	+1·1	+0·5	+0·2
STACKPOLE QUAY (7M W of Caldey Island)							
–0005	+0025	–0010	–0010	+0·9	+0·7	+0·2	+0·3

SHELTER Good, but hbr dries up to 5m; access HW±2½. Sheltered ⚓s, depending on wind direction, to NE in Tenby Roads, in Lydstep Haven (2·5M SW), and around Caldey Is as follows: Priory Bay to the N but shallow, Jone's Bay (NE), Drinkim Bay (E) or Sandtop Bay (W).

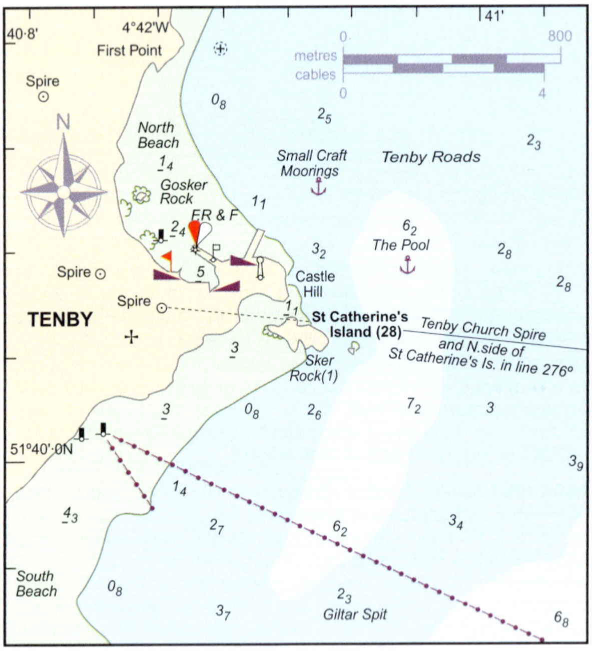

NAVIGATION WPT 51°40'·02N 04°38'·08W, 279°/2·2M to monument on Castle Hill. The ⊕ WPT (off chartlet) is 2ca W of DZ2 SPM lit buoy. Beware Woolhouse Rks (3·6m) 1·5M SExE of the Hbr, marked by lit SCM buoy; and Sker Rk (1m high) closer in off St Catherine's Island (28m). From the W, Caldey Sound is navigable with care between Eel Pt SHM and Giltar Spit PHM lit buoys. Approaching Tenby Roads, keep outside the line of mooring buoys. For adjacent Firing ranges, see overleaf. Caldey Island is private and no landing without permission from the Abbot.

LIGHTS AND MARKS See 4.3 and chartlet. Church spire transit N side of St Catherine's Is 276°. FR 7m 7M on pier hd. Inside hbr, FW 6m 1M marks landing steps PHM beacon (unlit) marks outcrop from Gosker Rk on beach close N of hbr ent. Hbr is floodlit.

R/T Ch 16, 80 (listening during HO).

TELEPHONE (Code 01834) HM ☎ 842717 (end May-end Sept), Mobile 07977 609947; MRCC (01646) 690909; Marinecall 09068 969649; Police (01437) 763355 ; Dr 844161; Ⓗ 842040.

FACILITIES **Hbr** AB, Slip (up to 4·2m). **Town** P & D (cans), ▣, CH, 🛒, R, Bar, Gas, ✉, Ⓑ, ⇌, ✈ (Swansea; and a small airfield at Haverfordwest).

OTHER ADJACENT HARBOURS (See AC *5620*)

SAUNDERSFOOT, Pembrokeshire, **51°42'·60N 04°41'·76W**. AC 1179, 1076, 1482. HW –0510 on Dover; ML 4·4m; Duration 0605. See 4.13. A half-tide hbr with good shelter, but there may be a surge in prolonged E winds. On appr, beware buoys marking restricted area (power boats, etc) between Coppett Hall Pt and Perry's Pt. AB may be available (see HM), or moorings in the middle. Pier hd lt Fl R 5s 6m 7M on stone cupola. VHF: HM 11 16. HM ☎ (01834) 812094/(Home 831389). Facilities: 6 AB, CH, FW (on SW wall), Slip, P & D (cans), ME, BH. **Town** 🛒, R, Bar, ✉, Ⓑ, ⇌ (Tenby/Saundersfoot).

CARMARTHEN, Carmarthenshire, **51°46'·27N 04°22'·53W**. AC 1179, 1076. HW –0455 on Dover. See 4.14. R Towy & Taf dry; access HW±2. Beware Carmarthen Bar in S winds F4 and over with strong sp streams. Nav info is available from Carmarthen Bar Navigation Committee ☎ (01267) 231250 or YC's. Appr on N'ly hdg toward Wharley Pt, leaving DZ8 & 9 buoys 5ca to stbd. Chan shifts frequently and is unmarked so local knowledge reqd unless conditions ideal. ⚓ in mid-stream or 🅐s at R Towy YC off Ferryside (7M below Carmarthen) or R Towey Boat Club 1M N on W bank. Access for both HW±2. 4 power lines cross in last 2·5M before Carmarthen, clearance 7·4m. **R Towy YC** ☎ (01267) 238356, M, FW, Bar. **R Towy BC** ☎ (01267) 238316. **Town** Ⓑ, Bar, Gas, ✉, 🛒, ⇌, ✈ (Cardiff).

MUMBLES HEAD TO CARDIFF

(AC 1165, 1182) Off Mumbles Hd (Lt, fog sig) beware Mixon Shoal (dries 0·3m), marked by PHM buoy. In good conditions pass N of shoal, 1ca off Mumbles Hd. Anch N of Mumbles Hd, good holding but exposed to swell. At W side of Swansea Bay, Green Grounds, rky shoals, lie in appr's to Swansea.

Scarweather Sands, much of which dry (up to 3·3m) with seas breaking heavily, extend 7M W from Porthcawl (4.15) and are well buoyed (AC 1161). There is a chan between the sands and coast to E, but beware Hugo Bank (dries 2·6m) and Kenfig Patches (0·5m) with o'falls up to 7ca offshore between Sker Pt and Porthcawl.

Nash Sands extend 7·5M WNW from Nash Pt. Depths vary and are least at inshore end (dries 3m), but Nash Passage, 1ca wide, runs close inshore between E Nash ECM buoy and ledge off Nash Pt. ► *On E-going stream there are heavy overfalls off Nash Pt and at W end of Nash Sands. Between Nash Pt and Breaksea Pt the E-going stream begins at HW Avonmouth +0535, and the W-going at HW Avonmouth –0035, sp rates 3kn. Off Breaksea Pt there may be overfalls.* ◄

From Rhoose Pt to Lavernock Pt the coast is fringed with foul ground. Lavernock Spit extends 1·75M S of Lavernock Pt, and E of the spit is main chan to Cardiff; the other side of the chan being Cardiff Grounds, a bank drying 5·4m which lies parallel with the shore and about 1·5M from it.

4.14 BURRY INLET

Carmarthenshire **51°40'·52N 04°14'·93W** (Burry Port) ❁❁◊◊✿

CHARTS AC 5620, 5608 1179, 1076, 1167; Imray C59, C60; Stanfords 14.

TIDES –0500 Dover; ML 4·7; Duration 0555

Standard Port MILFORD HAVEN (⟵)

Times				Height (metres)			
High Water		Low Water		MHWS	MHWN	MLWN	MLWS
0100	0800	0100	0700	7·0	5·2	2·5	0·7
1300	2000	1300	1900				
Differences BURRY PORT							
+0003	+0003	+0007	+0007	+1·6	+1·4	+0·5	+0·4
LLANELLI							
–0003	–0003	+0150	+0020	+0·8	+0·6	No data	
FERRYSIDE							
0000	–0010	+0220	0000	–0·3	–0·7	–1·7	–0·6
CARMARTHEN							
+0010	0000	Dries		–4·4	–4·8	Dries	

SHELTER Good in Burry Port via lock with flapgate controlled by R/G lts. Access HW±2 over sill depth 2m. Pontoons for visitors. Sp tides run hard. Note: If bad weather precludes access, see 4.13 for ⚓s around Caldey Island, especially in W'lies. Call Hbr Office (01554 835691 mob 07817 395710). Visitors welcome but few facilities.

NAVIGATION WPT 51°36'·37N 04°24'·38W, 087°/3·3M to Burry Holms, thence 4·5M to Burry Port.

Carmarthen Bar, extending from the R Towy entrance SE to Burry Holms, should not be attempted in W winds >F5 nor at night. Best entry is close NW of Burry Holms at HW–2; thence track 018° with Worms Hd on a transit astern (198°) between Burry Holms and Limekiln Pt. When Whiteford lighthouse (disused) bears about 082°, alter to approx 050° into deeper water and steer to leave the Barrel Post at least 1½ ca to port as a large sand bank has formed to E of it.

Near approaches to the harbour are marked by a buoyed channel (3.2m) access HW±2. Barrel Post now marks W end of new sandbank, only to be used as reference point – do not round close to. E end of this bank marked by unlit buoy PHM. Approach from here on NW'ly heading, channel marked by 3 pairs unlit buoys PHMs & SHMs beyond which 2 unlit PHMs in near appr to lock/flapgate. Chan is liable to shift. Before appr, check Firing Range activity (contact HM or Pendine Range Control, see above).

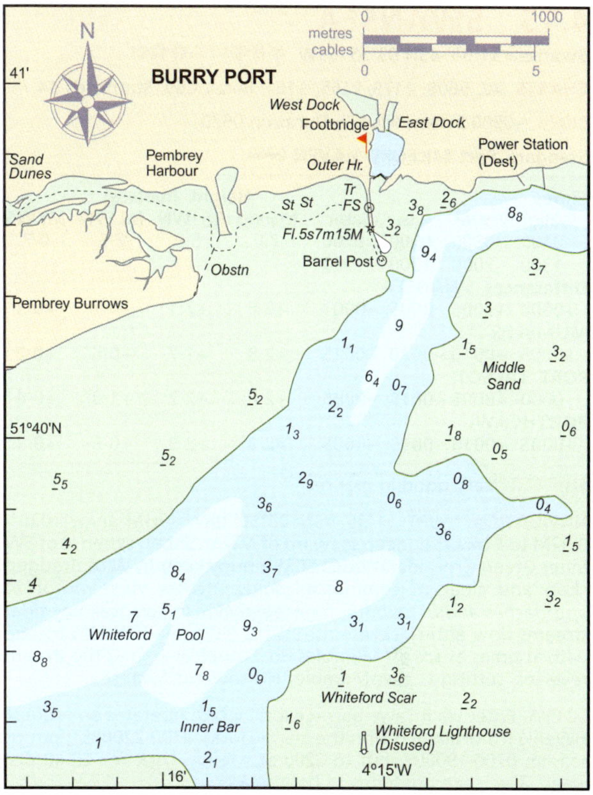

LIGHTS AND MARKS Whiteford lt ho is conspic, but no longer lit. On head of W bkwtr is Barrel post; 1½ca N is conspic old lt ho (W tr, R top) Fl 5s 7m 15M, and flagstaff.

R/T Ch M (Hbr Office), 18.

TELEPHONE (Code 01554); HM 835691, mob 07817 395710; MRCC (01792) 366534; Pendine Range (01994) 453243 Ext 240; Marinecall 09068 969649; Police 0845 3302000; Dr 832240.

FACILITIES Slip, M, L, CH; **E Pier** (small craft only): Slip; **Burry Port YC** Bar; **Services:** D, ME, El, ⚒, C, Gas. **Town** P, D, CH, 🛒, R, Bar, ✉, Ⓑ, ⇌, ✈ (Cardiff).

SEVERN ESTUARY

(AC 1176, 1166) Near the centre of Bristol Chan, either side of the buoyed fairway, are the islands of Flat Holm (Lt, fog sig) and Steep Holm. 7M SW of Flat Holm lies Culver Sand (0·9m), 3M in length, with W and ECM bys. Monkstone Rk (Lt, dries) is 2M NW of the buoyed chan to Avonmouth and Bristol. Extensive drying banks cover the N shore of the estuary, beyond Newport and the Severn bridges (AC 1176).

▶ *The range of tide in the Bristol Chan is exceptionally large, 12·2m sp and 6·0m np, and tidal streams are very powerful, particularly above Avonmouth. Between Flat Holm and Steep Holm the E-going stream begins at HW Avonmouth – 0610, sp 3kn, and the W-going at HW Avonmouth + 0015, sp 4kn.* ◀

The ent to the R Avon is just to the S of Avonmouth S Pier Hd. Bristol City Docks lie some 6M up-river. Approach the ent via King Road and the Newcombe and Cockburn lt buoys and thence via the Swash chan into the Avon. The ent dries at LW but the river is navigable at about half tide. ▶ *Tidal streams are strong in the approaches to Avonmouth, up to **5kn at sp**. The tide is also strong in the R. Avon which is best entered no earlier than HW Avonmouth – 0200.* ◀

From Avonmouth it is 16M to Sharpness which yachts should aim to reach at about HW Avonmouth. ▶ ***Spring streams can run 8kn at the Shoots, and 6kn at the Severn bridges**. At the Shoots the flood begins at HW Avonmouth –0430 and the ebb at HW Avonmouth + 0045. The Severn Bore can usually be seen if Avonmouth range is 13·5m or more.* ◀

4.15 SWANSEA

Swansea 51°36'·43N 03°55'·67W ❀❀❀◊◊◊✿✿✿

CHARTS AC 5608, 1179, 1165, 1161; Imray C59; Stanfords 14.

TIDES –0500 Dover; ML 5·2; Duration 0620

Standard Port MILFORD HAVEN (⟵)

Times				Height (metres)			
High Water		Low Water		MHWS	MHWN	MLWN	MLWS
0100	0800	0100	0700	7·0	5·2	2·5	0·7
1300	2000	1300	1900				
Differences SWANSEA							
+0004	+0006	–0006	–0003	+2·6	+2·1	+0·7	+0·3
MUMBLES							
+0005	+0010	–0020	–0015	+2·3	+1·7	+0·6	+0·2
PORT TALBOT							
0000	+0005	–0010	–0005	+2·8	+2·2	+1·0	+0·4
PORTHCAWL							
+0005	+0010	–0010	–0005	+2·9	+2·3	+0·8	+0·3

SHELTER Very good in marina.

NAVIGATION WPT 51°35´·53N 03°56´·08W (SHM buoy) 020°/0·92M to E bkwtr lt. Keep seaward of Mixon Shoal. When N of SW Inner Green Grounds (SWIGG) SCM lt buoy keep to W of dredged chan and clear of commercial ships. *Yachts must motor in approaches and in harbour*, max speed 4kn. In Swansea Bay tidal streams flow anti-clockwise for 9½ hrs (Swansea HW –3½ to +6), with at times a race off Mumbles Hd. From HW–6 to –3 the stream reverses, setting N past Mumbles Hd towards Swansea.

LOCKS Enter via R Tawe barrage lock, which operates on request HW±4½ (co-ordinated with the marina lock), 0700-2200BST; out of season, 0700-1900UT, but to 2200 at w/ends. Lock fee £2.40 per week. There are pontoons in both locks.

Yachts usually exit Tawe barrage lock at H+00, and enter at H+30. Locks are closed when ht of tide falls to 1·5m above CD, usually at MLWS. At sp, do not enter river until LW+1½. Two large Or holding buoys below barrage in mid-stream; also, at W side of barrage lock, a landing pontoon (dries, foul ground).

LIGHTS AND MARKS See 4.3 and chartlet. Mumbles Hd, Fl (4) 20s35m16M, is 3M SSW of hbr ent. A conspic TV mast (R lts) NNE of hbr is almost aligned with the fairway. Ldg lts 020° mark E side of chan dredged 3m. When N of Swansea Middle West (QR) and Swansea Middle East (QG) chan buoys stay inside dredged chan. Barrage lock lit by 2FR/FG (vert) to seaward.

Port Traffic sigs are conspic at W side of ent to King's Dock; there are 9 lts, 🔴 or 🟢, arranged in a 3 x 3 frame. Yachts arriving must obey the middle lt in left column:

- 🔴 = Do not enter the river; hold SW of W Pier.
- 🟢 = Yachts may enter the river, keeping to mid-chan, then to W of holding buoys.

Lock Master will advise on tfc movements Ch 18.
Lock sigs for barrage and marina locks alike are:

- 🔴🔴 = Lock closed. Do not proceed
- 🔴 = Wait
- 🟢 = Enter with caution
- 🔴🟢 = Free flow operating; proceed with caution

R/T Barrage, *Tawe Lock* Ch 18. *Swansea Marina* Ch **80**. For commercial docks call *Swansea Docks Radio* VHF Ch14 (H24).

TELEPHONE (Code 01792) HM 653787; Barrage 456014; MRCC 366534; Police 456999; Marinecall 09068 969649; Ⓗ 205666; Dr 653452; DVLA (for SSR) 783355.

FACILITIES **Swansea Marina** (340+50 Ⓥ) ☎ 470310, £1·85, Lock width 9m; D (no P), C (1 ton), BH (25 ton), ⚓, Gas, Gaz, Ice, CH, ME, ACA, SM, El, Ⓔ, ⚒, ▣, ♿, Bar, R.

Swansea Yacht & Sub Aqua Club (SY & SAC) ☎ 654863, No visitors, M, L, FW, C (5 ton static), R, Bar. **City** 🛒, R, Bar, ✉, Ⓑ, ⇌, ✈.

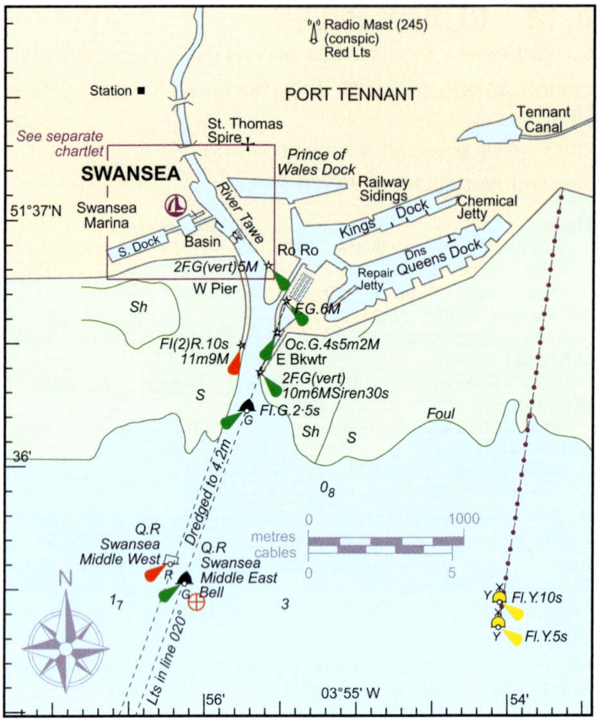

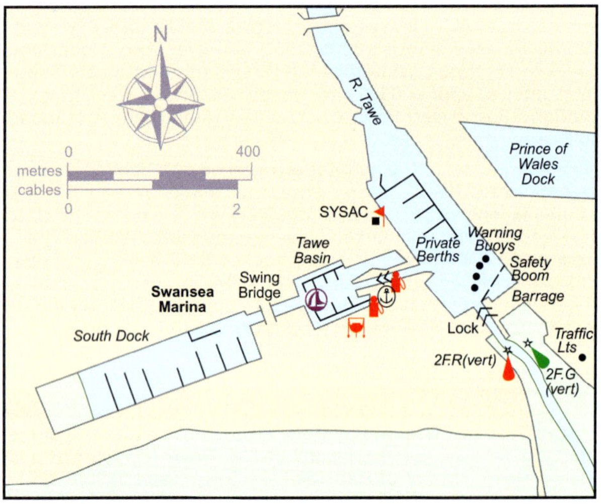

ADJACENT HARBOURS AND ANCHORAGES

Mumbles, 51°34'·2N 03°58'·2W. Good ⚓ in W'lies 5ca N of Mumbles Hd lt ho. **Bristol Chan YC** ☎ (01792) 366000, Slip, M; **Mumbles YC** ☎ 369321, Slip, M, L, FW, C (hire).

R Neath, 51°37'·88N 03°49'·97W. Ent over bar HW±2½ via 1·5M chan, marked/lit training wall to stbd. Tfc info from *Neath Pilot* VHF Ch 77, if on stn. **Monkstone Marina**, W bank just S of bridge, dries 4m: AB, 2 Y ⚓s, D, FW, Slip, BH (15 ton), R, Bar, Visitors welcome. **Monkstone C & SC**, ☎ (01792) 812229; VHF Ch M (occas).

PORTHCAWL, Bridgend, **51°28´·48N 03°42´·02W**. AC 1165, 1169. HW –0500 on Dover; ML 5·3m. See 4.15. A tiny drying hbr (access HW±2) protected by bkwtr running SE from Porthcawl Pt. Beware rk ledge (dries) W of bkwtr. Porthcawl lt ho, F WRG (see 4.3) in line 094° with St Hilary radio mast (QR & FR) leads through Shord chan. Tidal streams can reach 6kn at sp off end of bkwtr. 3 ⚓s or ⚓ approx 3ca SSE of lt ho. HM ☎ (01656) 782756. Facilities: **Porthcawl Hbr B C** ☎ 782342. **Town** P & D (cans), CH, 🛒, R, Bar, ✉, Ⓑ, ⇌ (Bridgend), ✈ (Cardiff).

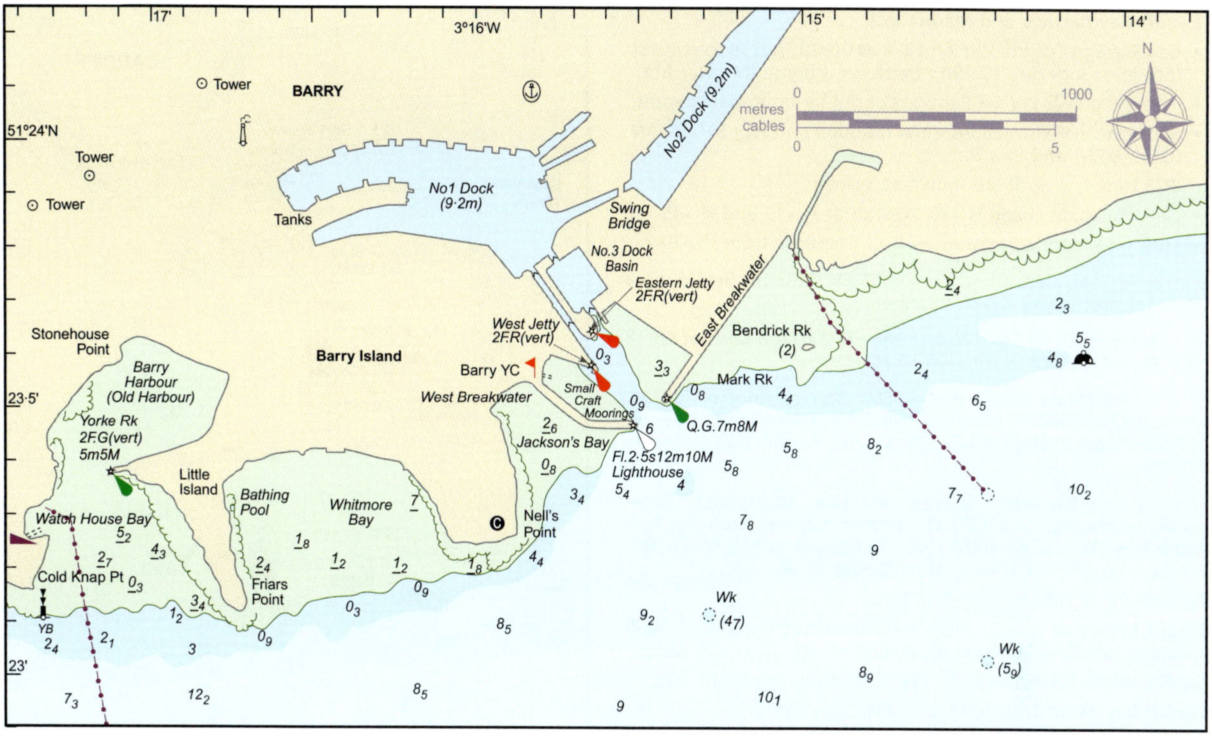

4.16 BARRY

Vale of Glamorgan **51°23'·48N 03°15'·45W**

CHARTS AC 5608, 1179, 1152, 1182; Imray C59; Stanfords 14.

TIDES –0423 Dover; ML 6·1; Duration 0630

Standard Port BRISTOL (AVONMOUTH) (⟶)

Times				Height (metres)			
High Water		Low Water		MHWS	MHWN	MLWN	MLWS
0600	1100	0300	0800	13·2	9·8	3·8	1·0
1800	2300	1500	2000				
Differences BARRY							
–0025	–0025	–0130	–0045	–1·6	–1·0	–0·2	0·0
FLAT HOLM							
–0015	–0015	–0035	–0035	–1·4	–1·0	–0·5	0·0
STEEP HOLM							
–0020	–0020	–0040	–0040	–1·7	–1·1	–0·5	–0·4

SHELTER Good, but in strong E/SE winds avoid Barry; No 1 Dock is not available for pleasure craft. Access H24 to the Outer hbr. No AB or ⚓, but Barry YC administers all moorings and welcomes visitors. Temporary mooring may be available from Bristol Pilots on request.

NAVIGATION WPT 51°23´·03N 03°15´·08W, 332°/0·53M to ent. Beware heavy commercial traffic. Approaching from E keep well out from the shore. Strong tidal stream across ent.

LIGHTS AND MARKS Welsh Water Barry West PHM buoy, Fl R 5s, and Merkur PHM buoy, Fl R 2·5s, lie respectively 217°/1·5M and 191°/1·65M from hbr ent. W bkwtr Fl 2·5s 10M. E bkwtr QG 8M.

R/T *Barry Radio* VHF Ch **11** 10 16 (HW–4 to HW+3); tidal info on request. *Bristol Pilot* via Ch 16 may advise on vacant moorings.

TELEPHONE HM 0870 609 6699; MRCC (01792) 366534; Marinecall 09068 969649; Police 01446 734451; Dr 01446 739543.

FACILITIES **Barry YC** (130) ☎ 735511, access HW±3½, Slip, M, Bar, FW, D, Gas, ME, El, ⚒, SM.
Town P (cans, 1M away), CH, 🛒, R, Bar, ✉, Ⓑ, ⇌, ✈ (Cardiff).

4.17 CARDIFF (PENARTH)

Vale of Glamorgan **51°26'·74N 03°09'·92W** (marina)

CHARTS AC 5608, 1179, 1176, 1182; Imray C59; Stanfords 14.

TIDES –0425 Dover; ML 6·4; Duration 0610

Standard Port BRISTOL (AVONMOUTH) (⟶)

Times				Height (metres)			
High Water		Low Water		MHWS	MHWN	MLWN	MLWS
0600	1100	0300	0800	13·2	9·8	3·8	1·0
1800	2300	1500	2000				
Differences CARDIFF							
–0015	–0015	–0100	–0030	–1·0	–0·5	0·0	0·0
NEWPORT							
–0020	–0010	0000	–0020	–1·1	–0·9	–0·6	–0·6
CHEPSTOW (River Wye)							
+0020	+0020	No data		No data		No data	

NOTE: At Newport the ht of LW does not normally fall below MLWS. Tidal hts are based on a minimum river flow; max flow may raise ht of LW by as much as 0·3m.

SHELTER Very good in marinas. See above for barrage locks. Waiting trot berths in outer hbr; or ⚓ off Penarth seafront in W'lies; in E'lies cramped ⚓ off Alexandra Dock ent in 2m.

NAVIGATION WPT 51°24´·03N 03°08´·81W (2½ca SW of S Cardiff SCM lt buoy), 349°/2·9M to barrage locks.

The outer approaches from W or SW are via Breaksea lt float and N of One Fathom Bk. Keep S of Lavernock Spit SCM lt buoy and NW of Flat Holm and Wolves NCM lt buoy drying rk. From NE, drying ledges and shoals extend >1M offshore. From E, appr via Monkstone Lt ho and S Cardiff SCM buoy. Ranny Spit (dries 0·4m) is 3½ca to the W, and Cardiff Grounds (dries 5·4m) 3½ca to the E.

The Wrach Chan is buoyed/lit and dredged 1·2m; it passes 1½ca E of Penarth Hd. The locks appr chan, buoyed, is dredged 0·7m below CD.

Do not impede merchant ships, especially those entering/leaving Alexandra Dock.

Cardiff Bay Barrage and Marina lock

- Call *Barrage Control* VHF Ch 18 or ☎ 02920 700234 to request lock-in or lock-out. Waiting berth on a barge in outer hbr.
- If entering near LW ask Barrage Control for up-to-date depths.
- Subject to VHF instructions, enter the outer hbr (Wpt 51°26'·71N 03°09'·84W) and lock in.
- IPTS (sigs 1, 2, 3, 5) are shown at lock ent.
- Departures on H and H +30. Arrivals at H +15 and H +45.
- Lock into marina operates H24 on free-flow from the bay.

LIGHTS AND MARKS Directional light, Oc WRG 10s 5m3M, on a W metal post marks Wrach Channel.

R/T Port VHF Ch **14** 16 (HW–4 to HW+3). *Barrage Control* Ch 18 H24. Penarth Quays marina Ch 80 H24.

TELEPHONE (Code 02920) HM 400500; Barrage control 700234; MRCC (01792) 366534; Marinecall 09068 969649; Weather Centre 397020; Police (01446) 734451; Dr 415258; Cardiff Bay Authority 877900.

FACILITIES **Penarth Quays Marina** ☎ 705021 H24, www.quaymarinas.com 350+ Ⓥ welcome, £2, max draft 3m, lock width 7·3m; Wi-fi, D&P (0930-1630, E pontoon), El, ME, ⚒, CH, BY, BH (20 ton), SM, C (20 ton), ACA, Ⓔ, Gas, ⊡, R.

Penarth YC ☎ 708196, Slip, FW, Bar.

Cardiff Marina ☎ 343459, www.cardiffmarina.com, 320 inc 50 Ⓥ welcome, £1.60, Wi-fi (free), D, ⚓, C (4·5 ton), 🛒 (short walk).

Cardiff YC ☎ 463697, Slip, M, FW, L (floating pontoon), Bar.

Cardiff Bay YC ☎ 226575, M, L, C, FW, Slip, Bar.

City 🛒, R, Bar, ✉, Ⓑ, ⇌, ✈ (15 mins).

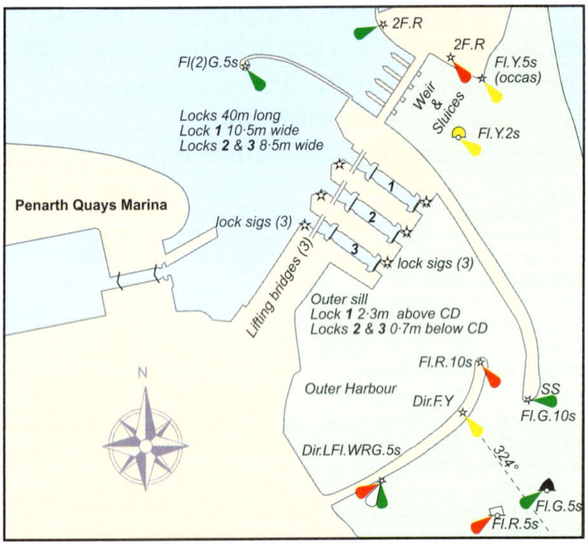

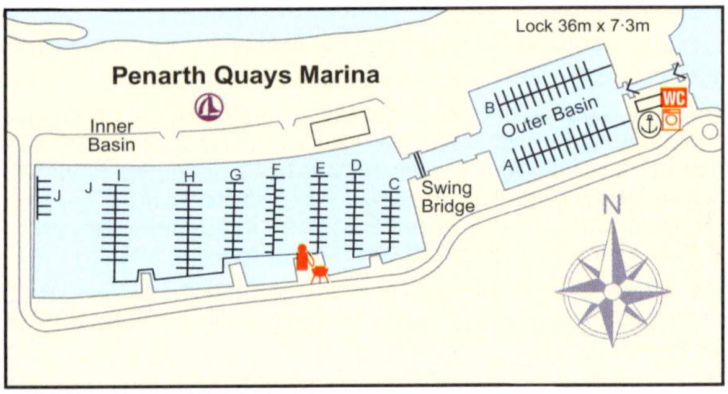

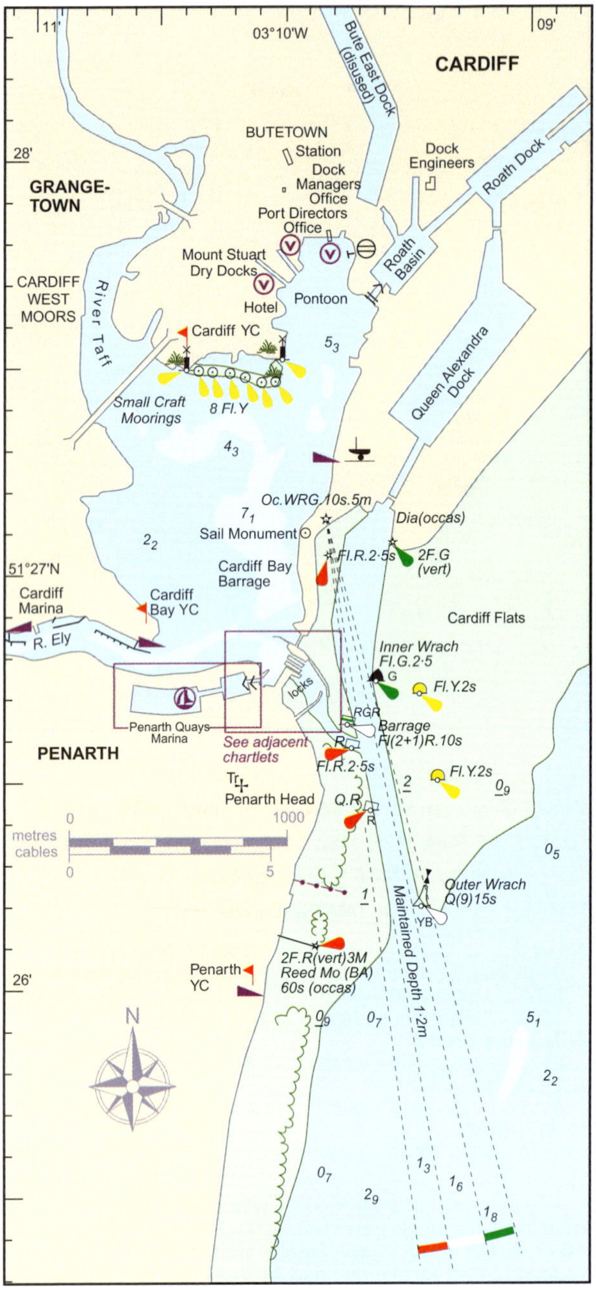

ADJACENT HARBOUR

NEWPORT, Newport, **51°32´·95N 02°59´·13W**. AC 5608, 1179, 1152, 1176. HW–0425 on Dover; ML 6·0m; Duration 0620. See 4.17. A commercial port controlled by ABP, but a safe shelter for yachts. Enter R Usk over bar (approx 0·5m) E of West Usk buoy, QR Bell) and follow buoyed and lit chan to S Lock ent; turn NE (ldg lts 062°) for yacht moorings on S side between power stn pier and YC. Beware overhead cables in Julian's Pill, clearance 3·8m.

Lights, see 4.3. East Usk lt ho Fl (2) WRG 10s. Ldg lts 062°, both FG. Alexandra Dock, S lock W pier head 2 FR (vert) 9/7m 6M. E pier head 2 FG (vert) 9/7m 6M.

Port VHF, *Newport Radio,* and VTS: Ch 09, **71**, 74 (HW ±4). HM (ABP) ☎ 0870 609 6699. Facilities: CH, El, ME, ⚒, Ⓔ. **Newport and Uskmouth SC** Bar, M. **Town** all facilities.

THE SEVERN BRIDGES (AC 1166) The Second Severn Crossing (37m clearance), from 51°34'·88N 02°43'·80W to 51°34'·14N 02°39'·82W, is 4M upriver from Avonmouth and 3M below the Severn Bridge.

The following brief directions, coupled with strong tidal streams and shifting banks, emphasise the need for local knowledge.

Going upriver, pass both bridges at about HW Avonmouth –1¾ (see also 4.18); max sp stream is 8kn at The Shoots and 6kn at the Severn Bridge, setting across the channel when the banks are covered.

Redcliffe F Bu ldg lts in transit with Charston Rock lt lead 013° through The Shoots, a narrow passage between English Stones (6·2m) and the rocky ledges (5·1m) off the Welsh shore. 5ca S of the Second Crossing, the chan is marked by Lower Shoots WCM bcn and Mixoms PHM bcn.

No vessel may navigate between the shore and the nearer Tower of the 2nd Crossing, except in emergency.

4ca N of the 2nd Crossing, leave the 013° transit before passing Old Man's Hd WCM bcn and Lady Bench PHM bcn. From abeam Charston Rk, keep Chapel Rk, Fl 2·6s, brg 050° until the E twr of Severn Bridge bears 068°; maintain this brg until Lyde Rk, QWR, bears about 355°, when alter 010° to transit the bridge (36m clearance) close to rks drying 1m.

Radar Warning. In certain conditions and tidal states, radar displays may show misleading echoes in the vicinity of the 2nd Severn Crossing. ***Racon (O)*** is at centre span of crossing.

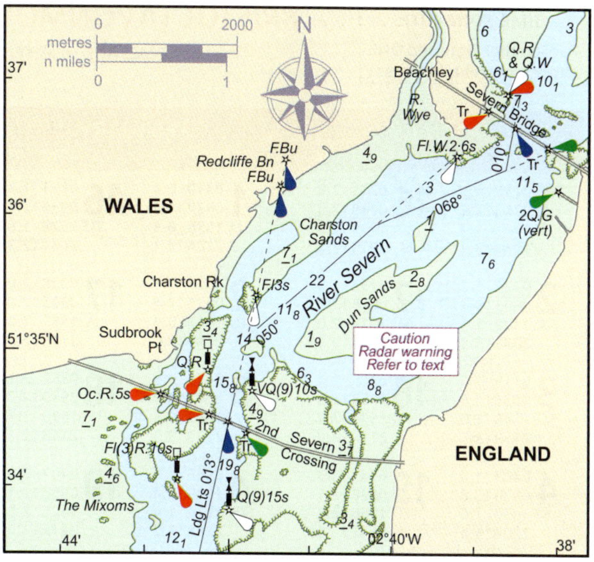

4.18 SHARPNESS

Gloucestershire **51°43'·03N 02°29'·08W**

CHARTS AC 5608, 1166, Imray C59; Stanfords 14.

TIDES –0315 Dover; Duration 0415. Note: The tidal regime is irregular and deviates from Avonmouth curve.

Standard Port BRISTOL (AVONMOUTH) (⟶)

Times				Height (metres)			
High Water		Low Water		MHWS	MHWN	MLWN	MLWS
0000	0600	0000	0700	13·2	9·8	3·8	1·0
1200	1800	1200	1900				
Differences SUDBROOK (Second Severn Crossing)							
+0010	+0010	+0025	+0015	+0·2	+0·1	–0·1	+0·1
BEACHLEY/AUST (Severn Bridge)							
+0010	+0015	+0040	+0025	–0·2	–0·2	–0·5	–0·3
INWARD ROCKS (River Severn)							
+0020	+0020	+0105	+0045	–1·0	–1·1	–1·4	–0·6
NARLWOOD ROCKS							
+0025	+0025	+0120	+0100	–1·9	–2·0	–2·3	–0·8
WHITE HOUSE							
+0025	+0025	+0145	+0120	–3·0	–3·1	–3·6	–1·0
BERKELEY							
+0030	+0045	+0245	+0220	–3·8	–3·9	–3·4	–0·5
SHARPNESS DOCK							
+0035	+0050	+0305	+0245	–3·9	–4·2	–3·3	–0·4
WELLHOUSE ROCK							
+0040	+0055	+0320	+0305	–4·1	–4·4	–3·1	–0·2

SHELTER Very good. The sea lock into the commercial dock is generally open HW–2 to HW but this depends on commercial shipping movements. The advice is plan your passage to arrive no sooner than HW–1 and no later than HW. For more detailed information on lock fees, canal licences and the passage from Avonmouth contact the HM at Sharpness on 01453 811862. The fog signal on Sharpness Point is available on request to Sharpness Radio on VHF channel 13 or 01453 511968.

NAVIGATION WPT 51°42´·83N 02°29´·28W, 028°/2ca to ent.

- Use transits shown on AC 1166. Request pilot notes from Sharpness HM in good time.
- Leave King Road, Avonmouth (17M downriver) not before HW Sharpness –3, to be off Hbr ent about HW –½. Stem strong flood S of F Bu lt; beware tidal eddy.
- Do not proceed above the Severn Bridge except HW±2. There is a 5H flood and a 7H ebb.

LIGHTS AND MARKS Lights as chartlet, but night passage not advised without local knowledge/pilot (07774 226143).

R/T Call *Sharpness Radio* VHF Ch 13 (HW –6 to +1) for lock. Gloucester and Sharpness Canal Ch 74 for bridges (no locks). Call *Bristol VTS* VHF Ch 12 when passing reporting points inwards/outwards: E/W Grounds PHM, Welsh Hook SCM and at Lower Shoots Bcn.

TELEPHONE (Code 01453) Pierhead 511968 (HW–5 to HW+1); HM 811862/64 (HO), 811863; Police (01452) 521201; Ⓗ 810777.

FACILITIES **Sharpness Marina** ☎ 811476. 170 inc 2 Ⓥ, £8 all LOA. El, D, ⚒, CH, Gas, ME, C. **Town** D (above Fretherne Bridge), R, Bar, ✉, Ⓑ (Berkeley), ⇌ (Stonehouse), ✈ (Bristol). Gloucester: D, ACA.

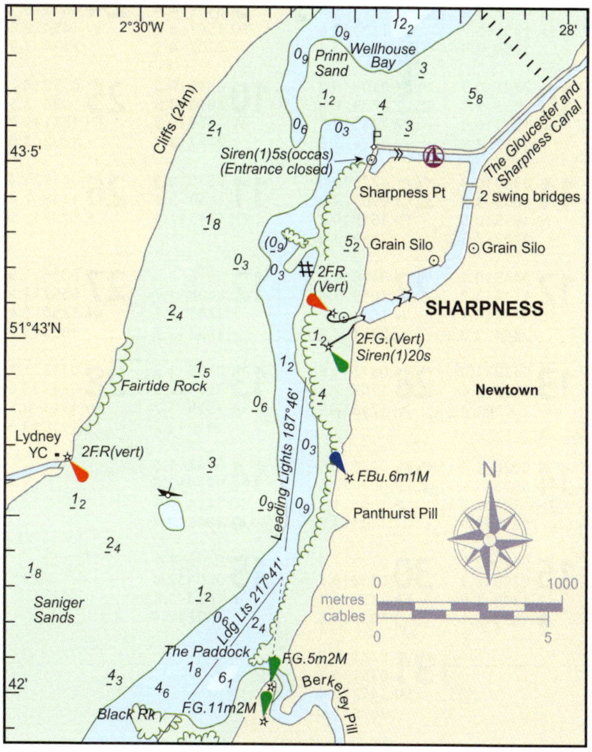

TIME ZONE (UT)
For Summer Time add ONE hour in **non-shaded areas**

BRISTOL (AVONMOUTH) LAT 51°30′N LONG 2°44′W

TIMES AND HEIGHTS OF HIGH AND LOW WATERS

Dates in red are SPRINGS
Dates in blue are NEAPS

YEAR **2010**

JANUARY

Date	Day	Time	m	Time	m	Time	m	Time	m
1	F	0136	1.5	0713	13.3	1407	1.4	1944	13.3
2	SA	0229	1.2	0802	13.7	1500	1.1	2033	13.5
3	SU	0319	1.0	0850	13.8	1548	1.0	2119	13.5
4	M	0403	1.0	0936	13.8	1630	1.0	2204	13.4
5	TU	0442	1.2	1021	13.5	1708	1.3	2246	12.9
6	W	0518	1.5	1104	12.9	1742	1.7	2329	12.3
7	TH	0554	2.0	1150	12.2	1817	2.3	◑	
8	F	0015	11.5	0633	2.6	1243	11.4	1858	2.9
9	SA	0112	10.7	0722	3.2	1350	10.7	1953	3.5
10	SU	0227	10.3	0832	3.7	1504	10.3	2117	3.9
11	M	0340	10.3	1003	3.7	1613	10.5	2242	3.6
12	TU	0443	10.7	1114	3.2	1713	10.9	2344	3.0
13	W	0539	11.3	1210	2.6	1805	11.4		
14	TH	0036	2.4	0626	11.9	1301	2.2	1851	11.9
15	F	0125	2.0	0709	12.3	1349	1.9	● 1933	12.1
16	SA	0211	1.8	0749	12.5	1433	1.9	2010	12.2
17	SU	0252	1.9	0825	12.5	1512	2.0	2044	12.1
18	M	0325	2.1	0858	12.3	1543	2.1	2114	12.0
19	TU	0349	2.3	0928	12.1	1606	2.3	2142	11.9
20	W	0406	2.3	0955	11.9	1626	2.3	2209	11.7
21	TH	0429	2.3	1023	11.7	1652	2.3	2239	11.5
22	F	0500	2.4	1057	11.4	1725	2.5	2316	11.2
23	SA	0536	2.7	1139	11.0	1805	2.9	◐	
24	SU	0002	10.7	0621	3.2	1234	10.4	1857	3.4
25	M	0104	10.2	0723	3.8	1347	10.1	2014	3.8
26	TU	0225	10.0	0901	3.9	1519	10.2	2159	3.6
27	W	0400	10.5	1042	3.4	1644	11.0	2321	2.9
28	TH	0513	11.6	1157	2.5	1748	12.0		
29	F	0026	2.0	0610	12.6	1301	1.7	1843	12.9
30	SA	0126	1.4	0702	13.5	1359	1.1	○ 1933	13.6
31	SU	0221	0.8	0751	14.1	1452	0.6	2020	14.0

FEBRUARY

Date	Day	Time	m	Time	m	Time	m	Time	m
1	M	0310	0.4	0837	14.4	1538	0.3	2104	14.1
2	TU	0353	0.3	0921	14.4	1617	0.4	2145	14.0
3	W	0429	0.5	1001	14.0	1649	0.8	2223	13.5
4	TH	0458	1.0	1039	13.4	1714	1.4	2258	12.7
5	F	0523	1.6	1116	12.4	1739	2.1	◑ 2334	11.7
6	SA	0552	2.4	1156	11.3	1810	2.8		
7	SU	0016	10.7	0630	3.2	1249	10.2	1854	3.7
8	M	0122	9.8	0728	4.0	1419	9.5	2003	4.4
9	TU	0304	9.5	0903	4.4	1547	9.6	2207	4.3
10	W	0419	10.0	1050	3.8	1653	10.3	2322	3.4
11	TH	0519	10.9	1150	2.9	1747	11.1		
12	F	0016	2.5	0608	11.7	1241	2.1	1832	11.8
13	SA	0105	1.9	0651	12.3	1329	1.7	1912	12.2
14	SU	0152	1.6	0729	12.6	1414	1.6	● 1949	12.4
15	M	0235	1.6	0804	12.6	1454	1.6	2022	12.4
16	TU	0311	1.7	0836	12.5	1528	1.8	2051	12.3
17	W	0338	2.0	0905	12.4	1551	2.0	2118	12.2
18	TH	0352	2.1	0930	12.3	1605	2.1	2143	12.1
19	F	0407	2.0	0958	12.1	1625	2.0	2212	12.0
20	SA	0433	2.0	1030	11.8	1654	2.1	2247	11.7
21	SU	0506	2.3	1110	11.3	1729	2.5	2330	11.1
22	M	0546	2.8	1200	10.6	1816	3.2	◐	
23	TU	0027	10.3	0641	3.6	1311	9.9	1925	3.9
24	W	0148	9.8	0815	4.1	1454	9.8	2134	3.9
25	TH	0339	10.2	1030	3.5	1631	10.7	2308	3.0
26	F	0459	11.4	1148	2.4	1737	11.9		
27	SA	0014	1.9	0557	12.6	1250	1.4	1829	13.0
28	SU	0112	1.1	0648	13.6	1344	0.7	○ 1916	13.8

MARCH

Date	Day	Time	m	Time	m	Time	m	Time	m
1	M	0205	0.4	0734	14.3	1434	0.2	2001	14.3
2	TU	0252	0.1	0818	14.6	1518	0.0	2042	14.4
3	W	0333	0.0	0859	14.5	1555	0.3	2120	14.1
4	TH	0406	0.4	0936	14.0	1623	0.8	2155	13.5
5	F	0432	1.0	1011	13.3	1642	1.5	2227	12.7
6	SA	0452	1.6	1043	12.2	1702	2.1	2258	11.7
7	SU	0516	2.3	1117	11.1	1730	2.9	◑ 2333	10.6
8	M	0552	3.2	1159	9.9	1809	3.7		
9	TU	0026	9.5	0645	4.1	1325	9.0	1915	4.6
10	W	0230	9.1	0814	4.6	1518	9.1	2119	4.6
11	TH	0352	9.6	1023	4.0	1626	9.9	2257	3.6
12	F	0452	10.6	1124	2.9	1720	10.9	2350	2.6
13	SA	0541	11.5	1214	2.1	1804	11.7		
14	SU	0038	1.9	0622	12.2	1301	1.6	● 1843	12.2
15	M	0124	1.6	0700	12.5	1346	1.4	1919	12.5
16	TU	0207	1.5	0735	12.6	1427	1.5	1952	12.5
17	W	0245	1.6	0808	12.6	1502	1.6	2023	12.5
18	TH	0315	1.8	0838	12.5	1527	1.9	2050	12.4
19	F	0332	2.0	0905	12.4	1542	1.9	2118	12.4
20	SA	0347	1.9	0935	12.3	1601	1.9	2149	12.2
21	SU	0412	1.9	1010	12.0	1630	2.0	2225	11.9
22	M	0445	2.1	1050	11.4	1705	2.4	2309	11.2
23	TU	0525	2.7	1141	10.6	1752	3.2	◐	
24	W	0006	10.4	0621	3.5	1253	9.8	1901	3.9
25	TH	0131	9.9	0800	4.0	1442	9.8	2121	3.9
26	F	0324	10.3	1017	3.3	1615	10.8	2249	2.8
27	SA	0440	11.5	1128	2.2	1717	12.0	2352	1.7
28	SU	0537	12.7	1226	1.2	1808	13.1		
29	M	0048	0.9	0626	13.6	1319	0.6	1853	13.8
30	TU	0139	0.4	0711	14.1	1407	0.2	○ 1936	14.1
31	W	0225	0.1	0754	14.3	1450	0.2	2016	14.1

APRIL

Date	Day	Time	m	Time	m	Time	m	Time	m
1	TH	0306	0.2	0834	14.1	1526	0.5	2053	13.8
2	F	0340	0.6	0911	13.6	1554	1.1	2127	13.2
3	SA	0405	1.2	0945	12.8	1612	1.7	2159	12.4
4	SU	0425	1.8	1016	11.9	1631	2.3	2228	11.5
5	M	0449	2.4	1047	10.9	1659	2.9	2302	10.5
6	TU	0524	3.1	1126	9.8	1736	3.6	◑ 2351	9.6
7	W	0616	3.9	1235	9.0	1838	4.4		
8	TH	0143	9.0	0737	4.4	1435	8.9	2019	4.6
9	F	0312	9.5	0917	4.0	1546	9.7	2212	3.9
10	SA	0412	10.3	1041	3.2	1640	10.6	2312	2.9
11	SU	0502	11.1	1135	2.4	1726	11.4		
12	M	0001	2.2	0545	11.8	1224	1.8	1806	12.0
13	TU	0048	1.8	0625	12.2	1309	1.6	1844	12.4
14	W	0132	1.6	0702	12.5	1351	1.5	● 1919	12.5
15	TH	0211	1.6	0737	12.5	1429	1.6	1953	12.6
16	F	0245	1.7	0811	12.5	1459	1.7	2025	12.6
17	SA	0311	1.8	0845	12.5	1523	1.8	2058	12.6
18	SU	0334	1.8	0920	12.4	1548	1.8	2134	12.4
19	M	0402	1.8	0958	12.0	1619	2.0	2214	12.0
20	TU	0437	2.1	1042	11.5	1657	2.4	2301	11.3
21	W	0521	2.6	1136	10.7	1747	3.1	◐	
22	TH	0000	10.6	0622	3.3	1248	10.2	1903	3.7
23	F	0125	10.3	0804	3.5	1425	10.2	2059	3.5
24	SA	0301	10.7	0946	2.9	1547	11.0	2218	2.6
25	SU	0412	11.6	1056	2.1	1649	11.9	2321	1.8
26	M	0510	12.5	1154	1.4	1740	12.8		
27	TU	0016	1.1	0559	13.1	1247	0.9	1826	13.3
28	W	0108	0.7	0645	13.5	1335	0.7	○ 1909	13.6
29	TH	0155	0.6	0729	13.5	1419	0.8	1949	13.5
30	F	0238	0.7	0810	13.3	1457	1.1	2028	13.2

Chart Datum: 6·50 metres below Ordnance Datum (Newlyn). HAT is 14·7 metres above Chart Datum; see 0.20

TIME ZONE (UT)
For Summer Time add ONE hour in **non-shaded areas**

BRISTOL (AVONMOUTH) LAT 51°30′N LONG 2°44′W

TIMES AND HEIGHTS OF HIGH AND LOW WATERS

Dates in red are SPRINGS
Dates in blue are NEAPS

YEAR **2010**

MAY

Day	Time	m	Time	m	Time	m	Time	m
1 SA	0314	1.1	0848	12.9	1528	1.5	2104	12.7
2 SU	0343	1.6	0924	12.3	1550	2.0	2137	12.1
3 M	0406	2.0	0956	11.6	1611	2.4	2209	11.4
4 TU	0432	2.5	1029	10.8	1639	2.8	2243	10.6
5 W	0507	2.9	1107	10.1	1716	3.3	2328	9.9
6 TH ◑	0555	3.4	1200	9.5	1809	3.9		
7 F	0040	9.4	0700	3.8	1321	9.2	1926	4.2
8 SA	0212	9.5	0814	3.8	1444	9.5	2049	4.0
9 SU	0318	10.0	0927	3.4	1546	10.2	2206	3.4
10 M	0413	10.7	1037	2.8	1639	10.9	2310	2.7
11 TU	0501	11.3	1135	2.3	1725	11.6		
12 W	0002	2.2	0545	11.8	1226	1.9	1807	12.1
13 TH	0050	1.9	0627	12.2	1313	1.7	1847	12.5
14 F	0135	1.7	0708	12.4	1356	1.6	● 1926	12.7
15 SA	0216	1.6	0749	12.6	1435	1.6	2006	12.8
16 SU	0255	1.6	0830	12.6	1511	1.6	2046	12.8
17 M	0330	1.6	0912	12.5	1545	1.7	2127	12.6
18 TU	0406	1.8	0956	12.2	1621	1.9	2212	12.2
19 W	0446	2.0	1043	11.8	1703	2.2	2301	11.8
20 TH	0533	2.3	1135	11.3	1755	2.7	◐ 2359	11.3
21 F	0632	2.7	1238	10.9	1903	3.0		
22 SA	0111	11.0	0746	2.8	1356	10.7	2024	3.0
23 SU	0230	11.1	0905	2.7	1510	11.0	2140	2.6
24 M	0338	11.4	1016	2.4	1614	11.5	2245	2.2
25 TU	0438	11.9	1118	2.0	1709	12.1	2343	1.7
26 W	0532	12.3	1213	1.6	1759	12.5		
27 TH	0036	1.4	0620	12.6	1304	1.4	○ 1844	12.8
28 F	0126	1.3	0706	12.7	1351	1.4	1927	12.8
29 SA	0212	1.3	0749	12.5	1433	1.6	2008	12.7
30 SU	0253	1.5	0830	12.3	1509	1.9	2046	12.4
31 M	0328	1.9	0908	11.9	1538	2.2	2122	12.0

JUNE

Day	Time	m	Time	m	Time	m	Time	m
1 TU	0356	2.2	0943	11.5	1601	2.5	2156	11.5
2 W	0423	2.4	1015	11.1	1628	2.7	2229	11.0
3 TH	0455	2.6	1050	10.7	1702	2.9	2307	10.6
4 F	0534	2.9	1130	10.3	1744	3.2	◑ 2353	10.2
5 SA	0623	3.1	1220	10.0	1838	3.5		
6 SU	0054	9.9	0721	3.3	1324	9.8	1945	3.7
7 M	0205	10.0	0826	3.3	1435	10.0	2058	3.6
8 TU	0311	10.3	0934	3.1	1542	10.5	2210	3.2
9 W	0412	10.8	1043	2.7	1641	11.1	2315	2.6
10 TH	0507	11.4	1144	2.2	1733	11.8		
11 F	0012	2.1	0557	11.9	1238	1.9	1820	12.4
12 SA	0104	1.8	0645	12.4	1329	1.6	● 1906	12.8
13 SU	0155	1.6	0733	12.6	1417	1.5	1952	13.0
14 M	0244	1.4	0820	12.8	1504	1.4	2038	13.1
15 TU	0331	1.4	0907	12.8	1547	1.4	2124	13.1
16 W	0414	1.4	0953	12.8	1629	1.5	2209	12.9
17 TH	0456	1.5	1039	12.5	1710	1.7	2257	12.5
18 F	0538	1.7	1126	12.1	1754	2.0	2347	12.1
19 SA ◐	0623	2.0	1218	11.6	1843	2.3		
20 SU	0045	11.5	0714	2.4	1320	11.1	1943	2.7
21 M	0153	11.2	0816	2.8	1429	10.9	2055	2.9
22 TU	0302	11.0	0931	3.0	1537	10.9	2208	2.9
23 W	0407	11.1	1042	2.8	1640	11.2	2313	2.5
24 TH	0507	11.4	1144	2.5	1735	11.7		
25 F	0010	2.1	0600	11.7	1238	2.1	1824	12.1
26 SA	0103	1.8	0649	12.0	1329	1.9	○ 1910	12.3
27 SU	0152	1.7	0734	12.1	1415	1.8	1952	12.4
28 M	0238	1.7	0816	12.1	1457	1.9	2032	12.3
29 TU	0318	1.9	0854	11.9	1531	2.1	2108	12.1
30 W	0350	2.1	0927	11.7	1557	2.3	2140	11.8

JULY

Day	Time	m	Time	m	Time	m	Time	m
1 TH	0416	2.3	0958	11.5	1619	2.4	2211	11.5
2 F	0441	2.3	1027	11.3	1644	2.5	2241	11.2
3 SA	0510	2.4	1059	11.0	1716	2.6	2316	10.9
4 SU	0546	2.6	1137	10.7	1756	2.9	◑ 2359	10.5
5 M	0631	2.9	1225	10.3	1847	3.3		
6 TU	0055	10.2	0727	3.3	1327	10.1	1955	3.7
7 W	0207	10.1	0839	3.4	1443	10.1	2118	3.6
8 TH	0324	10.3	0958	3.2	1600	10.6	2237	3.1
9 F	0434	10.9	1110	2.6	1704	11.4	2344	2.4
10 SA	0535	11.7	1212	2.1	1800	12.2		
11 SU	0044	1.9	0629	12.3	1311	1.7	● 1851	12.9
12 M	0143	1.5	0720	12.9	1407	1.3	1940	13.4
13 TU	0238	1.2	0810	13.2	1459	1.1	2028	13.7
14 W	0329	0.9	0858	13.4	1545	0.9	2114	13.7
15 TH	0413	0.8	0943	13.4	1626	0.9	2159	13.6
16 F	0451	0.9	1025	13.2	1703	1.1	2241	13.2
17 SA	0526	1.2	1107	12.7	1737	1.5	2325	12.6
18 SU ◐	0559	1.7	1150	12.0	1814	2.1		
19 M	0013	11.7	0636	2.4	1241	11.2	1857	2.8
20 TU	0113	10.9	0724	3.1	1348	10.5	2000	3.5
21 W	0228	10.3	0836	3.7	1505	10.2	2132	3.7
22 TH	0342	10.3	1012	3.7	1616	10.5	2250	3.3
23 F	0448	10.6	1121	3.1	1717	11.1	2351	2.6
24 SA	0545	11.2	1218	2.5	1809	11.8		
25 SU	0044	2.1	0634	11.7	1310	2.0	1855	12.3
26 M	0134	1.7	0718	12.1	1358	1.7	○ 1936	12.5
27 TU	0221	1.6	0759	12.2	1442	1.7	2015	12.6
28 W	0303	1.6	0834	12.2	1520	1.8	2048	12.4
29 TH	0338	1.8	0906	12.0	1549	2.1	2119	12.2
30 F	0404	2.1	0934	11.9	1607	2.3	2146	11.9
31 SA	0422	2.2	1000	11.7	1622	2.3	2212	11.6

AUGUST

Day	Time	m	Time	m	Time	m	Time	m
1 SU	0442	2.2	1027	11.5	1647	2.4	2241	11.3
2 M	0510	2.4	1059	11.2	1720	2.6	2318	10.9
3 TU ◑	0546	2.7	1141	10.7	1800	3.1		
4 W	0007	10.4	0633	3.2	1236	10.2	1856	3.7
5 TH	0115	9.9	0743	3.7	1352	9.9	2027	4.0
6 F	0245	9.9	0921	3.7	1527	10.2	2210	3.5
7 SA	0413	10.6	1047	3.1	1644	11.2	2329	2.7
8 SU	0520	11.5	1157	2.3	1745	12.3		
9 M	0034	1.8	0616	12.5	1259	1.6	1837	13.2
10 TU	0134	1.2	0707	13.2	1357	1.0	● 1926	13.8
11 W	0228	0.7	0755	13.7	1448	0.6	2013	14.2
12 TH	0317	0.4	0841	14.0	1533	0.4	2057	14.3
13 F	0359	0.4	0923	13.9	1612	0.5	2139	14.1
14 SA	0434	0.6	1003	13.6	1645	0.9	2219	13.5
15 SU	0503	1.2	1040	12.9	1712	1.5	2257	12.7
16 M	0527	1.9	1118	12.0	1739	2.2	◐ 2338	11.6
17 TU	0556	2.7	1201	11.0	1815	3.1		
18 W	0029	10.4	0636	3.5	1305	10.0	1909	4.0
19 TH	0158	9.6	0741	4.3	1441	9.6	2054	4.4
20 F	0324	9.6	0950	4.3	1557	10.0	2234	3.8
21 SA	0431	10.2	1104	3.4	1659	10.9	2334	2.8
22 SU	0527	11.0	1159	2.5	1750	11.7		
23 M	0024	2.0	0614	11.8	1248	1.8	1834	12.4
24 TU	0112	1.5	0656	12.3	1335	1.5	○ 1914	12.8
25 W	0158	1.3	0733	12.5	1420	1.4	1950	12.8
26 TH	0240	1.4	0807	12.4	1459	1.6	2022	12.6
27 F	0316	1.6	0838	12.3	1529	1.9	2052	12.4
28 SA	0343	2.0	0905	12.1	1548	2.2	2117	12.1
29 SU	0358	2.2	0929	11.9	1558	2.3	2142	11.9
30 M	0412	2.2	0955	11.8	1618	2.3	2210	11.6
31 TU	0437	2.3	1027	11.5	1648	2.5	2246	11.2

Chart Datum: 6·50 metres below Ordnance Datum (Newlyn). HAT is 14·7 metres above Chart Datum; see 0.20

TIME ZONE (UT)
For Summer Time add ONE hour in **non-shaded areas**

BRISTOL (AVONMOUTH)

LAT 51°30′N LONG 2°44′W

TIMES AND HEIGHTS OF HIGH AND LOW WATERS

Dates in red are SPRINGS
Dates in blue are NEAPS

YEAR **2010**

SEPTEMBER

Date	Time	m	Date	Time	m
1	0510	2.6	16	0556	3.8
	1107	10.9		1223	9.6
W	1724	3.0	TH	1831	4.3
◑	2333	10.5			
2	0552	3.2	17	0125	9.1
	1200	10.3		0659	4.7
TH	1814	3.7	F	1419	9.3
				2008	4.8
3	0038	9.8	18	0302	9.2
	0654	3.9		0929	4.7
F	1317	9.8	SA	1533	9.8
	1938	4.3		2213	4.0
4	0217	9.6	19	0407	10.0
	0852	4.1		1042	3.6
SA	1506	10.0	SU	1633	10.8
	2157	3.8		2309	2.9
5	0359	10.4	20	0500	10.9
	1034	3.3		1133	2.6
SU	1629	11.1	M	1723	11.7
	2320	2.7		2357	2.0
6	0506	11.6	21	0546	11.8
	1144	2.2		1220	1.8
M	1729	12.4	TU	1806	12.4
7	0021	1.6	22	0043	1.5
	0600	12.7		0625	12.3
TU	1244	1.3	W	1306	1.4
	1820	13.5		1843	12.8
8	0117	0.9	23	0128	1.3
	0648	13.6		0701	12.6
W	1338	0.7	TH	1349	1.4
●	1907	14.2	○	1919	12.8
9	0208	0.4	24	0209	1.3
	0734	14.1		0735	12.6
TH	1428	0.3	F	1429	1.6
	1952	14.5		1952	12.7
10	0255	0.2	25	0246	1.6
	0817	14.3		0806	12.5
F	1512	0.2	SA	1501	1.9
	2035	14.5		2022	12.5
11	0335	0.3	26	0315	1.9
	0858	14.1		0834	12.3
SA	1549	0.5	SU	1523	2.2
	2115	14.1		2049	12.3
12	0409	0.8	27	0332	2.2
	0936	13.6		0901	12.1
SU	1620	1.0	M	1535	2.3
	2153	13.4		2116	12.1
13	0433	1.5	28	0347	2.2
	1012	12.8		0929	12.0
M	1644	1.7	TU	1556	2.3
	2229	12.4		2147	11.8
14	0453	2.2	29	0412	2.3
	1046	11.8		1003	11.7
TU	1707	2.5	W	1625	2.5
	2305	11.2		2225	11.3
15	0518	3.0	30	0445	2.6
	1125	10.7		1045	11.1
W	1740	3.3	TH	1703	2.9
◐	2349	10.0		2313	10.6

OCTOBER

Date	Time	m	Date	Time	m
1	0527	3.2	16	0035	9.1
	1139	10.4		0625	4.6
F	1752	3.7	SA	1343	9.3
◑				1923	4.6
2	0018	9.8	17	0225	9.1
	0628	4.0		0804	4.8
SA	1256	9.9	SU	1458	9.7
	1915	4.3		2120	4.3
3	0159	9.6	18	0330	9.8
	0832	4.2		1001	4.0
SU	1448	10.2	M	1556	10.5
	2142	3.8		2230	3.3
4	0341	10.5	19	0423	10.7
	1016	3.3		1056	3.0
M	1608	11.3	TU	1646	11.4
	2259	2.6		2320	2.4
5	0446	11.7	20	0509	11.5
	1122	2.1		1144	2.3
TU	1707	12.5	W	1729	12.0
	2358	1.6			
6	0538	12.8	21	0006	1.8
	1219	1.3		0549	12.1
W	1758	13.5	TH	1229	1.8
				1809	12.5
7	0051	0.8	22	0051	1.5
	0625	13.6		0626	12.5
TH	1311	0.7	F	1313	1.6
●	1844	14.1		1846	12.6
8	0141	0.4	23	0133	1.5
	0709	14.1		0702	12.6
F	1400	0.4	SA	1353	1.7
	1928	14.4	○	1921	12.7
9	0226	0.4	24	0211	1.6
	0751	14.2		0736	12.6
SA	1444	0.4	SU	1429	1.9
	2011	14.3		1955	12.6
10	0307	0.6	25	0244	1.8
	0831	13.9		0808	12.5
SU	1523	0.7	M	1457	2.1
	2051	13.8		2027	12.4
11	0340	1.1	26	0309	2.0
	0910	13.4		0839	12.4
M	1554	1.3	TU	1519	2.2
	2129	13.1		2059	12.2
12	0405	1.8	27	0332	2.2
	0946	12.6		0913	12.2
TU	1619	2.0	W	1544	2.3
	2204	12.1		2135	11.9
13	0425	2.5	28	0400	2.3
	1020	11.7		0951	11.9
W	1643	2.7	TH	1617	2.5
	2239	11.0		2217	11.5
14	0451	3.1	29	0435	2.6
	1057	10.7		1036	11.4
TH	1716	3.4	F	1657	2.9
◐	2320	10.0		2306	10.9
15	0527	3.9	30	0520	3.2
	1151	9.7		1130	10.8
F	1804	4.2	SA	1750	3.5
			◑		
			31	0009	10.3
				0623	3.7
			SU	1244	10.4
				1911	3.9

NOVEMBER

Date	Time	m	Date	Time	m
1	0138	10.1	16	0231	9.6
	0807	3.9		0825	4.2
M	1421	10.6	TU	1505	10.1
	2106	3.5		2108	3.8
2	0311	10.7	17	0332	10.2
	0942	3.2		0946	3.7
TU	1539	11.4	W	1559	10.7
	2225	2.7		2221	3.1
3	0417	11.6	18	0424	10.9
	1050	2.3		1052	3.0
W	1639	12.3	TH	1647	11.3
	2326	1.9		2319	2.5
4	0511	12.5	19	0509	11.6
	1148	1.6		1144	2.4
TH	1732	13.1	F	1731	11.9
5	0020	1.2	20	0008	2.0
	0559	13.2		0551	12.1
F	1241	1.0	SA	1232	2.1
	1820	13.6		1813	12.3
6	0110	0.9	21	0054	1.8
	0644	13.6		0631	12.5
SA	1331	0.8	SU	1316	1.9
●	1905	13.8	○	1853	12.5
7	0157	0.8	22	0137	1.7
	0727	13.7		0709	12.7
SU	1417	0.8	M	1358	1.9
	1948	13.7		1932	12.6
8	0239	1.0	23	0217	1.7
	0808	13.5		0747	12.8
M	1458	1.1	TU	1437	1.9
	2030	13.3		2011	12.6
9	0316	1.5	24	0253	1.8
	0848	13.1		0826	12.7
TU	1533	1.6	W	1512	2.0
	2110	12.7		2051	12.5
10	0344	2.0	25	0326	2.0
	0926	12.5		0905	12.6
W	1602	2.2	TH	1547	2.1
	2147	11.9		2132	12.3
11	0407	2.6	26	0401	2.1
	1002	11.7		0948	12.4
TH	1628	2.7	F	1623	2.3
	2222	11.1		2215	12.0
12	0433	3.0	27	0439	2.4
	1039	11.0		1033	12.0
F	1700	3.2	SA	1705	2.5
	2300	10.4		2303	11.5
13	0508	3.5	28	0524	2.7
	1124	10.2		1125	11.5
SA	1743	3.7	SU	1755	2.9
◐	2349	9.7	◑	2358	11.1
14	0556	4.0	29	0620	3.1
	1232	9.7		1227	11.1
SU	1842	4.0	M	1858	3.2
15	0107	9.3	30	0107	10.7
	0704	4.4		0733	3.3
M	1401	9.7	TU	1345	11.0
	1952	4.1		2019	3.2

DECEMBER

Date	Time	m	Date	Time	m
1	0229	10.8	16	0211	9.8
	0858	3.2		0827	4.0
W	1502	11.2	TH	1453	10.1
	2141	3.0		2109	3.6
2	0341	11.2	17	0323	10.2
	1013	2.8		0943	3.7
TH	1608	11.7	F	1557	10.5
	2250	2.5		2222	3.2
3	0441	11.8	18	0425	10.8
	1116	2.2		1053	3.1
F	1706	12.3	SA	1653	11.2
	2349	2.0		2325	2.6
4	0534	12.4	19	0517	11.5
	1212	1.7		1152	2.5
SA	1758	12.7	SU	1743	11.8
5	0042	1.6	20	0019	2.1
	0622	12.9		0604	12.2
SU	1305	1.4	M	1245	2.1
●	1846	12.9		1829	12.3
6	0131	1.4	21	0109	1.8
	0707	13.1		0648	12.7
M	1354	1.4	TU	1335	1.8
	1931	13.0	○	1915	12.6
7	0217	1.4	22	0157	1.6
	0751	13.1		0732	13.0
TU	1439	1.5	W	1424	1.7
	2015	12.8		2000	12.8
8	0258	1.7	23	0243	1.6
	0832	12.9		0816	13.2
W	1519	1.7	TH	1510	1.7
	2056	12.5		2045	12.9
9	0333	2.0	24	0326	1.6
	0911	12.5		0900	13.1
TH	1552	2.1	F	1552	1.6
	2133	12.0		2128	12.9
10	0359	2.4	25	0406	1.6
	0948	12.0		0944	13.1
F	1619	2.4	SA	1631	1.7
	2206	11.6		2211	12.8
11	0423	2.7	26	0444	1.7
	1022	11.5		1027	12.9
SA	1647	2.7	SU	1708	1.8
	2239	11.1		2254	12.4
12	0452	2.9	27	0522	2.0
	1057	11.0		1113	12.5
SU	1721	2.9	M	1748	2.1
	2315	10.6		2340	11.9
13	0528	3.2	28	0605	2.3
	1139	10.5		1201	11.9
M	1803	3.2	TU	1833	2.5
◐	2359	10.1	◑		
14	0615	3.6	29	0033	11.3
	1232	10.1		0656	2.8
TU	1855	3.5	W	1306	11.3
				1928	3.0
15	0057	9.8	30	0142	10.8
	0714	3.9		0804	3.3
W	1342	9.9	TH	1422	10.9
	1958	3.7		2046	3.4
			31	0302	10.6
				0931	3.4
			F	1537	10.9
				2214	3.3

Chart Datum: 6·50 metres below Ordnance Datum (Newlyn). HAT is 14·7 metres above Chart Datum; see 0.20

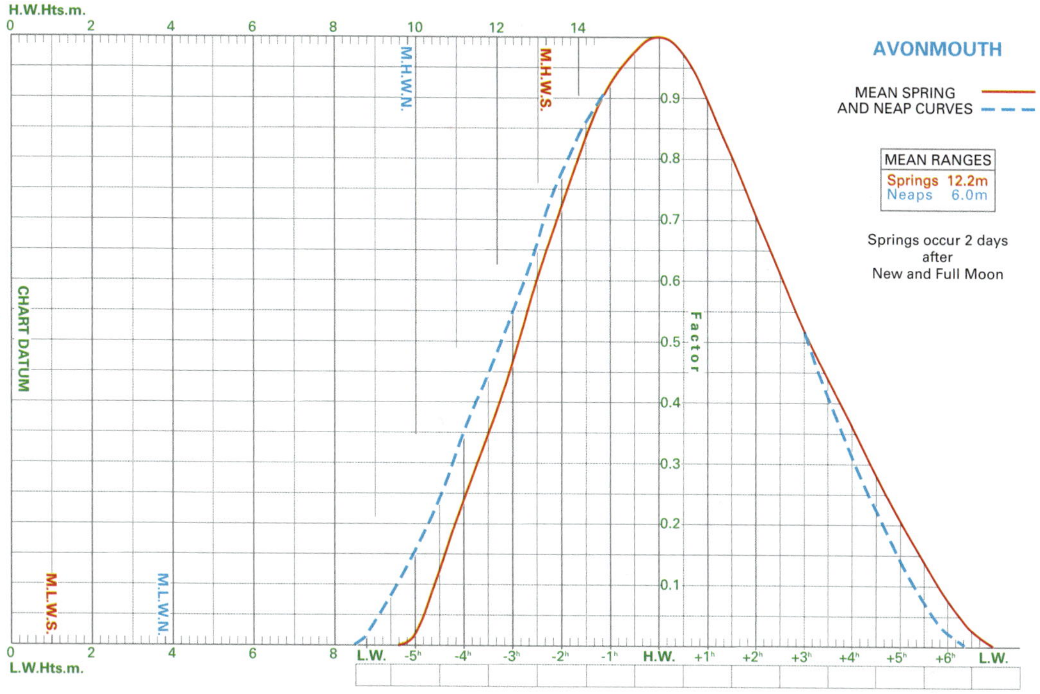

4.19 BRISTOL (CITY DOCKS)

Ent to R Avon **51°30'·44N 02°43'·31W**

CHARTS AC 5608, 1179, 1176, 1859; Imray C59; Stanfords 14.

TIDES –0410 on Dover; ML 7·0; Duration 0620. NB very large range

Standard Port BRISTOL (AVONMOUTH) (⟵)

Times				Height (metres)			
High Water		Low Water		MHWS	MHWN	MLWN	MLWS
0200	0800	0300	0800	13·2	9·8	3·8	1·0
1400	2000	1500	2000				
Differences SHIREHAMPTON (R Avon, 51°29'N 02°41'W)							
0000	0000	+0035	+0010	–0·7	–0·7	–0·8	0·0
SEA MILLS (R Avon, 51°29'N 02°39'W)							
+0005	+0005	+0105	+0030	–1·4	–1·5	–1·7	–0·1
CUMBERLAND BASIN (Ent)							
+0010	+0010	Dries		–2·9	–3·0	Dries	

SHELTER Excellent in Bristol Floating Harbour. Avonmouth and Royal Portbury Docks are prohib to yachts, except in emergency. If early/late on the tide, ⚓ as close inshore as depth allows in Portishead Pool between Portishead Dock and Royal Portbury Dock, but avoid in onshore winds.

NAVIGATION **From the south and west**: from Avon SHM buoy (51°27'·92N 02°51'·73W) stay well clear to the S of the Bristol Deep shipping channel and use the *Inshore Route* (see chartlet), passing close to Portishead Pt. If using the *Offshore Route* to the north, cross the shipping channel immediately E of Denny Shoal SCM Buoy (51°30'·15N 02°45'·45W) and Firefly SHM Buoy.

From the north: use the *Inshore Route*, passing close to the entrance to Avonmouth Docks but keeping clear of disused fuel pier 2ca NE.

- Beware large ships transiting and turning in the main channel.
- Beware ships and tugs leaving the docks at any time.
- When on passage up/down the Severn estuary without stopping at Bristol or Portishead, use the *Offshore Route*.

Entering R Avon keep N of shallows (Swatch Bank) between Royal Portbury Dock and Avonmouth Docks. Speed limit 6kn in river.

LIGHTS AND MARKS Ldg lts 127°, both Iso R 2s, to R Avon ent abeam S pier lt, Oc RG 30s. St George ldg lts 173°, both Oc G 5s, front R/Or post, rear W/Or chequers on Or post, clear Swash Bank (dries). Upriver, G or R ☆s mark the outside of bends.

Entry signals to Bristol Hbr may be shown from E bank, 1½ and 2½ca S of Clifton Suspension Bridge: ● = continue with caution; ● = stop and await orders.

LOCKS Floating Harbour (approx 7M upriver) is accessed via Entrance Lock into Cumberland Basin and Junction Lock into Floating Hbr. Aim to reach the Ent lock no later than HW -0015; waiting pontoon (dries). Ent lock opens approx HW –2½, –1½ and –¼hr for arrivals; departures approx 15 mins after these times. Plimsoll swing bridge opens in unison with lock, except weekday rush hours 0800-0900 and 1700-1800.

Junction lock is always open, unless ht of HW is >9·6m ('stopgate' tide) when it closes; read special instructions. If you miss the last lock-in, call Ch 12 for advice. Options: dry out in soft mud at pontoons, or on N Wall (bow abreast ladder No 4 Survey Mark; no nearer the lock gate). Other areas are foul.

BRIDGES Prince St Bridge usually opens H+15, 0915-2215 summer, by arrangement in winter; pre-notify Bridgemaster ☎ 9299338, Ch 73 or sound ·–·(R). Redcliffe Bridge, pre-arrange same ☎. Clearances above HAT: St Augustine's Reach 1·8m & 0·7m; Prince St 0·7m; Redcliffe 2·1m; Bristol 2·6m. The R Avon leads to Netham lock ☎ 9776590, Keynsham, Bath and the Kennett & Avon canal.

R/T **VTS Areas:** *Severn VTS* Ch **69**, W of Brean Down/Flatholm/Steepholm; *Bristol VTS* Ch **12**, East of *Severn VTS* area. *Bristol VTS* is friendly and helpful and will, on request, advise big ship movements and other MSI. If no radio, ☎ 0117 982 2257.

R/T procedures for R Avon and Bristol City Docks

- When inbound, call *Bristol VTS* with intentions at Welsh Hook PHM buoy and abeam Portishead Pt.
- This also applies to craft bound for Portishead marina.
- In R Avon at Nelson Point call *Bristol VTS* again, low power, confirming inbound to City Docks.
- At Black Rks (1M to run) call *City Docks Radio* Ch **14**, 11 low power, (HW–3 to HW+1) for locking instructions.
- For berth: *Bristol Hbr* Ch **73**, or Bristol Marina Ch **80** M.
- Departure procedure is the reverse.

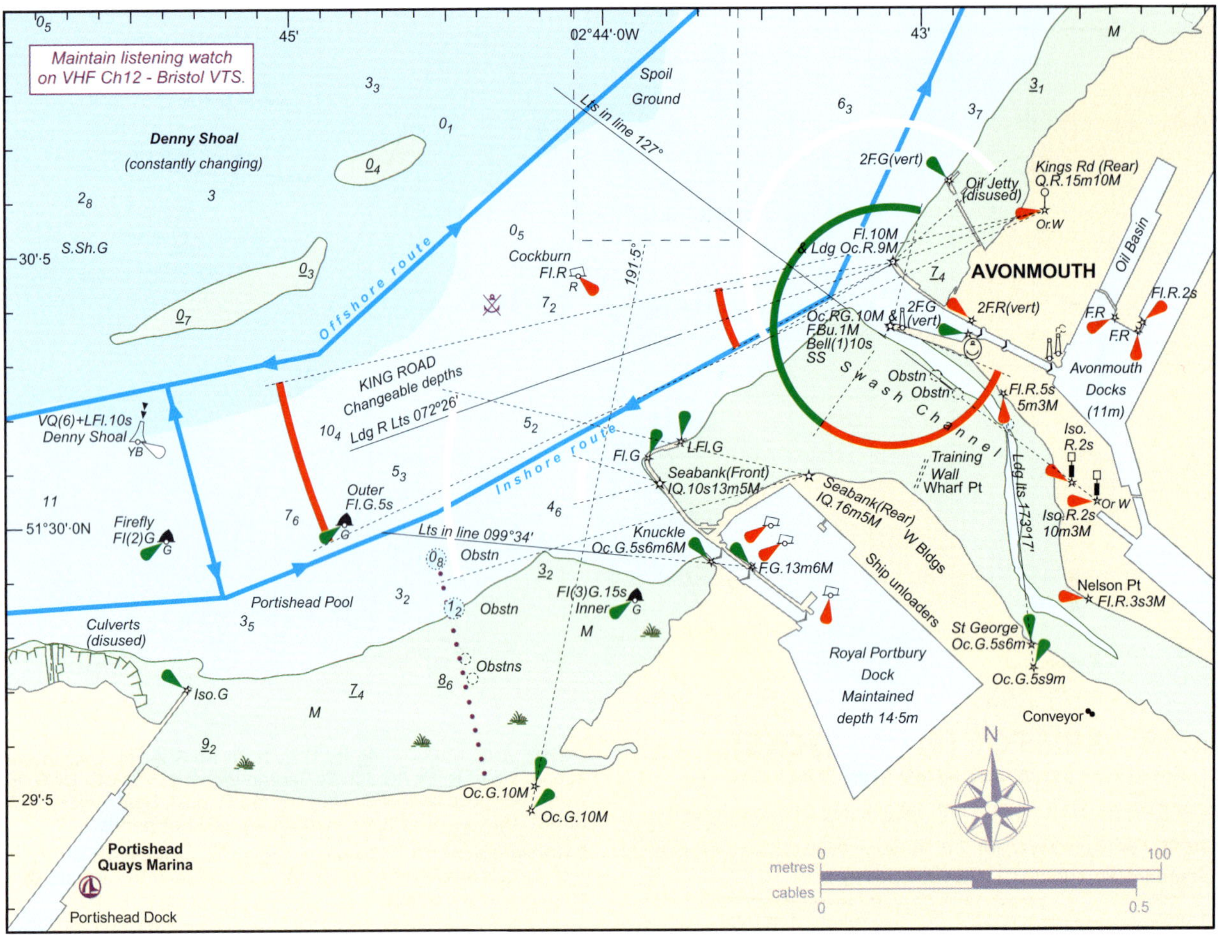

TELEPHONE (Bristol code 0117) Severn VTS 0845 6018870; Bristol VTS 982 2257; Dock Master (Cumberland Basin) 9273633; Bristol weather centre 927 9298; Swansea MRCC (01792) 366534; Marinecall 0891 500459; Police 9277777; Ⓗ 923 0000.

FACILITIES from seaward. **Portishead CC**, at Crockerne Pill, SW bank, 5ca upstream of the M5 motorway bridge; ☎ 01275 373988, www.portisheadcruisingclub.org.uk. Drying ⚓ (soft mud), Slip, grid (£5/day).

Bristol Hbr HM, Underfall Yard, Cumberland Rd, Bristol BS1 6XG. ☎ 9031484, www.bristol-city.gov.uk/bristolharbour Approx 40 Ⓥ AB near ent to St Augustine's Reach, £2.60 inc licence fee. FW, D, ⛽, ⚓, Slip (launching £9), CH, Gas, 🛒, R, Bar; ferries ply between various landing stages around the hbr.

Baltic Wharf Leisure Centre contact HM ☎ 9031484, Slip, L, Bar.

Bristol Marina ☎ 9213198. www.bristolmarina.co.uk Access HW–3 to +1. 100 AB, inc about 5 Ⓥ (20m max LOA), £1.97. D, ⚓, BY, El, Ⓔ, ME, ⚒, Gas, Gaz, SM, Wi-fi (some berths), Slip (£1.97/m), CH, C (9 & 12 ton), BH (50 ton), ♿, 🗑.

Bathurst Basin Shower block.

Cabot CC ☎ 9268318, AB, M, FW, Bar.

City All domestic facilities, ACA, ⇌, ✈.

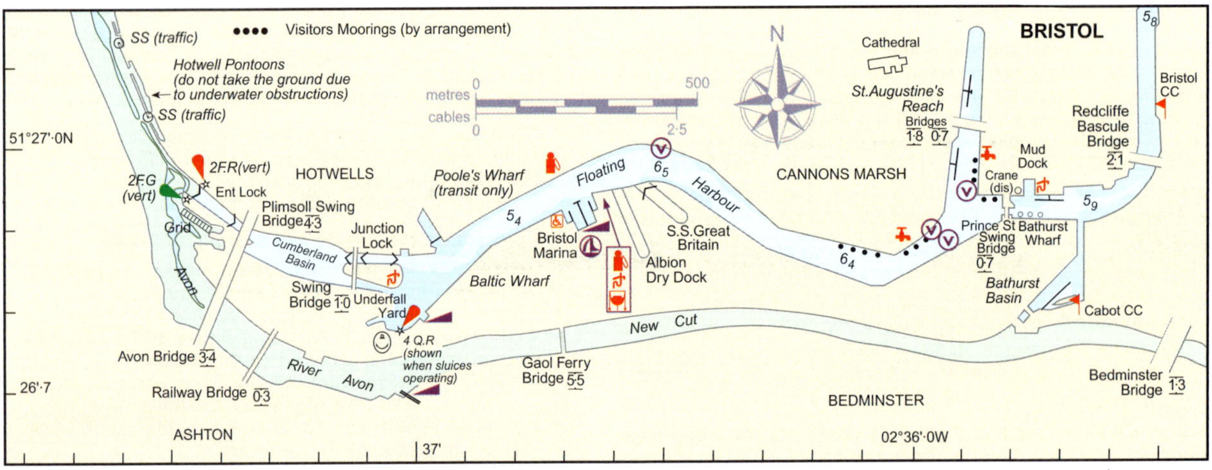

4.20 PORTISHEAD

Somerset **51°29'·56N 02°45'·41W** ❀❀◇◇◇✿✿✿

CHARTS AC 5608, 1176, 1859; Imray C59; Stanfords 14.

TIDES –0405 Dover; ML 6·8

Standard Port BRISTOL (AVONMOUTH) (⟵)

Times				Height (metres)			
High Water		Low Water		MHWS	MHWN	MLWN	MLWS
0200	0800	0300	0800	13·2	9·8	3·8	1·0
1400	2000	1500	2000				
Differences PORTISHEAD							
–0002	0000	No data		–0·1	–0·1	No data	
CLEVEDON							
–0010	–0020	–0025	–0015	–0·4	–0·2	+0·2	0·0
ST THOMAS HEAD							
0000	0000	–0030	–0030	–0·4	–0·2	+0·1	+0·1
ENGLISH AND WELSH GROUNDS							
–0008	–0008	–0030	–0030	–0·5	–0·8	–0·3	0·0
WESTON-SUPER-MARE							
–0020	–0030	–0130	–0030	–1·2	–1·0	–0·8	–0·2

SHELTER Good in marina. Access by lock 9m x 40m x 3·5m draft (5·5m by prior arrangement) HW ±4½ (nps) ±3¾ (sp). Ⓥ's available in marina. ⚓ 1ca NE of pier hd (sheltered from SE to W) to await the tide for marina or Sharpness.

NAVIGATION WPT 51°29´·96N 02°45´·35W, Firefly SHM lt buoy, 168°/500m to pier hd. Firefly Rks (0·9m) are close W of the 168° appr track. Appr's dry to mud and are exposed to N/NE winds. Close inshore a W-going eddy begins at HW –3 whilst the flood is still making E.

LIGHTS AND MARKS Portishead Pt, Q (3) 10s9m 16M, is 7ca W of Portishead pierhd, Iso G 2s 5m 3M. Lock ent has 2FG(vert) and 2FR(vert) lts.

R/T See 4.19. Monitor *Bristol VTS* Ch **12** for shipping movements. Portishead Quays Marina VHF Ch 80 24H.

TELEPHONE (Code 01275) MRCC (01792) 366534; Marinecall 09068 969649; Police 08454 567000; Health centre 08444 773283; Ⓗ (Clevedon) 01179 872212.

FACILITIES **Marina** (200+Ⓥ), £1.65 (min charge £16.50), ☎ 841941, www.quaymarinas.com; Wi-fi, BH (35 ton), Slip, P & D, El, ME, CH, BY, SM, Gas, ⊡. **Portishead Cruising Club** ☎ 373988, Bar **Town** ✉, Ⓑ, ⇌, ✈ (Bristol). 3M to Junction 19 of M5.

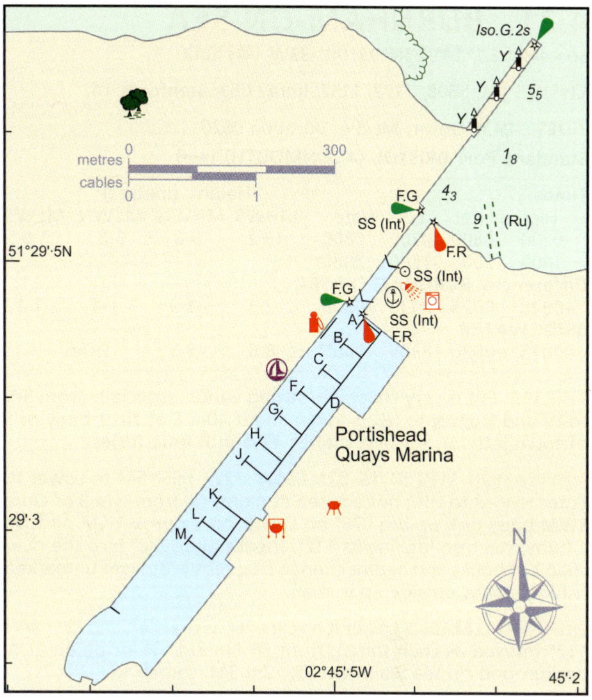

ADJACENT HARBOUR

WESTON-SUPER-MARE, Somerset, **51°21´·03N 02°59´·28W**. AC 5608, 1179, 1176,1152. HW –0435 on Dover; Duration 0655; ML 6·1m. See 4.20. Good shelter, except in S'lies, in Knightstone Hbr (dries) at N end of bay; access HW±1½. Causeway at ent marked by bn. Grand Pier hd 2 FG (vert) 6/5m. Or ⚓ in good weather in R Axe (dries), entry HW±2. Facilities: **Weston Bay YC** (located on beach) ☎ 01934 413366, M (lower R Axe), dry out on beach, FW, Bar, VHF Ch 80; **Services**: AB, CH, El, D, BH (10 ton), FW, Slip, ME, ⚒; **Uphill Boat Centre** ☎ 01934 418617 AB, slip, Gas, Gaz; **Town** Bar, Ⓑ, FW, P, ✉, R, ⇌, 🛒.

AVONMOUTH TO HARTLAND POINT

(AC 1152, 1165) From Avonmouth to Sand Pt, the part-drying English Grounds extend 3M off the S shore. Portishead Quays Marina offers good shelter. Extensive mud flats fill the bays S to Burnham-on-Sea. Westward, the S shore of Bristol Chan is cleaner than N shore. But there is less shelter since the approaches to harbours such as Watchet, Minehead, Porlock Weir and Watermouth dry out.

▶ *In bad weather dangerous overfalls occur NW and NE of Foreland Pt. 5M to W there is a race off Highveer Pt. Between Ilfracombe and Bull Point the E-going stream begins at HW Milford Haven + 0540, and the W-going at HW Milford Haven – 0025, sp rates 3kn. Overfalls occur up to 1·5M N of Bull Pt and over Horseshoe Rks, which lie 3M N. There is a dangerous race off Morte Pt, 1·5M to W of Bull Pt.* ◀

Shelter is available under the lee of Lundy Island; but avoid bad races to NE (White Horses), NW (Hen and Chickens), and SE; also overfalls over NW Bank. ▶ *W of Lundy streams are moderate, but strong around the island and much stronger towards the Bristol Channel proper.* ◀

Proceeding WSW from Rivers Taw/Torridge, keep 3M off to avoid the race N of Hartland Pt (Lt, fog sig, conspic radome). There is shelter off Clovelly in S/SW winds.

4.21 BURNHAM-ON-SEA

Somerset **51°14'·23N 03°00'·33W**

CHARTS AC 5608, 1179, 1152; Imray C59; Stanfords 14.

TIDES –0435 Dover; ML 5·4; Duration 0620

Standard Port BRISTOL (AVONMOUTH) (⟵)

Times				Height (metres)			
High Water		Low Water		MHWS	MHWN	MLWN	MLWS
0200	0800	0300	0800	13·2	9·8	3·8	1·0
1400	2000	1500	2000				
Differences BURNHAM-ON-SEA							
–0020	–0025	–0030	0000	–2·3	–1·9	–1·4	–1·1
BRIDGWATER							
–0015	–0030	+0305	+0455	–8·6	–8·1	Dries	

SHELTER Ent is very choppy in strong winds, especially from SW to W and from N to NE. ⚓ in 4m about 40m E of No 1 buoy or S of town jetty or, for best shelter, Ⓥ/🗘 in R Brue (dries).

NAVIGATION WPT 51°15'·32N 03°08'·22W, 095°/5M to Lower lt. Enter HW –3 to HW; not advised at night. Or from ½M S of Gore SWM buoy pick up brg 076° on Low lt ho. Approx 1½M past No 1 buoy, steer on ldg line/lts 112°; thence alter 180° into the river chan but banks and depths change frequently. Beware unmarked fishing stakes outside appr chan.

LIGHTS AND MARKS Lower lt ho Dir 076° as chartlet. Ldg lts/marks 112° (moved as chan shifts): front FR 6m 3M, Or stripe on □ W background on sea wall; rear FR 12m 3M, church tr.

R/T HM and Pilot VHF Ch 08 16 (when vessel expected).

TELEPHONE (Code 01278) HM 01938 822666, mob 0772 773469; harbour.master@ sedgemoor.gov.uk; Marinecall 09068 969649; Police 0845 456 7000; Ⓗ 782262.

FACILITIES **Burnham-on-Sea MB&SC** ☎ 781500, M, two drying pontoon berths in River Brue (£8), L, Bar; FW, D, 🛒. **Services:** ME, El, ⚒, ACA (Bridgwater). **Town** Gas, ✉, Ⓑ, ⇌ (Highbridge), ✈ (Bristol). Note: No access to Bridgwater marina from sea/R Parrett.

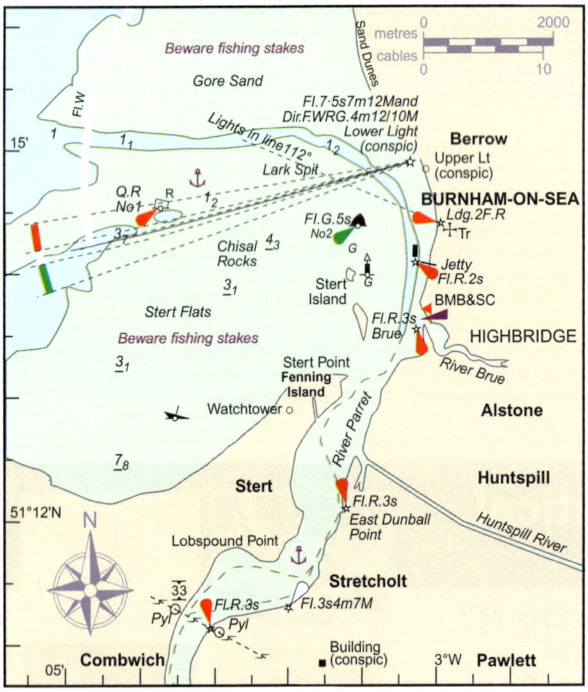

4.22 WATCHET

Somerset **51°11'·03N 03°19'·72W**

CHARTS AC 5608, 1179, 1152, 1160; Imray C59; Stanfords 14.

TIDES –0450 Dover; ML 5·9; Duration 0655

Standard Port BRISTOL (AVONMOUTH) (⟵)

Times				Height (metres)			
High Water		Low Water		MHWS	MHWN	MLWN	MLWS
0200	0800	0300	0800	13·2	9·8	3·8	1·0
1400	2000	1500	2000				
Differences HINKLEY POINT							
–0020	–0025	–0100	–0040	–1·7	–1·4	–0·2	–0·2
WATCHET							
–0035	–0050	–0145	–0040	–1·9	–1·5	+0·1	+0·1
MINEHEAD							
–0037	–0052	–0155	–0045	–2·6	–1·9	–0·2	0·0
PORLOCK BAY							
–0045	–0055	–0205	–0050	–3·0	–2·2	–0·1	–0·1
LYNMOUTH							
–0055	–0115	No data		–3·6	–2·7	No data	

SHELTER Good, but open to N and E winds. Outer hbr (controlled by HM on VHF) dries 6·5m, but has about 6m depth at MHWS; access approx HW±2½. Marina entered through a dropping sill gate (width 7m) which is open when the tide level is at or above CD +6.92m (retained water level). Min clearance over the gate is 2.5m. Approx gate opening times HW ±2½H sp, HW ±1½H np.

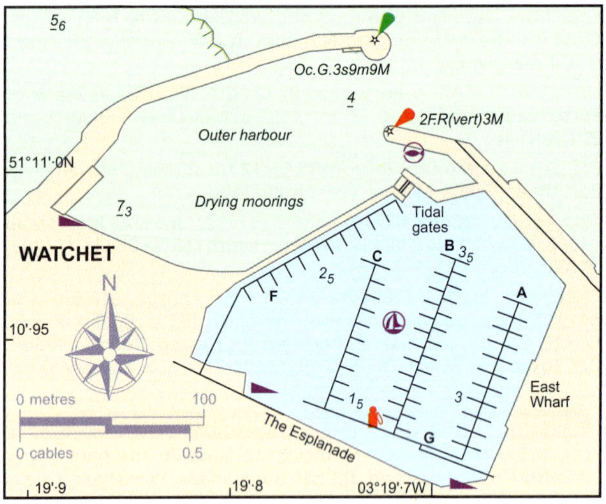

NAVIGATION WPT 51°12'·03N 03°18'·88W, 208°/1·1M to hbr ent. Rks/mud dry 5ca to seaward. Beware tidal streams 4-5kn at sp offshore and around W pier hd. Movement through the marina entrance is controlled by stop/go R/G lts. Entrance max width 8m. Min retained water depths vary 1.5–3.0m. Marina subject to constant silting and some berths may not be accessible at all times. 3kn speed limit in marina.

LIGHTS AND MARKS Two unlit radio masts (206m) bearing 208° 1·6M from hbr ent are conspic approach marks. Hinkley Pt nuclear power stn is conspic 7·5M to the E. W pier hd Oc G 3s 9m 9M on Red (R) tr. E pier hd 2 FR (vert) 3M.

R/T Outer Harbour VHF Ch 16 10 12 14; Marina VHF Ch 80.

TELEPHONE (Code 01984) HM 634562, mob 07739 958441; Watchet Boat Owners Association (01643) 702569; MRCC (01792) 366534; Marinecall 09068 969649; Police 0845 456 7000.

FACILITIES **Outer Harbour** 6 drying AB on W wall, £2, also used by commercial shipping. **Watchet Harbour Marina** ☎ 631264, www.watchet-harbour-marina.com, AB (250 inc Ⓥ) £2·54 inc ⚡, D, 🗑, CH, Gaz, ACA, BY, C (20 ton). **Town** ✉, Ⓑ, 🛒, R, Bar. At Williton (2M): Gas, D & P (cans); Ⓗ (Minehead 8M), ⇌ (Taunton 18M), ✈ (Bristol).

HARBOURS ON THE SOUTH SHORE OF THE BRISTOL CHANNEL

MINEHEAD, Somerset, **51°12′·79N 03°28′·37W**. AC 1179, 1165, 1160. HW –0450 on Dover. ML 5·7m. See 4.22. Small hbr, dries 7·5m; access HW±2. Good shelter within pier curving E and then SE, over which seas may break in gales at MHWS; exposed to E'lies. Best appr from N or NW; beware The Gables, shingle bank (dries 3·7m) about 5ca ENE of pier. Keep E of a sewer outfall which passes ½ca E of pierhd and extends 1¾ca NNE of it; outfall is protected by rk covering, drying 2·8m and N end marked by SHM Bn QG 6m 7M. There are 3 pairs of fore and aft R Ⓥs at hbr ent just seaward of 3 posts or drying alongside berth, £2, at inner end of pier. Hbr gets very crowded. Holiday camp is conspic 6ca SE. Pierhd lt Fl (2) G 5s 4M, vis 127°-262°. VHF Ch 16 12 14 (occas). HM ☎ (01984) 634562, Mob 07739 958441; Facilities: **Hbr** FW, Slip (launching £7.00). **Town** D, P, El, Gas, ME, ⚒, R, Bar, 🛒, ✉, Ⓑ, ⇌(Taunton).

PORLOCK WEIR, Somerset, **51°13′·17N 03°37′·64W**. AC 1179, 1165, 1160. HW –0500 on Dover; ML 5·6m. See 4.22. Access HW±1½. Ent chan (250°), about 15m wide marked by withies (3 PHM and 1 SHM), between shingle bank/wood pilings to stbd and sunken wooden wall to port is difficult in any seas. A small pool (1m) just inside ent is for shoal draft boats; others dry out on pebble banks. Or turn 90° stbd, via gates (but opening bridge usually closed), into inner drying dock with good shelter. No lts. HM ☎ 01643 863187 (not local). **Porlock Weir SC**. Facilities: FW and limited 🛒.

LYNMOUTH, Devon, **51°14'·16N 03°49'·79W**. AC 1160,1165. HW–0515 on Dover. See 4.22. Tiny hbr, dries approx 5m; access HW±1, but not with particularly low Nps, but only in settled offshore weather. Appr from Sand Ridge SHM lt buoy, 1·6M W of Foreland Pt and 9ca N of hbr ent. The narrow appr chan between drying boulder ledges is marked by 7 unlit posts. After first 2 posts keep 10m away from next SH post then next 2PH posts keep to middle of ent. Hbr ent is between piers, 2FR/FG lts, on W side of river course. Berth on E pier, which covers (beware) at MHWS. Resort facilities. Admin by Council ☎ 01598 752384.

WATERMOUTH, Devon, **51°13′·03N 04°04′·6W**. AC 1179, 1165. HW –0525 on Dover; ML 4·9m; Duration 0625. Use 4.23. Good shelter in drying hbr, but heavy surge runs in strong NW winds. Access HW±3 at sp; only as far as inner bkwtr at np. Dir lt 153° Oc WRG 5s 1m, W sector 151·5°-154·5°, W △ on structure, 1½ca inside ent on S shore. Bkwtr, covered at high tide, has Y poles along its length and a G pole with conical topmark at the end. 9 Y Ⓥs with B handles £6.50. HM ☎ (01271) 865422. Facilities: **Hbr** D (cans), FW (cans), CH, C (12 ton), Slip; **YC**, Bar. **Combe Martin** 1½M all facilities.

4.23 ILFRACOMBE

Devon **51°12'·65N 04°06'·65W** ✿✿✿✿✿

CHARTS AC 5608, *1179, 1165,* 1160; Imray C59; Stanfords 14.

TIDES –0525 Dover; ML 5·0; Duration 0625

Standard Port MILFORD HAVEN (⟵)

Times				Height (metres)			
High Water		Low Water		MHWS	MHWN	MLWN	MLWS
0100	0700	0100	0700	7·0	5·2	2·5	0·7
1300	1900	1300	1900				
Differences ILFRACOMBE							
–0016	–0016	–0041	–0031	+2·3	+1·8	+0·6	+0·3
LUNDY ISLAND							
–0025	–0025	–0020	–0035	+0·9	+0·7	+0·3	+0·1

SHELTER Good except in NE/E winds. SW gales can cause surge in hbrs, which dry. 8 Ⓥs in outer hbr, access HW±3. Or ⚓ clear of pier. Visitors AB on N snd S walls of Inner Hbr, access HW±2 or dry out on chains off foot of N Pier.

NAVIGATION WPT 51°13′·23N 04°06′·67W, 180°/0·55Mto pier hd. From E, beware Copperas Rks (4M to E), and tiderips on Buggy Pit, 7ca NE of ent. On entry keep toward Pier to clear drying ledges and lobster keep-pots obstructing Hbr ent on SE side.

LIGHTS AND MARKS See 4.3 and chartlet.

R/T Call: *Ilfracombe Hbr* VHF Ch 12 16 (when manned).

TELEPHONE (Code 01271) HM 862108 mob 07775 532606; MRCC (01792) 366534; Marinecall 09068 969649; Police 08705 777444; Dr 863119.

FACILITIES **Hbr** AB and Ⓥs £1·18 (inc use of showers), M, D, ⛽,(S Quay), FW, CH, Slip(launching £16·50/week), ME, El, ⚒; **Ilfracombe YC** ☎ 863969, M, 🗔, Bar, C (35 ton, as arranged) **Town** 🛒, R, Bar, ✉, Ⓑ, bus to Barnstaple (⇌), ✈ (Exeter).

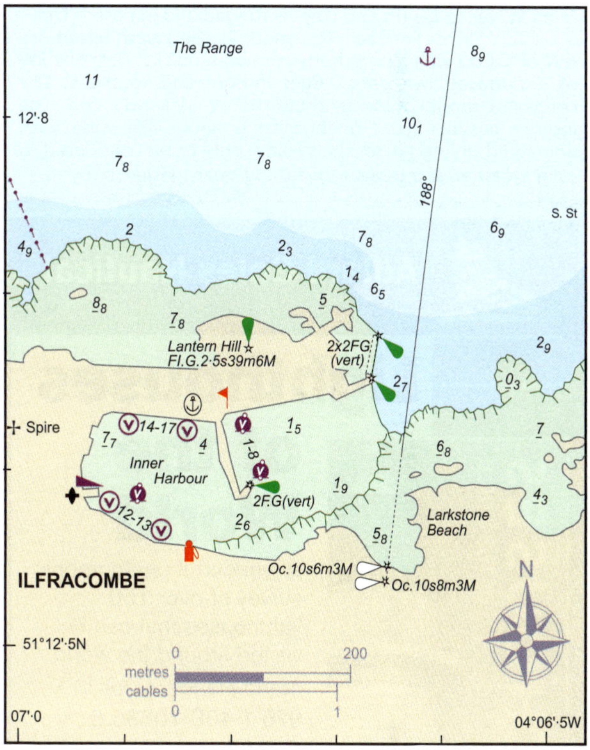

HARTLAND POINT TO LAND'S END

(AC 1156, 1149) The N coast of Cornwall and SW approaches to Bristol Chan are very exposed. Yachts need to be sturdy and well equipped since, if bad weather develops, no shelter may be at hand.

Bude dries, and is not approachable in W winds; only accessible in calm weather or offshore winds. Boscastle is a tiny hbr (dries) 3M NE of Tintagel Hd. Only approach in good weather or offshore winds; anch off or dry out alongside.

Padstow can be a refuge, but in strong NW winds the sea breaks on bar and prevents entry. Off Trevose Hd beware Quies Rks which extend 1M to W. From here S the coast is relatively clear to Godrevy Is, apart from Bawden Rks 1M N of St Agnes Hd. Newquay B is good anch in offshore winds, and the hbr (dries) is sheltered but uncomfortable in N winds. Off Godrevy Is are The Stones, drying rky shoals extending 1·5M offshore, marked by NCM lt buoy.

In St Ives Bay (AC 1168), Hayle is a commercial port (dries); seas break heavily on bar at times, especially with a ground swell. ► *Stream is strong, so enter just before HW.* ◄ The bottom is mostly sand. St Ives (dries) gives shelter from winds E to SW, but is very exposed to N; there is sometimes a heavy breaking sea if there is ground swell.

From St Ives to Land's End coast is rugged and exposed. There are o'falls SW of Pendeen Pt. Vyneck Rks lie awash about 3ca NW of C Cornwall. The Brisons are two high rky islets 5ca SW of C Cornwall, with rky ledges inshore and to the S. The Longships group of rks is about 1M W of Land's End. The inshore passage (001° on Brisons) is about 4ca wide with unmarked drying rks on the W side; only to be considered in calm weather and beware of fishing gear marker buoys.

4.24 RIVERS TAW and TORRIDGE

Devon **51°04'·37N 04°12'·88W** ❁❁◊◊✿✿✿

CHARTS AC 5608, 1179, 1164, 1160; Imray C58; Stanfords 14.

TIDES –0525 (Appledore) Dover; ML 3·6; Duration 0600

Standard Port MILFORD HAVEN (⟵)

Times				Height (metres)			
High Water		Low Water		MHWS	MHWN	MLWN	MLWS
0100	0700	0100	0700	7·0	5·2	2·5	0·7
1300	1900	1300	1900				
Differences APPLEDORE							
–0020	–0025	+0015	–0045	+0·5	0·0	–0·9	–0·5
YELLAND MARSH (R Taw)							
–0010	–0015	+0100	–0015	+0·1	–0·4	–1·2	–0·6
FREMINGTON (R Taw)							
–0010	–0015	+0030	–0030	–1·1	–1·8	–2·2	–0·5
BARNSTAPLE (R Taw)							
0000	–0015	–0155	–0245	–2·9	–3·8	–2·2	–0·4
BIDEFORD (R Torridge)							
–0020	–0025	0000	0000	–1·1	–1·6	–2·5	–0·7
CLOVELLY							
–0030	–0030	–0020	–0040	+1·3	+1·1	+0·2	+0·2

SHELTER Very well protected, but ent is dangerous in strong on-shore winds and/or swell. Yachts can ⚓ or pick up RNLI buoy (please donate to RNLI, Boathouse ☎ 473969) in Appledore Pool N of Skern Pt where spring stream can reach 5kn. Bideford quay dries to hard sand; used by commercial shipping.

NAVIGATION WPT 51°05´·43N 04°16´·11W, 118°/0·9M to Bar.

Bar and sands constantly shift; buoys are moved occasionally to comply. For advice on bar contact Bideford HM. Least depths over bar 0·1 and 0·4m. Estuary dries and access is only feasible from HW–2 to HW. Night entry not advised for strangers. Once tide is ebbing, breakers quickly form between Bideford Bar SHM lt buoy and Middle Ridge SHM lt buoy. Hold the ldg line 118° only up to Outer Pulley where chan deviates stbd toward Pulley buoy and Grey Sand Hill, thence to Appledore Pool. 2M passage to Bideford is not difficult. Barnstaple (7M): seek local advice or take pilot.

LIGHTS AND MARKS See 4.3 and chartlet. Ldg marks are W trs, lit H24. R Torridge: Lt QY at E end of Bideford bridge, 2FR vert & 2FG vert indicate preferred chan; then SHM bn, QG, on W bank.

R/T *2 Rivers Port/Pilots* VHF Ch 12 16 (From HW–2 occasional).

TELEPHONE Appledore/Bideford: Code 01237. Appledore HM 474569; Bideford HM/Pilot 475834, mob 07967 333725; Dr 474994. Instow/Barnstaple: Code 01271. Dr 372672 Common Nos: MRCC (01792) 366534; Marinecall 09068 969649; Police 08705 777444.

FACILITIES

APPLEDORE: no AB; slips at town quay. **Services:** CH, D, El, Ⓔ, BY, C (70 tons), Slip, ME, ⚒.

BIDEFORD: some AB (contact HM), FW, 🛒, R, Gas, Bar. Ferry to Lundy Is.

INSTOW: North Devon YC, ☎ 860367, FW, Slip, R, Bar; **Services:** AB and a few moorings, £5 via Instow Marine ☎ 861081, CH, D, ME, M, Ⓔ, C (4 ton). **Town** R, FW, Bar.

BARNSTAPLE: AB (free for short stay), 🛒, Bar, Gas. FW: limited facilities; P & D: small quantities in cans.

Towns ✉ (all four), Ⓑ (Barnstaple, Bideford), ⇄ (Barnstaple), ✈ (Exeter).

CLOVELLY, Devon, **51°00'·18N 04°23'·77W** ❁◊◊✿✿✿. AC 1164. Tides see above. HW –0524 on Dover. Tiny drying hbr, 5M E of Hartland Pt, is sheltered from S/SW winds; useful to await the tide into Bideford or around Hartland Pt. Some AB (max LOA 12m) £7 on pier, access only near HW; or ⚓ off in 5m. Lt Fl G 5s 5m 5M on hbr wall. HM ☎ (01237) 431761. Facilities: Slip, FW, ✉, limited 🛒, P, D.

RIVERS TAW & TORRIDGE *continued*

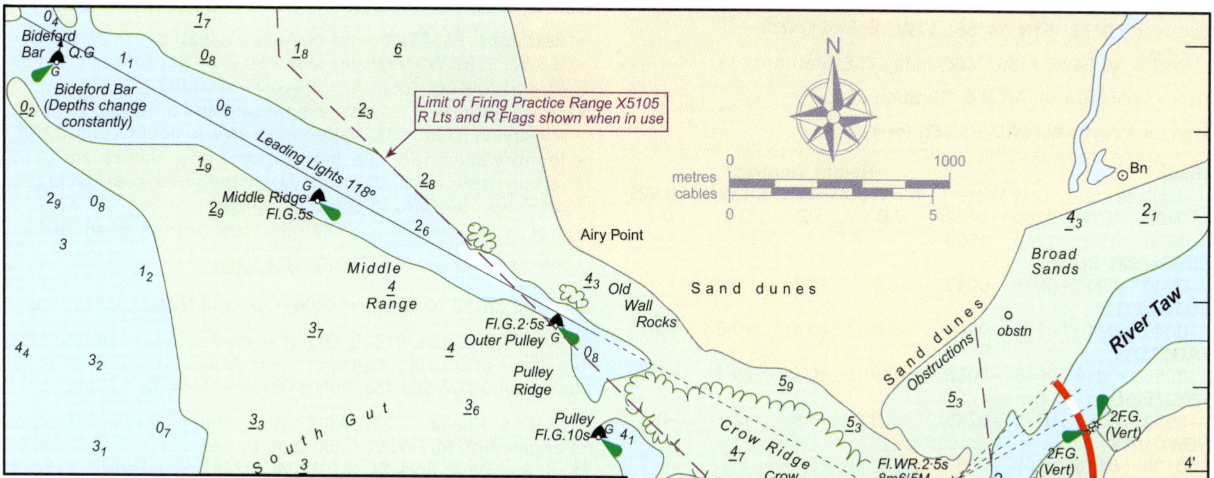
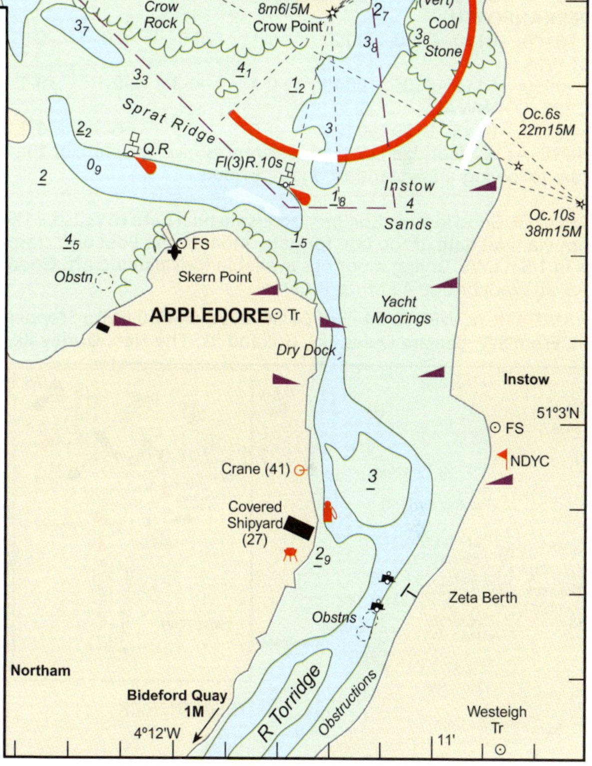

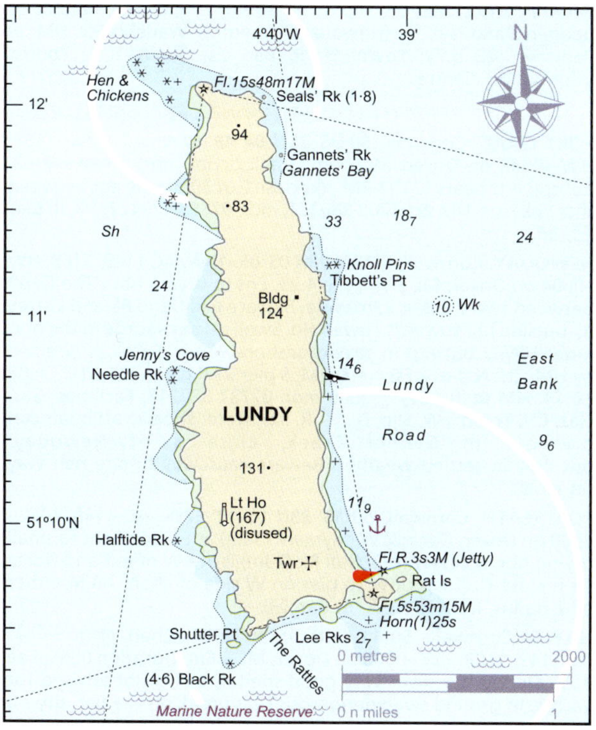

ISLAND IN BRISTOL CHANNEL, 10M NNW of Hartland Pt

LUNDY ISLAND, Devon, **51°09´·83N 04°39´·27W**. AC 5608, *1179, 1164*. HW –0530 on Dover; ML 4·3m; Duration 0605. See 4.23. Shore Office ☎ 01237 470074, Island ☎ 01237 431831. Beware bad tide races, esp on E-going flood, off the N and SE tips of the island; and to the SW on the W-going ebb. A violent race forms over Stanley Bank 3M NE of the N tip. Shelter good in lee of island's high ground (145m). In SSW to NW winds, usual ⚓ is close inshore to NW of SE Pt and Rat Island, clear of ferry. In N'lies ⚓ in The Rattles, small bay on S side. In E'lies Jenny's Cove is safe if no W'ly swell. Lts: NW Pt, Fl 15s 48m 17M, vis 009°-285°, W ○ tr. On SE Pt, Fl 5s 53m 15M, vis 170°-073°, W ○ tr, horn 25s. Two Historic Wrecks (see 0.29) lie on the E side of island, at 51°11'N 04°39'·4W, and 4ca further E. Facilities: Landing by the ⚓ off SE end of island or using N side of jetty to disembark passengers only, boats may not remain alongside; £5.00/person landing fee. The waters around Lundy are a Marine Nature Reserve. **Lundy Co**: Gas, Bar, limited stores, ✉.

MINOR HARBOURS ON THE NW COAST OF CORNWALL

BUDE, Cornwall, **50°49´·93N 04°33´·37W**. AC 5608, 1156. HW –0540 on Dover. Duration 0605. See 4.25. Limited shelter in drying hbr, access HW±2 in daylight, quiet weather, no swell conditions but sea-lock gives access to canal basin with 2m. Conspic W radar dish aerials 3·3M N of hbr. Outer ldg marks 075°, front W spar with Y ◊ topmark, rear W flagstaff; hold this line until inner ldg marks in line at 131°, front W pile, rear W spar, both with Y △ topmarks. There are no lts. VHF Ch 16 12 (when vessel expected). Advise HM of ETA with 24H notice ☎ (01288) 353111; FW on quay; **Town** (½M); Ⓑ, Bar, ✉, R, 🛒, Gas.

BOSCASTLE, Cornwall, **50°41'·48N 04°42·17W**. AC 5608, 1156. HW –0543 on Dover; see 4.25. A tiny, picturesque hbr, almost a land-locked cleft in the cliffs. Access HW±2, but not in onshore winds when swell causes surge inside. An E'ly appr, S of Meachard Rk (37m high, 2ca NW of hbr), is best. 2 short bkwtrs at ent; moor bows-on to drying S quay. HM ☎ 01840 250453.

4.25 PADSTOW

Cornwall **50°32'·51N 04°56'·17W** ❀❀⚘⚘✿✿✿

CHARTS AC 5608, 1156, 1168; Imray C58; Stanfords 13.

TIDES –0550 Dover; ML 4·0; Duration 0600

Standard Port MILFORD HAVEN (⟵)

Times				Height (metres)			
High Water		Low Water		MHWS	MHWN	MLWN	MLWS
0100	0700	0100	0700	7·0	5·2	2·5	0·7
1300	1900	1300	1900				
Differences BUDE							
–0040	–0040	–0035	–0045	+0·7	+0·6	No data	
BOSCASTLE							
–0045	–0010	–0110	–0100	+0·3	+0·4	+0·2	+0·2
PADSTOW							
–0055	–0050	–0040	–0050	+0·3	+0·4	+0·1	+0·1
WADEBRIDGE (R Camel)							
–0052	–0052	+0235	+0245	–3·8	–3·8	–2·5	–0·4
NEWQUAY							
–0100	–0110	–0105	–0050	0·0	+0·1	0·0	–0·1
PERRANPORTH							
–0100	–0110	–0110	–0050	–0·1	0·0	0·0	+0·1
ST IVES							
–0050	–0115	–0105	–0040	–0·4	–0·3	–0·1	+0·1
CAPE CORNWALL							
–0130	–0145	–0120	–0120	–1·0	–0·9	–0·5	–0·1

NOTE: At Wadebridge LW time differences give the start of the rise, following a LW stand of about 5 hours.

SHELTER Good in inner hbr 3m+, access via tidal gate HW±2 sp, ±1½ nps via tidal gate. If too late for gate, moor in the Pool or ⚓ close N in 1·5m LWS. Drying moorings available for smaller craft. Good AB at Wadebridge 4.5M up R Camel.

NAVIGATION WPT 50°34′·56N 04°56′·07W, 044°/ 0·6Mto Stepper Pt. From SW, beware Quies Rks, Gulland Rk, The Hen, Gurley Rk, Chimney Rks and a wreck 5ca W of Stepper Pt (all off the chartlet). From N, keep well off Newland Island and its offlying reef.

- Best appr HW–2½, do not try LW±1½; least depth on the bar is 0·5m at MLWS. Waiting ⚓s in Port Quin Bay in lee of Rumps Pt and Mother Ivey's Bay 3M WSW Stepper Pt.
- Shifting banks in estuary require care and a rising tide (ditto the drying R Camel to Wadebridge, 4M). In doubt, consult HM.
- Identify/align 180° the first 2 chan buoys before entry. In strong onshore winds or heavy ground swell, seas can break on Doom Bar and in the adjacent chan.
- S of St Saviour's Pt the chan lies very close to W shore.

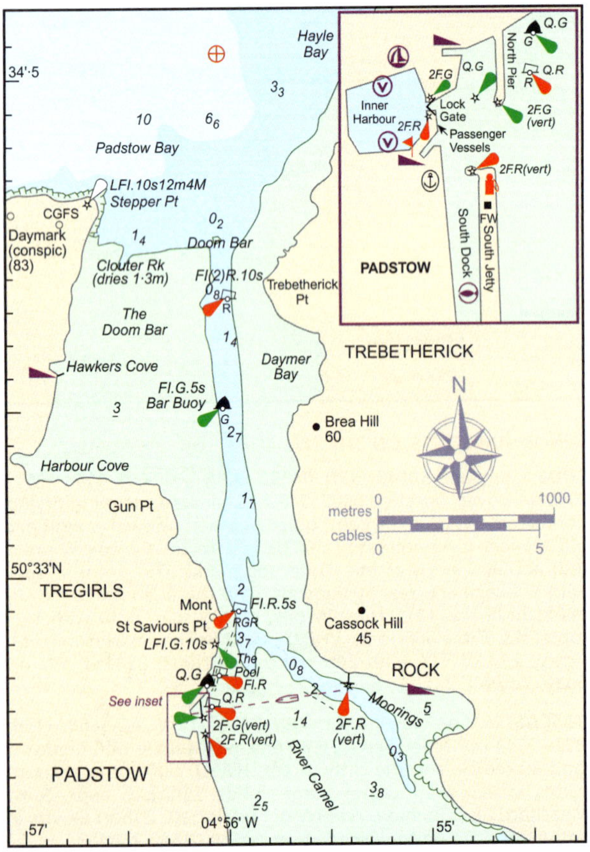

LIGHTS AND MARKS See 4.3 and chartlet.

R/T VHF Ch 12 16 (Mon-Fri 0800–1700 and HW±2). Water taxi.

TELEPHONE (Codes 01841; 01208 = Wadebridge) HM 532239; padstowharbour@btconnect.com; MRCC (01326) 317575; Marinecall 09068 500 458; Police 08705 777444; Dr 532346.

FACILITIES **Hbr** ☎ 532239, AB £1.40, ♿, Slip(£3.50/£5.00 depends on engine hp), M, FW, El, C (60 ton), D, Gas, Gaz, ME, 🗊, showers, 🛒, R, Bar, Wi-fi; **Rock SC** ☎ (01208) 862431, Slip; **Ferry 1** to Rock, also on request as water taxi, ☎ (01326) 317575 or VHF Ch 12 16. **Services:** BY, C, ME, CH, Slip, L, ⚒. **Town** 🗊, P, ✉, Ⓑ, ⇌ (bus to Bodmin Parkway), ✈ (Newquay/Plymouth). **Wadebridge** HM as Padstow; AB only; **Town** 🛒, R, Bar, ✉, Ⓑ, Wi-fi in Tourist Information Centre.

MINOR HBRS BETWEEN BOSCASTLE AND LAND'S END

PORT ISAAC, Cornwall, **50°35′·75N 04°49′·57W**. AC 1156, 1168. HW –0548 on Dover; ML 4·0m. Small drying hbr, access HW±2. Conspic ✠ tr bears 171°/1·3M. Rks close E of 50m wide ent between short bkwtrs. HM ☎ 01208 880321, mob 07855 429422; 🛒, R, Bar, ✉, LB.

NEWQUAY, Cornwall, **50°25′·06N 05°05′·19W**. AC 1149, 1168. HW –0604 on Dover; ML 3·7m; see 4.25. Ent to drying hbr ('The Gap') between two walls, is 23m wide. Beware Old Dane Rk and Listrey Rk outside hbr towards Towan Hd. Swell causes a surge in the hbr. Enter HW±2 but not in strong onshore winds. Berth as directed by HM. Lts: N pier 2 FG (vert) 2M; S pier 2 FR (vert) 2M. VHF Ch 08 16 14. HM ☎ (01637) 872809 mob 07737 387217. Facilities: Gas, Gaz, CH. **Town**; FW, Slip, D, 🛒, R, Bar. Note: Shoal draft boats can dry out in Gannel Creek, close S of Newquay, but only in settled weather. Beware causeway bridge half way up creek.

PORTREATH, Cornwall, **50°15′·88N 05°17′·57W**. AC 1149. HW –0600 on Dover. Conspic W daymark (38m) at E side of ent to small drying hbr, access HW±2. Gull Rk (23m) is 3ca W of ent and Horse Rk is close N. Keep close to pier on W side of chan. AB in either of 2 basins, both dry. 🛒, R, Bar, ✉.

HAYLE, Cornwall, **50°11′·84N 05°26′·19W** (Chan ent) ❀⚘✿. AC 1149, 1168. HW –0605 on Dover; ML 3·6m; Duration 0555. See 4.25. Drying hbr gives very good shelter, but is not advised for yachts. In ground swell dangerous seas break on the bar, drying 2·7m; approx 4m at ent @ MHWS. Cross the bar in good weather HW±1. Charted aids do not necessarily indicate best water. Ldg marks/lts 180°: both W □ R horiz band, ☆ FW 17/23m 4M. PHM buoy, QR is about 7ca N of the front ldg lt. Training wall on W side of ent chan is marked by 5 lit perches, all Oc G 4s. The hbr is divided by long central island (about 700m long, with lt bn QG at NW end) which should be left to stbd. Follow the SE arm of hbr to Hayle; the S arm leads to Lelant Quay. HM ☎ (01736) 754043, AB £5. Facilities: Ⓑ, Bar, FW (can), ⇌, R, 🛒, Gas, P & D (cans).

ST IVES, Cornwall, **50°12′·79N 05°28′·67W** ❀❀⚘⚘✿✿✿. AC 1149, 1168. HW –0610 on Dover; ML 3·6m; Duration 0555. See 4.25. Drying hbr with about 4·5m @ MHWS. Good shelter except in on-shore winds when heavy swell works in. Ⓐs and ⚓ in 3m between the hbr and Porthminster Pt to S and drying Or Ⓐs in hbr. From the NW beware Hoe Rk off St Ives Hd, and from SE The Carracks. Keep E of SHM buoy about 1½ ca ENE of E pier. Lts: E pier hd 2 FG (vert) 8m 5M. W pier hd 2 FR (vert) 5m 3M. VHF Ch 12 16 (occas). HM ☎ (01736) 795018. Facilities: Ⓐs £12.13; **E Pier** FW. **Town** Gas, Gaz, Ⓑ, 🗊, Bar, ✉, R, 🛒, ⇌.

Ireland

All Ireland

AREA 5 – SOUTH IRELAND

AREA 6 – NORTH IRELAND

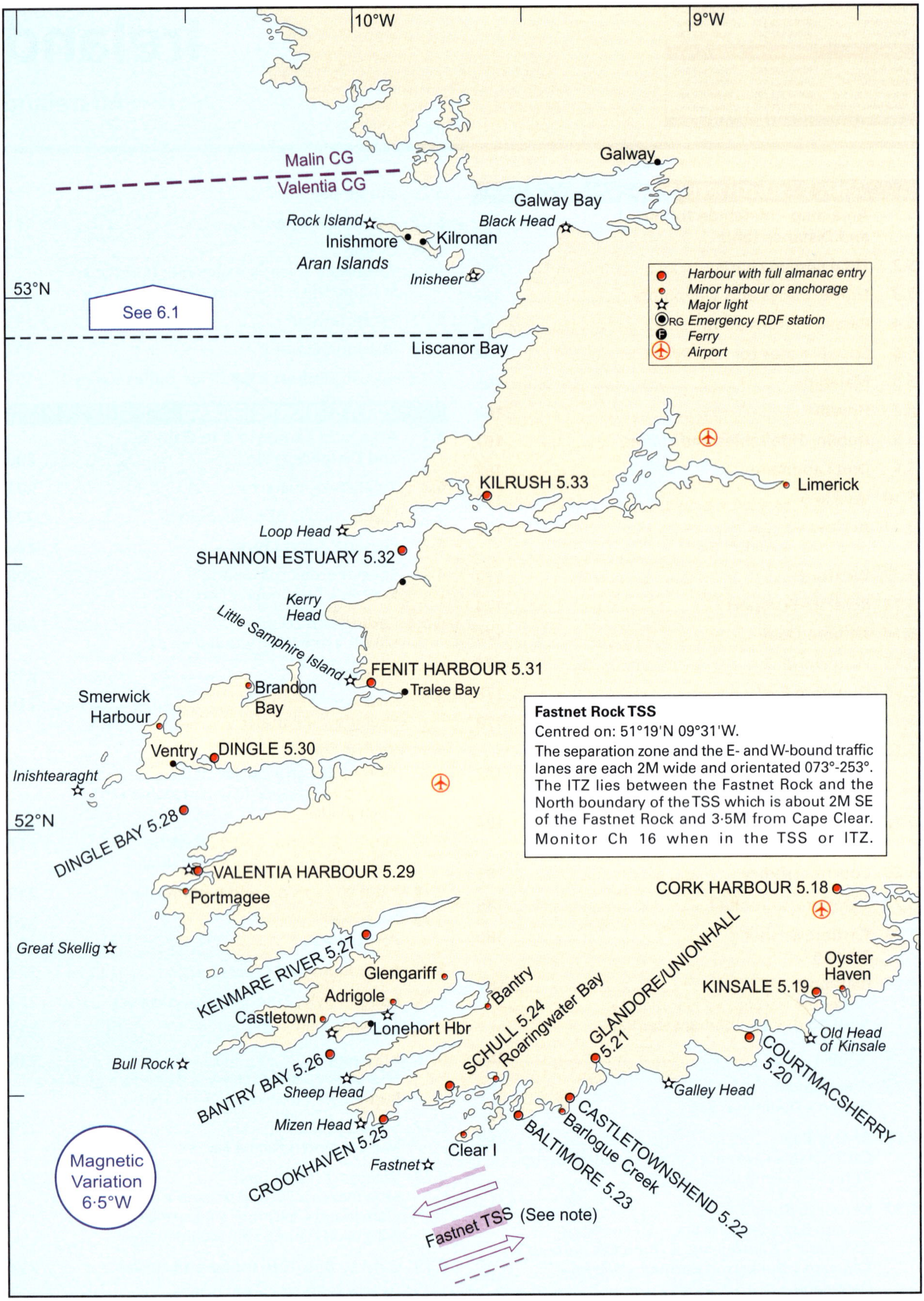
10°W
9°W
53°N
52°N
Malin CG
Valentia CG
Galway
Galway Bay
Black Head
Rock Island
Inishmore
Kilronan
Aran Islands
Inisheer
See 6.1
Liscanor Bay
Harbour with full almanac entry
Minor harbour or anchorage
Major light
RG Emergency RDF station
Ferry
Airport
KILRUSH 5.33
Limerick
Loop Head
SHANNON ESTUARY 5.32
Kerry Head
Little Samphire Island
FENIT HARBOUR 5.31
Tralee Bay
Brandon Bay
Smerwick Harbour
Ventry
DINGLE 5.30
Inishtearaght
DINGLE BAY 5.28
VALENTIA HARBOUR 5.29
Portmagee
Fastnet Rock TSS
Centred on: 51°19'N 09°31'W.
The separation zone and the E- and W-bound traffic lanes are each 2M wide and orientated 073°-253°. The ITZ lies between the Fastnet Rock and the North boundary of the TSS which is about 2M SE of the Fastnet Rock and 3·5M from Cape Clear. Monitor Ch 16 when in the TSS or ITZ.
CORK HARBOUR 5.18
Great Skellig
KENMARE RIVER 5.27
Glengariff
Adrigole
Castletown
Lonehort Hbr
Bantry
SCHULL 5.24
Roaringwater Bay
GLANDORE/UNIONHALL 5.21
KINSALE 5.19
Oyster Haven
Old Head of Kinsale
COURTMACSHERRY 5.20
Galley Head
Bull Rock
BANTRY BAY 5.26
Sheep Head
Mizen Head
CROOKHAVEN 5.25
Clear I
Fastnet
CASTLETOWNSHEND 5.22
Barlogue Creek
BALTIMORE 5.23
Fastnet TSS (See note)
Magnetic Variation 6·5°W

1. ***Carlingford Lough***	1																			
2. Howth	39	2																		
3. **Dun Laoghaire**	48	8	3																	
4. **Wicklow**	63	25	21	4																
5. **Arklow**	75	37	36	15	5															
6. **Tuskar Rock**	113	73	70	52	37	6														
7. **Rosslare**	108	70	66	47	34	8	7													
8. **Dunmore East**	139	101	102	84	69	32	32	8												
9. **Youghal**	172	134	133	115	100	63	65	34	9											
10. **Crosshaven**	192	154	155	137	122	85	85	59	25	10										
11. Kinsale	202	164	168	150	135	98	95	69	35	17	11									
12. **Baltimore**	239	201	196	177	164	128	132	102	70	54	42	12								
13. **Fastnet Rock**	250	212	207	189	174	137	144	112	78	60	49	10	13							
14. Bantry	281	243	241	223	208	171	174	146	112	94	83	42	34	14						
15. Darrynane	283	245	240	221	208	172	176	146	114	98	86	44	39	38	15					
16. Valentia	295	257	252	242	227	184	188	165	131	113	102	56	48	55	16	16				
17. Dingle	308	270	265	246	233	197	201	171	139	123	111	69	61	63	29	13	17			
18. Kilrush	361	323	318	299	286	250	254	224	192	176	164	122	114	116	82	66	64	18		
19. *Galway*	366	362	357	339	324	287	291	262	228	210	199	159	150	155	119	103	101	76	19	
20. *Slyne Head*	317	351	346	328	313	276	283	251	217	199	188	153	139	144	113	97	95	75	49	20

DISTANCE TABLE

Approximate distances in nautical miles are by the most direct route, whilst avoiding dangers and allowing for Traffic Separation Schemes. Places in *italics* are in adjoining areas; places in **bold** are in 0.32, Distances across the Irish Sea.

5.1

South Ireland

Malahide clockwise to Liscanor Bay

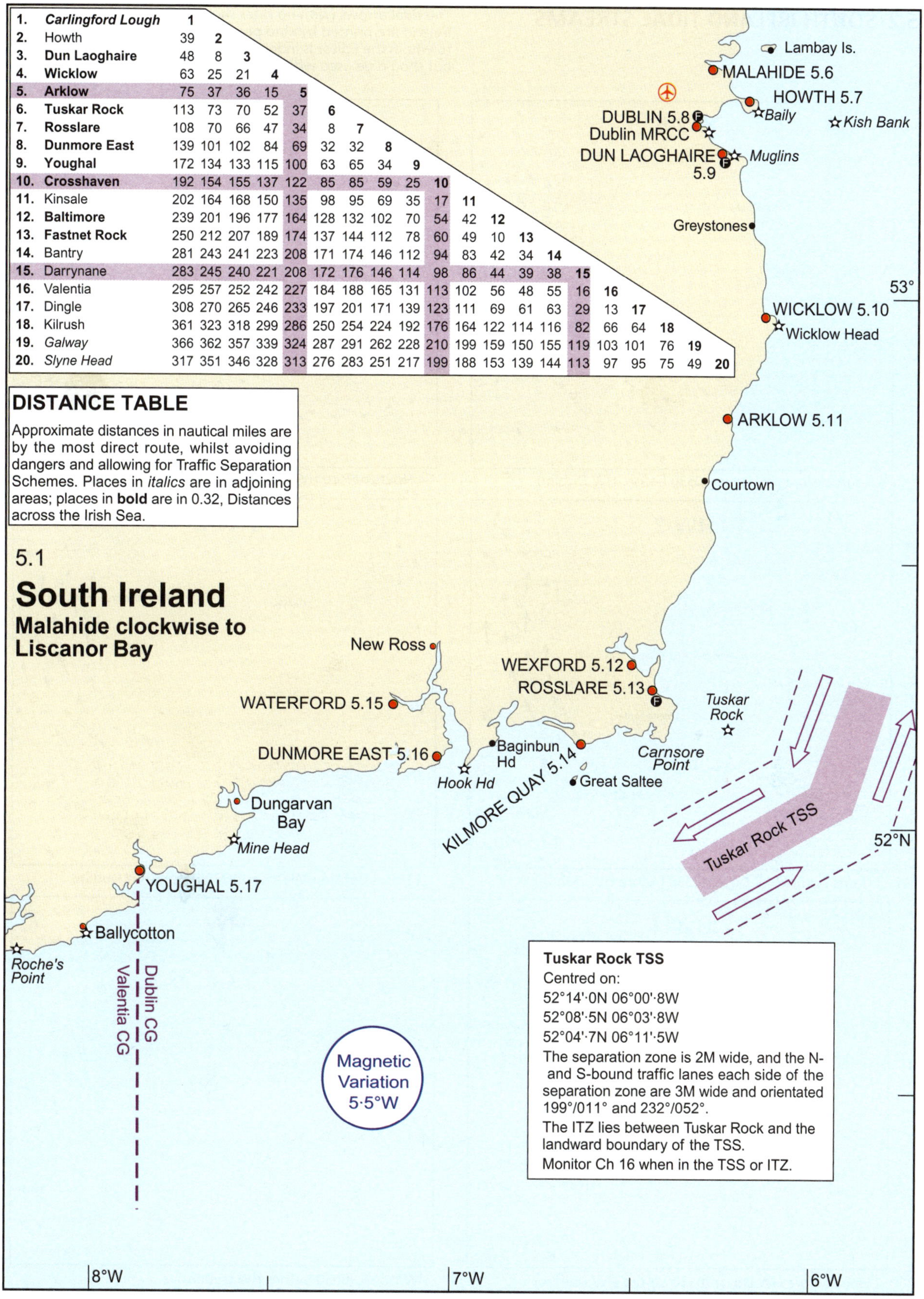

Tuskar Rock TSS

Centred on:

52°14'·0N 06°00'·8W

52°08'·5N 06°03'·8W

52°04'·7N 06°11'·5W

The separation zone is 2M wide, and the N- and S-bound traffic lanes each side of the separation zone are 3M wide and orientated 199°/011° and 232°/052°.

The ITZ lies between Tuskar Rock and the landward boundary of the TSS.

Monitor Ch 16 when in the TSS or ITZ.

5.2 SOUTH IRELAND TIDAL STREAMS

The tidal arrows (with no rates shown) off the S and W coasts of Ireland are printed by kind permission of the Irish Cruising Club, to whom the Editor is indebted. They have been found accurate, but should be used with caution.

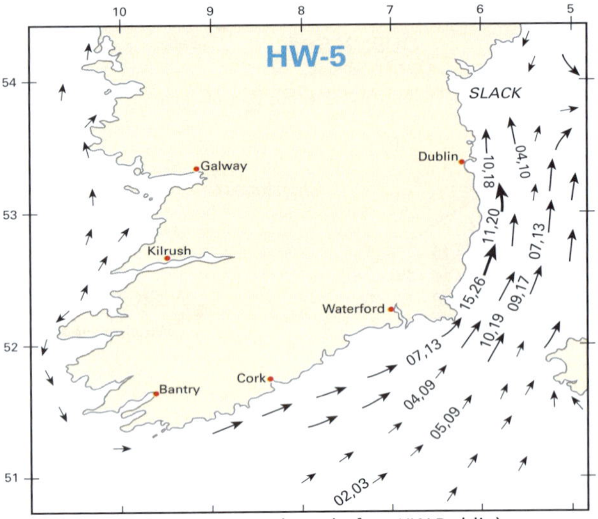

5 Hours before HW Dover (0530 before HW Dublin)

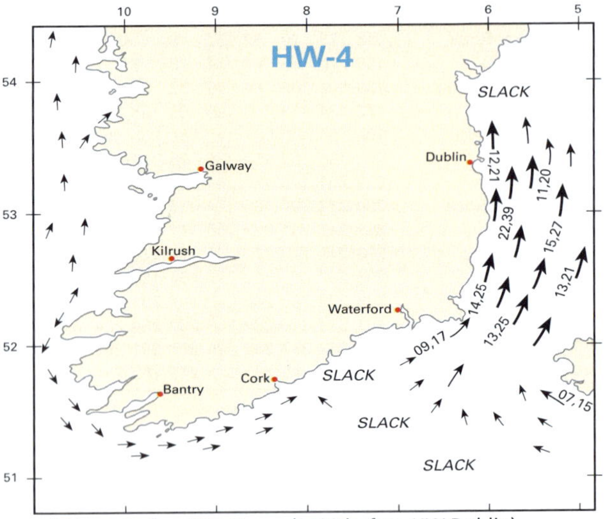

4 Hours before HW Dover (0430 before HW Dublin)

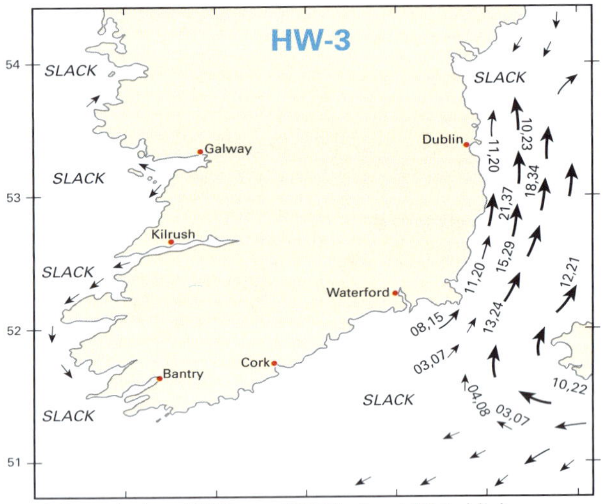

3 Hours before HW Dover (0330 before HW Dublin)

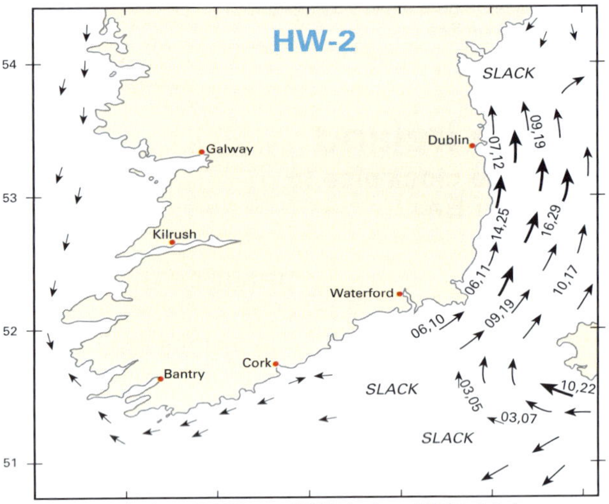

2 Hours before HW Dover (0230 before HW Dublin)

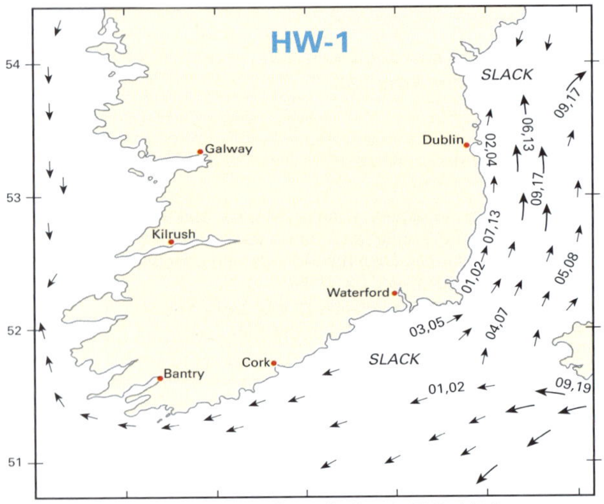

1 Hour before HW Dover (0130 before HW Dublin)

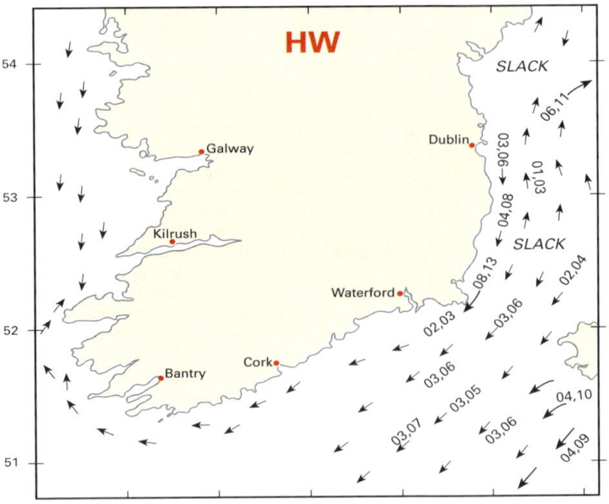

HW Dover (0030 before HW Dublin)

Northward 6.2 South Irish Sea 4.2

The tidal arrows (with no rates shown) off the S and W coasts of Ireland are printed by kind permission of the Irish Cruising Club, to whom the Editor is indebted. They have been found accurate, but should be used with caution.

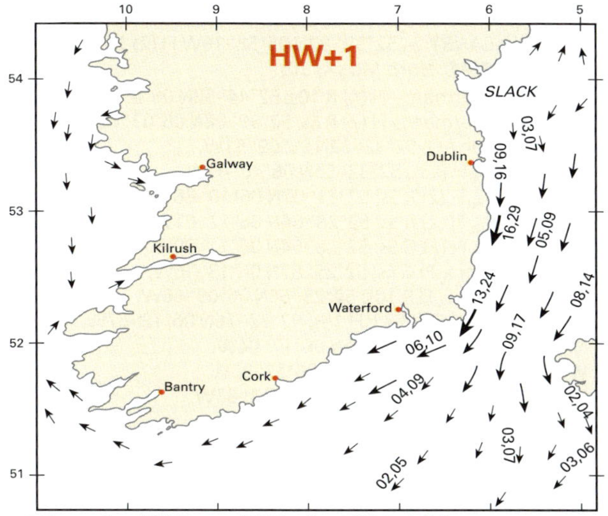

1 Hour after HW Dover (0030 after HW Dublin)

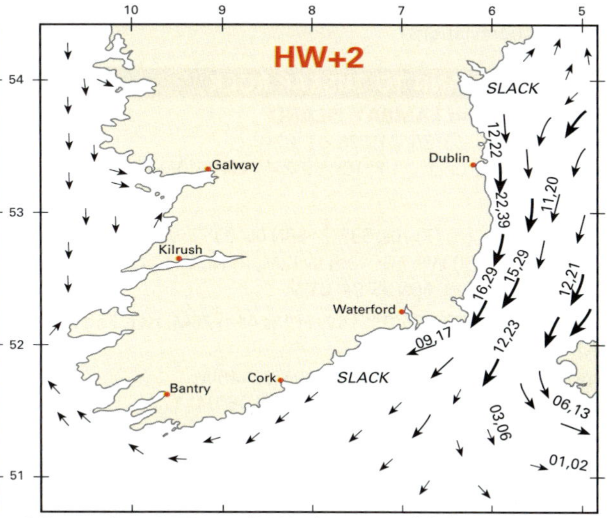

2 Hours after HW Dover (0130 after HW Dublin)

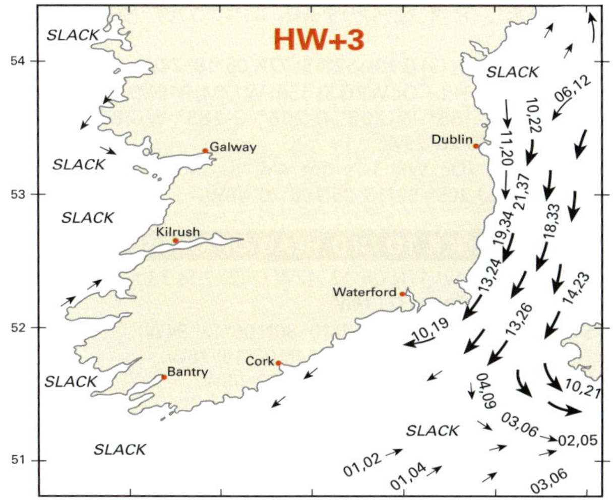

3 Hours after HW Dover (0230 after HW Dublin)

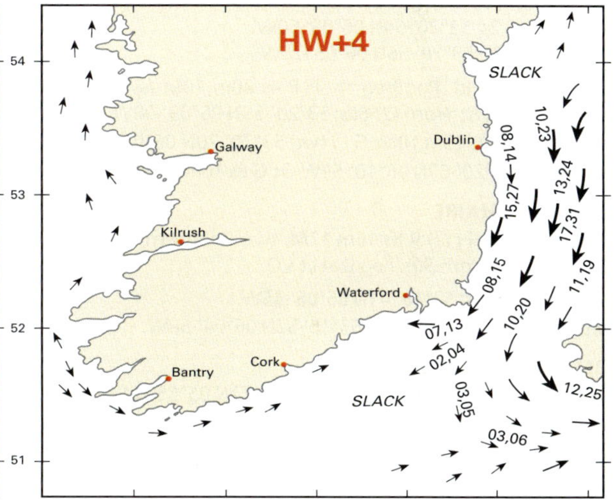

4 Hours after HW Dover (0330 after HW Dublin)

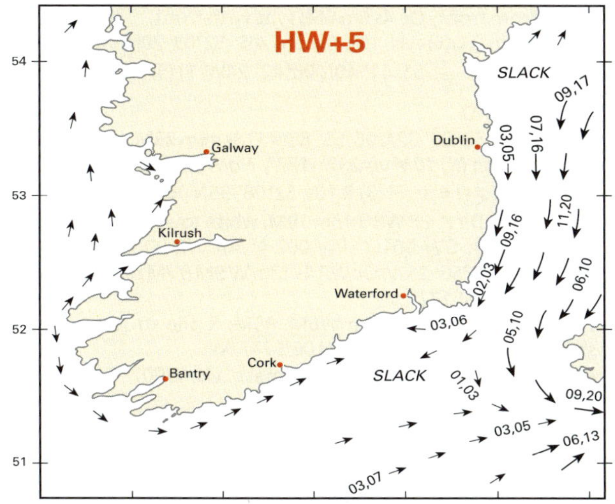

5 Hours after HW Dover (0430 after HW Dublin)

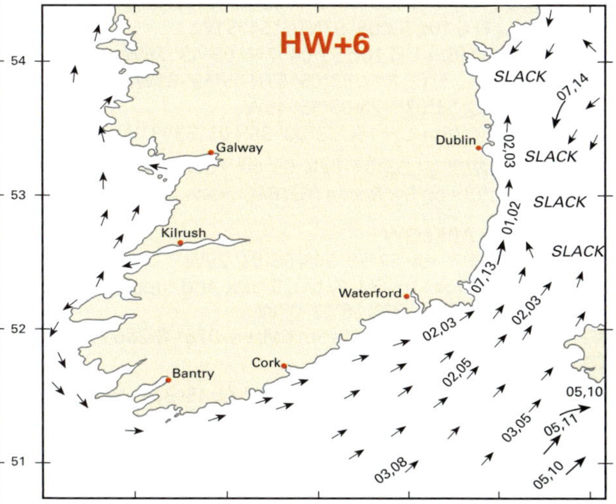

6 Hours after HW Dover (0530 after HW Dublin)

5.3 LIGHTS, BUOYS AND WAYPOINTS

Bold print = light with a nominal range of 15M or more. CAPITALS = place or feature. *CAPITAL ITALICS* = light-vessel, light float or Lanby. *Italics* = Fog signal. ***Bold italics*** = Racon. See 0.2 for Abbreviations.

LAMBAY ISLAND TO TUSKAR ROCK

MALAHIDE and LAMBAY ISLAND

Taylor Rks Q; 53°30'·21N 06°01'·87W.
Malahide approach L Fl 10s; 53°27'·12N 06°06'·87W.

HOWTH

Rowan Rocks Q (3) 10s; 53°23'·88N 06°03'·27W.
E Pier Hd Fl (2) WR 7·5s 13m W12M, R9M; W twr; vis: W256°-R295°-256°; 53°23'·66N 06°04'·03W.

Baily ☆ 53°21'·70N 06°03'·14W Fl 15s 41m **26M**; twr. Fog Det Lt VQ.

Rosbeg E Q (3) 10s; 53°21'·02N 06°03'·45W.
Rosbeg S Q (6) + L Fl 15s; 53°20'·22N 06°04'·17W.

PORT OF DUBLIN

Dublin Bay Mo (A) 10s; ***Racon (M);*** 53°19'·92N 06°04'·64W.
No. 1 Fl (3) G 5s; 53°20'·30N 06°05'·56W.
No. 3 IQ G; 53°20'·57N 06°06'·76W.
No. 4 IQ R; 53°20'·48N 06°06'·93W.
No. 5 Fl G 2s; 53°20'·64N 06°08'·60W.
No. 6 Fl R 2s; 53°20'·56N 06°08'·75W.

Great S Wall Hd Poolbeg ☆ Fl R 4s 20m 10M *(synchro with N.Bull)*; R ○ twr; *Horn (2) 60s*; 53°20'·53N 06°09'·08W

N Bull ☆ Fl G 4s 15m 10M; G ○ twr; 53°20'·70N 06°08'·98W.

N Bank ☆ 53°20'·69N 06°10'·59W Oc G 8s 10m **16M**; G □ twr.

DUN LAOGHAIRE

E Bkwtr Hd Fl (2) R 8s 16m **17M**; twr, R lantern; 53°18'·15N 06°07'·62W. *Horn 30s*. Fog Det Lt VQ.

Outfall Fl Y 5s; 53°18'·41N 06°08'·35W.
Muglins Fl R 5s 14m 11M; 53°16'·52N 06°04'·58W.

OFFSHORE MARKS

Bennett Bank Q (6) + L Fl 15s; 53°20'·17N 05°55'·11W.

Kish Bank ☆ 53°18'·64N 05°55'·48W Fl (2) 20s 29m **22M**; W twr, R band; ***Racon (T) 15M***; *Horn (2) 30s*. Fog Det Lt VQ.

N Kish VQ; 53°18'·56N 05°56'·44W.
E Kish Fl (2) R 10s; 53°14'·35N 05°53'·56W.
E Codling Fl (4) R 10s; 53°08'·54N 05°47'·11W.
W Codling Fl G 10s; 53°06'·97N 05°54'·51W.
S Codling VQ (6) + L Fl 10s; 53°04'·74N 05°49'·76W.
Breaches Shoal Fl (2) R 6s; 53°05'·67N 05°59'·81W.
North India Q; 53°03'·12N 05°53'·46W.
South India Q (6) + L Fl 15s; 53°00'·36N 05°53'·31W.

CODLING LANBY 53°03'·02N 05°40'·76W Fl 4s 12m **15M**; tubular structure on By; ***Racon (G)10M***; *Horn 20s*.

WICKLOW to ARKLOW

Wicklow Fl (4) Y 10s; 52°59'·54N 06°01'·29W.
E Pier Hd Fl WR 5s 11m 6M; W twr, R base and cupola; vis: 136°-R-293°-W-136°; 52°58'·99N 06°02'·07W.
W Packet Quay Hd Fl WG 10s 5m 6M; vis: 076°-G-256°-W-076°; 52°58'·88N 06°02'·08W.

Wicklow Head ☆ 52°57'·95N 05°59'·89W Fl (3) 15s 37m **23M**; W twr.

Horseshoe Fl R 3s; 52°56'·62N 05°59'·31W.
N Arklow Q; 52°53'·86N 05°55'·21W.
Arklow Bank Wind Farm from 52°48'·47N 05°56'·57W to 52°46'·47N 05°57'·11W, N and S Turbines Fl Y 5s14m 10M + Fl W Aero lts. AIS transmitters. Other turbines Fl Y 5s. See 5.4.

ARKLOW to WEXFORD

S Pier Hd Fl WR 6s 11m 13M; twr; vis: R shore- W223°- R350°-shore; 52°47'·61N 06°08'·22W.
Roadstone Bkwtr Hd QY; 52°46'·65N 06°08'·23W.
S Arklow VQ (6) + L Fl 10s; 52°40'·82N 05°59'·21W.

ARKLOW LANBY 52°39'·52N 05°58'·16W Fl (2) 12s 12m **15M**; ***Racon (O)10M***; *Horn Mo (A) 30s*.

No. 2 Glassgorman Fl (4) R 10s; 52°44'·52N 06°05'·36W.
No. 1 Glassgorman Fl (2) R 6s; 52°39'·08N 06°07'·42W.
N Blackwater Q; 52°32'·22N 06°09'·51W.
No. 6 Rusk Fl R 3s; 52°32'·65N 06°10'·41W.
No. 4 Rusk Fl (2) R 5s; 52°31'·07N 06°10'·86W.
No. 2 Rusk Fl (2) R 5s; 52°28'·64N 06°12'·61W.
No. 1 Rusk Fl (2) G 5s; 52°28'·54N 06°11'·80W.
W Blackwater Fl G 6s; 52°25'·87N 06°13'·56W.
SE Blackwater Fl R 10s; 52°25'·64N 06°09'·66W.
S Blackwater Q (6) + L Fl 15s; 52°22'·76N 06°12'·87W.
North Long Q; 52°21'·44N 06°17'·04W.
West Long QG; 52°18'·18N 06°17'·96W.
Lucifer VQ (3) 5s; 52°17'·02N 06°12'·67W.

ROSSLARE

S Long VQ (6) + L Fl 10s; 52°14'·84N 06°15'·64W.
Splaugh Fl (2) R 6s; 52°14'·37N 06°16'·76W.
South Holdens Fl G 3s; 52°15'·14N 06°17'·24W. (Synch with Calmines)
Calmines Fl R 3s; 52°15'·01N 06°17'·77W. (Synch with S Holdens)
W Holdens Fl (3) G 10s; 52°15'·77N 06°18'·74W.
Rosslare Pier Hd Oc WRG 5s 15m W13M, R10M, G10M; R twr; vis:098°-G-188°-W-208°-R-246°-G-283°-W-286°-R-320°; 52°15'·43N 06°20'·29W.
Ballygeary Oc WR 1·7s 7m 4M vis: shore-R-152°-W-200°-W(unintens)-205°; 52°15'·25N 06°20'·48W.

TUSKAR ROCK TO OLD HEAD OF KINSALE

Tuskar ☆ 52°12'·17N 06°12'·42W Q (2) 7·5s 33m **24M**; W twr; *Horn (4) 45s*, ***Racon (T) 18M***.

S Rock Q (6) + L Fl 15s; 52°10'·80N 06°12'·84W.
Fundale Fl (2) R 10s; 52°11'·04N 06°19'·78W.
Barrels Q (3) 10s; 52°08'·32N 06°22'·05W.

KILMORE

Kilmore Quay SWM Iso 10s; (Apr-Sep); 52°09'·20N 06°35'·30W.
Kilmore Bkwtr Hd Q RG 7m 5M; vis: 269°-R-354°-G-003°-R-077°; 52°10'·20N 06°35'·15W.
Ldg lts 007·9°, Front 52°10'·37N 06°35'·08W Oc 4s 3m 6M. Rear, 100m from front, Oc 4s 6m 6M; sync with front.
Coningbeg Q(6)+LFl 15s, Racon, AIS; 52°03'·20N 06°38'·57W.
'M5' ODAS 35 51°41'·40N 06°42'·24W; Fl (5) Y 20s.

WATERFORD

Hook Hd ☆ 52°07'·32N 06°55'·85W Fl 3s 46m **23M**; W twr, two B bands; ***Racon (K) 10M vis 237°-177°***; *Horn (2) 45s*. Fog Det Lt VQ.

Waterford Fl R 3s. Fl (3) R 10s; 52°08'·95N 06°57'·00W.

Duncannon Dir lt F WRG 13m 10M, white tower on fort, 359·5°-FG-001·2°-Alt GW-001·7°-FW-002·4°-Alt WR-002·9°-FR-004·5°; 52°13'·23N 06°56'·25W; Oc WR 4s 13m W 9M R 7M on same tower, 119°-R-149°-W-172°.
Passage Pt Fl WR 5s 7m W6M, R5M; R pile structure; vis: W shore- R127°-302°; 52°14'·26N 06°57'·77W.
Cheek Pt Q WR 6m 5M; W mast; vis: W007°-R289°-007°; 52°16'·12N 06°59'·38W.
Sheagh Fl R 3s 29m 3M; Gy twr; vis: 090°-318°; 52°16'·29N 06°59'·34W.
Snowhill Point Ldg lts 255°. Front, Fl WR 2·5s 5m 3M; vis: W222°-R020°- W057°-107°; 52°16'·39N 07°00'·91W. Rear, Flour Mill, 750m from front, Q 12m 5M.

Queen's Chan Ldg lts 098°. Front, QR 8m 5M; B twr, W band; vis: 030°-210°;52°15'·32N 07°02'·38W. Rear, 550m from front, Q 15m 5M; W mast.

Beacon Quay Fl G 3s 9m; vis: 255°-086°; 52°15'·50N 07°04'·21W.

Cove Fl WRG 6s 6m 2M; W twr; vis: R111°- G161°- W234°-111°; 52°15'·05N 07°05'·16W.

Smelting Ho Pt Q 8m 3M; W mast; 52°15'·15N 07°05'·27W.

Ballycar Fl RG 3s 5m; vis: G127°- R212°-284°; 52°15'·06N 07°05'·51W.

DUNMORE EAST

East Pier Head ☆ 52°08'·93N 06°59'·37W Fl WR 8s 13m **W17M**, R13M; Gy twr, vis: W225°- R310°-004°.

W Wharf Fl G 2s 6m 4M; vis: 165°-246°; 52°08'·97N 06°59'·45W.

DUNGARVAN

Ballinacourty Point Fl (2) WRG 10s 16m W10M, R8M, G8M; W twr; vis: G245°- W274°- R302°- W325°-117°; 52°04'·69N 07°33'·18W.

Helvick Q (3) 10s; 52°03'·61N 07°32'·25W.

Mine Head ☆ 51°59'·52N 07°35'·25W Fl (4) 30s 87m **20M**; W twr, B band; vis: 228°-052°.

YOUGHAL

Bar Rocks Q (6) + L Fl 15s; 51°54'·85N 07°50'·05W.

Blackball Ledge 51°55'·34N 07°48'·53W Q (3) 10s.

W side of ent ☆ 51°56'·57N 07°50'·53W Fl WR 2·5s 24m **W17M**, R13M; W twr; vis: W183°- R273°- W295°- R307°- W351°-003°.

BALLYCOTTON

Ballycotton ☆ 51°49'·52N 07° 59'·09W Fl WR 10s 59m **W22M, R18M**; B twr, within W walls, B lantern; vis: W238°- R048°-238°; *Horn (4) 90s*. Fog Det Lt VQ.

The Smiths Fl (3) R 10s; 51°48'·62N 08°00'·71W.

Power Q (6) + L Fl 15s; 51°45'·59N 08°06'·67W.

CORK

Cork L Fl 10s; ***Racon (T) 7M***; 51°42'·92N 08°15'·60W.

Daunt Rock Fl (2) R 6s; 51°43'·52N 08°17'·65W.

Fort Davis Ldg lts 354·1°. Front, 51°48'·82N 08°15'·80W Dir WRG 29m **17M**; vis: FG351·5°-AlWG352·25°-FW353°-AlWR355°-FR355·75°-356·5°. Rear, Dognose Quay, 203m from front, Oc 5s 37m 10M; Or 3, synch with front.

Roche's Point ☆ 51°47'·59N 08°15'·29W Fl WR 3s 30m **W20M, R16M**; vis: Rshore- W292°- R016°- 033°, W (unintens) 033°- R159°- shore.

Outer Hbr Rk E2 Fl R 2·5s; 51°47'·52N 08°15'·67W.

Chicago Knoll E1 Fl G 5s; 51°47'·66N 08°15'·54W.

W1 Fl G 10s; 51°47'·69N 08°16'·05W.

W2 Fl R 10s; 51°47'·69N 08°16'·34W.

White Bay Ldg lts 034·6°. Front, Oc R 5s 11m 5M; W hut; 51°48'·53N 08°15'·22W. Rear, 113m from front, Oc R 5s 21m 5M; W hut; synch with front.

Spit Bank Pile Iso WR 4s 10m W10M, R7M; W house on R piles; vis: R087°- W196°- R221°- 358°; 51°50'·72N 08°16'·45W.

KINSALE and OYSTER HAVEN

Bulman Q (6) + L Fl 15s; 51°40'·14N 08°29'·74W.

Charle's Fort Fl WRG 5s 18m W9M, R6M, G7M; vis: G348°- W358°- R004°-168°; H24; 51°41'·74N 08°29'·97W.

OLD HEAD OF KINSALE TO MIZEN HEAD

Old Head of Kinsale ☆, S point 51°36'·28N 08°32'·03W Fl (2) 10s 72m **20M**; B twr, two W bands; *Horn (3) 45s*.

COURTMACSHERRY

Barrel Rock 51°37'·01N 08°37'·30W.

Black Tom Fl G 5s; 51°36'·41N 08°37'·95W.

Wood Pt (Land Pt) Fl (2) WR 5s 15m 5M; vis: W315°- R332°-315°; 51°38'·16N 08°41'·00W.

Galley Head ☆ summit 51°31'·80N 08°57'·19W Fl (5) 20s 53m **23M**; W twr; vis: 256°-065°.

GLANDORE and CASTLETOWNSHEND

Reen Point Fl WRG 10s 9m W5M, R3M, G3M; W twr; vis: Gshore- W338°- R001°-shore; 51°30'·98N 09°10'·50W.

Kowloon Bridge Q (6) + L Fl 15s; 51°27'·58N 09°13'·75W.

BALTIMORE and FASTNET

Barrack Pt Fl (2) WR 6s 40m W6M, R3M; vis: R168°- W294°-038°; 51°28'·33N 09°23'·65W.

Loo Rock Fl G 3s; 51°28'·43N 09°23'·45W.

Fastnet ☆, W end 51°23'·35N 09°36'·19W Fl 5s 49m **27M**; Gy twr, *Horn (4) 60s*, ***Racon (G) 18M***. Fog Det Lt VQ.

SCHULL and LONG ISLAND CHANNEL

Ldg lts 346° Front, Oc 5s 5m 11M, W mast; 51°31'·68N 09°32'·43W. Rear, 91m from front, Oc 5s 8m11M; W mast.

CROOKHAVEN

Rock Is Pt L Fl WR 8s 20m W13M, R11M; W twr; vis: W over Long Is B to 281°-R-340°; inside harbour 281°-R-348°- towards N shore; 51°28'·59N 09°42'·29W.

MIZEN HEAD TO DINGLE BAY

Mizen Head ☆ 51°27'·00N 09°49'·24W Iso 4s 55m **15M**; vis: 313°-133°.

Sheep's Hd ☆ 51°32'·60N 09°50'·95W Fl (3) WR 15s 83m **W18M, R15M**; W bldg; vis: 007°-R-017°-W-212°.

BANTRY BAY, CASTLETOWN BEARHAVEN, WHIDDY ISLE, BANTRY and GLENGARIFF

Roancarrigmore ☆ 51°39'·19N 09°44'·83W Fl WR 3s 18m **W18M**, R14M; W □ twr, B band; vis: 312°-W-050°-R-122°-R (unintens)-242°-R-312°. Reserve lt W8M, R6M obsc 140°-220°.

Ardnakinna Pt ☆ 51°37'·11N 09°55'·08W Fl (2) WR 10s 62m **W17M**, R14M; W ○ twr; vis: 319°-R- 348°-W- 066°-R-shore.

Castletown Dir lt 024° Oc WRG 5s 4m W14M, R11M, G11M; W hut, R stripe; vis: 020·5°-G-024°-W-024·5°-R-027·5°; 51°38'·79N 09°54'·30W.

Castletown Ldg lts 010°. Front, Oc 3s 4m 1M; W col, R stripe; vis: 005°-015°; 51°39'·16N 09°54'·40W. Rear, 80m from front, Oc 3s 7m 1M; W with R stripe; vis: 005°-015°.

Bull Rock ☆ 51°35'·51N 10°18'·08W Fl 15s 83m **21M**; W twr; vis: 220°-186°.

KENMARE RIVER, DARRYNANE and BALLYCROVANE

Darrynane Ldg lts 034°. Front, Oc 3s 10m 4M; 51°45'·90N 10°09'·20W. Rear, Oc 3s 16m 4M.

Skelligs Rock ☆ 51°46'·12N 10°32'·51W Fl (3) 15s 53m **19M**; W twr; vis: 262°-115°; part obsc within 6M 110°-115°.

VALENTIA and PORTMAGEE

Fort (Cromwell) Point ☆ 51°56'·02N 10°19'·27W Fl WR 2s 16m **W17M, R15M**; W twr; vis: 304°-R-351°,102°-W-304°; obsc from seaward by Doulus Head when brg more than 180°.

Ldg lts 141°. Front, Oc WRG 4s 25m W11M, R8M, G8M; W twr, R stripe; vis:134°-G-140°-W-142°-R-148°; 51°55'·52N 10°18'·41W. Rear, 122m from front, Oc 4s 43m 5M; vis:128°-157·5° synch with front.

DINGLE BAY TO LOOP HEAD

DINGLE BAY, VENTRY and DINGLE

Ldg lts 182° Oc 3s. Front 52°07'·41N 10°16'·59W, rear 100m behind.

Inishtearaght ☆, W end Blasket Islands 52°04'·55N 10°39'·68W Fl (2) 20s 84m **19M**; W twr; vis: 318°-221°; ***Racon (O)***.

BRANDON BAY, TRALEE BAY and FENIT HARBOUR

Little Samphire Is ☆ 52°16'·26N 09°52'·91W Fl WRG 5s 17m **W16M**, R13M; G13M; Bu ○ twr; vis: 262°-R-275°, 280-R-090°-G-140°-W-152°-R-172°.

Great Samphire I QR 15m 3M; vis: 242°-097°; 52°16'·15N 09°51'·82W.

Fenit Hbr Pier Hd 2 FR (vert) 12m 3M; vis: 148°-058°; 52°16'·24N 09°51'·55W.

SHANNON ESTUARY

Ballybunnion VQ; ***Racon (M) 6M***; 52°32'·52N 09°46'·93W.
Kilstiffin Fl R 3s; 52°33'·80N 09°43'·83W.

Kilcredaune Head ☆ Fl 6s 41m **15M**; W twr; 52°34'·79N 09°42'·58W; obsc 224°-247° by hill within 1M.

Tail of Beal Q (9) 15s; 52°34'·39N 09°40'·75W.
Carrigaholt Fl (2) R 6s; 52°34'·92N 09°40'·51W.
Beal Spit VQ (9) 10s; 52°34'·82N 09°39'·98W.
Beal Bar Q; 52°35'·18N 09°39'·23W.
Doonaha Q (3) R 5s; 52°35'·46N 09°38'·50W.
Letter Point Fl R 7s; 52°35'·44N 09°35'·89W.
Asdee Fl R 5s; 52°35'·09N 09°34'·55W.
Rineanna QR; 52°35'·59N 09°31'·24W.
North Carraig Q; 52°35'·60N 09°29'·76W.

Scattery Is, Rineanna Pt Fl (2) 8s 15m 10M; W twr; vis: 208°-092°; 52°36'·32N 09°31'·03W.

KILRUSH

Marina Ent Chan Ldg lts 355°. Front, Oc 3s; 52°37'·99N 09°30'·27W. Rear, 75m from front, Oc 3s.
Tarbert Is N Point Q WR 4s 18m W14M, R10M; W ○ twr; vis: W069°- R277°- W287°-339°; 52°35'·52N 09°21'·83W.
Tarbert (Ballyhoolahan Pt) Ldg lts 128·2°. Front,Iso 3s 13m 3M; △ on W twr; vis: 123·2°-133·2°; 52°34'·35N 09°18'·80W. Rear, 400m from front, Iso 5s 18m 3M; G stripe on W Bn.

Garraunbaun Pt Fl (3) WR 10s 16m W8M, R5M; W □ col, vis: R shore - W072°- R242°- shore; 52°35'·62N 09°13'·94W.

Rinealon Pt Fl 2·5s 4m 7M; B col, W bands; vis: 234°-088°; 52°37'·12N 09°09'·82W.

FOYNES

W Chan Ldg lts 107·9° (may be moved for changes in chan). Front, Oc 4s 34m 12M;52°36'·91N 09°06'·59W . Rear, Oc 4s 39m 12M.

RIVER SHANNON

Beeves Rock Fl WR 5s 12m W12M, R9M; vis: 064·5°-W-091°-R-238°-W-265°-W(unintens)-064·5°; 52°39'·01N 09°01'·35W .
North Channel Ldg lts 093°. Front, Tradree Rock Fl R 2s 6m 5M; W Trs; vis: 246°-110°; 52°41'·00N 08°49'·87W. Rear 0·65M from front, Iso 6s 14m 5M; W twr, R bands; vis: 327°-190°.

N side, Ldg lts 061°. Front, 52°40'·72N 08°45'·27W, Crawford Rock 490m from rear, Fl R 3s 6m 5M. Crawford No. 2, Common Rear, Iso 6s 10m 5M; 52°40'·85N 08°44'·88W.
Ldg lts 302·1°, Flagstaff Rock, 670m from rear, Fl R 7s 7m 5M; 52°40'·66N 08°44'·40W.

Ldg lts 106·5°. Meelick Rk, Front Iso 4s 6m 3M; 52°40'·25N 08°42'·36W . Meelick No. 2, rear 275m from front Iso 6s 9m 5M; both W pile structures.

LOOP HEAD

Loop Head ☆ 52°33'·68N 09°55'·96W Fl (4) 20s 84m **23M**.

5.4 PASSAGE INFORMATION

The latest editions of the Irish Cruising Club (www.irishcruisingclub.com) Sailing Directions are strongly recommended for all Irish waters. Particularly useful on the W coast where other information is scarce, they are published in two volumes: *E and N coasts of Ireland* and *S and W coasts of Ireland*. See also *Cruising Cork and Kerry* (Graham Swanson/Imray). For notes on crossing the Irish Sea, see 6.4; and for Distances across it see 0.32.

More Passage Information is threaded between the harbours of this Area.

5.5 SPECIAL NOTES FOR IRELAND

Céad Míle Fáilte! One hundred thousand Welcomes!

Lifejackets: It is compulsory to wear lifejackets in Irish waters on all craft of <7m LOA. Children under 16 years must wear a lifejacket or personal flotation device at all times on deck when underway. Every vessel, irrespective of size, must carry a lifejacket or personal flotation device for each person on board. These regulations are mandatory.

Ordnance Survey map numbers refer to the Irish OS maps, scale 1:50,000 or 1¼ inch to 1 mile, which cover the whole island, including Ulster, in 89 sheets.

Irish Customs: First port of call should preferably be at Customs posts in one of the following hbrs: Dublin, Dun Laoghaire, Waterford, New Ross, Cork, Ringaskiddy, Bantry, Foynes, Limerick, Galway, Sligo and Killybegs. Yachts may, in fact, make their first call anywhere and if no Customs officer arrives within a reasonable time, the skipper should inform the nearest Garda (Police) station of the yacht's arrival. Only non-EC members should fly flag Q or show ● over ○ lts on arrival. Passports are not required by UK citizens. All current Northern Ireland 5 and 6 digit telephone numbers have become 8 digits **028 9012** 3456.

Telephone: To call the **Republic of Ireland (RoI)** from the UK, dial **00-353**, then the area code (given in UK ☎ directories and below) minus the initial 0, followed by the ☎ number. To call UK from the RoI: dial 00-44, followed by the area code minus the initial 0, then the number.

Salmon drift nets: Use of these is decreasing but may be encountered along the S and W coasts, off headlands and islands during the summer, especially May–Jul. They may be 1½ to 3M long and difficult to see. FVs may give warnings on VHF Ch 16, 06, 08.

Liquefied petroleum gas: In RoI LPG is supplied by Kosan, a sister company of Calor Gas Ltd, but the bottles have different connections, and the smallest bottle is taller than the normal Calor one fitted in most yachts. Calor Gas bottles can be filled in most larger towns. Camping Gaz is widely available. The abbreviation Kos indicates where Kosan gas is available.

Information: The Irish Cruising Club publishes 2 highly recommended books of Sailing Directions, one for the S and W coasts of Ireland, the other for the N and E coasts. All three are distributed by Imray. See also *Cruising Cork and Kerry* by Graham Swanson (Imray.com & Amazon). All three available from: Irish Sailing Association, 3 Park Road, Dun Laoghaire, Co Dublin, ☎ (01) 2800239, 📠 2807558; or the Irish Tourist Board, 150 New Bond St, London W1Y 0AQ, ☎ (020 7) 518 0800.

Useful websites:

Commissioners of Irish Lights	www.cil.ie
Irish Sailing Association	www.sailing.ie
Irish Tourist Board	www.discoverireland.com
Irish Met Service Sea Area Forecast	www.met.ie/forecasts/sea-area.asp

Currency is the Euro (€), cash is most readily available from ATMs. VAT is 21·5%.

Access by air: There are airports in RoI at Dublin, Waterford, Cork, Kerry, Shannon, Galway, Connaught, Sligo and Donegal/Carrickfin.

Northern Ireland: Belfast CG (MRCC) is at Bangor, Co Down, ☎ (028 91) 463933. HM Customs (⊜) should be contacted H24 on ☎ (028 90) 358250 at the following ports, if a local Customs Officer is not available: Belfast, Warrenpoint, Kilkeel, Ardglass, Portavogie, Larne, Londonderry, Coleraine. Northern Ireland's main airport is Belfast (Aldergrove).

5.6 MALAHIDE

Dublin **53°27'·20N 06°08'·90W** ⚙⚙⚓⚓⚓✿✿✿

CHARTS AC 1468, 633, 5621; Imray C61, C62.

TIDES +0030 Dover; ML 2·4; Duration 0615

Standard Port DUBLIN (NORTH WALL) (⟶)

Times				Height (metres)			
High Water		Low Water		MHWS	MHWN	MLWN	MLWS
0000	0700	0000	0500	4·1	3·4	1·5	0·7
1200	1900	1200	1700				
Differences MALAHIDE							
+0002	+0003	+0009	+0009	+0·1	−0·2	−0·4	−0·2

SHELTER Excellent in marina, dredged approx 2·3m. Access HW±4. Visitors berth on pontoon F. ⚓ between marina and Grand Hotel on S edge of fairway, clear of moorings.

NAVIGATION WPT: SWM LFl 10s 53°27'·12N 06°06'·87W. The approach channel lies between drying sandbanks. It is strongly recommended that visiting yachtsmen obtain up-to-date information by ☎ or VHF from the marina on the latest depths and buoyage and refer this to AC 633. The channel is marked by PHM and SHM perches which are lit.

Entry not advised in strong onshore winds against the ebb. The flood reaches 3kn sp, and the ebb 3½kn. Speed limit 10kn in fairway and 4kn in marina.

LIGHTS AND MARKS The marina and apartment blocks close S of it are visible from the WPT. The Grand Hotel is no longer conspic from seaward, due to trees and bldgs.

R/T Marina, *Call sign Malahide Marina*, Ch **M** 80 (H24). MYC, call *Yacht Base* Ch M (occas).

TELEPHONE (Code 01) Marina 8454129; MRCC 6620922/3; ⊜ 8746571; Police 666 4600; Dr 845 5994; Ⓗ 837 7755.

FACILITIES **Marina** (349) ☎ 8454129, Ⓥ (20) €3·90, ⛽ (€6·50) D(hose H24), P(cans H24), Wi-fi, Gas, BH (30 ton), BY, R, Bar, Ice, ⊡, WC, showers **Malahide YC** ☎ 8453372, Slip (for craft <5.5m, launching HW ±2), Scrubbing posts for <10m LOA; **Services:** Ⓔ, ⚒, Kos. **Town** ⊡, ✉, Ⓑ, ⇌, ✈ (Dublin).

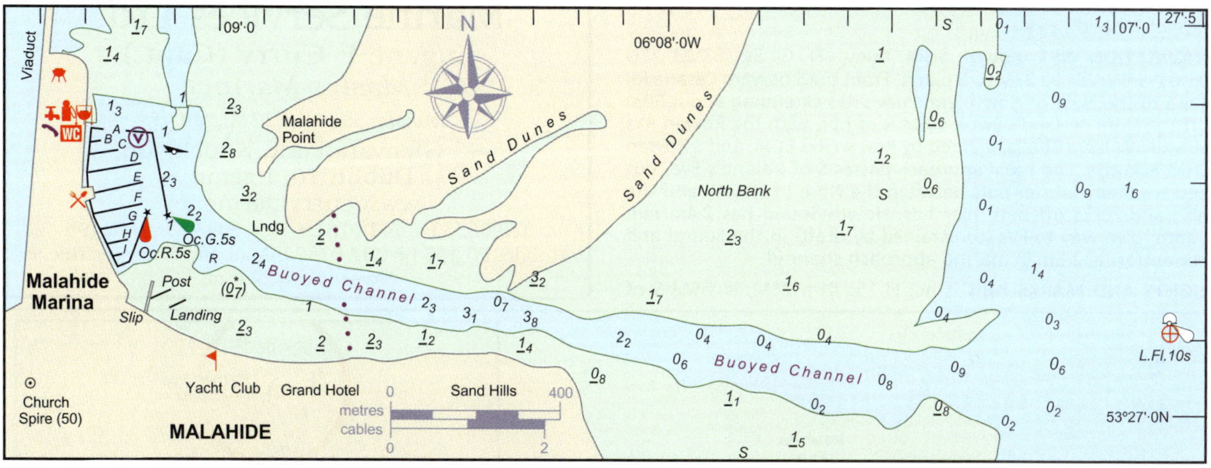

MALAHIDE TO TUSKAR ROCK

(AC 1468, 1787) Malahide, 4M from both Lambay Is and Howth, can be entered in most weather via a channel which constantly shifts through drying sandbanks. Ireland's Eye, a rky island which rises steeply to a height of 99m, lies about 7½ca N of Howth with reefs running SE and SW from Thulla Rk at its SE end. Ben of Howth, on N side of Dublin Bay, is steep-to, with no dangers more than 1ca offshore.

Rosbeg Bank lies on the N side of Dublin Bay. Burford Bank, on which the sea breaks in E gales, and Kish Bank lie offshore in the approaches. ▶ *The N-going stream begins at HW Dublin –0600, and the S-going at HW Dublin, sp rates 3kn.* ◀

From Dublin to Carnsore Pt as a cruising area, hbr facilities are being improved. The shallow offshore banks cause dangerous overfalls and dictate the route which is sheltered from the W winds. ▶ *Tidal streams run mainly N and S, but the N-going flood sets across the banks on the inside, and the S-going ebb sets across them on the outside.* ◀

Leaving Dublin Bay, yachts normally use Dalkey Sound, but with a foul tide or light wind it is better to use Muglins Sound. Muglins (lt) is steep-to except for a rk about 1ca WSW of the lt. Beware Leac Buidhe (dries) 1ca E of Clare Rk. The inshore passage is best as far as Wicklow.

Thereafter yachts may either route offshore, passing east of Arklow Bank and its Lanby to fetch Tuskar Rock or Greenore Pt, or keep inshore of Arklow Bank, avoiding Glassgorman Banks. Stay E of the Blackwater Bank to Lucifer ECM buoy then pass W of Tuskar Rock to round Carnsore Pt to the SW. Avoid the Rusk Channel except in settled weather. Arklow is safe in offshore winds; Wexford has a difficult entrance. Rosslare lacks yacht facilities, but provides good shelter to wait out a SW'ly blow.

Arklow Bank Wind Farm, 7 miles east of Arklow, has 7 wind turbines, each 72.8m high with 104m diameter blades. They are lit, N'most and S'most are fitted with AIS transmitters.

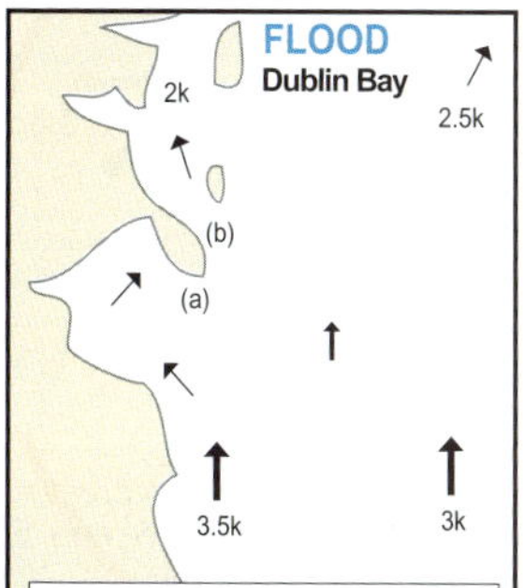

Tide between Rosbeg bank and Howth Hd (a) runs NE from HW Dublin +0300 for 9h30. In Howth Sd (b) the stream is NW going from +0430 to –0130.
New flood and ebb tides begin close to the S shore and N of Baily up to 1h before HW Dublin.

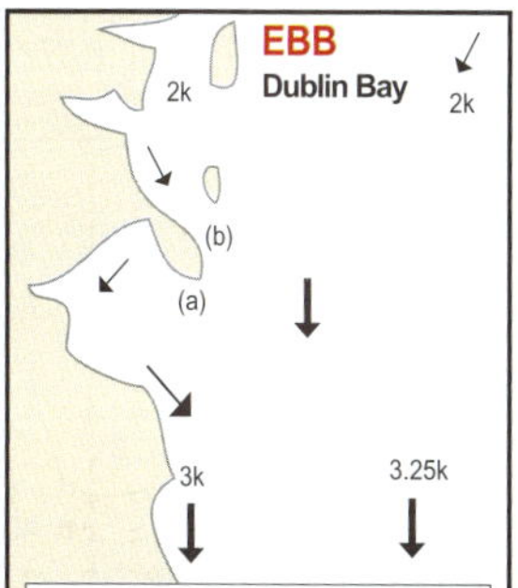

The tide between Rosbeg bank and Howth Hd (a) runs SW from HW Dublin for 3h. In Howth Sd (b) the stream is SE going from –0130 to +0430.
Strengths of streams increase S of Dublin Bay, and decrease N of it.

5.7 HOWTH

Dublin **53°23'·60N 06°04'·00W** ❁❁❁◊◊◊✿✿✿

CHARTS AC 1468, 1415, 5621; Imray C61, C62.

TIDES +0025 Dover; ML 2·4; Duration 0625

Standard Port DUBLIN (NORTH WALL) (⟶)

Times				Height (metres)			
High Water		Low Water		MHWS	MHWN	MLWN	MLWS
0000	0700	0000	0500	4·1	3·4	1·5	0·7
1200	1900	1200	1700				
Differences HOWTH							
−0007	−0005	+0001	+0005	0·0	−0·1	−0·2	−0·2

SHELTER Excellent in marina, available at all tides and in almost any conditions. After a severe ENE'ly storm, expect a dangerous scend in the app chan. Caution: many moorings in E part of outer hbr. No ent to FV basin for yachts. Inside the inner hbr keep strictly to chan to avoid drying shoals either side and a substantial wavebreak (gabion). Marina depth 2·2m. R PHM posts mark the outer limit of dredging around the marina. 4kn speed limit. There is a fair weather ⚓ in 2-3m at Carrigeen Bay, SW side of Ireland's Eye.

NAVIGATION WPT Howth SHM buoy, Fl G 5s, 53°23'·72N 06°03'·53W, 251°/0·27M to E pier lt. From the S beware Casana Rk 4ca S of the Nose of Howth and Puck's Rks extending about 50m off the Nose. Ireland's Eye is 0·6M N of hbr, with the Rowan Rks SE and SW from Thulla, marked by Rowan Rks ECM, and S Rowan SHM lt buoys. The usual approach passes S of Ireland's Eye, but beware many lobster pots between the Nose of Howth and the hbr, and rocks off both pier hds. Howth Sound has 2·4m min depth; give way to FVs (constrained by draft) in the Sound and hbr entrance. 2·5m in marina approach channel.

LIGHTS AND MARKS Baily lt ho, Fl 15s 41m 26M, is 1·5M S of Nose of Howth. Disused lt ho on E pier is conspic. E pier lt, Fl (2) WR 7·5s 13m 12/9M; 256°-W-295°, R elsewhere. W sector leads safely to NE pierhead which should be rounded 50m off. Ent to FV Basin has QR and Fl G 3s. The chan to marina is marked by 8 R & G floating perches (some lit) with W reflective tape (2 bands = port, 1 = stbd).

R/T Marina Ch M 80 (H24). HM VHF Ch 16 11 (Mon-Fri 0700–2300LT; Sat/Sun occas).

TELEPHONE (Code 01) HM 832 2252; MRCC 6620922/3; ⊖ 8746571; Police 666 4900; Dr 832 3191; Ⓗ 837 7755.

FACILITIES **Howth Marina** (350 inc Ⓥ) ☎ 8392777, www.hyc.ie; €2.75, Wi-fi, M, D (H24), P(cans), Slip(H24), C (15 ton), ⛽, ▣, ♿. **Howth YC** ☎ 832 2141, Scrubbing posts <20m LOA, R (☎ 839 2100), Bar (☎ 8320606), ▣, ♿. **Howth Boat Club** (no facilities). **Services:** LB, Gas, Kos, ME, SM, CH, El, Ⓔ. **Town** ✉, Ⓑ, ▣, ⇌, ✈ (Dublin).

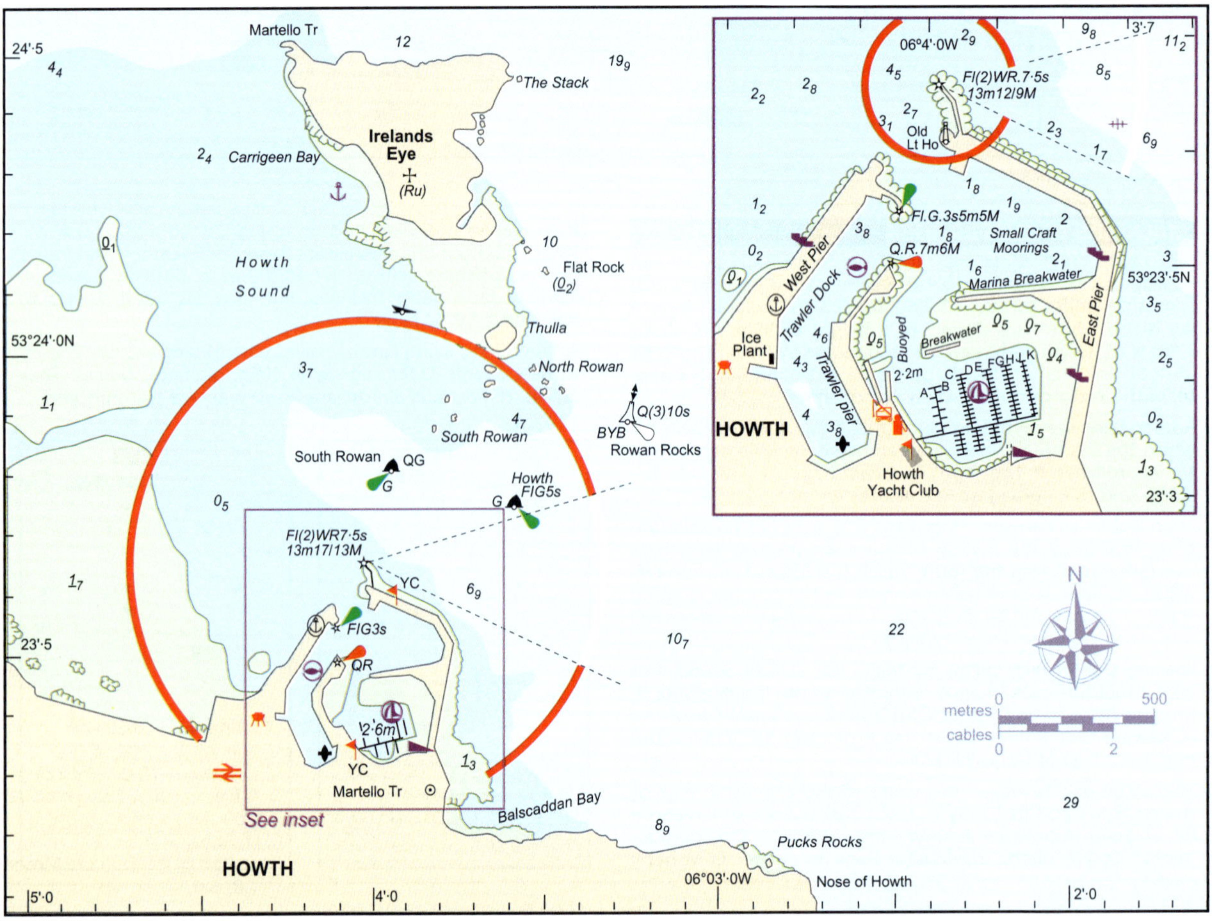

5.8 DUBLIN

Dublin **53°20'·85N 06°14'·80W**

CHARTS AC 1468, 1415, 1447, 5621; Imray C61, C62.

TIDES +0042 Dover; ML 2·4; Duration 0640

Standard Port DUBLIN (NORTH WALL) (⟶)

Times				Height (metres)			
High Water		Low Water		MHWS	MHWN	MLWN	MLWS
0000	0700	0000	0500	4·1	3·4	1·5	0·7
1200	1900	1200	1700				
Differences DUBLIN BAR and DUN LAOGHAIRE							
–0006	–0001	–0002	–0003	0·0	0·0	0·0	+0·1
GREYSTONES (53°09'N 06°04'W)							
–0008	–0008	–0008	–0008	–0·5	–0·4	No data	

SHELTER **Dublin Port,** excellent on N side 1ca below Matt Talbot Br on pontoons and Poolbeg YBC Marina, S of Alexandra Basin W.

NAVIGATION **Dublin Port** WPT 53°20'·50N 06°06'·71W, 275°/1·35M to hbr ent. Accessible H24, but the ent to R Liffey is rough in >E'ly F5 against ebb tide.

Note that Bull Wall covers 0.6 to 2.7m at HW. For clearance to enter call *Dublin Port Radio* Ch 12. Beware of shipping; small craft must keep outside fairway buoys. E Link Lifting Br (2·2m closed) opens 1100, 1500 and 2100, or on request HO and Bank Holidays. Call 00 353 1 855 5779.

LIGHTS AND MARKS Entance, N. Bull Lt Fl G 4s 15m 10M synchro with Gt. S. Wall Hd Poolbeg Lt Fl R 4s 20m 10M. Poolbeg power stn 2 R/W chimneys (VQ R) are conspic from afar.

R/T Call *Dublin Port Radio* Ch **12** 13 16 (H24). Lifting bridge (call *Eastlink*) Ch 12. *Poolbeg Marina* Ch **37** 12 16. Dublin Coast Radio Stn 16 67 83.

TELEPHONE (Code 00 353 1) HM Dublin 8748771; MRCC 6620922/3; Coast/Cliff Rescue Service 2803900; ⊖ 2803992; Weather 1550 123855; Police (Dublin) 6668000; Dr 2859244; ⊞ 2806901.

FACILITIES **Dublin City Moorings** ☎ 818 3300, mobile 086856 8113, 20 Ⓥ's AB in 3·3m,€3.25, FW, ⏚, Showers. **Poolbeg YBC Marina** ☎ 6604681, www.poolbegmarina.ie, 35 Ⓥs for 20m max LOA in 2.4m,€3.80, D, FW, ⏚, Showers, ▣, Slip, Bar, R. **Dublin City,** all needs, @ at library, ⇌, ✈. **Ferries:** Holyhead; 4/day; 3¼ hrs; Irish Ferries (www.irishferries.com). Liverpool; 2/day; 8 hrs; P&O (www.poferries.co.uk).

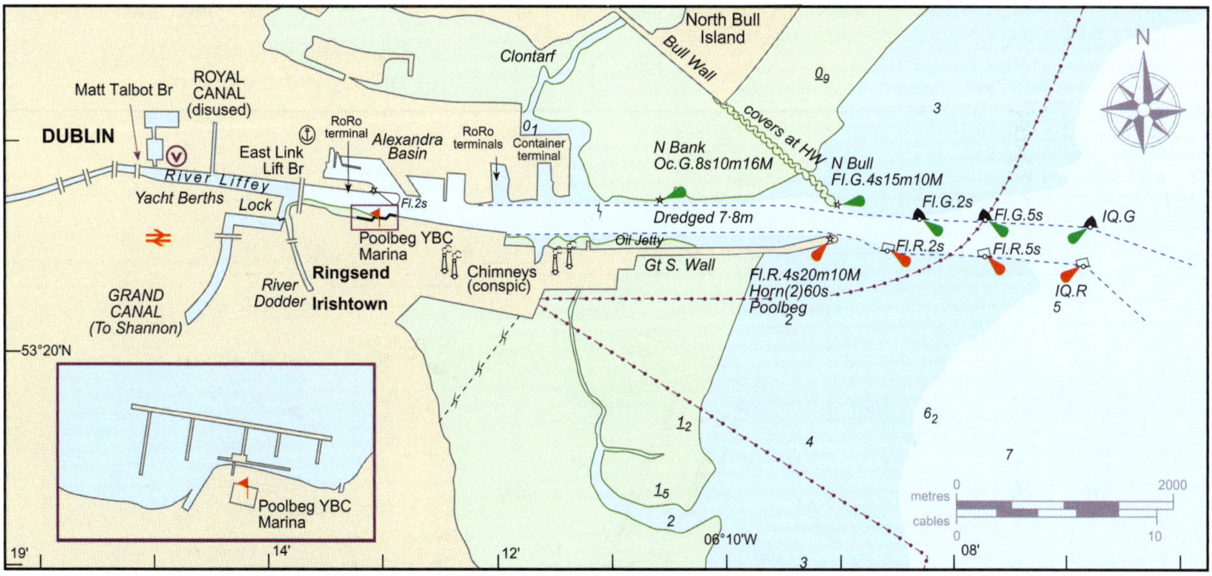

5.9 DUN LAOGHAIRE

Dublin (Port ent) **53°18'·16N 06°07'·68W**

CHARTS AC 1468, 1415, 1447, 5621; Imray C61, C62.

TIDES +0042 Dover; ML 2·4; Duration 0640

Standard Port DUBLIN (NORTH WALL) (⟶)

Times				Height (metres)			
High Water		Low Water		MHWS	MHWN	MLWN	MLWS
0000	0700	0000	0500	4·1	3·4	1·5	0·7
1200	1900	1200	1700				
Differences DUBLIN BAR and DUN LAOGHAIRE							
–0006	–0001	–0002	–0003	0·0	0·0	0·0	+0·1
GREYSTONES (53°09'N 06°04'W)							
–0008	–0008	–0008	–0008	–0·5	–0·4	No data	

SHELTER Excellent. Breakwaters within main hbr protect 800+ berth marina from ferry wash. Ⓥ berths on end of pontoons or as directed. Additional berths inside Western Marina Breakwater. All YCs advertise Ⓥs and/or pontoon berths.

NAVIGATION Dun Laoghaire is accessible H24, WPT 53°18'·40N 06°07'·00W, 240° 0·47M to ent. Keep clear of coasters, ferries/HSS, which turn off St Michael's Pier. Beware drying rocks approx 10m off E Pier Hd. See chartlet overleaf.

TSS: Two TSS ½M long, one at either end of the Burford Bank lead to/from an anti-clockwise circular TSS radius 2·3ca centred on Dublin Bay SWM lt buoy,(53°19'·90N 06°04'·58W, 2·5M NE of Dun Laoghaire/2·75M ESE of Dublin Port). Do not impede large vessels and keep clear of the TSS and fairway.

LIGHTS AND MARKS On Ro Ro Berth 2 x Fl.W = 'Large vessel under way; small craft keep clear of No 1 Fairway' (extends 600m seaward of ent). Traffic signals (Fl W) repeated at head of E Marina Breakwater when large vessels underway.

R/T *Dun Laoghaire Hbr* VHF Ch **14** 16 (H24); Marina Ch **M**; YCs Ch M. Dublin Coast Radio Stn 16 67 83.

TELEPHONE (Code 00 353 1) HM Dun Laoghaire 2801130; MRCC 6620922/3; Coast/Cliff Rescue Service 2803900; ⊖ 2803992; Weather 1550 123855; Police 6665000; Dr 2859244; ⊞ 2806901.

FACILITIES **Dun Laoghaire Hbr Marina** ☎ 2020040, hal@dlmarina.com, www.dlmarina.com, (800 AB inc 20Ⓥ) €4.00, BH, D&P, ▣, ♿, Wi-fi. **Yacht Clubs** (E to W): **National YC** ☎ 2805725, ℻ 2807837, Slip, M, L, C (12 ton), FW, D, R, Bar; **Royal St George YC** ☎ 2801811, ℻ 2843002, Boatman ☎ 2801208; AB by prior agreement, €3.00, Slip, M, D, L, FW, C (5 ton), R, Bar; **Royal Irish YC** ☎ 2809452, ℻ 2809723, Slip, M, D, L, FW, C (5 ton), R, Bar; **Dun Laoghaire Motor YC** ☎ 2801371, ℻ 2800870, Slip, FW, AB, Bar, R. **Services** SM, CH, ACA, ⚒, Ⓔ, El, Gas. **Irish National SC** ☎ 28444195. HSS to Holyhead.

WGS84 DATUM

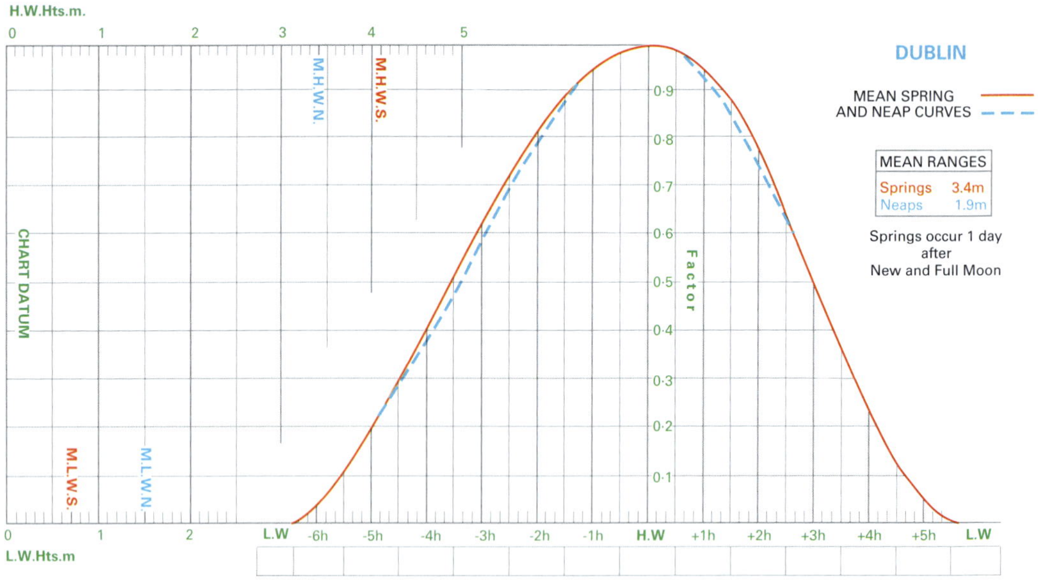
H.W.Hts.m.
CHART DATUM
M.H.W.N.
M.H.W.S.
M.L.W.S.
M.L.W.N.
Factor
L.W.Hts.m
L.W -6h -5h -4h -3h -2h -1h H.W +1h +2h +3h +4h +5h L.W
DUBLIN
MEAN SPRING AND NEAP CURVES
MEAN RANGES
Springs 3.4m
Neaps 1.9m
Springs occur 1 day after New and Full Moon

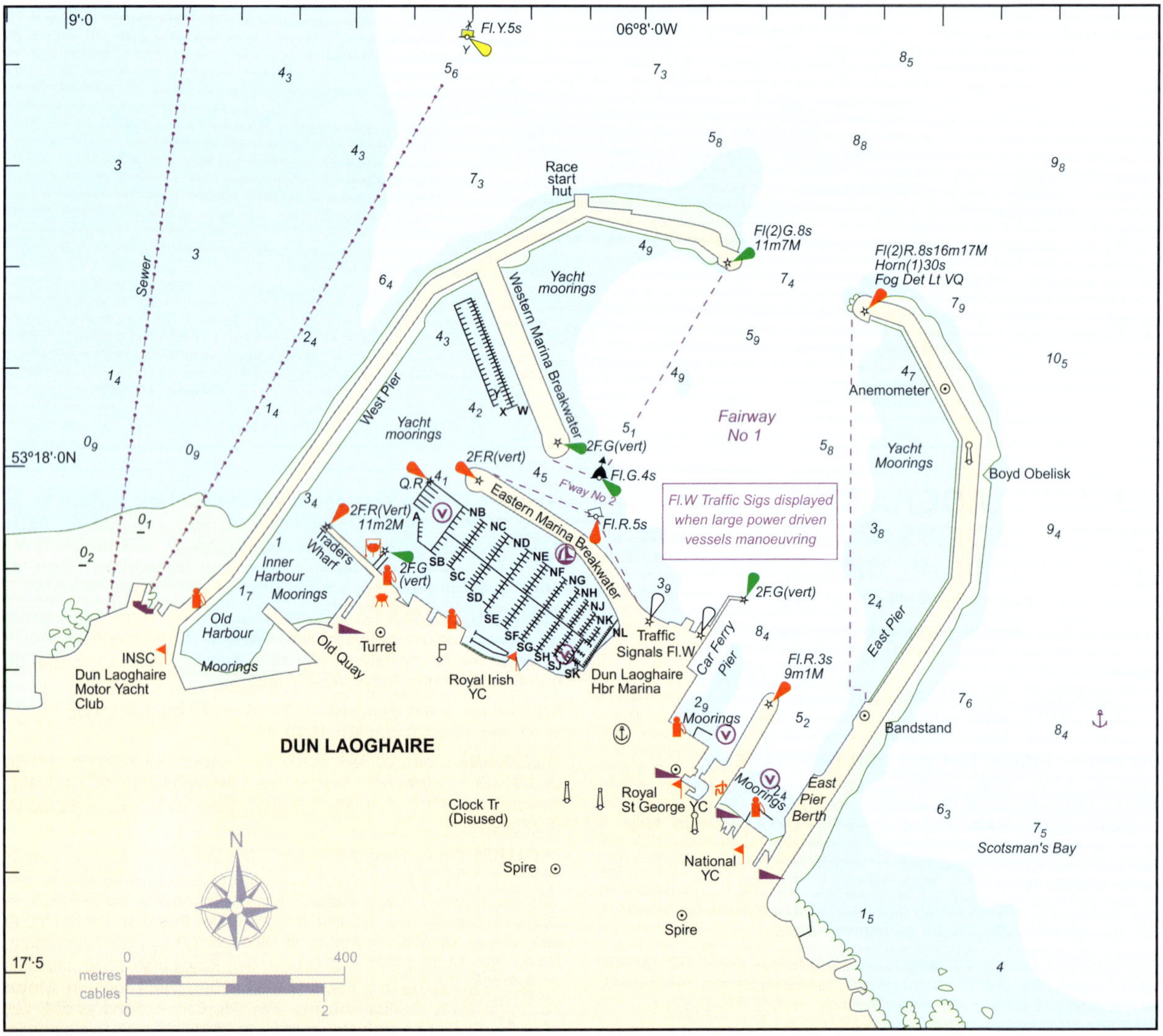
9'·0
06°8'·0W
53°18'·0N
17'·5
Fl.Y.5s
Race start hut
Fl(2)G.8s 11m7M
Fl(2)R.8s16m17M Horn(1)30s Fog Det Lt VQ
Yacht moorings
Western Marina Breakwater
West Pier
Sewer
Anemometer
Fairway No 1
Yacht Moorings
Boyd Obelisk
2F.G(vert)
Fl.G.4s
2F.R(vert)
Q.R
F'way No 2
Fl.R.5s
Eastern Marina Breakwater
Fl.W Traffic Sigs displayed when large power driven vessels manoeuvring
2F.R(Vert) 11m2M
Traders Wharf
Inner Harbour Moorings
2F.G (vert)
Old Harbour
Moorings
Old Quay
Turret
Traffic Signals Fl.W
Car Ferry Pier
East Pier
Fl.R.3s 9m1M
INSC
Dun Laoghaire Motor Yacht Club
Royal Irish YC
Dun Laoghaire Hbr Marina
Bandstand
DUN LAOGHAIRE
Moorings
East Pier Berth
Clock Tr (Disused)
Royal St George YC
Scotsman's Bay
Spire
National YC
metres
cables

TIME ZONE (UT)
For Summer Time add ONE hour in **non-shaded areas**

DUBLIN (NORTH WALL) LAT 53°21'N LONG 6°13'W

TIMES AND HEIGHTS OF HIGH AND LOW WATERS

Dates in red are SPRINGS
Dates in blue are NEAPS

YEAR **2010**

JANUARY

Date	Time	m	Date	Time	m
1 F	0451	0.8	16 SA	0007	3.7
	1133	4.3		0542	1.0
	1723	0.4		1211	4.0
				1811	0.9
2 SA	0003	4.1	17 SU	0036	3.7
	0535	0.7		0612	1.0
	1219	4.4		1242	4.0
	1809	0.3		1841	0.9
3 SU	0051	4.1	18 M	0106	3.7
	0620	0.7		0642	1.0
	1306	4.4		1314	4.0
	1859	0.3		1910	0.9
4 M	0140	4.1	19 TU	0139	3.7
	0708	0.8		0713	1.0
	1356	4.4		1350	3.9
	1950	0.4		1940	0.9
5 TU	0232	4.0	20 W	0215	3.6
	0759	0.9		0747	1.0
	1449	4.3		1428	3.9
	2044	0.5		2014	0.9
6 W	0327	3.8	21 TH	0254	3.6
	0855	1.0		0826	1.1
	1545	4.1		1510	3.8
	2140	0.7		2053	1.0
7 TH	0426	3.7	22 F	0338	3.5
	0955	1.2		0909	1.2
	1645	4.0		1554	3.7
	◑ 2239	1.0		2136	1.1
8 F	0529	3.6	23 SA	0427	3.4
	1100	1.4		0959	1.4
	1752	3.8		1644	3.5
	2343	1.2		◐ 2227	1.3
9 SA	0636	3.5	24 SU	0525	3.3
	1211	1.5		1100	1.5
	1902	3.6		1744	3.4
				2332	1.4
10 SU	0053	1.3	25 M	0635	3.3
	0741	3.5		1218	1.5
	1328	1.5		1858	3.4
	2012	3.6			
11 M	0206	1.4	26 TU	0052	1.5
	0845	3.6		0749	3.4
	1441	1.4		1335	1.4
	2119	3.6		2015	3.4
12 TU	0307	1.4	27 W	0207	1.4
	0942	3.7		0852	3.6
	1539	1.3		1441	1.1
	2217	3.6		2121	3.6
13 W	0356	1.3	28 TH	0307	1.1
	1030	3.8		0946	3.9
	1625	1.1		1537	0.8
	2302	3.6		2216	3.8
14 TH	0436	1.2	29 F	0357	0.9
	1109	3.9		1034	4.1
	1704	1.0		1626	0.5
	2338	3.7		2304	4.0
15 F	0511	1.1	30 SA	0441	0.7
	1141	4.0		1119	4.3
	1739	0.9		1711	0.2
	●			○ 2349	4.1
			31 SU	0523	0.5
				1203	4.4
				1755	0.1

FEBRUARY

Date	Time	m	Date	Time	m
1 M	0033	4.1	16 TU	0036	3.7
	0604	0.5		0613	0.8
	1248	4.5		1246	4.0
	1840	0.1		1834	0.7
2 TU	0117	4.1	17 W	0105	3.7
	0648	0.5		0641	0.8
	1334	4.4		1320	3.9
	1926	0.2		1902	0.7
3 W	0203	4.0	18 TH	0139	3.7
	0734	0.6		0713	0.8
	1423	4.3		1357	3.9
	2015	0.4		1936	0.8
4 TH	0251	3.8	19 F	0217	3.7
	0825	0.8		0751	0.9
	1515	4.1		1438	3.8
	2106	0.7		2015	0.8
5 F	0343	3.7	20 SA	0259	3.6
	0921	1.0		0833	1.0
	1611	3.8		1522	3.7
	◑ 2200	1.0		2058	1.0
6 SA	0442	3.5	21 SU	0346	3.5
	1023	1.3		0923	1.1
	1717	3.6		1612	3.5
	2259	1.3		2149	1.2
7 SU	0552	3.4	22 M	0442	3.3
	1133	1.4		1024	1.3
	1832	3.4		1712	3.3
				◐ 2253	1.4
8 M	0010	1.5	23 TU	0552	3.2
	0704	3.4		1146	1.4
	1301	1.5		1831	3.3
	1948	3.3			
9 TU	0139	1.6	24 W	0022	1.5
	0815	3.4		0718	3.3
	1428	1.4		1314	1.3
	2103	3.4		1958	3.3
10 W	0252	1.5	25 TH	0149	1.4
	0919	3.6		0831	3.5
	1527	1.3		1427	1.0
	2205	3.4		2107	3.6
11 TH	0341	1.3	26 F	0255	1.1
	1010	3.7		0929	3.8
	1611	1.1		1525	0.6
	2248	3.5		2203	3.8
12 F	0419	1.2	27 SA	0345	0.8
	1050	3.8		1019	4.1
	1646	0.9		1613	0.3
	2320	3.6		2249	4.0
13 SA	0452	1.0	28 SU	0427	0.6
	1122	3.9		1104	4.3
	1717	0.8		1656	0.1
	2346	3.6		○ 2331	4.1
14 SU	0521	0.9			
	1150	3.9			
	1745	0.8			
	●				
15 M	0011	3.7			
	0548	0.8			
	1217	4.0			
	1810	0.7			

MARCH

Date	Time	m	Date	Time	m
1 M	0507	0.4	16 TU	0520	0.7
	1146	4.4		1150	3.9
	1737	0.0		1736	0.6
2 TU	0011	4.1	17 W	0004	3.7
	0546	0.3		0544	0.6
	1229	4.4		1218	3.9
	1818	0.0		1759	0.6
3 W	0051	4.1	18 TH	0033	3.8
	0627	0.3		0612	0.6
	1312	4.3		1252	3.9
	1901	0.2		1829	0.6
4 TH	0132	4.0	19 F	0107	3.8
	0711	0.4		0645	0.6
	1358	4.2		1331	3.9
	1945	0.4		1905	0.7
5 F	0216	3.9	20 SA	0147	3.8
	0759	0.6		0725	0.7
	1447	3.9		1413	3.8
	2033	0.7		1946	0.8
6 SA	0303	3.7	21 SU	0230	3.7
	0853	0.9		0810	0.8
	1541	3.7		1500	3.7
	2124	1.1		2032	1.0
7 SU	0357	3.5	22 M	0319	3.6
	0953	1.1		0904	1.0
	1646	3.4		1552	3.5
	◑ 2221	1.4		2127	1.2
8 M	0506	3.3	23 TU	0415	3.4
	1101	1.3		1010	1.1
	1802	3.2		1656	3.3
	2328	1.6		◐ 2236	1.4
9 TU	0626	3.3	24 W	0527	3.3
	1226	1.5		1133	1.2
	1921	3.1		1818	3.3
10 W	0057	1.7	25 TH	0004	1.5
	0740	3.3		0653	3.3
	1401	1.4		1258	1.1
	2040	3.2		1942	3.3
11 TH	0224	1.6	26 F	0130	1.4
	0848	3.5		0808	3.5
	1501	1.2		1410	0.8
	2141	3.3		2051	3.5
12 F	0316	1.4	27 SA	0236	1.1
	0942	3.6		0909	3.8
	1544	1.0		1507	0.5
	2222	3.5		2146	3.8
13 SA	0354	1.1	28 SU	0326	0.8
	1023	3.7		1001	4.0
	1618	0.9		1554	0.3
	2252	3.6		2232	3.9
14 SU	0426	0.9	29 M	0410	0.5
	1056	3.8		1047	4.2
	1647	0.8		1637	0.1
	2319	3.6		2312	4.0
15 M	0454	0.8	30 TU	0450	0.4
	1124	3.9		1129	4.3
	1713	0.7		1717	0.1
	● 2342	3.7		○ 2349	4.0
			31 W	0529	0.3
				1211	4.2
				1757	0.2

APRIL

Date	Time	m	Date	Time	m
1 TH	0026	4.0	16 F	0004	3.8
	0609	0.3		0546	0.6
	1254	4.2		1229	3.9
	1837	0.3		1803	0.6
2 F	0106	4.0	17 SA	0042	3.9
	0653	0.4		0624	0.6
	1339	4.0		1310	3.8
	1920	0.6		1841	0.7
3 SA	0148	3.9	18 SU	0124	3.8
	0740	0.6		0708	0.6
	1426	3.8		1356	3.8
	2005	0.8		1926	0.8
4 SU	0233	3.7	19 M	0211	3.8
	0833	0.8		0759	0.7
	1519	3.6		1447	3.7
	2055	1.1		2017	1.0
5 M	0324	3.6	20 TU	0303	3.7
	0931	1.0		0859	0.9
	1620	3.3		1544	3.5
	2150	1.4		2118	1.2
6 TU	0427	3.4	21 W	0402	3.6
	1034	1.2		1008	1.0
	1731	3.1		1650	3.4
	◑ 2254	1.6		◐ 2228	1.4
7 W	0546	3.3	22 TH	0513	3.5
	1147	1.3		1123	1.0
	1846	3.1		1806	3.4
				2347	1.4
8 TH	0008	1.7	23 F	0631	3.5
	0701	3.3		1238	0.9
	1313	1.3		1922	3.4
	1958	3.1			
9 F	0134	1.6	24 SA	0103	1.3
	0807	3.4		0743	3.7
	1419	1.2		1345	0.7
	2057	3.3		2027	3.6
10 SA	0235	1.4	25 SU	0208	1.1
	0902	3.5		0846	3.8
	1505	1.0		1442	0.5
	2141	3.4		2123	3.7
11 SU	0317	1.2	26 M	0302	0.9
	0946	3.6		0941	4.0
	1540	0.9		1532	0.4
	2215	3.5		2211	3.8
12 M	0351	1.0	27 TU	0349	0.7
	1022	3.7		1030	4.1
	1610	0.8		1617	0.3
	2245	3.6		2253	3.9
13 TU	0421	0.8	28 W	0433	0.5
	1053	3.8		1115	4.1
	1636	0.7		1659	0.3
	2310	3.7		○ 2330	4.0
14 W	0448	0.7	29 TH	0515	0.5
	1121	3.8		1158	4.1
	1701	0.7		1738	0.4
	● 2334	3.8			
15 TH	0515	0.6	30 F	0007	4.0
	1152	3.8		0556	0.5
	1729	0.6		1240	4.0
				1817	0.6

Chart Datum: 0·20 metres above Ordnance Datum (Dublin). HAT is 4·5 metres above Chart Datum; see 0.20

TIME ZONE (UT)
For Summer Time add ONE hour in **non-shaded areas**

DUBLIN (NORTH WALL) LAT 53°21'N LONG 6°13'W

TIMES AND HEIGHTS OF HIGH AND LOW WATERS

Dates in red are SPRINGS
Dates in blue are NEAPS

YEAR **2010**

MAY

Date	Day	Time	m	Time	m	Time	m	Time	m
1	SA	0045	3.9	0639	0.5	1323	3.8	1858	0.7
2	SU	0126	3.9	0726	0.6	1409	3.7	1942	0.9
3	M	0210	3.8	0816	0.8	1458	3.5	2030	1.1
4	TU	0259	3.7	0910	0.9	1553	3.3	2123	1.3
5	W	0355	3.5	1007	1.1	1655	3.2	2222	1.5
6	TH	0502	3.4	1109	1.2	1803	3.1	◑ 2325	1.6
7	F	0614	3.3	1214	1.3	1907	3.1		
8	SA	0032	1.6	0719	3.3	1318	1.2	2004	3.2
9	SU	0136	1.5	0814	3.4	1411	1.1	2052	3.4
10	M	0227	1.3	0902	3.5	1453	1.0	2133	3.5
11	TU	0308	1.1	0943	3.6	1527	0.9	2206	3.6
12	W	0343	1.0	1019	3.7	1559	0.8	2236	3.7
13	TH	0415	0.8	1053	3.8	1630	0.7	2306	3.8
14	F	0449	0.7	1130	3.8	1705	0.7	● 2342	3.9
15	SA	0527	0.6	1211	3.9	1743	0.7		
16	SU	0022	4.0	0610	0.6	1256	3.9	1825	0.8
17	M	0108	4.0	0658	0.6	1345	3.8	1913	0.9
18	TU	0158	3.9	0753	0.6	1439	3.7	2008	1.0
19	W	0253	3.9	0854	0.7	1537	3.6	2108	1.1
20	TH	0352	3.8	0959	0.8	1640	3.6	◐ 2213	1.2
21	F	0458	3.8	1106	0.8	1748	3.5	2322	1.3
22	SA	0608	3.7	1213	0.8	1856	3.5		
23	SU	0032	1.2	0717	3.8	1317	0.8	2000	3.6
24	M	0138	1.2	0822	3.8	1416	0.7	2058	3.7
25	TU	0237	1.0	0921	3.9	1510	0.7	2150	3.8
26	W	0330	0.9	1016	3.9	1558	0.7	2235	3.8
27	TH	0419	0.8	1104	3.9	1642	0.7	○ 2315	3.9
28	F	0504	0.7	1147	3.9	1723	0.7	2351	3.9
29	SA	0547	0.7	1227	3.8	1801	0.8		
30	SU	0028	3.9	0629	0.7	1307	3.7	1840	0.9
31	M	0107	3.9	0712	0.8	1349	3.6	1920	1.0

JUNE

Date	Day	Time	m	Time	m	Time	m	Time	m
1	TU	0149	3.9	0758	0.8	1433	3.5	2004	1.1
2	W	0233	3.8	0845	0.9	1520	3.4	2052	1.2
3	TH	0320	3.7	0935	1.0	1611	3.3	2144	1.4
4	F	0413	3.5	1027	1.1	1708	3.2	◑ 2240	1.5
5	SA	0512	3.4	1121	1.2	1809	3.2	2339	1.5
6	SU	0616	3.4	1217	1.3	1908	3.2		
7	M	0037	1.5	0717	3.4	1311	1.3	2000	3.3
8	TU	0132	1.4	0812	3.4	1400	1.2	2047	3.5
9	W	0221	1.3	0901	3.5	1445	1.1	2128	3.6
10	TH	0305	1.1	0946	3.6	1526	1.0	2206	3.7
11	F	0347	0.9	1029	3.8	1605	0.9	2245	3.9
12	SA	0429	0.8	1113	3.9	1646	0.8	● 2325	4.0
13	SU	0512	0.6	1157	3.9	1728	0.7		
14	M	0008	4.1	0558	0.5	1244	3.9	1812	0.7
15	TU	0055	4.1	0648	0.5	1334	3.9	1900	0.8
16	W	0145	4.1	0742	0.5	1426	3.9	1953	0.9
17	TH	0238	4.1	0840	0.5	1521	3.8	2050	1.0
18	F	0335	4.0	0940	0.6	1619	3.7	2150	1.1
19	SA	0437	4.0	1041	0.7	1721	3.6	◐ 2253	1.2
20	SU	0543	3.9	1143	0.8	1826	3.6		
21	M	0000	1.3	0652	3.8	1248	0.9	1931	3.6
22	TU	0109	1.3	0800	3.8	1351	1.0	2033	3.6
23	W	0216	1.2	0905	3.7	1450	1.0	2130	3.7
24	TH	0317	1.1	1003	3.8	1543	1.0	2220	3.8
25	F	0410	1.0	1055	3.8	1628	1.0	2303	3.9
26	SA	0456	0.9	1138	3.7	1709	1.0	○ 2338	3.9
27	SU	0538	0.9	1215	3.7	1745	0.9		
28	M	0011	3.9	0616	0.8	1248	3.7	1820	1.0
29	TU	0046	3.9	0654	0.8	1323	3.6	1856	1.0
30	W	0123	3.9	0732	0.9	1401	3.6	1934	1.0

JULY

Date	Day	Time	m	Time	m	Time	m	Time	m
1	TH	0202	3.9	0812	0.9	1440	3.5	2014	1.1
2	F	0244	3.8	0852	1.0	1522	3.4	2057	1.2
3	SA	0328	3.7	0935	1.1	1607	3.4	2144	1.3
4	SU	0416	3.6	1022	1.2	1658	3.3	◑ 2237	1.4
5	M	0509	3.4	1114	1.3	1757	3.3	2336	1.5
6	TU	0612	3.4	1212	1.4	1901	3.3		
7	W	0038	1.5	0720	3.4	1312	1.4	2002	3.4
8	TH	0139	1.4	0825	3.4	1409	1.3	2055	3.6
9	F	0235	1.2	0921	3.6	1500	1.1	2142	3.8
10	SA	0326	1.0	1011	3.8	1547	1.0	2227	4.0
11	SU	0413	0.7	1058	3.9	1631	0.8	● 2310	4.1
12	M	0459	0.5	1143	4.0	1714	0.7	2353	4.3
13	TU	0545	0.3	1228	4.1	1757	0.6		
14	W	0037	4.3	0632	0.3	1315	4.0	1842	0.6
15	TH	0126	4.3	0723	0.3	1404	4.0	1931	0.7
16	F	0216	4.3	0816	0.4	1455	3.9	2024	0.8
17	SA	0310	4.2	0912	0.6	1549	3.8	2121	1.0
18	SU	0409	4.0	1010	0.8	1648	3.7	◐ 2222	1.2
19	M	0515	3.8	1111	1.0	1754	3.6	2329	1.3
20	TU	0628	3.7	1216	1.2	1903	3.5		
21	W	0043	1.4	0741	3.6	1327	1.3	2010	3.6
22	TH	0202	1.4	0852	3.6	1434	1.3	2112	3.7
23	F	0311	1.3	0954	3.6	1530	1.3	2206	3.8
24	SA	0403	1.1	1046	3.6	1615	1.1	2249	3.9
25	SU	0446	1.0	1127	3.7	1653	1.0	2323	3.9
26	M	0523	0.9	1158	3.7	1727	1.0	○ 2352	4.0
27	TU	0557	0.8	1225	3.6	1758	0.9		
28	W	0022	4.0	0628	0.8	1254	3.6	1829	0.9
29	TH	0055	4.0	0659	0.8	1326	3.6	1900	0.9
30	F	0130	3.9	0729	0.9	1401	3.6	1933	1.0
31	SA	0208	3.9	0802	0.9	1439	3.6	2010	1.1

AUGUST

Date	Day	Time	m	Time	m	Time	m	Time	m
1	SU	0249	3.8	0839	1.0	1520	3.5	2052	1.2
2	M	0334	3.6	0922	1.1	1606	3.4	2140	1.3
3	TU	0424	3.5	1012	1.3	1700	3.3	◑ 2237	1.5
4	W	0523	3.3	1114	1.4	1806	3.3	2350	1.5
5	TH	0638	3.3	1230	1.5	1922	3.3		
6	F	0107	1.5	0758	3.4	1342	1.4	2028	3.5
7	SA	0214	1.2	0902	3.5	1442	1.2	2122	3.8
8	SU	0311	0.9	0955	3.8	1532	1.0	2209	4.0
9	M	0400	0.6	1042	4.0	1616	0.7	2252	4.3
10	TU	0445	0.3	1126	4.1	1658	0.5	● 2335	4.4
11	W	0528	0.1	1208	4.1	1739	0.4		
12	TH	0017	4.5	0612	0.1	1252	4.1	1821	0.4
13	F	0102	4.4	0658	0.2	1336	4.1	1906	0.5
14	SA	0150	4.3	0748	0.4	1424	4.0	1956	0.7
15	SU	0242	4.2	0840	0.6	1515	3.8	2051	0.9
16	M	0339	3.9	0936	0.9	1611	3.7	◐ 2152	1.1
17	TU	0446	3.7	1036	1.2	1718	3.5	2300	1.4
18	W	0605	3.5	1143	1.4	1833	3.5		
19	TH	0021	1.5	0724	3.4	1302	1.5	1946	3.5
20	F	0153	1.4	0841	3.4	1418	1.5	2053	3.6
21	SA	0301	1.3	0944	3.5	1514	1.4	2149	3.8
22	SU	0350	1.1	1033	3.6	1557	1.2	2231	3.9
23	M	0428	0.9	1109	3.7	1632	1.0	2303	4.0
24	TU	0501	0.8	1136	3.7	1704	0.9	○ 2331	4.0
25	W	0531	0.8	1200	3.7	1733	0.8	2357	4.0
26	TH	0558	0.8	1225	3.7	1801	0.8		
27	F	0026	4.0	0622	0.8	1253	3.7	1827	0.8
28	SA	0059	4.0	0648	0.8	1326	3.7	1858	0.9
29	SU	0136	3.9	0720	0.9	1403	3.7	1934	0.9
30	M	0217	3.8	0757	1.0	1444	3.6	2015	1.1
31	TU	0301	3.7	0841	1.1	1529	3.5	2103	1.2

Chart Datum: 0·20 metres above Ordnance Datum (Dublin). HAT is 4·5 metres above Chart Datum; see 0.20

TIME ZONE (UT)
For Summer Time add ONE hour in **non-shaded areas**

DUBLIN (NORTH WALL) LAT 53°21'N LONG 6°13'W

TIMES AND HEIGHTS OF HIGH AND LOW WATERS

Dates in red are SPRINGS
Dates in blue are NEAPS

YEAR **2010**

SEPTEMBER

Day	Time	m	Day	Time	m
1	0350	3.5	16	0541	3.3
	0931	1.3		1109	1.6
W	1622	3.4	TH	1801	3.4
	◑ 2201	1.4		2356	1.5
2	0450	3.3	17	0702	3.3
	1035	1.5		1230	1.7
TH	1727	3.3	F	1916	3.5
	2319	1.5			
3	0609	3.2	18	0132	1.4
	1200	1.6		0822	3.3
F	1849	3.3	SA	1352	1.6
				2025	3.6
4	0045	1.4	19	0238	1.2
	0737	3.3		0924	3.5
SA	1321	1.5	SU	1449	1.4
	2003	3.5		2121	3.7
5	0159	1.1	20	0325	1.1
	0845	3.5		1008	3.6
SU	1426	1.2	M	1531	1.2
	2101	3.8		2204	3.9
6	0257	0.8	21	0401	0.9
	0939	3.8		1041	3.7
M	1516	0.9	TU	1606	1.0
	2150	4.1		2237	3.9
7	0345	0.4	22	0433	0.8
	1024	4.0		1108	3.7
TU	1559	0.7	W	1638	0.9
	2233	4.3		2306	4.0
8	0428	0.2	23	0500	0.8
	1106	4.1		1133	3.8
W	1639	0.4	TH	1706	0.8
	● 2315	4.5		○ 2332	4.0
9	0509	0.0	24	0525	0.8
	1146	4.2		1156	3.8
TH	1719	0.3	F	1733	0.8
	2356	4.5		2359	4.0
10	0551	0.0	25	0547	0.8
	1226	4.2		1222	3.8
F	1800	0.3	SA	1759	0.8
11	0040	4.4	26	0031	4.0
	0633	0.2		0613	0.8
SA	1309	4.1	SU	1255	3.8
	1844	0.4		1830	0.8
12	0126	4.3	27	0109	3.9
	0719	0.4		0646	0.9
SU	1354	4.0	M	1333	3.8
	1932	0.6		1907	0.9
13	0217	4.1	28	0151	3.8
	0809	0.7		0726	1.0
M	1443	3.9	TU	1416	3.7
	2027	0.9		1950	1.0
14	0313	3.8	29	0236	3.7
	0903	1.0		0811	1.1
TU	1537	3.7	W	1503	3.6
	2128	1.1		2041	1.2
15	0421	3.5	30	0329	3.5
	1003	1.3		0905	1.4
W	1643	3.5	TH	1556	3.5
	◐ 2236	1.3		2144	1.3

OCTOBER

Day	Time	m	Day	Time	m
1	0431	3.4	16	0629	3.2
	1013	1.5		1150	1.7
F	1701	3.4	SA	1838	3.5
	◑ 2302	1.4			
2	0551	3.3	17	0049	1.4
	1138	1.6		0743	3.3
SA	1820	3.4	SU	1310	1.7
				1945	3.6
3	0026	1.3	18	0159	1.3
	0715	3.4		0844	3.4
SU	1259	1.5	M	1412	1.5
	1934	3.6		2042	3.7
4	0139	1.0	19	0249	1.1
	0823	3.6		0929	3.6
M	1403	1.2	TU	1458	1.3
	2036	3.9		2128	3.8
5	0237	0.7	20	0327	1.0
	0918	3.8		1004	3.7
TU	1455	1.0	W	1536	1.1
	2128	4.1		2206	3.9
6	0325	0.4	21	0359	0.9
	1004	4.0		1035	3.8
W	1540	0.7	TH	1609	1.0
	2214	4.3		2238	3.9
7	0409	0.2	22	0427	0.9
	1046	4.1		1104	3.8
TH	1621	0.5	F	1639	0.9
	● 2257	4.4		2307	3.9
8	0450	0.1	23	0452	0.8
	1125	4.2		1129	3.9
F	1702	0.4	SA	1706	0.9
	2339	4.4		○ 2336	3.9
9	0531	0.2	24	0517	0.8
	1205	4.2		1156	3.9
SA	1744	0.4	SU	1735	0.8
10	0023	4.3	25	0009	3.9
	0612	0.3		0546	0.8
SU	1246	4.1	M	1230	3.9
	1827	0.5		1809	0.8
11	0109	4.2	26	0048	3.9
	0655	0.6		0622	0.9
M	1330	4.1	TU	1310	3.9
	1915	0.6		1849	0.9
12	0159	4.0	27	0132	3.8
	0743	0.9		0703	1.0
TU	1417	3.9	W	1355	3.9
	2008	0.9		1936	1.0
13	0254	3.7	28	0221	3.7
	0835	1.1		0751	1.2
W	1510	3.8	TH	1444	3.8
	2107	1.1		2030	1.1
14	0358	3.5	29	0316	3.6
	0933	1.4		0849	1.4
TH	1612	3.6	F	1539	3.7
	◐ 2211	1.3		2134	1.1
15	0512	3.3	30	0420	3.5
	1037	1.6		0957	1.5
F	1725	3.5	SA	1642	3.6
	2324	1.4		◑ 2247	1.2
			31	0533	3.4
				1114	1.5
			SU	1753	3.7

NOVEMBER

Day	Time	m	Day	Time	m
1	0002	1.1	16	0100	1.4
	0648	3.5		0749	3.4
M	1230	1.5	TU	1321	1.6
	1904	3.8		1954	3.6
2	0111	0.9	17	0200	1.3
	0755	3.7		0840	3.5
TU	1335	1.3	W	1416	1.5
	2008	3.9		2045	3.6
3	0211	0.7	18	0245	1.2
	0852	3.8		0923	3.7
W	1431	1.1	TH	1500	1.3
	2105	4.1		2129	3.7
4	0303	0.6	19	0322	1.1
	0942	4.0		1000	3.8
TH	1520	0.8	F	1537	1.2
	2156	4.2		2208	3.8
5	0350	0.4	20	0353	1.0
	1027	4.1		1033	3.9
F	1606	0.7	SA	1610	1.1
	2243	4.3		2242	3.8
6	0433	0.4	21	0422	1.0
	1108	4.2		1103	3.9
SA	1650	0.6	SU	1642	1.0
	● 2328	4.3		○ 2315	3.9
7	0514	0.5	22	0452	0.9
	1148	4.2		1134	4.0
SU	1733	0.6	M	1716	0.9
				2352	3.9
8	0012	4.2	23	0526	0.9
	0554	0.6		1210	4.0
M	1229	4.2	TU	1754	0.8
	1817	0.6			
9	0057	4.1	24	0033	3.9
	0636	0.8		0604	0.9
TU	1312	4.1	W	1252	4.1
	1903	0.7		1837	0.8
10	0145	3.9	25	0119	3.9
	0721	1.0		0648	1.0
W	1357	4.0	TH	1338	4.0
	1953	0.8		1926	0.8
11	0236	3.7	26	0209	3.8
	0810	1.2		0737	1.1
TH	1446	3.9	F	1429	4.0
	2047	1.0		2020	0.8
12	0333	3.5	27	0304	3.7
	0904	1.4		0834	1.2
F	1541	3.7	SA	1523	4.0
	2144	1.2		2120	0.9
13	0437	3.3	28	0404	3.7
	1003	1.6		0937	1.3
SA	1644	3.6	SU	1622	3.9
	◐ 2245	1.3		◑ 2224	1.0
14	0544	3.3	29	0509	3.6
	1107	1.7		1045	1.4
SU	1752	3.5	M	1726	3.9
	2351	1.4		2332	1.0
15	0650	3.3	30	0618	3.6
	1215	1.7		1156	1.4
M	1857	3.5	TU	1833	3.9

DECEMBER

Day	Time	m	Day	Time	m
1	0039	1.0	16	0053	1.5
	0724	3.7		0748	3.4
W	1304	1.3	TH	1323	1.6
	1940	3.9		1957	3.4
2	0144	0.9	17	0150	1.4
	0826	3.8		0839	3.5
TH	1407	1.2	F	1417	1.5
	2044	4.0		2050	3.5
3	0242	0.8	18	0239	1.3
	0921	3.9		0924	3.7
F	1504	1.1	SA	1503	1.4
	2143	4.0		2136	3.6
4	0333	0.8	19	0320	1.2
	1012	4.0		1003	3.8
SA	1555	0.9	SU	1544	1.2
	2235	4.0		2219	3.7
5	0420	0.8	20	0357	1.1
	1057	4.1		1040	3.9
SU	1643	0.8	M	1622	1.0
	● 2323	4.0		2258	3.8
6	0502	0.8	21	0433	1.0
	1137	4.1		1116	4.1
M	1727	0.7	TU	1701	0.8
				○ 2338	3.9
7	0006	4.0	22	0511	0.9
	0542	0.8		1154	4.2
TU	1216	4.2	W	1741	0.7
	1809	0.7			
8	0047	3.9	23	0020	4.0
	0621	0.9		0550	0.8
W	1255	4.1	TH	1236	4.2
	1852	0.7		1825	0.6
9	0129	3.8	24	0105	4.0
	0701	1.0		0634	0.8
TH	1337	4.1	F	1322	4.2
	1936	0.8		1912	0.5
10	0213	3.7	25	0153	4.0
	0744	1.1		0721	0.9
F	1420	4.0	SA	1411	4.2
	2022	0.9		2003	0.6
11	0300	3.6	26	0244	3.9
	0832	1.3		0813	1.0
SA	1507	3.9	SU	1503	4.2
	2110	1.1		2058	0.7
12	0351	3.4	27	0339	3.8
	0924	1.4		0911	1.1
SU	1557	3.7	M	1558	4.1
	2201	1.2		2157	0.8
13	0449	3.3	28	0439	3.7
	1021	1.6		1013	1.2
M	1652	3.6	TU	1657	4.0
	◐ 2256	1.4		◑ 2259	0.9
14	0551	3.3	29	0544	3.7
	1121	1.6		1121	1.3
TU	1755	3.5	W	1804	3.8
	2354	1.4			
15	0652	3.3	30	0006	1.1
	1222	1.7		0653	3.6
W	1858	3.4	TH	1234	1.4
				1917	3.8
			31	0116	1.2
				0800	3.7
			F	1346	1.4
				2028	3.7

Chart Datum: 0·20 metres above Ordnance Datum (Dublin). HAT is 4·5 metres above Chart Datum; see 0.20

5.10 WICKLOW

Wicklow **52°58'·98N 06°02'·70W**

CHARTS AC 1468, 633, 5621; Imray C61.

TIDES –0010 Dover; ML 1·7; Duration 0640

Standard Port DUBLIN (NORTH WALL) (⟵)

Times				Height (metres)			
High Water		Low Water		MHWS	MHWN	MLWN	MLWS
0000	0700	0000	0500	4·1	3·4	1·5	0·7
1200	1900	1200	1700				
Differences WICKLOW							
–0019	–0019	–0024	–0026	–1·4	–1·1	–0·4	0·0

SHELTER Very safe, and access H24. Outer hbr is open to NE winds which cause a swell. Moorings in NW of hbr belong to SC and may not be used without permission. 4 berths on E Pier (2·5m) are convenient except in strong winds NW to NE, with fender boards/ladders provided. W pier is not recommended. ⚓ in hbr is restricted by ships' turning circle. Inner hbr (river) gives excellent shelter in 2·5m on N and S Quays, which are used by FVs. Packet Quay is for ships (2·5m), but may be used if none due; fender board needed. Yachts should berth on N or S quays as directed and/or space available.

NAVIGATION WPT 52°59'·20N 06°01'·80W, 220°/0·27M to ent. Appr presents no difficulty; keep in the R sector of the E pier lt to avoid Planet Rk and Pogeen Rk.

LIGHTS AND MARKS No ldg marks/lts; lts are as on the chartlet. W pier head lt, Iso G 4s, is shown H24. ☆ Fl WG 10s on Packet Quay hd is vis 076°-G-256°-W-076°.

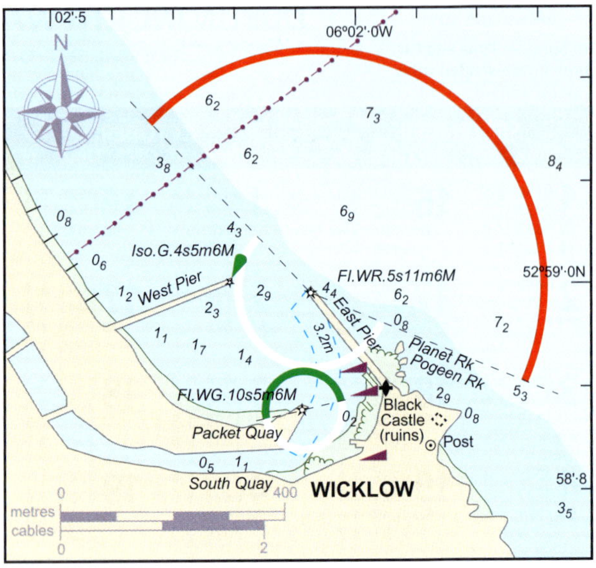

R/T VHF Ch 12, **14**, 16. Wicklow SC Ch M 16 (occas).

TELEPHONE (Code 0404) HM ☎ 67455; MRCC (01) 6620922; Coast/ Cliff Rescue Service 69962; ⊖ 67222; Police 67107; Dr 67381.

FACILITIES **East Pier, S and N Quays**, L, FW, AB €14.00/craft, reductions for longer stay, P & D (cans; bulk: see HM); **Wicklow SC** ☎ 67526, Slip (except LWS), M, L, FW, Bar; **Services**: ME, El, C, Kos, Gaz. **Town** CH, 🛒, R, Bar, ✉, Ⓑ, ⇌, ✈ (Dublin).

5.11 ARKLOW

Wicklow **52°47'·60N 06°08'·20W**

CHARTS AC 1468, 633, 5621; Imray C61.

TIDES –0150 Dover; ML 1·0; Duration 0640

Standard Port DUBLIN (NORTH WALL) (⟵)

Times				Height (metres)			
High Water		Low Water		MHWS	MHWN	MLWN	MLWS
0000	0700	0000	0500	4·1	3·4	1·5	0·7
1200	1900	1200	1700				
Differences ARKLOW (Note small Range)							
–0315	–0201	–0140	–0134	–2·7	–2·2	–0·6	–0·1
COURTOWN							
–0328	–0242	–0158	–0138	–2·8	–2·4	–0·5	0·0

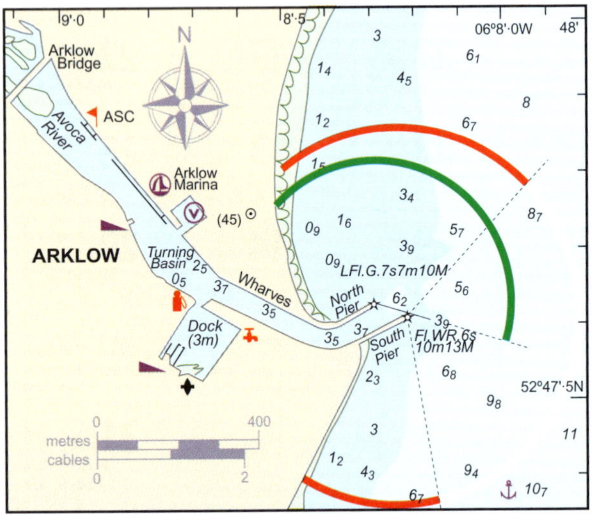

SHELTER Good, access H24.

- Entrance unsafe in strong or prolonged NE to SE winds, when seas break across the bar.

A 60 berth marina lies on NE side of river. Good ⚓ in bay; avoid whelk pots. One AB for Ⓥ (1.4m) at ASC quay. AB on SE wall of Dock (ent is 13·5m wide; 3m depth) in perfect shelter, but amidst FVs. **Arklow Roadstone Hbr**, 1M S of Arklow, is not for yachts.

NAVIGATION WPT 52°47'·60N 06°07'·50W, 270°/0·40M to ent. No navigational dangers, but beware ebb setting SE across hbr ent; give S pierhd a wide berth. Ent is difficult without power, due to blanking by piers. 3kn speed limit. Night entry, see below. Caution: Up-river of Dock ent keep to NE side of river.

LIGHTS AND MARKS No ldg lts/marks, see 5.3 and chartlet Conspic factory chy 2·5ca NW of piers.

- Beware the Pier Hd lts are very difficult to see due to powerful orange flood lts near the root of both piers shining E/ENE onto them (to assist pilotage of departing shipping).
- Best advice to visitors is to approach from the NE with R sector just showing, or enter by day.

R/T Marina Ch 16 12 (HJ); Arklow SC Ch 10.

TELEPHONE (Code 0402) HM 32466; MRCC (01) 6620922/3; Coast/ Cliff Rescue Service 32430; RNLI 32901; ⊖ 32553; Police 32304/5; Dr 32421.

FACILITIES (from seaward) **Dock** €15.00/craft (2nd day free), use showers and toilets in LB Hse, D (Dock ent, HO); **Marina** (60 inc Ⓥ €3·35), ☎ 39901/32610. **Arklow SC** (NE bank, 500m up-river from Dock), showers, pontoon €15.00, 1 Ⓥ. **Services:** FW, P & D (cans ½M), ME, El, ⚒, C (20 ton mobile), Kos. **Town** limited CH for yachts, 🛒, R, P & D (cans), Bar, ✉, Ⓑ, Wi-fi, @, ⇌, ✈ (Dublin).

MINOR HARBOURS S OF ARKLOW

COURTOWN, Wexford, **52°38'·55N 06°13'·50W**. AC 1787. 9.6M S of Arklow is feasible in settled weather and offshore winds. Caution: 10m wide ent; only 1m (maintained by local YC) at MLWS due to silting. AB on E wall or pick up vacant mooring.

MINOR HARBOURS S OF ARKLOW *continued*

POLDUFF PIER, Wexford, **52°34'·15N 06°11'·97W**. AC 1787. 14M S of Arklow. Pier, 100m long, extends in NE direction from shore. NW side of pier has slipway from shore and 1m depth alongside. Local moorings W of pier. Good shelter for small boats in S to W winds. Swell in winds E of S. Appr in daylight only. Appr is clear from NE to E. Rks extend from shore E'ward 200m N of pier but steering along line of pier will clear them. Pub near pier. Village (Ballygarrett) 1·25M W.

5.12 WEXFORD

Wexford **52°20'·10N 06°27'·00W** ☸⚓⚓✿✿

CHARTS AC 1787, 1772, 5621; Imray C61.

TIDES –0450 Dover; ML 1·3; Duration 0630

Standard Port COBH (⟶)

Times				Height (metres)			
High Water		Low Water		MHWS	MHWN	MLWN	MLWS
0500	1100	0500	1100	4·1	3·2	1·3	0·4
1700	2300	1700	2300				
Differences WEXFORD							
+0126	+0126	+0118	+0108	–2·1	–1·7	–0·3	+0·1

SHELTER 250m of AB available just below bridge. Sheltered ⚓ off town quays in 2·3m, but streams are strong. Some ⚓s are provided by WHBTC, close N of Ballast Bank. There are no commercial users other than FVs. Work continues on new waterfront on W side of river.

NAVIGATION Visitors are strongly advised to obtain up to date local information from the WHBTC. See www.whbtc.ie or ☎ 053 9122039.

- Entry is hazardous in strong winds between SE and NE when the sea breaks on the bar. Entry is also difficult at any time for vessels with a draft >1.3m. For strangers best entry is HW±2.
- From N make good 221° from North Long Buoy for approx 2·4M keeping outside 5m contour to avoid Slaney Wreck and Dogger Bank; from S make good 353° for approx 4M from West Holdens Buoy. PHM Bar Buoy (52°19'·57N 06°19·52W in 2009) on 10m contour marks the entrance.
- The narrow buoyed chan, which constantly shifts, starts approx 245°/8ca from Bar Buoy. Keep close to all PHM buoys. Beware the S training wall (covers) and pass well S of Black Man SHM Bn at end of N training wall.
- Proceed either to the quays or by arrangement (☎ 053 9122039 or Ch 16/69) to club visitor's mooring.

LIGHTS AND MARKS The marks and tracks on chartlet should be treated with great caution as the channel shifts continually. There are no ldg lts. The 2 church spires at Wexford give useful general orientation.

R/T Wexford Hbr BC VHF Ch 16 (best time to try 1000–1200 hrs).

TELEPHONE (Code 053) Wexford Hbr BC 9122039; MRCC (01) 6620922/3; ⊖ 9133116; Police 9122333; Dr 9131154; ⊕ 9142233.

FACILITIES Wexford Quays, AB (free), Slip, P, D, FW, ME, El, 🛒, CH; **Wexford Hbr Boat Club,** Slip, C (5 ton), Bar; **Town** ✉, Ⓑ, ≷, ✈ (Waterford).

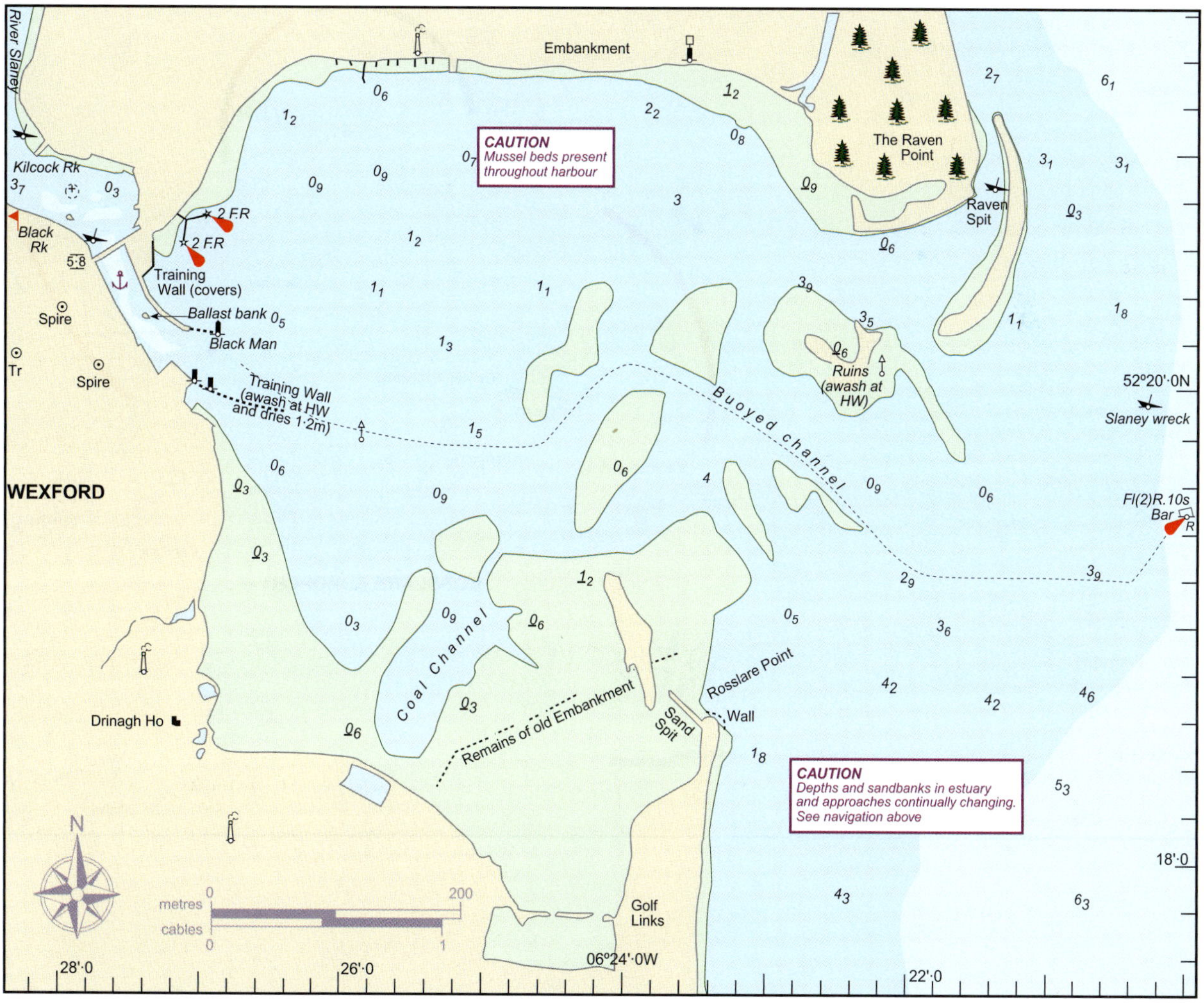

5.13 ROSSLARE EUROPORT

Dublin **52°15'·30N 06°20'·90W**

CHARTS AC 1787, 1772, 5621; Imray C61, C57.

TIDES –0510 Dover; ML 1·1; Duration 0640

Standard Port COBH (⟶)

Times				Height (metres)			
High Water		Low Water		MHWS	MHWN	MLWN	MLWS
0500	1100	0500	1100	4·1	3·2	1·3	0·4
1700	2300	1700	2300				
Differences ROSSLARE EUROPORT							
+0045	+0035	+0015	–0005	–2·2	–1·8	–0·5	–0·1

SHELTER Useful passage shelter from SW'lies, but few facilities for yachts which may berth on E wall of marshalling area (⛵ on the chartlet, 3·7m), or ⚓ about 0·5M W of hbr. ***Small craft harbour (5ca W) is not recommended. In winds from WNW-NNE it is often uncomfortable and, if these winds freshen, dangerous; leave at once, via S Shear***. Rosslare has 160 ferry/high-speed catamaran (41kn) movements per week.

NAVIGATION WPT 52°14'·82N 06°15·60W (abeam S Long SCM buoy, VQ (6)+L Fl 10s), 285°/2·92M to bkwtr lt. Main appr from E, S and W is via S Shear, buoyed/lit chan to S of Holden's Bed, a shoal of varying depth; the tide sets across the chan. From S, beware rks off Greenore Pt, and overfalls here and over The Baillies. From the N, appr via N Shear. Tuskar TSS is approx 8M ESE of hbr. Yachts, bound N/S, will usually navigate to the W of Tuskar Rk where the 3·5M wide chan lies to seaward of The Bailies. A passage inshore of The Bailies requires local knowledge and should not be attempted at night. In heavy weather or poor vis, passage E of Tuskar Rk is advised.

LIGHTS AND MARKS Tuskar Rk, Q (2) 7·5s 33m 28M, is 5·8M SE of hbr. Water tr (R lt, 35m) is conspic 0·8M SSE of hbr ent. Bkwtr lt, Oc WRG 5s 15m 13/10M, see 5.3. Its two W sectors (188°-208° and 283°-286°) cover N and S Shear respectively. Note: Powerful floodlights in the hbr make identification of navigational lights difficult.

R/T VHF Ch **12** (H24) before entering hbr.

TELEPHONE (Code 053) HM 9157921, mobile 087 2320251; MRCC (01) 6620922/3; LB Lookout Stn 9133205; ⊖ 9133116; Police 053 9165200; Dr 9131154; ⊕ 9142233.

FACILITIES Hbr Ops ☎ 9157929, No dues, P&D (cans), L, FW (by hose on Berths 2 and 3), ME, C, Divers, Kos, El. **Village**; 🛒, R, Bar, ✉, Ⓑ, ⇌, ✈ (Dublin). **Ferries:** Irish Ferries (www.irishferries.com): Pembroke Dock, daily, 3¾ Hrs; Cherbourg, 3/week, 18½ hrs; Roscoff, 2/week, 17 hrs. Stena (www.stenaline.co.uk): Fishguard, 2/day, 1¾ Hrs. LD Lines (www.ldlines.co.uk): Le Havre, Sat only, 20 hrs.

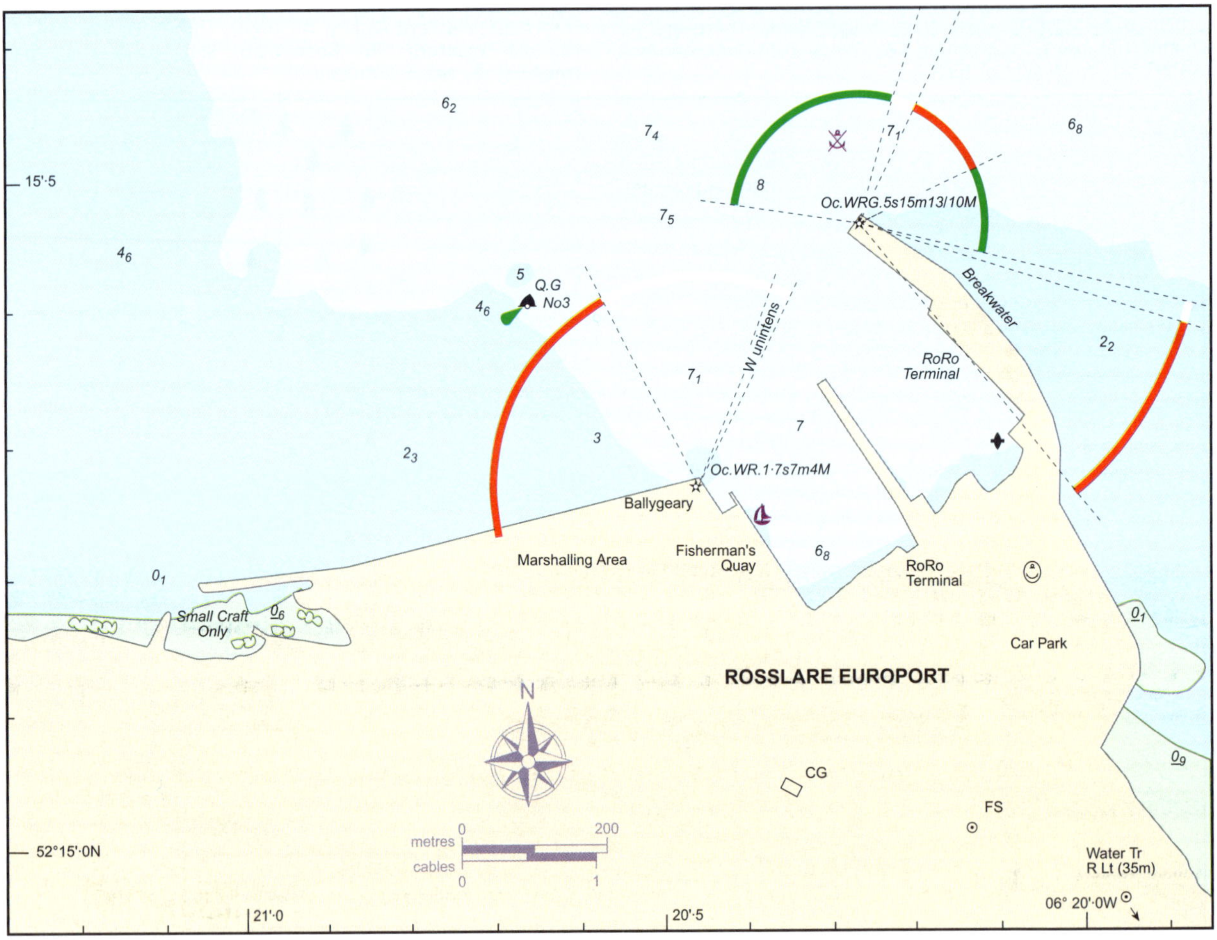

TUSKAR ROCK TO OLD HEAD OF KINSALE

(AC 2049) Dangerous rks lie up to 2ca NW and 6½ca SSW of Tuskar Rk and there can be a dangerous race off Carnsore Pt. In bad weather or poor visibility, use the Inshore Traffic Zone of the Tuskar Rock TSS, passing to seaward of Tuskar Rk (lt), the Barrels ECM lt buoy and Coningbeg buoy.

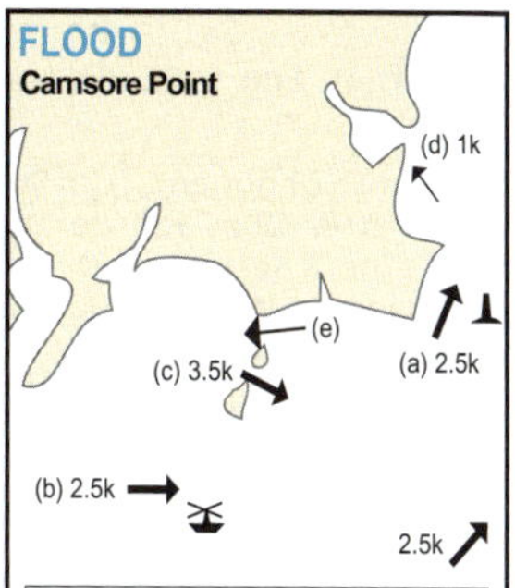

The tide turns to the NE or N (Irish Sea flood) as follows:
(a): HW Dover +0500;
(b): HW D +0520;
(c): HW D +0600;
(d): HW D –0600. NE going streams are shorter in duration and weaker than SE going - careful passage planning is essential.

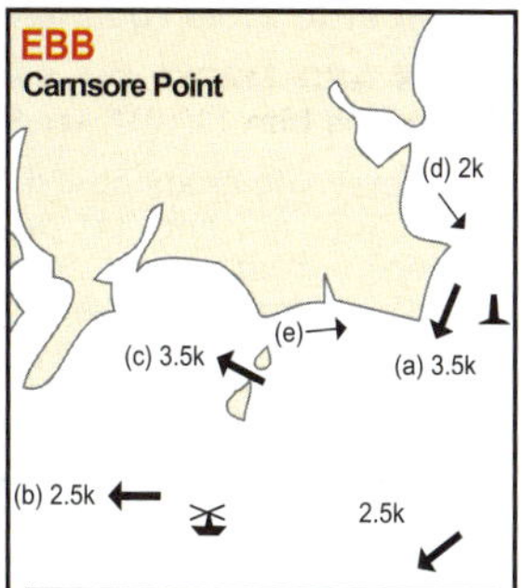

The tide turns to the SW or S as follows:
(a): HW Dover –0200;
(b): HW D –0020;
(c): HW D –0015;
(d): HW D –0300. Leaving Rosslare at HW D –0300 a yacht can carry a fair tide for about 8h until HW D +0515 off Hook Head.

NOTE: The tide turns on St Patrick's Bridge (e) up to 2 hours earlier than in Saltee Sound

If taking the inshore passage from Greenore Pt, stay inside The Bailies to pass 2ca off Carnsore Pt. Beware of lobster pots in this area. Steer WSW to pass N of Black Rk and the Bohurs, S of which are extensive overfalls. The small hbr of Kilmore Quay has been rebuilt with a new marina, but beware rks and shoals in the approaches.

Saltee Sound (AC 2740) is a safe passage, least width 3ca, between Great and Little Saltee, conspic islands to S and N. ▶ *Sebber Bridge extends 7½ca N from the NE point of Great Saltee and Jackeen Rk is 1M NW of the S end of Little Saltee, so care is needed through the sound, where the stream runs 3·5kn at sp.* ◀ There are several rks S of the Saltees, but clear passage between many of them. There are no obstructions on a direct course for a point 1M S of Hook Head, to avoid the overfalls and Tower Race, which at times extend about 1M S of the Head.

Dunmore East (AC 2046) is a useful passage port at the mouth of Waterford Hbr. To the W, beware Falskirt, a dangerous rk off Swines Pt. There are few offlying rks from Tramore Bay to Ballinacourty Pt on the N side of Dungarvan Bay (AC 2017). Helvick is a small sheltered hbr approached along the S shore of the bay, keeping S of Helvick Rk (ECM lt buoy) and other dangers to the N.

Mine Hd (lt) has two dangerous rks, The Rogue about 2½ca E and The Longship 1M SW. To the W is a subm'gd rk 100m SE of Ram Hd. ▶ *Here the W-going stream starts at HW Cobh + 0230, and the E-going at HW Cobh –0215, sp rates 1·5kn.* ◀ Pass 2ca off Capel Island; the sound between it and Knockadoon Hd is not recommended.

The N side of Ballycotton B is foul up to 5ca offshore. Ballycotton Hbr is small and crowded, but usually there is sheltered anch outside. Sound Rk and Small Is lie between the mainland and Ballycotton Is (lt, fog sig). From Ballycotton to Cork keep at least 5ca off for dangers including The Smiths (PHM lt buoy) 1·5M WSW of Ballycotton Island. Pass between Hawk Rk, close off Power Hd, and Pollock Rk (PHM lt buoy) 1.25M SE.

Near the easy entrance and excellent shelter of Cork Harbour (AC 1777), Ringabella Bay offers temp anch in good weather. 7ca SE of Robert's Hd is Daunt Rk (3·5m) on which seas break in bad weather; marked by PHM lt buoy. Little Sovereign on with Reanies Hd 241° leads inshore of it. The Sovereigns are large rks off Oyster Haven, a good hbr but prone to swell in S'lies. The ent is clear except for Harbour Rk which must be passed on its W side. Bulman Rk (SCM lt buoy) is 4ca S of Preghane Pt at the ent to Kinsale's fine harbour. ▶ *The tide on the Cork coast turns to the NE at HW Dover +0045. There is an eddy 5M ESE of Old Head of Kinsale at HW Dover +0400. The ingoing Cork Harbour tide begins at HW Dover +0055.*

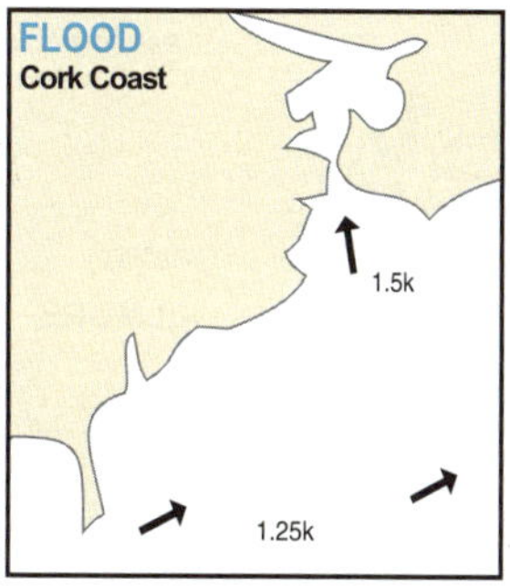

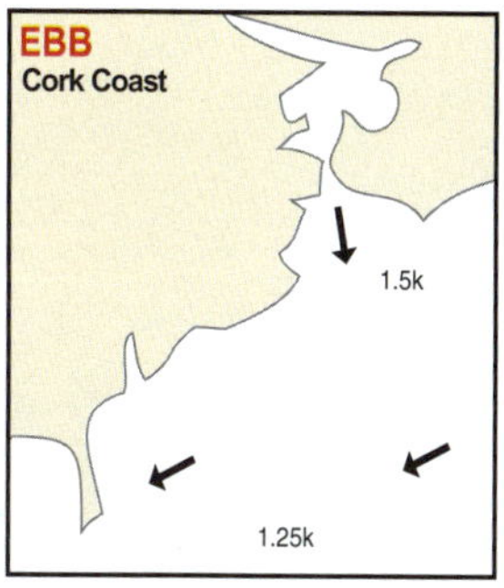

The tide turns SW at HW Dover +0500. The outgoing Cork Harbour tide begins at HW Dover –0540. Old Head of Kinsale (lt, fog sig) is quite steep-to, but a race extends 1M to SW on W-going stream, and to SE on E-going stream. ◀ There is an inshore passage in light weather, but in strong winds keep 2M off.

5.14 KILMORE QUAY

Wexford **52°10'·25N 06°35'·15W**

CHARTS AC 2049, 2740, 5621; Imray C61, C57.

TIDES –0535 Dover; ML No data; Duration 0605

Standard Port COBH (⟶)

Times				Height (metres)			
High Water		Low Water		MHWS	MHWN	MLWN	MLWS
0500	1100	0500	1100	4·1	3·2	1·3	0·4
1700	2300	1700	2300				
Differences BAGINBUN HEAD (5M NE of Hook Hd)							
+0003	+0003	–0008	–0008	–0·2	–0·1	+0·2	+0·2
GREAT SALTEE							
+0019	+0009	–0004	+0006	–0·3	–0·4	No data	
CARNSORE POINT							
+0029	+0019	–0002	+0008	–1·1	–1·0	No data	

SHELTER Excellent in marina (3·0m depth), but hbr ent is exposed to SE'lies. FVs berth on W and E piers, close S of marina.

NAVIGATION WPT 52°09'·22N 06°35'·32W, SWM buoy (Apr-Sep), 007°/1·0M to pier hd lt, on ldg line. Great (57m) and Little (35m) Saltee Islands lie 3M and 1·7M to SSW and S, respectively, of hbr, separated by Saltee Sound. From the E, safest appr initially is via Saltee Sound, then N to WPT. Caution: In bad weather seas break on the Bohurs and The Bore, rks 2M E of Saltee Islands. Beware Goose Rk (2·6m) close W of Little Saltee and Murroch's Rk (2·1m) 6ca NW of Little Saltee. St Patrick's Bridge, 650m E of the WPT, is a 300m wide E/W chan used by FVs and yachts, but carrying only 2·4m; care needed in strong onshore winds. It is marked by a PHM buoy, Fl R 6s, and a SHM buoy, Fl G 6s, (laid Apr to mid-Sep); general direction of buoyage is E. From the W, appr is clear but keep at least 5ca off Forlorn Pt to avoid Forlorn Rk (1·5m).

LIGHTS AND MARKS See 5.3 and chartlet. Ldg lts/marks lead 008° to the hbr.

- From W, ldg lts are obsc'd by piers until S of hbr ent. Turn 90° port into hbr ent, just past ☆ QRG at W Quay Hd; do not overshoot into shoal water ahead. The R sectors of this ☆ QRG warn of Forlorn Rock and The Lings to W of the ldg line and shingle banks drying 0·6m close E of the ldg line.

A white-gabled church is conspic from afar, as are two 20m high flood lt pylons on the E quay. A disused lt ship at the inner end of W quay is a museum of no navigational significance.

R/T VHF Ch 09 (occas).

TELEPHONE (Code 053) HM ☎ 9129955; ⊖ 9133741; MRCC (01) 6620922/3; Emergency/Dr/Police 999.

FACILITIES **Marina** Ch 09 16 (35+20 Ⓥ) ☎ 9129955, €2.20, Slip, D & P, El, ME, LB; **Village** Showers at Stella Maris (10 mins walk), Gaz, CH, ME, El, D & P (cans) is 3M away, R, Bar, ✉, Ⓗ (Wexford 15M).

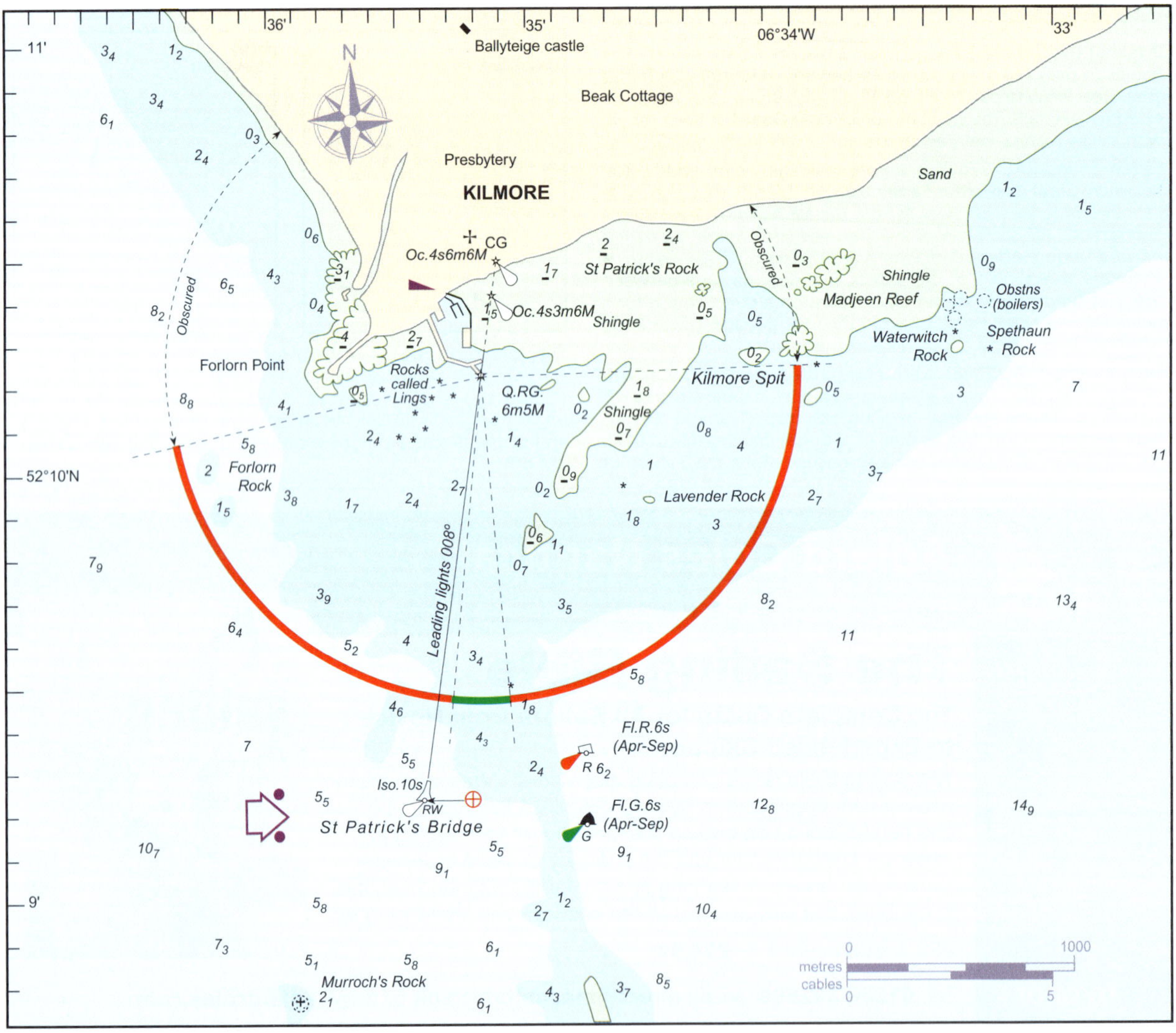

5.15 WATERFORD

Waterford **52°15'·50N 07°06'·00W** ❀❀❀◊◊✿✿

CHARTS AC 2049, 2046, 5621, 5622; Imray C57.

TIDES –0520 Dover; ML 2·4; Duration 0605

Standard Port COBH (⟶)

Times				Height (metres)			
High Water		Low Water		MHWS	MHWN	MLWN	MLWS
0500	1100	0500	1100	4·1	3·2	1·3	0·4
1700	2300	1700	2300				
Differences WATERFORD							
+0057	+0057	+0046	+0046	+0·4	+0·3	–0·1	+0·1
CHEEKPOINT							
+0022	+0020	+0020	+0020	+0·3	+0·2	+0·2	+0·1
KILMOKEA POINT							
+0026	+0022	+0020	+0020	+0·2	+0·1	+0·1	+0·1
NEW ROSS							
+0100	+0030	+0055	+0130	+0·3	+0·4	+0·3	+0·4

SHELTER Very good on 4 long marina pontoons after Nanny pontoon (first one/private) on S bank, abeam cathedral spire. Beware strong tidal stream. Up the estuary are many excellent ⚓s: off S side of R Suir in King's Chan (only to be entered W of Little Is); and up the R Barrow near Marsh Pt (about 2M S of New Ross) and 0·5M S of New Ross fixed bridge.

NAVIGATION WPT 52°06'·50N 06°58'·50W, 002°/6·7M to Dir lt at Duncannon. From the E, keep clear of Brecaun reef (2M NE of Hook Hd). Keep about 1·5M S of Hook Hd to clear Tower Race and overfalls, especially HW Dover ±2. From the W beware Falskirt Rk (3m), 2ca off Swine Head and 2M WSW of Dunmore East (5.16). Marine Farms off Creadan Hd and Broomhill Pt; cruise liners and large container ships go up to Waterford; beware ferry between Passage East and Ballyhack.

LIGHTS AND MARKS The estuary and R Suir are very well buoyed/lit all the way to Waterford. The estuary ent is between Dunmore East and Hook Hd. Duncannon dir lt, F WRG, leads 002° into the river. R Barrow is also well lit/marked up to New Ross. The railway swing bridge at the river ent opens at its W end. Call bridge-keeper VHF Ch 14.

R/T Waterford and New Ross VHF Ch **14** 16. No VHF for marina.

TELEPHONE (Code 051) Marina 309900, mobile 087 2384944; HMs Waterford 301400, Mob 08725 98297 or 08722 24961; New Ross 421303; MRCC (01) 6620922; ⊜ 832090; Police 305300; Dr 855411; Ⓗ 848000.

FACILITIES **Marina** FW, ⛽, AB €2.00. All tides access for 1·5m draft; showers (free) and ▣ at HM's office.

Services: ME, El, ⚒, C, BY (Ballyhack). **City** P, D (by arrangement with marina or from Dunmore East), Gaz, all facilities, Bus and ⇌ to Rosslare for UK ferries, ✈ (Cork) for UK/Continent, ✈ (Waterford) for Manchester and Luton and summer seasonal to Lorient.

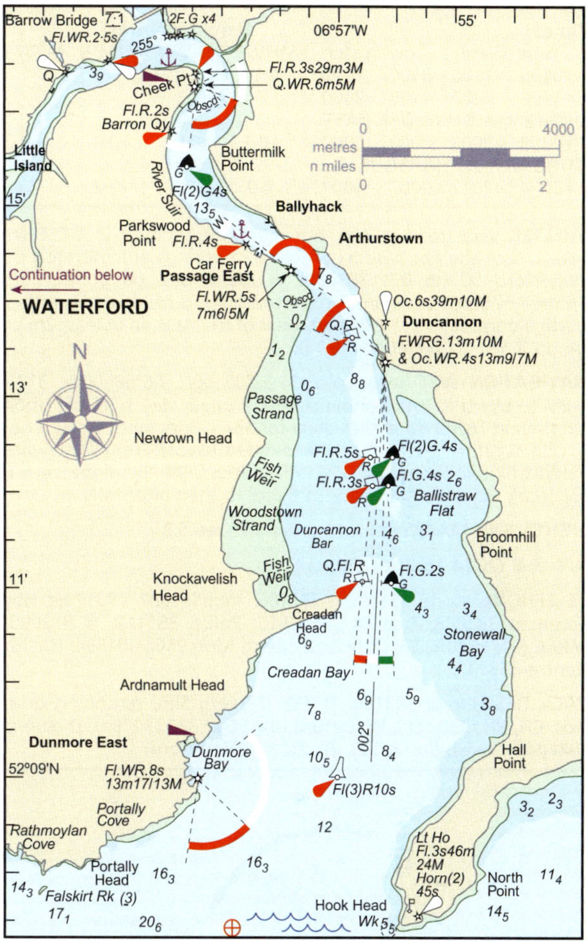

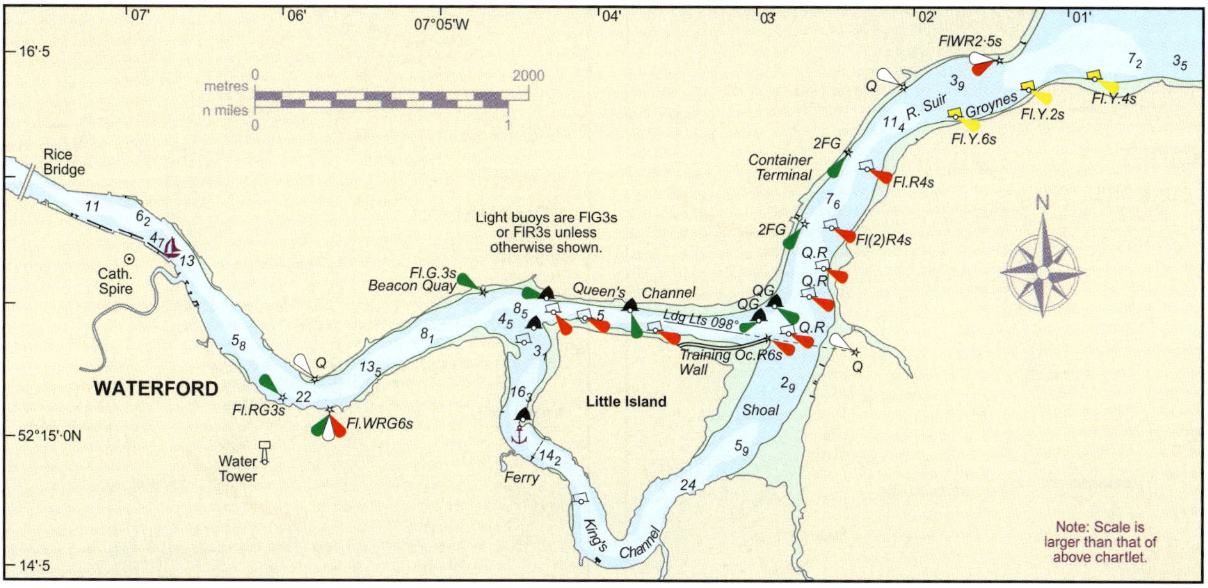

5.16 DUNMORE EAST

Waterford **52°08'·95N 06°59'·37W**

CHARTS AC 2049, 2046, 5621, 5622; Imray C57, C61.

TIDES –0535 Dover; ML 2·4; Duration 0605

Standard Port COBH (⟶)

Times				Height (metres)			
High Water		Low Water		MHWS	MHWN	MLWN	MLWS
0500	1100	0500	1100	4·1	3·2	1·3	0·4
1700	2300	1700	2300				
Differences DUNMORE EAST							
+0008	+0003	0000	0000	+0·1	0·0	+0·1	+0·2
DUNGARVAN HARBOUR							
+0004	+0012	+0007	–0001	0·0	+0·1	–0·2	0·0

SHELTER Very good in hbr, but moorings exposed in E-ESE'lies >F6. ⚓ N of the hbr. Visitors welcome, moorings administered by Waterford SC (☎ 051 383389). A useful passage port/refuge. Primarily a busy FV hbr and large cruise liners ⚓ off. In bad weather berth alongside FVs at W Wharf, clear of ice plant, in at least 2m or go up R Suir to Waterford (5.15).

NAVIGATION WPT (see also 5.15) 52°08'·00N, 06°58'·00W, 317°/1·2M to bkwtr lt. Enter under power. From E, stay 1·5M off Hook Hd to clear Tower Race; then steer for hbr in R sector of E pier lt ho. In calm weather Hook Hd can be rounded 1ca off. From W, beware Falskirt Rk (off Swines Hd, 2M WSW) dries 3·0m. By night track E for Hook Hd until in R sector of E pier lt, then alter to N.

LIGHTS AND MARKS Lts as chartlet and see 5.3.

R/T VHF Ch 14 16 (Pilot Station).

TELEPHONE (Code 051) HM 383166, mobile 087 7931705; Hbr Foreman 383688; Fuel 087 2503510; Police 383112; ⊖ 832090; MRCC (01) 6620922/3; Duty Coastguard Mob 0868 501764; Health Centre 383347.

FACILITIES Hbr ☎ 383166, D, FW (E pier), Slip, scrubbing grid, Kos, CH, BH (230 ton); **Waterford Hbr SC** ☎ 383230, Bar, showers; **Village** P (cans), Bar, R, 🛒, Ⓑ, ✉, ✈ (Waterford).

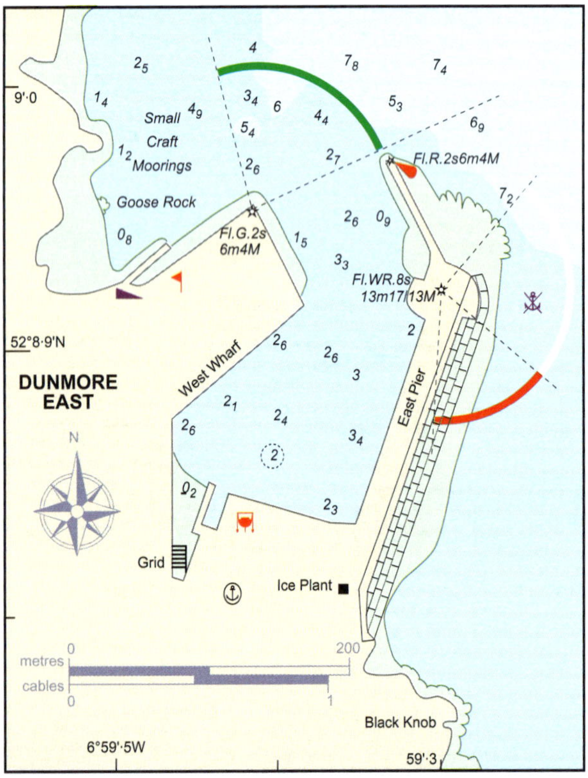

5.17 YOUGHAL

Cork **51°56'·54N 07°50'·20W**

CHARTS AC 2049, 2071, 5622; Imray C57.

TIDES –0556 Dover; ML 2·1; Duration 0555

Standard Port COBH (⟶)

Times				Height (metres)			
High Water		Low Water		MHWS	MHWN	MLWN	MLWS
0500	1100	0500	1100	4·1	3·2	1·3	0·4
1700	2300	1700	2300				
Differences YOUGHAL							
0000	+0010	+0010	0000	–0·2	–0·1	–0·1	–0·1

SHELTER Good, but strong S'lies cause swell inside the hbr. Possible AB in 1.3m (drying patches just off quay); seasonal short-stay pontoon, with FW, off landing jetty. ⚓ as chartlet; no dues. Strong tidal streams run throughout anchorages.

NAVIGATION WPT, East Bar, 51°55'·62N 07°48'·00W, 302°/1·8M to Fl WR 2·5s lt. Beware Blackball Ledge (ECM lt buoy) and Bar Rks (SCM lt buoy), both outside hbr ent in R sector of lt ho. From W, appr via West Bar (1·7m) is shorter route and E Bar has 2·0m.

- Both Bars in E to SSW'lies >F6 are likely to have dangerous seas.
- Beware salmon nets set during June-July, Mon-Thurs 0400-2100.
- Red Bank is continually changing, obtain local knowledge.

LIGHTS AND MARKS See 5.3 and chartlet. Water tr is conspic from seaward; clock tr and ✠ tr within hbr. Up-river, 175° transit of convent belfry tr/town hall clears W of Red Bank.

R/T VHF Ch 14 16 0900-1700 and when ships expected.

TELEPHONE (Code 024) HM Mobile 0872511143 MRCC (066) 9476109; Coast Guard 93252 or mob 0868 501769; ⊖ (021) 4325000; Police 92200; Dr 92702. Youghal Shipping 92577 (for poss AB).

FACILITIES Services: L, FW, Slip, AB (☎Youghal Shipping). **Town** P & D (cans), 🛒, R, Bar, ✉, Ⓑ, Bus (Cork/W'ford), ✈(Cork).

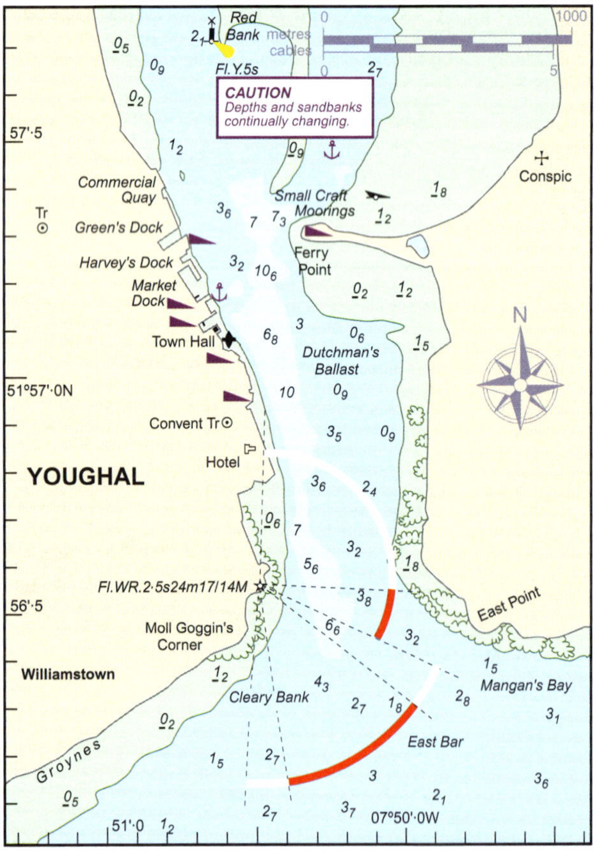

TIME ZONE (UT)
For Summer Time add ONE hour in **non-shaded areas**

COBH LAT 51°51′N LONG 8°18′W

TIMES AND HEIGHTS OF HIGH AND LOW WATERS

Dates in red are SPRINGS
Dates in blue are NEAPS

YEAR **2010**

JANUARY

Day	Time	m	Day	Time	m
1 F	0529 1202 1751	4.2 0.5 4.1	16 SA	0010 0605 1227 1817	0.7 4.1 0.8 3.9
2 SA	0019 0617 1249 1838	0.4 4.3 0.4 4.2	17 SU	0040 0639 1255 1847	0.7 4.1 0.8 3.9
3 SU	0105 0704 1335 1924	0.3 4.3 0.4 4.2	18 M	0108 0710 1325 1917	0.7 4.0 0.9 3.9
4 M	0152 0751 1421 2010	0.3 4.3 0.4 4.1	19 TU	0138 0741 1357 1949	0.8 4.0 0.9 3.9
5 TU	0239 0839 1508 2057	0.4 4.1 0.6 4.0	20 W	0211 0813 1432 2023	0.9 3.9 1.0 3.8
6 W	0328 0927 1557 2146	0.6 4.0 0.7 3.8	21 TH	0248 0848 1509 2100	1.0 3.9 1.1 3.8
7 TH	0418 1016 1648 ◑ 2237	0.7 3.8 0.9 3.7	22 F	0328 0927 1550 2142	1.1 3.8 1.2 3.7
8 F	0513 1110 1746 2334	0.9 3.6 1.1 3.5	23 SA	0414 1013 1637 ◐ 2233	1.2 3.6 1.3 3.5
9 SA	0615 1212 1851	1.1 3.5 1.2	24 SU	0511 1108 1741 2336	1.4 3.5 1.4 3.4
10 SU	0041 0725 1322 2002	3.4 1.2 3.4 1.3	25 M	0624 1216 1900	1.4 3.4 1.5
11 M	0155 0839 1431 2110	3.4 1.2 3.4 1.2	26 TU	0051 0743 1332 2018	3.4 1.4 3.4 1.3
12 TU	0303 0945 1533 2210	3.5 1.1 3.5 1.0	27 W	0211 0859 1448 2127	3.5 1.2 3.5 1.1
13 W	0400 1039 1624 2258	3.7 1.0 3.7 0.9	28 TH	0324 1005 1555 2228	3.7 0.9 3.8 0.7
14 TH	0448 1123 1707 2337	3.9 0.9 3.8 0.8	29 F	0425 1101 1650 2319	4.0 0.6 4.0 0.4
15 F	0529 1157 1745 ●	4.0 0.8 3.9	30 SA	0517 1150 1739 ○	4.2 0.3 4.2
			31 SU	0006 0603 1235 1823	0.2 4.4 0.2 4.3

FEBRUARY

Day	Time	m	Day	Time	m
1 M	0050 0648 1318 1906	0.1 4.4 0.2 4.3	16 TU	0045 0646 1300 1855	0.6 4.0 0.7 3.9
2 TU	0134 0731 1401 1949	0.1 4.3 0.2 4.2	17 W	0112 0713 1330 1923	0.7 4.0 0.7 3.9
3 W	0217 0814 1443 2031	0.2 4.2 0.4 4.1	18 TH	0143 0742 1402 1953	0.7 4.0 0.8 3.9
4 TH	0301 0857 1526 2114	0.4 4.0 0.6 3.9	19 F	0217 0814 1436 2026	0.8 3.9 0.9 3.8
5 F	0345 0940 1611 ◑ 2158	0.6 3.8 0.8 3.7	20 SA	0255 0851 1512 2105	0.9 3.8 1.0 3.7
6 SA	0433 1027 1701 2249	0.9 3.5 1.1 3.4	21 SU	0338 0934 1556 2153	1.1 3.6 1.2 3.6
7 SU	0529 1124 1803 2355	1.1 3.3 1.3 3.2	22 M	0432 1029 1657 ◐ 2257	1.3 3.4 1.4 3.4
8 M	0639 1240 1921	1.3 3.1 1.4	23 TU	0546 1140 1821	1.4 3.3 1.4
9 TU	0122 0805 1406 2045	3.2 1.4 3.1 1.3	24 W	0018 0713 1306 1949	3.3 1.4 3.2 1.3
10 W	0242 0928 1515 2155	3.3 1.2 3.3 1.1	25 TH	0149 0837 1431 2106	3.4 1.1 3.4 1.0
11 TH	0342 1026 1608 2244	3.5 1.0 3.5 0.9	26 F	0309 0947 1540 2209	3.6 0.8 3.7 0.6
12 F	0430 1108 1651 2323	3.8 0.8 3.7 0.7	27 SA	0409 1043 1634 2301	4.0 0.4 4.0 0.3
13 SA	0510 1141 1727 2354	3.9 0.7 3.9 0.6	28 SU	0459 1131 1721 ○ 2347	4.2 0.2 4.2 0.1
14 SU	0546 1208 1800 ●	4.0 0.7 3.9			
15 M	0020 0617 1233 1828	0.6 4.1 0.7 3.9			

MARCH

Day	Time	m	Day	Time	m
1 M	0544 1214 1804	4.4 0.0 4.3	16 TU	0550 1205 1802	4.0 0.6 3.9
2 TU	0030 0626 1256 1844	0.0 4.4 0.0 4.3	17 W	0017 0617 1232 1828	0.5 4.0 0.6 3.9
3 W	0112 0707 1337 1924	0.0 4.3 0.1 4.2	18 TH	0045 0643 1303 1856	0.6 4.0 0.6 3.9
4 TH	0153 0747 1417 2003	0.1 4.2 0.2 4.1	19 F	0117 0713 1335 1927	0.6 3.9 0.7 3.9
5 F	0234 0826 1457 2043	0.3 4.0 0.5 3.9	20 SA	0152 0746 1410 2001	0.7 3.9 0.8 3.9
6 SA	0316 0906 1539 2124	0.6 3.7 0.7 3.7	21 SU	0232 0825 1449 2042	0.8 3.8 0.9 3.7
7 SU	0401 0949 1627 ◑ 2211	0.8 3.4 1.0 3.4	22 M	0317 0910 1536 2132	1.0 3.6 1.1 3.6
8 M	0454 1041 1726 2315	1.1 3.2 1.3 3.1	23 TU	0414 1007 1638 ◐ 2237	1.2 3.4 1.2 3.4
9 TU	0601 1157 1844	1.4 2.9 1.4	24 W	0526 1120 1800 2359	1.3 3.2 1.3 3.3
10 W	0051 0727 1338 2014	3.0 1.4 3.0 1.3	25 TH	0652 1247 1927	1.2 3.2 1.2
11 TH	0217 0858 1451 2128	3.2 1.2 3.2 1.1	26 F	0132 0815 1412 2044	3.4 1.0 3.4 0.9
12 F	0317 0958 1544 2218	3.4 1.0 3.4 0.9	27 SA	0248 0924 1519 2147	3.6 0.7 3.7 0.5
13 SA	0404 1041 1626 2257	3.7 0.8 3.7 0.7	28 SU	0347 1020 1612 2240	3.9 0.4 4.0 0.3
14 SU	0444 1114 1702 2327	3.8 0.7 3.8 0.6	29 M	0437 1108 1659 2326	4.1 0.1 4.2 0.1
15 M	0519 1141 1734 ● 2352	4.0 0.6 3.9 0.5	30 TU	0521 1152 1742 ○	4.3 0.0 4.3
			31 W	0009 0602 1233 1821	0.0 4.3 0.0 4.3

APRIL

Day	Time	m	Day	Time	m
1 TH	0050 0642 1313 1900	0.0 4.2 0.1 4.2	16 F	0021 0617 1240 1834	0.5 3.9 0.6 3.9
2 F	0130 0720 1353 1938	0.2 4.1 0.3 4.0	17 SA	0057 0651 1316 1909	0.6 3.9 0.6 3.9
3 SA	0210 0758 1433 2017	0.4 3.9 0.5 3.9	18 SU	0136 0729 1356 1948	0.6 3.8 0.7 3.9
4 SU	0251 0837 1514 2057	0.6 3.6 0.7 3.6	19 M	0220 0812 1440 2033	0.7 3.7 0.8 3.8
5 M	0335 0918 1601 2143	0.9 3.4 1.0 3.4	20 TU	0309 0902 1532 2126	0.9 3.6 0.9 3.6
6 TU	0426 1007 1658 ◑ 2242	1.1 3.1 1.2 3.1	21 W	0408 1001 1634 ◐ 2231	1.0 3.4 1.0 3.4
7 W	0530 1115 1810	1.3 2.9 1.3	22 TH	0517 1111 1748 2348	1.1 3.3 1.1 3.4
8 TH	0011 0646 1255 1930	3.0 1.4 2.9 1.3	23 F	0635 1230 1907	1.0 3.3 1.0
9 F	0138 0805 1412 2040	3.1 1.2 3.1 1.1	24 SA	0111 0751 1347 2019	3.5 0.9 3.4 0.8
10 SA	0239 0908 1506 2133	3.3 1.0 3.3 0.9	25 SU	0222 0857 1451 2122	3.7 0.6 3.7 0.5
11 SU	0327 0955 1549 2215	3.5 0.8 3.5 0.7	26 M	0320 0953 1546 2216	3.9 0.4 3.9 0.3
12 M	0408 1032 1627 2249	3.7 0.7 3.7 0.6	27 TU	0411 1043 1635 2304	4.0 0.3 4.1 0.2
13 TU	0444 1104 1701 2319	3.8 0.6 3.8 0.6	28 W	0458 1129 1719 ○ 2348	4.1 0.2 4.1 0.2
14 W	0516 1134 1732 ● 2348	3.9 0.6 3.9 0.5	29 TH	0541 1211 1801	4.1 0.2 4.1
15 TH	0546 1206 1802	3.9 0.5 3.9	30 F	0029 0620 1253 1840	0.2 4.0 0.3 4.1

Chart Datum: 0·13 metres above Ordnance Datum (Dublin). HAT is 4·5 metres above Chart Datum; see 0.20

TIME ZONE (UT)
For Summer Time add ONE hour in **non-shaded areas**

COBH LAT 51°51′N LONG 8°18′W

TIMES AND HEIGHTS OF HIGH AND LOW WATERS

Dates in red are SPRINGS
Dates in blue are NEAPS

YEAR **2010**

MAY

Date	Day	Time	m
1	SA	0110 0658 1332 1918	0.4 3.9 0.4 4.0
2	SU	0149 0735 1412 1956	0.5 3.8 0.6 3.8
3	M	0229 0813 1454 2036	0.7 3.6 0.8 3.6
4	TU	0312 0854 1538 2121	0.9 3.4 1.0 3.4
5	W	0400 0941 1630 2213	1.1 3.2 1.1 3.2
6	TH	0456 1037 1732 ◑ 2320	1.2 3.1 1.2 3.1
7	F	0601 1150 1839	1.3 3.0 1.3
8	SA	0038 0707 1308 1942	3.1 1.2 3.1 1.2
9	SU	0144 0806 1409 2036	3.3 1.1 3.3 1.0
10	M	0236 0857 1459 2123	3.4 1.0 3.4 0.9
11	TU	0321 0943 1542 2205	3.6 0.8 3.6 0.8
12	W	0402 1024 1623 2245	3.7 0.7 3.7 0.7
13	TH	0441 1105 1701 2324	3.8 0.6 3.8 0.6
14	F	0519 1144 1739 ●	3.9 0.6 3.9
15	SA	0003 0557 1224 1818	0.5 3.9 0.5 4.0
16	SU	0045 0638 1306 1859	0.5 3.9 0.5 4.0
17	M	0128 0721 1350 1943	0.5 3.8 0.6 3.9
18	TU	0215 0808 1438 2031	0.6 3.8 0.6 3.8
19	W	0306 0900 1530 2126	0.7 3.6 0.7 3.7
20	TH	0403 0957 1628 ◐ 2226	0.8 3.5 0.8 3.6
21	F	0505 1059 1733 2333	0.9 3.5 0.9 3.5
22	SA	0614 1207 1843	0.9 3.4 0.8
23	SU	0044 0723 1316 1951	3.5 0.8 3.5 0.8
24	M	0151 0827 1419 2054	3.6 0.7 3.6 0.6
25	TU	0251 0925 1517 2152	3.7 0.6 3.8 0.5
26	W	0346 1019 1610 2243	3.8 0.5 3.9 0.5
27	TH	0436 1108 1659 ○ 2330	3.9 0.5 4.0 0.5
28	F	0521 1153 1743	3.9 0.4 4.0
29	SA	0012 0602 1235 1822	0.5 3.9 0.5 4.0
30	SU	0052 0640 1314 1901	0.6 3.8 0.6 3.9
31	M	0129 0717 1353 1938	0.7 3.7 0.7 3.8

JUNE

Date	Day	Time	m
1	TU	0207 0754 1432 2017	0.8 3.6 0.8 3.7
2	W	0246 0832 1512 2058	0.9 3.5 0.9 3.6
3	TH	0329 0915 1556 2143	1.0 3.4 1.0 3.4
4	F	0417 1002 1646 ◑ 2233	1.1 3.3 1.1 3.4
5	SA	0510 1055 1742 2330	1.2 3.3 1.2 3.3
6	SU	0609 1156 1842	1.2 3.2 1.2
7	M	0032 0708 1300 1939	3.3 1.2 3.3 1.1
8	TU	0133 0804 1400 2034	3.4 1.1 3.4 1.0
9	W	0228 0858 1455 2126	3.5 1.0 3.5 0.9
10	TH	0320 0950 1546 2216	3.6 0.9 3.7 0.8
11	F	0409 1040 1635 2304	3.7 0.7 3.8 0.6
12	SA	0457 1127 1721 ● 2350	3.8 0.6 3.9 0.5
13	SU	0543 1212 1807	3.9 0.5 4.0
14	M	0035 0628 1257 1851	0.4 3.9 0.4 4.0
15	TU	0121 0715 1343 1938	0.4 3.9 0.4 4.0
16	W	0208 0803 1431 2027	0.4 3.9 0.4 4.0
17	TH	0258 0853 1521 2117	0.5 3.8 0.5 3.9
18	F	0350 0944 1613 2211	0.6 3.7 0.6 3.8
19	SA	0445 1038 1710 ◐ 2308	0.7 3.6 0.7 3.6
20	SU	0545 1137 1813	0.8 3.6 0.8
21	M	0011 0649 1241 1919	3.6 0.9 3.5 0.9
22	TU	0117 0755 1347 2026	3.5 0.9 3.5 0.9
23	W	0222 0859 1451 2130	3.5 0.9 3.6 0.8
24	TH	0322 0959 1550 2227	3.6 0.8 3.7 0.7
25	F	0417 1052 1642 2316	3.7 0.7 3.8 0.7
26	SA	0505 1138 1727 ○ 2358	3.7 0.6 3.9 0.7
27	SU	0547 1218 1808	3.8 0.6 3.9
28	M	0034 0624 1256 1844	0.7 3.8 0.6 3.9
29	TU	0108 0659 1330 1920	0.7 3.8 0.7 3.9
30	W	0141 0733 1404 1955	0.8 3.7 0.7 3.8

JULY

Date	Day	Time	m
1	TH	0216 0808 1439 2031	0.9 3.7 0.8 3.7
2	F	0253 0846 1516 2109	0.9 3.6 0.9 3.6
3	SA	0334 0926 1556 2150	1.0 3.5 1.0 3.6
4	SU	0418 1010 1643 ◑ 2236	1.1 3.5 1.1 3.5
5	M	0509 1101 1739 2330	1.2 3.4 1.2 3.4
6	TU	0610 1200 1843	1.3 3.4 1.3
7	W	0032 0715 1306 1949	3.4 1.3 3.4 1.2
8	TH	0139 0819 1413 2053	3.4 1.2 3.5 1.1
9	F	0243 0921 1516 2152	3.5 1.0 3.6 0.9
10	SA	0344 1018 1614 2247	3.7 0.8 3.8 0.6
11	SU	0439 1110 1706 ● 2336	3.8 0.6 4.0 0.4
12	M	0529 1157 1754	4.0 0.4 4.1
13	TU	0022 0615 1243 1839	0.3 4.0 0.3 4.2
14	W	0108 0702 1329 1925	0.2 4.1 0.2 4.2
15	TH	0154 0748 1414 2011	0.3 4.0 0.2 4.1
16	F	0240 0834 1501 2058	0.3 4.0 0.3 4.0
17	SA	0327 0921 1549 2145	0.5 3.9 0.5 3.9
18	SU	0417 1010 1640 ◐ 2236	0.6 3.7 0.7 3.7
19	M	0510 1103 1737 2334	0.8 3.6 0.9 3.5
20	TU	0612 1205 1843	1.0 3.4 1.0
21	W	0042 0722 1318 1958	3.3 1.1 3.3 1.1
22	TH	0156 0836 1431 2113	3.3 1.1 3.4 1.0
23	F	0304 0944 1534 2216	3.4 1.0 3.6 0.9
24	SA	0402 1040 1627 2305	3.5 0.8 3.7 0.8
25	SU	0450 1125 1712 2344	3.7 0.7 3.9 0.7
26	M	0530 1202 1750 ○	3.8 0.6 3.9
27	TU	0016 0606 1235 1825	0.7 3.8 0.6 4.0
28	W	0044 0638 1304 1857	0.7 3.8 0.6 3.9
29	TH	0112 0709 1332 1928	0.7 3.8 0.7 3.9
30	F	0142 0740 1402 1959	0.8 3.8 0.8 3.8
31	SA	0216 0813 1435 2032	0.9 3.7 0.9 3.8

AUGUST

Date	Day	Time	m
1	SU	0253 0848 1512 2109	1.0 3.7 1.0 3.7
2	M	0332 0928 1554 2150	1.1 3.6 1.1 3.6
3	TU	0416 1014 1644 ◑ 2241	1.2 3.5 1.2 3.5
4	W	0513 1111 1751 2344	1.3 3.4 1.3 3.3
5	TH	0627 1222 1909	1.4 3.3 1.3
6	F	0058 0745 1340 2024	3.3 1.3 3.4 1.2
7	SA	0216 0855 1454 2131	3.4 1.1 3.6 0.9
8	SU	0324 0957 1556 2228	3.6 0.8 3.8 0.6
9	M	0421 1051 1648 2319	3.9 0.5 4.1 0.3
10	TU	0511 1139 1736 ●	4.1 0.2 4.2
11	W	0004 0557 1224 1820	0.2 4.2 0.1 4.3
12	TH	0048 0641 1308 1903	0.1 4.2 0.1 4.3
13	F	0132 0725 1352 1947	0.1 4.2 0.1 4.2
14	SA	0216 0809 1436 2031	0.2 4.1 0.2 4.1
15	SU	0300 0853 1521 2115	0.4 3.9 0.4 3.9
16	M	0346 0939 1609 ◐ 2202	0.6 3.7 0.7 3.6
17	TU	0437 1029 1702 2257	0.9 3.5 1.0 3.3
18	W	0537 1132 1808	1.1 3.3 1.2
19	TH	0009 0652 1255 1932	3.1 1.2 3.2 1.3
20	F	0136 0818 1416 2100	3.1 1.2 3.3 1.2
21	SA	0249 0932 1519 2203	3.3 1.0 3.5 1.0
22	SU	0345 1026 1609 2249	3.5 0.8 3.7 0.8
23	M	0431 1108 1651 2325	3.7 0.6 3.9 0.7
24	TU	0510 1142 1728 ○ 2353	3.8 0.6 4.0 0.6
25	W	0543 1209 1801	3.9 0.6 4.0
26	TH	0016 0613 1234 1829	0.7 3.9 0.6 4.0
27	F	0041 0641 1258 1857	0.7 3.9 0.7 3.9
28	SA	0109 0709 1327 1924	0.7 3.8 0.7 3.9
29	SU	0142 0738 1359 1955	0.8 3.8 0.8 3.9
30	M	0216 0812 1436 2030	0.9 3.8 0.9 3.8
31	TU	0254 0850 1517 2111	1.0 3.7 1.1 3.7

Chart Datum: 0·13 metres above Ordnance Datum (Dublin). HAT is 4·5 metres above Chart Datum; see 0.20

TIME ZONE (UT)
For Summer Time add ONE hour in **non-shaded areas**

COBH LAT 51°51′N LONG 8°18′W

TIMES AND HEIGHTS OF HIGH AND LOW WATERS

Dates in red are SPRINGS
Dates in blue are NEAPS

YEAR **2010**

SEPTEMBER

Date	Day	Time	m	Time	m	Time	m	Time	m
1	W	0337	1.2	0935	3.5	1607	1.2	◑ 2203	3.5
2	TH	0433	1.3	1034	3.4	1713	1.4	2308	3.3
3	F	0551	1.4	1149	3.3	1837	1.4		
4	SA	0029	3.2	0716	1.3	1316	3.3	1959	1.2
5	SU	0154	3.4	0832	1.1	1435	3.6	2109	0.9
6	M	0305	3.6	0936	0.7	1537	3.9	2208	0.6
7	TU	0401	3.9	1030	0.4	1628	4.1	2257	0.3
8	W	0450	4.2	1117	0.1	1714	4.3	● 2342	0.1
9	TH	0535	4.3	1202	0.0	1758	4.4		
10	F	0025	0.0	0618	4.3	1245	0.0	1839	4.3
11	SA	0108	0.1	0700	4.3	1328	0.1	1921	4.2
12	SU	0150	0.2	0742	4.1	1411	0.3	2002	4.0
13	M	0234	0.4	0825	3.9	1455	0.5	2045	3.8
14	TU	0319	0.7	0909	3.7	1541	0.8	2129	3.5
15	W	0409	0.9	0959	3.4	1634	1.1	◐ 2222	3.3
16	TH	0509	1.2	1103	3.2	1740	1.3	2336	3.0
17	F	0626	1.3	1233	3.1	1906	1.4		
18	SA	0113	3.0	0756	1.3	1356	3.2	2036	1.3
19	SU	0228	3.2	0908	1.1	1456	3.4	2137	1.0
20	M	0321	3.5	0959	0.8	1544	3.7	2220	0.9
21	TU	0405	3.7	1040	0.7	1624	3.9	2255	0.7
22	W	0442	3.8	1112	0.6	1700	4.0	2322	0.7
23	TH	0515	3.9	1138	0.6	1732	4.0	○ 2345	0.7
24	F	0545	3.9	1202	0.6	1800	4.0		
25	SA	0010	0.7	0611	3.9	1228	0.7	1825	4.0
26	SU	0040	0.7	0639	3.9	1257	0.7	1853	4.0
27	M	0113	0.8	0709	3.9	1332	0.8	1925	3.9
28	TU	0148	0.9	0743	3.8	1409	0.9	2002	3.8
29	W	0227	1.0	0823	3.7	1453	1.1	2045	3.7
30	TH	0314	1.1	0912	3.6	1546	1.2	2139	3.5

OCTOBER

Date	Day	Time	m	Time	m	Time	m	Time	m
1	F	0414	1.3	1013	3.4	1653	1.4	◑ 2247	3.3
2	SA	0530	1.4	1129	3.3	1815	1.4		
3	SU	0008	3.3	0653	1.3	1257	3.4	1937	1.2
4	M	0132	3.4	0809	1.0	1414	3.6	2046	0.9
5	TU	0242	3.7	0912	0.7	1514	3.9	2144	0.6
6	W	0338	4.0	1007	0.4	1605	4.2	2234	0.3
7	TH	0427	4.2	1056	0.2	1652	4.3	● 2320	0.2
8	F	0512	4.3	1141	0.1	1735	4.4		
9	SA	0003	0.1	0555	4.3	1225	0.1	1817	4.3
10	SU	0046	0.2	0637	4.3	1307	0.2	1857	4.2
11	M	0128	0.3	0719	4.1	1349	0.4	1937	4.0
12	TU	0211	0.5	0801	3.9	1433	0.7	2018	3.8
13	W	0257	0.8	0845	3.7	1518	0.9	2101	3.5
14	TH	0346	1.0	0934	3.5	1610	1.2	◐ 2151	3.3
15	F	0445	1.2	1036	3.2	1712	1.4	2258	3.1
16	SA	0556	1.4	1158	3.1	1830	1.5		
17	SU	0032	3.0	0716	1.3	1320	3.2	1950	1.4
18	M	0151	3.2	0825	1.2	1420	3.4	2051	1.2
19	TU	0245	3.4	0917	1.0	1508	3.6	2137	1.0
20	W	0329	3.6	0959	0.8	1550	3.8	2214	0.9
21	TH	0408	3.8	1034	0.7	1627	3.9	2245	0.8
22	F	0443	3.9	1105	0.7	1700	4.0	2314	0.7
23	SA	0515	4.0	1133	0.7	1730	4.0	○ 2344	0.7
24	SU	0545	4.0	1203	0.7	1759	4.0		
25	M	0017	0.7	0616	4.0	1237	0.8	1830	4.0
26	TU	0053	0.8	0650	4.0	1314	0.8	1906	3.9
27	W	0131	0.8	0728	3.9	1356	0.9	1946	3.9
28	TH	0215	1.0	0811	3.8	1443	1.0	2033	3.7
29	F	0305	1.1	0903	3.7	1537	1.2	2128	3.6
30	SA	0405	1.2	1004	3.6	1641	1.3	◑ 2234	3.4
31	SU	0515	1.2	1115	3.5	1756	1.3	2349	3.4

NOVEMBER

Date	Day	Time	m	Time	m	Time	m	Time	m
1	M	0631	1.2	1234	3.5	1913	1.1		
2	TU	0106	3.5	0744	1.0	1347	3.7	2021	0.9
3	W	0214	3.8	0848	0.7	1447	3.9	2119	0.7
4	TH	0312	4.0	0945	0.5	1541	4.1	2212	0.5
5	F	0404	4.2	1036	0.4	1630	4.2	2300	0.4
6	SA	0452	4.3	1123	0.3	1715	4.2	● 2345	0.3
7	SU	0537	4.3	1208	0.4	1758	4.2		
8	M	0028	0.4	0619	4.2	1250	0.4	1838	4.1
9	TU	0110	0.5	0701	4.1	1332	0.6	1917	3.9
10	W	0152	0.7	0742	4.0	1414	0.8	1956	3.8
11	TH	0236	0.8	0825	3.8	1457	1.0	2037	3.6
12	F	0323	1.0	0912	3.6	1545	1.2	2123	3.4
13	SA	0415	1.2	1004	3.4	1639	1.4	◐ 2217	3.2
14	SU	0516	1.3	1108	3.3	1742	1.5	2326	3.1
15	M	0623	1.4	1220	3.3	1850	1.4		
16	TU	0044	3.2	0727	1.3	1327	3.4	1951	1.3
17	W	0150	3.4	0822	1.2	1420	3.5	2043	1.2
18	TH	0242	3.5	0910	1.1	1507	3.7	2128	1.0
19	F	0326	3.7	0953	0.9	1549	3.8	2208	0.9
20	SA	0407	3.9	1033	0.9	1627	3.9	2247	0.8
21	SU	0446	4.0	1110	0.8	1704	4.0	○ 2324	0.8
22	M	0524	4.0	1148	0.8	1740	4.0		
23	TU	0002	0.7	0601	4.1	1226	0.7	1816	4.0
24	W	0042	0.7	0640	4.1	1307	0.8	1856	4.0
25	TH	0123	0.8	0721	4.0	1350	0.8	1939	3.9
26	F	0209	0.8	0807	4.0	1438	0.9	2028	3.8
27	SA	0259	0.9	0858	3.9	1530	1.0	2121	3.7
28	SU	0354	1.0	0955	3.8	1627	1.1	◑ 2220	3.6
29	M	0456	1.1	1057	3.7	1732	1.1	2325	3.6
30	TU	0604	1.1	1205	3.7	1843	1.1		

DECEMBER

Date	Day	Time	m	Time	m	Time	m	Time	m
1	W	0034	3.6	0714	1.0	1314	3.7	1952	1.0
2	TH	0142	3.7	0821	0.9	1418	3.8	2054	0.9
3	F	0245	3.9	0923	0.8	1517	3.9	2151	0.7
4	SA	0343	4.0	1019	0.7	1611	4.0	2243	0.6
5	SU	0436	4.1	1110	0.6	1700	4.1	● 2330	0.6
6	M	0523	4.2	1155	0.6	1744	4.1		
7	TU	0013	0.5	0606	4.2	1237	0.6	1823	4.0
8	W	0055	0.6	0647	4.1	1316	0.7	1901	3.9
9	TH	0134	0.7	0726	4.0	1355	0.9	1937	3.8
10	F	0214	0.8	0806	3.9	1433	1.0	2015	3.7
11	SA	0255	1.0	0847	3.8	1513	1.1	2055	3.6
12	SU	0338	1.1	0930	3.6	1558	1.3	2139	3.5
13	M	0426	1.3	1017	3.5	1648	1.4	◐ 2230	3.4
14	TU	0521	1.4	1111	3.4	1745	1.4	2329	3.3
15	W	0622	1.4	1212	3.4	1847	1.4		
16	TH	0035	3.3	0722	1.4	1316	3.4	1947	1.4
17	F	0141	3.4	0820	1.3	1415	3.5	2043	1.2
18	SA	0241	3.6	0914	1.2	1509	3.7	2135	1.1
19	SU	0334	3.8	1005	1.0	1558	3.8	2224	0.9
20	M	0422	3.9	1052	0.9	1643	3.9	2308	0.8
21	TU	0507	4.0	1136	0.7	1726	4.0	○ 2351	0.7
22	W	0550	4.1	1218	0.6	1808	4.1		
23	TH	0032	0.6	0632	4.2	1300	0.6	1849	4.1
24	F	0115	0.6	0715	4.2	1343	0.6	1933	4.1
25	SA	0200	0.6	0800	4.1	1428	0.7	2019	4.0
26	SU	0247	0.6	0848	4.0	1516	0.8	2107	3.9
27	M	0337	0.7	0938	3.9	1606	0.9	2159	3.8
28	TU	0430	0.9	1032	3.8	1702	1.0	◑ 2255	3.7
29	W	0530	1.0	1131	3.7	1806	1.1	2358	3.6
30	TH	0638	1.1	1238	3.6	1917	1.2		
31	F	0108	3.6	0751	1.1	1349	3.6	2028	1.1

Chart Datum: 0·13 metres above Ordnance Datum (Dublin). HAT is 4·5 metres above Chart Datum; see 0.20

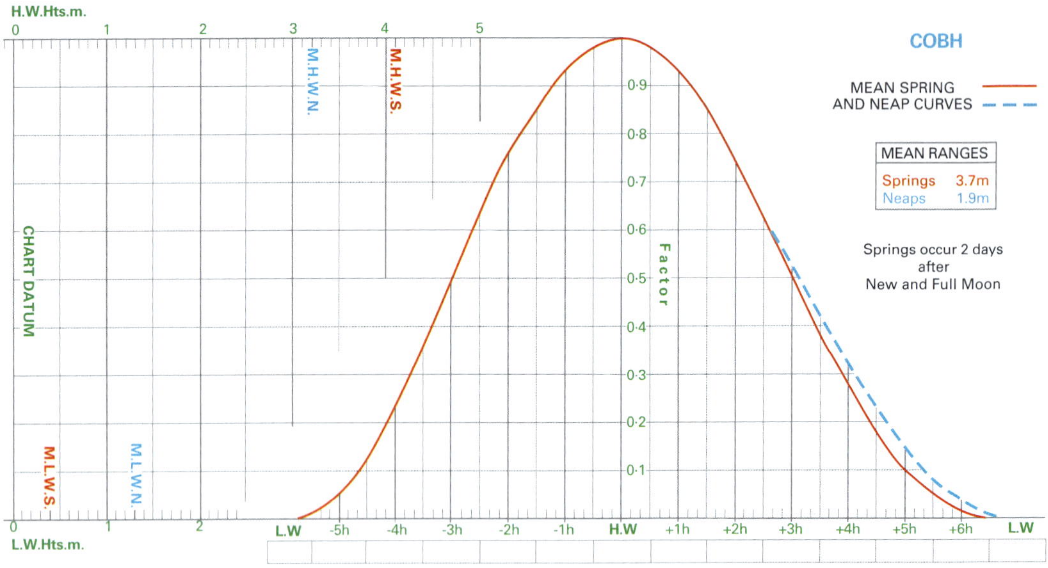

5.18 CORK HARBOUR

Cork **51°47'·50N 08°15'·54W** ❁❁❁◊◊◊✿✿✿

CHARTS AC 1765, 1777, 1773, 5622; Imray C57, C56.

TIDES –0523 Dover; ML 2·3; Duration 0555

Standard Port COBH (⟵)

Times				Height (metres)			
High Water		Low Water		MHWS	MHWN	MLWN	MLWS
0500	1100	0500	1100	4·1	3·2	1·3	0·4
1700	2300	1700	2300				
Differences BALLYCOTTON (15M ENE of Roche's Point)							
–0011	+0001	+0003	–0009	0·0	0·0	–0·1	0·0
RINGASKIDDY							
+0005	+0020	+0007	+0013	+0·1	+0·1	+0·1	+0·1
MARINO POINT							
0000	+0010	0000	+0010	+0·1	+0·1	0·0	0·0
CORK CITY							
+0005	+0010	+0020	+0010	+0·4	+0·4	+0·3	+0·2
ROBERTS COVE (approx 4M SW of Roche's Point)							
–0005	–0005	–0005	–0005	–0·1	0·0	0·0	+0·1

SHELTER Very good in all conditions, esp in Crosshaven and East Passage. There are 3 main marinas at Crosshaven (see Facilities), plus a small private marina and several ⚓s up the Owenboy River, in particular at Drake's Pool. There is a marina at E Ferry at the E end of Great Island. Cobh, Ringaskiddy and Cork City are commercial and ferry ports; contact Port Ops for advice on yacht berths.

NAVIGATION WPT 51°46'·57N, 08°15'·39W, 005°/1M to Roche's Pt lt; also on 354°ldg line. Safe hbr with no dangers for yachts; ent is deep and well marked. Sp rate is about 1½kn in ent. Main chan up to Cork and the chan to E Ferry are marked, but shoal outside navigable chan. Ent to Crosshaven/Owenboy River carries at least 3m at LWS, and the chan is buoyed.

LIGHTS AND MARKS See 5.3. The 24·5m high hammerhead water tr S of Crosshaven and the R/W power stn chy NE of Corkbeg Is are conspic from seaward. Two set Ldg lts/marks lead through The Sound, either side of Hbr Rk (5·2m), not a hazard for yachts; but do not impede merchant ships. The chan to Crosshaven is marked by C1 SHM lt buoy, C1A SHM lt buoy; C2A PHM lt buoy, C2 PHM lt buoy; and C4 PHM lt buoy.

R/T Call: *Cork Hbr Radio* (Port Ops) VHF Ch 12 14 16 (H24); *Crosshaven BY* Ch **M** (Mon–Fri: 0830–1730LT). *Royal Cork* YC Marina Ch **M** (0900–2359LT) and RCYC water taxi, *Salve Marine and East Ferry Marina* both Ch **M** 0830-1730.

TELEPHONE (Code 021) HM 4273125, info@portofcork.ie; Port Ops 4811380; MRSC (066) 9476109; IMES 4831448; ⊜ 4311024; Police 4831222; Dr 4831716; Ⓗ 4546400.

FACILITIES **Crosshaven BY Marina** (100 + 20Ⓥ) ☎ 4831161, cby@eircom.net, €2.50, BH (40 ton), C (1.5 tons), M, Ⓔ, CH, D, P (cans), El, Gaz, Kos, SM, ME, ⚒.

Salve Marine (45 + 12 Ⓥ) ☎ 4831145, AB €2.50, M, BY, El, ME, C, CH, R, D, P (cans), Slip.

Royal Cork YC Marina (170 + 30Ⓥ) ☎ 4831023, www.royalcork.com, €3.00, P , Bar, R, Slip, ♿.

Crosshaven Pier/Pontoon AB €21.00 any size.

East Ferry Marina (85 + 15Ⓥ) ☎ 4811342, €2.50, D, Bar, R, Slip; access all tides, max draft 5·5m.

Crosshaven Village FV pier in 3·5m at Town quay, L, Slip HW±4(for RIBs & small power craft), Grid, SM, Bar, Dr, ✉, R, 🛒 + ATM, 🗑.

Cork City All facilities. ⇌, ✈, **Ferries:** Roscoff; weekly; 13 Hrs; Brittany (www.brittany-ferries.co.uk).

MINOR HARBOUR 16M ENE of YOUGHAL

DUNGARVAN BAY, Waterford, **52°05'·15N 07°36'·70W.**❁❁◊◊✿✿. AC 2017, 5622. HW –0542 on Dover; Duration 0600. See 5.16. A large bay, drying to the W, entered between Helvick Hd to the S and Ballynacourty Pt to the N. Appr in W sector (274°-302°) of this lt to clear Carricknamoan islet to the N, and Carrickapane Rk and Helvick Rk (ECM buoy Q (3) 10s) to the S. 5ca W of this buoy are The Gainers, a large unmarked rky patch (dries 0·8m). Beware salmon nets. Off Helvick hbr are 8 Y 🅜s or ⚓ in approx 4m. Dungarvan town hbr is accessible HW+3, via buoyed (FlG/FlR) chan which shifts, the buoys being moved to suit. Appr is difficult in SE'lies >F6. ⚓ in the pool below the town or AB on pontoon (dries to soft mud), S bank below bridge; craft can stay overnight beyond double Y lines. Facilities: D & P (cans), Bar, Ⓑ, ✉, 🗑, R, 🛒, Kos.

MINOR HARBOUR 15M ENE of ROCHE'S POINT

BALLYCOTTON, Cork, **51°49'·70N 08°00·19W**. AC 2424, 5622. HW –0555 on Dover; Duration 0550. See above. Small, NE-facing hbr at W end of bay suffers from scend in strong SE winds; 3m in ent and about 1·5m against piers. Many FVs alongside piers, on which yachts should berth, rather than ⚓ in hbr, which is foul with old ground tackle. 6 Y 🅜s are outside hbr, or good ⚓ in offshore winds in 6m NE of pier, protected by Ballycotton Is. Lt ho Fl WR 10s 59m 21/17M, B tr in W walls; 238°-W-048°-R-238°; Horn (4) 90s. Facilities: FW on pier. **Village** Hotel, R, ✉, 🛒, LB, Kos.

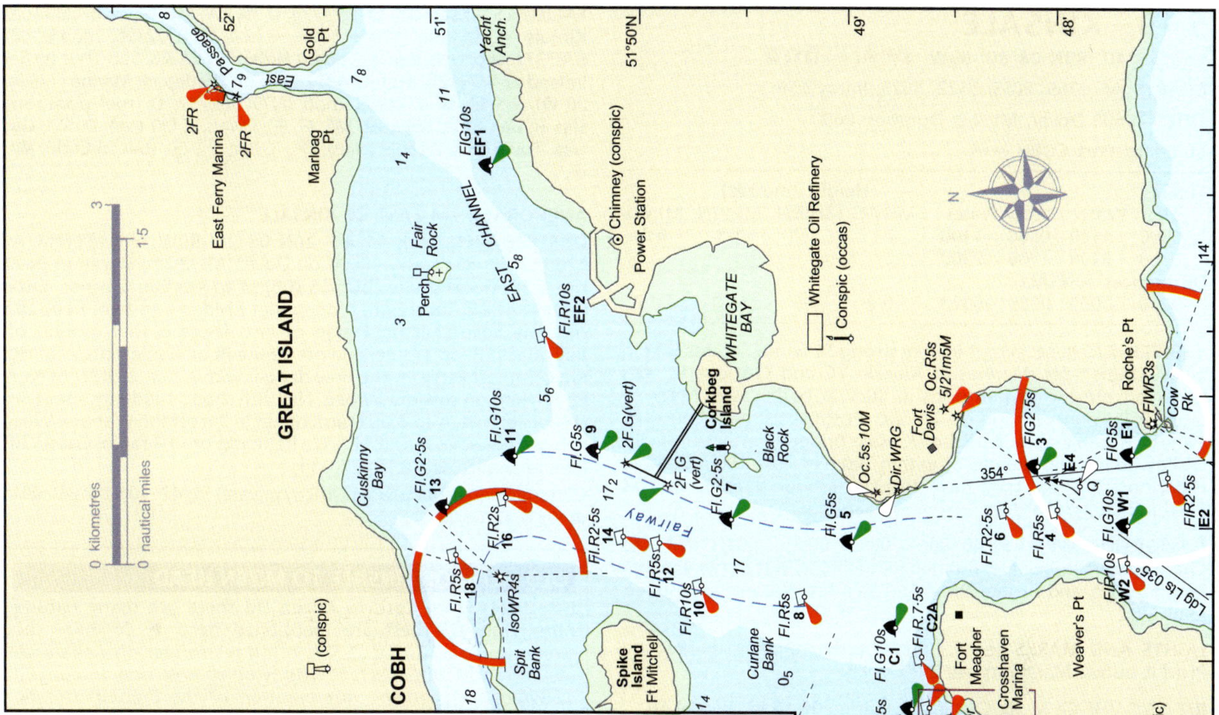
GREAT ISLAND
COBH
East Ferry Marina
2FR
Marloag Pt
Gold Pt
East Passage
Yacht Anch.
51°50'N
Fair Rock
Perch
EAST CHANNEL
Fl.G10s EF1
Fl.R10s EF2
Chimney (conspic)
Power Station
WHITEGATE BAY
Corkbeg Island
Cuskinny Bay
Fl.G2·5s 13
Fl.G10s 11
Fl.G5s 9
2F.G(vert)
Fl.R2s 16
Fl.R5s 18
IsoWR4s
Spit Bank
Fl.R2·5s 14
Fl.R5s 12
Fl.R10s 10
Fairway
Fl.G2·5s 7
Black Rock
Fl.G5s 5
Oc.5s.10M
Dir.WRG
Fort Davis
Oc.R5s 5/21m5M
Fl.G2·5s 3
E4
354°
Fl.G5s E1
Fl.G10s W1
Fl.R2·5s E2
Roche's Pt
FlWR3s
Cow Rk
Fl.R2·5s 6
Fl.R5s 4
Fl.R10s W2
Ldg Lts 035°
Spike Island
Ft Mitchell
Curlane Bank
Fl.R5s 8
Fl.G10s C1
Fl.R.7·5s C2A
Fl.G5s C1A
Fort Meagher
Crosshaven Marina
Weaver's Pt
Whitegate Oil Refinery
Conspic (occas)
(conspic)
kilometres
nautical miles
0
1·5
3
52'
51'
49'
48'
14'

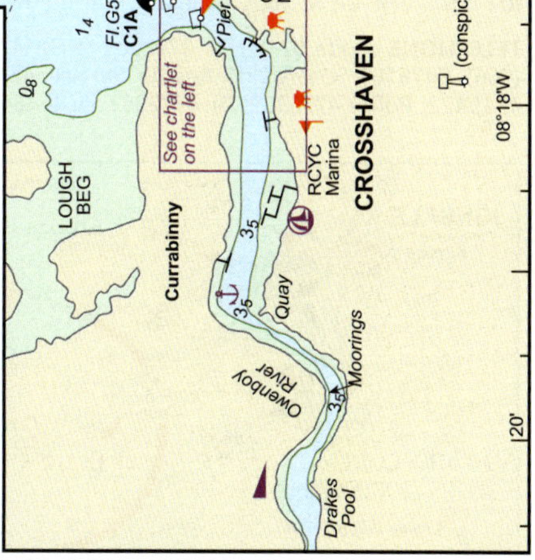
LOUGH BEG
Currabinny
CROSSHAVEN
See chartlet on the left
Pier
RCYC Marina
Quay
Moorings
Owenboy River
Drakes Pool
(conspic)
08°18'W
20'

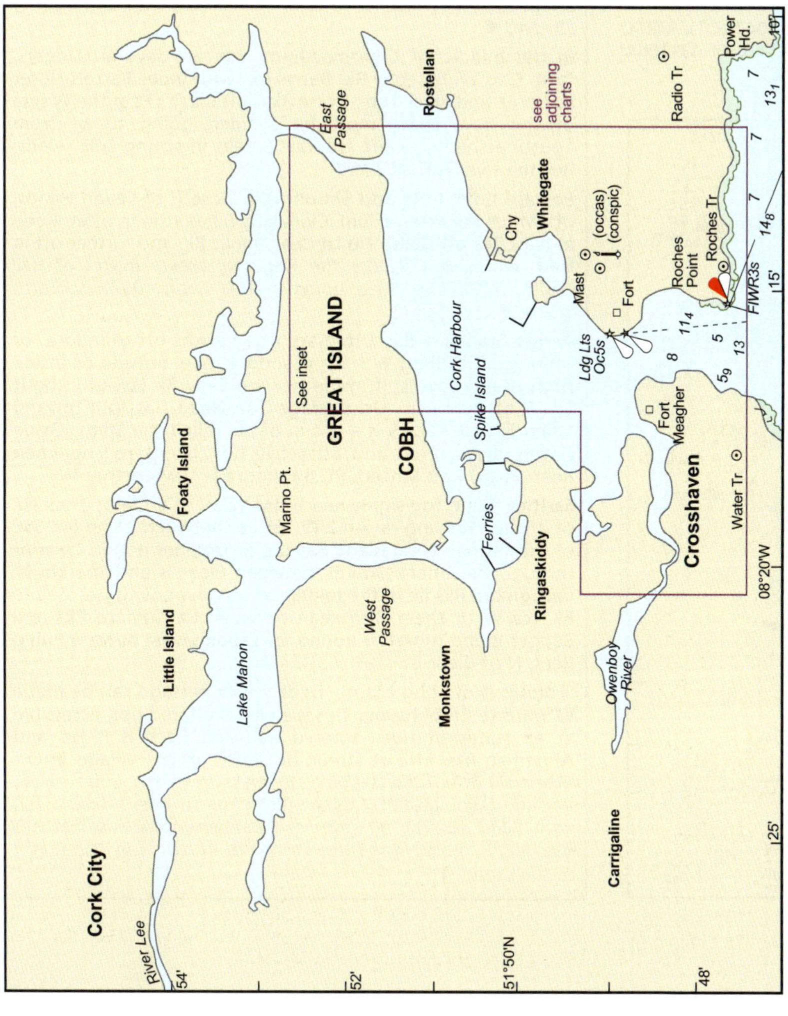
Cork City
River Lee
Little Island
Lake Mahon
Foaty Island
Marino Pt.
Monkstown
West Passage
Ringaskiddy
Ferries
Carrigaline
Owenboy River
Crosshaven
Water Tr
Fort Meagher
Spike Island
Cork Harbour
COBH
GREAT ISLAND
See inset
East Passage
Rostellan
see adjoining charts
Whitegate
Chy
Mast
Fort
(occas)
(conspic)
Ldg Lts Oc5s
Roches Point
Roches Tr
FlWR3s
Radio Tr
Power Hd.
51°50'N
08°20'W
54'
52'
48'
25'
15'
10'

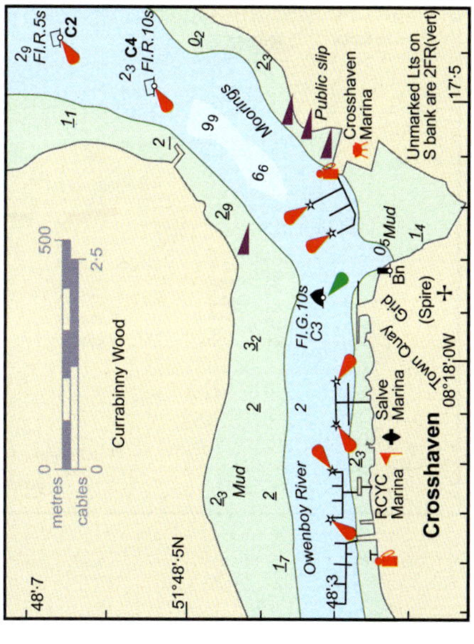
Fl.R.5s C2
C4 Fl.R.10s
Moorings
Public slip
Crosshaven Marina
Unmarked Lts on S bank are 2FR(vert)
Mud
Bn
Grid
(Spire)
Town Quay
Fl.G.10s C3
Salve Marina
RCYC Marina
Crosshaven
Owenboy River
Currabinny Wood
metres
cables
0
500
2·5
48'·7
51°48'·5N
48'·3
08°18'·0W
17'·5

5.19 KINSALE

Cork **51°40'·80N 08°30'·00W** ❀❀❀⛵⛵⛵✿✿✿

CHARTS AC 1765, 2053, 5622, 5623; Imray C56.

TIDES –0600 Dover; ML 2·2; Duration 0600

Standard Port COBH (⟵)

Times				Height (metres)			
High Water		Low Water		MHWS	MHWN	MLWN	MLWS
0500	1100	0500	1100	4·1	3·2	1·3	0·4
1700	2300	1700	2300				
Differences KINSALE							
–0019	–0005	–0009	–0023	–0·2	0·0	+0·1	+0·2

SHELTER Excellent, except in very strong SE winds. Access H24 in all weathers/tides. Marinas at Kinsale YC and Castlepark; Ⓥ's berth on outside of pontoons in 10m in both cases; NNW of latter is FV pontoon and no ⚓ area. Possible AB (Sun-Thurs) at Trident Hotel. 2 large Ⓥs NE of Kinsale Bridge (contact HM). No ⚓ allowed in main channel or within 700m of Town Pier. Contact HM prior to ⚓. All craft have to pay harbour dues as well as berthing/launching fees.

NAVIGATION WPT 51°40'·00N 08°30'·00W, 001°/1·7M to Charles's Fort lt. Beware: Bulman Rk (0·9m; SCM lt buoy) 4ca S of Preghane Pt; and Farmer Rk (0·6m) ¾ca off W bank. Hbr speed limit 6kn.

LIGHTS AND MARKS See 5.3 and chartlet. Chan is marked by PHM lt buoys. Marina lts are 2 FG or FR.

R/T KYC VHF Ch M 16. Castlepark marina 06 16 M. HM **14** 16.

TELEPHONE (Code 021) HM 4772503 (HO), 4773047 (OT); MRCC (066) 9476109; Coast/Cliff Rescue Service 4772346; ⊖ 4311044/4315422; Police 4772302; Dr 4772253; Ⓗ 4546400.

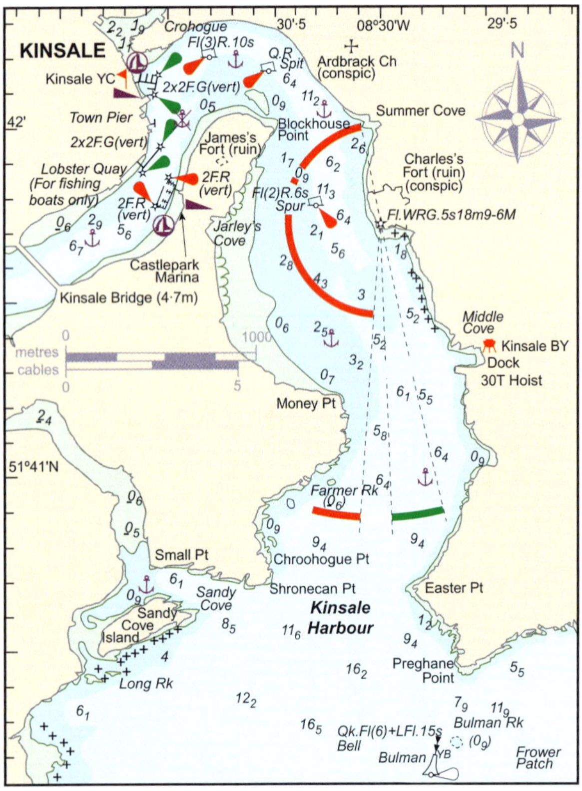

FACILITIES Kinsale BY, ☎ 4774774. D, Ⓥ, FW, ME, ⚒, El, BH (30 ton). **Kinsale YC Marina** (170 + 50Ⓥ), €3.20, ☎ 4772196, mobile 087 6787377, Slip, D, R, Bar, ♿; **Trident Hotel**, D, FW, AB, Sun-Thur try Sail Ireland ☎ 4772927, Mobile 0877 502737. **Castlepark Marina** (130 inc 20 Ⓥ), €5·50, ☎ 4774959, mob 0877 502737, D (fuel pontoon), Slip, R, Bar, El, ⊡. **Services:** ME, El, Ⓔ, Divers, C (30 ton), D, SM, Gas, Gaz. **Town** @ & Wi-fi, P (cans), 🛒, R, Bar, ✉, Ⓑ, (bus to Cork), ⇌, ✈.

ANCHORAGE 2M EAST OF KINSALE

OYSTERHAVEN, Cork, **51°41'·20N 08°26'·90W**. ❀❀⛵✿✿✿. AC 1765, 2053, 5622. HW –0600 on Dover; ML 2·2m; Duration 0600. Use 5.18. Good shelter but ⚓'s subject to swell in S winds. Enter 0·5M N of Big Sovereign, a steep islet divided into two. Keep to S of Little Sovereign on E side of ent. There is foul ground off Ballymacus Pt on W side, and off Kinure Pt on E side. Pass W of Hbr Rk (0·9m) off Ferry Pt, the only danger within hbr. ⚓ NNW of Ferry Pt in 4–6m on soft mud/weed. NW arm shoals suddenly about 5ca NW of Ferry Pt. Also ⚓ up N arm of hbr in 3m off the W shore. Weed in higher reaches may foul ⚓. No lts, marks or VHF radio. Coast/Cliff Rescue Service ☎ (021) 4770711.

Oysterhaven Yacht Harbour (strictly private) 51°42'·10N 08°26'·58W, ☎ (021) 4770878.

OLD HEAD OF KINSALE TO MIZEN HEAD

(AC 2424) From Cork to Mizen Hd there are many natural hbrs. Only the best are mentioned here. ▶ *Offshore the stream seldom exceeds 1·5kn, but it is stronger off headlands causing races and overfalls with wind against tide. Prolonged W winds increase the rate/duration of the E-going stream, and strong E winds have a similar effect on the W-going stream.* ◀

In the middle of Courtmacsherry Bay are several dangers, from E to W: Blueboy Rk, Barrel Rk (with Inner Barrels closer inshore), and Black Tom; Horse Rk is off Barry's Pt at the W side of the bay. These must be avoided going to or from Courtmacsherry, where the bar breaks in strong S/SE winds, but the river carries 2·3m.

Beware Cotton Rk and Shoonta Rk close E of Seven Heads, off which rks extend 50m. Clonakilty B has little to offer. Keep at least 5ca off Galley Hd to clear Dhulic Rk, and further off in fresh winds. ▶ *Offshore the W-going stream makes at HW Cobh +0200, and the E-going at HW Cobh –0420, sp rates 1·5kn.* ◀

Across Glandore Bay there are good anchs off Glandore, or Union Hall. Sailing W from Glandore, pass outside or inside High Is and Low Is; if inside beware Belly Rk (awash) about 3ca S of Rabbit Is. On passage Toe Head has foul ground 100m S, and 7½ca S is a group of rks called the Stags. Castle Haven, a sheltered and attractive hbr, is entered between Reen Pt (lt) and Battery Pt. Baltimore is 10M further W.

Fastnet Rk (lt, fog sig) is nearly 4M WSW of C Clear; 2½ca NE of it is an outlying rk. An E/W TSS lies between 2 and 8M SSE of the Fastnet. Long Island Bay can be entered from C Clear or through Gascanane Sound, between Clear Is and Sherkin Is. Carrigmore Rks lie in the middle of this chan, with Gascanane Rk 1ca W of them. The chan between Carrigmore Rks and Badger Island is best. If bound for Crookhaven, beware Bullig Reef, N of Clear Is.

Schull is N of Long Island, inside which passage can be made W'ward to Crookhaven. This is a well sheltered hbr, accessible at all states of tide, entered between Rock Is lt Ho and Alderman Rks, ENE of Streek Hd. Anch off the village. ▶ *Off Mizen Hd (lt ho) the W-going stream starts at HW Cobh +0120, and the E-going at HW Cobh –0500. The sp rate is 4kn, which with wind against tide forms a dangerous race, sometimes reaching to Brow Hd or Three Castle Hd, with broken water right to the shore.* ◀

5.20 COURTMACSHERRY

Cork **51°38'·22N 08°40'·90W**

CHARTS AC 2092, 2081, 5622, 5623; Imray C56.

TIDES HW –0610 on Dover; Duration 0545

Standard Port COBH (⟵)

Times				Height (metres)			
High Water		Low Water		MHWS	MHWN	MLWN	MLWS
0500	1100	0500	1100	4·1	3·2	1·3	0·4
1700	2300	1700	2300				
Differences COURTMACSHERRY							
–0025	–0008	–0008	–0015	–0·1	–0·1	0·0	+0·1

SHELTER Good shelter up-river, but in strong S/SE winds seas break on the bar (2·3m), when ent must not be attempted. Dry out in small inner hbr or AB afloat on jetty (FVs) or on yacht pontoon (18·5m). ⚓ NE of Ferry Pt in about 2·5m or N of pontoon. Weed may foul ⚓; best to moor using two ⚓s.

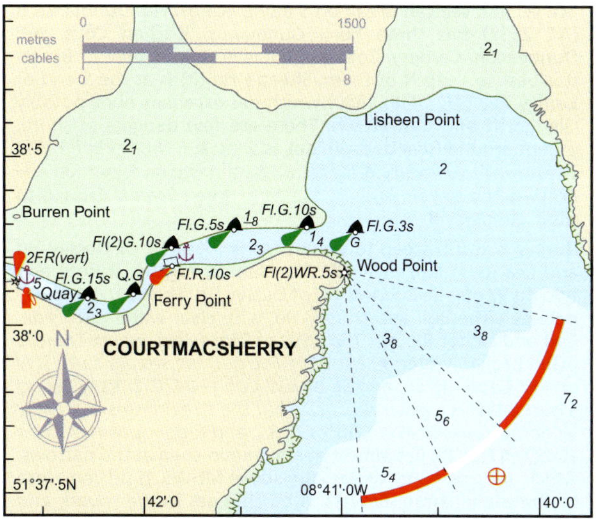

NAVIGATION WPT, 51°37'·50N 08°40'·17W, 324°/0·8M to Wood Pt. Appr in the W sector of Wood Pt lt, between Black Tom and Horse Rk (dries 3·6m); the latter is 3-4½ca E of Barry Pt on the W shore. Black Tom (2·3m), with SHM buoy Fl.G.5s 5ca SSE, is close NE of the appr. Further to NE, in centre of bay, Barrel Rk (dries 2·6m), has unlit perch (ruin). To NNW and E of it are Inner Barrels (0·5m) and Blueboy Rk. Hbr ent is between Wood Pt and SHM buoy 2ca NE, Fl G 3s. Chan (2m but 1·4m close inside ent) is marked by 5 SHM buoys and 1 PHM buoy (off Ferry Point). Keep close N of moorings on S side of harbour.

LIGHTS AND MARKS Wood Pt, Fl (2) WR 5s 15m 5M.

R/T None.

TELEPHONE (023) HM (Mob) 08610 40812; RNLI boathouse 8846600; Dr 8846186 (HN 1850 335999); Police 8846122; Coast Rescue Service (Mob) 08685 01806.

FACILITIES Quay AB (min €15/craft). ⛽, WC, FW, ♿, D (Pier 0930-1800 on request), Slip, LB, R. **Village**, Bar, R, 🛒, (bus to Cork), ⇄, ✈.

5.21 GLANDORE/UNIONHALL

Cork, **51°33'·70N 09°07'·20W**

CHARTS AC 2092, 5622, 5623; Imray C56.

TIDES Approx as for 5.21 Castletownshend

SHELTER Excellent. 12 Y Ⓥs or ⚓ 1½ca SW of Glandore Pier in 2m or 1ca NE of the New pier at Unionhall in 3m.

NAVIGATION WPT 51°32'·35N 09°05'·10W, 129°/1·2M to Outer Dangers. Approach between Adam Is and Goat's Hd, thence keep E of Eve Is and W of the chain of rocks: Outer, Middle and Inner Dangers and Sunk Rk. Before altering W for Unionhall, stand on to clear mudbank 1ca off S shore. Speed limit 3kn.

LIGHTS AND MARKS See 5.3. Galley Hd, Fl (5) 20s, is 5M E of ent. Outer Dangers are marked by GRG lt buoy, and PHM bn; Middle and Inner Dangers by 2 SHM bns; and Sunk Rk by a NCM lt buoy.

R/T HM Ch 06.

TELEPHONE (Code 028) HM Glandore/Unionhall 34737, mob 0866081944; Police (023) 23088; Dr 23456; Coast Rescue 33115.

FACILITIES **Glandore** GHYC, Ⓥs €14.00/craft (contact Glandore Inn ☎ 33468/33518), FW, ✉, R, Bar, Kos. **Unionhall** AB (outside of FVs/drying AB Old Quay) €15.00/craft, FW, D(occ quayside) or D & P (by cans from Leap 2M), ME, Gas, showers, WC, ✉, R, Bar, 🛒.

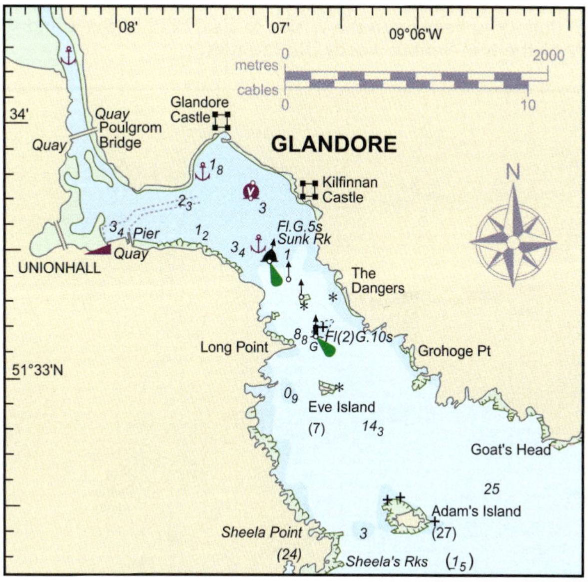

5.22 CASTLETOWNSHEND

Cork **51°30'·90N 09°10'·70W**

CHARTS AC 2092, 2129, 5623; Imray C56.

TIDES +0605 Dover; ML 2·2; Duration 0605

Standard Port COBH (⟵)

Times				Height (metres)			
High Water		Low Water		MHWS	MHWN	MLWN	MLWS
0500	1100	0500	1100	4·1	3·2	1·3	0·4
1700	2300	1700	2300				
Differences CASTLETOWNSHEND							
–0020	–0030	–0020	–0050	–0·4	–0·2	+0·1	+0·3
CLONAKILTY BAY (5M NE of Galley Head)							
–0033	–0011	–0019	–0041	–0·3	–0·2	No data	

SHELTER Excellent ⚓ in midstream SE of Castletownshend slip, protected from all weathers and available at all tides; but the outer part of hbr is subject to swell in S winds. Or ⚓ N of Cat Island, or upstream as depth permits. Caution: An underwater cable runs E/W across the hbr from the slip close N of Reen Pier to the slip at Castletownshend.

NAVIGATION WPT 51°30'·28N, 09°10'·26W, 351°/7ca to Reen Pt lt. Enter between Horse Is (35m) and Skiddy Is (9m) both of which have foul ground all round. Black Rk lies off the SE side of Horse Is and is steep-to along its S side. Flea Sound is a narrow boat chan, obstructed by rks. Colonel's Rk (0·5m) lies close to the E shore, 2ca N of Reen Pt. Beware salmon nets.

Continued overleaf

CASTLETOWNSHEND *continued*

LIGHTS AND MARKS Reen Pt, Fl WRG 10s; a small slender W bn; vis shore-G-338°-W-001°-R-shore. A ruined tr is on Horse Is.

R/T None.

TELEPHONE (Code 028) MRCC (066) 9746109; Coast/Cliff Rescue Service 21039; ⊜ Bantry (027) 50061; Police 36144; Dr 23456; Ⓗ 21677.

FACILITIES **Reen Pier** L, FW; **Sailing Club** ☎ 36100; **Castletownshend Village** Slip, Bar, R, 🛒, FW, ✉, Ⓑ (Skibbereen), ⇌, ✈ (Cork).

BARLOGE CREEK, Cork, **51°29'·57N 09°17'·58W**. AC 2129. Tides approx as Castletownshend. A narrow creek, well sheltered except from S/SE winds. Appr with Gokane Pt brg 120°. Enter W of Bullock Is, keeping to the W side to clear rks S of the island. ⚓ W of the Is in 3m but weedy. No facilities.

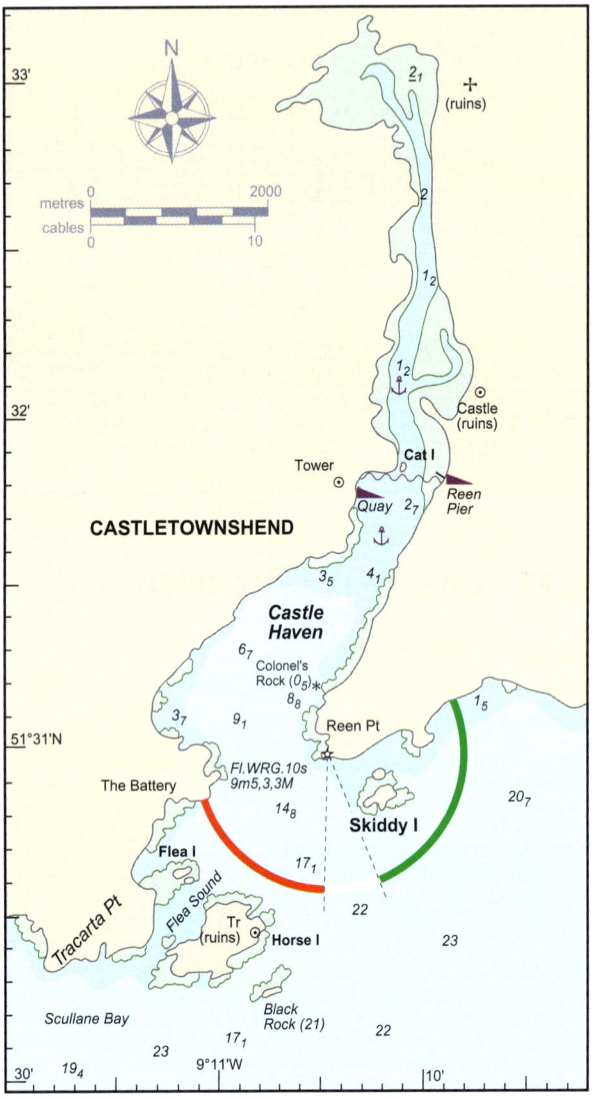

THE WEST COAST

This coast offers wonderful cruising, although exposed to the Atlantic and any swell offshore; but this diminishes mid-summer. In bad weather however the sea breaks dangerously on shoals with quite substantial depths. There is usually a refuge close by, but if caught out in deteriorating weather and poor vis, a stranger may need to make an offing until conditions improve, so a sound yacht and good crew are required. Even in mid-summer at least one gale may be met in a two-week cruise. Fog is less frequent than in the Irish Sea.

▶ *Tidal streams are weak, except round headlands.* ◀ There are few lights, so inshore navigation is unwise after dark, however coastal navigation is feasible at night in good visibility. Keep a good watch for lobster pots in inshore waters. Stores, fuel and water are not readily available.

MIZEN HEAD TO DINGLE BAY

(AC 2423) At S end of Dunmanus Bay Three Castle Hd has rks 1ca W, and sea can break on S Bullig 4ca off Hd. Dunmanus B (AC 2552) has three hbrs: Dunmanus, Kitchen Cove and Dunbeacon. Carbery, Cold and Furze Is lie in middle of B, and it is best to keep N of them. Sheep's Hd (lt) is at the S end of Bantry Bay (AC 1838, 1840) which has excellent hbrs, notably Glengariff and Castletown. There are few dangers offshore, except around Bear and Whiddy Islands. ▶ *Off Blackball Hd at W entrance to Bantry B there can be a nasty race, particularly on W-going stream against the wind. Keep 3ca off Crow Is to clear dangers.* ◀

Dursey Island is steep-to except for rk 7½ca NE of Dursey Hd and Lea Rk (1·4m)1½ca SW. The Bull (lt, fog sig, Racon) and two rks W of it lie 2·5M WNW of Dursey Hd. The Cow is midway between The Bull and Dursey Hd, with clear water each side. Calf and Heifer Rks are 7½ca SW of Dursey Hd, where there is often broken water. ▶ *2M W of The Bull the stream turns NW at HW Cobh +0150, and SE at HW Cobh –0420. Dursey Sound (chart 2495) is a good short cut, but the stream runs 4kn at sp; W-going starts at HW Cobh +0135, and E-going at HW Cobh –0450.* ◀ Flag Rk lies almost awash in mid-chan at the narrows, which are crossed by cables 25m above MHWS. Hold very close to the Island shore. Beware wind changes in the sound, and broken water at N entrance.

Kenmare R. (AC 2495) has attractive hbrs and anchs, but its shores are rky, with no lights. The best places are Sneem, Kilmakilloge and Ardgroom. Off Lamb's Head, Two Headed Island is steep-to; further W is Moylaun Is with a rk 300m SW of it. Little Hog (or Deenish) Island is rky 1·5M to W, followed by Great Hog (or Scariff) Is which has a rk close N, and a reef extending 2ca W.

Darrynane is an attractive, sheltered hbr NNW of Lamb Hd. The entrance has ldg lts and marks, but is narrow and dangerous in bad weather. Ballinskelligs Bay has an anch N of Horse Is, which has two rks close off E end. Centre of bay is a prohib anch (cables reported).

Rough water is met between Bolus Hd and Bray Hd with fresh onshore winds or swell. The SW end of Puffin Island is steep-to, but the sound to the E is rky and not advised. Great Skellig (lit) is 6M, and Little Skellig 5M WSW of Puffin Is. Lemon Rk lies between Puffin Is and Little Skellig. ▶ *Here the stream turns N at HW Cobh +0500, and S at HW Cobh –0110.* ◀ There is a rk 3ca SW of Great Skellig. When very calm it is possible to go alongside at Blind Man's Cove on NE side of Great Skellig, where there are interesting ruins.

5.23 BALTIMORE

Cork **51°28'·30N 09°23'·40W**

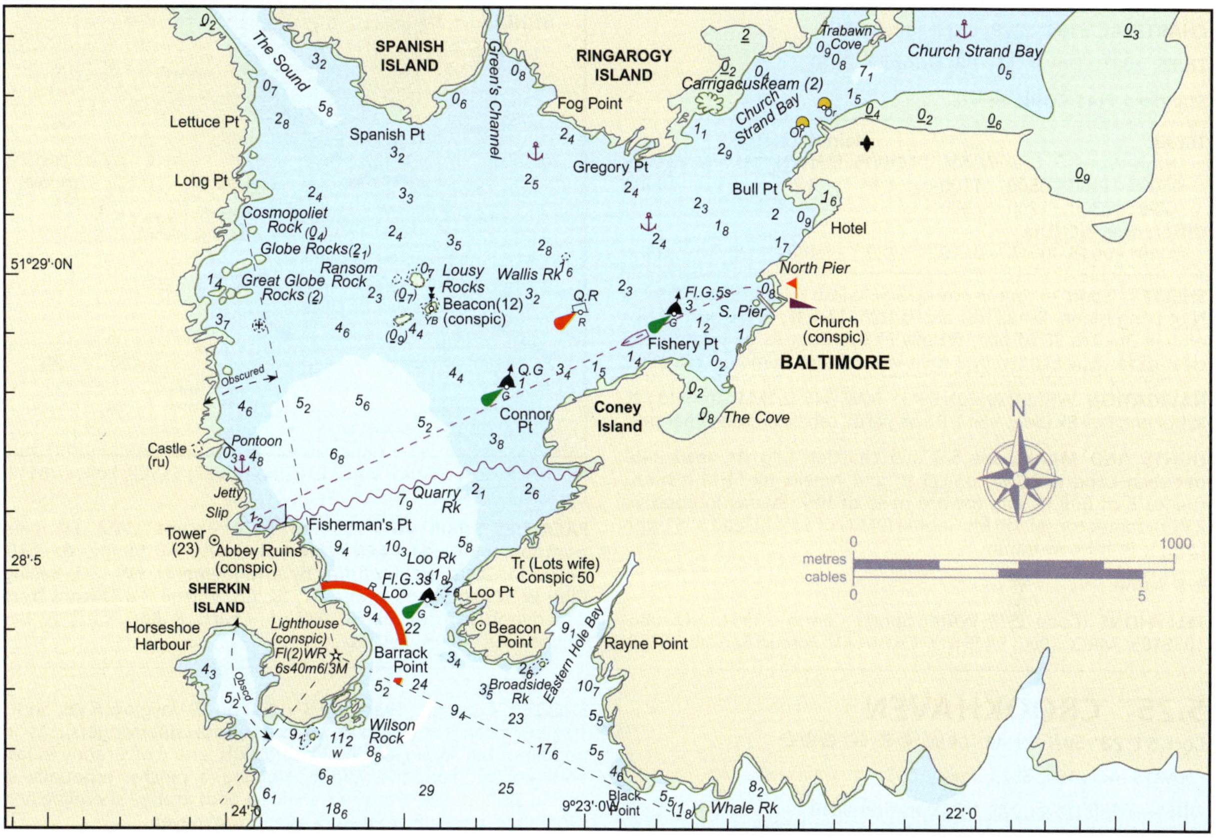

CHARTS AC 2129, 3725, 5623; Imray C56.

TIDES –0605 Dover; ML 2·1; Duration 0610

Standard Port COBH (⟵)

Times				Height (metres)			
High Water		Low Water		MHWS	MHWN	MLWN	MLWS
0500	1100	0500	1100	4·1	3·2	1·3	0·4
1700	2300	1700	2300				
Differences BALTIMORE							
–0025	–0005	–0010	–0050	–0·6	–0·3	+0·1	+0·2

SHELTER Excellent. Access H24 from the S. At Baltimore, pontoon (Apr-Sep) on S Pier, AB for up to 20 yachts in 2·4m depth. Inner Hbr, partly drying between N and S piers, mostly used by ferries, local boats and FVs; the latter also berth on N pier. ⚓ about 200m W of S pier, or about 200m N of N Pier. Beware extensive moorings. In strong NW'lies ⚓ in Church Strand Bay. lts are required. Do not ⚓ in dredged chan between Wallis Rk buoy and N Pier, or in chan to Church Strand Bay. In strong W winds ⚓ in lee of Sherkin Is off Castle ruins or berth on pontoon (see Adjacent Anchorages, Sherkin Island).

NAVIGATION WPT 51°27'·93N 09°23'·46W, 000°/5ca to Loo Rk SHM lt buoy. No passage between buoy and mainland. Beware Lousy Rks (SCM bn) and Wallis Rk (PHM lt buoy) in middle of the bay. From/to the N The Sound needs careful pilotage; AC 3725 and ICC SDs essential. R Ilen is navigable on the flood for at least 4M above The Sound. Speed limit 6kn in R Ilen and N/NE of Wallace Rock.

LIGHTS AND MARKS See 5.3 and chartlet. Ent easily identified by Barrack Pt lt ho and conspic W tr (Lot's Wife) on Beacon Pt.

R/T VHF (HM) Ch 09, 16.

TELEPHONE (Code 028) HM 087 2351485; MRCC and Coast/Cliff Rescue Service (066) 9476109; ⊜ (027) 53210; Police 20102; Dr 23456/after hrs 1850 335999, Ⓗ 21677.

FACILITIES Berthing: May-Sept from €20/craft, ☎ 22145, 0872 351485 or www.atlanticboat.ie; slip, AB, D (☎ 20106), FW on pontoon; **Baltimore SC,** ☎ 20426, visitors welcome, bar, showers; **Glenans Irish Sailing School** ☎ (01) 6611481, 028 20154; **Sherkin** Pontoon, FW, access to shore in season. Hotel ☎ 20361. **Services:** D (hose), BY (on R Ilen at Old Court), ME, El, CH, 🛒, Gas, Gaz, Kos, ACA; **Village:** Bar, ✉, bus to Cork for ≷, ✈.

ADJACENT ANCHORAGES

SHERKIN ISLAND on W side of harbour entrance. ⚓s: Horseshoe Harbour (keep well to the W in narrow entrance; unlit); and off Castle ruins, 5ca N, where there are also some AB on pontoons (FW and electricity) belonging to nearby Islander's Rest Hotel.

CLEAR ISLAND, N HARBOUR, 51°26'·60N 09°30'·20W. AC 2129, 5623. Tides approx as Schull, 5.23. A tiny, partly drying inlet on N coast of Clear Is, exposed to N'ly swell. Rks either side of outer appr 196°. Inside the narrow (30m), rky ent keep to the E. Lie to 2⚓s on E side in about 1·5m or drying berth in Inner Hbr clear of ferry bad weather berth. **Facilities** D & P (cans), FW, 🛒, ✉,email, R, Bar.

ROARINGWATER BAY, Long Island Bay AC 2129, 5623. Entered between Cape Clear and Mizen Hd and extends NE into Roaringwater Bay, beware extensive marine farms with narrow chans between them. Fastnet Rk/Lt Ho, is 4M to seaward. Safest appr, S of Schull, is via Carthy's Sound (51°30'N 09°30'W). From the SE appr via Gascanane Sound, but beware Toorane Rks, Anima Rk and outlying rks off many of the islands. Shelter in various winds at ⚓s clockwise from Horse Island: 3ca E and 7ca NE of E tip of Horse Is; in Ballydehob B 2m; Poulgorm B 2m; 5ca ENE of Mannin Is in 4m; 2ca SE of Carrigvalish Rks in 6m. Rincolisky Cas (ru) is conspic on S side of bay. The narrow chan E of Hare Is and N of Sherkin Is has two ⚓s; also leads via The Sound into Baltimore hbr. Local advice useful. Temp'y fair weather ⚓s in Carthy's Islands. Rossbrin Cove safe ⚓ 2·5M E of Schull, but many local moorings; no access from E of Horse Is due to drying Horse Ridge. Ballydehob has a good quay for tenders and most facilities.

5.24 SCHULL

Cork **51°30'·80N 09°32'·00W**

CHARTS AC 2184, 2129, 5623; Imray C56.

TIDES +0610 Dover; ML 1·8; Duration 0610

Standard Port COBH (⟵)

Times				Height (metres)			
High Water		Low Water		MHWS	MHWN	MLWN	MLWS
0500	1100	0500	1100	4·1	3·2	1·3	0·4
1700	2300	1700	2300				
Differences SCHULL							
−0040	−0015	−0015	−0110	−0·9	−0·6	−0·2	0·0

SHELTER Good, except in strong S/SE winds when best shelter is N of Long Island. Schull Hbr access H24. 12 Y ◉s in NE part of hbr or ⚓ in 3m 1ca SE of pier, usually lit by street lts all night; keep clear of fairway marked by 8 unlit lateral buoys (summer time only).

NAVIGATION WPT 51°29'·60N 09°31'·60W, 346°/2·1M to front ldg lt. In hbr ent, Bull Rk (dries 1·8m), R iron perch, can be passed either side.

LIGHTS AND MARKS See 5.3 and chartlet. Ldg lts, lead 346° between Long Is Pt, W conical tr, and Amelia Rk SHM lt buoy; thence E of Bull Rk and toward head of bay. By day in good vis 2 W radomes conspic on Mt Gabriel (2M N of Schull) lead 355° with Long Is Pt lt ho in transit.

R/T None.

TELEPHONE (Code 028) Water Sports Centre 28554; HM 086-1039105; MRCC (066) 9476109; Coast/Cliff Rescue Service 35318;

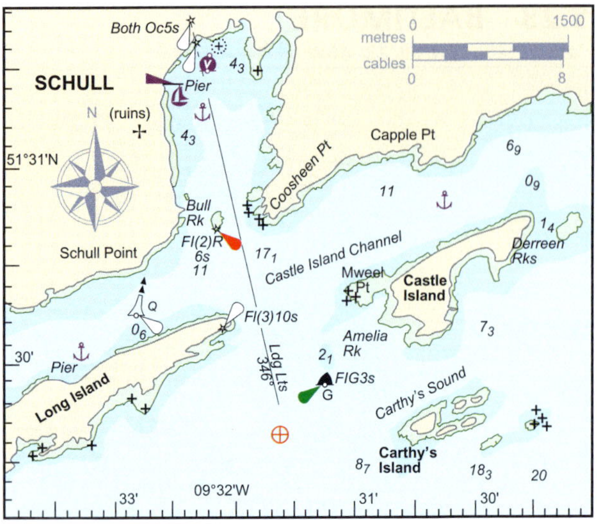

Inshore Rescue Service 086 236 0206; ⊖ (027) 51562; Police 28111; Dr 28311; ⊞ (027) 50133.

FACILITIES Schull Pier/Hbr Slip (H24 except LWS) FV pier/ pontoon for tenders (v.crowded at times), AB tempy, ◉s €10/ night, M, D (large quantities by arrangement), FW, SM; **Sailing Club** ☎ 37352; **Services:** Kos, BY, ⚒, CH. **Village** P & D (cans from Ballydehob 5M), ME, El, 🛒, @/Wi-fi, Charts, R, Bar, ⊡, ✉, Ⓑ, bus to Cork for: ⇌, ✈, Ferries.

5.25 CROOKHAVEN

Cork **51°28'·50N 09°42'·00W**

CHARTS AC 2184, 5623; Imray C56.

TIDES +0550 Dover; ML 1·8; Duration 0610

Standard Port COBH (⟵)

Times				Height (metres)			
High Water		Low Water		MHWS	MHWN	MLWN	MLWS
0500	1100	0500	1100	4·1	3·2	1·3	0·4
1700	2300	1700	2300				
Differences CROOKHAVEN							
−0057	−0033	−0048	−0112	−0·8	−0·6	−0·4	−0·1
DUNMANUS HARBOUR							
−0107	−0031	−0044	−0120	−0·7	−0·6	−0·2	0·0
DUNBEACON HARBOUR							
−0057	−0025	−0032	−0104	−0·8	−0·7	−0·3	−0·1

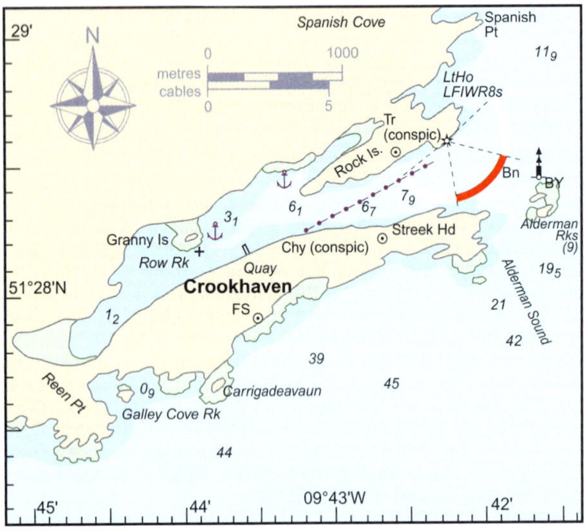

SHELTER Excellent. There are 8 Y ◉s and 10 dayglow R ◉s. Short stay pontoon for up to 4 boats (FW/stores/passengers). ⚓s in middle of bay in 3m; off W tip of Rock Is; and E of Granny Is; last two are far from the village. Holding is patchy, especially in strong SW'lies; beware weed, shellfish beds around shoreline and submarine pipeline from Rock Is to Crookhaven.

NAVIGATION WPT 51°28'·50N 09°40'·50W, 274°/1M to Rock Is lt ho. Ent between this lt and NCM bn on Black Horse Rks (3½ca ESE). From S, keep 1ca E of Alderman Rks and ½ca off Black Horse Rks bn. Passage between Streek Hd and Alderman Rks is not advised for strangers. Inside the bay the shores are steep to.

LIGHTS AND MARKS Lt ho on Rock Is (conspic W tr) L Fl WR 8s 20m 13/11M; vis outside hbr: W over Long Is Bay-281°-R-340°; vis inside hbr: 281°-R-348°-W-shore(N).

R/T None.

TELEPHONE (Code 028) HM (O'Sullivan's Bar) 35319; MRCC (066) 9476109; Coast/Cliff Rescue at Goleen 35318; ⊖ (027) 50061; Dr 35148; ✉ 35200.

FACILITIES Village ◉s €8.00, Bar, R, FW, 🛒, ✉, D (cans), ME, Ⓑ (Schull), taxi to Goleen then bus to Cork, ✈, ⇌.

ADJACENT HARBOURS

GOLEEN (Kireal-coegea), Cork, **51°29'·65N 09°42'·21W**. AC 2184, 5623. Tides as Crookhaven. A narrow inlet 6ca N of Spanish Pt; good shelter in fair weather, except from SE. 2 churches are easily seen, but ent not visible until close. Keep to S side of ent and anchor fore-and-aft just below quay, where AB also possible. Facilities: P, 🛒, Bar.

DUNMANUS BAY, Cork. AC 2552, 5623. Tides see 5.24. Appr between Three Castle Hd and Sheep's Hd, Fl (3) WR 15s 83m 18/ 15M; no other lts. Ent to **Dunmanus Hbr**, 51°32'·70N 09°39'·86W, is 1ca wide; breakers both sides. ⚓ in 4m centre of B. **Kitchen Cove**, 51°35'·50N 09°38'·05W, best of the 3 hbrs; enter W of Owens Is and ⚓ 1ca NNW of it or 2ca further N in 3m. Exposed to S, but good holding. Quay at Ahakista village: AB (drying) FW, ⛽, 🛒, R, Bar. **Dunbeacon Hbr**, 51°36'·35N 09°33'·60W, is shallow and rock-girt. Quay possible AB in 2m (used by FVs), Slip; anchorage E or SE of Mannion Is. Durrus (¾M): Fuel (cans), R, Bar.

5.26 BANTRY BAY

Cork **51°34'N 09°57'W** ❁❁❁◊◊✿✿✿

CHARTS AC 2552, 1840, 1838, 5623; Imray C56.

TIDES +0600 Dover; ML 1·8; Duration 0610

Standard Port COBH (⟵)

Times				Height (metres)			
High Water		Low Water		MHWS	MHWN	MLWN	MLWS
0500	1100	0500	1100	4·1	3·2	1·3	0·4
1700	2300	1700	2300				
Differences BANTRY							
−0045	−0025	−0040	−0105	−0·7	−0·6	−0·2	+0·1
CASTLETOWN (Bearhaven)							
−0048	−0012	−0025	−0101	−0·9	−0·6	−0·1	0·0
BLACK BALL HARBOUR (51°36N 10°02W)							
−0115	−0035	−0047	−0127	−0·7	−0·6	−0·1	+0·1

SHELTER/NAVIGATION Bantry Bay extends 20M ENE from Sheep's Hd, Fl (3) WR 15s 83m 18/15M. Access is easy, but the Bay is exposed to W'lies. The shore is clear everywhere except off Bear Is and Whiddy Is. Some of the many well sheltered ⚓s on the N shore are detailed on this page. The S shore has few ⚓s.

CASTLETOWNBERE 51°38'·80N 09°54'·45W. AC 1840, 5623. Sheltered ⚓ in 2·4m NW of Dinish Is, to E of 010° ldg line, but never far from FVs; also ⚓ at **Dunboy Bay,** W of Piper Sound (open to E). 4 Y Ⓜs are laid Apr-Sep 3ca E of Dinish Is. Lts: At W ent, Ardnakinna Pt, Fl (2) WR 10s 62m 17/14M, H24. At E ent to Bearhaven: Roancarrigmore, Fl WR 3s 18m 18/14M. Appr W of Bear Is on 024° Dir lt, Oc WRG 5s 4m 14/11M (024°-W-024·5°); then inner ldg lts 010°, both Oc 3s 4/7m 1M, vis 005°-015°, via ent chan which narrows to 50m abeam Perch Rk lt bn. Beware Walter Scott Rk (2·7m), SCM lt buoy, and Carrigaglos (0·6m high) S of Dinish Is. VHF Ch 14 16. HM ☎ (027) 70220. Facilities: FW & D on quay; BH on Dinish Is. **Town** El, ME, ⚒, P (cans), Bar, Ⓑ, ✉, 🛒, R, Kos.

LAWRENCE COVE MARINA 51°38'·28N 09°49'·28W; AC 1840, 5623. *See inset on chartlet below.* Good shelter on N side of Bear Island. Marina on S side of cove has NE/SW pontoon 90m long (40 AB in 3-3·5m). From E keep clear of Palmer Rock and a shoal patch, both 1·8m. ☎ 027 75044; VHF Ch 16 M. AB (€1.52), FW, ⛽, D, BH, 🅆. Friendly welcome at the only marina between Kinsale and Dingle. There are 4 yellow Ⓜs in 3m close S of Ardagh Point, or ⚓ in 4m to W of Turk Is. At Rerrin village: BY, Slip, Gaz, 🛒, R, Bar, ✉, storage facilities. Bus to Cork.

LONEHORT HARBOUR 51°38'·12N 09°47'·80W. AC 1840, 5623. At E tip of Bear Is, good shelter but keep S at ent to clear unmarked rks; then turn ENE to ⚓ in 2·7m at E end of cove. Be aware of Firing Practice Area to east of harbour entrance (full clear range procedure in force).

ADRIGOLE 51°40'·51N 09°43'·22W. AC 1840, 5623. Good shelter, but squally in W/N gales. Beware Doucallia Rk, dries 1·2m, 1M SSW of ent. Beyond the 2ca wide ent, keep E of Orthons Is (rks on W side). 7 Y Ⓜs NE of Orthons Is. ⚓s to suit wind direction: off pier on E shore 4m; N or NW of Orthons Is. Drumlave (½M E): Slip, FW, showers (sailing school), D (cans), Gaz, 🛒, ✉.

Trafrask Bay, 2M east, has Y Ⓜ at **51°40'·8N 09°40'·1W**; 🛒, Bar/R.

GLENGARRIFF 51°44'·20N 09°31'·90W. AC 1838, 5623. Tides as Bantry. Beautiful ⚓ S of Bark Is in 7-10m; or to NE in 3m, where there are 6 Y Ⓜs. Better for yachts than Bantry hbr. Ent between Big Pt and Gun Pt. No lts/marks. Keep 1ca E of rks off Garinish Island (Illnacullen) and Ship Is; beware marine farms. Rky chan W of Garinish, with HT cable 15m clearance, should not be attempted. Facilities: Eccles hotel, showers. **Village** FW (ferry berth 1800-1900), Bar, D & P (cans), ✉, R, 🛒, Kos.

BANTRY 51°40'·85N 09°27'·85W. AC 1838, 5623. Beware Gerane Rks ½M W of Whiddy Is. Appr via the buoyed/lit N chan to E of Horse and Chapel Is; keep 2ca off all islands to clear unlit marine farms. The S chan, fair weather only. Appr Relane Pt hdg 063° with HW mark S.Beach (seaward edge of airfield) ∅ Reenbeg Cliff (distant rounded hill) to clear Cracker Rk, then leave Blue Hill and S Beach to stbd. Ⓜ's call Bantry Hbr Ch 14 or ☎ 027 51253; VHF Ch 14 11 16 (H24). HM (027) 53277; ⊖ 50061; Police 50045; Dr 50405; Ⓗ 50133. MRCC (066) 9476109. Facilities: **Pier** AB(drying), L, FW, Gaz; **Bantry Bay SC** ☎ 50081 Ⓜs(free),Slip, L, FW, Showers; **Town** @ (Vickery's Inn), P & D (cans), Kos, ME, CH, 🛒, R, Bar, ✉, Ⓑ, bus to Cork.

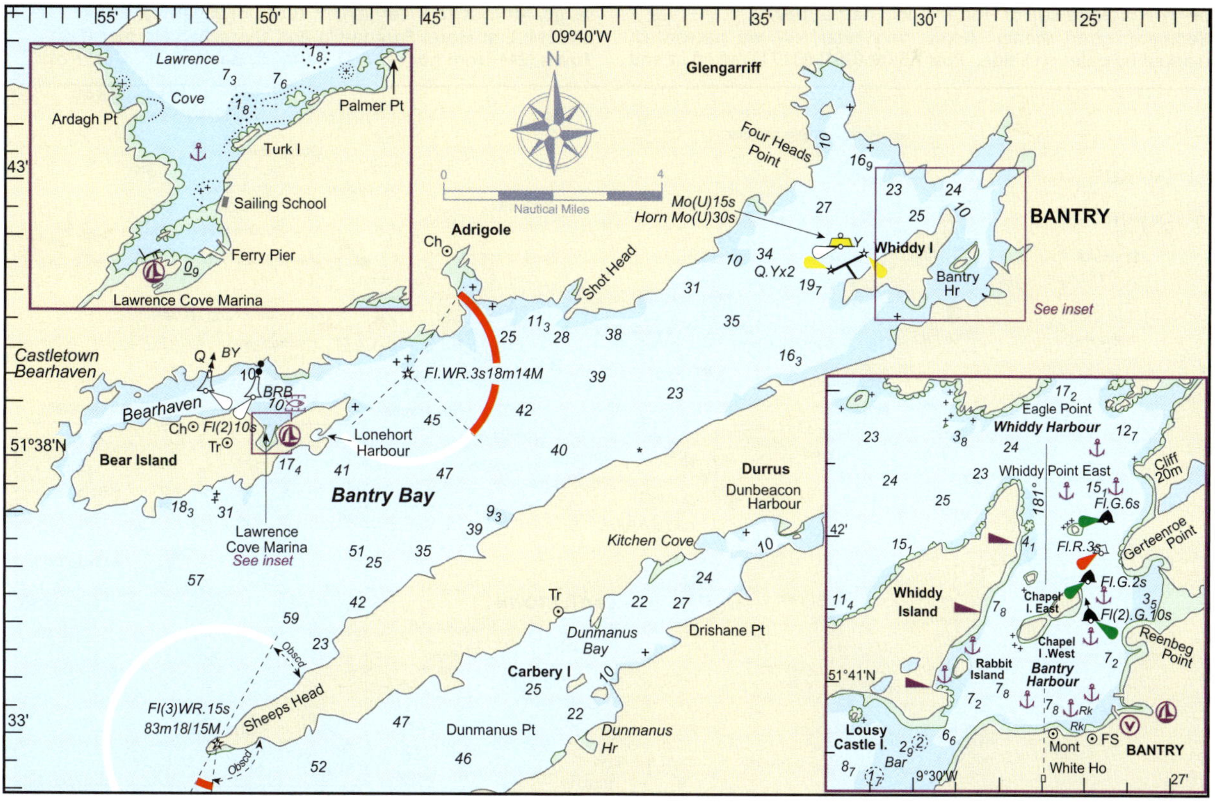

5.27 KENMARE RIVER

Kerry **51°45'·00N 10°00'·00W** ❀❀❀◊✿✿✿

CHARTS AC 2495; Imray C56.

TIDES +0515 Dover; Duration Dunkerron 0620

Standard Port COBH (⟵)

Times				Height (metres)			
High Water		Low Water		MHWS	MHWN	MLWN	MLWS
0500	1100	0500	1100	4·1	3·2	1·3	0·4
1700	2300	1700	2300				
Differences BALLYCROVANE HARBOUR (Coulagh Bay)							
−0116	−0036	−0053	−0133	−0·6	−0·5	−0·1	0·0
DUNKERRON HARBOUR							
−0117	−0027	−0050	−0140	−0·2	−0·3	+0·1	0·0
WEST COVE (51°46'N 10°03'W)							
−0113	−0033	−0049	−0129	−0·6	−0·5	−0·1	0·0
BALLINSKELLIGS BAY							
−0119	−0039	−0054	−0134	−0·5	−0·5	−0·1	0·0

SHELTER Garnish Bay (S of Long I): is only good in settled weather and W'ly winds. ⚓ either W or 1ca S of the Carrigduff concrete bn.

Ballycrovane: in NE of Coulagh B is a good ⚓, but open to W'ly swell which breaks on submerged rks in SE. N and E shores are foul 5ca NE of Bird Is.

Cleanderry: ent NE of Illaunbweeheen (Yellow Is) is only 7m wide and rky. ⚓ ENE of inner hbr. Beware marine farms.

Ardgroom: excellent shelter, but intricate ent over rky bar. Appr with B bn brg 135°; then 2 W bns (front on Black Rk, rear ashore) lead 099° through bar. Alter 206° as two bns astern come in transit. When clear, steer WNW to ⚓ 0·5 ca E of Reenavade pier; power needed. Beware marine farms off Ardgroom & Kilmakilloge.

Kilmakilloge: is a safe ⚓ in all winds. Beware mussel beds and rky shoals. On appr keep S side of ent, steer W of Spanish Is, but pass N of it. Bunaw Hbr ldg lts 041°, front Oc R 3s, rear Iso R 2s, (access only near HW; AB for shoal draft). Keep S side of ent; ⚓ 2ca W of Carrigwee bn; S of Eskadawer Pt; or Collorus Hbr W side only.

Ormond's Harbour: good shelter except in SW or W winds, but beware rk 2½ca ENE of Hog Is. ⚓ in S half of bay.

Kenmare: good shelter. Access only near HW via narrow ch marked by poles on S side. Poss AB (☎ (064) 83171) rafted at end of pier (FW available) at N side of river, just below town. ⚓ in pool (2.5m) just downstream of concrete suspension bridge. Beware very strong ebbs at springs and after heavy rains.

Dunkerron Harbour: ent between Cod Rks and The Boar to ⚓ 1ca NW of Fox Is in 3·2m; land at Templenoe pier. 4ca E of Reen Pt behind pier FW available.

Sneem: enter between Sherky Is and Rossdohan Is. Hotel conspic NE of hbr. 3 Y Øs and ⚓ NE of Garinish Is, but uncomfortable if swell enters either side of Sherky Is. Beware of marine farms.

Darrynane: 1½M NW of Lamb's Hd, is appr'd from the S between Deenish and Moylaun Islands, but not with high SW swell. Enter with care on the ldg marks/lts 034°, 2 W bns, both Oc 3s 10/16m 4M. 3 Y Øs (beware unmkd drying rk close N) and safe ⚓ (3m) NE of Lamb's Is. Also ⚓s in Lehid Hbr, R Blackwater, Coongar Hbr & W Cove.

NAVIGATION WPT 51°40'·00N 10°17'·20W, 065°/15·6M to 0.5M S of Sherky Island. From SW, keep NW of The Bull and Dursey Is. From SE, Dursey Sound is possible in fair weather but narrow (beware Flag Rk 0·3m) and with cable car, 21m clearance. To clear dangerous rks off Coulagh Bay, keep twr on Dursey Is well open of Cod's Head 220°. From NW, there are 3 deep chans off Lamb's Head: between Scarriff Is and Deenish Is which is clear; between Deenish and Moylaun Is which has rky shoals; and between Moylaun and Two Headed Is which is clear and 4½ca wide. A night appr into the river is possible, but close appr to hbrs or ⚓s is not advised. Up-river from Sneem Hbr, keep N of Maiden Rk, dries 0·5m, and Church Rks; also Lackeen Rks and Carrignarona beg. Beware marine farms, also salmon nets Jun-Sep. See 5.4.

LIGHTS AND MARKS On Dursey Is: Old Watch Twr (conspic) 250m. Eagle Hill (Cod's Hd) 216m. Lights are as on chartlet.

R/T None.

TELEPHONE (Code 064) MRCC (066) 9476109; Coast/Cliff Rescue Service (Waterville) (066) 74320; ⊜ Bantry (027) 50061; Ⓗ 4108; Police 41177.

FACILITIES

ARDGROOM Pallas Hbr: D & P (cans), 🛒, R, Bar, Kos, ✉ at Ardgoom village (2M SSW of Reenavade pier).

KILMAKILLOGE: Bunaw Pier, AB, 🛒, Bar/R; 2M to D(cans), Kos, ✉.

KENMARE: AB. **Town** D & P (cans), Kos, Gaz, R, 🛒, Bar, Ⓗ, ✉ inc @, Ⓑ, ⇌ (bus to Killarney), ✈ (Cork or Killarney).

SNEEM: L at Hotel Parknasilla and Oysterbed Ho pier (FW). **Town** (2M from hbr), P & D (cans), R, Bar, ✉, 🛒, Gaz, Kos.

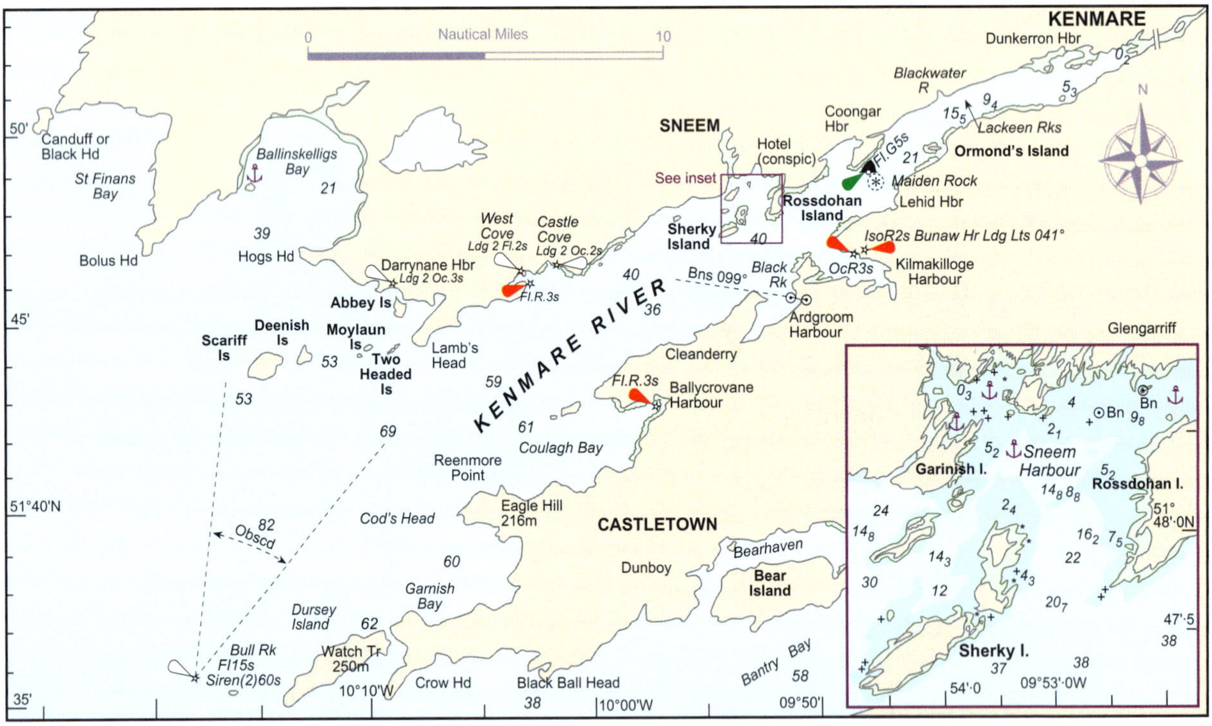

5.28 DINGLE BAY

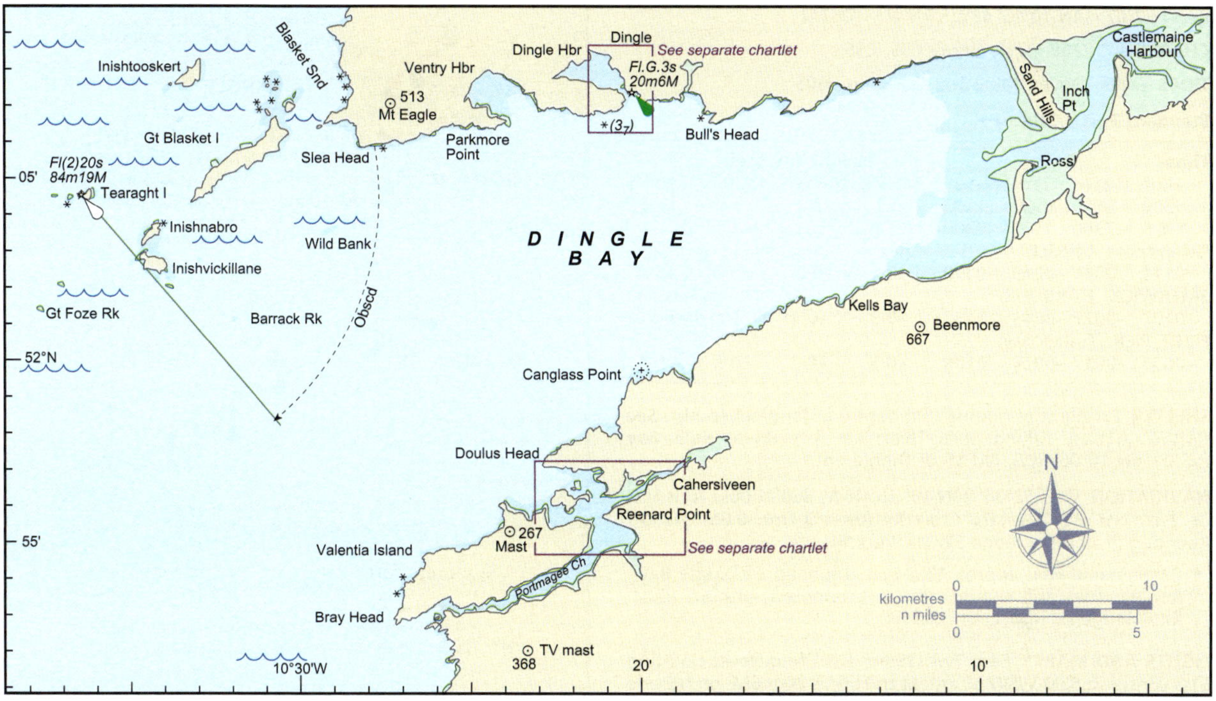

5.29 VALENTIA HARBOUR

Kerry **51°55'·7N 10°17'·1W**

CHARTS AC 2125; Imray C56.

TIDES +0515 Dover

Standard Port COBH (⟵)

Times				Height (metres)			
High Water		Low Water		MHWS	MHWN	MLWN	MLWS
0500	1100	0500	1100	4·1	3·2	1·3	0·4
1700	2300	1700	2300				
Differences VALENTIA HARBOUR (Knight's Town)							
–0118	–0038	–0056	–0136	–0·6	–0·4	–0·1	0·0

SHELTER Good ⚓s at: Glanleam B, 6ca S of Fort Pt in 4m; 1ca NW of LB slip in 2·5m, with 6 Y 🅥s (beware The Foot, spit drying 1·2m, marked by ECM lt buoy; SE of Ferry Pier at Knight's Town (E end of the island) in 4m; in bay on the S side of Beginish Is in 3m.

NAVIGATION Wpt 51°56'·84N 10°20'·15W 147°/1M to Fort Pt lt. Appr the NE end of Valentia Is, either via;

- Doulus Bay, N of Beginish Is (avoid if swell is running). Clear Black Rks by ½ca then head for E end of Beginish Is immediately Reenard Pt opens to port of it. When Lamb Is and the N point of Beginish are about to open astern, alter course to keep them so till Reenard Point opens to the E of Church Is. Then steer to pass 50m E of Church Is to avoid Passage Rk ($\underline{1}_5$) 1ca E of Is.
- Better ent, between Fort Pt and Beginish Is (easy access except in strong NW'lies). Beware Hbr Rk, 2·6m, 3ca SE of Fort Pt and 100m SW of ldg line and marked by ECM lt Bn.

For **Cahersiveen Marina** from Valentia Is start as early on the tide possible to cross the Caher Bar (buoyed WC, EC ,SH & PHMs), using the ldg lts/lines 019-199°, 100°-280°, 076°-256°, 053°-233°, 035°-215° and then keep to the middle of the river.

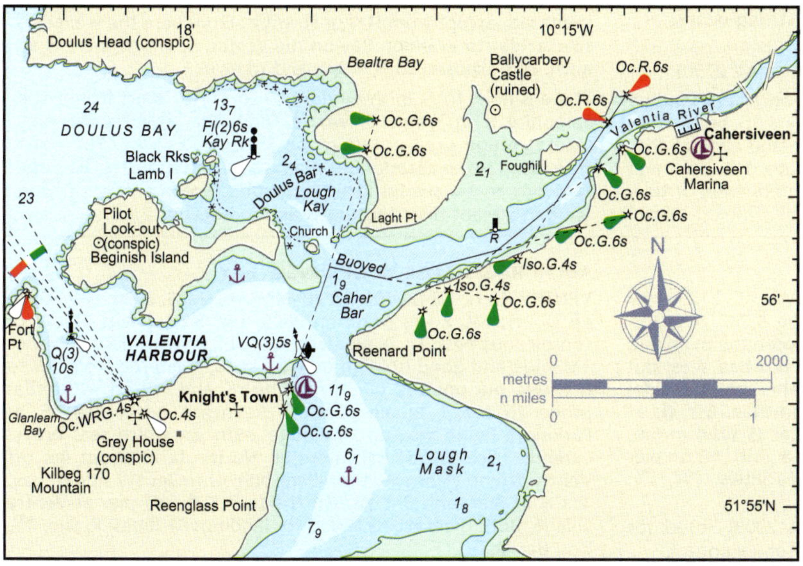

For appr S of Island via Portmagee chan see **Portmagee** overleaf for info on availability of the swing bridge across the chan.

LIGHTS AND MARKS See 5.3 and chartlet.

R/T Cahersiveen Marina VHF Ch 80.

TELEPHONE Knightstown HM (066) 9476124; CG 9476109; ⊜ 7128540; Dr 9472121; Police 9472111; Ⓗ 9472100; Cahersiveen Marina ☎ 947 2777, www.cahersiveenmarina.ie.

FACILITIES **Knight's Town**: 6 Y 🅥s; BY, ⚒, ME, Kos, 🛒, R, Bar, ▣. A new marina is under construction and should be available for Summer 2010 (see monthly online updates). Ferry/bus to Cahersiveen (2½M) for usual shops; Bus to ⇌ (Tralee and Killarney), ✈ (Kerry, Shannon, Cork). **Cahersiveen Marina** (2M upriver): (min depth 2.5m in basin, 93 incl Ⓥ) €2.50, BH(14T), ME, El, Ch, Ⓔ, ⚒, P & D, ▣, 🛒, Ⓑ, ✉, R, Bar.

5.30 DINGLE

Kerry **52°07'·14N 10°15'·48W** ❁❁❁◊◊✿✿✿

CHARTS AC 2789, 2790; Imray C55, C56.

TIDES +0540 Dover; ML 2·1m; Duration 0605

Standard Port COBH (⟵)

Times				Height (metres)			
High Water		Low Water		MHWS	MHWN	MLWN	MLWS
0500	1100	0500	1100	4·1	3·2	1·3	0·4
1700	2300	1700	2300				
Differences DINGLE							
−0111	−0041	−0049	−0119	−0·1	0·0	+0·3	+0·4
SMERWICK HARBOUR							
−0107	−0027	−0041	−0121	−0·3	−0·4	No data	
FENIT PIER (Tralee Bay)							
−0057	−0017	−0029	−0109	+0·5	+0·2	+0·3	+0·1

SHELTER Excellent at marina (5m depth) in landlocked hbr. *See RMWG.* A busy fishing port. There are 4 Y Ⓜs at **Kells Bay** (52°01'·6N 10°06'·3W), 8M SE of Dingle ent.

NAVIGATION WPT 52°06'·20N 10° 15'·48W, 360°/1·06M to lt Fl G 3s. Easy ent H24. Beware Crow Rk (dries 3·7m), 0·8M SW off Reenbeg Pt and rky ledge SW of Black Pt.

- **Castlemaine Hbr**, approx 15M E at the head of Dingle Bay, largely dries and should not be attempted without local knowledge or inspection at LW.

LIGHTS AND MARKS Eask Twr (195m, with fingerpost pointing E) is conspic 0·85M WSW of ent. Lt tr, Fl G 3s 20m 6M, on NE side of ent. Ent chan, dredged 2·6m, is marked by 5 SHM lt buoys and 3 PHM lt buoys, as chartlet. Ldg lts, both Oc 3s, (W ◊s on B poles) lead from astern 182° to hbr bkwtrs. Sectored lt Oc RWG 4s on W side of Main Pier.

R/T Ch **14** 16 M, but no calls required. Valentia Radio (Ch 24 28) will relay urgent messages to Dingle HM.

TELEPHONE (Code 066) HM 9151629; Coastguard (066) 9476109; ⊖ 7121480; Dr 9152225; Ⓗ 9151455; Police 9151522. All emergencies: 999 or 112.

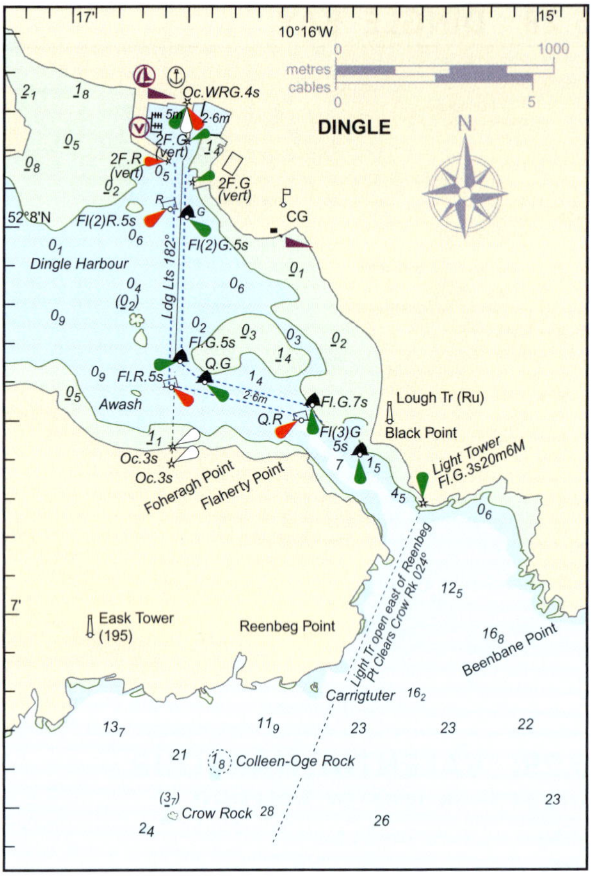

FACILITIES **Marina** (60+20 Ⓥ) ☎ 087 9254115, 1dingle @eircom.net, €2.50, D, Slip (launching €2.00), ⊡, ♿, C (hire). **Town** P (cans), Kos, ME, Ⓔ, Gas, Gaz, SM, ✉, R, Bar, 🛒, Ⓑ, ⇄ Tralee (by bus), ✈ (Kerry 30M).

DINGLE BAY TO LISCANNOR BAY

(AC 2254) Dingle Bay (AC 2789, 2790) is wide and deep, with few dangers around its shores. Cahersiveen and Dingle have small marinas. The best anchs are at Portmagee and Ventry. At the NW ent to the bay, 2·5M SSW of Slea Hd, is Wild Bank (or Three Fathom Pinnacle), a shallow patch with overfalls. 3M SW of Wild Bank is Barrack Rk, which breaks in strong winds.

The Blasket Islands are very exposed, ▶ *with strong tides and overfalls* ◀ but worth a visit in settled weather (AC 2790).

Great Blasket and Inishvickillane each have anch and landing on their NE side. Inishtearaght is the most W'ly Is (lt), but further W lie Tearaght Rks, and 3M S are Little Foze and Gt Foze Rks. Blasket Sound is the most convenient N-S route, 1M wide, and easy in daylight and reasonable weather with fair wind or tide; extensive rks and shoals form its W side. ▶ *The N-going stream starts at HW Galway + 0430, and the S-going at HW Galway – 0155, with sp rate 3kn.* ◀

Between Blasket Sound and Sybil Pt there is a race in W or NW winds with N-going tide, and often a nasty sea. Sybil Pt has steep cliffs, and offlying rks extend 3½ca.

Smerwick hbr, entered between Duncapple Is and the E Sister is sheltered, except from NW or N winds. From here the scenery is spectacular to Brandon Bay on the W side of which there is an anch, but exposed to N winds and to swell.

There is no lt from Inishtearaght to Loop Hd, apart from Little Samphire Is in Tralee B, where Fenit hbr provides the only secure refuge until entering the Shannon Estuary. The coast from Loop Hd to Liscanor Bay has no safe anchs, and no lts. Take care not to be set inshore, although there are few offlying dangers except near Mutton Is and in Liscanor Bay.

ANCHORAGE SW VALENTIA ISLAND

PORTMAGEE, Kerry, **51°53'·20N 10°22'·29W**. AC 2125. HW +0550 on Dover; ML 2·0m; Duration 0610; See 5.28. A safe ⚓ 2·5M E of Bray Head in Portmagee Sound between the mainland and Valentia Is. The ent to the Sound often has bad seas, but dangers are visible. Care required E of Reencaheragh Pt (S side) due rks either side. Deepest water is N of mid-chan. 6 Y Ⓜs at 51°53'·3N 10°22'·5W (N side), or ⚓ off the pier (S side) in 5m, opposite Skelling Heritage Centre (well worth a visit). AB on pier is not recommended due to strong tides. Facilities: FW, 🛒, showers (at hotel), R, Bar, Kos.

The swing bridge 1ca E of pier is currently (Feb 2009) closed; for further information check with Valentia RNLI or Valentia CG.

ANCHORAGE CLOSE W OF DINGLE BAY

VENTRY Kerry, **52°06·70N 10°20'·30W**. AC 2789, 2790. HW +0540 on Dover; ML 2·1m; Duration 0605; Use 5.29. Ent is 2M W of conspicuous Eask Tr. A pleasant harbour br with easy entrance 1M wide and good holding on hard sand; sheltered from SW to N winds, but open to swell from the SE, and in fresh westerlies prone to sharp squalls. Beware Reenvare Rocks 1ca SE of Parkmore Point; also a rocky ridge 2·9m, on which seas break, extends 2·5ca SSE of Ballymore Pt. No lts. ⚓s in about 4m off Ventry Strand (✠ brg W, the village NE); or in 3m SW side of bay, 1ca N of pier; also 3 Y Ⓜs. On N side 3 Y Ⓜs off pier at Ventry village. Both piers access HW±3 for landing. Facilities: P, Slip, 🛒, Kos, Bar, R, ✉.

ANCHORAGES BETWEEN THE BLASKETS AND KERRY HD

SMERWICK HARBOUR, Kerry, **52°13'·00N 10°24'·00W**. AC 2789. Tides 5.29. Adequate shelter in 1M wide bay, except from NW'ly when considerable swell runs in. Ent between The Three Sisters (150m hill) and Dunacapple Is to the NE. Beacon Fl.R.3s at pier end at Ballnagall Pt. ⚓s at: the W side close N or S of the Boat Hr in 3-10m; to the S, off Carrigveen Pt in 2·5m; or in N'lies at the bay in NE corner inside 10m line. Facilities at Ballynagall village on SE side: 4 Y 🅥s, pier (0·5m), limited 🛒, Bar, Bus.

BRANDON BAY, Kerry, **52°16'·10N 10°09'·92**W. AC 2739. Tides as Fenit 5.29. A 4M wide bay, very exposed to the N, but in moderate SW-W winds there is safe ⚓ in 6m close E of drying Brandon Pier, 2FG (vert). Cloghane Inlet in SW of Bay is not advised. Facilities at Brandon: limited 🛒, P (1M), ✉, R, Bar, bus.

TRALEE BAY, Kerry, **52°18'·00N 09°56'·00W**. AC 2739. HW –0612 on Dover; ML 2·6m; Duration 0605. See 5.29. Enter the bay passing 3M N of Magharee Islands. Pick up the W sector (W140°–152°) of Little Samphire Is lt, Fl WRG 5s 17m 16/13M; see 5.3 for sectors. Approach between Magharee Is and Mucklaghmore (30m high).

5.31 FENIT HARBOUR

Kerry **52°16'·20N 09°51'·61W** ✿✿✿

CHARTS AC 2254, 2739; Imray C55.

TIDES –0612 Dover; ML 2·6m; Duration 0605

Standard Port COBH (⟵)

Times				Height (metres)			
High Water		Low Water		MHWS	MHWN	MLWN	MLWS
0500	1100	0500	1100	4·1	3·2	1·3	0·4
1700	2300	1700	2300				
Differences FENIT PIER (Tralee Bay)							
–0057	–0017	–0029	–0109	+0·5	+0·2	+0·3	+0·1

SHELTER Good shelter in marina (2.7m depth), but a few berths exposed to SE'ly conditions.

NAVIGATION Appr on 146° to WPT 52°16'·00N 09° 53'·00W, Little Samphire Is, conspic lt ho, Fl WRG 5s 17m 16/13M, thence 7ca E to Samphire Is; lt QR 15m 3M vis 242°–097°. Fenit Pier Hd 2 FR (vert) 12m 3M, vis 148°–058°. Easy ent H24.

LIGHTS AND MARKS See 5.3 and chartlet.

R/T *Neptune* (Tralee SC) VHF Ch 14 16. Port Manager: VHF Ch 16 **14 M** (0900-2100UT).

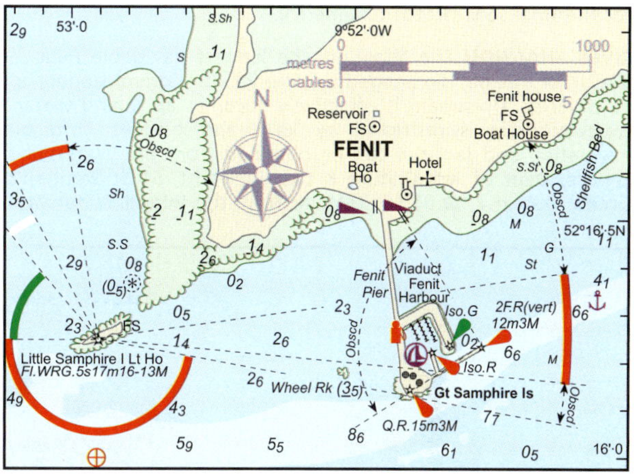

TELEPHONE (Code 066) Port Manager ☎ 7136231; ⊜ ☎ 7121480.

FACILITIES **Marina** (130 inc 15 🅥; max LOA 25m, €1.60 min €16.00/craft), FW, D, D, ⊡, ♿; For 🅥s call *Neptune* (Tralee SC); **Village** Slip, C, P (cans), ME, 🛒, Bar, R, ✉, Ⓑ, ⇌ Tralee (by bus), ✈ (Kerry 30M).

THE SHANNON ESTUARY

(AC 1819, 1547, 1548, 1549) The estuary and lower reaches of the Shannon are tidal for 50M, from its mouth between Loop Hd and Kerry Hd up to Limerick Dock, some 15M beyond the junction with R Fergus. ▶ *The tides and streams are those of a deep-water inlet, with roughly equal durations of rise and fall, and equal rates of flood and ebb streams. In the entrance the flood stream begins at HW Tarbert Is – 0555, and the ebb at HW Tarbert Is + 0015.* ◀

There are several anchorages available for yachts on passage up or down the coast. Kilbaha Bay (AC 1819) is about 3M E of Loop Hd, and is convenient in good weather or in N winds, but exposed to SE and any swell. Carrigaholt B (AC 1547), entered about 1M N of Kilcredaun Pt, is well sheltered from W winds and has little tidal stream. In N winds there is an anchorage SE of Querrin Pt (AC 1547), 4·5M further up-river on N shore. At Kilrush there is a marina and anchorages E of Scattery Is and N of Hog Is. ▶ *Note that there are overfalls 0·75M S of Scattery Is with W winds and ebb tide.* ◀

▶ *Off Kilcredaun Pt the ebb reaches 4kn at sp, and in strong winds between S and NW a bad race forms. This can be mostly avoided by keeping near the N shore, which is free from offlying dangers, thereby cheating the worst of the tide. When leaving the Shannon in strong W winds, aim to pass Kilcredaun Pt at slack water, and again keep near the N shore. Loop Hd (lt) marks the N side of Shannon Est, and should be passed 3ca off. Here the stream runs SW from HW Tarbert Is + 0300, and NE from HW Tarbert Is – 0300.* ◀

▶ *Above the junction with R Fergus (AC 1540) the tidal characteristics become more like those of most rivers, ie the flood stream is stronger than the ebb, but it runs for a shorter time. In the Shannon the stream is much affected by the wind. S and W winds increase the rate and duration of the flood stream, and reduce the ebb. Strong N or E winds have the opposite effect. Prolonged or heavy rain increases the rate and duration of the ebb.* ◀

The Shannon is the longest river in Ireland, rising at Lough Allen 100M above Limerick, thence 50M to the sea.

5.32 SHANNON ESTUARY

Clare (N); Kerry and Limerick (S) **52°35'·00N 09°40'·00W**

CHARTS AC 1819, 1547, 1548, 1549, 1540; L. Derg 5080; L. Ree 5078. Imray C55. The ICC's *Sailing Directions for S & W Ireland* and/or Admiralty *Irish Coast Pilot* are essential.

TIDES

HW at	HW Tarbert Is	HW Dover
Kilbaha & Carrigaholt	–0030	+0605
Coney Island	+0045	–0500
Foynes	+0030	–0515
Limerick	+0110	–0435

At Limerick strong S-W winds increase the height and delay the times of HW; strong N-E winds do the opposite.

SHELTER The Shannon Estuary is 50M long (Loop Hd to Limerick). For boats on passage N/S the nearest ⚓ is Kilbaha Bay, 3M inside Loop Hd; it has 🅥s sheltered in winds from W to NE, but is exposed to swell and holding is poor. 6M further E, Carrigaholt Bay has 🅥s and good shelter from W'lies; ⚓ just N of the new quay, out of the tide. Kilrush Marina (5.33) with all facilities is 7M further E. From Kilcredaun Head in the W to the R Fergus ent (about 25M) there are ⚓s or 🅥s, protected from all but E winds, at Tarbert Is, Glin, Labasheeda, Killadysert (pontoon) and among the islands in the Fergus mouth. There is a pontoon off the YC S of Foynes Is and drying quays at Ballylongford Creek (Saleen), Knock and Clarecastle (S of Ennis, off chartlet). Yachts may enter Limerick Dock, but this is a commercial port with usual problems; major improvements planned.

Continued overleaf

NAVIGATION WPT 52°32'·50N 09°46'·90W, Ballybunnion NCM By VQ, 064°/4·2M to Tail of Beal Bar buoy WCM, Q (9) 15s. For notes on ent and tidal streams see 5.4. The ebb can reach 4kn. Ldg lts, Oc. 5s, 046·4° on Corlis Pt. The lower estuary between Kerry and Loop Heads is 9M wide, narrowing to 2M off Kilcredaun Pt.

Here the chan is well buoyed in mid-stream and then follows the Kerry shore, S of Scattery Is. From Tarbert Is to Foynes Is the river narrows to less than 1M in places, before widening where the R Fergus joins from the N, abeam Shannon airport. Above this point the buoyed chan narrows and becomes shallower although there is a minimum of 2m at LWS. AC 1540 is essential for the final 15M stretch to Limerick.

RIVER SHANNON The Shannon, the longest navigable river in the UK or Ireland, is managed by Limerick Hbr Commissioners up to Limerick. Up-stream it effectively becomes an inland waterway; progress is restricted by locks and bridges. Info on navigation and facilities can be obtained from the Waterways Service, Dept of Art, Culture & the Gaeltacht, 51 St Stephen's Green, Dublin 2, ☎ 01-6613111; or from the Inland Waterways Association of Ireland, Kingston House, Ballinteer, Dublin 4, ☎ 01-983392; also from Tourist Offices and inland marinas.

LIGHTS AND MARKS See 5.3. There are QW (vert) aero hazard lts on tall chimneys at Money Pt power station 3M ESE of Kilrush. 2 chys at Tarbert Is are conspic (R lts).

R/T Foynes Ch 12 13 16 (occas). *Shannon Estuary Radio* Ch 12 13 16 (HO).

FACILITIES Marine facilities are available at several communities on the Shannon; M, P & D (cans), FW, 🛒, can be found at many villages. ⚓s are being laid at Labasheeda, Glin Pier (pontoon) and Foynes. E of Aughanish Is on S shore, R Deal is navigable 3M to Askeaton. Ent, marked by RW bn, is 8ca SE of Beeves Rk with 1m in buoyed chan. BY at Massey's Pier ☎ 069 73100, ⚓s, FW, C, CH, ⛭, D, Slip. Facilities at Foynes and Limerick include: **Foynes** Slip, L, AB, P & D (cans), FW, ✉, Ⓑ, Dr, 🛒, R, Bar; **Foynes YC** ☎ (069) 65261, AB (pontoon), Bar, R. **Limerick**: **Hbr Commission** ☎ (061) 315377; ⊜ ☎ 415366. **City** Slip, AB, L, FW, P & D (cans), Kos, Gas, Gaz, ME, El, Dr, Ⓗ, ✉, all usual city amenities, ≷, ✈ (Shannon).

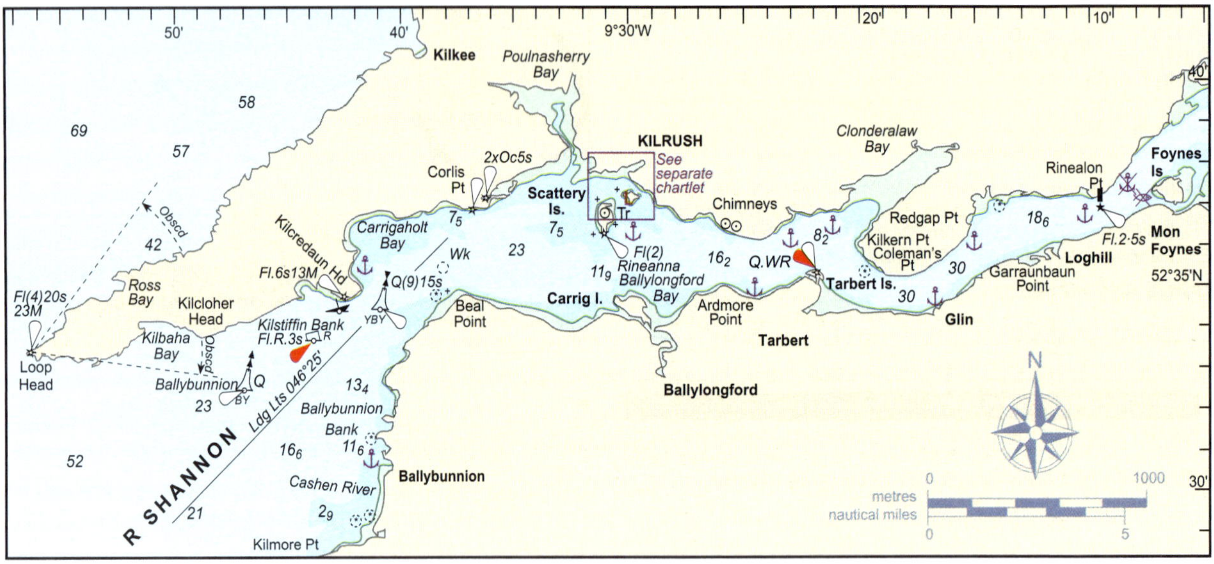

GAELIC

It helps to understand some of the more common words for navigational features (courtesy of the Irish Cruising Club):

Ail, alt	cliff, height	*Carrick*	rock	*Inish, illaun*	island	*More, mor*	big
Aird, ard	height, high	*Cladach*	shore	*Inver*	river mouth	*Rannagh*	point
Anna, annagh	marsh	*Cuan, coon*	harbour	*Keal, keel*	narrow place,	*Ron, roan*	seal
Ath	ford	*Derg, dearg*	red		sound	*Roe, ruadh*	red
Bal, Bally	town	*Drum*	hill, ridge	*Kill*	church, cell	*Scolt*	split, rky gut
Barra	sandbank	*Duff, dubh*	black	*Kin, ken*	promontory,	*Scrow*	boggy,
Bel, beal	mouth, strait	*Dun, doon*	fort		head		grassy sward
Beg	little	*Ennis*	island	*Knock*	hill	*Slieve*	mountain
Ben, binna	hill	*Fad, fadda*	long	*Lag*	hollow	*Slig*	shells
Bo	sunken rock	*Fan*	slope	*Lahan*	broad	*Stag, stac*	high rock
Boy, bwee	yellow	*Fin*	white	*Lea*	grey	*Tawney*	low hill
Bullig	shoal, round	*Freagh, free*	heather	*Lenan*	weed-	*Tigh, ti*	house
	rock, breaker	*Gall*	stranger		covered rock	*Togher*	causeway
Bun	end, river	*Glas, glass*	green	*Lis*	ancient fort	*Tra, traw*	strand
	mouth	*Glinsk*	clear water	*Long, luing*	ship	*Turlin*	boulder,
Caher	fort	*Gorm*	blue	*Maan*	middle		beach
Camus	bay, river	*Gub*	point of land	*Maol, mwee*	bare	*Vad, bad*	boat
	bend	*Hassans*	swift current	*Mara*	of the sea		

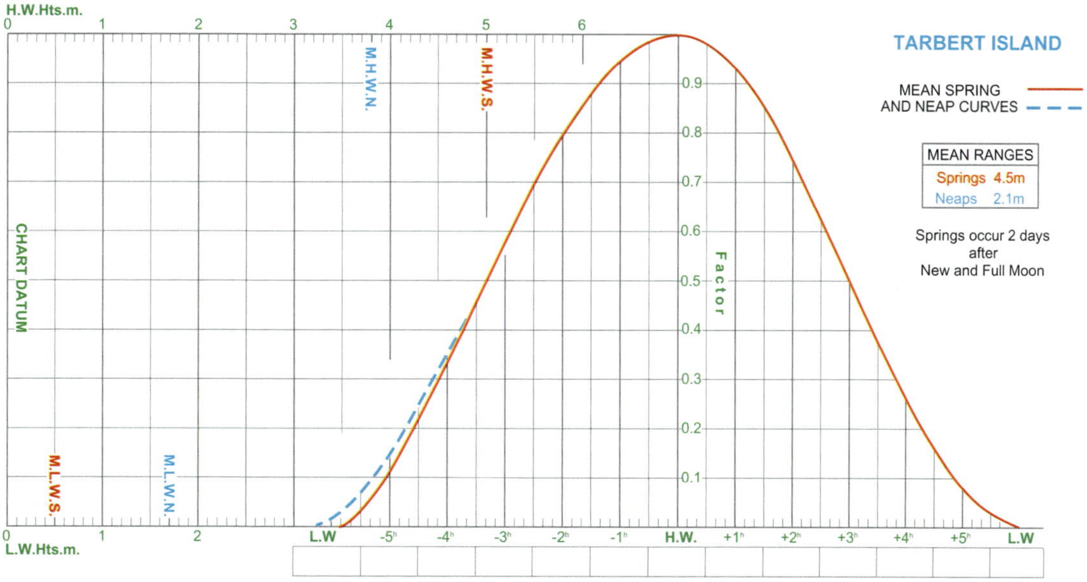

5.33 KILRUSH

Clare **52°37'·90N 09°29'·70W**

CHARTS AC 1819, 1547; Imray C55.

TIDES –0555 Dover; ML 2·6; Duration 0610

Standard Port TARBERT ISLAND (⟶)

Times				Height (metres)			
High Water		Low Water		MHWS	MHWN	MLWN	MLWS
0500	1000	0000	0600	5·0	3·8	1·7	0·5
1700	2200	1200	1800				
Differences KILRUSH							
–0010	–0010	–0005	–0005	0·0	–0·1	0·0	0·0

SHELTER Excellent in Kilrush Marina (2·7m), access via lock (width 9m) H24. Day ⚓ in lee of Scattery Is.

NAVIGATION WPT 52°37'·18N 09°31'·64W, 063°/1M to SWM buoy. From seaward usual appr is N of Scattery Is (conspic Round Twr, 26m); beware Baurnahard Spit and Carrigillaun to the N. Coming down-river between Hog Is and mainland, beware Wolf Rk.

LIGHTS AND MARKS SWM By L Fl 10s marks ent to buoyed chan (dredged 2·5m), with ldg lts 355°, both Oc 3s, to lock. Fl G 3s 2M, S side of lock.

R/T Marina Ch 80. Kilrush Ch 16, 12.

TELEPHONE (Code 06590) Marina 52072 Mobile 086 2313870; Lock 52155; MRCC (066) 9476109; Coast/Cliff Rescue Service 51004; ⊖ (061) 415366; Weather (061) 62677; Police 51017; Dr (065) 51581 also 51470.

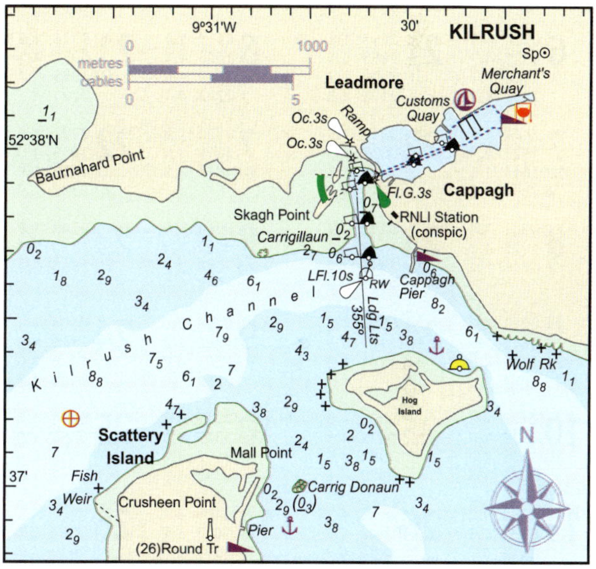

FACILITIES Marina (120 inc ⓥ) ☎ 52072, kcm@shannondev.ie. Lock 52155, €1.90, (minimum €16.00/craft), D, P (cans), Slip, BY, CH, Gas, Gaz, Kos, BH (45 ton), C (26 ton), ME, El, ⊡, 🛒; **Town** El, CH, 🛒, R, Bar, Dr, ✉, Ⓑ, ≷ (bus to Limerick), ✈ (Shannon).

TIME ZONE (UT)
For Summer Time add ONE hour in **non-shaded areas**

TARBERT ISLAND

LAT 52°35′N LONG 9°21′W

TIMES AND HEIGHTS OF HIGH AND LOW WATERS

Dates in red are SPRINGS
Dates in blue are NEAPS

YEAR **2010**

JANUARY

Date	Day	Time	m	Time	m	Time	m	Time	m
1	F	0537	5.0	1156	0.4	1811	4.9		
2	SA	0009	0.5	0624	5.1	1243	0.2	1858	5.0
3	SU	0055	0.5	0710	5.1	1327	0.2	1945	4.9
4	M	0139	0.5	0755	5.1	1412	0.3	2030	4.8
5	TU	0224	0.6	0841	4.9	1457	0.5	2117	4.7
6	W	0310	0.9	0929	4.7	1546	0.7	2207	4.4
7	TH	0401	1.1	1022	4.4	1641	1.1	◑ 2304	4.2
8	F	0501	1.4	1127	4.2	1744	1.4		
9	SA	0012	4.1	0610	1.6	1249	4.0	1852	1.5
10	SU	0126	4.1	0726	1.6	1408	4.0	2001	1.6
11	M	0233	4.2	0837	1.5	1513	4.1	2104	1.5
12	TU	0331	4.3	0939	1.3	1608	4.3	2158	1.4
13	W	0420	4.5	1029	1.1	1654	4.4	2244	1.2
14	TH	0503	4.6	1112	1.0	1735	4.5	2324	1.1
15	F	0541	4.8	1151	0.8	1811	4.6	●	
16	SA	0000	1.0	0615	4.8	1226	0.8	1843	4.6
17	SU	0032	1.0	0648	4.9	1258	0.8	1915	4.6
18	M	0102	1.0	0721	4.8	1327	0.9	1946	4.6
19	TU	0132	1.1	0753	4.8	1356	1.0	2018	4.5
20	W	0203	1.2	0825	4.7	1427	1.1	2051	4.4
21	TH	0237	1.3	0859	4.5	1503	1.3	2128	4.3
22	F	0316	1.5	0939	4.3	1544	1.5	2213	4.2
23	SA	0403	1.7	1031	4.1	1635	1.7	◐ 2311	4.0
24	SU	0502	1.8	1141	4.0	1741	1.8		
25	M	0023	4.0	0619	1.9	1301	3.9	1859	1.8
26	TU	0136	4.1	0748	1.7	1416	4.1	2018	1.6
27	W	0243	4.3	0906	1.4	1523	4.3	2126	1.3
28	TH	0343	4.6	1007	0.9	1621	4.6	2222	1.0
29	F	0437	4.9	1058	0.5	1712	4.9	2312	0.6
30	SA	0526	5.1	1144	0.2	1800	5.1	○ 2357	0.4
31	SU	0612	5.3	1228	0.0	1844	5.2		

FEBRUARY

Date	Day	Time	m	Time	m	Time	m	Time	m
1	M	0040	0.3	0655	5.4	1310	0.0	1926	5.2
2	TU	0122	0.3	0737	5.3	1351	0.1	2008	5.1
3	W	0202	0.4	0819	5.2	1431	0.4	2049	4.9
4	TH	0243	0.7	0903	4.9	1514	0.8	2132	4.6
5	F	0327	1.1	0950	4.5	1601	1.2	◑ 2221	4.3
6	SA	0418	1.4	1048	4.1	1659	1.6	2322	4.1
7	SU	0525	1.8	1208	3.9	1814	1.9		
8	M	0043	3.9	0653	1.9	1344	3.8	1939	1.9
9	TU	0207	4.0	0822	1.8	1501	4.0	2052	1.8
10	W	0315	4.2	0929	1.5	1557	4.2	2147	1.5
11	TH	0406	4.4	1017	1.2	1641	4.4	2230	1.3
12	F	0447	4.6	1056	1.0	1717	4.5	2307	1.1
13	SA	0522	4.8	1132	0.8	1750	4.6	2341	1.0
14	SU	0554	4.9	1204	0.7	1819	4.7	●	
15	M	0011	0.9	0624	5.0	1234	0.7	1847	4.8
16	TU	0040	0.9	0655	5.0	1301	0.8	1917	4.8
17	W	0108	0.9	0724	4.9	1328	0.9	1946	4.7
18	TH	0136	1.0	0754	4.9	1357	1.0	2017	4.7
19	F	0207	1.2	0825	4.7	1429	1.2	2050	4.5
20	SA	0243	1.3	0902	4.5	1506	1.4	2129	4.3
21	SU	0326	1.5	0950	4.2	1553	1.7	2221	4.1
22	M	0422	1.8	1059	4.0	1659	1.9	◐ 2337	3.9
23	TU	0543	1.9	1230	3.8	1830	2.0		
24	W	0104	4.0	0726	1.8	1400	4.0	2005	1.7
25	TH	0224	4.2	0854	1.3	1513	4.3	2117	1.3
26	F	0330	4.5	0954	0.8	1610	4.7	2211	0.9
27	SA	0424	4.9	1042	0.4	1658	5.0	2257	0.5
28	SU	0511	5.2	1126	0.1	1742	5.2	○ 2340	0.2

MARCH

Date	Day	Time	m	Time	m	Time	m	Time	m
1	M	0555	5.4	1207	-0.1	1824	5.4		
2	TU	0020	0.1	0636	5.5	1247	-0.1	1903	5.4
3	W	0100	0.2	0716	5.4	1326	0.1	1942	5.3
4	TH	0137	0.3	0756	5.2	1403	0.5	2020	5.0
5	F	0215	0.6	0837	4.9	1442	0.9	2059	4.7
6	SA	0256	1.0	0921	4.5	1525	1.3	2144	4.4
7	SU	0342	1.4	1014	4.1	1617	1.8	◑ 2239	4.0
8	M	0443	1.8	1133	3.7	1734	2.1	2359	3.8
9	TU	0616	2.0	1316	3.6	1917	2.1		
10	W	0132	3.8	0759	1.9	1441	3.8	2035	1.9
11	TH	0247	4.0	0906	1.6	1535	4.1	2126	1.6
12	F	0340	4.3	0952	1.3	1616	4.3	2206	1.3
13	SA	0419	4.5	1029	1.0	1650	4.5	2241	1.1
14	SU	0453	4.7	1103	0.8	1720	4.7	2313	0.9
15	M	0525	4.8	1134	0.7	1748	4.8	● 2344	0.8
16	TU	0555	4.9	1203	0.7	1817	4.9		
17	W	0013	0.8	0625	5.0	1232	0.7	1846	4.9
18	TH	0042	0.8	0654	5.0	1300	0.8	1916	4.9
19	F	0111	0.9	0726	4.9	1329	0.9	1947	4.8
20	SA	0142	1.0	0800	4.8	1401	1.1	2021	4.7
21	SU	0218	1.1	0840	4.5	1439	1.3	2102	4.4
22	M	0302	1.3	0929	4.2	1527	1.6	2153	4.2
23	TU	0359	1.6	1037	3.9	1635	1.9	◐ 2307	3.9
24	W	0523	1.7	1210	3.8	1814	1.9		
25	TH	0038	3.9	0708	1.6	1348	3.9	1952	1.7
26	F	0205	4.1	0833	1.2	1458	4.3	2059	1.2
27	SA	0311	4.5	0930	0.7	1551	4.7	2151	0.8
28	SU	0404	4.9	1018	0.3	1637	5.0	2237	0.4
29	M	0450	5.2	1102	0.1	1720	5.3	2319	0.2
30	TU	0534	5.3	1143	0.0	1800	5.4	○ 2358	0.1
31	W	0615	5.4	1222	0.1	1839	5.3		

APRIL

Date	Day	Time	m	Time	m	Time	m	Time	m
1	TH	0036	0.2	0655	5.3	1300	0.3	1916	5.2
2	F	0114	0.4	0734	5.1	1336	0.6	1954	5.0
3	SA	0151	0.6	0814	4.7	1414	1.0	2032	4.7
4	SU	0230	1.0	0857	4.4	1454	1.4	2114	4.3
5	M	0313	1.3	0946	4.0	1542	1.8	2204	4.0
6	TU	0407	1.7	1057	3.7	1649	2.1	◑ 2313	3.8
7	W	0527	1.9	1233	3.6	1831	2.1		
8	TH	0042	3.7	0705	1.8	1355	3.7	1953	1.9
9	F	0158	3.8	0817	1.6	1452	3.9	2047	1.7
10	SA	0254	4.1	0907	1.3	1535	4.1	2129	1.4
11	SU	0338	4.3	0947	1.1	1611	4.4	2205	1.1
12	M	0415	4.5	1023	0.9	1643	4.6	2240	0.9
13	TU	0449	4.7	1057	0.8	1714	4.7	2313	0.8
14	W	0522	4.8	1129	0.7	1745	4.9	● 2346	0.7
15	TH	0554	4.9	1201	0.7	1817	4.9		
16	F	0018	0.7	0628	4.9	1233	0.7	1850	4.9
17	SA	0051	0.7	0704	4.9	1306	0.8	1925	4.8
18	SU	0126	0.8	0744	4.7	1342	1.0	2004	4.7
19	M	0205	0.9	0829	4.5	1424	1.2	2048	4.5
20	TU	0252	1.1	0921	4.2	1516	1.4	2142	4.2
21	W	0351	1.3	1028	3.9	1627	1.7	◐ 2250	4.0
22	TH	0511	1.4	1154	3.8	1758	1.7		
23	F	0012	4.0	0641	1.3	1326	4.0	1925	1.4
24	SA	0138	4.1	0758	1.0	1433	4.3	2031	1.1
25	SU	0245	4.4	0857	0.7	1526	4.6	2124	0.7
26	M	0339	4.7	0948	0.4	1612	4.9	2211	0.5
27	TU	0427	4.9	1034	0.3	1656	5.1	2255	0.3
28	W	0511	5.0	1117	0.3	1737	5.2	○ 2336	0.3
29	TH	0554	5.1	1157	0.4	1817	5.1		
30	F	0016	0.3	0636	5.0	1236	0.5	1855	5.0

Chart Datum: 0·30 metres above Ordnance Datum (Dublin). HAT is 5·5 metres above Chart Datum; see 0.20

TIME ZONE (UT)
For Summer Time add ONE hour in **non-shaded areas**

TARBERT ISLAND LAT 52°35′N LONG 9°21′W

TIMES AND HEIGHTS OF HIGH AND LOW WATERS

Dates in red are SPRINGS
Dates in blue are NEAPS

YEAR **2010**

MAY

Date	Day	Time	m	Time	m	Time	m	Time	m
1	SA	0054	0.5	0716	4.8	1313	0.8	1933	4.9
2	SU	0131	0.7	0757	4.5	1350	1.1	2011	4.6
3	M	0209	0.9	0838	4.3	1429	1.3	2052	4.4
4	TU	0250	1.2	0924	4.0	1513	1.6	2137	4.1
5	W	0337	1.4	1020	3.7	1608	1.8	2232	3.9
6	TH	0437	1.6	1135	3.6	1724	2.0	◑ 2342	3.7
7	F	0554	1.7	1252	3.6	1847	1.9		
8	SA	0055	3.8	0708	1.6	1354	3.8	1949	1.7
9	SU	0157	3.9	0806	1.4	1443	4.0	2039	1.5
10	M	0247	4.1	0854	1.2	1524	4.2	2122	1.2
11	TU	0330	4.3	0936	1.0	1602	4.5	2203	1.0
12	W	0409	4.5	1017	0.9	1638	4.6	2242	0.8
13	TH	0448	4.6	1055	0.8	1715	4.8	2321	0.7
14	F	0527	4.7	1134	0.7	1752	4.9	● 2359	0.6
15	SA	0607	4.8	1212	0.7	1831	4.9		
16	SU	0037	0.5	0650	4.7	1252	0.7	1911	4.8
17	M	0118	0.5	0735	4.6	1334	0.8	1954	4.7
18	TU	0201	0.6	0823	4.5	1420	1.0	2041	4.6
19	W	0250	0.7	0916	4.3	1513	1.2	2134	4.4
20	TH	0347	0.9	1018	4.1	1618	1.3	◐ 2234	4.2
21	F	0455	1.0	1131	4.0	1734	1.4	2345	4.1
22	SA	0608	1.0	1252	4.1	1850	1.3		
23	SU	0102	4.1	0718	0.9	1401	4.3	1956	1.1
24	M	0213	4.3	0820	0.8	1457	4.5	2054	0.9
25	TU	0312	4.5	0916	0.7	1547	4.7	2146	0.7
26	W	0404	4.6	1006	0.6	1633	4.8	2234	0.6
27	TH	0452	4.7	1053	0.6	1717	4.9	○ 2319	0.5
28	F	0538	4.7	1137	0.7	1758	4.9		
29	SA	0000	0.5	0621	4.6	1218	0.8	1838	4.8
30	SU	0040	0.6	0702	4.5	1256	0.9	1916	4.7
31	M	0117	0.7	0742	4.4	1332	1.0	1954	4.6

JUNE

Date	Day	Time	m	Time	m	Time	m	Time	m
1	TU	0153	0.8	0821	4.2	1408	1.2	2033	4.4
2	W	0230	1.0	0901	4.1	1447	1.4	2113	4.3
3	TH	0310	1.2	0944	3.9	1531	1.6	2158	4.1
4	F	0355	1.3	1036	3.8	1624	1.7	◑ 2249	3.9
5	SA	0448	1.5	1139	3.7	1730	1.8	2349	3.8
6	SU	0552	1.5	1245	3.8	1842	1.8		
7	M	0052	3.8	0657	1.5	1344	3.9	1944	1.6
8	TU	0151	4.0	0756	1.4	1435	4.1	2038	1.4
9	W	0243	4.1	0849	1.2	1521	4.3	2128	1.2
10	TH	0332	4.3	0938	1.1	1606	4.5	2215	0.9
11	F	0419	4.5	1026	0.9	1649	4.7	2300	0.7
12	SA	0505	4.6	1112	0.7	1732	4.8	● 2344	0.5
13	SU	0552	4.7	1158	0.6	1816	4.9		
14	M	0028	0.4	0639	4.7	1243	0.6	1900	4.9
15	TU	0112	0.3	0727	4.7	1328	0.6	1945	4.9
16	W	0157	0.3	0816	4.6	1415	0.7	2032	4.8
17	TH	0244	0.4	0906	4.5	1505	0.8	2121	4.6
18	F	0334	0.5	1000	4.4	1600	1.0	2215	4.4
19	SA	0431	0.7	1102	4.2	1704	1.2	◐ 2316	4.2
20	SU	0534	0.9	1213	4.1	1814	1.3		
21	M	0027	4.1	0640	1.1	1326	4.2	1923	1.2
22	TU	0142	4.1	0746	1.1	1429	4.3	2028	1.1
23	W	0249	4.2	0849	1.1	1525	4.4	2127	1.0
24	TH	0347	4.3	0946	1.0	1616	4.6	2219	0.9
25	F	0439	4.4	1038	1.0	1702	4.7	2307	0.7
26	SA	0526	4.4	1124	0.9	1745	4.7	○ 2349	0.7
27	SU	0609	4.5	1205	0.9	1824	4.8		
28	M	0028	0.6	0648	4.4	1242	0.9	1901	4.7
29	TU	0104	0.7	0724	4.4	1316	1.0	1936	4.7
30	W	0137	0.8	0759	4.3	1348	1.1	2011	4.6

JULY

Date	Day	Time	m	Time	m	Time	m	Time	m
1	TH	0208	0.9	0833	4.3	1421	1.2	2047	4.4
2	F	0241	1.0	0909	4.1	1457	1.4	2124	4.3
3	SA	0317	1.2	0949	4.0	1539	1.5	2205	4.1
4	SU	0400	1.4	1038	3.9	1628	1.7	◑ 2255	4.0
5	M	0450	1.5	1138	3.9	1730	1.8	2355	3.9
6	TU	0550	1.6	1244	3.9	1844	1.8		
7	W	0100	3.9	0658	1.6	1348	4.0	1955	1.6
8	TH	0204	4.0	0806	1.5	1446	4.2	2059	1.4
9	F	0303	4.1	0908	1.3	1540	4.4	2155	1.0
10	SA	0358	4.3	1005	1.0	1630	4.6	2246	0.7
11	SU	0451	4.5	1058	0.7	1718	4.8	● 2333	0.4
12	M	0542	4.7	1147	0.5	1805	5.0		
13	TU	0018	0.2	0630	4.9	1233	0.4	1849	5.1
14	W	0102	0.0	0716	4.9	1318	0.3	1934	5.1
15	TH	0145	0.0	0802	4.9	1402	0.4	2018	5.0
16	F	0228	0.2	0848	4.8	1447	0.6	2104	4.8
17	SA	0314	0.4	0936	4.6	1536	0.8	2153	4.6
18	SU	0403	0.7	1030	4.4	1632	1.1	◐ 2249	4.3
19	M	0500	1.1	1135	4.1	1739	1.4	2358	4.0
20	TU	0607	1.4	1251	4.0	1856	1.5		
21	W	0119	3.9	0720	1.5	1407	4.1	2011	1.4
22	TH	0236	3.9	0833	1.5	1511	4.2	2117	1.2
23	F	0340	4.1	0937	1.3	1606	4.4	2211	1.0
24	SA	0433	4.2	1028	1.2	1652	4.6	2256	0.9
25	SU	0517	4.3	1112	1.0	1732	4.7	2337	0.7
26	M	0555	4.4	1151	0.9	1808	4.8	○	
27	TU	0013	0.7	0629	4.5	1225	0.9	1841	4.8
28	W	0046	0.7	0700	4.5	1255	0.9	1913	4.8
29	TH	0115	0.7	0731	4.5	1323	1.0	1945	4.7
30	F	0142	0.8	0801	4.5	1352	1.1	2017	4.6
31	SA	0210	1.0	0833	4.4	1424	1.2	2049	4.5

AUGUST

Date	Day	Time	m	Time	m	Time	m	Time	m
1	SU	0242	1.1	0906	4.3	1500	1.4	2125	4.3
2	M	0319	1.3	0946	4.1	1543	1.6	2209	4.1
3	TU	0403	1.5	1038	4.0	1638	1.8	◑ 2308	3.9
4	W	0500	1.7	1150	3.9	1751	1.9		
5	TH	0020	3.8	0613	1.8	1309	3.9	1920	1.8
6	F	0136	3.9	0736	1.7	1420	4.1	2040	1.4
7	SA	0245	4.1	0851	1.4	1522	4.4	2141	1.0
8	SU	0347	4.3	0954	1.0	1617	4.7	2233	0.6
9	M	0441	4.6	1047	0.7	1706	5.0	2319	0.2
10	TU	0530	4.9	1134	0.4	1752	5.2	●	
11	W	0003	-0.1	0616	5.1	1219	0.2	1835	5.3
12	TH	0045	-0.2	0700	5.2	1301	0.1	1917	5.3
13	F	0126	-0.1	0742	5.1	1342	0.2	2000	5.2
14	SA	0207	0.1	0825	5.0	1424	0.5	2043	5.0
15	SU	0248	0.5	0909	4.7	1509	0.8	2130	4.6
16	M	0333	0.9	0957	4.4	1600	1.2	◐ 2224	4.2
17	TU	0426	1.3	1058	4.1	1706	1.5	2334	3.9
18	W	0535	1.7	1220	3.9	1834	1.7		
19	TH	0104	3.7	0703	1.8	1349	3.9	2003	1.6
20	F	0229	3.8	0828	1.7	1500	4.1	2110	1.4
21	SA	0333	4.0	0930	1.5	1554	4.3	2159	1.1
22	SU	0421	4.2	1016	1.2	1637	4.5	2240	0.9
23	M	0500	4.4	1055	1.0	1713	4.7	2316	0.7
24	TU	0533	4.5	1130	0.9	1746	4.8	○ 2349	0.7
25	W	0603	4.6	1201	0.8	1816	4.9		
26	TH	0019	0.7	0630	4.6	1229	0.8	1845	4.9
27	F	0047	0.7	0659	4.7	1256	0.9	1915	4.8
28	SA	0113	0.8	0728	4.7	1324	1.0	1945	4.7
29	SU	0140	0.9	0757	4.6	1354	1.1	2016	4.6
30	M	0210	1.1	0828	4.5	1427	1.3	2051	4.4
31	TU	0244	1.3	0905	4.3	1508	1.5	2135	4.2

Chart Datum: 0·30 metres above Ordnance Datum (Dublin). HAT is 5·5 metres above Chart Datum; see 0.20

TIME ZONE (UT)
For Summer Time add ONE hour in **non-shaded areas**

TARBERT ISLAND LAT 52°35′N LONG 9°21′W

TIMES AND HEIGHTS OF HIGH AND LOW WATERS

Dates in red are SPRINGS
Dates in blue are NEAPS

YEAR **2010**

SEPTEMBER

Date	Day	Time	m	Time	m	Time	m	Time	m
1	W	0326	1.5	0952	4.1	1601	1.7	◑ 2234	3.9
2	TH	0423	1.8	1103	3.9	1717	1.9	2352	3.8
3	F	0544	1.9	1235	3.9	1858	1.7		
4	SA	0118	3.8	0719	1.7	1401	4.1	2027	1.4
5	SU	0235	4.1	0842	1.4	1508	4.4	2127	0.9
6	M	0336	4.4	0942	0.9	1602	4.8	2216	0.4
7	TU	0427	4.8	1032	0.5	1650	5.1	2300	0.1
8	W	0513	5.1	1117	0.2	1734	5.3	● 2343	-0.1
9	TH	0557	5.3	1159	0.0	1817	5.4		
10	F	0023	-0.2	0638	5.3	1240	0.0	1858	5.4
11	SA	0103	0.0	0719	5.2	1320	0.2	1940	5.2
12	SU	0142	0.3	0759	5.0	1400	0.5	2022	4.9
13	M	0222	0.7	0841	4.7	1443	0.8	2108	4.5
14	TU	0304	1.1	0926	4.4	1531	1.2	2201	4.1
15	W	0354	1.6	1024	4.0	1635	1.6	◐ 2312	3.7
16	TH	0503	1.9	1147	3.8	1809	1.8		
17	F	0044	3.6	0644	2.0	1322	3.8	1947	1.7
18	SA	0212	3.7	0813	1.8	1437	4.0	2049	1.4
19	SU	0312	3.9	0909	1.6	1529	4.2	2134	1.2
20	M	0356	4.1	0951	1.3	1610	4.5	2212	0.9
21	TU	0431	4.3	1027	1.1	1644	4.6	2246	0.8
22	W	0502	4.5	1100	0.9	1716	4.8	2318	0.7
23	TH	0530	4.6	1131	0.8	1746	4.9	○ 2348	0.7
24	F	0558	4.7	1201	0.8	1816	4.9		
25	SA	0016	0.7	0626	4.8	1230	0.8	1845	4.9
26	SU	0044	0.8	0656	4.8	1259	0.9	1917	4.8
27	M	0113	0.9	0727	4.7	1329	1.0	1951	4.6
28	TU	0144	1.1	0801	4.6	1404	1.1	2029	4.4
29	W	0219	1.3	0839	4.4	1446	1.3	2115	4.2
30	TH	0303	1.5	0928	4.2	1540	1.6	2215	3.9

OCTOBER

Date	Day	Time	m	Time	m	Time	m	Time	m
1	F	0402	1.7	1036	3.9	1659	1.7	◑ 2334	3.8
2	SA	0527	1.8	1208	3.9	1839	1.6		
3	SU	0104	3.8	0705	1.7	1341	4.1	2004	1.2
4	M	0221	4.2	0825	1.3	1449	4.4	2103	0.8
5	TU	0318	4.5	0922	0.8	1542	4.8	2152	0.4
6	W	0407	4.9	1011	0.5	1629	5.1	2236	0.1
7	TH	0452	5.1	1055	0.2	1714	5.3	● 2319	0.0
8	F	0534	5.3	1138	0.1	1757	5.3	2359	0.0
9	SA	0616	5.3	1218	0.1	1839	5.3		
10	SU	0039	0.2	0655	5.2	1259	0.3	1921	5.1
11	M	0118	0.5	0735	5.0	1339	0.5	2004	4.8
12	TU	0157	0.8	0816	4.7	1420	0.9	2049	4.4
13	W	0237	1.2	0900	4.4	1506	1.2	2140	4.0
14	TH	0324	1.6	0952	4.0	1603	1.5	◐ 2244	3.7
15	F	0425	1.9	1105	3.8	1726	1.7		
16	SA	0007	3.6	0557	2.0	1234	3.7	1857	1.7
17	SU	0128	3.6	0726	1.9	1350	3.8	2004	1.5
18	M	0229	3.8	0827	1.6	1446	4.1	2052	1.3
19	TU	0314	4.1	0911	1.4	1530	4.3	2132	1.1
20	W	0352	4.3	0950	1.2	1607	4.5	2207	0.9
21	TH	0424	4.5	1025	1.0	1641	4.6	2241	0.8
22	F	0455	4.6	1059	0.8	1714	4.8	2314	0.7
23	SA	0525	4.8	1133	0.8	1746	4.8	○ 2346	0.7
24	SU	0557	4.8	1206	0.8	1820	4.8		
25	M	0018	0.8	0630	4.8	1239	0.8	1855	4.8
26	TU	0051	0.9	0706	4.8	1313	0.9	1933	4.6
27	W	0126	1.0	0744	4.7	1351	1.0	2016	4.4
28	TH	0205	1.2	0826	4.5	1436	1.1	2105	4.2
29	F	0252	1.4	0916	4.2	1532	1.3	2204	4.0
30	SA	0352	1.6	1020	4.0	1645	1.4	◑ 2316	3.9
31	SU	0511	1.7	1141	4.0	1812	1.3		

NOVEMBER

Date	Day	Time	m	Time	m	Time	m	Time	m
1	M	0042	3.9	0639	1.5	1311	4.1	1930	1.1
2	TU	0156	4.2	0755	1.2	1422	4.4	2031	0.8
3	W	0253	4.5	0854	0.9	1517	4.7	2122	0.5
4	TH	0343	4.8	0946	0.6	1607	4.9	2209	0.3
5	F	0428	5.0	1033	0.4	1653	5.0	2254	0.3
6	SA	0512	5.1	1117	0.3	1738	5.1	● 2337	0.3
7	SU	0554	5.1	1200	0.3	1822	5.0		
8	M	0017	0.5	0635	5.0	1241	0.4	1905	4.8
9	TU	0057	0.7	0715	4.9	1321	0.6	1948	4.6
10	W	0135	0.9	0756	4.7	1402	0.8	2031	4.3
11	TH	0214	1.2	0838	4.4	1444	1.1	2117	4.1
12	F	0257	1.5	0925	4.2	1533	1.4	2210	3.8
13	SA	0347	1.7	1020	3.9	1634	1.6	◐ 2314	3.7
14	SU	0454	1.9	1131	3.8	1749	1.6		
15	M	0025	3.7	0615	1.9	1246	3.8	1858	1.6
16	TU	0129	3.8	0724	1.8	1349	3.9	1955	1.5
17	W	0221	4.0	0819	1.6	1441	4.1	2042	1.3
18	TH	0305	4.2	0906	1.3	1525	4.3	2125	1.1
19	F	0344	4.4	0949	1.1	1605	4.5	2204	1.0
20	SA	0420	4.6	1029	1.0	1643	4.6	2243	0.9
21	SU	0456	4.7	1109	0.8	1720	4.7	○ 2321	0.8
22	M	0533	4.8	1147	0.7	1759	4.7	2358	0.8
23	TU	0611	4.9	1225	0.7	1839	4.7		
24	W	0036	0.8	0650	4.8	1305	0.7	1921	4.6
25	TH	0116	0.9	0732	4.8	1346	0.7	2007	4.5
26	F	0158	1.0	0817	4.6	1432	0.8	2056	4.4
27	SA	0245	1.1	0906	4.5	1524	0.9	2150	4.2
28	SU	0341	1.3	1003	4.3	1626	1.1	◑ 2253	4.1
29	M	0448	1.4	1111	4.1	1738	1.1		
30	TU	0007	4.1	0604	1.4	1232	4.1	1849	1.1

DECEMBER

Date	Day	Time	m	Time	m	Time	m	Time	m
1	W	0121	4.2	0718	1.3	1349	4.3	1954	1.0
2	TH	0223	4.4	0823	1.1	1451	4.5	2052	0.8
3	F	0317	4.6	0921	0.9	1545	4.6	2144	0.7
4	SA	0407	4.8	1013	0.7	1636	4.7	2233	0.7
5	SU	0453	4.9	1101	0.6	1723	4.8	● 2319	0.7
6	M	0537	4.9	1146	0.5	1808	4.8		
7	TU	0001	0.7	0619	4.9	1229	0.5	1851	4.7
8	W	0041	0.8	0659	4.9	1308	0.6	1932	4.6
9	TH	0118	1.0	0739	4.8	1346	0.8	2012	4.4
10	F	0154	1.1	0818	4.6	1424	1.0	2051	4.3
11	SA	0231	1.3	0858	4.4	1503	1.2	2133	4.1
12	SU	0312	1.5	0942	4.2	1547	1.4	2219	3.9
13	M	0400	1.7	1034	4.0	1640	1.6	◐ 2315	3.8
14	TU	0500	1.8	1135	3.9	1744	1.7		
15	W	0018	3.8	0612	1.9	1244	3.9	1850	1.7
16	TH	0120	3.9	0722	1.8	1347	4.0	1950	1.6
17	F	0215	4.1	0822	1.6	1442	4.1	2042	1.4
18	SA	0304	4.3	0915	1.4	1530	4.3	2131	1.3
19	SU	0349	4.5	1003	1.2	1616	4.4	2216	1.1
20	M	0432	4.7	1049	0.9	1700	4.6	2300	0.9
21	TU	0514	4.8	1132	0.7	1743	4.7	○ 2343	0.8
22	W	0556	4.9	1214	0.6	1827	4.8		
23	TH	0025	0.7	0638	5.0	1256	0.5	1910	4.8
24	F	0107	0.7	0721	5.0	1338	0.4	1955	4.7
25	SA	0149	0.7	0805	4.9	1422	0.5	2041	4.7
26	SU	0234	0.8	0851	4.8	1508	0.6	2130	4.5
27	M	0323	1.0	0942	4.6	1601	0.9	2225	4.4
28	TU	0419	1.2	1041	4.3	1701	1.1	◑ 2328	4.2
29	W	0525	1.4	1152	4.2	1810	1.2		
30	TH	0040	4.2	0640	1.4	1315	4.1	1920	1.3
31	F	0152	4.2	0755	1.4	1429	4.2	2027	1.3

Chart Datum: 0·30 metres above Ordnance Datum (Dublin). HAT is 5·5 metres above Chart Datum; see 0.20

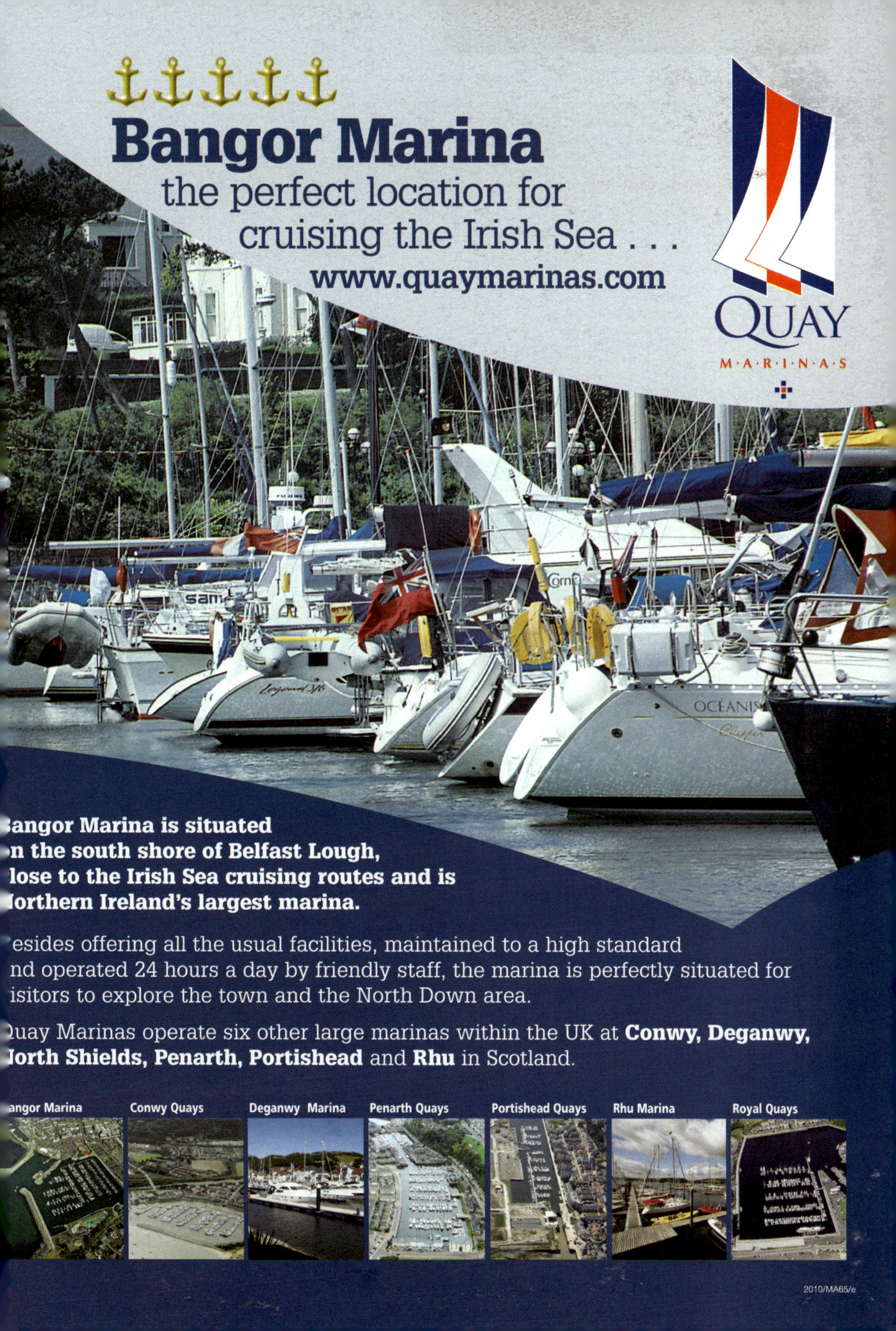
Bangor Marina
the perfect location for
cruising the Irish Sea . . .
www.quaymarinas.com
QUAY
MARINAS
angor Marina is situated
n the south shore of Belfast Lough,
lose to the Irish Sea cruising routes and is
lorthern Ireland's largest marina.
esides offering all the usual facilities, maintained to a high standard
nd operated 24 hours a day by friendly staff, the marina is perfectly situated for
isitors to explore the town and the North Down area.
luay Marinas operate six other large marinas within the UK at Conwy, Deganwy,
lorth Shields, Penarth, Portishead and Rhu in Scotland.
angor Marina
Conwy Quays
Deganwy Marina
Penarth Quays
Portishead Quays
Rhu Marina
Royal Quays
2010/MA65/e

1.	*Kilrush*	318	361	364	335	332	323	309	291	276	270	251	220	203	191	183	142	119	75	76	**1**
2.	Galway	348	366	338	309	307	297	284	266	253	245	227	192	178	166	163	104	94	49	**2**	
3.	Slyne Head	352	317	289	260	257	248	234	217	201	195	178	143	128	117	114	55	44	**3**		
4.	Westport	337	323	295	266	249	240	226	207	193	187	168	137	120	108	100	57	**4**			
5.	Eagle Island	297	262	234	205	198	193	175	162	147	136	123	88	72	62	59	**5**				
6.	Sligo	281	246	218	189	179	177	156	146	123	117	107	72	51	30	**6**					
7.	Killybegs	267	232	204	175	171	163	148	132	115	109	93	58	43	**7**						
8.	Burtonport	218	182	153	130	130	116	108	90	74	68	49	18	**8**							
9.	**Tory Island**	209	174	146	117	113	105	90	74	57	51	35	**9**								
10.	L Swilly (Fahan)	200	166	138	109	104	96	81	65	48	42	**10**									
11.	**Lough Foyle**	157	121	92	72	73	55	47	30	11	**11**										
12.	**Portrush**	150	115	87	58	60	48	35	19	**12**											
13.	Altacarry Head	135	102	74	45	45	31	21	**13**												
14.	**Carnlough**	118	78	50	25	26	11	**14**													
15.	**Larne**	108	73	45	16	16	**15**														
16.	**Carrickfergus**	101	66	39	6	**16**															
17.	**Bangor**	96	61	34	**17**																
18.	**Strangford Lough**	71	36	**18**																	
19.	**Carlingford Lough**	50	**19**																		
20.	***Dun Laoghaire***	**20**																			

DISTANCE TABLE

Approximate distances in nautical miles are by the most direct route, whilst avoiding dangers and allowing for Traffic Separation Schemes. Places in *italics* are in adjoining areas; places in **bold** are in 0.32, Distances across the Irish Sea.

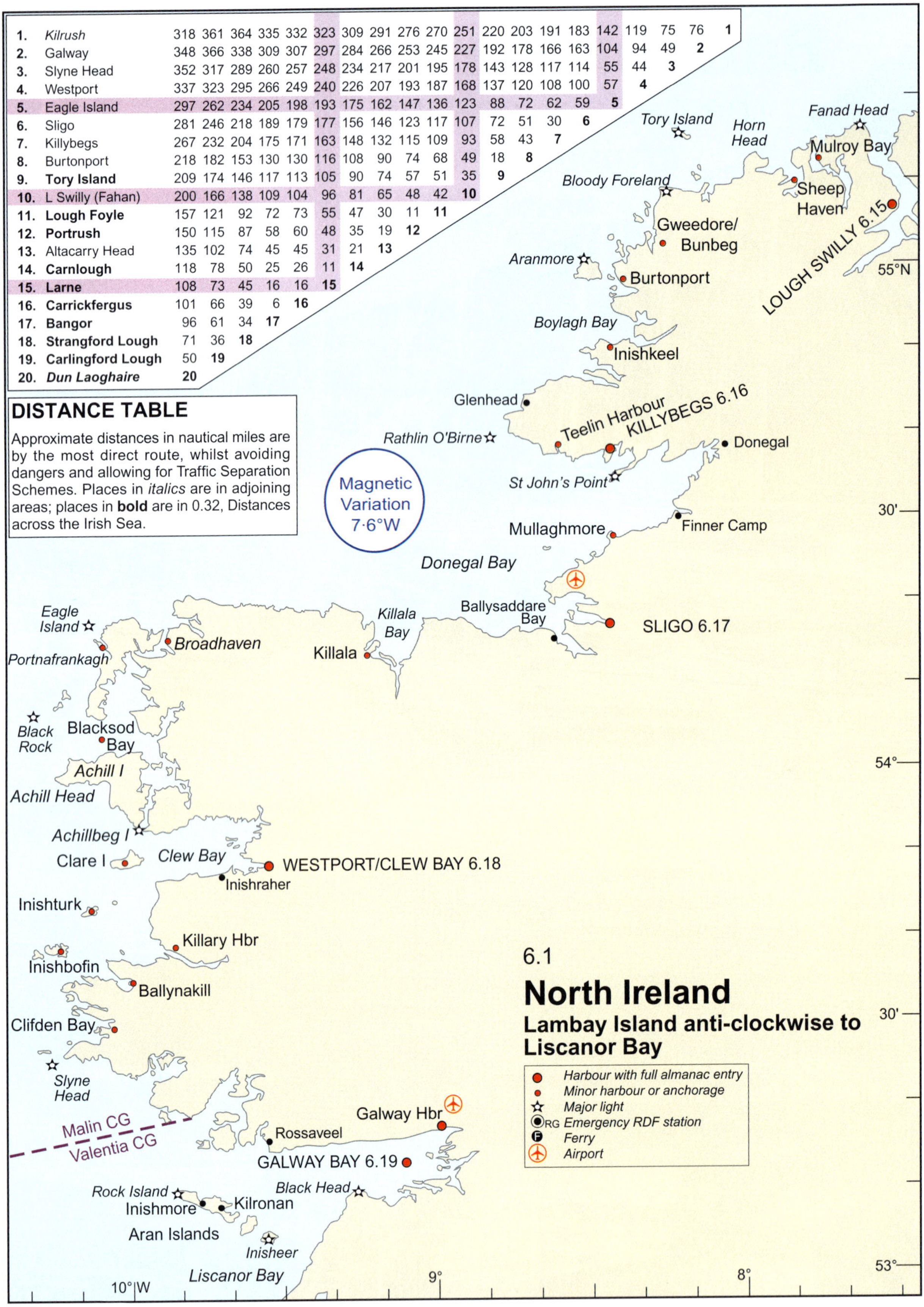

6.1

North Ireland

Lambay Island anti-clockwise to Liscanor Bay

Malin Head
Inishtrahull
MRCC
Malin CG
Belfast CG
Inishowen
Moville
LOUGH FOYLE 6.14
N Chan TSS (see 2.1)
Rathlin I
Fair Head
Ballycastle
RG
West Torr
PORTRUSH 6.12
Portstewart
RIVER BANN 6.13
Cushendun Bay
Red Bay
Carnlough
Glenarm
Campbeltown
Mull of Kintyre
Sanda I
Lamlash
Firth of Clyde
Troon
Ailsa Craig
55°N
Maidens
Loch Ryan
Portpatrick
LARNE 6.10
Black Head
BELFAST LOUGH 6.9
Carrickfergus
Lough Neagh
Belfast MRCC
Orlock Pt
Mew Island
Bangor
Donaghadee
Portavogie
Magnetic Variation 4·6°W
30'
STRANGFORD LOUGH 6.6
ARDGLASS 6.7
St John's Point
Dundrum Bay
Peel
I of Man
Annalong
Warrenpoint
CARLINGFORD LOUGH 6.6
Kilkeel
Port St Mary
Dundalk
Haulbowline
54°
Belfast CG
Dublin CG
Dunany Pt
Port Oriel
Clogher Head
Drogheda
R. Boyne
Balbriggan
Skerries
Rockabill
See 5.1
Off Skerries TSS (see 3.1)
30'
Lambay I
Malahide
Howth
Baily
The Skerries
Dublin
Kish Bank
Holyhead
Dun Laoghaire
Muglins
Magnetic Variation 4·5°W
53°
Wicklow
7°
6°
5°W

6.2 NORTH IRELAND TIDAL STREAMS

The tidal arrows (with no rates shown) off the S and W coasts of Ireland are printed by kind permission of the Irish Cruising Club, to whom the Editor is indebted. They have been found accurate, but should be used with caution.

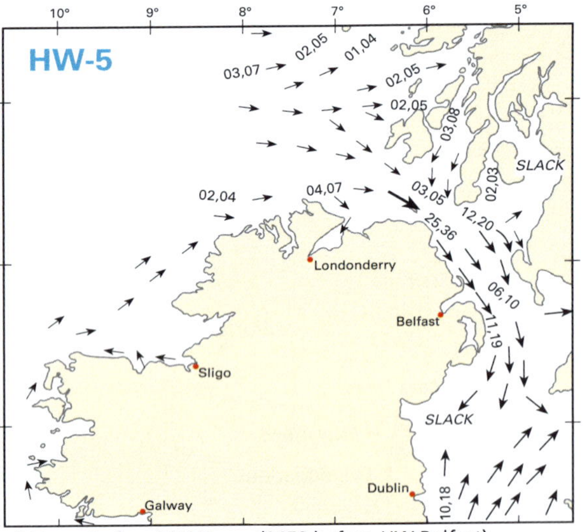

5 Hours before HW Dover (0450 before HW Belfast)

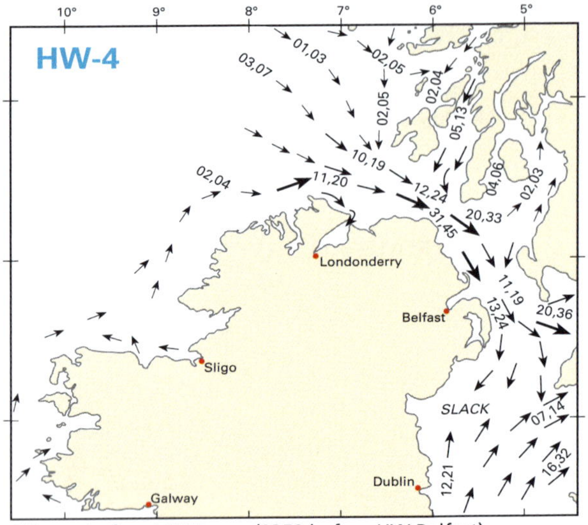

4 Hours before HW Dover (0350 before HW Belfast)

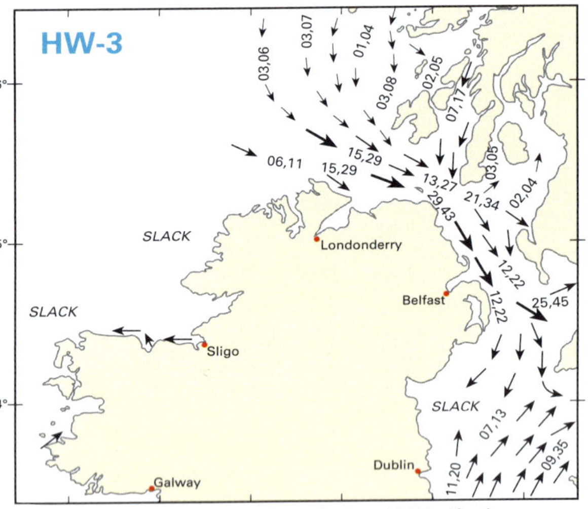

3 Hours before HW Dover (0250 before HW Belfast)

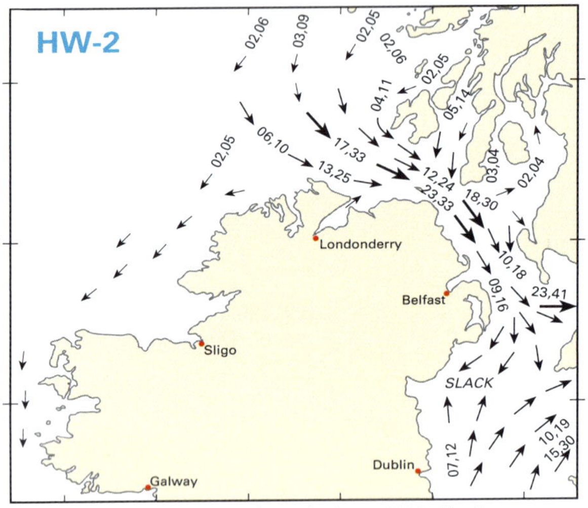

2 Hours before HW Dover (0150 before HW Belfast)

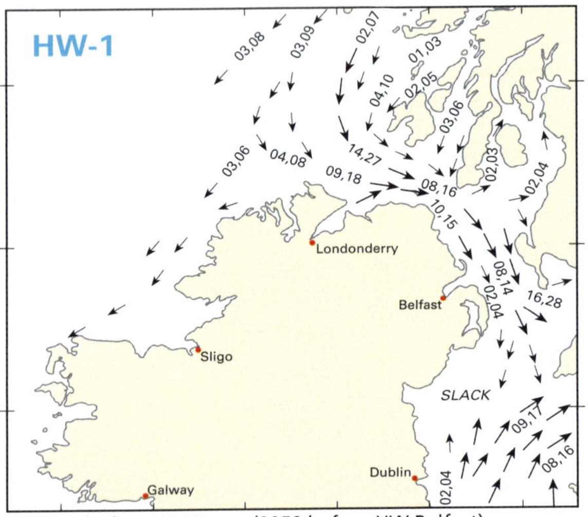

1 Hour before HW Dover (0050 before HW Belfast)

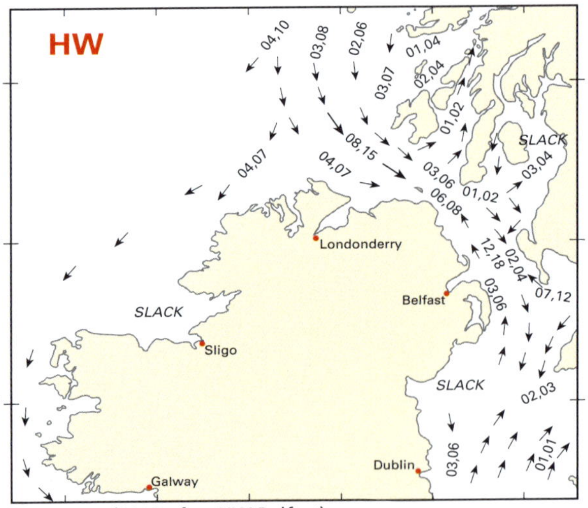

HW Dover (0010 after HW Belfast)

Rathlin Island 6.11
Mull of Kintyre 2.9
North Irish Sea 3.2

SW Scotland 2.2
South Ireland 5.2

The tidal arrows (with no rates shown) off the S and W coasts of Ireland are printed by kind permission of the Irish Cruising Club, to whom the Editor is indebted. They have been found accurate, but should be used with caution.

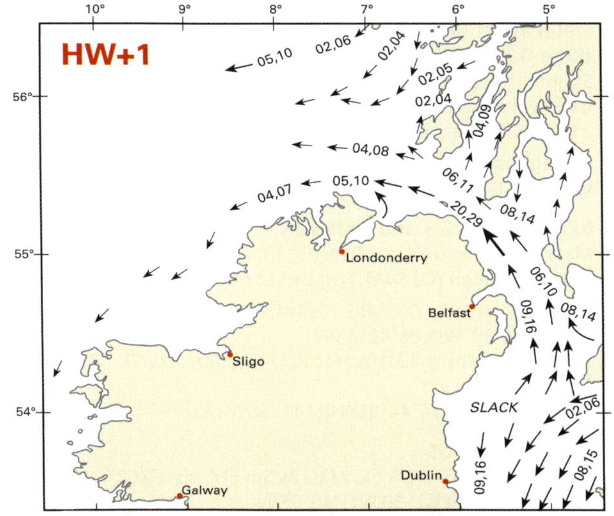

1 Hour after HW Dover (0110 after HW Belfast)

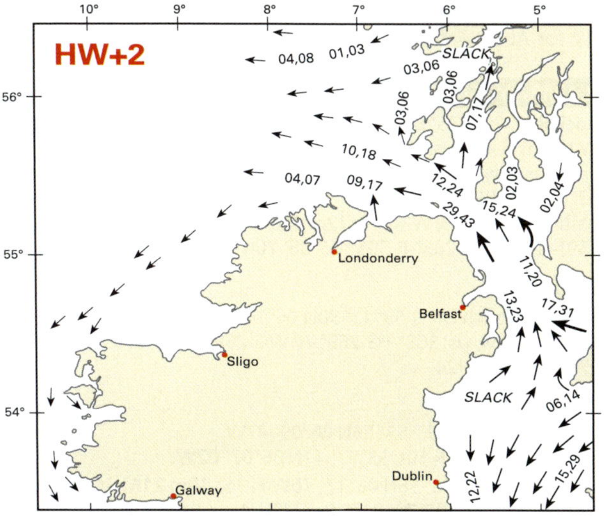

2 Hours after HW Dover (0210 after HW Belfast)

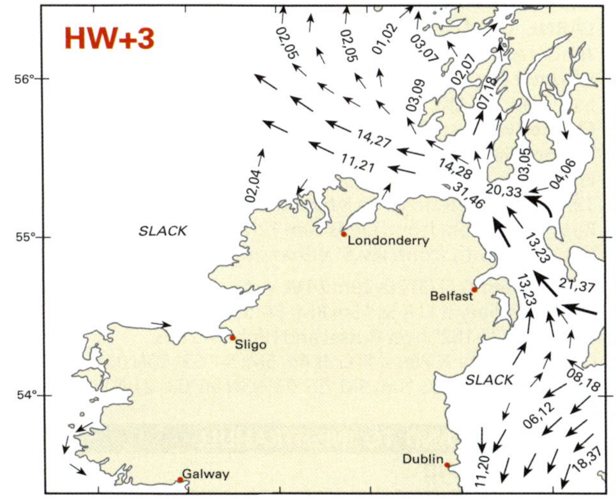

3 Hours after HW Dover (0310 after HW Belfast)

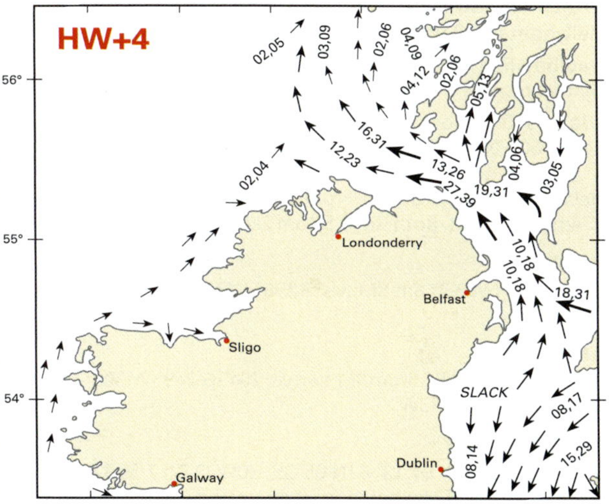

4 Hours after HW Dover (0410 after HW Belfast)

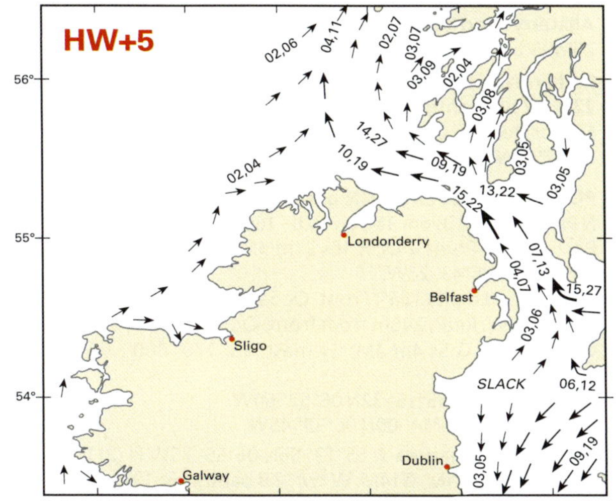

5 Hours after HW Dover (0510 after HW Belfast)

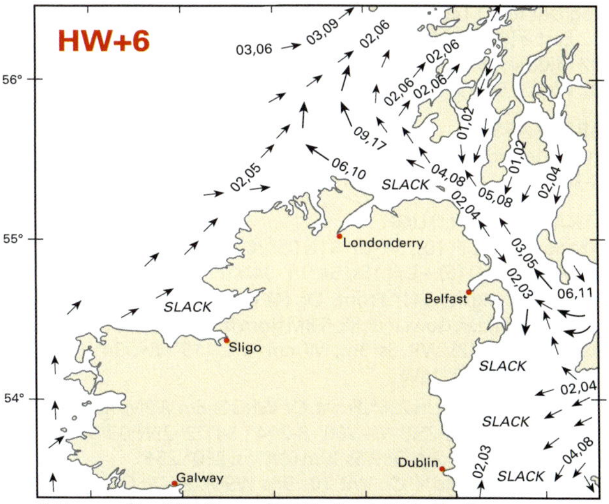

6 Hours after HW Dover (0610 after HW Belfast)

6.3 LIGHTS, BUOYS AND WAYPOINTS

Bold print = light with a nominal range of 15M or more. CAPITALS = place or feature. *CAPITAL ITALICS* = light-vessel, light float or Lanby. *Italics* = Fog signal. ***Bold italics*** = Racon. See 0.2 for Abbreviations.

LAMBAY ISLAND TO DONAGHADEE

Rockabill ☆ 53°35'·82N 06°00'·25W Fl WR 12s 45m **W17M, R13M;** W twr, B band; vis: 178°-W-329°-R-178°.
Skerries Bay Pier Hd ☆ Oc R 6s 7m 7M; W col; vis: 103°-154°; 53°35'·09N 06°06'·49W.
Balbriggan ☆ Fl (3) WRG 10s 12m W13M, R10M, G10M; W twr; vis: 159°-G-193°-W-288°-R-305°; 53°36'·76N 06°10'·80W.

DROGHEDA

Port Approach Dir lt 53°43'·30N 06°14'·73W WRG 10m **W19M, R15M**, G15M; vis: 268°-FG-269°-Al WG-269·5°-FW-270·5°-Al WR-271°-FR-272°; H24.

DUNDALK

Dunany Fl R 3s; 53°53'·56N 06°09'·47W.
Imogene Fl (2) R 10s; 53°57'·41N 06°07'·02W.
Pile Light ☆ 53°58'·56N 06°17'·70W Fl 15s 10m **21M**; W Ho; vis: 124°-W-151°-R-284°-W-313°-R-124°; *Horn (3) 60s*.

CARLINGFORD LOUGH and NEWRY RIVER

Hellyhunter Q (6) + L Fl 15s; ***Racon***; 54°00'·35N 06°02'·10W
Haulbowline ☆ 54°01'·19N 06°04'·74W Fl (3) 10s 32m **17M**; Gy twr; reserve lt 15M.
Ldg lts 310·4° Front, Oc 3s 7m 11M; R △ on twr; vis: 295°-325°; 54°01'·80N 06°05'·43W. Rear, 457m from front, Oc 3s 12m 11M; R ▽ on twr; vis: 295°-325°; both H24.
Newry River Ldg lts 310·4°. Front, 54°06'·37N 06°16'·51W. Rear, 274m from front. Both Iso 4s 5/15m 2M; stone cols.

KILKEEL

Pier Hd ☆ Fl WR 2s 8m 8M; vis: R296°-W313°-017°; 54°03'·46N 05°59'·30W.

ANNALONG

E Bkwtr Hd ☆ Oc WRG 5s 8m 9M; twr; vis: 204°-G-249°-W-309°-R-024°; 54°06'·51N 05°53'·73W.

DUNDRUM BAY

St John's Point ☆ 54°13'·61N 05°39'·30W Q (2) 7·5s 37m **25M**; B twr, Y bands; H24 when horn is operating. **Auxiliary Light** ☆ Fl WR 3s 14m **W15M**, R11M; same twr, vis: 064°-W-078°-R-shore; Fog Det lt VQ 14m vis: 270°; *Horn (2) 60s*.
DZ East 54°13'·51N 05°46'·23W.
DZ Middle 54°13'·01N 05°48'·57W.
DZ West 54°13'·35N 05°50'·07W.

ARDGLASS

Inner Pier Hd ☆ Iso WRG 4s 10m W8M, R7M, G5M; twr; vis: shore-G-308°-W-314°-R-shore; 54°15'·79N 05°36'·33W.

STRANGFORD LOUGH

Strangford L Fl 10s; 54°18'·61N 05°28'·67W.
Bar Pladdy Q (6) + L Fl 15s; 54°19'·34N 05°30'·51W.
Dogtail Pt Ldg lts 341° Front, Oc (4) G 10s 2m 5M; 54°20'·79N 05°31'·83W. Rear, Gowlands Rk, 0·8M from front, Oc (4) G 10s 6m 5M.
Swan Is ☆ Fl (2) WR 6s 5m; W col; vis: 115°-W-334°-R-115°; 54°22'·38N 05°33'·16W.
Strangford East Ldg lts 256°. Front, Oc WRG 5s 6m W9M, R6M, G6M: vis: 190°-R-244°-G-252°-W- 260°-R-294°; 54°22'·29N 05°33'·27W. Rear, 46m from front, Oc R 5s 10m 6M; vis: 250°-264°.
Portaferry Pier Hd ☆ Oc WR 10s 9m W9M, R6M; Or mast; vis: W335°- R005°- W017°-128°; 54°22'·82N 05°33'·03W.

SOUTH ROCK 54°24'·49N 05°22'·02W Fl (3) R 30s 9M; *Horn (3) 45s*, ***Racon (T) 13M***.

PORTAVOGIE, BALLYWATER and DONAGHADEE

Plough Rock 54°27'·40N 05°25'·12W Fl R 3s.
Outer Bkwtr Hd ☆ Iso WRG 5s 9m W10M, R8M, G8M; □ twr; vis: shore-G-258°-W-275°-R-348°; 54°27'·44N 05°26'·14W.
Skulmartin L Fl 10s; 54°31'·82N 05°24'·80W.
Ballywalter, Bkwtr Hd Fl WRG 1·5s 5m 9M; vis: 240°-G-267°-W-277°-R-314°; 54°32'·68N 05°28'·83W.
Donaghadee ☆, S Pier Hd 54°38'·70N 05°31'·86W Iso WR 4s 17m **W18M**, R14M; W twr; vis: shore-W-326°-R-shore; *Siren 12s*.

BELFAST LOUGH and BANGOR

Mew I ☆ NE end 54°41'·91N 05°30'·79W Fl (4) 30s 37m; B twr, W band; ***Racon (O) 14M***. Fog Det Lt VQ.
Bangor Dir lt 105°. Oc WRG 10s 1M; vis: 093°-G-104·8°-W-105·2°-R-117°; 54°39'·98N 05°40'·15W.
Belfast Fairway LFl10s;*Horn (1) 16s*; ***Racon (G)***; 54°41'·71N 05°46'·24W
Cloghan Jetty 54°44'·10N 05°41'·58W QG.

CARRICKFERGUS

Marina Ent Appr ☆ Dir Oc WRG 3s 5m 3M; vis: G308°- W317·5°-R322·5°-332°; 54°42'·58N 05°48'·78W.
Black Hd ☆ 54°45'·99N 05°41'·33W Fl 3s 45m **27M**; W 8-sided twr.

LARNE, CARNLOUGH and RED BAY

N Hunter Rock Q; 54°53'·04N 05°45'·13W.
S Hunter Rock VQ (6) + L Fl 10s; 54°52'·69N 05°45'·22W.
Larne No. 1 QG; 54°51'·68N 05°47'·67W.
Chaine Twr ☆ Iso WR 5s 23m **16M**; Gy twr; vis: 230°-W-240°-240°-R-shore; 54°51'·27N 05°47'·90W.
Ent Ldg lts 184°, No. 11 Front, 54°49'·60N 05°47'·81W Oc 4s 6m 12M; W 2 with R stripe on R pile structure; vis: 179°-189°. No. 12 Rear, 610m from front, Oc 4s 14m 12M; W 2 with R stripe on R □ twr; synch with front, vis: 5° either side of Ldg line.
East Maiden ☆ Fl (3) 20s 29m **24M**; W twr, B band; ***Racon (M) 11-21M***. Auxiliary lt Fl R 5s 15m 8M; 54°55'·74N 05°43'·65W; same twr; vis:142°-182° over Russel and Highland Rks.
Carnlough Hbr N Pier ☆ Fl G 3s 4m 5M; 54°59'·59N 05°59'·29W.
Red Bay Pier ☆ Fl 3s 10m 5M; 55°03'·93N 06°03'·21W.

RATHLIN ISLAND TO INISHTRAHULL

RATHLIN ISLAND

Rue Pt ☆ Fl (2) 5s 16m 14M; W 8-sided twr, B bands; 55°15'·53N 06°11'·47W.
Drake Wreck 55°17'·00N 06°12'·48W Q (6) + L Fl 15s.
Altacarry Head Rathlin East ☆ 55°18'·06N 06°10'·30W Fl (4) 20s 74m **26M**; W twr, B band; vis: 110°-006° and 036°-058°; ***Racon (G) 15-27M***.
Rathlin W 0·5M NE of Bull Pt ☆ 55°18'·05N 06°16'·82W Fl R 5s 62m **22M**; W twr, lantern at base; vis: 015°-225°; H24. Fog Det Lt VQ.
Manor House ☆ Oc WRG 4s 5M; vis: 020°-G-023°-W-026°-R-029°; 55°17'·52N 06°11'·73W.

PORTRUSH, RIVER BANN and COLERAINE

N Pier Hd ☆ Fl R 3s 6m 3M; vis: 220°-160°; 55°12'·34N 06°39'·58W.
Portstewart Point ☆ Oc R 10s 21m 5M; R □ hut; vis: 040°-220°; 55°11'·33N 06°43'·26W.
River Bann Ldg lts 165°. Front, Oc 5s 6m 2M; W twr; 55°09'·96N 06°46'·23W. Rear, 245m from front, Oc 5s 14m 2M; W □ twr.
W Mole ☆ Fl G 5s 4m 2M; Gy mast; vis: 170°-000°; 56°10'·25N 06°46'·45W.
Foyle L Fl 10s; 55°15'·32N 06°52'·60W.
Tuns Fl R 3s; 55°14'·00N 06°53'·46W.
Inishowen Dunagree ☆ 55°13'·56N 06°55'·75W Fl (2) WRG 10s 28m **W18M**, R14M, G14M; W twr, 2 B bands; vis: 197°-G-211°-W-249°-R-000°. Fog Det lt VQ 16m vis: 270°.

WGS84 DATUM

Plot waypoints on chart before use

LOUGH FOYLE

Greencastle S Bkwtr Dir lt 042·5°. Fl (2) WRG 3s 4m W11M, R9M, G9M; vis 307°-G- 040°-W-045°-R-055°; 55°12'·17N 06°59'·13W.
McKinney's Fl R 5s; 55°10'·9N 07°00'·5W.
Moville Fl WR 2·5s 11m 4M; W house on G piles vis: 240°-W-064°-R-240°; 55°10'·98N 07°02'·13W.

INISHTRAHULL TO BLOODY FORELAND

Inishtrahull ☆ 55°25'·86N 07°14'·62W Fl (3) 15s 59m **19M**; W twr; obscd 256°-261° within 3M; ***Racon (T) 24M 060°-310°***. Fog Det Lt VQ.

LOUGH SWILLY, BUNCRANA and RATHMULLAN

Fanad Head ☆ 55°16'·57N 07°37'·91W Fl (5) WR 20s 39m **W18M**, R14M; W twr; vis 100°-R-110°-W-313°-R-345°-W-100°.

Swilly More Fl G 3s; 55°15'·12N 07°35'·79W.

Dunree Fl (2) WR 5s 46m W12M, R9M; vis: 320°-R-328°-W-183°-R-196°; 55°11'·88N 07°33'·25W.
Buncrana Pier near Hd Iso WR 4s 11m W13M, R10M; R twr, W band; vis: R shore- over Inch spit, 052°-W-139°-R-shore over White Strand Rock; 55°07'·60N 07°27'·86W.
Rathmullan Pier Hd Fl G 3s 5M; vis: 206°-345°; 55°05'·70N 07°31'·66W.

MULROY BAY

Limeburner Q Fl; 55°18'·54N 07°48'·40W.
Ravedy Is Fl 3s 9m 3M; twr; vis: 177°-357°; 55°15'·14N 07°46'·90W.

SHEEPHAVEN to BLOODY FORELAND

Portnablahy Ldg lts 125·3°. Front Oc 6s 7m 2M; B col, W bands; 55°10'·79N 07°55'·65W. Rear, 81m from front, Oc 6s 12m 2M; B col, W bands.

Tory Island ☆ 55°16'·36N 08°14'·97W Fl (4) 30s 40m **27M**; B twr, W band; vis: 302°-277°; ***Racon (M) 12-23M***; H24.

West Town Ldg lts 001° Iso 2s 9m 7M △ on Y structure R stripe; 55°15'·79N 08°13'·50W. Rear Iso 2s 11m 7M ▽ ditto (synchronised)

Ballyness Hbr. Ldg lts 119·5°. Front, Iso 4s 25m 1M; 55°09'·06N 08°06'·98W. Rear, 61m from front, Iso 4s 26m 1M.
Bloody Foreland Fl WG 7·5s 14m W6M, G4M; vis: 062°-W-232°-G-062°; 55°09'·51N 08°17'·03W.

BLOODY FORELAND TO RATHLIN O'BIRNE

Glassagh. Ldg lts 137·4°. Front, Oc 8s 12m 3M; 55°06'·83N 08°18'·97W. Rear, 46m from front, Oc 8s 17m 3M; synch.

Inishsirrer, NW end Fl 3·7s 20m 4M; W □ twr vis: 083°-263°; 55°07'·40N 08°20'·93W.

BUNBEG, MULLAGHDOO and OWEY SOUND

Gola I s Ldg lts 171·2°. Front, Oc 3s 9m 2M; W Bn, B band; 55°05'·11N 08°21'·07W. Rear, 86m from front, Oc 3s 13m 2M; B Bn, W band; synch with front.
Cruit Is. Owey Sound Ldg lts 068·3°. Front, Oc 10s; 55°03'·06N 08°25'·85W. Rear, 107m from front, Oc 10s.
Rinnalea Point 55°02'·59N 08°23'·72W Fl 7·5s 19m 9M; □ twr; vis: 132°-167°.

Aranmore, Rinrawros Pt ☆ 55°00'·90N 08°33'·66W Fl (2) 20s 71m **27M**; W twr; obsc by land about 234°-007° and about 013°. Auxiliary lt Fl R 3s 61m 13M, same twr; vis: 203°-234°.

N SOUND OF ARAN and RUTLAND N CHANNEL

Ldg lts 186°. Front, Oc 8s 8m 3M; B Bn, W band; 54°58'·94N 08°29'·27W. Rear, 395m from front, Oc 8s 17m 3M; B Bn.
Inishcoo Ldg lts 119·3°. Front, Iso 6s 6m 1M; W Bn, B band; 54°59'·43N 08°29'·63W. Rear, 248m from front, Iso 6s 11m 1M.
Rutland I Ldg lts 137·6°. Front, 54°58'·97N 08°27'·68W Oc 6s 8m 1M; W Bn, B band. Rear, 330m from front, Oc 6s 14m 1M.

BURTONPORT

Ldg lts 068·1°. Front , FG 17m 1M; Gy Bn, W band; 54°58'·95N 08°26'·40W. Rear, 355m from front, FG 23m 1M; Gy Bn, Y band.

S SOUND OF ARAN and RUTLAND S CHANNEL

Wyon Point Fl (2) WRG 10s 8m W6M, R3M; W □ twr; vis: shore-G-021°-W-042°-R-121°-W-150°-R-shore; 54°56'·51N 08°27'·54W.

Rathlin O'Birne, W side ☆ 54°39'·80N 08°49'·94W Fl WR 15s 35m **W18M**, R14M; W twr; vis: 195°-R-307°-W-195°; ***Racon (O) 13M, vis 284°-203°***.

RATHLIN O'BIRNE TO EAGLE ISLAND

DONEGAL BAY, TEELIN and KILLYBEGS

St John's Pt Fl 6s 30m 14M; W twr; 54°34'·16N 08°27'·64W.
Bullockmore Qk Fl (9) 15s; 54°33'·98N 08°30'·14W.

Rotten I ☆ 54°36'·97N 08°26'·41W Fl WR 4s 20m **W15M**, R11M; W twr; vis: W255°- R008°- W039°-208°.

New Landing Dir lt 338°, Oc WRG 6s 17m; vis: 328°-G-334°-Al WG-336°-W-340°-Al WR-342°-R-348°; 54°38'·14N 08°26'·38W.

Killybegs Outer VQ (6) + L Fl 10s; 54°37'·92N 08°29'·15W.

SLIGO

Wheat Rock Q (6) + LFl 15s; 54°18'·84N 08°39'·10W.

Black Rock Fl WR 5s 24m 10/8M; vis: 130°-W-107°-R-130° (R sector covers Wheat and Seal rks); W twr, B band; 54°18'·45N 08°37'·06W.

Lower Rosses, (N of Cullaun Bwee) Fl (2) WRG 10s 8m 13 -10M; W hut on piles; vis: G over Bungar bank-066°-W-070°-R over Drumcliff bar; shown H24; 54°19'·72N 08°34'·41W.
Ldg lts 125°. Front, Metal Man Fl (3) 6s 13m 7M; 54°18'·24N 08°34'·56W. Rear, Oyster I, 365m from front, fL (3) 6s 13m 7M (synchronised); H24.

KILLALA

Inishcrone Pier Root Fl WRG 1·5s 8m 2M; vis: 098°-W-116°-G-136°-R-187°; 54°13'·21N 09°05'·79W.
Ldg lts 230°. Rinnaun Point, Front No. 1, Oc 10s 7m 5M; □ twr; 54°13'·21N 09°05'·79W. Rear, 150m from front, No. 2 Oc 10s 12m 5M; □ twr.
Dir lt 215°, Inch I, Fl WRG 2s 6m 3M; □ twr; vis: 205°-G-213°-W-217°-R-225°; 54°13'·29N 09°12'·30W.
Ldg lts 196°. Kilroe, Front, 54°12'·63N 09°12'·33W Oc 4s 5m 2M; □ twr. Rear, 120m from front, Oc 4s 10m 2M; □ twr.
Ldg lts 236°. Pier, Front, Iso 2s 5m 2M; W ◇ on twr; 54°13'·02N 09°12'·84W. Rear, 200m from front, Iso 2s 7m 2M; W ◇ on pole.

BROAD HAVEN BAY

Gubacashel Point Iso WR 4s 27m **W17M**, R12M; 110°-R-133°-W-355°-R-021° W twr; 54°16'·06N 09°53'·33W.
Rinroe Pt Fl (2) 10s 5m 3M; 54°17'·83N 09°50'·59W.

EAGLE ISLAND TO SLYNE HEAD

Eagle Is, W end ☆ 54°17'·02N 10°05'·56W Fl (3) 15s 67m **19M**; W twr.

Black Rock ☆ 54°04'·03N 10°19'·25W Fl WR 12s 86m **W20M, R16M**; W twr; vis: 276°-W-212°-R-276°.

BLACKSOD BAY

Carrigeenmore VQ(3) 5s 3M; 54°06'·56N 10°03'·4W.
Blacksod Q (3) 10s; 54°05'·89N 10°03'·01W.
Blacksod Pier Root Fl (2) WR 7·5s 13m W12M, R9M; W twr on dwelling; vis: 189°-R-210°-W-018°; 54°05'·91N 10°03'·63W.

ACHILL SOUND

Ldg lts 330°, 53°52'·50N 09°56'·91W Whitestone Point, Front and rear both Oc 4s 5/6m; W ◇, B stripe.
Achill I Ldg lts 310°, Purteen, Oc 8s 5m; 53°57'·83N 10°05'·93W (PA). Rear, 46m from front Oc 8s 6m.

CLEW BAY and WESTPORT

Achillbeg I S Point ☆ 53°51'·51N 09°56'·85W Fl WR 5s 56m **W18M, R18M, R15M**; W□ twr on □ building; vis: 262°-R-281°-W-342°-R-060°-W- 092°-R(intens)-099°-W-118°.

Cloughcormick Q (9) 15s; 53°50'·56N 09°43'·20W.

Roonagh Quay Ldg lts 144°. Front 53°45'·75N 09°54'·23W. Rear, 54m from front, both Iso 10s 9/15m.

INISHBOFIN and CLIFDEN BAY

Inishlyon Lyon Head Fl WR 7·5s 13m W7M, R4M; W post; vis: 036°-W-058°-R-184°-W-325°-R-036°; 53°36'·74N 10°09'·56W.

Gun Rock Fl (2) 6s 8m 4M; W col; vis: 296°-253°; 53°36'·59N 10°13'·23W.

Cleggan Point Fl (3) WRG 15s 20m W6M, R3M, G3M; W col on W hut; vis: shore-W-091°-R-124°-G-221°; 53°34'·49N 10°07'·73W.

Carrickrana Rocks Bn, large W Bn; 53°29'·24N 10°09'·48W.

Slyne Head, North twr, Illaunamid ☆ 53°23'·99N 10°14'·06W Fl (2) 15s 35m **19M**; B twr.

SLYNE HEAD TO BLACK HEAD

Inishnee Fl (2) WRG 10s 9m W5M, R3M, G3M; W col on W□ base; vis: 314°-G-017°-W-030°-R-080°-W-194°; 53°22'·75N 09°54'·53W.

Croaghnakeela Is Fl 3·7s 7m 5M; W col; vis: 034°-045°, 218°-286°, 311°-325°; 53°19'·40N 09°58'·21W.

GALWAY BAY and INISHMORE

Eeragh, Rock Is ☆ 53°08'·90N 09°51'·40W Fl 15s 35m **18M**; W twr, two B bands; vis: 297°-262°.

Straw Is ☆ 53°07'·06N 09°37'·85W Fl (2) 5s 11m **15M**; W twr.

Killeany Ldg lts 192°. Front, Oc 5s 6m 3M; W col on W□ base; vis: 142°-197°, 53°06'·25N 09°39'·74W. Rear, 43m from front, Oc 5s 8m 2M; W col on W□ base; vis: 142°-197°.

Inishmaan, Ldg lts 199°, Oc 6s 8M; 53°06'·08N 09°34'·77W.

KIGGAUL BAY, CASHLA BAY and SPIDDLE

Kiggaul Bay Fl WR 3s 5m W5M, R3M; vis: 329°-W-359°-R-059°, part obsc by W shore of bay; 53°14'·02N 09°43'·04W.

Cashla BayEnt, W side Fl (3) WR 10s 8m W6M, R3M; W col on concrete structure; vis: 216°-W-000°-R-069°; 53°14'·23N 09°35'·20W.

Lion Pt Dir lt Iso WRG 5s 6m (H24), G6M, W8M, R6M,(night), G2M, W3M, R2M(day); vis: 005°-G- 008·5°-W-011·5°-R-015°; 53°15'·84N 09°33'·95W.

Rossaveel Pier Ldg lts 116° Front, 53°16'·02N 09°33'·38W Oc 3s 7m 3M; W mast. Rear, 90m from front, Oc 3s 8m 3M.

Spiddle Pier Hd Fl WRG 3·5s 11m W6M, R4M, G4M; Y col; vis: 102°-G-282°-W-024°-R-066°; 53°14'·42N 09°18'·55W.

GALWAY

Margaretta Shoal Fl G 3s; *Whis;* 53°13'·68N 09°05'·99W.

Leverets Q WRG 9m 10M; B□ twr, W bands; vis: 015°-G-058°-W-065°-R-103°-G-143·5°-W-146·5°-R-015°; 53°15'·33N 09°01'·90W.

Rinmore Iso WRG 4s 7m 5M; W□ twr; vis: 359°-G-008°-W-018°-R-027°; 53°16'·12N 09°01'·97W.

Appr Chan Dir lt 325°, WRG 7m 3M; vis: 322·25°-FG-323·75°-AlGW-324·75°-FW-325·25°-AlRW-326·25°-FR-331·25°-FlR-332·25°; 53°16'·12N 09°02'·83W.

Black Hd Fl WR 5s 20m W11M, R8M, W □ twr; vis: 045°- R268°-276°; 53°09'·26N 09°15'·83W.

Finnis Rock Q (3) 10s; 53°02'·82N 09°29'·14W.

Inisheer ☆ 53°02'·78N 09°31'·58W Iso WR 12s 34m **W20M, R16M**; vis: 225°-W(partially vis >7M)-231°, 231°-W-245°-R-269°-W-115°; ***Racon (K) 13M***.

6.4 PASSAGE INFORMATION

The latest editions of the Irish Cruising Club (www.irishcruisingclub.com) Sailing Directions are strongly recommended for all Irish waters. Particularly useful on the N and W coasts where other information is scarce, they are published in two volumes: *E and N coasts of Ireland* and *S and W coasts of Ireland*. Admiralty Leisure Folio 5612 covers Carlingford Lough to Lough Foyle.

More Passage Information is threaded between the harbours of this Area.

CROSSING THE IRISH SEA

(AC 1123, 1121, 1411) Passages across the Irish Sea can range from the fairly long haul from Land's End to Cork (140M), to the relatively short hop from Mull of Kintyre to Torr Pt (11M). Such distances are deceptive, because the average cruising yacht needs to depart from and arrive at a reasonably secure hbr. ▶ *In the North Chan strong tidal streams can cause heavy overfalls.* ◀ Thus each passage needs to be treated on its merits. See 0.32 for distances across the Irish Sea.

Many yachts use the Land's End/Cork route on their way to (and from) the delightful cruising ground along the S coast of Ireland, see 5.4. Penzance Bay or one of the Scilly Is ⚓s are convenient places from which to leave, with good lights to assist departure.

▶ *Although the Celtic Sea is exposed to the Atlantic, there are no dangers on passage and the tidal streams are weak.* ◀ A landfall between Ballycotton and Old Hd of Kinsale (both have good lights) presents no offlying dangers, and in poor vis decreasing soundings indicate approach to land. There is a likelihood, outward bound under sail, that the boat will be on the wind – a possible benefit on the return passage. If however the wind serves, and if it is intended to cruise along the southern coast, a landfall at the Fastnet with arrival at (say) Baltimore will place the yacht more to windward, for little extra distance.

From Land's End the other likely destination is Dun Laoghaire. A stop at Milford Haven enables the skipper to select the best time for passing the Smalls or Bishops (see 4.4) and roughly divides the total passage into two equal parts. From S Bishop onwards there are the options of making the short crossing to Tuskar Rk and going N inside the banks (theoretically a good idea in strong W winds), or of keeping to seaward. ▶ *But in bad weather the area off Tuskar is best avoided; apart from the Traffic Separation Scheme, the tide is strong at sp and the sea can be very rough.* ◀

The ferry route Holyhead/Dun Laoghaire is another typical crossing, and is relatively straightforward with easy landfalls either end. ▶ *The tide runs hard round Anglesey at sp, so departure just before slack water minimises the set N or S.* ◀ Beware also the TSS off The Skerries.

The Isle of Man is a good centre for cruising in the Irish Sea, and its hbrs provide convenient staging points whether bound N/S or E/W.

CROSSING TO SCOTLAND

(AC 2198, 2199, 2724) Between Scotland and Northern Ireland there are several possible routes, but much depends on weather and tide. ▶ *Time of departure must take full advantage of the stream, and avoid tide races and overfalls* ◀ (see 2.4). **Conditions can change quickly, so a flexible plan is needed.**

▶ *From Belfast Lough ent, the passage distance to Mull of Kintyre is about 35M and, with a departure at local HW (also HW Dover) providing at least 6hrs of N-going tides, fair winds make it possible to get past the Mull or Sanda Is on one tide. But to be more confident of reaching Gigha or the small marina in Port Ellen, a departure from Glenarm Marina or Red Bay at HW makes a shorter passage with better stream advantage. The inshore side of the TSS coincides with the outer limit of the race S and SW off the Mull of Kintyre; this occurs between HW Dover + 0430 and + 0610 when a local S-going stream opposes the main N-going stream.* ◀

For information on submarine exercises/activity see Subfacts.

LAMBAY ISLAND TO FAIR HEAD

(AC 44, 2093, 2198/9) The coast is fairly steep-to except in larger bays, particularly Dundalk. ▶ *Streams offshore run up to 2·5kn as far as Rockabill, but are weaker further N until approaching Belfast Lough.* ◀ Lambay Island is private, and steep-to except on W side, where there can be overfalls. Skerries Islands (Colt, Shenick's and St Patrick's) are 1M E and SE of Red Island, to E of Skerries hbr. Shenick's Island is connected to shore at LW. Pass between Colt and St Patrick's Islands, but the latter has offliers 3ca to S. Rockabill, two steep-to rks with lt ho, is 2·5M E of St Patrick's Island.

NE'wds from Carlingford Lough, after rounding Hellyhunter SCM, there are no offshore dangers until Strangford Lough where ▶ *the tidal cycle is approx 3 hours later than in the N Channel. Flood runs for 6 hours from HW Belfast –0330 (HW Dover –0345), with a maximum rate of 7.5kn at Rue Point. The strong flow flattens the sea in onshore winds and entrance can be made in strong winds. The ebb runs for 6 hours from HW Belfast +0230 (HW Dover +0215), max rate 7.5kn, E of Angus Rk. If entering against ebb use West Channel with care. Smoothest water near Bar Pladdy Buoy when leaving.* ◀

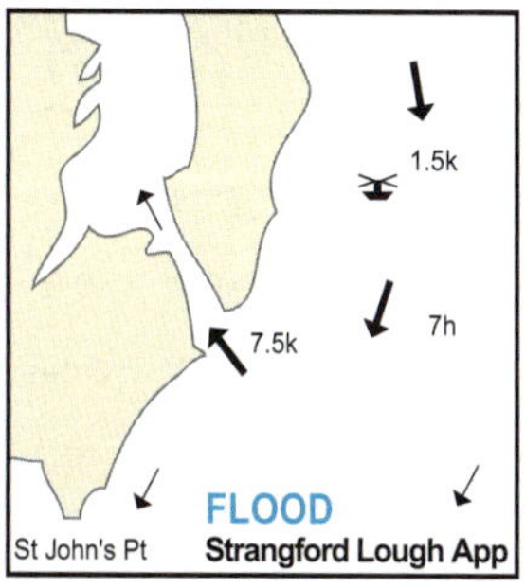

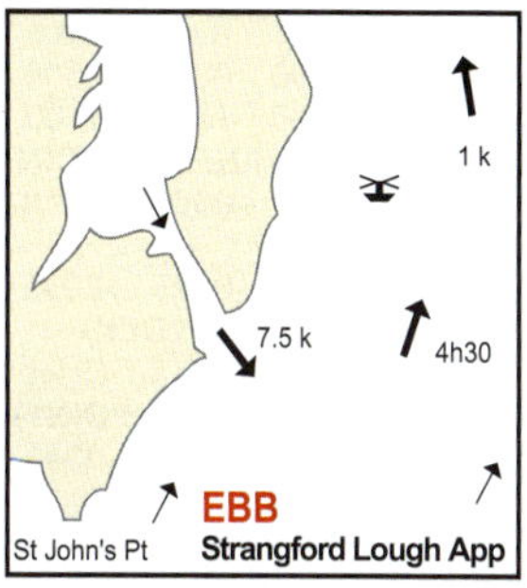

There is a marina at Ardglass. N of Strangford keep 5ca off Ballyquintin Pt. 3M to NE are Butter Pladdy Rks; keep to E of these. 2M further N is South Rk, with disused lt ho, part of group of rks to be avoided in poor vis or bad weather by closing South Rk superbuoy. In good vis pass inshore of South Rk, between it and North Rks (AC 2156), rounding South Ridge PHM buoy.

Three routes lead into Belfast Lough: **a.** E of Mew Is, but beware Ram Race (to the N on the ebb, and the S on the flood). **b.** Copeland Sound, between Mew Is and Copeland Is, is passable but not recommended; **c.** Donaghadee Sound is buoyed and a good short cut for small craft. ▶ *Here the stream runs SSE from HW Belfast + 0530 and NW from HW Belfast – 0030, 4·5kn max. An eddy extends S to Ballyferris Pt, and about 1M offshore.* ◀ For Donaghadee see AC 3709.

(AC 2198) N from Belfast L, Black Hd is steep-to as is Muck Is on its E side. Hunter Rk (0·8m), 2·5M NE of Larne, is marked by N & S cardinals. 2M further N are the Maidens, two dangerous groups of rks extending 2·5M N/S; E Maiden is lit.

Glenarm Marina provides good shelter for small craft and is useful for on passage to the W coasts of Scotland or Ireland. Other ⚓s in offshore winds are at Red Bay 5M further N, and in Cushendun B, 5M NNW of Garron Pt. All provide useful anch on passage to/from the Clyde or Western Is. Fair Hd is a bold 190m headland, steep-to all round, but with extensive overfalls in Rathlin Sound.

6.5 SPECIAL NOTES FOR IRELAND: See 5.5

MINOR HARBOURS AND ANCHORAGES BETWEEN LAMBAY ISLAND AND CARLINGFORD LOUGH

SKERRIES, Dublin, **53°35'·09N 06°06'·49W**. AC 633. Tides as Balbriggan, 6.6. E & SE of Red Island (a peninsula) lie Colt, Shenick's and St Patrick's Is, the latter foul to S and SW. Inshore passage between Colt and St Patrick's Is uses transit/brg as on chart to clear dangers. Good shelter and holding in 3m at Skerries Bay, W of Red Is. Appr from E or NE outside PHM buoy, Fl R 10s, off Red Is. ⚓ WNW of pier, Oc R 6s 7m 7M, vis 103°-154°; clear of moorings. Most facilities; Skerries SC ☎ 1-849 1233, Slip (HW±3). Rockabill Lt, Fl WR 12s 45m 22/18M, is conspic 2·4M ExN of St Patrick's Is.

BALBRIGGAN, Dublin, **53°36'·76N 06°10'·84W**. AC 44, 1468. Tides see 6.6. Good shelter in small hbr, dries about 0·9m, access approx HW ±2. Hbr unattractive, mainly FV's. Appr on SW, to open the outer hbr which is entered on SE; thence to inner hbr and AB on SE quay. Beware shoaling on both sides of outer hbr. Lt, Fl (3) WRG 10s 12m 13/10M, conspic W tr on E bkwtr head, vis 159°-G193°-W-288°-R-305°. Facilities: FW, D (by tanker from Skerries), Gas, Slip (HW±2), R, Bar, 🛒.

PORT ORIEL, Louth, **53°47'·94N 06°13'·37W**. AC 44. Tides see 6.6 (Dunany Pt). Good shelter, except in strong NW'lies, in small new fishing harbour. Appr from NE on ldg marks 179°, Fl 3s; Pier Hd Lt Mo(A) R 9s. AB on pier in 4m or dry out in inner hbr. HM ☎ 087 2628777. D by tanker, 🛒 in Clogher Hd village (1·2M).

6.6 CARLINGFORD LOUGH

Louth/Down **54°01'·25N 06°04'·30W** ☸☸🚿🚿✿✿✿

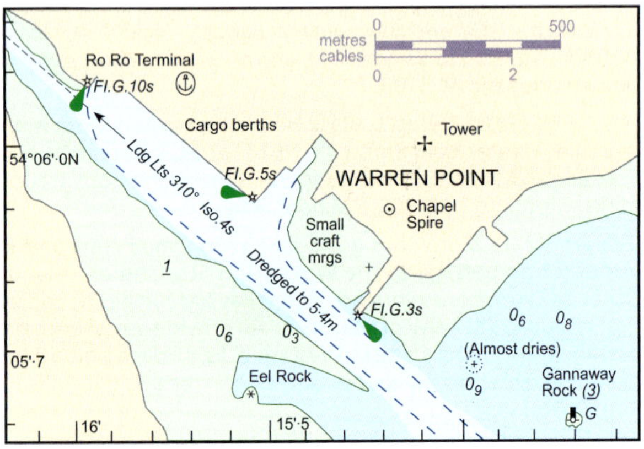

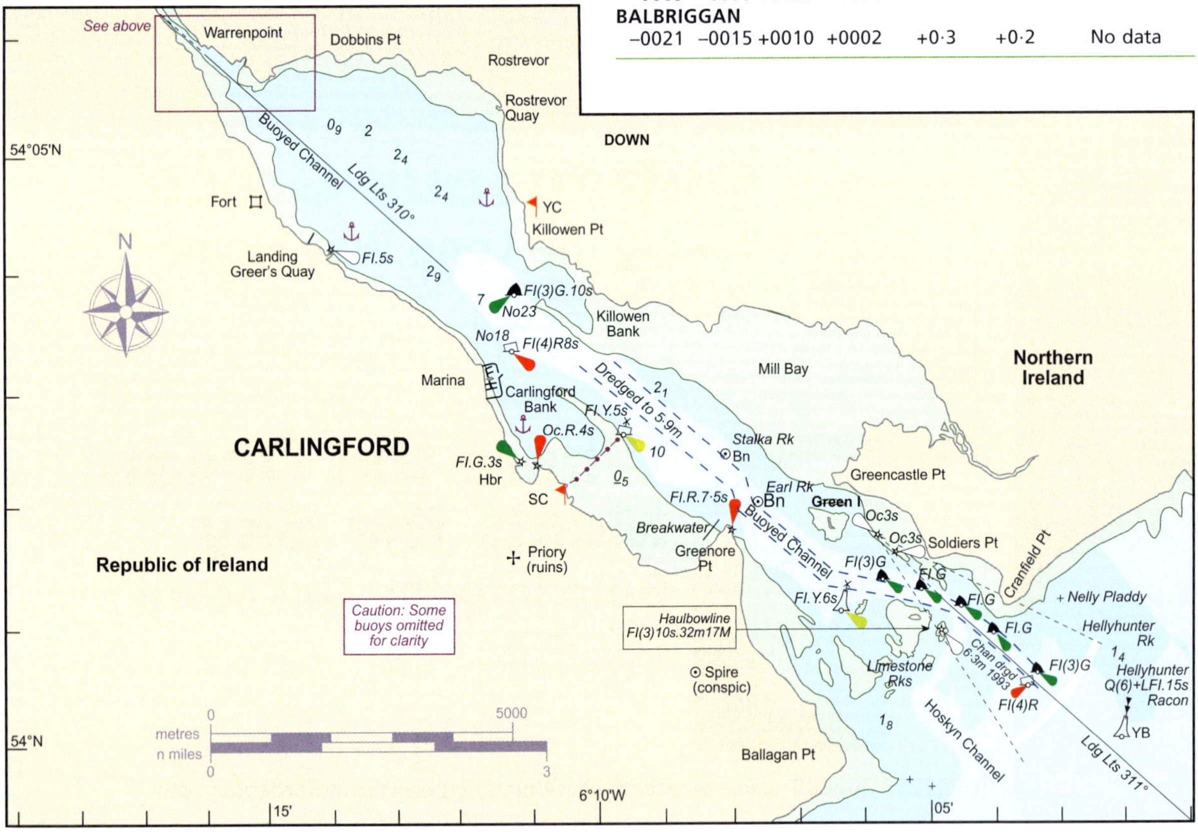

CHARTS AC 44, 2800, 5621, 5612; Imray C62.

TIDES Cranfield Pt +0025 and Warrenpoint +0035 Dover; ML 2·9; Duration Cranfield Pt 0615, Warrenpoint 0540

Standard Port DUBLIN (NORTH WALL) (⟵)

Times				Height (metres)			
High Water		Low Water		MHWS	MHWN	MLWN	MLWS
0000	0700	0000	0500	4·1	3·4	1·5	0·7
1200	1900	1200	1700				
Differences CRANFIELD POINT							
−0027	−0011	+0005	−0010	+0·7	+0·9	+0·3	+0·2
WARRENPOINT							
−0020	−0010	+0025	+0035	+1·0	+0·7	+0·2	0·0
NEWRY (VICTORIA LOCK)							
−0005	−0015	+0045	Dries	+1·2	+0·9	+0·1	Dries
DUNDALK (SOLDIERS POINT)							
−0010	−0010	0000	+0045	+1·0	+0·8	+0·1	−0·1
DUNANY POINT							
−0028	−0018	−0008	−0006	+0·7	+0·9	No data	
RIVER BOYNE BAR							
−0005	0000	+0020	+0030	+0·4	+0·3	−0·1	−0·2
BALBRIGGAN							
−0021	−0015	+0010	+0002	+0·3	+0·2	No data	

SHELTER **Carlingford Marina** is protected on S side by sunken barge; depths 1·4m–3·5m (check with Marina). Appr from N with Nos 18 and 23 buoys in transit astern 012°, to clear the tail of Carlingford Bank (dries) and beware of marine farms in vicinity.

Carlingford Hbr (dries 2·2m), AB at piers.

Warrenpoint has pontoons on NW side of breakwater (Fl G 3s); access dredged 1·1m. ⚓s clockwise from ent include: off Greenore Pt, between SW end of quay and bkwtr, in 3m clear of commercial traffic; off Greer's Quay in 2m; off Rostrevor Quay, Killowen Pt (YC) and off derelict pier at Greencastle Pt (beware rks). Limited space may be available for short-stay visiting craft in the mussel fishing complex (approx £15/night). Call at least 24 hours before arrival.

NAVIGATION WPT 54°00'·09N 06°02'·00W, (2½ ca S of Hellyhunter SCM lt buoy) 311°/1M to first chan buoys. The main chan is Carlingford Cut (6·3m), about 3ca SW of Cranfield Pt, and passing 2ca NE of Haulbowline lt ho. Drying rocks and shoals obstruct most of the entrance. Small craft should at all times keep clear of commercial shipping in the narrow dredged channel. The ent is impassable in strong on-shore winds. The NE bank is **Northern Ireland**, SW bank is **Republic of Ireland**.

The lough becomes choppy in S'ly winds and, due to the funnelling effect of the mountains, NW winds can cause a higher sea state within the lough than outside it.
Tides run up to 5kn off Greenore Pt and entry is impracticable against the ebb. Beware sudden squalls and waterspouts.

Extensive shellfish beds exist along the NE side of the lough; beware fishing vessels on both sides of the channel, and give them a wide berth.

LIGHTS AND MARKS Haulbowline Fl (3) 10s 32m 17M; granite tower. Ldg lts 310°26': both Oc 3s 7/12m 11M, vis 295°-325°; R △ front, ▽ rear, on framework trs. Greenore Pier Fl R 7·5s 10m 5M. Newry R: Ldg lts 310°, both Iso 4s 5/15m 2M, stone columns. Channel from Green Is to Warren Pt marked by lit lateral buoys.

R/T Greenore (*Ferry Greenore*) Ch 12 16 (HJ). Carlingford Marina Ch M 16. Warrenpoint Ch 12 16 (H24); call Ch 12 at By No. 23 to enter dredged chan. Dundalk Ch 14 16 (HW±3).

TELEPHONE (Code Greenore/Carlingford 042; Warrenpoint 028). MRCC (01) 6620922/3 or (02891) 463933; Irish ⊖: Dundalk (042) 34114; Marinecall 09068 969655; Dr (042) 73110; Ⓗ Newry (028) 3026 5511, Dundalk (042) 34701; Police (042) 9373102, (028) 4172 2222.

FACILITIES

Carlingford Marina ☎ 042 9373073, mob 0872 321567. 290 inc Ⓥ, €4.00 (min€20/craft), short stay <5hrs€12.50/craft, D (0900-

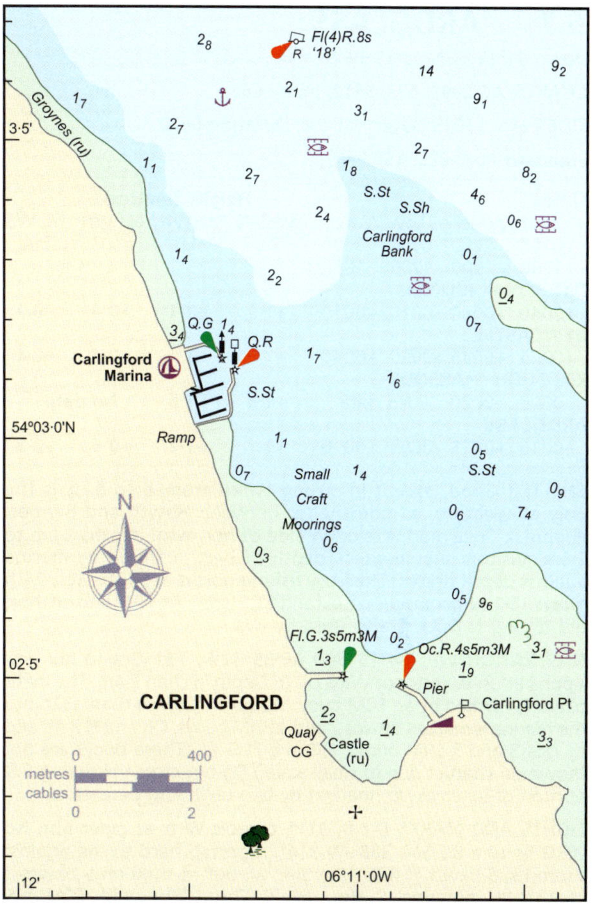

2100), C, CH, BH (50T), ME ☎ 0872 301319, Rigger ☎ (048)44 828882, Divers, Slip, ⊡, Bar, R, Wi-fi + @. **Carlingford YC** ☎ (041) 685 1951, Slip, Bar, M, FW.

Village P (cans), 🛒, R, Bar, Ⓑ, ✉. **Hbr** AB, Slip, ME, El, ⚒, Kos, Gas. **Warrenpoint** HM ☎ (02841) 752878; AB, M (but no access at LW), FW, P, D, ✉ also at Rostrevor, Ⓑ also Dundalk, ⇌ (Dundalk, Newry), ✈ (Dublin).

MINOR HARBOURS NORTH OF CARLINGFORD LOUGH

KILKEEL, Down, **54°03'·47N 05°59'·26W**. AC 44, 2800, 5612. HW +0015 on Dover; ML 2·9m; Duration 0620. See 6.7. Inner basin is completely sheltered, but gets crowded by FVs; depth off quays approx 1m. Secure in inner basin and see HM. There are drying banks both sides of ent chan and SW gales cause a sandbank right across ent. This is dredged or slowly eroded in E winds. S bkwtr lt Fl WR 2s 8m 8M, 296°-R-313°-W-017°, storm sigs. Meeney's pier (N bkwtr) Fl G 3s 6m 2M. VHF Ch **12** 14 16 (Mon-Fri: 0900-2000). HM ☎ (028 417) 62287; Facilities: FW on quay, BY (between fish market and dock), El, ME, ⚒, Slip. **Town** (¾M) Bar, ✉, R, 🛒, Gas, ⊡.

ANNALONG HBR, Down, **54°06'·50N 05°53'·65W**. AC 44, 5621, 5612. Tides as Kilkeel, see 6.7. Slight silting rep't 2006. Entry HW ±2. Excellent shelter in small drying hbr, dredged to 1·5m 80m beyond pier with 30m pontoon (£12/craft), FW. Appr in W sector of S breakwater light, Oc WRG 5s 8m 9M, vis 204°-G-249°-W-309°-R-024°. Hug N side of the breakwater to avoid rocky shore to starboard. Surge gate at harbour entrance may be closed in SE winds (3R lts vert shown). IPTS shown at entrance. HM ☎ mob 07739 527036 Facilities: 🛒, Bar, ✉.

DUNDRUM BAY, Down. AC 44, 5612. Tides see 6.7. This 8M wide bay to the W of St John's Pt is shoal to 5ca offshore and unsafe in onshore winds. The small drying hbr at **Newcastle** (54°11'·8N 05°53'·0W) is for occas use in fair weather. HM ☎ (02843) 722804, mob 07803 832515. **Dundrum Hbr** (**54°14'·2N 05°49'·4W**) No longer used by commercial tfc, provides ⚓ in 2m for shoal draft; the bar carries about 0·3m. A steep sea can run at the bar in onshore winds. HW Dundrum is approx that of HW Liverpool; see also 6.7 Newcastle. *The Irish Cruising Club's Sailing Directions* are essential for the 1M long, buoyed approach channel. 3 unlit DZ buoys offshore are part of the Ballykinler firing range, 2M E of hbr; R flag/lts indicate range active.

6.7 ARDGLASS

Down 54°15′·63N 05°35′·96W ❀❀❀◊◊✿✿

CHARTS AC 2093, 633, 5612; Imray C62.

TIDES HW +0025 Dover; ML 3·0; Duration 0620

Standard Port BELFAST (⟶)

Times				Height (metres)			
High Water		Low Water		MHWS	MHWN	MLWN	MLWS
0100	0700	0000	0600	3·5	3·0	1·1	0·4
1300	1900	1200	1800				
Differences KILKEEL							
+0040	+0030	+0010	+0010	+1·2	+1·1	+0·4	+0·4
NEWCASTLE							
+0025	+0035	+0020	+0040	+1·6	+1·1	+0·4	+0·1
KILLOUGH HARBOUR							
0000	+0020	No data		+1·8	+1·6	No data	
ARDGLASS							
+0010	+0015	+0005	+0010	+1·7	+1·2	+0·6	+0·3

SHELTER Good, except in strong winds from E to S. It is the only all-weather, all-tide shelter between Howth and Bangor. Phennick Cove marina is on W side of hbr, with depths 1·0m to 2·8m. Visitors should check depth of berth offered by marina against depth drawn. The busy fishing port is in South Hbr, with quays (2·1m) on inside of extended S pier. At NW end of hbr, old drying N Dock is also used by FVs.

NAVIGATION WPT 54°15′·30N 05°35′·32W, 131°/5ca to hbr ent. Appr 311° in W sector of WRG Dir lt. Depth in chan 2·4m. The inner bkwtr is marked by an ECM buoy, VQ (3) 4s. Thence chan 232° into the marina is marked by Nos 2 and 4 PHM buoys, QR and Fl R 4s; and by Nos 3 and 5 SHM buoys, QG and Fl G 4s. (These buoys are not shown on chartlet due to small scale.) Do not cross the drying SW portion of inner bkwtr, marked by two unlit SCM perches.

LIGHTS AND MARKS Dir lt, 311°, conspic W tr at inner hbr, Iso WRG 4s 10m 8/7/5M, 308°-W-314°; reported hard to see against shore lts. S bkwtr Fl R 3s 10m 5M. W roof of shed on S bkwtr is conspic. If entering S Hbr, avoid Churn Rk, unlit SCM bn. Entrance to marina is buoyed. Castle, spire and water tr (off plan) are conspic to W.

R/T Hbr VHF Ch 12 14 16. Marina Ch M, 80.

TELEPHONE (Code 028) HM 4484 1291, mob 07790 648274; MRCC 9046 3933; Marinecall 09068 969655; Police 4461 5011; Dr 9084 1242.

FACILITIES **Phennick Cove Marina** (55 inc 30Ⓥ £1.60), ☎ 44842332, www.ardglassmarina.co.uk; Slip(£3.00), D, P (cans), ⊡, ♿. **Town** P (cans), Bar, ✉, R, 🛒, Gas.

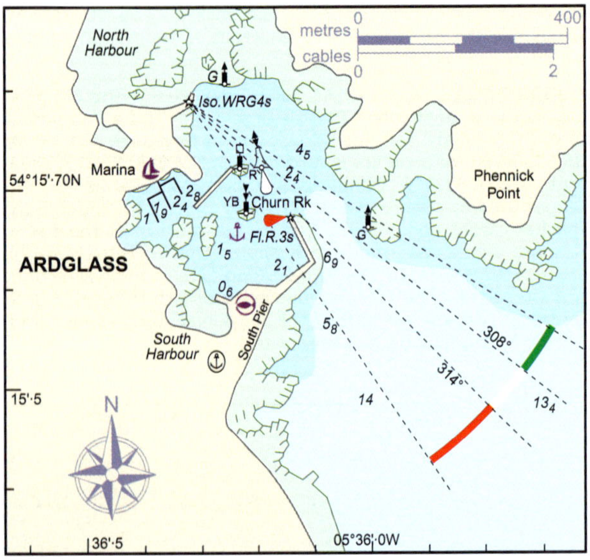

6.8 STRANGFORD LOUGH

Down **54°19'·33N 05°30'·85W** (Narrows) ❀❀◊◊✿✿✿

CHARTS AC 2156, 2159, 5612; Imray C62.

TIDES Killard Pt 0000, Strangford Quay +0200 Dover; ML 2·0; Duration 0610

Standard Port BELFAST (⟶)

Times				Height (metres)			
High Water		Low Water		MHWS	MHWN	MLWN	MLWS
0100	0700	0000	0600	3·5	3·0	1·1	0·4
1300	1900	1200	1800				
Differences STRANGFORD (The Narrows)							
+0147	+0157	+0148	+0208	+0·1	+0·1	–0·2	0·0
KILLARD POINT (Entr)							
+0011	+0021	+0005	+0025	+1·0	+0·8	+0·1	+0·1
QUOILE BARRIER							
+0150	+0200	+0150	+0300	+0·2	+0·2	–0·3	–0·1
KILLYLEAGH							
+0157	+0207	+0211	+0231	+0·3	+0·3	No data	
SOUTH ROCK							
+0023	+0023	+0025	+0025	+1·0	+0·8	+0·1	+0·1
PORTAVOGIE							
+0010	+0020	+0010	+0020	+1·2	+0·9	+0·3	+0·2

SHELTER Excellent; largest inlet on E coast. Good ⚓s in the Narrows at Cross Roads; in Strangford Creek (NW of Swan Island, which is marked by 3 lt bns to S, E and N); in Audley Rds and Ballyhenry Bay. 3 Ⓜs at Strangford. Portaferry has a small marina with a few visitors' berths. Many good ⚓s and some Ⓜs up the lough, by villages and YCs; dues, if applicable, are seldom collected.

NAVIGATION WPT Strangford SWM buoy, L Fl 10s, 54°18′·63N 05°28′·62W, 306°/2·05M to Angus Rk lt tr.

Strangers should use the E Chan. Beware St Patricks Rk, Bar Pladdy and Pladdy Lug; also overfalls in the SE apprs and at the bar, which can be dangerous when ebb is against strong onshore winds.

During flood the bar presents no special problem, preferable to enter on the young flood or at slack water. Strong (up to 7kn at sp) tidal streams flow through the Narrows. The flood starts in the Narrows at HW Belfast –3½ and runs for about 6 hrs; the ebb starts at HW Belfast +2½. Beware car ferry plying from Strangford, S and E of Swan Is, to Portaferry.

Swan Island, seen as a grassy mound at HW, is edged with rks and a reef extends 32m E ending at W bn, Fl (2) WR 6s. Further up the lough, AC 2156 is essential. Pladdies are drying patches, often un-marked.

LIGHTS AND MARKS An IDM, red and black bands, Fl(2) 10s 13m 3M, 54°22′·12N 05°32′·77W (off Strangford) marks a submerged tidal turbine, 3·1m below CD.

R/T HM at Strangford Ferry Terminal Ch 12 14 16 M (Mon-Fri 0900-1700LT). Some YCs Ch **80** M.

TELEPHONE (Code 028) Strangford HM 4488 1637; MRCC 9146 3933; Marinecall 09068 969655; Police 4461 5011; Medical Clinic 4461 3016; Casualty 4461 3311.

FACILITIES Strangford, Portaferry and Killyleagh are easy to access and offer good shops, pubs and restaurants.
STRANGFORD 3 Ⓜs SE of Swan Is. **Islander Marine** ☎ 4488 1449: FW, Slip, El, Ⓔ, ⚒, D (cans). Village: 🛒, R, Bar, ✉.
PORTAFERRY: Marina, ☎ 42729598, mobile 07703 209780; barholm.portaferry@virgin.net. AB(limited) £1.50, Gas, Gaz, P & D (cans), 🛒, R, Bar, ✉, Ⓑ, aquarium. **Cook St Pier** (2ca S), limited AB, FW.
QUOILE RIVER: **Quoile YC** ☎ 4461 2266. AB, M, Slip, FW.
KILLYLEAGH: M, P & D (cans), L, CH, SM (Irish Spars & Rigging ☎ 4482 8882), El, ME, 🛒, Gas, Gaz, Kos, R, Ⓑ, Bar, ✉; **Killyleagh YC** ☎ 4482 8250; N of village, **East Down YC** ☎ 4482 8375, AB (about 1M NE of town).
RINGHADDY QUAY: CC, M, AB drying, FW, Slip.
SKETRICK ISLAND: In White Rk B, **Strangford Lough YC,** ☎ 9754 1883, L, AB, FW, BY, CH, R, Bar. To the NW in the Dorn, **Down CC**, (Old Lightship) FW, D, Bar.
KIRCUBBIN (tidal): Gas, P & D (cans), Ⓑ, R, Bar, 🛒, ✉.

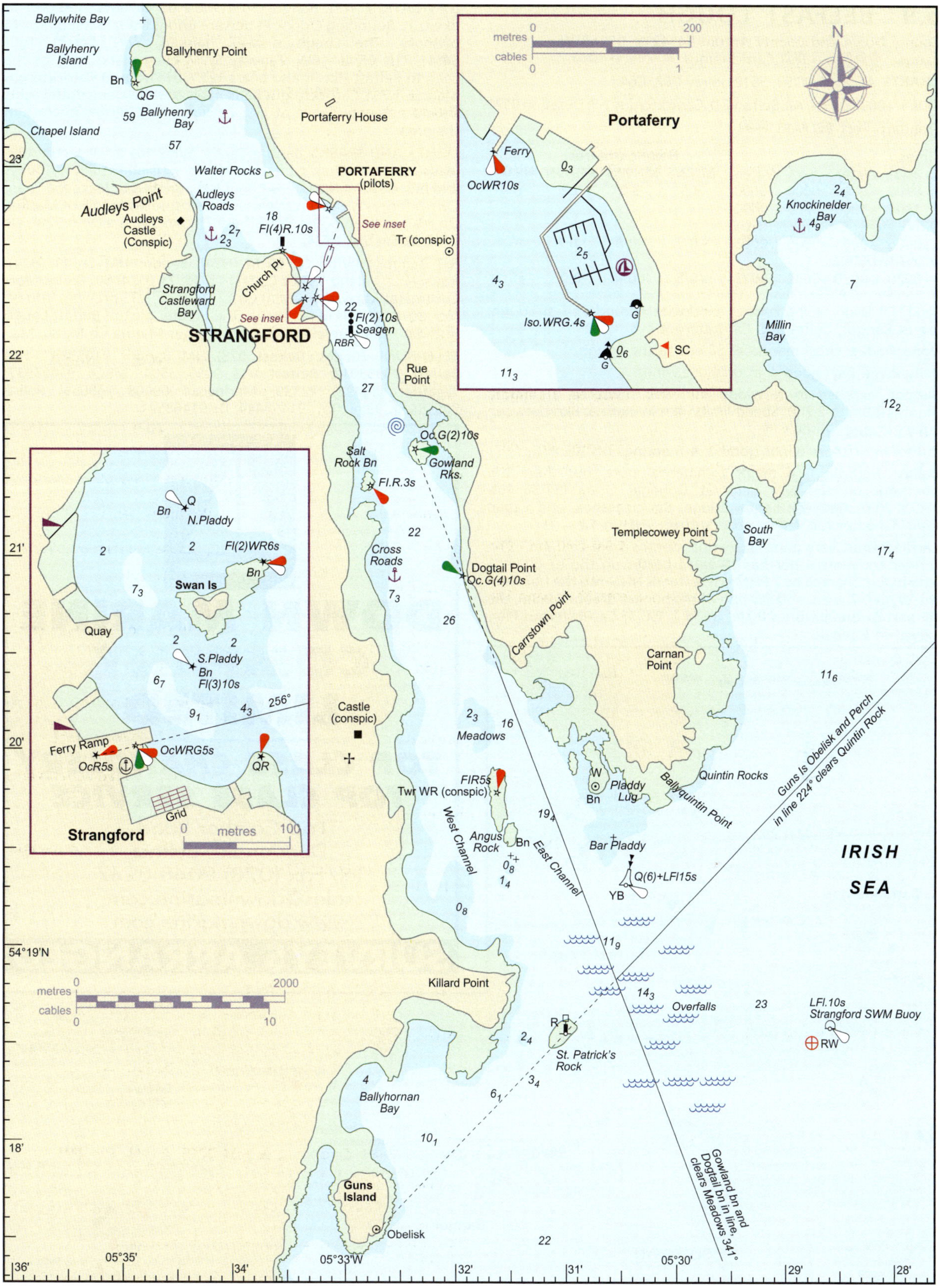
Ballywhite Bay
Ballyhenry Island
Bn
QG
Ballyhenry Point
59
Ballyhenry Bay
Chapel Island
57
Portaferry House
Walter Rocks
PORTAFERRY
(pilots)
Audleys Point
Audleys Roads
Audleys Castle (Conspic)
18
Fl(4)R.10s
See inset
Tr (conspic)
Church Pt
Strangford Castleward Bay
See inset
22
Fl(2)10s
Seagen
RBR
STRANGFORD
Rue Point
27
Oc.G(2)10s
Salt Rock Bn
Gowland Rks.
Fl.R.3s
22
Cross Roads
Dogtail Point
Oc.G(4)10s
26
Carrstown Point
Castle (conspic)
16
Meadows
FlR5s
Twr WR (conspic)
West Channel
Angus Rock
Bn
East Channel
Bar Pladdy
Q(6)+LFl15s
YB
Pladdy Lug
Bn
W
Ballyquintin Point
Quintin Rocks
Carnan Point
Templecowey Point
South Bay
Millin Bay
Knockinelder Bay
Guns Is Obelisk and Perch in line 224° clears Quintin Rock
IRISH SEA
Overfalls
23
LFl.10s
Strangford SWM Buoy
RW
St. Patrick's Rock
R
Killard Point
Ballyhornan Bay
Guns Island
Obelisk
22
Gowland bn and Dogtail bn in line, clears Meadows 341°
metres
cables
0
2000
10
54°19'N
23'
22'
21'
20'
18'
36'
05°35'
34'
05°33'W
32'
31'
05°30'
29'
28'
N
Portaferry
metres
cables
200
1
Ferry
OcWR10s
Iso.WRG.4s
G
SC
Bn
Q
N.Pladdy
Fl(2)WR6s
Swan Is
Quay
S.Pladdy
Bn
Fl(3)10s
256°
Ferry Ramp
OcR5s
OcWRG5s
QR
Grid
Strangford
metres
100

6.9 BELFAST LOUGH

County Down and County Antrim **54°42'N 05°45'W**
Bangor ; Carrickfergus

CHARTS AC 2198, 1753, 5612; Imray C62, C64

TIDES +0007 Dover; ML Belfast 2·0, Carrickfergus 1·8; Duration 0620

Standard Port BELFAST (⟶)

Times				Height (metres)			
High Water		Low Water		MHWS	MHWN	MLWN	MLWS
0100	0700	0000	0600	3·5	3·0	1·1	0·4
1300	1900	1200	1800				
Differences CARRICKFERGUS							
+0005	+0005	+0005	+0005	–0·3	–0·3	–0·2	–0·1
DONAGHADEE							
+0020	+0020	+0023	+0023	+0·5	+0·4	0·0	+0·1

SHELTER Main sailing centres, clockwise around Belfast Lough, are at Bangor, Cultra and Carrickfergus.

Donaghadee: small marina at SE ent to the Lough.

Ballyholme Bay: good ⚓ in offshore winds.

Bangor: exposed to N winds, but well sheltered in marina (depths 2·9m to 2·2m). Speed limits: 4kn in marina, 8kn between Luke's Pt and Wilson's Pt.

Cultra: in offshore winds good ⚓ & moorings off RNoIYC.

Belfast Harbour is a major commercial port, but there are pontoons on the NW bank at Donegal Quay (54°36'·16N 05°55'·20W) between Lagan Bridge, 8m clearance, and Lagan Weir. To enter call *Belfast Port Control* VHF Ch **12**.

Carrickfergus: very good in marina, depths 1·8m to 2·3m. The former commercial hbr has 10 yacht berths on the W quay. A stub bkwtr, marked by 2 PHM bns, extends NNE into the hbr from the W pier. The ent and SW part of the hbr are dredged 2·3m; the NE part of the hbr dries 0·7m. Good ⚓ SSE of Carrickfergus Pier, except in E winds.

NAVIGATION WPT Bangor 54°41'·00N 05°40'·00W, 190°/1M to bkwtr lt. Rounding Orlock Pt beware Briggs Rocks extending ¾M offshore. The Lough is well marked. WPT Carrickfergus 54°41'·71N 05°46'·16W, Fairway SWM buoy marks start of the chan to Belfast Hbr. It also bears 121°/301° from/to Carrickfergus Marina, 1.7M. Carrickfergus Bank liable to shift. Deep draft yachts should not enter/leave at LW±2. High speed ferries operate in the area.

LIGHTS AND MARKS Bangor Dir Oc WRG 10s lt; W sector 105° leads into ent. Chan to Belfast Hbr is well marked/lit by buoys and bns. Beyond No 12 PHM bn it is dangerous to leave the chan. Carrickfergus is easily recognised by conspic castle to E of Marina. On Marina Bkwtr, 30m W of the ☆ QR 7m 3M, is a Dir lt 320°, Oc WRG 3s 5m 3M, (H24).

R/T Bangor Marina Ch **80** M (H24); Bangor HM Ch 11 (H24). Royal N of Ireland YC (at Cultra) Ch **16**; 11 (H24) 80. *Belfast Port Control* (at Milewater Basin) Ch **12** 16 (H24); VTS provides info on request to vessels in port area. The greater part of Belfast Lough is under radar surveillance. Carrickfergus Marina Ch M, 80, M2.

TELEPHONE (Codes: Belfast 028) HM Bangor 91453297; HM Belfast 90553012; Belfast VTS 9055 3504; MRCC 91463933; Weather (08494) 22339; Marinecall 09068 969655; Police 90558411, 93362021, 91454444; Dr 91468521.

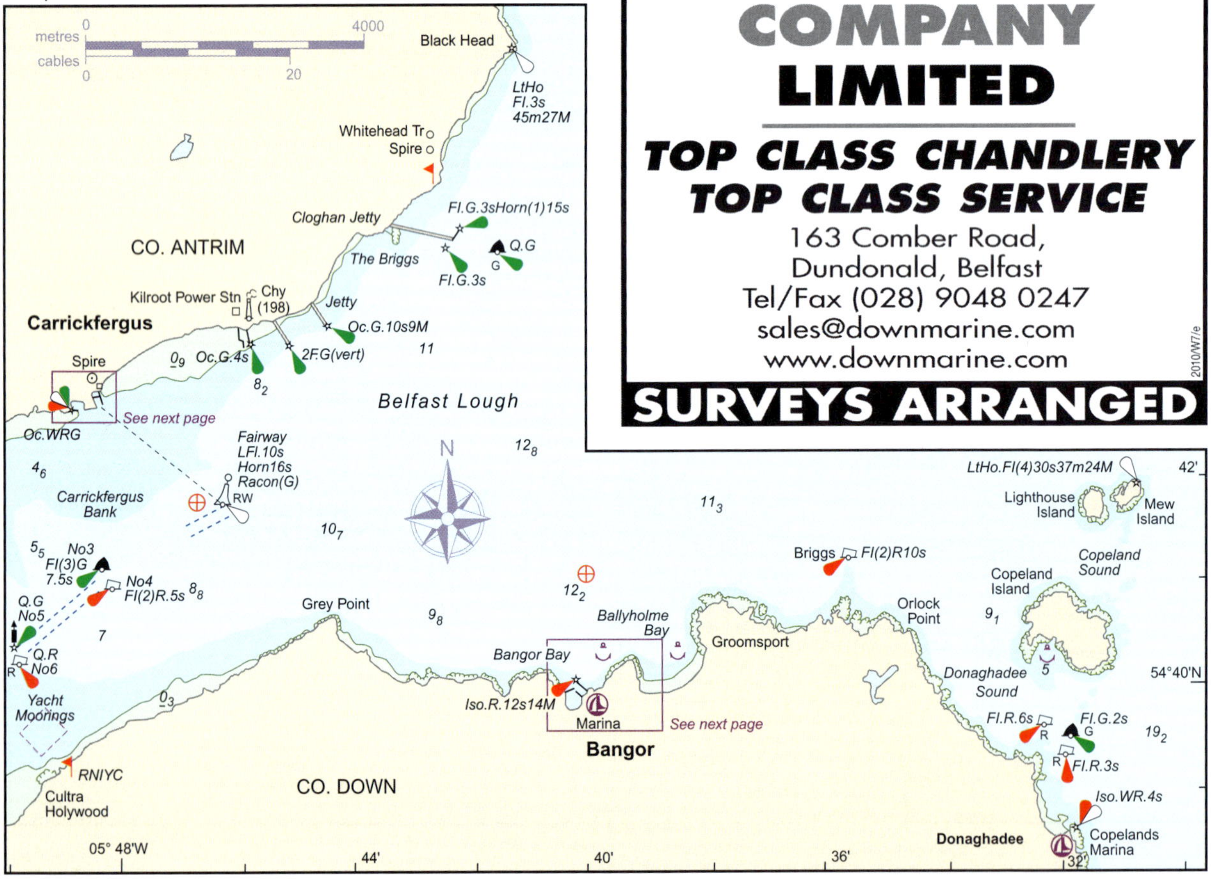

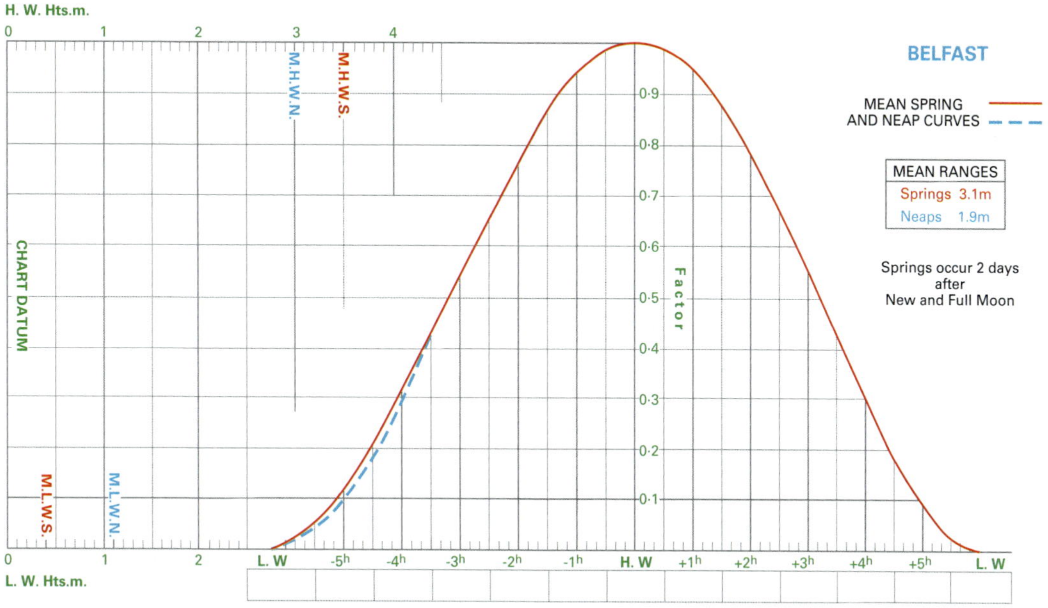

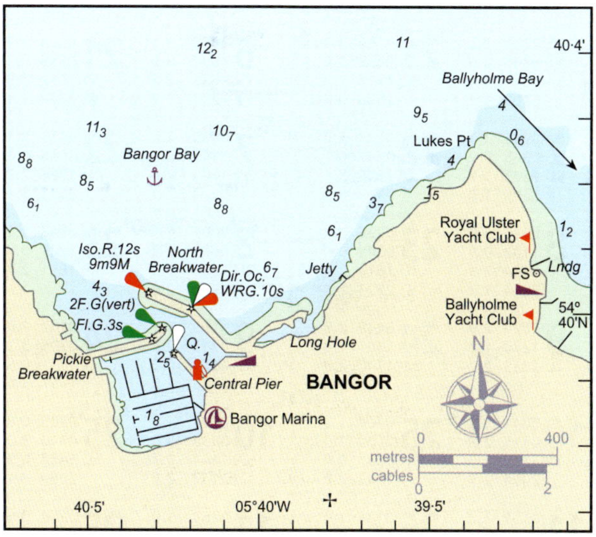

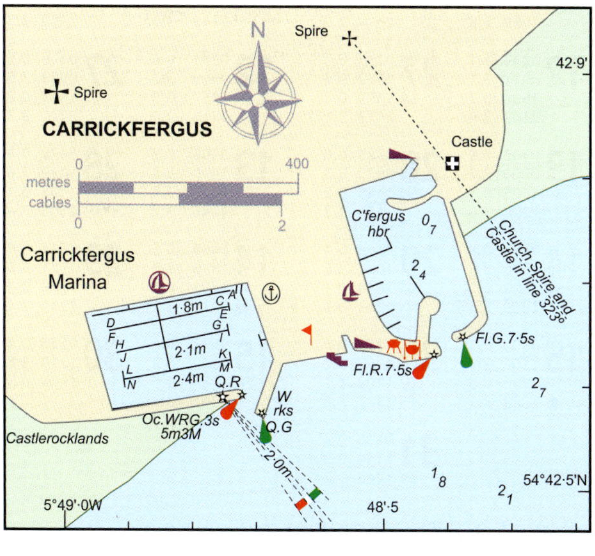

BELFAST River Manager ☎ 90328507, AB, P, D, FW, ME, El, ⚒, CH, C (200 ton), SM, Gas. **City** EC Wed; all facilities, ⇌, ✈. **Ferries:** Stranraer; 6/week; 2½ Hrs; Stena (www.stenaline.co.uk.). Liverpool; 2/day; 10 Hrs; Norfolk Line (www.norfolkline.com).

CARRICKFERGUS Marina (300 inc Ⓥ) ☎ 93366666, www.carrickfergus.org/site/marina; £2.15 (2nd night free), short stay £0.78 (min £5.88), Wi-fi, El, ⚒, Rigging, ME, Ⓔ. **Carrick SC** ☎ 351402, M, L, FW, C, AB. **Hbr**: 10 AB, D, BH (45 ton). **Town**: 🛒, R, Ⓑ, ✉, ⇌, ✈ (Belfast).

HARBOURS BETWEEN STRANGFORD AND BELFAST LOUGHS

PORTAVOGIE, Down, **54°27´·45N 05°26´·08W**. ✿✿✿✿✿. AC 2156, 5612. HW +0016 on Dover; ML 2·6m; Duration 0620. See 6.8. Good shelter, but hbr so full of FVs as to risk damage; best only for overnight or emergency. Entrance dangerous in strong onshore winds. Beware Plough Rks to SE marked by PHM buoy, Fl (2) R 10s, and McCammon Rks to NE of ent. Keep in W sector of outer bkwtr lt, Iso WRG 5s 9m 9M, shore-G-258°-W-275°-R-348°. Inner bkwtr 2 FG (vert) 6m 4M. VHF Ch 12 14 16 (Mon-Fri: 0900-1700LT). HM ☎ (028) 4277 1470. Facilities: Slip, FW (on central quay) ⚒, ME, El. **Town** CH, D & P (cans), ✉, R, Gas, 🛒.

DONAGHADEE, Down, **54°38´·71N 05°31´·85W**. ✿✿✿✿✿✿✿. AC 1753, 3709, 5612. HW +0025 on Dover; see 6.9; ML no data; Duration 0615. Excellent shelter and basic facilities in tiny marina, access HW±4 over sill; covers approx 1.1m at half tide. Appr on about 275° on ldg marks, orange △s to tricky ent with sharp 90° port turn into marina (pilots available). Appr in strong winds or at night not advised. 3ca to the N, the Old Hbr is small and very full; scend often sets in. Beware rocky reef with less than 2m extends 1·5ca ENE from S pier hd. Max depth in hbr is approx 2·5m, dries at SW end; best berth alongside SE quay. S pier lt, Iso WR 4s 17m 18/14M, W shore–326°, R326°–shore. HM ☎ (028) 9188 2377. Police 9188 2526. Facilities: **Copelands Marina** ☎ 9188 2184, mobile 07802 363382; VHF Ch **16** 11 80; AB for 6 Ⓥ, D, C (20 ton). **Old Hbr** AB £4. **Town** Bar, D, P, Gas, ✉, R, 🛒, Ⓑ, ⇌ (Bangor), ✈ (Belfast).

TIME ZONE (UT)
For Summer Time add ONE hour in **non-shaded areas**

BELFAST LAT 54°36′N LONG 5°55′W

TIMES AND HEIGHTS OF HIGH AND LOW WATERS

Dates in red are SPRINGS
Dates in blue are NEAPS

YEAR **2010**

JANUARY

Date	Day	Time	m	Time	m	Time	m	Time	m
1	F	0453	0.7	1106	3.7	1719	0.4	2334	3.5
2	SA	0539	0.7	1152	3.8	1805	0.3		
3	SU	0024	3.4	0625	0.7	1241	3.9	1851	0.3
4	M	0116	3.4	0713	0.7	1330	3.9	1940	0.3
5	TU	0209	3.3	0803	0.7	1422	3.8	2031	0.4
6	W	0304	3.2	0856	0.8	1514	3.8	2126	0.5
7	TH	0359	3.2	0952	0.9	1609	3.6	◑ 2225	0.7
8	F	0456	3.1	1055	1.0	1709	3.4	2330	0.8
9	SA	0558	3.0	1204	1.1	1816	3.3		
10	SU	0036	1.0	0706	3.0	1314	1.1	1931	3.2
11	M	0141	1.0	0812	3.1	1422	1.0	2038	3.2
12	TU	0240	1.1	0910	3.2	1524	0.9	2134	3.2
13	W	0332	1.0	1000	3.4	1614	0.8	2222	3.2
14	TH	0414	1.0	1043	3.5	1655	0.7	2303	3.2
15	F	0450	0.9	1121	3.5	1728	0.7	● 2340	3.2
16	SA	0523	0.9	1156	3.6	1758	0.7		
17	SU	0013	3.2	0555	0.8	1228	3.5	1828	0.7
18	M	0045	3.1	0629	0.8	1256	3.5	1900	0.7
19	TU	0116	3.1	0703	0.8	1325	3.5	1933	0.7
20	W	0150	3.1	0739	0.8	1356	3.5	2008	0.7
21	TH	0228	3.1	0818	0.8	1432	3.4	2047	0.7
22	F	0309	3.1	0900	0.9	1513	3.3	2131	0.8
23	SA	0356	3.1	0948	1.0	1601	3.2	◐ 2223	1.0
24	SU	0453	3.0	1044	1.2	1703	3.1	2326	1.1
25	M	0559	2.9	1154	1.2	1821	3.0		
26	TU	0054	1.1	0706	3.0	1329	1.2	1936	3.0
27	W	0211	1.0	0812	3.1	1440	0.9	2044	3.1
28	TH	0308	0.9	0911	3.3	1535	0.6	2143	3.2
29	F	0357	0.7	1002	3.5	1623	0.4	2233	3.3
30	SA	0442	0.6	1050	3.7	1708	0.2	○ 2321	3.4
31	SU	0526	0.5	1136	3.8	1751	0.1		

FEBRUARY

Date	Day	Time	m	Time	m	Time	m	Time	m
1	M	0008	3.4	0609	0.5	1224	3.9	1835	0.1
2	TU	0057	3.4	0654	0.5	1313	3.9	1919	0.2
3	W	0147	3.3	0739	0.5	1402	3.8	2005	0.3
4	TH	0235	3.3	0827	0.6	1452	3.7	2053	0.5
5	F	0324	3.2	0919	0.7	1542	3.6	◑ 2146	0.7
6	SA	0413	3.1	1019	0.8	1635	3.3	2249	0.9
7	SU	0508	3.0	1133	1.0	1737	3.1		
8	M	0003	1.1	0621	2.9	1248	1.1	1904	2.9
9	TU	0114	1.2	0748	2.9	1401	1.0	2024	2.9
10	W	0220	1.1	0852	3.1	1508	0.9	2121	3.0
11	TH	0316	1.0	0943	3.2	1600	0.7	2207	3.0
12	F	0358	0.9	1025	3.4	1637	0.6	2246	3.1
13	SA	0431	0.8	1103	3.4	1705	0.6	2321	3.1
14	SU	0501	0.7	1137	3.4	1732	0.5	● 2352	3.1
15	M	0532	0.7	1205	3.4	1801	0.5		
16	TU	0019	3.1	0604	0.6	1226	3.4	1831	0.5
17	W	0042	3.1	0636	0.6	1249	3.4	1902	0.5
18	TH	0111	3.2	0709	0.6	1321	3.4	1934	0.6
19	F	0146	3.2	0745	0.6	1358	3.4	2011	0.6
20	SA	0226	3.2	0825	0.7	1439	3.3	2053	0.7
21	SU	0310	3.1	0911	0.8	1527	3.2	2143	0.9
22	M	0404	3.0	1007	1.0	1630	3.0	◐ 2246	1.1
23	TU	0516	2.9	1118	1.1	1754	2.8		
24	W	0024	1.2	0634	2.9	1314	1.0	1916	2.8
25	TH	0156	1.0	0748	3.0	1426	0.8	2031	3.0
26	F	0254	0.8	0852	3.3	1520	0.5	2130	3.1
27	SA	0343	0.6	0944	3.5	1607	0.2	2218	3.3
28	SU	0427	0.5	1032	3.7	1651	0.1	○ 2303	3.3

MARCH

Date	Day	Time	m	Time	m	Time	m	Time	m
1	M	0509	0.4	1118	3.8	1732	0.0	2348	3.4
2	TU	0550	0.3	1204	3.8	1813	0.1		
3	W	0034	3.4	0631	0.3	1252	3.8	1854	0.2
4	TH	0120	3.3	0714	0.3	1340	3.7	1936	0.3
5	F	0205	3.3	0759	0.4	1427	3.6	2020	0.5
6	SA	0250	3.3	0848	0.6	1515	3.4	2108	0.7
7	SU	0336	3.1	0945	0.7	1605	3.1	◑ 2205	1.0
8	M	0426	3.0	1102	0.9	1704	2.9	2324	1.2
9	TU	0529	2.9	1220	1.0	1833	2.7		
10	W	0041	1.3	0715	2.8	1333	1.0	2004	2.7
11	TH	0150	1.2	0827	2.9	1440	0.8	2059	2.8
12	F	0249	1.1	0917	3.1	1530	0.7	2143	2.9
13	SA	0332	0.9	0959	3.2	1605	0.5	2220	3.0
14	SU	0404	0.8	1036	3.3	1633	0.5	2253	3.1
15	M	0435	0.7	1108	3.3	1701	0.5	● 2323	3.1
16	TU	0506	0.6	1134	3.3	1732	0.5	2346	3.1
17	W	0538	0.6	1150	3.3	1802	0.5		
18	TH	0008	3.2	0609	0.5	1217	3.4	1832	0.5
19	F	0039	3.2	0641	0.5	1252	3.4	1905	0.5
20	SA	0115	3.3	0718	0.5	1332	3.3	1942	0.6
21	SU	0156	3.3	0759	0.6	1416	3.2	2026	0.8
22	M	0241	3.2	0847	0.7	1508	3.1	2118	0.9
23	TU	0336	3.0	0945	0.9	1617	2.9	◐ 2223	1.1
24	W	0448	2.9	1101	1.0	1740	2.8		
25	TH	0004	1.2	0609	2.9	1256	0.9	1903	2.8
26	F	0134	1.0	0727	3.0	1405	0.6	2018	2.9
27	SA	0233	0.8	0832	3.3	1459	0.3	2113	3.1
28	SU	0323	0.6	0925	3.5	1545	0.2	2159	3.2
29	M	0408	0.4	1012	3.6	1628	0.1	2243	3.3
30	TU	0450	0.3	1058	3.7	1708	0.1	○ 2327	3.4
31	W	0530	0.3	1144	3.7	1748	0.2		

APRIL

Date	Day	Time	m	Time	m	Time	m	Time	m
1	TH	0010	3.4	0611	0.3	1231	3.7	1828	0.3
2	F	0054	3.4	0653	0.3	1317	3.6	1909	0.5
3	SA	0137	3.4	0736	0.4	1403	3.4	1951	0.6
4	SU	0220	3.3	0823	0.5	1450	3.2	2037	0.8
5	M	0304	3.2	0919	0.7	1539	3.0	2130	1.1
6	TU	0353	3.1	1032	0.9	1635	2.8	◑ 2241	1.2
7	W	0450	2.9	1147	0.9	1745	2.6		
8	TH	0001	1.3	0603	2.8	1254	0.9	1926	2.6
9	F	0108	1.2	0743	2.9	1355	0.8	2023	2.8
10	SA	0206	1.1	0839	3.0	1444	0.7	2107	2.9
11	SU	0253	1.0	0922	3.1	1523	0.6	2143	3.0
12	M	0331	0.8	0959	3.2	1557	0.5	2216	3.1
13	TU	0406	0.7	1030	3.2	1629	0.5	2246	3.2
14	W	0439	0.6	1056	3.3	1701	0.5	● 2313	3.2
15	TH	0512	0.6	1120	3.3	1733	0.5	2341	3.3
16	F	0545	0.5	1151	3.3	1807	0.6		
17	SA	0015	3.4	0620	0.5	1231	3.3	1843	0.6
18	SU	0055	3.4	0659	0.5	1315	3.3	1924	0.7
19	M	0138	3.4	0743	0.5	1405	3.2	2011	0.8
20	TU	0227	3.3	0834	0.6	1503	3.0	2107	1.0
21	W	0324	3.2	0936	0.7	1612	2.9	◐ 2214	1.1
22	TH	0431	3.1	1056	0.8	1731	2.8	2341	1.1
23	F	0548	3.1	1229	0.7	1851	2.8		
24	SA	0102	1.0	0705	3.2	1337	0.5	1957	3.0
25	SU	0205	0.8	0810	3.3	1432	0.3	2050	3.1
26	M	0258	0.6	0904	3.5	1520	0.2	2138	3.3
27	TU	0346	0.5	0953	3.6	1603	0.2	2222	3.3
28	W	0430	0.4	1039	3.6	1645	0.3	○ 2306	3.4
29	TH	0513	0.4	1125	3.6	1726	0.4	2349	3.4
30	F	0556	0.4	1210	3.5	1806	0.5		

Chart Datum: 2·01 metres below Ordnance Datum (Belfast). HAT is 3·8 metres above Chart Datum; see 0.20

TIME ZONE (UT)
For Summer Time add ONE hour in **non-shaded areas**

BELFAST LAT 54°36'N LONG 5°55'W

TIMES AND HEIGHTS OF HIGH AND LOW WATERS

Dates in red are SPRINGS
Dates in blue are NEAPS

YEAR **2010**

MAY

Date	Day	Time	m	Time	m	Time	m	Time	m
1	SA	0030	3.4	0638	0.4	1255	3.4	1847	0.7
2	SU	0112	3.4	0720	0.5	1340	3.3	1928	0.8
3	M	0154	3.4	0805	0.6	1425	3.1	2012	0.9
4	TU	0237	3.3	0856	0.7	1513	3.0	2101	1.1
5	W	0324	3.2	0957	0.8	1606	2.8	2157	1.2
6	TH	0416	3.1	1105	0.9	1704	2.7	◑ 2307	1.2
7	F	0515	2.9	1209	0.9	1809	2.7		
8	SA	0016	1.2	0621	2.9	1307	0.8	1915	2.8
9	SU	0116	1.2	0730	2.9	1357	0.8	2008	2.9
10	M	0208	1.1	0826	3.0	1440	0.7	2052	3.0
11	TU	0253	0.9	0910	3.1	1520	0.6	2132	3.2
12	W	0333	0.8	0948	3.2	1556	0.6	2209	3.3
13	TH	0411	0.7	1023	3.3	1632	0.6	2244	3.3
14	F	0448	0.6	1057	3.3	1709	0.6	● 2320	3.4
15	SA	0527	0.5	1135	3.3	1747	0.6	2358	3.5
16	SU	0607	0.5	1218	3.3	1829	0.7		
17	M	0041	3.5	0650	0.4	1306	3.3	1914	0.7
18	TU	0128	3.5	0737	0.4	1359	3.2	2005	0.8
19	W	0218	3.5	0831	0.5	1459	3.1	2102	0.9
20	TH	0313	3.4	0932	0.5	1606	3.0	◐ 2206	1.0
21	F	0415	3.3	1043	0.6	1718	2.9	2316	1.0
22	SA	0525	3.3	1158	0.6	1828	2.9		
23	SU	0026	0.9	0639	3.3	1305	0.5	1930	3.0
24	M	0132	0.8	0745	3.3	1402	0.5	2025	3.1
25	TU	0231	0.7	0843	3.4	1454	0.5	2116	3.2
26	W	0325	0.6	0935	3.5	1541	0.5	2203	3.3
27	TH	0415	0.6	1024	3.5	1626	0.5	○ 2248	3.4
28	F	0501	0.5	1109	3.4	1708	0.6	2331	3.4
29	SA	0544	0.5	1153	3.3	1749	0.7		
30	SU	0011	3.5	0626	0.5	1235	3.3	1828	0.8
31	M	0051	3.5	0706	0.5	1317	3.2	1907	0.9

JUNE

Date	Day	Time	m	Time	m	Time	m	Time	m
1	TU	0131	3.5	0745	0.6	1400	3.1	1947	0.9
2	W	0212	3.4	0826	0.7	1446	3.0	2030	1.0
3	TH	0256	3.3	0912	0.7	1535	2.9	2117	1.0
4	F	0342	3.2	1004	0.8	1627	2.9	◑ 2208	1.1
5	SA	0433	3.1	1105	0.9	1720	2.9	2305	1.2
6	SU	0528	3.0	1208	0.9	1815	2.9		
7	M	0009	1.2	0626	3.0	1306	0.9	1909	3.0
8	TU	0113	1.1	0725	3.0	1357	0.8	2001	3.0
9	W	0210	1.0	0821	3.1	1443	0.8	2050	3.2
10	TH	0301	0.9	0911	3.2	1527	0.7	2136	3.3
11	F	0347	0.8	0957	3.2	1609	0.7	2219	3.4
12	SA	0430	0.6	1040	3.3	1650	0.6	● 2301	3.5
13	SU	0513	0.5	1123	3.3	1733	0.6	2344	3.6
14	M	0557	0.4	1208	3.3	1818	0.7		
15	TU	0028	3.6	0642	0.3	1258	3.3	1905	0.7
16	W	0117	3.7	0730	0.3	1351	3.2	1956	0.7
17	TH	0207	3.6	0821	0.3	1449	3.1	2050	0.8
18	F	0300	3.6	0918	0.4	1551	3.1	2147	0.8
19	SA	0357	3.5	1019	0.5	1654	3.0	◐ 2249	0.8
20	SU	0459	3.4	1126	0.6	1757	3.0	2354	0.9
21	M	0608	3.3	1232	0.6	1900	3.0		
22	TU	0102	0.9	0719	3.3	1335	0.7	2000	3.1
23	W	0208	0.8	0824	3.3	1432	0.7	2056	3.2
24	TH	0309	0.7	0921	3.3	1524	0.7	2148	3.3
25	F	0404	0.7	1012	3.3	1611	0.7	2235	3.4
26	SA	0451	0.6	1057	3.3	1653	0.8	○ 2317	3.4
27	SU	0533	0.5	1139	3.2	1732	0.8	2355	3.5
28	M	0611	0.5	1217	3.1	1808	0.8		
29	TU	0032	3.5	0645	0.6	1254	3.1	1843	0.8
30	W	0108	3.5	0718	0.6	1333	3.1	1919	0.9

JULY

Date	Day	Time	m	Time	m	Time	m	Time	m
1	TH	0145	3.4	0752	0.6	1415	3.0	1957	0.9
2	F	0223	3.4	0829	0.7	1459	3.0	2039	0.9
3	SA	0303	3.3	0910	0.7	1546	3.0	2123	1.0
4	SU	0345	3.2	0956	0.8	1635	3.0	◑ 2212	1.0
5	M	0433	3.1	1051	0.9	1727	3.0	2307	1.1
6	TU	0531	3.0	1157	1.0	1822	3.0		
7	W	0013	1.2	0635	2.9	1312	1.0	1918	3.0
8	TH	0130	1.1	0740	3.0	1413	0.9	2014	3.1
9	F	0235	1.0	0841	3.1	1505	0.8	2107	3.3
10	SA	0329	0.8	0935	3.2	1551	0.7	2155	3.4
11	SU	0416	0.5	1023	3.3	1635	0.6	● 2241	3.6
12	M	0501	0.4	1109	3.3	1719	0.6	2326	3.7
13	TU	0544	0.2	1155	3.3	1803	0.6		
14	W	0012	3.7	0628	0.2	1244	3.3	1849	0.6
15	TH	0101	3.8	0714	0.2	1335	3.3	1937	0.6
16	F	0151	3.8	0802	0.2	1430	3.2	2027	0.6
17	SA	0242	3.7	0853	0.3	1524	3.2	2120	0.7
18	SU	0335	3.6	0949	0.5	1620	3.1	◐ 2219	0.8
19	M	0432	3.4	1052	0.7	1719	3.0	2326	0.9
20	TU	0536	3.2	1202	0.8	1826	3.0		
21	W	0038	0.9	0653	3.1	1311	0.9	1937	3.0
22	TH	0151	0.9	0809	3.0	1415	0.9	2040	3.1
23	F	0259	0.8	0910	3.1	1511	0.9	2134	3.3
24	SA	0356	0.7	1001	3.1	1558	0.9	2221	3.4
25	SU	0442	0.6	1045	3.1	1637	0.8	2302	3.4
26	M	0519	0.5	1123	3.1	1711	0.8	○ 2339	3.4
27	TU	0549	0.5	1158	3.1	1743	0.8		
28	W	0012	3.4	0617	0.6	1230	3.1	1815	0.8
29	TH	0042	3.4	0646	0.6	1302	3.1	1848	0.8
30	F	0112	3.4	0717	0.6	1337	3.1	1923	0.8
31	SA	0143	3.4	0750	0.6	1416	3.1	2001	0.8

AUGUST

Date	Day	Time	m	Time	m	Time	m	Time	m
1	SU	0217	3.3	0826	0.7	1457	3.1	2043	0.8
2	M	0255	3.3	0908	0.8	1543	3.1	2128	0.9
3	TU	0339	3.1	0956	0.9	1635	3.0	◑ 2220	1.1
4	W	0437	3.0	1055	1.0	1736	2.9	2324	1.2
5	TH	0553	2.9	1221	1.1	1839	3.0		
6	F	0056	1.1	0708	2.9	1350	1.0	1942	3.1
7	SA	0217	0.9	0817	3.0	1447	0.9	2041	3.2
8	SU	0313	0.7	0916	3.1	1535	0.7	2133	3.4
9	M	0401	0.4	1006	3.3	1619	0.6	2220	3.6
10	TU	0444	0.2	1051	3.3	1701	0.5	● 2306	3.7
11	W	0526	0.1	1137	3.4	1743	0.5	2353	3.8
12	TH	0608	0.1	1224	3.4	1827	0.4		
13	F	0041	3.8	0650	0.1	1313	3.3	1912	0.5
14	SA	0131	3.8	0735	0.2	1404	3.3	1959	0.5
15	SU	0221	3.7	0822	0.4	1454	3.3	2050	0.6
16	M	0312	3.6	0913	0.6	1545	3.2	◐ 2148	0.8
17	TU	0406	3.3	1013	0.8	1641	3.1	2300	0.9
18	W	0507	3.1	1130	1.1	1748	3.0		
19	TH	0018	1.0	0628	2.9	1247	1.2	1913	3.0
20	F	0134	1.0	0756	2.9	1357	1.1	2023	3.1
21	SA	0247	0.8	0858	2.9	1457	1.0	2117	3.2
22	SU	0344	0.7	0946	3.0	1543	0.9	2202	3.4
23	M	0426	0.6	1026	3.1	1617	0.9	2241	3.4
24	TU	0456	0.5	1102	3.1	1646	0.8	○ 2316	3.4
25	W	0520	0.6	1134	3.1	1715	0.8	2347	3.4
26	TH	0546	0.6	1202	3.1	1746	0.7		
27	F	0010	3.4	0614	0.6	1227	3.2	1817	0.7
28	SA	0033	3.4	0643	0.6	1256	3.2	1850	0.7
29	SU	0103	3.4	0714	0.6	1331	3.2	1926	0.7
30	M	0138	3.4	0748	0.7	1410	3.2	2006	0.8
31	TU	0217	3.3	0829	0.8	1453	3.2	2051	0.9

Chart Datum: 2·01 metres below Ordnance Datum (Belfast). HAT is 3·8 metres above Chart Datum; see 0.20

TIME ZONE (UT)
For Summer Time add ONE hour in **non-shaded areas**

BELFAST LAT 54°36′N LONG 5°55′W

TIMES AND HEIGHTS OF HIGH AND LOW WATERS

Dates in red are SPRINGS
Dates in blue are NEAPS

YEAR **2010**

SEPTEMBER

Date	Day	Time	m	Time	m	Time	m	Time	m
1	W	0302	3.2	0917	0.9	1546	3.1	◑ 2144	1.0
2	TH	0400	3.0	1015	1.1	1654	3.0	2249	1.1
3	F	0523	2.8	1134	1.2	1806	3.0		
4	SA	0029	1.1	0643	2.8	1328	1.2	1915	3.1
5	SU	0157	0.9	0758	2.9	1427	0.9	2018	3.3
6	M	0253	0.6	0859	3.1	1516	0.7	2112	3.5
7	TU	0341	0.3	0948	3.3	1559	0.6	2159	3.7
8	W	0423	0.2	1032	3.4	1640	0.5	● 2245	3.8
9	TH	0503	0.1	1116	3.4	1720	0.4	2332	3.9
10	F	0543	0.1	1202	3.5	1802	0.4		
11	SA	0021	3.8	0624	0.2	1249	3.4	1846	0.4
12	SU	0110	3.8	0707	0.3	1337	3.4	1932	0.5
13	M	0200	3.7	0752	0.5	1425	3.4	2022	0.6
14	TU	0250	3.5	0840	0.8	1514	3.3	2120	0.8
15	W	0342	3.2	0936	1.0	1606	3.2	◐ 2234	0.9
16	TH	0440	3.0	1054	1.2	1709	3.0	2354	1.0
17	F	0602	2.8	1217	1.3	1841	3.0		
18	SA	0109	1.0	0737	2.8	1329	1.3	1958	3.1
19	SU	0221	0.9	0836	2.9	1431	1.2	2052	3.2
20	M	0317	0.7	0922	3.0	1517	1.0	2136	3.3
21	TU	0355	0.7	1000	3.1	1549	0.9	2214	3.4
22	W	0421	0.6	1034	3.2	1618	0.8	2248	3.4
23	TH	0446	0.6	1105	3.2	1648	0.8	○ 2316	3.4
24	F	0514	0.6	1131	3.3	1718	0.7	2335	3.4
25	SA	0543	0.7	1154	3.3	1750	0.7	2357	3.4
26	SU	0612	0.7	1222	3.4	1822	0.7		
27	M	0030	3.4	0643	0.7	1258	3.4	1857	0.7
28	TU	0109	3.4	0718	0.8	1337	3.4	1938	0.8
29	W	0152	3.3	0800	0.9	1422	3.3	2024	0.9
30	TH	0240	3.2	0849	1.0	1514	3.2	2119	1.0

OCTOBER

Date	Day	Time	m	Time	m	Time	m	Time	m
1	F	0343	3.0	0950	1.2	1621	3.1	◑ 2227	1.1
2	SA	0504	2.8	1109	1.3	1737	3.1		
3	SU	0004	1.0	0624	2.9	1259	1.2	1850	3.2
4	M	0131	0.8	0740	3.0	1402	1.0	1956	3.4
5	TU	0227	0.6	0839	3.2	1452	0.8	2051	3.6
6	W	0314	0.4	0928	3.4	1536	0.6	2140	3.7
7	TH	0357	0.3	1012	3.5	1618	0.5	● 2227	3.8
8	F	0437	0.2	1056	3.5	1659	0.5	2314	3.9
9	SA	0518	0.3	1140	3.6	1741	0.5		
10	SU	0001	3.8	0559	0.4	1226	3.6	1825	0.5
11	M	0050	3.7	0642	0.6	1312	3.6	1911	0.6
12	TU	0139	3.6	0726	0.8	1358	3.5	2001	0.7
13	W	0228	3.4	0814	1.0	1445	3.4	2057	0.8
14	TH	0319	3.2	0907	1.2	1536	3.3	◐ 2208	1.0
15	F	0415	3.0	1015	1.4	1633	3.1	2323	1.1
16	SA	0524	2.8	1137	1.4	1745	3.0		
17	SU	0031	1.1	0658	2.8	1247	1.4	1914	3.1
18	M	0135	1.0	0800	2.9	1347	1.3	2015	3.2
19	TU	0228	0.9	0847	3.0	1436	1.2	2101	3.3
20	W	0309	0.8	0925	3.2	1514	1.0	2140	3.3
21	TH	0341	0.7	1000	3.3	1548	0.9	2215	3.4
22	F	0412	0.7	1032	3.4	1620	0.9	2244	3.4
23	SA	0443	0.7	1101	3.4	1653	0.8	○ 2308	3.4
24	SU	0515	0.8	1128	3.5	1727	0.8	2334	3.4
25	M	0547	0.8	1159	3.5	1801	0.7		
26	TU	0009	3.4	0621	0.8	1236	3.6	1838	0.7
27	W	0051	3.4	0659	0.9	1318	3.5	1920	0.8
28	TH	0138	3.3	0743	1.0	1404	3.5	2009	0.8
29	F	0230	3.2	0835	1.1	1457	3.4	2105	0.9
30	SA	0333	3.1	0936	1.2	1559	3.3	◑ 2213	1.0
31	SU	0447	3.0	1052	1.3	1710	3.2	2336	0.9

NOVEMBER

Date	Day	Time	m	Time	m	Time	m	Time	m
1	M	0606	3.0	1218	1.2	1825	3.3		
2	TU	0054	0.8	0717	3.1	1327	1.1	1932	3.4
3	W	0154	0.6	0816	3.2	1423	0.9	2030	3.6
4	TH	0245	0.5	0907	3.4	1512	0.7	2122	3.7
5	F	0331	0.5	0953	3.5	1559	0.6	2211	3.8
6	SA	0415	0.5	1038	3.6	1643	0.6	● 2258	3.8
7	SU	0458	0.6	1122	3.7	1728	0.6	2345	3.7
8	M	0540	0.7	1207	3.7	1813	0.6		
9	TU	0032	3.6	0622	0.8	1251	3.7	1858	0.6
10	W	0119	3.5	0706	0.9	1335	3.6	1945	0.7
11	TH	0206	3.3	0751	1.1	1420	3.6	2036	0.8
12	F	0255	3.2	0840	1.2	1508	3.4	2135	0.9
13	SA	0347	3.0	0936	1.3	1600	3.3	◐ 2240	1.0
14	SU	0443	2.9	1042	1.4	1657	3.2	2344	1.1
15	M	0546	2.9	1152	1.4	1802	3.1		
16	TU	0043	1.1	0653	2.9	1255	1.4	1910	3.1
17	W	0136	1.0	0751	3.0	1349	1.3	2010	3.2
18	TH	0222	1.0	0838	3.2	1436	1.2	2057	3.3
19	F	0303	0.9	0920	3.3	1517	1.0	2138	3.3
20	SA	0340	0.9	0959	3.4	1555	0.9	2215	3.4
21	SU	0416	0.8	1035	3.5	1633	0.9	○ 2248	3.4
22	M	0452	0.8	1109	3.6	1710	0.8	2320	3.4
23	TU	0529	0.8	1143	3.7	1749	0.7	2358	3.4
24	W	0608	0.9	1221	3.7	1829	0.7		
25	TH	0040	3.4	0649	0.9	1304	3.7	1913	0.7
26	F	0128	3.3	0736	1.0	1351	3.7	2001	0.7
27	SA	0221	3.2	0827	1.0	1442	3.6	2056	0.7
28	SU	0320	3.1	0925	1.1	1539	3.5	◑ 2159	0.8
29	M	0428	3.1	1031	1.2	1644	3.4	2308	0.8
30	TU	0541	3.1	1142	1.2	1755	3.4		

DECEMBER

Date	Day	Time	m	Time	m	Time	m	Time	m
1	W	0018	0.8	0650	3.1	1252	1.1	1906	3.5
2	TH	0122	0.7	0751	3.2	1355	1.0	2010	3.5
3	F	0219	0.7	0847	3.4	1452	0.9	2106	3.6
4	SA	0311	0.7	0937	3.5	1545	0.7	2159	3.6
5	SU	0359	0.7	1025	3.6	1634	0.7	● 2247	3.6
6	M	0444	0.8	1110	3.7	1720	0.6	2333	3.5
7	TU	0527	0.8	1153	3.7	1805	0.6		
8	W	0018	3.5	0608	0.9	1235	3.7	1847	0.6
9	TH	0101	3.4	0649	1.0	1316	3.7	1928	0.7
10	F	0144	3.3	0729	1.0	1358	3.6	2010	0.8
11	SA	0229	3.2	0811	1.1	1441	3.5	2053	0.9
12	SU	0316	3.1	0856	1.2	1527	3.4	2142	0.9
13	M	0405	3.0	0945	1.2	1616	3.3	◐ 2237	1.0
14	TU	0457	3.0	1041	1.3	1710	3.2	2340	1.1
15	W	0552	3.0	1146	1.4	1807	3.1		
16	TH	0041	1.1	0648	3.0	1255	1.3	1907	3.1
17	F	0137	1.1	0746	3.1	1355	1.3	2008	3.1
18	SA	0227	1.0	0840	3.3	1448	1.1	2103	3.2
19	SU	0313	0.9	0928	3.4	1534	1.0	2149	3.3
20	M	0355	0.9	1011	3.5	1617	0.8	2230	3.4
21	TU	0436	0.8	1050	3.6	1658	0.7	○ 2309	3.4
22	W	0516	0.8	1128	3.7	1738	0.6	2348	3.4
23	TH	0557	0.8	1207	3.8	1820	0.5		
24	F	0030	3.4	0640	0.8	1251	3.8	1904	0.5
25	SA	0117	3.3	0725	0.8	1337	3.8	1951	0.5
26	SU	0208	3.3	0814	0.8	1427	3.7	2041	0.5
27	M	0303	3.2	0907	0.9	1520	3.7	2137	0.6
28	TU	0402	3.2	1005	1.0	1619	3.6	◑ 2238	0.7
29	W	0507	3.1	1110	1.0	1724	3.4	2346	0.8
30	TH	0616	3.1	1222	1.1	1838	3.4		
31	F	0054	0.9	0726	3.1	1333	1.0	1951	3.3

Chart Datum: 2·01 metres below Ordnance Datum (Belfast). HAT is 3·8 metres above Chart Datum; see 0.20

6.10 LARNE

Antrim **54°51'·20N 05°47'·50W** ✵✵✵◊◊✿✿

CHARTS AC 2198, 1237, 5612; Imray C62, C64.

TIDES +0005 Dover; ML 1·6; Duration 0620

Standard Port BELFAST (⟵)

Times				Height (metres)			
High Water		Low Water		MHWS	MHWN	MLWN	MLWS
0100	0700	0000	0600	3·5	3·0	1·1	0·4
1300	1900	1200	1800				
Differences LARNE							
+0005	0000	+0010	−0005	−0·7	−0·5	−0·3	0·0
RED BAY							
+0022	−0010	+0007	−0017	−1·9	−1·5	−0·8	−0·2
CUSHENDUN BAY							
+0010	−0030	0000	−0025	−1·7	−1·5	−0·6	−0·2

SHELTER Secure shelter in Larne Lough or ⚓ overnight outside hbr in Brown's Bay (E of Barr Pt) in 2-4m. Hbr can be entered H24 in any conditions. Larne is a busy commercial and ferry port; W side is commercial until Curran Pt where there are two YCs with congested moorings. ⚓ S of Ballylumford Power Stn. No AB available for visitors. Yachts should not berth on any commercial quays, inc Castle Quay, without HM's permission. Boat Hbr (0·6m) 2ca S of Ferris Pt only for shoal draft craft.

NAVIGATION WPT 54°51'·70N 05°47'·47W, 184°/2·1M to front ldg lt. Beware Hunter Rk 2M NE of hbr ent. Magnetic anomalies exist near Hunter Rk and between it and the mainland. Inside the narrow ent, the recommended chan is close to the E shore. Tide in the ent runs at up to 3½kn.

LIGHTS AND MARKS No1 SHM Q G 1½ca off chartlet N edge; Ldg lts 184°, Oc 4s 6/14m 12M, synch and vis 179°-189°; W ◊ with R stripes. Chaine Tr and fairway lts as chartlet. Note: Many shore lts on W side of ent may be mistaken for nav lts.

R/T VHF Ch **14** 11 16 *Larne Port Control*. Traffic, weather and tidal info available on Ch 14.

TELEPHONE (Code 02828) HM 872100; MRCC 9146 3933; Pilot 273785; Marinecall 09068 969655; Dr 275331; Police 272266.

FACILITIES **Pier** ☎ 27 9221, M, L, FW, C (33 ton); **E Antrim Boat Club** ☎ 277204, Visitors should pre-contact Sec'y for advice on moorings; Slip, L, 🛒, FW, Bar; **Services:** D, Gas, ⚒, El. **Town** P & D (delivered, tidal), CH, 🛒, R, Bar, ✉, Ⓑ, ⇌, **Ferries:** Cairnryan; 8/day; 1¾ Hrs; P&O (www.poferries.co.uk). Fleetwood; 20/week; 9 Hrs; Stena (www.srenaline.co.uk). Troon; 17/week; 1¾ Hrs; P&O. ✈ (Belfast City and Belfast/Aldergrove).

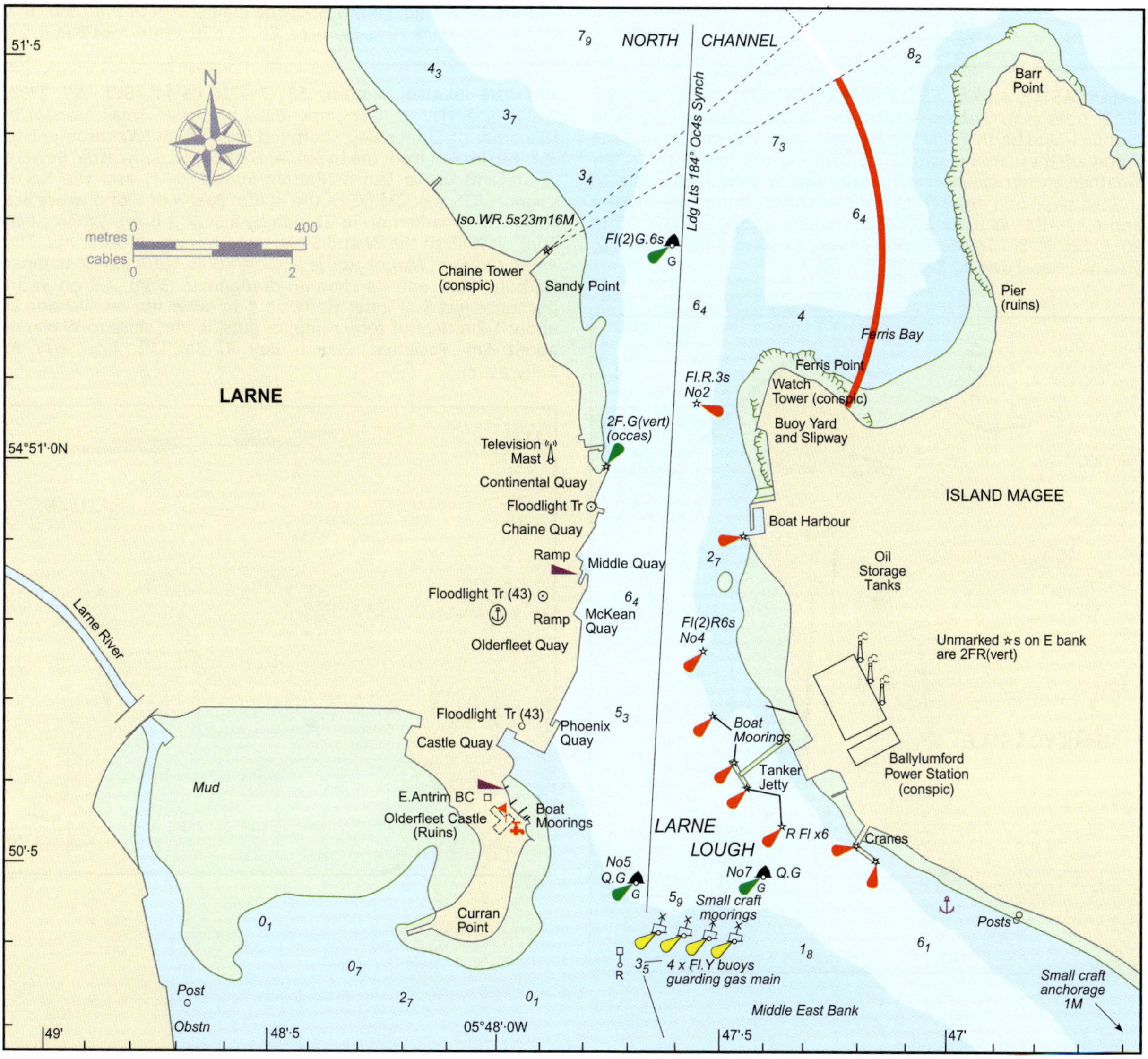

HARBOURS & ANCHORAGES BETWEEN LARNE & PORTRUSH

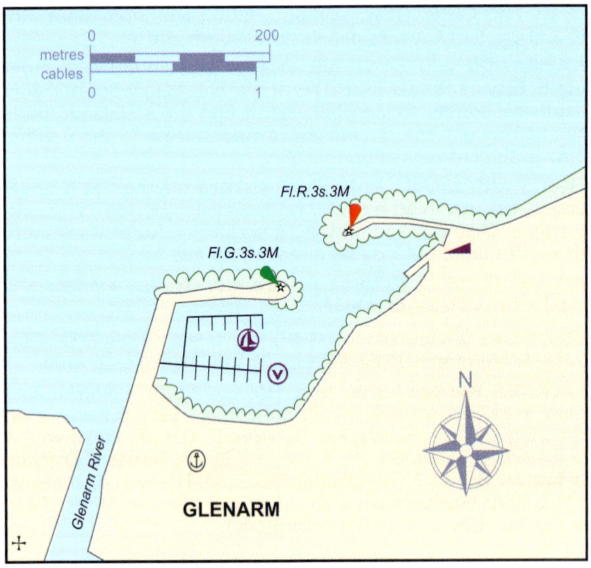

GLENARM, Antrim, **54°58′N 05°57′W**. AC 2198, 2199, 5612. HW +0006 on Dover, +0005 on Belfast; HW –1·6m on Belfast; ML no data; Duration 0625. Good shelter in marina. Hbr ent lts Q.G.3s3M and Q.R.3s3M. HM and Marina ☎ 028 2884 1285, Mob 07703 606763. **Marina** 40 AB inc Ⓥ in 4-6m, £1.00, FW, D, ⊣D⟩. **Village** 🛒, P (cans).

CARNLOUGH HARBOUR, Antrim, **54°59′·87N 05°59′·20W**. AC 2198, 5612. HW +0006 on Dover, +0005 on Belfast; HW –1·6m on Belfast; ML no data; Duration 0625. Good shelter, except in SE gales; do not enter in fresh/strong onshore winds. Entrance shoaling due to build up of kelp, minimum depth 1m (2004). Ldg marks 310°, Y ▽s on B/W posts. N pier lt, Fl G 3s 4m 5M; S pier Fl R 3s 6m 5M, both lts on B/W columns. Beware fish farms in the bay marked by lt buoys (unreliable); and rks which cover at HW on either side of ent. Small harbour used by yachts and small FVs; visitors welcome. HM ☎ (Mobile) 07703 606763. Facilities: **Quay** AB £1, AC (see HM), D (by arrangement), FW, Slip. **Town** P (cans), Gas, Gaz, ✉, R, 🛒, Bar, ♿.

RED BAY, Antrim, **55°03′·91N 06°03′·13W**. AC 2199, 5612. HW +0010 on Dover; ML 1·1m; Duration 0625. See 6.10. Good holding, but open to E winds. Beware rks, 2 ruined piers W of Garron Pt and fish farms, marked by lt buoys, on S side of bay, approx ½M from shore. Glenariff pier has lt Fl 3s 10m 5M. In S and E winds ⚓ 2ca off W stone arch near hd of bay in approx 3·5m; in N or W winds ⚓ S of small pier in 2–5m, ½M NE of Waterfoot village. **Facilities: Cushendall** (1M N of pier) Bar, D & P (cans), ✉, R, 🛒, Gas. **Services:** CH, El, Slip. **Waterfoot** Bar, R, ✉.

BALLYCASTLE, Antrim, **55°12′·47N 06°14′·27W**. AC 2798, 2494, 5612. Tides as for Rathlin Is; ML 0·8m; –0320 on Dover. Ferries to Rathlin Island berth inside the N breakwater. The marina is in the S part of the harbour with 2·3m. Outside the harbour is a fair weather anchorage clear of strong tidal streams, but liable to sudden swell and exposed to onshore winds. Lights: see chartlet and 6.3. HM ☎ (028) 20768525, mobile 07803 505084; CG ☎ 20762226; Ⓗ 20762666. **Marina** 74 AB , £2·00 <9·14m. El, Slip, D, P (cans), Gas. **Town** R, Bar, 🛒, ✉, Ⓑ, ♿.

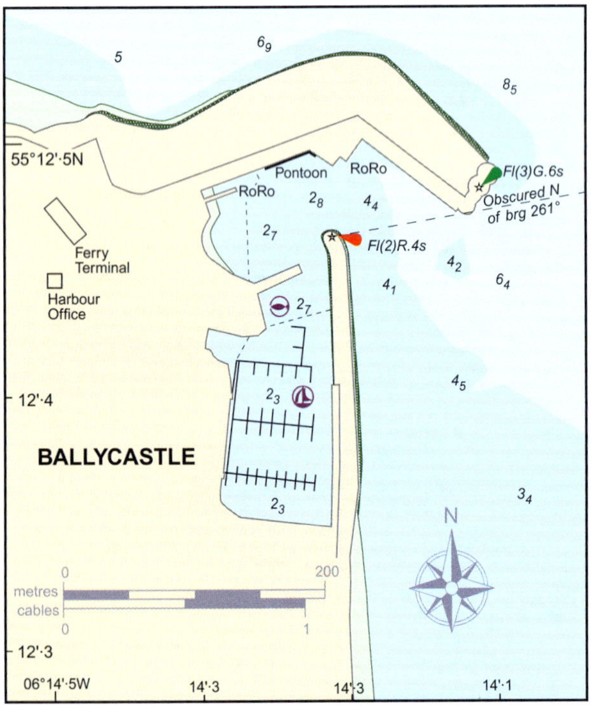

RATHLIN ISLAND, Antrim, **55°17′·47N 06°11′·78W**. AC 2798, 2494, 5612. HW sp –0445, nps –0200 on Dover. Small harbour in NE corner of Church Bay, sheltered from winds NW through E to SSE. Ferries run from the the Inner Harbour to Ballycastle. Beware sp streams up to 6kn in Rathlin Sound (6.11) and the North Channel TSS, just 2M NE of the island. Pass N or E of a wreck 6ca SW of hbr, marked on its SE side by a SCM lt buoy. When clear, appr on NNE to the W and S piers which form an outer hbr. The white sector of Manor House lt, Oc WRG 4s, leads 024·5° to Inner Harbour (2m) ent via channel dredged to 3·5m. AB on yacht pontoons just S of Inner Harbour. ⚓ in outer hbr on NW side in about 1.2m clear of ferry ramp; or outside hbr, close to W pier in about 5m. **Facilities**: Church Bay R, Bar, 🛒, ✉, ferry to Ballycastle.

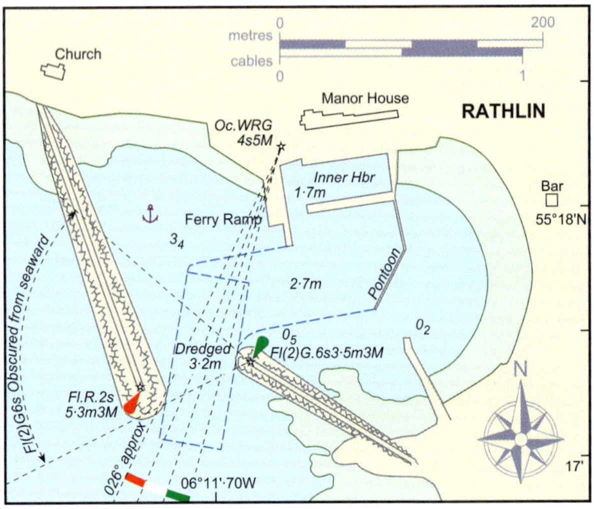

6.11 TIDAL STREAMS AROUND RATHLIN ISLAND

North Ireland 6.2
North Irish Sea 3.2
Off Mull of Kintyre 2.9
SW Scotland 2.2
South Ireland 5.2

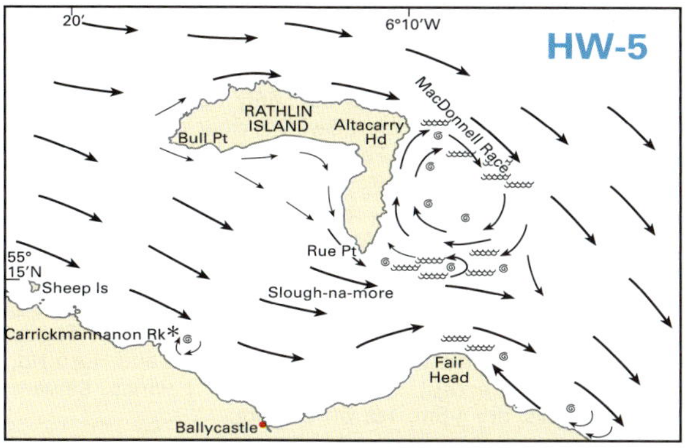

5 Hours before HW Dover (0605 after HW Greenock)

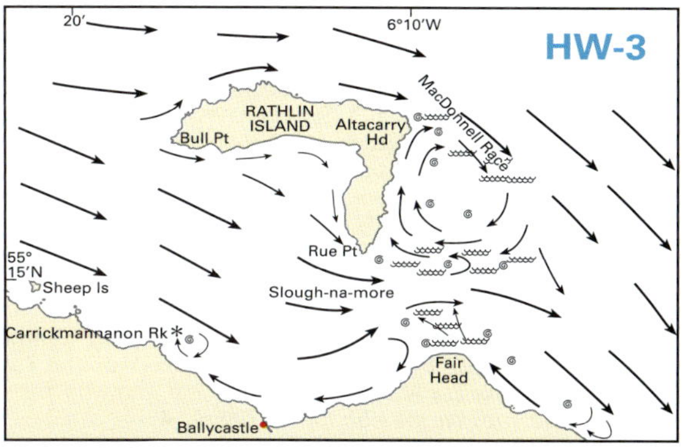

3 Hours before HW Dover (0420 before HW Greenock)

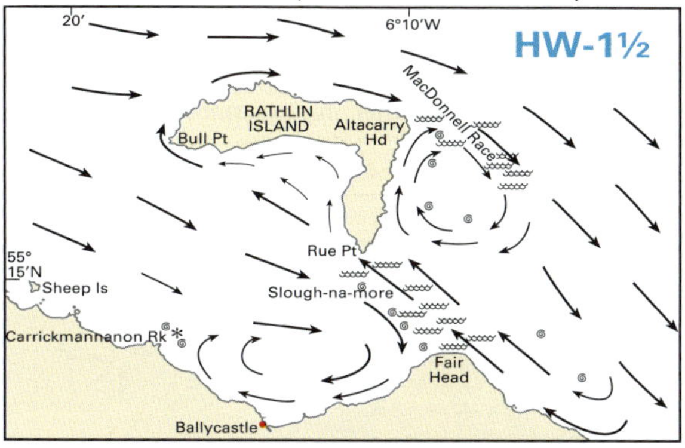

1½ Hours before HW Dover (0250 before HW Greenock)

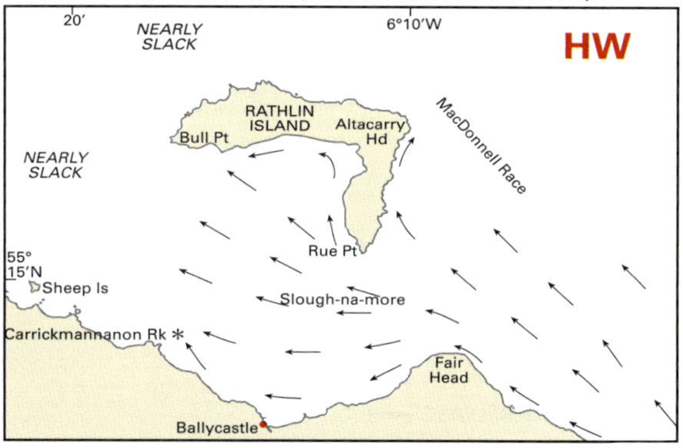

HW Dover (0120 before HW Greenock)

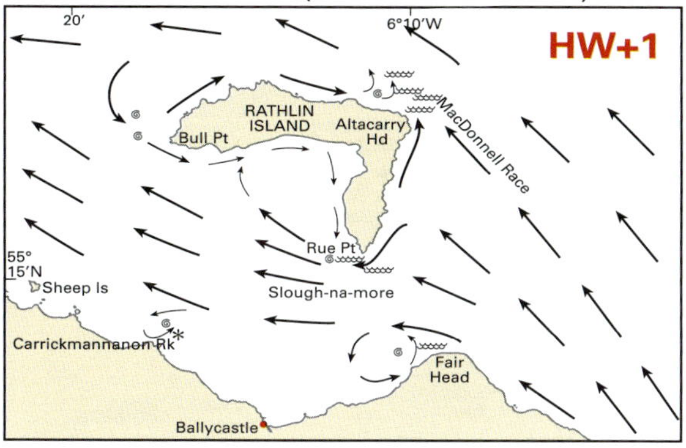

1 Hour after HW Dover (0020 before HW Greenock)

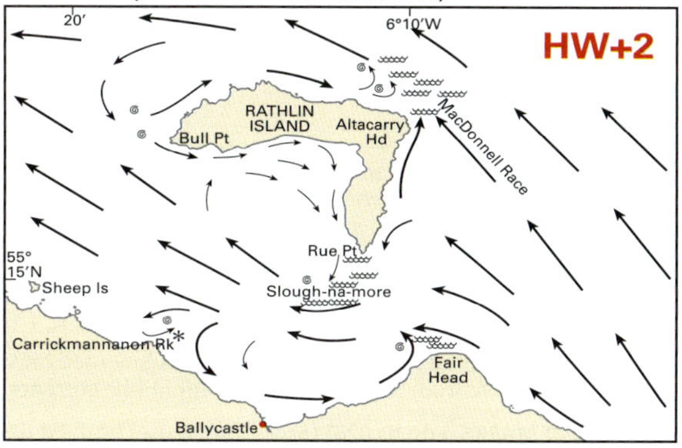

2 Hours after HW Dover (0040 after HW Greenock)

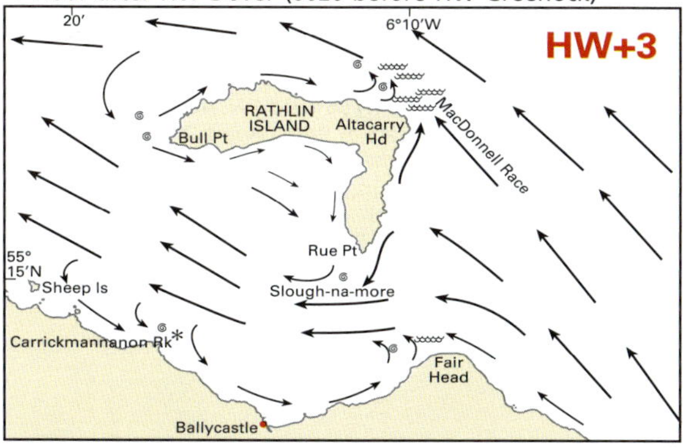

3 Hours after HW Dover (0140 after HW Greenock)

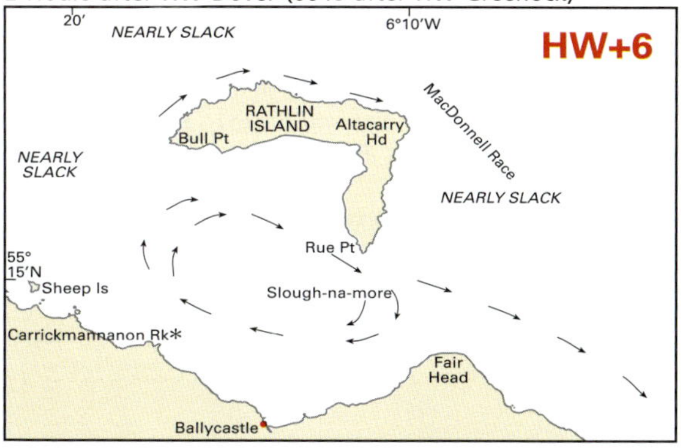

6 Hours after HW Dover (0440 after HW Greenock)

FAIR HEAD TO BLOODY FORELAND

(AC 2723, 5612) This is a good cruising area, under the lee of land in SW'lies, but very exposed to NW or N. Beware fishing boats and nets in many places and the North Channel TSS.

▶ ***A fair tide is essential through Rathlin Sound, as sp rates reach 6kn, with dangerous overfalls.*** *The main stream sets W from HW Dover +0030 for 5 hrs, and E from HW Dover –0530 for 5 hrs. The worst overfalls are S of Rue Pt (Slough-na-more) from HW Dover +0130 to +0230, and it is best to enter W-bound at the end of this period, on the last of fair tide. E-bound enter the Sound at HW Dover –0500. Close inshore between Fair Hd and Carrick-mannanon Rk a counter eddy runs W from HW Dover –0030, and an E-going eddy runs from HW Dover +0200 to +0300.* ◀ Pass outside Carrickmannanon Rk (0·3m) and Sheep Is. There are small hbrs in Church Bay (Rathlin Is) and at Ballycastle.

Proceeding to Portrush, use Skerries Sound in good weather. ▶ *Enter Lough Foyle by either the North Chan W of The Tuns, or S chan passing 2ca N of Magilligan Pt and allowing for set towards The Tuns on the ebb (up to 3·5kn).* ◀

Tor Rks, Inishtrahull and Garvan Is lie NE and E of Malin Hd. In bad weather it is best to pass at least 3M N of Tor Rks. Inishtrahull is lit and about 1M long; rks extend N about 3ca into Tor Sound. ▶ *Inishtrahull Sound, between Inishtrahull and Garvan Is, is exposed; tidal streams up to 4kn sp can raise a dangerous sea with no warning. Stream also sets hard through Garvan Isles, S of which Garvan Sound can be passed safely in daylight avoiding two sunken rks, one 1½ca NE of Rossnabarton, and the other 5ca NW. The main stream runs W for only 3 hrs, from HW Galway –0500 to –0200. W of Malin Hd a W-going eddy starts at HW Galway +0400, and an E-going one at HW Galway – 0300.* ◀

W of Malin Hd the direction of buoyage changes to E. From Malin Hd SW to Dunaff Hd, at ent to Lough Swilly, keep 5ca offshore. Trawbreaga Lough (AC 2697) gives shelter, but is shallow, and sea can break on bar; only approach when no swell, and at half flood. Ent to L Swilly is clear except for Swilly Rks off the W shore, SSE of Fanad Hd.

W from Lough Swilly the coast is very foul. Beware Limeburner Rk (2m), 6·8M WNW of Fanad Hd. Mulroy Bay has good ⚓s but needs accurate pilotage (see ICC SDs).

Between Mulroy B and Sheephaven there is an inshore passage S of Frenchman's Rk, and between Guill Rks & Carnabollion, safe in good weather; otherwise keep 1M offshore. Sheep Haven B is easy to enter between Rinnafaghla Pt and Horn Hd, and has good ⚓s except in strong NW or N winds. Beware Wherryman Rks, dry 1·5m, 1ca off E shore.

Between Horn Hd and Bloody Foreland (AC 2752) are three low-lying islands: Inishbeg, Inishdooey and Inishbofin. The latter is almost part of the mainland; it has a temp anch on S side and a more sheltered ⚓ on NE side in Toberglassan B. 6M offshore is Tory Is (lt, fog sig, RC) with rks for 5ca off SW side. Temp anch in good weather in Camusmore B. ▶ *In Tory Sound the stream runs W from HW Galway +0230, and E from HW Galway –0530, sp rates 2kn.* ◀

6.12 PORTRUSH

Antrim **55°12'·34N 06°39'·49W** ❁❁✿✿✿✿

CHARTS AC 2798, 2499, 49, 5612; Imray C53, C64.

TIDES –0400 Dover; ML 1·1; Duration 0610

Standard Port BELFAST (⟵)

Times				Height (metres)			
High Water		Low Water		MHWS	MHWN	MLWN	MLWS
0100	0700	0000	0600	3·5	3·0	1·1	0·4
1300	1900	1200	1800				
Differences PORTRUSH							
–0433		–0433		–1·6	–1·6	–0·3	0·0

SHELTER Good in hbr, except in strong NW/N winds. Berth on N pier or on pontoon at NE end of it and see HM. A ◉ may be available, but very congested in season. ⚓ on E side of Ramore Hd in Skerries Roads 1ca S of Large Skerrie gives good shelter in most conditions, but open to NW sea/swell.

NAVIGATION WPT 55°13'·00N 06°41'·00W, 128° to N pier lt, 1·1M.

Ent with onshore winds >F 4 is difficult. Beware submerged bkwtr projecting 20m SW from N pier. Depth is 2·8m in hbr entrance.

LIGHTS AND MARKS Ldg lts 028° (occas, for LB use) both FR 6/8m 1M; R △ on metal bn and metal mast. N pier Fl R 3s 6m 3M; vis 220°-160°. S pier Fl G 3s 6m 3M; vis 220°-100°.

R/T VHF Ch 12 16 (0900-1700LT, Mon-Fri; extended evening hrs June-Sept; Sat-Sun: 0900–1700, June-Sept only).

TELEPHONE (Code 028) HM 7082 2307; MRCC 9146 3933; Marinecall 09068 969655; Police 7034 4122; Dr 7082 3767; Ⓗ 7034 4177.

FACILITIES Hbr AB £14, D(0900-1800), FW, M, Slip (launching £3), Gas, El, Ⓔ, ♿; Portrush YC ☎ 7082 3932, Bar; **Town** @ Library, 🛒, R, Bar, ⊡, D & P (cans), ✉, Ⓑ, ⇌, ✈ (Belfast). Giant's Causeway is 10M ENE.

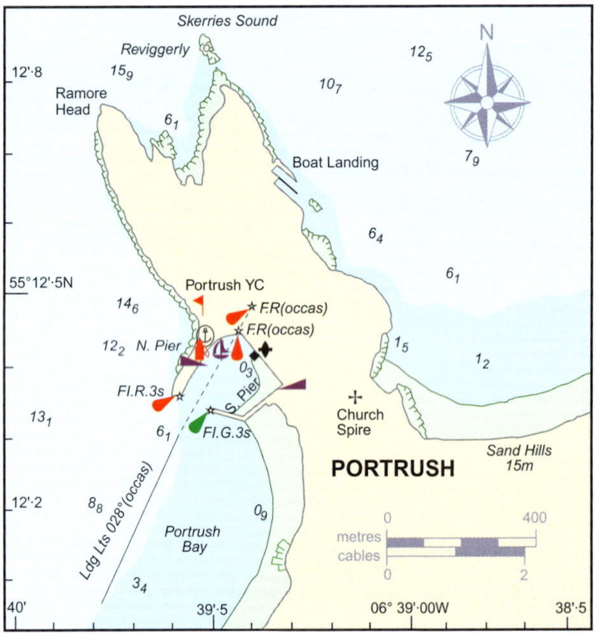

Portstewart, Antrim, **55°11'·21N 06°43'·21W**. AC 49, 5612. Tides as for Portrush. A tiny hbr 1·1ca S of Portstewart Pt lt, Oc R 10s 21m 5M, vis 040°–220°, obscd in final appr. A temp, fair weather berth (£10) at S end of inner basin in 0·8–1·7m; the very narrow ent is open to SW wind and swell. Visitors should obtain fuel at Portrush before proceeding to Portstewart. Beware rocks close to S bkwtr.

Facilities: @ Library, FW, Gas, Slip, Bar, 🛒, R.

6.13 RIVER BANN and COLERAINE

Londonderry/Antrim **55°10'·32N 06°46'·35W**

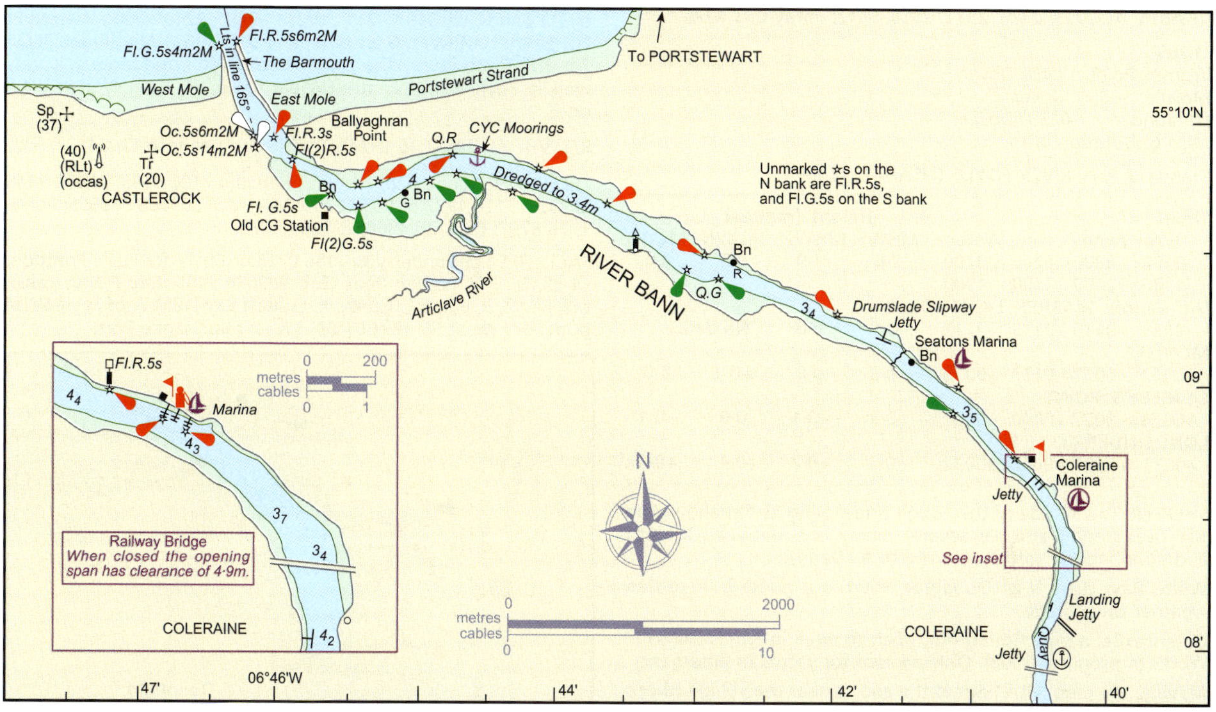

CHARTS AC 2723, 2798, 2494, 5612; Imray C64.

TIDES –0345 Dover (Coleraine); ML 1·1; Duration 0540

Standard Port BELFAST (⟵)

Times				Height (metres)			
High Water		Low Water		MHWS	MHWN	MLWN	MLWS
0100	0700	0000	0600	3·5	3·0	1·1	0·4
1300	1900	1200	1800				
Differences COLERAINE							
–0403		–0403		–1·3	–1·2	–0·2	0·0

SHELTER Good, once inside the river ent (The Barmouth) between 2 training walls, extending 2ca N from the beaches. Do not try to enter in strong on-shore winds or when swell breaks on the pierheads. If in doubt call Coleraine Hbr Radio or ring HM. ⚓ upstream of old CG stn, or berth at Seaton's or Coleraine marinas, 3½M & 4½M from ent, on NE bank.

NAVIGATION WPT 55°11'·00N, 06°46'·65W, 165°/0·72M to ent. Appr from E of N to bring ldg lts into line at bkwtr ends. The sand bar is constantly moving but ent is dredged to approx 3·5m. Beware commercial traffic.

LIGHTS AND MARKS Ldg lts 165°, both Oc 5s 6/14m 2M, front on W pyramidal metal tr; rear W □ tr. Portstewart Pt, Oc R 10s, is 2M ENE.

R/T Coleraine Hbr Radio Ch 12 (Mon-Fri: HO and when vessel due). Coleraine Marina Ch M.

TELEPHONE (Code 028) HM 70342012; MRCC 91463933; Marinecall 09068 969655; Rly Bridge 70325400; Police 70344122; Ⓗ 70344177; Dr 70344831.

FACILITIES **Seatons Marina** ☎ 70832086, mobile 07733100915, BH (14 ton), Slip (£3), D. **Coleraine Hbr** ☎ 7034 2012, BH (35 ton); **Coleraine Marina** (90+5Ⓥ), ☎ 70344768, £20, ME, (by arrangement), ⚒, 🛒, Slip, D(H24), R, BH (12.5 ton); **Coleraine YC** ☎ 70344503, Bar, M; **Services**: Gas, Kos, El, Ⓔ. **Town** P & D (cans), 🛒, R, ✉, Ⓑ, ≷, ✈ (Belfast).

6.14 LOUGH FOYLE

Londonderry/Donegal **55°14'N 06°54W** ❁❁❁⚓⚓✿✿

CHARTS AC 2723, 2798, 2511, 2510, 5612; Imray C53, C64.

TIDES
Warren Point: –0430 Dover
Moville: –0350 Dover
Londonderry: –0255 Dover
ML 1·6; Duration 0615

Standard Port RIVER FOYLE (LISAHALLY) (⟶)

Times				Height (metres)			
High Water		Low Water		MHWS	MHWN	MLWN	MLWS
0100	0800	0200	0700	2·6	1·9	0·9	0·4
1300	2000	1400	1900				
Differences WARREN LIGHTHOUSE							
–0055	–0115	–0155	–0117	–0·3	0·0	No data	
MOVILLE							
–0042	–0057	–0127	–0058	–0·3	0·0	+0·1	0·0
QUIGLEY'S POINT							
–0020	–0027	–0040	–0027	–0·3	–0·1	0·0	–0·1
LONDONDERRY							
+0033	+0035	+0032	+0032	+0·1	+0·2	+0·3	+0·2

SHELTER The SE side of the Lough is low lying and shallow. The NW rises steeply and has several village hbrs between the ent and Londonderry (often referred to as Derry).

White Bay: close N of Dunagree Point is a good ⚓ in settled weather on passage.

Greencastle: a busy fishing hbr, open to swell in winds SW to E. Works in progress (2008). Only advised for yachts in emergency.

Moville: the pier, with 1·5m at the end, is near the village (shops closed all day Wed), but is much used by FVs. ⚓ outside hbr is exposed; inside hbr for shoal draft only. 8 Y 🅐s are about 600m up-stream.

Carrickarory: pier/quay is used entirely by FVs. ⚓ in bay is sheltered in winds from SW to NNW. Plans for possible new marina.

Culmore Bay: good shelter. ⚓ 1½ca W of Culmore Pt in pleasant cove, 4M from Londonderry.

Londonderry, Foyle Pontoon: AB, £12-£17/night, adjacent to the centre of historic city or ⚓ close below Craigavon Bridge clearance 1·7m. Commercial operations are now at Lisahally (55°02'·6N 07°15'·6W).

NAVIGATION WPT Tuns PHM buoy, Fl R 3s, 55°14'·00N 06°53'·49W, 235°/2·5M to Warren Pt lt, 2·5M. The Tuns bank lies 3M NE of Magilligan Pt and may dry. The main or N Chan, ¾M wide, runs NW of The Tuns; a lesser chan, min depth 4m, runs 3ca off shore around NE side of Magilligan Pt. Beware commercial traffic. Foyle Bridge at Rosses Pt has 31m clearance. In June and July the chan is at times obstructed by salmon nets at night. N Chan tides reach 3½kn, and up-river the ebb runs up to 6kn.

LIGHTS AND MARKS Inishowen Fl (2) WRG 10s 28m 18/14M; W tr, 2 B bands; vis G197°–211°, W211°–249°, R249°–000°. Warren Pt Fl 1·5s 9m 10M; W tr, G abutment; vis 232°–061°. Magilligan Pt QR 7m 4M; R structure. The main chan up to Londonderry is very well lit. Foyle Bridge centre FW each side; VQ G on W pier; VQ R on E.

R/T VHF Ch 14 12 16 (H24). Traffic and nav info Ch 14.

TELEPHONE (Code 028) HM (at Lisahally) 7186 0555; MRCC 9146 3933; ⊜ 7126 1937 or 9035 8250; Marinecall 09068 969655; Police 7776 6797; Dr 7126 4868; Ⓗ 7034 5171.

FACILITIES Londonderry ☎ 7186 0313 or Ch 14 for Foyle Pontoon, £1·39, M, FW; **Prehen Boat Club** ☎ 7034 3405. **City** P & D (cans), ME, El, 🛒, R, Bar, ✉, Ⓑ, ⇌, ✈. **Culdaff Bay** (10M W of Foyle SWM buoy) 6 Y 🅐s at 55°18'N 07°09'·1W, off Bunnagee Port.

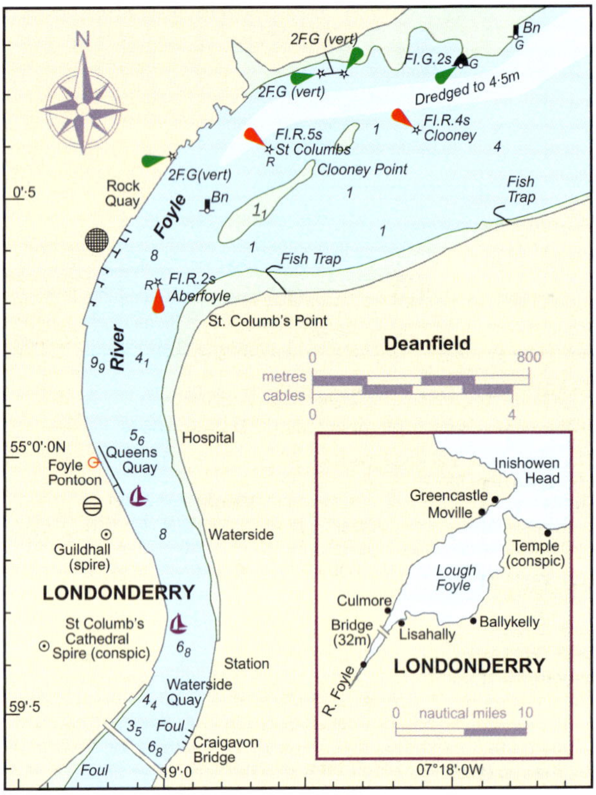

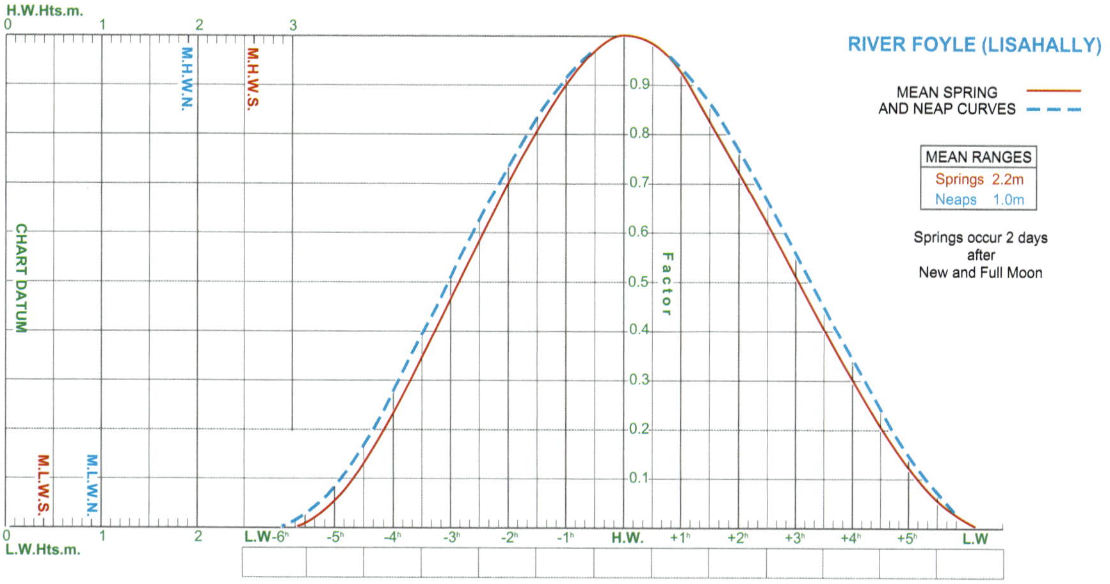
H.W.Hts.m.
0 1 2 3
M.H.W.N.
M.H.W.S.
CHART DATUM
M.L.W.S.
M.L.W.N.
0 1 2
L.W.Hts.m.
0.9
0.8
0.7
0.6
0.5
0.4
0.3
0.2
0.1
Factor
L.W-6h -5h -4h -3h -2h -1h H.W. +1h +2h +3h +4h +5h L.W
RIVER FOYLE (LISAHALLY)
MEAN SPRING AND NEAP CURVES
MEAN RANGES
Springs 2.2m
Neaps 1.0m
Springs occur 2 days after New and Full Moon

TIME ZONE (UT)
For Summer Time add ONE hour in **non-shaded areas**

RIVER FOYLE LAT 55°03′N LONG 7°16′W

TIMES AND HEIGHTS OF HIGH AND LOW WATERS

Dates in red are SPRINGS
Dates in blue are NEAPS

YEAR **2010**

JANUARY

Date	Day	Time	m	Time	m	Time	m	Time	m
1	F	0140	0.5	0744	2.9	1428	0.5	2012	2.7
2	SA	0225	0.4	0828	3.0	1518	0.5	2059	2.7
3	SU	0309	0.3	0912	3.0	1606	0.5	2144	2.6
4	M	0351	0.3	0958	2.9	1652	0.5	2229	2.5
5	TU	0433	0.4	1045	2.8	1740	0.6	2315	2.3
6	W	0515	0.5	1137	2.6	1831	0.8		
7	TH	0005	2.2	0601	0.7	1242	2.4	◑ 1929	0.9
8	F	0110	2.0	0658	0.9	1405	2.2	2037	1.0
9	SA	0229	1.9	0812	1.0	1530	2.2	2149	1.0
10	SU	0349	2.0	0945	1.0	1648	2.2	2252	0.9
11	M	0459	2.2	1106	1.0	1746	2.2	2343	0.8
12	TU	0551	2.3	1202	0.9	1830	2.2		
13	W	0027	0.7	0632	2.5	1248	0.8	1907	2.3
14	TH	0107	0.6	0708	2.6	1328	0.8	1939	2.3
15	F	0145	0.6	0742	2.6	1405	0.8	● 2006	2.3
16	SA	0220	0.5	0814	2.7	1440	0.7	2032	2.3
17	SU	0252	0.5	0845	2.7	1511	0.7	2059	2.3
18	M	0322	0.5	0917	2.6	1542	0.7	2129	2.3
19	TU	0350	0.6	0951	2.5	1614	0.7	2202	2.2
20	W	0422	0.6	1027	2.4	1651	0.7	2236	2.1
21	TH	0457	0.7	1106	2.3	1732	0.7	2315	2.0
22	F	0540	0.8	1154	2.2	1821	0.8		
23	SA	0002	1.9	0635	0.9	1258	2.1	◐ 1919	0.9
24	SU	0116	1.8	0746	1.0	1418	2.0	2022	0.9
25	M	0255	1.9	0904	1.0	1534	2.1	2130	0.9
26	TU	0418	2.0	1033	0.9	1644	2.2	2243	0.8
27	W	0520	2.2	1147	0.8	1744	2.3	2349	0.7
28	TH	0610	2.4	1244	0.6	1835	2.4		
29	F	0043	0.5	0653	2.7	1335	0.4	1921	2.6
30	SA	0131	0.4	0734	2.9	1422	0.3	○ 2003	2.6
31	SU	0215	0.2	0816	3.0	1507	0.2	2044	2.7

FEBRUARY

Date	Day	Time	m	Time	m	Time	m	Time	m
1	M	0256	0.2	0856	3.0	1549	0.3	2123	2.6
2	TU	0336	0.2	0938	3.0	1629	0.4	2201	2.6
3	W	0414	0.2	1019	2.8	1707	0.5	2240	2.4
4	TH	0452	0.4	1104	2.6	1748	0.7	2322	2.2
5	F	0534	0.6	1156	2.3	1837	0.9	◑	
6	SA	0015	2.0	0625	0.8	1323	2.0	1942	1.1
7	SU	0145	1.9	0737	1.0	1517	1.9	2111	1.1
8	M	0325	1.9	0936	1.1	1646	1.9	2225	1.0
9	TU	0444	2.1	1107	1.0	1742	2.0	2321	0.9
10	W	0538	2.2	1159	0.9	1824	2.1		
11	TH	0007	0.7	0619	2.4	1240	0.8	1858	2.1
12	F	0049	0.6	0654	2.5	1317	0.7	1928	2.2
13	SA	0128	0.5	0725	2.5	1351	0.6	1952	2.2
14	SU	0204	0.4	0754	2.6	1423	0.6	● 2012	2.3
15	M	0237	0.4	0822	2.6	1451	0.5	2035	2.3
16	TU	0305	0.4	0851	2.6	1518	0.5	2103	2.4
17	W	0332	0.4	0923	2.5	1546	0.5	2132	2.3
18	TH	0401	0.5	0957	2.5	1617	0.5	2204	2.3
19	F	0434	0.6	1034	2.3	1653	0.6	2238	2.2
20	SA	0514	0.7	1117	2.2	1735	0.7	2318	2.0
21	SU	0605	0.9	1213	2.0	1829	0.8		
22	M	0015	1.9	0716	1.0	1340	1.9	◐ 1937	0.9
23	TU	0207	1.8	0846	1.0	1520	1.9	2054	0.9
24	W	0358	1.9	1039	0.8	1639	2.0	2221	0.8
25	TH	0506	2.2	1146	0.6	1739	2.1	2335	0.7
26	F	0555	2.4	1237	0.4	1826	2.3		
27	SA	0028	0.4	0637	2.6	1324	0.2	1907	2.5
28	SU	0114	0.3	0717	2.8	1406	0.1	○ 1944	2.6

MARCH

Date	Day	Time	m	Time	m	Time	m	Time	m
1	M	0156	0.1	0755	3.0	1446	0.1	2020	2.7
2	TU	0236	0.0	0834	3.0	1523	0.1	2056	2.7
3	W	0314	0.1	0913	2.9	1558	0.3	2131	2.6
4	TH	0351	0.2	0953	2.7	1631	0.4	2208	2.4
5	F	0429	0.3	1034	2.4	1706	0.6	2247	2.2
6	SA	0511	0.6	1120	2.1	1748	0.8	2337	2.0
7	SU	0602	0.8	1237	1.8	1846	1.0	◑	
8	M	0112	1.9	0715	1.0	1452	1.7	2022	1.1
9	TU	0300	1.9	0928	1.0	1621	1.7	2151	1.0
10	W	0414	2.0	1050	0.9	1719	1.8	2251	0.8
11	TH	0510	2.2	1137	0.8	1801	1.9	2340	0.7
12	F	0553	2.3	1216	0.7	1836	2.0		
13	SA	0023	0.5	0628	2.4	1252	0.6	1904	2.1
14	SU	0103	0.4	0658	2.4	1325	0.5	1926	2.2
15	M	0139	0.4	0726	2.5	1356	0.4	● 1945	2.3
16	TU	0211	0.3	0753	2.5	1424	0.4	2008	2.4
17	W	0240	0.3	0823	2.5	1449	0.3	2034	2.4
18	TH	0308	0.4	0856	2.5	1516	0.3	2104	2.4
19	F	0339	0.4	0931	2.5	1546	0.4	2136	2.4
20	SA	0414	0.5	1009	2.3	1620	0.4	2211	2.3
21	SU	0455	0.6	1053	2.1	1700	0.6	2252	2.1
22	M	0547	0.8	1149	1.9	1749	0.7	2349	1.9
23	TU	0703	0.9	1317	1.7	1857	0.9	◐	
24	W	0139	1.8	0845	0.9	1503	1.7	2023	0.9
25	TH	0333	2.0	1025	0.7	1621	1.9	2156	0.8
26	F	0439	2.2	1127	0.5	1720	2.1	2309	0.6
27	SA	0530	2.4	1216	0.3	1805	2.2		
28	SU	0002	0.4	0613	2.6	1301	0.1	1844	2.4
29	M	0048	0.2	0653	2.8	1341	0.1	1920	2.5
30	TU	0130	0.1	0732	2.8	1419	0.1	○ 1954	2.6
31	W	0211	0.0	0810	2.8	1453	0.1	2029	2.6

APRIL

Date	Day	Time	m	Time	m	Time	m	Time	m
1	TH	0249	0.1	0849	2.7	1526	0.2	2104	2.6
2	F	0328	0.2	0929	2.5	1558	0.4	2142	2.5
3	SA	0407	0.4	1011	2.2	1632	0.6	2223	2.3
4	SU	0451	0.6	1056	1.9	1711	0.7	2314	2.1
5	M	0545	0.8	1202	1.7	1802	0.9		
6	TU	0048	1.9	0658	0.9	1403	1.5	◑ 1923	1.0
7	W	0226	1.9	0843	0.9	1528	1.5	2106	0.9
8	TH	0333	2.0	0959	0.8	1635	1.6	2212	0.8
9	F	0428	2.1	1052	0.7	1724	1.7	2304	0.6
10	SA	0514	2.1	1135	0.6	1801	1.9	2349	0.5
11	SU	0551	2.2	1214	0.5	1830	2.0		
12	M	0029	0.4	0622	2.3	1250	0.4	1852	2.1
13	TU	0106	0.4	0651	2.4	1322	0.3	1914	2.2
14	W	0139	0.4	0722	2.4	1351	0.3	● 1940	2.4
15	TH	0210	0.3	0755	2.5	1420	0.3	2009	2.5
16	F	0243	0.4	0832	2.5	1450	0.3	2041	2.5
17	SA	0319	0.4	0912	2.4	1523	0.3	2117	2.4
18	SU	0359	0.5	0955	2.3	1559	0.4	2156	2.3
19	M	0447	0.6	1043	2.1	1640	0.5	2243	2.2
20	TU	0545	0.7	1142	1.9	1729	0.6	2346	2.0
21	W	0703	0.7	1303	1.8	1833	0.7	◐	
22	TH	0130	2.0	0832	0.7	1433	1.8	1957	0.8
23	F	0301	2.1	0950	0.6	1546	1.8	2124	0.7
24	SA	0406	2.2	1052	0.4	1647	2.0	2235	0.5
25	SU	0500	2.4	1145	0.3	1737	2.2	2331	0.4
26	M	0547	2.5	1230	0.2	1818	2.3		
27	TU	0020	0.2	0630	2.6	1312	0.2	1855	2.5
28	W	0105	0.2	0710	2.6	1350	0.2	○ 1931	2.5
29	TH	0146	0.2	0750	2.6	1425	0.2	2007	2.6
30	F	0227	0.2	0831	2.5	1459	0.3	2044	2.6

Chart Datum: 1·37 metres below Ordnance Datum (Belfast). HAT is 3·1 metres above Chart Datum; see 0.20

TIME ZONE (UT)
For Summer Time add ONE hour in **non-shaded areas**

RIVER FOYLE LAT 55°03'N LONG 7°16'W

TIMES AND HEIGHTS OF HIGH AND LOW WATERS

Dates in red are SPRINGS
Dates in blue are NEAPS

YEAR **2010**

MAY

Date	Day	Time	m	Time	m	Time	m	Time	m
1	SA	0308	0.3	0912	2.3	1532	0.4	2123	2.5
2	SU	0350	0.5	0954	2.1	1606	0.5	2206	2.3
3	M	0436	0.6	1040	1.9	1643	0.6	2257	2.1
4	TU	0529	0.8	1133	1.7	1727	0.7		
5	W	0011	2.0	0632	0.8	1252	1.5	1827	0.8
6	TH	0139	1.9	0745	0.8	1415	1.5	◑ 1956	0.9
7	F	0244	1.9	0852	0.8	1526	1.5	2120	0.8
8	SA	0338	2.0	0949	0.7	1627	1.6	2220	0.7
9	SU	0424	2.0	1041	0.6	1714	1.7	2308	0.6
10	M	0505	2.1	1127	0.5	1748	1.9	2350	0.5
11	TU	0541	2.2	1207	0.4	1817	2.1		
12	W	0028	0.5	0616	2.3	1245	0.4	1845	2.2
13	TH	0105	0.4	0653	2.4	1319	0.3	1916	2.4
14	F	0143	0.4	0733	2.4	1354	0.3	● 1950	2.5
15	SA	0224	0.4	0815	2.5	1430	0.3	2027	2.5
16	SU	0308	0.4	0900	2.4	1508	0.3	2107	2.5
17	M	0356	0.4	0948	2.3	1548	0.3	2152	2.4
18	TU	0449	0.5	1040	2.2	1631	0.4	2244	2.3
19	W	0549	0.5	1137	2.0	1720	0.5	2348	2.2
20	TH	0656	0.6	1242	1.9	1819	0.6	◐	
21	F	0110	2.1	0805	0.6	1355	1.8	1931	0.6
22	SA	0228	2.2	0911	0.5	1505	1.8	2049	0.6
23	SU	0333	2.2	1013	0.5	1610	1.9	2201	0.6
24	M	0432	2.3	1111	0.4	1708	2.1	2303	0.5
25	TU	0525	2.3	1201	0.4	1755	2.2	2356	0.4
26	W	0613	2.4	1245	0.3	1836	2.4		
27	TH	0044	0.4	0657	2.4	1326	0.3	○ 1914	2.5
28	F	0129	0.4	0739	2.3	1404	0.3	1952	2.5
29	SA	0212	0.4	0820	2.3	1440	0.3	2030	2.5
30	SU	0255	0.5	0901	2.2	1514	0.4	2110	2.5
31	M	0338	0.6	0941	2.0	1548	0.4	2152	2.4

JUNE

Date	Day	Time	m	Time	m	Time	m	Time	m
1	TU	0423	0.6	1022	1.9	1623	0.5	2238	2.2
2	W	0509	0.7	1104	1.8	1700	0.6	2330	2.1
3	TH	0559	0.7	1150	1.7	1745	0.7		
4	F	0034	2.0	0652	0.7	1248	1.6	◑ 1844	0.8
5	SA	0142	1.9	0747	0.7	1358	1.5	1957	0.8
6	SU	0239	1.9	0841	0.7	1509	1.6	2111	0.8
7	M	0329	2.0	0936	0.6	1613	1.7	2215	0.7
8	TU	0416	2.0	1031	0.6	1704	1.8	2307	0.7
9	W	0502	2.1	1123	0.5	1745	2.0	2354	0.6
10	TH	0547	2.2	1210	0.4	1822	2.2		
11	F	0040	0.5	0632	2.3	1254	0.4	1859	2.4
12	SA	0126	0.5	0718	2.4	1337	0.3	● 1938	2.5
13	SU	0215	0.4	0805	2.4	1419	0.3	2019	2.6
14	M	0306	0.4	0854	2.4	1501	0.2	2103	2.6
15	TU	0358	0.4	0942	2.4	1543	0.2	2150	2.6
16	W	0449	0.4	1031	2.3	1626	0.3	2240	2.5
17	TH	0541	0.4	1121	2.2	1711	0.3	2336	2.4
18	F	0636	0.4	1214	2.0	1802	0.5		
19	SA	0042	2.3	0734	0.5	1315	1.9	◐ 1902	0.6
20	SU	0155	2.2	0835	0.6	1424	1.8	2014	0.7
21	M	0305	2.1	0938	0.6	1535	1.9	2131	0.7
22	TU	0413	2.1	1041	0.6	1644	2.0	2243	0.6
23	W	0516	2.1	1137	0.5	1741	2.1	2344	0.6
24	TH	0610	2.2	1226	0.5	1827	2.3		
25	F	0035	0.6	0656	2.2	1310	0.4	1906	2.4
26	SA	0122	0.5	0737	2.2	1350	0.4	○ 1944	2.5
27	SU	0207	0.5	0816	2.1	1427	0.4	2021	2.5
28	M	0249	0.6	0851	2.1	1502	0.3	2058	2.5
29	TU	0329	0.6	0925	2.1	1534	0.4	2135	2.4
30	W	0406	0.6	0958	2.0	1605	0.4	2213	2.3

JULY

Date	Day	Time	m	Time	m	Time	m	Time	m
1	TH	0443	0.6	1033	1.9	1637	0.5	2253	2.2
2	F	0523	0.6	1110	1.9	1714	0.6	2339	2.1
3	SA	0607	0.6	1153	1.8	1800	0.7		
4	SU	0034	2.0	0655	0.6	1248	1.7	◑ 1859	0.8
5	M	0139	1.9	0748	0.7	1400	1.6	2009	0.9
6	TU	0240	1.9	0844	0.7	1518	1.7	2121	0.8
7	W	0338	2.0	0942	0.6	1627	1.8	2232	0.8
8	TH	0434	2.0	1044	0.6	1723	2.0	2334	0.7
9	F	0529	2.1	1144	0.5	1808	2.2		
10	SA	0028	0.6	0621	2.2	1237	0.4	1849	2.4
11	SU	0121	0.5	0710	2.3	1325	0.3	● 1930	2.5
12	M	0213	0.4	0758	2.4	1410	0.2	2012	2.7
13	TU	0303	0.3	0844	2.4	1453	0.1	2055	2.8
14	W	0350	0.2	0928	2.4	1535	0.1	2138	2.8
15	TH	0436	0.2	1011	2.4	1615	0.1	2223	2.7
16	F	0521	0.3	1054	2.3	1655	0.2	2312	2.5
17	SA	0608	0.4	1140	2.1	1739	0.4		
18	SU	0009	2.3	0659	0.6	1235	2.0	◐ 1831	0.6
19	M	0122	2.1	0800	0.7	1345	1.9	1940	0.8
20	TU	0246	2.0	0908	0.8	1508	1.8	2110	0.8
21	W	0409	2.0	1018	0.7	1632	1.9	2239	0.8
22	TH	0520	2.0	1119	0.7	1736	2.1	2343	0.7
23	F	0613	2.0	1209	0.6	1822	2.3		
24	SA	0033	0.7	0656	2.1	1254	0.4	1900	2.4
25	SU	0118	0.6	0733	2.1	1335	0.4	1935	2.5
26	M	0159	0.6	0806	2.1	1413	0.3	○ 2008	2.5
27	TU	0237	0.5	0834	2.1	1448	0.3	2039	2.5
28	W	0311	0.5	0900	2.1	1519	0.3	2111	2.5
29	TH	0343	0.5	0928	2.1	1546	0.3	2143	2.4
30	F	0413	0.5	0959	2.1	1615	0.4	2218	2.3
31	SA	0446	0.5	1032	2.0	1647	0.5	2257	2.2

AUGUST

Date	Day	Time	m	Time	m	Time	m	Time	m
1	SU	0524	0.6	1109	1.9	1726	0.7	2343	2.0
2	M	0609	0.6	1152	1.8	1818	0.8		
3	TU	0044	1.9	0701	0.7	1256	1.7	◑ 1927	0.9
4	W	0200	1.9	0800	0.7	1434	1.7	2046	0.9
5	TH	0312	1.9	0903	0.7	1602	1.8	2215	0.9
6	F	0419	1.9	1013	0.7	1708	2.0	2330	0.7
7	SA	0521	2.1	1125	0.6	1757	2.2		
8	SU	0025	0.5	0614	2.2	1223	0.4	1838	2.4
9	M	0116	0.4	0701	2.3	1312	0.3	1917	2.7
10	TU	0203	0.2	0744	2.4	1356	0.1	● 1956	2.8
11	W	0249	0.2	0825	2.5	1438	0.0	2036	2.9
12	TH	0331	0.1	0904	2.6	1517	0.0	2117	2.9
13	F	0412	0.2	0943	2.5	1555	0.0	2159	2.8
14	SA	0452	0.3	1023	2.4	1634	0.2	2243	2.6
15	SU	0533	0.5	1105	2.3	1715	0.4	2335	2.3
16	M	0620	0.7	1156	2.1	1805	0.6	◐	
17	TU	0051	2.0	0720	0.8	1313	1.9	1914	0.9
18	W	0238	1.9	0840	0.9	1453	1.9	2107	1.0
19	TH	0407	1.9	0956	0.8	1620	2.0	2242	0.9
20	F	0513	1.9	1058	0.7	1722	2.2	2339	0.8
21	SA	0602	2.0	1148	0.6	1807	2.3		
22	SU	0023	0.7	0641	2.1	1234	0.4	1843	2.4
23	M	0103	0.6	0715	2.1	1315	0.3	1916	2.5
24	TU	0140	0.5	0744	2.2	1352	0.3	○ 1945	2.5
25	W	0214	0.5	0807	2.2	1427	0.3	2013	2.5
26	TH	0245	0.5	0829	2.3	1457	0.3	2041	2.5
27	F	0312	0.5	0855	2.3	1523	0.3	2111	2.5
28	SA	0338	0.5	0924	2.3	1549	0.4	2144	2.4
29	SU	0407	0.5	0955	2.2	1620	0.5	2220	2.3
30	M	0442	0.6	1027	2.1	1657	0.7	2301	2.1
31	TU	0523	0.6	1104	2.0	1744	0.8	2356	1.9

Chart Datum: 1·37 metres below Ordnance Datum (Belfast). HAT is 3·1 metres above Chart Datum; see 0.20

TIME ZONE (UT)
For Summer Time add ONE hour in **non-shaded areas**

RIVER FOYLE

LAT 55°03′N LONG 7°16′W

TIMES AND HEIGHTS OF HIGH AND LOW WATERS

Dates in red are **SPRINGS**
Dates in blue are **NEAPS**

YEAR **2010**

SEPTEMBER

Date	Day	Time	m	Time	m	Time	m	Time	m
1	W	0613	0.8	1155	1.8	1853	1.0	◑	
2	TH	0122	1.8	0715	0.8	1345	1.7	2023	1.0
3	F	0256	1.8	0826	0.9	1540	1.8	2215	0.9
4	SA	0409	1.9	0946	0.8	1647	2.1	2322	0.7
5	SU	0510	2.1	1105	0.6	1735	2.3		
6	M	0013	0.5	0559	2.2	1203	0.4	1816	2.6
7	TU	0059	0.3	0642	2.4	1250	0.3	1855	2.8
8	W	0143	0.2	0721	2.5	1333	0.1	● 1933	2.9
9	TH	0224	0.1	0758	2.6	1414	0.0	2012	3.0
10	F	0303	0.1	0836	2.7	1453	0.0	2051	3.0
11	SA	0341	0.2	0913	2.7	1532	0.1	2132	2.8
12	SU	0417	0.4	0952	2.6	1611	0.3	2216	2.6
13	M	0454	0.6	1034	2.4	1653	0.5	2305	2.2
14	TU	0537	0.8	1125	2.2	1743	0.8		
15	W	0023	1.9	0635	0.9	1251	2.0	◐ 1857	1.0
16	TH	0222	1.8	0804	1.0	1435	2.0	2105	1.0
17	F	0345	1.8	0926	0.9	1552	2.1	2226	0.9
18	SA	0448	1.9	1028	0.8	1652	2.2	2317	0.8
19	SU	0536	2.0	1120	0.6	1738	2.4	2357	0.7
20	M	0615	2.1	1205	0.5	1816	2.4		
21	TU	0034	0.6	0647	2.2	1247	0.4	1847	2.5
22	W	0109	0.5	0713	2.2	1325	0.4	1915	2.5
23	TH	0142	0.5	0734	2.3	1359	0.3	○ 1941	2.6
24	F	0211	0.5	0756	2.4	1428	0.4	2009	2.6
25	SA	0236	0.4	0822	2.5	1455	0.4	2039	2.6
26	SU	0302	0.4	0851	2.5	1523	0.5	2113	2.5
27	M	0331	0.5	0922	2.4	1556	0.6	2150	2.4
28	TU	0405	0.5	0955	2.3	1634	0.7	2232	2.2
29	W	0444	0.7	1033	2.2	1722	0.9	2326	2.0
30	TH	0532	0.8	1123	2.0	1831	1.0		

OCTOBER

Date	Day	Time	m	Time	m	Time	m	Time	m
1	F	0050	1.8	0632	0.9	1258	1.9	◑ 2010	1.0
2	SA	0233	1.8	0749	0.9	1506	2.0	2153	0.8
3	SU	0346	2.0	0913	0.8	1613	2.2	2257	0.6
4	M	0445	2.1	1032	0.7	1704	2.4	2348	0.4
5	TU	0535	2.3	1132	0.5	1749	2.7		
6	W	0033	0.3	0616	2.5	1222	0.3	1829	2.9
7	TH	0115	0.2	0655	2.6	1306	0.2	● 1908	3.0
8	F	0154	0.2	0732	2.8	1348	0.1	1948	3.0
9	SA	0232	0.2	0809	2.8	1428	0.1	2028	2.9
10	SU	0308	0.3	0847	2.8	1509	0.3	2109	2.7
11	M	0343	0.5	0927	2.7	1550	0.4	2152	2.5
12	TU	0419	0.6	1010	2.5	1634	0.7	2241	2.2
13	W	0500	0.8	1102	2.3	1727	0.9	2352	1.9
14	TH	0551	0.9	1226	2.1	1840	1.0	◐	
15	F	0141	1.8	0707	1.0	1403	2.1	2029	1.1
16	SA	0301	1.8	0843	1.0	1513	2.2	2144	1.0
17	SU	0407	1.8	0950	0.9	1611	2.3	2235	0.9
18	M	0459	1.9	1045	0.8	1659	2.3	2318	0.8
19	TU	0540	2.0	1132	0.7	1739	2.4	2356	0.7
20	W	0612	2.2	1214	0.6	1812	2.5		
21	TH	0032	0.6	0638	2.3	1252	0.5	1839	2.5
22	F	0105	0.5	0701	2.4	1325	0.5	1907	2.6
23	SA	0134	0.5	0726	2.5	1356	0.5	○ 1938	2.6
24	SU	0202	0.5	0754	2.6	1426	0.5	2012	2.6
25	M	0231	0.5	0826	2.6	1500	0.6	2049	2.6
26	TU	0303	0.5	0900	2.6	1537	0.7	2130	2.5
27	W	0340	0.5	0937	2.5	1621	0.8	2216	2.3
28	TH	0420	0.6	1019	2.4	1714	0.9	2311	2.1
29	F	0507	0.7	1113	2.3	1823	0.9		
30	SA	0027	2.0	0603	0.8	1238	2.2	◑ 1950	0.9
31	SU	0158	1.9	0715	0.9	1425	2.2	2114	0.8

NOVEMBER

Date	Day	Time	m	Time	m	Time	m	Time	m
1	M	0311	2.0	0837	0.9	1535	2.4	2221	0.7
2	TU	0413	2.2	0954	0.7	1631	2.5	2315	0.5
3	W	0505	2.3	1059	0.6	1721	2.7		
4	TH	0003	0.4	0550	2.5	1153	0.5	1805	2.8
5	F	0046	0.3	0631	2.7	1241	0.4	1847	2.9
6	SA	0126	0.3	0710	2.8	1325	0.3	● 1928	2.9
7	SU	0205	0.4	0748	2.9	1408	0.4	2009	2.8
8	M	0241	0.4	0827	2.9	1450	0.5	2051	2.6
9	TU	0317	0.5	0908	2.8	1533	0.6	2134	2.4
10	W	0353	0.6	0952	2.6	1618	0.8	2220	2.2
11	TH	0431	0.8	1042	2.5	1709	0.9	2314	1.9
12	F	0514	0.9	1148	2.3	1809	1.0		
13	SA	0033	1.8	0607	1.0	1313	2.2	◐ 1923	1.1
14	SU	0157	1.7	0723	1.1	1424	2.2	2038	1.0
15	M	0306	1.7	0853	1.0	1523	2.2	2137	1.0
16	TU	0407	1.8	1000	1.0	1613	2.3	2227	0.9
17	W	0456	2.0	1053	0.9	1656	2.3	2311	0.8
18	TH	0534	2.1	1137	0.8	1732	2.4	2350	0.7
19	F	0604	2.3	1216	0.7	1805	2.5		
20	SA	0026	0.6	0632	2.4	1252	0.7	1837	2.6
21	SU	0101	0.6	0701	2.6	1328	0.7	○ 1913	2.6
22	M	0134	0.5	0734	2.7	1405	0.6	1952	2.6
23	TU	0209	0.5	0809	2.7	1446	0.7	2034	2.6
24	W	0246	0.5	0847	2.7	1530	0.7	2119	2.5
25	TH	0326	0.5	0929	2.7	1618	0.7	2207	2.4
26	F	0408	0.6	1015	2.6	1712	0.8	2300	2.3
27	SA	0454	0.6	1109	2.5	1813	0.8		
28	SU	0002	2.1	0545	0.7	1218	2.4	◑ 1922	0.8
29	M	0115	2.1	0647	0.8	1344	2.4	2033	0.8
30	TU	0229	2.1	0800	0.9	1459	2.4	2141	0.8

DECEMBER

Date	Day	Time	m	Time	m	Time	m	Time	m
1	W	0336	2.1	0917	0.8	1603	2.5	2243	0.7
2	TH	0436	2.3	1029	0.8	1700	2.6	2336	0.6
3	F	0528	2.4	1131	0.7	1750	2.6		
4	SA	0023	0.5	0613	2.6	1223	0.6	1835	2.7
5	SU	0106	0.5	0655	2.7	1311	0.6	● 1918	2.6
6	M	0145	0.5	0735	2.8	1356	0.6	1959	2.6
7	TU	0223	0.5	0815	2.9	1439	0.7	2039	2.5
8	W	0259	0.6	0855	2.8	1521	0.7	2119	2.3
9	TH	0334	0.6	0936	2.7	1603	0.8	2158	2.2
10	F	0409	0.7	1019	2.6	1645	0.9	2237	2.1
11	SA	0444	0.8	1106	2.4	1731	1.0	2319	1.9
12	SU	0525	0.9	1201	2.3	1822	1.0		
13	M	0012	1.8	0615	1.0	1313	2.2	◐ 1918	1.0
14	TU	0133	1.7	0720	1.1	1421	2.1	2018	1.0
15	W	0253	1.8	0837	1.1	1519	2.1	2117	0.9
16	TH	0359	1.9	0954	1.0	1609	2.2	2214	0.9
17	F	0452	2.0	1054	1.0	1654	2.3	2306	0.8
18	SA	0533	2.2	1142	0.9	1736	2.4	2351	0.7
19	SU	0609	2.4	1226	0.8	1817	2.5		
20	M	0034	0.6	0644	2.5	1310	0.7	1858	2.5
21	TU	0115	0.5	0721	2.7	1355	0.7	○ 1941	2.6
22	W	0156	0.5	0759	2.8	1442	0.6	2025	2.6
23	TH	0237	0.4	0840	2.9	1528	0.6	2111	2.6
24	F	0319	0.4	0923	2.9	1615	0.6	2156	2.5
25	SA	0401	0.4	1008	2.8	1703	0.6	2243	2.4
26	SU	0443	0.5	1056	2.7	1753	0.7	2333	2.3
27	M	0529	0.6	1152	2.6	1849	0.8		
28	TU	0031	2.2	0621	0.7	1302	2.4	◑ 1952	0.9
29	W	0142	2.1	0726	0.8	1425	2.3	2103	0.9
30	TH	0259	2.1	0843	0.9	1543	2.3	2214	0.9
31	F	0412	2.2	1008	0.9	1653	2.3	2316	0.8

Chart Datum: 1·37 metres below Ordnance Datum (Belfast). HAT is 3·1 metres above Chart Datum; see 0.20

6.15 LOUGH SWILLY

Donegal **55°17'N 07°34'W** ❁❁❁◊◊✿✿✿

CHARTS AC 2697; Imray C53

TIDES –0500 Dover; ML 2·3; Duration 0605

Standard Port GALWAY (⟶)

Times				Height (metres)			
High Water		Low Water		MHWS	MHWN	MLWN	MLWS
0200	0900	0200	0800	5·1	3·9	2·0	0·6
1400	2100	1400	2000				
Differences INISHTRAHULL							
+0100	+0100	+0115	+0200	–1·8	–1·4	–0·4	–0·2
TRAWBREAGA BAY							
+0115	+0059	+0109	+0125	–1·1	–0·8	No data	
FANAD HEAD							
+0115	+0040	+0125	+0120	–1·1	–0·9	–0·5	–0·1
RATHMULLAN							
+0125	+0050	+0126	+0118	–0·8	–0·7	–0·1	–0·1
MULROY BAY (BAR)							
+0108	+0052	+0102	+0118	–1·2	–1·0	No data	
SHEEP HAVEN (DOWNIES BAY)							
+0057	+0043	+0053	+0107	–1·1	–0·9	No data	

SHELTER Good, but beware downdrafts on E side. ⚓s N of 55°05'N may suffer from swell. ⚓s from seaward: Ballymastocher Bay, also 8 Y 🅥s, but exposed to E'lies; inside Macamish Pt, sheltered from SE to N; Rathmullan Roads N of pier, where yacht pontoon lies N/S in 3·6m MLWS; Fahan Creek and marina ent at HW–1.

NAVIGATION WPT 55°17'·50N 07°34'·50W, 172°/5·7M to Dunree Hd lt. Ent is easy and main chan is well lit/buoyed. Beware: off W shore, Swilly More Rks, Kinnegar Spit and Strand; off E shore, Colpagh Rks and Inch Flats. These dangers are buoyed, as is Fahan Creek. There are many marine farms and shellfish beds S from Scraggy Bay (☎ 074 50172/59071 for permission to use pier).

LIGHTS AND MARKS Fanad Hd lt, Fl (5) WR 20s 38m 18/14M, touching Dunree Hd lt, Fl (2) WR 5s 46m 12/9M, leads 151° into the Lough. Thence Ballygreen Pt and Hawk's Nest in line at 202°.

R/T None.

TELEPHONE (Codes: both sides of lough 074) Rathmullan Pontoon 9158131, 9158315 (eves); MRCC 9370243; Police 9153114 (Milford) and 9361555 (Buncrana); Dr 9158416 (Rathmullan), 1850 400911(out of hours), and 9363611 (Buncrana).

FACILITIES **Rathmullan** Pontoon (Easter–October) ☎ 087 2480132 €10/craft/day, €20/craft/overnight, FW, slip, ▣, R, Hotel, Bar, D & P (cans), Kos, 🛒, ✉. **Ramelton** AB (drying),

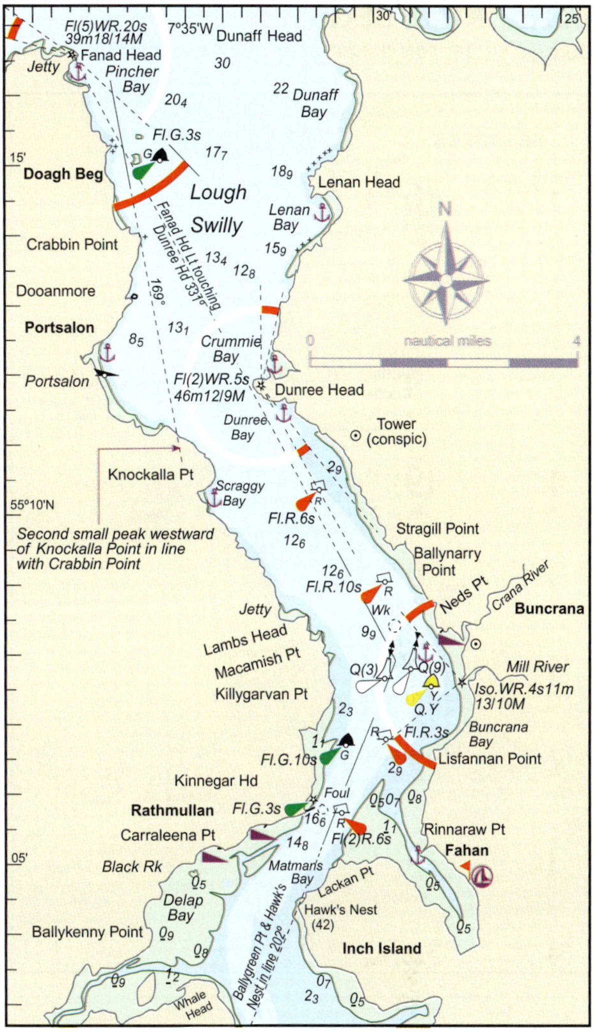

BY ☎ 9151082, Bar, R, D & P (cans), FW, Kos, 🛒, ✉. **Lough Swilly Marina** ☎ 086 1082111, some 🅥, €2/m. **Fahan**, Slip, FW, Bar, R, ✉, **Lough Swilly YC** www.loughswillyyc.com. Services (1M SE): 🛒, D & P (cans), ⇌, ✈ (Londonderry 10M bus/taxi). **Buncrana** AB (congested), Hotel, R, Bar, Ⓑ, ✉, 🛒, ▣, D & P (cans), Kos.

BLOODY FORELAND TO EAGLE ISLAND

(AC 2725) Off low-lying Bloody Foreland (lt) there is often heavy swell. The coast and islands 15M SW to Aran Is give good cruising (AC 1883). An inshore passage avoids offlying dangers: Buniver and Brinlack shoals, which can break; Bullogconnell 1M NW of Gola Is; and Stag Rks 2M NNW of Owey Is. ⚓s include Bunbeg and Gweedore Hbr, and Cruit B which has easier access. Behind Aran Is are several good ⚓s. Use N ent, since S one is shallow (AC 2792). Rutland N Chan is main appr to Burtonport.

Boylagh B has shoals and rks N of Roaninish Is. Connell Rk (0·3m) is 1M N of Church Pool, a good ⚓, best approached from Dawros Hd 4·5M to W. On S side of Glen B a temp ⚓ (but not in W or NW winds) is just E of Rinmeasa Pt. Rathlin O'Birne Is has steps E side; anch SE of them 100m offshore. Sound is 5ca wide; hold Is side to clear rks off Malin Beg Hd.

In Donegal B (AC 2702) beware uncharted rks W of Teelin, a good natural hbr but exposed to S/SW swell. Killybegs has better shelter and is always accessible. Good shelter with fair access in Donegal Hbr (AC 2715). Good ⚓ or 🅥 via YC at Mullaghmore in fair weather; sea state is calm with winds from SE through S to NW. Inishmurray is worth a visit in good weather, anch off S side. There are shoals close E and NE of the Is, and Bomore Rks 1·5M to N. Keep well clear of coast S to Sligo in onshore winds, and beware of lobster pots.

Killala B has temp ⚓ 1M S of Kilcummin Hd, on W side. Proceeding to Killala beware St Patrick's Rks. Ent has ldg lts and marks, but bar is dangerous in strong NE winds.

The coast W to Broadhaven is inhospitable. Only Belderg and Portacloy give a little shelter. Stag Rks are steep-to and high. Broadhaven (AC 2703) is good ⚓ and refuge, but in N/NW gales sea can break in ent. In approaches beware Slugga Rk on E side with offlier, and Monastery Rk (0·3m) on S side.

6.16 KILLYBEGS

Donegal **54°36'·90N 08°26'·80W** ❀❀❀◊◊◊✿✿✿

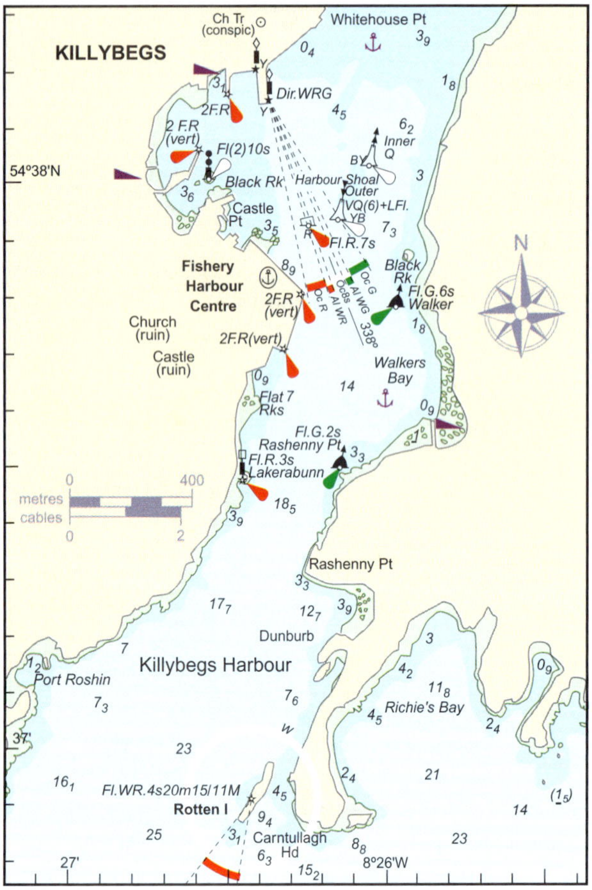

CHARTS AC 2702, 2792; Imray C53

TIDES –0520 Dover; ML 2·2; Duration 0620

Standard Port GALWAY (⟶)

Times				Height (metres)			
High Water		Low Water		MHWS	MHWN	MLWN	MLWS
0600	1100	0000	0700	5·1	3·9	2·0	0·6
1800	2300	1200	1900				
Differences KILLYBEGS							
+0040	+0050	+0055	+0035	−1·0	−0·9	−0·5	0·0
GWEEDORE HARBOUR							
+0048	+0100	+0055	+0107	−1·3	−1·0	−0·5	−0·1
BURTONPORT							
+0042	+0055	+0115	+0055	−1·2	−1·0	−0·6	−0·1
DONEGAL HARBOUR (SALTHILL QUAY)							
+0038	+0050	+0052	+0104	−1·2	−0·9	No data	

SHELTER Secure natural hbr, but some swell in SSW winds. A busy major FV port, H24 access. ⚓ about 2½ca NE of the Pier, off blue shed (Gallagher Bros) in 3m, clear of FV wash. Or contact HM and berth at pier. **Bruckless Hbr**, about 2M E at the head of McSwyne's Bay, is a pleasant ⚓ in 1·8m but is severely restricted due to fish cages, sheltered from all except SW winds. Ent on 038° between rks; ICC SDs are essential.

NAVIGATION WPT 54°36´·00N 08°27´·00W, 022°/0·94M to Rotten Is lt. From W, beware Manister Rk (covers at HW; dries at LW) off Fintragh B. Keep mid chan until off new Killybegs Fishery Centre, then follow the Dir lt or Y ◊ ldg marks 338° into hbr.

LIGHTS AND MARKS Rotten Is lt, Fl WR 4s 20m 15/11M, W tr, vis W255°-008°, R008°-039°, W039°-208°. Dir lt 338°, Oc WRG 6s 17m; W sector 336°-340° (see 6.3). Harbour Shoal (2·3m) is marked by a SCM and NCM lt buoy.

R/T HM Ch **14**; essential to request a berth.

TELEPHONE (Code 07497) HM 31032; MRCC (01) 6620922/3; Bundoran Inshore Rescue ☎ (071) 9841713; ⊖ 31070; Police 31002; Dr 31148 (Surgery).

FACILITIES **Town Pier** ☎ 31032, AB (free), M, D & P (cans), FW, ME, El, CH ⚒, C (12 ton), Kos, Ⓔ, Slip, 🛒, R, Bar.
Black Rock Pier AB, M, Slip, D.
Town ✉, Ⓑ, ⇌ (bus to Sligo), ✈ (Strandhill).

OTHER HARBOURS AND ANCHORAGES IN DONEGAL

MULROY BAY, Donegal, **55°15´·30N 07°46´·30W**. AC 2699; HW (bar) –0455 on Dover. See 6.15. Beware Limeburner Rk, (NCM buoy, Q) 3M N of ent & the bar which is dangerous in swell or onshore winds. Obtain local advice as the depths on the bar change considerably. Ent at half flood (not HW); chan lies between Bar Rks and Sessiagh Rks, it is rep'd to run along the alignment of the charted drying spit thence through First, Second and Third Narrows (with strong tides) to Broad Water. HW at the head of the lough is 2¼ hrs later than at the bar. ⚓s: Close SW of Ravedy Is (Fl 3s 9m 3M); Fanny's Bay (2m), excellent; Rosnakill Bay (3·5m) in SE side; Cranford Bay; Milford Port (3 to 4m). Beware power cable 6m, over Moross chan, barring North Water to masted boats. Facilities: **Milford Port** AB, FW, 🛒; **Fanny's Bay** ✉, Shop at Downings village (1M), hotel at Rosepenna (¾M).

SHEEP HAVEN, Donegal, **55°11´·00N 07°51´·00W**. AC 2699. HW –0515 on Dover. See 6.15. Bay is 2M wide with many ⚓s, easily accessible in daylight, but exposed to N winds. Beware rks off Rinnafaghla Pt, and further S: Black Rk (6m) and Wherryman Rks, which dry, 1ca off E shore. ⚓ or 8 Y ⓜs in Downies Bay to SE of pier; in Pollcormick inlet close W in 3m; in Ards Bay for excellent shelter, but beware the bar in strong winds. Lts: Portnablahy ldg lts 125°, both Oc 6s 7/12m 2M, B col, W bands; Downies pier hd, Fl R 3s 5m 2M, R post. Facilities: (Downies) EC Wed; 🛒, FW, P (cans 300m), R, Bar; (Portnablahy Bay) 🛒, P (cans), R, Bar.

GWEEDORE HBR/BUNBEG, Donegal, **55°03'·75N 08°18'·87W**. AC 1883. Tides see 6.16. Gweedore hbr, the estuary of the R Gweedore, has sheltered ⚓s or temp AB at Bunbeg Quay, usually full of FVs. Apprs via Gola N or S Sounds are not simple especially in poor visibility. N Sound is easier with ldg lts 171°, both Oc 3s 9/13m 2M, B/W bns, on the SE tip of Gola Is. (There are also ⚓s on the S and E sides of Gola Is.) E of Bo Is the bar 0·4m has a Fl G 3s and the chan, lying E of Inishinny Is and W of Inishcoole, is marked by a QG and 3 QR. A QG marks ent to Bunbeg. Night ent not advised. Facilities: FW, D at quay; 🛒, ✉, Ⓑ, Bar at village ½M.

BURTONPORT, Donegal, **54°58´·93N 08°26´·60W**. AC 1879, 2792. HW –0525 on Dover; ML 2·0m; Duration 0605. See 6.16. Only appr via N Chan. Ent safe in all weathers except NW gales. Hbr very full, no space to ⚓; berth on local boat at pier or go to Rutland Hbr or Aran Roads: 6 Y ⓜs 250m NE of Black Rks, Fl R 3s. Ldg marks/lts: N Chan ldg lts on Inishcoo 119·3°, both Iso 6s 6/11m 1M; front W bn, B band; rear B bn, Y band. Rutland Is ldg lts 138°, both Oc 6s 8/14m 1M; front W bn, B band; rear B bn, Y band. Burtonport ldg lts 068°, both FG 17/23m 1M; front Gy bn, W band; rear Gy bn, Y band. HM ☎ (075) 42155 (43170 home); VHF Ch 06, 12, **14**, 16. Facilities: D (just inside pier), FW (root of pier), P (½M inland). **Village** Bar, ✉, R, 🛒, Kos.

INISHKEEL, Donegal, **54°50´·82N 08°26´·50W**. AC 2792. 6 Y ⓜs in Church Pool, 3ca E of Inishkeel. Open to N/NE'lies.

TEELIN HARBOUR, Donegal, **54°37'·50N 08°37'·87W**. AC 2792. Tides as 6.16. A possible passage ⚓, mid-way between Rathlin O'Birne and Killybegs. But Hbr is open to S'ly swell and prone to squalls in NW winds. Ent, 1ca wide, is close E of Teelin Pt lt, Fl R 10s, which is hard to see by day. 4 Y ⓜs and ⚓ on E side in 3m to N of pier, or ⚓ on E side near pier. Many moorings and, in the NE, mussel rafts. Facilities: possible FW, D, 🛒 at Carrick, 3M inland.

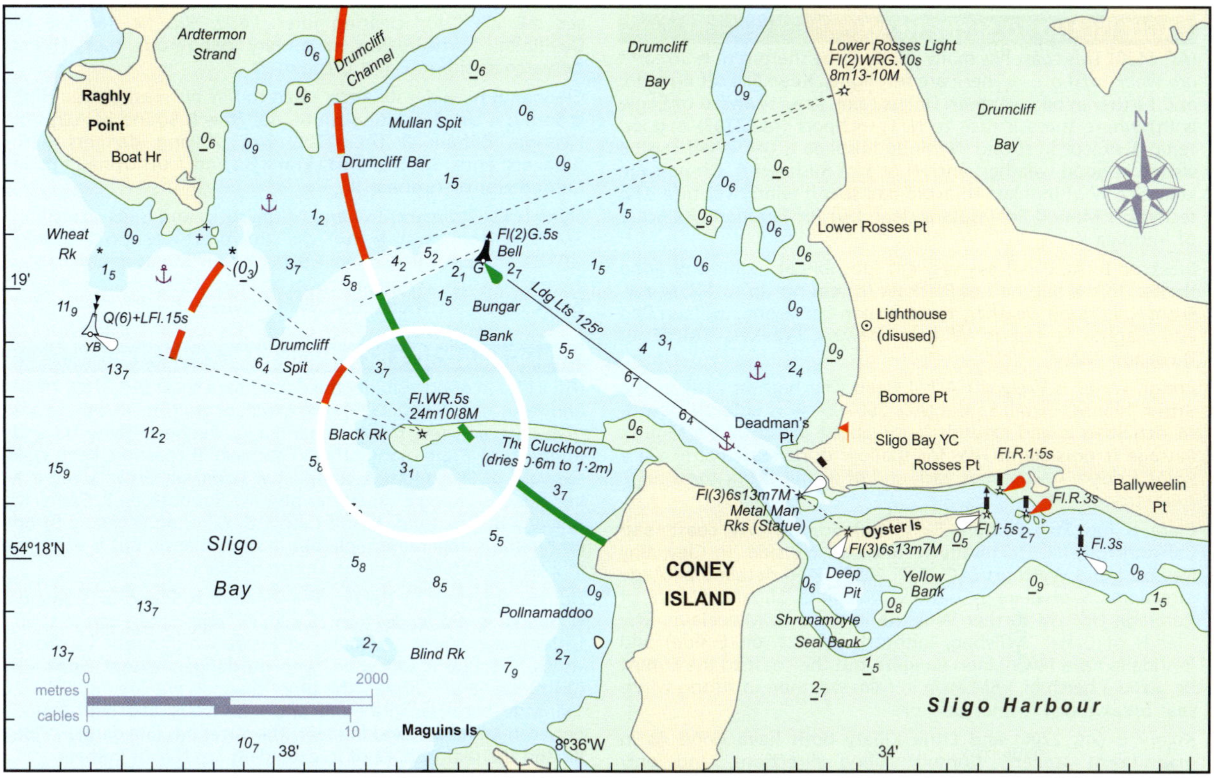

6.17 SLIGO

Sligo **54°18'·30N 08°34'·70W**

CHARTS AC 2767, 2852; Imray C54.

TIDES –0511 Dover; ML 2·3; Duration 0620

Standard Port GALWAY (⟶)

Times				Height (metres)			
High Water		Low Water		MHWS	MHWN	MLWN	MLWS
0600	1100	0000	0700	5·1	3·9	2·0	0·6
1800	2300	1200	1900				
Differences SLIGO HARBOUR (Oyster Is)							
+0043	+0055	+0042	+0054	–1·0	–0·9	–0·5	–0·1
MULLAGHMORE							
+0036	+0048	+0047	+0059	–1·4	–1·0	–0·4	–0·2
BALLYSADARE BAY (Culleenamore)							
+0059	+0111	+0111	+0123	–1·2	–0·9	No data	
KILLALA BAY (Inishcrone)							
+0035	+0055	+0030	+0050	–1·3	–1·2	–0·7	–0·2

SHELTER The lower hbr is fairly exposed; ⚓ along N side of Oyster Island, or proceed 4M (not at night) up to the shelter of Sligo town; 2nd berth below bridge for yachts.

NAVIGATION WPT 54°19'·15N 08°36'·77W, 125°/1·6M to front ldg lt.

- The passage between Oyster Island and Coney Island is marked 'Dangerous'.
- Pass N of Oyster Is leaving Blennick Rks to port. Passage up to Sligo town between training walls. Appr quays at HW–3 or higher.
- Some perches are in bad repair. Pilots at Raghly Pt and Rosses Pt. *Tide Tables* (based on Inishraher/Inishgort, published by Westport Hbr Comm.) available locally.

LIGHTS AND MARKS See 6.3 and chartlet. Channel to Sligo Deepwater Quay is well marked by lit bcns.

R/T Pilots VHF Ch 12 16. HM Ch 16.

TELEPHONE (Code 071) Hbr Office ☎ 9153819, mob 086 0870767; MRCC (01) 6620922/3; ⊜ 9161064; Police 9157000; Dr 9142886; Ⓗ 9171111.

FACILITIES **No 3 berth** (next to bridge) AB 20-30ft €19.00, P & D (in cans), FW, ME, El, ⚒, CH, C (15 ton); **Sligo YC** ☎ 9177168, Ⓐs, FW, Bar, Slip. **Services:** Slip, D, ME, El, ⚒, SM, Gas; **Town** 🛒, R, Bar, ✉, Ⓑ, ⇌ Irish Rail ☎ 9169888, Bus ☎ 9160066, ✈ (Strandhill) ☎ 9168280.

MINOR HARBOUR ON S SIDE OF DONEGAL BAY

MULLAGHMORE 54°27'·90N 08°26'·80W. AC 2702. Tides see 6.17. Pierhead lit Fl G 3s 5m 3M. Fair weather ⚓ in 2-3m off hbr ent, sheltered by Mullaghmore Head, except from N/NE winds. For Ⓐs near hbr ent, call Liam Carey at BY, ☎ 071 66106, mobile ☎ 087 2574497. Keep close to N pier to avoid shingle bank drying 1m, ⅔ of the way across the ent toward the S pier. Take the ground or dry out against the piers inside hbr berth on pontoon on bkwtr (min 1m at MLWS). Access approx HW±2 when least depth is 2m. VHF Ch 16, 8, 6. Facilities: FW at S Pier and on bkwtr, BY, ⚒, D (cans), 🛒, R, Bar.

MINOR HARBOUR/ANCHORAGE TO THE WEST

KILLALA BAY, Sligo/Mayo, **54°13'·02N 09°12'·80W**. AC 2715. Tides, see 6.17. The bay, open to the N-NE, is entered between Lenadoon Pt and Kilcummin Hd, 6M to the W. 1·1M W of Kilcummin Hd are 8 Y Ⓐs off Rathlackan pier, well sheltered from W'lies. Carrickpatrick ECM lt buoy, in mid-bay marks St Patrick's Rks to the W. Thence, if bound for Killala hbr, make good Killala SHM lt buoy, 7½ca to the SSW. The Round Tr and cathedral spire at Killala are conspic. Four sets of ldg bns/lts lead via a narrow chan between sand dunes and over the bar (0·3m) as follows:

- 230°, Rinnaun Pt lts Oc 10s 7/12m 5M, □ concrete trs.
- 215°, Inch Is, □ concrete trs; the rear has Dir lt Fl WRG 2s.
- 196°, Kilroe lts Oc 4s 5/10m 2M, W □ trs, which lead to ⚓ in Bartragh Pool, 6ca NE of Killala hbr; thence
- 236°, Pier lts Iso 2s 5/7m 2M, W ◊ daymarks, lead via narrow, dredged chan to pier where AB is possible in about 1·5m.

Facilities: FW, P & D (cans), 🛒 in town ½M.
Other hbrs in the bay: R Moy leading to Ballina should not be attempted without pilot/local knowledge. Inishcrone in the SE has a pier and lt; see 6.3.

EAGLE ISLAND TO SLYNE HEAD

(AC 2420) This coast has many inlets, some sheltered. ▶ *Streams are weak offshore.* ◀ There are few lights. Keep 5ca off Erris Hd, and further in bad weather. Unless calm, keep seaward of Eagle Is (lt) where there is race to N. Frenchport (AC 2703) is good temp ⚓ except in strong W winds. Inishkea Is (AC 2704) can be visited in good weather; anch N or S of Rusheen Is. On passage keep 5ca W of Inishkea to avoid bad seas if wind over tide. The sound off Mullett Peninsula is clear, but for Pluddany Rk 6ca E of Inishkea N.

Blacksod B (AC 2704) has easy ent (possible at night) and good shelter. In the approaches Black Rk (lt) has rks up to 1·25M SW. From N, in good weather, there is chan between Duvillaun Beg and Gaghta Is, but in W gales beware breakers 1M SE of Duvillaun More.

Rough water is likely off Achill Head (the highest cliffs in the British Islands). Achill Sound (ACs 2667/2704) is entered close N of Achillbeg Is and extends N for about 8M to Bull's Mouth. Passage is possible at HW for shallow draft craft (<2m) via a swing bridge. Anchorages each end of Sound, ▶*but the stream runs strongly.* ◀

Clare Is has Two Fathom Rk (3·4m) 5ca off NW coast, and Calliaghcrom Rk 5ca to the N; anch on NE side. In Clew Bay Newport and Westport (AC 2667, 2057) need detailed pilotage directions. S of Clare Is beware Meemore Shoal 1·5M W of Roonagh Hd. 2M further W is the isolated rk Mweelaun. The islands of Caher, Ballybeg, Inishturk (with ⚓ on E side) and Inishdalla have few hidden dangers, but the coast to the E must be given a berth of 1·5M even in calm weather; in strong winds seas break much further offshore.

Killary B (AC 2706) and Little Killary both have good ⚓s in magnificent scenery. Consult sailing directions, and only approach in reasonable weather and good vis.

Ballynakill Hbr (AC 2706), easily entered either side of Freaghillaun South, has excellent shelter; Tully mountain is conspic to N. Beware Mullaghadrina and Ship Rk in N chan. ⚓ in Fahy, Derryinver or Barnaderg B. There is ⚓ on S side of Inishbofin (lt), but difficult access/exit in strong SW wind or swell. Rks and breakers exist E of Inishbofin and S of Inishshark; see AC 2707 for clearing lines. Lecky Rks lie 1M SSE of Davillaun. Carrickmahoy is a very dangerous rock (1·9m) between Inishbofin and Cleggan Pt.

Cleggan B is moderate anch, open to NW but easy access. High Is Sound is usual coasting route, not Friar Is Sound or Aughrus Passage. Clifden B (AC 2708) has offlying dangers with breakers; enter 3ca S of Carrickrana Bn and ⚓ off Drinagh Pt, in Clifden Hbr or Ardbear B.

Slyne Hd Lt Ho marks SW end of the rocks and islets stretching 2M WSW from coast. ▶ *Here the stream turns N at HW Galway – 0320, and S at HW Galway + 0300. It runs 3kn at sp and in bad weather causes a dangerous race; keep 2M offshore.* ◀ Seas break on Barret Shoals, 3M NW of Slyne Hd.

SLYNE HEAD TO LISCANNOR BAY

(AC 2173) In good visibility the Connemara coast (AC 2709, 2096) and Aran Islands (AC 3339) give excellent cruising. But there are many rks, and few navigational marks. Between Slyne Hd and Roundstone B are many offlying dangers. If coasting, keep well seaward of Skerd Rks. A conspic twr (24m) on Golan Head is a key feature. Going E the better hbrs are Roundstone B, Cashel B, Killeany B, Greatman B and Cashla B. Kilronan (Killeany B) on Inishmore is only reasonable hbr in Aran Islands, but is exposed in E winds. Disused lt ho on centre of island is conspic.

Normal approach to Galway B is through N Sound or S Sound. N Sound is 4M wide from Eagle Rk and other dangers off Lettermullan shore, to banks on S side which break in strong winds. S Sound is 3M wide, with no dangers except Finnis Rk (0·4m) 5ca SE of Inisheer. The other channels are Gregory Sound, 1M wide between Inishmore and Inishmaan, and Foul Sound between Inishmaan and Inisheer. The latter has one danger, Pipe Rk and the reef inshore of it, extending 3ca NW of Inisheer.

The N side of Galway Bay is exposed, with no shelter. Galway is a commercial port, with possible marina plans. 3M SE, New Hbr (AC 1984) is a more pleasant anch with moorings off Galway Bay SC. Westward to Black Hd there are many bays and inlets, often poorly marked, but providing shelter and exploration. The coast SW to Liscannor Bay is devoid of shelter. O'Brien's Twr is conspic just N of the 199m high Cliffs of Moher.

6.18 WESTPORT (CLEW BAY)

Mayo **53°47'·85N 09°35'·40W** ❀❀◊◊✿✿✿

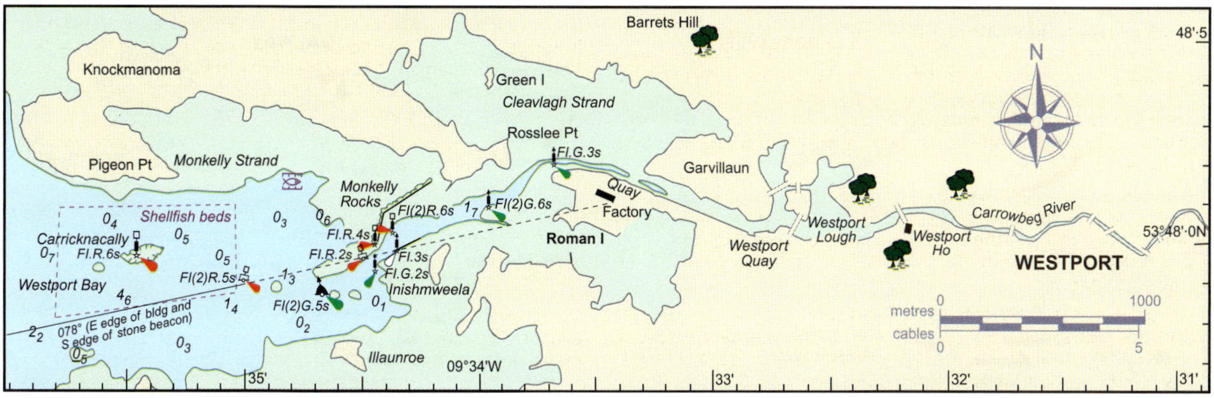

CHARTS AC 2667, 2057; Imray C54.

TIDES –0545 Dover; ML 2·5; Duration 0610

Standard Port GALWAY (⟶)

Times				Height (metres)			
High Water		Low Water		MHWS	MHWN	MLWN	MLWS
0600	1100	0000	0700	5·1	3·9	2·0	0·6
1800	2300	1200	1900				
BROADHAVEN							
+0040	+0050	+0040	+0050	–1·4	–1·1	–0·4	–0·1
BLACKSOD QUAY							
+0025	+0035	+0040	+0040	–1·2	–1·0	–0·6	–0·2
CLARE ISLAND							
+0015	+0021	+0039	+0027	–0·6	–0·4	–0·1	+0·2
INISHGORT/CLEW BAY							
+0035	+0045	+0115	+0100	–0·7	–0·5	–0·2	+0·2
KILLARY HARBOUR							
+0021	+0015	+0035	+0029	–1·0	–0·8	–0·4	–0·1
INISHBOFIN HARBOUR							
+0013	+0009	+0021	+0017	–1·0	–0·8	–0·4	–0·1
CLIFDEN BAY							
+0005	+0005	+0016	+0016	–0·7	–0·5	No data	

SHELTER Secure ⚓s amongst the islands at all times, as follows: E of Inishlyre in 2m; 2ca NE of Dorinish More, good holding in lee of Dorinish Bar (dries); 6 Ⓜs in Rosmoney Hbr 53°49'·75N 09°37'·34W; Westport Quay HW±1½, to dry out on S side; Newport Hbr (dries) can be reached above mid-flood with careful pilotage (AC 2667); dry out against N quay or ⚓ at E end of Rabbit Is.

NAVIGATION WPT 53°49'·20N 09°42'·10W, 071°/1·2M to Inishgort lt ho. Contact Tom Gibbons (Inishlyre Is) ☎ (098) 26381 for pilotage advice. Approaches to Westport Channel between Monkellys Rks and Inishmweela are well marked by lit PHMs and SHMs. Beware fish farms E of Clare I and in Newport Bay. Do not anchor or ground in the Carricknacally Shellfish Bed Area.

LIGHTS AND MARKS Westport Bay entered via Inishgort lt, L Fl 10s 11m 10M (H24), and a series of ldg lines, but not advised at night. Final appr line 080° towards lt bn, Fl 3s. but beware of drying patches on this lead inwards from Pigeon PHM. Chan from Westport Bay to Westport Quay, 1½M approx, is marked by bns.

R/T None.

TELEPHONE (Code 098) MRCC (01) 6620922/3; ⊜ (094) 9021131; Police 9025555; Ⓗ (094) 9021733.

FACILITIES **Westport Quays** M, AB free, Slip, 🛒, R, Bar; **Services:** Kos, El, Ⓔ; **Town** P & D (cans), ✉, Ⓑ, ⇌, ✈ (Galway/Knock). **Mayo SC Rosmoney** ☎ 9026160, Slip, Bar; **Glénans Irish SC** ☎ 9026046 on Collanmore Is.

OTHER ANCHORAGES FROM EAGLE IS TO SLYNE HEAD

BROAD HAVEN, Mayo, **54°16'·00N 09°53'·20W**. AC 2703. A safe refuge except in N'lies. Easy appr across Broad Haven Bay to the ent between Brandy Pt and Gubacashel Pt, Iso WR 4s27m 12/9M, W tr. 7ca S of this lt is Ballyglas Fl G 3s on W side. ⚓ close N or S of Ballyglas which has pier (2m) and 8 Y Ⓜs. In E'lies ⚓ 3ca S of Inver Pt out of the tide. Further S off Barrett Pt, the inlet narrows and turns W to Belmullet. Facilities: 🛒, ✉.

PORTNAFRANKAGH Mayo, **54°14'·95N 10°06'·00W**. AC 2703. Tides approx as Broad Haven. A safe passage ⚓, close to the coastal route, but swell enters in all winds. Appr toward Port Pt, thence keep to the N side for better water; middle and S side break in onshore winds. ⚓ in 4–5m on S side, close inshore. L and slip at new pier. Unlit, but Eagle Is lt, Fl (3) 10s 67m 26M H24, W tr, is 2M N. No facilities; Belmullet 4M, 🛒.

BLACKSOD BAY, Mayo, **54°05'·00N 10°02'·00W**. AC 2704. HW –0525 on Dover; ML 2·2m; Duration 0610. See 6.18. Easy appr, accessible by night. Safe ⚓s depending on wind: NW of Blacksod Pt 6 Y Ⓜs in 3m; at Elly B in 1·8m; Elly Hbr 6 Y Ⓜs; Saleen Bay (ldg lts 319°, both Oc 4s, lead to pier); N of Claggan Pt. Beware drying rk 3·5ca SSE of Ardmore Pt. Lts: Blacksod Pt, Fl (2) WR 7·5s 13m 9M, see 6.3. ECM buoy Q (3) 10s. Ldg lts 181°, Oc W 5s, lead to Blacksod pier hd. Few facilities; nearest town is Belmullet.

CLARE ISLAND, Mayo, **53°48'·1N 09°56'·7W**. 6 Ⓜs on SE side untenable in E winds. Hotel, Bar, some 🛒, Wi-fi.

INISHTURK, Mayo, **53°42'·3N 10°05'·2W**. 8 Y Ⓜs Garranty Hbr. sheltered SW to NNW winds. Slip, quay, Bar, R, ✉, 6 Ⓜs on E side.

KILLARY HARBOUR, Mayo/Galway, **53°37'·83N 09°54'·00W**, 4ca W of Doonee Is. AC 2706. Tides 6.18. A spectacular 7M long inlet, narrow and deep. Caution fish farms, some with Fl Y lts. Appr in good vis to identify Doonee Is and Inishbarna bns, both LFl G, ldg 099° to ent. ⚓s off Dernasliggaun, Bundorragha and, at head of inlet, Leenaun with 8 Y Ⓜs. (Village: L, 🛒, Bar, hotel, Wi-fi). Enter **Little Killary Bay** 4ca S of Doonee Is; drying rks at ent. Good ⚓ in 3m at head of bay.

BALLYNAKILL, Galway, **53°34'·95N 10°03'·00W**. AC 2706. Tides as Inishbofin/Killary. Easy appr between Cleggan Pt, Fl (3) WRG 15s and Rinvyle Pt. Then pass N of Freaghillaun South Is, E of which is good passage ⚓ in 7m. Further E, Carrigeen and Ardagh Rks lie in mid-chan. Keep N for ⚓ in Derryinver B. S chan leads to ⚓s: off Ross Pt; S of Roeillaun; in Fahy Bay with 8 Y Ⓜs sheltered by bar dries 0·2m. No facilities.

INISHBOFIN, Galway, **53°36'·60N 10°13'·20W**. AC 1820, 2707.HW –0555 on Dover; ML 1·9m. Very safe once inside narrow ent. 2 conspic W trs and Dir RWG lt lead 032°. ⚓ between new pier and Port Is. Old pier to the E dries. Gun Rock, Fl (2) 6s 8m 4M, vis 296°-253°. Slip, FW (on both piers), R, Bar, 🛒, Wi-fi, Hotel ☎ (095) 45803.

CLIFDEN BAY, Galway, **53°29'·40N 10°05'·90W**. AC 1820, 2708. HW –0600 on Dover; Duration 0610. Tides at 6.18. Before entering identify the conspic W bn on Carrickrana Rks. To the E keep clear of Coghan's Rks and Doolick Rks. Ldg marks: W bn at Fishing Pt on 080° with Clifden Castle (ruin); caution bar 2·4m off Fishing Pt. 8 Y Ⓜs are 3ca S of Castle ruins, or ⚓ NE of Drinagh Pt. In the drying creek to Clifden beware ruined trng wall; dry out against the quay. Or enter Ardbear Bay to ⚓ SE of Yellow Slate Rks in 3·4m. Keep clear of fish farms. Facilities: **Town** Bar, Ⓑ, CH, D, P, ✉, R, 🛒, Kos, FW, 🛒, R, Dr, Ⓗ. Bus to Galway.

6.19 GALWAY BAY

Galway **53°12'N 09°08'W** ❀❀❀◊◊✿✿✿

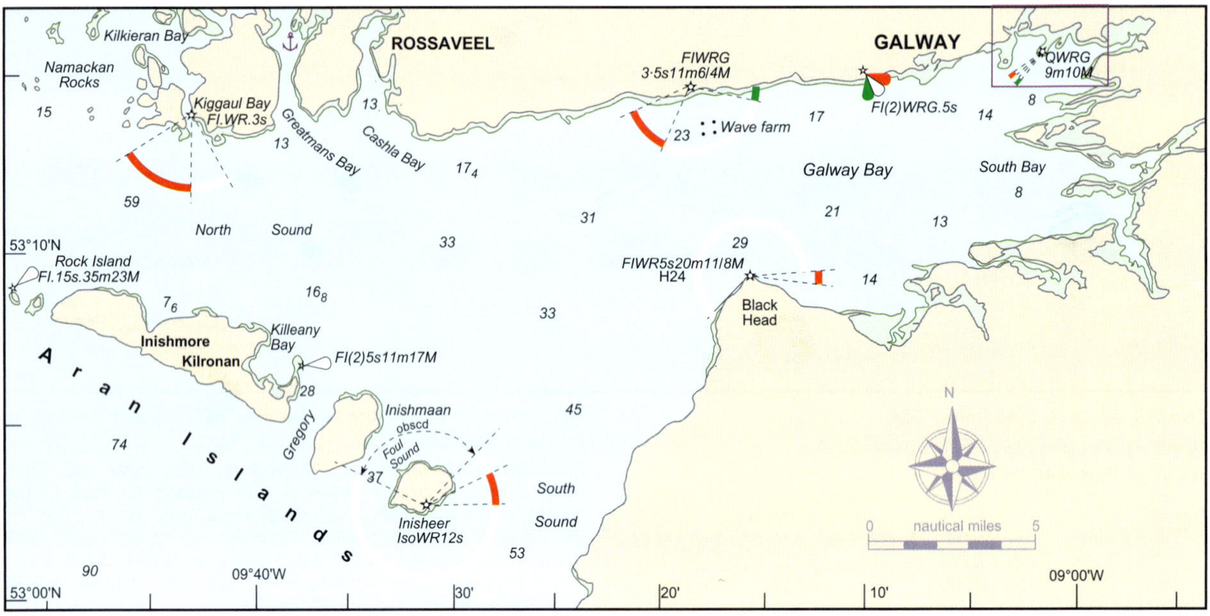

CHARTS AC 2173, 3339, 1984,1904; Imray C55.

TIDES –0555 Dover; ML 2·9; Duration 0620

Standard Port GALWAY (⟶)

Times				Height (metres)			
High Water		Low Water		MHWS	MHWN	MLWN	MLWS
0600	1100	0000	0700	5·1	3·9	2·0	0·6
1800	2300	1200	1900				
Differences KILKIERAN COVE							
+0005	+0005	+0016	+0016	–0·3	–0·2	–0·1	0·0
ROUNDSTONE BAY							
+0003	+0003	+0008	+0008	–0·7	–0·5	–0·3	–0·1
KILLEANY BAY (Aran Islands)							
–0008	–0008	+0003	+0003	–0·4	–0·3	–0·2	–0·1
LISCANNOR							
–0003	–0007	+0006	+0002	–0·4	–0·3	No data	

SHELTER Galway Bay is sheltered from large swells by Aran Is, but seas get up in the 20M from Aran Is to Galway. Beware salmon drift nets in the apps to many bays. The better ⚓s from Slyne Head and clockwise around Galway Bay are:

Bunowen Bay: (53°24'·6N 10°06'·9W). Sheltered in W-NE winds; unsafe in S'ly. Easy appr with Bunowen House brg 000°, leaving Mullauncarrickscoltia Rk (1·1m) to port. ⚓ in 3-4m below conspic Doon Hill.

Roundstone Bay: AC2709 (Off chartlet at 53°23'N 09°54'·5W). Safe shelter/access, except in SE'ly. 4 Y 🅐s are 5ca SSE of Roundstone, or ⚓ in 2m off N quay. There are other ⚓s E'ward in Bertraghboy and Cashel Bays.

Kilkieran Bay: Easy ent abm Golam Tr (conspic). 12 Y 🅐s off Kilkieran. Many ⚓s in 14M long, sheltered bay.

Kiggaul Bay: Easy ent, H24; ⚓ close W/NW of lt Fl WR 3s 5/3M. Depth 3 to 4m; exposed to S/SE winds.

Greatman Bay: Beware English Rk (dries 1·2m), Keeraun Shoal (breaks in heavy weather), Arkeena Rk, Trabaan Rk, Rin Rks and Chapel Rks. ⚓ off Natawny Quay (E side), or on 4 Y 🅐s off Maumeen Quay (dries), AB possible.

Cashla Bay: Easiest hbr on this coast; ent in all weather. ⚓ and 8 Y 🅐s off Sruthan Quay. Rossaveel, on E side, is a busy fishing and ferry hbr.

Note: There is no safe hbr from Cashla to Galway (20M).

Bays between Black Hd and Galway have rocks and shoals, but give excellent shelter. Kinvarra B, Aughinish B, South B and Ballyvaghan B are the main ones. Enter Kinvarra B with caution on the flood; beware rks. Berth in small drying hbr. Beware fish farm in South B. Ballvaghan B, entered either side of Illaunloo Rk, leads to two piers (both dry) or ⚓ close NE in pool (3m). Best access HW±2.

NAVIGATION Enter the Bay by one of four Sounds:

- North Sound between Inishmore and Golam Tr (conspic), 4½M wide, is easiest but beware Brocklinmore Bank in heavy weather.
- Gregory Sound between Inishmore and Inishmaan, is free of dangers, but give Straw Island a berth of 2-3ca.
- Foul Sound between Inishmaan and Inisheer; only danger is Pipe Rock (dries) at end of reef extending 3ca NW of Inisheer.
- South Sound between Inisheer and mainland. Only danger Finnis Rock (dries 0·4m) 4½ca SE of E point of Inisheer (marked by ECM buoy Q (3) 10s). From S, beware Kilstiffin Rocks off Liscanor Bay.

LIGHTS AND MARKS Roundstone Bay: Croaghnakeela Is Fl 3·7s 7m 5M. Inishnee lt Fl (2) WRG 10s 9m 5/3M, W sector 017°-030°. Kiggaul Bay: Fl WR 3s 5m 5/3M, 329°-W-359°-R-059°. Cashla Bay: Killeen Pt Fl (3) WR 10s 6/3M; Lion Pt Dir lt 010°, Iso WRG 4s 8/6M, 008·5°-W-011·5°. Rossaveel ldg lts 116°, Oc 3s. Black Head lt Fl WR 5s 20m 11/8M H24, vis 045°-W-268°-R (covers Illanloo Rk)-276°.

FACILITIES

Bunowen Bay: No facilities.
Roundstone Bay: 🛒, FW, Bar, ✉, Bus to Galway.
Kilkieran Bay: Bar, ☎, P, 🛒, Bus to Galway.
Kiggaul Bay: Bar (no ☎), shop at Lettermullen (1M).
Greatman Bay: Maumeen 🛒, P (1M), Bar.
Cashla Bay: **Carraroe** (1M SW) 🛒, Hotel, ☎; **Rossaveel** HM ☎ 091 572108, FW, D, ME; **Costelloe** (1½M E), Hotel, ✉, Gge.

ARAN ISLANDS Beware marine farm activity, only reasonable shelter is off Inishmore in Killeany Bay, but exposed to E/NE winds and crowded with FVs. HM ☎ 099 20946; 8 Y 🅐s available; or ⚓ S of Kilronan pier; or ⚓ E of Killeany Pt; or in good weather ⚓ at Portmurvy. Kilronan, facilities: 8🅐s, 🛒, D, FW, ✉; Ferry to Galway, ✈ to Galway from airstrip on beach. **Lights and marks**: Inishmore: Eeragh Island (Rk Is) Fl 15s 35m 23M, W tr, B bands. Killeany Bay: Straw Is, Fl (2) 5s 11m 17M. Ldg lts 192° both Oc 5s for Killeany hbr. Inishmaan Ldg lts 199°, both Oc 6s 8M. New harbour being constructed (2009). Inisheer: Iso WR 12s 34m 20/16M, Racon, vis 225°-W-245° (partially obscd 225°-231° beyond 7M), R sector covers Finnis Rk.

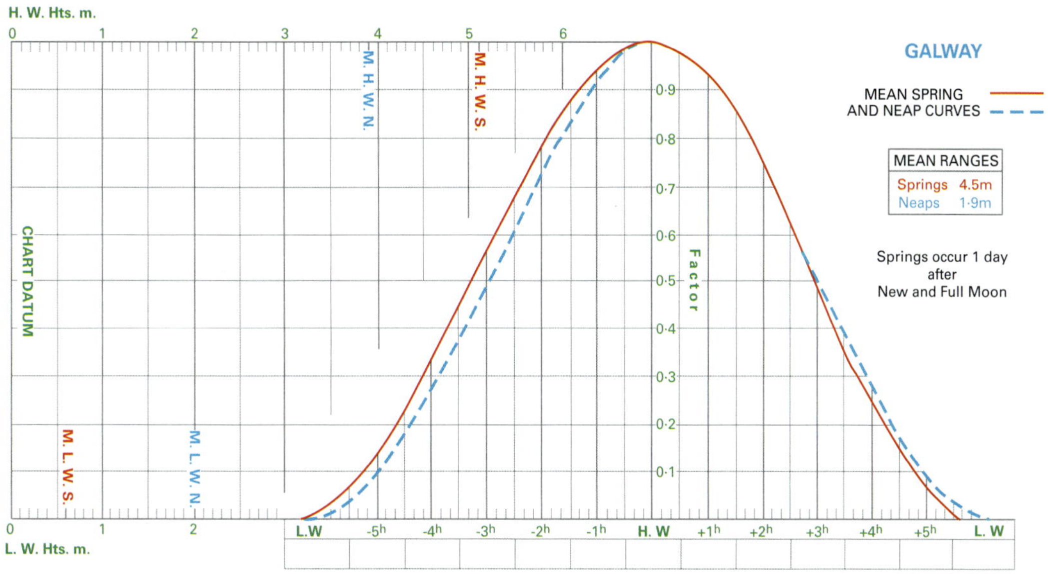

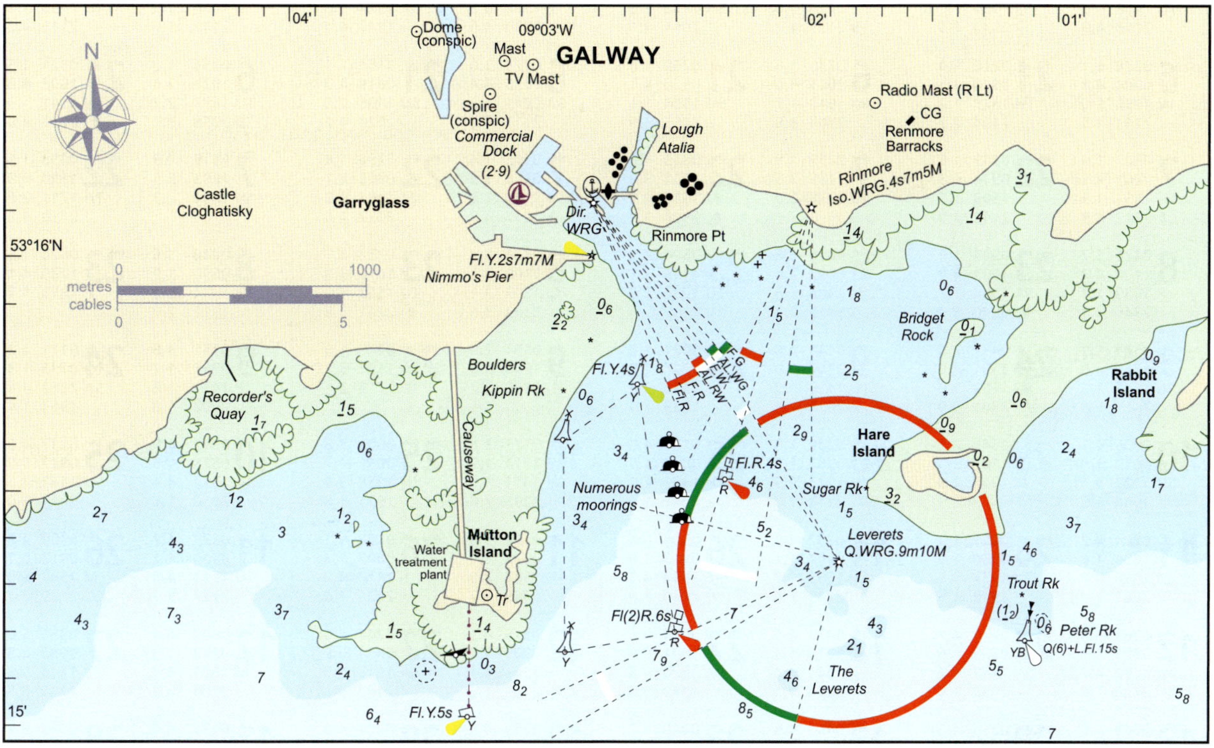

GALWAY HARBOUR 53°16'·07N 09°02'·74W

SHELTER Very good in Galway hbr, protected from SW'lies by Mutton Island. Dock gates open HW–2 to HW, when min depth is 6m. Enter Galway Dock and secure in SW corner of basin where there is a 25-berth marina, or ask HM for waiting berth on lead-in pier. It is dangerous to lie in the 'Layby' (a dredged cut NE of New pier) when wind is SE or S; if strong from these points, seas sweep round the pierhead. New Harbour (2·5M ESE and home of Galway Bay SC) is nearest safe ⚓ to Galway. 5 Y 🅐s in lee of Mutton Island causeway in 2-4m.

NAVIGATION Galway WPT 53°14'·80N 09°03'·40W, 061°/1·1M to Leverets lt. Tidal information see www.gsmtides.com. Shipping information see www.aislive.com.

LIGHTS AND MARKS See 6.3 and chartlet. Leverets Q WRG 9m 10M; B tr, W bands; Rinmore Iso WRG 4s 7m 5M; W □ tr . Appr chan 325° is defined by a Dir lt WRG 7m 3M on New Pier.

R/T Call *Galway Harbour Radio* VHF Ch **12** 16 (HW–2½ to HW+1). Call Galway Pilots on VHF Ch **12** in case ship movements are imminent or under way and follow their instructions on berthing.

TELEPHONE (Code 091) HM 561874; MRCC (066) 9476109; Coast/Cliff Rescue Service (099) 61107; Police 538000; Dr 562453.

FACILITIES **Dock** AB €15 if space available, FW, D (by r/tanker not small quantities), El, ME, ⚒, C (35 ton), CH, LB, PV, SM, 🛒, R, Bar; **Galway YC** M, Slip, FW, C, CH, Bar; **Galway Bay SC** ☎ 794527, M, CH, Bar; **Town** P, D, ACA, Gas, Gaz, Kos, 🛒, R, Bar, ✉, Ⓑ, ⇌, ✈ Carnmore (6M to the E of Galway City direct flights to UK see www.aerann.com). The nearest D by pump is Rossaveal.

TIME ZONE (UT)
For Summer Time add ONE hour in **non-shaded areas**

GALWAY LAT 53°16′N LONG 9°03′W

TIMES AND HEIGHTS OF HIGH AND LOW WATERS

Dates in red are SPRINGS
Dates in blue are NEAPS

YEAR **2010**

JANUARY

Date	Time	m	Date	Time	m
1 F	0504 1110 1735 2323	5.2 0.5 5.1 0.7	16 SA	0548 1141 1813 2354	4.8 0.9 4.6 1.1
2 SA	0553 1155 1822	5.3 0.3 5.2	17 SU	0625 1215 1848	4.8 0.8 4.6
3 SU	0009 0639 1239 1909	0.6 5.3 0.2 5.1	18 M	0028 0701 1249 1923	1.1 4.8 0.8 4.6
4 M	0055 0726 1323 1956	0.6 5.3 0.3 5.0	19 TU	0102 0735 1321 1957	1.1 4.8 0.9 4.5
5 TU	0140 0813 1408 2046	0.8 5.1 0.6 4.8	20 W	0136 0808 1354 2030	1.2 4.6 1.0 4.3
6 W	0228 0904 1456 2141	1.1 4.8 1.0 4.5	21 TH	0210 0840 1428 2104	1.4 4.5 1.2 4.2
7 TH	0322 1001 1551 ◑ 2242	1.4 4.5 1.3 4.3	22 F	0249 0916 1508 2146	1.6 4.3 1.5 4.0
8 F	0426 1104 1659 2346	1.7 4.2 1.7 4.1	23 SA	0334 1003 1554 ◐ 2240	1.9 4.1 1.7 3.9
9 SA	0541 1212 1827	1.9 4.0 1.9	24 SU	0431 1101 1652 2341	2.0 4.0 1.9 3.9
10 SU	0055 0657 1328 1944	4.1 1.9 4.0 1.9	25 M	0546 1207 1807	2.1 3.9 2.0
11 M	0204 0806 1438 2041	4.2 1.8 4.0 1.8	26 TU	0051 0730 1327 1949	3.9 1.9 3.9 1.8
12 TU	0301 0901 1532 2125	4.3 1.6 4.2 1.6	27 W	0211 0838 1447 2053	4.1 1.6 4.2 1.5
13 W	0348 0946 1617 2205	4.5 1.4 4.3 1.4	28 TH	0315 0931 1545 2143	4.5 1.1 4.5 1.1
14 TH	0430 1027 1658 2242	4.6 1.2 4.4 1.3	29 F	0407 1017 1636 2228	4.8 0.6 4.9 0.7
15 F	0510 1105 1736 ● 2319	4.7 1.0 4.5 1.2	30 SA	0455 1100 1723 ○ 2312	5.1 0.3 5.1 0.4
			31 SU	0542 1142 1808 2355	5.4 0.0 5.3 0.2

FEBRUARY

Date	Time	m	Date	Time	m
1 M	0627 1223 1851	5.4 -0.1 5.3	16 TU	0005 0639 1222 1857	0.7 4.9 0.6 4.7
2 TU	0038 0710 1304 1934	0.2 5.4 0.1 5.1	17 W	0037 0711 1251 1927	0.8 4.8 0.7 4.6
3 W	0120 0753 1344 2018	0.4 5.2 0.3 4.9	18 TH	0107 0740 1322 1953	0.9 4.7 0.8 4.5
4 TH	0204 0838 1427 2105	0.7 4.8 0.8 4.5	19 F	0139 0808 1355 2018	1.1 4.5 1.0 4.3
5 F	0251 0927 1514 ◑ 2159	1.1 4.4 1.3 4.2	20 SA	0216 0840 1433 2054	1.3 4.3 1.3 4.1
6 SA	0346 1025 1612 2303	1.5 4.0 1.7 3.9	21 SU	0259 0926 1518 2151	1.6 4.1 1.6 3.9
7 SU	0459 1135 1738	1.9 3.7 2.0	22 M	0353 1031 1615 ◐ 2304	1.8 3.9 1.9 3.8
8 M	0020 0622 1303 1915	3.8 2.0 3.6 2.1	23 TU	0504 1144 1732	2.0 3.7 2.0
9 TU	0145 0747 1428 2027	3.8 1.9 3.7 1.9	24 W	0021 0714 1310 1939	3.8 1.9 3.8 1.9
10 W	0249 0852 1523 2113	4.0 1.7 3.9 1.7	25 TH	0156 0826 1437 2042	4.0 1.5 4.1 1.4
11 TH	0337 0934 1605 2149	4.2 1.4 4.2 1.4	26 F	0304 0917 1534 2130	4.4 1.0 4.5 1.0
12 F	0417 1010 1643 2224	4.5 1.1 4.4 1.1	27 SA	0354 1001 1620 2213	4.8 0.5 4.9 0.5
13 SA	0455 1044 1718 2259	4.6 0.9 4.5 0.9	28 SU	0440 1042 1704 ○ 2255	5.2 0.1 5.2 0.2
14 SU	0531 1118 1753 ● 2333	4.8 0.7 4.6 0.8			
15 M	0606 1150 1826	4.8 0.6 4.7			

MARCH

Date	Time	m	Date	Time	m
1 M	0525 1122 1747 2336	5.4 -0.1 5.3 0.0	16 TU	0541 1121 1758 2338	4.8 0.6 4.8 0.6
2 TU	0608 1201 1829	5.5 -0.1 5.3	17 W	0613 1151 1827	4.8 0.6 4.8
3 W	0017 0650 1240 1909	0.0 5.4 0.0 5.2	18 TH	0009 0644 1221 1854	0.7 4.8 0.6 4.7
4 TH	0058 0730 1319 1949	0.2 5.2 0.4 4.9	19 F	0039 0713 1252 1920	0.8 4.7 0.8 4.6
5 F	0139 0812 1358 2030	0.5 4.8 0.8 4.6	20 SA	0113 0744 1326 1947	0.9 4.6 1.0 4.4
6 SA	0223 0856 1441 2117	1.0 4.4 1.3 4.2	21 SU	0151 0819 1406 2024	1.1 4.3 1.3 4.2
7 SU	0315 0948 1534 ◑ 2217	1.4 3.9 1.8 3.8	22 M	0236 0908 1452 2122	1.4 4.1 1.6 4.0
8 M	0426 1100 1703 2343	1.8 3.6 2.1 3.6	23 TU	0331 1016 1552 ◐ 2241	1.7 3.8 1.9 3.8
9 TU	0551 1240 1840	2.0 3.4 2.2	24 W	0445 1131 1717	1.9 3.7 2.1
10 W	0121 0714 1411 2001	3.6 1.9 3.6 2.0	25 TH	0003 0655 1258 1921	3.8 1.7 3.9 1.8
11 TH	0228 0828 1503 2049	3.9 1.7 3.9 1.7	26 F	0138 0803 1420 2021	4.1 1.3 4.2 1.4
12 F	0315 0909 1543 2125	4.1 1.4 4.1 1.4	27 SA	0244 0854 1513 2109	4.5 0.9 4.6 0.9
13 SA	0355 0942 1619 2159	4.4 1.1 4.4 1.1	28 SU	0334 0938 1558 2152	4.9 0.5 5.0 0.5
14 SU	0431 1016 1653 2233	4.6 0.8 4.6 0.8	29 M	0419 1019 1641 2233	5.2 0.2 5.2 0.3
15 M	0507 1049 1726 ● 2306	4.7 0.7 4.7 0.7	30 TU	0503 1059 1723 ○ 2314	5.3 0.1 5.3 0.1
			31 W	0546 1138 1803 2355	5.4 0.1 5.3 0.1

APRIL

Date	Time	m	Date	Time	m
1 TH	0628 1216 1843	5.3 0.3 5.2	16 F	0616 1151 1824	4.8 0.7 4.8
2 F	0036 0708 1254 1922	0.3 5.0 0.6 5.0	17 SA	0015 0651 1226 1856	0.7 4.7 0.8 4.7
3 SA	0118 0749 1332 2003	0.6 4.7 1.0 4.6	18 SU	0053 0728 1305 1932	0.8 4.6 1.0 4.6
4 SU	0201 0832 1414 2047	1.0 4.3 1.4 4.3	19 M	0135 0810 1348 2015	1.0 4.4 1.3 4.4
5 M	0251 0922 1506 2142	1.4 3.9 1.9 3.9	20 TU	0223 0902 1438 2115	1.3 4.2 1.6 4.2
6 TU	0359 1027 1633 ◑ 2258	1.8 3.6 2.2 3.7	21 W	0321 1008 1541 ◐ 2231	1.5 4.0 1.9 4.0
7 W	0519 1203 1801	1.9 3.5 2.2	22 TH	0438 1120 1711 2350	1.6 3.9 2.0 4.0
8 TH	0040 0630 1334 1911	3.6 1.9 3.6 2.0	23 F	0626 1238 1853	1.5 4.1 1.7
9 F	0151 0735 1431 2008	3.8 1.7 3.8 1.8	24 SA	0111 0733 1352 1954	4.2 1.3 4.4 1.4
10 SA	0242 0826 1512 2050	4.0 1.5 4.1 1.5	25 SU	0217 0827 1447 2044	4.5 1.0 4.7 1.0
11 SU	0323 0906 1547 2127	4.2 1.2 4.3 1.2	26 M	0309 0913 1533 2129	4.8 0.7 5.0 0.7
12 M	0400 0942 1621 2203	4.4 1.0 4.5 0.9	27 TU	0356 0955 1616 2211	5.0 0.5 5.2 0.5
13 TU	0435 1016 1653 2237	4.6 0.8 4.7 0.8	28 W	0440 1035 1657 ○ 2253	5.1 0.5 5.2 0.4
14 W	0509 1049 1723 ● 2310	4.7 0.7 4.8 0.7	29 TH	0524 1115 1739 2336	5.1 0.5 5.2 0.5
15 TH	0543 1120 1754 2342	4.8 0.7 4.8 0.7	30 F	0607 1154 1819	5.0 0.7 5.1

Chart Datum: 0·20 metres above Ordnance Datum (Dublin). HAT is 5·6 metres above Chart Datum; see 0.20

TIME ZONE (UT)
For Summer Time add ONE hour in **non-shaded areas**

GALWAY LAT 53°16'N LONG 9°03'W

TIMES AND HEIGHTS OF HIGH AND LOW WATERS

Dates in red are SPRINGS
Dates in blue are NEAPS

YEAR 2010

MAY

Day	Time	m	Day	Time	m
1 SA	0017	0.6	16 SU	0634	4.8
	0648	4.8		1209	0.9
	1233	0.9		1841	4.9
	1900	4.9			
2 SU	0100	0.8	17 M	0041	0.7
	0730	4.6		0716	4.7
	1312	1.2		1252	1.0
	1941	4.7		1924	4.8
3 M	0143	1.1	18 TU	0126	0.8
	0813	4.3		0802	4.6
	1353	1.5		1338	1.2
	2025	4.4		2012	4.6
4 TU	0232	1.4	19 W	0216	1.0
	0900	4.0		0855	4.4
	1442	1.8		1430	1.4
	2116	4.1		2111	4.4
5 W	0330	1.6	20 TH	0313	1.2
	0957	3.7		0955	4.2
	1552	2.1		1531	1.7
	2217	3.9		◐ 2219	4.3
6 TH	0438	1.8	21 F	0422	1.4
	1106	3.6		1102	4.2
	1715	2.2		1650	1.8
	◑ 2331	3.7		2330	4.3
7 F	0543	1.8	22 SA	0547	1.4
	1226	3.6		1210	4.2
	1821	2.1		1818	1.7
8 SA	0048	3.8	23 SU	0041	4.3
	0641	1.8		0659	1.3
	1336	3.8		1319	4.4
	1919	1.9		1925	1.5
9 SU	0150	3.9	24 M	0148	4.5
	0736	1.6		0758	1.2
	1427	4.0		1419	4.6
	2009	1.7		2019	1.2
10 M	0239	4.0	25 TU	0244	4.6
	0823	1.4		0848	1.1
	1507	4.2		1508	4.8
	2052	1.4		2107	1.0
11 TU	0320	4.2	26 W	0334	4.8
	0905	1.2		0933	1.0
	1542	4.4		1553	4.9
	2131	1.2		2152	0.8
12 W	0358	4.4	27 TH	0421	4.8
	0942	1.1		1015	0.9
	1614	4.6		1636	5.0
	2208	1.0		○ 2236	0.8
13 TH	0435	4.6	28 F	0506	4.8
	1018	0.9		1056	1.0
	1647	4.8		1718	5.0
	2244	0.8		2319	0.8
14 F	0513	4.7	29 SA	0550	4.7
	1052	0.9		1136	1.0
	1723	4.8		1800	4.9
	● 2320	0.7			
15 SA	0552	4.8	30 SU	0002	0.8
	1129	0.8		0632	4.6
	1801	4.9		1215	1.1
	2359	0.7		1841	4.8
			31 M	0044	0.9
				0714	4.5
				1254	1.3
				1923	4.7

JUNE

Day	Time	m	Day	Time	m
1 TU	0126	1.0	16 W	0118	0.5
	0755	4.3		0751	4.8
	1334	1.5		1330	0.9
	2006	4.5		2003	4.8
2 W	0208	1.2	17 TH	0205	0.6
	0838	4.2		0840	4.6
	1417	1.7		1418	1.1
	2051	4.3		2058	4.7
3 TH	0254	1.4	18 F	0256	0.9
	0925	4.0		0935	4.5
	1507	1.9		1513	1.3
	2141	4.1		2159	4.5
4 F	0346	1.6	19 SA	0355	1.1
	1016	3.9		1036	4.3
	1611	2.0		1619	1.6
	◑ 2234	3.9		◐ 2305	4.3
5 SA	0443	1.7	20 SU	0504	1.3
	1110	3.8		1139	4.2
	1722	2.1		1737	1.6
	2328	3.8			
6 SU	0542	1.8	21 M	0011	4.2
	1208	3.8		0620	1.5
	1826	2.0		1246	4.2
				1853	1.6
7 M	0027	3.8	22 TU	0120	4.2
	0639	1.8		0729	1.5
	1313	3.9		1351	4.3
	1924	1.9		1958	1.5
8 TU	0133	3.9	23 W	0223	4.3
	0736	1.7		0827	1.4
	1411	4.0		1448	4.5
	2015	1.6		2051	1.3
9 W	0231	4.0	24 TH	0318	4.4
	0826	1.5		0915	1.3
	1457	4.2		1537	4.6
	2100	1.4		2138	1.1
10 TH	0319	4.2	25 F	0408	4.5
	0910	1.3		0959	1.3
	1537	4.5		1621	4.7
	2142	1.1		2223	1.0
11 F	0404	4.4	26 SA	0453	4.5
	0952	1.1		1040	1.2
	1617	4.7		1704	4.8
	2224	0.9		○ 2306	0.9
12 SA	0449	4.6	27 SU	0537	4.5
	1033	0.9		1120	1.2
	1659	4.9		1746	4.8
	● 2306	0.7		2347	0.8
13 SU	0534	4.8	28 M	0618	4.5
	1115	0.8		1158	1.1
	1744	5.0		1826	4.8
	2349	0.5			
14 M	0620	4.9	29 TU	0026	0.8
	1159	0.8		0657	4.5
	1829	5.0		1235	1.2
				1906	4.7
15 TU	0033	0.5	30 W	0103	0.9
	0704	4.9		0735	4.4
	1244	0.8		1312	1.2
	1915	5.0		1945	4.6

JULY

Day	Time	m	Day	Time	m
1 TH	0140	1.0	16 F	0146	0.3
	0814	4.3		0819	4.9
	1349	1.4		1400	0.7
	2024	4.4		2036	4.8
2 F	0218	1.1	17 SA	0232	0.6
	0852	4.2		0908	4.6
	1428	1.5		1448	1.1
	2105	4.3		2132	4.5
3 SA	0257	1.3	18 SU	0324	1.0
	0933	4.1		1003	4.4
	1511	1.7		1546	1.4
	2149	4.1		◐ 2235	4.2
4 SU	0341	1.5	19 M	0425	1.4
	1015	3.9		1105	4.1
	1602	1.9		1657	1.7
	◑ 2236	3.9		2342	4.0
5 M	0429	1.7	20 TU	0541	1.7
	1102	3.9		1213	4.0
	1709	2.0		1822	1.8
	2328	3.8			
6 TU	0527	1.8	21 W	0055	3.9
	1155	3.8		0701	1.8
	1830	2.0		1328	4.0
				1941	1.7
7 W	0027	3.8	22 TH	0209	4.0
	0637	1.9		0808	1.7
	1259	3.9		1435	4.2
	1940	1.8		2042	1.5
8 TH	0138	3.8	23 F	0309	4.1
	0749	1.7		0900	1.6
	1410	4.1		1527	4.4
	2037	1.5		2129	1.2
9 F	0246	4.0	24 SA	0358	4.2
	0846	1.5		0944	1.4
	1507	4.3		1612	4.5
	2125	1.2		2210	1.0
10 SA	0341	4.3	25 SU	0442	4.4
	0935	1.2		1023	1.2
	1556	4.6		1652	4.7
	2210	0.8		2248	0.9
11 SU	0431	4.6	26 M	0522	4.5
	1020	0.9		1101	1.1
	1643	4.9		1731	4.8
	● 2254	0.5		○ 2326	0.7
12 M	0519	4.8	27 TU	0600	4.5
	1104	0.7		1137	1.0
	1730	5.1		1809	4.8
	2337	0.2			
13 TU	0605	5.0	28 W	0001	0.7
	1148	0.5		0636	4.6
	1816	5.2		1212	0.9
				1845	4.8
14 W	0020	0.1	29 TH	0035	0.7
	0649	5.1		0711	4.6
	1232	0.4		1245	1.0
	1901	5.2		1920	4.7
15 TH	0103	0.1	30 F	0108	0.8
	0734	5.0		0746	4.5
	1315	0.5		1318	1.1
	1948	5.1		1955	4.6
			31 SA	0141	0.9
				0818	4.4
				1352	1.3
				2028	4.4

AUGUST

Day	Time	m	Day	Time	m
1 SU	0216	1.1	16 M	0252	1.1
	0850	4.2		0927	4.4
	1427	1.5		1513	1.4
	2105	4.2		◐ 2201	4.1
2 M	0252	1.4	17 TU	0349	1.5
	0926	4.1		1026	4.0
	1508	1.7		1622	1.7
	2151	4.0		2314	3.8
3 TU	0336	1.6	18 W	0508	1.9
	1011	3.9		1141	3.8
	1601	2.0		1754	1.9
	◑ 2247	3.8			
4 W	0428	1.9	19 TH	0036	3.7
	1107	3.8		0636	2.0
	1713	2.1		1310	3.8
	2349	3.7		1930	1.8
5 TH	0537	2.0	20 F	0159	3.8
	1211	3.8		0749	1.9
	1914	1.9		1423	4.0
				2040	1.6
6 F	0102	3.7	21 SA	0259	4.0
	0721	1.9		0843	1.7
	1330	3.9		1514	4.3
	2021	1.6		2117	1.3
7 SA	0225	3.9	22 SU	0343	4.2
	0829	1.6		0924	1.4
	1448	4.2		1556	4.5
	2111	1.1		2151	1.0
8 SU	0326	4.3	23 M	0423	4.4
	0920	1.2		1001	1.2
	1542	4.6		1634	4.7
	2155	0.7		2224	0.8
9 M	0415	4.6	24 TU	0500	4.5
	1005	0.8		1037	1.0
	1629	5.0		1711	4.8
	2237	0.3		○ 2258	0.7
10 TU	0501	4.9	25 W	0536	4.6
	1048	0.5		1112	0.8
	1714	5.2		1746	4.9
	● 2319	0.0		2332	0.6
11 W	0546	5.2	26 TH	0611	4.7
	1131	0.2		1145	0.8
	1759	5.4		1820	4.9
12 TH	0000	-0.1	27 F	0004	0.6
	0629	5.2		0643	4.7
	1213	0.2		1217	0.8
	1843	5.4		1853	4.8
13 F	0041	-0.1	28 SA	0035	0.7
	0711	5.2		0714	4.6
	1254	0.2		1247	0.9
	1926	5.2		1923	4.6
14 SA	0122	0.2	29 SU	0106	0.9
	0753	5.0		0743	4.5
	1336	0.5		1318	1.1
	2011	4.9		1953	4.5
15 SU	0205	0.6	30 M	0138	1.1
	0837	4.7		0810	4.3
	1421	0.9		1352	1.3
	2100	4.5		2026	4.3
			31 TU	0214	1.4
				0840	4.2
				1432	1.6
				2112	4.0

Chart Datum: 0·20 metres above Ordnance Datum (Dublin). HAT is 5·6 metres above Chart Datum; see 0.20

N Ireland

TIME ZONE (UT)
For Summer Time add ONE hour in **non-shaded areas**

GALWAY LAT 53°16'N LONG 9°03'W

TIMES AND HEIGHTS OF HIGH AND LOW WATERS

Dates in red are SPRINGS
Dates in blue are NEAPS

YEAR **2010**

SEPTEMBER

Date	Time	m	Date	Time	m
1	0257	1.7	16	0443	2.1
	0926	4.0		1108	3.8
	W 1522	1.9		TH 1726	2.0
	◑ 2215	3.8			
2	0351	2.0	17	0017	3.6
	1031	3.8		0611	2.2
	TH 1629	2.1		F 1247	3.8
	2324	3.7		1904	1.9
3	0502	2.1	18	0143	3.8
	1140	3.8		0722	2.0
	F 1856	2.0		SA 1401	4.0
				2025	1.7
4	0040	3.7	19	0239	4.0
	0706	2.0		0816	1.8
	SA 1303	4.0		SU 1452	4.2
	2003	1.6		2053	1.4
5	0207	4.0	20	0320	4.3
	0812	1.6		0858	1.5
	SU 1431	4.3		M 1533	4.5
	2051	1.1		2123	1.1
6	0307	4.4	21	0357	4.5
	0901	1.2		0935	1.2
	M 1525	4.7		TU 1610	4.7
	2134	0.6		2155	0.9
7	0354	4.8	22	0432	4.6
	0945	0.7		1010	1.0
	TU 1610	5.1		W 1645	4.8
	2215	0.2		2228	0.8
8	0438	5.1	23	0507	4.8
	1027	0.4		1044	0.9
	W 1654	5.4		TH 1719	4.9
	● 2255	0.0		○ 2300	0.7
9	0521	5.3	24	0540	4.8
	1109	0.1		1117	0.8
	TH 1738	5.5		F 1752	4.9
	2336	-0.1		2331	0.7
10	0604	5.4	25	0611	4.8
	1150	0.1		1147	0.8
	F 1821	5.5		SA 1823	4.8
11	0016	0.0	26	0001	0.8
	0645	5.3		0641	4.7
	SA 1231	0.2		SU 1217	0.9
	1903	5.3		1853	4.7
12	0057	0.3	27	0032	1.0
	0726	5.1		0709	4.6
	SU 1313	0.5		M 1249	1.1
	1945	5.0		1924	4.6
13	0138	0.7	28	0106	1.2
	0807	4.8		0737	4.5
	M 1356	0.9		TU 1326	1.3
	2032	4.5		2000	4.4
14	0223	1.3	29	0145	1.5
	0853	4.4		0809	4.3
	TU 1445	1.4		W 1408	1.5
	2129	4.1		2048	4.1
15	0319	1.8	30	0230	1.8
	0948	4.1		0857	4.1
	W 1553	1.8		TH 1458	1.8
	◐ 2246	3.7		2154	3.9

OCTOBER

Date	Time	m	Date	Time	m
1	0327	2.1	16	0538	2.3
	1006	4.0		1205	3.8
	F 1605	2.0		SA 1812	2.0
	◑ 2306	3.8			
2	0444	2.2	17	0106	3.8
	1120	4.0		0643	2.2
	SA 1828	1.9		SU 1322	4.0
				1922	1.8
3	0022	3.9	18	0206	4.0
	0645	2.0		0740	1.9
	SU 1242	4.1		M 1418	4.2
	1936	1.6		2011	1.6
4	0143	4.2	19	0249	4.3
	0748	1.6		0826	1.7
	M 1406	4.5		TU 1502	4.4
	2026	1.1		2048	1.4
5	0242	4.6	20	0326	4.5
	0838	1.2		0905	1.4
	TU 1502	4.9		W 1539	4.6
	2110	0.7		2123	1.2
6	0329	5.0	21	0400	4.7
	0922	0.8		0942	1.2
	W 1548	5.2		TH 1614	4.7
	2151	0.4		2156	1.0
7	0412	5.3	22	0434	4.8
	1004	0.5		1016	1.0
	TH 1632	5.5		F 1648	4.8
	● 2231	0.2		2229	1.0
8	0455	5.5	23	0506	4.8
	1046	0.3		1049	1.0
	F 1715	5.5		SA 1720	4.9
	2311	0.2		○ 2300	1.0
9	0537	5.5	24	0537	4.9
	1128	0.2		1121	0.9
	SA 1758	5.5		SU 1754	4.9
	2351	0.4		2331	1.0
10	0619	5.4	25	0609	4.9
	1209	0.4		1153	1.0
	SU 1841	5.3		M 1829	4.8
11	0032	0.6	26	0005	1.1
	0700	5.2		0642	4.8
	M 1252	0.6		TU 1229	1.1
	1924	4.9		1905	4.7
12	0114	1.0	27	0044	1.3
	0742	4.9		0717	4.7
	TU 1335	1.0		W 1309	1.2
	2010	4.5		1946	4.5
13	0159	1.5	28	0126	1.5
	0827	4.5		0756	4.5
	W 1424	1.4		TH 1353	1.4
	2103	4.1		2037	4.3
14	0254	1.9	29	0214	1.8
	0920	4.2		0845	4.4
	TH 1526	1.8		F 1445	1.6
	◐ 2215	3.8		2140	4.1
15	0415	2.2	30	0313	2.0
	1030	3.9		0951	4.2
	F 1650	2.0		SA 1551	1.8
	2345	3.7		◑ 2249	4.1
			31	0430	2.1
				1103	4.2
				SU 1733	1.8

NOVEMBER

Date	Time	m	Date	Time	m
1	0001	4.2	16	0111	4.0
	0612	2.0		0655	2.1
	M 1218	4.3		TU 1323	4.0
	1902	1.6		1917	1.8
2	0113	4.4	17	0205	4.1
	0719	1.7		0747	1.9
	TU 1335	4.6		W 1417	4.2
	1957	1.2		2006	1.7
3	0213	4.8	18	0247	4.3
	0812	1.3		0832	1.7
	W 1435	4.9		TH 1501	4.3
	2044	0.9		2047	1.5
4	0303	5.1	19	0324	4.5
	0859	1.0		0913	1.5
	TH 1525	5.2		F 1540	4.5
	2127	0.7		2125	1.3
5	0347	5.3	20	0359	4.7
	0943	0.7		0950	1.3
	F 1610	5.3		SA 1616	4.7
	2208	0.6		2200	1.2
6	0431	5.4	21	0432	4.8
	1026	0.6		1026	1.1
	SA 1655	5.4		SU 1652	4.8
	● 2249	0.6		○ 2234	1.1
7	0514	5.4	22	0507	4.9
	1109	0.6		1101	1.0
	SU 1739	5.3		M 1730	4.8
	2330	0.8		2310	1.1
8	0557	5.3	23	0545	5.0
	1152	0.6		1138	0.9
	M 1823	5.1		TU 1810	4.9
				2348	1.1
9	0012	1.0	24	0624	5.0
	0640	5.2		1217	0.9
	TU 1235	0.8		W 1852	4.8
	1907	4.9			
10	0055	1.3	25	0030	1.2
	0723	4.9		0704	4.9
	W 1319	1.1		TH 1300	1.0
	1952	4.6		1936	4.7
11	0139	1.6	26	0116	1.3
	0807	4.7		0748	4.8
	TH 1405	1.4		F 1345	1.1
	2042	4.2		2026	4.6
12	0230	1.9	27	0205	1.5
	0856	4.4		0837	4.7
	F 1457	1.7		SA 1435	1.3
	2142	4.0		2123	4.4
13	0334	2.2	28	0300	1.8
	0953	4.1		0936	4.5
	SA 1602	1.9		SU 1534	1.5
	◐ 2253	3.8		◑ 2228	4.3
14	0451	2.3	29	0408	1.9
	1100	4.0		1043	4.4
	SU 1714	2.0		M 1646	1.6
				2334	4.4
15	0005	3.9	30	0529	1.9
	0557	2.2		1152	4.4
	M 1214	3.9		TU 1817	1.6
	1819	2.0			

DECEMBER

Date	Time	m	Date	Time	m
1	0041	4.5	16	0055	3.9
	0645	1.7		0701	2.1
	W 1304	4.5		TH 1304	3.9
	1927	1.4		1916	1.9
2	0145	4.7	17	0156	4.1
	0746	1.5		0757	2.0
	TH 1410	4.7		F 1411	4.0
	2021	1.3		2011	1.8
3	0239	4.9	18	0245	4.3
	0839	1.3		0846	1.7
	F 1505	4.9		SA 1503	4.2
	2108	1.1		2057	1.6
4	0327	5.1	19	0326	4.5
	0926	1.1		0929	1.4
	SA 1554	5.0		SU 1548	4.4
	2151	1.0		2138	1.4
5	0413	5.2	20	0406	4.7
	1012	0.9		1010	1.2
	SU 1640	5.0		M 1630	4.6
	● 2233	1.0		2218	1.2
6	0457	5.2	21	0446	4.9
	1056	0.8		1050	0.9
	M 1726	5.0		TU 1713	4.8
	2315	1.1		○ 2259	1.0
7	0542	5.2	22	0528	5.0
	1139	0.8		1130	0.7
	TU 1810	4.9		W 1757	4.9
	2357	1.1		2340	0.9
8	0625	5.1	23	0612	5.1
	1222	0.9		1210	0.6
	W 1853	4.8		TH 1840	5.0
9	0038	1.3	24	0023	0.9
	0707	5.0		0654	5.1
	TH 1303	1.0		F 1252	0.6
	1936	4.6		1924	4.9
10	0120	1.5	25	0107	0.9
	0750	4.8		0738	5.1
	F 1344	1.2		SA 1335	0.6
	2020	4.4		2010	4.8
11	0203	1.7	26	0153	1.1
	0833	4.6		0824	4.9
	SA 1426	1.4		SU 1421	0.9
	2107	4.2		2102	4.6
12	0251	1.9	27	0243	1.3
	0919	4.3		0917	4.7
	SU 1513	1.6		M 1512	1.1
	2200	4.0		2200	4.5
13	0348	2.1	28	0341	1.6
	1008	4.2		1018	4.5
	M 1607	1.8		TU 1611	1.4
	◐ 2256	3.9		◑ 2304	4.3
14	0455	2.2	29	0449	1.7
	1059	4.0		1124	4.4
	TU 1709	2.0		W 1725	1.6
	2354	3.9			
15	0600	2.2	30	0010	4.3
	1155	3.9		0607	1.8
	W 1814	2.0		TH 1235	4.3
				1854	1.7
			31	0118	4.4
				0722	1.7
				F 1348	4.3
				2003	1.6

Chart Datum: 0·20 metres above Ordnance Datum (Dublin). HAT is 5·6 metres above Chart Datum; see 0.20